FERTILITY, FOOD AND FEVER

for my wife Agustina

with love and gratitude

for all she has given, and forgiven, to make this book possible

VERHANDELINGEN
VAN HET KONINKLIJK INSTITUUT
VOOR TAAL-, LAND- EN VOLKENKUNDE

201

DAVID HENLEY

FERTILITY, FOOD AND FEVER

Population, economy and environment in
North and Central Sulawesi, 1600-1930

KITLV Press
Leiden
2005

Published by:
KITLV Press
Koninklijk Instituut voor Taal-, Land- en Volkenkunde
(Royal Netherlands Institute of Southeast Asian and Caribbean Studies)
P.O. Box 9515
2300 RA Leiden
The Netherlands
website: www.kitlv.nl
e-mail: kitlvpress@kitlv.nl

KITLV is an institute of the Royal Netherlands Academy of Arts and Sciences
(KNAW)

Cover: Creja Ontwerpen, Leiderdorp

ISBN 90 6718 209 5

© 2005 Koninklijk Instituut voor Taal-, Land- en Volkenkunde

Printed in the Netherlands

Contents

List of figures, maps and tables   vii

Acknowledgements   xi

I	Introduction	1
II	Economic patterns	51
III	Interpreting the demographic data	101
IV	Population data, Sangir and Talaud	127
V	Population data, peninsular North Sulawesi	165
VI	Population data, Central Sulawesi	213
VII	Death and disease	249
VIII	Disease control	289
IX	The food supply	317
X	Reproductive fertility	363
XI	Demographic patterns	403
XII	The causes of population growth	435
XIII	Vegetation and deforestation	469
XIV	The making of the landscape	515
XV	Population and environment	567

Appendices
A	Abbreviations	612
B	Glossary	613
C	Weights and measures	614
D	Areas of major islands and 1930 administrative divisions	616
E	The Edeling fertility survey, Minahasa, 1874	618
F	The Kruyt fertility survey, Poso area, 1902	620
G	The Tillema fertility survey, Central Sulawesi, 1924	622
H	The Kündig fertility and mortality survey, Minahasa, 1930-1932	623
I	Land use in Minahasa, 1862	625

J   Land use in Minahasa, 1919   626
K   Areal foodcrop yields in Minahasa   627

Bibliography   629

General index   697

Index of geographical names   703

List of plates, figures, maps and tables

Plates

1   Lowland rainforest on the Tomori Bay (eastern Central Sulawesi),
as sketched by a Dutch sea captain in 1850   17
2   Minahasan (Bantik) farmer in working dress with bark-cloth tunic,
circa 1890   18
3   Toraja (Pamona) woman in formal dress, with imported heirloom
sarong and bark-cloth jacket, circa 1920   22
4   Pagan uplanders ('Alfurs') of eastern Central Sulawesi, with elevated
pile-dwellings in background, as sketched in 1850   25
5   Swidden burn in Talaud, 1979   52
6   Hillside swiddens in Talaud, 1979   55
7   Wet ricefields in Kulawi, with swidden-fallow vegetation
on adjacent slopes, circa 1913   56
8   Water buffalo driven through wet ricefields to turn the soil, western
Central Sulawesi, circa 1913   57
9   Extraction of palm pith for sago manufacture, Talaud, 1979   61
10   Nineteenth-century model of a *kora-kora* vessel from Talaud   89
11   Toraja village (Buyu mBajau, To Pebato area) in defensive
hilltop site, circa 1905   102
12   Swidden houses in the upper Bongka Valley (To Wana area),
circa 1975   103
13   New model village, Central Sulawesi, circa 1920   229
14   *Raja* of Banggai, blind and with skin disease, 1678   282
15   Funeral feast in the Poso area with animals awaiting slaughter,
circa 1918   348
16   Men (dibbling) and women (sowing) plant rice on a newly cleared
and burned swidden complex, Central Sulawesi, 1912   420
17   Tondano town from the lake, 1679   425
18   Public market in Tomohon (Minahasa), 1945   451
19   Rattan being dried for export, Gorontalo, circa 1930   458
20   A colonial survey expedition crossing the Pada grassland, 1910   479
21   The Bada Valley, circa 1912   481
22   The Palu Valley with the deforested western range in
the background, 1910   483
23   The Palu Valley, showing cultivated fields on the lower part of
the valley floor and grasslands on the adjacent porous sediments, 1944   485

24 Deforested landscapes around the Bay of Palu (Kaili), as seen from
   a VOC ship in 1669   488
25 Part of the central plateau of Minahasa to the west of Lake Tondano,
   with grassland much in evidence, 1920   497
26 Siau in 1677, showing coconut stands   511
27 A taro swidden on Talaud, 1979   516
28 Swidden landscapes, I: Sonder (Minahasa), 1824   522
29 Swidden landscapes, II: the Gorontalo trench, circa 1880   522
30 Swidden landscapes, III: northeast coast of Minahasa, 1944   523
31 Permanent and short-fallow unirrigated fields near Tomohon
   (Minahasa), 1944   524
32 Artist's view of Lake Tondano with deer and meadow in
   the foreground, circa 1870   536
33 Part of southeastern Minahasa between Belang and Ratahan,
   showing continuous coconut plantations near the coast and
   grassy hills inland, 1944   549
34 Unforested, steeply-incised stream valley on the western flank of
   the Palu Trench, circa 1913   558
35 Burning lignite outcrop near Tomata on the Pada grassland, 1910   564
36 Sustainable land use, 1945: wet ricefields (with ox-drawn plough)
   and coconut groves in Minahasa   569
37 Unsustainable land use, 1945: deforested, eroded limestone hills
   between Gorontalo town and the Gulf of Tomini coast   571
38 Women transplanting rice seedings on an irrigated field,
   Minahasa, 1945   590

Figures
1 Average monthly rainfall at selected locations in northern Sulawesi   15
2 Copra exports and rice imports, residency of Manado, 1875-1938   84
3 Monthly rainfall distribution and variability in Tomohon
   (Minahasa), 1895-1907   329
4 Food production and mortality in Minahasa, 1854-1872   335
5 Staple food production in Minahasa, 1854-1872   336
6 Growth curves for infants on Greater Sangir and elsewhere, ca 1948   346
7 Minahasa: imports by value, 1840-1900   355
8 Recorded crude birth and death rates, Minahasa, 1849-1872   365
9 Female fertility and the labour burden of compulsory coffee
   cultivation in some Minahasan districts, 1874   387
10 Child mortality and the labour burden of compulsory coffee
   cultivation in some Minahasan districts, 1874   391
11 Household size and the labour burden of compulsory coffee
   cultivation in some Minahasan districts, 1874   394
12 Female fertility and income from compulsory coffee cultivation
   in some Minahasan districts, 1873-1874   395
13 Compulsory coffee cultivation in Minahasa, 1834-1892   396
14 Population density and island size, 1930   413
15 Population growth in Minahasa, 1860-1930   447
16 Annual rainfall at Masarang (Minahasa), 1882-1933   582

Maps
1   Northern Sulawesi: geographical   10-11
     Northern Sulawesi: soils   12
3   Northern Sulawesi: rainfall   14
4   Northern Sulawesi: aspects of political geography, 1750-1880   32
5   To Pamona (in Poso and Mori): ethnic subgroups   36
6   Minahasa: geographical   38
7   Minahasa: linguistic and administrative divisions   40
8   Northern Sulawesi: aspects of economic geography, circa 1850   54
9   Northern Sulawesi: subregions for demographic analysis   124
10   Minahasa: population distribution, circa 1940   182
11   Bolaang Mongondow: population distribution, circa 1940   194
12   The Limboto Depression ('Sketch map of the districts around
     Gorontalo town'), circa 1890   209
13   Western Central Sulawesi: population distribution, circa 1920   223
14   Northern Sulawesi: vegetation cover according to G.G.G.J. van Steenis
     in 1932   471
15   Northern Sulawesi: vegetation cover according to G.G.G.J. van Steenis
     in 1958   472
16   Northern Sulawesi: vegetation cover, circa 1985   473
17   'Sketch map of the eastern part of Central Sulawesi travelled through
     by Dr N. Adriani and Albert C. Kruyt', 1899   478
18   Minahasa: vegetation cover in 1895 according to S.H. Koorders   496
19   Minahasa: vegetation cover according to a military reconnaissance
     study, 1944   498

Tables
1   Recorded gold exports, Gorontalo, 1737-1848   98
2   Class composition of the Gorontalo population according to
     Dutch sources, 1820-1860   108
3   Implied size of some conventional units of demographic
     measurement, 1695-1908   120
4   Population data, Tagulandang, 1669-1930   128
5   Population data, Siau, 1564-1930   135
6   Population data, Greater Sangir, 1591-1930   146
7   Population data, Talaud, 1656-1930   156
8   Population data, Minahasa, 1568-1930   167
9   Population data, Bolaang Mongondow, 1563-1930   185
10   Population data, Gorontalo, 1591-1930   198
11   Population data, Buol and Tolitoli, 1591-1930   214
12   Population data, Tomini, 1591-1930   219
13   Population data, Poso, Tojo and Lore, 1863-1930   224
14   Population data, Banggai, 1679-1930   236
15   Population data, Luwuk Peninsula, 1705-1930   240
16   Population data, Tobungku, 1678-1930   244
17   Mortality variations by administrative division in Minahasa, 1849-1872 299
18   Extreme weather, food shortages and disease in Gorontalo, 1820-1869   321

19	Extreme weather, epidemic disease, food production and mortality in Minahasa, 1849-1872	332
20	Reported fertility and child survival rates among four Pamona subgroups in the Poso area, 1924	371
21	Reported fertility and child survival rates among four ethnic groups in the Poso area, 1902	374
22	Reported sex ratios in the child population, Minahasa and Gorontalo, 1823-1870	376
23	Long-term mean population estimates by subregion, 1600-1930	405
24	Approximate average population density, selected subregions, 1850-1930	408
25	Mean annual precipitation and interannual rainfall variation at 16 locations in northern Sulawesi	418
26	Reported dimensions of Lake Limboto, 1682-1993	492
27	Swidden cycle data, Minahasa, 1821-1901	501
28	Reported extent of irrigation in northern Sulawesi, 1926	517
29	Swidden cycle data for areas outside Minahasa, 1825-1949	518
30	Expansion of irrigation in Minahasa, 1860-1920	526
31	Reported livestock numbers, Minahasa, 1850-1920	538
32	Reported livestock numbers, Gorontalo, 1860-1930	541
33	Approximate copra exports (tonnes) by subregion, 1939	548

Acknowledgements

This work was produced under the auspices of the EDEN (Ecology, Demography and Economy in Nusantara) research project of the Royal Institute of Southeast Asian and Caribbean Studies (KITLV) in Leiden. Research in the National Archives of Indonesia (ANRI) in Jakarta was made possible by a grant from the Netherlands Foundation for the Advancement of Tropical Research (WOTRO), and by the support of the Lembaga Ilmu Pengetahuan Indonesia (LIPI, Indonesian Institute of Sciences).

Peter Boomgaard inspired and supported my work throughout; without him it would never have been possible. Jouke Wigboldus generously granted me access to his important unpublished book on the history of Minahasa from 1680 to 1825, and supplied many other crucial references, observations and ideas. Mieke Schouten, as always, gave freely of her valuable time and advice. I am also very grateful to Hendrik E. Niemeijer for allowing me to make advance use of his forthcoming source publications on the history of the Moluccas under the Dutch East Indies Company.

Numerous other people provided vital help and information at various stages. They include H.S. Ahimsa Putra, Dr Johanna Barten, David Cole, Jaap Erkelens, Menno Hekker, Dr Rahayu S. Hidayat, Professor H.J. van der Kaay, H. Kosam Ribarawa, Tania Li, Eddy and Tine Mambu, Anke Niehof, Halid Payu, Gary Rose, Professor R. Schefold, Sugeha W. Jusuf, Leo and Stien Supit, Dr Thee Kian Wie, Nani Tuloli, Alex Ulaen, Alex Velberg, Frans Watuseke, and Professor H. Waworuntu. Hans Borkent painstakingly prepared the maps. My thanks are also due to the staff of the Arsip Nasional Republik Indonesia (ANRI) in Jakarta, especially Oloan Marpaung and Langgeng Sulistyo Budi, to Peter Levi of the Royal Tropical Institute (KIT) in Amsterdam, to Ms A. Werner and Ms M. Dirkzwager formerly of the Hendrik Kraemer Instituut in Oegstgeest, and to all of my colleagues at the KITLV.

CHAPTER I

Introduction

This book combines historical geography with historical demography, and was conceived as a study in environmental history, a discipline encompassing every aspect of the relationship between man and the natural world. The particular aspects of that relationship which have attracted attention recently as far as Indonesia is concerned, like the general upsurge of interest in the environmental history of Southeast Asia as a whole, reflect current concerns with nature conservation and environmental politics. A large proportion of the essays in the recent volumes edited by Boomgaard, Colombijn and Henley (1997), King (1998), and Grove, Damodaran and Sangwan (1998), for instance, deal either with state politics (forestry, agrarian, and conservation policies, and the struggles against them) or with the impact of human exploitation on particular populations of vulnerable wild animals and plants (large mammals, commercial fish stocks, plants yielding useful forest products). Other writers have scoured the historical record for the origins of urban pollution in Indonesia (Nagtegaal 1995), or in search of indigenous precedents for modern environmental law (Von Benda-Beckmann and Brouwer 1995). My own study concentrates on two interconnected themes which, although perhaps no less relevant to current concerns, also lie closer to the core of the relationship between man and environment in past times: the size, distribution, and growth of the human population, and its effect on the landscape, particularly in terms of the destruction or modification of natural vegetation.

Before the advent of mechanized logging and industrial pollution, the human impact on the natural environment in Indonesia consisted largely of agricultural deforestation. The extent of this deforestation, and its further consequences in terms of faunal change, soil erosion, and hydrology, were determined by the size of the population and by the specific farming techniques employed. Agricultural practices, in turn, were themselves conditioned partly by population densities, while the rate of demographic change was affected both by the amount of food available and by the amount of labour involved in producing it. In this book I examine the interconnected questions of Indonesian demographic and landscape history in the light of a favourable combination of historical and ethnographic evidence from northern Sulawesi, an area corresponding to the colonial residency of Manado or the two modern provinces of North and Central Sulawesi.[1] Particular attention is given to the ways in which environmental factors (climate, soils, and disease) affected the size and distribution of the population and the extent to which it altered its habitat. In the course of my research, however, it became obvious that factors less closely connected with the natural environment – most importantly the extent of trade and commodity production, but also a range of political and cultural variables – were often crucial determinants of demographic change. Any meaningful examination of the relationship between population and environment in northern Sulawesi, then, would have to encompass a good deal of social, political, and economic history. Some information has also been included regarding traditional resource management systems, the question of agricultural sustainability, and the human impact on wild animal populations.

Indonesia: historical demography

The significance of demography in Indonesian history, of course, extends far beyond questions of environmental change. The general sparsity of the population in precolonial times, for instance, has been invoked to help explain the weakness of most precolonial states in Indonesia and elsewhere in Southeast Asia, on the basis that oppressed or dissatisfied subjects always had the option of flight to uninhabited areas (Adas 1981:232-3; Gullick 1958: 28-9). An abundance of land relative to population has also been seen as one reason for the emphasis on control of human resources (especially slaves), rather than land, in traditional political systems (Booth 1988:67-8; Reid 1988-93, I:129). Rapid population growth, conversely, has often been blamed for economic difficulties during and after the colonial period (Geertz 1963:70; Ricklefs 2001:197, 240, 344).

Yet much of the demographic history of Indonesia still remains to be described as well as explained. Its broad outlines in the early twentieth century (Gooszen 1994, 1999), and the dimensions of the population boom in nineteenth-century Java (Boomgaard 1989a), admittedly, are now quite well documented. Ricklefs (1986) has also assembled some indirect statistical evidence on the population of Java in the seventeenth and eighteenth centuries, while Knaap (1987:99-123, 1995) provides a detailed reconstruction of the

---

[1]   The residency of Manado, that is, as it was constituted after 1924, when the east coast subdivisions of Banggai, Tobungku, and Mori were added to it (*Koloniaal verslag* 1925:26), and the provinces North and Central Sulawesi as they were until Gorontalo was separated from the remainder of North Sulawesi to become a separate province in 2001.

demography of the part of Ambon under Dutch rule in the years 1670-1695, together with some fragmentary data from earlier in the same century. In quantitative terms, however, almost nothing is known about the population of other parts of the archipelago before 1800.[2] Outside Java the nineteenth century also remains mysterious in demographic terms, although attempts have been made to discern the general patterns in parts of the Lesser Sundas (Fox 1977:149-76), Sumatra (Reid 1997:70-5), and Kalimantan (Knapen 2001: 106-14, 135-6).

If a consensus can be detected in the existing studies, it is that most parts of Indonesia, historically, were sparsely populated (despite some dense local concentrations) even by contemporary Asian standards, and saw very little long-term population increase until they were brought under stable European government, whereupon sustained growth often set in. The first area in which this took place was Java, where the population, according to Ricklefs (1986:30), 'was almost certainly growing at a rate in excess of 1% per annum' in the third quarter of the eighteenth century, following the cessation of civil war and the partition of the island between the Verenigde Oost-Indische Compagnie (VOC, Dutch East Indies Company) and two Javanese vassal states.[3] Demographic growth in the nineteenth century was not limited to Java; the population of Southeast Kalimantan, according to Knapen (2001:135), doubled between 1830 and 1900 following colonial paci-fication and associated economic changes. In the seventeenth century, by contrast, the data from Java and the Moluccas suggest a net demographic decline, a development for which there is also some parallel evidence from the Philippines.[4] Whereas in Java this decline continued into the eighteenth century, in Ambon the population had recovered by 1690, but subsequently seems to have remained more or less stable until the second half of the nine-teenth century (Knaap 1987:122-3).

The only systematic attempt to explain low population growth in preco-lonial Indonesia remains a well-known essay by Reid (1987), and the reasons for the subsequent population boom also remain surprisingly controversial. What might be described as the 'traditional' interpretation emphasizes mor-tality to the exclusion of fertility, attributes the slowness of population increase to war, disease and hunger, and credits European intervention with the sup-

[2]   An exception here is the demographic component of archaeological research by Bulbeck (1992:456-63) on the town and immediate hinterland of Makassar in the seventeenth century and before. The early European demographic record from some parts of the Philippines, by compari-son, is more complete (Cullinane and Xenos 1998; Newson 1998; Vandermeer 1967).

[3]   In the Spanish Philippines, too, sustained growth seems to have set in during the eighteenth century or earlier (Cullinane and Xenos 1998:94; Vandermeer 1967:334).

[4]   Newson 1998:26; Reid 1990:649. Other data presented by Newson (1998:21) for Luzon sug-gest that this decline was already well underway in the sixteenth century.

pression of all three, respectively by means of pacification, health care, and improved food distribution (Fisher 1966:172-3; Palte and Tempelman 1978: 55-6). 'A combination of war, pestilence and famine', agrees Metzner (1982: 90-1) in his study of agriculture and population pressure on Flores, kept population growth at bay until 'the Dutch abandoned their policy of non-interference in native affairs and put an end to tribal wars', whereupon 'population figures soared' (see also Seavoy 1986:129). The various Malthusian 'positive checks' to population growth (Malthus 1976:36) continue to figure prominently in recent analyses of Indonesian demographic history. Knapen (1998) and Boomgaard (1989a:187-92, 197, 1996b:13), for instance, have both emphasized the devastating impact of lethal diseases on precolonial populations, while some studies also indicate a strong link between mortality levels and poor foodcrop harvests (Boomgaard 2001; Henley 1997a). Reid (1990: 656) suggests that a series of abnormally dry years, associated with a period of global cooling and leading to food shortages and disease outbreaks, was partly responsible for demographic decline in the seventeenth century.[5]

In general, however, Reid (1987, 1988-93, I:17-8), like Metzner, gives pride of place to warfare – or rather to the disruptive effects of war on food supplies, health conditions, and patterns of marriage and reproduction. Population change before colonialism, in his analysis, was characterized by spurts of growth during periods of peace, interspersed – and in the long run, all but cancelled out – by wartime mortality crises.

> The demographic pattern of pre-colonial Southeast Asia, it would appear, was very far removed from the smooth but shallow growth curve resulting from backward projections. When conditions of reasonable stability prevailed, the combination of early marriage, abundant food and relative health probably gave rise to quite rapid population growth, at least among the wet-rice cultivators and urban traders of the lowland and coast. Population must have declined equally sharply when these areas were laid waste by the movement of armies, however. (Reid 1987:43.)

The subsequent shift to sustained population growth, accordingly, was brought about in the first place by the *pax imperica*. Reid also notes, nevertheless, that upland, swidden-farming populations in twentieth-century Southeast Asia, in contrast to most of their lowland, wet rice-farming neighbours, have often been found to display low birth rates as well as high mortality.[6] This suggests that besides colonial pacification, another stimulus to population growth may have been provided by 'changes in values and practices which accompanied the movement of animist swidden cultiva-

---

[5]   Knaap (1995:239), however, doubts whether this applies in the Moluccan case.
[6]   Reid 1987:39-42, 1988-93, I:160-2, 2001:56-7.

tors into the orbit of the world religions centred in the cities and lowlands'
(Reid 1987:43). Traditional practices depressing fertility among such 'animist'
groups include abortion (deliberately induced by massage or by drugs), and
the custom of breast-feeding infants for long periods, which has a contraceptive effect (lactational amenorrhoea).

At this point Reid's account overlaps with a strand of demographic explanation which stresses changes in fertility rather than mortality, and which
emerged in the 1970s as a reaction against the assumption that population
growth in nineteenth-century Java must have reflected the benevolence of
Dutch rule. Inspired partly by White (1973), who observed that rapid growth
during the period of the Cultivation System (1830-1870) coincided with a
dramatic increase in the labour burden imposed on Javanese households by
the colonial state, Alexander and Alexander (1979) proposed that women,
in order to meet this labour demand, deliberately altered their reproductive
behaviour in such a way as to increase the size of their families.[7] Traditional
practices restricting fertility which were amenable to relaxation in order
to achieve this, they suggested, might have included late marriage, abortion, and infanticide, as well as prolonged breast-feeding (Alexander and
Alexander 1979:24-5). Boomgaard (1989a:176, 186) later confirmed that when
demographic and economic statistics for 19 different Javanese residencies
in the period 1830-1880 were compared, a significant correlation emerged
between local fertility rates and the percentage of the population subject to
Cultivation System labour services.[8]

Distancing himself from the calculating interpretation of reproductive
behaviour implicit in his original argument, Paul Alexander (1984, 1986) later
came to favour a modified version of the labour-demand theory in which
conscious agency was no longer involved. The 'increased participation of
women in arduous and sustained work' under the Cultivation System, he
proposed, left them less time for breast-feeding and forced them to wean
their children more quickly (Alexander 1986:257). This led automatically to
shorter intervals between successive pregnancies, partly because of reduced
lactational amenorrhoea, but mainly due to a custom, well documented in
modern Java, of avoiding sexual intercourse for as long as breast-feeding continues. Boomgaard (1989a:197), by contrast, interprets the correlation between

---

[7]   White himself initially believed that child mortality, rather than female fertility, was the factor adjusted (by means of food redistribution within the family) to promote population growth
in response to labour demand. Having more use for their children under the Cultivation System,
in other words, the Javanese allowed fewer of them to die. In subsequent work, however, White
(1976:400-20) stressed fertility control as a factor affecting household size.

[8]   Boomgaard (1989a:197) nevertheless denies that the overall average fertility level rose
over this period, arguing that the observed population growth must be attributed primarily to
reduced mortality.

labour demand and fertility in terms of a conscious and positive response to 'the growth of the non-agricultural sectors of the Javanese economy, generated by the Cultivation System, which created new economic opportunites with higher returns to labour'.[9] A complementary factor was that the additional income provided by these same opportunities also allowed people 'to marry earlier than they could have done if they had had to wait for a piece of land'. In a more recent publication, Boomgaard (1996b:18) again stresses the link between fertility and age at marriage, maintaining, in contrast to Reid (1987:38), that 'early and universal marriage may well be a relatively recent phenomenon in many Indonesian societies'.[10] While the causes, mechanisms, and even directions of fertility change in particular contexts remain controversial, it has become obvious that no interpretation of Indonesian demographic history can afford to ignore variations in the birth rate.[11]

At the end of the colonial period the botanist P.M.L. Tammes (1940:196-7), in a pioneer study of the historical demography of North Sulawesi, claimed that the population of certain parts of this region had remained more or less stable for long periods at levels determined by the productivity of local farming systems. Later authors, not least because of their greater awareness that both mortality and fertility are affected by many factors which bear no immediate relation to the existing food supply, have mostly been less willing to speculate about the existence of systematic relationships between agricultural production and population change. Theoretical advances in the study of 'carrying capacity' – the supposed maximum or optimal population density which can be supported by a given farming system – have also played a role here. Even under pre-industrial conditions, it seems, food production per unit area of land could almost always be increased to accommodate a growing population if farmers were prepared to adopt more labour-intensive cultivation methods (Bayliss-Smith 1980; Boserup 1965). Given the likelihood of cultural and other resistance to such intensification (Brookfield 1972:35), and the fact that beyond a certain point, per capita foodcrop yields do tend to

[9]   The fertility control mechanisms implicated here include late marriage, frequent divorce, prolonged breast-feeding, contraceptive rotation of the uterus, and abortion (Boomgaard 1989a: 192-5).
[10] Reid (1987:38) initially stated that age at marriage 'must be dismissed' as a factor suppressing the birth rate in precolonial Southeast Asia, although elsewhere (Reid 1988-93, I:158-60) he qualifies this standpoint to some extent.
[11] Knapen (2001:392-6) speculates that population growth in Southeast Kalimantan during the nineteenth century involved an increase in natality which was both a conscious and an unconscious response to changing economic conditions. Growing involvement by men in commercial activities, first of all, led to harder female labour in food production, raising fertility via the unconscious mechanism of reduced lactational amenorrhoea. The elimination of warfare, secondly, made children less of a liability in the fields, and therefore increased their economic value, so that parents were also less inclined to apply conscious means of birth control.

decline as population density and labour inputs increase (Metzner 1982:240), it nevertheless remains possible that the kind of balance between demography and resources described by Tammes sometimes existed. Knaap (1987: 121-2, 1995:239) has seen the apparent stabilization of the Ambonese population after 1690 as evidence for just such an equilibrium, which could have been maintained, in theory, either by mortality and emigration (the mechanisms favoured by Tammes) or by the 'preventive check' (Malthus 1976:34) of fertility control.[12] One type of fertility limitation which has often acted to adjust population to agrarian resources, both in European history and in developing countries (Pirie 1984:122), is the postponement of marriage when the availability of farmland is limited.

Tammes (1940:196-7) also argued that trade and the cultivation of cash crops, as well as improvements in the productivity of subsistence agriculture, had sometimes led to episodes of population growth before either colonial pacification or the introduction of modern medical treatments.[13] Recent work by Heersink (1998), on the distribution of the population in South Sulawesi before 1930, points in the same direction, indicating that thanks to compensatory specialization in trade, shipbuilding, and cotton and coconut cultivation, areas poorly suited for foodcrop farming were often among the most densely populated (see also Heersink 1999:321-5). Boomgaard (1989a:191-8) sees commercial expansion and the creation of new economic opportunities as key reasons for both declining mortality and (as already noted) rising fertility in nineteenth-century Java, and Reid (2001:51) has recently supplemented his analysis of precolonial demography by suggesting (although without specifying the mechanisms involved) that population numbers in Southeast Asia were always sensitive to commercial as well as political and environmental conditions. The demographic 'crisis' of the seventeenth century, it appears, coincided with a marked downturn in the volume of maritime trade (Reid 1988-93, II:286-91), while population growth in late eighteenth and early nineteenth-century Java came during a period of expanding international commerce (Bulbeck et al. 1998:15). The direction of causality here, however, is ambiguous, and the idea that long-distance trade was one factor causing the population to increase sits rather uneasily with Reid's observation (1997) that at this time much, if not most, of the Indonesian population lived in upland rice-farming valleys remote from trading ports.

---

[12]   Fox (1977:17, 23, 157) also uses the concept of carrying capacity in relation to emigration, as well as agricultural intensification, on Sawu and Roti in the Lesser Sundas.
[13]   Tammes believed that the positive influence of commerce on population growth operated entirely via reductions in mortality, but an alternative possibility, along the lines proposed by Boomgaard for nineteenth-century Java, is that fertility increased in response to economic opportunity.

Indonesia: landscape history

Although there is an increasing awareness of the antiquity of forest clearance in certain parts of Indonesia (Boomgaard 1997a:10-5; Brookfield 1997), the literature on this subject still tends to portray early instances of deforestation as anomalies requiring highly specific historical or ecological explanations. Precolonial Southeast Asia, according to Reid, was 'a region of forest and water' in which the two main causes of local deforestation were 'the elaboration of permanent irrigated rice fields in upland valleys', and the spread of smallholder cash crops like sugar, cloves, coffee, and especially pepper.[14] For the rest, the relationship between humans and forests 'was primarily one of interdependence' (Reid 1995:93). Boomgaard (1998a:23, 26) agrees that '80 or 90' percent of Southeast Asia was still under forest cover on the eve of the European period, and that the system of shifting (swidden) cultivation by which most crops were then produced 'is only harmful to the natural environment if the fallow period is too short'.[15] The colonial stereotype of swidden agriculture as 'axiomatically destructive of plant growth, soil, and other resources' (Spencer 1966:3) is in danger of being replaced by an assumption that the continuous recycling of fallow land which usually characterized this type of farming in its traditional form 'should probably not be considered deforestation at all' (Calkins 1994:52); Cribb (2000:23), for instance, doubts 'whether it was any more significant than natural destructive forces such as landslides and lightning strikes'.

The role of population growth in the deforestation of colonial Java, where permanent-field farming methods were common and which had already lost almost three quarters of its natural forest cover by the end of the nineteenth century (Boomgaard 1998a:21), is well known (Donner 1987:53-115; Smiet 1990). Where deforestation is discussed with reference to Java before the colonial population boom, however, it is usually in the narrower context of timber exploitation by the teak and shipbuilding industries (Boomgaard 1988:62-73, 1998b:389-90; Durand 1994:201-11). For parts of Sumatra, comparably, Colombijn (1997a, 1997b, 1997c) identifies tin mining, early commercial logging, and the use of firewood in gambir processing as the principal causes of deforestation prior to the twentieth century.[16] The ecological studies on Timor and the Lesser Sundas by Ormeling (1955), Metzner (1977), and Dove

---

[14] Reid (1995:93, 104) does add, however, that sandalwood and sappan exploitation, and possibly the deliberate creation of grasslands for horses and game animals, were also significant locally.

[15] 'Until very recent times', agrees Falkus (1990:68), 'almost all of Southeast Asia was extensively covered by natural forest, a factor which in itself permitted long-term frontier development and the continuance of shifting cultivation'.

[16] Gambir, used as an ingredient of the betelnut chewing quid, in medicine, and as a tanning agent in the leather industry, is extracted from the leaves of the shrub *Uncaria gambir*.

(1984), by contrast, stress the deliberate creation of grasslands as pasture
for livestock, in combination with population pressure and the unusually
dry climatic conditions which prevail in this corner of Indonesia. The possibility that early deforestation also occurred in more routine ways, even in
generally wet climates and at low population densities, is better reflected
in the literature on Kalimantan (Brookfield, Potter and Byron 1995:179-203).
Here, swidden farming and the use of fire to maintain pastures for game and
domesticated animals (Potter 1987; Seavoy 1975) seem to have combined
with natural fires (Goldammer and Seibert 1989) to push back the forest
boundary in some areas well before the twentieth century. The significance
of this finding, however, has perhaps been obscured by the fact that until
recently the proportion of unforested land in Kalimantan, although higher
(at an estimated 18 percent in 1941) than sometimes assumed, was still lower
than on any other large Indonesian island (Boomgaard 1996a:165).

The best-known man-made landscapes of the archipelago are those resulting from *sawah* (wet rice) and *ladang* (swidden) agriculture, the 'two types of
ecosystems' identified by Geertz (1963:12-37) with 'inner Indonesia' (Java and
Bali) and the outer islands respectively; the real distribution of these systems,
of course, was always more complex. Although by, say, African standards it
may be true to say that premodern Indonesia had 'no substantial grasslands'
(Reid 1988-93, I:5), large expanses of grassy and savanna vegetation resulting
from human activities existed from an early date in many parts of the archipelago (Terra 1952:171), including South Sulawesi (Heersink 1995:77), North
Sumatra (Sherman 1980:119-23), and upland Java (Nibbering 1997:164) as well
as Kalimantan and the Lesser Sundas. The extent of permanently cultivated
but unirrigated farmland of various types (Boomgaard 1989a:78-9; Vink 1941:
149-57) is less clear. This study attempts to reconstruct the past landscapes
of one part of the archipelago, and to explain them with reference to agriculture and other human activities. Of particular interest here is the relationship
between population growth, changes in farming techniques, and the stability
or sustainability of agricultural production. In some times and places, population growth among swidden cultivators has been associated with declining
fertility and soil erosion as a result of excessively short fallow periods (Dobby
1956:349; Ormeling 1955:286); in others, it has been the trigger for the adoption
of alternative techniques, such as irrigation (Conelly 1992:206-12) or the terracing and manuring of permanent dry fields (Nibbering 1997:165-9), which not
only involve less land, but also carry with them less risk of land degradation.[17]

---

[17]   Fox (1977:50-3) also describes a case of agricultural intensification as a result of population
growth which seems to have occurred without conscious intent. On Roti and Sawu, the natural
appearance of fire-resistant *lontar* (*Borassus sundaicus*) palms on man-made savannas associated
with swidden farming paved the way for a productive new subsistence economy based on the
extraction of sugar from this tree.

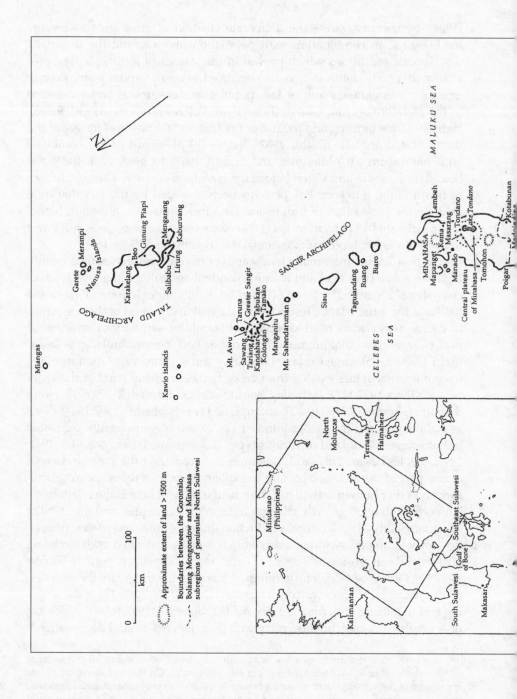

MALUKU SEA

Miangas

Garete Merampi
Narusa Islands
Karakelang Beo
Gunung Piapi
Saibabu Mengarang
Lirung Kaburuang

TALAUD ARCHIPELAGO

Kawio islands

Taruna
Sawang Greater Sangir
Tariang Tabukan
Kandahar Tamako
Kolongan
Mt. Awu Manganitu

SANGIR ARCHIPELAGO

Mt. Sahendaruman

Siau

Tagulandang
Ruang
Biaro

CELEBES SEA

Lembeh
MINAHASA
Mapanget Kema
Masarang
Manado Tondano
Central plateau Lake Tondano
of Minahasa
Tomohon
Poigar Kotabunan

Approximate extent of land > 1500 m

Boundaries between the Gorontalo,
Bolaang Mongondow and Minahasa
subregions of peninsular North Sulawesi

0   100
|——————|
km

N

North
Moluccas
Ternate
Halmahera

Mindanao
(Philippines)

Kalimantan

South Sulawesi
Gulf
of Bone
Southeast Sulawesi

Makasar

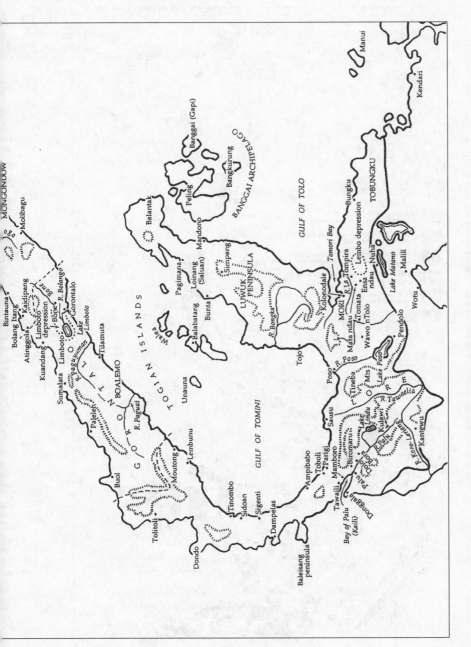

Map 1. Northern Sulawesi, geographical

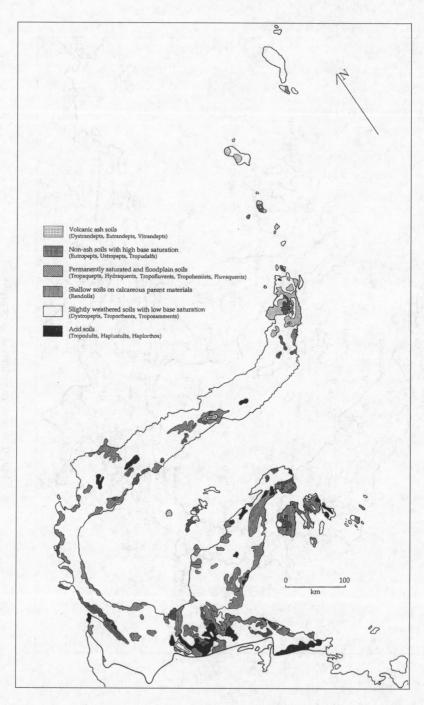

Map 2. Northern Sulawesi: soils (redrawn from RePPProT 1990b: Map 8)

The demographic, environmental, and cultural factors affecting the choice and environmental impact of farming systems will be an important theme of my concluding chapter.

Northern Sulawesi: geography

Northern Sulawesi covers a land area of some 90,000 km², or a little more than Central and East Java combined, and stretches over a maximum straight-line distance (from Palu to Talaud) of more than 1,000 km, roughly the length of Java from tip to tip. It comprises two of Sulawesi's four peninsular arms, the long northern peninsula and the shorter eastern or Luwuk Peninsula, together with a little less than half of the island's central heartland (Map 1). Four major groups of outlying islands are also included in the region as defined here: the Banggai Archipelago in the Maluku Sea, the Togian Islands in the Gulf of Tomini between the eastern and northern arms, and the Sangir and Talaud groups in the far north between Sulawesi and the Philippines. Despite its sinuous form and the fact that no place within it lies more than 90 km from the sea, northern Sulawesi is very mountainous. Approximately half of its land area lies at altitudes above 500 metres, and perhaps one fifth at over 1,000 metres.[18] The coastal plain, correspondingly, is seldom more than a few kilometres wide, but the very long coastline means that its total area is nevertheless great. Rivers are generally small and steeply graded, without large deltas, and only in the geological trench to the south of Palu does a major lowland valley penetrate far into the interior.[19] The greatest expanses of relatively level terrain are found in inland basins and plateaux, although here too the landscape is usually accidented in detail. On the northern arm the most important of these basins are the plateaux of Minahasa and Mongondow near the tip of the peninsula, and the low-lying Limboto Depression around the lake of the same name in Gorontalo. In Central Sulawesi they include the upper Bongka Valley on the Luwuk Peninsula, the basin of the La River to the west of Kolonodale, the depression surrounding the Poso lake and river in the centre of the island, and a number of smaller valleys in the western highlands.

The geology of the region is very complex (R.W. van Bemmelen 1949, I:389-413; Koperberg 1929) and lies largely outside the scope of this book. Of

[18]   RePPProT 1988, I:258; Whitten, Mustafa and Henderson 1987:497. These figures refer to Sulawesi as a whole, but it is unlikely that the proportions are lower in northern Sulawesi alone. The highest single peak, near the base of the Luwuk Peninsula between Tojo and the Bongka River, reaches 2,865 m (*Peta rupabumi Indonesia* 1992).
[19]   The Koro-Lariang (known in its upper reaches as the Tawaelia) is fully 225 km long due to its eccentric course, but this is exceptional (Whitten, Mustafa and Henderson 1987:258).

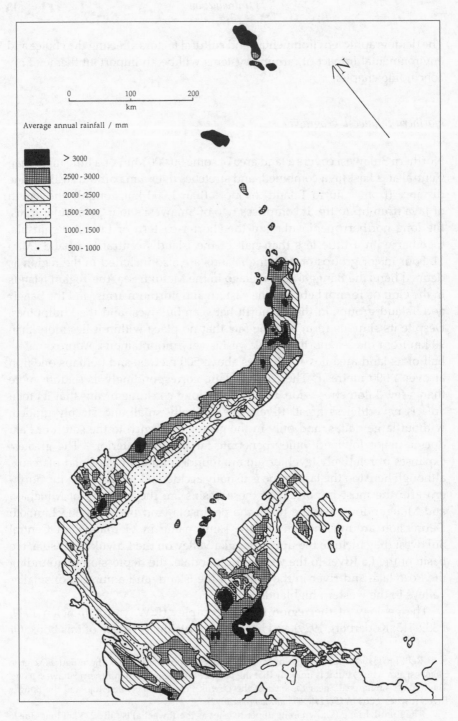

0   100   200
km

Average annual rainfall / mm

> 3000
2500 - 3000
2000 - 2500
1500 - 2000
1000 - 1500
500 - 1000

Map 3. Northern Sulawesi: rainfall (redrawn from Fontanel and Chantefort 1978: Indonésie III)

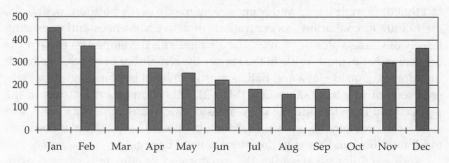

West monsoon maximum: Mapanget (west coast of Minahasa)

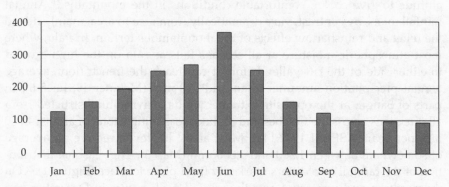

East monsoon maximum: Banggai

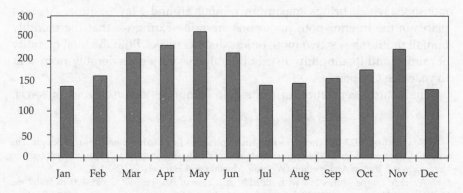

Double maximum: Kantewu (upland western Central Sulawesi)

Figure 1. Average monthly rainfall (mm) at selected locations in northern Sulawesi. Sources: ASEAN 1982:15, 152 (Mapanget, Banggai); Kornrumpf 1935:61 (Kantewu).

considerable significance for agriculture and demography, however, is the fact that the Sangir Island and Minahasa, at the tip of the northern peninsula, are unique in containing concentrations of active volcanoes and consisting largely of young volcanic rocks.[20] The alkaline soils developed on these rocks are generally the most fertile in the region, the remainder of which, like much of Indonesia outside Java and Bali, is mostly covered by thin, slightly weathered soils of low base saturation (Map 2). Other important features of the regional soil map include the large areas of calcareous (limestone) and acid soils (both problematic types for farming purposes) between Lake Poso and the Tomori Bay, and the thin limestone soils of Banggai.

Northern Sulawesi straddles the equator and its climate is tropical, with high temperatures throughout the year at sea level, falling predictably with altitude to give cooler, comfortable conditions in the mountains.[21] Annual rainfall totals, by contrast, vary dramatically from area to area, mainly due to the relief and rainshadow effects of the mountainous terrain. In Palu, where most atmospheric moisture at all seasons falls as rain on the high ground to either side of the rift valley before it can reach the trench floor, average annual precipitation amounts to an arid 550 mm (Metzner 1981a:45-6). In parts of Sangir, at the opposite extreme, winds arriving unobstructed from all directions across the Celebes and Maluku seas bring a total of almost 4,000 mm per year (ASEAN 1982:144). Most areas, however, receive an average of somewhere between 1,500 and 3,000 mm (Map 3). The seasonal distribution of the rainfall also differs markedly from place to place (Figure 1).[22] On the northern and western coasts the rainfall peak occurs in December and January, when the prevailing winds in the region blow from the northwest. On the eastern coasts, by contrast, the wettest period is that of the southeast monsoon, which brings maximum rainfall around May or June. At most places in the interior both monsoons are rain-bearing, so that the monthly rainfall profile shows two more or less distinct peaks. Both the total quantity of rainfall and its monthly distribution always vary considerably from year to year (see Chapters IX, XI).

The natural vegetation of the region comprises diverse types of forest,

---

[20]   Kemmerling 1923-24. There are five such volcanoes in Minahasa, and four in Sangir. The whole of the remainder of the region contains only two, one in Mongondow and another on Unauna in the Togian Archipelago (Whitten, Mustafa and Henderson 1987:10).

[21]   Average temperatures fall with altitude at a rate of 0.6° or 0.7° C per 100 m (Whitten, Mustafa and Henderson 1987:499), so that elevated areas like the Tondano plateau in Minahasa (700 m) have temperatures of about 25° C by day and at 19° C at night (Smits 1909:92; Van der Stok 1900:65).

[22]   See also Boerema 1933; Fontanel and Chantefort 1978: Indonésie III (map); Kornrumpf 1935:60-1, 75-6, 78-9, 83-4; Oldeman and Darmiyati Sjarifuddin 1977:4-8; Whitten, Mustafa and Henderson 1987:21.

Plate 1. Lowland rainforest on the Tomori Bay (eastern Central Sulawesi), as
sketched by a Dutch sea captain in 1850 (Van der Hart 1853: Plate 9)

from forty-metre tall evergreen rain forest in wet lowland areas (Plate 1) to
light, predominantly deciduous monsoon forest in the driest locations; specialized variants occupy unusual local environments such as karst (limestone
with underground drainage) and swampy terrain (Whitten, Mustafa and
Henderson 1987:338-543). The typical number of tree species found within
a 0.5-hectare plot of natural vegetation ranges from fewer than 10 in coastal
mangrove swamps, to almost 60 in the most fertile lowland forests; hill forests vary on the same scale from 30 to 50 species, and monsoon forests have
about 20.[23] Grasses, shrubs, and other pioneer species, rare or absent under
a closed canopy, temporarily colonize the gaps created when large trees die
or fall as a result of storms, landslides, or forest fires. The possible extent of
permanent non-arboreal vegetation under conditions of zero human interference will be discussed in Chapter XIV.

[23]   Whitten, Mustafa and Henderson 1987:33. These figures refer only to trees of 15 cm or more
in diameter at breast height.

Plate 2. Minahasan (Bantik) farmer in working dress with bark-cloth tunic, circa 1890 (KITLV Photograph 4548)

Northern Sulawesi: society

The indigenous population of northern Sulawesi, numbering a little more than 1.1 million in 1930 (*Volkstelling* 1933-36, V:123), belongs to the same broad Austronesian linguistic and genetic grouping which also encompasses the rest of Indonesia west of the Moluccas, and its ancestors are thought to have been present on the island for several thousand years (Bellwood 1997: 118). In the following outline I attempt to identify some characteristic features of its traditional social organization, and also to give an impression of the local diversity which it always displayed. Agriculture and other economic activities will be sketched in Chapter II, while many further details on those aspects of social behaviour relevant to demographic change appear elsewhere in the book.

Early European accounts of the societies in the region portray the same paradoxical combination of political decentralization and social mobility on the one hand, with inequality and slavery on the other, which was characteristic to a greater or lesser degree of all parts of precolonial Southeast Asia, and which made a particularly baffling impression on Spanish observers in the Philippines (Reid 1988-93, I:120; W.H. Scott 1985:96-7). An acute concern with status and hierarchy, it appeared, went hand in hand with a remarkably democratic political process. In Minahasa, for instance, local decisions were said to be taken 'by majority verdict' (Padtbrugge 1866:314), and leaders elected 'by majority vote'.[24] Yet in other respects, the society was far from egalitarian. 'Contrasts between superiors and inferiors', in fact, were 'a guiding principle in Minahasan thought and action' (Schouten 1998:32).

> Although anyone may be chosen to exercise power among the Alfurs [uplanders] of Minahasa, they are certainly not indifferent to whether an individual belongs to the *pahangaranan* (from *ngaran*, name or repute), the *ahakai um banua* (elite of the village), the *suruh ne pahangaranan* (nobility in general), or to the *ata* (slaves) or *suruh ne ata* (descendants of slaves) (Riedel 1872b:565).

Individuals and kin groups struggled constantly to improve their position (and to some extent that of their descendants) within this hierarchy by achieving success in agriculture or war, by attaching themselves to influential patrons, or by otherwise accumulating enough resources to hold potlatch-like, status-boosting feasts of merit (Schouten 1998:22-38). While the degree and rigidity of social stratification varied somewhat from area

---

[24] AR Manado to Gov. Moluccas, 10-6-1832 and 1-10-1832 (ANRI Manado 77). Also Besluiten Res. Manado, 20-3-1834 and 5-5-1834 (ANRI Manado 70). To some extent, it should be added, these descriptions may already reflect the influence of European norms; older sources, however, suggest a similar pattern (Riedel 1872b:525; Watuseke and Henley 1994:369).

to area, the structure was always flat-topped rather than pyramidal. In the more centralized or state-like polities, power was usually shared by an oligarchy of nobles referred to in Malay as the *bangsa*.[25] These appointed one or more of their number as *raja* or 'king' to adjudicate disputes between them, to represent them on diplomatic occasions, and also to perform certain ceremonial or religious functions: in many areas, for instance, the leader, as guardian of the fertility of the land, played a central role in agricultural ritual (A.C. Kruyt 1938, I:502, 508; Nourse 1989:5-6). Such *raja* typically had 'just so much influence over their subjects as is necessary in order to resolve the most minor conflicts which arise among them'; as soon as one party in a more serious dispute refused to accept the royal judgement, noted a Dutch official in 1840, 'the distinction between prince and subject disappears, and both stand as equals' (R. Scherius 1847:400). In Gorontalo, the two paramount *raja* (*olongiya*) were elected from a number of genealogically eligible candidates by a council of more than a hundred local chiefs.[26]

> The relationship of the *negeri* [village or domain] heads to the *raja* was not one of subordinate chiefs to their king, but that of lesser *raja* to a paramount chief whom they had chosen themselves. Indeed, the four most prominent *olongiya* [...] were actually equal in rank to the raja, who likewise bore the title of *olongiya*. The *raja*, then, was no more than a *primus inter pares*. (Von Rosenberg 1865:18.)

The main source of noble power, as in other parts of Southeast Asia (Reid 1988-93, I:120-1), was not state office, but access to political backing and labour resources in the form of kin, personal followers, and especially slaves. In 1830 a Dutch official stationed in Gorontalo complained 'that it makes little difference to the chiefs whether or not they are dismissed from office, since they always retain their hereditary slaves [*erfslaven*], who provide them with income and assure them of an idle and independent existence'.[27]

Slave status, besides being hereditable, could also be acquired as a result of debt, crime, or capture in war.[28] 'Among all of the tribes', notes an early description of Central Sulawesi, 'it is possible for nobles and commoners to fall into slavery' (Riedel 1886:83). Most slaves spent only a part of their working time serving their masters, and European observers usually regard-

[25]   Different members of the *bangsa* bore different titles borrowed from foreign languages, but there was little or no functional differentiation between them (Adriani and Kruyt 1898:406; A.C. Kruyt 1938, I:42).

[26]   AR Gorontalo to Res. Manado, 16-8-1830 (ANRI Manado 115), 11-6-1836 (ANRI Manado 116).

[27]   AR Gorontalo to Res. Manado, 26-1-1830 (ANRI Manado 115).

[28]   Hissink 1912:107-10, A.C. Kruyt 1911, 1938, I:512-21, R. Scherius 1847:402-3, Schouten 1998: 31-2, and Steller 1866:40-4 provide general accounts of slavery in (respectively) the Palu Valley, western Central Sulawesi and the Poso area, Gorontalo, Minahasa, and Sangir.

ed their treatment as mild.[29] Where taxes or labour services were levied by chiefs or *raja*, moreover, slaves, as a rule, were not directly liable, their only obligations being to their owners (Sarasin and Sarasin 1905, I:172; Wilken and Schwarz 1867c:383). Slaves, on the other hand, were sometimes killed at élite funerals or other ceremonies demanding human sacrifice (A.C. Kruyt 1911: 64, 73-4; Schouten 1998:32). In most areas some slaves were also sold on occasion for export, although the perception that this was an extravagant waste of resources (Adriani 1915:468) tended to restrict the scale of slave trading, as did the fact that in many cases the rights to a single slave were shared by the members of a whole kin group, among whom a consensus had to be reached before the individual in question could be disposed of.[30] The capture of slaves was a common aim of local warfare (Adriani and Kruyt 1912-14, I:87; Graafland 1867-69, I:272, 286), while more or less commercial slave raiding by pirates originating from outside the region formed a constant danger for coast-dwellers until the second half of the nineteenth century (Chapter XI).

Descent in these societies was traced along both male and female lines, so that each individual was regarded as belonging to a number of descent groups, rather than exclusively to a single lineage or clan. In many areas, however, the female line was more significant than the male in terms of inheritance and residence patterns. Among the inhabitants of the Poso Valley, for instance, the principal corporate kinship group consisted of 'a set of siblings (*to saana*, children of one mother) and their families who shared an undivided inheritance of exchange goods'; this inheritance, made up of water buffalo, valuable textiles, and brassware, 'was managed by the co-resident matrifocal stem family on behalf of its non-resident kin for several generations' (Schrauwers 1997: 365). Such a stem family comprised between four and sixteen matrilaterally related households, all living in a single large house called a *banua*.[31] Upon marriage, a man left his own *banua* and went to live in that of his wife's family. In Buol, patterns of residence after marriage likewise showed a 'strong matrilocal tendency' and the 'very large' traditional dwellings always housed 'a to a greater or lesser degree matrilineal kin group' (Van Wouden 1941:392). In Sangir and Talaud, too, a 'big house' or *bale* was 'occupied by a traceable exogamic matrilineal kinship group, that is, husband and wife with children, grandchildren and great-grandchildren in the female line'.[32] The number of

---

[29]   Adriani 1901:240-1; Adriani and Kruyt 1912-14, I:161-2; Van Delden 1844:6-7; Encyclopaedisch Bureau 1912a:25; Gonggrijp 1915:1363; Hissink 1912:107; A.C. Kruyt 1895-97, II:122, 1911:72; Steller 1866:43; Vosmaer 1839:98; Wilken and Schwarz 1867c:383-4.

[30]   A.C. Kruyt 1911:74, 1938, I:516; R. Scherius 1847:403; Steller 1866:44.

[31]   Schrauwers (2000:104) specifies 'from four to six' households, but Adriani and Kruyt (1912-14, II:148) state that although this was the norm, the largest house which they saw contained sixteen families.

[32]   H.Th. Chabot 1969:95. Many sources mention that on marriage, men in Sangir and Talaud

Plate 3. Toraja (Pamona) woman in formal dress, with imported heirloom sarong and bark-cloth jacket, circa 1920 (Adriani and Kruyt 1950-51: Plate 114)

matrilaterally related households in a single *bale* ranged from five to thirty or more.[33]

Partly in connection with these matrifocal aspects of the kinship system, the 'distinctive Southeast Asian pattern' (Reid 1988-93, I:146) of female autonomy in economic and social life was much in evidence. While the formal head of a Sangirese *bale* was always male, 'the women also managed affairs' (H.Th. Chabot 1969:98), and in Central Sulawesi it was typically the senior female members of the matrifocal kin group who controlled its collective inheritance.[34] A seventeenth-century Dutch East Indies Company official warned his successor in office against being 'taken advantage of by the women' in diplomatic negotiations with local communities in North Sulawesi; in the past, he recalled, it had often happened 'that a toothless old woman, even the least respected, suddenly and unexpectedly overturns a good and considered decision which the menfolk are on the point of making' (Van Dam 1931:66). While women mostly exerted their political influence in an indirect way (A.C. Kruyt 1937:20), some also occupied formal leadership positions, up to and including that of *raja*.[35]

In many cases, female authority was linked with the fact that women played a prominent role in pagan religious practice (Adriani 1917; Schouten 1998:34-5). Traditional religion, oriented toward the procurement of long life, fertility, status, and prosperity, involved women as augurers, ritual experts, and communicators with the ancestral and supernatural world.[36]

> The Toraja of Central Sulawesi, in the ideal state of their society, would have been a people of [warrior-]heroes and priestesses. It was the men in their role as head-hunters, and the women as priestesses, who brought back the booty of health and longevity to the members of their tribe from outside its territory. To this end they made long and dangerous journeys: the headhunters to the hostile regions of this Middle World, the priestesses to the Upper- or Underworld. (Adriani 1917:453.)

Women's role in producing the more mundane necessities of life was also great. Clearing and fencing the swidden fields at the beginning of each

---

moved to the house and family of their wife (Encyclopaedisch Bureau 1912a:26; Frieswijck 1902: 431; Hickson 1887:138, 1889:167, 197).

[33]   H.Th. Chabot 1969:95, 98; Van Dinter 1899:360; Hickson 1887:140; Roep 1917:420; Steller 1866:30.

[34]   Acciaioli 1989:xviii; Adriani 1919:40, 1921b:12; Adriani and Kruyt 1912-14, I:153, 1950-51, I: 148; A.C. Kruyt 1938, III:154; Schrauwers 1995b:23; Tillema 1926:221.

[35]   AV Midden Celebes 1906 (ANRI Manado 30); Bleeker 1856:135; Van Hoëvell 1893b:9; A.C. Kruyt 1908:1311-2, 1937:22; *Koloniaal verslag* 1906:59; Nourse 1999:236; Riedel 1870a:108, 1886:83; Von Rosenberg 1865:121; Schrauwers 2000:65, 249.

[36]   Key aspects of indigenous religion, some of which have survived the processes of formal conversion to Christianity and Islam, are summarized by Aragon (1992:228-71, 2000:157-274), Atkinson (1989), Downs (1956), Hekker (1988, 1991), Nourse (1989, 1999), Tauchmann (1968), and Van Wylick (1941:17-80, 104-64).

agricultural season (see Chapter II) were male tasks, and men often participated in sowing too, making planting holes with dibbling sticks while the
women followed behind them with seed (Chapter XI, Plate 16).[37] Women
and girls, however, were largely responsible for weeding, guarding the
crops against pests, harvesting, and threshing and hulling the rice, while the
majority of domestic handicraft activities, most importantly the production
of clothing, were likewise female preserves. 'The men', complained a seventeenth-century Jesuit missionary on Siau (Sangir), 'do no work to speak
of; they only make war, fish, cut wood, and build huts; everything else is
left to the women'.[38] The relatively heavy female workload, on the other
hand, reflected a high degree of economic independence (Aragon 2000:79).
Combined with the help which a woman could always expect from her co-
resident blood relatives, it meant that 'up to a certain point, she can say that
she does not need a man', and gave her 'a feeling of independence, so that
she does not regard herself as the servant of her husband' (A.C. Kruyt 1938,
III:133). Marriage gifts flowed mainly (although not exclusively) from the
kin of the groom to that of the bride (bride price), and partly for this reason,
prospective parents reported either neutral attitudes regarding the gender of
their children (Graafland 1867-69, I:302; Woensdregt 1929b:357), or a positive
preference for girls.[39]

Despite the individualistic tenor of the culture, individual property rights,
as already indicated with respect to slaves and inherited prestige goods, were
weakly developed. Over large parts of Central Sulawesi, for example, all of the
swidden fallow land controlled by a single village was 'owned' collectively
by all of the villagers, and redistributed in a different way each year (Adriani
and Kruyt 1950-51, III:24-7). Even where farmland was hereditable within
smaller kin groups, as in more densely populated areas like Minahasa and
Sangir, it was seldom divided up among its inheritors with the passing of each
generation, but instead remained subject to multiple claims, typically recon-
ciled by rotation of use rights among the entitled households.[40] Periodically,
a more permanent division would nevertheless become inevitable as a result
of mutual disagreement, population growth, or the dissolution of the descent
group as a corporate unit (A.C. Kruyt 1938, III:154); in Minahasa the result

---

[37]   Adriani and Kruyt 1912-14, II:249-50, 253; A.C. Kruyt 1900a:227-8, 1930b:541, 1932d:481, 1934:
131, 1937:14; J. Kruyt 1924:152; Padtbrugge 1866:324; Stokking 1922a:247; Woensdregt 1928:200.
[38]   Jacobs 1974-84, III:476; C. Wessels 1935:108. Many later observers also made almost identical comments regarding Sangir (Van der Crab 1875:338; Van Delden 1844:380; Van Dinter
1899:344; *Generale missiven* IX:530; Steller 1866:28, 35-6).
[39]   Adriani and Kruyt 1912-14, II:41, 1950-51, II:336; Van Doren 1854-56, II:142; A.C. Kruyt
1903b:195, 1933b:70, 1938, II:191.
[40]   Van Dinter 1899:352; Holleman 1930:56, 72; Li 1991:42; *Rapport* 1910:5; Tergast 1936:134;
G.A. Wilken 1873:112.

Plate 4. Pagan uplanders ('Alfurs') of eastern Central Sulawesi, with elevated pile-
dwellings in background, as sketched in 1850 by Van der Hart (1853: Plate 6)

seems to have been a 'perpetual alternation between individual and collective ownership of land' (*Rapport* 1910:59) which continued, despite Dutch
attempts to standardize the former, until the end of the colonial period.[41]

Houses and other structures, almost without exception, were built of
wood and bamboo and elevated above the ground on piles, sometimes to
a floor height of four metres or more (Plate 4).[42] The houses in the nuclear
settlements, as already noted with respect to Poso and Sangir, were typically
large, containing, as a Portuguese description from the mid-sixteenth century already records, 'a whole kinship group [*toda huma parentera*], divided
into compartments [*cellas*] on both sides of a central corridor'.[43] On Talaud

[41]   Holleman 1930:44-59; Van Marle 1922, I:68, 73. There is evidence, however, that both corporate kin groups and patterns of collective land ownership had been more stable in the precolonial
past (see Chapter XII).
[42]   Graafland 1898, I:173; Riedel 1872b:493, 1872c:193, 1886:80; Tillema 1922:230-1; Wanner
1914:80. A floor height of about 2 m, however, seems to have been more usual (Adriani and
Kruyt 1912-14, II:151; Hickson 1887:140). Kaudern (1925) provides a general survey of traditional
architecture in the western part of Central Sulawesi.
[43]   De Sá 1955:328. See also Van der Capellen 1855:359, 362; De Clercq 1872, 1883:119; *Fragment* 1856:27; Graafland 1867-69, I:270, II:55; Van Hoëvell 1892:357; Olivier 1834-37, I:317;

these big houses apparently featured a modular construction and could be extended to accommodate new households in the manner of a Borneo longhouse (Hickson 1887:140), although this was not typical for the region as a whole. Many other local variations also existed. Whereas it was usual, for instance, for each nuclear family either to have its own cooking-place or to share this with one other, the 'four to six families' which shared a house in some parts of western Central Sulawesi also shared a single communal hearth (Aragon 1992:39). Smaller single- or double-hearth dwellings, in the nuclear settlements as well as scattered among the swidden fields, were also reported from several other parts of the region prior to the colonial intervention which eventually made this pattern almost universal.[44]

Despite some recurrent patterns, it must be stressed, northern Sulawesi was always characterized by great cultural diversity, so that almost no ethnographic generalization is valid for the whole region. While slavery was a characteristic institution, for instance, there were nevertheless some groups in Central Sulawesi which included almost no slaves (Adriani and Kruyt 1912-14, I:156-7; A.C. Kruyt 1938, I:512). Whereas in most areas residence after marriage, in accordance with the usual Southeast Asian pattern (Reid 1988-93, I:147), was traditionally uxorilocal, among at least one of the Minahasan ethnic groups (the Tombulu) it seems to have been virilocal, in a house containing many nuclear families related on the male rather than the female side – the patrilineal mirror image, in other words, of the Toraja *banua* or the Sangirese *bale* as described above.[45]

This last contrast in social organization was probably related to variations in the extent of male absence. The limited demand for male labour in agriculture after the planting season meant that men typically had much time for other activities, and in many areas this was largely spent away from home on military and commercial expeditions. 'While the women are harvesting',

---

Padtbrugge 1866:321; Pietermaat, De Vriese and Lucas 1840:135; Riedel 1864b:276, 1870a:128, 1872b:493, 1872c:193; Tillema 1922:231; Wilken and Schwarz 1867c:331-2.

[44]   Adriani and Kruyt 1950-51, I:183-4; AV Manado 1833 (ANRI Manado 48); *Fragment* 1856:73; A.C. Kruyt 1930a:370, 1932a:345, 1932b:31, 1932c:76; Pietermaat, De Vriese and Lucas 1840:135; A.J.F. Jansen, 'Missive Sangir en Talaud Eilanden', 26-8-1857 (ANRI Manado 166); Scalliet 1995: 409-10; Schouten 1998:20; Schrauwers 2000:247; Schwarz 1903:122; Van de Velde van Cappellen 1858-59:329.

[45]   Padtbrugge 1866:321; Riedel 1872b:505-6; G.A. Wilken 1883:732, 734-5. Another source for the Tombulu even describes a duolocal (natolocal) system in which husband and wife continued to live apart, in their respective patrifocal big houses, after marriage (Riedel 1895a:93). Among the neighbouring Tontemboan and Bantik, by contrast, marriage traditionally seems to have been neolocal following a temporary uxorilocal phase (Mandagi 1914:61-2; Schouten 1978: 18-9). Recent accounts which identify neolocal marriage as the traditional pattern throughout Minahasa (S. van Bemmelen 1987:189; Hekker 1993:67) overlook the fact that at least among the Tombulu and Tondano, large multiple-hearth houses were the norm in precolonial times.

noted the missionary A.C. Kruyt (1938, IV:158) in one of his ethnographies of Central Sulawesi, 'the men go on journeys: in olden times to trade or to make war on enemies, in recent times to earn money by gathering and selling forest products, making salt, building boats, and suchlike'. In Sangir, likewise, sea-borne trading expeditions took many men away from home for long periods (Steller 1866:36-7). In Minahasa, by contrast, temporary or seasonal male emigration was never so common, and men spent much more time at home. The direction of causality in the relationship between economic and kinship patterns is unclear; while the uncomfortable degree of subservience which Toraja men were expected to show to the affinal relatives in whose houses they lived was said to be one direct reason for the custom of seasonal emigration (A.C. Kruyt 1938, III:134), it is also possible that the predominance of the matriline in Central Sulawesi and Sangir was itself a consequence of frequent male absence. Patrilocal residence in Minahasa, conversely, may have been related either to the limited economic need for male emigration in this area of relatively abundant agricultural resources (see Chapter XI), or to the use of unusually labour-intensive farming techniques (see Chapter XV) which required the men to stay at home in order to boost the agricultural workforce.[46]

If patterns of gender relations varied between pagan groups, conversion to the world religions (of which more below) was associated with deeper changes in the position of women. Muslim immigrants and converts tended to promote the ideal of female domesticity, even seclusion, which prevailed in the Bugis-Makasar world of South Sulawesi.[47] Women in Gorontalo, the part of the region with the longest history of Islamization, were reported in the 1820s to take 'no part whatsoever' in agricultural work, 'not even in winnowing the *padi*'.[48] Later sources from Gorontalo confirm that rice harvesting is a male task (Riedel 1870a:82), and that 'only men' work in the *sawah* fields.[49] In the Islamic trading settlements of Central Sulawesi, likewise, female workloads were said to be lighter than in the uplands, since 'women are more respected by the Muslims than by the unconverted Toraja, among

[46] Boomgaard (1999) discusses similar difficulties of interpretation with respect to the kinship and migration patterns of various ethnic groups in Sumatra.
[47] H.Th. Chabot 1950:143-5; Pelras 1996:161-2. In Tolitoli in the early twentieth century, Bugis immigrants, unlike indigenous pagan men, were reported to 'keep their wives in the home if this is at all possible' (Kortleven 1927:69).
[48] AV Gorontalo 1829 (ANRI Gorontalo 3). A complication here, however, is that many Gorontalese women specialized at this period in the weaving of cotton cloth for export (see Chapter II), so that Islam was not the only factor behind their 'domestication'.
[49] Morison 1931:51. These statements may, however, be somewhat exaggerated; my own inquiries (interviews, Gorontalo, October 1994) suggest that only well-to-do men could afford to spare their wives all work in the fields. Harvesting, in most other areas, was a female affair, although in Minahasa (Francis 1860:348) and Mori (A.C. Kruyt 1900a:228), both men and women participated.

whom they have to work hard' (A.C. Kruyt 1903b:198). The price of this less arduous life, on the other hand, was a loss of personal autonomy; a pagan woman who married a lowlander and adopted Islam, in the words of the missionary-linguist Adriani (1901:220), 'exchanges the independent position which she would enjoy in a marriage with a member of her own tribe for a much more modest status in the Islamized *padangka* [trader] society'. Christian missionaries themselves, while denying any interest in lowering the status of indigenous women, also tended to favour a more exclusively domestic role for their female converts (Bickmore 1868:365; Schouten 1995b), although for a long time the burden of compulsory labour services imposed by the colonial state made this impossible in Minahasa (Chapter X).

Northern Sulawesi: political and ethnic geography

The societies of the region, it has been noted, were competitive and fractious; 'eternal rivalry', a phrase chosen by Schouten (1988) to convey the flavour of Minahasan social and cultural life down the centuries, also seems appropriate to other groups.[50] In Central Sulawesi, according to Kruyt (1938, I:524), prominent individuals constantly tested the limits of their influence by accusing their rivals of insulting or injurious behaviour, and demanding recompense in the form of brassware or livestock. Adjudication of such disputes, here and elsewhere in the region, was one of the most important functions of political leaders, a substantial part of whose income often came from the share which they received in any fines paid.[51]

The principal source of solidarity in this fissiparous society was kinship. In Central Sulawesi, declared Adriani (1901:220), 'the bond of kinship is the sole source of security among the native population'; on Sangir, traditionally, the multiple-hearth, matrilineally-structured 'big house' group 'was often compared with a prau: a rift in the family would have the same effect as a prau which breaks in half and sinks; in common opinion, one of the most terrible things that can happen' (H.Th. Chabot 1969:95). Superimposed on the kinship-based pattern of social organization, in most areas, there was also a system of spatial organization into village units, each usually consisting of a localized nuclear settlement and an extended agricultural territory (see Chapter III). The village formed a defensive and ritual unit, regulated disputes among its inhabitants, and was led or represented by a chief or chiefs chosen from among the heads of its major

---

[50]   H.Th. Chabot 1969:95; Cuarteron 1855:103; Henley 1993:41, 44.
[51]   Aragon 1992:54; Van Delden 1844:14, 17, 378; Godée Molsbergen 1928:189; Goedhart 1908: 460; Hissink 1912:99; A.C. Kruyt 1932:341; *Landschap Donggala* 1905:525; Riedel 1872b:512; Steller 1866:27; Watuseke and Henley 1994:370-71.

constituent kin groups.[52] The exact relationship between the village and the corporate kin groups varied from area to area. In Sangir, each of the large villages (*soa*) was in principle an endogamous community, its *bale* or big houses (of which there were typically eight) intermarrying mainly with each other (H.Th. Chabot 1969:95). In the Poso area, by contrast, the two to ten (generally smaller) *banua* (Adriani 1916:110) making up a single village (*lipu*) each formed the core of a spatially extended kin group (*santina*) which also included members living in neighbouring villages.[53]

> For a man to marry in his own village is often impossible; the girls there are either his sisters, or his cousins and nieces, which amounts to almost the same thing. He marries, then, with a girl from another village of his own tribe. Understandably, marriages often take place repeatedly between men and women from the same pairs of villages. Sometimes it is a complex of three or four villages which constantly intermarry with each other in this way. (Adriani 1916:109.)

In Minahasa it was a larger cluster of a dozen or so villages (*ro'ong, wale, wanua*), known collectively as a *walak*, which formed the endogamous unit; as in Poso, such an intermarrying village cluster also featured some degree of central political and ritual leadership.[54] Adriani (1916:110) believed that this kind of incipient political integration was a straightforward consequence of intermarriage. 'If stronger family ties have given rise to more intimate contact between particular villages', he wrote, 'the heads of those villages inevitably have more to do with one another; they then organize themselves automatically, and one becomes the foremost among them'. Where larger units like the *walak* are concerned, however, it seems equally likely that political or economic circumstances favoured the establishment of marriage ties. Factors potentially conducive to the emergence of political communities encompassing more than one village, other than frequent intermarriage, included shared origins as recalled in foundation myths or folk memories (Schouten 1998:19), occasional military cooperation against common enemies (Adriani and Kruyt 1912-14, I:121-2, 124-5), and mutual trade (Schrauwers 1997:370-5). Indigenous classification systems sometimes also facilitated the stable coexistence of equally-matched rival groups, if not their actual unification, by allowing the relationship between them to be

[52]   In Minahasa, until the traditional system was altered by the Dutch administration, most villages had two paramount chiefs (Graafland 1898, I:71; 'Memorie door den afgaande Manados onderprefect Carl Christoph Prediger', 15-9-1809, in ANRI Manado 61).
[53]   In the Poso area, each village as a whole was conceived (or idealized) as a corporate kin group (Adriani and Kruyt 1950-51, I:103-6).
[54]   Schouten 1998:19. According to the earliest reasonably complete village list, which dates from 1849, the largest Minahasan *walak* (district), Tonsea, comprised 32 villages, and the average number was 10 (AV Manado 1849, in ANRI Manado 51).

conceived in terms of sexual complementarity.[55]

Political organization above the level of the kin group and the village was typically loose. The anthropologist Acciaioli (1989:66) agrees with his colonial predecessor Albert C. Kruyt (1938, I:38) that even the 'kingdoms' of the Palu Valley, large and relatively integrated polities by regional standards, were actually 'village clusters' composed of 'independent communities' which 'recognized one of the local village heads as foremost among them'.[56] Further centralization of power, on the whole, was impeded by fierce personal and intercommunal rivalries, rather high levels of local economic self-sufficiency (see Chapter II), and the tendency, well described by Adas (1981) in the context of larger states in Java and Burma, for people to seek less demanding masters (Van Dam 1931:66; A.C. Kruyt 1911:74-5) or less accessible places to live (Adriani 1916:119; Von Rosenberg 1865:18) rather than submit to unwanted authority. Endemic warfare, underpinned by hereditary feuds (Adriani and Kruyt 1912-14, I:202-6; A.C. Kruyt 1938, I:168) and by headhunting traditions with powerful ritual and religious overtones (Downs 1955:40-51; Schouten 1992), prevailed in most parts of the region up to the establishment of Dutch rule.

The most common type of 'petty kingdom' (*rijkje*), as the Dutch called most of the larger indigenous polities, consisted in the first place of a small coastal trading community headed by one or more elected *raja*, but also exercised a certain restricted authority over a larger semi-independent farming population in the adjacent interior. Upland chiefs, for instance, would be chosen by their peers, but receive their formal investiture from the lowland *raja* or his representatives.[57] The sources of this authority (and of much of the income of the coastal elite) were essentially twofold: trade (the supply of valuable imported goods in return for produce of the land), and limited intervention in the conflicts arising among the upland communities, which were exploited either by using (allowing) one group to discipline another (A.C. Kruyt 1938, I:256; Schrauwers 1997:371-2), or by offering relatively

---

[55]   In Minahasa, for instance, the two largest ethnic groups, the Tombulu and Tontemboan, seem to have been categorized in ritual terms as male and female respectively (Henley 1996:47), and the same was true of the 'twin kingdoms' of Gorontalo and Limboto (Korn 1939:77-84). The relationship between the sexes provided a rare model for cooperation between equals among people for whom, as in South Sulawesi as described by Hendrik Chabot (1950:102), equality otherwise tended to be synonymous with rivalry. Upstream/downstream and interior/exterior dualisms, however, were also involved here (Bastiaans 1939:26-8). Leonard Andaya (1993:54-5) describes a similar relationship between binary symbolism and decentralized political organization in the North Moluccas.

[56]   Knaap (1987:10-2) comes to a similar conclusion regarding the 'early states' of the precolonial South Moluccas, which he characterizes as 'village federations'.

[57]   A.C. Kruyt 1930a:359, 1938, I:187. In Minahasa, a version of this practice continued to exist in colonial times (Riedel 1872b:525; Watuseke and Henley 1994:369).

impartial arbitration between the opposing parties.[58] Such upland/lowland political systems, consisting of an often Islamic or Christian coastal capital and a loosely subordinated pagan hinterland, were found in Minahasa and Bolaang Mongondow until the nineteenth century, and in most parts of Central Sulawesi until the early twentieth.[59] Among the lowlanders, and among contemporary European observers, the pagan peoples of the interior were variously known as *alifuru* (in European sources, 'Alfurs'), apparently from a Halmahera (Moluccan) word meaning 'wilderness' (*Encyclopaedie* 1917-39, I:30), by the Bugis term *toraja*, 'uplander' (Adriani and Kruyt 1912-14, I:2), or occasionally by its Malay equivalent *dayak*, more commonly used in Kalimantan (Kortleven 1927:17; A.C. Kruyt 1898:10-1). Where a more precise ethnic specification is unnecessary or impossible, the word Toraja, although technically obsolete except as an ethnonym for the Sa'dang people of South Sulawesi (Schrauwers 1995b:15-6), has been retained in this book with reference to the interior populations of Central Sulawesi.

Besides small village confederacies and upland/lowland political systems, there were also places in the region where something more clearly akin to 'state-formation' took place during precolonial times. By the beginning of the nineteenth century, some 80,000 people in the Gorontalo area lived under the authority of a single political federation known as the Lima lo Pohala'a, variously translated as 'Five Brothers' or 'Five Alliances'.[60] The bipartite core of this polity was formed by the big twin kingdoms of Gorontalo and Limboto, each in itself a complex federation of chiefdoms surmounted by a dual monarchy.[61] Although personal dependency relationships, as already noted, continued to provide its economic foundations, the Gorontalo state also featured a rather sophisticated system of taxation linked with 'public' office rather than personal service. Its various officials, for instance, were reportedly entitled to a tenth part of all the rice and maize harvested by its subjects, together with regular corvée labour services from the free population and, on a more continuous basis, the labour of a special group of royal slaves which served the incumbent political leaders regardless of their identity.[62] Private slave-owners, moreover, had lost the right to exclusive control over their own slaves, one category of which (called *mongoohule*) was obliged to perform the same

[58]   A.C. Kruyt 1938, I:177; Watuseke and Henley 1994:360. B.W. Andaya (1993a:95, 1993b:31-2) describes similar bases for royal (downstream) authority in precolonial Sumatra.
[59]   In the case of Minahasa, however, the position of the indigenous *raja* was taken over by Dutch VOC representatives in the late seventeenth century (Henley 1996:31-4).
[60]   Riedel 1870a:46; Nur 1979:51. The number is conventional or symbolic; in reality there appear to have been six component states (see Chapter V).
[61]   Bastiaans 1938, 1939; Haga 1931; Korn 1939:74-97; Nur 1979; Riedel 1870a.
[62]   AV Gorontalo 1841-1843 (ANRI Manado 50), 1845 (KITLV H 111); Reinwardt 1858:510-1; Riedel 1870a:66, 74-5; Von Rosenberg 1865:25-6; R. Scherius 1847:403. There were also certain monopoly trade privileges, and a tax on the fish catch from Lake Limboto.

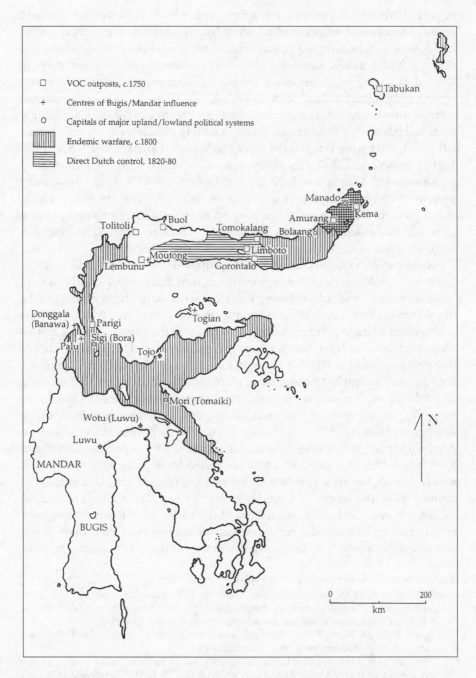

Map 4. Northern Sulawesi: aspects of political geography, 1750-1880

state corvée duties as free commoners.[63] Reid (1983:19, 1988-93, I:132) identifies this kind of restriction on private slavery as a key index of state formation
in Southeast Asian societies. Another such index, arguably, is the elimination
of internal warfare. Although a headhunting tradition does originally seem
to have existed in Gorontalo (Bastiaans 1938:228), and a series of destructive
local wars, exacerbated by the interference of outside powers, was fought
there in the middle of the seventeenth century (Bastiaans 1938:232-6; Tiele and
Heeres 1886-95, III:358-9, 388-90), this area was consistently free from serious
internal violence after the conclusion of a formal treaty of alliance between
Gorontalo and Limboto in 1673.[64]

The Sangir Archipelago, another area of sizeable indigenous kingdoms
without a clearly distinct 'Alfur' or tribal population, was also substantially
at peace from about 1680 onward, despite the fact that in this case no formal
overcapping federation was formed. Banggai, the site of an important indigenous state since the sixteenth century or earlier (L.Y. Andaya 1993:85-6; A.C.
Kruyt 1931), was a third part of the region where nineteenth- and early twentieth-century visitors detected no headhunting (Bosscher and Matthijssen
1854:97; A.C. Kruyt 1932c:249). Assuming that this peace was also of long
standing, the approximate distribution of zones of endemic warfare around
1800 is reconstructed, along with other aspects of the political geography
of the region in the eighteenth and nineteenth centuries, on Map 4.[65] In
Bolaang Mongondow, finally, a late episode of indigenous state-formation
occurred in the middle of the nineteenth century, not long before the onset
of direct colonial intervention. This development, parallelling (and perhaps
partly inspired by) contemporary changes in neighbouring Dutch Minahasa,
involved a rapid consolidation of the power of the coastal (Bolaang) chiefs
over the upland (Mongondow) interior, and was reflected in the cessation of
internal warfare (De Clercq 1883:121; Veenhuizen 1903:74), the construction
of new unfortified settlements in accessible locations (Schwarz and De Lange
1876:162-4, 178; Wilken and Schwarz 1867c:293), and the formulation or revision of a written legal code (Dunnebier 1949:256-8; Menopo 1893).

---

[63]   'Pengatoran pusaka di Gorontalo', 29-4-1828 (ANRI Gorontalo 18).
[64]   Bastiaans 1938:219. Although Dutch officials, in later times, were inclined to take the credit
for this peace (AV Gorontalo 1852, in ANRI Gorontalo 3), it was established well before the
arrival of a Dutch garrison in Gorontalo in 1729. External relationships between the Lima lo
Pohala'a and its neighbours, it should be added, were anything but peaceful; the relatively high
levels of cooperation prevailing within the federation, indeed, enabled it to augment its population by organizing effective slave raids against the kingdoms around the Gulf of Tomini (Riedel
1870b:556-8; Tacco 1935:79).
[65]   The position of Buol and Tolitoli, shown here as peaceful in 1800, is somewhat unclear: a
source from 1745 mentions human sacrifice in Tolitoli (*Corpus diplomaticum* V:394), but headhunting was said to be rare in Buol by 1831 (AR Gorontalo to Res. Manado, 21-10-1831, in ANRI
Manado 115).

While cause and effect are hard to disentangle in the complex processes of precolonial state formation (a thorough analysis of which is in any case well beyond the scope of this study), it can be concluded that the consolidation of larger political units was usually associated with a relatively intensive involvement in commerce.[66] In the sixteenth century, for instance, it was the sultanate of Banggai which controlled the trade in iron, probably Sulawesi's oldest major export product (see Chapter II), from Tobungku and Mori (Reid 1988-93, I:110). Gorontalo and Sangir, from an almost equally early date, exported gold and coconut oil respectively.[67] The late episode of indigenous state formation in Bolaang Mongondow occurred during a period when Mongondow was exporting increasing quantities of cocoa, and probably also coffee (Riedel 1864b:275, 277). In Parigi on the south coast of the Gulf of Tomini, conversely, an episode of political disintegration toward the end of the nineteenth century (Adriani and Kruyt 1898:390-4, 399; A.C. Kruyt 1892:247-8), leading to the dispersal of the population and the abandonment of irrigated ricefields (Engelenberg 1906:10-1; *Koloniaal verslag* 1906:59), coincided with the rise of Gorontalo (Van Hoëvell 1891:42-3; Van Musschenbroek 1880:97), largely at Parigi's expense, as the dominant commercial entrepôt for the lands around the Gulf.[68]

Although explicit historical clues are scarce, it is useful to note some of the ways in which trade might have been conducive both to pacification and to the establishment of relatively centralized political authority. The link between indebtedness and slavery, firstly, has already been noted, and it appears that debt was also associated with other forms of hierarchy: in 1809, a Dutch official in Manado wrote that 'at least nine tenths of the natives are in debt to one or another of their *hukum* [chiefs]'.[69] If indebtedness led to political dependency, then any small group which could secure preferential access to scarce and desirable foreign goods was no doubt in a position to consolidate its power.[70] In some cases the additional labour demand created

[66] Junker (1999:3-28) discusses the relationship between foreign trade and 'sociopolitical evolution' with special reference to the precolonial Philippines, where the political situation was very similar to that in northern Sulawesi. Also W.H. Scott 1994:129.

[67] Dutch conflict mediation, on the other hand, also played a role in the pacification of Sangir (*Corpus diplomaticum* III:88, 96, 108-9, 363, V:64, 473, 569, 579, 596; Lobs 1686; Van Schoonderwoerdt 1766).

[68] By 1911 the overland trade route across the base of the northern peninsula, on which the wealth of Parigi had been based (see Chapter II), was said to have 'not the slightest economic significance' (Boonstra van Heerdt 1914b:759).

[69] 'Memorie door den afgaande Manados onderprefect Carl Christoph Prediger', 15-9-1809 (ANRI Manado 61). In nineteenth-century Gorontalo, comparably, the production of cotton textiles for export (see Chapter II) was undertaken largely by the wives of debt-bondsmen, 'who, thanks to what is often a petty debt, remain in lifelong servitude to their creditors' (AV Gorontalo 1854, in ANRI Gorontalo 3).

[70] This, of course, raises the question of how such exclusivity could be maintained, an issue to which I will return in Chapter XII.

by commercial activities, as Warren (1981, 1998) has argued in the context of the Sulu sultanate and the collection and processing of *tripang* (edible sea cucumbers) for export, may also have increased the incentive for such leaders to concentrate large numbers of people in their vicinity; the availability of trade wealth to distribute among followers and henchmen, meanwhile, both encouraged voluntary immigration (even at the cost of political submission) and eased the organizational problems involved in mounting slave-raiding expeditions.[71]

On a more benign note, a relatively strong political leadership often played a facilitating or functional role in the independent commerce of its subjects by providing military protection for traders and by helping to guarantee (unwritten) trade contracts – an important service given that most trade was based on long-term credit.[72] But is also likely that as Dobbin (1983:123-8, 135) has argued in the case of eighteenth-century West Sumatra, trade tended to exert a pacifying influence even in the absence of political hierarchy. By common consent of the Toraja tribes, according to one account of the boom in commercial forest products which took place in Central Sulawesi toward the end of the nineteenth century (see Chapter II), the Sumara Valley in Mori (eastern Central Sulawesi) was declared 'neutral territory', and placed out of bounds for headhunters, when it became the main route via which these products were exported (A.C. Kruyt 1930b:505). In many cases, commerce probably also pacified simply by taking up time which would otherwise have been spent on violence. The traditional swidden-farming economies of the region, it has been noted, featured considerable underemployment of male labour. Among the Toraja, according to Kruyt (1938, II:55), war was just one of the activities (others included hunting and gambling) which 'filled up in an exciting way the time in which the men's labour was not required in agriculture'. When profitable alternatives such as forest product collection became available, then, interest in headhunting probably declined to some extent for reasons of time allocation alone.

The three-way correlation between religious conversion, pacification, and commerce, finally, also deserves attention here. Gorontalo, where Islam was apparently introduced from Ternate in the late sixteenth century (Bastiaans 1938:231-2), was the first part of the region to undergo such a conversion.[73] In Sangir, a large part of the population was formally converted to Christianity

---

[71]   Both coerced and voluntary immigration were involved, for instance, in the consolidation of the Lima lo Pohala'a during the eighteenth century (see Chapters V and VI).

[72]   Adriani and Kruyt 1912-14, II:302; 1950-51, III:341; NA VOC 1775:225-6; De Clercq 1883: 118.

[73]   The Islamization of Gorontalo, nevertheless, was a long process which did not approach completion until the end of the nineteenth century (Riedel 1870a:98-9; Gonggrijp 1915:1366; Van Hoëvell 1891:31).

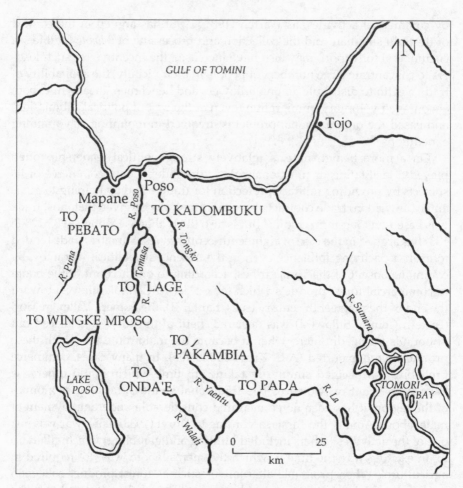

Map 5. To Pamona (in Poso and Mori): ethnic subgroups

by Spanish and Dutch missionaries in the course of the seventeenth century.[74]
The Palu Bay, another concentration of relatively large indigenous polities, was
the site of an Islamic enclave by the 1790s (Woodard 1969:107-8). Although
occasional wars continued to be fought in the Palu area during the nineteenth
century, Europeans who visited it on the eve of the colonial conquest observed
that ritual headhunting had ceased, and that the village temples or *lobo*, in
which pagan groups elsewhere displayed skulls and other trophies of war,
had been replaced by mosques and Muslim prayer-houses (*Landschap Donggala*
1905:519; Sarasin and Sarasin 1905, II:9). Mongondow, still pagan at the begin-

---

[74]   The Christianization of Sangir and Talaud is described by Coolsma (1893, 1901:633-73),
Brilman (1938:94-183), and C. Wessels (1935:100-34).

ning of the nineteenth century, became substantially Muslim during the period of its political integration between 1830 and 1900.[75] Although detailed information is often lacking, most of these conversions were associated either directly or indirectly with trade. In the nineteenth century, Muslim traders of Bugis, Arab, and Minangkabau descent were the main groups responsible for spreading Islam in Central Sulawesi and Bolaang Mongondow.[76] If only by weakening the pagan conviction that bloodshed (including headhunting and human sacrifice) was an intrinsic source of well-being, conversion to Islam or Christianity probably reinforced the transition to more peaceful conditions which was also promoted by other changes associated with commerce.[77]

The pattern of indigenous ethnic identities and boundaries was complex. In the Poso area, the 'tribes' referred to by Adriani represented geographical subdivisions of a single language group (the speakers of Pamona, or Bare'e as it was known in colonial times), each occupying a territory which in many cases coincided with a single river valley (Schrauwers 2000:65). Map 5 shows the approximate locations, as described in sources from the end of the nineteenth century and the beginning of the twentieth, of those Pamona subgroups which are mentioned in the following chapters.[78] Although most were acephalous in political terms, the villages and village federations which made up each one shared common genealogical origins as remembered in oral tradition (Adriani and Kruyt 1912-14, I:119-20). In multilingual Minahasa, by comparison, the principal foci of ethnic identity above and beyond the *walak* or 'districts' (of which there were 27 in the first half of the nineteenth century) were provided by the eight local language groups, four of which also became the bases for colonial administrative divisions. The political and ethnic geography of Minahasa, an area which figures prominently throughout this book, is sketched in Maps 6 and 7.[79]

Although all belong to the same branch of the Austronesian language

---

[75] De Clercq 1883:121, 125; Schwarz and De Lange 1876:163, 172-3; Riedel 1864b:277-8; Sarasin and Sarasin 1905, I:86; Wilken and Schwarz 1867b:276-83.

[76] Adriani and Kruyt 1912-14, I:298-9; A.C. Kruyt 1938, III:3; Wilken and Schwarz 1867b:276-7. In the case of Sangirese Christianity, admittedly, this connection is less obvious or direct. It is interesting to note, nevertheless, that in the eighteenth century both the Christian schoolteachers appointed by the Dutch on Sangir, and the clergymen who supervised them, were involved in trade (Buddingh 1860:352).

[77] Nominally Muslim populations sometimes continued to engage in headhunting (Adriani and Kruyt 1912-14, I:360; A.C. Kruyt 1900a:222; Vosmaer 1839:105), but the signs are that they did so less often, and in a context of inter-state conflict rather than individual revenge or village ritual. A Dutch source from 1831, for instance, states that in Buol it is 'not customary for the natives to hunt heads unless they are ordered to do so by their ruler – at least, that is, among the Muslims' (AR Gorontalo to Res. Manado, 21-10-1831, in ANRI Manado 115).

[78] Their names were prefixed 'To', a common word for 'people' in the languages of the region.

[79] Several of the *walak* (Klabat, Tondano, Tombasian, Rumo'ong) had both an upland (*atas*) and a coastal (*bawah*) centre of settlement (Map 6).

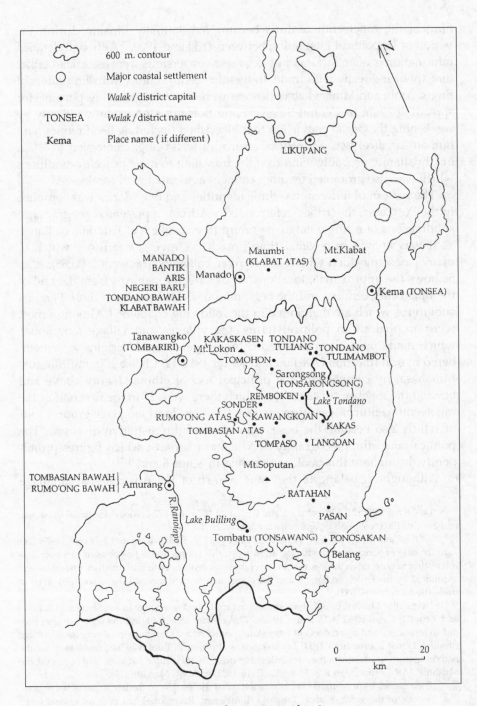

600 m. contour

○ Major coastal settlement

• *Walak* / district capital

TONSEA *Walak* / district name

Kema Place name (if different)

N

LIKUPANG

Maumbi
(KLABAT ATAS)

Mt.Klabat

MANADO
BANTIK
ARIS
NEGERI BARU
TONDANO BAWAH
KLABAT BAWAH

Manado

Kema (TONSEA)

Tanawangko
(TOMBARIRI)

KAKASKASEN   TONDANO
Mt.Lokon   TULIANG   TONDANO
      TOMOHON   TULIMAMBOT

Sarongsong
(TONSARONGSONG)

REMBOKEN   Lake Tondano
SONDER
RUMO'ONG ATAS   KAWANGKOAN
TOMBASIAN ATAS   KAKAS
         TOMPASO   LANGOAN

Mt.Soputan

TOMBASIAN BAWAH
RUMO'ONG BAWAH Amurang

R.Ranoiapo

RATAHAN

PASAN

Lake Buliling

Tombatu (TONSAWANG) • PONOSAKAN

Belang

0   20
     km

Map 6. Minahasa: geographical

family, about 40 distinct languages were (and are) spoken in northern Sulawesi.[80] This diversity reflected the general condition of political fragmentation. In those localities where some degree of political integration existed, conversely, the linguistic situation tended to be relatively homogeneous. A single Sangirese language, for instance, was spoken by more than 50,000 people throughout the Sangir Islands in the mid-nineteenth century, while the great majority of the population of the Lima lo Pohala'a spoke Gorontalese.[81] Dialects of the Kaili language, likewise, were spoken throughout the Palu Valley, and in neighbouring mountain areas as far south as Kulawi (Noorduyn 1991:76-80). The Palu (Ledo) dialect of Kaili was also in use over a much larger area of western Central Sulawesi as a lingua franca for trading purposes.[82] In North Sulawesi, the Moluccan dialect of Malay played the same role.[83]

More difficult to explain in political or commercial terms is the wide distribution of the Pamona language. Approximately 40,000 Pamona-speakers, at the beginning of the twentieth century, inhabited a large part of stateless upland Central Sulawesi, including the whole of the Poso Depression and considerable areas to its south and east.[84] Probably the homogeneity of this group, as well as its wide distribution, had to do with an unusual degree of geographical mobility. Farmers in most parts of the region, as in most parts of Indonesia as a whole, had 'permanent villages and fixed, delineated village territories' (Dove 1985a:9) within which they rotated their swidden fields (see Chapter II). In the Poso Valley, however, a permanent rotation, for reasons discussed in Chapters XIV and XV, was often unsustainable, so that whole villages periodically shifted to new locations. Occasional village movements did also occur elsewhere for political reasons or in response to epidemics, and migration between existing population centres was certainly always a significant aspect of the demographic scene. There is little sign in

---

[80]   Sneddon 1981. This total includes the language spoken by the Bajo 'sea people', but not the Malay (Indonesian) lingua franca or the languages of allochthonous Indonesian groups like the Bugis and Mandar. Noorduyn (1991:9-113) provides a survey of the extensive literature on the languages of North and Central Sulawesi.
[81]   Several minor languages were spoken in peripheral parts of the Gorontalo area, but it is likely that as in recent times (Departemen Pendidikan dan Kebudayaan 1983:17), their speakers were also fluent in Gorontalese.
[82]   Adriani and Kruyt 1912-14, III:350; Esser 1934:1; Boonstra van Heerdt 1914b:753; A.C. Kruyt 1938, I:46; Noorduyn 1991:78.
[83]   Henley 1996:26, 86. In Sangir, where Malay was also the medium of instruction in the Christian schools established during the VOC era, about half of the population (and implicitly all of the men) were said to understand it in the mid-nineteenth century (Van de Velde van Cappellen 1857:55).
[84]   Pamona, moreover, was also widely spoken as a second language in Mori (Adriani and Kruyt 1900:152; A.C. Kruyt 1900a:216).

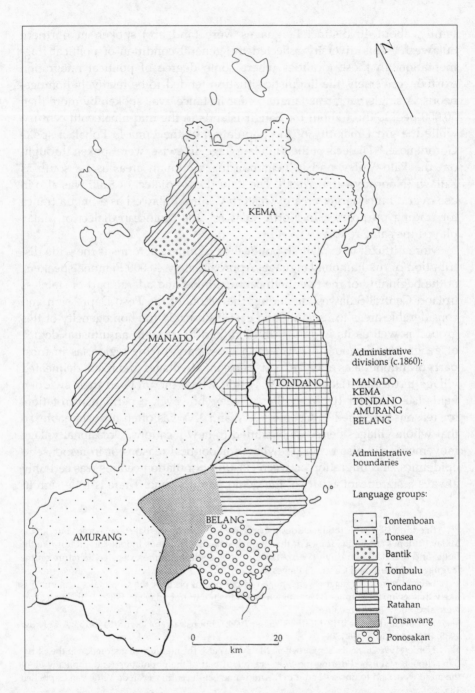

N

KEMA

MANADO

TONDANO

Administrative
divisions (c.1860):

MANADO
KEMA
TONDANO
AMURANG
BELANG

Administrative _____
boundaries

Language groups:

	Tontemboan
	Tonsea
	Bantik
	Tombulu
	Tondano
	Ratahan
	Tonsawang
	Ponosakan

BELANG

AMURANG

0°

0   20
        km

Map 7. Minahasa: linguistic and administrative divisions

the 400-year historical record from northern Sulawesi, however, of the kind of 'waves of migration', involving the permanent displacement of whole ethnic groups, which are described in the literature on Kalimantan.[85]

Northern Sulawesi: European expansion

In the sixteenth and seventeenth centuries northern Sulawesi, despite its rather limited economic significance, saw intervention of various kinds by a number of rival foreign powers (Henley 1993). These included both European (first Portuguese, later Spanish and Dutch) traders based in the nearby Moluccan Spice Islands, and the two most powerful indigenous states of eastern Indonesia, Makassar in South Sulawesi and Ternate in the North Moluccas. Minahasa and parts of Sangir were the targets of considerable Catholic mission activity during this period of competitive intervention, and also hosted an intermittent Spanish military presence (C. Wessels 1933, 1935). Dutch ascendancy, however, was established with the foundation of a permanent VOC (Dutch East Indies Company) fort at Manado in 1657 (Godée Molsbergen 1928:15), and in 1677 the last Spanish stronghold, on the island of Siau in Sangir, was captured by a joint Dutch-Ternatan expedition (Robidé van der Aa 1867). Makassar, meanwhile, had been conquered by the VOC and its Bugis allies in 1669 (L.Y. Andaya 1981:117-36), and Ternate lost the last of its already waning influence in North Sulawesi after an unsuccessful revolt against the Dutch in 1679-1681 (L.Y. Andaya 1993:181-6). Ternate retained nominal sovereignty, however, over Tobungku, Banggai and part of the Luwuk Peninsula, which areas were not transferred to more direct Dutch rule until 1908 (*Koloniaal verslag* 1908:62-3).

In the course of the eighteenth century the Company consolidated its influence in the region by establishing a series of new outposts – beginning in 1729 with Gorontalo (*Generale missiven IX*:9) – which were intended mostly to control gold exports (Map 4).[86] From 1747 to 1795 there was even a Dutch fort in remote Parigi, collecting gold panned in the mountains of western Central Sulawesi (Adriani and Kruyt 1898:410; Colenbrander 1898). This expansion, however, was never very successful in either economic or military terms, and by the time the VOC went bankrupt at the end of the eighteenth century and

---

[85]   Knapen 2001:77-101; MacKinnon et al. 1996:60, 360-1. While many people moved (or were moved) from the coasts of the Tomini Gulf to Gorontalo in the eighteenth century (see Chapters V and VI), for instance, their settlements of origin continued to exist, and remain identifiable on recent maps.

[86]   Henley 1997b:425. It is likely that the sudden Dutch interest in Sulawesi gold, already a significant export product since much earlier times, was related to declining VOC gold exports from Japan in the same period (Glamann 1981:68-9).

its possessions were inherited by the colonial state, all Dutch establishments outside Minahasa had been either destroyed by Indonesian enemies, or withdrawn. Except perhaps for the religious conversions on Sangir, the social impact of European expansion prior to 1800 was limited. In Minahasa, which remained almost entirely pagan, the VOC seems to have inherited the economic and judicial roles of an indigenous coastal kingdom displaced by its arrival – most importantly, the purchase of surplus rice from upland farmers in exchange for imported textiles, and the provision of impartial arbitration between opposing parties in their continuing headhunting wars (Watuseke and Henley 1994:359-61).

The situation in Minahasa was to change dramatically, however, following the collapse of the VOC and two short interludes of British administration between 1797 and 1817.[87] Now this agriculturally productive area became the scene of a dramatic colonial transformation involving complete pacification, the compulsory cultivation of coffee under a state monopoly system, and the construction of a dense road network using corvée labour. Between 1831 and 1891, moreover, the Minahasan population was almost entirely converted to Protestantism under the influence of the Nederlandsch Zendelinggenootschap (NZG, Netherlands Missionary Society).[88] Concurrent changes, later repeated to a greater or lesser degree elsewhere in the region, included the partial dissolution of corporate kin groups larger than the nuclear family (Hekker 1993: 63-72), the provision (and acceptance) of Western-style schooling (Kroeskamp 1974:99-296), the incorporation of political leaders into the colonial state bureaucracy (Schouten 1998:75-104, 127-45), and the regrouping of the population, partly under direct Dutch guidance and partly as a spontaneous response to pacification, in new villages located on the newly-built roads.[89] A permanent Dutch presence was also re-established after the British period in Gorontalo, where the compulsory gold deliveries initiated in VOC times continued (and were replaced in 1850 by a monetary head tax). Most of the region, however, was little affected by the colonial presence until much later in the nineteenth century (Map 4), and the interior of Central Sulawesi was not brought under Dutch control until a series of military actions in the years 1903-1907.[90] Still predominantly pagan at the time of this conquest, from 1909 onward its Toraja populations were gradually converted to Christianity by various Protestant missionary organizations.[91]

---

[87]   Manado was in British hands from 1797 to 1803 (Leupe 1865:287; *Overname van Ternate* 1879: 221-2) and again from 1810 to 1817 (Godée Molsbergen 1928:171-82).
[88]   Coolsma 1901:560-611; Gunning 1924; Henley 1996:52-4; Schouten 1998:105-25.
[89]   *Fragment* 1856:27, 69; Graafland 1867-69, II:10; J.J. ten Siethoff, 'Topografische schetsen van een gedeelte der residentie Manado, 1845' (ANRI Manado 46); Teysmann 1861:350.
[90]   Arts and Van Beurden 1982:99-105; *Koloniaal verslag* 1906:62-3, 1907:67-70, 1908:62-6.
[91]   Aragon 1992:142-83; Adriani 1919:206-58; De Vreede 1950:10, 12-16. In the centre and east of

Another important change associated with the expansion of colonial rule was the abolition of slavery, which took place in different areas at different dates, beginning with Minahasa in 1819. In later chapters I will argue that given the importance of slavery in indigenous social systems, its disappearance was probably often brought about more by concurrent economic and social changes than by the formal prohibition itself; one Dutch resident of Manado commented in 1833 that it was 'solely thanks to the good nature [*goeden aard*] of the population' that this measure had not caused political difficulties for the administration.[92] In Minahasa the ban itself, however enforced, nevertheless seems to have had some effect; when it was issued in 1819, an old man from Tondano later recalled, 'the rich people and the chiefs lost a great deal' (Graafland 1867-69, I:286). The abolition of slavery in Gorontalo in 1859 was followed by considerable emigration of freed slaves from the Limboto Depression (Chapters V, XV), and in the second half of the nineteenth century, efforts were certainly made to identify and punish those violating the bans on slave ownership (and debt-bondage) in Dutch-controlled areas.[93]

Northern Sulawesi: historical sources

Much of the information on which this book is based, and almost all of the statistical material in particular, was originally obtained, often by indigenous investigators acting on European instructions, from indigenous informants. However, the absence (except in Gorontalo) of a significant written historical tradition, together with the inadequacy and opacity of oral history as a guide to such areas as demography, agriculture, or health, means that the sources actually cited here are almost exclusively European.[94] What makes northern Sulawesi especially suitable for the purposes of a study like this is the great number and variety of the relevant European sources available, some of which date back as far as the sixteenth century. Copious administrative statistics on population and food production are complemented by missionary accounts of those aspects of indigenous society (family life and sexual behaviour, for instance) which tended to escape the attention of government officials and explorers.

Central Sulawesi (as in Minahasa) the leading role was played by the NZG, in western Central Sulawesi by the Salvation Army, and in Luwuk and Banggai by the Protestant state church of the Netherlands Indies, the Indische Kerk.

92   AV Manado 1833 (ANRI Manado 48).
93   'Stukken pandelingschap 1850-1882', in ANRI Manado 13.
94   Bastiaans (1938:218, 232, 1939:24) and Nur (1979:4) give some information on the manuscript tradition of Gorontalo, which is mainly concerned with genealogical and dynastic history.

The nineteenth century is in many ways the most richly documented period, thanks in the first place to the 67 metres of administrative records preserved in what remains of the Manado *residentie archief* (residency archive) at the Arsip Nasional Republik Indonesia (ANRI, Indonesian National Archive) in Jakarta.[95] The bulk of this collection dates from the period 1819-1895, and includes extensive general reports (*algemene* or *administratieve verslagen*, AV) on the state of the whole residency in the years 1824, 1825, 1829, 1833, and 1849-1894 inclusive, together with even more detailed monthly reports (*maand verslagen*, MV) for many years after 1853, annual 'cultivation reports' (*cultuur verslagen*, CV) on agriculture in the region for almost every year from 1853 to 1895, an enormous quantity of general correspondence, and a number of important special reports on remote areas not yet under direct Dutch control. Among the valuable quantitative data extracted from the residency archive was a wealth of demographic records, including an almost complete series of birth and death statistics for Minahasa in the period 1849-1872.

Residency records, generally speaking, were only transferred to what is now the Arsip Nasional once they reached the age of 50 years, and were therefore considered to have outlived their usefulness to local administrators.[96] Most archival material dating from after 1892, consequently, was still in the regions when the Japanese invaded in 1942, and almost without exception this has been lost. The most useful surviving administrative sources from the early twentieth century are the *memories van overgave* or 'memoirs of transfer' written by departing Dutch residents and lower-level administrators (assistant residents, *controleurs*, *gezaghebbers*) for the benefit of their successors. Many (though not all) of these were sent to the Netherlands, where they are now available at the Nationaal Archief (NA) in The Hague.[97] The archive collection of the Hendrik Kraemer Instituut (Archief van de Raad voor de Zending, ARZ) in Oegstgeest (since 1999, Utrecht) contains documents on Protestant missionary activities in northern Sulawesi in both the nineteenth and twentieth centuries. Numerous published sources are also very important for reconstructing the late colonial history of the region; one of these is the annual *Koloniaal Verslag* ('Colonial Report') for Indonesia as a whole, which includes synopses of events and developments in the residency

---

[95] References to this collection ('ANRI Manado') in the present book will specify the catalogue number of the document bundle (*bundel*) in which the cited source was found. Part of the archive material for Gorontalo is kept in a small separate collection referred to here as 'ANRI Gorontalo'. Unlike the residency archive, this boasts a published inventory (*Inventaris Arsip Gorontalo* 1976).

[96] M. Lohanda, interview, 23-3-96.

[97] These are grouped into two microfiche collections under the location codes MMK and KIT, the latter referring to the Koninklijk Instituut voor de Tropen (in Amsterdam) where this collection was originally housed. *Memories van overgave* are referred to in this book by the names of their authors, and listed under those names in the bibliography.

of Manado for every year from 1848 to 1941.

The period before 1800, by contrast, is less well served in the published literature, although Jacobs (1974-84) has edited the relevant Jesuit mission accounts of the sixteenth and seventeenth centuries, and Godée Molsbergen (1928) a selection from the VOC archive documentation on Minahasa. The published *Generale missiven* (1960-97) or 'General missives' of the VOC also contain some information on Dutch activities in northern Sulawesi up to 1750. Two forthcoming source publications edited by H.E. Niemeijer make available the *memories van overgave* written by VOC governors of Ternate (North Sulawesi fell under the administrative authority of Ternate until a separate residency of Manado was created in 1824), and the 'visitation reports' compiled by Dutch Protestant church ministers on their occasional journeys to Sangir and other Christian enclaves in North Sulawesi during the VOC period.[98] Most other information from this period was extracted, in some cases with the help of source indications provided by Wigboldus (1988, 1996a, 1996b), from the huge collection of VOC *overgekomen brieven en papieren* ('letters and papers sent over here') held at the NA.

A few of the most important individual authors of published and unpublished sources on northern Sulawesi are worth introducing at this stage. Among the early writers it is Robert Padtbrugge (1637-1703), a Leiden-trained physician turned VOC administrator (Pabbruwe [1994]), who stands out for the detail and insight of his descriptions. Padtbrugge made three journeys to northern Sulawesi during his five-year period as governor of Ternate (1677-1682); extracts from the official diaries of two of these expeditions were published in the nineteenth century (Robidé van der Aa 1867; Padtbrugge 1866), while his *memorie van overgave* of 1682 was incorporated into Pieter van Dam's 1701 *Beschrijvinghe van de Oostindische Compagnie* (Van Dam 1931:62-107), and also drawn upon extensively by François Valentijn (Keijzer 1856) in the first volume of *Oud en nieuw Oost-Indiën*, originally published in 1724. Besides the writings of Padtbrugge, some early descriptions by Catholic missionaries are also informative. Foremost among these is a late sixteenth-century portrait of Siau and its people by the Jesuit priest Antonio Marta, based on information obtained from the Flemish missionary Rogier Berwouts who lived on that island in the years 1585-1588 (Jacobs 1974-84, II:18, 32, 261-8). A lively account of the Palu area and its inhabitants by David Woodard, an American sea captain accidentally stranded there in 1793, illu-

---

[98]   Where archival documents are included in these source publications (entitled *Memories van overgave van gouverneurs van de Molukken (Ternate) in de zeventiende en achttiende eeuw* and *Bronnen betreffende de Protestantsche kerk in de Molukken, 1605-1795*), I refer to the (forthcoming) published text. Each document, however, is listed in the bibliography under its author's name, and the original source location is also mentioned. The writing of *memories van overgave* was a VOC custom which fell into disuse after 1800 and was revived toward the end of the nineteenth century.

minates the end of the eighteenth century, a period rich in routinized VOC administrative correspondence but otherwise very poor in useful geographic or ethnographic descriptions.[99]

Two nineteenth-century colonial administrators whose writings will be much cited in this study are J.G.F. Riedel (1832-1911) and F.S.A. de Clercq (1842-1906). Riedel, born in Minahasa as the son of an NZG missionary, worked there for more than a decade as a *controleur* (1853-1864) and subsequently for an equal period in Gorontalo as assistant resident (1864-1875), writing prolifi-cally on both areas and on others which he visited. De Clercq, a *controleur* in Minahasa from 1866 to 1872, provided detailed descriptions of agriculture, social life and material culture there and in Bolaang Mongondow.[100] Another local official, A.J. van Delden, wrote a useful account of the Sangir Islands in 1825 (Van Delden 1844), and several nineteenth-century residents of Manado, especially J. Wenzel, D.F.W. Pietermaat, and A.J.F. Jansen (in office 1825-1826, 1826-1831 and 1853-1859 respectively), also left administrative reports and descriptions of particularly high value.[101] In the middle of the century two Dutch diplomatic missions to the Ternatan possessions on the east coast of Central Sulawesi produced important descriptions of these otherwise little-documented areas; one, by C. Bosscher and P.A. Matthijssen, was published soon afterwards (1854), while the other, by A.F.J.J.G. Revius, remains an unpublished archival document.[102] A crucial source on demography and agri-culture in Minahasa is the voluminous *Memorie omtrent de Minahasa* compiled in 1875 by A.C.J. Edeling, one of a long series of 'commissioners' (investiga-tors) sent by the central government in Batavia to review the economic and political situation in the residency of Manado.[103] Of the twentieth-century *memories van overgave*, those by residents A.Ph. van Aken (1932) and M. van Rhijn (1941) stand out as exceptionally informative.

The importance of missionary authors for this study has already been noted. Among the Minahasa missionaries it is Nicolaas Graafland (1827-

[99] A reprint of the second edition of Woodard's account, originally published in 1805, appeared in 1969 (Woodard 1969).
[100] *Encyclopaedie* 1917-39, I:493-4, III:602-3. Later, as resident of Ternate, De Clercq (1890:123-46) also described the eastern part of Central Sulawesi.
[101] Wenzel's uniquely detailed annual residency report of 1825 was later published, with annotations, by Riedel (1872b). Pietermaat's almost equally useful report on the state of the resi-dency in 1833 (in ANRI Manado 48) has never been published, but information from it was later incorporated into a joint article by Pietermaat, De Vriese and Lucas (1840) and into publications by Van Doren (1854-56, 1857-60). Jansen produced many important documents including the first systematic *cultuur verslag* for the residency, which was later published (A.J.F. Jansen 1861), and unpublished reports on Mongondow and Talaud (in ANRI Manado 166, 167). Schouten (1998: 281) provides a list of all Dutch residents of Manado from 1819 to 1942.
[102] 'Algemeen Verslag omtrent de Oostkust van Celebes', 10-2-1851 (ANRI Ternate 180).
[103] NA V 17-4-1877/20. An much-abridged version of this report was later published (Edeling 1919).

1898), mainly thanks to his detailed regional monograph *De Minahassa* (Graafland 1867-69, 1898), who will be referred to most often.[104] Two others, N.P. Wilken and J.A. Schwarz, produced an extensive description of neighbouring Bolaang Mongondow in 1866; in the same year their colleagues F. Kelling and E. Steller wrote useful notes on Sangir.[105] As in the present chapter, however, the most frequently cited sources will be the prolific writings of the well-known pioneers of the Protestant mission in Central Sulawesi, the NZG missionary-anthropologist Albert Kruyt (1869-1949) and his colleague, the Nederlandsch Bijbelgenootschap (Dutch Bible Society) linguist Nicolaus Adriani (1865-1926). Arriving in Poso in 1892 and 1895 respectively, Kruyt and Adriani lived and travelled in Central Sulawesi for more than a decade before it was brought under Dutch rule, observing and documenting its indigenous societies with a view to converting them to Christianity. Their strongest interests, accordingly, were in language, religion, and magic, but their many published ethnographic works are also rich sources of information on subjects relating to demography and agriculture. The same is true of the less extensive writings of two other NZG missionaries: Jacob Woensdregt, who worked in the Bada Valley of western Central Sulawesi from 1916 to 1928, and Albert Kruyt's son Jan, who likewise began work in 1916 (J. Kruyt 1970:374-5). In 1924, Kruyt senior organized an important statistical survey of fertility and mortality patterns in Central Sulawesi, the results of which were later published by the hygiene expert H.F. Tillema (1926:26-48).

Besides Kruyt and Adriani, a number of European ethnographers and naturalists also travelled in Central Sulawesi before or immediately after the colonial conquest, most importantly the Swiss explorers Paul and Fritz Sarasin in 1893-1896 and 1902-1903.[106] Earlier too there had been visits to more accessible parts of the region by professional scientists of various kinds, notably C.J.C. Reinwardt in 1821, C.B.H. von Rosenberg in 1863, and the British naturalists Alfred Russel Wallace in 1859 and Sydney Hickson in 1885-1886 – all of whom, like the Sarasins, published their observations in major monographs.[107] Important specialist publications of the early twentieth century include the results of a big geological and geographical survey expedition to Central Sulawesi in 1909-1910 (Abendanon 1915-18); the many articles by foresters P.K. Heringa and F.K.M. Steup on the vegetation of the

---

104 *Encyclopaedie* 1917-39, I:815. Graafland lived in Minahasa from 1850 to 1895.
105 F. Kelling, 'Het eiland Taghoelandang en zijn bewoners' [1866] (ARZ NZG 43-2); Steller 1866; Wilken and Schwarz 1867a-c.
106 Kotilainen (1992:17-32) gives a useful overview of all the important writers on Central Sulawesi in this period, including the missionaries, and their principal publications.
107 Hickson 1889; Reinwardt 1858; Von Rosenberg 1865; Sarasin and Sarasin 1901, 1905; Wallace 1986. Meyer and Wiglesworth (1898:2-10) give a much more complete list of the many European naturalists who visited Sulawesi (mostly North Sulawesi) in the course of the nineteenth century.

region; the exhaustive geographic and economic description of Minahasa and Bolaang Mongondow compiled by V.J. van Marle (1922) in 1920 (as part of a feasibility study for a local railway which was never built); and the results of some remarkable medical and demographic research conducted by government doctor A. Kündig in Minahasa at the beginning of the 1930s (Kündig 1934). In 1940, finally, the botanist P.M.L. Tammes, then head of the coconut research establishment (*klapperproefstation*) in Manado, published an article on 'The biological background to the population question in North Sulawesi' which in many respects foreshadows the present study.

In addition to the contemporary sources, this book has also benefited from the results of a number of field studies carried out in various parts of the region since the end of the colonial period. A dissertation on liver disease in Sangir in the late 1940s, by the medical doctor David Blankhart (1951), provides much useful information on dietary and health conditions, as does a nutritional survey of part of Central Sulawesi carried out in the same period by J.F. de Wijn (1952), a military physician. After a short stay on Siau in 1952-1953 the anthropologist Hendrik Chabot, better known for his work on South Sulawesi, made an invaluable attempt to reconstruct vanished features of the indigenous social order which are not fully described in any historical source (H.Th. Chabot 1969). Albert Schrauwers (1995a, 1995b, 1997, 1998, 2000), following more extensive fieldwork in 1990-1993, has recently done the same for the Pamona of the Poso area. Also useful for the purposes of reconstructing past conditions is recent anthropological research by Tania Li (1991, 1996a, 1996b, 2001) and Jennifer Nourse (1989, 1999) on the Lauje, an upland group inhabiting the hinterland of Tinombo on the neck of the northern peninsula, and by Greg Acciaioli (1989) and Lorraine Aragon (1992, 2000) on two different communities in the interior of western Central Sulawesi. The publications of Mieke Schouten, above all her definitive monograph on leadership and social mobility in Minahasa (1998), combine thorough historical research with insights obtained from long periods of anthropological fieldwork. The work of Jouke Wigboldus – both published (1979, 1987) and unpublished (1988, 1996a, 1996b) – on the agrarian and demographic history of Minahasa (and adjacent parts of North Sulawesi) forms, together with that of Tammes, the immediate background to my own study.[108] For topics relating to the natural environment, finally, my guide in the first instance was always the invaluable *Ecology of Sulawesi* compiled by Whitten, Mustafa and Henderson (1987, 2002).

---

[108]   These are the only historical studies to date on the human ecology of the region, although a monograph by Gavin Jones (1977) deals with the demography of North Sulawesi in the period 1920-1971.

The structure of this book

Both the cutoff date for this study, 1930, and the geographical cutoff at the border with South and Southeast Sulawesi were determined in the first place by the nature and organization of the source materials, and are necessarily somewhat arbitrary. The region under study, in effect, is defined by a colonial administrative boundary – although whether a different boundary or an island-wide study would have produced a more coherent study is an open question (Henley 1989), and the environmental and social diversity encompassed within North and Central Sulawesi is already sufficient to permit some illuminating comparative analysis. The chronological boundary was chosen because it corresponds both with the date of the first reliable, comprehensive population census, the definitive Netherlands Indies *volkstelling* of 1930, and with the age of the materials used to compile the earliest available vegetation map of the whole region. With the necessary caution, however, considerable use will also be made of later sources. The limitations of the sources and the problems of interpreting them, unfortunately, will be a recurrent theme in the following chapters. In many contexts, particularly with reference to landscape history, it will sometimes be necessary to make use of backwards extrapolation from better-documented later periods rather than attempt to infer a complete picture from fragments of contemporary evidence.

After a brief overview of the agricultural and economic history of the region in Chapter II, Chapters III-XI deal with its demography. Chapter III establishes a general methodology for reconstructing past population levels on the basis of the problematic sources available for this purpose, and Chapters IV-VI apply it in turn to each of three major sub-regional divisions: the Sangir and Talaud Islands, peninsular North Sulawesi, and Central Sulawesi. Chapters VII-X examine four general categories of factors affecting population change: mortality levels, with special reference to disease; disease control; the food supply; and patterns of reproductive fertility. In the next two chapters I attempt to relate the interplay of these factors to the reconstructed patterns of demographic history; Chapter XI deals mainly with the geographical distribution of the population, and Chapter XII with changes over time. In Chapter XIII, the focus shifts to landscape history and the reconstruction of past patterns of vegetation cover. Chapter XIV examines the causes of deforestation: foodcrop agriculture, cash crop cultivation, animal husbandry, timber exploitation, and natural fires. Chapter XV, finally, assesses the factors affecting the sustainability of farming practices, examines the question of agricultural intensification, and summarizes the main conclusions of the book regarding the relationship between population, economy and environment.

CHAPTER II

Economic patterns

This chapter provides, as essential background to many of the demographic and landscape processes to be discussed later, a concise overview of the economic history of northern Sulawesi up to 1930. Throughout the period under study here, most people in this region were in the first place subsistence farmers. The following notes, accordingly, deal first with the agricultural backbone of the economy, and subsequently with trade and exchange. Some further analysis of the factors affecting economic behaviour in different historical situations will be attempted in Chapter XV.

Subsistence agriculture

Most food was grown on dry fields under a system of swidden (*ladang*) cultivation involving a fallow rotation. Each year the trees and other vegetation covering a section of the arable land were felled and slashed, and the cut material left to dry out before being burned (Plate 5). This was done during the driest season, the timing of which varied from area to area. In the uplands of Minahasa the swidden burn typically took place in June, July, or August (Graafland 1864:8, 19; N.P. Wilken 1870:375), but in Mori and Banggai, where these months were still wet (Chapter I, Figure 1), not until October or November (A.C. Kruyt 1900a:227, 1932d:477). The resulting swidden clearings were planted with main foodcrops for one or two years (occasionally longer), then allowed to revert gradually to secondary forest before being re-opened for the next cultivation cycle. The purpose of the fallow interval was twofold. As Padtbrugge (1866:324) already observed in 1679, firstly, the ash from the fired secondary vegetation acted as a fertilizer, and fields were opened 'in a new place each year, or one which has again become thick bush [*digt bosch*], in order to have more ash and a more fertile soil'.[1] The second reason for felling and burning 'dense woods', later sources add, was that

---

[1]   Whether soil nutrient depletion was also the proximate reason for the cessation of main crop cultivation on the typical swidden after one or two years, as Reid (1988-93, I:20) and many

Plate 5. Swidden burn in Talaud, 1979 (YMB Talaud/Minahasa Photograph II.A.21)

'weeds do not proliferate so rapidly there'.[2] Invading weeds, the removal of which is often the most labour-intensive aspect of swidden cultivation (Clark and Haswell 1967:39, 44-5), became progressively more troublesome after the opening of a new field, but were killed by the shade of the regenerating leaf canopy during the reversion to secondary forest (Seavoy 1973a). The swidden burn itself also served to destroy remaining seeds of unwanted vegetation (Tonelli 1992:7).

The length of the fallow period, examined in detail in Chapters XIII and XIV, varied considerably, but most often fell within the range of 6-10 years described by Boserup (1965:16) as 'bush-fallow', resulting in a low but dense secondary vegetation cover. Occasionally a very short grassland fallow was

others have assumed, is uncertain. Research on swidden farms in Kalimantan has shown that 'after the usual occupation period of two or three years the surface soil is even richer in available plant nutrients than at the beginning of cultivation' (Driessen, Buurman and Permadhy 1976: 113). This finding supports the 'shading cycle' model developed by Seavoy (1973a), in whose view weed proliferation, rather than soil depletion, typically determines the duration of cultivation on a single swidden. Soil nutrient replenishment, nevertheless, is certainly a major consideration when it comes to the duration of the fallow interval (Dove 1985b:82, 391).

[2]   AV Manado 1833 (ANRI Manado 48); Riedel 1872b:540.

employed, but this entailed more intensive weeding, and often also the equally laborious extraction of subterranean grass rhizomes.[3] While the nutrient supply was augmented by the swidden burn prior to planting, variations in natural soil conditions also affected crop yields, and farmers were skilled in the recognition of favourable and unfavourable soil properties.[4] In eastern Central Sulawesi, for instance, the thin acidic soils developed on ultrabasic rocks were carefully avoided wherever possible (Whitten, Mustafa and Henderson 1987:463).

Throughout the period for which historical documentation is available, rice (*Oryza sativa*) and maize (*Zea mays*) were the two principal foodcrops in most parts of the region. Many other crops, however, were always planted alongside these on the same swidden fields.[5] Crop diversity was particularly pronounced in Sangir and Talaud, where tubers and bananas played a major role in the diet:

> In the first instance they plant rice, often mixed with some maize and sorghum; frequently bananas are also planted out at the same time. In some cases a second rice crop follows, but the usual practice after the first harvest of rice and maize is to plant a jumbled mixture of all possible crops, including sweet potatoes, bananas, *Colocasia* [taro], cassava, peanuts, *kacang ijo* [mung beans], maize, sorghum; sometimes also *wijen* [sesame], sugar cane, various vegetables (such as *sesawi* [*Brassica* species], *bayem* [*Amaranthus* species], onions, chilli peppers, *kacang panjang* [long beans, *Vigna sinensis*] and brown beans [*Phaseolus vulgaris*]), and papaya. The *ladang*, correspondingly, generally make a disorderly impression. After the annual crops among this second planting have been harvested, cassava, colocasia and above all bananas continue to be collected for several years. (Tergast 1936:136.)

Much diversity was also found within individual foodcrop species. In Gorontalo at least 21 distinct varieties of rice were cultivated in the nineteenth century (Riedel 1870a:81-2), and in Minahasa reportedly more than a hundred (Graafland 1898, I:35; II:xlix), with ripening periods ranging from four to seven months.[6] While indigenous statements regarding the advan-

---

[3]   Wilken and Schwarz (1867c:366) noted that in Bolaang Mongondow, where there was less grassland than in Minahasa, 'the work involved in maize and *padi* cultivation, especially the weeding, is much less heavy'. Grassland swiddens could be cultivated either by levering out the grass root system, as in Minahasa (N.P. Wilken 1870:376), or by leaving it in the ground and weeding continuously 'in order to stay in control of the stubbornly sprouting grass', as in Mori (J. Kruyt 1924:144). Potter (1987:169) describes the equivalents of both systems in the interior of South Kalimantan.

[4]   Adriani and Kruyt 1950-51, III:25; A.C. Kruyt 1932d:479, 1938, III:36; Woensdregt 1928:149.

[5]   Adriani and Kruyt 1950-51, III:147-68; Francis 1860:349; A.C. Kruyt 1938, IV:278-85; N.P. Wilken 1870:374.

[6]   De Clercq 1871d. De Clercq gives individual descriptions of 57 varieties grown on dry fields alone.

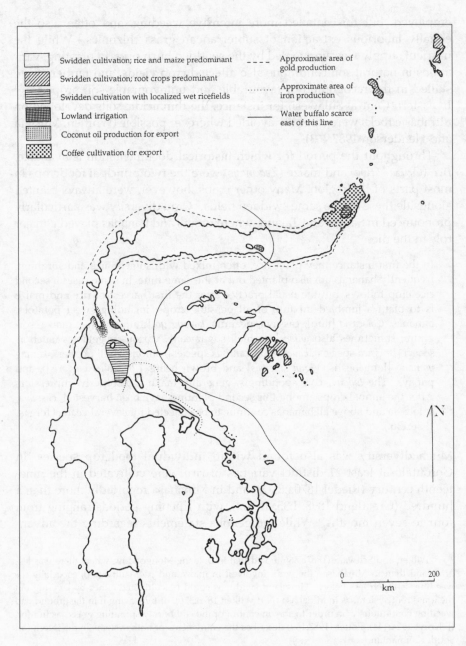

Swidden cultivation; rice and maize predominant

Swidden cultivation; root crops predominant

Swidden cultivation with localized wet ricefields

Lowland irrigation

Coconut oil production for export

Coffee cultivation for export

Approximate area of gold production

Approximate area of iron production

Water buffalo scarce east of this line

N

0   200
km

Map 8. Northern Sulawesi: aspects of economic geography, circa 1850

Plate 6. Hillside swiddens in Talaud, 1979 (YMB Talaud/Minahasa Photograph
II.A.14)

tages of maintaining such diversity are not available, it seems clear that as
in similar systems elsewhere (Marten and Saltman 1986:41-2), the reduction
of risk was an important consideration: if some crops or varieties failed due
to pests or adverse weather (see Chapter IX), others were likely to be less
affected. The Minahasan farmer, noted Graafland (1864:22), often 'takes two
chances, and sows early and late rice in different places'; in Central Sulawesi,
comparably, a single household frequently opened two small swidden fields
simultaneously, each in a different soil and relief environment or planted
with a different combination of crops (Adriani and Kruyt 1912-14, II:239; A.C.
Kruyt 1932d:476).

Hillside slopes, which ensured good drainage and facilitated the tasks
of clearing and weeding, were usually the preferred locations for swiddens
(Plate 6).[7] In most places these dry fields were the only type present, but in
upland Minahasa, and in parts of western Central Sulawesi (Map 8), they
were complemented by wet ricefields located on or around the adjacent

---

[7]   Adriani and Kruyt 1912-14, II:231; Aragon 1992:39; Boonstra van Heerdt 1914b:727; CV
Sangir en Talaud 1884 (ANRI Manado 146); Van Dam 1931:97; Kaudern 1925:36; A.C. Kruyt
1895-97, III:129, 1900a:227; *Landschap Donggala* 1905:516; Steller 1866:17; Tergast 1936:131; Tillema
1922:211.

Plate 7. Wet ricefields in Kulawi, with swidden-fallow vegetation on adjacent slopes,
circa 1913 (Abendanon 1915-18, II: Plate CLVIII)

valley floors (Plate 7).[8] In 1857, when Dutch efforts to promote irrigation
had only just begun, 21 percent of the total reported Minahasan rice harvest
already came from wet fields; within the Tondano administrative division,
where most of the *sawah* were concentrated, the proportion was 35 percent.[9]
Three types of wet rice farming were in fact indigenous to Minahasa.[10] The
simplest of these was practised on the 'muddy lands, more or less thickly
overgrown with water plants' (Worotikan 1910:154), which straddled the
seasonally fluctuating margins of Lake Tondano.[11]

[8]   AV Manado 1833 (ANRI Manado 48); Van der Capellen 1855:360; Edeling 1919:58; Francis
1860:344-8; A.J.F. Jansen 1861:232-5; A.C. Kruyt 1938, IV:18-227; P.A. van Middelkoop, 'Memorien
ten vervolge van het Algemeen Verslag van de commissie naar de Moluksche eilanden', 30-9-
1818 (NA Schneither 128); Van Thije 1689; N.P. Wilken 1870:373-4; Woensdregt 1928.
[9]   CV Manado 1857 (ANRI Manado 52).
[10]   Wet rice farming in Minahasa dates back at least to the seventeenth century, when the VOC
official Van Thije (1689) recorded that the people of Tondano 'cultivate the land [...] by flooding
or draining it at will'. In recent times its introduction has often been attributed to a group of
Javanese political exiles resettled by the Dutch near Tondano in 1830, a confusion which probably
results in part from the fact that these immigrants did pioneer the use of the plough in Minahasa
(Babcock 1989:38-9).
[11]   Also *Adatvonnissen* 1914:84. In Mori, too, some rice was planted on land inundated by

Plate 8. Water buffalo driven through wet ricefields to turn the soil, western Central Sulawesi, circa 1913 (ARZ photograph collection, Land- en Volkenkunde Celebes 360)

> If the south wind blows for a long period, these fall dry, and people who have established rights there clear them for the purpose of extending [adjacent] rice-fields or planting sago trees. Most of the time, however, they lie under water, and return to their primitive state, so that all signs of cultivation disappear. (Worotikan 1910:154.)

The rice planted during dry spells on the exposed lake margins was naturally irrigated when the water level rose, and a reference to *padi* with 'a straw of six to seven feet long' near Tondano in 1845 presumably refers to floating or swamp rice grown in this way.[12] The second traditional method of wet rice farming in Minahasa was practised further from the lake, on dyked fields fed with water redirected from small streams by 'dams constructed from wood and earth'.[13] These true irrigated *sawah* were seeded by broadcast sowing,

---

natural means (J. Kruyt 1924:144). On Talaud (Lam 1932:52) and elsewhere, similar naturally swampy areas were often used for the cultivation of sago and taro.

[12] J. Grudelbach, 'Gevoelen over de topografische schetsen van den Luitenant J.J. ten Siethoff', 24-12-1846 (ANRI Manado 46). Hanks (1972:33-6) describes similar systems of broadcast-sown swamp rice cultivation in Thailand.

[13] AV Manado 1833 (ANRI Manado 48). Another report from the same period mentions 'water channels' constructed by some *walak* in order to irrigate their *sawah* (AV Manado 1829, in KITLV H 70).

without separate nursery beds or systematic transplanting of the young rice plants (although some seedlings were shifted as they grew in order to even out the distribution of the crop in the field), and cultivated without the plough, although some working and levelling of the soil was carried out using hand tools (Francis 1860:347). Around Tonsawang in the south of Minahasa, thirdly, a similar degree of water control was combined with seedbeds and transplanting, although here too no use was made of draught animals.[14] In this last respect, Central Sulawesi was different: whereas wet rice farmers in Minahasa relied exclusively on human labour, their counterparts in Lore and the Palu Valley drove herds of water buffalo through their fields in order to turn the soil by trampling in preparation for planting (Plate 8).[15] Another difference was that transplanting was much more widespread in Central Sulawesi than in Minahasa, although broadcast sowing was also practised in Tawaelia (A.C. Kruyt 1938, IV:97).

Wet ricefields could be cultivated on an annual basis, without fallowing, because immersion both suppressed weed growth (Furukawa 1994:123; Padoch 1985:279, 284) and helped to maintain soil fertility (Geertz 1963:29-31; Grist 1955:172-4). In the uplands, as Reid (1997:78) has observed of comparable systems in Sumatra, wet and dry fields typically 'operated together as part of a spectrum of different agricultural strategies'.[16] The two rice crops, for instance, were often staggered such that the wet rice was planted and harvested later in the year – a practice which, together with the additional diversity provided by the double system itself, must have reduced the risk of food shortages as well as making for an efficient calendrical distribution of labour. In Minahasa, swidden rice was typically planted in December or January to be harvested between April and August, while wet rice was planted in February or March to be harvested between August and November.[17]

Swidden farming, together with supplementary upland irrigation sys-

---

[14]   AV Manado 1833 (ANRI Manado 48); Francis 1860:347, 354. The use of seedbeds did not become widespread in Minahasa until the twentieth century (CV Manado 1879, in ANRI Manado 86; A.C.J. Edeling, 'Memorie omtrent de Minahasa', 13-8-1875, in NA V 17-4-1877/20; Van Geuns 1906:80; *Zending* 1895:358).

[15]   Padtbrugge stated in 1682 that farmers in upland Central Sulawesi 'plough the land with buffalo' (Van Dam 1931:93), but while this may be regarded as good evidence for the antiquity of wet rice farming there, it probably should not be taken literally; at the beginning of the twentieth century, the plough was said to be unknown even in the Palu Valley (Hissink 1912:121).

[16]   Kaudern (1925:34) states that dry and wet rice-farming settlements in Central Sulawesi are distinct, but A.C. Kruyt (1938, IV:18-227) and Woensdregt (1928) both describe an agricultural calendar in which activities on swiddens and irrigated fields interlock.

[17]   Francis 1860:346; Graafland 1864:8; MV Manado 1868-1869 (ANRI Manado 54). Most irrigated fields in the region produced a single rice crop each year. Two harvests per year were said to be possible from *sawah* in the Palu Valley at the end of the eighteenth century (NA VOC 1775: 110), but this was exceptional; in Minahasa, a double harvest was still uncommon even in the early twentieth century (Van Marle 1922, I:73, 75).

tems of various technically simple kinds, typified agriculture in the region throughout the period up to 1930. These were not, however, the only systems present. The Limboto Depression in Gorontalo, for example, contained in the mid-nineteenth century an enclave of land-, labour-, and even capital-intensive irrigated farming, featuring water diversions from substantial rivers and the use of a buffalo-drawn plough.[18] In this area there were also many continuously cultivated dry fields, some of which, uniquely in northern Sulawesi, were manured as well as ploughed to maintain their fertility.[19] The causes of this and other cases of agricultural intensification will be addressed in Chapter XV; the historical origins of lowland irrigation are also touched upon in the following discussion of changes in the foodcrop assemblage.

Variations in foodcrop patterns

That patterns of subsistence agriculture in the region were not static is immediately apparent from the fact that one of the two main foodcrops of the historical period, maize, is a New World domesticate introduced only after European contact in the sixteenth century. Wigboldus (1979) has discussed the earliest report of maize cultivation in the region (and one of the earliest in Indonesia as a whole), which forms part of Marta's description of Siau in the 1580s (Jacobs 1974-84, II:262). A century later Minahasans were growing maize 'in great abundance', and it was also present in Gorontalo.[20] The drought-tolerance and short maturation period of maize made it an ideal complement to rice as a swidden crop, and both were typically planted on the same land in the same year, the sequence of cultivation varying from area to area. In upland Minahasa, as in parts of the North Moluccas (Visser 1989:32), the main maize crop was customarily planted and harvested before the rice was sown, while a second was planted at greater intervals interspersed with the rice (Graafland 1898, I:151-2; N.P. Wilken 1870:375, 379, 381). In the Palu area, by contrast,

---

[18]   AV Gorontalo 1854 (ANRI Gorontalo 3); CV Gorontalo 1854 (ANRI Gorontalo 3); Francis 1860:344, 346-7; MV Gorontalo March-May 1868, April and May 1869; Riedel 1870a:82-3; R. Scherius 1847:414. Von Rosenberg (1865:28), however, states that the rice was sown by broadcasting and that no seedbeds were used; in reality no doubt a mixture of more and less intensive systems was present.

[19]   Most nineteenth-century descriptions of agriculture in Gorontalo imply that permanent-field maize cultivation existed on the plain alongside swidden farming on the surrounding slopes, and one (CV Gorontalo 1863, in ANRI Manado 134) states explicitly that 'many dry fields have been planted year in, year out with maize'. Van Hoëvell (1891:35) describes the ploughing of dry maize fields, while Von Rosenberg (1865:27) mentions manuring.

[20]   Van Dam 1931:78, 97. The earliest specific mention of maize in Central Sulawesi, on the other hand, dates only from 1793, when this was an important crop in the Palu area (Woodard 1969:90-1).

maize was first planted together with the rice, and then again after the rice harvest (A.C. Kruyt 1938, IV:230; Ter Laag 1920:41). In two particularly dry subregions, Gorontalo (Reinwardt 1858:513; Von Rosenberg 1865:27) and the Donggala area (Boonstra van Heerdt 1914b:728; *Landschap Donggala* 1905:516), maize ultimately overtook rice to become the staple food.

There is an influential theory, classically expounded by Spencer (1963, 1966:110-9), to the effect that only since the beginning of the sixteenth century has rice itself become important in eastern Indonesia, where it is therefore barely older than maize.[21] Even Bellwood (1997:245), one of the foremost proponents of the idea that the earliest Austronesian colonists of Indonesia were already rice-growers, supposes that they subsequently 'dropped rice to the scale of a very minor crop' in Sulawesi and the eastern part of the archipelago, gradually reverting to rice cultivation after 1500 at the expense of other staples such as yams, taro, bananas, and sago.

In the colonial period, NZG missionaries certainly believed that there was legendary and ritual evidence in Central Sulawesi for an ancient 'yam era' terminated by the arrival of the 'rice-bringers', a foreign people remembered in oral tradition as gods.[22] At the end of the nineteenth century, moreover, old people in parts of western Central Sulawesi also claimed that 'many more tubers' than at present had still been cultivated and eaten there 'in their young years'.[23] The available historical sources, on the other hand, show that any general replacement of root crops by rice must have been well underway at a very early date. Rice, for instance, was grown on a large scale in Tobungku in the 1540s (Abendanon 1915-18, IV:1768), and on a smaller scale in Sangir in the 1580s (Jacobs 1974-84, II:262). At the beginning of the seventeenth century it was already the most important crop in both ritual and commercial terms in Minahasa (Godée Molsbergen 1928:14; Pérez 1913-14, IV:433), and a few decades later Balantak, on the Luwuk Peninsula, was also exporting surplus rice to the Moluccas.[24] In 1682, Padtbrugge reported (albeit at second hand) that 'an abundance of rice' was grown in the upland

[21]   See also Hutterer 1984:96; Knapen 2001:205-15; Macknight 1983:97; Slamet-Velsink 1995:22; Visser 1989:38-9. Spencer's sole historical source regarding Sulawesi, quoted at second hand from Burkill (1935, I:828), was Rumphius (1750, V:347), who stated that '*ubi* cultivation begins in earnest in Celebes and Buton, and goes on through the Moluccas, Ambon, Banda, and all the southeastern islands to New Guinea'.

[22]   A.C. Kruyt 1924:33-9. Woensdregt (1928:125-7) records similar evidence from myth and ritual. In Minahasan mythology, comparably, rice was stolen from the gods (Schefold 1995) at a time when the staple food, according to one ethnographic source, was the fruit of the liana *Gnetum latifolium* (Schwarz 1907, III:244).

[23]   A.C. Kruyt 1938, IV:279. In many parts of Central Sulawesi, interestingly, maize was said to be an older crop than rice (A.C. Kruyt 1938, IV:230; Woensdregt 1928:128). As Kruyt suggested, however, this may have reflected the replacement by maize of an indigenous crop, Job's tears.

[24]   NA VOC 1359:153v; Van Dam 1931:99; *Generale missiven* III:171, 184; Keijzer 1856:221.

Plate 9. Extraction of palm pith for sago manufacture, Talaud, 1979 (YMB Talaud/ Minahasa Photograph 280). The starch grains will be leached out of the pulverized pith with water over a sieve, and the starch recovered from the slurry passing through the sieve by letting it settle.

interior of Central Sulawesi (Van Dam 1931:93). In South Sulawesi, finally, archaeologists have found remains of rice husks 'believed to be 1500 years old' (Whitten, Mustafa and Henderson 1987:74), and rice was certainly a very important crop (and export product) by the early sixteenth century according to European historical sources (Pelras 1981:156).

Not quite all early descriptions of northern Sulawesi, admittedly, mention rice. A brief Portuguese account from 1561 lists only bananas (*figos*, literally 'figs'), coconuts, and yams (*ynhames*) as food crops in the 'Celebes' (De Sá 1955: 328). In the sixteenth century, however, the term Celebes encompassed everything from North Sulawesi to Mindanao (Abendanon 1915-18, IV:1896-8), and this source may well refer to the Sangir Archipelago, where rice cultivation was to remain limited, and local diets based mainly on tubers, cooked bananas, and sago, for the next four centuries.[25] Comparably, a comment in a Dutch

[25]   Robidé van der Aa 1867:254; E. Francis, 'Aantekeningen van den kommissaris voor Menado 1846' (ANRI Manado 167); Blankhart 1951:95; Coolsma 1901:640, 649; Van Dam 1931:70; Van Delden 1844:20; Van Dinter 1899:337-40; Frieswijck 1902:434-6; Van Geuns 1906:74; F. Kelling,

report from 1670 that the inhabitants of Buol and Tolitoli are 'sago-eaters, for they have no rice' (Noorduyn 1983:117) concerns an area where sago was still the staple food in the late nineteenth century (Riedel 1872a:191, 200).

Much of the variation in farming systems within the region, in other words, was geographical rather than chronological. Like the Sangirese, farmers in the Talaud and Banggai Islands were always heavily dependent on root crops (Map 8).[26] On Banggai, in fact, almost no rice was grown even in 1930; here yams (*Dioscorea* species) provided the staple food, supplemented by taro (*Colocasia esculenta*) grown in the wetter valley-floor locations (A.C. Kruyt 1932d:475). In rainy Sangir and Talaud, by contrast, *Colocasia* was more important than yams, while the giant aroid *Alocasia macrorrhizos* and (in parts of Talaud) the 'swamp taro' *Cyrtosperma merkusii* were also grown.[27] Smaller enclaves of root crop cultivation existed on the mainland too. At the beginning of the twentieth century, according to A.C. Kruyt (1926:532, 1938, IV: 3, 279), tubers were still more significant than rice in the Pekawa area to the west of the Palu Trench (Chapter VI, Map 13), while taro remains the staple crop today in parts of the uplands behind Tinombo in Tomini (Li 1991:39).

Another important non-grain food was sago, the starch extracted from the trunks of certain palms (Plate 9), both wild (*Nota Toli-Toli* 1912:52; Tergast 1936:137) and cultivated (Adriani and Kruyt 1912-14, II:203-4; Kortleven 1927:90). The main sago-yielding trees in the region were the true sago palm (*Metroxylon sagu*) and the sugar or *aren* palm (*Arenga pinnata*). A third species, *Arenga microcarpa*, the *sagu baruk* or 'Magindanao sago tree' (E. Steller 1866: 17), was also important on Sangir.[28] Although the primary use of sago in most areas was as a fallback or emergency food (see Chapter IX), there were some localities where it provided the mainstay of the diet in late colonial times. Besides coastal Buol and Tolitoli, these included the Togian Islands, parts of the Tobungku coast, Tonsawang in the south of Minahasa, and Manganitu on Greater Sangir.[29] *Aren* sago also seems to have been very important, alongside rice and maize, in nineteenth-century Bolaang Mongondow.[30]

'Taghoelandang en zijn bewoners' [1866] (ARZ NZG 43.2); Steller 1866:18, 20; Van de Velde van Cappellen 1857:48.

[26]   A.C. Kruyt 1932d:473; Pennings 1908:14; Roep 1917:432; Stokking 1922a:253; Keijzer 1856: 175.

[27]   Blankhart 1951:95; Van Dinter 1899:340; Frieswijck 1902:436; Lam 1932:52; Tergast 1936:131, 136-7; Vorderman 1899. The last source translates the principal indigenous crop names. Taro, *Alocasia* and yams were also present in Minahasa in the nineteenth century, although here they were much less important in dietary terms (De Clercq 1873:265-6; Van Spreeuwenberg 1845-46:311).

[28]   CV Sangir en Talaud 1884, 1887 (ANRI Manado 146); Tammes 1936a; Tergast 1936:138.

[29]   Avink 1935; Bleeker 1856, I:73; *Een en ander* 1908:1047; Goedhart 1908:518; Graafland 1867-69, I:182, 1898, II:33; Van Hoëvell 1893b:7; A.J.F. Jansen 1861:233; A.C. Kruyt 1895-97, V:36; Riedel 1872b:495; Van Spreeuwenberg 1845-46:311; Tammes 1936a:43.

[30]   De Clercq 1883:122; Wilken and Schwarz 1867c:327, 360; Riedel 1864b:276. A report from

Two definite episodes of 'rizification' did take place in lowland areas during the late seventeenth and early eighteenth centuries, and in both cases they were associated with irrigation. When the Spanish priest Domingo Navarrete visited the Palu (Kaili) area in 1657, firstly, he reported that its population lived on bananas, 'without sowing Rice or any other Grain' (Cummins 1962, I:110). Just 25 years later, by contrast, Padtbrugge wrote that the Palu Valley contained 'a multitude of fertile [wet] paddy fields which are worked using buffalo, and not in the way that is customary on the stony soils in those parts [swidden cultivation]' (Van Dam 1931:91). Travelling from Limboto to Gorontalo in 1677, secondly, Padtbrugge recorded in his diary that although the land was 'everywhere entirely suitable for the cultivation of rice', none was grown, and the only 'properly tended' crops to be seen were banana trees (Robidé van der Aa 1867:164). Since Rumphius (1750, V:198) mentions that small quantities of (wet) rice were exported from Gorontalo in the seventeenth century, this observation cannot be entirely accurate. In the first half of the eighteenth century, nevertheless, new irrigated ricefields were certainly laid out in the Limboto Depression on a large scale (Riedel 1870a:110; Tacco 1935:107-8).

At no stage were the plains of Palu and Limboto, both located in areas of unusual climatic aridity (Chapter 1, Map 3) yet also periodically subject to periodic flooding, favoured as sites for dry rice cultivation.[31] 'On the valley floor', wrote a Dutch *controleur* of Palu in the 1930s, 'rice can be grown only on *sawah*' (Vorstman 1935a:19). In nineteenth-century Gorontalo, comparably, all ricefields in the depression were apparently irrigated, and dry rice was found only in the surrounding upland districts.[32] The fact that no rice was seen in these areas prior to irrigation, then, does not necessarily mean that none was present in the adjacent hills. In his *memorie van overgave* of 1682, indeed, Padtbrugge reveals that Gorontalo farmers are not entirely without rice after all, but rather 'prefer to plant the little *padi* which they grow on the slopes of the mountains in the Moluccan fashion' – that is, in swidden fields.[33]

If lowland plains were often unsuitable for swidden rice farming, the size of the rivers flowing across them also made them much more difficult and laborious to irrigate than upland valleys. Dams and channels had to be bigger,

---

the beginning of the twentieth century that sago was the staple in Mori (Goedhart 1908:539), however, appears to be erroneous (A.C. Kruyt 1900b:459; J. Kruyt 1924:143).

[31]   Abundant, steady and reliable rainfall during the growing season is the most essential and demanding environmental precondition for the cultivation of rice without irrigation, making this type of farming most suitable for ever-wet rainforest areas (Uhlig 1990:379).

[32]   Gov. Moluccas to GG, 3-7-1824 (KITLV H 142); MV Manado June 1863 (ANRI Manado 54). Maize, like bananas, was apparently less vulnerable to frequent flooding (Riedel 1870a:78).

[33]   Van Dam 1931:97. The comment in his 1677 travel diary that the terrain 'can always be reliably supplied with water' confirms that in lamenting the absence of rice, Padtbrugge was thinking only of the prospects for irrigated farming on the plain (Robidé van der Aa 1867:164).

and required constant maintenance due to frequent flood damage (Lanting 1939:69). The irrigation of the Limboto Depression, for example, involved the excavation of a major canal in 1744.[34] A century later a Dutch official in Gorontalo complained that smaller waterworks could be constructed 'only on a temporary basis; the slightest high water destroys these immediately'.[35] The rivers of the Palu Valley, likewise, frequently swept away the 'unprotected diversions' constructed by local farmers, sometimes altering their courses in the process to flow permanently along what had been man-made irrigation channels (Vorstman 1935a:3). Lowland irrigation, consequently, was never widespread, and tended to be practised only where trade and state forma-tion made it particularly desirable or necessary (see Chapter XV). Outside the Palu Valley and the Limboto Depression, the only other example prior to the twentieth century was found on the coastal plain of Parigi (Map 8).[36]

Rice is identified as the most socially prestigious food in most areas even in early sources, and when large quantities of this grain began to be imported from outside the region in the twentieth century, there was certainly a shift away from other foods.[37] The propagation of irrigated farming within the region by the colonial government (Chapter XV), beginning in the 1850s in Minahasa, had a similar effect. Countervailing trends, however, were not unknown. In the Napu Valley of western Central Sulawesi, the importance of tubers relative to rice seems to have increased in the late nineteenth century when rice cultivation was 'neglected' as a result of emigration. 'Ultimately', reported Adriani and Kruyt (1912-14, II:203), 'rice was eaten only by the elite, and the common people and slaves had to make do with root crops'. Here again the crucial variable was irrigation, the extent of which declined more sharply than that of swidden cultivation in Napu over the period concerned (A.C. Kruyt 1908:1313). Whereas tubers, bananas, and vegetables were always planted on swidden fields even where rice and maize were the main crops, irrigated fields, due to imperfect drainage or deliberate inundation (to prevent weed growth) in the off-season, mostly produced only rice.[38] This meant that any increase in the area under irrigation automatically led to a

---

34   NA VOC 2649:111.
35   CV Gorontalo 1854 (ANRI Gorontalo 3).
36   CV Gorontalo 1864 (ANRI Manado 44); Engelenberg 1906:11; Van Hoëvell 1893a:71; RPR Ternate 19-5-1787 (ANRI Ternate 26).
37   NA VOC 1359:153v; VOC 1775:110; Morison 1931:51; Vorstman 1935a:19.
38   CV Manado 1862 (ANRI Ambon 1563), 1876, 1888 (ANRI Manado 86); Dirkzwager 1912:1163; Francis 1860:346; A.J.F. Jansen 1861:235; Kortleven 1927:95; A.C. Kruyt 1938, IV:78; Stuurman 1936:68; Von Rosenberg 1865:28; N.P. Wilken 1870:374. In Gorontalo and the Palu Valley, however, maize was sometimes grown on off-season *sawah* (CV Gorontalo 1854, in ANRI Gorontalo 3; CV Gorontalo 1863, in ANRI Manado 134; Hissink 1912:121; Morison 1931:49; Riedel 1870a:84; Stap 1919:812). In Minahasa this occurred for the first time, 'by way of experiment', in 1895 (CV Manado 1895, in ANRI Manado 86).

greater emphasis on rice relative to other crops.[39]

There are, then, reasons to be sceptical of the 'rizification' hypothesis insofar as this implies a general transition from non-rice to rice farming, independent of changes in the extent of irrigation. At the same time, however, it must be acknowledged that the earlier sources on agriculture in the region are not so numerous or detailed that such a transition can be ruled out. The situation with respect to the New World crops provides a salutary warning against too rigorously positivistic an approach here. Given the virtual ubiquity of maize in historical descriptions of agriculture in the region, a researcher who did not know from other sources that this was a post-Columbian introduction would almost certainly conclude that it was an indigenous crop of long-standing importance.[40] The same goes for another New World domesticate, the sweet potato (*Ipomoea batatas*), which was probably cultivated on Siau by the 1650s (Colin 1900-02, I:110) and which seems to have become almost as important as taro in Sangirese agriculture by the nineteenth century.[41] If only because of these two crucial introductions, it is clear that something approaching a revolution in subsistence agriculture must in fact have taken place in northern Sulawesi during the late sixteenth or early seventeenth centuries, just out of sight of all but the oldest European sources.[42] It therefore remains possible that this early period also saw an increase in the importance of rice with respect to root crops, sago, bananas, or to non-rice grains such as sorghum (*Andropogon sorghum*), foxtail millet (*Setaria italica*), and Job's tears (*Coix lachryma-jobi*), all of which were still grown in small quantities as swidden crops in colonial times.[43]

One reason why such a change might have taken place, some writers have suggested, is an increasing involvement in long-distance trade (Knapen 2001:

---

[39] Exceptionally, however, one source (A.C. Kruyt 1938, IV:279) refers to an oral tradition from Kantewu in western Central Sulawesi according to which 'in olden times, irrigated terraces were built upon which only *Colocasia* was grown'.

[40] The only source on any part of the region which explicitly states that maize is *not* present seems to be a Portuguese account of Tobungku dating from 1544 (Abendanon 1915-18, IV:1768).

[41] There is some doubt, however, whether the term used by Colin in 1660, *camotes*, permits a definite identification as sweet potato (W.H. Scott 1994:42). Later sources from Sangir refer to *batatas* (Van Dam 1931:56; Van Delden 1844:7, 18; Van Dinter 1899:340; Frieswijck 1902:436; Lam 1932:51; E. Steller 1866:17; Tergast 1936:131, 137; E. Francis, 'Aantekeningen van den kommissaris voor Manado 1846', in ANRI Manado 167; CV Manado 1895, in ANRI Manado 86). Another introduced root crop, cassava, is first mentioned from Minahasa in 1877 ('Stukken voedingsmiddelen in de Minahassa 1877-78', in ANRI Manado 37), and later became very common, alongside the existing tubers, in Sangir and Talaud (Blankhart 1951:86; Tergast 1936:136).

[42] Other significant New World crop introductions of this period included tomato, papaya, chilli peppers, pineapple, and also tobacco, which was in use on Siau by 1629 (Jacobs 1974-84, III:477).

[43] Adriani and Kruyt 1950-51, III:152-3; Koorders 1898:278; A.C. Kruyt 1938, IV:271; Tergast 1936:136.

225; Visser 1989:20, 38-9). The established external demand for rice, combined with its good storage and transport properties, could have made it attractive in the first place as a commercial rather than a subsistence crop. One indigenous account of Minahasan history, written down at the beginning of the twentieth century, also takes this view, arguing that rice initially became popular because it could be used to purchase foreign textiles and firearms (Worotikan 1910:157). Minahasa certainly exported much rice to the Moluccas from the beginning of the seventeenth century onward, and this was one of the main reasons for early Spanish and Dutch political intervention there; the European garrisons in the Moluccas had difficulty obtaining food supplies locally, and looked to fertile Minahasa, 300 km to the west, for a solution. The first Dutch ship loaded rice in Manado in 1608 (Van Dijk 1862: 268), and the first Spanish expedition in 1610 (Bohigian 1994:185). Whether the Minahasa rice trade preceded European involvement is not known.

In the mid-nineteenth century one Minahasan ethnic group, the Tonsawang, apparently grew rice almost exclusively for export, while feeding itself mainly with sago.[44] At least by this period, however, the bulk of the rice grown in Minahasa as a whole was certainly consumed locally. Farmers, complained Resident Pietermaat in 1830, did not begin to deliver their rice to the government warehouses as soon as it was harvested, but rather 'store it until they are sure of having a good harvest, out of fear that otherwise they will not have enough to meet their own needs'.[45] Over the years 1828-1845, for which period a continuous record can be reconstructed, the total quantity of hulled rice delivered annually by Minahasan farmers averaged 1,470 tonnes.[46] This comprised the bulk of the traded surplus, including not only the rice exported to Ternate, but also most of that purchased by the population of Manado and other coastal settlements within Minahasa.[47] In the decade 1853-1862, by comparison, the first ten systematic attempts to measure the overall size of the Minahasan rice harvest indicated an average of 14,550 tonnes, almost ten times the amount sold to the government before

[44]   De Clercq 1873:262; A.J.F. Jansen 1861:233. Uniquely in Minahasa, the rice grown in Tonsawang was planted exclusively on wet fields.
[45]   Res. Manado to Gov. Moluccas, 3-4-1830 (ANRI Manado 76).
[46]   Calculated from: Res. Manado to Gov. Moluccas, 3-4-1830 (ANRI Manado 76); Van Doren 1854-56, I:260; 'Opgave van in 's Lands Pakhuis jaarlijks geleverde rijst' [1840-45], in KITLV H 142. In the years 1815 and 1816, by comparison, deliveries averaged 1,600 tonnes (P.A. van Middelkoop to A.A. Buijskens, 4-10-1817, in NA Schneither 128), in 1821 about 1,500 tonnes (Reinwardt 1858:585), and in 1822-1824 the average was 1,280 tonnes (Olivier 1834-37, II:29).
[47]   More than half of the government rice was re-sold locally (Van Doren 1857-60, II:362-3; Res. Manado to Gov. Moluccas, 3-4-1830, in ANRI Manado 76). Exports through private channels, permitted on a limited scale after 1828, totalled only about 150 tonnes in 1833 (AV Manado 1833, in ANRI Manado 48), although in later years they may have been more significant (Francis 1860: 351).

1845.[48] While this figure may be somewhat exaggerated (see Chapter XI), it does not seem likely that the proportion of the rice harvest entering any kind of long-distance trade in the first half of the nineteenth century was greater than 15 or 20 percent.

Some earlier Dutch sources on rice cultivation in Minahasa, by contrast, do suggest a stronger commercial orientation. When the VOC fort was established at Manado in 1657, the Minahasan chiefs reportedly undertook to supply it with 'one third of their whole harvest' each year in exchange for imported textiles.[49] In 1660, a Dutch governor of Ternate implied that the sale of rice was a high priority for Minahasan farmers when he wrote that 'if they do not sell part of their harvest in the beginning, they consume it later in feasts and other celebrations'.[50] According to other sources, however, it was usually old reserve *padi* on the verge of decay which was delivered to the Dutch (Van Dam 1931: 79; Van Thije 1689). Fragments of quantitative evidence from this period, moreover, suggest that the actual proportion of the harvest sold to the VOC was not as great as one third. In 1680, for instance, the Dutch requirement stood at 350 tonnes of unhusked *padi*, but Padtbrugge remarked that Minahasan farmers always kept 'more than' 1,500 tonnes in storage for their own use.[51] The 300-400 tonnes of husked rice which the VOC was exporting from Minahasa annually by the middle of the eighteenth century were likewise thought to be 'a small quantity in comparison with the whole crop' (Van Brandwijk van Blokland 1749). The VOC, on the other hand, was never the sole exporter of Minahasan rice. Private (mostly ethnic Chinese) traders were already buying rice in Manado in the seventeenth century (Hustaart 1656; Padtbrugge 1866: 308), and after 1700 their numbers increased.[52] Not until 1810 did the Minahasa rice trade become a state monopoly (Godée Molsbergen 1928:173-4).

Rice, it should be added, was not the only foodstuff for which a commercial demand existed. Due to its equally good storage properties, sago too was 'eminently suitable as an item of trade' (Ellen 1979:53); in the seventeenth century, some sago was also exported from North Sulawesi (*Historische verhael* 1646:70) and Banggai (Van Leur 1960:116) to the Moluccas, while Gorontalo imported considerable quantities from nearby Paguat.[53] Later sources, in fact, suggest that sago, rather than rice, was the most important

48 Calculated from: CV Manado 1853-62 (ANRI Ambon 1543, 1563; Manado 48, 51, 52, 95).
49 NA VOC 1328:163r.
50 NA VOC 1233:224r.
51 NA VOC 1359:153v. Padtbrugge later claimed that more than 4,500 tonnes of *padi* were destroyed in a single fire in Tomohon in 1682, although this may well have been an exaggeration (Van Dam 1931:78).
52 Wigboldus 1988:37, 51. A source from 1792 suggests that by this date, private trade accounted for more than half of the Minahasan rice exported to Ternate (NA VOC 3957:196).
53 NA VOC 1366:569; Van Dam 1931:95; Keijzer 1856:218.

food item in intra-regional seaborne trade. Produced in surplus quantities
only in certain coastal areas where environmental conditions were particularly suitable for the *Metroxylon sagu* palm, sago was traded extensively around
the Gulf of Tomini, between the Banggai Islands and the Luwuk Peninsula,
along the west coast of Central Sulawesi, and from Greater Sangir to Siau
and Tagulandang.[54]

Hunting, animal husbandry, and fishing

While the collection of commercial forest products was often an important
off-season activity for farmers, there is no historical evidence for the existence in northern Sulawesi of specialized hunter-gatherer groups like the
Punan of Borneo or the 'Negritos' of the Philippines.[55] Wild foodstuffs, in
this region, were collected mainly in times of crop failure, and the hunting
and trapping of deer, wild pigs and other game, although a popular male
pastime, seldom seems to have been very important in economic or dietary
terms (Chapter IX). 'Hunting', noted a Dutch official in Gorontalo in the
early twentieth century, 'is engaged in exclusively for amusement, and cannot be regarded as a means of survival [*middel van bestaan*]' (Dutrieux 1930:
23). Because it often involved the use of fire to create pasture for deer, hunting, together with animal husbandry, nevertheless had a significant impact
on the landscape (Chapter XIV). Large game was most often hunted using
dogs and spears, small animals with blowpipes shooting poisoned darts; in
the nineteenth century, the use of firearms for hunting purposes also became
widespread.[56]

The two most important domesticated animals, historically speaking,
were the water buffalo and the pig. Already mentioned in early European
sources from Sangir and Minahasa (Padtbrugge 1866:326; De Sá 1955:328),
domesticated pigs were found in all parts of the region except Saluan on the
Luwuk Peninsula (A.C. Kruyt 1930a:377), although conversion to Islam tend-

[54]   AV Gorontalo 1824, 1829 (ANRI Gorontalo 3); AV Manado 1854 (ANRI Manado 51); Bleeker
1856:135; Boonstra van Heerdt 1914b:741; Bosscher and Mathijssen 1854:99; De Clercq 1890:133;
Van Delden 1844:17; Goedhart 1908:483; Van der Hart 1853:215, 225; Van Hoëvell 1893b:11; F.
Kelling, 'Taghoelandang en zijn bewoners' [1866] (ARZ NZG 43.2); A.C. Kruyt 1932c:257. In
Banggai, some tubers were also traded by sea (Goedhart 1908:483).
[55]   The Austronesians are thought to have practised agriculture, including rice farming,
since before their arrival in Indonesia (Bellwood 1997:249-50). Pre-Austronesian archaeological
remains from about 6,000 BC found in Minahasa, by contrast, suggest a hunter-gatherer population (Bellwood 1976:283).
[56]   Bow and arrow were in use only on the east coast of Central Sulawesi (Chapter I, Plate 4),
apparently as a result of Moluccan influence. Pleyte (1891:269-71) discusses the historical distribution of blowpipe and bow in Sulawesi.

ed to result in their local replacement by goats or sheep.[57] The distribution of the water buffalo, by contrast, was more restricted. Although present in Central Sulawesi and Gorontalo since the seventeenth century or earlier (Van Dam 1931:91, 93, 97), this animal never became common to the north and east of the 'buffalo line' shown on Map 8 (that is, on the Luwuk Peninsula or in North Sulawesi east of Gorontalo), and always remained absent from the Banggai, Sangir and Talaud islands.[58] Horses, variously used for transport, sport, and food (Van Hoëvell 1905), were present in the seventeenth century in the Palu Valley (Van Dam 1931:91) and presumably in Minahasa, where in later times they were regarded as a Spanish introduction (Graafland 1867-69, I:43). Padtbrugge noticed no horses in Gorontalo in 1677 or 1681, but they were certainly present in this area by 1729.[59] For reasons discussed in Chapter XIV, cattle, originally restricted to the Palu Valley (Van Dam 1931:91; Woodard 1969:94), quickly became the dominant livestock type in Gorontalo and Minahasa after 1850. On the Luwuk Peninsula, finally, young *anoa* or dwarf buffalo (*Bubalus depressicornis*, a wild indigenous herbivore) were often captured alive by hunters and reared in captivity.[60]

Some livestock were kept primarily as working animals (Tillema 1926:221) or as prestige and exchange items, and even when they were raised for slaughter, their meat was typically consumed only on ceremonial occasions (Chapter IX).[61] More significant in terms of its contribution to the routine diet, typically, was fish. Sea fishing, although constrained until late in the nineteenth century by the prevalence of seaborne violence, was always very important in the Sangir, Talaud, and Banggai Islands.[62] Elsewhere inland fisheries, particularly in lakes, tended to predominate. In Gorontalo, much of the population was said to have 'no need' for sea fish because of the plentiful supply from Lake

[57]   *Fragment* 1856:78; Wilken and Schwarz 1867c:338. Gorontalo, for instance, had only sheep and goats in the 1670s (Robidé van der Aa 1867:167), but its inhabitants remembered that their ancestors had kept pigs (NA VOC 1366:733).

[58]   Beyond the buffalo line, small numbers of buffalo were present in the nineteenth century in the Bongka Valley (Adriani and Kruyt 1912-14, II:170, 252), on the south coast of the Luwuk Peninsula (Bosscher and Matthijssen 1854:100; Goedhart 1908:485), in the southeastern corner of Minahasa (Graafland 1898, II:V), and in Mongondow (Riedel 1864b:271; Wilken and Schwarz 1867c:289).

[59]   Robidé van der Aa 1867:166-7, Van Dam 1931:97; NA VOC 2132:217.

[60]   A.C. Kruyt 1930a:377, 1932a:355, 1934:131.

[61]   In Bada and Napu (Lore), but apparently not elsewhere, water buffalo milk and cheese were also consumed (A.C. Kruyt 1938, IV:301-2).

[62]   Colin 1900-02, I:110; Van Delden 1844:22; Van Dinter 1899:353; Encyclopaedisch Bureau 1912a:46-7; Frieswijck 1902:477; A.C. Kruyt 1932c:268; Schrader 1941:127; E. Steller 1866:39. In Gorontalo, the size of the sea fish catch was said to vary in inverse proportion to the amount of pirate activity in the Gulf of Tomini (AV Gorontalo 1841-43, in ANRI Manado 50; AV Gorontalo 1845, in KITLV H111).

Limboto.[63] Much fishing was also done in rivers (Adriani and Kruyt 1950-51, III:381; Van Spreeuwenberg 1845-46:195), while artificial fishponds for fresh-water (not seawater) aquaculture were common in Gorontalo, Minahasa, and probably also Mongondow, although apparently not elsewhere.[64] Fishing tools included lines, nets, traps, harpoons, and also vegetable poisons, which were used both in rivers and on coral reefs (Adriani and Kruyt 1950-51, III:392; Van Dinter 1899:355). Despite the economic importance of fishing, the number of professional fishermen always seems to have been small.[65] Although 'thou-sands' of people, according to a nineteenth-century source, were involved in the Lake Limboto fishery, a later report emphasizes that only 'a very small number' of these actually fished for a living; 'normally, fishing only provides a supplementary source of income'.[66] This lack of occupational specialization, it will be shown below, was a recurrent feature of economic life in the region.

Trade and industry

At the most local level, the scope for trade tended to be restricted by the 'moral economy' of kinship. 'Nobody can refuse a request for something from a member of his tribe – that is, his kinsman', wrote Adriani and Kruyt, 'so any attempt at trading would end with the trade goods being given away as gifts' (Adriani and Kruyt 1912-14, II:299). Individuals who defied public opinion on this point became objects of resentment and risked, according to one Minahasan informant, being poisoned by their neighbours (Graafland 1867-69, I:220). Would-be traders, accordingly, were 'quickly bankrupt' (*Brieven*, 29-10-1909) unless they restricted their commercial exchanges to relative strangers. The feasibility of commerce, on the other hand, increased with distance, and a wide range of goods, including pottery, textiles, palm sugar, tobacco, livestock and slaves, as well as rice, sago and other foodstuffs, were traded between communities within the region on a regular basis. One trade item, iron, was vital to food production, since axes and chopping knives were essential for clearing the vegetation before planting crops on swidden fields. Forged locally from readily-smelted ore found at or near the ground

[63]　Van Doren 1857-60, II:352; R. Scherius 1847:416. In the early twentieth century, the supply of sea fish in many parts of the residency was said to be inadequate to meet local demand (Boonstra van Heerdt 1914b:728; Kornrumpf 1935:85; *Koloniaal verslag* 1908:66; Ter Laag 1920:54).
[64]　Gorontalo: Van Doren 1857-60, II:351. Minahasa: AV Manado 1853 (ANRI Manado 51); Schwarz 1907, III:266. Mongondow: Wilken and Schwarz 1867a:238. The absence of reports of fishponds from other areas may sometimes reflect the inadequacy of the relevant sources; in the Palu Valley, how-ever, there were definitely no fishponds at the time of the Dutch conquest (Hissink 1912:125).
[65]　Bleeker 1856:39-40; Li 1991:17; Logeman 1922:71; Riedel 1872b:546.
[66]　AV Gorontalo 1864 (ANRI Gorontalo 3); Edie 1923:24.

surface in many parts of eastern Central Sulawesi (A.C. Kruyt 1901b), iron was also one of the region's oldest export products.[67] Padtbrugge even wrote that the mountains behind Tobungku were 'as rich in iron and steel as any land could be'.[68] For centuries, this area supplied iron tools and weapons not only to other parts of Sulawesi, but also to Java and the Moluccas.[69] Banggai, the polity which originally controlled most of the iron trade, was mentioned as early as the fourteenth century both by Chinese sources (Ptak 1992:29, 31) and in the Javanese poem *Nāgarakṛtāgama* (Robson 1995:34).

A second mineral of great historical importance was gold, a product for which northern Sulawesi was already well known in the sixteenth century (Cortesão 1944:221-2; Tiele 1877-86, II:39). Mined by both hydraulic and underground techniques from numerous alluvial and bedrock deposits scattered along the northern peninsula and in parts of western Central Sulawesi (Henley 1997b), most of the gold produced in the region was either exported by Indonesian traders, or, after 1729, subject to compulsory purchase by the Dutch authorites in Gorontalo and elsewhere (Chapter I). Coconut oil, used mainly for cooking and lighting, was traded from Sangir to the Moluccas (Hustaart 1656) and from the Palu Valley to Makasar (Cummins 1962:110) from the middle of the seventeenth century onward.[70] Also significant from an early date were a range of valuable, compact sea and forest products, including turtleshell, beeswax, shark fin, mother-of-pearl, edible birds' nests, and sandalwood. One manufactured item, cloth made from pounded tree bark (*fuya*), was also exported to Java and other islands in the seventeenth century as bed hangings or paper (Cummins 1962:110; Padtbrugge 1866: 326), and later for use in shipbuilding (Adriani and Kruyt 1912-14, II:326). *Tripang*, sea cucumbers which commanded high prices as culinary delicacies in China, became a key export after 1700.[71] All of these products were exchanged, down the centuries, for foreign manufactured goods – in the first

[67]   Some iron, nevertheless, was also imported from outside the region. In Minahasa, where iron was a commodity of 'the greatest value' (Colin 1900-02, I:111) in the seventeenth century, knives were manufactured from 'pieces of Chinese pans' (Padtbrugge 1866:325), and later from other scrap iron obtained through Dutch channels (Godée Molsbergen 1928:102).

[68]   NA VOC 1345:286.

[69]   Abendanon 1915-18, IV:1766, 1768-9; Adriani 1913b:859; Lapian 1980:24; L.Y. Andaya 1993:87; Bosscher and Matthijssen 1854:77-8; Cortesão 1944:215-6; Van Dam 1931:93; M.L. Dames 1921:205; *Generale missiven* V:441; Van der Hart 1853:83; Van Hoëvell 1893b:27; Van Musschenbroek 1880:96; Noorduyn 1983:104; Reid 1988-93, I:110; Riedel 1886:79-80; Rumphius 1705:205, 213; De Sá 1955:394; Sarasin and Sarasin 1905, I:312; A. Revius, 'Algemeen verslag omtrent de oostkust van Celebes', 10-2-1851 (ANRI Ternate 180); Vosmaer 1839:107.

[70]   Later in the seventeenth century, Kaili also traded oil and coconuts to Dutch Batavia (*Daghregister* 1676:247, 318, 1677:246, 283, 1678:411, 619, 1679:281, 388, 550).

[71]   The earliest report of *tripang* collection which I have come across for northern Sulawesi dates from 1695 (NA VOC 1579:171).

place textiles, but also brassware, porcelain, opium, and firearms.[72]

The most important single concentration of trade, historically, was the narrow base of the northern peninsula, where gold and other products were carried overland from the Gulf of Tomini, from the long coasts of which they had been brought together by sea, to the Palu Bay, itself an important producer of coconut oil and a gateway to the interior of western Central Sulawesi. From here the produce of the region was exported to Makasar, Java, and the Malaka Straits (especially, after its foundation in 1819, Singapore).[73] The shortest route across the peninsula at this point ended in the west at Tawaeli, the ruler of which was described by Padtbrugge as the most powerful chief in the Bay (Van Dam 1931:89-90), while the Tomini Gulf terminus of the same crossing was controlled by the important kingdom of Parigi (Bleeker 1856:134; Van der Hart 1853:205). In eastern Central Sulawesi there was no such single central trade node, the valuable iron produced in this area being exported variously via the Tomori Bay (Van der Hart 1853:83), Bungku and neigbouring settlements on the Tobungku coast (Bosscher and Matthijssen 1854:77), or Wotu and Luwu on the Gulf of Bone in South Sulawesi (Reid 1988-93, I:110). On the northern peninsula, Gorontalo and Manado were the most historically important of the many local entrepôts.

Media of exchange

Until late in the nineteenth century, most trade in northern Sulawesi took the form of barter. Some money did circulate in the region from much earlier periods: VOC soldiers, for instance, used cash to buy food in Manado in the seventeenth century, and silver coins were in demand in Parigi around 1750.[74] Copper currency also came into use in Gorontalo during the 1820s, and in Bolaang Mongondow by the 1850s.[75] In Sangir and Talaud, on the other hand, little money of any kind appeared before 1860.[76] Around the

---

[72]   Although the import of firearms and opium may have increased in later times, both were already present in the region in the seventeenth century (Padtbrugge 1866:317; Keijzer 1856:211; Wessels 1935:108).

[73]   NA VOC 1366:694, 919-20; VOC 1775:232-5; AV Ternate 1807 (ANRI Ternate 141); AV Manado 1854 (ANRI Manado 51); Van Dam 1931:90-1; A.J. van Delden, 'Nota', 1-7-1846 (KITLV H142); Van Doren 1857-60, II:354; Noorduyn 1983:116; RPR Ternate 19-5-1787 (ANRI Ternate 26); Riedel 1872b:548; C.L. Wieling, 'Berigt omtrent het al of niet bezitten van Gorontalo', 6-2-1806 (ANRI Manado 165); Woodard 1969:81, 85-6.

[74]   NA VOC 1366:553; VOC 2882:315-6.

[75]   AV Gorontalo 1823 (ANRI Gorontalo 3); Riedel 1864b:277, 283.

[76]   AV Manado 1853 (ANRI Manado 51); Buddingh 1860:336-7; Cuarteron 1855:10, 23; Van Delden 1844:23; E. Francis, 'Aantekeningen van den kommissaris voor Manado 1846' (ANRI Manado 167); A.J.F. Jansen, 'Rapport betrekkelijk het oppergezag over en den toestand van de Talaut Eilanden', 12-8-1857 (ANRI Manado 166); Van de Velde van Cappellen 1857:51.

Gulf of Tomini, traders generally worked without cash throughout the nine-teenth century (Broersma 1931b:231), and Kruyt claimed that when he first arrived in the interior of Central Sulawesi in 1892, coins still had 'no value' there except as jewelry.[77] Earlier sources confirm that even where money was present, it did not necessarily function as a medium of exchange. Woodard (1969:119) observed in 1793 that although the 'Malays' of Palu 'set a great value on all coined money', they 'keep it in store, and do not part with it even when they want to purchase any thing'. 'Their chief trade', instead, was 'for gold dust and barter'.[78] In Minahasa at the same period, the Dutch were said to 'gain much on their copper money, which going amongst the highland-ers, and often worn as ornament (by the children especially), never returns' (Forrest 1792:86). In Central Sulawesi, some copper coinage was actually melted down and recast as jewellry (A.C. Kruyt 1900b:460). Exchange rates between different types of coinage varied widely from area to area even at the end of the nineteenth century (Adriani and Kruyt 1912-14, II:312; A.C. Kruyt 1892:375). Weights and measures were correspondingly diverse; in Gorontalo, for instance, the *gantang* used for measuring rice was six times smaller than in Minahasa.[79]

In many parts of the region it was imported textiles, rather than money as such, which long provided the closest approximation to a standardized currency. Clothing for everyday use was mostly manufactured within the region, from locally-grown cotton or abaca (Manila hemp), from the pounded bark of certain trees, or from pineapple and bamboo fibres, the pre-ferred materials varying from area to area.[80] Foreign (mostly Indian) woven textiles, however, were also important from early times as prestige goods.[81] These luxury cloths were seldom worn, but rather stored as a form of capital (Adriani and Kruyt 1912-14, II:188, 311; Steller 1866:25). Minahasans, in the early nineteenth century, were reported to 'measure the value of everything

[77]   A.C. Kruyt 1923:150. Elsewhere Kruyt qualified this view to some extent, although it remains clear that money played a subsidiary role in exchange in the interior (Adriani and Kruyt 1912-14, II:312).
[78]   This reference to gold as a medium of exchange is unusual; both silver and copper were preferred over gold for this purpose in the nineteenth century (AV Manado 1854, in ANRI Manado 51).
[79]   AV Gorontalo 1841-1843 (ANRI Manado 50); Riedel 1872b:542. De Clercq (1871b:27) and Logeman (1922:69) give similar examples of discordant local measuring systems.
[80]   Except for pineapple (*Ananas sativa*) fibre cloth, briefly discussed by Martin (1993:378), descriptions of the main indigenous weaving technologies of northern Sulawesi are given in the standard work by Jasper and Pirngadie (1912:19, 37, 54-60, 143-7, 180-82, 230, 236, 270-74, 294-300). Bark cloth is dealt with by, among many other writers, Adriani and Kruyt (1901) and Aragon (1990).
[81]   Silk *patola* cloths from India, for instance, were already present on Siau in the sixteenth century (C. Wessels 1933:390).

in terms of pieces of cloth' (Pietermaat, De Vriese and Lucas 1840:144), particularly the Indian weavings known as *salempuris*, 'which have been familiar
to the natives of Manado for many years, and are therefore accepted just like
money for the purposes of sale and exchange'.[82] In Palu at the beginning of
the eighteenth century another type of Indian cloth, from Bengal, was reportedly the standard measure of comparative value.[83] Not all prestige textiles
had such distant origins; 'money cloths' woven on the island of Buton in
southeastern Sulawesi (A.C. Kruyt 1933b) played a similar role in parts of
Mori and Tobungku in the nineteenth century, and on the Luwuk Peninsula
until the early twentieth.[84]

The role of textiles as units of comparative value was sometimes taken
over by other commodities.[85] On Banggai in the mid-nineteenth century,
according to Revius, the price of 'any article whatsoever' was 'always
expressed as a certain number of slaves'; one slave, moreover, was also
regarded as having a monetary value of 20 silver *rijksdaalders* (rix-dollars)
or pieces of eight.[86] Before money actually began to circulate in large quantities in the Gulf of Tomini, comparably, it was already common for the value
of trade goods to be 'expressed in *ringgit* [dollars, rix-dollars], even though
the *rijksdaalders* themselves were seldom seen' (Broersma 1931b:232). The
distinction between monetized and non-monetized exchange, then, was
never absolute, and neither was the extensive monetization of the late colonial period (a development outlined in Chapter IX) irreversible. During the
economic depression of the 1930s, when cash incomes temporarily declined
following the collapse of copra prices (Henley 1996:127), there was an almost
complete reversion to barter in some areas as cash disappeared from circulation (A.Ph. van Aken 1932:22; Avink 1935). The volume of local commerce,
however, remained considerable, and in Palu one Dutch official commented
that people 'would be entirely content in this money-less society were it
not for the troublesome government, which demands taxes in hard cash'
(Vorstman 1936:40).

Slaves and imported textiles represented large units of value, and mainly
seem to have been used, along with livestock and brassware, for making
brideprice payments and rendering substantial fines. Significant quantities of

---

[82]   Res. Manado to Directeur 's lands producten Batavia, 15-10-1832 (ANRI Manado 77).
[83]   NA VOC 1775:232.
[84]   Van der Hart 1853:73; A. Revius, 'Algemeen verslag omtrent de oostkust van Celebes', 10-
2-1851 (ANRI Ternate 180); A.C. Kruyt 1930a:357. Cotton cloths from Gorontalo may have had a
similar function in Poso (Adriani 1913b:857).
[85]   Brass ornaments, for instance, may have been a more important exchange item than textiles
in parts of the interior of Central Sulawesi at the turn of the century (Sarasin and Sarasin 1905,
II:69).
[86]   'Algemeen verslag omtrent de oostkust van Celebes', 10-2-1851 (ANRI Ternate 180).

cloth and other prestige goods were also buried with the dead, disappearing permanently from circulation.[87] Such goods were nevertheless also exchange-able, in principle, for less valuable items like foodstuffs, and although some European accounts emphasize the irrational and ritual aspects of indigenous barter trade (Graafland 1867-69, I:157; A.C. Kruyt 1923), others portray a practical system of predictable exchange rates.

> The value of the goods on offer [in local trade among the Toraja] was quite well established. A complete set of brass bracelets or anklets, for instance, was equiva-lent to one buffalo; in rice, a buffalo was worth 500 sheaves; in salt, two pieces of about 75 cm in length and with the girth of a man's waist. If the place to which the salt was carried lay far from the coast, on the other hand, one such piece of salt was sufficient to purchase a buffalo. (Adriani and Kruyt 1912-14, II:301.)

Most labour, in agriculture and other activities, was supplied from within the household, or by slaves, or on the basis of reciprocal exchange.[88] Labour hire, however, also occurred, even in substantially non-monetized contexts. In early nineteenth-century Minahasa, for instance, the densely-populated Tondano area formed an exception to the local rule of limited demographic mobility, displaying a pattern of seasonal male emigration predicated on the existence of a market for labour in neighbouring districts.

> And because the people of Tondano possess more water than land, so that food-stuffs are relatively scarcer there than elsewhere, each year the greater part hire themselves out all over the rest of the country of Manado, building or repairing houses, opening and clearing swiddens, cutting planks and timber, burning lime, and generally doing any work which people will pay them for. In this way they earn their keep, and also obtain cloths [*lijnwaden*] and other items, with which they return to their wives when their work is done.[89]

Until the establishment of internal peace in 1809, some Tondano men also hired out their services as headhunters (Mangindaän 1873:366). Besides labour, farmland in Minahasa could likewise be hired and, at least within the bounds of the *walak* or village federation, sold (Riedel 1872b:538, 542; Van Spreeuwenberg 1845-46:326). Where this was not the case, as in the Poso and Balantak areas (A.C. Kruyt 1924:49-50, 1934:125), it was usually where popu-lation densities were lower, and land correspondingly more abundant.

---

[87]   Jacobs 1974-84, II:266; Schrauwers 1997:371; Van Wylick 1941:48, 109, 197.
[88]   The literature on the best-documented type of traditional labour exchange in the region, the Minahasan *mapalus*, is surveyed by Hekker (1988:108-14); Schrauwers (1995a:342, 346, 1998:116) describes its Pamona equivalent, *pesale*, and Li (1991:15-16) gives information on modern labour exchange practices among the Lauje.
[89]   P.A. van Middelkoop, 'Memorien ten vervolge van het Algemeen Verslag van de Commissie naar de Moluksche eilanden', 30-9-1818 (NA Schneither 128).

The social context of trade

Trade, traditionally, seldom took place in the context of permanent or periodic markets at which many buyers and sellers regularly came together. In
Central Sulawesi before the colonial conquest, for instance, marketplaces of
any sort were seen only in the Palu Valley and a part of Mori.[90] In the Poso
area only funeral feasts were 'sometimes reminiscent of markets', guests
from distant villages taking advantage of the security and sociability which
prevailed at these ceremonial occasions to barter goods with one another
(Adriani and Kruyt 1912-14, II:304). On Siau, according to Van Delden (1844:
23), the only marketplace in all of Sangir was abolished at some point prior
to 1823 by a *raja* who 'managed to achieve a monopoly on trade, and strictly
forbade anybody to buy or sell anything except from and to himself' (Van
Delden 1844:23).

A proportion of trade was always embedded in political monopolies of
this kind. The various *raja* of the Sangir Islands, for example, all had vassals
in Talaud whom they prohibited from sailing to any destination other than
Sangir.[91] According to one source, this ban was enforced 'on pain of death'.[92]
Trade between the two island groups, as Resident Jansen observed, took the
form of a 'privileged exchange' [*gepriviligeerde ruilhandel*] involving political as well as commercial commodities.[93] Honorific titles were conferred on
Talaud leaders by their Sangirese overlords upon payment of a *harga pangkat*
or 'price of office', consisting of ten slaves or the equivalent value in abaca
textiles, rattan mats, and sometimes gongs or other brassware. At their investiture, the recipients were also presented with foreign goods, imported via
Sangir, which were regarded as the material attributes of the rank conferred.
For a Talaud *raja* in 1825, the 'complete clothing and equipment necessary for
that office' were specified as 'one to two fathoms of black and white linnen,
two or three handspans of rod iron, and two fathoms of brass wire'.[94]

Political leaders were almost always traders. The ruler of Tojo was described
at the end of the nineteenth century as 'more a merchant than a *raja*', and said
to spend most of his time 'trading with the Alfurs in the interior of his territo-

---

[90]   Adriani and Kruyt 1898:489, 1900:171, 1912-14, II:303-4, 344; A.C. Kruyt 1900b:461, 1926:
529-30, 1938, I:24, 75-6, 119; *Landschap Donggala* 1905:517; Sarasin and Sarasin 1905, II:68.
[91]   Cuarteron 1855:9, 22-3; A.J.F. Jansen, 'Missive Sangir en Talaut Eilanden', 26-8-1857;
'Rapport betrekkelijk het oppergezag over en den toestand van de Talaut Eilanden', 12-8-1857
(ANRI Manado 166).
[92]   E. Francis, 'Aantekeningen van den kommissaris voor Menado 1846' (ANRI Manado 167).
[93]   'Rapport betrekkelijk het oppergezag over en den toestand van de Talaut Eilanden', 12-8-
1857 (ANRI Manado 166).
[94]   Van Delden 1844:5. The granting of honorific titles in return for payment was also reported
from other parts of the region (De Clercq 1883:123; 'Memorie door den afgaande Manados onderprefect Carl Christoph Prediger', 15-9-1809, in ANRI Manado 61; Riedel 1872b:535).

ry'.[95] The chiefs in Bolaang Mongondow, complained the missionaries Wilken and Schwarz (1867c:296) in 1866, were 'all traders, as a result of which the population is more or less obliged to buy at outrageously high prices'. Political leaders in Banggai and Tobungku told Revius that their status entitled them 'to purchase all goods at reduced value as a form of taxation'.[96] Commerce and taxation, in fact, were not distinct, and even labour services performed for political leaders were often (partially) remunerated in trade goods.

> In Sigi the common people worked a large expanse of *sawah*, from which 10,000 sheaves of rice could be harvested, for the king. Groups of boys took turns to graze the numerous royal buffalo, receiving clothing and food from the king for as long as they were so employed. In other areas too, noblemen usually gave something in return for services rendered and gifts offered to them: salt, a chopping knife, a clay cooking pot. (A.C. Kruyt 1938, I:508.)

Most forms of precolonial tribute or taxation probably involved some such element of direct reciprocity.[97] In the case of the 'privileged exchange' between Sangir and remote, relatively inaccessible Talaud, it is possible that the reverse was also true: that is, that most trade took place in a political context.[98] Sheer decentralization of political power, however, probably meant that exclusive monopolies, although many may have aspired to them in principle, were not very common in practice.[99] In Central Sulawesi, where tribute from upland groups to coastal *raja* was typically paid only at intervals of several years (Adriani and Kruyt 1912-14, I:131; A.C. Kruyt 1938, I:176), it is likely that as Aragon (1992:119) suggests, 'such nominal or periodic tribute gifts were made with the aim of establishing good enough relations to open opportunities in external trade markets'.[100] In the Poso area, trade

[95] Jellesma 1903:214. Many other *raja*, at least partly in connection with their trading activities, were likewise peripatetic (Bastiaans 1938:227; Van der Hart 1853:113; Henley 1996:30; Van Hoëvell 1892:357; *Koloniaal verslag* 1874:20; Riedel 1864b:277; Sarasin and Sarasin 1905, I:91; Steller 1866:36-7; Velthoen 1997b:373).
[96] 'Algemeen verslag omtrent de oostkust van Celebes', 10-2-1851 (ANRI Ternate 180). W.H. Scott (1994:129) describes similar systems in the pre-Hispanic Philippines.
[97] Some foreign observers were either unaware of this, or thought it too obvious to be worth mentioning explicitly. In the seventeenth century, for instance, Navarette stated only that the inhabitants of the Palu Valley paid an annual 'tribute' in coconut oil to the kingdom of Makasar (Cummins 1962:110), whereas the Dutch admiral Speelman later described the same transaction as a purchase in exchange for Indian textiles (Noorduyn 1983:116).
[98] Even in Talaud, however, there were also some direct contacts with Mindanao (Cuarteron 1855:23; 'Rapport betrekkelijk het oppergezag over en den toestand van de Talaut Eilanden', 12-8-1857, in ANRI Manado 166) and with foreign traders sailing directly from Ternate (Valckenaer 1778).
[99] Heersink (1999:43), comparably, concludes that on Selayar in South Sulawesi, a royal trade monopoly could not have been effective 'given the internal political fragmentation on the island'.
[100] Aragon's characterization of tribute as a form of 'gift', on the other hand, seems questionable given that non-payment could lead to punitive raids (Aragon 1992:128; A.C. Kruyt 1938, I: 184, 271).

conducted on disadvantageous terms within the context of a tributary relationship was known as *mobalu sala* or 'not really selling' (Adriani and Kruyt
1912-14, I:132, 136, 138), already implying a contrast with 'real' trade based
on equal exchange. In one early field report, in fact, Albert Kruyt (1894:13)
states explicitly that after the Poso Toraja have delivered their annual rice
tribute to the kingdom of Parigi in exchange for a few pieces of cotton cloth,
they are free to sell rice to others 'at the normal market prices'. Having paid
an 'anchorage charge' in trade goods to the *raja*, likewise, foreign traders
arriving at harbour settlements were usually able to deal directly with his
subjects.[101]

During anthropological fieldwork in the Tinombo area in 1990, Li (1991:8-
9, 16, 22, 26, 62-3) observed extensive non-market, non-monetized exchange
between the inhabitants of adjacent 'agro-ecological zones', including the
'middle hills', characterized by swidden agriculture based on rice and maize;
and the 'inner hills', where the most important subsistence crops were taro
and cassava.

> Middle hill people most commonly go inland to seek food from the inner hills
> when they experience a prolonged drought and are unable to grow the customary
> two to three corn crops per year. In this case, they go seeking food in large groups,
> since everyone is hungry. Middle hill farmers also go seeking food from inner
> hill people when they have suffered from an individual disaster such as a crop
> ravaged by wild pigs, or a shallot crop that was diseased. The inner hill people
> usually give them taro and cassava, unless they happen to have had a good crop
> of rice or corn. In the latter case, the middle hill farmers hearing about an abun-
> dant harvest may take major trade goods such as sarongs or parangs [chopping
> knives] with them, and make several trips or go with many family members so
> that they can carry home enough corn or rice to see them through several weeks.
> (Li 1991:63.)

Although facilitated under modern conditions by the absence of violence or
political trading privileges, in other respects this may well provide a good
model for traditional patterns of local exchange. Trading contacts are made
on a person-to-person basis as the need arises, and the distribution of manufactures like iron and cloth is carried out by farmers themselves as one part
of an exchange system which, as a whole, is oriented as much toward the
maintenance of food security as toward the maximization of income.

---

[101] Lapian 1980:147; Bosscher and Matthijssen 1854:87-8; De Clercq 1883:118; Van der Hart
1853:73, 100; Steller 1866:37. In Central Sulawesi, some professional traders penetrated the interior themselves (A.C. Kruyt 1909:371).

An unspecialized economy

Except on a gender basis, any kind of permanent division of labour was always unusual.[102] Almost every Sangirese male, for instance, was traditionally 'a farmer, a fisherman, and from time to time also a trader' (Van de Velde van Cappellen 1857:50).

> No craftsmen [*ambachtslieden*] are found on Sangir. None, that is, unless we regard as such a small number of men who are more skilled than others in blacksmithing and carpentry, and who are referred to as *tukang* (master), but who most of the time are nevertheless fishermen, traders and farmers in one person just like the rest, and who only occasionally work iron or wood. (Steller 1866:39.)

Even in the parts of eastern Central Sulawesi which were renowned for the manufacture and export of iron weapons, according to Kruyt (1901b:150), there were no professional blacksmiths at the end of the nineteenth century. Handicraft production and trade, along with hunting, fishing, gambling, feasting, and war, were typically part-time activities engaged in by farmers during periods when their labour was not required in food production.[103] Salt, too, was produced mostly by its consumers themselves, who trekked to the coast in the dry season to manufacture it by boiling brine.[104] Nor did high social status necessarily bring freedom from agricultural labour. 'Everybody, from *raja* to slave', wrote the missionary Kelling on Tagulandang (Sangir), 'is employed in farming'.[105] Among the Toraja, likewise, the chiefs (and their wives) all grew their own food (Adriani 1913b:861).

> The Toraja are without exception farmers, from the most distinguished chief to the humblest slave. All adhere to the philosophy that each must supply his own food. Besides growing rice and maize, in his spare time the Toraja also manufactures palm sugar, fishes, works iron, builds boats, and searches for *damar* and rattan. But he never lives from these activities; he lives from his ricefield. (Adriani and Kruyt 1912-14, II:229.)

At the same period even the paramount *raja* of Mori, one of the most influential chiefs in the whole region, was reported to 'work his swidden [*tuin*]

---

102 Adriani and Kruyt 1912-14, II:301; AV Manado 1833 (ANRI Manado 48); Van Dinter 1899: 332; Graafland 1867-69, II:250; Van Hoëvell 1891:41; Van Kol 1903:335; Riedel 1870b:66; Tendeloo 1873:28; Van de Velde van Cappellen 1857:50; Wilken and Schwarz 1867c:376.
103 Trading expeditions were often combined with hunting (Adriani and Kruyt 1912-14, II:301).
104 Adriani and Kruyt 1912-14, II:338-41; Nourse 1989:74; Padtbrugge 1866:325. Some salt, however, was also traded between the coast and the interior (Aragon 1992:130; Graafland 1898, II:131; A.C. Kruyt 1938, I:128, 325; Res. Manado to Gov. Moluccas, 27-7-1842, in ANRI Manado 80; Riedel 1864b:276, 1869b:509).
105 F. Kelling, 'Het eiland Taghoelandang en zijn bewoners' [1866] (ARZ NZG 43.2).

just as well as his subjects'.[106] Despite rather sustained economic growth and commercialization in the first decades of the twentieth century, low levels of occupational specialization remained typical of the region throughout the colonial period; 'almost all Minahasans', for example, were still said to be farmers in the 1920s.[107]

The fact that most people grew most of their own food, however, should not be interpreted as an indication that other economic activities were insignificant.[108] Dove (1983b:93) has rightly warned against 'the misconstrual of swidden farming as not just the focus but the sum total of the economy', a mistake which tends to result in the false assumption that swidden farmers must be 'without ties to broader trading and commercial networks'. Indeed, the relatively light labour demands of this type of cultivation (Boserup 1965: 44-8; Hanks 1972:65) tended, other things being equal, to permit a more extensive part-time involvement in commercial activities than was possible among farmers who depend for their food on more labour-intensive technologies. In Bolaang Mongondow during the nineteenth century, off-season gold mining by swidden farmers appeared to rival agriculture itself in economic significance.[109]

> The inhabitants of Mongondow are farmers and miners. After the dry *padi* fields are cleared and fenced, the men normally go to the mines of Dolangon, Mintu and other places to collect gold. This metal is later sold to the Bugis and other traders at Kotabunan, or exchanged for cloths and iron. Each year the *raja*, in addition to his half *gantang* [10 kg] of rice and two guilders in copper coins from each household, also receives a *duit* or $^1/_9$ *reaal* [3 grammes] of gold from each miner. (Riedel 1864b:276-7.)

The extent to which farmers engaged in part-time commercial activities, as already noted (Chapter I), varied considerably from area to area. In Minahasa (except Tondano), the pattern of seasonal male emigration found elsewhere was never strongly developed, and lulls in agricultural work were filled mostly with elaborate ceremonial events and feasting (Schouten 1998:22-4; Tauchmann 1968:196-245). Sangirese men, by contrast, were described by the

---

[106] Adriani and Kruyt 1900:165. Elsewhere, however, there may have been some *raja* who lived entirely from tribute and the labour of others (Aragon 1992:50; Nourse 1989:56-7).
[107] Eibergen 1928:237. Also Graafland 1898, II:338; Kielstra 1921:41; Van Marle 1922, I:53; Tendeloo 1873:28.
[108] Some accounts, in fact, do not even put farming at the head of the list of economic activities. 'The natives', wrote the botanist Lam (1932:49) after a visit to Miangas (Talaud) in 1926, 'are fishermen, traders and agriculturalists and it may be suggested that any individual can take up these professions as opportunity affords'.
[109] A similar pattern of seasonal gold mining persists up to the present in some parts of the region (Aragon 1992:73).

missionary Steller (1866:36-7) as possessing an 'inborn' inclination to trade, groups of up to a thousand spending months at a time away from home on expeditions to Manado, Ternate and Talaud. Resident Jansen admired the courage with which they 'defied the perils of the sea' to bring coconut oil for sale in Manado, commenting that this indicated 'no lack of entrepreneurial spirit [*ondernemingsgeest*]'.[110] Despite the absence of either money or local marketplaces, accordingly, the domestic economy of the Sangirese farmer was always quite closely integrated into long-distance commerce.

> Farming provides him with coconut oil in such quantities that he is able to supply Manado and Ternate with a large part of the lamp oil which they need. Seldom does a year go by in which he does not sell a few *pikul* of rice at a good price. His cacao trees, although they have been ailing somewhat in the last four years, also bring him a reasonable profit now and then. His daily food costs him no money, and indeed little effort, to produce. His *kofo* [*Musa textilis*, abaca] (a sort of banana plant), thanks to its silvery fibres and the diligence of his wife, provides him and his whole family with plenty of cloth for clothing. He builds *prahu*, forges his iron weapons and tools, manufactures his fishing nets, and makes the best brass wire available in Manado or Ternate, to which places he takes any surplus of these articles which he has. In this way he obtains cotton textiles, pots and pans, brass, iron, firearms, and anything else which he needs or desires. Seldom, however, does he acquire money; his trade is predominantly barter. (Van de Velde van Cappellen 1857:50-1.)

In addition to coconut oil and cocoa, turtleshell, birds' nests, and abaca cloth (*kofo*) were also exported from Sangir at this period. Of the 'thousands' of pieces of *kofo* shipped each year to Manado and Ternate (Buddingh 1860:45), some ultimately found their way to buyers in more distant areas such as New Guinea (Martin 1993:377).

The limited division of labour within each community did not preclude the emergence of product specialization on a geographical basis. Cotton textiles woven by women in Gorontalo, for instance, were long traded to the lands around the Gulf of Tomini (Riedel 1870a:91; R. Scherius 1847:416-7), partly in exchange for *fuya* (bark cloth), used by the Gorontalese in boatbuilding and as ceremonial clothing, produced in the Toraja uplands, where no weaving was practised (Adriani and Kruyt 1912-14, II:326). The inhabitants of the Nanusa Islands, small outliers of the Talaud group, specialized from an early date in the manufacture of boats, which they exported to the rest of Talaud, to Sangir, and sometimes even to peninsular North Sulawesi and Ternate, probably in return for foodstuffs.[111] The island of Manui, off

---

[110]   AV Manado 1853 (ANRI Manado 51).
[111]   AV Manado 1906 (ANRI Manado 30); Cuarteron 1855:22; Van Delden 1844:28; Ebbinge Wübben 1888:137, 1889:209; Forrest 1779:317; *Generale missiven* VII:84; A.J.F. Jansen, 'Rapport betrekkelijk het oppergezag over en den toestand van de Talaut Eilanden', 12-8-1857 (ANRI Manado 166); *Koloniaal verslag* 1891:18; *Nanoesa-eilanden* 1905:315; Stokking 1910:17.

the southern coast of Tobungku, also exported boats (Van der Hart 1853:72; Vosmaer 1839:109). Other areas, particularly Tinombo (*Landbouw in Gorontalo* 1871:364; Riedel 1870a:89), became specialized in the cultivation of tobacco, a common item in intra-regional trade by the nineteenth century. The highest degree of either local or occupational specialization at any time prior to 1930 was probably found in the most important ironworking centre, Matano (just over the 'border' with South Sulawesi on the lake of the same name), during the seventeenth century, before the Indonesian iron industries began to decline as a result of competition from foreign imports (Reid 1988-93, I: 112). Rumphius (1705:213) wrote of Matano in this period that 'almost the whole *negeri* consists of blacksmiths', and although it is likely that the iron founders were in fact also engaged in farming, Padtbrugge agreed that the population of this area 'makes its living mostly by mining and forging iron' (Van Dam 1931:93).

Cash crops and forest products

Besides allowing time for supplementary commercial activities, swidden farming also provided opportunities to plant commercial tree crops, without (at least in the short term) much additional investment of labour, on the newly-abandoned swiddens after the last foodcrop harvest.[112] The rapid expansion of smallholder cocoa production during the early nineteenth century, stimulated by a lucrative market in the Philippines, illustrates how effectively people could made use of these opportunities when sufficient commercial demand existed. In 1804 it was reported that cocoa grew well in Minahasa, but that the indigenous population understood neither its value nor the correct cultivation methods (Watuseke and Henley 1994: 381-3). By the late 1840s, however, there were estimated to be more than a million cocoa trees in Minahasa, and 'almost every native' was said to have planted some.[113] Meanwhile the crop had also spread to Gorontalo and to areas outside direct Dutch control, including the Sangir Islands and Bolaang Mongondow. Had it not been for a destructive pod-borer pest which spread

---

112   Clarence-Smith (1998b:99), extrapolating from experience in other parts of the world, argues that cocoa was usually planted on virgin land cleared specifically for that purpose. Contemporary descriptions, however, portray mixed stands of cocoa and other trees (CV Manado 1859, in ANRI Ambon 1543), and Resident Jansen (1861:239) identified 'fallow land covered with brushwood [*kreupelhout*]' as 'most suitable for cocoa planting' in Minahasa. Virgin forest, admittedly, was cleared on quite a large scale for coffee cultivation at the same period, but this took place in a context of political compulsion (Schouten 1998:58).
113   A.J.F. Jansen, 'Aantekeningen betreffende de kakao-kultuur in de residentie Menado', 23-4-1859' (ANRI Manado 167); AV Manado 1849 (ANRI Manado 51).

inexorably through North Sulawesi from 1841 onward (Clarence-Smith 1998b:101), cocoa would probably have become the region's primary export crop. Coffee cultivation in Minahasa, likewise, was initiated by Minahasans themselves at the beginning of the nineteenth century, and expanded quickly on a voluntary basis.[114] Some 200,000 coffee trees had already been planted by the time coffee exports were monopolized by the government, and compulsory cultivation introduced, in 1822.[115]

Toward the end of the nineteenth century, people in many parts of the region were also quick to respond to a sudden expansion in international demand for two local forest products. Rattan, long an important raw material for indigenous handicrafts, became a major export commodity in the lands around the Gulf of Tomini during the 1870s, prompting an 'amazing' increase (Van Hoëvell 1891:42) in the volume of trade passing through the port of Gorontalo.[116] The other ingredient of this forest product boom was *damar*, the resin of conifers of the genus *Agathis*, used for manufacturing varnishes.[117] *Damar* production was concentrated in the eastern part of Central Sulawesi, where a completely new entrepôt, attracting seasonal resin collectors from as far afield as Bada in the western highlands, sprang up at Watambayoli in the Sumara Valley on the Gulf of Mori around 1885 (Adriani and Kruyt 1900:153; 1950-51, III:346). Existing harbour settlements also grew – Tojo, for instance, from some 450 souls around 1890 to about 900 in 1898 (Adriani and Kruyt 1899:18; Van Hoëvell 1893a:69). In the year 1900 almost 3,500 tonnes of rattan and more than 1,300 tonnes of resin were exported from the Dutch-controlled harbours of the region alone (*Statistiek* 1900:265-6); the real totals, especially of *damar*, must have been considerably higher (Schrauwers 1997:373).

The product which really began to shake the regional economy loose from its foundations in subsistence agriculture, however, was copra (dried coconut flesh), in the second half of the nineteenth century an increasingly

---

[114] Riedel 1872b:566; L. Wessels 1891:50-3. The earliest references to coffee in the region date from the 1740s, when the VOC encouraged its cultivation in Bolaang Mongondow (NA VOC 2649:85-6). While there is no record that this policy was effective at the time, European visitors to Mongondow were surprised to find coffee growing extensively there in 1857 (Riedel 1864b:275), and although a source from the 1860s states that Mongondow coffee served only for domestic consumption (Wilken and Schwarz 1867c:287), it was certainly being exported by 1880 (Matthes 1881). In the first half of the nineteenth century some coffee was also exported from Donggala in western Central Sulawesi (Crawfurd 1856:194).

[115] AV Manado 1833 (ANRI Manado 48).

[116] AV Gorontalo 1872 (ANRI Manado 9); AV Manado 1883 (ANRI Manado 52); Van der Crab 1875:443.

[117] *Damar*, used locally for lighting (A.C. Kruyt 1931:618; Van der Vlies 1940:622), in boatbuilding (Woodard 1969:121), and as a varnish for pottery (Graafland 1867-69, I:226, Van Son 1935: 12), was a minor trade product long before the boom, which began in about 1865 (Goedhart 1908:521). A sixteenth-century Portuguese map already labels northern Sulawesi as an 'Island of Damar' (Henley 1995:32).

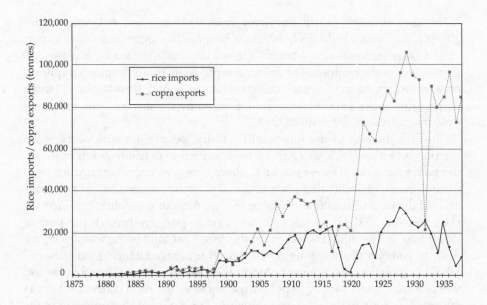

Figure 2. Copra exports and rice imports, residency of Manado, 1875-1938.
Sources: De Clerq 1891:221 (1875, 1878); *Statistiek handel* 1879-1900; W.H.M. Jansen
1990, Bijlage 2 (1901-38).

important raw material for the European and North American food, soap,
and lubricant industries (Heersink 1999:160-63). Copra first became important in those areas where coconuts were already cultivated on a commercial
basis for their oil: Sangir, where copra production was pioneered during the
1860s on Siau (Van Dinter 1899:334), and Kaili, where the seventeenth-century visitor Navarrete had already found it 'wonderful to see the Coco-trees
there are about the Fields' (Cummins 1962:110), and where copra was 'an
important export article' by the 1890s.[118] The new industry, however, quickly
also spread to other parts of the region, where millions of coconut trees
were planted from about 1880 onward.[119] While most coconuts were planted
spontaneously, the Dutch added an element of compulsion in some areas
around the turn of the century.[120] Chinese traders, by lending money and

[118]   *Landschap Donggala* 1905:516. Copra production, apparently, is less labour-intensive than the
manufacture of coconut oil (Heersink 1999:174), and this no doubt accelerated the transition.
[119]   Minahasa, for instance, had fewer than half a million coconut trees in 1860 (CV Manado
1861, in ANRI Manado 95), but at least 6 million by 1938 (Weg 1938:144). Around the Gulf of
Tomini and on the Togian Islands, where there were only 100,000 trees according to a rough estimate made in the 1860s (CV Gorontalo 1864, in ANRI Manado 44), 'millions' had been planted
by 1915 (À Campo 1992:167). Further statistics on coconut cultivation are given in Chapter XIV.
[120]   Van Hengel 1910:26; Hissink 1912:122; À Campo 1992:167.

goods against the future yield of trees which they obliged their borrowers to plant, also contributed indirectly to the expansion of this crop (Peddemors 1935:25). Copra was the most important single item of trade in Manado by 1892 (*Koloniaal verslag* 1893:24), and in the 1920s it accounted for as much as 87 percent (by value) of all exports from the residency.[121] The 100,000 tonnes or so of copra exported annually from northern Sulawesi around 1930 generated sufficient income to buy, among other things, some 25,000 tonnes of imported rice (Figure 2), enough to feed more than 20 percent of the total population of the residency (Chapter IX). By the end of the colonial period there were reportedly many farmers in the region who had 'little or no interest in *ladang* cultivation' (M. van Rhijn 1941:42) and 'only made *ladang* in order to plant coconuts on them later' (Lanting 1939:65).

Trading minorities

While full-time traders and other professionals were all but absent in upland areas and on the northern islands, some were always present in the coastal trading entrepôts of the Sulawesi mainland, especially in Central Sulawesi where the commercial hinterlands of the interior were relatively large in area. 'Many rich black [Indonesian] merchants', according to Woodard (1969:85), lived in Palu at the end of the eighteenth century, and despite a dramatic recent downturn caused by local wars, the volume of trade passing through the capital of Tobungku in 1850 was reportedly 'still sufficient to provide a living for hundreds of people [*toch nog genoegzaam dat honderden mensen daarin hun bestaan vinden*]'.[122] In the Muslim harbour settlements of the Tomini coasts during the *damar* boom of the late nineteenth century, likewise, 'little was done in the way of agriculture', and the population was 'largely dependent on the Toraja for rice and maize' (Adriani and Kruyt 1912-14, II:230).

Most professional traders always belonged to trade-specialized ethnic minorities. This pattern, it is worth noting, preceded colonialism: the merchants of Palu at the beginning of the eighteenth century, for instance, were almost all (Indonesian) foreigners, the local population itself possessing 'no sailing vessels, or at any rate very few'.[123] In Tojo during the *damar* boom, royal trading privileges were already farmed out to Chinese professionals prior to the Dutch occupation (A.C. Kruyt 1893:110). Foremost among the

---

[121]   W.H.M. Jansen 1989:72. The figures for each decade of the early twentieth century were as follows: 1900-1909: 44%; 1910-1919: 76%; 1920-1929: 87%; 1930-1938: 71%.

[122]   A. Revius, 'Algemeen verslag omtrent de oostkust van Celebes', 10-2-1851 (ANRI Ternate 180).

[123]   NA VOC 1775:235.

trading minorities, historically speaking, were communities of Bugis and
Mandar immigrants from South Sulawesi, whose success reflected not only
their commercial and nautical skills, but also their willingness and ability to
fight in order to advance their economic interests.[124] The Dutch sea captain
Van der Hart (1853:244), circumnavigating Sulawesi in 1850, described the
Bugis as 'masters of all the trade in these regions'. From the late seventeenth century onward, successive waves of migrants from the south of the
island came 'searching for good fortune' (Acciaioli 1989) in the north. Many
achieved political as well as commercial supremacy in the areas where
they settled; the royal dynasties of Tojo and Moutong, for instance, were
founded respectively by Bugis and Mandar settlers during the eighteenth
century.[125]

By contrast a second major entrepreneurial group, the ethnic Chinese,
generally 'did not appear in an area where they had no security of residence
or property', but rather 'waited until the Dutch government was sufficiently
represented there'.[126] Their earliest and most important field of activity, correspondingly, was Minahasa, although a few, based in Gorontalo, ventured into
the uncolonized Tomini Gulf from 1857 onward (Adriani and Kruyt 1912-14,
II:326). Also significant as traders and craftsmen in areas under Dutch control
were the *burgers* or *borgo*, a mestizo group descended from VOC 'citizens'
or 'freemen' (*mardijkers*).[127] Hadhrami Arabs, although later eclipsed by the
Chinese, were very active in regional commerce during the mid-nineteenth
century (Clarence-Smith 1998a). Not all such groups originated from outside
the region; in eastern parts of Central Sulawesi at the beginning of the twentieth century, some resident traders were 'domestic' migrants from Gorontalo,
Minahasa and the Palu Bay.[128] The Bajo (Bajau) or 'sea people' (*orang laut*),
although distributed far beyond Sulawesi (Pelras 1972; Sopher 1965), might

[124]   The sword, together with the tongue (persuasion) and the penis (intermarriage), was one of
the 'three tips' (*tellu cappa*) by means of which the Bugis, according to their own tradition, managed to achieve power and wealth outside their homeland (Acciaioli 1989:139).
[125]   Adriani and Kruyt 1912-14, I:76; A.C. Kruyt 1938, I:198; AV Manado 1854 (ANRI Manado
51); Bleeker 1856:130-36; Blok 1848:63; *Corpus diplomaticum* V:93; Van Dam 1931:90, 92; *Generale
missiven* IX:145; Jellesma 1903:218-25; Riedel 1870b.
[126]   Broersma 1931a:1039. There were always individual exceptions to this rule, however
(Adriani and Kruyt 1900:153; Forrest 1779:160, 317; A.C. Kruyt 1893:106, 1900a:215). In 1708, for
example, two ethnic Chinese traders from Dutch Makasar had settled in Palu to escape unpaid
debts (NA VOC 1775:114).
[127]   AV Manado 1829 (KITLV H70), 1833 (ANRI Manado 48); *Fragment* 1856:7-8; Edeling 1919:
87-8; Francis 1860:376-7; Graafland 1898, I:109-11; Riedel 1872b:548-9. The ancestors of the *burgers*
of North Sulawesi included Portuguese mestizos and freed Asian slaves imported by the VOC
from the Moluccas; many people of local origin, however, were also absorbed into this group
during the eighteenth and early nineteenth centuries (Schouten 1999:253-6).
[128]   Adriani 1915:464; Adriani and Kruyt 1898:441, 1912-14, II:304; Goedhart 1908:473, 475, 487;
A.C. Kruyt 1908:1322; *Koloniaal verslag* 1908:62; Logeman 1922:70; F.J. Nieboer 1929:80.

also be regarded as a kind of indigenous trading minority. Living either at sea or in coastal villages scattered throughout the region, they specialized in fishing and the collection of commercial sea products like turtleshell and *tripang*, purchasing much of their food from shore-dwellers.[129]

While there were many professional trading groups, none of them was ever very large in demographic terms. Trade in early nineteenth-century Gorontalo, for instance, was 'exclusively in the hands of the Bugis' (R. Scherius 1847:413), yet the total population of the local Bugis *kampung* in 1824, including women and children, was 691, against an indigenous population of at least 50,000, and probably closer to 80,000.[130] In Minahasa in 1821, comparably, there were 281 Bugis, 231 Chinese and 1,516 *burgers* (Reinwardt 1858:583) against perhaps 90,000 Minahasan farmers (Chapter V). In 1930, after several decades of sustained economic growth, there were just over 25,000 'foreign orientals' (ethnic Chinese and Arabs) in the region as a whole, just over 30,000 people (many of them recently arrived coconut-planting settlers rather than traders) who identified themselves as Bugis, Mandar or Makasarese, and just over 9,000 Bajo.[131] These three groups combined accounted for 5.7 percent of the total population.

Impediments to trade

Like the combination of irrigated with shifting cultivation in the uplands, or the diversity of foodcrops typically grown on swidden fields, the production of cash crops and other goods for exchange partly reflected a habit of spreading one's economic assets. 'Cocoa, banana, coconut, *pinang* [Areca nut] and *saguer* [sugar palm] trees', notes one nineteenth-century report on agriculture in Gorontalo, 'are usually planted very close together in mixed stands, on the assumption that if one type fails, another will surely succeed'.[132] The same concern to limit risks, however, usually meant that households and settlements avoided becoming too dependent upon outsiders for their supply of

---

[129]   Van Dam 1931:80-83; De Clercq 1873:255; Godée Molsbergen 1928:42-3; Lapian 1987:142-213; Riedel 1872c:196; Van Spreeuwenberg 1845-46:35-41; Velthoen 1997a; Van Verschuer 1883; Vosmaer 1839:113-28; Zacot 1978.

[130]   AV Gorontalo 1824 (ANRI Gorontalo 3). Total population estimates for Gorontalo are given in Chapter V.

[131]   *Volkstelling* 1933-36, V:123, 169-70. No earlier figures, unfortunately, are available regarding the Bajo, although in 1681 there were reportedly 'six or seven hundred' Bajo boats in the waters of North Sulawesi (NA VOC 1366:575), and 'hundreds' were said to be present off eastern Central Sulawesi in the first half of the nineteenth century (A. Revius, 'Algemeen verslag omtrent de oostkust van Celebes', 10-2-1851, in ANRI Ternate 180).

[132]   CV Manado 1859 (ANRI Ambon 1543).

essential items, especially food.[133] Even those coastal communities which were oriented primarily toward commerce, and which obtained much of their food from the uplands in payment for trade goods, also tended to grow at least some of their own.[134] While large numbers of people participated to some extent in commerce, the unspecialized character of the economy also limited the scope and necessity for exchange at the local level. The absence of markets in most parts of Central Sulawesi, claimed Adriani and Kruyt (1912-14, II:303) in an exaggerated but not entirely misleading passage, reflected the fact that each Toraja 'makes and grows everything he needs, and so is not obliged to go to others for it'. 'Since everybody generally produces the same products', echoed Van de Velde van Cappellen (1857:51) on Sangir, trade among local farmers themselves (as opposed to the purchase of foreign goods) was necessarily 'limited to minor exchanges'.

Violence, and the threat of it, was no doubt one reason for the general reluctance to abandon self-sufficiency. Although trade, as noted in Chapter I, was often an agent of pacification in its own right, violence, where this had not yet been eliminated, was also a serious impediment to trade. Small parties of traders, for instance, were favourite targets for headhunters.[135] In Central Sulawesi, consequently, a trading expedition 'seldom included fewer than ten members, one or more of whom, if possible, carried a gun over his shoulder' (Adriani and Kruyt 1912-14, II:301). In Mori, where regular marketplaces already existed in precolonial days, they were nevertheless liable to disappear in times of war (Goedhart 1908:542; A.C. Kruyt 1900b:461). Revius, visiting the east coast of Central Sulawesi during a particularly violent period, complained that commerce between neighbouring settlements was 'entirely insignificant', so that 'trade objects like tobacco, cotton and rice often lie stacked up in one village, while another in the immediate vicinity is short of everything'.[136] Besides the 'not really selling' which took place in a context of political compulsion but without overt violence, there was also some open theft and extortion by marauders operating under the protection of influential chiefs (Schrauwers 1997:374). 'Security of persons and property', at least according to Dutch reports, was precarious even in non-

---

[133]   Swidden farmers, as Heersink (1998:95) has observed in the context of South Sulawesi, were 'always quick to occupy new economic niches', but only provided that the activities involved did not interfere with 'their time allocation for subsistence cultivation'.

[134]   Adriani 1901:219; Adriani and Kruyt 1912-14, I:82, II:230; Van der Hart 1853:71; Li 1991:22; CV Belang 1873 (ANRI Manado 19). The seagoing Bajo, comparably, were capable of subsisting on sago from coastal forests (Van Dam 1931:82), and sometimes even planted their own crops (L.Y. Andaya 1993:87; Encyclopaedisch Bureau 1912b:103; Kortleven 1927:23).

[135]   Adriani and Kruyt 1912-14, I:179, 203, II:301-2; Boonstra van Heerdt 1914a:621-2; A.C. Kruyt 1911:65, 1930b:505, 1938, I:166, 179, 292, 303, 317, II:56; Wanner 1914:79; Wichmann 1890:989.

[136]   A. Revius, 'Algemeen verslag omtrent de oostkust van Celebes', 10-2-1851 (ANRI Ternate 180).

Plate 10. Nineteenth-century model of a *kora-kora* vessel from Talaud (Horridge 1978: 17). Note: outriggers are missing. Reproduced by permission of Adrian Horridge.

headhunting areas like Gorontalo and Sangir.[137] One consequence was that women, in contrast to a widespread pattern of female commercial activity in more peaceful Southeast Asian societies (Reid 1988-93, I:163-5), could play little or no role in trade; many, indeed, never left their home villages.[138]

Poor transport facilities were a third major problem for traders. Northern Sulawesi was never as hospitable to sailors as its deep bays and long island chains would suggest. Piracy, a particular scourge during the slave-raiding heyday of the Sulu sultanate from about 1770 to 1860 (Warren 1981), was one reason for this.[139] Another was the pattern of dangerously strong seasonal winds. Depending on the direction of the monsoon, vessels sailing along the

[137]   AV Gorontalo 1854, 1864 (ANRI Gorontalo 3); A.J.F. Jansen, 'Missive Sangir en Talaut Eilanden', 26-8-1857 (ANRI Manado 166).
[138]   Adriani and Kruyt 1912-14, II:301. The wives of political leaders, however, did play a trading role in Gorontalo (Reinwardt 1858:510).
[139]   In 1825, for instance, 'many native traders' in Manado were said to be unemployed as a result of the pirate threat (Res. Manado to Gov. Moluccas, 25-1-1825, in ANRI Manado 74). In Sangir, a number of vessels often sailed together in convoy for protection against pirates (A.J.F. Jansen, 'Missive Sangir en Talaut Eilanden', 26-8-1857, in ANRI Manado 166).

exposed coasts of the northern peninsula risked either being blown out to sea (Wilken and Schwarz 1867a:20, 1867c:359) or driven onto rocky shores between widely-spaced bays and harbours (De Clercq 1873:251). In 1932, one of the last Dutch residents of Manado was still concerned to correct a widespread 'misunderstanding' to the effect that there was 'no particularly urgent need for roads along the coasts of Sulawesi, since the *prahu* traffic there was so busy'.

> Now this absolutely does not apply to North Sulawesi, where most of the coastal settlements are inaccessible to *prahu* for half of the year and where, probably as a consequence of this, a *prahu* trade like that of South Sulawesi is not much in evidence even during the other half. The usable anchorages lie tens of kilometres apart, and must therefore be linked with each other by roads. (A.Ph. van Aken 1932:22).

The region shared in the ancient boatbuilding traditions of eastern Indonesia (Horridge 1978:16-7) – archaic *kora-kora* designs, for instance, surviving up to recent times in Talaud (Plate 10). The Sangirese in particular were always known for their seafaring skills (Van Delden 1844:378; Keijzer 1856:198), and in the seventeenth century some of their voyages extended as far as Ambon and Manila (Van Dam 1931:65, 71; Henley 1993:46, 52). Even within Sangir, nevertheless, it was 'downright impossible' to sail from one coastal village to another at certain times of year, so that local sea communications were 'totally paralyzed' on a regular basis (Van Dinter 1899:329). The seasonal constraints upon longer journeys, of course, were more serious still. The voyage between Sangir and Talaud, on the edge of the open Pacific, was perilous during both monsoons, and best attempted at the short periods of transition between them.[140] Because the working lifetime of locally-built boats was short, Talaud islanders were actually obliged to build a new one for each of their annual tributary and trading expeditions to Sangir and back (Stokking 1922b:150).

The difficulties of sea travel were compensated to some extent by the use of overland trade routes. Footpaths, for instance, traversed the northern peninsula at each of its narrowest points (Boonstra van Heerdt 1914b:758-65; *Generale missiven* IX:146), allowing access from either coast depending on the season.[141] In the heart of Central Sulawesi, where overland distances were greater, the geologist Koperberg (1929:6) observed at the beginning of the twentieth century that 'connecting paths traverse the country in all directions'. A certain amount of 'public' transport infrastructure, moreover, existed even in stateless areas. Padtbrugge, climbing from Manado to the uplands

[140]   A.J.F. Jansen, 'Rapport betrekkelijk het oppergezag over en den toestand van de Talaut Eilanden', 12-8-1857 (ANRI Manado 166).
[141]   When, for instance, the port of Manado was unsafe for anchored vessels (as opposed to boats small enough to be drawn up on the beach) during the northwest monsoon, Kema on the east coast of Minahasa was used instead (Buddingh 1860:31; Graafland 1898, I:24-5), people and goods travelling overland between the two settlements.

of Minahasa in 1679, was impressed by the 'well-built bamboo bridges' along
the way, and by the fact that wooden steps had been built into steep sections
of the path.[142] Relatively centralized indigenous polities achieved more still
in this respect: when European visitors reached the Mongondow plateau in
the 1850s and 1860s, they were surprised to find bridges which, like those
in neighbouring Minahasa, were roofed for protection against the elements,
and which formed part of a network of narrow (2.5 metre) but well-main-
tained 'roads'.[143] In general, however, bridle paths like these were rare prior
to colonial intervention, and roads suitable for wheeled traffic probably
unknown.[144] The great bulk of goods moving overland was carried by men
on foot, a 'very serious disincentive' (Reinwardt 1858:585), especially given
the mostly mountainous terrain, to trade in all but the lightest and most valuable commodities. Before the construction of vehicular roads in Minahasa,
for example, an upland farmer could spend 'three days and more' delivering
just 20 kg of rice to the nearby coast for sale.[145]

Despite the existence of such more or less structural impediments to
trade, the success with which they were often overcome when sufficiently
lucrative markets beckoned suggests that where there was not much commercial activity, a large part of the problem was often simply a lack of economic products in which the outside world was sufficiently interested.[146]
Where export opportunities were still restricted to the kind of 'splendid and
trifling' goods – beeswax, turtleshell, sandalwood, gold, and the like – which
Van Leur (1960:70) characterized as typical of early Indonesian trade, the
scope for commercial growth was inevitably limited. The emergence of a foreign market on an industrial scale for local products such as *damar* or copra,
however, could quickly change things, as Riedel, writing on Central Sulawesi
in the early 1880s, already appreciated.

> Trade – the exchange of gold, brass, pottery and textiles for unworked iron, weap-
> ons, wax, rice, tobacco and maize, sometimes also horses, buffalo, pigs, sheep and

---

142   NA VOC 1345:539-40.

143   De Clercq 1883:121; Riedel 1864b:278. The access paths between Mongondow and the coast,
by contrast, were very poor, and Resident Jansen speculated that they were kept so deliberately
in order to discourage foreign visitors ('Uittreksel uit het dagboek gehouden [...] op zijne reis
naar de landen op de noord en westkust van Celebes [...] September en Oktober 1857', in ANRI
Manado 167).

144   Water buffalo, however, were used as a means of transport in seventeenth-century
Gorontalo (Van Dam 1931:97) and a bridle path, which could be traversed in 24 hours, existed
along the key trade route between the Palu Bay and the Gulf of Tomini in 1850 (Van der Hart
1853:205).

145   Graafland 1867-69, I:81. Other sources specify similar (Wilken and Schwarz 1867a:225) or
even lighter (Schrauwers 1997:373; Veenhuizen 1903:37) man-loads.

146   Touwen (2001) effectively makes the same argument with respect to the Indonesian outer
islands as a whole in the period 1900-1942.

goats – remains very inconsequential, and is engaged in by everybody [sic]. As soon as people begin to collect forest products like rattan and *damar*, however, commerce will flourish. (Riedel 1886:80.)

This optimism was borne out by the subsequent boom in forest product exports; the simultaneous spread of commercial copra cultivation in the lowlands, which likewise took place largely outside the colonial sphere, also confirmed the responsiveness of indigenous societies to market opportunities.

Commerce and colonialism

With respect to problems of security and transport, European government did ultimately make an important difference to the prospects for trade. While neither the establishment of peace and order nor the provision of transport infrastructure was beyond the capacity of indigenous institutions, the colonial state did both with much greater efficiency. The Dutch, for instance, were able and willing to mobilize local labour on an unprecedented scale for the purpose of roadbuilding: in Minahasa, more than 1,000 km of vehicular roads (suitable for ox-carts) were built using corvée labour between the years 1840 and 1875.[147] At sea, the introduction of scheduled steamship services from 1852 onward freed an increasing proportion of trade from the constraints of wind and weather.[148] One reason for the dramatic rise of the rattan and *damar* trade in the Gulf of Tomini during the 1870s was that in 1873, Gorontalo became a regular port of call for steamers of the Royal Dutch Packet-Boat Company (*Koloniaal verslag* 1874:101). Piracy, too, yielded to European technology, beginning in 1856 when a steam gunboat succeeded for the first time in cornering a fleet of raiding vessels off the coast of Minahasa (Graafland 1867-69, I:33). Internal war in Minahasa, although still common during the eighteenth century when the VOC played no more than a mediating role in local conflicts (Godée Molsbergen 1928:98-101, 124-7, 132, 135-9, 143, 145, 153; Schouten 1998:49), all but ceased after the military defeat of an anticolonial rebellion in Tondano in 1809.[149] On Talaud (Weber-Van Bosse 1904:124) and throughout Central Sulawesi all warfare ended with the imposition of

[147]   A.C.J. Edeling, 'Memorie omtrent de Minahasa', 13-8-1875 (NA V 17-4-1877/20).
[148]   A regular civilian steamship service from Batavia to Manado, via Makasar and Ternate, began in 1852 (À Campo 1992:43), and thereafter many of the smaller ports were gradually also included in steamship networks (Encyclopaedisch Bureau 1912a:21, 1912b:90, 137).
[149]   Supit n.d., 1986:154-94. Another crucial event occurred sometime between 1812 and 1815, when on the orders of Resident J.A. Neijs, all trophy heads which could be found in Minahasa were brought to the fort in Manado and burned (Roorda van Eysinga 1831:106). By 1822, according to the same source, the custom of headhunting had already 'fallen completely into disuse'. Occasional headhunts, however, did in fact continue after this date (Graafland 1867-69, I:128,

Dutch rule at the beginning of the twentieth century.[150]

In other respects, however, the European presence long remained a serious burden in economic terms. Until the mid-nineteenth century in the cases of rice, gold, and coconut oil, and until the end of that century in the case of coffee, the Dutch authorities in northern Sulawesi pursued policies of contractual or compulsory trade (comparable to the 'not really selling' required by many indigenous *raja* of their subjects) in which the government (originally, the Company) paid a low standard price to the producers or suppliers of commodities which it demanded in lieu of taxation. The state was never the only potential outlet for these goods, and in the early nineteenth century the ratio between the prices which it paid for gold and coffee, and those available for the same products from independent traders, was typically about 2: 3, and sometimes lower (Van Doren 1857-60, II:371; L. Wessels 1891:51, 56). During the VOC era, the saving grace of this system was that like most of its indigenous counterparts, it seldom amounted to a state monopoly. The rice trade between Minahasa and the Moluccas, for instance, although dominated by the Company, also remained open to private traders throughout the eighteenth century, a circumstance which was partly to thank for the considerable economic expansion which appears to have occurred in Minahasa during that period (Chapter XII).[151] When the VOC authorities in Batavia ordered in 1729 that all gold mined in Gorontalo was to be sold to the new Company outpost there at *f* 10 per *real*, the governor of the Moluccas immediately warned that since 'the Gorontalese are astute enough to understand that a *real* of pure gold is worth a great deal more', much evasion was to be expected (*Corpus diplomaticum* V:93). A formal monopoly was established nevertheless, and remained technically in force in various forms for the next 120 years, but the consistently low official price, combined with corruption among the resident European officials, ensured – fortunately for the producers – that most Gorontalo gold was always exported by Bugis 'smugglers'.[152]

In nineteenth-century Minahasa, by contrast, the economic grip of the colonial state, manifest above all in a 77-year (1822-1899) regime of compulsory coffee cultivation involving a near-watertight government monopoly, became far stronger. Enforced where necessary by violent means (Graafland

286-7; Pietermaat, De Vriese and Lucas 1840:130), the last on record taking place as late as 1862 (De Clercq 1870b:5).

[150] A last (failed) headhunt was reported from Parigi in 1914 (*Koloniaal verslag* 1915:35).

[151] Compulsory coconut oil deliveries from Sangir, likewise, only made up a part of the total quantity exported (AV Ternate 1807, in ANRI Ternate 141; Riedel 1872b:547; Van Delden 1844:22).

[152] *Corpus diplomaticum* V:92-3, VI:397; Consideratieën P.J. Valckenaar 1775 (ANRI Ternate 90). In 1774 the gold supplied to the VOC was thought to be 'perhaps not even one eighth of what Sulawesi produces', and in 1846 the total gold production of the Gorontalo mines alone, including the quantity smuggled to Singapore, was estimated at four times the amount delivered to the Dutch (Consideratie J.J. Craan, 15-2-1774, in ANRI Ternate 90; Francis 1860:339).

1898, I:186; Riedel 1872b:566), this regime, analogous to the contemporary 'Cultivation System' of Java, produced a rapid expansion of coffee planting despite reduced profits and considerable passive resistance among the growers (Schouten 1998:72-4). In the first three years of compulsory planting the number of coffee trees in Minahasa rose from 200,000 to more than 600,000 (Riedel 1872b:543), and by 1865 it had reached 6.4 million.[153] At the same period rice exports, as already noted, also became a state monopoly (superseded in 1852 by a monetary head tax), and the Minahasan population was subjected to a very heavy burden of entirely unpaid roadbuilding labour (see Chapter X).

In the long run, it will be argued in Chapter IX, the forcible mobilization of underexploited labour reserves, the enormous investment in transport infrastructure, and the sustained injection of cash from coffee payments contributed to a marked acceleration of both domestic and import/export commerce, leading to an improvement in food security and material standards of living.[154] These effects, however, did not become visible until the 1860s; in the short term, the diversion of labour into unpaid or relatively unprofitable activities apparently led to diminishing welfare as well as social dislocation. Imports of foreign goods, for instance, seem to have stagnated in the first half of the nineteenth century. Although import statistics are not available from before 1840, in 1825 it was reported that shipping activity in Manado had remained at the same level 'for many years' (Riedel 1872b:549), and between 1840 and 1853 the trend in the total value of imports into Minahasa was, if anything, downwards (Chapter IX, Figure 7). Two sources from this period, moreover, refer explicitly to the 'poverty' of the Minahasan population.[155] In the 1850s, tellingly, some areas outside Dutch control made a more prosperous impression than Minahasa even on the Dutch themselves. 'It cannot be denied', conceded Resident Jansen in 1857, 'that the Sangirese, despite the lack of adequate security for their persons and property, already enjoy a certain degree of welfare'.[156] Parigi, likewise, was an 'apparently prosperous land'.[157] On a visit to the Mongondow plateau, Jansen even declared himself

[153] A.C.J. Edeling, 'Memorie omtrent de Minahasa', 13-8-1875 (NA V 17-4-1877/20).
[154] Elson (1994:317-20) makes the same argument in more detail for the Cultivation System itself.
[155] J. Gansneb Tengnagel, 'Beknopte nota betrekkelijk de residentie Manado', 16-3-1848 (ANRI Manado 168); Riedel 1872b:549. By what criteria this poverty was judged, on the other hand, is not clear. Many traditional prestige goods, including Indian textiles, gold and brass jewelry, and gongs, were certainly sold and disappeared from circulation (Graafland 1867-69, II:195-6), but cultural changes associated with conversion to Christianity (see Chapter I) may have been involved here as well as economic difficulties. In later periods, 'the possession of much clothing made from European fabrics' (Sarasin and Sarasin 1905, I:313) was often regarded by European observers as an indication of prosperity among indigenous groups.
[156] 'Missive Sangir en Talaut Eilanden', 26-8-1857 (ANRI Manado 166).
[157] AV Manado 1854 (ANRI Manado 51).

'amazed at the prosperity and order prevailing in this country'.[158]

A side effect of the corvée and coffee labour burden in Minahasa was to reduce the amount of time left over for trade, displacing commerce out of the peasant sector and into the hands of those for whom it was a core activity rather than a dispensable sideline: Chinese and *burger* traders, who also enjoyed the advantage of being exempt from compulsory labour themselves.[159] This helps to explain why the growth of the ethnic Chinese community in Minahasa between 1820 and 1850, from about 250 persons to over 900, was out of proportion to that of the local economy.[160] Whether for political, cultural, or organizational reasons, the size and commercial importance of the Chinese and other Asian trading minorities in the region continued to grow up to the end of the colonial period. European business, by contrast, was important only in mining, and that only during an abortive gold rush around the turn of the century (Henley 1997b:429); the 3,146 Europeans (about 0.3 percent of the population) living in the residency of Manado in 1930 (*Volkstelling* 1933-36, V:123) were mostly civil servants of various kinds.[161] Agriculture, including the lucrative copra industry, remained overwhelmingly the preserve of indigenous smallholders (Henley 1996:71); in 1923, only three percent of the copra exported from the residency was produced on company plantations.[162] By this date, greatly reduced taxation (see Chapter X) and ready access to copra marketing channels had brought conspicuous prosperity to areas where the coconut palm grew well, such as Tonsea in the north of Minahasa.[163]

[158] 'Uittreksel uit het dagboek gehouden op zijne reis naar de landen op de noord en westkust van Celebes [...] September en Oktober 1857' (ANRI Manado 167).

[159] The *burgers* were obliged only to perform periodic military service, while the Chinese paid a head tax and a variety of levies on their businesses (Bleeker 1856:30, 40, 123).

[160] Reinwardt 1858:583; AV Manado 1850 (ANRI Manado 51). Other factors here included the mobility restrictions imposed on Minahasan farmers by the colonial government (Henley 1996: 38). Similar restrictions were later applied in Central Sulawesi (Adriani 1915:473).

[161] A substantial proportion, it is perhaps worth adding, were also of mixed (Eurasian) descent (Henley 1996:67-74).

[162] W.H.M. Jansen 1990:15. Chinese and European commercial plantations, established on land leased from the colonial state, were most significant in Minahasa, where there were 22 of them in 1900 (*Koloniaal verslag* 1901: Bijlage ZZ) and 40 in 1920 (Van Marle 1922, II:92-8). The majority, however, were very small; in 1928 their combined area amounted to 106 km^2, of which 85 km^2 were planted with coconuts and the remainder with coffee, rubber, nutmeg, or oil palms (Verkuyl 1938:105).

[163] Dirkzwager 1912:1166; Henley 1996:70-1; Van Marle 1922, I:96-7; Schouten 1998:170.

Some evidence on the scale of trade and industry: Gorontalo, circa 1700-1850

To conclude the present chapter, it is useful to examine some fragmentary quantitative evidence regarding the significance of trade and industry relative to subsistence agriculture during the eighteenth and early nineteenth centuries. A set of surviving customs records for the port of Gorontalo in the years 1828-1846, first of all, provides a rare statistical glimpse of the intra-regional commerce in foodstuffs and textiles.[164] In this period Gorontalo imported rice from the south coast of the Gulf of Tomini and sago, in what was described as the 'most important branch of trade', from Paguat and the Togian Islands.[165] Annual rice imports over the 19 years in question averaged 26 tonnes, and in the five years 1841-1845, when sago imports were also recorded, these averaged 68 tonnes per year. In relation to the population of the Gorontalo hinterland, numbering at that time somewhere between 50,000 and 80,000 (see Chapter V), both figures represent tiny quantities of food, equivalent to perhaps 500 grammes of rice and one kilogramme of sago per person per year. In 1866, by comparison, the first Dutch attempt to estimate domestic rice production within Gorontalo yielded a figure equivalent to more than 4,000 tonnes (Riedel 1870a:83). Even allowing for some incompleteness in the import data, then, it is clear that during the early nineteenth century, this part of the region was almost completely self-sufficient in food.[166]

The corresponding statistics regarding Gorontalo's main intra-regional export product, cotton textiles, tell a similar story.[167] In the years 1828-1846 an average of 6,625 pieces of cotton cloth (mostly sarongs, but also including smaller headcloths) were exported annually from Gorontalo to Minahasa and the lands around the Gulf of Tomini.[168] In 1840 it was estimated that a Gorontalese weaver, starting with raw cotton, could complete a single sarong in 12-15 days if she had no other work to perform (R. Scherius 1847: 416). On this basis, the recorded textile exports represented a labour input of approximately 100,000 woman-days per year. Since the adult population of the Gorontalo area cannot have included fewer than 10,000 women,

---

[164]   'Journaal van inkomende en uitgaande regten' (ANRI Gorontalo 8, 9).
[165]   AR Gorontalo to Res. Ternate, 12-3-1820 (ANRI Ternate 153).
[166]   Although there was some smuggling over the hills to the west of Gorontalo (AR Gorontalo to Res. Manado, 20-8-1826, in ANRI Manado 114), most of the trade in rice and sago (relatively bulky goods) probably passed through this harbour; no import duties, significantly, were paid on food. The unofficial export of gold, by contrast, mostly took place directly from peripheral mining sites.
[167]   Horses, 54 of which were shipped to Minahasa on average each year over the period 1828-1846, were another significant export. When the first livestock statistics became available in 1864, however, there were (at least) 4,694 horses in Gorontalo (CV Gorontalo 1864, in ANRI Manado 44), suggesting an export rate of less than 2% per year.
[168]   'Journaal van inkomende en uitgaande regten' (ANRI Gorontalo 8, 9).

Table 1. Recorded gold exports, Gorontalo, 1737-1848

Period	Average annual exports (kg)
1737-1749	47.9
1749-1755	61.2
1758-1766	54.7
1771-1778	42.4
1784-1789	12.7
1820-1827	11.3
1828-1838	34.2
1838-1848	13.6

Sources: AV Manado 1829 (KITLV H70); W.J. Cranssen, 'Consideratie nopens het al of niet bezetten van Gorontalo', 31-5-1806 (ANRI Manado 66); Van Mijlendonk 1756; Schoonderwoert 1766; 'Staat goud leverantie der onder de afdeling Gorontalo sorterende rijkjes' 1828-1848 (ANRI Gorontalo 14); Valckenaer 1778; C.L. Wieling, 'Berigt omtrent het al of niet bezetten van Gorontalo', 6-2-1806 (ANRI Manado 165).

this means that no more than three percent of the potential three million or so woman-days per year were spent on weaving for export.[169] Even if the labour required for the cultivation of the cotton is also taken into account, this must still have been a rather marginal industry as far as the mass of the population was concerned.

It seems doubly unlikely, on the face of it, that the same could be said of gold mining, one of Sulawesi's historic export industries and the main reason for the long Dutch involvement in Gorontalo. Nineteenth-century accounts, indeed, emphasize the extent to which seasonal mining expeditions interfered with agricultural production (Francis 1860:289, 295, 340), and the heavy loss of life to 'fevers' in the malarial mining areas (R. Scherius 1847:407). The sources from this period, nevertheless, also consistently put the number of gold miners (almost all of whom were short-term or seasonal migrants from the Limboto Depression) in the order of hundreds rather than thousands, suggesting that no more than 10 percent of the adult male population was involved in mining at any one time.[170]

[169] Only Gorontalo proper, in fact, exported part of its textile production; Limboto and the other satellite kingdoms produced cloth only for local use (AV Gorontalo 1841-1843, in ANRI Manado 50).
[170] In 1821, for instance, 300-500 miners were thought to be working in Paguat, the most important mining area, each year (Bik 1845:91; Van Doren 1857:368). In 1828, following heavy pressure from the Dutch authorities to increase gold deliveries, 'more than 1200' were sent to the mines, but by October 1830, sickness and desertion had brought down the total number at work to a little more than 500 (AR Gorontalo to Res. Manado, 29-1-1829 and 6-10-1830, in ANRI Manado 115). Estimates of the average amount of time spent away from home by each individual miner range from 4 months to more than a year (Bik 1845:91; Francis 1860:294; R. Scherius 1847:407).

As in Minahasa, on the other hand, the early nineteenth century was a period of economic depression in Gorontalo; commerce in general, and gold production in particular, had been more important here in earlier times. Because extensive smuggling of gold always took place, the official Dutch statistics regarding exports of this precious metal unfortunately have little value in absolute terms. It must, nevertheless, be significant that whereas in the period 1737-1778 the VOC had exported an average of more than 50 kg of gold from Gorontalo each year, the recorded annual average over the years 1820-1848 was only just over 20 kg (Table 1). The numbers of people involved in gold mining, correspondingly, were probably also greater in the eighteenth-century heyday of the industry, when the mines were reportedly worked 'without intermission' and when Paguat, later inhabited only on a seasonal basis, was the permanent site of 'several populous *negeri*'.[171] Exhaustion of what had been some of the richest mines (Henley 1997b:430) led to a general decline in gold exports after about 1780, and this trend was exacerbated after 1835 by counterproductive Dutch interference in the organization of mine labour.[172] At the same time, moreover, the introduction of customs duties in 1828 (to which we owe the existence of the trade statistics cited above) seems to have caused much of the transit trade of the Tomini Gulf, previously focused upon Gorontalo, to shift to the Togian Islands, which were still outside Dutch control.[173] The local weaving industry, thirdly, was probably affected by incipient competition from European factory textiles. In the 1820s, luxury cloths like Indian *salempuris* and 'fine Java batiks' were still the main types of foreign textile arriving in Gorontalo and Manado.[174] By 1840, however, their place was being taken by European cloths which competed more directly with the simple cotton sarongs woven by Gorontalese women.[175] For all of these reasons, the 1840s in particular were a decade of declining prosperity in the Gorontalo area.[176]

It is possible that the decline of commerce had already begun in much earlier times. In the 1720s, rice imports to Gorontalo were apparently cut off when Togian and the south coast of the Gulf of Tomini came under Bugis

---

[171] NA VOC 3357:204; AR Gorontalo to Res. Manado, 5-1-1835 (ANRI Manado 116).
[172] AV Gorontalo 1845 (KITLV H111).
[173] E. Francis, 'Aantekeningen van den kommissaris voor Menado 1846' (ANRI Manado 167). Indonesian goods originating from outside the residency of Manado were taxed on arrival at 6% of their estimated value, Asian goods from outside Indonesia (Indian and Chinese textiles, for example) at 12%, and European manufactures at a full 35% ('Journaal van inkomende en uitgaande regten' 1828-1846, in ANRI Gorontalo 8, 9).
[174] AV Gorontalo 1829 (ANRI Gorontalo 3); Res. Manado to Directeur 's Lands Producten Batavia, 16-4-1829 (ANRI Manado 76).
[175] 'Opgave te Manado ingevoerde goederen 1840-1845' (ANRI Manado 50); R. Scherius 1847: 417.
[176] AV Gorontalo 1841-1843 (ANRI Manado 50); 1845 (KITLV H111).

and Mandar control (*Corpus diplomaticum* V:93; *Generale missiven* IX:145). Although this trade was later re-established, two circumstances suggest that its volume may have been greatest before the interruption. Vessels with a capacity of some 60 tonnes (40 *lasten*), firstly, were reportedly used to ship the rice to Gorontalo at the beginning of the eighteenth century.[177] Except for a single schooner of European design, this is considerably larger than any of the boats sailing the Gulf a century later.[178] The fact that irrigated rice cultivation spread in the Limboto Depression at approximately the same time as the import of rice was interrupted, secondly, suggests that the two events were related, in which case the significance of food imports relative to local production prior to the change was presumably considerable.[179] Both the decline in food imports and the transition to *sawah* cultivation probably reduced the availability of labour for non-agricultural activities, so that food and gold production became less mutually compatible than in, say, swidden-farming Bolaang Mongondow. The picture of an overwhelmingly subsistence-orientated economy emerging from the early nineteenth-century quantitative sources for Gorontalo, in conclusion, is probably atypical insofar as these happen to refer to a period of commercial stagnation, and to a population which was less than usually involved in non-agricultural activities.

Summary

Most people in northern Sulawesi, in the period before 1930, were in the first place subsistence farmers, cultivating a wide variety of foodcrops on swidden fields periodically reopened by cutting and burning under a system of bush-fallow rotation. Rice and maize, the latter a New World introduction, were the most important of these crops in most parts of the region after 1600, although root crops (principally taro, yams, and sweet potato), together with bananas and sago, always predominated in Banggai, Sangir, and Talaud. It is possible that these non-grain foods were also more significant in mainland

---

[177] NA VOC 2132:260.

[178] Captained by a trader of Arab descent, this schooner, the *Pakalombian*, had a capacity of about 90 tonnes. In the year 1830 the port of Gorontalo was visited by 55 vessels, three of which (including the *Pakalombian*) were schooners of 60 tonnes or more; three others large Bugis *paduakang* of about 30 tonnes, and the rest much smaller boats with an average capacity of 5-6 tonnes ('Journaal van inkomende en uitgaande regten' 1830, in ANRI Gorontalo 8). These figures apply to the 48 vessels for which a cargo capacity is specified. Of the 55 captains, 45 were Indonesians, at least 21 of them Bugis.

[179] Other possible factors here, however, include an increase in population (see Chapter V) and an episode of political centralization (see Chapter XV), both perhaps associated with the establishment of a permanent Dutch presence in 1729.

areas toward the beginning of the historical period, but the evidence here is inconclusive. The two instances in which rice definitely spread at the expense of other crops, in Palu during the late seventeenth century and Gorontalo in the early eighteenth, were associated with the construction of irrigated rice-fields in lowland valley locations unsuitable for the cultivation of swidden rice. In the uplands of Minahasa and western Central Sulawesi, by contrast, many farmers were able to cultivate both dry and wet fields as part of a spectrum of agricultural strategies. Protein to supplement the vegetable foods came from (inland and marine) fisheries, and to a lesser extent from animal husbandry and hunting.

Although the economy was subsistence-oriented, it was also diversified. While there were few professionals of any kind, and most households probably produced most of their own food and clothing, a great many were also involved, on a part-time or seasonal basis, in the production of textiles, metals, and forest or farm produce for sale and exchange. Despite numerous impediments to trade (low levels of monetization, few regular markets, endemic insecurity, poor transport facilities, political interference from both indigenous and European quarters, and obligations to share resources with kin without regard for immediate profit), an impressive range of goods was always traded both within and beyond the region. In the late nineteenth century, commercial activity increased dramatically as a result of rising international demand for *damar*, rattan, and above all copra. The demographic evidence presented in later chapters suggests that even before this development, patterns of population change were already responsive to the extent of non-agricultural activity and income.

CHAPTER III

Interpreting the demographic data

Reid (1988-93, I:11) calls population 'the most difficult problem of quantifica-tion' for the historian of precolonial Southeast Asia; Caldwell (2001:20) notes with no less accuracy that although demographic history has an 'enormous intellectual attraction', the process of reconstructing it from raw population data is 'tedious, labour-intensive and expensive'. The demographic source materials for northern Sulawesi, it has been noted, are relatively abundant over an unusually long period – longer, indeed, than for any other Indonesian region outside the Moluccas. Making use of them, however, is difficult and frustrating, not only because they are widely scattered and often cryptic, but also because many of them are probably only just reliable enough to make demographic reconstruction possible at all, and then only on the basis of very careful consideration and comparison. An extreme example of the problems involved is provided by two widely divergent population estimates for the kingdom of Tojo, as quoted in a report published as late as 1893 by the great-est European authority of the time on this part of Sulawesi, G.W.W.C. van Hoëvell.[1]

> Although it is possible to estimate with some accuracy how many Bugis and people of Bugis descent live in the various hamlets and *kampung* along the coast, the number of Alfurs who inhabit the interior can only be given by approxima-tion. When asked about the size of the population, various people who had traded for many years in the Tojo kingdom consistently put this at 90,000 or more. The ruler [*vorst*], however, gave a figure of just ± 10,000. (Van Hoëvell 1893b:3.)

The first task, then, is to establish some general procedures for the presentation and interpretation of this kind of problematic data.[2] The uncertainties inherent in most early population estimates can be divided into two main categories.

---

[1]   Van Hoëvell (assistant resident of Gorontalo, 1886-1891) had made 17 journeys into the Gulf of Tomini (Van Hoëvell 1893a:64).

[2]   Although recent authors on the historical demography of Indonesia have addressed the same issues in passing (Boomgaard and Gooszen 1991:14-16; Elson 1994:278-84; Knaap 1987: 279-82, 1995:228-33; Ricklefs 1986), no systematic treatment of this subject seems to have been attempted in the Indonesian context.

Plate 11. Toraja village (Buyu mBajau, To Pebato area) in defensive hilltop site,
circa 1905 (Adriani and Kruyt 1912-14: Plate 43)

The first concerns the scope of the available figures, whether in geographic
terms (the areas to which they refer) or in social terms (the proportion of the
actual population which they include). Many population counts not only
encompassed indefinite geographical areas, but also systematically excluded
particular sections of their population (most commonly women, children, and
slaves). The second source of uncertainty lies in the accuracy of each estimate,
in the strict sense of its fidelity within the parameters set by its scope and units
of measurement. While levels of accuracy can never be reconstructed with
certainty, they can often be assessed indirectly in terms of the way in which an
estimate was arrived at and the purpose for which it was intended, as well as
the personal judgement of the individual who made or recorded it.

Problems of scope

Part of the confusion regarding the population of Tojo in 1893 probably
stemmed from the fact that what the traders meant by Tojo was different from
what the *raja* himself understood as such. Although Tojo was at that time the
most important political centre on the south coast of the Gulf of Tomini, most

Plate 12. Swidden houses in the upper Bongka Valley (To Wana area), circa 1975
(Atkinson 1989: Photograph 2)

of the adjacent interior to its south and west, where the traders based there probably also operated, did not recognize its suzerainty. The higher estimate of 90,000 people, then, most likely refers not only to Tojo proper, but also to a much larger part of Central Sulawesi. Comparison with other estimates from the same period (Chapter VI) shows that in this context, it is essentially credible. Similar difficulties are involved in interpreting many of the population figures for Bolaang Mongondow, where the *raja* based at coastal Bolaang exercised an indeterminate authority over the Mongondow hinterland; several population estimates for the kingdoms of Sangir, likewise, may or may not include their vassals in the outlying Talaud Islands (Chapters IV and V). A related problem in some sources may be that of overlapping or multiple political allegiances. At the fringes of Tojo's sphere of influence, for instance, there were vassal groups which rendered tribute both to it and to other overlords (A.C. Kruyt 1895-97, II:113; J. Kruyt 1933:44). Bada, further west, was 'the slave of three masters: Luwu, Sigi, and Palu' (Sarasin and Sarasin 1905, II:101). In Minahasa, on a smaller scale, some individuals and groups were regarded as belonging to two districts or *walak* (village federations), rendering labour services to the chiefs of both (G.A. Wilken 1873:118-9).

Another problem of geographical scope relates to the patterns of settlement found in the region. In most areas there were two main types of settlement: nucleated political and ritual centres, typically fortified for defence (Plate 11), and much less conspicuous, but often very numerous, swidden houses or small hamlets scattered in the surrounding farmland and secondary forest (Plate 12).[3] The former figure prominently in Dutch reports as *dorpen*, *kampung* or *negeri* (villages), but while some foreign observers recognized that these 'can also be regarded as districts, since they have many small settlements or hamlets under them' (De Clercq 1890:141), others ignored the dispersed part of the population entirely. One quite common type of population estimate, in fact, was obtained simply by multiplying the number of villages thought to be present in a given area by an estimate of the average number of houses per village, and then by a guess at the number of people living in each house.

The accuracy of this procedure, of course, depended on whether or not the number of inhabitants calculated for each house was high enough to allow for those people who normally lived outside the village. In many areas the inhabitants of the dispersed swidden houses did come together on regular occasions in the nuclear settlements for ritual or defensive purposes,

---

[3]	There were also a few areas, notably Peling in Banggai and some other parts of eastern Central Sulawesi, where nuclear settlements of any size were scarce, and most of the population lived permanently in dispersed swidden houses (Van der Hart 1853:70; A.C. Kruyt 1932a:341-2, 1932b:71).

so that the village structures had to be large enough to accommodate them all.[4] But where conditions were more peaceful and social stratification more pronounced, the dispersed pattern was more permanent, and the inhabitants of the nuclear and scattered settlements formed two distinct groups. In Gorontalo, for example, it was reported in 1854 that 'concentrated settlements (*kampung* or *negeri*), with few exceptions, are inhabited only by the *raja*, the chiefs [*rijksgroten*] and other nobles', together with a small number of slaves, while 'the mass of the free population, and most of the slaves, live scattered over the whole countryside'.[5] An accurate census would only be possible in Gorontalo once the whole population was forcibly concentrated in the vicinity of the capital settlements; as things stood, many farmers deliberately put as much distance as possible between themselves and the *negeri* in order to minimize the tax and labour impositions upon them.[6]

In many cases it is not clear to what extent the population was permanently dispersed. On Siau in the late nineteenth century, according to Chabot, the nuclear settlements (*soa*) with their big houses (*bale*) were located on the coast, while the swidden houses (*daseng*), each occupied by just one or two households, 'were scattered throughout the hills and belonged to a big house, being built on land owned by one of the big house kinship groups'.[7] The two groups formed a single social unit, 'the big house in this sense also including inhabitants of the garden houses connected to it' (H.Th. Chabot 1969:96-7). 'At any festivity', Chabot claimed, the 'garden [swidden] house people' were to be found at 'their' big house in the *soa*. According to another source, however, there were also people on Siau who 'almost never visited the main *kampung*' (Encyclopaedisch Bureau 1912a:13), and early population figures for this and other parts of Sangir, referring only to *dorpen* or *negeri*, are often suspiciously low in comparison with more painstaking later counts.[8] When Padtbrugge attempted to estimate the population of Minahasa in 1679, comparably, he warned that many of its inhabitants could not be included, since 'because

[4]   Adriani and Kruyt 1912-14, II:164-5; Aragon 1992:39; Atkinson 1989:2; Goedhart 1908:534; Hofman 1906:336; A.C. Kruyt 1898:100, 1908:1286, 1297, 1930b:459, 1938, I:158, 1938, II:136-7; *Nota berglandschappen* 1912:5, 9; Sarasin and Sarasin 1905, II:46; Steller 1866:30; Tillema 1926:206; Wilken and Schwarz 1867a:9, 1867c:332. Adriani (1919:10), referring to the Poso area, claimed that if the garden houses were included in the count, there were 'twice as many houses as were necessary to accommodate the population'.

[5]   Res. Manado to Gov. Moluccas, 29-11-1854 (ANRI Gorontalo 18).

[6]   AV Gorontalo 1845 (KITLV H111).

[7]   Brilman (1938:31) noted that toward the end of the colonial period, 'only a small part of the population' on Sangir lived in the villages.

[8]   A VOC source from the late seventeenth century notes that despite decades of Spanish and Dutch presence, 'it is said that there are people on this small island who have never yet seen Europeans' (Van Thije 1689). The missionary Van de Velde van Cappellen (1857:72) reported in 1855 that 'many households have established their permanent homes far outside the *negeri*'.

they live scattered far and wide in the forests and swiddens, it is impossible to know their exact number'.[9] In 1908, not long after the Dutch conquest of Central Sulawesi, Albert Kruyt (1908:1309) commented that the initial military population estimate for the Napu Valley 'seems to me to be much too low; and indeed in the present situation of dispersed settlement it is not possible to count all the women and children'. As late as 1932, the head of a village in the interior of the Luwuk Peninsula apparently gave a figure for the number of taxable men under his authority which still did not include 'the people who make their swiddens a long distance away' (J. Kruyt 1933:44).

The question of whether a given estimate encompassed the dispersed as well as the concentrated part of the population is typically one of social as well as spatial scope. The two types of house on Siau were, as Chabot put it, 'indicative of the people who lived in them'. The inhabitants of the big houses, called *tau soa* or 'village people', occupied a social position above that of their dispersed dependants, whom they referred to as *tau ruku* ('swidden people') or, more simply, as their slaves.[10] Early population counts, particularly the many Dutch estimates expressed as numbers of *weerbare mannen* or 'fighting men', often excluded slaves as an irrelevant category. Padtbrugge's 1679 estimate for Minahasa, for instance, took this form, and he appended to it a note that in addition to the men included in the count, 'women, children *and slaves* are present here in great numbers' (my emphasis).[11] When Van Delden (1844:372) attempted to derive a population total for the Sangir Islands from *weerbare mannen* figures provided by the local *raja* in 1825, he too qualified his final estimate with the disconcerting note: 'not yet including the numerous slaves'.[12] Knaap (1987:278) confirms that in Ambon, enumerations of fighting men generally excluded slaves as well as women and children. The same limitation apparently applied to figures given in *hombres de armas*, the Spanish equivalent of *weerbare mannen*. The early seventeenth-century Spanish writer Argensola (1992:82), who provides important statistics regarding the numbers of fighting men in several parts of Sulawesi who are obedient to the sultan of Ternate, notes that these represent only 'the regular militia', and include neither 'the numerous irregulars' nor 'the multitude of slaves'.

---

[9]   NA VOC 1345:474-5.
[10]   H.Th. Chabot 1969:97, 99; Van Dinter 1899:345. Chabot translates *tau ruku* as 'grass people', but Van Dinter (1899:338) notes that the meaning of *ruku* is *tuin* (swidden).
[11]   One exception to this implicit rule, his figure for the *negeri* of Manado, is annotated 'with slaves and all' (NA VOC 1345:474-5).
[12]   The way in which the problems of establishing slave numbers are discussed elsewhere in the same report confirms that slaves were not included in the lists of *onderdanen* or 'subjects' supplied by the *raja* (Van Delden 1844:4, 368, 370). These problems are described as stemming from the fact that 'the *raja* own very many themselves, and would not welcome an investigation into the way in which their slaves became such, since this could lead to immediate manumission'.

Slaves, of course, are not by definition unable to bear arms; in northern Sulawesi, indeed, they often took part in fighting (Hissink 1912:109; A.C. Kruyt 1899a:151), and among one group, the warlike To Napu, some even became distinguished military leaders (A.C. Kruyt 1908:1310). It follows that the term *weerbare mannen* and its equivalents in the European sources should not be interpreted literally. While the original indigenous expressions which they translate do not seem to have been preserved in any instance, and may not have been uniform in meaning, it is likely that their primary significance was fiscal rather than military. The adult men included in most early population counts, both indigenous and European, were those liable (or potentially liable) to pay tribute or render labour services to an overlord, so that their number represented a measure of economic rather than military potential. Reid (1987:33) agrees that it was people exempt from corvée, including slaves, religious officials and 'outlaws', who were typically excluded from precolonial Southeast Asian population counts. The fact that privately-owned slaves were normally exempt from any direct tax and corvée impositions, then, explains their otherwise puzzling exclusion from enumerations of so-called 'fighting men'.[13]

The proportion of the population made up of slaves varied greatly from place to place, even over short distances and between communities which otherwise had a great deal in common. Among the Pamona-speakers at the beginning of the twentieth century, for instance, the To Pebato held almost no slaves, yet on the other side of the Poso River among the To Lage, there were villages in which slaves accounted for more than half of the population (Adriani and Kruyt 1912-14, I:156-7; A.C. Kruyt 1911:64-5). In some areas, moreover, it was difficult to identify a clear-cut slave class or *slavenstand*. 'There are slaves who are slaves of other slaves', wrote Resident Jansen regarding Sangir, 'and chiefs who, being descended from slaves, are dismissed as slaves by other slaves'.[14] This recalls the observation by Chabot (1950:114), in South Sulawesi, that slavery was a relational rather than an absolute category, and that the slave status of individuals 'can only be established in the context of their relationships with their masters'. It also shows that slavery was sometimes a disputed status, so that the reported size of the slave group might depend upon the identity of the informant.[15]

Another problem here is that slavery often came in a number of types or gradations. Nineteenth-century sources on Gorontalo, by far the best documented area in this respect, appear to distinguish no fewer than five: *budak*

---

[13]   Individuals sometimes gambled themselves deliberately into slavery in order to avoid paying tax and performing labour services (Sarasin and Sarasin 1905, I:172-3).

[14]   AV Manado 1853 (ANRI Manado 51).

[15]   H.Th. Chabot (1969:96, 99) confirms, for instance, that the status of children of marriages between free men and female slaves on Siau was uncertain.

Table 2. Class composition of the Gorontalo population according to Dutch sources, 1820-1860

Year	Slaves (% of total population)	Groups included in the slave category	Nobles (% of total population)	Groups included in the noble category
1820[1]	15	'persons reduced [through debt] to slavery' and *pandelingen* only	–	–
1843[2]	33	all 'who are considered to a greater or lesser extent as slaves and must perform services as such'	–	–
1846[3]	36	*mongoohule, budak di muka* and *ilapita*	–	–
1849[4]	17	not specified	18	'chiefs and *negeri* officials'
1852[5]	13	*budak di muka* only	–	–
1854[6]	13	not specified	11	not specified
1854[7]	20	*budak di muka, budak pembelian* and *pandelingen* only	29	'aristocracy (*bangsa*), including *raja, rijksgroten*, lesser chiefs and a swarm of idlers without official functions'
1856[8]	14	not specified	25	not specified
1858a[9]	33	not specified	–	–
1858b[10]	14	not specified	25	not specified
1860[11]	16	not specified	27	not specified

[1]   Res. Gorontalo to Res. Ternate, 5-5-1820 (ANRI Ternate 153); percentage calculated using the total population estimate in AV Gorontalo 1823 (ANRI Gorontalo 3).
[2]   AV Gorontalo 1841-43 (ANRI Manado 50).
[3]   'Tulisan djiwa deri parentahan di Gorontalo', 7-11-1846; 'Tulisan djiwah derij parentahan di Limbotto', 5-11-1846 (KITLV H142). Unlike the others used in this table, this estimate includes only the two main chiefdoms of Gorontalo and Limboto, and not the smaller satellite polities.
[4]   'Staat van de gedane zielsbeschrijving onder ultimo Augustus 1849' (ANRI Gorontalo 18).
[5]   AV Gorontalo 1852 (ANRI Gorontalo 3).
[6]   AV Gorontalo 1854 (ANRI Gorontalo 3).
[7]   Res. Manado to Gov. Moluccas, 29-11-1854 (ANRI Gorontalo 18).
[8]   AV Manado 1856 (ANRI Manado 51).
[9]   Van Baak 1919:112 ('about one third' of the population consists of slaves).
[10]   AV Manado 1858 (ANRI Manado 52).
[11]   AV Manado 1860 (ANRI Manado 52).

di muka (also known as *budak pusaka* or *erfslaven*, 'hereditary slaves'), who were the personal property of their masters and could be bought and sold at will within the community; *mongoohule* or '*kampung* slaves', who had a semi-free status and could not be traded; *ilapita* or royal slaves, who served the incumbent political leaders; *pandelingen* or debt slaves; and a small number of registered *koopslaven* (*budak pembelian*), the only slave category legally recognized as such by the colonial government.[16] Because members of the local political elite, or even the whole of the *bangsa* or 'nobility' where such a group existed, were often also exempt from tribute and labour services, it is possible that some *weerbare mannen* counts exclude this group as well as the slaves.[17] In Gorontalo the nobles, like the slaves, were divided into a number of substrata (Riedel 1870a:65-6; R. Scherius 1847:402). Differences in the number of subgroups included in both slave and noble categories undoubt-edly explain most of the wide variation in the proportion of the Gorontalo population falling into these categories according to diverse Dutch sources from the nineteenth century (Table 2).

Taken as a whole, this table suggests that servile groups in the broadest sense (Table 2: 1843, 1846, 1858b) accounted for about a third of the population in Gorontalo, and the noble class – again in the broadest sense (Table 2: 1854, 1856, 1858b, 1860) – for at least another quarter, leaving the free commoner population at barely 40 percent of the total. Even if the *mongoohule* (who, unlike other slaves, were obliged to perform *herendienst* and other labour services) are subtracted from the slave total, and a minimal definition of the *bangsa* (1849, 1854) is employed, the '*weerbaar*' group in the economic sense indicated above still does not exceed 75 percent of the total population.[18]

Dutch proto-censuses for parts of Sangir and the north coast of North Sulawesi in the period 1855-1859 also provide some information on class

16   Besides the sources referred to in Table 2 below, information on categories of slaves in Gorontalo was drawn from: R. Scherius 1847:402-3; Res. Manado to Gov. Moluccas, 17-1-1828 (ANRI Gorontalo 18); E. Francis, 'Aantekeningen van den kommissaris voor Menado 1846' (ANRI Manado 167). Except for the Gorontalese term *mongoohule*, all of the names given here for slave categories are either Malay or Dutch. The most common general terms for 'slave' in the indigenous languages of the region were variants of *ata* (*wato*, *batua*), although in Sangirese, slaves were usually called *ellang* (Steller and Aebersold 1959:572).

17   At least one VOC census of Minahasa, from 1695, certainly lists the *bobato* or *regenten* (chiefs) of each division separately from the *weerbare mannen*, although they are recombined the final total (NA VOC 1579:216-28). In the nineteenth century, even figures expressed in the apparently more neutral unit of *dapur* or 'hearths' (see below) sometimes excluded the families of chiefs and officials who were exempt from taxation (*Fragment* 1856:96; Wilken and Schwarz 1867c:285).

18   The one estimate which gives specific figures for the *mongoohule*, that of 1846, suggests that these alone accounted for fully 26% of the population, or 21% in Gorontalo and 43% in Limboto ('Tulisan djiwa deri parentahan di Gorontalo', 7-11-1846 and 'Tulisan djiwah derij parentahan di Limbotto', 5-11-1846 (KITLV H142). For unknown reasons, however, the census table for Limboto does not include *budak di muka*, so that this figure is probably exaggerated.

composition.[19] These suggest that here the free commoner class was generally larger, accounting for between 70 and 92 percent of the total population.[20]
The reliability of this information, however, is low. 'The number of slaves on
these islands', wrote the missionary Steller (1866:40) from Greater Sangir a
few years later, 'is unknown, since the Sangirese often do not know it themselves, and also do their utmost to conceal the truth on this point'.[21] Steller
also noted that while most of the slaves 'live scattered on the mountains and
islands', a smaller number, used for domestic services, stayed under the same
roof as their masters.[22] This raises the worrying possibility that some of the
population counts of the 1850s included only the latter category, and ignored
the 'garden house' slave population (that is, the 'swidden people') altogether.
More likely still is that the same applies to the many seventeenth- and eighteenth-century population statistics from Sangir which include only baptized
Christians; the particular problems of interpreting these church records will
be addressed in Chapter IV.

Problems of inaccuracy

Besides the question of its uncertain geographical scope, the low population
figure quoted by the *raja* of Tojo in the introductory example above may also
have reflected both incomplete information and deliberate inaccuracy. It was
'common knowledge', according to Van Hoëvell (1893b:3), 'that none of the
rulers here has ever carried out a census, and that when asked for a population figure, they always give one which is very low'.[23] A rare general report
on problems of inaccuracy in population statistics collected in Indonesia
was produced by the colonial civil servant T.J. Willer in 1861. Dutch officials
in the outer islands, Willer noted, usually depended for their demographic
information on indigenous informants whose reports, for political as well as

[19]   AV Manado 1855 (Siau), 1857 (Bolang Itang, Kaidipang, Siau, Manganitu), 1858 (Siau), and
1859 (Siau, Taruna, Tabukan), in ANRI Manado 51 and 52.
[20]   The first figure is from Kaidipang and the second from Bolang Itang, both on the north coast
of the peninsula. The equivalents for the Sangir chiefdoms ranged from 78% to 89%.
[21]   Steller was paraphrasing the earlier account by Van Delden (1844:4), but evidently believed
that the same was also true in his own time.
[22]   Steller 1866:42. This is probably analogous to the distinction between the *mongoohule* and
budak di muka in Gorontalo, the *batua ri gimba* and the *batua ri abu* in the Palu Valley (Hissink
1912:107), or the *alipin namamahay* (house-owning slaves) and *alipin sa gigilid* (hearth slaves) in
the Tagalog Philippines (W.H. Scott 1985:107). Ruibing (1937:30-8) notes that similar distinctions
existed throughout Indonesia.
[23]   A Dutch government count in 1909, on the other hand, also put the population of Tojo at
just 9,800 (Adriani and Kruyt 1912-14, I:89), and even in 1930 it was still only 14,691 (*Volkstelling*
1933-36, V:134).

practical reasons, they were unable to verify or control. Any open attempt to check the accuracy of such information tended to be perceived 'as a piece of offensive European arrogance, a deliberate humiliation of the population and the chiefs'. At best, Dutch administrators could make use of figures supplied 'by chiefs who are able and willing to count the population *in their own way*' (original emphasis). At worst, they had to depend on statements 'which, as a result of fear, prejudice or uncooperative attitudes, are evidently either evasive or false'.[24] In Minahasa, according to Graafland (1867-69, I:265), some village headmen kept two different population registers: one, showing a misleadingly small number of households, for inspection by government officials, and a more accurate list 'for their own use'.

The importance of manpower as a source of prestige and an economic and military resource, as Gooszen (1994:38) points out, makes it unlikely that many indigenous political leaders in Indonesia ever actually had no insight into the size of the population under their influence. Local chiefs in northern Sulawesi, despite Van Hoëvell's suggestion to the contrary, were certainly interested in keeping demographic records. In Gorontalo, and apparently also in Sangir, written population registers of sorts were compiled more or less independently of the Dutch administration in the early nineteenth century.[25] Elsewhere, purely oral registers existed which represented considerable feats of memory as well as research. One of the last and most impressive of these, recited in 1906 by the paramount *raja* of Mori in eastern Central Sulawesi and compared by its publishers to the famous Javanese *volkstelling* obtained by Rycklof van Goens at the court of Mataram in 1654, listed a total of exactly 4,761 *weerbare mannen* divided over 44 'tribes' (*stammen*) and no fewer than 119 named *kampung*.[26]

Van Hoëvell, nevertheless, was not the only experienced Dutch official who gave credence to protestations of demographic ignorance on the part of local leaders.[27] Resident Jansen, for instance, even found it 'believable' that chiefs on Sangir did not know the number of their own slaves.[28] If so, this was most probably because they were deliberately misinformed by the intermediaries whom, according to Van Delden (1844:7), they appointed to collect payments (in foodstuffs and coconut oil) from the dispersed slave

---

[24]   Willer 1861:4, 7. It is worth adding with Elson (1994:280) that quite apart from any errors of enumeration, many Dutch population tables also incorporate errors of simple arithmetic.
[25]   'Pengatoran pusaka di Gorontalo', 29-4-1828 (ANRI Gorontalo 18); Van Delden 1844:371. Little is known about these records, and none have survived. In Gorontalo they appear to have been an indigenous innovation associated with taxation and the competition for control over manpower between royal and local authorities; in Sangir they may have been based on Dutch models.
[26]   Maengkom 1907:864-8. A comparably detailed census of Talaud was recited by a Magindanao chief in 1775 (Forrest 1779:315-7).
[27]   Others included De Clercq (1883:118) and Van Delden (1844:4).
[28]   Res. Manado to Gov. Moluccas, 26-8-1857 (ANRI Manado 166).

population.[29] If Javanese officials always had a strong economic incentive to establish the number of people under their authority, notes Ricklefs (1986:9), then by the same token 'they usually wished also to diminish that number when reporting it to those above them'. Assuming that the size of the tribute demand on Sangir was connected with the number of slaves known to be present, then the interests of the intermediate chiefs (whether in order to reduce the burden on their subordinates, to spare themselves work, or to retain more of the rendered tribute for themselves) must have lain in understating the slave population.

The best concrete evidence for this practice of defensive understatement in northern Sulawesi comes from enumerations organized by the Dutch authorities themselves. An early example is the count carried out in Minahasa by Padtbrugge, who was under no illusions regarding its reliability and who recognized that besides the problem of incomplete scope, there was also one of deliberate undercounting. The Minahasans, he wrote, 'become suspicious when anyone tries to find out their exact strength, thinking that this is being done in order to harm them, and this fear is the reason why they conceal the truth from us in this matter'.[30] In his *memorie van overgave* (Van Dam 1931: 75) he speculated that the real number of *weerbare mannen* in Minahasa might well amount to double the total of 3,990 indicated by his own survey, and Valentijn (Keijzer 1856:201) was later to take him literally by suggesting a figure of 8,000 men. When Van Delden (1844:368) attempted to elicit demographic statistics from the various *raja* of the Sangir Islands in 1825, he too 'ran up in all cases against extreme reticence and mistrust'.

> When I asked the *raja* how many subjects they had, they usually replied that they did not know, stated that they were not in the habit of conducting accurate counts and that many people had died, and finally gave an approximate figure which was too obviously false to place any trust in. In response I feigned indifference and asked them, without giving the impression that I found the matter very important, to order a population count. The results always far exceeded their initial estimates, even though (as I was able to establish on many occasions, and as their apologies confirmed) they continued to conceal a proportion of the total. (Van Delden 1844:368.)

Undeterred, and not apparently worried about offending the *raja*, Van Delden set out to correct for the resulting under-registration by modifying their fig-

---

[29]   Another possibility is that they never dared to make enquiries on this subject. Willer (1861:5) noted that in Kalimantan it was not only the Dutch who had to proceed with caution when investigating the size of the population; attempts by indigenous chiefs to obtain accurate demographic information from their subordinates also tended to generate 'resentment and suspicion'.

[30]   NA VOC 1345:474-5.

ures on the basis of what he called 'trustworthy information collected in the places themselves'. The sources of this information included a schoolmaster, subordinate chiefs, and, in one case, a written census compiled by the *raja* a year earlier and perhaps not intended for European eyes (Van Delden 1844: 370-1). The resulting estimates for each kingdom ranged up to 42 percent higher than the figures offered by the *raja*, and the overall correction factor for all kingdoms combined was 28 percent.[31] The revised total, he noted, still 'cannot be entirely accurate, but is more likely to lie below the true figure than above it' (Van Delden 1844:370).

At least where information supplied by indigenous chiefs already under Dutch authority was concerned, most European observers agreed that the stated figures tended to be too low.[32] Sometimes this habit of underestimation was attributed partly to 'superstition' (Van Doren 1854-56, I:266; Riedel 1872b: 478), but the more usual and credible interpretation was that by understating their labour resources, local leaders hoped to minimize existing economic impositions and avoid new ones. Van Delden (1844:369), for instance, attributed the evasiveness of the Sangir *raja* in the first place to their suspicion that population figures would be used as a basis for recruitment of a proportion of the male workforce for compulsory military service elsewhere in Indonesia, 'by which the *raja* and chiefs naturally stand to lose, since they live off the population'.[33] They were also reluctant to reveal the size of the coconut oil tribute which they collected from their subjects each year at the rate of about five litres per man, fearing that this would lead to increased compulsory purchases of oil by the Dutch. Far from being 'obtuse and stupid', as Padtbrugge claimed,[34] such behaviour was prudent given that the collection of population statistics by the European authorities was almost always connected with the extraction, either potential or imminent, of tax or labour services. In at least one case from the end of the eighteenth century, even the enumeration itself was an occasion for extortion by the enumerators from the population which they were counting (Godée Molsbergen 1928:150).

The commonest problem of deliberate distortion in population statistics,

---

[31] Van Delden 1844:370-2. The smallest kingdom, Kandahar, was actually upgraded by a full 190%, but this has been ignored here (and excluded from the calculation of the overall correction ratio) because the indigenous estimate for Kandahar apparently contained an error. Not all of the original estimates, it should be added, were so dramatically revised. The 'corrected' population for Tabukan, for instance, represented an increase of less than 2% (although even here the *weerbare mannen* figure, as opposed to those for women and children, was raised by 19%).

[32] AV Manado 1824 (ANRI Manado 101), 1829 (KITLV H 70), 1861, 1862 (ANRI Manado 52); De Clercq 1883:118; Van Doren 1854-56, I:266, 1857-60, II: 318; Van Hoëvell 1893b:3; Riedel 1872b:478.

[33] An attempt at such compulsory recruitment, accompanied by a superficial demographic survey, had indeed been made by the Dutch 17 years earlier (C. Mesman, 'Journaal [...] recrutee-ring naar de Zangers' [May-December 1808] (ANRI Manado 62).

[34] NA VOC 1345:474.

then, was defensive deflation in the face of actual or anticipated fiscal pressures. This accords with the predominant pattern identified in the demographic literature on other parts of colonial Indonesia, particularly Java.[35] It is not, however, the whole story. Not all population figures, first of all, where obtained in a fiscal context. Some, like the high figure of 90,000 people quoted above for Tojo, were supplied by traders rather than political leaders, or recorded by missionaries and non-Dutch European visitors rather than by representatives of the colonial power. Particularly for groups not yet subject to foreign authority, secondly, the logic of understatement did not always apply even in the political sphere. Independent kingdoms, in fact, may sometimes have had an interest in exaggerating their demographic strength, whether in order to impress with their labour resources in the hope of securing military protection, or, conversely, in order to intimidate the Europeans into keeping their distance. The figures in *hombres de armas* recorded at the beginning of the seventeenth century by Argensola (1609:82-3) may well provide one example of such defensive or boastful inflation, since they were obtained from Ternatan sources and specify the extent of Ternate's power at a time when it had briefly shaken off European interference (L.Y. Andaya 1993: 132-43; Jacobs 1974-84, II:304). Population statistics provided by the Ternate sultanate, the territories of which included Banggai and Tobungku in Central Sulawesi, were reportedly still subject to deliberate inflation in the 1850s. 'The vanity of the rulers', it was said, 'usually leads them to exaggerate these figures'.[36] At the turn of the century, comparably, Adriani and Kruyt (1898: 501) dismissed as 'certainly exaggerated' local claims that the population of Kulawi (in western Central Sulawesi) comprised 1,000 'men'.

In extreme cases boastful exaggeration, fuelled by status rivalry between indigenous groups or leaders, could occur even when it had higher taxation as a direct consequence.[37] Chabot, writing on Siau, described an example:

> In about 1900, the Government started to levy taxes at the rate of 20 cents per employable man per year. The head of one of the principal big houses, Radjah Rumah ['king of the house'] as they were known, paid the sum of 20 guilders without demur, thus showing that his group consisted of 100 men of working age, an unusually large number. The payment of a high tax thus served to show the superiority of his kinship group over others. (H.Th. Chabot 1969:97.)

Similar practices, although undoubtedly less common than defensive under-

[35]   Boomgaard and Gooszen 1991:14-6; Elson 1994:208; Gooszen 1994:39.
[36]   Quarles van Ufford 1856:65. Wigboldus (personal communication) suggests that in some cases, even Dutch officials were pleased to exaggerate the population of the regions under their authority in order to underline the importance of their own position.
[37]   In Central Sulawesi not long after the establishment of colonial rule, many well-to-do Toraja were said to be proud to be able to pay the maximum *f* 5 head tax (*Brieven*, 20-3-1911).

statement, were also recorded from other parts of colonial Indonesia.[38] A final type of demographic exaggeration which deserves mention here concerns the vague global estimates which European visitors sometimes wrote down in the absence of verifiable local informaton. Remote but relatively populous areas often attracted this kind of guesswork, which might be based on heresay, intuition or general impressions, and which tended to result in very large round figures. At periods when they were little known to Europeans, both Minahasa and the highlands around Lake Poso were said to be inhabited by 'more than 100,000 souls'.[39] The fact that such a figure is not beyond the bounds of possibility in these particular cases may well be coincidental, since a sort of 'Shangri-La' hyperbole is known to have affected similar second-hand accounts of other regions during the early stages of their exploration by Europeans. When Dutch soldiers and officials first arrived in the high, isolated valley of Kerinci (southwestern Sumatra) in 1903, they were surprised to find that its real population was scarcely a quarter of the 200,000 souls previously suggested by 'reports which had reached their administrators on the West Coast' (Watson 1992:11-2). High first-contact population estimates for many of the Pacific Islands, similarly, although long taken seriously as evidence for a spectacular demographic collapse in the early years of European rule, were later reinterpreted by some experts as impressionistic exaggerations with little foundation in fact (Brookfield and Hart 1971:66-7; Bushnell 1993).

Presenting the quantitative data

Whatever is to be made of problematic demographic sources like those quoted above, it is clear that they cannot be taken as literally as some authors have presumed.[40] The Spanish *tributos* statistics presented by Reid (1990:649-50) and Newson (1998:21, 26) to support the idea of a dramatic population decline in the Philippines between 1550 and 1650, for example, undoubtedly need to be examined in the same fiscal context in which they were obtained – that is, in the light of changes in the scope of European political influence

[38]   Gooszen (1994:39-40) quotes a source from 1907 which states that during population counts, the inhabitants of upland Seram in the South Moluccas sometimes 'exaggerate the size of their tribe due to the tendency to grandiloquence which is common among the Alfurs'.
[39]   Blair and Robertson 1903-09, XXXV:122; Jacobs 1974-84, I:538; Riedel 1886:77. Newson (1998:21) quotes a similar statement referring to part of the Philippines.
[40]   Tammes (1940) wrote his pioneering study of demography and environment in North Sulawesi almost without questioning the reliability of the population figures at his disposal, and the earliest detailed study of the demographic history of Minahasa, Edeling's *memorie* of 1875 (NA V 17-4-1877/20), is equally naive in this respect.

and taxation over the period in question.[41] In one particularly powerful dem-
onstration of how changing fiscal circumstances could affect demographic
statistics, the recorded population of Minahasa rose immediately by fully
28 percent when an unpopular rice tax calculated on a demographic basis
was discontinued in 1824 (Chapter V) The strength of the incentive for indigenous informants to lie about the size of the population, clearly, sometimes
rivalled the real size itself as a determinant of the figures written down by
European officials.

Given that understatement is the most common form of inaccuracy in
the available data, it is tempting to select a 'correction factor' to compensate for this, and apply it consistently to all (presumably) deflated figures
as they occur in the sources. Since the most sophisticated contemporary
attempt to correct such figures on the basis of field evidence was that made
by Van Delden on Sangir in 1825, his correction of 28 percent – augmented,
perhaps, by another factor to allow for the slave component of the population which even his corrected count did not claim to include – would seem
to be the obvious starting point. Faced with the large scale of the uncertainties involved, in an earlier exploratory paper I simply resorted to a round 50
percent 'upwards adjustment'.[42] When other accuracy indications are absent,
this may indeed serve by default as a first approximation. Considering, however, the number and complexity of the factors affecting the degree of understatement, the way in which they can combine with problems of uncertain
scope, and the existence of some factors conducive to inflation rather than
deflation of population figures, it is obviously too simplistic to apply such a
correction indiscriminately.

The crudity of a standard adjustment is particularly highlighted by the
problem of deciding at what chronological point to stop applying it. Elson
has pointed out that even in Java, the means by which demographic data
were obtained often did not change dramatically in the course of the nineteenth century. Since 'the information was still collected by the village chiefs
and passed up through the indigenous and Dutch administrative hierarchy',
he argues, at least for the period up to 1870 there is 'no reason to think that
the improvement in the quality of figures was a radical one'.[43] Yet it would
certainly be misleading to treat an estimate for, say, Minahasa in 1870 as inac-

[41]   The same applies to the comparison made by Knaap (1987:100, 277-8) between early and
late seventeenth-century Dutch population figures for the South Moluccas.
[42]   Henley 1994:7. For the VOC period even this is perhaps too conservative a standard; Dutch
writers in the seventeenth and eighteenth centuries, as we have seen in the case of Padtbrugge,
were more inclined to double the figures supplied by local informants (also Roselaar 1706;
Keijzer 1856:201).
[43]   Elson 1994:282. Boomgaard (1989a:165-71) provides a more detailed analysis of accuracy
variations and improvements in population figures from Java in the nineteenth century.

curate in the same degree as one for Minahasa in 1830. The number, knowledge and discipline of the local colonial administrators did increase over the intervening period, giving them a better chance of detecting faulty enumerations, while qualitative innovations like standard data forms and village birth and death registers were also introduced to help them (see Chapter V). The increase in accuracy, however, must have been gradual, and can only be assessed with careful attention to the administrative and fiscal context.

The sobering conclusion here is that figures which are inaccurate in diverse ways and degrees can best be presented as they stand in the original sources, and any attempts at correction or quantitative tinkering relegated to a separate interpretative discussion also encompassing all other available figures for the region to which they refer. What can and must be included in the data tables, however, is as full as possible a range of that contextual information which is relevant for the assessment and interpretation of each figure. In the first place, it is important to reproduce any indication of what the people who actually collected or recorded the statistics thought about their accuracy; such contemporary judgements may not always have been correct, but ours are not always likely to be better. Secondly, each tabulated statistic will also be accompanied by a summary of other circumstantial clues to its reliability, including the number and type of components (geographical, ethnic, or otherwise) into which it is divided, the degree to which the figures appear to have been rounded off, the identity of the author and his informants, and any recent administrative or fiscal changes which might have affected the quality of the data.

Regarding rounded and unrounded statistics, it is worth noting that a high degree of precision (figures quoted to the single 'fighting man', for instance) may indicate absolute fidelity to misleading indigenous sources rather than a high level of accuracy as such. Other things being equal, in fact, the most accurate estimate is likely to be one which combines statistical imprecision with social and spatial detail – that is, one which is composed of a large number of approximate-looking subtotals and shows no obvious omissions, whether geographical (subregions) or social (for instance, slaves). The author of such an estimate probably had a good knowledge of the area in question, and was at the same time experienced enough not to take local statements too literally. The pre-interpretation inherent in this kind of material, on the other hand, is a potential source of error in its own right, and here again it is important to include as many contextual details as possible. Finally, and most obviously, it is also necessary to establish the spatial and social scope of each estimate with as much exactitude as possible.

Translating the partial and collective units of measurement

One aspect of the problem of establishing the social scope of a given estimate is often that of interpreting the units of measurement in which it is expressed. If standardization is usually futile where levels of under-registration are concerned, some attempt to standardize our interpretation of these units remains a practical necessity. While many of the later figures (and also a few of the earliest, particularly in Catholic missionary sources) purport to represent the whole population of the area to which they refer, including women and children, figures in *weerbare mannen* were more common before the nineteenth century. When attempting to derive equivalent all-in population totals from such figures, different writers have applied different conversion factors. Valentijn, for instance, generally took a ratio of three to one as his rule of thumb, but later authors typically multiplied by four or even five.[44] Other units of indirect demographic measurement sometimes found in the sources include *wapendragende mannen* ('men at arms'), *werkbare mannen* ('working' or able-bodied men), and *belasting betalende mannen* ('taxpaying men'), all presumably comparable to *weerbare mannen*. Rather more problematic is the *huisgezin* or 'household' – also referred to as *dapur* or (in Dutch sources on Minahasa) *combuis*, both literally meaning 'hearth' or 'cooking-place'.[45] This unit was already in occasional use in the seventeenth century, but became particularly popular in the early nineteenth.

The best way to assess how figures expressed in the various collective and partial units of measurement should be translated into total population estimates is to examine those cases from the historical record in which both types of figure are given side by side with respect to the same population, and the total figure is not obviously just an arithmetical derivation of its partial counterpart. Table 3 shows ratios between the total population and the number of *huisgezinnen*, *weerbare mannen* and so on – that is, the implied conversion ratios for these units – as calculated from sources containing such parallel estimates.

As usual, the picture here is one of great variation. Even for *weerbare mannen* and its equivalents alone, the recorded ratio ranges from 2.5 (Napu 1908) to 4.7 (Minahasa 1846). In some cases, moreover, the aggregate figures conceal even greater local contrasts. The 1695 VOC Minahasa count which produced the low overall ratio of 2.7 also gave figures for individual districts (*walak*)

---

[44]   Adriani 1913a:860; Knaap 1987:104, 278; Graafland 1898, I:115; Tammes 1940:184-90; Keijzer 1856:201, 214. Kruyt (1909:351), however, applies a factor of only 3.0 in the case of a recently colonized part of Central Sulawesi at the beginning of the twentieth century.
[45]   The indigenous Minahasan equivalent was *awu*, which designated a family group sharing one of the hearths in a Minahasan house (Godée Molsbergen 1928:150; Schouten 1998:20); the Spanish equivalent was *familia* (Colin 1900-02, III:815).

ranging from an even lower 2.0 (Rumo'ong) to a very high 7.4 (Manado).[46] Possibly this contrast indicates that slaves were included in the overall population count for Manado, but not for the *walak* in the hinterland, among which the highest individual ratio was 3.7 (Tonsea).[47] The average ratio for Minahasa in 1695, at 2.7, is similar to those obtained for *weerbare mannen* equivalents in Central Sulawesi two centuries later (To Bau 1899, Mata ndau 1906, Napu and Besoa 1908), which range from 2.5 to 3.6. Comparable ratios from other areas (including Minahasa) in the nineteenth and early twentieth centuries, however, are consistently higher, ranging from 3.8 to 4.7 (Greater Sangir, Siau and Tagulandang 1825, Minahasa 1846, Bolaang Mongondow 1904). To some extent this probably indicates a greater proportion of children in the population, but it may also reflect more complete counting of the population as a whole.

Knaap (1987:278) notes that in the uniquely accurate and detailed VOC population counts from Ambon in the late seventeenth century, the ratio of *weerbare mannen* to total population (including slaves) 'lies between 1:3 and 1:3.5'. The average of all such ratios for *weerbare mannen* and equivalent units in the data from northern Sulawesi, as listed in Table 3, is 3.6.[48] On the face of it, then, we will probably not be too far wrong in general if we follow Knaap (1987:103-4, 278) by taking 3.5 as a realistic standard multiplication factor for converting from figures in *weerbare mannen* to total population estimates. The average proportion of slaves in the population of the region covered by the Moluccan VOC enumerations, however, was only 12-13 percent (Knaap 1987:128), a low figure by the standards of many parts of northern Sulawesi. Where it is suspected that the slave population was proportionally larger than this, a somewhat higher conversion ratio is likely to produce a better first approximation.

The number of individuals per 'household' (*dapur*, *huisgezin*) was apparently higher still, ranging from 4.5 (Siau 1856, Minahasa 1821) to 6.2 (Minahasa 1846), and the fact that the latter figure is given alongside a lower one in *werkbare mannen* proves that the two units were not always synonymous.[49] The average ratio of households to total population, according to Table 3, was 5.2, which accords well with the standard assumption among contemporary Dutch observers that the average household contained five

---

[46]   NA VOC 1579:216-28.

[47]   Excluding, that is, the *walak* known as Negeri Baru (also in Manado), with a ratio of 4.2. It is probably significant that Manado, as noted above, was also the only part of Minahasa for which slaves were included in Padtbrugge's *weerbare mannen* count of 1679.

[48]   This average includes the ratios, 10 in all, for *weerbare mannen*, *werkbare mannen*, *wapendragende mannen* and *belasting betalende mannen*.

[49]   In the *dapur* count for Gorontalo in 1849, on the other hand, slaves are included as part of their masters' *dapur*, suggesting a closer equivalence between *dapur* and *weerbare mannen*.

Table 3. Implied size of some conventional units of demographic measurement, 1695-1908

Area	Year	Type of count	Type of unit	Persons per unit	Other details
Greater Sangir[1]	1825	indigenous count as 'corrected' by A.J. van Delden[2]	weerbare mannen	4.0	-
Siau[3]	1825	as above[4]	weerbare mannen	3.8	-
Siau[5]	1856	count carried out by indigenous political leaders on Dutch orders	dapur	4.5	slave and non-slave dapur listed separately (that is, slaves not included as part of their master's dapur)[6]
Tagulandang	1825	indigenous count as 'corrected' by A.J. van Delden	weerbare mannen	4.3	-
Minahasa[7]	1695	VOC count	weerbare mannen	2.7	chiefs (bobato) included as weerbare mannen
Minahasa[8]	1821	Dutch administrative count	huisgezinnen	4.5	count dates from after official abolition of slavery
Minahasa[9]	1829	Dutch administrative count	dapur or huisgezinnen	5.0	count dates from after official abolition of slavery
Minahasa[10]	1840	Dutch administrative count	dapur or huisgezinnen	5.0	count dates from after official abolition of slavery
Minahasa[11]	1846	Dutch administrative count	werkbare mannen	4.7	werkbare mannen total includes those officially exempt from labour services (mostly chiefs); count dates from after official abolition of slavery
Minahasa[12]	1846	Dutch administrative count	dapur or huisgezinnen	6.2	count dates from after official abolition of slavery
Bolaang Mongondow[13]	1904	Dutch administrative count	huisgezinnen	5.6	-
Bolaang Mongondow[14]	1904	Dutch administrative count	werkbare mannen	4.5	-

	Year	Type of count	Category	Ratio	Notes
Gorontalo[15]	1849	Dutch administrative count	*dapur*	5.7	slaves included as part of their master's *dapur*
To Bau (eastern Central Sulawesi)[16]	1899	rough estimate based on personal observation	'men at arms'	2.5	'considering that there are many unmarried people among them, so that the assumption of 5 souls per *huisgezin* is not applicable' (Adriani and Kruyt)
Mata ndau, Mori, (eastern Central Sulawesi)[17]	1906	indigenous count or in situ estimate by visiting colonial official	*weerbare mannen*	3.6	refers to a single settlement (a major political centre)
Napu (Lore, Central Sulawesi)[18]	1908	Dutch military count	taxpaying men	2.5	figure for taxpaying men 'will not be far from the truth, but the total population figure seems much too low to me' (A.C. Kruyt)
Besoa (Lore, Central Sulawesi)[19]	1908	Dutch military count	taxpaying men	3.0	as above

1   Van Delden 1844:371-2.
2   This ratio refers to the 'corrected' totals. Where both uncorrected figures are given for the same kingdom, the ratio varies (leaving aside the eccentric data for Kandahar) between 3.3 (Manganitu) and 3.9 (Tabukan).
3   Van Delden 1844:370.
4   According to the original figures as supplied by local informants, the ratio was 5.4.
5   AV Manado 1856 (ANRI Manado 51).
6   For the slaves alone, the multiplication factor is 5.0.
7   NA VOC 1579:216-28.
8   Reinwardt 1858:583.
9   Van Doren 1854-56, I:267.
10 Van Doren 1854-56, I:267.
11 Francis 1860:280-1.

12 Francis 1860:280.
13 Encyclopaedisch Bureau 1912b:145.
14 Encyclopaedisch Bureau 1912b:145.
15 'Staat van de gedane zielsbeschrijving onder ultimo Augustus 1849' (ANRI Gorontalo 18).
16 Adriani and Kruyt 1900:138.
17 Maengkom 1907:863.
18 A.C. Kruyt 1908:1309.
19 A.C. Kruyt 1908:1337.

individuals.[50] All of the available figures, however, date from the nineteenth century, so that this ratio may well be inapplicable to earlier conditions because it refers to an unusually juvenile population.[51] Fortunately there are few earlier sources in which figures in *huisgezinnen* or an equivalent unit occur, and when they do, they appear from contextual evidence to be more or less equivalent to *weerbare mannen*.

Indirect and non-quantitative evidence

Besides quantitative material, the European sources also contain many impressionistic statements regarding population size, density, growth and decline. While these have not been incorporated into the demographic tables, they are included where appropriate in the accompanying discussions. Two indirect or surrogate indices of population density will also be invoked on occasion to support or modify conclusions drawn from the quantitative evidence. A high incidence of land or boundary disputes, first of all, can usually be interpreted as an indication of population pressure.[52] While the societies of northern Sulawesi were probably often prone to seek conflict with each other whether or not economic issues were at stake, such conflicts were more likely to take a territorial form where land was a relatively scarce resource. Thanks to the mediating and judicial role which the Dutch authorities came to play in some areas with respect to indigenous society, territorial disputes tend to be quite well reflected in the historical record. Levels of deforestation, secondly, also provide clues to historical demography. Because swidden agriculture was always the economic mainstay of the majority of the population, a high population density was usually reflected in the landscape by extensive clearance of primary forest. Evidence of this type, however, has to be treated with caution, since the areal intensity of farming systems varied, and since agriculture was not the only cause of deforestation. European observers, moreover, sometimes mistook secondary forest regrowth on temporarily abandoned swiddens for natural vegetation, and concluded that the country was less intensively cultivated than it actually was. A full discussion

---

50   Adriani and Kruyt 1900:138; Van de Velde van Cappellen 1858-59:325; De Clercq 1883:118; Graafland 1867-69, I:147; Wilken and Schwarz 1867c:285.

51   Household size, it should be added, may also have been susceptible to historical change for other reasons. The fact that the compulsory rice purchases made by the Dutch authorities in Minahasa until 1852 were imposed on a household basis, according to one later source, encouraged older and married children to continue to live with their parents 'in order to be regarded as a single family [*gezin*]' (Worotikan 1910:157).

52   This correlation is explicitly noted in some Dutch sources (Van Andel and Monsjou 1919: 118-9; Tergast 1936:134).

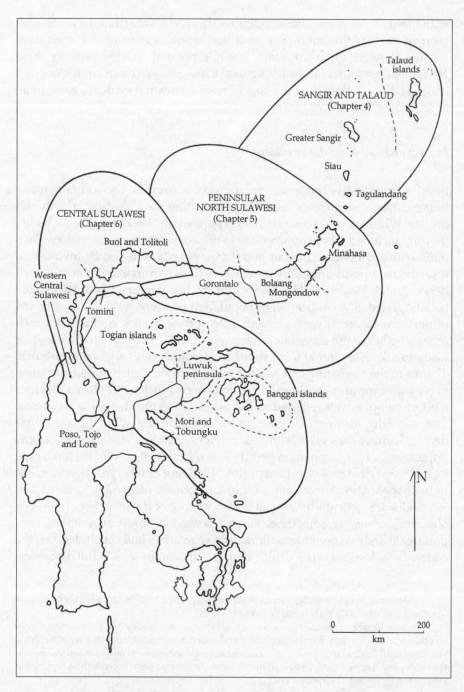

Talaud
islands

SANGIR AND TALAUD
(Chapter 4)

Greater Sangir

Siau

Tagulandang

PENINSULAR
NORTH SULAWESI
(Chapter 5)

CENTRAL SULAWESI
(Chapter 6)

Buol and Tolitoli

Minahasa

Western
Central
Sulawesi

Gorontalo

Bolaang
Mongondow

Tomini

Togian islands

Luwuk
peninsula

Banggai islands

Poso, Tojo
and Lore

Mori and
Tobungku

N

0   200
km

Map 9. Northern Sulawesi: subregions for demographic analysis

of the pattern of deforestation and its relationship to demographic variables appears in Chapters XIII and XIV.[53]

Map 9 shows the three major geographical divisions, and the 15 smaller subregions, into which the demographic information has been divided for presentation and analysis in Chapters IV-VI.[54] The data series presented in these chapters do not in themselves add up to detailed demographic histories of each subregion, but rather provide a basis on which to draw general conclusions regarding patterns of population distribution and long-term trends of growth and decline. At least until the late nineteenth century the available population totals, for reasons which should be clear after my survey of the many types of uncertainty and inaccuracy which they incorporate, are mostly too approximate (and in many cases also too widely spaced in time) to illustrate even the rather dramatic fluctuations which tended to characterize demographic change in the short term. Data on mortality and population decline as a result of specific short-run demographic crises, except where such crises are immediately evident from changes in the total population figures or overwhelmingly important for the interpretation of those figures, will be presented in Chapters VII-IX, which deal with the factors affecting the death rate.

[53]   Knapen (2001:109-14) uses another surrogate demographic indicator, the scale of annual salt imports, to reconstruct demographic change in Southeast Kalimantan during the nineteenth century. It is not possible to apply this technique to northern Sulawesi, where most salt was manufactured locally and no overall import statistics exist. As Knapen concedes, moreover, the income-elasticity of per capita salt purchases makes the procedure unreliable even where total consumption figures can be estimated.
[54]   The Togian Islands, for which few population data are available, are not treated as a separate unit in Chapter VI, although more is said about their early twentieth-century demography in Chapter XI.

CHAPTER IV

Population data, Sangir and Talaud

Geographically compact, clearly bounded by sea and with a long history of European contact, Sangir (comprising the large islands of Tagulandang, Siau and Greater Sangir) and Talaud offer the most concrete and complete series of early population estimates available for northern Sulawesi. Best of all are the records for Siau and Greater Sangir, which include early first-hand Hispanic missionary estimates as well as diverse Dutch data. I begin, however, with the more straightforward case of Tagulandang, the closest major island to Manado, and proceed from south to north.

Tagulandang

Tagulandang (Table 4), the centre of a single kingdom of the same name, came under VOC influence in the 1640s, and for two separate periods during the seventeenth century (but not thereafter) it was the site of a small Dutch military outpost (Van Dam 1931:71; Tiele and Heeres 1886-95, III:387). Its chiefs, formerly Muslim, converted to Protestantism at the beginning of the Dutch period, whereupon churches and schools, run by local or Ambonese schoolmasters, were established on the island under the occasional supervision of Dutch Reformed Church ministers based in Ternate. The written church rolls kept by the schoolmasters, as inspected by the European clergymen during their periodic 'visitations', form the basis for many of the statistics presented in Table 4. Approximately the same ecclesiastical situation persisted until 1858, when Tagulandang became a permanent Protestant mission post (Coolsma 1893:226), although the church registers seem to have fallen into disuse at the end of the eighteenth century (Steller 1866:31). From 1771 until 1829 the Sangirese kingdoms, including Tagulandang, were each obliged to sell a fixed quantity of coconut oil to the Dutch authorities each year.[1] Thereafter they were free from any kind of colonial taxation until 1860, and subject only to a relatively light nominal head tax assessment from 1860 to

---

[1] Kartodirdjo 1973:397; *Corpus diplomaticum* VI:337; Riedel 1872b:547.

Table 4. Population data, Tagulandang, 1669-1930

Year	Figure	Type of estimate	Other accuracy indications
1669	350 *weerbare mannen*[1]	VOC military estimate	'This island can supply [...]'; single undivided figure
1682	500 'armed men'[2]	estimate by Padtbrugge	'This island can supply only [...]'; single undivided figure
1695	1,764 Christians[3]	contemporary inspection of local church registers	aggregate figure only available
1696	1,390 Christians[4]	contemporary inspection of local church registers	2 *negeri* distinguished; figures unrounded; 'but since there have been many births and deaths, and the schoolmaster has not taken these into account, the true number remains uncertain'
1702	1,683 Christians[5]	contemporary inspection of local church registers	2 *negeri* distinguished
1705	1,910 Christians[6]	contemporary inspection of local church registers	2 *negeri* distinguished; figure reproduced as total population estimate by VOC governor of the Moluccas P. Roselaar (1706)
1707	1,572 Christians[7]	contemporary inspection of local church registers	2 *negeri* distinguished
1720	4,188 Christians[8]	contemporary inspection of local church registers	2 *negeri* distinguished
1724	1,724 Christians[9]	contemporary inspection of local church registers	2 *negeri* distinguished
1726	1,853 Christians[10]	contemporary inspection of local church registers	2 *negeri* distinguished
1728	1,650 Christians[11]	contemporary inspection of local church registers	capital *negeri* only
1762	2,391 Christians[12]	contemporary inspection of local church registers	3 *negeri* distinguished; men/women/children distinguished
1769a[13]	'about 600 *weerbare mannen*'[14]	estimate by VOC resident of Manado (1763-1769) B.S. Seydelman	single undivided figure
1769b	2,236 Christians[15]	contemporary inspection of local church registers	2 *negeri* distinguished; men/women/children distinguished

Year	Figure	Source	Notes
1774	1,912 Christians[16]	contemporary inspection of local church registers	3 *negeri* distinguished; men/women/children distinguished
1781	1,689 Christians[17]	contemporary inspection of local church registers	2 *negeri* distinguished; men/women/children distinguished
1808	293 'men and youths [*jongelingen*]'[18]	count obtained by Dutch envoys in connection with planned military recruitment[19]	3 *negeri* distinguished
1824	1,200 people[20]	estimate by resident of Manado	single undivided figure
1825	1,300[21]	estimate by A.J. van Delden based on 'correction' of an estimate by the *raja* (1,132)	'I estimate the population at [...]'; single undivided figure; excludes slaves
1846	± 2,000'[22]	estimate by Dutch government investigator (E. Francis)	single undivided figure
1848	3,000[23]	second-hand estimate by Spanish adventurer (C. Cuarteron)	single undivided figure
1858	3,000[24]	Protestant missionary estimate	single undivided figure
1860	3,114[25]	estimate obtained through 'personal investigation' by 'the missionaries now established on the Sangir Islands'	'deserves rather more credibility than former estimates'; single undivided figure[26]
1866	'more than 3,000'[27]	in situ estimate by Protestant missionary	3 *negeri* distinguished
1872	2,000[28]	Protestant missionary estimate[29]	single undivided figure
1884	'about 4,000'[30]	second-hand estimate by visiting Dutch trader	single undivided figure
1890	5,600[31]	in situ estimate by Protestant missionary	single undivided figure; includes smaller neighbouring island Biaro
1900	'more than 6,000'[32]	in situ estimate by Dutch official (*controleur* Sangir-Talaud, 1899-1900)	single undivided figure

Year	Figure	Type of estimate	Other accuracy indications
1906	'about 6,500'[33]	Dutch administrative estimate	–
1920	9,573[34]	Dutch administrative count	–
1930	9,950[35]	Netherlands Indies census	includes 383 'foreign orientals'

1   De Jongh 1669; also reproduced by Van Dam (1931:56).
2   Van Dam 1931:71.
3   Buddingh 1860:333; Coolsma 1893:202; Keijzer 1856:596.
4   Stampioen 1696.
5   Noot 1703.
6   Buddingh 1860:333; Roselaar 1706; Keijzer 1856:197, 601.
7   Van Wely 1707.
8   Cluijsenaer 1720.
9   Sell 1724.
10 Molt 1726.
11 Werndly 1729.
12 Van Sinderen 1901:395-6.
13 It is also possible that this figure, like those given by the same source for Greater Sangir, dates from 'before the smallpox epidemic', which other sources place in 1763-1764 (Gov. Ternate to GG, 25-7-1763 and 30-7-1764, in NA VOC 3119).
14 Seydelman 1769.
15 Wiltenaar 1769.
16 Tenckink 1774.
17 Lakehinila 1782.
18 'Lijst der verdeling over de gantsche Sangireese eilanden der te leveren recruten' [1808] (ANRI Manado 64).
19 The plan was to draft one in every 15 able-bodied males into the colonial army to assist in the defence of Java against the British.
20 AV Manado 1824 (ANRI Manado 101).
21 Van Delden 1844:370. The same estimate was repeated by visiting missionaries in 1832 (Coolsma 1893:211-2, 1901:628).
22 Francis 1860:296.
23 Cuarteron 1855:27.
24 Brilman 1938:140; Coolsma 1901:640.
25 AV Manado 1860 (ANRI Manado 52); also reproduced by Van der Crab (1862:385).
26 AV Manado 1860 (ANRI Manado 52).
27 F. Kelling, 'Het eiland Taghoelandang en zijn bewoners' [1866] (ARZ NZG 43.2).

28   Brilman 1938:147; Coolsma 1901:634.

29   The origin of this estimate is not explicitly stated in the sources which quote it, but in both cases it is mentioned in the context of missionary activity, and it does not appear in administrative sources for the same period, which continue to cite the estimate of 1867.

30   De Vries 1996:117.

31   Coolsma 1901:652.

32   Frieswijck 1902:470.

33   Van Geuns 1906:72.

34   Pottinga, 'Nota van toelichting betreffende het landschap Tagulandang' (administrative document, 1922) quoted by Tammes (1940:188).

35   *Volkstelling* 1933-36, V:12. The higher figure (11,401) given elsewhere in the census results (*Volkstelling* 1933-36, V:135) includes the smaller neighbouring islands of Ruang and Biaro. The latter is seldom mentioned in early estimates or descriptions, while Ruang was uninhabited in 1705 (Roselaar 1706) and contained only temporary settlements around 1910 (Encyclopaedisch Bureau 1912a:9).

1899.[2] In principle this should mean that the incentive to provide deflated population statistics was weak. Like the other Sangir kingdoms, Tagulandang possessed political dependencies in the Talaud Islands; population estimates which definitely include these have been omitted from Table 4.

At first sight the figures up to 1872, applying a multiplication factor of 3.5 to those expressed in *weerbare mannen* and assuming that the discordantly high count of 1720 is erroneous, are fairly consistent. Almost all correspond to a population of between 1,200 and 3,000, and if the 1808 figure is slightly lower, this is not surprising given the context in which it was obtained. There is some apparent growth up to 1762, followed by a downturn and then a slow recovery by 1860, although the 1872 figure is out of line here. After 1872, however, a more rapid increase sets in, and the population appears to double or even treble in the next three decades, after which growth slows down again, all but ceasing after 1920. The population density on this small (62 km^2) island was a high 159 persons per km^2 at the 1930 census.[3]

One piece of qualitative evidence supports the picture of rapid population growth during the last decades of the nineteenth century. 'Until about 40 years ago', wrote a Dutch official at the beginning of the twentieth century, 'a large part of Tagulandang was covered with virgin forest, but the increasing population meant that more and more forest needed to be felled and land cleared', so that the whole island had now become 'a continous patchwork' of woodland, farmland and coconut stands (Frieswijck 1902:427, 433). Details from earlier descriptions, on the other hand, suggest that considerable deforestation had already occurred well before 1860. Van Delden (1844:362) wrote in 1825 that Tagulandang, like neighbouring Siau, was 'for the most part well cultivated', and in 1846 the *raja* complained to the government commissioner Francis that his subjects were 'constantly' at odds with each other over questions of land ownership.[4] A missionary who visited the island in 1855 described it as 'strewn, as it were, with swidden houses' (Van de Velde van Cappellen 1857:54).

Most of the estimates from the period 1800-1860 were made at long range and show little geographical detail, both good reasons to treat them with caution, and the same goes for the *weerbare mannen* estimates of the VOC period. The church registers of 1695-1781 are more detailed – always, for instance, including women (the sex ratio in these sources, where specified, is balanced), and often also children. These too, however, may be a poor

---

2   AV Manado 1860 (ANRI Manado 52); Van der Crab 1862:386; Encyclopaedisch Bureau 1912a:38.
3   *Volkstelling* 1933-36, V:8. It is not clear how the different figure presented by Tammes (1940: 188) was calculated.
4   E. Francis, 'Aantekeningen van de kommissaris voor Manado 1846' (ANRI Manado 167).

indication of the total population. One source from the end of the seventeenth century does state that the population of Tagulandang 'is said to
consist entirely of Christians' (Van Dam 1931:56), and some nineteenth-century observers even reported that the whole population of Sangir regarded
itself as Christian.[5] The missionary Steller (1866:43-4), however, observed
that Sangirese slave-owners 'prevent their slaves from attending church,
school and religious instruction', and when his colleague Kelling arrived on
Tagulandang in 1858, he found that only a quarter to a third of its inhabitants
had been baptized.[6] In 1899 the number of 'native Christians' on this island,
according to church figures, was still only 3,304, against a total population
of perhaps 6,000 (Coolsma 1901:653). From the following sections on Siau
and Greater Sangir it will be evident that almost all of the earlier figures can
in fact be regarded as minima, and that the demographic growth in the late
nineteenth century, although undoubtedly real, was not as dramatic as the
raw figures suggest.

Siau

Before its conquest by Ternate and the Dutch in 1677 (Chapter I), the island
kingdom of Siau (Table 5) had already been the target of Catholic missionary
activity for more than a century.[7] Thereafter its (now Protestant) population, like that of Tagulandang, was regularly visited by Dutch clergymen
who recorded the contents of the local church registers. Apart from being
more numerous, the pre-nineteenth century estimates for Siau must also be
regarded as potentially more reliable than their equivalents for other parts of
Sangir. Many of them, for instance, reflected extended personal observation
by Catholic missionaries living on the island itself. Even in the Dutch period,
secondly, Siau probably remained the most thoroughly Christianized of the
Sangir Islands, so that the discrepancy between its total population and the

---

[5]   Van Delden 1844:381; Res. Manado to Gov. Moluccas, 26-8-1857 (ANRI Manado 166).
[6]   Brilman 1938:140; Coolsma 1893:238. In 1854 the proportion had apparently been lower still
(Coolsma 1901:629). In the eighteenth century, thanks to more frequent visits by European clergymen, it may well have been higher. Before Kelling's arrival in 1858, Tagulandang (and the rest
of Sangir) had apparently received only four visits from ordained ministers since 1789 (although
the last, in 1854, had been quite recent). It is not entirely clear, on the other hand, whether such
a visit was a precondition for baptism; the whole population of Siau was said to be baptized in
1832 despite the fact that no clergyman had been there for 11 years (Coolsma 1901:627-9). In the
VOC period, according to a later account, visiting clergymen had apparently been in the habit
of baptizing any Sangirese who paid them a small fee in coconut oil and agricultural produce
(Buddingh 1860:352).
[7]   Since the end of the sixteenth century (C. Wessels 1933:393) it had also hosted an intermittent Spanish military presence.

number of people listed in its church registers must have been smaller than elsewhere.[8] At least in the early nineteenth century, the Christians on Siau certainly included slaves.[9] Beginning in 1855, finally, the *raja* of Siau, unlike his counterpart on Tagulandang, responded cooperatively to an attempt by Resident Jansen to have detailed demographic information collected on standard 'census' forms provided for that purpose. Jansen noted in 1857 that of all the kingdoms instructed to do so, Siau had submitted 'the best and most accurate population table'.[10] Unfortunately this particular practice fell into disuse after Jansen's transfer to another residency in 1859, but the number and chronological depth of the available estimates for Siau still makes its population record one of the most complete for any part of the region.

The Siau kingdom included two sets of exclave territories outside the eponymous island: one in the southern part of Greater Sangir, comprising the territories of Tamako and Dago (referred to in many sources, and in Table 5, as Tamako for short), and another in Talaud. Undifferentiated population estimates which definitely include the Talaud dependencies have been omitted here, while those of which the scope is unclear, or which include the territories on Greater Sangir, have been identified as such in the table. According to the geographically very detailed proto-census of 1855, which has survived in its entirety, the combined population of Tamako and Dago in that year was 2,124, while that of Siau proper was more than five times larger at 11,718.[11] The proportion of the population subject to Siau living on the Talaud Islands cannot be reconstructed, but must have been considerably greater.

Leaving aside the first figure (1564), which may reflect inflation for political purposes or include exclaves outside Siau proper, all estimates in Table 5 up to that of 1846 suggest a population of somewhere between 2,000 and 7,000 people. The late sixteenth and early seventeenth centuries (1588, 1594, 1612) appear to have been a period in which the population was relatively small, and since at least one of the relevant estimates (1588) has every appearance of reliability, this is unlikely to be an illusion. As in the case of Tagulandang there is some indication of demographic growth in the mid-eighteenth

---

[8] Spanish missionaries claimed by the 1660s that the whole population was Catholic (C. Wessels 1935:118-9), and two decades after their departure a VOC resident of Manado agreed that 'almost all' were Christian even in the interior of the island (Van Thije 1689). At the end of the nineteenth century, on the other hand, only 8,000 of the approximately 24,000 islanders were said to be Christians (Van Dinter 1899:344).

[9] When the pioneer missionary Joseph Kam (1821:284) visited Siau in 1817, according to his own account, the *raja* 'requested that I would baptize a considerable number of the slaves, both men and women, who had been instructed in the doctrines of Christianity'. This must have been an unusual event, for Kam praised 'the excellent character of this good man' and wrote that he had 'little expected to be the instrument of introducing into the church of Christ so large a number of his slave servants'.

[10] AV Manado 1857 (ANRI Manado 52).

[11] AV Manado 1856 (ANRI Manado 51).

Table 5. Population data, Siau, 1564-1930

Year	Figure	Scope	Type of estimate	Other accuracy indications
1564	20-25,000 souls, including 6,000 fighting men[2]	possibly includes vassals on other islands[1]	estimate by Jesuit missionary (D. de Magalhães) in Manado, apparently based on information from *raja* of Siau[3]	Siau *raja* 'has 6,000 *homens de peleja*, and on the island there are perhaps 20-25,000 souls'; information probably based in the context of a request for missionary attention
1588	2,300-2,400 souls[4]	'around the island, on the sea coast, and in the interior' (whole population)	Jesuit estimate based on in situ information from missionary (R. Berwouts, on Siau 1585-1888)[5]	Christians/pagans distinguished; includes population of 'about 14 places, besides many houses which stand dispersed'
1594	'up to 600 men'[6]	Siau Island only	Jesuit missionary estimate	Siau, 'on which there could be [...]'; single undivided figure; no missionary stationed on Siau at this date[7]
1612	3,000 souls[8]	'on the island of Siau'	Jesuit missionary estimate	single undivided figure; no missionary stationed on Siau at this date[9]
1630	'not more than 7,000 people'[10]	Siau Island only	in situ estimate by Jesuit missionary (M. de Faria, on Siau 1629-1930)	single undivided figure
ca 1644	'more than 3,000' people[11]	Siau Island only	estimate by Jesuit missionary writer (A. Lopes) in Malabar	single undivided figure; reports 'more than 3,000 Christians', but claims that the whole island is Christian; 'The numbers of Christians seem somewhat arbitrary [comments Jesuit historian H. Jacobs] and one does not know on what sources Lopes bases his statements.'[12]
ca 1650	2,500-3,000 people[13]	'vassals and natives' of the *Reyno de Siao*	Franciscan missionary estimate	single undivided figure

Year	Figure	Scope	Type of estimate	Other accuracy indications
1669	'about 1,400' weerbare mannen[14]	'the whole island'	VOC military estimate	single undivided figure
1675	5,500 souls[15]	Siau Island only	Jesuit missionary estimate based on in situ presence (1655-1675)[16]	single undivided figure
1681	3,933 Christians[17]	Siau Island only	contemporary inspection of local church registers	2 negeri distinguished; men/women/children distinguished
1682	1,500 'armed men'[18]	Siau Island only	estimate by Padtbrugge	island 'can send to sea, at a guess, [...]'; single undivided figure
1695	3,934 Christians[19]	Siau Island only	contemporary inspection of local church registers	aggregate figure only available
1702	2,828 Christians[20]	Siau Island only	contemporary inspection of local church registers	4 negeri distinguished
1705a	1,070 'armed men'[21]	Siau Island only	estimate from VOC source reproduced by Valentijn	4 negeri distinguished; some figures rounded to 50 or 100
1705b	3,298 Christians[22]	Siau Island only	contemporary inspection of local church registers	4 negeri distinguished; figures un-rounded; Valentijn regarded this as equivalent to the total population[23]
1706	2,728 Christians[24]	Siau Island only	figure given by VOC governor of Ternate (1701-1706) P. Roselaar	4 negeri distinguished; figures rounded to 10; author claims inhabitants of listed places are 'all Christians', but only 'principal' settlements apparently included
1707	2,979 Christians[25]	Siau Island only	contemporary inspection of local church registers	4 negeri distinguished
1720	4,045 Christians[26]	Siau Island only	contemporary inspection of local church registers	4 negeri distinguished
1726	2,891 Christians[27]	Siau Island only	contemporary inspection of local church registers	4 negeri distinguished

Year	Figure	Scope	Source / method	Categories
1728	2,939 Christians[28]	Siau Island only	contemporary inspection of local church registers	4 *negeri* distinguished
1734	3,150 Christians[29]	Siau Island only	contemporary inspection of local church registers	4 *negeri* distinguished
1761	4,597 Christians[30]	Siau Island only	contemporary inspection of local church registers	3 *negeri* distinguished; men/women/children distinguished
1769a[31]	'about 2,000 *weerbare mannen*'[32]	Siau Island only	estimate by VOC resident of Manado (1763-1769) B.S. Seydelman	single undivided figure
1769b	4,940 Christians[33]	Siau Island only	contemporary inspection of local church registers	4 *negeri* distinguished; men/women/children distinguished
1774	4,194 Christians[34]	Siau Island only	contemporary inspection of local church registers	2 *negeri* distinguished; men/women/children distinguished
1808	631 'men and youths [*jongelingen*]'[35]	Siau Island only (?); definitely excludes Tamako	count obtained by Dutch envoys in connection with planned military recruitment	2 *negeri* distinguished
1824	2,000 people[36]	not specified includes Tamako; excludes slaves	estimate by resident of Manado	single undivided figure
1825	at least 5,000[37]		estimate by Dutch official (A.J. van Delden) based on 'correction' of indigenous estimate (4,506)	single undivided figure
1846	'± 6,000'[38]	unspecified, but does not include Talaud dependencies	estimate by visiting Dutch government investigator (E. Francis)	single undivided figure
1848	8,000[39]	Siau Island only	second-hand estimate by Spanish adventurer (C. Cuarteron)	single undivided figure
1855	11,718[40]	Siau Island only[41]; includes slaves	count by indigenous chiefs on Dutch orders (full original census table preserved)	6 *negeri* (districts) distinguished; men/women/m. and f. children distinguished and *dapur* totals given for each of the categories: nobles/free Christians/free Muslims/slaves; 'although they do not deserve any great trust', the figures

Year	Figure	Scope	Type of estimate	Other accuracy indications
1855	25-30,000[42]	unspecified; probably includes Talaud dependencies	second-hand Dutch administrative estimate	'nevertheless seem worth mentioning as approximations' (resident of Manado); single undivided figure
1857	14,019[43]	includes Tamako; includes slaves	count by indigenous chiefs on Dutch orders using standard 'census' tables	nobility / free commoners / slaves distinguished; 'can be regarded as a very close approximation to the true population' (resident of Manado)
1858	13,964[44]	includes Tamako; includes slaves	count by indigenous chiefs on Dutch orders using standard 'census' tables	nobles / free commoners / slaves distinguished
1859	14,275[45]	includes Tamako; includes slaves	count by indigenous chiefs on Dutch orders using standard 'census' tables	nobles / free commoners / slaves distinguished
1860	11,715[46]	Siau Island only	estimate obtained through 'personal investigation' by 'the missionaries now established on the Sangir Islands'[48]	single undivided figure; 'deserves rather more credibility than previous estimates'[47]
1861	'at least 15,000'[49]	unspecified	personal estimate by *raja*	single undivided figure; 'But not much faith can be placed in any of these figures [...]'
1872	20-25,000[50]	includes Tamako	Protestant missionary estimate[51]	single undivided figure
1880	30,000[52]	probably includes Talaud dependencies[53]	official estimate in *Koloniaal verslag*	single undivided figure

1898	24,000[54]	Siau Island only	in situ estimate by Dutch official (*controleur* Sangir-Talaud, 1898)	'can be estimated at [...]'; single undivided figure
1907	'± 28,000'[55]	Siau Island only	in situ estimate by Protestant missionary	single undivided figure
ca 1918	'about 40,000'[56]	Siau Island only includes 730 'foreign orientals' and Europeans	Dutch administrative estimate	single undivided figure
1930	30,858[57]		Netherlands Indies census	–

1 Tammes 1940:187; Tiele 1877-86, IV:419. One Dutch mission historian describes this figure as 'certainly too high for that period' (C. Wessels 1933: 373), and another ignores it completely (Jacobs 1992:33).

2 Jacobs 1974-84, I:414; Tiele 1877-86, IV:419. A twentieth-century administrative document quoted by Tammes (1940:187), which states that the *raja* of Siau had 6,000 warriors in 1542, probably refers to this source.

3 The Siau *raja* was in Manado at the time and was baptized by Magalhães.

4 Jacobs 1974-84, II:262.

5 Jacobs 1974-84, II:18, 32.

6 Jacobs 1974-84, II:399.

7 Jacobs 1974-84, II:18.

8 Jacobs 1974-84, III:237.

9 Jacobs 1974-84, III:17.

10 Jacobs 1974-84, III:476.

11 Jacobs 1974-84, III:549.

12 Jacobs 1974-84, III:547. The author claims that two missionaries are stationed on Siau, but Jacobs (1974-84, III:18, 547) notes that this 'does not give the actual situation of 1644'.

13 Colin 1900-02, I:110.

14 De Jongh 1669; also reproduced by Van Dam (1931:56).

15 Jacobs 1974-84, III:694.

16 According to Jacobs (1974-84, III:18), there was a continuous Jesuit presence on Siau in this period.

17 *Generale missiven* III:509.

18 Van Dam 1931:70.

19 Buddingh 1860:333; Coolsma 1893:204; Keijzer 1856:596.

20 Noot 1703; also reproduced by Valentijn (Keijzer 1856:196).

21 Keijzer 1856:196.

22 Buddingh 1860:333-4; Coolsma 1893:204; Keijzer 1856:601.

23 Keijzer 1856:196.

24 Roselaar 1706.

25 Van Wely 1707. L. van Rhijn (1851:287) gives a rounded verson of the same statistic.

26 Cluijsenaer 1720.

27 Molt 1726.

28 Werndly 1729.

29 J. Scherius 1735.

30 Van Sinderen 1901:369-71.

31 It is also possible that this figure, like those given by the same source for Greater Sangir, dates from 'before the smallpox epidemic', which other sources place in 1763-1764.

32 Seydelman 1769.

33 Wiltenaar 1769.

34 Tenckink 1774.

35 'Lijst der verdeeling over de gantsche Sangireese eilanden der te leveren recruten' [1808] (ANRI Manado 64).

36 AV Manado 1824 (ANRI Manado 101).

37 Van Delden 1844:370.

38 Francis 1860:297.

39 Cuarteron 1855:27.

40 AV Manado 1856 (ANRI Manado 51).

41 The subtotals for Tamako and Dago have been subtracted.

42 Fragment 1856:141.

43 AV Manado 1857 (ANRI Manado 52).

44 AV Manado 1858 (ANRI Manado 52).

45 AV Manado 1859 (ANRI Manado 52).

46 AV Manado 1860 (ANRI Manado 52); also reproduced by Van der Crab (1862:385).

47 AV 1860 (ANRI Manado 52).

48 Four Protestant missionaries had arrived in the Sangir archipelago in 1857, of whom one lived on Siau (Brilman 1938:137, 139-40; Coolsma 1901:634; Van der Crab 1862:385).

49 AV Manado 1861 (ANRI Manado 52).

50 Brilman 1938:147; Coolsma 1901:634; Encyclopaedisch Bureau 1912a:57.

51 The origin of this estimate is not explicitly stated in the three sources which quote it, but in all cases it is mentioned in the context of missionary activity, and it does not appear in administrative sources for the same period, which continue to cite the estimate of 1867.

52 Koloniaal verslag 1882, Bijlage A:5.

53 The same source locates only an improbably low 5,000 of the estimated 80,000-strong population of Sangir-Talaud on the Talaud Islands.
54 Van Dinter 1899:344.
55 Kelling 1907:6.
56 Encyclopaedie 1917-21, III:689.
57 Volkstelling 1933-36, V:12. The 1920 census, unfortunately, does not include a regional breakdown of the Sangir archipelago (Uitkomsten 1922, II:218-9).

century, followed by a possible decline in the years around 1800. Here too, however, it should be noted that the 1808 figure is certainly deflated, and that of 1824 a very crude long-range estimate. After 1846 the reported population totals suddenly rise, and the 1857 'census', in what Jansen regarded as 'a very close approximation to the true population', counted more than 14,000 Siau subjects including those in Tamako, corresponding to a total of about 12,000 on Siau alone. Despite what has been said about the comparative reliability of the earlier figures for Siau, it can still be assumed that this jump reflects the unprecedented accuracy of the data from the years 1855-1859. Jansen's figures are very detailed in geographical terms, and explicitly include slaves.[12] They also agree well with the in situ missionary estimate of 1860.

Between 1860 and 1920, as in the case of Tagulandang, the picture emerging from the rather scanty data (setting aside the disproportionate estimate of 1880, which probably includes the Talaud dependencies) is one of rapid and sustained growth. If the real population in 1860 was about 15,000, then the annual growth rate over the last four decades of the nineteenth century averaged around 1.2 percent. A description from 1898 confirms that the population of the island 'is constantly increasing at a rapid rate' (Van Dinter 1899:344). In the 1920s, by contrast, there was apparently some demographic decline, although it should be noted that the high rough estimate from circa 1918 may well be exaggerated.

Siau was described in 1588 as a place where there was 'commonly a shortage of foodstuffs' (Jacobs 1974-84, II:261), in 1614 as a 'bare island' (*kaal eyland*), the inhabitants of which 'can obtain the necessities of life only with great difficulty' (Tiele and Heeres 1886-95, I:134), and around 1650 as 'a poor kingdom, the only asset of which is its vassals and natives' (Colin 1900-02, I:110); these comments already suggest a high ratio of population to agricultural resources. Padtbrugge, writing in 1682, also found Siau a 'very poor and needy' island (Van Dam 1931:70), and VOC sources from the beginning of the eighteenth century describe it as 'populous' (Claaszoon 1710; *Generale missiven* VII:7). In 1866 the missionary Steller (1866:17) wrote that 'the size of the population on Siau is much greater in relation to the land area than on any of the other [Sangir] islands', and Kelling even referred to the 'overpopulated island of Siau'.[13] From 1880 onward the term 'overpopulation' occurs repeatedly in descriptions of this island.[14] The figures presented

---

[12]   The proportion of the population listed as slaves is low: 9% in 1855 and 1857, and 8% in 1858 and 1859. In this case, however, it seems that the 'swidden people' (see Chapter III) were included with the free population. Slavery was officially abolished on Siau, as in the rest of Sangir and Talaud, in 1889 (Van Dinter 1899:343; Encyclopaedisch Bureau 1912a:25).
[13]   'Het te zeer bevolkte eiland Siau' ('Taghoelandang en zijn bewoners' [1866], in ARZ NZG 43.2).
[14]   *Koloniaal verslag* 1882, Bijlage A:5; Van Dinter 1899:343; Kelling 1907:6.

above certainly reflect high population densities. The population of about 15,000 indicated by the counts of the 1850s already corresponds to a density of about 95 people per km^2, and the figure was a remarkable 197 per km^2 in 1930.[15]

Landscape descriptions from all periods also confirm that despite its very mountainous terrain, almost the whole area of Siau was settled and cultivated. In the 1580s the 'wooded interior' (*matto dentro*) of the island was inhabited as well as the coastlands (Jacobs 1974-84, II:262), and a century later a Dutch resident of Manado wrote that many of its inhabitants lived permanently 'in the woods, close to their swiddens' (Van Thije 1689). Van Delden (1844:370), writing in 1825, identified Siau as the most intensively cultivated of all the Sangir Islands. 'It is indeed amazing', he wrote (in spite of his relatively low population estimate), 'how the natives on Siau work their gardens on mountains and slopes, and on and between rocks where one would think hardly a tree or a plant could gain a hold'.[16] By 1898 the island was 'almost completely devoid of forest' (Van Dinter 1899:332), and in 1910 there was said to be 'no durable timber' left, so that wood for the construction of a new church had to be imported from an islet located twelve hours away by sea.[17]

At the end of the nineteenth century, according to a local Dutch official, initial attempts by the colonial government to stimulate migration from 'over-populated' Siau found no favour with the local population, most of which showed a strong attachment to its home island (Van Dinter 1899:344). An only slighter later source, however, states that because Siau is 'too small for the number of people who live on it', emigration to other islands has taken place 'from former times up to the present' (Kelling 1907:7). The Sangirese migrants who settled in Minahasa during the late nineteenth century (see below) probably included many from Siau.[18] By the 1930s spontaneous emigration from this island was certainly common (Tergast 1936:128) due to the 'pressing' shortage of land (Tammes 1940:189), and Siau families also joined government transmigration schemes in Bolaang Mongondow (Hoff 1938:31; Weg 1938:162). The demographic stagnation or decline between 1918 and 1930 was probably the result of accelerating emigration. In earlier times, conversely, there seems

---

[15]   *Volkstelling* 1933-36, V:8. The derivation of the figure of 260 people per km^2 given by Tammes (1940:188) is unclear.
[16]   Van Delden 1844 I:362. This statement was also repeated almost word for word by Steller in the 1860s (Steller 1866:17). 'The whole island', wrote another missionary in 1906, is dotted with native houses' (Kelling 1907:6-7).
[17]   *Geestelijke en stoffelijke dingen* 1911:3.
[18]   There was also some emigration during the seventeenth century. A number of Siau Islanders settled in Manila during the period of Spanish control before 1677, and others joined them there after the fall of the island to the Dutch (Blair and Robertson 1903-09, 29:257, 42:124-5, 44:29).

to have been considerable immigration. The author of the comparatively high population estimate from 1630, for instance, observed that 'a great multitude of people have moved in from surrounding islands recently' (Jacobs 1974-84, III:476), and the continual import of slaves from Talaud in the eighteenth and early nineteenth centuries will be discussed below.

The estimates in Table 5 are generally too crude and too widely spaced to reflect the impact of individual demographic events such as epidemics or wars. A notorious forced deportation of almost 450 Siau Islanders by the VOC in 1615, for example, is completely invisible in this record, which suggests only growth between 1612 and 1630.[19] Most of the fluctuations which do appear in the figures, conversely, can be dismissed as statistical 'noise', although with the help of other information it is possible to identify one exception. In 1723, according to a contemporary Dutch report, Siau was hit by a 'great drought' in which 'all the grain in the fields was scorched by the sun', accompanied by 'a deadly sickness or *rode loop* [dysentery], which persisted for several months and killed more than 800 people, as a result of which what crops remained in the swiddens could not be guarded for lack of hands, and fell prey to wild animals' (*Generale missiven* VII:694). At almost the same time, moreover, a devastating smallpox epidemic, more details on which are given below with respect to Greater Sangir, swept through the whole region. The large drop in the number of Christians counted on Siau between 1720 and 1726 no doubt reflects this mortality crisis. What accounts for the almost equally great increase in the reported size of the Christian population between 1709 and 1720, on the other hand, remains a mystery. Such idiosyncracies mean that figures like these are useful only in large numbers and for interpreting long-term trends and patterns.

Greater Sangir

Although its early European contacts were less extensive than those of Siau, Greater Sangir (Table 6) was also the scene of intermittent Catholic missionary efforts from 1640 until the departure of the Spanish in 1677 (C. Wessels 1935:111-22). Thereafter it too (except for the small northern kingdom of Kandahar, which was largely Muslim) converted to Protestantism, obtaining churches and schools run by local or Ambonese schoolmasters and periodically inspected by Dutch clergymen based in Ternate. From 1711 until the end of the eighteenth century, a small VOC military outpost also existed in

---

[19]   Tiele 1877-86, VIII:297-8; Tiele and Heeres 1886-95, I:132-63. The Company intended the islanders to provide forced labour for its nutmeg plantations on Banda in the South Moluccas.

Tabukan on the east coast.[20] Two Protestant mission posts were established on the island in 1857 (Coolsma 1893:225), and the first Dutch government official to be stationed anywhere in Sangir during the nineteenth century arrived in Tabukan in 1882 (Encyclopaedisch Bureau 1912a:39).

Greater Sangir presents a more complex picture than Siau and Tagulandang in that it was divided between a number of indigenous polities. Some proportional details, therefore, will be useful regarding internal subdivions. The political geography of Sangir in the sixteenth and early seventeenth centuries is obscure, but from about 1660 until the end of the nineteenth century there were always five main units: the kingdoms of Tabukan, Manganitu, (Kolongan-)Taruna and Kandahar, and the Siau dependency of Tamako in the south.[21] According to Van Delden (1844:370-3) in 1825, Tabukan had a population of 7,100, Manganitu 4,350, Taruna 3,700 and Kandahar 545. For Tamako, which Van Delden lumped with Siau, later sources from 1846 and 1848 give figures of 500 and 1,000 respectively.[22] A combination of these estimates indicates that in the early nineteenth century Tabukan accounted for 43 percent of the total population, Manganitu 26 percent, Taruna 22 percent, Kandahar three percent, and Tamako five percent.[23]

Prior to 1867 the figures in Table 6 show much variation, indicating, at first glance, population totals ranging from fewer than 6,000 (1726) to more than 20,000 (1775). A feature of the earlier data, however, is that more than in the cases of Tagulandang or Siau, there is a consistent discrepancy between the population figure according to the church records and that suggested by contemporary estimates in *weerbare mannen* or equivalents. Whereas the 'fighting men' figure of 1763 and the 'males, who wear breeches' estimate of 1775 both imply, applying a multiplication factor of 3.5, a total population of 20,000 or more, the church registers of the same period listed only between 8,000 and 14,000 Christians. The military-fiscal estimates of 1669, 1681, 1706 and 1705-1711 are also relatively high. There are other indications, too, that the church registers on Greater Sangir were a particularly poor guide to the total population. At the end of the seventeenth century, for instance, the island was still said to contain many 'heathens and unbaptized people who

[20]   Positieve order Gov. Ternate, 12-1-1711 (ANRI Ternate 62); AV Ternate 1807 (ANRI Ternate 141). In 1776 this outpost consisted of 'a sergeant and ten or twelve soldiers' (Forrest 1779:310).
[21]   Colin 1900-02, III:814; C. Wessels 1935:113; Laarhoven 1989:51, 100, 116-7. The sultan of Ternate created a separate chiefdom at Sawang (formerly part of Taruna) in 1675, and at least two other minor schisms occurred at around the same date, but all were resolved as a result of Dutch intervention in 1678 (Van Dam 1931:51, 73; Keijzer 1856:180).
[22]   E. Francis, 'Aantekeningen van den kommissaris voor Menado 1846' (ANRI Manado 167); Cuarteron 1855:12.
[23]   An 'average' figure of 750 has been assumed for Tamako. Francis gives similar ratios (44:26: 22:3:5). The figures for 1848 and 1860, however, accord a greater majority to Tabukan (59% and 55% respectively).

Table 6. Population data, Greater Sangir, 1591-1930

Year	Figure	Scope	Type of estimate	Other accuracy indications
1591	3,000 men[1]	possibly refers to Tabukan only	estimate by Jesuit missionary in Ternate, probably based on Ternatan source	single undivided estimate of the men 'serving' the 'king of Sangir'
1640	16,000 souls[2]	'the whole of this island'	in situ estimate by Franciscan missionary	'[...] or a little more or fewer'; single undivided figure
ca 1655	5-6,000 people[3]	possibly refers only to Kalongan-Taruna	estimate by Jesuit writer in 1660, probably from Jesuit missionary sources[4]	'hasta [...]'; single undivided figure
1669	'about 4,000[5] weerbare mannen'	excludes Tamako and Kandahar	estimate by VOC governor of the Moluccas (1667-1669) M. de Jongh after personal visit to Sangir in situ estimate by Padtbrugge	separate figures given for Tabukan, Manganitu, Taruna and Sawang, all rounded to 100
1677	7,000 souls[6]		in situ estimate by Padtbrugge	'at a rough estimate'; single undivided figure
1681[7]	4,190 huisgezinnen[8]		figures given by Padtbrugge in his memorie van overgave (1682)	13 dorpen distinguished; figures rounded to 10 or 100
1694	> 8,310 Christians[9]		contemporary inspection of local church registers	11 negeri distinguished
1695	11,034 Christians[10]		contemporary inspection of local church registers	aggregate figure only available
1696	> 8,904 Christians[11]		contemporary inspection of local church registers	10 negeri distinguished
1702	10,313 Christians[12]		contemporary inspection of local church registers	11 negeri distinguished
1705	10,116 Christians[13]		contemporary inspection of local church registers	11 negeri distinguished; figures mostly rounded to 10 or 100
ca 1706	4,590 huisgezinnen[14]		estimate by VOC governor of Ternate (1701-1706) P. Roselaar	13 negeri distinguished; figures rounded to 10 or 100

Year	Figure		Source	Notes
1705-11[15]	12,810 souls or 4,080 weerbare mannen[16]	–	compiled from unspecified VOC sources by Valentijn	13 dorpen distinguished; most figures rounded to 10 or 100; not all zielen subtotals are derived from weerbare mannen figures
1707	11,770 Christians[17]	–	contemporary inspection of local church registers	11 negeri distinguished; figures mostly unrounded
1720	11,479 Christians[18]	–	contemporary inspection of local church registers	10 negeri distinguished
1724	8,124 Christians[19]	–	contemporary inspection of local church registers	11 negeri distinguished
1726	5,563 Christians[20]	–	contemporary inspection of local church registers	8 negeri distinguished
1728	8,468 Christians[21]	–	contemporary inspection of local church registers	11 negeri distinguished
1734	>5,959 Christians[22]	–	contemporary inspection of local church registers	8 negeri distinguished
1757	13,304 Christians[23]	–	contemporary inspection of local church registers	12 negeri distinguished; men/women/children distinguished
1761-62	13,958 Christians[24]	–	contemporary inspection of local church registers	12 negeri distinguished; men/women/children distinguished
1763[25]	5,650 weerbare mannen[26]	–	estimate by VOC resident of Manado (1763-1769) B.S. Seydelman	12 negeri distinguished; men/women/children distinguished; separate figures given for Tabukan, Taruna, Manganitu, Kandahar, and Tamako; figures rounded to 50, 100 or 1000 and all qualified 'approximately' or 'at least'
1769	10,366 Christians[27]	–	contemporary inspection of local church registers	12 negeri distinguished; men/women/children distinguished
1774	10,428 Christians[28]	–	contemporary inspection of local church registers	12 negeri distinguished; men/women/children distinguished

Year	Figure	Scope	Type of estimate	Other accuracy indications
1775	'about 6,000 males, who wear breeches'[29]	–	second-hand estimate by British sea captain (T. Forrest), probably from Magindanao source[30]	'Sangir contains many Nigris [...] in all of which are reckoned [...]'; single undivided figure
1780	9,631 Christians[31]	–	contemporary inspection of local church registers	11 *negeri* distinguished; men/women/children distinguished
1781	8,142 Christians[32]	excludes Kandahar and parts of Manganitu and Taruna	contemporary inspection of local church registers	9 *negeri* distinguished; men/women/children distinguished
1808	3,014 'men and youths [jongelingen]'[33]	–	count obtained by Dutch officials in connection with military recruitment	12 *negeri* distinguished
1824	8,000 people	excludes Tamako	estimate by resident of Manado	Tabukan, Manganitu, Taruna and Kandahar distinguished; figures rounded to 500
1825	15,695 people[34]	excludes Tamako; excludes slaves	in situ estimate by Van Delden, based on adjusted local counts	individual estimates given for Manganitu, Taruna, Kandahar and Tabukan; figures rounded to 100; total 'more likely to lie below the true figure than above it'
1846a	4,500 souls plus 2,000 *huisgezinnen*[35]	Tamako, Manganitu and Taruna only	in situ estimate by visiting Dutch government investigator (E. Francis)	separate estimates given for 3 kingdoms (that in *huisgezinnen* is for Manganitu)
1846b[36]	15,990 souls[37]	excludes Tamako; includes slaves	later estimate by E. Francis, basis unknown[38]	4 kingdoms distinguished; figures rounded to 10 or 100
1848	13,000 souls[39]	excludes Kandahar	second-hand estimate by Spanish adventurer (C. Cuarteron)	Tabukan, Tamako, Manganitu and Taruna distinguished; figures rounded to 500 or 1000
1854	17,550 Christians and Muslims[40]	–	estimates by visiting Dutch Protestant minister	7 subunits distinguished; figures mostly rounded to 100 or 500

Year	Population	Notes	Source/method	Remarks
1859	14,428 people[41]	Tabukan, Taruna and Kandahar only; includes slaves	counts by local *raja* using Dutch standard 'census' forms	separate estimates from each kingdom; nobles/free commoners/slaves distinguished; figures 'can only be regarded as approximations'[42]
1860	16,469[43]	excludes Tamako	estimates obtained through 'personal investigation' by 'the missionaries now established on the Sangir Islands'[44]	Tabukan, Manganitu, Taruna and Kandahar distinguished; figures unrounded; results 'deserve rather more credibility than former estimates'[45]
1867	17,090[46]	–	estimate from special report by resident of Manado to governor-general	single undivided figure; 'It is difficult to determine whether these figures indicate the correct size of the population'
1872	25,000[47]	excludes Tamako	Protestant missionary estimate[48]	single undivided figure
1880	'about 45,000'[49]	may include dependencies on Talaud[50]	Dutch administrative estimate	single undivided figure
1892	70,000[51]	–	estimate by Dutch visitor, basis unknown	single undivided figure
1899	60,000[52]	–	estimate by Dutch visitor, basis unknown	single undivided figure
1905	'about 76,000'[53]	–	Dutch administrative estimate	single undivided figure
ca 1910	57,434[54]	excludes Tamako	Dutch administrative count	3 *landschappen* (Kandahar-Taruna, Manganitu and Tabukan) distinguished
ca 1918	60,000[55]	–	Dutch administrative estimate	single undivided figure
1930	79,537[56]	includes 1,545 Europeans and 'foreign orientals'	Netherlands Indies census	–

1 Argensola 1992:83; dated by Jacobs (1974-84, II:304).
2 Pérez 1913-14, V:638.
3 Colin 1900-02, I:110.
4 A Jesuit mission post existed in Kalongan in 1655 (C. Wessels 1935:114).
5 De Jongh 1669; *Generale missiven* III:678; also reproduced by Van Dam (1931:56).
6 Robidé van der Aa 1867:254.
7 Padtbrugge last visited Sangir in 1680 (NA VOC 1366).
8 Van Dam 1931:68-69.
9 G. van Aken 1694. For one *negeri*, Tabukan, only a minimum estimate of 2,000 Christians was available.
10 Keijzer 1856:596; Coolsma 1893:207.
11 Stampioen 1696. As in 1694, the register for Tabukan was incomplete.
12 Noot 1703.
13 Coolsma 1893:207; Keijzer 1856:662. The equivalent figures listed by Buddingh (1860:333-4) amount to a slightly different total.
14 Roselaar 1706.
15 These are the earliest and latest dates mentioned in association with population figures in Valentijn's account of Sangir (Keijzer 1856:177-93).
16 Keijzer 1856:192-3.
17 Van Wely 1707.
18 Cluijsenaer 1720.
19 Sell 1724.
20 Molt 1726.
21 Werndly 1729.
22 J. Scherius 1735. The figure for one *negeri*, Taruna, is a minimum estimate.
23 À Besten 1757.
24 Van Sinderen 1901:381-93.
25 The figures date from 'before the smallpox epidemic', which other sources place in 1763-1764.
26 Seydelman 1769.
27 Wiltenaar 1769.
28 Tenckink 1774.
29 Forrest 1779:312.
30 See the entry for Talaud at the same date (Table 4.4).
31 Huther 1781.
32 Lakehinila 1782.
33 'Lijst der verdeeling over de gantsche Sangireese eilanden der te leveren recruten' [1808] (ANRI Manado 64).
34 Van Delden 1844:370-2. Also reproduced by Coolsma (1901:628, referring to 1832) and many other later authors.

35 'Aantekeningen van den kommissaris voor Menado 1846' (ANRI Manado 167).

36 The figures are presumed to apply to the year in which Francis visited Manado and Sangir.

37 From a report written by Francis in 1847 and quoted by Jansen in 1857 ('Missive Sangir en Talaut Eilanden', 26-8-1857, in ANRI Manado 166); also published by Francis (1860:296-7).

38 The component figures for Tamako, Manganitu and Taruna are different from those noted by Francis in his first in situ estimate.

39 Cuarteron 1855:12.

40 Buddingh 1860:330, 336, 339, 341. The Muslims, in Kandahar, numbered only 300.

41 AV Manado 1859 (ANRI Manado 52).

42 In a separate report on Sangir and Talaud from 1857 (ANRI Manado 166), Resident Jansen remarks that the stated numbers of slaves in particular are 'far below the true figures'.

43 AV Manado 1860 (ANRI Manado 52); Van der Crab 1862:385.

44 Four Protestant missionaries had arrived in the Sangir archipelago in 1857; two of these lived on Greater Sangir, one in Tabukan and one in Manganitu (Brilman 1938:137, 144; Coolsma 1901:634; Van der Crab 1862:385).

45 AV Manado 1860 (ANRI Manado 52).

46 AV Manado 1867 (ANRI Manado 53).

47 Brilman 1938:147; Coolsma 1901:634; Encyclopaedisch Bureau 1912a:57.

48 The origin of this estimate is not explicitly stated in the three sources which quote it, but in both cases it is mentioned in the context of missionary activity, and it does not appear in administrative sources for the same period, which continue to cite the estimate of 1867.

49 Koloniaal verslag 1882, Bijlage A:5.

50 The same source locates only an improbably few 5,000 of the estimated 80,000-strong population of Sangir-Talaud on the Talaud Islands.

51 De Vries 1996:262.

52 Weber-Van Bosse 1904:117.

53 'According to the algemene memorie' (Tammes 1940:187). I have not been able to identify this source.

54 Encyclopaedisch Bureau 1912a:27.

55 Encyclopaedie 1917-21, III:689.

56 Volkstelling 1933-36, V:12. The higher figure of 90,241 given elsewhere (Volkstelling 1933-36, V:135) includes the population of some smaller nearby islands.

152 *Fertility, food and fever*

live in the forests' (Stampioen 1696), and in 1788 the *raja* of Taruna report-edly prevented a visiting Dutch clergyman from baptizing his subjects.[24] The adventurer Cuarteron (1855:13) reported that in 1848 there were still pagans on Greater Sangir 'in the interior of the island in the slave hamlets [*nelle capanne degli schiavi*]'. The only guide to the size of the slave group as such is provided by two of the 'census' counts ordered by Resident Jansen in the late 1850s, according to which slaves made up three percent of the population in Manganitu, seven percent in Tabukan, and 18 percent in Taruna.[25] These proportions are very probably understated, however, since as Van Delden (1844:4, 368-70) observed, slavery was a sensitive issue in the relationship between the Dutch and the *raja*. Even in 1899, when other sources suggested a total population of 60-70,000, church reports indicated only 31,800 'native Christians' on Greater Sangir.[26]

As in the case of Siau, one early fluctuation indicated here which can be regarded as real is the population decline of the 1720s. When the clergyman Dominicus Sell inspected the church and school at Tabukan in 1724, he was told that 1,435 Christians had recently died there in a smallpox epidemic, against 2,716 still living; elsewhere on the island, the mortality rate had apparently been even higher (Sell 1724). Sell also mentioned that 'other dis-eases' had been involved alongside smallpox, and it is likely that crop failure and dysentery, as on Siau, had contributed to the crisis. The subsequent visi-tation report, written two years later, also refers to many deaths as a result of disease (Molt 1726). The impact of another smallpox epidemic, in 1763-1764, is likewise visible in the figures obtained from the local church registers. Less clear here, particularly given that the estimate from 1781 is geographically incomplete, is the more sustained population decline toward the end of the eighteenth century which is suggested by the data from Tagulandang, and to a lesser extent from Siau. A qualitative source from 1807, however, confirms that while the Sangir Archipelago was formerly populous, 'a number of erup-tions of the volcano on Greater Sangir, the resulting epidemics, the smallpox, and constant slave raiding by the Magindanao have reduced the population enormously, especially on Sangir itself [Greater Sangir]'.[27] In 1821, the Sangir Islands as a whole were still said to be in a 'state of depopulation'.[28]

[24] RPR Ternate, 8-10-1788 (ANRI Ternate 27).
[25] AV Manado 1857 (Manganitu), 1859 (Tabukan, Taruna), in ANRI Manado 52.
[26] Coolsma 1901:653. In 1930, by comparison, 71% of the population was Christian, 20% pagan, and 9% Muslim (*Volkstelling* 1933-36, V:92).
[27] AV Ternate 1807 (ANRI Ternate 141). Siau, according to this source, had been less affected, so that it had now overtaken Tabukan as the most populous of the Sangir kingdoms. Van Delden (1844:372) also mentions the 'terrible ravages of the smallpox' in Sangir in 1792.
[28] Van Graaff and Meijlan 1856:359. Also P. Merkus, 'Aanteekeningen nopens den staat en tegenwoordige gesteldheid der Moluksche Eilanden' [1822] (NA MvK 2954).

Demographic growth on Greater Sangir in the second half of the nine-teenth century, if Table 6 is taken at face value, was phenomenal. The record-ed population more than tripled in the period 1867-1900, corresponding to an unrealistic annual growth rate of 3.8 percent per year, and confirming that the level of underestimation in the sources from the mid-nineteenth century had been severe. Except for the 'corrected' estimate by Van Delden (and even this excludes slaves), most of these sources were probably based directly on oral statements by the local *raja*.[29] In 1854 the kingdoms of Greater Sangir, like those of Siau and Tagulandang, were instructed 'to complete and main-tain registers of population, births and deaths according to model forms sent to them for that purpose'; a year later, however, Resident Jansen complained that although some tables had been returned, they were 'so incorrectly completed that they could not be used'.[30] 'An accurate population count', confirmed the missionary Van de Velde van Cappellen (1857:46) in 1857, 'has never yet been held here'. Barely had Jansen's efforts begun to show results in 1859 when he left the residency and his census procedure fell into disuse, leaving his successors to guess or to rely on missionary estimates. At no point before the twentieth century were detailed village-level population counts produced like those recorded on Talaud (see below).

If Jansen's partial 'census' result of 1859 (14,428) is raised in the ratio of 100:68 (in accordance with the regional proportions established above) to allow for the missing territories of Manganitu and Tamako, it suggests a total population of about 21,000. Applying a similar procedure to the in situ esti-mates for Manganitu, Taruna and Tamako obtained by commissioner Francis in 1846, and using a multiplication factor of 3.5 for the figure in *huisgezinnen*, we obtain a 'real' total of 22,000 instead of the 16,000 indicated by his second and geographically complete estimate (1846b). Both figures correspond quite well with the highest (and presumably best) *weerbare mannen* estimates from the eighteenth century (1763, 1775). Raising them again by our arbitrary 'standard' 50 percent to allow for underestimation produces a hypothetical population of 30-35,000 souls for Greater Sangir in the middle of the nine-teenth century. This may still be somewhat too low, since it corresponds to a growth rate in the period 1860-1900 (from, say, 35,000 to 60,000) of over 1.3 percent per annum, slightly higher than on Siau. It does enable us to conclude, however, that around 1850 the island probably supported 60 inhabitants per km^2; by 1930 this figure had risen to 141 per km^2 (*Volkstelling* 1933-36, V:8).

The *negeri* mentioned in European descriptions of Greater Sangir were all located on the coasts of the island.[31] Early church visitation reports, how-

[29]   One source (AV Manado 1861, in ANRI Manado 52) suggests that even the first missionary estimates of 1860 were obtained in this way.
[30]   AV Manado 1854, 1855 (ANRI Manado 51).
[31]   Van Delden 1844:361; Steller 1866:29; Van de Velde van Cappellen 1857:54.

ever, already mention extensive settlement in the interior (G. van Aken 1694; Werndly 1729), and in 1857 the missionary Van de Velde van Cappellen (1957:54) confirmed that Greater Sangir, like Siau and Tagulandang, was 'everywhere inhabited, even outside the *negeri*'. Resident Jansen agreed in the same year that 'a large part of the population' lived in dispersed houses and hamlets.[32] Many seventeenth- and eighteenth-century Dutch sources mention land disputes and precise definition of territorial boundaries on the island, both indicative of a high population density.[33]

Emigration from Sangir to Talaud may have a long history, since in 1886 the population of 'many of the coast places' in Talaud was described by Hickson (1887:139) as 'unmixed Sengirese'.[34] Given, however, the long-standing political supremacy of Sangir over Talaud and the commerce (see below) between them, this could equally have been the result of local acculturation. What is certain is that the growth of the population on Sangir toward the end of the nineteenth century coincided with a new movement to Minahasa, where Sangirese migrants were working as hired labourers by 1880 (Matthes 1881; Schouten 1998:169). By 1901 there was a constant stream of emigrants to the peninsula from Greater Sangir as well as Siau (Frieswijck 1902:470). Some established new Sangirese farming villages on the coastlands of Minahasa (Tergast 1936:128; Worotikan 1910:155), and in the 1920s many were employed harvesting coconuts for Minahasan smallholders.[35] The initial causes of this migration are not recorded, but by the 1930s the shortage of agricultural land on the home island was certainly an important factor (Bastiaan 1930:4; Tammes 1940:189). At the 1930 census more than 24,000 ethnic Sangirese were reported to be living in Minahasa (*Volkstelling* 1933-36, V:22), and by the late 1940s the total number in peninsular North Sulawesi was thought to have reached 50,000.[36] According to Boomgaard and Gooszen (1991:46) the combined population of Sangir and Talaud declined, presumably in connection with this massive emigration, in the years 1934-1938 – an observation which lends credibility to the indication in Table 5 that the population of Siau was already falling in the 1920s.

<hr />

[32]   'Missive Sangir en Talaut Eilanden', 26-8-1857 (ANRI Manado 166).
[33]   Brandwijk van Blokland 1749; *Corpus diplomaticum* III:109; V:51, 61, 63, 569, 578, 597; *Generale missiven* VI:349, XI:512; Pielat 1731.
[34]   Se also Encyclopaedisch Bureau 1912a:27.
[35]   A.Ph. van Aken 1932:108; NA MR 779x/20; Departement van Landbouw, Nijverheid en Handel 1925:17.
[36]   Blankhart 1951:89. The 1930 census results, however, are not consistent on this point (*Volkstelling* 1933-36, V:33, 49). A proportion of the 'Sangirese' emigrants may in fact have been Talaud islanders (see below).

Talaud

The Talaud Islands (Table 7), at the extreme margin of European contact, were visited by occasional military and missionary expeditions from the seventeenth century onward, but did not become the site of a Dutch government outpost until 1888 (Encyclopaedisch Bureau 1912a:39). Protestant missionaries, although active here since 1859 (Coolsma 1903:273), do not seem to have produced any useful population estimates for this group. Talaud consists of three main islands, Karakelang, Salibabu and Kaburuang, together with the smaller Nanusa islets and the remote outlier of Miangas, off the coast of Mindanano in the far north. Several of the estimates in Table 7 omit Miangas, but the population of this island, at least in the late nineteenth and early twentieth centuries, probably did not amount to more than three percent of the Talaud total.[37]

Almost as dramatically as in the case of Tojo, with which I introduced Chapter III, the data for Talaud illustrate the difficulties involved in interpreting even late-colonial population statistics. The *Koloniaal verslag* for 1889, for instance, first mentions a population of 60,000, only to add in a footnote that an alternative figure of 35,000 can be found 'elsewhere' for the same islands.[38] Another official estimate from the same period, omitted here, even puts the total population at just 5,000 souls (*Koloniaal verslag* 1882, Bijlage A: 5). Talaud, however, demonstrates the rewards as well as the frustrations of historical demography. Apart from the censuses of the early twentieth century, two estimates in Table 7, those of 1775 and 1848, do appear to stand out for their potential reliability. Both are extremely detailed and realistically rounded, and both were made, with the benefit of first-hand experience of the islands, by Europeans who also enjoyed the rare advantage of not being directly associated with the colonial power. Both, however, indicate a disconcertingly large population. Cuarteron, whose calculation included women and children, arrived at a sum total of 37,700 souls in 1848, while Forrest's figure of 13,410 'men who wear breeches', applying our standard 'fighting men' multiplication factor of 3.5, and even without allowing for possible undercounting, would suggest a total population of almost 47,000 in 1775.

On the face of it, these figures are hard to accept given the much lower totals indicated by all twentieth century data (including the censuses of 1920

---

[37]   The population of Miangas was about 1,000 in 1885, and 450 in 1905 (Lam 1932:46-7).

[38]   *Koloniaal verslag* 1891, Bijlage A:5. The former estimate probably represents informed guesswork, and the latter the result of a lost official population count for the Sangir kingdoms which was completed in 1888 (*Koloniaal verslag* 1890, Bijlage A:5).

Table 7. Population data, Talaud, 1656-1930

Year	Figure	Scope	Type of estimate	Other accuracy indications
1656	11,000 souls[1]	possibly only that part of Talaud under the control of Siau[2]	Jesuit missionary estimate	*hasta* [...]; single undivided figure
1701	2,325 *weerbare mannen*[3]	excludes Miangas	compiled from the diary of a journey to Talaud by VOC envoys	33 *negeri* distinguished; most figures rounded to 10 or 100; governor of Ternate P. Roselaar comments (1706): 'but in my opinion there are probably more than twice as many'
1689-1705[4]	2,900 *weerbare mannen* (9,030 souls)[5]	excludes Miangas	compiled from various VOC sources by Valentijn	24 *dorpen* distinguished; *weerbare mannen* figures rounded to 10 or 100; whole population totals apparently derived from these via a multiplication factor of around 3.0
1769	'20,000 souls'[6]	–	estimate by VOC resident of Manado (1763-1769) B.S. Seydelman	single undivided figure
1775	13,410 'men who wear breeches'[7]	excludes Miangas	recorded by British sea captain (T. Forrest) from a Magindanao chief who 'kept a register, which I took down from his mouth', and from a Chinese trader in Talaud[8]	69 villages distinguished; figures rounded to 10, 50 or 100
1846	13,650 souls[9]	–	in situ estimate by visiting Dutch government investigator (E. Francis) using local information	single-unit approximation based on total of 64 *negeri* with estimated average of 42 *huisgezinnen* each, at an assumed 5 individuals per *huisgezin*

1848	37,700 (see text)[10]	–	in situ estimate by Spanish adventurer (C. Cuarteron) using local sources	'notes which I acquired from the natives of the Talaud Islands regarding the number of settlements [...] and an approximate calculation of the number of inhabitants of each, during the 8 months for which I stayed on those islands'; 79 villages distinguished; adults/children and males/females distinguished; most figures rounded to 10 or 50
1854[11]	> 13,650[12]	–	modification of 1846 estimate by resident Jansen on basis of brief visit to Talaud	'In my opinion this figure can be regarded as a minimum. There are more *negeri* than the [...] commissioner mentioned.'
1857	12-15,000[13]	–	second estimate by Jansen in general report on Sangir and Talaud	single undivided figure; 'As long as no population count has been carried out, all figures remain assumptions [...] However we will probably not be far from the truth if we estimate [...]'
1860a	15,000[14]	–	estimate by resident of Manado	'according to most visitors'; 'without any fear of exaggeration'
1860b	15-20,000[15]	excludes Nanusa	second-hand estimate by Dutch investigator in Manado	'accurate information regarding the number of the population is completely unavailable'
1867	'approximately 41,000'[16]	–	estimate from special report for central government by resident of Manado	single undivided figure

Year	Figure	Scope	Type of estimate	Other accuracy indications
1889a	60,000[17]	–	Dutch administrative estimate (see text)	single undivided figure
1889b	35,000[18]	–	Dutch administrative estimate (see text)	single undivided figure
1890	50,000[19]	–	Dutch administrative estimate	'based on pure guesswork'; single undivided figure
1895a	35,000[20]	–	derived from Dutch administrative estimate for Sangir and Talaud together[21]	single undivided figure
1895b[22]	'about 25,000'[23]	–	estimate by resident of Manado, basis unclear	4 islands or island groups distinguished; figures rounded to 500
1911[24]	18,992[25]	excludes immigrants from outside Talaud and Sangir[26]	Dutch administrative count	aggregate figure only available
1917	'± 20,000'[27]	–	in situ estimate by Dutch official in Talaud	single undivided figure
1920	21,025[28]	includes 172 Chinese and Europeans	Netherlands Indies census	5 districts distinguished
1930	23,825[29]	includes 264 'foreign orientals' and Europeans	Netherlands Indies census	3 districts distinguished

1 From a report on the Jesuit mission province of Ternate, as reproduced by Blair and Robertson (1903-1909 XXVIII: 101), Colin (1900-02, III 814), and Pastells (1936:CCXXIII).

2 The original source, which is ambiguous, discusses Talaud in the context of its subordination to, or alliance with, Siau. Wessels (1935:118), however, interprets the figure as an estimate for the whole Talaud group.

3 Roselaar 1706 (sum corrected for an arithmetical error).

4 These are the earliest and latest dates mentioned for Dutch visits in Valentijn's account of Talaud (Keijzer 1856:171-6).

5 Keijzer 1856:175, 192. Valentijn himself quotes a total of 2,600 *weerbare mannen* and 8,010 *zielen*, but information reproduced elsewhere in the same work (Keijzer 1856:601-2), as Wigboldus (1996a:29) has pointed out, shows that in the case of the island Kaburuang Valentijn misinterprets his own sources to the tune of 1,020 people and about 300 *weerbare mannen*.

6   Seydelman 1769.

7   Forrest 1779:315-17. I am grateful to Jouke Wigboldus for drawing my attention to this crucial source.

8   The Magindanao chief, 'Dato Woodine', had been sent to Talaud in connection with rights over part of it which Magindanao claimed to have inherited from Sangir as the result of a royal marriage (Forrest 1779:311-4). The trader ('the blind Chinese, who came on board to visit me, when I went into the harbour of Leron [Lirung]') provided supplementary information on the outlying Nanusa group, enabling Forrest to produce a figure for the whole Talaud archipelago. The explicit units of the Nanusa estimate were 'male inhabitants' (Forrest 1779:317).

9   'Aantekeningen van den kommissaris voor Menado 1846' (ANRI Manado 167); Francis 1860:297.

10 Cuarteron 1855, Quadro 4.

11 Jansen visited Talaud in 1854, and wrote this report in 1857.

12 A.J.F. Jansen, 'Rapport betrekkelijk het oppergezag over en den toestand van de Talaut Eilanden', 12-8-1857 (ANRI Manado 166).

13 A.J.F. Jansen, 'Missive Sangir en Talaut Eilanden', 26-8-1857 (ANRI Manado 166).

14 AV Manado 1860, 1862 (ANRI Manado 52).

15 Van der Crab 1862:386.

16 AV Manado 1867 (ANRI Manado 53). Lumped together with the estimates for Sangir, Siau and Tagulandang in the same source, this appears to form the basis of the figures reproduced in the Koloniale verslagen for the years 1869-1887.

17 As above, alternative figure.

18 Koloniaal verslag 1891, Bijlage A:5.

19 Koloniaal verslag 1892, Bijlage A:5.

20 Koloniaal verslag 1897, Bijlage A:5.

21 The combined Sangir-Talaud figure here is 15,000 lower than in the previous report (when the estimate for Talaud was still 50,000), and the accompanying text states that this difference is 'presumably' due to 'more accurate figures from the Talaud Islands'.

22 This information was published in 1911, but it is not clear to what year it refers. The author, E.J. Jellesma, was resident of Manado between 1892 and 1903, and the most likely date for the figure is 1895, when Jellesma himself visited Talaud (Lam 1932:39).

23 Jellesma 1911:1237.

24 Or 1910 (Encyclopaedisch Bureau 1912a:68).

25 Encyclopaedisch Bureau 1912a:27.

26 These were probably very few in number.

27 Roep 1917:428-9.

28 Uitkomsten 1922, II:218.

29 Volkstelling 1933-36, V:123, 135.

and 1930), and given the fact that the latter appear to be corroborated by the low figures of 1846, 1854, 1857, and 1860.[39] The estimates from the beginning of the eighteenth century, even if doubled as recommended by the VOC governor of Ternate in 1706, also indicate a population closer to 20,000 than 40,000, and Seydelman's figure from 1769 is in line with this too. When I was still unaware of Forrest's account and had not yet worked in the Jakarta archives, my instinct was to reject Cuarteron's total as erroneous on the grounds that his figures for the male and female children in each community are in every case identical to those which he gives for the adult men and women respectively, suggesting a misunderstanding between him and his informants (Henley 1994:9). In the light of the corroborating evidence from 1775 and 1867, however, this no longer seems reasonable. The way in which Cuarteron estimated the juvenile population may have been crude, but it was almost certainly no misunderstanding. Forrest, too, was well aware that his figures indicated an unusually dense population, and noted that the Talaud Islands, 'being well cultivated, abound with inhabitants and provisions'.[40] 'This much is certain', echoed Jansen after his own visit in 1854: 'that the Talaud Islands, like the Sangirs, are densely populated'.[41]

As Wigboldus (1996a) has pointed out, moreover, there are other reasons to accept that Talaud saw a real and dramatic demographic decline after about 1875. Like the rest of North Sulawesi, first of all, Sangir and Talaud were hit in 1877-1878 by perhaps the worst drought of the nineteenth century, accompanied by harvest failure, 'quite general shortages of foodstuffs', and 'persistent fevers' (*Koloniaal verslag* 1878:27, 1879:24). In 1885 a devastating cholera outbreak, accompanied by epidemic malaria, also took place on Talaud. 'Out of a population of nearly nine thousand in the neighbourhood', a local chief told the naturalist Sydney Hickson (1889:169) in Beo (Karakelang) at the end of that year, 'no fewer than three thousand had died within the space of a few months'. When a Dutch warship carrying food and medicine reached Beo in April 1886, the *raja* told the members of the relief expedition 'that his *negeri* was now almost uninhabited due to the terrible number of lives taken by

[39]   The 1854 and 1857 estimates, however, are simply qualifications of that of 1846, and those of 1860 are very probably based on the same source. The method by which Francis arrived at his estimate in 1846, moreover, was crude, and he almost certainly underestimated the size of the 'average' *negeri*. 'Numbers of *negeri* and houses within them', as Jansen was later to observe, 'cannot serve as a guideline, because a large part of the population lives dispersed' ('Missive Sangir en Talaut Eilanden', 26-8-1857, in ANRI Manado 166).
[40]   Forrest 1779:160. It should be added, however, that Forrest's count also features a worrying ambiguity in that his unit of measurement is alternately identified as 'men who wear breeches' and simply 'inhabitants'. Only for the Nanusa group is the estimate unambiguously identified as a number of 'male inhabitants'.
[41]   'Rapport betrekkelijk het oppergezag over en den toestand van de Talaut Eilanden', 12-8-1857 (ANRI Manado 166).

cholera and fevers, so that the maize fields could not be cultivated, and many of those recovering from the sickness itself had died of hunger'. At Lirung on Salibabu, likewise, 'most of the inhabitants were still too weak to work their gardens' (Ebbinge Wübben 1889:206-7), and famine conditions also prevailed on Nanusa and Miangas (Ebbinge Wübben 1888:137; Lam 1932:47). The food crisis did not pass until the following year.[42]

The Dutch authorities estimated the death toll for Talaud in 1885-1886 at 'about one quarter of the population' (*Koloniaal verslag* 1886:13). In 1888 there was again 'harvest failure and [...] famine [*hongersnood*]' on Talaud (Van Hogendorp 1890:121), and the *Koloniaal verslag* of that year noted that the existing population estimates for Sangir-Talaud as a whole would have to be revised 'because the population there must have been significantly thinned out in recent years by epidemics'.[43] Another episode of hunger, this time associated with drought and 'stomach disease', occurred in Talaud in 1895-1896.[44] In 1915 and 1916 a brief attempt was made by the Dutch to keep birth and death registers on the Talaud Islands; in the first year, apparently as a result of epidemic malaria, there were 845 deaths against only 544 births, and in the second the number of births exceeded that of deaths by just three (Roep 1917:429).

An indirect demographic effect of the 1885 epidemic was to accelerate a wave of emigration, possibly facilitated by a weakening of Sangirese political control over Talaud (Jellesma 1911:1236-7), which would continue into the twentieth century.[45] At the time of the disaster, some Talaud islanders were already working as labourers on small European plantations in Minahasa and on Bacan (in the North Moluccas).[46] Thereafter, the developing copra boom created an ever-increasing demand for hired Talaud labour from Minahasan coconut smallholders.[47] From 1892 onward, service in the Dutch colonial military provided another channel for emigration (Encyclopaedisch Bureau 1912a:27). In later years Talaud islanders also became 'well-known throughout Sulawesi and Ternate as the best timbermen, and in particular the best cutters of ebony trees' (Heringa 1921b:742). By 1906 the Dutch authorities in Manado were worried that the exodus of young Talaud men, 'who have a tendency to leave their homeland in order to free themselves from constricting family ties', was becoming excessive in view of 'the scanty population of the Talaud Islands',

---

[42] CV Sangir en Talaud eilanden 1887 (ANRI Manado 146).
[43] *Koloniaal verslag* 1888, Bijlage A:5. The famine coincided with the arrival of the missionary Ottow, which Coolsma (1893:291) places in 1888.
[44] CV Manado 1896 (ANRI Manado 86); *Koloniaal verslag* 1896:30, 1897:28; Tammes 1940:185-7.
[45] In the wake of the disaster, a plantation company on Bacan offered an advance payment in rice to hungry coolie recruits (Ebbinge Wübben 1888:138).
[46] Hickson 1889:65; Ebbinge Wübben 1888:138, 1889:209; Matthes 1881; Schouten 1998:169.
[47] Departement van Landbouw, Nijverheid en Handel 1925:17; Van Kol 1903:246; Stakman 1893:90.

and decided 'to discourage it as much as possible' (Van Geuns 1906:74). In 1911 a missionary on Talaud also recommended a ban on 'the recruitment of coolies from these already sparsely-populated islands' (*Zegeningen Gods* 1911:5). But in practice emigration does not seem to have slowed down until the economic depression of the 1930s, when falling copra prices reduced the demand for labour from coconut growers (Tergast 1936:128).

There remain some facts which appear to cast doubt on the credibility of a demographic collapse in Talaud at the end of the nineteenth century. Emigration from these islands, first of all, was not a new phenomenon. At least since the beginning of the eighteenth century, and probably earlier, the annual tribute paid by Talaud chiefs to their overlords in Sangir had included slaves.[48] The tribute-collecting expedition which returned from Talaud to Siau in 1848, according to Cuarteron's eye-witness account, comprised five *korakora* vessels, suggesting a cargo of perhaps 50 slaves – or, by way of crude extrapolation, a total of 300 per year for all the six Sangir kingdoms combined.[49] At least in the second half of the eighteenth century, some Talaud slaves were also exported to Ternate by Chinese private traders (Valckenaer 1778). In the late nineteenth century, secondly, Talaud shared its experience of sustained emigration and natural disasters with Sangir, which also suffered several episodes of epidemic disease and food shortages (as well as a volcanic eruption in 1892 which killed 2,000 people outright) without showing any signs of demographic decline.[50] The census of 1930, finally, did not reveal very large numbers of Talaud islanders outside Talaud, although this may well have been because most of the emigrants preferred to identify themselves as Sangirese, a better known and more prestigious ethnicity.[51]

All things considered, however, it still seems reasonable to assume that Forrest and Cuarteron were right and that the Talaud Islands, with 24,000 inhabitants – fewer than 20 per km^2 – in 1930, had once supported 40-50,000, or 30-40 per km^2. This is a surprising conclusion. Tammes, in his pioneering 1940 article on population and environment in North Sulawesi, concluded that Talaud represented a classic example of precolonial demographic 'equilibrium'. His sources for Talaud were limited to twentieth-century statistical

[48] The first explicit record of this compulsory slave trade dates from 1731, when a VOC governor of Ternate noted that the 'income' of the Sangir kings included 'a quantity of slaves, which they obtain from their respective territories in the Talaud Islands each year' (Pielat 1731).

[49] Cuarteron 1855:116-7. A Sangirese *kora-kora* was propelled by 24 oarsmen and was said to be little different from its Ternatan equivalent, which could carry 50 people (Van de Velde van Cappellen 1857:28-30). Cuarteron himself only states that there were 'many' slaves, and implies that all five vessels were loaded with them.

[50] Coolsma 1901:645; CV Manado 1896 (ANRI Manado 86); *Koloniaal verslag* 1861:22, 1862:28, 1863:18, 1878:27, 1879:24, 1892:21, 1893:24, 1896:30; *Nanoesa-eilanden* 1905:315.

[51] Only 9% of the Talaud ethnic group, according to the 1930 census, were living outside the home islands (*Volkstelling* 1933-36, V:22, 47).

material together with Valentijn, whose figures which he took rather literally, so that his impression was one of a small, stable population from the beginning of the eighteenth century right up to about 1920, with slow growth thereafter.[52] Like at least one other observer of his time (Tergast 1936:125), Tammes (1940:189-90) attributed the relatively sparse population of these islands partly to the infertility of their soils, particularly compared with those of the volcanic Sangir group. In the light of the additional data examined here, however, such an argument, at least as it stands, becomes untenable. The speed and magnitude of the late nineteenth-century collapse, moreover, indicates that the demographic situation was far more volatile than Tammes suspected.

Summary

The Sangir and Talaud Islands were densely populated. In the middle of the nineteenth century there were probably 35,000 people, or 60 per km^2, on Greater Sangir, and about 15,000, or 95 per km^2, on Siau. The best of the older statistics suggest that in the early and mid-eighteenth century, the figures had probably been similar. The beginning of the seventeenth century, by contrast, seems to have been a period in which the population was relatively small, as does the beginning of the nineteenth. Despite the limitations of the data, it can be concluded that all of the Sangir Islands saw rapid population growth in the second half of the nineteenth century and the beginning of the twentieth, followed by stabilization (with much emigration) after 1920. By contrast Talaud, with perhaps 40-45,000 people around 1850, saw a rather sustained demographic decline, apparently caused partly by natural disasters and partly by emigration, in the period 1870-1910, its population density falling from at least 30 persons per km^2 to fewer than 20. Serious mortality crises, especially following epidemics, also affected other areas from time to time. All parts of the major islands were always inhabited, but the large nuclear settlements were all coastal. These conclusions will be reiterated in more detail, along with equivalent summaries from other subregions, in Chapter XI.

---

[52]   Tammes 1940:185-6. Tammes multiplied the *weerbare mannen* figures by 5 rather than by the factor of 3 favoured by Valentijn himself, but otherwise assumed that they were reliable.

CHAPTER V

Population data, peninsular North Sulawesi

Although the earliest demographic data for the northern peninsula are not as impressive as their counterparts for Sangir, those from the nineteenth century, when an intensive colonial administration operated in Minahasa (and to a lesser extent in Gorontalo), are much better. The very detailed information which is available for Minahasa from about 1850 onward will also provide some of the most important points of reference when it comes to analysing the factors affecting demographic change (Chapters VII-X).

Minahasa

Minahasa (Table 8) originally consisted of twenty-odd village federations or *walak*, suzerainty over which was claimed by a *raja* who controlled the port settlements of Manado and Amurang on the west coast. In the course of the seventeenth century this claim was contested first by the Spanish, who exported rice from the area and supported ineffective efforts by Franciscan and Jesuit missionaries to convert its population to Catholicism, and later by the Dutch, who were interested in rice and the departure of their Spanish rivals. Spanish soldiers and missionaries were intermittently present in Minahasa from 1606 until 1657 (C. Wessels 1935:83-99), when they were expelled for the last time during a local revolt prompted by the establishment of a Dutch fort at Manado in 1656.[1] By 1679, when Governor Padtbrugge concluded a definitive treaty with the *walak* chiefs in the name of the VOC (Godée Molsbergen 1928:50-8), the influence of the *raja* had also been excluded from Minahasa and restricted to neighbouring Bolaang Mongondow, where his descendants continued to rule until the beginning of the twentieth century. In Minahasa itself, a rather stable political system emerged in which the VOC authorities took over the traditional royal functions of trade and political arbitration (Chapter I). Following military pacification in 1809, Minahasa was divided

---

[1]   NA VOC 1225:393v-5r.

into 27 administrative districts, each corresponding to a precolonial *walak*, and containing between them a total of about 300 villages. Eurasian *opzieners* ('supervisors') formed the main link between the Dutch resident in Manado and the various district (*walak*) chiefs.[2] The number of *opzieners*, surprisingly, was reduced in 1827 from eight to five, and in 1832 there were only four administrative divisions above the district level; in 1853, however, the number of divisions rose again to five (Chapter I, Map 7), and in 1857 the *opzieners* were replaced by European *controleurs*.[3]

The principal minority groups mentioned under the 'scope' heading in Table 8 are the ethnic Chinese and the *burgers*. Chinese traders were already shipping rice from Minahasa to Ternate in the seventeenth century (Chapter II), but do not seem to have settled permanently in Manado until the 1770s.[4] In the nineteenth century their numbers grew, partly due to immigration from Chinese communities in the Philippines (Van Spreeuwenberg 1845-46:43). In 1900 the 3,145 Chinese in Minahasa, together with 327 other 'foreign orientals' (mostly people of Arab descent) and 897 (mostly Eurasian) Europeans, made up about 2.5 percent of the total population (*Koloniaal verslag* 1902, Bijlage A:7). The *burgers* of Minahasa (including traders, fishermen, and craftsmen) continued to enjoy a separate legal status until 1929 (Brouwer 1936:113-4). Slavery was officially abolished as far as the indigenous population was concerned in 1819 (Graafland 1898, I:422), and Minahasan slaves are not explicitly mentioned in any population count. Those referred to in nineteenth-century estimates were mostly of Papuan origin and belonged to Europeans, Chinese and *burgers*, who were permitted to own slaves until 1859.[5] Two of the early population counts (1669b, 1679) exclude what I have called 'southern Minahasa': the *walak* Tonsawang, Ratahan, Pasan and Ponosakan, which were not brought under full Dutch control until the end of the seventeenth century. In more geographically complete VOC estimates (1644b, 1695, 1769), these account for 43, 15 and 10 percent of the population respectively; the first of these figures is probably exaggerated. Table 8 is selective after 1860.

[2]   'Nominative staat der in de residentie Manado zich bevindende lands dienaren', 1-1-1832 (ANRI Manado 88); J. Gansneb Tengnagel, 'Beknopte nota betrekkelijk de residentie Menado', 16-3-1848 (ANRI Manado 168); Pietermaat, De Vriese and Lucas 1840:147.
[3]   AV Manado 1853 (ANRI Manado 51); Adam 1925a:422; Res. Manado to Gov. Moluccas, 18-11-1845 (KITLV H70); 'Nominative staat der in de residentie Menado zich bevindende lands dienaren', 1-1-1832 (ANRI Manado 88).
[4]   No Chinese residents are mentioned in the *memorie van overgave* by Seydelman (1769), or in earlier sources, but by 1782 there were 'many Chinese in Manado' (Gov. Moluccas to GG, 28-9-1782 in ANRI Ternate 91).
[5]   Riedel 1872b:561; J.J. ten Siethoff, 'Topographische schetsen van een gedeelte der residentie Menado, 1845' (ANRI Manado 46).

Table 8. Population data, Minahasa, 1568-1930

Year	Figure	Scope	Type of estimate	Other accuracy indications
1568	'more than 100,000 souls'[1]	unknown	estimate by indigenous envoys to Jesuit missionary in Manado	estimate made in context of request for evangelical attention; possibly refers to Gorontalo rather than Minahasa[2] single aggregate figure
1642a	more than 15,000 people[3]	–	estimate by Franciscan missionary J. Iranzo, in Manado since 1640	
1642b	'more than 100,000 souls'[4]	possibly includes some areas outside Minahasa	alternative estimate by other Spaniards in Manado	'[...] who desire to be Christian'; single aggregate figure
1644a[5]	30-40,000 people[6]	–	Spanish missionary estimate	single undivided figure
1644b	9,880 weerbare mannen[7]	–	estimate acquired by VOC military mission from Ternate; source unclear	16 dorpen (walak) distinguished; figures rounded to 100
1644c	'more than 10,000 indios'[8]	–	estimate by Spanish missionary (J. Iranzo) of number involved in revolt against Spanish garrison	single undivided figure; probably refers to weerbare mannen only
1669a	2,780 weerbare mannen[9]	excludes several walak[10]	VOC count	16 negeri (walak) distinguished; figures rounded to 10 or 100
1669b	4,400 weerbare mannen[11]	excludes southern Minahasa	VOC military estimate	distinguishes two groups (3,000 and 1,400 weerbare mannen), for and against the Company
1670	80,000 familias[12]	'Manados; a big island almost continuous with Makasar'	Jesuit missionary estimate from a relación compiled in Manila	'hasta 40,000 families which live in poblados on the coast, and about the same number again in the mountains'

Year	Figure	Scope	Type of estimate	Other accuracy indications
1672	4-5,000 'adult men'[13]	–	VOC estimate	'[...] are said to live in that area'; single undivided figure
1679	3,990 *weerbare mannen*[14]	excludes southern Minahasa	figures obtained by Padtbrugge during 5-day journey in interior	18 *negeri* distinguished; figures rounded to 10 or 100; 'but it is said that there are twice as many'[15]
1695	23,703 people (8,790 *weerbare mannen*)[16]	–	figures obtained by VOC envoy (P. Alsteijn) on 19-day journey in interior	24 *dorpen* (*walak*) distinguished; figures unrounded; chiefs / *weerbare mannen* / women and children distinguished
1706	more than 10,000[17] *weerbare mannen*	–	estimate by VOC governor of Ternate (1701-1706) P. Roselaar	'at a rough guess'; single undivided figure
1769	20,350 *mannen*[18]	excludes 'more than 60' *burgers*	count by VOC resident of Manado (1763-1769) B.S. Seydelman	18 *landschappen* (*walak*) distinguished; 102 constituent villages also named; figures rounded to 50 or 100 and qualified 'approximately [...]'
1792	20-30,000 *combuizen* (households)[19]	–	estimate by resident of Manado (1792-1803) G.F. Duhr, in context of attempt to predict income from proposed rice tax	'at least 200 *negeri* which exist in this land, each containing, on average, 100 *combuizen* [...] but this is only a rough calculation, and people who know the size of the population of this land better than myself assure me that the annual yield, even at just half a *gantang* [10 kg] of rice per *combuis*, would not be much less than 200 *lasten* [300 tonnes, implying 30,000 households]'

Year	Figure		Method	Remarks
1804	7,909 *combuizen* (households)[20]	–	Dutch count in connection with rice tax	27 districts (*walak*) distinguished; figures unrounded
1807	'60-70,000 people, if not more'[21]	–	estimate by resident of Ternate (1804-1809) C.L. Wieling	single undivided figure
1817a	58,635[22]	–	Dutch administrative count	aggregate figure only available
1817b	'More than 100,000'[23]	'Alvoors' who 'dwell on the north-west coast of Celebes, under the Dutch government'	second-hand estimate by visiting missionary in Manado	single undivided figure
1821	56,236[24]	includes 244 Chinese and Europeans, 1,516 Christian *burgers*, 281 'Mohamedans and Bugis', 499 slaves	Dutch administrative count	–
1823	57,130[25]	–	Dutch administrative count	aggregate figure only available
1824a	73,364[26]	–	Dutch administrative count	aggregate figure only available; resident comments: 'one of the main causes of this increase [since 1823] is the discontinuation of the former compulsory [rice] contribution for the *kora kora* [...] The second is the rising level of trust among the population [...]'; actual population 'is to my mind larger still'
1824b	'more than 80,000 souls'[27]	–	estimate recorded by visiting governor-general (G.A.G.P. van der Capellen)	single aggregate figure; 'The population of this residency is roughly estimated at [...]'
1825	73,088[28]	–	Dutch administrative count	7 administrative units (supervised by *opzieners*) distinguished; figures unrounded

Year	Figure	Scope	Type of estimate	Other accuracy indications
1829	76,311[29]	includes 264 Chinese, 451 slaves	Dutch administrative count	men/women/m. and f. children distinguished
1832	83,000[30]	includes 512 Chinese, 2,875 *burgers*, 510 slaves	Dutch administrative count	aggregate figure only available
1840a	82,355[31]	includes 512 Chinese, 2,637 *burgers*, 416 slaves	Dutch administrative count	men/women/m. and f. children distinguished
1840b	88,272[32]	includes 510 Chinese, 2,875 *burgers*		aggregate figure only available
1842	92,332[33]	–	Dutch administrative count	aggregate figure only available
1845	92,350[34]	includes 830 Chinese	Dutch administrative count	aggregate figure only available
1846	91,664[35]	includes 1,040 Chinese[36]	Dutch administrative count	29 districts distinguished; figures unrounded
1847	91,857[37]	–	Dutch administrative count estimate in *Koloniaal verslag*	aggregate figure only available
1848	85,000[38]	–		single undivided figure
1849	95,662[39]	includes 889 Chinese, 649 Europeans, 3,433 *burgers*, 380 slaves	Dutch administrative count	272 villages distinguished; men/women/m. and f. children distinguished
1850	96,815[40]	includes Chinese, Europeans, *burgers* and slaves	Dutch administrative count	village by village enumeration
1851	99,256[41]	includes Chinese, Europeans, *burgers* and slaves	Dutch administrative count	village by village enumeration
1852	99,588[42]	includes Chinese, Europeans, *burgers* and slaves	Dutch administrative count	village by village enumeration
1853	99,588[43]	includes Chinese, Europeans, *burgers* and slaves	Dutch administrative count	village by village enumeration; figures 'do not warrant the credibility which they should'

Year	Number	Composition	Source	Notes
1854	92,544[44]	includes Chinese, Europeans, *burgers* and slaves	Dutch administrative count	village by village enumeration
1855	93,273[45]	includes Chinese, Europeans, *burgers* and slaves	Dutch administrative count	village by village enumeration; 'Although these figures cannot be regarded as fully accurate, they will nevertheless not be far from the truth. Generally speaking the native chiefs perform their duty to record changes in the population reasonably well.'
1856	93,885[46]	includes Chinese, Europeans, *burgers* and slaves	Dutch administrative count	village by village enumeration
1857	95,070[47]	includes Chinese, Europeans, *burgers* and slaves	Dutch administrative count	village by village enumeration; increase since 1856 'partly due to better counting in some districts'
1858	96,749[48]	includes Chinese, Europeans, *burgers* and slaves	Dutch administrative count	village by village enumeration
1859	99,337[49]	includes Chinese, Europeans, *burgers* and slaves	Dutch administrative count	figures based on new population register held by each village; resident comments: 'I believe I can give an assurance that they are fully reliable'
1860	100,308[50]	includes 1,272 Chinese, 609 Europeans, 3,887 *burgers*	Dutch administrative count	data based on new village registers
1870	115,007[51]	includes 1,619 Chinese, 778 Europeans, 4,255 *burgers*	Dutch administrative count	–
1880	134,362[52]	includes 2,251 'foreign orientals', 700 Europeans	Dutch administrative count	–

Year	Figure	Scope	Type of estimate	Other accuracy indications
1890	148,300[53]	includes 3,260 'foreign orientals', 871 Europeans	Dutch administrative count	–
1900	182,704[54]	includes 3,472 'foreign orientals', 897 Europeans	Dutch administrative count	–

1 Jacobs 1974-84, I:538.
6 Wessels (1933:379) assumes that this estimate refers to Minahasa. Jacobs (1974-84, I:525-6, 538) however, points out that another letter, by a colleague of the Manado missionary, refers specifically to envoys from Gorontalo.
3 Blair and Robertson 1903-09, XXXV:122; C. Wessels 1935:95.
4 Blair and Robertson 1903-09, XXXV:122.
5 The date is approximate. Franciscan missionaries were present in Minahasa from 1640 to 1645 (C. Wessels 1935:94-6).
6 Colin 1900-02, I:111.
7 *Daghregister* 1644:118.
8 Pérez 1913-14, V:641.
9 De Jongh 1669.
10 Wigboldus (1996b:11) has argued that the figure of 1,500 *weerbare mannen* listed by this source for 'Monondo or Mangondo' actually refers to the *walak* in the Amurang area, which were then still under the control of the Manado *raja* rather than the VOC. Monondo, however, is described as lying 'on the Bulan [Bolaang] River, the far boundary of his kingdom in the south', and for this reason I have treated it as referring not to Minahasa, but to that part of modern Mongondow then under the control of the *raja*. The *walak* missing from the estimate, Kawangkoan, Sonder, Romo'ong, Tompaso and Tombasian, accounted for 17% and 35% of the population according to the 1695 and 1769 counts respectively.
11 NA VOC 1271:597v.
12 Pastells 1936:CCXXIV-CCXXV; Colin 1900-02, III:815.
13 Godée Molsbergen 1928:30.
14 NA VOC 1345:474.
15 Van Dam 1931:75.
16 NA VOC 1579:216-28.
17 Roselaar 1706.
18 Seydelman 1769. I am grateful to Jouke Wigboldus for drawing my attention to this important source.
19 Res. Manado to Gov. Moluccas, 20-10-1792 (NA COIHB 86).
20 'Memorie door den afgaande Manados onderprefect Carl Christoph Prediger', 15-9-1809 (ANRI Manado 51). Only the total is reproduced here, but a later source provides a complete breakdown (Res. Manado to Gov. Ambon, 25-10-1810, in ANRI Manado 62). The latter gives a slightly different

total of 7,911 families, but is almost certainly based on the same count of 1804.

21 AV Ternate 1807 (ANRI Ternate 141).
22 Reinwardt 1858:582.
23 Kam 1821:281.
24 Reinwardt 1858:582-3.
25 AV Manado 1824 (ANRI Manado 101).
26 AV Manado 1824 (ANRI Manado 101).
27 Van der Capellen 1855:360.
28 Riedel 1872b:478.
29 Van Doren 1854-56, I:266.
30 Bleeker 1856:32.
31 Van Doren 1854-56, I:266. The figures are for 1 January 1840. The total has been corrected for an arithmetical error. Pietermaat, De Vriese and Lucas (1840:112) provide another set of figures for 1840 which differ from these only as far as the *burgers* (2,865) and slaves (510) are concerned (total population: 82,657).
32 Bleeker 1856:32. Presumably a second count from the end of the year.
33 Bleeker 1856:32; Van Spreeuwenberg 1845-46:190.
34 J.J. ten Siethoff, 'Topografische schetsen van een gedeelte der residentie Menado, 1845' (ANRI Manado 46).
35 Francis 1860:279-80.
36 Francis 1860:405.
37 *Koloniaal verslag* 1852:9.
38 *Koloniaal verslag* 1848:31.
39 AV Manado (ANRI Manado 51).
40 AV Manado 1850 (ANRI Manado 51).
41 AV Manado 1851 (ANRI Manado 51).
42 AV Manado 1852 (ANRI Manado 51).
43 AV Manado 1853 (ANRI Manado 51). This is not a duplication of the result from 1852; the constituent figures are different.
44 AV Manado 1854 (ANRI Manado 51).
45 AV Manado 1855 (ANRI Manado 51).
46 AV Manado 1856 (ANRI Manado 51).
47 AV Manado 1857 (ANRI Manado 52).
48 AV Manado 1858 (ANRI Manado 52).
49 AV Manado 1859 (ANRI Manado 52).
50 AV Manado 1860 (ANRI Manado 52).
51 AV Manado 1870 (ANRI Manado 53).
52 *Koloniaal verslag* 1882, Bijlage A:5.

53 *Koloniaal verslag* 1892, Bijlage A:5.
54 *Koloniaal verslag* 1902, Bijlage A:7.
55 *Uitkomsten* 1922: 216-19.
56 *Volkstelling* 1933-36, V:135.

The population estimates from the seventeenth century, as they stand, range from the equivalent of fewer than 15,000 people (1669a, using a multiplication factor of 3.5 to convert from *weerbare mannen* and allowing an extra 30 percent for the missing *walak*) to more than 100,000 (1642b, 1670). Obviously not all can be taken seriously. The substantial difference between the two *weerbare mannen* counts of 1669, together with Padtbrugge's admission that his own survey in 1679 might have missed half of the population, also provide ample warning that not even geographically detailed estimates from this period can be taken literally. It is striking, however, that a number of the early sources (1644b, 1644c, 1695, 1706, and also 1679 if this estimate is doubled as Padtbrugge suggested) give a figure somewhere in the region of 10,000 *weerbare mannen*, – corresponding, if the number of slaves was small, to a total population of perhaps 35,000 people. At least at the time of the abolition of slavery in 1819, however, 'a large number of slaves was found in the possession of the chiefs and some well-to-do natives' in Minahasa.[6] The eighteenth-century evidence discussed below, moreover, suggests that the earlier figures were in fact severe underestimates. On balance, a figure of 50,000 can probably be regarded as a safe minimum for the size of the whole population at the beginning and end of the seventeenth century. Between 1644 and 1679 there may have been a decline, an idea consistent both with the idea that Southeast Asia as a whole experienced a demographic 'crisis' in the mid-seventeenth century (Reid 1990:649-52), and with the likelihood that a major smallpox epidemic affected northern Sulawesi in the early 1650s (Chapter VII). Particularly considering that no such crisis was evident in the contemporary data from Sangir (Chapter IV), however, the especially low figures of 1669 and 1672 (but not the inflated Spanish estimate of 1670) might also be interpreted in terms of the increased incentive to defensive understatement provided by the consolidation of VOC power in Minahasa after 1657.[7]

The one estimate from before 1800 which stands out as potentially reliable is that of 1769. Resident Seydelman's enumeration is not only detailed, geographically inclusive, and realistically rounded, but also comes complete with a list of more than 100 named villages, indicating that his knowledge of Minahasa was much greater than that of earlier authors. His figure of 20,350 *weerbare mannen*, correspondingly, is much higher than its predecessors, and higher also than those from the first part of the nineteenth century, although

---

[6] AV Manado 1833 (ANRI Manado 48).
[7] Reid (2001:49) has interpreted two of these estimates (1644b, 1669a), which I presented in isolation in an exploratory paper (Henley 1994:12), as supporting the idea of a 'drastic drop in population' in the mid-seventeenth century. Viewed in the fuller context of Table 8, however, the evidence for a demographic 'seventeenth-century crisis' in Minahasa is less strong.

when multiplied by 3.5 it tallies well with the colonial population counts
from 1824 onward. It is also supported by the cruder estimate of 1792, which
(again multiplying by 3.5) likewise corresponds to a total of at least 70,000
Minahasans, and perhaps as many as 105,000.

The much lower figure of 1804, by contrast, is certainly misleading. Shortly
after Duhr made his high estimate in 1792, Minahasa was subjected for the
first time to a form of taxation calculated on an explicitly demographic basis.
This consisted of a 'contribution' in rice from each *combuis* or household to
help meet the costs of the Ternatan *kora-kora* vessels stationed there to ward
off pirates (Godée Molsbergen 1928:155). Unlike the collective rice deliveries
which each *walak* had long been obliged to make each year, this was not paid
for in any way, and inevitably led to energetic evasion of population counts.[8]
The household enumeration of 1804 was the last to take place before the British
occupation of 1810, and in 1809 it was reported that 'the correct population of
each village [...] would now be very difficult to establish, since the natives
will certainly try to conceal this information as much as possible because of
the annual contribution'.[9] The impressionistic estimate of 1807, according to
which Minahasa might contain more than 70,000 people, was certainly more
accurate than the official counts of the same period. When the rice tax was
discontinued in 1824, the recorded population of Minahasa rose immediately
by 28 percent.[10] In 1825, moreover, Resident Wenzel complained that the new
figure was still too low because 'the chiefs have always understated the population because of the contribution for the *kora-kora*', and 'a single year is naturally too short to put an end to such ingrained habits' (Riedel 1872b:478).

Most of the apparent growth in the second quarter of the nineteenth century, in fact, can safely be ascribed to progressively better counting. In 1849
Resident Scherius went so far as to claim that where demography was concerned, 'the absence of fully correct statistics, in a residency almost devoid
of European civil servants, and where the chiefs are not salaried officials
like their counterparts elsewhere, makes statistical comparisons between the
present and the past illusory'.[11] Most Dutch observers of this period had the
impression that the Minahasan population was increasing either very slowly,
or not at all.[12] Indeed, given that some earlier estimates (1792, 1817b) sug-

---

[8]   The collection of this tax was also an occasion for additional, illicit extortion by officials
(Van der Capellen 1855:363).
[9]   'Memorie door den afgaande Manados onderprefect Carl Christoph Prediger', 15-9-1809
(ANRI Manado 61).
[10]   AV Manado 1824 (ANRI Manado 101).
[11]   AV Manado 1849 (ANRI Manado 51).
[12]   AV Manado 1833 (ANRI Manado 48), 1852, 1853, 1856 (ANRI Manado 51); J. Gansneb
Tengnagel, 'Beknopte nota betrekkelijk de residentie Manado', 16-3-1848 (ANRI Manado 168);
Bleeker 1856:32, 85; Van Doren 1857-60, II:361-2; *Fragment* 1856:22; Graafland 1867-69, I:174-9; De
Lange 1897:686; Wallace 1987:197.

gest a total of some 100,000 people, and that at least 15,000 are known from other sources to have been killed by a smallpox epidemic in 1819 (Reinwardt 1858:582; Riedel 1872b:478), it seems quite likely that the population of Minahasa was larger in 1800 than in 1850.

The evidence for growth in the course of the eighteenth century, by contrast, is rather strong despite the scarcity of data from this period. While the figure for 1769 is undoubtedly based on much more complete information than any of its predecessors, the fact that it is fully twice as large as those from 1695 and 1706 is still striking. Even if the latter are raised by a 'standard' 50 percent to allow for undercounting, and the former is regarded as fully accurate, half of the apparent growth still remains unaccounted for. Only six years before Seydelman's count, moreover, Minahasa was hit by a major smallpox epidemic, prior to which the total population must have been even greater. In this area, then, demographic stagnation in the first part of the colonial period was apparently preceded, as Wigboldus (1988:36) observes, by considerable population growth in an era before pacification, vaccination, or famine relief.

Between 1850 and 1860 the quality of the administrative population counts in Minahasa improved to the point where many Dutch officials regarded them as accurate. In 1849, birth and death registers were introduced alongside the 'census' forms distributed to the village heads.[13] In 1854 the authorities were apparently able to detect and correct an error of just 15 households in their head tax assessment, and in 1855 the census results were described for the first time as 'not far from the truth'.[14] Beginning in 1859, each village was also required to complete a standardized annual register listing every inhabitant by name, and in that year it was even claimed that the figures collected were 'fully reliable'.[15] In 1860 the population data were described as 'obtained by means of a nominative count carried out in each village by the *hukum tua* [village head], and checked by the district heads and district clerks' – although not, apparently, by the *controleurs*.[16]

While this improvement did not lead to a sudden jump in the recorded

---

[13] The *opzieners*, however, were given virtually no instructions regarding how the enumeration should be carried out (residency secretary to *opzieners*, 15-12-1849 and 12-2-1850, in ANRI Manado 102; internal residency correspondence concerning the population counts, 1853-1854, in ANRI Manado 27).

[14] AV Manado 1854, 1855 (ANRI Manado 51).

[15] AV Manado 1858, 1859 (ANRI Manado 52). In 1860, however, the recorded population growth since 1859 according to the census was still 396 greater than the recorded surfeit of births over deaths. The resident admitted that immigration could not fully account for this discrepancy, since in the course of the year the number of new immigrants (mainly from Sangir, Gorontalo, Mongondow, Ternate and Tidore) had not exceeded 100 (AV Manado 1860, in ANRI Manado 52).

[16] AV Manado 1860 (ANRI Manado 52).

population like that of 1824, it is clearly reflected in the increasing sensitivity of the count to demographic crises. Whereas the 15,000 or more smallpox
deaths of 1819 had barely led to the slightest dip in the reported total population (1817, 1821), an epidemic of dysentery, cholera and measles which killed
around 10,000 people in 1854 caused this to fall immediately by over 7,000.[17]
Although *controleur* De Clercq (1871c:216) claimed in 1870 that the population of Minahasa was still 'known only by approximation', it is likely that the
figures from the second half of the nineteenth century give a realistic picture
of sustained population growth. The average annual rate of increase between
1860 and 1900, according to the reported figures, was 1.5 percent, increasing
to 1.7 percent after the turn of the century, so that the total population of
Minahasa tripled between 1860 and 1930.

The number of Minahasan villages explicitly mentioned in Dutch sources
rose from 102 in 1769 to 230 in 1809 and 272 in 1849.[18] Given that the total
population does not seem to have grown to a similar extent over the same
period, however, it is far from certain that this increase reflected anything
more than improving accuracy. Lists of *dorpen* or *negeri* in seventeenth-century
reports (1644b, 1669a, 1679, 1695), by comparison, usually included only the
capital settlement of each *walak*, but this did not mean that no others existed.
The Franciscan missionary Juan Iranzo, who lived in Minahasa from 1640 to
1645, wrote soon after his arrival that 'more than 50 villages, large and small,
have been discovered' and that 'the people are numerous, for counting men,
women and children, they number more than fifteen thousand'.[19] Leaving
aside his probable underestimation of both the population and the number
of villages, this would already suggest differentiation within the *walak* and an
average population per village of some 300 people, roughly the same as in the
nineteenth century. Padbrugge's reference in 1679 to dependants 'scattered far
and wide in the forests and swiddens' also confirms that the pattern was not as
simple as his list of *negeri* implies.[20] Even Seydelman (1769) admitted that his
own rather impressive village list did not include 'some smaller hamlets'.

[17]   The monthly residency reports for 1854 (in ANRI Manado 54) indicate at least 9,456 epidemic deaths, while the decline in the recorded population total was 7,044. Reported overall
fertility and mortality in 1854 were 3,348 and 12,821 respectively, indicating a rather greater
decline of 9,473. The resident of Manado attributed this discrepancy to 'a more accurate population count at the end of 1854' (AV Manado 1854, in ANRI Manado 51).
[18]   Seydelman 1769; 'Memorie door den afgaande Manados onderprefect Carl Christoph
Prediger', 15-9-1809 (ANRI Manado 61); AV Manado 1849 (ANRI Manado 51).
[19]   From an excerpt from a letter from the Spanish governor of Ternate, received in Manila
sometime before July 1642, reproduced by Blair and Robertson (1903-09, XXXV:122). In 1619, a
Minahasan chief told another missionary that two particular *walak* already contained 'more than
20 *pueblos*' between them (Pérez 1913-14, IV:435).
[20]   NA VOC 1345:474.

The oral history of Minahasa as recorded in the nineteenth and twentieth centuries is replete with stories in which new villages are founded, but in general it is difficult to relate these to historical events within the period of European contact.[21] More interesting is the specific evidence for several important new village foundations – at Tanawangko on the west coast (*Generale missiven* VIII:21), around Likupang in the far north (Waworoentoe 1894:95), and in the southern part of Minahasa beyond the Ranoiapo River (Graafland 1867-69, II:8) – during the period of apparent demographic growth in the eighteenth century. One source, moreover, explicitly mentions population pressure (alongside political conflict) as a reason for this early emigration from the central plateau (Ulfers 1868:14-5). On the edge of the plateau itself, the *walak* (later district) of Sonder seems to have separated from that of Kawangkoan around 1750 (Schwarz 1907, II:193), and while the immediate cause of this fission was apparently political, it is possible that here too population growth played a role.

If nothing else, the higher and more impressionistic of the sixteenth- and seventeenth-century estimates (1568, 1644b, 1670) indicate that Minahasa was a populous area by regional standards. This is confirmed by contemporary qualitative descriptions. In 1617 the Jesuit missionary Joannes Scalamonti reported that the Alfurs in the hinterland of Manado were 'very numerous, and distributed over various villages' (Van Aernsbergen 1925: 19). 'The country was very pleasing to me for its abundance of provisions and its population of many and large *pueblos*', echoed Iranzo – despite his relatively low initial population estimate – in a *relación* describing his experiences in the 1640s.[22] In 1660 the Jesuit historian Colin (1900-02, I:111), albeit probably basing himself partly on Iranzo, also described the 'Provincia de Manados', with its supposed 30-40,000 inhabitants, as '*muy poblada de gente*'. Later Dutch observers agreed (Godée Molsbergen 1928:30, 114), one describing the 'upland villages of Manado' at the end of the eighteenth century as 'crawling with people'.[23]

At least until the twentieth century, the average population density in Minahasa as a whole was nevertheless much lower than those of the neighbouring Sangir and Talaud Islands. Around 1850, it was concluded in the previous chapter, Greater Sangir probably supported 60 inhabitants per km^2, and Siau as many as 95 per km^2. With its total population of about 100,000 and its much larger land area of more than 5,000 km^2, the equivalent figure

[21]   Domsdorff 1937:344-52; Graafland 1898, I:80-1, 206; Schwarz 1907, II:184-229. Local tradition also pointed to some shrunken and vanished villages, although these were not very numerous (Graafland 1898, I:206, 308; *Rapport* 1910:155; Worotikan 1910:155, 168).

[22]   Pérez 1913-14, V:639. Iranzo, moreover, had also visited Greater Sangir without making any such comment about this undoubtedly populous island (Pérez 1913-14, V:638).

[23]   NA VOC 3957:196.

at the same period was only about 20 per km² for Minahasa.²⁴ Nineteenth-century colonial writers, correspondingly, often bemoaned the fact that large parts of Minahasa were either uninhabited, or only under very extensive forms of cultivation.²⁵ While their lack of appreciation for swidden farming inclined them to exaggerate this point, the internal distribution of the population was certainly very uneven.

> As a whole, Minahasa could easily feed twice its present number of inhabitants. Although there are some areas where the population is densely concentrated, especially in the uplands around Lake Tondano and to its south and west as far as Langoan, Sonder and the foot of Mount Lokon, there are many others outside this zone where the density is only moderate, and others still – on the far side of the Ranoiapo River, in the district of Tombariri, and above all in Tonsea and Likupang – where uninhabited land is available in abundance. (Graafland 1867-69, II:247.)

'If people remark that Minahasa is sparsely populated', wrote another observer in 1855, 'then they are certainly not talking about the Tondano plateau' (Bleeker 1856:90). In earlier years the concentration of population on the plateau had apparently been even more marked, for in 1872, well into the period of sustained population growth, the Minahasa-born ethnographer G.A. Wilken (1873:118) wrote that the district of Tomohon had been 'more heavily populated in the past than it is now', many people subsequently migrating to other districts. Sources from the beginning of the nineteenth century confirm that because Tomohon had 'many people but little land', it was constantly involved in territorial conflicts with neighbouring *walak*.²⁶ In Chapter II it was noted that Tondano was also short of farmland at this period, so that many of its male inhabitants were obliged to hire themselves out as labourers in other districts. Scalamonti, writing in 1617, already observed that 'the greatest part' of the Minahasan population lived 'on the shores of the [Tondano] lake' (Van Aernsbergen 1925:19).

Minahasa, in fact, provides a classic example of a common pattern in Indonesian demographic history, described by Reid (1997) for several parts of Sumatra, in which the bulk of the population was originally concentrated in

---

²⁴ Even in 1930, Minahasa, with 58 inhabitants per km², was still much less densely populated than Siau in 1850.
²⁵ Bleeker 1856:29-30; CV Manado 1862, 1863 (ANRI Manado 52, Ambon 1563); De Clercq 1883:118; Francis 1860:319; *Fragment* 1856:151; A.J.F. Jansen 1861:222; Olivier 1834-37, II:35-6; Matthes 1881; Pietermaat, De Vriese and Lucas 1840:114; J.J. ten Siethoff, 'Topografische schetsen van een gedeelte der residentie Menado, 1845' (ANRI Manado 46).
²⁶ 'Memorie door den afgaande Manados onderprefect Carl Christoph Prediger', 15-9-1809 (ANRI Manado 61); Res. Manado to Res. Ternate, 15-9-1809 (ANRI Manado 64); Watuseke and Henley 1994:378. A source from 1778 also mentions frequent disputes over agricultural land in Minahasa (Godée Molsbergen 1928:132).

high inland valleys and plateaux, while the coastlands are sparsely settled. In the mid-nineteenth century the low-lying northern administrative division of Tonsea, covering almost a third of the total area of Minahasa (Chapter I, Map 7), contained only 16 percent of its population (Bleeker 1856:101, 109), while on the east coast there was only a single village between Kema in the north and Belang in the south.[27] As in Sumatra, this pattern began to change toward the end of the colonial period. The centrifugal migration already noted by Wilken accelerated when the rise of the copra trade gave coastal areas, where the coconut palm grew best, a new economic significance (Schouten 1995a:13, 1998:170, 181). Coconut picking in Tonsea and other lowland districts also provided work both for seasonal migrants from the upland districts, and for long-term immigrants from Sangir, Talaud and Gorontalo.[28] In the early twentieth century there was also both spontaneous and government-sponsored migration from the central plateau to the south of Minahasa beyond the Ranoiapo.[29]

At the same time, nevertheless, population pressure in central Minahasa continued to rise (De Clercq 1898:847; Van Kol 1903:242). In 1920 Van Marle (1922, I:48) calculated that the Tondano plateau had 169 inhabitants per km^2 – a density, he noted, 'reminiscent of many parts of Java'. By 1930 the local density was about 200 per km^2 in Tomohon, and as high as 400 per km^2 in the area of irrigated farming around Kakas to the south of Lake Tondano (Tammes 1940:191) – a locality described by Kündig (1934:168), along with Tondano itself, as 'badly overpopulated'. Despite the recent changes, the original pattern of concentration in the central uplands is still very clear on the demographic sketch-map of Minahasa prepared by Tammes in 1940 (Map 10). With its densely-populated interior and empty coastlands, this area presents a dramatic contrast with the more even distribution, and the many big coastal settlements, described in Chapter IV for the Sangir Islands to its north.

Minahasans, in accordance with their predominantly inland pattern of settlement, were traditionally orientated toward the land rather than the sea, and except in Tondano they did not have a custom of seasonal emigration like that which existed in Gorontalo and some parts of Central Sulawesi. In the course of the nineteenth century, however, many began to migrate to other parts of Indonesia in Dutch service, either as soldiers of the colonial

[27] Graafland 1867-69, II:164. It is possible that the coastal population, due to depletion by slave raids (Chapter XI) in the late eighteenth and early nineteenth centuries, was formerly larger. Earlier Dutch sources, however, do not suggest this; the southwestern quarter between Amurang and the modern border with Bolaang Mongondow, for instance, was described by Padtbrugge in 1682 as 'uninhabited' (Van Dam 1931:84).

[28] A.Ph. van Aken 1932:108; NA MR 779x/20; Departement van Landbouw, Nijverheid en Handel 1925:17; Kündig 1934:183; Schouten 1995a:13-4, 1998:170.

[29] A.Ph. van Aken 1932:112-23; Van Marle 1922, I:66; Tideman 1926:86-8; Tillema 1926:205-6.

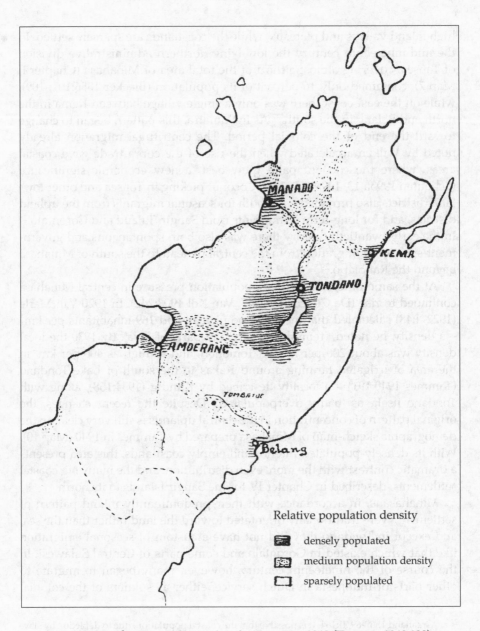

Map 10. Minahasa: population distribution, circa 1940 (Tammes 1940:190)

army or as teachers, overseers or clerks (Henley 1996:81-2). During the second half of the century an average of 100 or more young men enlisted in military service annually (Schouten 1998:123), but in some years the number was much greater (Van Kol 1903:303), and by the 1920s the average recruitment rate had risen to 15 per month.[30] At the 1930 census about 12 percent of ethnic Minahasans, some 35,000 people in all, lived outside Minahasa.[31] This outflow, however, was almost exactly counterbalanced by immigration from neighbouring areas, the reasons for which are discussed elsewhere. In 1930 there were almost 24,500 ethnic Sangir and Talaud islanders and 10,500 Gorontalese in Minahasa, together making up 11 percent of the population (*Volkstelling* 1933-36, V:22, 32-3).

Bolaang Mongondow

Besides the kingdom of the same name, consisting of the north coast harbour settlement of Bolaang together with its hinterland, Mongondow, in the interior of the peninsula, this colonial administrative unit also encompassed the smaller north coast polities of Kaidipang, Bolang Itang, Bintauna and Bolang Uki (Bolango).[32] Several of the estimates reproduced in Table 9 refer exclusively to Bolaang Mongondow proper, but given the relatively small size of the other units, this is less of a problem than it might appear. At the first reasonably complete colonial population count in 1904, Bolaang Mongondow, with some 41,000 souls, accounted for 76 percent of the total population, Kaidipang and Bolang Itam for about seven percent (4,000) each, and Bolang Uki and Bintauna for about ten percent (5,000) between them (Encyclopaedisch Bureau 1912b:145). Only for the very beginning of the documented period, when

---

[30]   Bouvy 1924:380. Departing soldiers, if married, took their wives and families with them (AV Manado 1855, in ANRI Manado 51).

[31]   Almost half of these, however, had been born overseas (*Volkstelling* 1933-36, V:22, 49).

[32]   Kaidipang and Bolang Itam were treated by the European authorities at some periods as a single kingdom (*Encyclopaedie* 1917-21, II:248; Roselaar 1706; A.J. van Delden, 'Verslag van de Rijkjes en Negorijen ten westen van Menado gelegen, 1833', in ANRI Manado 48). Bintauna first appears in historical sources as a minor chiefdom in Gorontalo. By 1755, however, it also had a satellite *negeri* at the newly-discovered Sangkup gold mine on the north coast, and in 1769 this was recognized by the VOC as an independent kingdom (*Corpus diplomaticum*, V:226-7, VI:66, 311). Bolang Uki was the main political centre of the Bolango, a small footloose ethnic group which formed dispersed colonies in several parts of peninsular North Sulawesi (Riedel 1871: 296-8). At the beginning of the nineteenth century some of the Bolango in Gorontalo migrated to Bolang Bangka, near the mouth of the Mongondow river, subsequently moving again to the bay of Bolang Uki, 30 km further west (A.J. van Delden, 'Verslag van de Rijkjes en Negorijen ten westen van Menado gelegen, 1833', in ANRI Manado 48; Wilken and Schwarz 1867a:35). Others settled on the south coast at Molibagu, which later became the capital of the Bolango kingdom (*Encyclopaedie* 1917-21, I:343).

Kaidipang appears to have been larger and more important, is there strong reason to suppose that the proportions were very different.

Despite its proximity to Minahasa, in Bolaang Mongondow Dutch influence was very indirect until a *controleur* was posted there in 1901 (Encyclopaedisch Bureau 1912b:143). Bolaang and the neighbouring coastal kingdoms, nominally Christian during the VOC period, were included in the church and school inspection tours periodically made by the Dutch Protestant ministers based in Ternate. The numbers of Christians included in the church registers according to the inspection reports, however, are so small that they cannot bear any relation to the total population, and have not been included here.[33] In the early nineteenth century, these Christian enclaves were converted to Islam (Wilken and Schwarz 1867a:44-5, 1867b: 276). Fiscal obligations to the Dutch government consisted of fixed deliveries of gold, which was mined at several locations in the area. In the years 1855-1858 this compulsory gold trade was replaced by a monetary tax or *hasil* of four guilders per household per year.[34]

The only feasible place to begin the interpretation of this erratic series is close to the end, with the first population counts supervised directly by the colonial administration at the beginning of the twentieth century. These indicate a total population of about 55,000, with no significant growth between 1904 and 1920. Since, however, the concentration of the population in nuclear settlements did not begin until after 1906 (Dunnebier 1907a:8), it is likely that the 1904 and 1906 counts were still somewhat incomplete and that Riedel's global estimate (1900) of 60,000 was closer to the truth. In that case the population was possibly slightly smaller in 1920 than in 1900, an idea which derives credibility from a report that the influenza pandemic of 1918 took 'many hundreds' of lives in Bolaang Mongondow, killing one twelfth of all adults in some villages (Dunnebier 1919). Between the 1920 and 1930 censuses, on the other hand, there was strong growth, most of it probably real.

The nineteenth-century estimates, ranging from fewer than 5,000 souls (1833, 1857a) to 50,000 or more (1866c, 1895), obviously present greater problems. An accurate population count, judged the missionaries Wilken and Schwarz after their visit to Bolaang Mongondow in 1866, 'is probably impossible for the present, since there are still many people who live a wandering life in the swiddens and forests and who marry, have children, and die without the government knowing anything about them'. Informants, moreover,

---

[33]   In 1761, for instance, one such church inspection recorded just '559 [Christian] souls' in Bolaang (Van Sinderen 1901:361).

[34]   Encyclopaedisch Bureau 1912b:141-2; Wilken and Schwarz 1867c:291. Of this tax, 10% was officially destined for the *raja* and other chiefs, the rest for the Dutch government (Wilken and Schwarz 1867c:295).

Table 9. Population data, Bolaang Mongondow, 1563-1930

Year	Figure	Scope	Type of estimate	Other accuracy indications
1563	'12-15,000 souls' under Bolaang, plus (at least) '3,000 men' in Kaidipang[1]	'7 or 8 places' under the ' king of Bolaang', and 6 places on the coast in Kaidipang	in situ estimate by Jesuit missionary	two undivided figures; 'they say that they may have [...]' (Bolaang); *obra de tres mil homens* came to the shore three times asking to be baptized (Kaidipang)[2]
1591[3]	7,000 *hombres de armas*[4]	Kaidipang only	estimate by Jesuit missionary in Ternate, probably based on Ternatan source	single undivided figure
ca 1650	6-8,000 people[5]	'kingdom of Bolaang' (including Mongondow) and Kaidipang	Spanish missionary estimates	two undivided figures (2-3,000 and 4-5,000 respectively)
1669	1,500 *weerbare mannen*[6]	Mongondow only	included in VOC population estimate for Minahasa	single undivided figure
1670	5,000 families[7]	Kaidipang only	Jesuit missionary estimate from a *relación* compiled in Manila	single undivided figure
1682	'4,000 strong'[8] (probably *weerbare mannen*)[9]	Mongondow only	estimate by Padtbrugge	'but not more than 900 are fully obedient to the king of Bolaang'
1769	5,500 *weerbare mannen*[10]	Bolaang, Mongondow, Kaidipang and Bintauna	estimates by VOC resident of Manado (1763-1769) B.S. Seydelman	rounded figures for each unit (300, 3,000, 2,000 and 200 respectively); estimate for Mongondow refers to '77 *negeri*'
1824	12,300 souls (of which 7,000 in Bolaang Mongon-dow)[11]	–	estimate by resident of Manado (1825-1826) J. Wenzel	'according to information acquired, the population [...] can probably be put at [...]'; 4 kingdoms distinguished; figures rounded to 100

Year	Figure	Scope	Type of estimate	Other accuracy indications
1829	6,520 souls[12]	'small kingdoms along the N.E. coast of Celebes' (probably including Buol and Tolitoli)	Dutch administrative estimate	single aggregate estimate only available
1833	3,940 people (of which 'not more than 2,000 souls' in Bolaang Mongondow)[13]	excludes the Bolango in Molibagu ('whose number is very small')	estimates by 'persons familiar with that area' as recorded by Van Delden	5 kingdoms distinguished; figures rounded to 100; 31 named *negeri* listed (without individual population figures) for Bolaang Mongondow, where 'many people are also scattered here and there in the mountains, so that even the *raja* can only give very unreliable information regarding the number of his subjects'
1846	27,800 (of which about 25,000 in Bolaang Mongondow)[14]	–	second-hand estimates by government investigator L. Francis	'plus or minus'; 'with a population, it is said, of [...]' (Bolaang Mongondow); 5 kingdoms distinguished; figures rounded to 100; of the Bolaang Mongondow population 'a total of hardly 3,000 souls shows a minimal obedience to its chiefs'
1852a	31,280 (of which 25,000 in Bolaang Mongondow)[15]	–	Dutch administrative estimate	5 kingdoms distinguished; figures rounded to 100; 'An accurate census of the small kingdoms belonging to this residency is not possible except on the basis of earlier reports and information which I have been able to find [...]'[16]
1852b	at least 3,615 *dapur* [hearths][17]	(part of) Mongondow only	indigenous census recited by 'a native from Mongondow'	29 *negeri* distinguished; figures rounded to 10 or 100; 'the native

Date	Figure	Scope	Source	Comments
			to Dutch engineer (S.H. de Lange) in Kotabunan	assured us that the figures were too low rather than too high'; 'he claimed that he could only name fewer than half of the *negeri* found in Mongondow'
1852c	'more than 36,000'[18]	Mongondow only	'corrective' modification of official 1852 estimate for Bolaang Mongondow (25,000) by Dutch government investigator (P. Bleeker) based on findings of De Lange (1852b)	dismisses original estimate as 'much too low' and substitutes figure based on indigenous census (3,615 *dapur*), assuming 5 persons per *dapur* and 50 percent coverage
1857a	3,336 souls[19]	Bolaang Mongondow only	count compiled by Bolaang chiefs on Dutch orders[20]	19 settlements or areas distinguished; men/women/m. and f. children distinguished; resident of Manado comments: 'It is beyond doubt that these figures are incorrect'
1857b	'about 12,000 souls'[21]	Bolaang Mongondow only	in situ estimate by resident Jansen 'in connection with the number of houses which I personally counted'	1,000 houses, assuming 2 households per house, 5 people per household, and 2,000 'people living dispersed'[22]
1857c	'about 30,000 souls'[23]	Bolaang Mongondow only	in situ estimate by Dutch visitor (J.G.F. Riedel)	single figure, but broken down elsewhere into 4 regional subunits[24]
1860	24,344 people (of which 20,816 in Bolaang Mongondow)[25]	—	Figures supplied by chiefs [*rijksbesturen*] of each kingdom in context of Dutch administrative count	5 kingdoms distinguished; figures unrounded; 'an estimate which approaches reality somewhat more closely than previous estimates'
1864-94	24,000 people[26]	'small kingdoms on the north coast of Sulawesi' (presumably including Buol)[27]	official estimate in *Koloniaal verslag*	single undivided figure

Year	Figure	Scope	Type of estimate	Other accuracy indications
1866a	1,116 *huisgezinnen*[28]	Bolaang Mongondow only	'official estimate according to which the *hasil* is calculated'	single undivided figure; 'does not include the nobility and slaves, who pay no tax'; 'if a significantly larger total were admitted to, the *hasil* might be increased, which the chiefs do not wish to see happen'[29]
1866b	7,000 *huisgezinnen*[30]	Bolaang Mongondow only[32]	estimate supplied by *kapitan laut* (a high indigenous official) of Bolaang to visiting Protestant missionaries[33]	single figure for 'whole kingdom'[31]
1866c	50,000 souls (10,000 *huisgezinnen*)[34]	Bolaang Mongondow only	in situ estimate by visiting colonial official (F.S.A. de Clercq)	'There is little certainty regarding the size of the population [...] I received information which led me to suspect a total of [...]; broken down elsewhere into 4 regional units'[35]
1893	16,134 people (of which 8,374 in Bolaang Mongondow)[36]	excludes Bolang Uki	'figures obtained from the native rulers'	'still incomplete'; 4 kingdoms distinguished; figures unrounded
1895	58,500 (of which 50,000 in Bolaang Mongondow)[37]	–	official Dutch administrative estimates in connection with political contracts	5 kingdoms distinguished; figures rounded to 500 or 1,000
1900	'circa 60,000'[38]	Mongondow only	rough estimate by knowledgeable Dutch official (J.G.F. Riedel)	single undivided figure
1904	54,755 (of which 41,417 in Bolaang Mongondow)[39]	–	Dutch administrative count	5 kingdoms distinguished; figures unrounded
1906	41,140[40]	Bolaang Mongondow only	Dutch administrative count	76 villages distinguished

| 1920 | 55,910[41] | includes 459 'foreign orientals' and Europeans | Netherlands Indies census | – |
| 1930 | 71,989[42] | includes 1,356 'foreign orientals' and Europeans | Netherlands Indies census | – |

1 Judging by the original text (Jacobs 1974-84, I:414), there is a possibility that the first figure actually refers to Tolitoli rather than Bolaang, although Wessels (1933:373) does not think so.

2 Wessels (1933:373), however, interprets the latter figure as the total population of Kaidipang.

3 Dated by Jacobs (1974-84, II:304).

4 Argensola 1992:83.

5 Colin 1900-02, I:111.

6 De Jongh 1669.

7 Colin 1900-02, III:815; Pastells 1936:CCXXV.

8 Van Dam 1931:84.

9 Valentijn (Keijzer 1856:207), however, interpreted this as an estimate of the total population.

10 Seydelman 1769.

11 AV Manado 1824 (ANRI Manado 101).

12 Van Doren 1854-56, I:266.

13 A.J. van Delden, 'Verslag van de Rijkjes en Negorijen ten westen van Menado gelegen, 1833' (ANRI Manado 48). One estimate, for Bolang Bangka (Bolango), is expressed in *huisgezinnen*, and has been multiplied here by 3.5. The same figures are also reproduced by Pietermaat, De Vriese and Lucas (1840:160-1).

14 Francis 1860:283-4.

15 AV Manado 1852 (ANRI Manado 51).

16 The figures are probably from an 1848 report, by the government investigator A.L. Weddik, which is mentioned later in the same source.

17 De Lange 1853:177.

18 Bleeker 1856:127.

19 AV Manado 1857 (ANRI Manado 52).

20 The original Malay-language census table has survived (*Daftar akan menjatakan babarapa kabanjakan issij djitwa manuwsija adanja*, in 'Aanteekeningen Mongondo' [1857], in ANRI Manado 168).

21 AV Manado 1857 (ANRI Manado 52).

22 The number of houses is implied rather than stated. In his diary of the journey in question, Jansen lists a total of 700 houses, but this excludes Bolaang and the other lowland settlements ('Uittreksel uit het dagboek [...] gehouden op zijne reis naar de landen op de noord en westkust van Celebes [...] September en Oktober 1857', in ANRI Manado 167).

23 Riedel 1864b:267.

24 Riedel 1864b:279.

25 AV Manado 1860 (ANRI Manado 52).

26 *Koloniaal verslag* 1864, Bijlage A:17 (and subsequent *Koloniale verslagen*).

27 Tolitoli, the other such kingdom, was detached from Manado and made part of the residency of Makasar in 1857 (Van der Crab 1862:383).

28 Wilken and Schwarz 1867c:285, 330.

29 The Dutch authorities were aware that this figure was too low, but nevertheless tolerated it for many years as a basis for the *hasil* assessment (Van der Crab 1862:384). Following the first more complete count in 1904, however, the size of the *hasil* for Bolaang Mongondow as a whole was raised in one jump from ƒ 4,000 (a nominal ƒ 4 per *huisgezin*) to ƒ 12,000 (Encyclopaedisch Bureau 1912b:146).

30 Wilken and Schwarz 1867b:285. The authors, using a high conversion factor of 5 persons per family, equate this with a total population of 35,000.

31 Individual estimates for a few specified components of this population are given by the same authors elsewhere (Wilken and Schwarz 1867a:9, 13, 40-1). The population of Bolaang, for instance, is estimated at 1,200.

32 Elsewhere the same authors also give separate estimates for two of the other kingdoms: Bolang Uki (including its dependency on the south coast at Molibagu) with 50-60 *huisgezinnen*, and Bintauna with about 100 *huisgezinnen* (Wilken and Schwarz 1867a:33, 40).

33 The missionaries, N.P. Wilken and J.A. Schwarz of the NZG, were on a reconnaissance trip from Minahasa with a view to extending their activities to Bolaang Mongondow.

34 De Clercq 1883:118.

35 De Clercq 1883:118, 120, 124.

36 *Koloniaal verslag* 1895, Bijlage A:5.

37 Encyclopaedisch Bureau 1912b:91.

38 Veenhuizen 1903:66. The same figure is given by Van Kol (1903:350) for 1902.

39 Encyclopaedisch Bureau 1912b:91, 145; Van Geuns 1906:34; Tammes 1940:194.

40 Dunnebier 1907b.

41 *Uitkomsten* 1922, II:218-9.

42 *Volkstelling* 1933-36, V:122.

showed 'the greatest reticence and suspicion' when questioned about the size of the population (Wilken and Schwarz 1867c:285-6, 330). Even Tammes (1940:194), who took every available piece of historical population data for Sangir, Talaud and Minahasa quite literally, decided to dismiss all estimates for Bolaang Mongondow before 1906 as 'untrustworthy' on the grounds that until the beginning of the twentieth century, 'the interior was still too little known'.

Used with discrimination, some of the older data are nevertheless informative. The figures from the period 1846-1895 can be divided into two main categories: unrounded indigenous fiscal enumerations which are obviously too low (1857a, 1860, 1866a, 1893), and rounded impressionistic estimates of uncertain derivation which may or may not be more accurate (1846, 1852a, 1857c, 1864-1894, 1866b, 1866c, 1895). The fiscal count of 1866, at just 1,116 households or the equivalent of about five thousand people (1866a), explicitly excludes both nobles and slaves, regarding the proportional numbers of which there is no further information for Bolaang Mongondow. It was also more or less officially acknowledged at the time to be a defensive underestimate. Both limitations must also apply to the comparable but even lower fiscal figure for 1857, ironically the most promising estimate of all in terms of geographical resolution and social detail (1857a). Slightly better is the less detailed but apparently more inclusive administrative count of 1860, which the Dutch described as approaching reality 'somewhat more closely than previous estimates'. This provides a reliable minimum population figure with its exact total of 24,344 souls.

The rounded approximations, by comparison, range from 24,000 to 50,000 – or if the first figure, repeated for fully 30 years in the Koloniaal verslag but usually qualified there as 'pure guesswork' (berustende op loutere gissing) – is ignored, from 30,000 to 50,000.[35] None of these approximations stands out as potentially more reliable than the others on grounds of scope or detail, but the figure of 7,000 households (1866b), obtained directly from a presumably knowledgeable indigenous official in a non-fiscal context, is perhaps relatively free from distortion. This corresponds to a total of perhaps 35,000 people in Bolaang Mongondow proper, or about 46,000 altogether (including the minor chiefdoms) according to the proportional breakdown of 1904. A valuable cross-check is provided by the extrapolation (1852c) of a uniquely detailed indigenous dapur (hearth) count recited in a non-fiscal context but covering only part of Mongondow (1852b).[36] This suggests a population of

[35]   That the Koloniaal verslag figure cannot be taken seriously is confirmed by the fact that it technically includes Buol as well as Bolaang Mongondow, yet is lower than the 1860 population count for the latter alone.
[36]   In principle, Jansen's 'house count' calculation (1857b) provides another potential cross-check here. Like the similarly-derived totals for the Talaud Islands (Chapter IV, Table 7:1846,

'more than' 36,000 for the kingdom of Bolaang Mongondow alone, or close to 50,000 for the whole area, which agrees well with the 1866 *huisgezinnen* estimate. Despite the many misleading data which imply rapid growth, then, it can be concluded that the population of Bolaang Mongondow was probably only slightly (if at all) smaller in the mid-nineteenth century than at the beginning of the twentieth.

The stated or implied population totals from 1833 and earlier years range from fewer than 10,000 (1650, 1669, 1829, 1833) to more than 20,000 (1591, 1670, 1769), without showing any obvious chronological trend. A careful comparison of the contextual details of these and later counts suggests one reason for their wide variation. In 1846 it was noted that of the 25,000 or so people thought to inhabit Bolaang Mongondow proper, 'a total of hardly 3,000 souls shows a minimal obedience to its chiefs'. In 1682, similarly, Padtbrugge wrote that 'not more than 900' of the 4,000 *weerbare mannen* in Bolaang Mongondow were 'fully obedient to the king of Bolaang'. The estimate for 1833, while not itself broken down in this way, is accompanied by a list of settlements in which nine *negeri* 'belonging under Bolaang' are clearly distinguished from 22 others. Possibly, then, the strikingly low figure of 'not more than 2,000 souls' for the kingdom of Bolaang Mongondow in 1833 actually refers only to the former group of *negeri*, and the same may be true of the other low estimates too.[37] The results of early population estimates for this area must have depended partly upon the uncertain (and probably fluctuating) political influence of Bolaang in its Mongondow hinterland.

Considering this, and the many other uncertainties involved, it is probably not wise to draw any conclusions regarding population change in Bolaang Mongondow prior to the mid-nineteenth century. Earlier qualitative sources indicate that this was always a 'populous' (*volkrijk*) area by regional standards.[38] A population figure of 50,000, nevertheless, corresponds to an average density of only six persons per km^2, much lower than those of either Minahasa or Sangir-Talaud in the same period. But as the demographic insignificance of the north coast kingdoms already suggests, the population of this area, even more than that of Minahasa, was unevenly distributed.[39] Of the

---

1854), however, this can be dismissed as a severe underestimate, not least because Jansen assumed an average of just two households per dwelling, whereas Wilken and Schwarz (1867c: 331-2) put the figure at between 4 and 10.

[37] Whether the distinction between 'obedient' and independent parts of the population could always be expressed in such clear geographic terms is uncertain, since it is tempting to equate the first category with the 'fiscal' population of the lower mid- and late nineteenth-century estimates, one of which (1857a) divides its 3,336 souls over fully 19 separate settlements or districts.

[38] AV Ternate 1807 (ANRI Ternate 141); Claaszoon 1710; 'Memorie van den oud Manados resident George Frederik Duhr', 26-11-1803 (ANRI Manado 165).

[39] The south coast was even more sparsely populated. In 1682, according to Padtbrugge, there were only two settlements 'worth mentioning' along the whole southern coastline between

10,000 households which *controleur* De Clercq (1883:118, 120, 124) estimated the kingdom of Bolaang Mongondow to contain in 1866, no fewer than 8,000 lived in the interior. Wilken and Schwarz (1867c:293) observed in the same year that even the largest coastal settlements, Bolaang and Kotabunan, were 'very small', and that most of the population was concentrated on the narrow Mongondow plateau around Kotabangon, where 'all of the *negeri* lie close to one another'.

This densely settled and cultivated plain, likened by Riedel (1864b:275) in 1857 to 'a huge, impressive garden, surrounded on all sides by beautiful mountain terraces', covered only about 300 km^2 (Van Marle 1922, I:49), less than five percent of the area of the Bolaang Mongondow administrative division as a whole. Other parts of the interior, including the borderlands on the Minahasan side as well as the Dumoga Valley and surrounding mountains to the west, were either sparsely populated, or uninhabited.[40] By 1906, according to the administrative count of that year, the proportion of the population living in the interior was somewhat lower at 64 percent (26,380 people out of 41,140) for Bolaang Mongondow proper, or perhaps 50 percent for the area as a whole.[41] It is likely that some centrifugal migration had taken place by this stage in connection with coconut cultivation and the decline of coastal piracy, and this movement certainly continued thereafter (Tammes 1940:194). The population density on the Mongondow plateau, nevertheless, remained high: an estimated 82 persons per km^2 in 1920, and 100 per km^2 in 1940.[42] As in the case of Minahasa, the original pattern of concentrated upland settlement, with separate, smaller inhabited strips along some stretches of the coastline, is still clearly evident on Tammes' 1940 demographic sketch-map (Map 11).

Population movements into and out of Bolaang Mongondow never seem to have been very significant.[43] Dutch sources from the eighteenth and nine-

---

Gorontalo and the border with Minahasa (Van Dam 1931:98). Tammes (1940:194), more than two and a half centuries later, still noted only four small enclaves of 'moderately dense population' on the south coast of Bolaang Mongondow.

[40]   Sarasin and Sarasin 1905, I:79-85, 97-9, 111-5, 121-6, 149-64; Schwarz and De Lange 1876:157; Tammes 1940:193-4; Veenhuizen 1903:37.

[41]   Dunnebier 1907b. These figures, too, refer exclusively to the kingdom of Bolaang Mongondow. All villages in Pasi and Lolayan have been counted here as highland settlements, the remainder as lowland villages.

[42]   Van Marle 1922, I:49; Tammes 1940:194. The density in the settled coastal strip around Bolaang, by comparison, was about 30 per km^2 in 1920 (Van Marle 1922, I:50), and that of the Bolaang Mongondow administrative division as a whole, as in earlier times, about 6 per km^2.

[43]   Some slaves, however, were apparently exported from Bolaang Mongondow in the nineteenth century (Van Doren 1857-60, II:337; J.J. ten Siethoff, 'Topografische schetsen van een gedeelte der residentie Menado, 1845', in ANRI Manado 46), and some emigration to Minahasa also occurred at various times (Tammes 1940:194; Worotikan 1910:155).

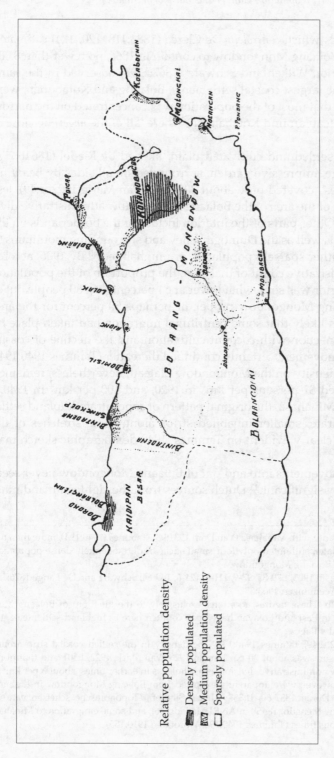

Relative population density

▨ Densely populated
▨ Medium population density
☐ Sparsely populated

Map 11. Bolaang Mongondow: population distribution, circa 1940 (Tammes 1940:194)

teenth centuries make much of occasional flows of Minahasan refugees into the neighbouring territory during periods of violence or harsh compulsory labour regimes north of the border (Henley 1996:33-4), but although few of these emigrants ever returned home, their numbers remained relatively small. According to the village-by-village population count of 1906, the five settlements in Bolaang Mongondow inhabited by Minahasans and their descendants contained a total of 1,952 people, or five percent of the total recorded population.[44]

Gorontalo

Originally vassal states of Ternate, Gorontalo and Limboto, the two main indigenous kingdoms of the Gorontalo area (Table 10), were contested between Ternate and Makasar in the mid-seventeenth century (Henley 1993:45) before coming under VOC suzerainty in 1677 (*Corpus diplomaticum* III:56-7). Shortly afterward they joined Ternate in its abortive rebellion against the Dutch, and were defeated in 1681 by a military expedition under the command of Padtbrugge (*Daghregister* 1681:374-5; Godée Molsbergen 1928:83-4). A permanent VOC outpost, however, was not established in Gorontalo until 1729, when the Dutch developed an interest in the gold produced from many small mines in the area (*Generale missiven* IX:9; Henley 1997b:425). This garrison was withdrawn in 1797, then re-established during the British interregnum of 1810-1817.[45] At most periods there were actually two Dutch outposts, one at Gorontalo town and another in Limboto. In 1864 the European administration was intensified with the assignment of *controleurs* to Bone in the east, Kuandang on the north coast, and Paguat in the west (De Clercq 1871b:25), but in 1880 two of these were withdrawn (*Regeringsalmanak* 1879:241, 1880:247), and by 1930 the Gorontalo administrative division once more contained only two subdivisions (*Volkstelling* 1933-36, V:134).

In principle, Gorontalo as defined here encompasses only the area covered by the administrative unit of that name in the twentieth century, consisting of the northern peninsula of Sulawesi between Moutong and Kaidipang, excluding Buol and Paleleh on the north coast (Chapter III, Map 9). Originally, however, the kingdoms of Gorontalo and Limboto also included extensive dependencies around the Gulf of Tomini, and early sources do

---

[44]   Dunnebier 1907b. In 1866, by comparison, the 'total number of all refugees combined' was reported to be 7-800 souls (Wilken and Schwarz 1867a:13).
[45]   AV Ternate 1807 (ANRI Ternate 141); 'Extract uit het register der handelingen en besluiten van commissarissen tot overname der Molukse eilanden', 22-3-1817 (ANRI Manado 34). Van Doren (1857-60, II:319) erroneously states that Gorontalo was not reoccupied until the Dutch restoration.

not always make a clear distinction between these and the peninsular core area.[46] The influence of the twin kingdoms in the Gulf was eroded in the course of the eighteenth century by Bugis and Mandar intervention; Limboto seems to have lost any remaining control of its overseas exclaves around the year 1790, and both had certainly done so by 1807.[47]

Besides Gorontalo proper, with its capital near the south coast in the narrow trench between the Limboto Depression and the sea, and Limboto, centred in the depression itself to the north of the eponymous lake, peninsular Gorontalo also encompassed the three satellite kingdoms of Bone (Suwawa), Atinggola, and Boalemo.[48] Together, these five polities made up the *Lima lo Pohala'a* federation described in Chapter I. Until the mid-nineteenth century there was also a sixth kingdom, Bolango, the capital of which was transferred in 1862 from the eastern part of the Limboto Depression to Bolang Uki in Bolaang Mongondow (Von Rosenberg 1865:16). According to the colonial population count of 1867, the last to specify the distribution among the old indigenous political units, Gorontalo proper accounted for 63 percent of the indigenous population (excluding Bugis immigrants and *burgers*), Limboto for 24 percent, Bone for eight percent, and the other kingdoms together for the remaining five percent.[49] Gorontalo and Limboto, then, contained the great majority of the population, and the former was more than twice as populous as the latter.[50] Of the other kingdoms, only Bone was more than marginally significant in demographic terms.

The population of the Bugis *kampung* in Gorontalo rose from a reported 691 in 1824 to 1,217 in 1843, fell again to 750 in 1852, and had recovered to 1,823 by 1865. The numbers of *burgers* in the same years were 203, 282, 325, and 663 respectively.[51] Neither allochthonous group, then, apparently constituted more than five percent of the total recorded population in this period, although both were no doubt counted much more comprehensively

---

[46]   These dependencies are specified in a VOC contract of 1765 (*Corpus diplomaticum* VI:254), according to which Gorontalo controls the western half of the Gulf as far south as Sausu, and Limboto the areas from Sausu to the Togian Islands.

[47]   AV Gorontalo 1854 (ANRI Gorontalo 3); AV Ternate 1807 (ANRI Ternate 141).

[48]   The capital of Gorontalo was originally located some distance from the coast, just inside the Limboto Depression, for security. It was moved to its present coastal location in the 1750s, following the completion of a stone VOC fort there (Bastiaans 1939:25; Von Rosenberg 1865:17).

[49]   Riedel 1870a:150. The earliest differentiated statistics tend to show a slightly greater majority for Gorontalo – 73%, for instance, in 1829, with Limboto at 21% and Bone at 3% (AV Gorontalo 1829, in ANRI Gorontalo 3). This difference, however, is most probably an illusion created by the fact that at that stage the accuracy of the count was highest close to the centre of Dutch power in Gorontalo town.

[50]   In 1776, Limboto claimed that Gorontalo was four times more populous (*Corpus diplomaticum* VI:399).

[51]   AV Gorontalo 1824, 1852, 1865 (ANRI Gorontalo 3), 1841-1843 (ANRI Manado 50).

than the indigenous element. Slavery was formally abolished in Gorontalo in 1859 (Riedel 1870a:66), whereafter slaves were no longer distinguished in population counts. An additional incentive to demographic understatement was provided in 1850 by the introduction of a head tax in place of the former compulsory gold purchases, which had been organized on a basis of fixed minimum deliveries for each kingdom as a collectivity.[52] Table 10 is selective after 1865.

The *weerbare mannen* data for Gorontalo in the seventeenth and eighteenth centuries are few and opaque. The rise of Dutch power here, in the years around 1680, coincided with attempts by Gorontalo and Limboto to boost their populations by forcing groups from elsewhere to resettle in their vicinity (*Generale missiven* IV:325). In 1678, Dutch envoys counted some 2,500 Tomini men, women and children living in captivity in the Gorontalo hinterland, while another 'whole villageful, no fewer than 300 people' had recently been relocated from Sidoan (near Tinombo).[53] In 1681, a further 250-300 captured slaves were imported from Buol.[54] The two estimates in Table 10 from 1676, however, probably still refer mainly to the population of exclave territories on the Gulf of Tomini coasts. When Padtbrugge visited Gorontalo for the first time in 1677, he noted that the local chiefs, when asked for information about the extent of their territories, 'deliberately mixed up the names of the interior, landward villages with those of villages located further afield' (Robidé van der Aa 1867:165). His own impression was that the indigenous population of Gorontalo and Limboto was very small ('about 300 men'), and that only a fraction of their overseas vassals had yet been resettled in the peninsular heartland. This is consistent with the fact that immigration, prompted by fear of Mandar slave raiders as well as by direct coercion, and encouraged also by the additional security provided by the existence of a Dutch garrison in Gorontalo after 1729, continued during the eighteenth century.[55] In later times, many of the villages of the Limboto Depression still bore the names of the settlements on the shores of the Gulf of Tomini from which their founders had come (Van Hoëvell 1891:32; Riedel 1870b:556, 558).

[52]   Kartodirdjo 1971:158, 1973:376-80; AV Gorontalo 1852 (ANRI Gorontalo 3); *Corpus diplomaticum* VI:317, 320, 396, 399, 505, 585.
[53]   NA VOC 1345:311, 333, 412. In earlier times, the tribute paid by Tomini chiefs to Gorontalo and Limboto had already included slaves (Robidé van der Aa 1867:165; NA VOC 1320:144r, 148v).
[54]   NA VOC 1366:169; *Generale missiven* III:511.
[55]   This movement is described by Riedel (1870b:556-8), and mentioned in many contemporary sources (Chapter VI). Toward the end of the eighteenth century there was also some movement of population from Tolitoli to Kuandang (*Corpus diplomaticum* VI:466). Immigration was to some extent offset, it should be added, by emigration from Gorontalo to the Tomini coastlands (*Corpus diplomaticum* VI:168; *Generale missiven* XI:648; Riedel 1870b:556).

Table 10. Population data, Gorontalo, 1591-1930

Year	Figure	Scope	Type of estimate	Other accuracy indications
1591	10,000 *hombres de armas*[1]	Gorontalo and Limboto	estimate by Jesuit missionary in Ternate, probably from Ternatan source	single undivided figure
1676a	7,730 *weerbare mannen*[2]	Gorontalo and Limboto dependencies in (originating from?) Gulf of Tomini	estimate by VOC envoy to Gorontalo	49 'provinces' or villages distinguished; figures rounded to 10 or 100
1676b	7,000 *weerbare mannen*[3]	Gorontalo and Limboto	estimate by Dutch official in Ternate	single undivided figure; probably a rounded restatement of (1676a), but describes this population simply as 'Alfur' subjects without specifying location
1677	'about 300 men', plus (at least) 2,000 souls transported from Gulf of Tomini[4]	Gorontalo and Limboto	in situ estimate by Padtbrugge	'We could not observe that more than 6 or 7 villages stood under Gorontalo and Limboto, and about 300 men, not counting women and children; all the rest were Tomini or Gulf villages.'
1778	5,000 *weerbare mannen*[5]	Gorontalo only	estimate by VOC governor of the Moluccas (1771-1778) P.J. Valckenaer	single undivided figure; 'that nation is populous, and to my mind can raise [...]'
1797[6]	'6,000 men'[7]	Gorontalo only	estimate by Dutch official in Ternate (1806), source probably as for 1805 below	single undivided figure
1805	'12,000 men'[8]	Gorontalo only	figure stated by Gorontalo envoys to Dutch officials in Ternate	single undivided figure
1821	52,000 people[9]	–	estimate by visiting European naturalist (C.J.C. Reinwardt), using information from Dutch resident of Gorontalo[10]	sum of rounded estimates for Gorontalo (30,000) Limboto (20,000) and Bone (2,000)

Year	Population	Exclusions	Source	Comments
1823	25,172 people[11]	–	Dutch administrative count	6 kingdoms distinguished; Limboto figures rounded to 100, others unrounded; men/women/m. and f. children distinguished
1824	26,541[12]	excludes Limboto[13]	Dutch administrative count	6 kingdoms distinguished; figures unrounded; men/women/m. and f. children distinguished; 'The reasons for this increase [since 1823] are to be sought simply in the abolition of a number of compulsory services and oppressive taxes, [and to] the end of the recruitment – or rather conscriptiom – in Gorontalo; the people who returned [to their homes] had been living as refugees in the woods and the surrounding country.'
1824	'not more than 20,000 souls'[14]	excludes Limboto	Estimate by governor of the Moluccas (1822-1829) P. Merkus, basis unknown	single undivided figure
1829	35,700[15]	excludes Bugis, *burgers*, Atinggola, and possibly western districts from Paguyaman to Paguat[16]	Dutch administrative count	'at a guess'; 'only a casual estimate by the [various] *raja*'; 'only Gorontalo can give a systematic estimate'; 5 kingdoms distinguished; all figures rounded to 50 or 100
1840	31,700[17]	excludes Bugis and *burgers*	Dutch administrative count	'The population must amount to approximately [...]'; 6 kingdoms distinguished; all figures rounded to 100 or 1000
1843	30,106[18]	–	Dutch administrative count	6 kingdoms distinguished; figures unrounded

Year	Figure	Scope	Type of estimate	Other accuracy indications
1845	31,577[19]	–	Dutch administrative count; for Gorontalo a written 'register of chiefs and population' now existed on which this figure (presumably) was partly based[20]	figure inaccurate 'since many natives live scattered in the forests'; 6 kingdoms distinguished
1846a	31,684[21]	–	Dutch administrative count requested from 'the respective *raja* [...] according to the model form provided'[22]	6 kingdoms distinguished
1846b	26,219[23]	Gorontalo and Limboto only	Dutch administrative count at village level (sole surviving village-by-village record)[24]	covers Gorontalo (124 *kampung*) and Limboto (71 *kampung*); men/women/m. and f. children, and free population/3 categories of slaves distinguished
1846c	30,000[25]	excludes Boalemo	estimate by visiting government investigator (E. Francis) on basis of Dutch count[26]	'plus or minus'; 5 kingdoms distinguished; all figures rounded to 100
1847	30,055[27]	?	figure given by visiting government investigator (A.L. Weddik), basis unknown; no further details	?
1849	39,129[28]	excludes Bugis and *burgers*	Dutch administrative count, 'confirmed under oath by the kings and chiefs [*rijksbesturen*]'	6 kingdoms distinguished; men/women/m. and f. children/m. and f. slaves distinguished; *dapur* or *huisgezinnen* totals specified for chiefs and 'labouring classes'
1852	38,688[29]	–	Dutch administrative count	6 kingdoms distinguished; men/women/m. and f. children and free population/slaves dis-

				tinguished; possibly excludes chiefs and their families, with the addition of which the total would be 'significantly higher'[30]
1853	33,913[31]	—	Dutch administrative count	6 kingdoms distinguished
1854	38,491[32]	—	Dutch administrative count	'according to information provided by the kings and chiefs [rijksbesturen] of the various kingdoms, the accuracy of which cannot be vouched for'; 6 kingdoms distinguished; nobles/free population/slaves distinguished
1856	41,053[33]	includes 16 Chinese and Europeans; excludes burgers	Dutch administrative count	'estimated'; 6 kingdoms distinguished; men/women/m. and f. children and nobles/free population/slaves distinguished
1858	42,617[34]	includes 8 Chinese and Europeans; excludes burgers	Dutch administrative count	6 kingdoms distinguished; nobles/free population/slaves distinguished
1860a	53,616[35]	includes 33 Chinese and Europeans	administrative count 'according to the kings and chiefs [rijksbesturen]'	6 kingdoms distinguished; nobles/free population/slaves distinguished; 'According to the assistant resident of Gorontalo these figures, which already differ substantially from those for 1858, [...] are still not accurate.'
1860b	80,163[36]	—	'corrective' personal estimate by the same official who recorded 1860a (B. van Baak, assistant resident 1859-1864)	'According to the official in question the population [...] is much more numerous, and can be approximately specified as follows [...]'; 6 kingdoms distin-

Year	Figure	Scope	Type of estimate	Other accuracy indications
				guished; most figures rounded to 500 or 1000
1863	55,060[37]	excludes Atinggola and Boalemo	estimate by visiting Dutch researcher, figures 'drawn from official sources'	sum of separate estimates for Gorontalo, Limboto, Sumalata [a north coast mining district under Limboto] and Bone; most figures rounded to 100; results 'must be regarded as approximations only'[38]
1863	47,324[39]	excludes Bugis and *burgers*	Dutch administrative count	5 kingdoms distinguished
1864	62,288[40]	includes 59 Chinese and Europeans	Dutch administrative count	new administrative organization in 5 divisions and 21 districts; men/women/m. and f. children distinguished; 'This increase [since 1863] must be attributed mainly to better recording of the population in the course of the year.'
1865	63,090[41]	includes 54 Chinese and Europeans	Dutch administrative count	'still far below the real figure', especially in Gorontalo 'where a much larger population is present'; 5 divisions and 21 districts; men/women/m. and f. children distinguished
1877	95,152[42]	includes 167 'foreign orientals' and Europeans	Dutch administrative count	'These figures are the result of a *telling* [count of individuals?] and deserve some confidence'; 14 subdivisions
1884	96,000[43]	–	Dutch administrative count	'acquired by approximation' (*bij benadering verkregen*)

Year				'acquired by survey' (*bij opneming verkregen*) based on a village-by-village count
1885	79,058[44]	—	Dutch administrative count	'acquired by survey' (*bij opneming verkregen*)
1890	81,777[45]	includes 349 'foreign orientals' and Europeans	Dutch administrative count	based on a village-by-village count
1900	111,229[46]	includes 1,780 'foreign orientals' and Europeans	Dutch administrative count	—
1920	134,307[47]	includes 2,084 'foreign orientals' and Europeans	Netherlands Indies census	—
1930	186,038[48]	includes 2,982 'foreign orientals' and Europeans	Netherlands Indies census	—

1 Argensola 1992:83; tentatively dated by Jacobs (1974-84, II:304).
2 NA VOC 1320:151.
3 NA VOC 1320:112v.
4 Robidé van der Aa 1867:158, 165.
5 Valckenaer 1778.
6 The figure is assumed to refer to the year in which the Dutch abandoned their post in Gorontalo.
7 G.F. Durr to C.L. Wieling, 10-1-1806 (ANRI Manado 165).
8 G.F. Durr to C.L. Wieling, 10-1-1806 (ANRI Manado 165).
9 Reinwardt 1858:512, 515, 520.
10 Reinwardt 1858:512.
11 AV Gorontalo 1823 (ANRI Gorontalo 3).
12 AV Gorontalo 1824 (ANRI Gorontalo 3). Figure corrected for an arithmetical error.
13 The resident of Manado guessed that the population of Limboto was about 8,000 (AV Manado 1824, in ANRI Manado 101); in 1829 it was a reported 7500.
14 Gov. Moluccas to GG, 3-7-1824 (KITLV H142).
15 AV Gorontalo 1829 (ANRI Gorontalo 3).
16 The combined population of the western districts is estimated elsewhere in the same report at 950.
17 AV Gorontalo 1838-1840 (ANRI Gorontalo 3); reproduced by R. Scherius (1847:399) and Van Doren (1857-60, II:318).
18 AV Gorontalo 1841-1843 (ANRI Manado 50). An arithmetical error has been corrected.
19 AV Gorontalo 1845 (KITLV H111).
20 'Dagregister van den civiele gezaghebber te Gorontalo', 19-5-1845 (ANRI Manado 118).
21 AV Gorontalo 1854 (ANRI Gorontalo 3).

22 'Dagregister van den civiele gezaghebber te Gorontalo', 20-8-1846 (ANRI Manado 5).

23 'Tulisan djiwa deri parentahan di Gorontalo', 7-11-1846; 'Tulisan djiwah derij parentahan di Limbotto', 5-11-1846 (KITLV H142).

24 The total figures indicated by this village census are slightly different from those given for Gorontalo and Limboto in the general population count for the same year (1846a).

25 Francis 1860:290.

26 Francis received the more 'precise' 1845 census from the assistant resident (total population: 31,577) and rounded it down to the stated figure ('Aantekeningen van den kommissaris voor Menado 1846', in ANRI Manado 167; 'Dagregister van den civiele gezaghebber te Gorontalo', 4-11-1846, in ANRI Manado 146).

27 Res. Manado to GG, 30-9-1849 (ANRI Gorontalo 18).

28 'Staat van de gedane zielsbeschrijving onder ultimo Augustus 1849' (ANRI Gorontalo 18).

29 AV Gorontalo 1852 (ANRI Gorontalo 3); reproduced by Bleeker (1856:127).

30 Bleeker 1856:128. This author used the figures only at second hand, and may have misinterpreted them here. The enumeration of 1849 explicitly did include chiefs and their families (which it indicates constituted some 14% of the population) without producing a result substantially different from that for 1852. It is true, however, that the original table includes no specific category of chiefs or 'nobility'.

31 AV Gorontalo 1854 (ANRI Gorontalo 3).

32 AV Gorontalo 1854 (ANRI Gorontalo 3); figure corrected for an arithmetical error.

33 AV Manado 1856 (ANRI Manado 51).

34 AV Manado 1858 (ANRI Manado 52).

35 AV Manado 1860 (ANRI Manado 52). Van der Crab (1862:379) reproduces part of this table.

36 AV Manado 1860 (ANRI Manado 52).

37 Von Rosenberg 1865:15, 69, 89, 102

38 Von Rosenberg 1865:15.

39 AV Gorontalo 1864 (ANRI Gorontalo 3).

40 AV Gorontalo 1864 (ANRI Gorontalo 3). The population of the Togian Islands and the Gulf of Tomini districts (included under Paguat) has been subtracted. Riedel (1870a:65) reproduces the same figure.

41 AV Gorontalo 1865 (ANRI Gorontalo 3). The population of the Togian Islands has been subtracted. Riedel (1870a:65) gives the figure 63090, which is based on the same source but includes Europeans and ethnic Chinese.

42 'Ass. Residentie Gorontalo, Algemeene Bevolking Staat 1877' (ANRI Manado 53).

43 Koloniaal verslag 1886, Bijlage A:5.

44 Koloniaal verslag 1887, Bijlage A:5.

45 Van Hoëvell 1891:32.

46 Koloniaal verslag 1902, Bijlage A:5.

47 Uitkomsten 1922:221. The population of Buol, temporarily part of the Gorontalo assistant residency at this period, has been subtracted.

48 Volkstelling 1933-36, V:122

The apparent jump in population between 1797 and 1805 must be regarded with scepticism, since the envoys from Gorontalo who provided both figures, insisting 'that their numbers had increased, and that instead of 6,000 men they now made up 12,000', were keen to see the abandoned Dutch outpost restored, and therefore had a special incentive to emphasize their labour resources.[56] As in Minahasa, however, the eighteenth century as a whole does seem to have been a period of overall population growth – albeit this time at least partly as a result of immigration, a factor not significant in the Minahasan case. Whereas VOC reports from 1733 state that Gorontalo 'is not sufficiently populous to consume a large quantity of textiles' (*Generale missiven* IX:488, 529), by the 1770s it was regarded as a large 'nation' (Table 10:1778), and in 1806 a Dutch governor of Ambon even described its population as 'perhaps the most considerable anywhere in these quarters'.[57]

The evidence for a converse process of depopulation in the mid-seventeenth century, along the lines of Reid's 'seventeenth-century crisis', is stronger here than in the cases of Sangir or Minahasa. The figure of 10,000 fighting men from 1591, like those given by the same source (Argensola) for other areas, may well be exaggerated. It is nevertheless striking that this estimate specifically excludes Tomini, for which there is a separate figure of no fewer than 12,000 *hombres de armas* (Chapter VI, Table 11), and that the total population which it implies, at about 35,000, is comparable with those given in Table 10 for the early nineteenth century. Accounts of a raid on Gorontalo by Ternatan and Dutch forces in 1647, moreover, mention as many as 4,000 local people killed and another 4,000 enslaved and deported – losses already equivalent in themselves to more than twice the total population of Gorontalo and Limboto as reported by Padtbrugge in 1677.[58] It is not clear whether other factors besides this raid, and the domestic wars of the same period (Bastiaans 1938:231-3), were also responsible for the apparently depopulated condition of the area in the late seventeenth century.

Except perhaps for those of 1805 and 1821, all of the figures from the early nineteenth century are severe underestimates. More isolated than their colleagues in Manado, and always weaker in political influence, the Dutch in Gorontalo were entirely dependent on the knowledge and cooperation of

56   G.F. Durr to C.L. Wieling, 10-1-1806 (ANRI Manado 165).
57   Gov. Ambon to Res. Ternate, 25-5-1806 (ANRI Manado 60). Elsewhere in the same letter, Gorontalo is described as 'amazingly populous', and a year later the resident of Ternate agreed that it had 'no lack of hands to work the fields' (AV Ternate 1807, in ANRI Ternate 141).
58   NA VOC 1170:764, VOC 1320:150; Tiele and Heeres 1886-95, III:358-9, 388-90. It remains possible, however, that Padtbrugge underestimated the population of the area, perhaps partly because tubers and bananas played a major role in its agricultural system (Chapter II), so that the landscape in the vicinity of the settlements appeared to him to be 'little cultivated' (Van Dam 1931:97).

the indigenous chiefs when it came to obtaining demographic information. In 1824 Limboto, at odds with the government over an abortive attempt to introduce compulsory coffee cultivation, simply refused to supply any figure, whereupon the assistant resident declined even to hazard a guess at its population.[59] In 1829 his successor reported that Gorontalo proper was still the only group for which anything more than demographic guesswork was possible, 'since the other kingdoms, whether out of fear, indifference or bad will, do not supply systematic estimates'.[60] 'Having tried for seven months to obtain some clarity regarding the number and composition of the population of this division', complained another official, W.A. van der Horst, in 1854, 'I have so far made no progress at all, and am therefore obliged to reproduce global figures which seem to me to be beside the truth'.[61]

In some respects, such protestations were exaggerated. Gorontalo, unlike Minahasa, possessed an indigenous writing tradition, and it appears that in connection with the delicate balance of power between the *raja* and the village élites with respect to control of manpower resources, each *kampung* kept a written record of the dependency status of its inhabitants.[62] This tradition was probably built on by the Dutch administration when it compiled the village-by-village population counts of which a single complete example survives (Table 10: 1846b).[63] The concrete and detailed character of these counts means that at the very least, they provide dependable minimum estimates. Since many specifically include slaves, moreover, there is no danger that only the elite strata of the population were counted. After 1850, an increasingly intensive European administration also did much to improve data collection. Especially striking is the jump between 1863 and 1864, when the area was reorganized into five new administrative divisions, each under the direct supervision of a *controleur*, in place of the former kingdoms.[64] At the same time, however, it is impossible to ignore the consistency with which the officials who recorded the indigenous figures dismissed them as far too low, or the fact that the 'corrective' Dutch estimate for 1860 is fully 50 percent higher than the official count for the same

---

59   AR Gorontalo to Res. Manado, 14-3-1825 (ANRI Manado 114).
60   AV Gorontalo 1829 (ANRI Gorontalo 3).
61   AV Gorontalo 1854 (ANRI Gorontalo 3). His superior, Resident Jansen, wrote that existing population figures from Gorontalo 'do not deserve any confidence, and are only useful insofar as they provide an approximate indication of the relative strength of the population of the various kingdoms' (AV Manado 1855, in ANRI Manado 51).
62   'Pengatoran pusaka di Gorontalo', 29-4-1828 (ANRI Gorontalo 18). This document claims that the arrangements to which it refers have existed 'since ancient times'.
63   The population lists were written down by *jurutulis* (clerks) employed by the *raja* (AR Gorontalo to Res. Manado, 1-2-1844, in ANRI Manado 118).
64   Riedel 1870a:72. Like their indigenous predecessors, however, these officials remained responsible for taxation as well as data collection, presumably with comparable consequences for the accuracy of that data.

year (1860a, 1860b). The figure of more than 80,000 people produced by this attempt at correction, moreover, is by no means incredible given that in 1877, the first count which the colonial authorities regarded as reasonably accurate revealed a total population of more than 95,000.[65]

Later in the century, as the sudden decline between the 'approximation' of 1884 and the *telling* ('census') of 1885 shows, inaccuracies persisted, although it should be noted that the high 1884 figure was probably based upon an unwarranted extrapolation of earlier data rather than an incorrect new count. The figure for 1877, by contrast, is unlikely to be an exaggeration, since the data for that year are given as exact figures without rounding, and the assistant resident expressed unusual confidence in them. A large part of the decline between 1877 and 1885, which corresponds to 17 percent of the population, must in fact be regarded as real. Gorontalo experienced a serious drought in 1877-1878, with accompanying disease outbreaks and heightened infant mortality (*Koloniaal verslag* 1878:27), followed by a smallpox epidemic in 1883-1884 'which killed thousands of children, and also many adults' (AV Manado 1884, in ANRI Manado 52). In 1885-1886, many also died of cholera (Van Hoëvell 1891:34). Like Talaud, then, but unlike Minahasa, Gorontalo in this period saw a rather protracted mortality crisis and an absolute demographic decline. By the turn of the century, however, a sustained growth trend seems to have been established; the apparent average rate of increase over the period 1900-1930 is 1.7 percent per year, although this is probably exaggerated due to residual undercounting in the figure for 1900.

Prior to 1877, the recorded population totals were not yet accurate enough to register even major short-term crises.[66] Qualitative sources reveal that the years 1853-1855, here as in Minahasa, were a time of drought and epidemics, while stomach disease in the wake of a dry spell had also caused a 'tremendous number of deaths' in 1846.[67] Smallpox, likewise, killed a reported 3,000 people in Gorontalo in 1859-1860 (Van der Crab 1862:379), yet the official population count for 1860 still indicates 11,000 more inhabitants than in 1858. Given the evident insensitivity of the data, and assuming a substantial degree of underenumeration, relatively constant up to about 1845 but decreasing thereafter, the figures as they stand do not warrant any firm conclusions regarding the overall direction of demographic change in the period

---

[65] It is also significant that the figure for 1865 was considered especially inaccurate for Gorontalo proper, which indicates that the undercounting was most serious not on the remoter fringes of the region, but rather in the very heartland of the village census.
[66] The considerable fluctuations which do appear in the figures from the mid-nineteenth century, as Van der Horst observed in 1854, 'must be ascribed less to external causes than to inaccurate enumeration' (AV Gorontalo 1854, in ANRI Gorontalo 3).
[67] AV Gorontalo 1854 (ANRI Gorontalo 3); MV Manado April 1854-December 1855 (ANRI Manado 54); Res. Manado to Gov. Moluccas, 15-4-1846 (ANRI Manado 83).

1800-1865. At least up to 1854, however, most Dutch observers believed that the general trend, due to disease, emigration, and slave raiding, was downward, and that the area had been more populous in the past.[68] By 1863, the population was thought to be increasing again (Von Rosenberg 1865:31).

Regarding the absolute size of the population in the first half of the nineteenth century, unfortunately, it can be concluded only that this probably lay somewhere between 50,000 and 80,000 (Table 10:1821, 1860b) – most likely closer to the latter figure. This would correspond to an average density of about seven persons per km^2, or roughly the same as that of Bolaang Mongondow. Once again, however, this low figure conceals a very uneven distribution.[69] The floor of the Limboto Depression immediately to the east of the lake, as a late nineteenth-century map shows (Map 12), was 'covered with villages and fields of rice and maize' (Riedel 1870a:78), but outside this heartland, densities were much lower. Van der Horst noted in 1854 that while Gorontalo proper was 'very populous in relation to its limited area', even the immediately neighbouring kingdoms of Limboto and Bone were much less so and had surplus agricultural land which was hired out to landless Gorontalese farmers.[70] Further afield, the north coast near Kuandang was 'sparsely populated', and Sumalata, a little further west, 'one great forest from the shore to the mountaintops'.[71] The Paguat area, stretching along the Tomini coast as far as Moutong, also had a very small population, only six percent of the total in 1865.[72] At the 1930 census, the assistant residency of Gorontalo contained two administrative subdivisions of roughly equal size: Gorontalo proper, covering the central depression together with a section of the north coast, and Boalemo, covering Paguyaman and Paguat to the west. In the Gorontalo division the average population density was 38 persons per km^2, but in Boalemo just three per km^2 (*Volkstelling* 1933-36, V:156).

Besides the regular seasonal exodus of gold miners described in Chapter II, Gorontalo also had a long history of permanent emigration. Oral history as recorded in the nineteenth century indicated that the subjugation of the Tomini lands, besides the relocation of Tomini people to Gorontalo, had also involved migration of Gorontalo *onderhoofden* ('sub-chiefs') and 'fortune-

[68]   'Aantekeningen van den kommissaris voor Menado 1846' (ANRI Manado 167); Van Graaff and Meijlan 1856:257; AV Gorontalo 1829, 1852, 1854 (ANRI Gorontalo 3), 1841-1843 (ANRI Manado 50); Francis 1860:289, 295, 344; Gov. Moluccas to GG, 3-7-1824 (KITLV H142; Reinwardt 1858:534; R. Scherius 1847:401.
[69]   Bik 1864:155; Van Höevell 1891:32; Reinwardt 1858:509, 523; Riedel 1870a:68, 78, 96; Von Rosenberg 1865:6-7, 58.
[70]   AV Gorontalo 1854 (ANRI Gorontalo 3). In some districts of Gorontalo there was 'a constant shortage of farmland' (CV Gorontalo 1867, in ANRI Manado 3).
[71]   Von Rosenberg 1865:82, 90. Earlier sources also describe the Kuandang area as virtually uninhabited (NA VOC 2649:21; AV Ternate 1807, in ANRI Ternate 141; Keijzer 1856:598).
[72]   AV Gorontalo 1865 (ANRI Gorontalo 3).

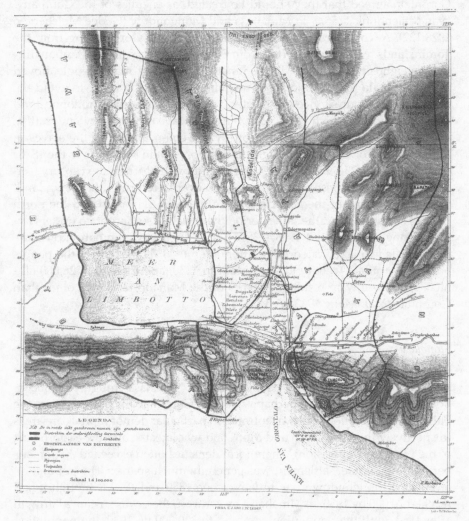

Map 12. The Limboto Depression ('Sketch map of the districts around
Gorontalo town'), circa 1890 (Van Hoëvell 1891: Map 1)

seekers' to Tomini (Riedel 1870b:556). In 1756 the Dutch complained of
Gorontalo 'vagrants' – probably political or fiscal refugees, since the kings of
Gorontalo agreed that they should be treated 'as enemies of the Company'
(Van Mijlendonk 1756) – in Minahasa and Mongondow (Godée Molsbergen
1928:122). A 'considerable' number of slaves, possibly originating from the
Tomini lands, were also exported from Gorontalo to Ternate and Ambon during the eighteenth century.[73] In the nineteenth century, many people moved
from Gorontalo to Buol and other neighbouring areas in order to avoid the
compulsory labour services associated with the Dutch gold monopoly, and
later the head tax which replaced it.[74] A new wave of voluntary emigration,
discussed in Chapter XV, was set off by the emancipation of the slaves in
1859. Colonies of Gorontalo emigrants were present in Minahasa in the 1870s
(De Clercq 1873:254, 259; Matthes 1881), and by the turn of the century 'settlements of Gorontalese who have no plan ever to return to their own land'
were found in 'all of the *landschappen* on the Gulf of Tomini and the north
coast of Sulawesi'.[75] At the same period there were also Gorontalo traders living in Banggai (Goedhart 1908:473, 475, 487). Increased population pressure
probably led to accelerated emigration after 1900; 11 percent of the people
born in Gorontalo were living outside it in 1930, and more than 26,000 ethnic Gorontalese were resident in parts of the Manado residency other than
Gorontalo (*Volkstelling* 1933-36, V:22, 47).

Summary

Around 1850 about 100,000 people lived in Minahasa, roughly 55,000 in
Bolaang Mongondow, and perhaps 75,000 in Gorontalo. In all three cases the
bulk of the population was concentrated in particular demographic core areas
(respectively the Minahasan and Mongondow plateaux, and the eastern part
of the Limboto Depression) where local densities often exceeded 50 persons
per km^2; elsewhere, settlement was generally much sparser. The population
of Bolaang Mongondow grew little between 1850 and 1920, although it had
reached 70,000 by 1930. In Minahasa, by contrast, there was sustained growth
after 1860, with the population climbing to 300,000 by 1930; the population

---

[73]   W.J. Cranssen, 'Consideratie nopens het al of niet bezetten van Gorontalo', 31-5-1806 (ANRI
Manado 66). Riedel (1870a:67, 1870b:556) also mentions this slave trade. Some slaves were still
being exported in secret as late as 1845 (J.J. ten Siethoff, 'Topografische schetsen van een gedeelte
der residentie Manado, 1845', in ANRI Manado 46).

[74]   AV Gorontalo 1852, 1854, 1864 (ANRI Gorontalo 3).

[75]   Jellesma 1903:206. In 1865 it was a Gorontalese man living in Poso, on the south side of the
Gulf of Tomini, who guided the *controleur* Van der Wyck on the overland journey which made
him the first European to reach Lake Poso (Adriani 1913a:850).

of Gorontalo, despite a serious mortality crisis in the years around 1880, also more than doubled between 1850 and 1930.

Developments prior to 1850 are much more difficult to reconstruct, and only for Minahasa are usable quantitative data available. In both Minahasa and Gorontalo, however, the eighteenth century appears to have been a period of considerable population growth, and the first half of the nineteenth century one of stasis or decline. In the case of Gorontalo migration was probably an important factor here, but in Minahasa, the population of which can tentatively be estimated at 55,000 in 1700 and 100,000 in 1800, the growth during the eighteenth century was endogenous. Gorontalo almost certainly saw a marked demographic decline in the middle of the seventeenth century, and the same may also be true of Minahasa, although the evidence for this is not conclusive.

CHAPTER VI

Population data, Central Sulawesi

The quantitative data for Central Sulawesi are nowhere near as complete as those for the north, and in reconstructing its historical demography, even in relatively shallow chronological depth, it is often necessary to rely heavily on indirect evidence. The attempt is worthwhile, however, because this section of the island remained almost entirely outside European political influence until the beginning of the twentieth century, and also because parts of it show evidence of long-term depopulation which will be significant for the discussion of the causes of demographic change in Chapters XII and XV.

Buol and Tolitoli

The northwestern corner of Sulawesi (Table 11) figures in some of the earliest European sources on the island, and was already visited by Portuguese ships in the sixteenth century (Jacobs 1974-84, I:67, 413-6; C. Wessels 1933:371, 373). For a brief period at the end of the seventeenth (Van Dam 1931:87-8; Keijzer 1856:211-2), and again in connection with the gold trade after 1734 (Buol) and 1737 (Tolitoli), it was also the site of permanent VOC outposts (*Corpus diplomaticum* V:253; *Generale missiven* IX:600). All this early European contact, however, yielded little useful demographic information, and in fact the best available population figure for Buol and Tolitoli prior to the nineteenth century is probably a Ternatan estimate reproduced by Argensola in 1609 (Table 11:1591). After the capture of Tolitoli and Buol by Mandar and Bugis 'pirates' in 1756 and 1763 respectively (Van Mijlendonk 1756; Schoonderwoert 1766), a full century passed in which the only European visitors were occasional envoys from Manado or Ternate, or naval expeditions like the one from Makasar which destroyed a Magindanao pirate colony in Tolitoli in 1822 (Pietermaat, De Vriese and Lucas 1840:164; Vosmaer 1839:130). It was not until 1862 that a Dutch *posthouder* was once again stationed in Tolitoli, and not until 1893 that a *controleur* arrived in Buol (Encyclopaedisch Bureau 1912b:142; *Nota Toli-Toli* 1912:40). For the period 1858-1905 there is the added complication that between these years Tolitoli, but not Buol, fell under the

Table 11. Population data, Buol and Tolitoli, 1591-1930

Year	Figure	Scope	Type of estimate	Other accuracy indications
1591	6,700 soldados[1]	Tolitoli, Buol and Dondo	estimate by Jesuit missionary in Ternate, probably based on Ternatan source	Tolitoli and Buol (6,000) lumped together, Dondo (700) distinguished; military estimate of forces under Ternatan control
1681	1,050 people[2]	Buol only	implicit VOC estimate	Gorontalo and Limboto have 'killed 200 Buol people and carried off 250, so that only about 600 are left'
1682	'not more than 400 men with shield and sword'[3]	Tolitoli only	estimate by Padtbrugge	'the guess is that it could supply only six kora-kora for the Company, and [...]'; probably refers only to seaborne military strength[4]
1824	7,500 (Buol 7,000, Tolitoli 500)	–	estimate by resident of Manado	'according to information acquired, the population [...] can probably be put at [...]'; two undivided estimates
1833	at least 5,500 (Buol 4,000, Tolitoli 1,500)[5]	–	estimates by 'persons familiar with that area' as recorded by Dutch government investigator (A.J. van Delden)	'estimated at [...]'; Tolitoli population 'cannot really be assessed, since part of it lives in the mountains, and many households which rebelled against the raja have emigrated'; two undivided estimates
1846	> 8,000[6]	–	second-hand estimate by government investigator (L. Francis)	Buol circa 4,000; Tolitoli, 'not including the mountain-dwellers, who are subject to no authority and live in a wild state', also circa 4,000
1852	8,100 (Buol 7,550, Tolitoli 550)[7]	–	Dutch administrative estimate	'An accurate census of the kingdoms belonging to this residency is not possible except on the basis of earlier reports and information which I have not been able to find [...]'[8]
1870	5,795[9]	Buol only; excludes women and children	Dutch administrative count	'A population count, carried out as accurately as possible, which I organized in the middle

Year	Figure			
	of 1,566 'foreign' (non-Buol) men[10]			of 1870' (J.G.F. Riedel, assistant resident of Gorontalo 1864-1875); 34 kampung and 7 ethnicities distinguished
1893	6,225[11]	Buol only	Dutch administrative count	'fairly accurate' but 'still not complete' total, based on 'information from the native authorities concerned'
ca 1912	'about 8,538'[12]	Tolitoli only	Dutch administrative count	count probably carried out in connection with tax assessment; 21 kampung (plus ethnic Arabs and Chinese) distinguished
1920	35,709[13]	includes 845 'foreign orientals'[14]	Netherlands Indies census	–
1930	49,048[15]	includes 1,659 'foreign orientals'[16]	Netherlands Indies census	–

1 Argensola 1992:83; dated by Jacobs (1974-84, II:304).
2 Generale missiven IV:511.
3 Van Dam 1931:89; figure repeated (and multiplied by 3 to give a putative total population figure) by Valentijn (Keijzer 1856:213, 215).
4 In his estimates of seaborne strength for Sangir, however, Padtbrugge assumes a complement of 50 men for each kora-kora, whereas here the ratio is higher (Van Dam 1931:72).
5 A.J. van Delden, 'Verslag van de Rijkjes en Negorijen ten westen van Menado gelegen, 1833' (ANRI Manado 48).
6 Francis 1860:283.
7 AV Manado 1852 (ANRI Manado 51).
8 The figures are probably from an 1848 report, mentioned later in the same source, by the government investigator A.L. Weddik.
9 Riedel 1872a:196.
10 Including men of Gorontalo, Limboto, Kaili, Bugis, Tolitoli, Mandar, and Arab descent or origin.
11 Koloniaal verslag 1895, Bijlage A:5.
12 Nota Toli-Toli 1912:37.
13 Uitkomsten 1922:220-1.
14 And 25 Europeans.
15 Volkstelling 1933-36, V:12.
16 And 5 Europeans.

administration of Makasar rather than Manado, so that no parallel estimates are available for both kingdoms (and in fact none at all, to my knowledge, for Tolitoli).[1] Proximity and small size, nevertheless, make it practical to combine the two sets of data.[2]

The social elite in Tolitoli and Buol was nominally Christian during the VOC period, and its numbers are recorded in many of the contemporary church visitation reports. As in the case of Bolaang Mongondow, however, these figures bear little relation to the size of the population as a whole. When a VOC governor of Ternate quoted a figure of 1,618 Buol Christians from one such report in 1706, he noted that it referred only to the *negeri*-dwellers as opposed to the dispersed part of the population – the equivalent, in other words, of the 'big house people' as opposed to the 'swidden people' on Siau (Chapter III). 'The rest of the subjects of this kinglet', he reported, 'are Moors and heathens, and live in hamlets or small neighborhoods in the interior' (Roselaar 1706). The data in the visitation reports, accordingly, have been omitted from Table 11. Buol and Tolitoli were subject to a largely ineffectual regime of compulsory gold deliveries until 1858, when the introduction of a head tax (Encyclopaedisch Bureau 1912b:142) should in principle have increased the incentive to underenumeration. Slavery, as elsewhere in Central Sulawesi, was not abolished until 1907 (Kortleven 1927:30), but none of the population estimates lists slaves specifically. In 1930 the recorded population was evenly distributed between the two kingdoms, although some older sources suggest that Buol was the more populous.

Many of these estimates, unfortunately, are useful only for illustrating the shortcomings of early demographic sources. The entry for 1681 is probably just as selective as those which appear in the church visitation reports, and that for 1682, which apparently refers only to seaborne military strength, is likewise best ignored. The sources from the years 1824-1912, taken at face value, suggest a combined population for Buol and Tolitoli of between 5,500 (1833) and 15,000 (1893 and 1912 together). Argensola's estimate from 1591, on the other hand, implies (multiplying by 3.5) a population of at least 23,000. Most of the nineteenth-century counts, it should be noted, either feature a disproportionately low figure for Tolitoli, or explicitly exclude a significant part of its population, or both. While the distribution of the population in Buol, at least by the end of the colonial period, was predominantly coastal

---

[1]   AV Manado 1857 (ANRI Manado 52); Encyclopaedisch Bureau 1912b:173-4; Kortleven 1927:109-10.

[2]   Also included here is Dondo, a small polity to the southwest of Tolitoli which is listed as a separate unit in the 1591 estimate, but appears in subsequent sources as a tributary either of Tolitoli or of Banawa (Donggala), a Kaili kingdom with its capital in the Palu Bay. Padtbrugge reported in 1682 that Dondo had been 'completely destroyed' by Mandar marauders backed by Tolitoli (Van Dam 1931:88).

(Van Wouden 1941:334), in Tolitoli, as some nineteenth-century observers were already aware (Table 11: 1833, 1846), the interior was also inhabited. The *controleur* Kortleven (1927:17-22) believed in the 1920s that the upland 'Dayak' of Tolitoli were few in number (hundreds rather than thousands) and that most had already been resettled on or near the coast. It is possible, however, that as on the opposite side of the peninsula in Tinombo (see below), some were in fact still living undetected in the mountains. According to the 1930 census, the population density of Buol and Tolitoli as a whole was just under seven persons per km[2]. Padtbrugge wrote in 1682 that 'good timber' was the most useful thing which Buol produced (Van Dam 1931:87), and both areas were still heavily forested in the late nineteenth and early twentieth centuries.[3]

Migration was an important factor in the historical demography of Buol and Tolitoli. Buol is mentioned in the late seventeenth century, and again in the late nineteenth, as a source of exported slaves.[4] In the eighteenth century the VOC attempted (although without permanent success) to relocate the inhabitants of these remote and vulnerable dependencies to Kuandang on the north coast of Gorontalo, where they could more easily be controlled.[5] In 1853, conversely, the population of Buol was said to be 'increasing by the year as a result of migration from the Gorontalo area'.[6] Tolitoli, for its part, saw considerable immigration from Mindanao and Sulu during the heyday of Philippine piracy in the late eighteenth century, and at the time of the British interregnum the pirate colony there was reported to be 3,000 strong.[7] In the early twentieth century, thousands of Bugis settlers (already a significant component of the population in earlier times) arrived to plant coconuts, a single twenty-kilometre strip of the coastal plain reportedly attracting 200 new immigrants each year in the 1920s (Kortleven 1927:6). By 1930 there were almost 9,000 Bugis in Tolitoli, making up more than a third of the total reported population (*Volkstelling* 1933-36, V:29).

---

[3] Boonstra van Heerdt 1914b:729, 744, 750, 759; Van der Hart 1853:251; *Nota Toli-Toli* 1912:31; Riedel 1872a:191; Sarasin and Sarasin 1905, I:187. 'Forest', wrote Kortleven (1927:11), 'dominates the landscape of Tolitoli to an overwhelming degree'.
[4] NA VOC 1345:463-4; AV Gorontalo 1864 (ANRI Gorontalo 3).
[5] Breton 1767; *Corpus diplomaticum* VI:466, 474; Valckenaer 1778.
[6] AV Manado 1853 (ANRI Manado 51).
[7] J. Hunt 1837:51; Warren 1981:164. More than a century later, oral tradition also recalled that before their defeat by the Dutch there had been 'thousands' of Magindanao in Tolitoli (Kortleven 1927:50). Some local people, conversely, were probably exported as slaves in this period by the pirates (Kortleven 1927:51).

Tomini

This subregion (Table 12) corresponds to the prewar administrative division of Parigi, extending from Moutong (on the border with Gorontalo) in the north to Sausu in the south (Chapter III, Map 9). Its most important indigenous political units were Tomini, Parigi, and in the nineteenth century also Moutong, founded by Mandar settlers in the 1780s (Jellesma 1903:222). The first Dutch outpost in the area was established at Sidoan (near Tinombo) as early as 1672 (Jellesma 1903:220), and in the mid-eighteenth century there were two, one at Lembunu to the west of Moutong, and one at Parigi in the south, both intended primarily to collect gold (Riedel 1870b:559). Perhaps partly because this was an exceptionally violent and demographically fluid region, however, only one population estimate is available from the VOC period (Table 12:1676). By 1800, Lembunu had been sacked and Parigi withdrawn. Although political contracts were re-established with the indigenous rulers of Moutong and Parigi in 1831-1832, it was not until 1908 that Parigi once again became the *standplaats* of a Dutch official (Kartodirdjo 1973:394; Arts and Van Beurden 1982:69). The record for the nineteenth century, consequently, is also rather skeletal.[8]

Long intervals between successive estimates, uncertain political boundaries, and the fact that none of the data include any details regarding social scope and exclusions, all make it difficult to draw any significant conclusions from these figures. Van Hoëvell's estimates from around 1890, however, are geographically inclusive and accord well with the result of the 1930 census, suggesting a population of about 40,000 souls. The figures from 1911 and 1920, by contrast, are considerably lower, but both are probably incomplete. Van Hoëvell (1892:354, 356) believed that there were at least 18,000 'Alfurs' living in the interior of the peninsula: 8,000 in the Moutong area, and 10,000 near Tinombo.[9] The military officer Boonstra van Heerdt (1914b:752, 754), who surveyed the area two decades later and published the figures for 1911, thought that almost the whole population had now been resettled, 'where necessary by force', in new villages on the coast, and that earlier claims

---

[8]   One Dutch report from 1854 warns that any attempt to estimate the population 'would only be misleading', and another from a year later states that no figure can be given 'even by approximation' (AV Gorontalo 1854, in ANRI Gorontalo 3; AV Manado 1855, in ANRI Manado 51).

[9]   The information given by Van Hoëvell for the stretch from Ampibabo to Moutong is somewhat confusing. The '± 10,000' Alfurs (or *Lado-Lado*) which he initially locates in the interior near Tinombo are not included in his subsequent summary table, which lists only 2,000 Alfurs other than the '± 8,000' in Moutong. In Table 12 I have assumed that the figure of 2,000 here refers to separate groups not included in the first 10,000, so that the total number of Alfurs is 20,000. I am grateful to Tania Li for drawing my attention to the incompleteness of Van Hoëvell's summary table.

Table 12. Population data, Tomini, 1591-1930

Year	Figure	Scope	Type of estimate	Other accuracy indications
1591	12,000 *hombres de armas*[1]	'Tomini'	estimate by Jesuit missionary in Ternate, probably from Ternatan source	single undivided figure
1676	6,080 *weerbare mannen*[2]	'Alfur' vassals of Gorontalo and Limboto; possibly includes some settlements on south side of Gulf of Tomini in Poso/Tojo area; part of the specified population possibly relocated to Gorontalo	estimate by VOC envoy to Gorontalo	44 units distinguished; figures rounded to 10 or 100[3]
1829	7,200 people[4]	Moutong, Tomini (including Tinombo) and Parigi only	Dutch administrative estimate	4 units distinguished; figures rounded to 100 or 1,000
1852	22,000 people[5]	'the kingdoms of Moutong and Parigi'	Dutch administrative estimate	single undivided figure; 'estimated by calculation, since census figures are completely impossible to obtain'
1865	6,000 souls[6]	Sausu only	Dutch estimate 'according to the information provided by the chiefs'	'Our knowledge regarding the size of the population in these lands is still very uncertain. The available means of obtaining good statistical data are still inadequate, while the native chiefs concerned are not in a position to provide accurate information on this point themselves.'
ca 1890	37,865[7]	–	combination of several estimates by assistant resident of Gorontalo (1886-1891) G.W.W.C. van Hoëvell	Sausu (1,250, 3 units), Parigi ('± 9,000', undivided figure), and the rest from Ampibabo to Moutong (27,615 in 12 units, mostly rounded to 10 or 100)

Year	Figure	Scope	Type of estimate	Other accuracy indications
1911	25,504[8]	Parigi administrative division (whole subregion)	Dutch administrative count	7 landschappen distinguished; m/f adults and children distinguished
1920	28,258[9]	includes 18 'foreign orientals' and Europeans	Netherlands Indies census	–
1930	43,003[10]	includes 658 'foreign orientals' and Europeans	Netherlands Indies census	breakdown: Moutong 10,248, Tinombo 14,796, North Parigi 7,969, South Parigi 9,990

1   Argensola 1992:83; dated by Jacobs (1974-84, II:304).
2   NA VOC 1320:151v.
3   Not all of the 49 toponyms included in the original list can be identified, but those which definitely lie outside the reference area have been excluded.
4   AV Gorontalo 1829 (ANRI Gorontalo 3).
5   AV Gorontalo 1852 (ANRI Gorontalo 3).
6   AV Gorontalo 1872 (ANRI Manado 9).
7   Van Hoëvell 1892:354, 356 (Moutong to Ampibabo), 1893a:72 (Parigi), 1893b:40 (Sausu).
8   Boonstra van Heerdt 1914b:754.
9   Uitkomsten 1922:221.
10 Volkstelling 1933-36, V:122, 134.

regarding the population of the interior had in any case been 'much exaggerated'. On the basis of recent oral history research, however, anthropologist Tania Li suggests that Van Hoëvell was in fact right, and that at least in the Tinombo area, most of the uplanders subsequently succeeded in avoiding resettlement and taxation.[10] In contrast to the situation in many other parts of Central Sulawesi, there was no missionary activity in this area to concentrate European attention on such peripheral groups. If some of them were also missed by the 1930 census, then the average population density in that year must have been rather higher than the recorded figure of just under seven persons per km^2. It is also possible, however, that the total population did decline around the turn of the century as a direct result of the Dutch resettlement policy (Nourse 1999:65). In many other parts of Central Sulawesi, as detailed below, the same policy led to heightened mortality as a result of malaria and other epidemics.

The existence of a significant population centre in the hinterland of Tinombo accords with the former political importance of the kingdom of Tomini, which gave its name to the whole Gulf, and with the substantial military strength attributed to this kingdom in 1591. The modern settlement of Tomini lies about 30 km northeast of Tinombo, and the first VOC outpost in the area, at Sidoan, was located just a short distance to its south. Nineteenth-century accounts, moreover, indicate that the Tomini lands had been more populous in earlier periods. 'The people of the kingdom of Tomini', states one Dutch source from 1829, 'are regarded as the oldest inhabitants of this Gulf, and in former times they were very numerous and much renowned; constant emigration, however, has reduced the kingdom to its present insignificant state'.[11] In 1855, another official was told of 'a once-numerous tribe of Alfurs', the remnants of which 'can still be found today in the mountains of Ampibabo and Sigenti' (Bleeker 1856:130). During the seventeenth and eighteenth centuries, as noted in Chapter V, large numbers of Tomini people moved to Gorontalo, whether under direct pressure from the Gorontalese or in search of safety from other aggressors.[12] On the basis of later oral history, Riedel (1870b:556) claimed that 'thousands of captured men, women and children were exported as slaves', to Ternate as well as to Gorontalo itself, during the period of Gorontalese ascendancy in the Gulf.

---

[10]   Personal communication, 11-8-1999. Even in 1990, observed Li (1991:38), a proportion of the 'inner hill' population of Tinombo 'are not registered in any village and do not possess indentity cards'.

[11]   AV Gorontalo 1829 (ANRI Gorontalo 3).

[12]   *Corpus diplomaticum* V:91; *Generale missiven* VI:419, 534, 757-8, IX:23, 140-1, 145, 149, 262, 295-6, 488, 569, XI:35, 241, 648; Van Mijlendonk 1756.

Poso, Tojo, and Lore

This subregion (Table 13), the colonial administrative division of Poso, encompasses three fairly distinct areas: the basin of the Poso lake and river in the geographical centre of the island; the hinterland of Tojo (including the Bongka River basin) further east; and the smaller highland depressions of Tawaelia, Napu, Besoa, and Bada, collectively known since 1916 as Lore (*Koloniaal verslag* 1917:35), in the west (Map 13). Although the coastlands around Poso and Tojo had some contact with the VOC outpost at Parigi until its withdrawal in 1795, nothing significant is known about their demography in this period. Dutch vessels began to make occasional visits to the south coast of the Gulf of Tomini once more after 1830, and in 1865 and 1869 Dutch *controleurs* even made brief overland journeys to Lake Poso, providing the first global population estimates (Adriani 1913a, 1913b). It was not until 1894, however, that a colonial official was permanently stationed in Poso (Arts and Van Beurden 1982:88). Napu and Besoa were first visited by Europeans during their military subjugation in 1905, while Bada, further south, was reached by the explorers Paul and Fritz Sarasin in 1902 (A.C. Kruyt 1908:1275; Sarasin and Sarasin 1905, II:95-116). Between 1905 and 1907 a series of military operations brought the whole area under colonial control (Adriani 1919:186-8; Arts and Van Beurden 1982:100-3), whereafter population figures of increasing reliability became available.

The most striking thing about this series of figures is the disproportionate size of the earlier estimates. Even if the first 1865 figure is taken to include – like Riedel's a few years later (Table 13: ca 1870) – part of what I have considered here as part of western Central Sulawesi, the contrast with the sober estimates by Kruyt and Adriani around the turn of the century, and with all of the colonial population counts, is sharp. Summarily put, the early twentieth-century sources indicate a total of 40-50,000 people, while the nineteenth-century estimates suggest a population more than twice as large. The earlier figures, of course, are the less reliable, and Van der Wijck's calculation on the basis of a global estimate of the number of villages (1865a) is particularly crude. Since they refer to the period before the establishment of colonial control and taxation, they may also have been subject to defensive or boastful inflation on the part of indigenous informants. When Kruyt and Adriani began to explore the interior in the 1890s, they found what they regarded as a very sparsely populated country.[13] Adriani in particular (1919: 126) was convinced that the high early estimates had indeed been completely mistaken, belonging to a time when Central Sulawesi 'was still believed to be exceptionally fertile and densely populated'. This perception had indeed

---

[13]   Adriani and Kruyt 1898:390, 1912-14, I:84-5; A.C. Kruyt 1898:33-4, 1903b:190-1.

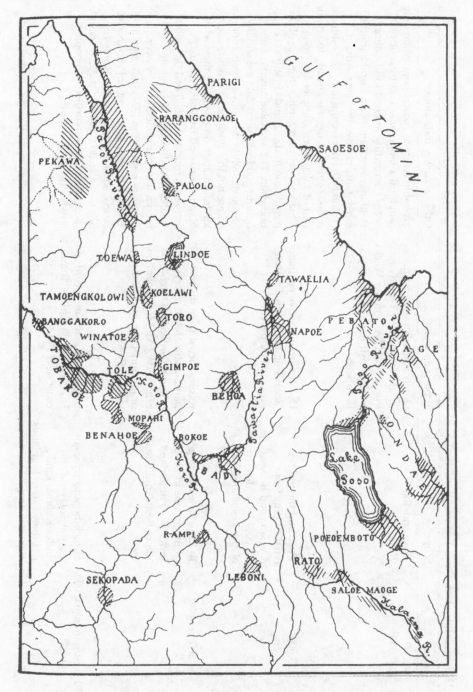

Map 13. Western Central Sulawesi: population distribution, circa 1920 (Kaudern 1925:33)

Table 13. Population data, Poso, Tojo and Lore, 1863-1930

Year	Figure	Scope	Type of estimate	Other accuracy indications
1863	30,000[1]	'Poso and Tojo'	Dutch administrative estimate in situ estimate by Dutch *controleur* (J.C.W.D.A. van der Wijck) on first visit to Lake Poso by a European	probably refers to coastal population only rough calculation based on total of 1,000 *negeri* ('according to good information') at 40 *weerbare mannen* each and a (high) 5 inhabitants per *weerbare man*; Adriani (1913b:860) later comments: 'The estimate of 200 souls per *negeri* is already too high; that of 1,000 *negeri* completely wrong.'
1865a	200,000[2]	'Poso'		
1865b	113,000[3]	'Poso and the interior' plus 'Tojo, Ampana and Bongka' (23,000); excludes Napu, Besoa and Bada	Dutch administrative estimate 'according to the information provided by the chiefs'	'Our knowledge regarding the size of the population in these lands is still very uncertain. The available means of obtaining good statistical data are still inadequate, while the native chiefs concerned are not in a position to provide accurate information on this point themselves.'
1869	64,500 people[4]	To Lage (one of 4 largest ethnic groups in Poso[5]), Torau (Tojo hinterland), Napu, Besoa and Bada	reconstructed from diverse partial estimates of uncertain origin recorded by Dutch official (W.J.M. Michielsen) on, or in connection with, journey to Lake Poso	Napu, Besoa and Bada: individual estimates rounded to 500 or 1,000, joint total 23,500; To Lage: 43 *kampung* mentioned, multiplied here by average *kampung* population (374) indicated in same source for area west of Poso (Napu, Besoa, Bada, Paibatu, Lindu, Kulawi, Sigi), = ca 16,000; To Rau: ca 25,000 people
ca 1870	'more than 100,000 souls'[6]	'autochthonous tribes of Central Sulawesi'; includes Kulawi, Lindu and the western highlands; excludes Tojo	indigenous estimate recorded by J.G.F. Riedel on Gulf of Tomini coast near Poso	'according to trustworthy old people'; single undivided figure

Year	Figure	Groups	Source	Notes
ca 1890	'at least 90,000'[7]	'the number of Alfurs who live in the interior' of the Tojo kingdom; probably also includes hinterland of Poso	estimate by traders, recorded at Tojo by assistant resident Gorontalo (1886-1891) G.W.W.C. Baron van Hoëvell	'When asked about the size of the population, various people who had traded for years in the Tojo kingdom consistently replied: [...]'; single undivided figure
1900	'±25,000'[8]	'Poso' (interior and coast); probably excludes Napu, Besoa and Bada	estimate by A.C. Kruyt	'A total of [...] is according to him [Kruyt] not too low an estimate.'
1905-09	38,676[9]	Poso (1908), Tojo (1909), Napu (ca 1908), Besoa (ca 1908), Bada (1905)	first official population counts after Dutch conquest	Poso 21,977, Tojo 9,800 (m/f adults and m/f children distinguished; male adults referred to as 'taxpaying men'); Bada 'a little under 4,000', based on 931 registered men; Napu 1,486 (but 'seems much too low' to Kruyt); Besoa 1,413 (also 'probably too low')
1913	< 50,000[10]	'Bare'e [Pamona]-speaking Toraja' (Poso, Tojo and some groups in Mori and over the 'border' in South Sulawesi, but not Napu, Besoa, or Bada)	in situ estimate by Adriani	'The number of Bare'e-speaking Toraja certainly does not exceed 50,000.'
1915	< 40,000[11]	'Bare'e [Pamona]-speaking Toraja'	second estimate by Adriani	'certainly no stronger than about 40,000 souls'
1920	46,298[12]	Poso, Tojo, Napu, Besoa and Bada, plus Togian Islands[13]; includes 223 'foreign orientals' and Europeans	Netherlands Indies census	aggregate figure only available

Year	Figure	Scope	Type of estimate	Other accuracy indications
1930	50,566[14]	Poso, Tojo, Napu, Besoa and Bada; includes 690 'foreign orientals' and Europeans	Netherlands Indies census	Poso 26,128; Tojo 14,691; Napu, Besoa and Bada together 9,747

1   AV Gorontalo 1864 (ANRI Gorontalo 3).
2   Adriani 1913b:860.
3   AV Gorontalo 1872 (ANRI Manado 9).
4   Adriani 1913a:1617-8.
5   According to Kruyt at the turn of the century, each of these four major groups had a population of 4-6,000 (Gallas 1900:812).
6   Riedel 1886:77.
7   Van Hoëvell 1893b:3.
8   Gallas 1900:813.
9   Adriani and Kruyt 1912-14 I:88-9; A.C. Kruyt 1908:1309, 1337, 1909:351.
10 Adriani 1913:860.
11 Adriani 1915:458.
12 *Uitkomsten* 1922:221.
13 The population of the Togian Islands in 1920 was reportedly about 7,000 (*Encyclopaedie* 1917-21, IV:389); some other figures for this archipelago, not examined here as a separate subregion, are provided in Chapter XI.
14 *Volkstelling* 1933-36, V:134.

been widespread among Dutch officials in the mid-nineteenth century.[14] In 1930, the reported population density for the subregion as a whole was just over five persons per km².

The twentieth-century figures, however, certainly underestimate the population to some extent, which has the effect of exaggerating the discontinuity with respect to earlier data. Kruyt acknowledged this under-registration himself with respect to the military counts of 1905-1909 (Table 13), and even in 1930 there must have been some peripheral groups, particularly among the remote To Wana on the upper reaches of the Bongka River, which were not included in the census.[15] More importantly, Kruyt and Adriani confirmed that during and immediately preceding the period of their presence there, the population of Central Sulawesi had indeed been declining.[16] The most dramatic cause of this decline had been a very serious smallpox epidemic in 1884, from which blow, wrote the two missionaries more than a generation later, 'the population still does not seem to have recovered' (Adriani and Kruyt 1912-14, I:87). Other factors, they suggested, had included a series of destructive wars during the second half of the nineteenth century.[17] Emigration – to the Palu Valley, to Parigi, to the Togian Islands, and to Mori on the east coast – also seemed to have played a part.[18] In some cases these population movements were triggered by war, but they were also stimulated by the rise of the export trade in *damar*, focused on coastal trading settlements like the new entrepôt of Watambayoli, near the mouth of the Sumara River in Mori (see Chapter II).[19] While seasonal male emigration in connection with war, salt manufacture, trade, and hunting was an established part of Toraja life, the increased commercial demand for forest products, as Kruyt observed in Bada, made it more common for men to spend longer periods away from home.

[14]   AV Manado 1852, 1854 (ANRI Manado 51); AV Gorontalo 1854 (ANRI Gorontalo 3); Van Hoëvell 1893b:21; 'Aantekeningen van den kommissaris voor Menado, 1846' (ANRI Manado 167); Von Rosenberg 1865:47.

[15]   A.C. Kruyt 1930b:404-5. In relation to the earliest colonial counts, based partly on tax registers, it is also worth noting that some adults were exempt from taxation (Adriani 1919:57).

[16]   Adriani and Kruyt 1912-14, I:87-8, 1950-51, I:76-8; A.C. Kruyt 1903b:203-4.

[17]   Some earlier sources support the idea that this was a particularly violent period (Adriani 1913a:862; Van Hoëvell 1893a:65).

[18]   Adriani and Kruyt 1912-14, I:72-3, 122; A.C. Kruyt 1908:1337, 1909:349-50.

[19]   Adriani and Kruyt 1912-14, II:306, 1950-51, III:346; Encyclopaedisch Bureau 1912b:102; A.C. Kruyt 1900b:437, 1911:83. In 1899 the number of *damar* collectors in the Sumara area alone was estimated at 1,500 (Kruyt 1900b:462), and although this was the most important collection point, there were also many others (Adriani and Kruyt 1912-14, II:306, 308). Kruyt (1908:1337) wrote that the population of distant Besoa would 'increase greatly' if all the Besoa men in Sumara were to return home. Descriptions of the multi-ethnic immigrant community of Watambayoli are given by Adriani and Kruyt (1900:150) and Abendanon (1915-17, II:646, 650).

Many boys and young men leave their land for years on end to gather riches [*schatten*] by searching for rattan and *damar* in areas close to the sea (usually Mamuju on the Makasar Strait, the Palu Valley, or Sumara on the Mori Bay). When they reach a mature age, most of them return to their country and settle there. (A.C. Kruyt 1909:372.)

The idea of a substantial demographic decline in the Poso area during the nineteenth century is supported by the large number of abandoned settlement sites mentioned by Kruyt and Adriani in their descriptions of the country, and by a level of deforestation (especially in the Poso Depression) which, by the standards of other parts of the region, was high in relation to the existing population. These features, and their implications, will be discussed in Chapters XIII-XV.

Abandoned *sawah* fields were another aspect of the local landscape at the beginning of the twentieth century which suggested that the population had been larger, or at least denser, in the past. These were found in greater or smaller numbers in three of the four valleys of Lore where irrigated rice cultivation was already practised prior to the Dutch occupation: Tawaelia, Napu, and Besoa.[20] Missionary observers attributed their abandonment partly to the recent exodus of much of the male population in connection with the *damar* boom (Kruyt and Kruyt 1921:409). Disease among the water buffalo used to work the wet fields, or political factors, may also have played a role. Particularly in the case of Napu, however, it seems likely that a long-term demographic change was involved.

> As a whole, this land must have been much more densely populated in the past. An example is the Hambu plain. In the north of this plain lies Tamaduë, but otherwise there are no settlements here at present – a remarkable fact, given that this is one of the most fertile parts of Napu. And indeed things were not always so, because the *sawah* dikes which are visible on both sides of the river show that thousands of people once grew their rice here. A long, low hill on the plain still bears the name 'rice-drying place'; this is where the rice sheaves were brought in from the surrounding country to be dried after the harvest. The old people insist that it was not their ancestors who laid out these *sawah*, but others. The giant trees which stand here and there on the abandoned fields prove that they have not been worked in a long time. (Kruyt and Kruyt 1921:407.)

Another possible piece of evidence for long-term depopulation comes from Padtbrugge's *memorie van overgave* of 1682. While neither Padtbrugge nor any other European of his time had actually seen the interior of Central Sulawesi, informants had told him that in the hinterland of Poso (including Lore) there were 'fine plains in or beyond the mountains, and these are so populous that

---

[20]   A.C. Kruyt 1908:1313-5, 1334, 1938, I:195, 219, 228, 232, IV:18; Kruyt and Kruyt 1921:406-9; Schuyt 1911:15.

Plate 13. New model village, Central Sulawesi, circa 1920 (Tillema 1922:17). Compare Chapter III, Plate 11.

in many places there is even a shortage of firewood around the villages'. He also recorded that most of these villages were said to lie on the 'enormous lake' which was the source of the Poso River (Van Dam 1931:93) – an observation no longer valid two centuries later (A.C. Kruyt 1894:17), but consistent with local oral tradition, according to which Lake Poso had been the original centre of population dispersal in Central Sulawesi, and its shores fabulously populous (Adriani and Kruyt 1912-14, I:5; A.C. Kruyt 1898:17).

That upland Central Sulawesi has a very long and interesting history of human habitation is confirmed by the large stone megaliths – urns, statues, and what appear to be mortars for grinding or pounding – which European explorers were surprised to find in Besoa, Bada and Napu at the beginning of the twentieth century.[21] These objects were no longer being manufactured, and indeed the inhabitants of the localities in which they occurred professed to have no knowledge of their origins. Most authorities have thought them to

---

[21] Kiliaan (1908) details the earliest finds, while Kaudern (1938) and A.C. Kruyt (1938, I:331-498) provide overviews. Megaliths were also present the Palu, Kulawi and Gimpu Valleys of western Central Sulawesi (A.C. Kruyt 1938, I:332-47) and in the Yaentu Valley of Mori, although not in the immediate vicinity of Lake Poso.

be very old, the archaeologist Bellwood (1997:306) noting that 'the apparent absence of Chinese pottery' in their vicinity 'can only suggest a date older than 500 years'. While it would be rash to link these monuments directly with modern demographic or deforestation patterns, they do suggest that the interior of Central Sulawesi, so peripheral in the twentieth century, was the site of relatively dense settlement at one or more periods in the distant past. Many of the montane basins identified by Reid (1997:67-77) as the oldest agricultural hearths and population concentrations in Sumatra also contain megalithic remains like those of Central Sulawesi (Schnitger 1989:126-54).

If at least one episode of depopulation occurred in precolonial times, there was another dramatic, if temporary, increase in mortality in many parts of upland Central Sulawesi immediately following the colonial conquest. This resulted from the harsh Dutch policy of regrouping the whole population, which had formerly lived partly in dispersed swidden houses and partly in small fortified villages on defensible hilltops, into a smaller number of new planned villages in more accessible sites on flat land (Plate 13).[22] Adriani and Kruyt (1950-51, I:78) attributed the 'many' deaths which occurred in the new settlements to a 'spiritual depression' which rendered the population 'susceptible to disease', but other sources indicate that exposure to malaria, the incidence of which varied greatly from place to place (Chapter VII), was the chief factor.[23] The hygiene expert H.F. Tillema (1926:48), who visited Central Sulawesi in 1924, even saw one *kampung* 'which had been relocated three times because its inhabitants were mown down by malaria'. The greater size of the new villages may also have led to more frequent infection by other diseases, such as cholera and tuberculosis (Tillema 1922:208). The number of people who died as a result of colonial resettlement policies in Central Sulawesi is not known, but even the muted missionary sources concede that for a period after 1905 there was an absolute population decline.[24] The pan-Indonesian influenza epidemic of 1918 also caused many deaths in the area. The recorded population of Napu, for instance, fell from 3,250 in 1917 to 2,365 in 1923.[25] The period of depopulation suggested by the nineteenth-century sources, then, may well have continued at least up to 1920.

---

[22]   Adriani 1915:469-70, 1919:193-4; Adriani and Kruyt 1912-14, I:149, 1950-51, I:78; A.C. Kruyt 1930b:404; *Koloniaal verslag* 1907:70; Tillema 1922:205-8, 1926:48, 211.
[23]   Tillema 1922:205, 208, 1926:48-9. Some coastal villages, on the other hand, were moved a few hundred metres inland in a deliberate attempt to protect them from this disease (Tillema 1922:210), and in the 1920s the whole resettlement policy was relaxed to some extent (A.C. Kruyt 1930b:404, 1938, I:123, 154, 262, 278; Vorstman 1935a:13).
[24]   Adriani and Kruyt (1950-51, I:78) imply that this decline was limited to the years 1905 and 1906, but other sources suggest that much of the population was relocated only after 1907 (Adriani 1919:193-4; Tillema 1922:206).
[25]   A.C. Kruyt 1938, I:242-3. Also Adriani 1919:258; Adriani and Kruyt 1950-51, I:77.

In 1930 more than half of the population of the Poso area lived in the drainage basin of the Poso lake and river, where it was fairly evenly distributed. In precolonial times, prior to forced concentration, the settlement pattern here must have been even more dispersed. In Tojo, by contrast, most of the population lived either on the coast, or along the upper reaches of the Bongka River in the interior; elsewhere, large areas were uninhabited (Adriani and Kruyt 1912-14, I:85, 89). In Lore, comparably, the population was heavily concentrated in the four upland valleys. These were densely settled, and in fact Bada, according to Grubauer (1913:508), had the highest population density of any part of the Central Sulawesi interior. In absolute terms, however, the population of Bada was not particularly large – the highest early twentieth-century estimates suggest a total of about 6,000 people (Adriani 1919:27; Encyclopaedisch Bureau 1912b:102) – and in 1930 the recorded population of Lore as a whole was only about 10,000 (Table 13). Much of this area, correspondingly, was also uninhabited (Adriani and Kruyt 1912-14, I:85; A.C. Kruyt 1903b:190-1).

Western Central Sulawesi

The one subregion (other than Togian) for which no table of population figures will be presented here is the western part of Central Sulawesi, comprising the west coast of the neck of the northern peninsula, the bay and valley of Palu, and the mountainous interior on both sides of the Palu Trench as far south as the latitude of Bada and Lake Poso (Chapter III, Map 9). In precolonial times this area was dominated by a number of kingdoms centred in the Palu area, the most important of which were Banawa (Donggala), Tawaeli, Palu, Dolo, and above all Sigi (Bora/Biromaru), which held nominal sovereignty over a large part of the interior.[26] In 1930 the recorded population of the whole subregion was just under 124,000.[27] At the 1920 census the equivalent figure was 82,000 (*Uitkomsten* 1922:221), but the growth of 4.1 percent per year which this suggests for the period 1920-1930 is already far too high to be credible, and the quality and geographical coverage of the earlier figures for western Central Sulawesi is such that even the most heavily annotated and qualified table would give a misleadingly concrete impression.

Although an important trading centre (Chapter II), the Palu Bay was

---

[26] A.C. Kruyt 1938, I:25-7. Banawa (Donggala) and Tawaeli were located on the shores of the bay and controlled the west coast, while the others lay in the valley and had their dependencies in the interior.

[27] *Volkstelling* 1933-36, V:156 (*onderafdelingen* Palu and Donggala combined). The population figure includes 1991 'foreign orientals' and Europeans (*Volkstelling* 1933-36, V:122).

visited only by a handful of VOC vessels before 1800. Ambassadors from the
kingdoms of Banawa and Palu signed a treaty with the Netherlands Indies
government in 1824, whereafter an influential Bugis trader was appointed
to represent Dutch interests in the area (Kartodirdjo 1973:276-7), but a permanent colonial administrative post was not established there until 1891
(*Landschap Donggala* 1905:529). The first Europeans to travel in the interior of
western Central Sulawesi were Adriani and Kruyt, who visited Kulawi and
Lindu in 1897. Gimpu, and the other remoter parts of the Palu Trench, were
first reached by the Sarasins in 1902, while the area to the west of the trench
was explored only in the years 1905-1912, during and immediately after the
Dutch military conquest.[28]

Adriani and Kruyt identified the Palu area as the sole exception to their
generalization that the population of Central Sulawesi was very sparse.[29] The
shores of the bay, wrote Albert Kruyt (1903b:191) after their first visit in 1897,
were 'quite thickly strewn with large villages', while the 'densely populated
Palu Valley' (Adriani and Kruyt 1898:483) was an almost completely deforested patchwork of settlements, grasslands and irrigated ricefields (Chapter
XIII). The 'town of Palu' alone, they were surprised to find, was larger than
Palopo, capital of Luwu, the powerful Bugis state on the Gulf of Bone which
claimed suzerainty over much of the Poso interior (Adriani and Kruyt
1898:454, 529). Captain Woodard (1969:28) had described Palu in 1793 as 'a
fine town, containing perhaps five hundred houses', and in 1850 the Dutch
naval captain Van der Hart (1853:264) agreed that it was 'a quite extensive
place'. Palu, moreover, was only one of a number of similar population concentrations in its immediate vicinity, including Dolo, which, according to the
Sarasins (1905, II:74), could 'almost be called a town' in 1902.

Argensola (1992:83), writing at the beginning of the seventeenth century,
attributed the considerable military strength of 10,000 *soldados* to the kings of
'Pulo and Yacua' on Sulawesi – very probably a reference to Palu and one of
its near neighbours. A VOC document from 1674 states that 'Kaili' – a loose
collective designation for the kingdoms of the Palu Bay and valley (A.C.
Kruyt 1938, I:46) – 'is said to be 7,000 *weerbare mannen* strong'.[30] Padtbrugge,

[28]   Adriani and Kruyt 1898; Boonstra van Heerdt 1914a:618; Encyclopaedisch Bureau 1912b:
157-60; Sarasin and Sarasin 1905, II:82-93.
[29]   Adriani and Kruyt 1898:453, 464, 483, 1912-14 I:85; A.C. Kruyt 1903b:191.
[30]   *Generale missiven* III:932. Kaili originally seems to have been the name of a village near
Tawaeli (A.C. Kruyt 1938, I:46), and Navarrete, writing in 1657, refers to a 'Kingdom of Caile'
(Cummins 1962:109). Padtbrugge (Van Dam 1931:89) and Valentijn (Keijzer 1856:213), however,
use Kaili as a name for the whole Palu Bay, and an eighteenth-century VOC source notes that
as an ethnic designation it also encompasses all of 'the peoples which live between Palu and
Tolitoli' (Seydelman 1769). In modern usage, Kaili refers in the first place to the major language
of lowland western Central Sulawesi (see Chapter I).

who sent a VOC soldier to explore the overland crossing between the Palu Bay and the Gulf of Tomini in 1681, put the figure at 4,000 men, inhabiting 31 'villages' divided between the spheres of influence of Tawaeli and Palu.[31] In 1747 there was a rumour that a military expedition comprising fully 10,000 Kaili men was on its way to attack Tolitoli (*Generale missiven* XI:512). In 1759 a Dutch governor of Makasar, Roelof Blok (1848:63), wrote that according to VOC officials who had been there Kaili was 'very populous and fertile in *padi*'. Nineteenth-century Dutch reports show the same vague but strong conviction that the area is densely populated. In 1829 a resident of Manado wrote that the population of 'Palu', while impossible to estimate, was by all accounts 'very large'.[32] Later writers, who likewise had not been there themselves, guessed that it might amount to 20,000 or more (Bleeker 1856:15; Francis 1860:283). Perhaps slightly better founded is a statement by the *controleur* Michielsen, after his visit to Lake Poso (but not the Palu area itself) in 1869, that 'the notable tribe of Sigi', located 'between Parigi and Palu' and north of Kulawi, 'certainly numbers more than 13,000 inhabitants, in about 25 *kampung*' (Adriani 1913b:1617).

Despite the dense concentration in the Palu area, the recorded average population density in western Central Sulawesi in 1930, at 12 persons per km^2, was no higher than the average for northern Sulawesi as a whole. Outside the Palu Valley, correspondingly, settlement was generally sparse. Large stretches of Donggala/Banawa north of the Palu Bay, for instance, were uninhabited in 1911 (Boonstra van Heerdt 1914:727, 729, 747, 750). The mountainous interior south of Palu, likewise, always seems to have been less populous than the valley.[33] Of the 31 Kaili settlements listed by Padtbrugge in 1682, only five were identified as 'mountain' villages.[34] Apart from the 'tribe of Sigi' in the Palu Valley, Michielsen includes only two other groups from western Central Sulawesi in his population estimates of 1869: Lindu, with 1,300 inhabitants, and Kulawi, with approximately 1,000 (Adriani 1913b: 1617). The latter figure, admittedly, is probably too low; Adriani and Kruyt

[31]   That is, 3,000 'armed men' under Tawaeli, and 1,000 under Palu (Van Dam 1931:90-1). Separate estimates for each 'village' are not given. These figures are also reproduced by Valentijn (Keijzer 1856:213-5), who multiplies them by 3 to arrive at a total population of 12,000 people.
[32]   AV Manado 1829 (KITLV H70).
[33]   Oral history as recorded in the early twentieth century, on the other hand, suggests that the inhabitants of the Palu Valley originally lived in the uplands, and one tradition (A.C. Kruyt 1938, I:48) associates the movement to the lowlands with the arrival of Bugis immigrants, which some authors (Acciaioli 1989:66; Metzner 1981a:47) have dated to the end of the seventeenth century. The shores of the Palu Bay, however, were already well populated at the time of Navarrete's visit in 1657 (Cummins 1962:109-10).
[34]   Van Dam 1931:90-1. Acciaioli (1989:70) raises this figure to 7 and suggests that the list included places as far away as Bada and Napu, but his toponymn identifications are contentious.

(1898:501) estimated the population of Kulawi at 2,200 in 1897, and in 1919 it was apparently about 3,000 (Kruyt and Kruyt 1920:196). There were also several other upland population centres not mentioned by Michielsen, including the mountain territory of Raranggonao to the east of the Palu Valley, which was described as 'well populated' (A.C. Kruyt 1938, I:98) on the eve of the Dutch conquest, and the valley of the Tewulu, a tributary of the Koro-Lariang in the highlands west of the trench, which also had a 'large population' in 1911 (Abendanon 1915-18, II:801). The upland population, nevertheless, must still have been small by the standards of Minahasa or Mongondow. As in Lore further east, much of it was concentrated in small enclaves of intensive agriculture: the five-square kilometre basin of Kulawi was likened in 1912 to 'one great *sawah* field', and irrigation was also present in Lindu in the nineteenth century (Adriani and Kruyt 1898:512; *Nota berglandschappen* 1912:2). Map 13 shows the population distribution as sketched by the anthropologist Kaudern around 1920.

As in the Poso area, there is some evidence for a demographic decline in western Central Sulawesi both before and immediately after the Dutch conquest. Although early European explorers noted few abandoned settlement sites here, and the extent of deforestation also appeared more in keeping with observed population densities than in Poso (Chapter XIII), abandoned *sawah* fields like those seen in Lore were also reported at the turn of the century in the Palu, Kulawi and Lindu Valleys.[35] While the possibility once again exists that this disintensification of agriculture was caused by livestock disease, war, or political change, its very wide distribution perhaps supports the idea that a general demographic decline was involved. Kulawi certainly saw substantial emigration in the last decades of the nineteenth century, at least partly in connection with the *damar* boom.[36] After the conquest, secondly, the population of the Palu area was subjected to the same policy of compulsory resettlement also applied elsewhere in Central Sulawesi, and with similar consequences in terms of health and mortality as relocated groups were exposed to new disease environments.[37] In at least one case, food shortages at the new village sites also played a role here. When uplanders from the Pekawa area west of Palu were relocated to the valley floor in the years 1912-1915, 'hundreds' died after a local famine was followed by a dysentery epidemic (A.C. Kruyt 1926: 542). The Raranggonao population, meanwhile, was said to have been 'much

[35]   Palu Valley: Abendanon 1915-17, II:906; Grubauer 1913:576; Hissink 1912:63; Kruyt and Kruyt 1920:215; Steup 1929:587-8; Tillema 1926:222; Lindu: Adriani and Kruyt 1898:512; Boonstra van Heerdt 1914a:626; Kulawi: Schuyt 1913:365-6.
[36]   Adriani and Kruyt 1898:501, 1912-14, I:87; Boonstra van Heerdt 1914a:623, 1914b:728; A.C. Kruyt 1903b:203, 1938, I:126; *Nota berglandschappen* 1912:25.
[37]   Boonstra van Heerdt 1914b:727; A.C. Kruyt 1926:542, 1938, I:97-8, 122-4, 262; *Koloniaal verslag* 1911:46-7, 1914:23, 1915:34; Schuyt 1913:371.

reduced' as a result of the 'difficult life' led by many members of this group in the 'inaccessible places in the forests' to which they fled after refusing to submit to Dutch authority (A.C. Kruyt 1938, I:98). The influenza epidemic of 1918, finally, was as serious in western Central Sulawesi as anywhere in the region; in Kulawi, some 400 of the 3,000 or so inhabitants died (Kaudern 1940:102).

Banggai

Moving to the opposite coast of Central Sulawesi, the available data for Banggai (Table 14), where there was no permanent Dutch presence until 1880 (De Clercq 1890:186), are almost as limited as those for the Palu area.[38] The figures which do exist, however, are highly interesting. The Banggai Archipelago consists of Banggai proper (also known as Gapi or Bolukan), where the political capital was always located, together with the much larger island of Peling and a number of smaller outliers. The kingdom of Banggai also possessed vassal territories on the Luwuk Peninsula; these will be dealt with separately below, and are not included in Table 14.

The most striking feature here is the disproportionate size of the second estimate (circa 1706). Applying our standard multiplication factor of 3.5 to this *weerbare mannen* figure produces a total population of almost 75,000. If the rate of underestimation is assumed to be one third, then the reconstructed total rises to 110,000 – although since the rounded figures of the original estimate suggest a higher level of accuracy than in the hypothetical standard case (Chapter III), such a large upwards adjustment may well be inappropriate. Even allowing for the tell-tale signs of underestimation and incomplete scope in the much lower nineteenth-century enumerations, which consist of unrounded figures collected exclusively from the paramount political leaders on Banggai proper, these are clearly far out of line with the very high 1706 estimate.[39] The latter, on the other hand, derives credibility from the surprising result of the 1930 census: a population of nearly 50,000, almost three times larger than that suggested by the last *weerbare mannen* count only 24 years earlier.[40]

[38] A VOC outpost, however, existed on Banggai for a brief period in the 1740s (*Corpus diplomaticum* V:332; *Generale missiven* IX:513).

[39] 'The population', wrote Resident De Clercq (1890:129), 'is divided into Muslims, who live on the coast, and Alfurs, who stay in their swiddens or in the forests'; possibly the nineteenth-century figures only refer to the former group.

[40] In the early twentieth century, moreover, many Banggai villages had been forcibly relocated from the interior to 'the unhealthy coastlands' (De Vreede 1950:9), presumably with heightened mortality as a result. Andaya (1993:86), evidently regarding Roselaar's figures for Peling as

Table 14. Population data, Banggai, 1679-1930

Year	Figure	Scope	Type of estimate	Other accuracy indications
1679	10,000 *weerbare mannen*[1]	probably includes dependencies on Luwuk Peninsula	in situ estimate by Padtbrugge on Banggai proper	'The number of inhabitants still belonging under Banggai is estimated at [...]'[2]; single undivided figure
ca 1706	21,560 'men'[3]	complete and exclusive[4]	reproduced by VOC governor of Ternate (1701-1706) P. Roselaar, from unspecified sources[5]	24 *negeri* distinguished; figures rounded to 100
1808	3,745 people[6]	possibly excludes (at least) Bangkurung and other smaller islands	'general survey or *zielsbeschrijving*' obtained from local informants on Banggai by Dutch envoys from Ternate	21 *negeri* distinguished; figures unrounded; males/females, adults/children and free population/slaves distinguished
1853	7,017 people[7]	geographically complete	recorded from local sources on Banggai by Dutch envoys from Ternate, who add: 'partly also obtained from a count carried out on our orders'	28 'districts' distinguished; figures mostly unrounded; m. adults/f. adults/children distinguished
ca 1888	15,500 souls[8]	complete	estimate by resident of Ternate (1885-1888) F.S.A. de Clercq[9]	*kampung* population (with island breakdown), Alfurs (total only), and Bajo (one settlement) distinguished; Alfur group 'estimated at ± 10,000 souls, because according to the chiefs their number is not small'; other subtotals rounded to 100 or 1,000 and qualified 'at least' or 'around'[10]
1906	5,210 *weerbare mannen*[11]	geographically complete	report by a Dutch government investigator; most components 'the result of a specially-held census', a few (for parts of Peling) 'obtained by estimation'	28 'districts' distinguished; 'Thanks to my visits to various Banggai districts, I am in a position to provide trustworthy information regarding the size of the population.'

| 1930[12] | 49,836 people[13] | includes 634 'foreign orientals' and Europeans | Netherlands Indies census | 7 districts distinguished |

1   NA VOC 1345:223; also reproduced by Andaya (1993:86).
2   This is a reference to the fact that Banggai had apparently controlled a larger area in the past (NA VOC 1345:222).
3   Roselaar 1706.
4   Banggai and Peling; other islands reported to be uninhabited.
5   Probably, as in the case of the parallel estimate for Mandono (Table 15), as investigated by knowledgeable people in Banggai in 1705'.
6   P. Landauw and J.A. Veldhuis to C.L. Wieling, 10-11-1808 (ANRI Ternate 116).
7   Bosscher and Matthijssen 1854:94.
8   De Clercq 1890:127-32.
9   This author had visited the Ternatan possessions on Sulawesi at least twice (De Clercq 1890:145).
10 In adding up the subtotals, no allowance has been made for the fact that some Alfurs ('200 at most') are included in the cited *kampung* population figure for Peling (De Clercq 1890:129).
11 Goedhart 1908:481-2.
12 The published results of the 1920 census, unfortunately, do not distinguish between the population of the archipelago and that of Banggai's Peninsular dependencies (*Uitkomsten* 1922:228-9).
13 *Volkstelling* 1933-36, V:122, 134.

The great bulk of the Banggai population (over 90 percent in 1706, according to the breakdown provided by Governor Roselaar) lived on Peling, where (at least according to later descriptions) it was scattered mainly in small hamlets in the interior (De Clercq 1890:128; A.C. Kruyt 1932c:71, 249, 268). A VOC *memorie van overgave* from 1710 notes that of the large number of inhabitants counted four years earlier, 'the majority, on the populous island of Peling, could not be brought to full obedience' by the kingdom of Banggai due to their fear of being abducted as slaves (Claaszoon 1710). In this light it is likely that many of the later figures, and also that recorded by Padtbrugge in 1679, included only a fraction of the people actually present on Peling.[41] There is no strong reason, then, to dismiss the high 1706 estimate as fantastic, or to wonder whether it actually represents a total population count rather than an enumeration of fighting men. Although the complete demographic collapse suggested by the estimates of 1808-1906 is no doubt illusory, it does seem likely that Banggai was more populous at the end of the seventeenth century than in 1930.

Local oral tradition, as recorded at the beginning of the twentieth century, supports the conclusion that Banggai had once had a larger population. According to one story the island of Banggai proper, originally called Gapi, 'was subsequently named Banggai by the Ternatans, because at that time it was so densely populated that it resembled a cluster of maggots (*banga gaai* in Ternatan, later contracted to Banggai)' (Goedhart 1908:442). Albert Kruyt (1931:505), some years later, was likewise told that 'in olden times the islands had a very dense population, so that the Ternatans spoke of them as *bagai*, "like worms", after the way they crawled with people, a term later bastardized to *banggai*'. The figure from 1706, it is also worth noting, does not indicate an unrealistically high population density. A reconstructed population of between 75,000 and 110,000 corresponds to a density of between 24 and 35 inhabitants per km^2, which is certainly high by regional standards, but probably no higher than that of, say, Talaud in the middle of the nineteenth century. In 1930 the average population density for the Banggai Archipelago was 16 persons per km^2 – still the highest in Central Sulawesi for an area of its size, but again similar to that of Talaud at the same date.

The demographic parallel between Banggai and Talaud is interesting in that both island groups also featured farming systems in which tubers

---

incredible, ignores them. Padtbrugge, to add to the confusion, described the Banggai Archipelago in 1682 as 'abandoned and depopulated' as a result of depredations by Bugis allies of the VOC during or after the Makasar War (Van Dam 1931:99). Banggai had been conquered by Makasar between 1632 and 1635, and was officially returned to Ternatan rule in 1667 (*Corpus diplomaticum* II:376; *Generale missiven* I:495).

[41]   In his accompanying description, strikingly, Padtbrugge does not even mention Peling by name.

played an unusually prominent role (see Chapter II). A further similarity is that Peling, like Talaud, is mentioned in all periods as a source of exported slaves.[42] 'Hundreds of these unfortunate individuals', claimed Revius in 1850, were shipped from the island each year, some destined for neighbouring areas like Banggai proper, the Luwuk Peninsula and Tobungku, others for Bone and Mandar in South Sulawesi, and Ternate in the Moluccas.[43] While violence and commerce, as in many other contexts, are not easy to distinguish here, it appears that this movement involved both raiding and the commercial purchase of slaves from local chiefs.

The Luwuk Peninsula

This subregion encompasses only that eastern part of the peninsula, beyond the Bongka River basin, which fell within the political orbit of Ternate up to 1908.[44] Except for the census of 1930 (and even that may not have been free from omissions in the interior), it is impossible to tell exactly how much of this area each of the estimates in Table 15 includes. None mention toponyms identifiable as places on the north coast to the west of Balantak (the mushroom-shaped terminus of the peninsula), and it seems probable that in most cases the scope was limited to the Banggai dependencies on the south coast (most importantly Mandono, the area directly opposite Peling) and their subjects among the 'Alfurs' of the interior.

Here again, one older estimate towers above the others and accords well with the results of the 1930 census. This time, however, the high figure is from 1850, probably originated from a rough guess by traders, and may be exaggerated. The *weerbare mannen* figure from 1705, by contrast, corresponds to a rather modest total of 10-15,000 people.[45] As in Banggai, however, there are indications that the comparatively large population suddenly revealed by the 1930 census was not a recent development. The Banggai dependencies on the peninsula were described in 1853 (albeit at second hand) as 'much more prosperous, more fertile, and more densely populated' than their southern neighbour Tobungku, and Mandono in particular was said to be 'a thriving land, inhabited by a large, prosperous [...] population'.[46] Loinang,

---

42   NA VOC 1345:463, 1366:698, 704, 710-1, 835, 916; Bleeker 1856:264; Bosscher and Matthijssen 1854:106; Claaszoon 1710; *Generale missiven* V:780; Knaap 1985:132; A.C. Kruyt 1931:612, 1932a:341, 1932c:251; 'Manados dagregister', 2-5-1682 (NA VOC 1392); Roselaar 1706.
43   'Algemeen verslag omtrent de Oostkust van Celebes', 10-2-1851 (ANRI Ternate 180).
44   AV Manado 1854 (ANRI Manado 51); *Koloniaal verslag* 1908:63.
45   Applying, that is, the multiplication factor of 3.5 and allowing for a possible underestimation of up to one third.
46   Bosscher and Matthijssen 1854:90-1. Also Van der Hart 1853:113.

Table 15. Population data, Luwuk Peninsula, 1705-1930

Year	Figure	Scope	Type of estimate	Other accuracy indications
1705	*sterk van manschap* 2,940[1]	probably south coast only	estimate obtained 'from knowledgeable people' by VOC mission	8 *negeri* distinguished; figures rounded to 100
1808	4,993 people[2]	probably south coast only	'general survey or *zielsbeschrijving*' obtained from local informants in Banggai by Dutch envoys from Ternate	47 *kampung* distinguished; figures unrounded; males/females, adults/children and free population/slaves distinguished
1850	40-50,000 people[3]	'Balantak and Mandono'	estimate by Dutch government investigator (C. van der Hart), probably on the basis of information from Bugis traders[4]	single undivided figure
1853	9,843 people[5]	Batui (Mandono) only	obtained from local sources on Banggai by Dutch envoys from Ternate	8 *negeri* distinguished; figures mostly unrounded; m. adults/f. adults/children distinguished; information obtained 'only with difficulty'[6]
ca 1888	'at least 3,000 souls'[7]	coastal population (*strandbevolking*) only; includes north coast of Balantak	estimate by resident of Ternate (1885-1888) F.S.A. de Clercq	single undivided estimate; 'a figure for the upland population [*bergbewoners*] can not be given even by approximation'
1906	2,512 *weerbare mannen*[8]	probably south coast only	'the result of a specially-held population count' ordered by Dutch government investigator	12 'districts' distinguished; 'Thanks to my visits to various Banggai districts I am in a position to provide trustworthy information regarding the size of the population.'
1930	45,679[9]	includes 1,389 'foreign orientals' and Europeans	Netherlands Indies census[10]	7 districts distinguished

1   Roselaar 1706.
2   P. Landauw and J.A. Veldhuis to C.L. Wieling, 10-11-1808 (ANRI Ternate 116).
3   Van der Hart 1853:113.
4   Van der Hart 1853:112.
5   Bosscher and Matthijssen 1854:94.
6   Bosscher and Matthijssen 1854:90.
7   De Clercq 1890:133.
8   Goedhart 1908:482. The peninsular districts were identified using the list provided by Goedhart (1908:454) elsewhere.
9   Volkstelling 1933-36, V:122, 134.
10   The 1920 census, unfortunately, gives only a combined figure for Luwuk and Banggai (Uitkomsten 1922:228-9).

an area located not far inland on the northern side of the Luwuk Peninsula and now known as Saluan (Aragon 1992:38), was described in 1854 as 'strong in population' and in 1863 as 'one of the most populous and best cultivated areas in the Gulf [of Tomini]'.[47] Just as the name Banggai is supposed to indicate dense settlement, finally, it is said that an alternative name for Balantak, Pokobondolong, originally meant 'very many people'.[48] In 1930, nevertheless, the average population density for the Luwuk area as a whole was only just over five persons per km^2.

Significant emigration from the Luwuk Peninsula, and especially from the Boalemo area on the north coast of Balantak, seems to have taken place from the seventeenth century onward. Ethnic Boalemo ('Tambelders') were present in Gorontalo and Buol, presumably as captives, in the 1680s, and probably also earlier.[49] More apparently joined them in Gorontalo after a Ternatan attack on their homeland in the second half of the eighteenth century (A.C. Kruyt 1930a:342, 352-3, 1932a:328). In the nineteenth century most of the Boalemo in Gorontalo settled in Tilamuta, on the south coast to the west of the capital (Riedel 1885b:519), subsequently giving their name to this area (and ultimately to the whole western half of the Gorontalo administrative area, including Paguat). Slaves, meanwhile, were exported or abducted on a regular basis from several parts of the Luwuk Peninsula in the mid-nineteenth century.[50] At least partly as a result of slave raiding, the population distribution around 1900 featured two long inhabited strips running parallel to the coast on both sides of the peninsula, but separated from it by five to ten kilometres of forest.[51] A similar pattern of coastal avoidance was found in Tobungku, in which context more will be said about it below.

Tobungku and Mori

Eastern Central Sulawesi – the prewar administrative subdivision of Kolonodale – comprised two large contiguous kingdoms: Tobungku (also known as Tombuku) on the east coast, and Mori (also known as Tomaiki)

[47]   AV Gorontalo 1854 (ANRI Gorontalo 3); Von Rosenberg 1865:53.
[48]   A.C. Kruyt 1932a:329. Like that of Banggai, this name was apparently bestowed by the Ternatans, who as nominal masters of the whole area had a strong interest in its manpower resources.
[49]   *Generale missiven* IV:511; Riedel 1885b:501. Riedel refers to Boalemo involvement in a war between Limboto and Gorontalo which other sources locate in the 1640s (*Corpus diplomaticum* III:56; Tiele and Heeres 1886-95, III:389-90).
[50]   Lapian 1980:145; AV Gorontalo 1865 (ANRI Gorontalo 3); Van der Hart 1853:106, 114; A.C. Kruyt 1930a:360, 1932a:342.
[51]   Van Musschenbroek 1880:96; Van Vuuren 1920, I:275; Wanner 1914:136. In Balantak, however, the distribution was more even (A.C. Kruyt 1932a:342).

in the interior. At the 1930 census, their combined population was just under 42,000 and their combined average population density very low at just over three persons per km^2 (*Volkstelling* 1933-36, V:156). No colonial official was stationed in this area until 1901 (Goedhart 1908:497). Mori was an independent state until its military conquest by the Dutch in 1907, and Tobungku technically a vassal of the Ternate sultanate until the transfer of both territories to the 'Government of Celebes and dependencies' (Makasar) in 1908 (*Koloniaal verslag* 1908:62-3). Not until 1924 did they officially become part of the residency of Manado (*Koloniaal verslag* 1925:26). The demographic record for Tobungku, nevertheless, stretches back to the seventeenth century, and benefits from the fact that this was a coastal polity without substantial dependencies inland. The Dutch envoys Bosscher and Matthijssen (1854:65) described it in 1853 as 'a narrow strip of land, washed to the east by the sea', and in 1906 its chiefs told another investigator that their authority reached only 24 hours' travel into the interior, or 'as far as the eye can see', before giving way to that of Mori and various tributaries of Luwu in South Sulawesi (Goedhart 1908:494). Despite fluctuations at its northern and southern extremities and uncertainty regarding the status of the central Tomori Bay, which at some periods formed an enclave controlled by Mori, its extent also seem to have been relatively constant.[52] Quantitative population data for Mori became available only at the beginning of the twentieth century and are too meagre, at three entries, to be worth tabulating. The figures for Tobungku will therefore be presented first (Table 16), followed by some shorter notes on Mori.

As in the case of Banggai (Table 14), the implication in Table 16 is a large population of perhaps 50,000 people at the end of the seventeenth century (the figure from circa 1706, when multiplied by 3.5, agrees quite well with that of 1678), declining substantially by 1850, and making only a very partial recovery by 1930. Qualitative sources support this picture of long-term demographic decline. At the beginning of the seventeenth century, Argensola (1992:83) wrote that the *gente de guerra* belonging to Tobungku (and Banggai) 'cannot be reduced to numbers'. But in 1851, Revius believed that Tobungku had a 'numerically weak population'.[53] Padtbrugge, in the diary of his sea journey along part of the Tobungku coast in 1678, wrote that he 'saw people and houses everywhere, and the land was for the most part planted and cultivated'.[54] Nineteenth-century accounts, by contrast, imply sparse settle-

---

[52]   De Clercq (1890:145-6) and Goedhart (1908:489) describe border disputes with Banggai and Kendari, Bosscher and Matthijssen (1854:65), Goedhart (1908:494, 522) and A.C. Kruyt (1900b: 448) the changing or uncertain status of the Tomori Bay. In 1853, the island of Manui was the southernmost Tobungku possession (Bosscher and Matthijssen 1854:71).
[53]   'Algemeen verslag omtrent de oostkust van Celebes,' 10-2-1851 (ANRI Ternate 180).
[54]   NA VOC 1345:284.

Table 16. Population data, Tobungku, 1678-1930

Year	Figure	Scope	Type of estimate	Other accuracy indications
1678	ca 43,000 people[1]	–	reconstruction from list of 'villages', with approximate sizes, compiled in situ by Padtbrugge[2]	'and this is very much believable, since we saw people and houses everywhere'; 65 villages distinguished, single average village size given for each of 3 groups (2-3,000 people, 100-200 *weerbare mannen*, 300-500 people)
ca 1706	13,500-14,500 *weerbare mannen*[3]	–	estimate by VOC governor Ternate (1701-1706) P. Roselaar, from unspecified sources[4]	11 *negeri* and one group of *negeri* distinguished; figures rounded to 100
1853	15,050 people[5]	southern Tobungku only; for the north 'the chiefs could give neither the names of the *negeri* (if any exist) nor the size of the population'	count carried out by order of Dutch envoys from Ternate (C. Bosscher and P.A. Matthijssen) by 'the various *sengaji* (*negeri* chiefs) in Tobungku	figures unrounded; 45 *negeri* distinguished; men/women/children distinguished; house numbers also given; 'We do not dare to decide whether these figures are entirely correct.'
1855	8,172 people[6]	–	figure supplied to Dutch by sultan of Ternate	single undivided figure; 'Not much value can be attached to the population figures for the territory of the sultans. [...] The vanity of these kings usually means that such figures are inflated.'
1865	7,987[7]	–	probably as above	single aggregate figure
1870	7,934[8]	–	probably as above	single aggregate figure
1872	7,891[9]	–	probably as above	single aggregate figure
1906[10]	3,416 *weerbare mannen*[11]	includes 200-250 Bajo, ±325' Bugis/Makasar and 278 other nonindigenous Indonesian men; excludes about 20 'foreign orientals'	figures obtained in situ by visiting Dutch investigator (indigenous count)	38 subdistricts and 6 foreign ethnic groups distinguished; figures mostly unrounded

1930[12]	26,548[13]	includes 259 'foreign orientals'
		Netherlands Indies census

1 NA VOC 1345:282-4.
2 8 *dorpen* at 2,500 people each, plus 23 at 150 *weerbare mannen* each (multiplied here by 3.5 to convert to total population), plus 27 at 400 people each.
3 Roselaar 1706.
4 Probably, however, from the same sources on Banggai which supplied the accompanying estimate for Mandono (Luwuk) in 1705 (Roselaar 1706).
5 Bosscher and Matthijssen 1854:71-2; also reproduced by Bleeker (1856:267-9).
6 Quarles van Ufford 1856:65.
7 AV Ternate 1865 (ANRI Ternate 162).
8 AV Ternate 1870 (ANRI Ternate 162).
9 AV Ternate 1872 (ANRI Ternate 162).
10 Date according to Goedhart (1908:473).
11 Goedhardt 1908:514-18.
12 The 1920 census, unfortunately, gives only a combined figure for Bungku and Mori (*Uitkomsten* 1922:228-9).
13 *Volkstelling* 1933-36, V:134.

ment and describe the hills behind the coast as 'inhospitable and infertile' (Bosscher and Matthijssen 1854:67).

In the nineteenth century only a minority of the population, despite its generally coastal distribution, lived directly by the sea. Of the 36 *kampung* listed in a description of the kingdom by De Clercq (resident of Ternate, 1885-1888), two were said to lie on offshore islands, eight on the coast, two 'in the mountains', and fully 24 'a short distance inland' (De Clercq 1890:142-3). This habit of keeping a certain distance from the shore had also been noted by Bosscher and Matthijssen, who explained it in terms of coastal malaria.

> The population is sparse and lives mostly in the hills; a few *negeri* are found on the coast, but these are relocated from time to time when the sicknesses typical of these swampy areas have raged for a time with unusual strength and decimated the population, instilling in it an aversion to its existing place of residence. (Bosscher and Matthijssen 1854:67.)

Another factor here was seaborne violence. A series of rebellions by the *raja* of Tobungku and Banggai against the sultan of Ternate, and the establishment of Magindanao and Tobelo pirate colonies in the area, had made the coasts of eastern Central Sulawesi increasingly dangerous places to live in the first decades of the nineteenth century.[55] By the time Van der Hart (1853:268) circumnavigated the island in 1850, the whole stretch of coast from Kendari to Balantak appeared to him to be 'completely deserted, the population having withdrawn into the interior or moved elsewhere'. In the same year, Revius was shown patches of 'open terrain' on the shores of the Tomori Bay where villages had stood until quite recently.[56]

In view of this evidence for demographic movement, it is reasonable to ask whether the depopulation of Tobungku between 1706 and 1853 can be explained in terms of migration to Mori, the population of which was described in the 1850s as very large compared to that of its coastal neighbour.[57] Many people certainly seem to have been forcibly displaced from Tobungku to Mori during wars between the two kingdoms in the mid-nineteenth century (Lapian 1980:134; Uhlenbeck 1861:4). An inland polity located in the La and Lembo basins between Tobungku and the Poso Valley, Mori is seldom mentioned in European sources from before 1900, although in 1856 it was the target of a Dutch military expedition launched at the request of Tobungku (Uhlenbeck 1861; Weitzel 1883). In 1906, on the eve of its definitive conquest by the Dutch,

---

[55]   AV Manado 1852 (ANRI Manado 51); A. Revius, 'Algemeen verslag omtrent de oostkust van Celebes', 10-2-1851 (ANRI Ternate 180); Bleeker 1856:264-70; De Clercq 1890:174-8; Van der Hart 1853:106, 218; Velthoen 1997b:374-5, 378-82.

[56]   'Algemeen verslag omtrent de oostkust van Celebes', 10-2-1851 (ANRI Ternate 180).

[57]   'Algemeen verslag omtrent de oostkust van Celebes', 10-2-1851 (ANRI Ternate 180); Uhlenbeck 1861:51; Weitzel 1883:35.

it yielded two remarkably detailed indigenous population counts. The first was recited by Marundu, the paramount *raja* of Mori, to a Minahasan colonial official; this specified a total of 4,761 *weerbare mannen* (Maengkom 1907:864-8). The second, elicited by a Dutch investigator partly from Marundu and partly from other chiefs, indicated a total of 4,060 indigenous fighting men, together with about another 1,150 Bugis and other foreign Indonesians.[58] Both results, multiplied by 3.5, suggest a total population of around 17-18,000 people – slightly more than at the 1930 census, which counted just over 15,000.[59]

Since the same harsh resettlement policy applied in other parts of Central Sulawesi was also followed in Mori after the conquest of 1907 (Tillema 1922:231), it is not surprising that there was some decline over this period. Given earlier reports of a large population, and the claim by Albert Kruyt in 1908 that Mori was 'much more densely populated' than the Poso Valley (*Brieven*, 2-11-1908), it is in fact tempting to conclude that the two 1906 figures were much too low. The Dutch official who recorded one of them, however, also took the rare precaution of attempting to verify it, both 'with the help of Bugis traders who have often been in the Mori interior', and 'by personally asking some tribal chiefs to give the names of their subjects'. The outcome, he claimed, 'spoke for the reliability of the information provided to me by Marundu and the others'.[60] If this is correct, then the average population density in Mori was only about three persons per km^2 at the turn of the century.[61] Some localities, notably the Lembo Depression and the hills separating it from the valley of the River La, were no doubt more densely settled (J. Kruyt 1924:34-5, 57-8), but there were also large areas of wilderness (Adriani 1919:30). The northernmost part of Mori, for instance, seems to have been uninhabited until the *damar* trading boom made its forests attractive to resin collectors around 1870 (Goedhart 1908:521; A.C. Kruyt 1900b:437). It is unlikely, then, that the long-term depopulation of Tobungku can be accounted for simply by a redistribution of the population in favour of Mori and the interior. The combined population of Tobungku and Mori together in 1930, at just under 42,000, was still smaller than that of Tobungku alone according to the estimates of 1678 and circa 1706 in Table 16. Nor, to my knowledge, is

[58] Goedhart 1908:532-6. The foreign Indonesians were mostly temporary migrants collecting *damar* in the forests. As published by Goedhart, this count specified only a few broad ethnic categories. In its original form, however, it was probably as detailed as that described by Maengkom.

[59] *Volkstelling* 1933-36, V:134. This figure includes 181 'foreign orientals' and Europeans.

[60] Goedhart 1908:536. A few years earlier, Kruyt and Adriani had also commented on the 'great accuracy which characterized the statements by the king of the country, Marundu, which we were able to check' (Kruyt 1900b:436).

[61] This calculation assumes a total of 5,000 *weerbare mannen* (x 3.5 = 17,500 people), and an area equivalent to that of the modern *kecamatan* of Lembo, Petasia and Mori Atas combined, or 5,462 km^2 (*Sulawesi Tengah* 1992:6-7).

there any evidence that large numbers of people emigrated to more distant areas in the intervening period. Depopulation, then, must have been the result of in situ processes affecting fertility and mortality.

Summary

Except for Banggai and the Palu Valley, Central Sulawesi at the beginning of the twentieth century was less densely populated than North Sulawesi, and much less so than Sangir and Talaud. As in the north, the population distribution was very uneven; here, however, important demographic concentrations were found not only in upland valleys and on offshore islands, but also in coastal lowland areas. Several parts of Central Sulawesi had been more populous in the more or less distant past: the population of Banggai, for instance, was larger in 1700 than in 1930, and that of Tobungku probably twice as large. The Tomini coastlands, too, saw considerable depopulation during the eighteenth century, although in this case migration (to Gorontalo) was a key factor. The population of the central uplands, and particularly the Poso Valley, seems to have declined in quite a sustained way in the second half of the nineteenth century, and qualitative evidence suggests that this was the continuation of a much older depopulation trend.

CHAPTER VII

Death and disease

Chapters IV-VI aimed to reconstruct the general patterns of demographic history in each part of the region; a recapitulation of the results will appear, together with a global attempt to explain them, in Chapters XI and XII. First, however, it is necessary to take a systematic look at the direct historical evidence regarding the factors controlling rates of demographic change. Chapters VII-IX, accordingly, deal with mortality and its determinants, and Chapter X with patterns of reproductive fertility.

Sources

A reasonably long series of annual birth and death statistics, it must be said at the outset, is available only for Minahasa, where these were collected by the Dutch authorities from 1849 onward.[1] Even here, moreover, the surviving record becomes incomplete beyond 1872, and all data from the early twentieth century have been lost. This deficiency, however, is compensated to some extent by a separate demographic (and medical) survey of five Minahasan districts organized by the physician Kündig in the years 1930-1932, the results of which are reproduced here as Appendix H. Three earlier Dutch investigations into the reproductive history of indigenous women, meanwhile, also shed light on patterns of both fertility and child mortality. The comprehensive report on the economic situation in Minahasa produced by A.C.J. Edeling in 1875, firstly, includes a survey of the numbers of children ever-born, and still living, among a sample of more than 8,500 households distributed over 14 named districts (Appendix E). While it is not clear exactly how these figures were obtained, they provide vital clues to

---

[1]   In 1925 an attempt was also made to introduce birth and death registers in all other parts of the region. Most areas, however, were found to be 'not yet ripe' for this, and in 1930 it was discontinued except for Minahasa and the port settlements of Gorontalo, Taruna (Greater Sangir), and Donggala (A.Ph. van Aken 1932:211). None of the resulting figures, unfortunately, are available today.

the causes of population growth in the colonial period.[2] In 1902, secondly, Albert Kruyt (1903b:197-8) or his assistants questioned nearly 500 post-meno-pausal women in Poso and Tojo regarding the number of children which they had borne and the proportion of these which had died 'as small children' (Appendix F). In 1924, finally, the same procedure was repeated, this time by mission schoolteachers, with almost all of the married women (nearly 12,000 of them in total, spread over 181 villages) living in that part of Central Sulawesi where the NZG was active. A small selection from the results of this very extensive survey, organized at the request of visiting hygiene expert H.F. Tillema, is reproduced here as Appendix G.[3]

The Edeling, Kruyt, Tillema, and Kündig reports, together with the vital rate statistics from Minahasa in the years 1849-1872, provide key points of reference for my examination of the factors affecting birth and death rates. Most often, however, it is not possible to investigate these factors on a strict-ly statistical basis, and the discussion in this and the following chapters is organized thematically rather than as an analysis of data series. The factors affecting the death rate can be divided into four categories: natural hazards, human violence, disease, and nutrition. The first three of these are dealt with in that sequence below, while Chapter VIII deals with the impact of colonial medicine and other forms of disease control, and Chapter IX with the food supply.

Natural hazards

Minahasa and the Sangir Islands, it was noted in Chapter I, both contained concentrations of active volcanoes. Those of Minahasa were seldom very dangerous to human life – although a VOC document does record that in 1694 the mountain Dua Saudara, on the northeast coast, erupted with a blast that was audible in Ambon, 'throwing out over all the lands of Manado such a quantity of ash that the roofs of many houses collapsed' (Godée Molsbergen 1928:89). The volcanoes of Sangir, by contrast, regularly took many lives. An eruption of Mount Awu on Greater Sangir in 1711, accord-

---

[2]   Edeling himself notes only that 'these statistics were collected only in a small number of places', suggesting that in most districts only a few villages were sampled ('Memorie omtrent de Minahasa', 13-8-1875, in NA V 17-4-1877/20). The total number of people (including children) covered by the survey was approximately 40,000; the total population of Minahasa at the same date, by comparison, was just over 120,000.
[3]   Adriani and Kruyt 1950-51, II:339; Tillema 1926:25-47. Of the *kampung* included in this sur-vey, 64 lay beyond the boundary of the residency of Manado and technically outside the scope of this study. Their inhabitants, however, were related to the other Toraja groups in ethnic terms, and all have been included in my calculations in order to keep the database large.

ing to a VOC sergeant who witnessed it, killed almost 3,000 people (Keijzer 1856:190-1); in 1812 the same volcano claimed perhaps another thousand victims, in 1856 a reported 2,806, and in 1892 at least 1,532.[4] In 1912 a subsidiary peak of the dormant volcano Sahendaruman, in the southern part of Greater Sangir, erupted and buried a nearby village, killing 117 people (*Koloniaal verslag* 1913:26). In 1871, an eruption of the island volcano Ruang generated a giant wave which drowned more than 400 people on the coasts of nearby Tagulandang.[5] The volcanoes of Sangir and Minahasa, on the other hand, were great assets in terms of their contribution to soil fertility (Chapter XI), and the fact that both areas were densely populated suggests that the destruction which they periodically brought about was not a particularly important demographic factor.

Earthquakes are frequent in most parts of the region, but do not often seem to have caused great numbers of human casualties. In Minahasa the most severe earthquake of the nineteenth century, that of 1845, killed 'about 100 people' in collapsing houses – although many more would have died if it had happened at night.[6] Miangas and Nanusa, in the far north, lay just within the Philippine typhoon belt and were occasionally hit by destructive storms, one of which killed about 30 people and caused much damage to crops and houses in 1904.[7] Flooding sometimes caused loss of life, and frequently crop and livestock losses, in low-lying areas like the Limboto Depression.[8] There were no tigers or other dangerous carnivorous mammals in Sulawesi, but bathers and fishermen were regularly killed by crocodiles in river mouths and in the Limboto and Poso lakes, where these animals were particularly common.[9] The most important natural hazard, however, was the unpredictability of the weather and its effects upon crop yields, which will be considered separately in Chapter IX.

---

[4]   Van Delden 1844:372; A.J.F. Jansen 1856:379; Steller 1866:12; Kemmerling 1923-24, I:24-9; *Koloniaal verslag* 1893:24.

[5]   Coolsma 1901:642-3; Kemmerling 1923-24, I:78; *Koloniaal verslag* 1871:13.

[6]   J.J. ten Siethoff, 'Topografische schetsen van een gedeelte der residentie Manado, 1845' (ANRI Manado 46). In western Central Sulawesi – also a very earthquake-prone area – most houses, apparently for extra stability (Boonstra van Heerdt 1914a:628; Schuyt 1913:365), were elevated on frames of horizontal logs rather than on the more conventional vertical piles.

[7]   *Koloniaal verslag* 1905:67; Lam 1932:43; *Nanoesa-eilanden* 1905:314.

[8]   *Koloniaal verslag* 1907:70, 1920:126; Moolenburgh 1921:4; Morison 1931:8.

[9]   Graafland 1898, I:48; A.C. Kruyt 1935:3-7; Van Doren 1857-60, II:375; Von Rosenberg 1865: 52, 68. Coastal settlements, apparently, were sometimes moved due to the frequency of crocodile attacks in their vicinity (Wilken and Schwarz 1867a:7, 35). Large pythons, in addition, occasionally killed children, and often livestock, in Minahasa (Graafland 1898, I:46; MV Manado April 1861, in ANRI Manado 54).

Warfare and ritual killing

Northern Sulawesi was a violent place in precolonial times. Only three parts of the region, Sangir (but not Talaud), Gorontalo, and Banggai, seem to have enjoyed freedom from internal war in the first part of the nineteenth century (Chapter I); in the case of Banggai, moreover, the absence of organized headhunting may have been compensated to some extent by the frequency of other forms of violence associated with individual and family feuding (A.C. Kruyt 1932c:249-53, 1932f:739-41). In the stateless areas, most nuclear settlements were built in strategic locations and more or less permanently fortified.[10] The villages of the Poso Valley, for instance (Chapter III, Plate 11), were each located 'on the ridge of a hill, with a difficult access path' (Adriani 1913b:860), and resembled 'great crows' nests' (Van Höevell 1893b:20). Sometimes even individual swidden houses were made defensible (A.C. Kruyt 1930a:431). Adult men carried weapons whenever they left their houses.[11] This habit persisted in pacified Minahasa until the 1870s (Tendeloo 1873:16-7), although it had apparently disappeared by the 1890s (Sarasin and Sarasin 1905, I:47).

On the basis of his early impressions in Central Sulawesi, Albert Kruyt (1903b:192) initially concluded that the general sparsity of the population 'must be attributed in the first place to the many wars which were fought here in the past'. Local oral history related numerous episodes in which settlements, and even whole ethnic groups, were said to have been wiped out in conflicts with their neighbours.[12] On closer inspection, however, the number of casualties caused by headhunting wars turned out to be smaller than such stories suggested. The largest number of skulls which Adriani and Kruyt (1900:207) ever found in a single *lobo* or village temple was fourteen. In a decade of continuous conflict between the To Napu (in Lore) and the To Onda'e (on the eastern shore of Lake Poso) over the period 1892-1902, the two missionaries counted a total of 194 deaths on both sides.[13] On an annual basis, this corresponds to about three deaths for every thousand members of the groups involved: a significant depletion, but still a surprisingly low mortality

---

[10]   Adriani and Kruyt 1912-14, I:149, 214-5, II:165; Graafland 1867-69, I:69, 271-2; *Fragment* 1856: 27, 69; Kaudern 1925:376-80; Kortleven 1927:52; A.C. Kruyt 1900b:459, 1938, II:1, 136-7; Riedel 1872d:156, 1886:81; J.J. ten Siethoff, 'Topografische schetsen van een gedeelte der residentie Manado, 1845' (ANRI Manado 46); Watuseke and Henley 1994:372.

[11]   AV Gorontalo 1841-1843 (ANRI Manado 50); Cuarteron 1855:101; Van Delden 1844:380; Goedhart 1908:537; Graafland 1867-69, I:311; Grubauer 1913:386; Pietermaat, De Vriese and Lucas 1840:136; Van Thije 1689; Vosmaer 1839:94; Wilken and Schwarz 1867c:349.

[12]   Adriani 1913b:862; Adriani and Kruyt 1912-14:29, 37, 40, 43-5, 73, 85-6, 120, 138, 227-8, 1950-51, I:77, 331; Engelenberg 1906:10; Goedhart 1908:535; Van Hoëvell 1891:29-30; A.C. Kruyt 1900: 462, 1903:191-2, 1908:1278-9, 1322, 1338, 1909:367, 1938, I:94-6, 196, 202-3, 211, 236-7, 256.

[13]   Adriani and Kruyt 1950-51, I:330. This war finally ended in 1905 (A.C. Kruyt 1908:1274).

rate for a war which local people insisted had been 'one of the bloodiest'.[14] Half a century earlier, Revius had also observed that the domestic wars of Central Sulawesi, although frequent, tended not to be very bloody.

> They are constantly at war with their neighbours, robbing and plundering each other, so that security is an unknown concept. Yet in recent years there have been few examples of complete conquest and subjugation of one kingdom by another. For this their military strength is insufficient, and their subjects too unwilling to engage in lengthy wars, restricting themselves instead to occasional raids and expeditions lasting a few days.[15]

Throughout the region pitched battles, although not unknown, were said to be rare.[16] The typical conflict, observed Kruyt (1895-97, II:109), 'resembles a guerilla war'. In view of such observations, he and Adriani later revised their original view on the demographic impact of warfare in Central Sulawesi. 'War and headhunting', concluded Adriani in 1915 and Kruyt in 1950, 'were not as important as one might imagine as direct reasons for the sparseness of the population, because the battles were seldom bloody and if ten people died as a result of a headhunt, that was already a large number'.[17]

Where settlements had indeed vanished as a result of warfare, most of their inhabitants had probably fled elsewhere or been taken into captivity. During the conflict between Mori and Tobungku in the 1850s, Mori warriors reportedly 'carried away the population of whole *kampung* into the interior as slaves'.[18] While adult male prisoners were usually killed, women and children were typically spared, and either incorporated into the victors' communities as slaves, or returned to their own in exchange for a ransom, itself often also paid in slaves.[19] Since polygamy was everywhere permissible (see Chapter X), the fact that most of those killed were men makes it particularly unlikely that battle casualties as such had much demographic impact. Another convention, according to Padtbrugge's description of seventeenth-century Minahasa, even protected stored food supplies:

[14]   Adriani and Kruyt 1912-14, I:227. Although contemporary figures are not available, the population of Napu at that time was probably at least 4,000 (Adriani 1919:23), and that of Onda'e perhaps 2,500 (*Volkstelling* 1933-36, V:134).
[15]   'Algemeen Verslag omtrent de oostkust van Celebes', 10-2-1851 (ANRI Ternate 180).
[16]   Adriani and Kruyt 1912-14, I:218-9; Goedhart 1908:538; Graafland 1867-69, I:274; A.C. Kruyt 1938, II:142-3; Padtbrugge 1866:319.
[17]   Adriani 1915:459; Adriani and Kruyt 1950-51, I:77. The first edition of *De Bare'e-sprekende Torajas* (Adriani and Kruyt 1912-14, I:85-6) still repeats Kruyt's original view.
[18]   Lapian 1980:134. Another source, however, states that it was customary for victors to enslave only 'five or six persons in every hundred' (Riedel 1886:90).
[19]   NA VOC 1366:160; Adriani and Kruyt 1912-14, I:220-23, 1950-51, I:339-42; A.C. Kruyt 1908: 1292, 1938, II:156-9. Older women, however, were also killed (Adriani and Kruyt 1912-14, I: 221).

The defeated party becomes completely subject to the victors and must dance to their tune, retaining only the rice which it has stored in its houses, while any standing crops are destroyed. The winners, however, take great care not to destroy the stored rice and will therefore also refrain from burning down defeated villages, which if it does happen is usually the work of Europeans participating in the attack. Women and children, finally, are carried away as prisoners, but readily freed again, with or without a ransom payment, once peace is restored. Any men who do not manage to escape, however, are killed, regardless of age. (Padtbrugge 1866:318.)

'Rules of engagement' like these, admittedly, must be interpreted as normative ideals rather than binding restrictions; *controleur* De Clercq (1870b:5), while claiming that in principle the killing of women in war had always been 'absolutely forbidden' by Minahasan custom, noted that it had sometimes happened nonetheless. Many other sources from Minahasa and elsewhere, moreover, indicate that women were in fact regarded as legitimate targets for headhunters, and that villages were frequently burned down.[20] On occasion, the loss of life was undoubtedly significant for individual communities. In 1789 one Minahasan village lost 62 men, apparently more than two thirds of its adult male population, in a headhunting war (Godée Molsbergen 1928: 136). But on the whole it still seems clear that wars in northern Sulawesi were much less destructive than their counterparts in Java and mainland Southeast Asia, upon which Reid (1987:42-3, 1988-93, I:17-18) bases his conclusion that warfare was the most important factor limiting population growth in precolonial Southeast Asia.

The extent to which small-scale violence nevertheless contributed indirectly to high death rates, by causing or exacerbating shortages of food and outbreaks of disease (effects emphasized by Reid), is difficult to judge. In the conflict between Napu and Onda'e, certainly, lives were lost 'both to the sword of the enemy and to the famine which resulted from that war' (Adriani and Kruyt 1912-14, I:87), and in 1708, 'all the coconuts' in the Palu Valley were reported to have been consumed as famine food during a local war.[21] The typical headhunting conflict, however, was a seasonal affair, 'a sort of sport', engaged in when 'the rice barns had just been filled after the harvest' (A.C. Kruyt 1938, II:56, 141). Disease and lack of water (in many

---

[20]   Adriani 1913b:862; A.C. Kruyt 1899b:185, 1912-14, I:213, II:398, 1950-51, I:244, 317; Van der Crab 1875:365; Gallas 1900:813; Godée Molsbergen 1928:124; *Generale missiven* III:327; A.C. Kruyt 1938, I:56, 77, 81, 108, 129, 300, 302; Padtbrugge 1866:319; Sarasin and Sarasin 1905, II:90; Vosmaer 1839:87, 106.

[21]   NA VOC 1775:107. Many Dutch sources from Minahasa also mention reduced food production as a result of warfare (NA VOC 1221:219r, 3119:32; Godée Molsbergen 1928:32, 157; Van Mijlendonk 1756; Watuseke and Henley 1994:372), although it is likely that these actually relate in the first place to disruption of rice transport between the uplands and the fort at Manado.

cases, no doubt, related problems) were sometimes reasons for the surrender of a besieged village, and hygiene in the fortified hilltop settlements was problematic even during peacetime (Chapter VIII). But no major epidemic in the historical record seems to have been triggered by war. Routine food production may well have been depressed to some extent: the continual threat of war, according to Adriani (1915:459), 'prevented people from devoting themselves fully to agriculture'. Sago and coconut trees, for instance, could be planted only in the immediate vicinity of the fortified villages, since at any outbreak of violence, 'the first work of the enemy was to destroy his opponent's plantations'.[22] However, the fact that Minahasa was already the region's major exporter of food (rice) at a time when it was still in a state of endemic war (Chapter II) weakens this argument, at least as a generalization. To the extent that war and commerce were alternative ways for male swidden farmers to fill up their 'free' time, conflict was arguably more a result than a cause of limited commercial opportunities (Chapter I). Doubts regarding the demographic significance of war, finally, are strengthened by the fact that the long-term population trends reconstructed in Chapters IV-VI show little association with conditions of war and peace; this argument will be presented in Chapter XII.

Closely connected with the ritual aspects of war was human sacrifice, practised following harvest failures and other disasters, during the construction of important new buildings, to mark the conclusion of peace agreements and alliances, or, most often, in connection with the funerals or other life-cycle ceremonies of members of the social elite.[23] If the relatives of a dead Minahasan chief, for instance, could not obtain enemy heads to accompany him in his grave, they killed one or more of their own slaves instead (Pietermaat, De Vriese and Lucas 1840:130). Judging by later evidence from Central Sulawesi (A.C. Kruyt 1911:64, 1938, I:513), sacrificial victims were usually individuals recently purchased from other groups for that purpose. When one of the first European visitors to Sulawesi, the Spaniard Andrés de Urdaneta, arrived in Banggai from the Moluccas in 1532, he found that the local ruler (a woman) had recently died, and 'in the 40 days or so that I stayed there they killed more than 150 men and women, saying that these were

[22] Adriani and Kruyt 1950-51, III:211. In the Palu Valley where timber was scarce (Chapter XIII), large numbers of coconut trees were also felled in times of war for their wood which was used to build fortifications (Blok 1848:63).
[23] NA VOC 1758:454, 2099:1030, 1049; Adriani 1901:241; Adriani and Kruyt 1912-14, I:139, II: 74, 105-9, 1950-51, I:346, II:523-7, III:75; *Corpus diplomaticum* V:394; Van Dinter 1899:379; Godée Molsbergen 1928:91, 138-9, 143-4; Graafland 1867-69, I:286-7; Kaudern 1940:96; A.C. Kruyt 1908:1302, 1909:366, 380, 1938, I:513, III:464, 476-92, IV:131-4; *Nota berglandschappen* 1912:11-2; Pietermaat, De Vriese and Lucas 1840:118, 130; Riedel 1872b:504; Sarasin and Sarasin 1905, II:45-6, 54, 78, 80, 83, 113-4, 123-5; Tauchmann 1968:188-96; Watuseke and Henley 1994:373; Woensdregt 1928:248.

needed to accompany the queen in the other world' (De Urdaneta 1837:437). This, however, was an extreme case. In Minahasa at the beginning of the nineteenth century, even according to later hearsay evidence, twelve victims was already 'an exceptionally large number' to join a chief in the afterlife.[24] Marta, describing Siau in the 1580s, stated only that the death of a principal was followed by the sacrifice of 'one of his or her slaves' (Jacobs 1974-84, II:266), and Woodard (1969:116), describing Kaili in the 1790s, agreed that it was customary to kill 'a [one] woman or girl' at the funeral of a *raja*.[25]

Another common type of violence was the killing of those individuals, referred to in the Dutch sources as 'witches' and 'werewolves', who were believed to have harmed their neighbours by magical means. On Banggai the killing of witches was said to have been 'the order of the day' in precolonial times (A.C. Kruyt 1932c:249), and on Talaud they were customarily buried alive.[26] Adriani (1901:245) judged that the witchcraft trials of the Toraja, while 'less notorious than their headhunts', nevertheless took 'many more lives'. In the small Tongko River basin east of Poso (Chapter I, Map 5), according to Kruyt (1899d:558), four werewolves were executed in the month of February 1897 alone. In later publications, nevertheless, the two missionaries concluded that such executions were 'still not so numerous that the population was perceptibly reduced as a result' (Adriani 1915:459; Adriani and Kruyt 1950-51, I:77). In the absence of further data, this judgement cannot be contested.

The expansion of Dutch power in northern Sulawesi, although partly based on military capability, was a mostly peaceful process driven by indigenous rivalries and the local desire for protection against domestic and external enemies.[27] Except during the Tondano War of 1808-1809, there was little violence between the Dutch and their subjects in those areas directly under their control.[28] Naval expeditions, occasionally sent out to punish nominal vassals further afield who failed to honour the terms of their political contracts, seldom succeeded in doing more than burning down empty coastal settlements; these were typically evacuated as soon as the attackers approached, and

---

[24]   Van Doren 1854-56, II:113. Other writers agree that the typical number was much lower (Pietermaat, De Vriese and Lucas 1840:130; Van Spreeuwenberg 1845-46:306; Van Thije 1689). Bickmore (1868:375), on the other hand, states on the basis of retrospective local accounts that 30-40 heads were sometimes taken for a single 'festive occasion'.

[25]   Aragon (1992:57), during her fieldwork among the Tobaku (western Central Sulawesi) in the 1980s, was told that human sacrifice had formerly been practised only once every 10-20 years. In a nearby area, Sarasin and Sarasin (1905, II:125) reported one ritual killing per year.

[26]   Cuarteron 1855:9; Hickson 1889:167; Jellesma 1911:1239; Weber-Van Bosse 1904:124.

[27]   Henley 1993; Schrauwers 1997:375-6; Watuseke and Henley 1994:359-60.

[28]   In 1827, 11 people died during the capture of a rebel noble and his retinue in Gorontalo (AR Gorontalo to Res. Manado, 3-11-1827, in ANRI Manado 114). In 1893, what was likewise regarded as a fairly serious local revolt on Karakelang in Talaud collapsed after the loss of only 3 lives to Dutch bullets (*Koloniaal verslag* 1894:29).

rebuilt after they left (R. Scherius 1847:401; *Zakelijk verslag* 1860:116-7). When military confrontations did occur, conversely, the organizational, technological, and often (thanks to local allies and auxiliaries) numerical superiority of the Dutch forces usually gave them a swift victory without much loss of life on either side. When a VOC force of more than 1,300 (mostly Indonesian) men conquered rebellious Gorontalo in 1681, only 29 defenders and four attackers died.[29] In 1856 the fortress of Ensa ndau in Mori was captured in a single day's fighting by an expeditionary force of some 900 men (again, only 30 of them Europeans), apparently with the loss of only four dead (and eight wounded) among its defenders, and one soldier dead on the Dutch side.[30]

There were some exceptions to this rule of not very bloody colonial expansion. A raid on Gorontalo by the Dutch and their Ternatan allies in 1648, as noted in Chapter V, apparently killed as many as 4,000 local people.[31] The Minahasan revolt at the beginning of the nineteenth century cost many lives, the defenders of the besieged water village at Tondano enduring nine months of Dutch attacks, and ultimately also famine, before their defeat.[32] In February 1809, just two months into the siege, it was reported that 'more than 100 people have already died in the *negeri*' (Godée Molsbergen 1928:168), and an unknown number of men and women were 'cruelly massacred' by Ternatan troops during the final Dutch attack.[33] The final military subjugation of Central Sulawesi in the years 1905-1907 was also relatively violent; in the Poso area a total of 38 people were killed and 50 wounded, in Mori about 100 died, and in the Palu Valley about 60.[34] For the most part, however, the scale of colonial violence in the region does not seem to have exceeded that already prevalent in indigenous society.

---

[29]   NA VOC 1366:871; *Daghregister* 1681:587; *Generale missiven* IV:514; Godée Molsbergen 1928:84. A 'large number' of people were also wounded.

[30]   Weitzel 1883:36, 49, 52-3. Another source, however, mentions a preliminary clash in which 'considerable' losses were inflicted by the Dutch force (Uhlenbeck 1861:48).

[31]   NA VOC 1170:763v, VOC 1320:150; Tiele and Heeres 1886-95, III:358-9, 388-90.

[32]   Godée Molsbergen 1928:165-9; Mambu 1986:56-81; Mangindaän 1873:367-9; Supit 1986:154-94.

[33]   L. Weintre to Res. Ternate, 7-8-1809 (ANRI Manado 61).

[34]   Arts and Van Beurden 1982:102; Coté 1996:97; *Koloniaal verslag* 1908:63. It is not clear whether the figures given by Coté for Poso include another 7 killed and 2 wounded in a previous incident (*Koloniaal verslag* 1906:62). A total of 16 people had also been killed in 1902 during resistance to the establishment of Dutch power in Bolaang Mongondow (*Koloniaal verslag* 1903:91).

Health and stature

In rejecting disease as a major reason for low population growth in precolonial Southeast Asia, Reid (1987:37-8) points out that European travellers
frequently commented on the large stature and healthy appearance of its
inhabitants. Early European visitors to Kalimantan, confirms Knapen (2001:
155), typically encountered 'stout and healthy men and women'. Comments
of this type are not hard to find in early accounts of northern Sulawesi either.
The 'people of Celebes' were described by a Portuguese Jesuit in 1576 as
'large and well-built' (C. Wessels 1933:381), the Sangirese by another missionary in 1631 as 'very vigorous and strong' (Jacobs 1974-84, III:476), and the
Minahasans by Padtbrugge (1866:309) in 1679 as 'strong and sound of limb'.

In colonial times, Minahasa in particular continued to enjoy a reputation
for the good health of its population.[35] In 1821, the naturalist Reinwardt
(1858:582) described Minahasans as 'generally very healthy, robust and
strong'.[36] Wallace (1987:185, 197), in 1859, likewise found them a 'stout and
well-made' people, inhabiting a 'beautiful and healthy country'. In 1824
another European visitor had even claimed that in Minahasa 'one never sees
a hunchbacked, stooped, crooked, disformed, lame, twisted or in any other
way disfigured person', and that its population was 'little subject to disease
or any form of illness' (Olivier 1834-37, II:37). Several other areas also made
a healthy impression at this period, at least on visitors seeing them for the
first time. On an expedition to the interior of Mongondow in 1857, Riedel
(1864b:281-3) admired the 'fine physiques' and 'healthy appearance' of its
inhabitants, reporting that neither epidemics nor 'ordinary sicknesses' were
common there.[37] In Central Sulawesi, he later wrote, Toraja men were also
'strongly built', reaching a height of 168 cm, and Toraja women, at 156 cm,
'slim and well-formed'.[38] At the beginning of the twentieth century the first
colonial administrators of the Palu area found that in the valley the health
situation was 'generally good' (Hissink 1912:80), while in the surrounding
mountains it even left 'little to be desired'.[39] The Sarasins (1905, II:19) also
judged the population of the upland part of the Palu Trench through which

[35]　Bik 1864:169; Bleeker 1856:23; Van Doren 1854-56, I:267-8, II:111; Francis 1860:310; Van der
Hart 1853:172; Kam 1821:281; Kükenthal 1896:236; Pietermaat, De Vriese and Lucas 1840:117; L.
van Rhijn 1851:279, 393; J.J. ten Siethoff, 'Topografische schetsen van een gedeelte der residentie
Menado, 1845' (ANRI Manado 46); Van Spreeuwenberg 1845-46, II:307; Van de Velde 1845:50.
[36]　'Diseases', this source adds, 'are little known among them; the only ailments to which they
are subject seem to be a number of skin diseases' (Reinwardt 1858:597).
[37]　In Buol too, according to Riedel, the population was 'generally healthy' and 'strong, slim
and well-built' (Riedel 1872a:197, 201).
[38]　Riedel 1886:78. It is not clear whether these figures represent averages or maxima.
[39]　*Nota berglandschappen* 1912:8. 'Their modes of life are simple, and their disorders are few',
Woodard (1969:100) had written in the 1790s.

they passed in 1902 to be 'strong, healthy and well-nourished'.

Even at first sight, on the other hand, not all parts of the region struck colonial observers as equally fortunate in this respect. On their visit to eastern Central Sulawesi in 1852, Bosscher and Matthijssen (1854:74) found that while the health situation in the interior was 'not unfavourable', that of the coastal population, which suffered heavily from 'stomach diseases, skin ailments, and intermittent fevers [malaria]', was 'the more deplorable'. Conditions on the Banggai Islands were particularly bad:

> On Banggai [proper], which consists almost entirely of swamp, malevolent fevers reign almost the whole year round, killing many of the inhabitants and giving others a sickly and weak appearance. The inhabitants of Peling, where there is an almost complete lack of good drinking water (what there is is brackish and turbid), are much afflicted by stomach illness [buikloop] and plagued by skin diseases, which give both men and women a repulsive appearance. (Bosscher and Matthijssen 1854:96-7.)

Van Delden's description of the Sangirese in 1825, while more nuanced, also paints a much less positive picture than do the accounts of Minahasa, Mongondow and western Central Sulawesi cited above.[40]

> Their height is moderate [matig] and they appear to have quite a strong physique. They are susceptible, however, to a variety of illnesses, such as hot and cold fevers, bloedpersingen [dysentery], and especially the skin disease bori, called kaskado in Malay [Tinea imbricata, a fungal infection], and usually also afflicted by kibo and stempang, which I believe are called boba and kudis in Malay [yaws and scabies respectively], and which cover the whole body with sores and wounds. (Van Delden 1844:374.)

As assistant resident of Gorontalo the 1860s, Riedel was struck by the unhealthy appearance of its population compared to the 'Alfurs' of Minahasa and Mongondow. The Gorontalese physique, he wrote, was 'generally small and weak, the arms and legs usually thin, the muscles little developed'. The men, consequently, were 'unable to endure much fatigue' and 'unsuitable for carrying heavy loads'. Eye and skin diseases, rheumatism, yaws, malaria and diarrhoea were common, while epidemics of smallpox, measles and cholera raged from time to time 'in the most terrible way' (Riedel 1870a:68-9, 101-2). Twentieth-century colonial officials agreed that the population of Gorontalo made a 'physically inferior' impression (Moolenburg 1922:23; Morison 1931: 58).

Partly, no doubt, as a result of contemporary increases in stature among

---

[40] Identification of the skin diseases mentioned in this and other passages was provided by the following sources: Aragon 1992:342; Brilman 1938:41; Echols and Shadily 1992:84; Kamus besar 1988:470; Kopstein 1926:44; Logeman 1922:76.

Europeans (Reid 1988-93, I:47), positive comments by foreign writers regarding the size of any of the indigenous peoples of the region became progressively less common after the middle of the nineteenth century. By 1920, the Swedish anthropologist Kaudern (1940:31) could write that 'all Toraja tribes' were 'rather small in stature'. Not every early source, on the other hand, suggests a population which is tall by European standards. 'The men and women of the island of Celebes', wrote captain Woodard (1969:97) after his stay in Donggala and Palu in 1793, 'are not tall, nor handsome in their persons, but short and thick set'.

In view of the inherent subjectivity of such statements, and considering that adult body height does give a good indication of both the disease history and the nutritional status of an individual during his or her growing years (Cuff 1995; Floud, Wachter and Gregory 1990:245-51), it is useful to review what little quantitative data exists regarding the stature of the various population groups.[41] The inhabitants of Minahasa, in accordance with their reputation for good health, were the tallest people in Sulawesi at the end of the nineteenth century, when Fritz Sarasin (1906:99) measured average heights of 165 and 154 cm among small samples of Minahasan men and women respectively.[42] British men, by comparison, had been about 165 cm tall in the second half of the eighteenth century; by 1900 they were considerably larger (Floud, Wachter and Gregory 1990:138). Earlier estimates from Minahasa give comparable or slightly higher figures: 167 cm (average) for men and 157 cm (maximum) for women in 1833, and a range (for men?) of 157-173 cm in 1845.[43] By contrast the Gorontalese, at least by the end of the century, were considerably smaller. Samples of 20 men and 15 women from the immediate vicinity of Gorontalo town, examined by a Dutch military doctor in 1892, had average heights of 158 and 149 cm respectively, while four adult men measured there by the Sarasins a few years later stood just 155 cm tall on average (Lubbers 1893, Bijlage 4; Sarasin 1906:93).

There is some impressionistic evidence, reviewed in Chapter XII, that the inhabitants of Gorontalo declined in height as a result of deteriorating health and nutrition in the course of the nineteenth century, in which case the contrast with Minahasans had previously been less marked. Strong variations in stature between the populations of neighbouring areas, on the other hand, were probably not unusual. In Central Sulawesi, later and closer observers than Riedel (whose 1886 account, with its male height estimate of 168 cm,

---

[41]   Body size, of course, also reflects genetic factors, but these are less important than is commonly supposed (Floud, Wachter and Gregory 1990:4-5).
[42]   Most of the individuals measured came from the central plateau of Minahasa.
[43]   AV Manado 1833 (ANRI Manado 48); Van Doren 1854-56, I:267; J.J. ten Siethoff, 'Topografische schetsen van een gedeelte der residentie Menado, 1845' (ANRI Manado 46). In the original units (Rhineland feet and inches): 5'4" and 5' (1833); 5'-5'6" (1845).

was based largely on second-hand information) agreed with him that some Toraja groups – specifically, those living in the highland basins of Lore – were physically large (Adriani and Kruyt 1912-14, I:89; Sarasin 1906:74). The Bada Valley in particular, according to Kruyt (1909:369), was inhabited by 'a fine-looking people, tall and well-built'. In the adjacent Poso Depression at the same period, however, most people were reportedly small by comparison.[44] While no figures are available to confirm this particular contrast, some other upland groups in Central Sulawesi were certainly small in stature during the early twentieth century. In 1925 the average height of 27 adult men from Simpang, a remote Loinang (Saluan) settlement in the interior of the Luwuk Peninsula, was 155 cm (Kleiweg de Zwaan 1929:787). A larger sample of 78 men from the Pekawa uplands to the west of the Palu Trench measured just under 153 cm on average in 1936 (Tesch 1939:2375), making them even smaller than their counterparts in Gorontalo at the turn of the century.[45]

Longevity and infant mortality

The often healthy appearance of the adult population concealed high levels of mortality at younger ages. Dr de Wijn (1952:168) emphasized that Mori adults, although heavier and taller on average than most Indonesians, were all exceptionally fit 'survivals' of an 'appallingly high death rate among the younger people'. The four groups of post-menopausal women interviewed by Kruyt in different parts of the Poso area in 1902 told him that respectively 18, 23, 25 and 56 percent of their offspring had died 'as small children'; the overall average was 25 percent (Appendix F). According to Tillema's much larger survey of 1924 (Appendix G), 20 percent of all children borne by the post-menopausal women interviewed had died before reaching the age of two, and 36 percent before reaching adulthood. The reason for the scarcity of handicapped adults, Adriani and Kruyt (1950-51, I:79) surmised, was simply that 'children who are not born healthy and whole quickly die'.[46] These results are the more striking considering that they certainly underestimate the real infant mortality rate; in many cases, children who died soon after birth were not included in the count by their mothers (Adriani and Kruyt 1950-51, II:339; Kaudern 1940:48). No such specific statistics are available

---

44   Adriani and Kruyt 1912-14, I:89; A.C. Kruyt 1903b:199; Sarasin 1906:73.
45   Measurements of 20 men from a village on Lake Lindu, on the other hand, produced a taller average of almost 160 cm (Tesch 1939:2382).
46   A survey of more than 13,000 adults carried out in the Poso area in 1908-1909 found only 36 handicapped or seriously disfigured individuals (Adriani and Kruyt 1912-14, I:89-90, 1950-51, I:79).

for other precolonial or recently colonized areas, but on Sangir and Talaud, according to the missionary writer Brilman (1938:176), infant mortality had stood at 'more than 40 percent' until the arrival of Western health care at the beginning of the twentieth century; in the Netherlands in 1933, by comparison, the figure was just over four percent.

In 1874, turning to Minahasa, 32 percent of all the children reported as ever-born into Edeling's sample households had subsequently died (Appendix E). Qualitative sources on Minahasa in the nineteenth and early twentieth centuries also repeatedly mention high infant mortality rates.[47] Kündig's medical survey in the years 1930-1932, admittedly a period of temporarily enhanced infant mortality due to a combined dysentery and measles epidemic in 1930, revealed that 18 percent of all children born in his five Minahasan districts (against, for instance, fewer than 7 percent of Europeans born in Indonesia) still were not surviving their first year of life (Appendix H).[48] The most important reported causes of infant deaths, overall, were respiratory diseases (mostly pneumonia and influenza), followed by tetanus and navel infections, 'fever' (mostly malaria), gastroenteritis, measles, and dysentery (Kündig 1934: 177-8). A more impressionistic report by the missionary Woensdregt (1930:328) at the same period specified 'malaria, dysentery and respiratory diseases' as the most important contributors to the 'very high' infant mortality in Bada.

A number of sources from the nineteenth century suggest that those inhabitants of northern Sulawesi who did survive to adulthood tended to be long-lived.[49] Riedel (1870a:57), for instance, wrote that the number of old people in Gorontalo was 'remarkable', and Resident Pietermaat claimed that individuals of 70-80 years were 'often' encountered in the Minahasan uplands.[50] Some valuable perspective on such statements, however, is provided by Resident Wenzel's uniquely detailed report on Minahasa in 1825. 'The age which the native generally seems to reach', Wenzel judged, 'is about 50 years or a little more'. 'I have also seen other much older people', he added, 'but I believe these to be exceptional' (Riedel 1872b:481). 'The usual age reached by the

---

[47]   AV Manado 1853, 1856 (ANRI Manado 51); Bierens de Haan 1893:73; Bleeker 1856, I:85-6; Bouvy 1924:380, 384; *Fragment* 1856:23; Graafland 1867-69, I:174-6, 1898, I:302-5; Guillemard 1886:173-4; A.J.F. Jansen 1861:230; Van Kol 1903:324-5; De Lange 1897:687; Van Marle 1922, I:56; Wallace 1987:197.

[48]   The same survey, moreover, indicated that the death rate increased in the last quarter of the first year of life, and probably remained very high in the second year due to the dangers (accidents, infections) associated with the increasing mobility of children of that age (Kündig 1934:176). In Central Sulawesi, Kruyt (1903b:198) likewise judged that because children received less parental attention and protection once they were able to crawl, the second year of life was the most dangerous.

[49]   Van Doren 1854-56, I:267; Reinwardt 1858:597; Woodard 1969:98; E. Francis, 'Aantekeningen van den kommissaris voor Manado, 1846' (ANRI Manado 50).

[50]   AV Manado 1833 (ANRI Manado 48).

islanders here', echoed Van Delden (1844:374) from Sangir in 1825, 'is 40 to 50 years'. 'Very old people', reported Kruyt (1903b:204-5) from Poso at the end of the century, 'are seldom seen, while people with grey hair are also scarce'.[51] In 1930 the proportion of the indigenous population over the age of 50 was 11 percent in Minahasa, 8 percent in Sangir and 10 percent in Talaud, compared to 17 percent in the Netherlands (*Volkstelling* 1933-36, V:62). In 1951, De Wijn (1952:169) estimated the average life-span of the adult rural population in Central Celebes at 45 years.

Epidemic disease

Besides hiding high infant mortality rates, the healthy appearance of much of the adult population in normal years was also misleading in that it did not reflect the periodic impact of lethal epidemics. Hickson (1889:159), visiting Talaud in the wake of a depopulating cholera and malaria epidemic in 1886 (Chapter IV), described even the noble ambassadors who came on board his vessel off Karakelang as 'miserable-looking, half-starved individuals'. Riedel (1886:93), describing the tall, athletic Toraja, did not neglect to add that they were nevertheless afflicted by regular outbreaks of smallpox, 'fevers', and stomach and respiratory disease. Although Adriani (1915:458) later claimed that epidemics were 'not very frequent' in Central Sulawesi, in the first two decades of the twentieth century alone the Poso Toraja were in fact hit successively by cholera (1902-1903), smallpox (1908-1909), an unidentified respiratory disease (1911-1912), cholera again (1915-1916), and influenza (1918-1919), besides numerous local malaria outbreaks.[52] Epidemic mortality rates were high; in 1911, for instance, an average of 10 percent of the population of the affected villages around Lake Poso was reported to be dying of lung disease.[53] The early twentieth century, admittedly, was a period of enhanced mortality due to population movements and social dislocation (Chapter VI); more serious still, nevertheless, had been the catastrophic smallpox epidemic of 1884, during which people 'died in droves' (A.C. Kruyt 1893:107), and as a result of which the country underwent 'a complete transformation' as afflicted settlements were abandoned and left to decay (A.C. Kruyt 1895-97, II:117).

[51] In one of the western highland basins, Tawaelia, there were even said to be 'no old people' (A.C. Kruyt 1908:1331).
[52] Adriani 1915:459; Adriani and Kruyt 1950-51, I:77, II:207; *Brieven*, 3-1909; *Koloniaal verslag* 1903:92, 1910:51, 1912:53, 1913:26, 1914:26, 1915:35, 1916:34, 1917:35, 1919:75, 1920:126.
[53] *Koloniaal verslag* 1912:34. 'The Toraja are a healthy people', wrote Adriani (1915:458), 'but they are not strong; an illness which hardly does us any harm renders them unable to work'.

A plea by the missionary Graafland for more European medical care in Minahasa, written in the 1860s, reveals that here too the population, however robust and healthy it appeared in good years, was in fact plagued by lethal disease.

> I need hardly expand on how important this is for a land where in thirty years no fewer than six disastrous epidemics have raged, above and beyond the endemic diseases and the annual fevers which come with the changing of the seasons. Sufficient to say that some of those epidemics, including the fever of 1832 and the dysentery of 1854, claimed ten to twelve thousand victims each, that outbreaks of sickness sometimes reduce the population of a village by up to a third, and that disease is one of the main reasons why the birth rate in some places barely exceeds the death rate, or even falls below it. (Graafland 1867-69, II:157.)

Important epidemic diseases in nineteenth-century Minahasa, other than dysentery, included cholera and malaria. Cholera, at least in its most virulent form, was a new disease imported to Indonesia only in 1821. Thanks to vaccination, on the other hand, colonial Minahasa was spared from serious attacks of the most feared epidemic, smallpox, which during its last full-scale visitation in 1819 had killed approximately one sixth of the population. Here and elsewhere, however, the most destructive single disease was probably malaria, which occurred in both epidemic and endemic forms.

Malaria

Early twentieth-century sources from almost every part of northern Sulawesi identify malaria as the most serious health problem.[54] Besides causing many direct casualties, malaria also reduced the resistance of the population to other diseases, with which it often occurred in combination.[55] Widespread malaria infection, for example, was seen as one reason for the high death toll taken in the residency of Manado by the influenza pandemic of 1918-1919 (Logeman 1922:74). Nineteenth-century sources, although they do not always distinguish between malaria and other types of 'fever', suggest a similar pattern.[56] Graafland (1867-69, II:158, 249) put 'fevers' at the head

---

[54] AV Midden Celebes 1906 (ANRI Manado 30); Avink 1935; Hissink 1912:80; Korn 1939:58; Roep 1917:426; Stuurman 1936:105; Weg 1938:194.

[55] AV Manado 1906 (ANRI Manado 30); Boonstra van Heerdt 1914b:727.

[56] Only when these sources refer specifically to 'intermittent' fevers is the identification with malaria reasonably certain (AV Manado 1859, 1860, in ANRI Manado 52; Bosscher and Matthijssen 1854:74; Riedel 1870a:102). In many other cases, however, it can be inferred from contextual details.

of his list of the 'most prevalent diseases' in Minahasa, noting that besides having a 'very debilitating effect upon the population', they could also 'assume a malevolent character, in which case they kill their victims in the space of one to two days'. The government investigator Francis (1860:307) noted in 1846 that the fevers of Minahasa were particularly deadly to children. Sources from the VOC period also mention the prevalence of 'hot' (Padtbrugge 1866:328; Schoonderwoert 1766) or 'burning' (Lobs 1686) fevers in Minahasa.

In most parts of the region, malaria was essentially a disease of the coast-lands (Logeman 1922:74). In coastal Tolitoli 'almost the whole population' was sick with malaria 'several times each year' (Kortleven 1927:89), and in nearby Buol the disease was likewise prevalent 'in almost all *kampung*' (W.C. Klein 1932:6). In Gorontalo, the coastal lowlands of Paguat were particularly dangerous.[57] A spleen examination carried out among schoolchildren here in 1929 indicated that every child was infected.[58] Universal spleen enlargement was also reported in settlements on the south coast of the Luwuk Peninsula in the same period (Broersma 1931a:1045). Almost the whole coastal area of Tobungku, where villages with a 90 percent infection rate were 'not uncommon', was said to 'labour under the calamitous influences of malaria'.[59] On the Banggai Islands too, 'most places' were 'notorious' for the disease (A.Ph. van Aken 1932:216). The capital, on Banggai proper, was described as 'one of the most unhealthy places in the Indies' (A.C. Kruyt 1931:527). Among the northern islands it was low-lying Talaud, especially Karakelang, which suffered most (Cuarteron 1855:10; Tammes 1940:185). A government doctor who carried out a health survey of the Talaud Islands in 1914 concluded that 'almost 50 percent of the population is suffering from malaria' (Roep 1917:426).

The Sangir Islands were less affected than Talaud, but except for Siau (see Chapter XI) they too had malarial pockets on their coasts.[60] Here, as elsewhere, this normally endemic disease periodically flared up in epidemic

---

[57]   Morks 1931:30. Kuandang, on the north coast, had also been notorious for its unhealthy 'climate' since VOC times (Breton 1767; Valckenaer 1778).

[58]   Dutrieux 1930:24. The spleen rate (the proportion of individuals in a population or sample showing enlarged spleens) is not always a good index of the prevalence of malaria in a given location, since adults who have developed malaria immunity as a result of repeated infection do not display this symptom. Children under the age of 9, however, have enlarged spleens even in 'holoendemic' areas (Bruce-Chwatt 1980:147).

[59]   Nouwens 1932:5. Also Avink 1935; Van der Hart 1853:69. In the Palu area, too, malaria was predominantly a coastal disease, although here its effects seem to have been less severe (Van den Berg 1935:7; Ter Laag 1920:21, 56-7).

[60]   Frieswijck 1902:472; F. Kelling, 'Het eiland Taghoelandang en zijn bewoners' [1866] (ARZ NZG 43.2); Tammes 1940:187; Van de Velde van Cappellen 1857:46. A survey of schoolchildren in 77 Greater Sangir *kampung* soon after the Second World War found 5 villages in which the spleen index exceeded 75%, and 11 in which it stood at between 50 and 75% (Blankhart 1951:88).

form.[61] One such epidemic is graphically described in a VOC expedition diary from the late seventeenth century. Visiting Greater Sangir in November 1680, Padtbrugge found that Tabukan (on the east coast) had recently been struck by 'the punishing hand of God, the hot fevers'. There had been 'a great number of deaths', and the sick were so numerous that 'every house was like a hospital'. Padtbrugge prayed 'that they may once again breath healthier air as before'. 'It was nonetheless also evident', he added, 'that the surrounding villages were not so badly affected'; except for one other coastal settlement, Taruna, the health situation elsewhere on the island was surprisingly normal.[62] Two and a half centuries later, colonial sources confirmed that malaria on Greater Sangir was found mainly in 'certain *kampung* on the east coast' (Tammes 1940:187), and also on the opposite coast at Taruna, where 'every few years a serious malaria epidemic takes place' (A.Ph. van Aken 1932:217). After one such epidemic in 1930 – not very different, no doubt, from that witnessed by Padtbrugge – the government responded by attempting to provide improved tidal access to a nearby brackish lagoon suspected as the breeding place of the mosquito vector (A.Ph. van Aken 1932:218).

In many areas the malarial zone did not extend far into the interior. In 1925, the residency medical officer Weck recorded a dramatic contrast in health conditions between upland and littoral settlements on the Luwuk Peninsula. In Simpang, at an altitude of about 1,500 metres in the interior, he found what he described as 'a vigorous and (in so far as I could judge from the part of it which I saw) healthy population, with a fine and well-built physique'. Here there was 'practically no malaria'.[63] Less than 30 km away on the north coast in the settlements around Bunta, by contrast, 'very severe endemic malaria' prevailed. 'Every individual which I saw from these *kampung*', wrote Weck, 'was sick, without exception from malaria' (A.C. Kruyt 1930a:338-9). Minahasa provides another example of a pattern of almost exclusively coastal malaria, this time already well documented in nineteenth-century sources. Here Manado (especially the Chinese quarter of the town), Kema and Likupang in Tonsea, and the Belang area in the southeast, all located in the vicinity of coastal swamps, were notorious for their 'hot fevers'.[64] All places

61   Van Andel (1921:6), Avink (1935) and Kündig (1934:179) mention periodic exacerbations of the malaria problem in endemic areas elsewhere in the region. In some cases, examples of which are discussed below, such fluctuations had to do with the biology of the mosquito vector. The incidence of malaria in a community, however, depends upon a complex balance between the numbers of vectors, the numbers of parasites, and the level of immunity among the human host population, so that it is seldom entirely constant (Bruce-Chwatt 1980:134-5).
62   NA VOC 1366:113, 119, 127.
63   In Simpang, Weck inspected some 30 adult men and an indeterminate number of children (A.C. Kruyt 1930a:338).
64   AV Manado 1853, 1859 (ANRI Manado 51, 52); De Clercq 1873:256; *Fragment* 1856:94; Graafland 1867-69, II:66, 213, 249, 1898, I:25; II:61, 336; Kielstra 1921:39; Riedel 1872b:462.

more than about 10 km ('six to eight *palen*') from the coast, by contrast, were regarded as healthy (Riedel 1872b:462). Life expectancy, correspondingly, was thought to be shorter in the lowlands than in the interior.[65]

Not all coastal settlements, on the other hand, were malarial: in Minahasa, the port of Amurang was an exception to the rule (Graafland 1898, I:493; Stuurman 1936:105). Outside Minahasa, conversely, the disease was not restricted to the coastlands. The Dumoga Valley in upland Bolaang Mongondow was heavily malarial, and even the densely populated Mongondow Plateau not free from the disease (Tammes 1940:194-5; Weg 1938:197). In Gorontalo, besides malarial strips on the north and south coasts, there were also inland pockets of endemic malaria in the upper Bone Valley (the Bawangio Plateau) to the east of the capital, in the western part of the Limboto Depression beyond the lake, and in the Paguyaman Basin, where attempts at commercial sugar cultivation in the 1930s had to be abandoned due to the prevalence of the disease among the plantation workers.[66]

In parts of Central Sulawesi, in fact, the pattern was reversed, and malaria became characteristically a disease of the interior. In Mori, coastal Kolonodale (on the Tomori Bay) was free of malaria, while the population of two inland settlements in the La River basin displayed spleen indices of 56 and 80 percent in 1935.[67] In the Poso area, likewise, the disease was found 'primarily in the mountain districts' (*Algemeene memorie Poso* 1925:5), while the highland basins of western Central Sulawesi were plagued by what one resident of Manado described as 'very severe chronic-endemic malaria' (A.Ph. van Aken 1932:214). In one of these basins, Tawaelia, Albert Kruyt had identified the malaria problem at the beginning of the twentieth century as a key reason for low population growth.

> It is said that the population of this little group can never rise above 100; as soon as this total is exceeded, a spate of deaths brings it back to a lower figure. I have made efforts to discover the reason for this demographic stasis among the inhabitants of Tawaelia. I found that the 27 married men now present, more than half of whom are still in the prime of life and so can be expected to produce more children in future, had so far fathered by 37 women (10 of the men had had two wives, or still did) a total of 126 children, 42 of which had died. This means that the slow growth of the population cannot be attributed to low fertility. The real culprit is undoubtedly malaria, which kills many of them at an early age. Old people, by their own testimony, are not to be found; among the men we saw several with distended abdomens resulting from a swollen spleen. (A.C. Kruyt 1908:1331.)

[65]   AV Manado 1833 (ANRI Manado 48); Van Doren 1854-56, I:267.
[66]   Edie 1923:25; Korn 1939:4, 58; MV Manado November 1864 (ANRI Manado 54); Von Rosenberg 1865:109, 111.
[67]   Avink 1935. Three decades earlier, Maengkom (1907:863) had noted that 'most' of the inhabitants of Mata ndau, the inland capital of Mori, suffered from 'fevers'.

In 1924, the post-menopausal To Tawaelia women interviewed as part of the Tillema survey reported that 46 percent of their offspring had died before reaching adulthood (Tillema 1926:39). Malaria was also rife in the other highland basins: in Kulawi there were 'innumerable' sufferers (Boonstra van Heerdt 1914a:622), and enlarged spleens were 'the order of the day' in Lindu.[68] Schistosomiasis, which was endemic in Lindu, Napu and Tawaelia (see below), also causes spleen enlargement (Strickland and Abdel-Wahab 1991:794), and early reports by medically untrained observers (including Kruyt) regarding the severity of malaria in these areas were probably exaggerated to some extent as a result. The 1937 publication announcing the discovery of schistosomiasis in Lindu, however, confirms that malaria too is common there (Müller and Tesch 1937:2144), and an earlier medical investigation ordered by Dr Kündig into the 'great mortality among the population' in Napu had concluded that malaria was the chief culprit (Platt 1933:13).

Migration epidemics

While occasional or seasonal malaria peaks occurred even among static populations in endemic areas, the most spectacular were associated with movement of people from relatively healthy to malarial locations. In Central Sulawesi, as noted in Chapter VI, malaria was probably the chief cause of the great increase in mortality which followed the forced relocation of upland villages to more accessible new sites after the imposition of Dutch rule. The same problem had afflicted some newly laid-out villages in nineteenth-century Minahasa (Schouten 1998:69). 'Severe fevers broke out', recalled Graafland (1867-69, I:177) in the 1860s, 'and the population of such villages was often reduced in a few years to less than half of its original number'.[69] Similar disasters, as the diary of a VOC expedition to the Gulf of Tomini in 1680 illustrates, sometimes also occurred under precolonial conditions.

> The king of Lembunu replied that the place [near Paguat] belonged to him, and that it was the most fertile sago-growing area in the whole Gulf. For this reason many attempts had been made to establish villages there, but the people dispatched to that end repeatedly perished or became gravely ill. It was therefore concluded that the area was the home of ghosts or evil spirits, and further migrations were postponed.[70]

[68]   *Nota berglandschappen* 1912:9. Also A.C. Kruyt 1938, I:152; Grubauer 1913:406, 546; Sarasin and Sarasin 1905, II:66.
[69]   Wiersma (1871:227) describes a similar event in the district of Ponosakan.
[70]   NA VOC 1359:207v.

When an inland group from the neighbourhood of Lake Matano was forced to resettle on the Tobungku coast as the result of a local war shortly before the end of the nineteenth century, many of its members likewise 'fell victim to murderous fevers' (Goedhart 1908:504).

Temporary migration could also result in malaria infection. 'Most of the people who become sick here', reported a Dutch official from malaria-free Tondano in 1846, 'bring the seeds of their sickness with them from the low-lands when they have had to go there to perform some work; this sickness consists of hot and cold fevers, from which most of them die for want of treatment' (Grudelbach 1849:405). Resident Wenzel noted in 1825 that upland Minahasans were reluctant to visit the coast because if they did so they invariably contracted the 'hot fevers', from which 'a speedy return to the uplands is the only possible cure'.[71] In 1925, likewise, Dr Weck reported that the inhabitants of Simpang 'were very susceptible to malaria and therefore afraid to travel to the coast, since they often return from it mortally ill, or not at all'.[72] The incidence of malaria as a result of temporary migration almost certainly increased in nineteenth-century Minahasa as a result of growing commerce, improving communications, and also corvée labour, which some-times involved a considerable journey to the work site.[73] In Central Sulawesi in the twentieth century, the collection of forest products was also a factor favouring infection (Nouwens 1932:5; Tillema 1926:212).

Not all types of temporary migration to malarial areas were new develop-ments. In Gorontalo, gold mining had long involved the seasonal migration of part of the male population from the agricultural heartland of Gorontalo and Limboto, where malaria was uncommon, to remote mining sites located mostly in malarial areas near the coast. As early as 1734, the Dutch in Ternate noted that gold deliveries from Gorontalo had fallen 'as a result of the deaths of many miners in the wet season' (*Generale missiven* IX:589). Another source from the same period claims that as many as four out of every ten gold miners typically died.[74] Paguat, the most important single mining area, was

[71]   Riedel 1872b:462, 465-6. See also Francis 1860:307; J.J. ten Siethoff, 'Topografische schetsen van een gedeelte der residentie Menado, 1846' (ANRI Manado 46).
[72]   Kleiweg de Zwaan 1929:783. The To Loinang believed that people returning sick from the coast had been possessed by the 'spirit of the sea' (A.C. Kruyt 1930a:396).
[73]   Schouten 1998:69. Grudelbach ('Gevoelen over de topographische schetsen van den Luitenant J.J. ten Siethoff', 24-12-1846, in ANRI Manado 46) specifically mentions malaria deaths as a consequence of *herendienst* performed by uplanders in Manado. Movement between upland and lowland areas probably explains how the military doctor Bouvy (1924:387) could declare in the 1920s that no place in Minahasa was free from malaria, and that most of the population caught the disease as children and carried it for the rest of their lives. A decade later, Kündig (1934:178-9, 183) showed that although most of the central uplands of Minahasa were definitely free from endemic malaria, there were numerous imported cases.
[74]   NA VOC 2099:944.

particularly notorious for its 'deadly climate' and the 'innumerable' lives lost there in the quest for gold.[75] Some figures from the early nineteenth century confirm the scale of the problem. Of the 800 miners who left Gorontalo for Paguat in March 1828, only 200 were still working at the beginning of 1829; of the rest, 260 had died, 200 were sick, and another 140, understandably enough, had 'deserted'.[76] A striking characteristic of the Paguat 'fevers' was that they seemed to affect only the temporary, immigrant population of gold miners. Among the small number of people who lived permanently in the vicinity of the mines, the mortality rate did not appear to be higher than elsewhere (Van Schelle 1890:122). Nineteenth-century Dutch officials explained this in terms of the fact that the permanent residents were 'accustomed to the local climate'.[77]

Malaria ecology

Malaria, stressed the British malariologist Bruce-Chwatt (1980:129), 'is essentially a focal disease, since its transmission depends greatly on local environmental and other conditions'. Foremost among these localizing conditions is the distribution of the *Anopheles* mosquitos which carry the disease, and which are seldom found more than two or three kilometres from their breeding places. By the Second World War 14 *Anopheles* species had been identified in the northern Sulawesi region (Allied Geographical Section 1945:155), most of them known malaria vectors. Three species, however, appear to have been particularly important: *A. subpictus*, *A. minimus*, and *A. maculatus*.[78]

Each of these dangerous types prefers a different habitat. *A. subpictus*, like the notorious *A. sundaicus* of Java and Sumatra, is typically a mosquito of the coastal lowlands, where it breeds in still pools of either fresh or salt water (Bonne-Wepster and Swellengrebel 1953:417, 431). This species was the main malaria vector in coastal settlements like Tolitoli, Belang, and Kema.[79] *A. min-*

---

[75]   R. Scherius 1847:407. Francis (1860:295) also observed that Paguat was 'extremely unhealthy', and that 'each year many of the mine workers die'. Van Schelle (1890:121), a mining engineer, even wrote that each spell in the mines tended to last either 'until the required amount of gold had been acquired, or until the fevers and numerous deaths which usually occurred made it necessary to return home'.

[76]   Res. Manado to *Raja* Gorontalo, 19-2-1829 (ANRI Manado 76).

[77]   AR Gorontalo to Res. Manado, 5-1-1835 (ANRI Manado 116).

[78]   A.Ph. van Aken 1932:213. *A. subpictus* is referred to in this source by its synonym *A. rossi*. A fourth species, *A. sundaicus*, apparently spreading from South Sulawesi, seems to have joined these three as a key vector in the period immediately after 1930 (Allied Geographical Section 1945:155).

[79]   A.Ph. van Aken 1932:215-6; Weg 1938:196. *A. subpictus* was also found in Sangir (Blankhart 1951:88).

imus, the feared upland mosquito of the Philippines (De Bevoise 1995:143-4), prefers gently-flowing fresh water (Bonne-Wepster and Swellengrebel 1953: 369, 374-5, 391) and is usually found further inland, although in Sulawesi its distribution overlapped with that of *A. subpictus*. The single most important vector in Minahasa and Bolaang Mongondow (Kündig 1934:179; Weg 1938: 195-7), *A. minimus* was also found in Sangir (Blankhart 1951:88; Brug 1926: 526), Banggai (A.Ph. van Aken 1932:217), and probably Palu (Cross et al. 1975:372). Although it is a hill mosquito rather than a strictly coastal species, and never breeds in brackish water, *A. minimus* is not normally found at altitudes of over 600 metres.[80] This explains why most of the central plateau of Minahasa was free from endemic malaria (Chapter I, Map 6). *A. maculatus*, another upland species, is not subject to this limitation, and it was *maculatus* which was blamed for the severe endemic malaria in the mountains of western Central Sulawesi.[81] Living in streams, pools and irrigated ricefields (Bonne-Wepster and Swellengrebel 1953:457), *maculatus* larvae 'abhor the shade' (Swellengrebel 1937:43) and must have thrived in the wet, heavily deforested and partly irrigated conditions of the western highland basins.

Research in late colonial times also shed light on the puzzle of malaria on Talaud, where in 1917 a Dutch administrator was unable to find a single *Anopheles* among the abundant local mosquitos, and where the distribution of endemic malaria seemed to bear no relation to that of swamps or other obvious breeding places.[82] Entomological survey results published in 1926 revealed *A. leucosphyrus*, not a common mosquito elsewhere in the region, as the sole *Anopheles* species present in the vicinity of the administrative capital of Talaud, Beo.[83] A dangerous malaria vector, this type typically breeds not in coastal swamps but in pools along streams in 'deep jungle', where it is 'difficult to detect'. Adults of the species, moreover, 'are seldom found in houses on account of the very late hours they choose for their meals and the habit of leaving the human habitation immediately afterwards' (Bonne-Wepster and Swellengrebel 1953:283-4).

[80] Bonne-Wepster and Swellengrebel 1953:375; Takken and Knols 1990:33. These sources refer to the variant *A. minimus var. flavirostis* (now classed as a separate species, *A. flavirostis*), which is the chief vector in the Philippines. Most colonial sources do not distinguish between *minimus* proper and *flavirostis*, although the latter was certainly present in Minahasa (Bonne-Wepster and Swellengrebel 1953:371) and Sangir (Blankhart 1951:88).
[81] A.Ph. van Aken 1932:214. Malarial Napu lies at an altitude of over 1,000 m, Bada at about 750 m.
[82] Roep 1917:430. Since only mosquitos of the genus *Anopheles* transmit malaria, there was little correlation between the incidence of malaria and the abundance of mosquitos in general. By the banks of malaria-free Lake Tondano, Hickson (1889:224) observed that in some places 'the water was quite black with mosquito and gnat larvae'.
[83] Rodenwaldt 1926:108 (table). *A. leucosphyrus* was also present in Bolaang Mongondow (M. van Rhijn 1941:136).

Nineteenth-century observers noted that besides the geographical pattern, a seasonal rhythm was also evident in the occurrence of malaria in Minahasa. Outbreaks were most likely during the transitional period or *kentering* between the two monsoons.[84] The same phenomenon was observed in Sangir (Van Delden 1844:361) and Gorontalo (Riedel 1870a:102), and on the east coast of Central Sulawesi (Vosmaer 1839:95). In due course, this too was explained in terms of vector ecology:

> The prime vector is *Anopheles minimus*, a [...] mosquito which prefers to breed in clear, slow-flowing streams or similar watercourses (irrigation ditches, millstreams and the like). This characteristic explains the seasonality of the malaria, spates of which occur especially at the beginning and the end of the rainy season. In the middle of the wet season the larvae are killed by the *banjir* [runoff peaks], while in the dry season the drying up of the stream beds produces the same effect. (Weg 1938:195.)

The epidemics associated with the establishment of new settlements may have been caused partly by the creation of new mosquito breeding sites such as fishponds, irrigated ricefields, sunlit pools of standing water, or stream margins cleared of forest.[85] It should be noted, however, that this common argument (Boomgaard 1987:56-7; Knapen 2001:161-2) is not complete in itself, since in most cases the areas from which the migrants originated also contained such environments. The implicit assumption here is that the mosquito population undergoes a temporary boom before being brought back under control by predation or vegetation regrowth (Meade 1976:431-2). Such a process would certainly account for the claim by Graafland (1867-69, I:177) and others that it was the immediate occupation of newly-cleared village sites, rather than migration as such, which was deadly. The population of the Poso area referred to migration-related malaria as 'the sickness caused by the rotting of the roots of the felled trees' (Tillema 1922:205), and Revius warned in 1850 that any new site for the capital of Tobungku should be located on ground already long cleared of forest, so that 'the lives and health of the inhabitants will not be placed in the balance'.[86] Many migration epidemics, however, simply reflected a combination of two more straightforward factors: the uneven distribution of the vector mosquitos, and the phenomenon of acquired malaria immunity. 'People who were already used to living in the area', noted Graafland (1867-69, I:205)

---

[84]   Francis 1860:307; Graafland 1867-69, II:158, 1898, II:197.

[85]   Tillema (1926:206) and Van Aken (1932:213) both noted the role of fishponds in facilitating malaria transmission in local transmigration sites in the south of Minahasa.

[86]   'Algemeen verslag omtrent de oostkust van Celebes', 10-2-1851 (ANRI Ternate 180). Van der Hart (1853:61), who likewise visited Tobungku in 1850, also mentions 'persistent fevers and sicknesses which were ascribed to the malevolent vapours released by the clearance of virgin lands'.

regarding the effects of the relocation of the Minahasan village of Sonder in 1847, 'held out fairly well, but among the new immigrants there was always a great number of fever sufferers, and many died'.

Lethal malaria is caused by the protozoa *Plasmodium falciparum*. Unless the disease is effectively treated, this organism always kills a substantial proportion of those people who are infected by it repeatedly and without prior immunity; according to an authoritative medical source, *P. falciparum* 'may kill up to 25% of non-immune adults within two weeks of a primary attack' (Strickland 1991:599). Those susceptible, moreover, include not only adults arriving from malaria-free areas, but also all infants, who may be protected for the first three to six months of life by immunity acquired from their mothers, but become vulnerable thereafter. Van der Brug (1995:74), in his study of malaria and its effects in VOC Batavia, claims that where *falciparum* malaria is always present, the mortality rate 'during the first years of life' is typically as high as 50 percent. Survivors of repeated infections, however, gradually acquire a large degree of immunity (although this is gradually lost again if regular infection ceases). The population of a 'holoendemic' malaria zone, then, suffered a high infant mortality rate, but its adult members were mostly immune. Adults living elsewhere, by contrast, were at risk both when, like Gorontalese gold miners, they travelled to endemic areas, and when, as in parts of Minahasa and Sangir, periodic increases in the vector population led to malaria epidemics.

Not all of the historical evidence from northern Sulawesi supports the conclusion that malaria was a chief cause of infant mortality. Edeling's 1874 survey (Appendix E), for instance, suggests no strong connection between death rates among Minahasan children and the malaria situation in each district. Although the (mainly) coastal districts of Bantik, Ponosakan and Tombariri showed the three highest reported rates of child mortality (43, 42 and 40 percent), they were immediately followed by Tomohon and Sarongsong (both 35 percent) on the highest part of the central plateau, while malarial Likupang and Manado (24 and 27 percent) both reported lower rates than any of the upland districts. The health survey conducted in Minahasa by Dr Kündig almost 60 years later, by contrast, did reveal a difference in infant mortality rates between the district of Airmadidi in Tonsea, where malaria was present, and the four upland districts included in his study. Here too, however, the contrast was not as dramatic as the reported lethality of *P. falciparum* would imply: in Airmadidi the death rate in the first year of life was 22.1 percent, while on the plateau the average was 17.3 percent.[87] No regional breakdown,

---

[87]   Calculated from the figures given in Appendix H (Tondano, Kawangkoan, Kakas, and Langoan combined: 8,073 births and 1,395 infant deaths in all registered years). The diffence, however, would have been rather larger had it not been for an epidemic of measles in Tondano in 1930.

unfortunately, is given for deaths among older children.[88]

Although Airmadidi lay well within the altitude range of *A. minimus*, and Kündig (1934:179) attributed the relatively high infant mortality there specifically to malaria, it was not among those localities notorious for the disease; Graafland (1898, II:291), in fact, called it 'one of the healthiest places in Minahasa'. As far as the Edeling statistics are concerned, it is also possible that reporting of infant deaths was particularly incomplete in the malarial districts, where such deaths were more routine. Another part of the explanation, however, is certainly that much of the malaria present in Minahasa, and elsewhere in the region, was not in fact caused by *Plasmodium falciparum* but by its less deadly cousin *Plasmodium vivax*. In the 1920s the military doctor Bouvy (1924:387) noted that 'all types' of malaria were found in Minahasa, and Tillema (1926:207) that the malaria prevalent in the coastal town of Poso was 'not the dangerous type which often causes sudden deaths, but the most dragging third-day fevers' – that is, the 'tertian' malaria caused by *P. vivax*. Dr Blankhart (1951:88) wrote at the end of the 1940s that 'most' of the malaria on Sangir was of the tertian type, and medical surveys carried out in several parts of Central Sulawesi in the 1970s also detected *P. vivax* as well as *P. falciparum* infections.[89] *Plasmodium* species other than *falciparum* (in Indonesia, *P. vivax* and more rarely *P. malariae*) are seldom lethal in themselves. In children, however, they do 'undermine the general defences of the growing organism and aggravate other intercurrent diseases' (Bruce-Chwatt 1980:43), and in adults they may cause protracted debility and anaemia as a result of relapses. 'Such a sickness', observed Tillema (1926:207), 'undermines the vitality, the strength, and the will to work and act'. Another indirect effect of all types of malaria is to increase the frequency of miscarriages, stillbirths, and neonatal deaths (Bruce-Chwatt 1980:39, 44-5; Strickland 1991:599). When assessing the evidence for malaria mortality in the times of Edeling and Kündig, finally, the impact of colonial medicine and public health measures, discussed in Chapter VIII, must also be taken into account.

Smallpox

If malaria was the most common serious disease, smallpox, caused by the virus *Variola major*, was the most feared.[90] Contagious, disfiguring, and above

---

[88]   Children in areas of endemic malaria remain at risk until the age of about 5 years (Bruce-Chwatt 1980:43).

[89]   Carney, Putrali and Caleb 1974:372-3; Cross et al. 1975:370, 372; Putrali et al. 1977:377, 379.

[90]   In Tinombo it was known as the 'supreme' or 'golden' disease, 'the lord of all diseases' (Nourse 1999:168).

all deadly, its sudden epidemic appearances caused the most spectacular of all mortality crises. In 1819 the last smallpox epidemic to hit Minahasa before the introduction of vaccination killed a reported 15,857 people (Reinwardt 1858:582), a figure which Graafland (1898, I:86) later equated, probably quite accurately, with one sixth of the population; according to Wenzel, the real death toll had been higher still (Reidel 1872b:478). In the following year an estimated 9-10,000 died in Gorontalo – 'which is the more terrible', commented Reinwardt (1858:514), 'since many adults (especially among the labouring class), even more than children, perished of it'. Here, moreover, the epidemic was followed by a 'very great' famine, caused by the inability of the sick to perform agricultural work, in which starvation led to additional loss of life.[91] Wigboldus (1988:36) has interpreted a passage in a VOC document from 1763 as indicating that 22,800 people, or at least 20 percent of the population (see Chapter V), died of smallpox around the beginning of that year in Minahasa.[92] The inspection report of a VOC church minister who visited the Sangir Islands in 1724 suggests that one earlier pre-vaccination epidemic took an even heavier toll: in Tabukan, according to the local church registers, 1,435 of the 4,151 Christians, or 35 percent, had recently died, in Tamako 41 percent, in Manganitu 51 percent, and in Taruna fully 60 percent (Sell 1724). Dysentery (*Generale missiven* VII:694) and 'other diseases' (Sell 1724), however, were also involved in this case.

As far as can be ascertained from the historical record, the region was struck by major smallpox epidemics in the years 1669-1670, 1700-1703, 1724-1726, 1763-1764, 1792, 1819-1823, 1839-1841, 1859-1861, 1883-1884, and 1908-1909.[93] In 1651 an epidemic consisting 'primarily of smallpox' was reported to be raging 'throughout the Moluccas' (*Generale missiven* II:490), and it is likely that this too affected northern Sulawesi.[94] Beyond that date the histori-

---

91   Res. Gorontalo to Res. Ternate, 18-3 and 24-4-1820; *Raja* Gorontalo to Res. Gorontalo, 18-3-1820 (ANRI Ternate 153).
92   The original source states that according to the resident of Manado, 'in the 76 *negeri*, in some more and in others fewer, 300 people had died [76 x 300 = 22,800]' (NA VOC 3119:43). During the next smallpox epidemic, in 1792, 'about 6,000' people died in Minahasa (RPR Ternate, 12-7-1792, in ANRI Ternate 30).
93   1669-1670: NA VOC 1275:627r, 642r; 1700-1703: NA VOC 1647:18, 75, 151; *Generale missiven* VI:220; 1724-1726: NA VOC 2050:146, 322, 325, 594; Sell 1725; 1763-1764: NA VOC 3119:29, 35, 43-4, 54, 153; Godée Molsbergen 1928:121, 127; Schoonderwoert 1766; 1792: NA VOC 3957:73, 191-2, 196; VOC 3958:104, 191-2, 196; Res. Gorontalo to Gov. Moluccas, 31-5-1792 (NA COIHB 86); Colenbrander 1898:588; Van Delden 1844:372; Godée Molsbergen 1928:153; RPR Ternate, 12-7-1792 (ANRI Ternate 30); 1819-1823: see text; 1839-1841: R. Scherius 1847:401-2, 407; De Clercq 1890:177, 1859-1861: Van der Crab 1862:379, 385-6; Steller 1866:31; *Koloniaal verslag* 1860:20, 22, 1861:22, 1862:28; 1883-1884: *Koloniaal verslag* 1884:22, 1885:24; 1908-1909: Adriani and Kruyt 1950-51, II:204-207; Guillemard 1886:210; A.C. Kruyt 1938, II:310; Tammes 1940:187-8; *Koloniaal verslag* 1908:66, 1909:74, 1910:52, 1911:48.
94   In the Moluccas, according to this source, it killed 'as much as one third of the population'.

cal record peters out, although oral tradition from Minahasa as recorded in the nineteenth century also recalled one smallpox epidemic at the time of the foundation of Tondano, not later than 1600 (Mangindaän 1873:365). The indigenous population was aware that smallpox tended to recur approximately once in every generation (Adriani and Kruyt 1912-14, I:417; Hissink 1912:81). At the beginning of the twentieth century a shaman in the Poso area stated that the smallpox spirit had warned him after the epidemic of 1883-1884: 'When the child of your child is born, I will come again' (Adriani and Kruyt 1950-51, II:204).

Epidemic cycles of smallpox reflect the immunity acquired by survivors of the disease. This protects individuals from subsequent re-infection, but is not passed on to their children, who remain vulnerable to the following outbreak. The interval between successive epidemics is related to the size, density and accessibility of the affected population; a long cycle is generally associated with a small, sparse, or isolated population, with a low absolute birth rate and a limited volume of interpersonal contacts (local or external) to facilitate infection (Fenner et al. 1988:196-7; Hopkins 1983:8). The average interval between pan-regional outbreaks in northern Sulawesi was 26 years, indicating, not surprisingly, a population smaller than that of Java in the seventeenth century, where the usual period between epidemics was seven to eight years, but denser and more accessible than that of some areas in the interior of Sumatra and Borneo, which in precolonial times were affected only once every 30-60 years.[95] The fact that the interval did not shorten substantially between 1650 and 1908 suggests that the population of northern Sulawesi – or at least, the part of it which had no artificial protection against smallpox – did not grow much over that period.[96]

Most smallpox epidemics spread to almost all parts of the region within a year or so of their first appearance. During every outbreak, however, there were always a few localities which escaped infection. The names of eight villages in the Poso area which were spared the ravages of the 1883-1884 epidemic were still remembered there many years later (Adriani and Kruyt 1912-14, I:417). In 1860 it was reported that the disease had not been seen on

---

In 1653 a 'certain infectious sickness', not further identified, was reported to be prevalent in Minahasa (NA VOC 1199:869v). Most smallpox epidemics in northern Sulawesi were more or less synchronized with similar outbreaks in Ternate.

[95]   Boomgaard 2003:596; Reid 1988-93, I:59. In the northern Philippines during the eighteenth century, by comparison, the interval was about 20 years (Newson 1998:29).

[96]   In the second half of the seventeenth century it was 25 years, in the eighteenth century 31 years, and in the nineteenth century 23 years. In parts of Java, by contrast, the frequency seems to have increased to one epidemic every 2-3 years by 1800 (Boomgaard 2003:596), and Knapen (2001:143) shows that in coastal Southeast Kalimantan the average interval fell from about 12 years in the eighteenth century to 6 years in the nineteenth.

the Togian Islands for 60 years, implying that Togian had been untouched by the previous two outbreaks. In such cases the lack of acquired immunity among the inhabitants ensured that when an epidemic finally did arrive, its impact was particulary severe. In May 1860 smallpox broke out on Togian 'with extreme violence', killing, according to a contemporary Dutch source, 'more than 900 people' among a population of which the total size had been estimated in 1854 at just 750, and of which a reported 400 were left in 1863.[97] Napu, in the interior of Central Sulawesi, was the only part of the region said to be safe from all smallpox epidemics.[98] The inhabitants of this remote valley regarded themselves as having a special pact with the smallpox spirit, claiming that if infected people passed the magical barriers which were set up on the path between Napu and neighbouring Besoa when epidemics reached Besoa from the south, the disease 'dies (loses its strength) on the way' (A.C. Kruyt 1938, II:310).

One smallpox epidemic, that of 1859-1860, is particularly well documented in Dutch sources, and although substantially moderated by vaccination (the history and impact of which are described in Chapter VIII), this epidemic gives an impression of how earlier outbreaks must have developed and spread in the region. In December 1859, after unconfirmed rumours of smallpox cases on the north coast of the northern peninsula, the disease broke out on a large scale in Gorontalo. By the end of May 1860, when it finally began to wane here, it had killed almost 2,800 people; the ultimate death toll in the Gorontalo area amounted to some 3,000.[99] In February 1860, meanwhile, the epidemic had spread to Siau and Greater Sangir, where the population was still largely unvaccinated. By the time an emergency supply of vaccine reached Sangir by steamship on 18 March, 288 of the 'approximately 600' inhabitants of the *negeri* Taruna were already dead.[100] The total death toll on the Sangir Islands was later estimated at 6,000; the real figure must have been considerably higher.[101] In June the smallpox reached Talaud, where there was no history of past vaccination, and where none was apparently attempted during this epidemic either. 'Hundreds have already died', reported a missionary from Salibabu in October, 'and it is said that there are some villages where almost the whole population is dead'. Agricultural work, moreover, came to a halt, so that the epidemic was followed by a famine which did not wane until May 1862 (Coolsma 1901:655).

[97]   MV Manado, May and September 1860 (ANRI Manado 54); Bleeker 1856:135; Von Rosenberg 1865:121.
[98]   A.C. Kruyt 1908:1289; E. Gobée, 'Aanteekeningen naar aanleiding van een reis door de Pososche berglandschappen', 7-3-1926 (ARZ NZG 101A-7-2).
[99]   MV Manado, December 1859 to May 1860 (ANRI Manado 54); Van der Crab 1862:379.
[100]   MV Manado, April 1860 (ANRI Manado 54).
[101]   Van der Crab 1862:385-6; Steller 1866:31; *Koloniaal verslag* 1861:22, 1862:28.

Cholera

Another lethal epidemic disease, Asiatic cholera, arrived in the region for the first time in the early nineteenth century. Although at least one intestinal disease closely resembling cholera was already endemic in Indonesia (Boomgaard 1987:52-3; Semmelink 1885), the global pandemic which began in Bengal in 1817 had a dramatic impact.[102] In 1821 the virulent new disease arrived in Semarang on Java, where it killed more than 1,000 people in 11 days (Boomgaard 1987:53). In 1823 it reached Makasar (Heersink 1995:69), and in 1828 Kendari, on the east coast of Sulawesi south of Tobungku (Vosmaer 1839:123). In June 1830 the *Cholera morbus*, as it was known, finally broke out in Minahasa, immediately killing 'more than 480 people in the various districts'.[103] By the beginning of 1834 it formed part of a mixed epidemic, also described as involving 'gall fever' (*galkoorts*) and dysentery, which affected the whole northern peninsula from Manado to Palu.[104]

Regional cholera epidemics subsequently recurred in 1852-1854, 1866-1867, 1874, 1885-1886, 1901-1903, and 1914-1915.[105] The second of these is particularly well described in contemporary Dutch sources. At the beginning of October 1866 there was a violent cholera outbreak in Gorontalo; by the end of the year 6,331 people in that area had been affected, of whom 1,438, or 23 percent, had died.[106] The epidemic continued on a smaller scale, but killing a rather higher proportion of those affected, until October 1867, by which time the recorded death toll in the Gorontalo area was 1,980, or perhaps three percent of the population, and the average case fatality rate for the whole outbreak 28 percent.[107] Meanwhile the disease had spread throughout the residency. By April 1867 it was estimated to have taken 1,000 lives in Moutong and adjacent parts of the Tomini coast, and in May it was 'raging

---

[102]   Reid (1988-93, I:61), however, argues that Asiatic cholera may already have been present in Indonesia in the seventeenth century. No identifiable reference to cholera occurs in the record for northern Sulawesi before 1830.

[103]   Res. Manado to Gov. Moluccas, 20-8-1830 (ANRI Manado 76). The first outbreak in Ternate also seems to have occurred in 1830 (De Clercq 1890:176).

[104]   Res. Manado to GG, 13-2-1834 (ANRI Manado 77).

[105]   1852-1854: Bosscher and Matthijssen 1854:71; MV Manado, September and December 1854 (ANRI Manado 54); 1866-1867: see text; 1874: AV Manado 1874 (ANRI Manado 53); Van der Crab 1875:5; Schwarz and De Lange 1876:158, 165; 1885-1886: Ebbinge Wübben 1889:201; Graafland 1898, I:96; Van Hoëvell 1891:34; *Koloniaal verslag* 1888:15; Lam 1931:43; 1901-1903: Engelenberg 1906:8; Van Kol 1902:334, 347; Pennings 1908:15; 1914-1915: *Koloniaal verslag* 1915:35, 1916:34. More localized outbreaks occurred near Parigi in 1891 (A.C. Kruyt 1892:249) and in Buol in 1911 (*Koloniaal verslag* 1912:34). By the beginning of the twentieth century the indigenous population was aware that cholera, like smallpox, exhibited a more or less regular epidemic cycle (Hissink 1912:81).

[106]   AV Manado 1866 (ANRI Manado 52).

[107]   Calculated from: AV Manado 1866 (ANRI Manado 52); MV Manado, January-October 1867 (ANRI Manado 54). The data are not entirely consistent, however, since for the months October-

fiercely' around Parigi in Central Sulawesi. In June it broke out in Kema and the Chinese quarter of Manado, although the rest of Minahasa seems to have been spared. By August the whole north coast of the peninsula was affected as far as Buol in the west, as were Sangir and Talaud, where the ultimate death toll was estimated at more than 1,500.[108] These figures indicate that while cholera was a formidable disease with a high case fatality rate, it did not kill on the same scale as smallpox.[109] In Gorontalo and Talaud, both areas of relatively dense population where the drinking water supply was often problematic (Chapter VIII), cholera and malaria nevertheless seem to have been the main components of a severe epidemic crisis, leading to significant depopulation, in the 1880s (Chapters IV and VI).[110] Caused by the bacterium *Vibrio cholerae*, cholera is transmitted mainly via water polluted by the faeces of infected individuals (Nalin and Morris 1991:367).

Other lethal diseases

While smallpox, malaria and cholera were the most prominent epidemic killers, others were also significant. After the smallpox epidemic of 1819, the most serious episode of lethal disease in Minahasa during the nineteenth century was probably that of 1853-1854, which began with an outbreak of 'epidemic stomach sickness' and developed into a multiple epidemic involving dysentery and measles as well as cholera and malaria; about 10 percent of the population died (see Chapter V). Contemporary observers stated that dysentery was unknown in Minahasa before this epidemic, but became endemic thereafter.[111] In 1679, however, Padtbrugge (1866:328) had already listed *bloedloop* or dysentery as one of the diseases 'by which these Manadonese are tormented and cut down', and *rode loop* is also mentioned in early sources from other parts of the region.[112] During the mixed epidemic of 1830-1834, moreover, the resident of Manado referred to *dysenterie* by name.[113] Dysentery epidemics were still common, especially in Gorontalo

---

December 1866 the sum of the fatality and recovery figures is not equivalent to the recorded total number of cholera cases.

[108]   MV Manado April-August 1867 (ANRI Manado 54), AV Manado 1867 (ANRI Manado 53).

[109]   In 1874, comparably, about 600 people died in the whole of Minahasa (AV Manado 1874, in ANRI Manado 53; Van der Crab 1875:5, 138), and in 1914 a total of 160 in Bolaang Mongondow (*Koloniaal verslag* 1915:35).

[110]   Together, these two diseases were also responsible for a significant rise in mortality on Java at the same period (Gardiner and Oey 1987:71, 77).

[111]   *Fragment* 1856:22; Graafland 1867-69, II:158. Local people, Graafland adds, was also of this opinion, refering to dysentery as *sakit baharu*, the 'new sickness'.

[112]   Duhr 1781:113; *Generale missiven* VII:694; Godée Molsbergen 1928:44; Keijzer 1856:571.

[113]   Res. Manado to GG, 13-2-1834 (ANRI Manado 77).

and on the Togian Islands, toward the end of the colonial period.[114] In 1934 an outbreak of bacillary dysentery also 'cost hundreds of lives' in eastern Central Sulawesi (Avink 1935). Measles is not reported in sources from before 1854, but recurred in at least two less serious epidemics in the second half of the nineteenth century.[115] Twentieth-century sources mention epidemic measles as a significant cause of infant deaths (Kündig 1934:173, 177-8; Stuurman 1936:105).

Tuberculosis, recognized during the nineteenth century as a significant killer in Minahasa (Graafland 1867-69, II:158-9), was later found to be endemic throughout the region.[116] Bubonic plague, which arrived on Java in 1910 (Hull 1987:210), apparently never reached this part of Sulawesi. The impact of the notorious 1918 global influenza pandemic, by contrast, was great.[117] In Donggala and around the Palu Bay about six percent of the population reportedly died, in Gorontalo 10 or 11 percent, in Kulawi at least 13 percent, and in Besoa perhaps as many as 17 percent.[118] In Buol, however, the same epidemic 'took a mild course, and only a very few deaths occurred' (Van Andel 1921:6), and although Dr Bouvy (1924:386) compared his memory of the outbreak in Minahasa to 'an oppressive dream', here too the number of fatalities seems to have been small. In a milder form, influenza had already been present in the region before 1918 (*Koloniaal verslag* 1901:36, 1914:26); in later reports it is mentioned as an endemic disease subject to epidemic exacerbations, and as a cause of infant deaths.[119]

Not all of the lethal diseases which appear in the historical record can readily be identified. In 1817 mysterious 'cold fevers' (Van Delden 1844:373), described in another source as 'a liver sickness' (Kam 1821:298), reportedly killed 3,376 people on Greater Sangir. Most of the many references in archival sources to epidemics of 'stomach disease' (*buikziekte*) also remain indeterminate. Typhoid fever, which caused devastation on Java in the years 1846-1851 (Boomgaard 1987:59-60), is not specifically mentioned in any nineteenth-

[114]   Kelling 1906:14; *Koloniaal verslag* 1910:51, 1912:34, 1913:26, 1915:35, 1917:35, 1918:31, 1923:23, 1925:26, 1929:23; A.Ph. van Aken 1932:219; Ansingh 1937:7; Dutrieux 1930:24; Hoff 1938:55; Korn 1939:58; Kündig 1934:173, 176-8; Logeman 1922:76; Platt 1933:14; Stuurman 1936:106; Tillema 1922:180, 1926:223; Weg 1938:197, 219. In 1946, according to Blankhart (1951:100), a dysentery epidemic on Sangir 'caused the death rate in that year to double'.

[115]   AV Manado 1865, 1884 (ANRI Manado 52); Graafland 1898, I:96.

[116]   Avink 1935; Blankhart 1951:89; Brilman 1938:41; Korn 1939:58; Kortleven 1927:89; Moolenburg 1922:23; Tillema 1926:223; De Wijn 1952:167. In 1930-1932, 16 percent of all adult deaths in the part of Minahasa studied by Kündig (1934:182) were caused by tuberculosis.

[117]   Throughout Indonesia, this killed 'at least 1.5 million people' (Brown 1987:235).

[118]   Kaudern 1940:102; A.C. Kruyt 1938, I:278; Ter Laag 1920:21; Moolenburgh 1922:13; Stap 1919:811.

[119]   Ansingh 1937:7; Eckenhausen 1930:10; Hoff 1938:54; Kündig 1934:173, 178; Logeman 1922: 75; M. van Rhijn 1941:134; Van Son 1935:12; Stuurman 1936:106.

century source from northern Sulawesi, but given the imprecision of many complaints about 'fevers', it may well have been present on a smaller scale. *Typhus abdominalis* certainly seems to have been endemic (although without causing a great number of deaths) in Minahasa, Bolaang Mongondow and Gorontalo in the 1920s and 1930s.[120]

Debilitating diseases

Besides those diseases which were commonly lethal in themselves, many others debilitated the population on a large scale and reduced its resistance to further infection, sickness, and hunger. *Vivax* ('benign tertian') malaria, probably the most important of these, has already been discussed. Another serious and extremely widespread debilitating disease was yaws (*Framboesia tropica*).[121] A nineteenth-century observer reported that in Minahasa, yaws 'spares neither old nor young people, and those affected by it sometimes continue to suffer for three to four years'.[122] Among the indigenous population of Central Sulawesi, according to Adriani and Kruyt (1912-14, I:407), it was accepted wisdom 'that every person must inevitably catch *Framboesia'*. A later report ranks yaws alongside malaria as one of the two 'foremost diseases' (*voornaamste ziekten*) in the Poso area (*Algemeene memorie Poso* 1925:5). A 'protracted and severe' health problem (Adriani and Kruyt 1912-14, I:407), yaws made it difficult for sufferers to walk or work, while the open sores which it caused on the skin facilitated other infections.[123] On occasion it also resulted in blindness (Adriani and Kruyt 1950-51, II:199). On the Banggai Islands many people showed symptoms closely resembling those of the yaws-related disease known in Latin America as pinta, whereby large patches of the skin become depigmented (Van Rootselaar 1957). Leprosy, a still more disfiguring disease, was widespread in the region, although the number of sufferers was relatively small.[124]

---

[120]   A.Ph. van Aken 1932:211, 219; Bouvy 1924:389; Hoff 1938:56; Stuurman 1936:106; Weg 1938:197-8. Bouvy and Hoff refer only to 'typhus', but it is clear that they mean typhoid fever rather than louse-borne typhus.
[121]   AV Manado 1833 (ANRI Manado 48); Ansingh 1937:7; Avink 1935; Brilman 1938:30, 41; Coolsma 1901:664; Van Dinter 1899:345; Van Doren 1854-56, I:268; Dutrieux 1930:24; Edie 1923:25; Frieswijck 1902:472; Korn 1939:58; Kortleven 1927:89; A.C. Kruyt 1930a:339; Lam 1932:50; Moolenburgh 1922:23; Roep 1917:426; Tillema 1926:204, 222.
[122]   Van Doren 1854-56, I:268. Also AV Manado 1833 (ANRI Manado 48); Graafland 1867-69, I:176.
[123]   Graafland 1867-69, I:176; Perine 1991:306-7; Netherlands Indies Medical and Sanitary Service 1929:62.
[124]   Adriani and Kruyt 1912-14, I:414-5, 1950-51, II:195-7; Ansingh 1935; Cuarteron 1855:10; Edie 1923:25; Hissink 1912:80; Hoff 1938:57; Korn 1939:58; Kortleven 1927:89; Logeman 1922:75;

Plate 14. *Raja* of Banggai, blind and with skin disease, 1678 (NA VOC 1345:193)

Skin disease was another very visible health problem (Plate 14). 'When we arrived in Central Sulawesi', remembered Adriani and Kruyt (1950-51, II:198), 'perhaps half of the population was afflicted by a scaly skin disease'.[125] In the Palu Valley, according to Tillema (1926:222) in 1924, 'practically everybody' suffered from scabies (*schurft*). The lowland population of eastern Central Sulawesi was also heavily affected:

> Skin diseases like scabies, *Dajakse schurft* [*Tinea imbricata*] and other fungal skin infections are part of the normal equipment of the population here. Fairly harmless in themselves, they contribute via numerous scratching effects to the danger of secondary infection with all its consequences (sores, abscesses, blood poisoning). Yaws, too, finds ready access to the body through the damaged skin. (Avink 1935.)

Moolenbergh 1922:23; M. van Rhijn 1941:142-3; Riedel 1870a:101; Stuurman 1936:105; Tesch 1936; Tillema 1926:222; Weg 1938:200.
[125]   Also Abendanon 1915-18, II:686; Adriani and Kruyt 1898:503, 1950-51, II:172, 198; A.C. Kruyt 1909:372; *Nota berglandschappen* 1912:9; Wichmann 1890:984.

On Banggai a slave without skin disease commanded double the price of a *kalanding*, as those with scaly skin were called.[126] The populations of other parts of the region, including Minahasa and Bolaang Mongondow, were all affected to a greater or lesser degree.[127] Most notorious in this respect, however, were Sangir and Talaud, where the spectacular fungal infection *Tinea imbricata* was particularly common. 'I truly believe', wrote Van Delden (1844:376) in 1825, 'that there is no other place where this disease is found so frequently as on the Sangir Islands'.[128] In 1914, a visiting government doctor estimated that on Talaud 'more than 90 percent of the population is suffering from various kinds of skin disease' (Roep 1917:426).

Intestinal parasite infections were also extremely common.[129] In Tondano in 1931, 63 percent of the population was found to be infected with hookworm and 27 percent with roundworm; in Sangir the proportions were 33 percent and 54 percent respectively.[130] Earlier research on Minahasan soldiers and their families had even indicated that more than 80 percent suffered from hookworm infections (Bouvy 1924:392), the symptoms of which include anaemia (Pearson and Guerrant 1991:704). 'It is unbelievable', wrote Dr Bouvy (1924:394) of patients treated for hookworm, 'how the appearance improves, and the vitality and will to work return, after completion of the cure'. Filarial parasite infections (transmitted, like malaria, by mosquitos) were also widespread, sometimes leading to elephantiasis.[131]

In western Central Sulawesi, uniquely in Indonesia, there were two areas of endemic schistosomiasis (bilharzia): one, identified at the end of the colonial period (Bonne et al. 1942a; Müller and Tesch 1937), around Lake Lindu, and another in the Napu and Tawaelia valleys which was not discovered by medical science until the 1970s.[132] In Lindu, echinostomiasis was also endemic.[133] Both of these debilitating diseases are caused by parasitic flatworms (trematodes) which have freshwater molluscs as intermediate hosts.

---

[126] A.C. Kruyt 1932c:251. Also Bosscher and Matthijssen 1854:97; A.C. Kruyt 1932e:150. It is possible that some of these descriptions refer to pinta (see above), which is easily mistaken for a fungal skin disease (Van Rootselaar 1957:44).
[127] AV Manado 1833 (ANRI Manado 48); Bouvy 1924:382; Edie 1923:25; Gallois 1892:44; Graafland 1867-69, II:159, 1898, II:198; Logeman 1922:76; Riedel 1870a:102; Wilken and Schwarz 1867c:328.
[128] Also Brilman 1938:41; Van Dinter 1899:345; F. Kelling, 'Het eiland Taghoelandang en zijn bewoners' [1866] (ARZ NZG 43-2); Frieswijck 1902:472; Lam 1932:51; Steller 1866:31; Van de Velde van Cappellen 1857:46.
[129] A.Ph. van Aken 1932:218; Avink 1935; Blankhart 1951:88; Bouvy 1924:392; Brilman 1938:30; Eckenhausen 1930:10; Hoff 1938:56; Logeman 1922:76; M. van Rhijn 1941:143; Stuurman 1936:105; Tillema 1926:223.
[130] A.Ph. van Aken 1932:218. Avink (1935) and Blankhart (1951:88) give comparable figures.
[131] Ansingh 1937:7; Avink 1935:8; Logeman 1922:76; Riedel 1870a:101-2; Vorstman 1935a:29.
[132] Carney et al. 1974. Also Sudomo and Carney 1974; Carney et al. 1975.
[133] Bonne 1941; Bonne et al. 1942b; Brug and Tesch 1937.

Schistosomiasis is contracted when a free-swimming stage of the parasite, shed into water by snails, penetrates the skin. In the case of echinostomiasis the human host must ingest the molluscs in which the pre-adult trematode stage develops; in Lindu this link was provided by freshwater mussels, which played an important role in the diet of the local population (Bonne and Sandground 1939).

Goitre, resulting from a deficiency of iodine in the diet, was very common in the mountain interior of western Central Sulawesi, where in some localities half of the population was said to be affected.[134] In some individuals, the symptoms included cretinism (Vorstman 1935a:29). Goitre was also reported in the early twentieth century from upland Minahasa (Bouvy 1924:390), and from the Pada area in the interior of eastern Central Sulawesi.[135] Another widespread deficiency disease was beriberi, caused by an inadequate intake of vitamin B_1 (thiamine). In 1934 a 'quite serious beriberi epidemic' took place in Tobungku (De Haze Winkelman 1935:7). The Dutch authorities noted that this was an area where, partly because rice production had recently been reduced by a series of harvest failures and by heavy involvement of the male population in forest product collection, more sago than rice was eaten.[136] Since rice, provided it is not too highly milled or polished, is a good source of vitamin B_1, it made sense to conclude that this epidemic resulted from 'the absence of the locally-grown rice, which should have provided a safe defence against the feared disease' (De Haze Winkelman 1935:8). Beriberi, however, was not restricted to sago-eating groups: in 1909, epidemics were reported both in 'the interior' of eastern Central Sulawesi (Mori?), and in Gorontalo (*Koloniaal verslag* 1910:50-1). Some sources also mention beriberi in Minahasa.[137] Kidney stones, an unusually frequent complaint in Minahasa, were later linked with a possible deficiency of vitamin A in the diet (Kisman 1941:2685).

---

[134] Tillema 1926:223; Abendanon 1915-18, II:602; Adriani and Kruyt 1898:503; Boonstra van Heerdt 1914a:628-9; E. Gobée, 'Aanteekeningen naar aanleiding van een reis door de Pososche berglandschappen', 7-3-1926 (ARZ NZG 101A-7-2); A.C. Kruyt 1908:1334-5, 1909:372; Logeman 1922:76; *Nota berglandschappen* 1912:9; Riedel 1886:93; Sarasin and Sarasin 1905, II:92; Vorstman 1935a:29. Kruyt (1900b:459) also mentions goitre in Mori.

[135] Avink 1935. In the Poso Valley, by contrast, goitre was said to be rare (A.C. Kruyt 1908:1335). In the endemic areas, most sufferers were women (Boonstra van Heerdt 1914a:628; A.C. Kruyt 1909:372).

[136] Avink 1935; De Haze Winkelman 1935:8, 14. Until the economic depression of 1930, it was reported, much rice had been imported to compensate for local underproduction. When the prices paid for forest products fell, however, 'people in some *kampung* lived [...] on the edge of vitamin deficiency, because their food consisted mainly of sago' (Avink 1935).

[137] AV Manado 1833 (ANRI Manado 48); Van Doren 1854-56, I:268; Van Kol 1903:303; *Koloniaal verslag* 1891:17. In 1891 a Dutch doctor even claimed that beriberi was a 'common' disease in Minahasa (Gallois 1892:44).

Although Reid (1987:41-2, 1988-93, I:161) has suggested that gonorrhoea was a significant cause of low fertility among Southeast Asian tribal populations, this was almost certainly not the case in northern Sulawesi. In the 1860s, Graafland (1867-69, II:159) reported that venereal disease had been introduced to Minahasa only recently by Europeans. Some women in the coastal trading settlements of Central Sulawesi had become sterile as a result of sexually transmitted diseases by the beginning of the twentieth century (see Chapter X), but such diseases were 'still entirely unknown' in the pagan interior (A.C. Kruyt 1903:198), and in 1924 only 4.2 percent of the almost 12,000 post-menopausal Toraja (upland) women included in the Tillema survey were reported to be sterile for any reason (Tillema 1926:47). In 1901 venereal disease was still 'extremely rare' on the readily accessible island of Tagulandang (Frieswijck 1902:472). As late as the 1930s it remained 'very rare' in Bolaang Mongondow (Hoff 1938:57) and 'virtually unknown' in eastern Central Sulawesi except in 'the more civilized places' on the coast (Avink 1935). In the 1940s syphilis, at least, was still completely absent from the upland populations of the Poso and Mori areas 'thanks to their isolation' (De Wijn 1952:166). Strikingly, it was precisely among such remote populations untouched by sexually transmitted diseases that the birth rate was lowest (Chapter X). Sources from other parts of Indonesia confirm that in the more isolated areas (as opposed to the major states and trading ports) these diseases became prevalent only at a late date, and therefore cannot be implicated in long-term patterns of low population growth (Knapen 2001, 156; Van der Sterren, Murray and Hull 1997:203-7).

Conclusion

Although the evidence is limited, it does not appear that war was a very important impediment to population growth in the region prior to European rule. While wars and other types of human violence were frequent in most areas, the numbers of war casualties and sacrificial or judicial killings were seldom large. The disruptive impact of war upon agriculture, the disease environment, and trade may have been more significant in demographic terms, but these effects are difficult to isolate, and no major epidemics, or episodes of more than very local famine, can be linked with warfare. Natural hazards, other than those affecting the food supply (see Chapter IX), were likewise a minor factor in the demographic equation.

Disease and poor health, by contrast, were crucial. At least a fifth of all children born – usually more – died in infancy, and at least a third before reaching adulthood. Most of those who did reach adulthood probably died in their 50s or younger. Once in every generation a smallpox epidemic killed about one person in every six, and sometimes more. In those places where malaria was highly endemic, it pushed the child mortality rate up beyond 40 percent; where it occurred in the form of occasional epidemics, it weakened the adult population and increased the frequency of abortions and stillbirths; and individuals brought up in places where it was absent always risked their lives if they travelled elsewhere. Dysentery and other gastro-enteritic diseases, tuberculosis, goitre, and beriberi were all common, while almost everyone was affected by yaws at some point in his or her life. In some areas most of the population was also permanently infected with hookworm and afflicted by chronic skin disease. While not all of the significant diseases can be traced back further than the nineteenth century in the historical record, in most cases this probably results simply from the less detailed character of the earlier sources. The advent of Asiatic cholera in 1830, on the other hand, did lead to a significant exacerbation of the disease environment; the extent to which this deterioration was compensated by improvements in medicine and hygiene will be examined in Chapter VIII.

The populations of upland areas, generally speaking, made a healthier and stronger impression than those of the coastlands (De Clercq 1873:258; Riedel 1870a:69), but this correlation was not universal. In nineteenth-century Minahasa the Bantik, inhabiting the coastal lowlands around Manado, were described as even more strongly built than the mountain-dwellers (Graafland 1867-69, II:262; Schippers 1886:94). In the Palu Valley, 105 adult male Kaili lowlanders measured by the military medical officer Tesch (1939: 2375) in 1936 were on average slightly taller, rather than smaller (155 against 153 cm), than their Pekawa neighbours from the mountains to the west of the valley.[138] On the opposite side of Central Sulawesi the upland Saluan, although apparently healthier than their malaria-ridden coastal neighbours, were remarkably small in stature (Kleiweg de Zwaan 1929:787). Due to the variety of mosquito vectors present in the region, it should be noted in this context, the distribution of malaria was complex, and not always restricted to the coastal lowlands. The relatively populous highland basins of western Central Sulawesi were areas of endemic malaria (as well as schistosomiasis), and this took its toll in terms of high infant and child mortality despite the tall, healthy appearance of much of the adult population.

Early European accounts emphasizing the good health of Southeast Asians (Reid 1987:37-8), in my opinion, need to be interpreted with caution as they are based largely on the appearance of active adults, a group whose condition may be a poor guide to that of the population as a whole (Schefold 1988:

---

[138]   Among the valley-dwellers themselves, Tesch (1939:2377) also reported, the inhabitants of coastal settlements like Palu were 'somewhat taller on average than is the case further inland'.

69-70). Because infant and child mortality accounted for much of the death rate in precolonial times, the relationship between overall mortality and the appearance of the surviving adults was not straightforward. 'The conditions under which the Kalinga live', observed the anthropologist Dozier (1966:42) of this isolated Philippine people around 1960, 'tend to eliminate all but the exceptionally fit'; the adult part of the Kalinga population, accordingly, was 'of magnificent physique, but the toll of those who do not make it into adult life is great.' In this perspective the surprising thing about European and Southeast Asian stature in the early modern period is perhaps not so much that Southeast Asian adults were taller than their European counterparts, but rather that so many small and weak Europeans were able to survive childhood and reach the other side of the world to compare themselves with Southeast Asia's surviving fittest.

The proposition that disease was a key population control in precolonial Indonesia is supported by the relevant literature on other parts of the country. 'Endemic and epidemic diseases', states Knapen (1998:87), 'seem to be the predominant factor in explaining low population growth on Borneo and the concomitant modest human impact on the environment before the twentieth century'. Ormeling (1956:180) reached the same conclusion for Timor, as did anthropologist Schefold (1988:21, 67-70), on the basis of fieldwork rather than historical research, for the still essentially 'precolonial' Sakuddei of Mentawai, whose population density remained very low despite an estimated average completed fertility rate of six births per woman.

CHAPTER VIII

Disease control

This chapter examines methods of disease control, including both indigenous and Western medicine, together with some other aspects of the social and domestic environment which, whether by intent or coincidence, may have affected the spread of disease. In order to assess the impact of colonial medicine and public health efforts on the rate of population growth, an attempt is made to relate documented changes in the medical and hygiene situation to what is known about mortality trends.

Indigenous medicine and disease prevention

Indigenous medicines, usually derived from plant products, are often mentioned in the colonial literature on northern Sulawesi.[1] The 1898 standard work by the botanist S.H. Koorders on the flora of Minahasa, to take the most detailed example, lists 20 different species yielding products with indigenous medicinal applications, including laxatives, a purgative, an antidote for poison bites and stings, and treatments for external wounds, eye and throat infections, gonorrhoea, thrush, intestinal worms, and 'abdominal and stomach diseases'.[2] The leaves of one vegetable, the bitter gourd (*Momordica charantia*), are also described (Koorders 1898:481) as *koortsverdrijvend* or febrifugal ('fever-expelling'). Resident Wenzel, writing in 1825, likewise claims that Minahasans have a medicine which 'often cures them' from the (malarial) 'fevers' which he calls the 'usual diseases found among the population'.

---

[1]   Adriani and Kruyt 1950-51, II:181-207, 194; Bosscher and Matthijssen 1854:74; De Clercq 1873:265; Van Doren 1854-56, I:268; Graafland 1867-69, I:202, 324-6; Grubauer 1913:376; Hickson 1889:196, 294-5; Hissink 1912:80-1; A.C. Kruyt 1930b:472, 1938, II:316-20; Padtbrugge 1866:328; Pennings 1908:16. Most of these accounts, however, are very sketchy. 'Their medicines', states Resident Pietermaat shortly, 'consist mainly of garlic, ginger, *daun kelur* (the leaves of a certain tree), and lemon' (AV Manado 1833, in ANRI Manado 48).

[2]   Koorders 1898:462, 481, 490, 510, 513, 545, 549, 561, 564, 568, 573, 582-3, 585, 588-9, 595, 604, 611. Indigenous informants provided much of the information from which this work was compiled.

According to his account this is derived not from a vegetable, but from 'the bark of a type of wild rattan' (Riedel 1872b:481). Van Delden (1844:375), in his account of the Sangir Islands at the same date, lists five plant medicines used to treat 'fevers', including, according to later identifications by Hickson (1889:196), the fungus *Pachyma* [*Lentinus*] *Tuber-regium*, and a boiled essence of leaves of the deciduous tree *Crataeva magna*. In Gorontalo the bark of the *kayu mas* (*Nauclea orientalis*) was prized as a febrifuge.[3] In Bolaang Mongondow, the seeds of a fruiting swamp-forest tree (genus *Xylocarpus*) were identified in 1933 as a traditional malaria remedy (Steup 1933:47).

How many of these indigenous medicines were effective, however, is another question. 'Despite all the miraculous stories told about them', noted Dr Bouvy (1924:375) after four years in Manado, 'I have not seen any such miracles myself'. The existence of an effective traditional malaria treatment seems particularly doubtful. The bitter gourd mentioned by Koorders has been shown to contain a mild laxative, but not a substance active against malaria or other 'fevers'.[4] Koorders himself (1898:291-2, 295), conversely, describes 16 useful rattan (*Calamus* and *Korthalsia*) species from Minahasa without mentioning the medicinal application described by Wenzel.[5] The fact that many of the supposed fever remedies were bitter in taste suggests that they may have been selected simply on the grounds of this superficial similarity to quinine.[6] When assessing the likely effectiveness of indigenous medicines, it is also important to note that most, including many of those used against malaria and other internal complaints, were not in fact swallowed, but only applied externally.[7]

> As we have seen, illnesses are generally ascribed to external [supernatural] causes. For this reason the treatment of a sick person is also wholly external; the concept of 'taking' medicines was originally alien to the Toraja. The medicine is applied to

[3]   Res. Manado to AR Gorontalo, 7-7-1858 (ANRI Manado 53).
[4]   Siemonsma and Kasem Piluek 1994:207. The fruit of this plant is also useful for the treatment of diabetes.
[5]   Neither are medicinal uses mentioned by De Clercq (1909:188-9, 217, 264) in his descriptions of Indonesian rattan (*Calamus*, *Korthalsia*, *Daemonorops*) species.
[6]   Heyne (1950, I:682, 888) mentions that the bark of *Creativa magna* contain 'a sharp, bitter substance' used for (external) treatment of fevers, and that *Xylocarpus* seeds also have a very bitter taste. Adriani and Kruyt (1950-51, II:197) mention another bitter antimalarial medicine. The association of bitterness with medicine, on the other hand, may predate the use of quinine: in Tobungku and Banggai in the mid-nineteenth century, 'many bitter plants' were already being used against 'the fever' (Bosscher and Matthijssen 1854:74).
[7]   Adriani and Kruyt (1950-51, II:197) and Hissink (1912:80) describe the external application of medicines against malaria. There were exceptions, however, to the rule of external treatment. In his account of traditional medicine in western Central Sulawesi, Kruyt (1938, II:316-20) mentions three remedies for stomach and digestive problems which were ingested. Bouvy (1924:376) also notes the internal use of plant medicines.

the outside of those parts of the body which are sick. The most common way of doing this is to chew it and then spit it, or rather sneeze it (*mosupa*), onto the body. In this way the medicine is mixed with the saliva and breath of the curer, which makes it even more effective. (Adriani and Kruyt 1950-51, II:188.)

At least where external complaints were concerned, Europeans were usually prepared to keep an open mind about the usefulness of traditional medicines. In 1901, Albert Kruyt sent 'a number of samples of tubers and roots' to the government health laboratory in Batavia for chemical analysis after observing 'that they are used by the Toraja of Central Sulawesi to heal wounds'.[8] One tuber did prove to contain some tannin, but not, it was thought, in sufficient quantity to have much medicinal effect. Kruyt and Adriani therefore attributed the reported efficacy of the treatment mainly to the bathing of the wound which it coincidentally involved. Local remedies for skin diseases, the missionaries concluded (not surprisingly in view of the prevalence of those diseases) also had 'little effect' (Adriani and Kruyt 1912-14, I:406, 415).

Only a few local medicines, on the other hand, were ever investigated in a scientific way, and it is possible that more thorough research would have yielded some surprises.[9] Certainly it is not the case that all medical techniques other than those introduced by the Dutch were useless. The practice of variolation to prevent smallpox, for instance, will be discussed below, and a similar type of pre-emptive infection was apparently also used in order to reduce the impact of yaws. 'Children', reported Adriani and Kruyt (1950-51, II:199), 'are sometimes deliberately infected with this disease so that they will not catch it later as adults'. Indigenous healers could also set broken bones using splints, and lance and cuarterize abscesses (Adriani and Kruyt 1950-51, II:193-4).

Certain aspects of traditional house design must have had a prophylactic effect against malaria. Because *Anopheles* mosquitos habitually fly close to the ground, firstly, the elevated pile-dwellings which were universal in the region automatically afforded their inhabitants some protection from mosquito bites.[10] In some places the mosquito nuisance was explicitly cited by local people as one of the reasons for building elevated houses.[11] There

---

8   Chef Geneeskundigen Dienst to Res. Manado, 2-2-1902 (ARZ NZG 101A). Bouvy (1924: 375-6) also mentions tests on indigenous medicines, including a putative cure for beriberi.
9   Some traditional medicines from Kalimantan (Knapen 1998:76) and peninsular Malaysia (Baer 1999:92) have recently been shown to have an effective anti-malarial action.
10   Baer 1999:92; Van der Brug 1995:81; Knapen 1998:76. Most *Anopheles* mosquitos, it should be added, bite only after nightfall.
11   Grubauer 1913:79. This source refers in the first place to the population of the area around Lake Matano, and I have found no reports of other similar statements regarding stilt-houses as such. On the southern shore of Lake Poso, however, Adriani and Kruyt (1912-14, II:148) did come across tree huts belonging to 'fishermen who, wishing to spend the night on the lakeshore, built themselves such high sleeping-places in order to avoid the numerous mosquitos'.

is no evidence that the specific connection between mosquitos and malaria was understood. Minahasans often attributed malaria attacks to the eating of certain fruits (Schouten 1998:69), a folk aetiology still popular today (Van Eeuwijk and Van Eeuwijk 1993-94:448). The ethnographer Grubauer (1913: 79), nevertheless, referred to 'the fact, certainly not unknown to the natives, that in houses built at ground level they are much more liable to fever attacks'. In the Poso area prior to Dutch rule, 'curtains of *fuya* [bark cloth] or cotton' were often hung around the sleeping compartments inside the houses 'against the cold or the mosquitos' – that is, as the functional equivalent of mosquito nets (Adriani and Kruyt 1912-14, II:187). A local name for these curtains, *kuyambu*, is clearly cognate with *kelambu*, the modern Malay word for the mosquito net proper. It is not clear, however, that they closed off the sleeping compartment from above as well as from the sides, and their main purpose, as assumed by authors describing similar hangings on Sangir and Talaud, may well have been to provide privacy.[12] The lack of windows or ventilation in most houses, finally, made for a permanently smoky interior, which also served to repel mosquitos.[13]

The most effective indigenous method of disease control was probably the prevention of contact between infected and uninfected people. During smallpox epidemics in the Poso area, ritual specialists were said to 'forbid any kind of intercourse with an infected village; if any person from such a village is encountered, one must pass him by with one's head turned away'.[14] 'When a whole *kampung* is affected by disease', states a later report from Tolitoli, 'it is closed off for a week, a condition indicated by white flags; nobody may then enter or leave it'.[15] Another common response to the approach of an epidemic was to abandon nuclear settlements for the dispersed swidden houses in their neighbourhood, or even take flight into the wilderness beyond.[16] In extreme cases, such as that of the 1884 smallpox epidemic in Central Sulawesi, whole villages were permanently deserted following epidemic attacks. Isolation of sufferers was probably typical only in

[12]   Van Dinter 1899:360; Roep 1917:420; Steller 1866:30; Tillema 1922:180-2.
[13]   Adriani and Kruyt 1950-51, II:201; Van Dinter 1899:359-60; Tillema 1922:181, 218, 230. A disadvantage of the fact that people lived 'a great part of their lives in the smoke of the hearth' was a high incidence of conjunctivitis and other eye problems (Adriani and Kruyt 1950-51, II: 201), and probably also respiratory disease (Feachem 1977:139, 173-4, 177).
[14]   *Brieven*, March 1909. Against an actual smallpox attack, it should be noted, there was no remedy, either in the indigenous pharmacopoeia (A.C. Kruyt 1938, II:310) or in European medicine (Breman 1991:168).
[15]   Kortleven 1927:84. In some sources, however, these flags are interpreted purely as magical barriers against the sickness itself (Grubauer 1913:578; A.C. Kruyt 1938, II:310).
[16]   Adriani and Kruyt 1912-14, I:206, 417; *Brieven*, March 1909; A.C. Kruyt 1893:107, 1938, I:115, II:310; Res. Manado to GG, 13-1-1840 (ANRI Manado 79); Schwarz and De Lange 1876:158; N.P. Wilken 1849:392.

response to highly contagious diseases like smallpox or cholera; gregarious family visits to the sick, in fact, may well have helped to spread less serious illnesses (Graafland 1867-69, I:177; Kündig 1934:176). Flight from epidemics, moreover, often served only to exacerbate their effects, since some of the fugitives were already infected (A.C. Kruyt 1893:107), and others sometimes died of hunger in the forests.[17] Significant protection against infectious diseases, nevertheless, may have been achieved locally. In Kendari (Southeast Sulawesi) in the 1830s, local people told the adventurer Vosmaer (1839:95-6) that thanks to the strict local custom of 'abandoning each sufferer to his fate, without concerning themselves with him in the least', only sporadic cases of smallpox had ever been known there.[18]

Malaria control in the colonial era

Colonial policies of population concentration and village relocation, as already noted, often led to serious exacerbations of malaria mortality. During the late nineteenth and early twentieth centuries, nevertheless, significant attempts to control this important disease were also made by the Dutch authorities. The idea of draining swamps to combat malaria, firstly, was already current among Europeans in northern Sulawesi long before the nature of the link between the two phenomena was understood. After a journey to Bolaang Mongondow in 1866, the missionaries Wilken and Schwarz (1867a:50) remarked that the health situation in Bolaang could be improved 'if a muddy pool in the vicinity of the *negeri* were to be cleaned up'. Graafland, at the same period, believed that a similar swamp was responsible for the severe malaria in Kema on the east coast of Minahasa, where people suffering from the so-called 'Kema fevers' were found in 'every house'. 'The cause', he wrote, 'was well-known: a swamp, which filled up with water and then partly emptied again twice each day, ran along the beach behind a raised dike, and spread pestilential vapours over the place whenever a sea wind blew' (Graafland 1898, II:307). The health problems in Kema, agreed Resident Jansen in 1853, 'could surely be much reduced, if not entirely eliminated, by draining the pools and providing better outlet channels for the water'.[19]

The projected cost of this undertaking proved prohibitively high, and nothing was done (De Clercq 1873:256). Three decades later, however, the malaria

---

[17]   MV Manado September 1860 (ANRI Manado 54).
[18]   Isolation of individual houses is also mentioned by Adriani and Kruyt (1912-14, I:396) for Central Sulawesi, and by Hunt (1837:52) for Sulu.
[19]   AV Manado 1853 (ANRI Manado 51). Graafland (1867-69, II:268) also suggested that a similar swamp on the opposite coast of Minahasa should be converted into irrigated ricefields as a means of malaria control.

problem in Kema suddenly solved itself in a case of environmental sanitation by accidental, natural means which seemed to confirm the potential of the technique. After a heavy storm one night in December 1882, the river which flows into the sea at Kema burst its banks and deposited a metre-thick layer of sand and clay over the lower ground in the vicinity of the settlement, including the coastal swamp. Whether or not the swamp itself had indeed been the mosquito breeding place (*A. minimus* breeds only in fresh water, and *A. subpictus* prefers a less strongly tidal environment), this event seems to have been responsible for the effective eradication of the local vector. While residents, on the basis of the contemporary European theory that a 'miasma' emanating from muddy terrain was the cause of the fevers, had expected them to intensify as a result of the flood, instead they disappeared. Attendance at the mission school increased dramatically, the children took on a 'healthy, vigorous' appearance, and from then on Kema, like Amurang (see Chapter VII), was counted 'among the healthy coastal settlements' (Graafland 1898, II:307).

At around the same time, the colonial authorities began to put some of their long-standing sanitation plans into practice. In 1883 an abandoned arm of the Manado River was drained (Wattendorff 1883), partly to permit expansion of the adjacent Chinese quarter of Manado town, but partly also on the grounds that this would be an important improvement 'from the point of view of hygiene' (Matthes 1881). On Sangir and Talaud at the beginning of the 1890s, attempts were made to relocate some *kampung* away from the 'swampy coasts' (*Koloniaal verslag* 1892:21), and from 1897 onward, 'much work' (*Koloniaal verslag* 1901:36) was made of marsh drainage in these islands.[20] Later, after the dynamics of malaria transmission via Anopheline mosquitos became understood as a result of the discoveries made by Ronald Ross in India in 1898, species-specific sanitation projects were also carried out at a number of places on the mainland of North and Central Sulawesi, and in Banggai.[21]

Few of the deliberate sanitation attempts, however, seem to have fulfilled the promise held out by the accidental case of Kema in 1882. In 1902, for instance, malaria was still common in Manado – especially, as before, in the Chinese quarter, at least part of which was still subject to flooding (Van Kol 1903:300). At local transmigration settlements established in the south of Minahasa during the 1920s, the draining of fishponds, identified as breeding sites for *A. minimus*, resulted only in an increased concentration of the same species in nearby natural streams (A.Ph. van Aken 1932:213). Another species sanitation programme, aimed at eliminating *A. subpictus* from the vicin-

---

[20]   Encyclopaedisch Bureau 1912a:55; *Koloniaal verslag* 1898:22, 1901:36; Roep 1917:430.
[21]   E. Gobée, 'Bestuurs-memorie over de afdeeling Poso', 28-3-1926 (ARZ NZG 101A.7); Hirschmann 1934:36; A.C. Kruyt 1931:527; Netherlands Indies Medical and Sanitary Service 1929: Fig. 8; Stuurman 1936:105; Tammes 1940:195; Tideman 1926:191.

ity of the administrative capital on Banggai, had already cost ƒ 50,000 before a persistently high rate of infection alerted researchers to the fact that two other vectors, *A. punctulatus* (a dangerous species in the Moluccas) and *A. minimus*, were also present (A.Ph. van Aken 1932:216-7). In 1927 the capital of Tolitoli was completely rebuilt two kilometres from its original location in an attempt to escape the disease, but the new site turned out to be just as malarial as the old one. Sanitation of the 'extensive brackish swamps' where the local *A. subpictus* population bred, meanwhile, was judged prohibitively expensive, especially since there was a possibility that *A. minimus* was also involved (A.Ph. van Aken 1932:215-6; Hirschmann 1934:36).

Elsewhere too, sanitation often proved impossible for economic or technical reasons. On the coasts of Minahasa, strong winds and high surf made it impractical to keep brackish lagoons open to the tides as a means of controlling *A. subpictus* (Weg 1938:196). In 1941 the penultimate Dutch resident of Manado complained that even the comparatively simple environmental measure recommended to combat *A. minimus* in the Minahasan interior – the preservation of shade trees along the banks of the clear streams in which this species, given plenty of sunlight, preferred to breed – was not practicable except in the vicinity of a few major settlements. The total length of such streams in the area was too great, and local people, who used their water, too much in the habit of clearing paths along their banks for access (M. van Rhijn 1941:136). In the highlands of western Central Sulawesi, likewise, any kind of sanitation of the marshes harbouring *A. maculatus* was found to be 'completely out of the question'.[22]

Malaria control in northern Sulawesi at the end of the colonial period, in fact, was still based much less on species sanitation than on the antimalarial drug quinine. Even in Minahasa, probably the part of the region where sanitation efforts had been most intensive, a Dutch official could still write in 1936 that the campaign against malaria 'principally came down to the distribution of quinine' (Stuurman 1936:105). Almost everywhere in the region, colonial officials and doctors distributed this drug in large quantities during the early twentieth century.[23] Immediately following the Dutch conquest of Central Sulawesi, for instance, 'depots' were established where 'tablets from the Bandung quinine factory' were 'made available at cost price (one cent per tablet), or at no charge to the poor'.[24] 'After the arrival of the government',

---

[22]   A.Ph. van Aken 1932:214. Also Avink 1935; Blankhart 1951:88.
[23]   A.Ph. van Aken 1932:215; Ansingh 1937:7; Hoff 1938:54; *Koloniaal verslag* 1913:26; Logeman 1922:74; Platt 1933:13; Roep 1917:427; Stokking 1910:16; 'Propaganda for quinine use', adds Hoff (1938:54), was also disseminated 'on a large scale'.
[24]   AV Midden Celebes 1906 (ANRI Manado 30). Distribution at no charge, or cost price at the most, was also standard policy elsewhere in the residency (A.Ph. van Aken 1932:215; Hoff 1938: 54; Logeman 1922:74; Platt 1933:13; Roep 1917:427).

Adriani and Kruyt (1950-51, II:198) later wrote, 'quinine quickly became a familiar and accepted item among the Toraja [*heeft de kinine al spoedig burger-recht onder de Toradjas gekregen*]'. In 1934 'the entire population' of the area around Lake Lindu 'was subjected to a four-day course' of quinine tablets by a government doctor.[25] Missionaries, where present, provided a second channel of quinine distribution.[26] In Central Sulawesi they provided it free to all comers, regardless of income, until 1924.[27] At least by the 1920s, finally, quinine was also available commercially on the open market; a residency *memorie van overgave* from 1922 notes that when free quinine is provided by the government, 'the population is spared from having to buy expensive and inferior tablets in the *kampung*' (Logeman 1922:74).

On a smaller scale, the use of this drug can also be traced back far into the nineteenth century. The earliest explicit mentions of quinine in Minahasa date from 1860, when 'most' of the 500 people affected by a 'fever' epidemic in Tonsea were said to have 'recovered quickly when treated with *sulph. chinini* [quinine (bi)sulphate]'.[28] Reports that fever sufferers had been treated successfully using medicines supplied by the government, however, began in 1855, and it is likely that these too refer to quinine.[29] In this early period the drug was distributed, apparently free of charge, by the military doctor based in Manado (who toured the interior during epidemics), by a number of *dokter Jawa* (indigenous medical assistants trained by the colonial government in Java), and by the Protestant missionaries resident in various districts of Minahasa.[30] In addition, some of the Minahasan chiefs received supplies for distribution among their subjects.[31] Later in the century, the drug also came into use elsewhere in the residency. In 1872 it was 'liberally distributed among the population' in Gorontalo.[32] During the epidemic of malaria and cholera on Talaud in 1886, a 'considerable quantity' was delivered to the stricken area together with a Minahasan medical assistant instructed to 'administer it daily to the sick' (Ebbinge Wübben 1889:206). The reputation of the drug spread widely; in the 1890s, Europeans travelling in areas far outside Dutch control were asked for quinine by local people (A.C. Kruyt 1898:5; Sarasin and Sarasin 1905, I:94).

[25]   Vorstman 1935a:29. The effectiveness of this treatment, unfortunately, is not recorded.
[26]   Aragon 1992:178; Dunnebier 1907a:16; J. Kruyt 1970:239; Roep 1917:427; Stokking 1910:16.
[27]   J. Kruyt 1970:239. Thereafter, they continued to distribute it free 'in some remote areas where not much money was yet in circulation'.
[28]   MV Manado February 1860 (ANRI Manado 54).
[29]   MV Manado November, December 1855, January, February, October 1856 (ANRI Manado 54); AV Manado 1857, 1858 (ANRI Manado 52); this last source refers to 'European medicines'.
[30]   In 1860 there were 3 *dokter Jawa* and 7 Protestant missionaries in Minahasa (Van der Crab 1862:342; Gunning 1924:455).
[31]   MV Manado January 1856 (ANRI Manado 54).
[32]   AV Gorontalo 1872 (ANRI Manado 9).

Quinine, in colonial times the sole available antimalarial medication, is a powerful one still used today for the emergency treatment of severe *falciparum* malaria.[33] At least compared to its modern counterparts, however, it is not particularly effective as a prophylactic drug (Bruce-Chwatt 1980:177), and for this reason, together with doubts regarding the scale on which it was distributed and the regularity with which it was consumed, recent writers have generally been sceptical regarding its impact in Indonesia during the colonial period. Elson (1994:285), for example, denies that there is 'any clear evidence that quinine was used effectively against malaria' on Java before 1870, and Gardiner and Oey (1987:80) doubt whether it had 'much effect' even in the twentieth century. Boomgaard (1987:59), while acknowledging that the drug was distributed in large quantities during epidemics after 1870, is likewise reluctant to draw any firm conclusion regarding its effectiveness.

Colonial medical opinion in the early twentieth century, certainly, was often pessimistic regarding the effectiveness of all but the most systematic and intensively monitored programmes of quinine distribution (Netherlands Indies Medical and Sanitary Service 1929:19; Terburgh 1919). Local observers in Sulawesi, on the other hand, had a more positive impression. Minahasans were said in 1938 to be 'very well aware of the beneficial effects of quinine, so that increases in mortality as a result of malaria occur only very infrequently' (Weg 1938:196). At local transmigration sites in southern Minahasa, 'liberal' use of quinine reportedly succeeded in suppressing the migration epidemics against which species sanitation had failed.[34] Albert Kruyt (1938, I:195), recounting in the 1930s how much the inhabitants of Tawaelia suffered from malaria, added that this had been so 'at least in the old time, when there was still no quinine'. That quinine distribution did eventually make a significant difference to mortality rates is also strongly suggested by an account of what happened on Greater Sangir when, after the Japanese invasion in 1942, the virtual cessation of shipping activity meant that all medical supplies were suddenly cut off.

In normal times, large quantities of quinine are made available in the event of a malaria epidemic. In 1943 this was not possible, so that the malaria raged

---

[33] Gilles and Warrell 1993:167. It is less effective, however, against the less virulent *P. vivax* and *P. malariae* species. In its unrefined form, as the powdered bark of certain South American trees of the genus *Chinchona*, quinine was already available in small quantities in Batavia during the eighteenth century (Van der Brug 1995:75-6). In 1820 the active component was isolated, and in 1854 the establishment of chinchona plantations on Java made possible mass production of quinine both for Indonesia and for the world market (Boomgaard 1987:58).

[34] A.Ph. van Aken 1932:213-4. At a planned colony of Sangirese emigrants founded in 1938 on the north coast of Bolaang Mongondow, 'regular quinine distribution' reportedly ensured that 'not only are mortality increases prevented, but even the ability of the population to work is practically unaffected' (Weg 1938:197).

unchecked, killing many children and also attacking a number of formerly malaria-free villages in the interior, where it claimed hundreds of victims among the non-immune population. The total mortality for the whole island in that year was 5.6 percent, three to four times the death rate in normal periods. (Blankhart 1951:100.)

After the occupation, according to the same account, malaria mortality fell again as quinine imports resumed. While other factors, including malnutrition, no doubt also contributed to the wartime mortality crisis, it still seems unlikely, given the known effectiveness of quinine as a malaria treatment and the scale on which it was used in 'normal' times, that there is no truth in this analysis. In 1949, 10,000 people on Greater Sangir were treated with quinine by government polyclinics alone (Blankhart 1951:88).

Quinine did not, and probably could not, eliminate malaria from the areas in which it had always been endemic. It could, however, save the lives of people exposed only to single or occasional *Plasmodium falciparum* infections, and by the end of the colonial period it was apparently used by such people on a large enough scale to suppress periodic epidemics which would otherwise have been much more lethal. By the same token, it must often have cured potentially fatal malaria infections acquired in endemic zones by non-immune visitors from malaria-free areas. A Dutch observer noted that in Tomohon, on the central plateau of Minahasa near Tondano, 'fevers occur, but do not usually persist for more than one or two days, and can easily be treated with quinine' (Van der Stok 1900:70). Possibly the successful treatment of imported malaria cases was the main contribution made by quinine to mortality decline during the initial stages of its use in Minahasa, which would help to explain why some of the greatest mortality improvements over the period 1849-1872 took place in the Tondano administrative division (see Chapter I, Map 7) rather than around the malarial administrative capital, Manado. Table 17 shows the recorded average crude death rates (CDR) by division in the two successive twelve-year periods 1849-1860 (excluding 1854, in which there was a severe epidemic mortality crisis caused mainly by dysentery and measles) and 1861-1872.

It is also possible that quinine ultimately reduced the death rate even in endemic areas like Belang and Kema by helping more infants, and long-term migrants from elsewhere, to survive the perilous process of acquiring natural immunity.[35] Certainly the drug was often given to children (*Brieven*, 10-10-1910; Hoff 1938:54), a practice facilitated when sugar-coated quinine tablets became available from about 1910 onward.[36] By 1941, 'immediate

---

[35]   Quinine delays the immunization process, but does not halt it. Treatment during severe fever attacks, meanwhile, can save infant lives which would otherwise be lost as part of the price paid by a population inhabiting a highly malarial locality.

[36]   The fact that most of the children involved were probably no longer in their infancy does

Table 17. Mortality variations by administrative division in Minahasa, 1849-1872

	CDR 1849-1860 (excluding 1854)	CDR 1861-1872	Mortality decline (in annual deaths per 1,000 inhabitants)
Manado	30.7	29.9	0.8
Kema	28.9	24.3	4.6
Tondano	27.1	23.1	4.0
Amurang	27.5	26.4	1.1
Belang	34.7	28.5	6.2
Minahasa	28.6	25.7	2.9

Sources: AV Manado 1849-1872 (ANRI Manado 51, 52, 53)

administration of quinine to children for a period of five days' was standard procedure during epidemics (M. van Rhijn 1941:136).

Besides species sanitation measures and the distribution of quinine, a third, less important, method of malaria control attempted by the Dutch toward the end of the colonial period was the distribution of mosquito nets. In Central Sulawesi after 1928 this occurred on the same basis as quinine distribution (free to the very poor, at cost price to others), and the nets were reportedly popular.[37] It is doubtful, however, whether they were very effective in practice. In the early 1920s, Dr Bouvy (1924:381) reported that although mosquito nets were already common in Minahasan houses, most were in a damaged state and served 'only for decoration'.

Smallpox vaccination and variolation

If the effectiveness of malaria control is debatable, that of another colonial medical intervention, smallpox vaccination, is beyond doubt. The regional smallpox epidemic of 1859-1860, as described in Chapter VII, was already substantially moderated by vaccination. In Gorontalo, where a part of the population was protected, only 3,000 people died, compared to perhaps 10,000 in 1819-1820. 'Those people who have been vaccinated', confirmed the assistant resident of Gorontalo at the height of the epidemic, 'remain free from the disease, or suffer only to a mild degree'.[38] In Sangir, too, mortality

not necessarily eliminate this possibility, since the period of high vulnerability before immunity is acquired begins only at the age of 6 months, and lasts up to 5 years (Bruce-Chwatt 1980:43-4).

[37]   Adriani and Kruyt 1950-51, II:198; Avink 1935; De Haze Winkelman 1935:11; J. Kruyt 1970: 237; Platt 1933:13.

[38]   MV Manado February 1860 (ANRI Manado 54).

was attenuated by the efforts of two medical officials (a government vaccinator and a *dokter Jawa*) sent there in response to the outbreak. Managing to
reach some localities in advance of the epidemic, these paramedics reported
vaccinating more than 14,000 Sangirese in the space of six months.[39] Minahasa,
with the highest level of prior vaccination coverage, was almost completely
untouched by the epidemic which raged all around it in 1860. Here only 62
cases (of which 24 fatal), most of them in unvaccinated immigrants, were
reported among a total population of some 100,000 people.[40]

The smallpox vaccine, known in the nineteenth century as 'cowpox' and
subsequently as Vaccinia, was discovered in Britain in 1796 and introduced
to Java as early as 1804 (Boomgaard 1989b:118; Fenner et al. 1988:258).
Vaccination in Minahasa began in 1822, and was immediately popular. In the
year 1824 a reported 3,823 children (about four percent of the total population)
were treated by 15 vaccinators, and Resident Wenzel wrote that 'no prejudices
against, or obstacles to, this beneficial treatment exist'.[41] As the memory of the
disastrous 1819 outbreak faded, both Dutch commitment and local enthusiasm for the vaccine also waned to some extent.[42] In the years 1843-1845, for
instance, only three vaccinators were active in Minahasa, and the average
number of children inoculated annually was 1,404 (Francis 1860:393). At mid-
century, however, the programme was revitalized, and from 1850 to 1856 an
average of 3,096 children and previously untreated adults were vaccinated
each year.[43] The average registered birth rate in Minahasa over the same
period, by comparison, was only slightly higher at 3,187. Beginning in 1854,
moreover, the vaccinators were instructed 'to inoculate not only those adult
men and women who had not previously been vaccinated, but also those
who had'.[44] By this stage it was known that the immunity conferred by the
vaccine, unlike that acquired as a result of an actual smallpox infection, was
not always lifelong, so that occasional revaccination was necessary in order
to maintain resistance (Fenner et al. 1988:271).

In 1860, the year in which Minahasa escaped unscathed from a major
regional epidemic, resident of Manado C. Bosscher went so far as to claim
that the level of cowpox inoculation there was 'as high as could be wished

[39]   MV Manado October 1860 (ANRI Manado 54).
[40]   AV Manado 1860 (ANRI Manado 52).
[41]   AV Manado 1824 (ANRI Manado 101); Riedel 1872b:482.
[42]   In 1833 the programme was still being 'continued with good results' in Minahasa, but now
a degree of compulsion was often necessary to overcome 'great indifference' among the parents
(AV Manado 1833, in ANRI Manado 48).
[43]   AV Manado 1850-56 (ANRI Manado 51). This figure includes only the successful vaccinations.
[44]   AV Manado 1854 (ANRI Manado 51). In the years 1854-1856 an annual average of 5,729 successful revaccinations was carried out in Minahasa (AV Manado 1854-56, in ANRI Manado 51).

for in any civilized country', and that no more than 'three in every thousand inhabitants above the age of one year' were unprotected.[45] At the same date, another observer reported that 'vaccination and revaccination take place on a regular basis, and are eagerly requested by the natives' (Van der Crab 1862: 342). The last regional smallpox epidemic to affect Minahasa to any significant degree, in fact, was that of 1839-1841, when mortality already seems to have been low compared with death tolls of at least 5,000 in Gorontalo and 6,000 in Banggai.[46] Late nineteenth-century sources make almost no mention of the disease in Minahasa, although Dr Bouvy (1924:366) later stated that '20 to 200 and more' cases occurred 'every year' until 1908.[47] This form of small-scale endemic smallpox, 'with a much lower case-fatality rate than before, and a different and milder symptomatology' (Fenner et al. 1988:272), was also observed among substantially protected populations in Europe when the rate of adult revaccination was less than optimal.[48] After 1908 it too was eliminated, as Bouvy recalled, by intensified revaccination:

> In 1911 there was not a single case, and so it continued until 1916, in which year there was a small epidemic, confined to a single village, which I remember very clearly. In a few days we inoculated 10,000 people, surrounding the disease hearth with a 'wall', as it were, of newly revaccinated people. Only one case occurred outside this wall, a lonely old man who had never been vaccinated, living miles away in the middle of the forest. (Bouvy 1924:366.)

At the same time an important improvement was made in the method of vaccination. In the nineteenth century the vaccine had usually been stored and transported in the bodies of living human subjects, and inoculation took place directly from person to person.[49] As a result, Dutch officials complained, the cowpox sometimes 'degenerated' or was contaminated with lethal smallpox, while the spread of other diseases was also facilitated.[50] From 1910 onward, however, vaccination was carried out exclusively with preserved animal vac-

[45] AV Manado 1860 (ANRI Manado 52).
[46] De Clercq 1890:177; R. Scherius 1847:402, 407, 409, 411; Res. Manado to GG, 13-1-1840, 17-3-1840 (ANRI Manado 79); Res. Manado to Gov. Moluccas, 15-2-1843 (ANRI Manado 80).
[47] 'Sporadic' cases were, however, reported in Minahasa during the regional epidemic of 1883-1884 (AV Manado 1883, in ANRI Manado 52). In this period, vaccination was made a precondition for admission of children to the mission and government schools in Minahasa (Graafland 1898, I:118).
[48] In 1897, 'benign' (*goedaardig*) smallpox was also reported on the Togian Islands (*Koloniaal verslag* 1898:22). In 1929, likewise, a local outbreak on Greater Sangir 'spread over the whole *landschap* of Tabukan', yet 'claimed few victims' (*Koloniaal verslag* 1930:26).
[49] On occasion, however, vaccine preserved in glass tubes was also used (AV Gorontalo 1869, in ANRI Manado 9; MV Manado September 1860, in ANRI Manado 54).
[50] AV Gorontalo 1854 (ANRI Gorontalo 3); Res. Manado to Res. Ternate, 27-2-1832 (ANRI Manado 77); Steller 1866:31.

cine (Bouvy 1924:366).

Outside Minahasa, vaccination coverage prior to the twentieth century was more limited. In Gorontalo, where the vaccine was likewise introduced in 1822, it seems to have met with much greater local resistance.[51] The Gorontalese were temporarily 'cured of their prejudice' during the epidemic of 1839-1841, when 'everybody wanted to be vaccinated' (R. Scherius 1847:420), but enthusiasm quickly faded again, and in 1841-1845 there were still only 423 reported vaccinations per year.[52] In 1855 the Dutch authorities decided to recruit new vaccinators from among local Islamic religious officials, who were thought to enjoy the particular trust of the population.[53] There followed a reassuring stream of reports suggesting more than a thousand inoculations each year, but in 1860 it was revealed that the chief vaccinator 'had simply fabricated the figures, and vaccinated nobody'.[54] The 1859-1860 epidemic, like its predecessor, provoked an immediate revival in the popularity of the treatment.[55] During the epidemic of 1883-1884, nevertheless, 'thousands of children, and also many adults' once more died in the Gorontalo area.[56] A British visitor was even led to conclude that the Dutch 'have not introduced vaccination here as they have in Minahasa'.[57] Small-scale attempts at vaccination in Bolaang Mongondow, from 1858 onward, seem to have had equally little effect.[58]

In contrast to the population of Gorontalo, the Sangirese, perhaps partly because Christianity gave them a greater affinity with the Dutch, began to adopt vaccination quite spontaneously as soon as some of them 'observed its beneficial effects in Manado and Ternate' (Van Delden 1844:376).

> In 1823, when smallpox was raging on the island of [Greater] Sangir, a large number of people on Siau were inoculated by Prince Taba, the son of the deceased *raja* there, initially using cowpox material brought over from Ternate, and subsequently using the natural pox. This worked well on healthy individuals, and had the result that people on the former island also began to practise it. (Van Delden 1844:376.)

[51]   'Extract uit het register der besluiten van den gouverneur der Moluksche eilanden', 19-9-1821 (ANRI Gorontalo 17), AV Gorontalo 1829 (ANRI Gorontalo 3), 1841-1843 (ANRI Manado 50); R. Scherius 1847:420.

[52]   AV Gorontalo 1841-43 (ANRI Manado 50), 1845 (KITLV H111).

[53]   AV Manado 1855 (ANRI Manado 51).

[54]   AV Manado 1860 (ANRI Manado 52).

[55]   AV Manado 1861 (ANRI Manado 52).

[56]   AV Manado 1884 (ANRI Manado 52).

[57]   Guillemard 1886:210. In 1908-1909, by contrast, Gorontalo, like Minahasa, saw only 'sporadic' cases of smallpox (*Koloniaal verslag* 1908:66, 1909:74, 1910:52).

[58]   AV Manado 1858, 1860 (ANRI Manado 52); MV Manado July 1859, September 1860 (ANRI Manado 54); Van der Crab 1860:384. During the epidemic of 1908-1909 there were 7,800 smallpox cases in Bolaang Mongondow, compared with only 144 in neighbouring Minahasa (Bouvy 1924:366).

Despite this promising start, a missionary who visited Sangir in 1855 reported strong resistance to a proposed re-introduction of the vaccine under government auspices (Van de Velde van Cappellen 1857:39). Not until the epidemic of 1860 did vaccination begin again on a large scale. This time, however, acceptance was complete and a professional vaccinator was stationed on Greater Sangir, where by 1864 the vaccine was reported to be 'permanently established'.[59] Despite the fact that a Dutch *controleur* was posted in Taruna from 1882 onward, I have found no record that Sangir was affected by the regional smallpox epidemic of 1883-1884; presumably this was at least partly a consequence of good vaccination coverage.[60]

In the early twentieth century, effective smallpox protection was gradually extended to all parts of the region. In Central Sulawesi state vaccination was introduced in 1906, and in 1909 an emergency campaign by two government vaccinators, assisted by missionaries and mission schoolteachers, reportedly saved most of the population of the Poso area from the disease when two infected travellers arrived overland from the south (Adriani and Kruyt 1912-14, I:418; *Brieven*, March 1909). In 1925 a new integrated inoculation system was introduced in which the residency was divided into 20 'vaccine districts', each with its own vaccinator. The whole population of each district was to be revaccinated, village by village, every six years, with repeat visits to every village where the initial turnout had failed to reach 80 percent (A.Ph. van Aken 1932: 209). Only in Tolitoli and Banggai, and among remote highland groups like the To Wana of the upper Bongka River, was there any significant resistance to vaccination by this period (A.Ph. van Aken 1932:209; Avink 1935). Despite the fact that the population was now larger and potentially more accessible to infection than ever before, there were no more major smallpox epidemics after 1909.

In some parts of the region a simple form of smallpox protection, variolation, was already in use before the introduction of vaccination by the Dutch. This involved the inoculation of healthy individuals, either by inhalation or via a skin wound, with pus or scabs from smallpox sufferers. When successful, it resulted in a mild, non-lethal form of the disease which nevertheless conferred immunity from subsequent infection.[61] In Sangir, as described

59   MV Manado December 1864 (ANRI Manado 54).
60   It is also possible, on the other hand, that the Sangir Islands, like Togian in 1819-1823 and 1839-1841, would have been spared from this epidemic even in the absence of vaccination; they were definitely affected to some extent by the following outbreak in 1908-1809 (*Koloniaal verslag* 1909:74, 1910:52; Tammes 1940:187-8). The situation on Talaud, where vaccination began only in 1890, is unclear (*Koloniaal verslag* 1891:18).
61   Fenner et al. 1988:245-58. Smallpox infection by natural means also occurred by inhalation, but whereas the material used in nasal variolation apparently lodged in the nose or throat, the smaller airborne droplets involved in natural transmission were deposited in the lungs (Hopkins 1983:3, 114).

above, vaccination seems to have preceded, and inspired, variolation. In
Central Sulawesi, however, variolation was introduced by immigrants from
other parts of Indonesia well in advance of vaccination.[62]

> During the epidemic in 1883 or 1884, Bugis and other foreigners travelled through
> the land and vaccinated the Toraja with material from pocks. People claim that
> the individuals inoculated in this way did catch smallpox, but did not die of it.
> (Adriani and Kruyt 1912-14, I:418.)

'To prevent the disease', confirms an early twentieth-century source on
traditional medicine in the Palu Valley (where Bugis influence was strong),
'material from the pocks of a sufferer is transferred to unaffected people'.[63] Variolation, however, was dangerous, often resulting in fatal smallpox
(Fenner et al. 1988:246), and never became as popular or widespread as the
artificial vaccine. One reason why the Sangirese became wary of vaccination
after the 1820s was a belief, probably resulting from its combination and confusion with variolation, that the cowpox vaccine itself could cause smallpox
epidemics (Van de Velde van Cappellen 1857:39).

Other medical interventions

The two most significant medical innovations of the colonial era, quinine and the smallpox vaccine, have already been discussed. In the early
twentieth century there were also several others, albeit directed against
debilitating rather than lethal diseases. Beginning in 1919, a very effective treatment for yaws became available in the form of the drug (neo-)
salvarsan.[64] Salvarsan injections, like quinine tablets, were made available
by the colonial government at a low price, or free to the very poor, and their
rapid, consistent and visible effects quickly made them very popular.[65] At the
beginning of the 1930s, Resident Van Aken (1932:212) could already claim that
as a result of the injection programme, '*Framboesia tropica* is now significant

---

[62]   Variolation seems to have been introduced to Indonesia in the eighteenth century, either
from China (Knapen 1998:79) or by Europeans (Boomgaard 1989b:117-8, 2003:603).
[63]   Hissink 1912:81. It is possible that knowledge of variolation contributed to the Bugis political ascendancy in Central Sulawesi during the eighteenth and early nineteenth centuries (see
Chapter II).
[64]   *Koloniaal verslag* 1922:119, 1923:23; Netherlands Indies Medical and Sanitary Service 1929:61.
[65]   Adriani and Kruyt 1950-51, II:200; M. van Rhijn 1941:138; Frohwein 1933:34; Vorstman
1935a:29. Sufferers often approached government doctors spontaneously to request injections
(Dutrieux 1931a:15). Van Rhijn (1941:138) complained that many people did not complete the recommended course of three weekly injections, but Bouvy (1924:391) noted that 'dazzling results
can be obtained even with a single salverson injection'.

only in relatively inaccessible areas'. 'Thanks to regular neo-salvarsan injections', agreed a *controleur* in Bolaang Mongondow a few years later, 'yaws in its eruptive phase is seldom seen any more' (Hoff 1938:54). Even in remote parts of Central Sulawesi, the disease had by this stage become 'much less frequent thanks to the salversan therapy' (Avink 1935). In the same period *kacang ijo* (mung bean, *Vigna radiata*), a thiamine-rich food, was distributed by the government in a reportedly successful endeavour to combat beriberi (Avink 1935; Tillema 1926:223), and iodized salt in an attempt to eliminate goitre (Vorstman 1935a:29). The popularity of the wound treatments available from missionaries and government doctors suggests that these were superior to indigenous remedies (Adriani and Kruyt 1950-51, II:195), and the reduction in the incidence of skin disease noted below in relation to hygiene improvements was probably also partly due to medical treatment.[66]

In terms of hospital facilities and numbers of personnel, Dutch medical services in the region nevertheless remained minimal. Until the middle of the nineteenth century a single military surgeon, already part of the Manado garrison since VOC times, provided the only Western medical care (other than smallpox vaccination) available in the whole residency.[67] The opening of a government training school for indigenous medical assistants (called, regardless of their ethnicity, *dokter Jawa* or 'Javanese doctors') in Batavia in 1851 (De Moulin 1989:24) provided an opportunity to improve this situation at low cost, and the first two Minahasans were sent there for instruction in 1855.[68] By 1860 three *dokter Jawa* were working in Minahasa, by 1875 five, and in 1890 six.[69] In 1873 one was posted to Gorontalo (Van der Crab 1875: 445), and after the turn of the century *dokter Jawa* were also stationed in more remote parts of the residency (Van Geuns 1906:49; Van Hengel 1910:41). Not until 1872, however, did a second European doctor arrive in Manado, and a civilian hospital, with an initial capacity of 50 beds, was not completed until after the turn of the century.[70] In 1931 there were still just 14 fully-qualified doctors – about one for every 80,000 people – in the whole residency, running between them a total of 18 hospitals of various (mostly very primitive) kinds,

---

[66]   Adriani and Kruyt 1950-51, II:199; J. Kruyt 1970:239. This reduction took place in Minahasa (Stuurman 1936:105) as well as in Central Sulawesi. Other medicaments distributed by missionaries included iodine, laxatives, bandages, aspirin, and drugs against intestinal parasites (Aragon 1992:178; J. Kruyt 1970:239).

[67]   Bleeker 1856:84. Early in the nineteenth century, Minahasans were apparently already accustomed to bring seriously wounded people to Manado for treatment by this medical officer (AV Manado 1829, in KITLV H70).

[68]   MV Manado February 1855 (ANRI Manado 54).

[69]   Van der Crab 1862:342, 1875:264; Gallois 1892:45.

[70]   Bouvy 1924:368, 374; Van der Crab 1875:264; Van Kol 1903:299. This hospital was enlarged and modernized at the beginning of the 1920s (Bouvy 1924:371).

together with 36 'polyclinics' where basic medicines were dispensed.[71]

Although Graafland claimed that they were 'reasonably well trained to treat most ordinary cases of illness', the main task of the *dokter Jawa* in the nineteenth century, other than dealing with accidents and distributing quinine and a few less effective medicaments, seems to have been one of surveillance, reporting details of disease outbreaks to the Dutch doctor in Manado (Graafland 1867-69, I:178, II:157-8). While details are not available, it is likely that this occurred in the context of attempts to prevent the spread of epidemic diseases by isolating affected individuals and communities. By 1921 it was said that in Minahasa, 'epidemics seldom acquire the same proportions [...] as they do among other native peoples, because the regulations for controlling them are better understood and followed' (Kielstra 1921:39-40). In the early twentieth century, the quarantine measures taken by the residency authorities during cholera outbreaks certainly had some success. During the epidemic of 1914, a woman suffering from cholera who arrived by sea in Buol was immediately isolated, together with everyone who had been in contact with her, in a specially built barrack, and the local population was not infected (Van Andel 1921:6). In 1915, and again in the following year, it was claimed that 'tough measures' taken by the government had limited the spread of cholera in Central Sulawesi.[72] While such claims may have been exaggerated, the incidence of this disease definitely declined throughout Indonesia toward the end of the colonial period: between 1921 and 1927, in fact, there was apparently 'not a single case of cholera in the whole of the Archipelago'.[73]

Another area in which colonial intervention may have been significant was that of childbirth, a dangerous event both for the mother – Brilman (1938: 176) wrote that on Sangir, 'the delivery room supplied a large contingent for the graveyard' – and for the child, not least because it was customary to cut the umbilical cord with a non-sterile bamboo knife.[74] Dr Kündig (1934:177-8) found that 'tetanus and navel complications' were still a significant cause of

[71] A.Ph. van Aken 1932:202-8. Ten of the hospitals were run by the state, the other 8 by mission and church institutions. Confidence in Western medicine was reportedly very high in Minahasa at the end of the colonial period (Weg 1938:193), although distrustful attitudes persisted elsewhere (Van den Berg 1935:7; Frohwein 1933:34; Morison 1931:59).

[72] *Koloniaal verslag* 1916:34, 1917:35. The precise nature of these measures is not clear, but they seem to have involved the isolation of whole infected localities. In October 1910 the port of Donggala had 'had to be declared contaminated' following a cholera outbreak, 'but as early as December the declaration could be revoked' (*Koloniaal verslag* 1911:47).

[73] Netherlands Indies Medical and Sanitary Service 1929:56. The Dutch government attributed this success partly to the use, from 1912 onward, of an anti-cholera vaccine. More recent sources, however, indicate that such vaccination is not effective (Nalin and Morris 1991:374).

[74] Adam 1925b:461; Adriani 1918:387; Adriani and Kruyt 1912-14, II:48; Van Dinter 1899:368; A.C. Kruyt 1900a:235, 1930a:465, 1930b:578, 1932b:47, 1933:70, 1938, III:228; Nourse 1999:83; Riedel 1870a:138, 1895a:96; Veenhuizen 1903:70; Woensdregt 1929b:360.

infant mortality in Minahasa at the beginning of the 1930s. 'Among the factors which hold back the growth of the population in Minahasa', Resident Jansen had judged in 1855, 'belongs in particular the extremely dangerous and careless way in which the women give birth'.[75] In the following year, accordingly, the first two Minahasan women were sent to Java for training as midwives.[76] By 1875 there were five qualified midwives in Minahasa, and in 1936 ten (Van der Crab 1875:265; Stuurman 1936:113). Beginning in 1873, midwives were also posted elsewhere in the residency.[77] Initially less appreciated than the *dokter Jawa* (Van der Crab 1875:265), by the 1920s their services, at least in Minahasa, were said to be in demand (Bouvy 1924:373). In Christianized areas, mission influence may also have led to some improvement in the care and diet of infants, deficiencies in which were sometimes identified as factors contributing to the high infant mortality rate.[78] Most complaints about inadequate care, however, are unspecific; poor hygiene (see below) and heavy female workloads (see Chapter X) usually seem to have been the main problems.[79]

Hygiene

In the early modern period, according to Reid (1988-93, I:50), the fact that Europeans 'distrusted water' meant that Southeast Asians, who did not share this distrust, tended to be clean by Western standards. Where water was plentiful and accessible, bathing was certainly always a common activity in Sulawesi. Woodard (1969:102) observed at the end of the eighteenth century that the people of the Palu valley bathed 'twice a day in fresh water', and even the nineteenth-century missionary Steller (1866:31) conceded that adults on Sangir made 'quite some use' of water for bathing. At the same time, however, Steller also wrote that infants experienced 'far-reaching uncleanliness' until they were old enough to bathe themselves, accused the Sangirese of 'carelessness regarding their own persons, clothing, and food', and noted that the open space beneath their houses served as 'a living area

---

75   AV Manado 1855 (ANRI Manado 51).
76   MV Manado February 1856 (ANRI Manado 54).
77   A.Ph. van Aken 1932:208; Van der Crab 1875:445; Van Geuns 1906:49; Ter Laag 1920:56.
78   AV Manado 1853, 1877 (ANRI Manado 51, 53); Bouvy 1924:384; Brilman 1938:176; *Fragment* 1856:22-3, 150; Graafland 1898, I:302-05; Kündig 1934:178; Van Son 1935:12; Woensdregt 1930:328.
79   De Clercq (1870a:126) wrote that the 'child torture' implied by some commentators was probably 'imaginary'. It is interesting to note that while Graafland (1867-69, I:175-6) referred to injuries caused by falls from stilt houses as a significant cause of death among young children in Minahasa, Adriani and Kruyt (1912-14, II:190) describe the use of baby fences to prevent such falls in Central Sulawesi. The question of infant diets will be examined in Chapter IX.

for goats, pigs and chickens, which, rooting in the mud for food, exacerbate the lack of cleanliness and make life in the house above neither healthier, nor more pleasant for the olfactory organs' (Steller 1866:29, 31).

No European of the colonial period, in fact, was impressed by local standards of either personal or public cleanliness in northern Sulawesi.[80] Many blamed shortcomings in these areas for the prevalence of infectious disease, especially skin disease, and some associated low population growth directly with 'the poor hygiene situation' (Adriani and Kruyt 1950-51, I: 76; Brilman 1938:176). Graafland (1867-69, I:256) – writing, like Steller, in the 1860s – expressed the general view when he declared that 'the pagan Alfur [Minahasan] is dirty to a grave degree'. As late as the 1920s Dr Bouvy (1924:382) claimed that 'as far as cleanliness and concepts of hygiene are concerned, even the most cultivated among them stand miles below what in Western culture was already regarded a century ago as the minimum civilized level'. Clothes, for instance, were seldom cleaned, and a child without head lice was 'an exception'. 'Bathing', Bouvy added, 'is done for refreshment, not for cleanliness'. 'Cleaning of the body after defaecation', noted Tillema (1922:198) at the same period on the basis of correspondence with missionaries and colonial officials, 'generally does not occur'. In Bada, as in Sangir, infants were seldom bathed by their parents, and appeared, according to Woensdregt (1930:327), 'unspeakably dirty'.

The unhygienic state of traditional houses, both internally and externally, also attracted much attention.[81] While Bouvy (1924:381-2) admitted that pile-dwellings as such were advantageous from a hygienic point of view in so far as 'much dirt ends up under the house which would otherwise have remained inside it', the reaction of the naturalist Hickson, visiting the village of Karaton in Nanusa (Talaud) in 1886, was more typical.

Each house accommodated several families, and I was told that in some cases as many as five hundred individuals were crowded into one of these dwellings. They were built upon wooden piles, many of them seven feet above the level of the ground, and the refuse of the kitchen and all manner of filth had accumulated for years beneath each house so as to diffuse a stench which is beyond my powers of description. Had the village been visited by a sanitary inspector with the necessary powers instead of by a resident without, there can be no doubt of the

[80]   Adam 1925b:434; Adriani 1915:458; Adriani and Kruyt 1950-51, II:201; Aragon 1992:168; Bouvy 1924:382; Van der Crab 1875:449-50; Van Delden 1844:376; *Fragment* 1856:27; Frieswijck 1902:472; Gallois 1892:44; Graafland 1867-69, I:256, 1898, I:384,II:35-6; F. Kelling, 'Het eiland Taghoelandang en zijn bewoners' [1866] (ARZ NZG 43.2); *Landschap Donggala* 1905:523; M. van Rhijn 1941:138; Roep 1917:415; Van Son 1935:12; Tillema 1922:230.
[81]   Adriani and Kruyt 1912-14, II:165; Bouvy 1924:382; Graafland 1867-69, I:256-7, 271, 1898, I: 384-5, 406; A.C. Kruyt 1895-97, IV:123; Ter Laag 1920:18; Roep 1917:416; Steller 1866:29-30; Tillema 1922:208, 216-7, 219.

first step he would have taken to restore the village to a fairly sanitary condition. (Hickson 1889:160.)

This may in fact have been an extreme case, not only because the houses on Talaud were large even by northern Sulawesi standards, but also because Hickson arrived there in the wake of a cholera and malaria epidemic. Healthy adults in Sangir and Talaud, according to other sources, normally defaecated 'in the woods', in streams, or, in coastal villages, on the beach, where the results were washed away by the tide; only the sick, together with children and old people, habitually did so at home through holes in the floor platform.[82] Similar patterns were reported elsewhere in the region.[83] Sarasin and Sarasin (1897:278) even claimed at one point that the ground underneath pile-dwellings in Sulawesi was typically 'kept entirely clean of faecal matter, except for that originating from domestic animals'. Evidently there was much variation here, however, for elsewhere on the same page they reported having 'reason to suspect that on occasion, the inhabitants of a village are obliged by the accumulated dirt to set up their houses in a new location'. Among some groups, including the Sea-Sea of Peling in Banggai, human faeces were systematically deposited underneath the house as food for pigs.

> These people live in rather large isolated houses on piles; the space underneath the house is used as a pigsty, to which end it is entirely fenced in. All domestic waste without exception, including faeces, is cast down through the floor as pig fodder. A thick layer of manure is found underneath such a house, and the resulting stench is already unbearable even at a considerable distance. (Tillema 1922:236.)

In Minahasa too, according to Tillema (1922:188), it was an 'old custom' to defaecate at night into 'the pigsty, which is constructed partly under the house'. In the Palu Valley people did so into the space where sheep and goats were penned overnight, an arrangement prohibited after the imposition of Dutch rule on the grounds that 'these spaces under the houses formed veritable breeding-places for vermin and dirt, and were the origin of many diseases' (Hissink 1912:82-3). Even where defaecation mainly occurred outside the village, finally, sanitary conditions still left much to be desired, human waste typically creating a 'stinking mess' in the undergrowth (Tillema 1922:217) while pollution of streams affected downriver settlements.[84]

---

[82]   Lam 1932:51; Roep 1917:417-8; Steller 1866:30; Tillema 1922:179. Healthy people, however, sometimes also defaecated in the house at night (Roep 1917:417; Tillema 1922:179, 198).
[83]   Graafland 1867-69, I:177, 1898, I:306; Tillema 1922:197-8, 217, 236-7. Again, however, Tillema (1922:188, 198) also notes defaecation from the house in Minahasa and in Central Sulawesi.
[84]   Roep 1917:414; Tillema 1922:208. Duhr (1781:113) refers to muddy water downstream of hydraulic gold mines which 'causes diarrhoea, or even dysentery, in those who are careless enough to drink it'.

In many places the availability of water for washing, and even drinking, was inherently limited. The scattered hillside swidden houses where people spent much of their lives were not always close to streams, and in the nuclear settlements, many of which were built on hilltops for defensive purposes, access to water, and hygiene in general, could be even more problematic.

> Here there was little space and the houses stood crowded together; the ground was almost completely covered with refuse, and the closest water source was usually at the foot of the hill. On these hilltops, moreover, people were very much exposed to wind and rain, against which the poorly-built houses offered little protection. These conditions, direct consequences of warfare, were more harmful to the population than war itself. (Adriani and Kruyt 1950-51, I:77.)

In pre-pacification Minahasa, likewise, problems of hygiene were 'exacerbated by lack of water, since the villages, because they were built in high places, were everywhere distant from rivers and streams' (*Fragment* 1856:27). Drinking water in coastal and lowland areas came from streams and shallow wells, the level of which was liable to run low in times of dry weather. Probably because this led to intensified water pollution, such areas were often particularly subject to outbreaks of stomach disease. On the low-lying Talaud Islands, with their partly coralline rocks and thin soils, droughts were regularly followed by drinking water shortages and epidemics.[85] In the early twentieth century, poor drinking water was also blamed for generally poor health conditions in Donggala (Grubauer 1913:579), Togian (Van Son 1935: 12), Tagulandang (Frieswijck 1902:472), and especially Gorontalo (A.Ph. van Aken 1932:219). 'It seems to me', wrote one Dutch official in Gorontalo town in 1923, 'that a piped water supply must be regarded as an even more important need than a hospital' (Edie 1923:27). The connection proposed by many colonial observers between poor hygiene and skin disease is perhaps supported by the fact that some of the areas where skin problems were particularly prevalent, including Talaud, Banggai and parts of Sangir, were also areas where, for geological and topographic rather than climatic reasons, there was a local or seasonal shortage of water.[86]

At first sight, there is little reason to suppose that the sanitary situation in the region changed much before 1930. Not until 1931 were professional demonstrators (a grand total of three of them, two in Minahasa and one in the Kolonodale area) appointed by the government to disseminate 'medical hygiene propaganda'.[87] The construction of latrines – holes in the ground

---

[85]   Ebbinge Wübben 1889:207; Jellesma 1911:1242; *Overzicht* 1914:14-5.
[86]   Bosscher and Matthijssen 1854:96-7; Van Delden 1844:376; Frieswijck 1902:472; Ferguson 1912:8; F. Kelling, 'Het eiland Taghoelandang en zijn bewoners' [1866] (ARZ NZG 43.2); Schrader 1941:108; Tillema 1922:236; Van de Velde van Cappellen 1857:46.
[87]   A.Ph. van Aken 1932:212, 219; M. van Rhijn 1941:134-5; Weg 1938:206.

which were periodically to be filled up, and the huts above them shifted to new sites – was ordered in some parts of the region earlier in the century, but there were many complaints that in practice these sanitary innovations were little used (Tillema 1922:179, 188, 217, 236). Even in the capital, sewerage and drinking water arrangements remained primitive until a very late date. 'My impression as far as urban hygiene is concerned', wrote Tillema (1926:200) after visiting Manado in 1924, 'can be expresed in one word – deplorable!'. Shortly afterwards a municipal piped water system was completed in this town (Bouvy 1924:385; Tideman 1926:109), but in 1930 it was still the only one in the residency. In Gorontalo town, the 'very inadequate water supply (artesian wells, the yield from which has greatly declined)' was still thought to be partly to blame for 'the regular and very frequent incidence of stomach diseases (dysentery and typhus)' (A.Ph. van Aken 1932:211).

Some colonial policies may nevertheless have had a positive effect on the hygiene situation. Beginning in Minahasa in the 1840s, first of all, the traditional multiple-hearth houses, partly on Dutch orders, were gradually replaced by smaller dwellings (see Chapter I). By the 1920s, houses every-where in the region typically contained between one and three nuclear families (Tillema 1922:194, 219, 231; 1926:203). Dutch officials argued that the big, crowded traditional houses were unhealthy as well as uncivilized, giving rise to 'all kinds of infectious diseases'.[88] Post-war research in New Guinea (Feachem 1977:173-4) demonstrated a significant correlation between the average number of people sharing a house and the prevalence of respiratory and skin disease, so that Resident Jansen may well have been right to argue that the replacement of the old houses by 'small hygienic dwellings' would promote population growth.[89] The concentration of larger numbers of people in single nuclear villages, on the other hand, probably had the opposite effect in health terms (Tillema 1922:208).

The relocation of the nuclear settlements from defensive hilltop sites to valley floors, although it often increased the malaria risk, was a hygienic advance in so far as it tended to improve access to water.[90] Certain measures taken to keep the new settlements clean may also have been significant. In terms of external appearances, the results were certainly impressive. Tondano, for instance, was described by Hickson (1889:213) in 1886 as con-sisting of 'rows of pretty little houses, each one – almost a model of neatness and cleanliness – surrounded by a garden of flowers and shrubs'. 'Nothing',

[88]   J. Gansneb Tengnagel, 'Beknopte nota betrekkelijk de residentie Menado', 16-3-1848 (ANRI Manado 168).
[89]   AV Manado 1857 (ANRI Manado 52). Alexander and Alexander (1993:258) also take this seriously as a factor promoting disease infection in Borneo longhouses.
[90]   Adriani 1915:469. In Bada, for instance, the new villages were built 'as much as possible in the vicinity of rivers' (Tillema 1922:208).

echoed another British visitor of the same period, 'can be more absolutely neat and clean than these Minahasa villages'.[91] By the second decade of the twentieth century strict sanitary regulations, not all of them cosmetic, were being enforced even in remote places like Talaud.[92]

> The external order and neatness of the villages is thus generally very adequate, and certainly not inferior to that of many Dutch country villages. If a *kampung* head allows his village to become neglected he is punished, in an extreme case dismissed, and if the compound of a house is not properly maintained the owner is fined, or, if he repeats the offence, imprisoned. As already noted, the level of order and cleanliness inside the houses, so important for health, does leave much to be desired. In times of emergency, however, intervention extends indoors. Last year, for instance, when dysentery was prevalent, the authorities [...] issued an order that nobody should drink other than boiled water. Those caught breaking this regulation were summarily punished by the native judge. (Roep 1917:419.)

Although little was done, on the whole, in the field of public waterworks, improved wells were provided by the government in some places (Hoff 1938:54; *Koloniaal verslag* 1898:22). Despite the continuing cynicism of Dutch observers like Bouvy, finally, there is also some evidence that standards of personal hygiene improved during the colonial period. In the mission schools of nineteenth-century Minahasa, according to Graafland (1867-69, I:257), children learned 'to clean themselves properly on the order of the schoolmaster', while cleanliness in clothing and cooking also improved in spontaneous imitation of European norms.[93] A few decades later in Central Sulawesi, it was reported that 'people are gradually becoming ashamed' of skin disease, 'as a result of which the population diligently helps to cure it by using soap, so that the number of people affected has fallen significantly'.[94] Another improvement was the increased use of footwear, which reduced the risk of hookworm infection (Bouvy 1924:394; Tillema 1922:196).

As Knapen (1998:89-90) has recently emphasized, on the other hand,

[91] 'Indeed', this writer added, 'their perfection of tidiness would be almost irritating were it not for the beauty of the flowers and the tropical vegetation' (Guillemard 1886:171).

[92] Tillema (1922:197-8, 237) gives examples of similar regulations elsewhere in the region.

[93] Training in cleanliness was an important aspect of mission education in nineteenth-century Minahasa (Graafland 1898, I:522; Kroeskamp 1974:117, 151; Schouten 1995b:10, 12). Kielstra (1921:39) later reported that hygiene in Minahasa was 'generally better than elswhere', partly thanks to 'the level of education among the population', and the *controleur* Roep (1917:415) claimed that bathing had recently become more frequent on Talaud due to 'the influence of mission and government'.

[94] Adriani and Kruyt 1950-51, II:199. This must have been a late development, however, because in 1918 Kruyt wrote to Tillema (1922:219) that in terms of personal and domestic hygiene, 'no improvement can yet be observed'. Coconut oil, it may be noted, was already used as shampoo in precolonial times (Adriani and Kruyt 1950-51, III:212; Riedel 1886:79; Van Spreeuwenberg 1845-46:34).

not all of the changes instituted by the colonial government in the name of hygiene had the desired effect. The penning of pigs in areas where they had traditionally been allowed to roam freely (Tillema 1922:217, 219), for instance, may well have allowed mosquitos to breed in pools which would otherwise have been disturbed by these animals. Dutch insistence on good ventilation, as contemporary studies of 'improved' houses on Java showed (Snellen 1990:120-27), also increased the danger of malaria by making the living area less smoky, and it is possible that an order 'to provide every house with large window openings' (Roep 1917:425) was a factor behind a series of malaria epidemics which took place on Talaud in the years 1912-1915.[95]

Conclusion

The most obvious improvement in the health situation during the nineteenth and early twentieth centuries was the virtual elimination of smallpox as a result of vaccination. Minahasa, where systematic inoculation began in 1822, suffered only light mortality during the epidemic of 1839-1841, and was almost entirely protected thereafter. Several other areas also enjoyed partial protection from 1860 onward, and after 1900 full vaccination coverage was gradually extended throughout the region. A second advance was the introduction of quinine, used on a large scale against malaria at the beginning of the twentieth century, and in some places much earlier. Toward the end of the colonial era, these two fundamental improvements were also complemented to some extent by better midwifery, hygiene, and quarantine arrangements, together with new treatments for yaws and other debilitating diseases.

In other respects, however, there was a simultaneous deterioration in the disease environment. Just as vaccination against smallpox began to take effect, another lethal epidemic disease, Asiatic cholera, arrived in the region in 1830; from 1850 onward, regular cholera epidemics swept through the region every 10-15 years. Measles and dysentery also seem to have become more common after 1850, and like cholera these could not be treated effectively. Just as quinine came into use against malaria in Minahasa, moreover, an intensification of internal population movements almost certainly also

---

[95] *Koloniaal verslag* 1913:26, 1914:26, 1915:35, 1916:34. The construction of separate kitchen spaces behind the houses (Roep 1917:425) probably had a similar effect, although Tillema (1922: 218) noted that in Central Sulawesi many people had simply taken to sleeping in the kitchen 'in order to protect themselves to some extent against the mosquito plague'. Another negative change mentioned by Knapen, the replacement of stilt houses by houses built on ground level, was less common in northern Sulawesi, since most of the new houses were still of elevated design. The height of the floor platform above the ground, however, did tend to decrease (Adam 1925b:429; Graafland 1898, I:172-3; Van Spreeuwenberg 1845-46:316).

increased the need for it. While the relocation of villages brought hygienic advantages in terms of access to water, at the same time it too often increased the malaria threat, as did concurrent changes in house design. Trade (see Chapter II), bringing 'great advantages, but also disadvantages in the form of infectious diseases' (Tillema 1922:212), probably increased the potential for disease transmission throughout the region during the boom in forest product and copra exports; venereal disease was one health problem which certainly intensified in the most accessible areas (Minahasa and Gorontalo) as a result of more frequent external contacts.[96]

Yet the data from Minahasa, incomplete though they are, leave no room for doubt that the death rate did fall after the middle of the nineteenth century. The combined epidemic of dysentery, cholera, measles and malaria in 1853-1854, when about 10 percent of the population died, was the last great mortality crisis of its kind in Minahasa, which thereafter was apparently spared not only the ravages of smallpox, but also any significant depopulation as a result of other epidemics. Where dysentery and measles are concerned, there is evidence (see Chapter VII) that the disappearance of periodic mortality peaks partly reflected a transition from epidemic to endemic status (presumably as a result of population growth and improved communications, which facilitated continuous transmission).[97] This was certainly not true, however, in the case of cholera, yet when cholera (and malaria) cut back the population in Gorontalo and Talaud in 1885-1886, the corresponding cholera outbreak in Minahasa was 'only sporadic, and did not last long' (Graafland 1898, I:96), so that demographic growth continued almost uninterrupted. While epidemic crises were damped, moreover, 'background' mortality in relatively normal years, far from rising as diseases which had been occasional visitors became endemic, also showed a clear downward trend (Chapter X, Figure 8). Even when the crisis year of 1854 is excluded from the calculation, the average recorded crude death rate over the period 1861-1872, at 25.7 per thousand, is still 2.9 per thousand lower than in the years 1849-1860 (this chapter, Table 17).[98]

How closely the decline in mortality was related to medical or hygiene improvements is ultimately impossible to say. With regard to the use of qui-

---

[96]   Bouvy 1924:391; Graafland 1867-69, II:159; Van Hoëvell 1891:35; Logeman 1922:75; Riedel 1870a:102; Tillema 1926:204, 223.

[97]   The periodicity of measles, like that of smallpox, is particularly dependent on the number of people living in close contact with one another. To sustain continuous transmission, 'at least 200,000 persons are needed to provide an adequate number of new susceptibles' (Breman 1991:163).

[98]   While an increasingly juvenile population composition, resulting from rising fertility (see Chapter X), may have played some role here alongside changes in health conditions, it should be noted that the death rate declined in absolute as well as proportional terms (Henley 1997a:117-20).

nine, the local variations in mortality reduction shown in Table 17 are inconclusive: very marked improvements took place in both malaria-endemic and malaria-free areas (Belang and Tondano respectively), while neither malarial Manado nor the relatively healthy Amurang administrative division saw much change. The remarkably limited impact of cholera and other non-smallpox epidemics in Minahasa after 1854, which cannot be explained in terms of medical treatment as such, makes it tempting to conclude that behavioural changes with respect to disease and hygiene must have played a key role.

Economic factors, however, also need to be taken into account when attempting to explain mortality trends. While the first half of the nineteenth century, as noted in Chapter II, was a period of static or diminishing prosperity in Minahasa, the second half, despite continuing pressures of un- and underpaid compulsory labour, saw a sustained increase in both domestic and external trade. Hickson (1889:208, 214), visiting the area in 1886, was impressed by what he saw as its 'very considerable [...] commercial prosperity', and in particular by 'the general condition of [...] prosperity of the country on the Tondano Lake'. Thanks to peace, order, and the new road network, he also observed, Minahasans were now 'able to send their corn, their chickens, and other produce to the markets' without any hindrance (Hickson 1889:208). In the following chapter I will argue that besides medical, epidemiological, and sanitary conditions, the size and accessibility of the food supply, whether from subsistence agriculture or via trade, was always another key determinant of disease mortality rates.

CHAPTER IX

The food supply

This chapter examines the relationship between mortality and the food supply. Special attention is given to the effects of climatic variation on subsistence production, and to food trade and exchange. Although disease was always far more significant than hunger in terms of the number of direct victims which it claimed, levels of disease mortality were determined partly by nutritional factors, and the mortality crises which periodically affected the population often involved a combination of food scarcity and disease. In the late nineteenth and early twentieth centuries, both peak and background mortality rates were reduced by greater food production, more effective food distribution, and the import of rice from outside the region.

One regional mortality crisis: 1853-1855

The earliest systematic monthly reports (*maandverslagen*) on the state of affairs in the residency of Manado, initiated in August 1853, provide a detailed description of one pronounced mortality crisis which affected many parts of the region. The exceptionally dry, hot weather which had set in around the middle of 1853 was very disadvantageous for the wet rice crop in Gorontalo, the harvest of which, in August and September, was 'for the most part a failure'.[1] By the end of October the onset of the northwest monsoon was also overdue, and in Minahasa the main maize crop, planted immediately after the opening of new swidden fields at the beginning of the dry season, was suffering from lack of rain.[2] In November some rain began to fall in Minahasa, but elsewhere the drought only deepened, and in December the assistant resident of Gorontalo reported that 'in the lands around the

---

[1]   MV Manado October 1853 (ANRI Manado 54).
[2]   In some parts of Minahasa the dry weather earlier in the year had also affected the swidden rice harvest in May, June and July. The Dutch resident, however, reported taking measures to supply the affected districts with rice from elsewhere, and insisted that there need be 'no fear of shortages' (MV Manado August 1853, in ANRI Manado 54).

Gulf of Tomini, famine [*hongersnood*] reigns everywhere as a result of the long drought and the resulting crop failure'.[3] In Moutong the food shortage was alleviated by sago imported from the Togian Islands, where there was so little water in the streams that instead of being processed in the normal way using a settling tank, the sago palm trunks had to be chopped up and shipped in dry form like timber. In Gorontalo itself, 'the scarcity and high price of foodstuffs put the population under great pressure'.[4]

The effects of the drought were now compounded by disease. At the end of August 1853 an 'epidemic stomach sickness' had broken out in the Minahasan district of Tomohon, where within a month it had claimed 107 lives and begun to spread to neighbouring areas. 'The long drought and intense heat', wrote the Resident in October, 'are surely one, if not the only, cause of the disease'.[5] In December, with the coming of the rains, it was thought to be on the wane, but in the first months of 1854 there was a resurgence of the epidemic, now identified as dysentery in combination with measles and *hete koorts* (malaria). The three diseases 'usually occurred in combination or succession in the same patient'.[6] By the end of July, when they finally began to subside in Minahasa, they had killed at least 9,456 people, about 10 percent of the Minahasan population.[7] By incapacitating many more for long periods, they also interfered seriously enough with agricultural activities to affect the foodcrop harvest in 1854.[8]

In May 1854 the same combined epidemic was also reported from the Tomini lands and from Gorontalo, where the number of sufferers was 'extremely high' and the death rate in some places 'very considerable'.[9] Here the outbreak coincided with a dramatic end to the drought in the form of a major flood on 17 May, in which 57 people and 1,200 head of livestock died and 112 houses were destroyed. Perhaps partly because of sanitation problems in the wake of this flooding, the epidemic in Gorontalo now acquired a fourth component, cholera.[10] In July the weather there was still abnormally wet, and in August rice was once again reported to be in short supply, as was maize in December. The epidemic, meanwhile, continued to rage; in the last

3   MV Manado January 1854 (ANRI Manado 54). Where the word 'famine' is used here and below in quotations, it always translates the Dutch term *hongersnood*.
4   MV Manado April 1854 (ANRI Manado 54). By now the continuing drought had also destroyed two successive plantings of cotton, a crop particularly resistant to dry conditions, in Gorontalo.
5   MV Manado October 1853 (ANRI Manado 54).
6   MV Manado March 1854 (ANRI Manado 54).
7   MV Manado September 1853-July 1854 (ANRI Manado 54).
8   CV Manado 1854 (ANRI Manado 51).
9   MV Manado May 1854 (ANRI Manado 54).
10   MV Manado September and December 1854 (ANRI Manado 54).

part of the year it was killing 40-50 people every month, a level of mortality which the assistant resident described as 'very high in relation to the size of the population, and far in excess of the birth rate'.[11] Not until February 1855 did the sickness subside in the Gorontalo area. In July 1854 it was reported to have broken out in Bolaang Mongondow, and by September the north coast of the peninsula and the Sangir Archipelago were also affected. In Sangir, as in Gorontalo, deaths continued into the following year.[12]

In the first quarter of 1855 there was a welcome return to more normal weather conditions, with plenty of rain for the young rice crop. In March the Minahasan swiddens seemed to promise a good harvest, while in Gorontalo the irrigated fields were planted on schedule and maize was in 'abundant' supply.[13] The respite, however, was only temporary; the rains ended early, and there were widespread crop failures in Minahasa due to heat, drought and pests. The maize hastily planted to compensate also failed repeatedly.[14] In Gorontalo it was the same story, with both rice and maize in short supply. For the first time there were now also reports of food shortages on Sangir, where the drought had caused 'great damage to trees and crops'.[15]

In October 1855 it seemed for a short time as if the northwest monsoon rains had begun on schedule, but in November the drought set in again. In Minahasa the number of fatal cases of malaria increased alarmingly, and rice rose to twice its normal price. In Gorontalo there was now a general subsistence crisis, and 'a large part of the population was searching for food in the forest'.[16] Part of the already limited rice reserve in Manado was exported 'to other parts of the residency where the results of the long and intense drought were even more serious for the rice crop than in Minahasa'.[17] Drier than average weather continued to prevail until the end of January 1856, but enough rain fell from December onward to ensure a good late maize crop and end the immediate crisis. The dry season of 1856 was again unusually rainy and caused some crop losses in Minahasa, but the total yield was still far better than in the previous year. In Gorontalo the rice harvest even 'produced an exceptionally favourable result, so that there was an abundance of food'.[18]

---

11 MV Manado December 1854 (ANRI Manado 54).
12 MV Manado July-September 1854, January 1855 (ANRI Manado 54).
13 MV Manado March 1855 (ANRI Manado 54).
14 CV Manado 1855 (ANRI Manado 51).
15 MV Manado September 1855 (ANRI Manado 54).
16 MV Manado December 1855 (ANRI Manado 54).
17 CV Manado 1855 (ANRI Manado 51).
18 MV Manado October 1856 (ANRI Manado 54).

Gorontalo

Nineteenth-century Dutch records from Gorontalo, a subregion particularly prone to natural disasters, provide a good view of the incidence and impact of subsistence crises over a longer period. Located partly in the extended rainshadow cast by the highlands of Central Sulawesi on the other side of the Tomini Gulf during the southeast monsoon, Gorontalo is significantly drier than the more easterly parts of North Sulawesi (Chapter I, Map 3). In the town itself, partly due to local orographic effects, the average annual precipitation is a low 1,211 mm (Braak 1946:75), although Kuandang on the north coast receives an average of 2,725 mm (ASEAN 1982:137). As the Dutch Assistant Resident Van Hoëvell noted in 1891, however, the most striking thing about the rainfall pattern in Gorontalo is its unpredictability.

> For places which lie as close to the equator as Gorontalo, it is extremely difficult to say with any certainty when the east and west monsoons will begin and end. The amount of rainfall is also very variable. While there are some very dry years (such as 1888, when the precipitation in Gorontalo [town] was just 710 mm), the lowest in all the outer islands, there are others in which rainfall is abundant throughout the year. For four years running I have even noted the highest water levels in the months of July and August, the heart of the east monsoon. (Van Hoëvell 1891:34.)

Variability in the timing of the seasonal rains had dissuaded Van Hoëvell from attempting to regulate the rice farming timetable by instruction, as was the practice in some other parts of Indonesia. 'Even after almost five years of experience and careful observation', he admitted, 'I am not able to say with any certainty in which month the preparation of the *sawah* can begin, and everything must be left to chance' (Van Hoëvell 1891:36). The impact of this unpredictability is evident in the archival chronicle of the extreme climatic events, food shortages and epidemics affecting Gorontalo over a timespan of half a century (Table 18). Many of the bad years, including those of the 1853-1855 crisis described above, corresponded to the global climatic perturbations now known as El Niño/Southern Oscillation (ENSO) events, and a record of these, as reconstructed from a variety of historical sources by Quinn (1992:129-30), has been included in the table.

Geographers Allen, Brookfield and Byron (1989:294) have warned that Dutch colonial officials suffered from a 'tendency to hyperbole' when it came to disasters.[19] Even allowing for a certain amount of hyperbole, however, the chronicle as a whole still presents a rather convincing picture of a society close to the limits of its food-producing capacity, and with evident demographic

---

[19]   Others, however, believe that the opposite was true and that officials tended to play down the magnitude of problems, even natural problems, in the areas for which they were responsible.

Table 18. Extreme weather, food shortages and disease in Gorontalo, 1820-1869

Year	ENSO events	Extreme weather	Food shortages	Epidemic disease
1820	?	–	'very great' famine, 'caused by the smallpox' (March-September),[2] food import[3]	smallpox epidemic[1]
1821	?	'severe drought', April-September[4]	by September 'the whole rice crop had completely failed, to the great disadvantage of the inhabitants who were thereby threatened with famine. Fruit and vegetables were unavailable. [...] Already some poor people had [..] died of hunger',[5] Dutch resident forbids export of foodstuffs[6]	–
1822	?	n.a.	n.a.	n.a.
1823	?	wet year (?); floods (October, November)[7]	'not only rice, but all necessities scarce' (June),[8] 'the rice crop here has failed' (November),[9] food export forbidden; rice imported from Manado	–
1824	strong	drought[10]	'prevailing lack of foodstuffs' (August); sago and rice imported,[11] indigenous claims of deaths by hunger denied by Dutch assistant resident[12]	–
1825	strong	–		–
1826	–	'great drought'[13]	'famine owing to the great drought (which went so far that the natives gathered all sorts of roots and leaves with which to feed themselves, and people even died of hunger)'; coconut oil unavailable because nuts serving as famine food[14]	–
1827	strong +	–	–	–
1828	strong +	–	–	–
1829	–	–	–	–

Year	ENSO events	Extreme weather	Food shortages	Epidemic disease
1830	medium	–	–	cholera[15]
1831	–	?	'poor rice harvest'[16]	–
1832	strong +	drought [17]	–	'malevolent fevers'[18]
1833	–	drought[19]	–	dysentery, cholera and other fevers[20]
1834	–	–	–	–
1835	medium	–	–	–
1836	medium	–	–	–
1837	strong	–	–	–
1838	strong	–	–	–
1839	strong	'long drought'[21]	famine[22]	smallpox (December), buikloop (dysentery?) and 'fever'[23]
1840	–	–	–	smallpox (January-February),[24] at least 5,000 dead[25]
1841	–	'long drought'[26]	'famine of more than six months'[27]	–
1842	–	heavy rains and flooding in July[28]	–	–
1843	–	continuous drought, May-September[29]	rice and maize harvest 'very unfavourable'; 'great scarcity of foodstuffs' in Gorontalo town (September)[30]	–
1844	very strong	–	–	–
1845	very strong	'tremendous rains' in January-March; 'unbroken drought of almost seven months', April-November[33]	drought 'destroyed more than two thirds of the rice and maize fields', so that 'the price of foodstuffs climbed to an extraordinary level';[32] 'pressing food shortage, so that the people are incapable of performing any work' (November)[34]	many deaths among livestock (water buffalo)[31]

1846	very strong	renewed drought, January–April[36]	famine (January),[35] 'total absence' of rice in Limboto, so that seed rice had to be imported (February);[37] 'lack of proper food over a period of several months, as a result of the intense heat and absence of rain' (April),[39] seed rice still short in December[40]	'stomach disease' causes a 'tremendous number of deaths' in first part of year[38]
1847	–	continuous heavy rains, February–July[41]	'repeated crop failures' in northern and eastern districts; foodstuffs short and many people searching for sago in forests on north coast (July)[42]	–
1848	–	–	–	–
1849	–	–	–	–
1850	strong	heavy rain in first half of year interferes with planting on wet fields;[45] drought in second half[46]	'almost complete harvest failure' in second half of year;[43] 'lack of foodstuffs', sago and rice imported[44]	n.a.
1851	–	n.a.	February: part of the population 'dispersed in the forests due to the failure of its crops and the resulting famine',[47] harvest for this year also 'very unfavourable';[48] sago and rice imported[49]	n.a.
1852	medium	n.a.	sago and rice imported[50]	n.a.
1853	medium	'continuous, unusually intense drought' in second half of year[51]	rice harvest 'for the most part a failure, and measures have had to be taken to prevent shortages of rice'[52]	–
1854	strong	drought, January–April;[53] heavy rain and flooding, May–July[54]	drought conditions 'very unfavourable for the rice crop, so that the shortage and high price of foodstuffs [...] put the population under great pressure' (March);[55] rice still in short supply in August;[57] maize shortage	'measles, and above all dysentery, have claimed many victims',[56] cholera also reported;[58] mortality

Year	ENSO events	Extreme weather	Food shortages[59]	Epidemic disease
1855	strong	exceptional drought and heat in second half of year[61]	in November;[59] rice and maize affected by drought in September, 'so that scarcity of food made itself felt';[62] by December 'food was short everywhere, and a large part of the population was searching for foodstuffs in the forest'[64]	'exceptionally high' and 'far in excess of fertility';[60] dysentery epidemic continues until February;[63] 'epidemic fevers of a catarrhal and gastric nature', August-September[65]
1856	–	much rain in 'dry' season[66]	–	disease outbreak kills > 500 water buffalo[67]
1857	medium +	n.a.	n.a.	n.a.
1858	medium +	n.a.	n.a.	n.a.
1859	medium +	–		smallpox (December)[68]
1860	medium	–	food import[69]	smallpox, January-May: about 3,000 dead[70]
1861	–	wet year; flooding (June-November)[71]	rice and maize scarce and expensive (November)[72]	–
1862	medium -	–	rice and maize scarce and expensive (January-April)[73]	–
1863	–	–	–	severe fevers (January-April)[74]
1864	strong +	harsh dry season[75]	rice scarce and expensive, June-September; rice and sago imported[76]	–
1865	medium +	harsh dry season[77]	partial rice crop failure; sago imported[78]	–
1866	medium +	–	–	cholera (from October onward); 1,438 deaths reported[79]

1867	strong +	unusually wet year; rain and floods destroy part of rice and maize crop[80]	–	cholera, 'fevers' and *buikloop* (dysentery?), January-September; another 542 reported dead[81]
1868	strong +	–	–	–
1869	strong +	–	–	–

1   Res. Gorontalo to Res. Ternate, 18-3 and 10-9-1820 (ANRI Ternate 153).
2   Res. Gorontalo to Res. Ternate, 18-3 and 24-4-1820 (ANRI Ternate 153).
3   Res. Gorontalo to Res. Ternate, 30-9-1820 (ANRI Ternate 153).
4   Reinwardt 1858:512; Res. Gorontalo to Res. Ternate, 23-9-1821 (ANRI Ternate 153).
5   Reinwardt 1858:512.
6   Res. Gorontalo to Res. Ternate, 26-9-1821 (ANRI Ternate 153).
7   Res. Gorontalo to Res. Ternate, 20-2-1824 (ANRI Gorontalo 1).
8   Res. Gorontalo to Res. Ternate, 22-6-1823 (ANRI Gorontalo 1).
9   Res. Gorontalo to Res. Ternate, 22-11-1823 (ANRI Gorontalo 1).
10 Res. Gorontalo to Res. Manado, 26-9-1824 (ANRI Manado 114).
11 Res. Gorontalo to Res. Manado, 26-9-1824 (ANRI Manado 114).
12 Res. Gorontalo to Res. Manado, 6-10-1824 (ANRI Manado 114).
13 AR Gorontalo to Res. Manado, 8-12-1826 (ANRI Manado 114).
14 AR Gorontalo to Res. Manado, 8-12-1826 (ANRI Manado 114).
15 AR Gorontalo to Res. Manado, 6-10-1830 (ANRI Manado 115).
16 AR Gorontalo to Res. Manado, 13-9-1831 (ANRI Manado 115).
17 AR Gorontalo to Res. Manado, 20-10-1832 (ANRI Manado 115).
18 AR Gorontalo to Res. Manado, 20-10-1832 (ANRI Manado 115).
19 Res. Manado to GG, 19-10-1833 (ANRI Manado 77).
20 Res. Manado to GG, 19-10-1833 (ANRI Manado 77).
21 AR Gorontalo to Res. Manado, 25-11-1841 (ANRI Manado 116).
22 AR Gorontalo to Res. Manado, 11-1-1840 and 25-11-1841 (ANRI Manado 116).
23 AR Gorontalo to Res. Manado, 14-1-1840 (ANRI Manado 116).
24 AR Gorontalo to Res. Manado, 20-2-1841 (ANRI Manado 116).
25 Scherius 1847:401-2, 407.

26   AR Gorontalo to Res. Manado, 25-11-1841 (ANRI Manado 116).

27   AV Gorontalo 1841-1843 (ANRI Manado 50); AR Gorontalo to Res. Manado, 25-11-1841 (ANRI Manado 116).

28   AR Gorontalo to Res. Manado, 10-7-1842 (ANRI Manado 117).

29   AR Gorontalo to Res. Manado, 22-9-1843 (ANRI Manado 117).

30   AR Gorontalo to Res. Manado, 22-9-1843 (ANRI Manado 117).

31   'Dagregister van den civiele gezaghebber te Gorontalo', 7-9-1846 (ANRI Manado 5).

32   AV Gorontalo 1845 (KITLV H111).

33   AV Gorontalo 1845 (KITLV H111).

34   'Dagregister van den civiele gezaghebber te Gorontalo', 20-11-1845 (ANRI Manado 172).

35   AR Gorontalo to Res. Manado, 17-1-1846 (ANRI Manado 119).

36   Res. Manado to Gov. Moluccas, 15-4-1846 (ANRI Manado 83); 'Dagregister van den civiele gezaghebber te Gorontalo', 21-3-1846 (ANRI Manado 172).

37   AR Gorontalo to Res. Manado, 2-1-1846 (ANRI Manado 119).

38   Res. Manado to Gov. Moluccas, 15-4-1846 (ANRI Manado 83); also 'Dagregister van den civiele gezaghebber te Gorontalo', 21-3-1846 (ANRI Manado 172).

39   Res. Manado to Gov. Moluccas, 15-4-1846 (ANRI Manado 83).

40   'Dagregister van den civiele gezaghebber te Gorontalo', 9-12-1846 (ANRI Manado 5).

41   AR Gorontalo to Res. Manado, 31-7-1847 (ANRI Manado 119).

42   AR Gorontalo to Res. Manado, 31-7-1847 (ANRI Manado 119).

43   AV Manado 1850 (ANRI Manado 51); AV Gorontalo 1852 (ANRI Gorontalo 3).

44   Res. Manado to Gov. Moluccas, 21-10-1854 (ANRI Gorontalo 18).

45   'Dagregister van den civiele gezaghebber te Gorontalo', first and second quarter 1850 (ANRI Manado 27, 120).

46   Drought inferred from crop failure (AV Gorontalo 1852, in ANRI Gorontalo 3), and from reports of a 'long, intense drought' in Java in the same year (W. van Bemmelen 1916:163). Except for 1835, all other drought years listed by Van Bemmelen for Java in the period 1833-1869 also correspond to droughts in Gorontalo.

47   A.J.F. Jansen, 'Nota omtrent het tweehoofdig bestuur in de landschappen Gorontalo, Limbotto, en Boalemo', 17-12-1855 (ANRI Gorontalo 18).

48   AV Gorontalo 1952 (ANRI Gorontalo 3).

49   Res. Manado to Gov. Moluccas, 21-10-1854 (ANRI Gorontalo 18).

50   Res. Manado to Gov. Moluccas, 21-10-1854 (ANRI Gorontalo 18).

51   AV Manado 1853 (ANRI Manado 51); MV Manado October 1853 (ANRI Manado 54).

52   MV Manado October 1853 (ANRI Manado 54).

53   MV Manado April and May 1854 (ANRI Manado 54).

54   MV Manado May and September 1854 (ANRI Manado 54).

55 MV Manado April 1854 (ANRI Manado 54).
56 AV Gorontalo 1854 (ANRI Manado 54).
57 MV Manado September 1854 (ANRI Manado 54).
58 MV Manado September and December 1854 (ANRI Manado 54).
59 MV Manado December 1854 (ANRI Manado 54).
60 AV Gorontalo 1854 (ANRI Manado 54); MV Manado December 1854 (ANRI Manado 54).
61 MV Manado September and December 1855 (ANRI Manado 54).
62 MV Manado September 1855 (ANRI Manado 54).
63 MV Manado February and March 1855 (ANRI Manado 54).
64 MV Manado December 1855 (ANRI Manado 54).
65 MV Manado September 1855 (ANRI Manado 54).
66 MV Manado July and October 1856 (ANRI Manado 54).
67 MV Manado October 1856 (ANRI Manado 54).
68 MV Manado December 1859 (ANRI Manado 54).
69 MV Manado November 1860 (ANRI Manado 54).
70 MV Manado May 1860 (ANRI Manado 54);Van der Crab 1862:379.
71 MV Manado August and December 1861 (ANRI Manado 54).
72 MV Manado December 1861 (ANRI Manado 54).
73 MV Manado January and June 1862 (ANRI Manado 54).
74 MV Manado January and June 1863 (ANRI Manado 54).
75 CV Gorontalo 1864 (ANRI Manado 44).
76 CV Gorontalo 1864 (ANRI Manado 44).
77 CV Manado 1865 (ANRI Manado 52).
78 CV Manado 1865 (ANRI Manado 52).
79 MV Manado March 1867 (ANRI Manado 54).
80 MV Manado October 1867 and January 1868 (ANRI Manado 54).
81 MV Manado January and October 1867 (ANRI Manado 54).

consequences. In some cases, like that of the smallpox epidemic in 1820, food shortages were the result, rather than the cause, of disease outbreaks, which rendered people unable to perform agricultural work. More often, however, epidemics followed (rather than preceded) food shortages clearly brought on by unfavourable weather (Table 18: 1839, 1846, 1854, 1855). Some of the Dutch sources are explicit regarding the direction of causality here: during the disastrously dry 'wet' season of 1845-1846, the assistant resident of Gorontalo described the 'tremendous number of deaths to stomach disease' as 'a result of lack of proper food over a period of several months due to the intense heat and absence of rain'.[20] It is possible that such reports underestimated more direct connections between drought and disease via poorer than usual hygiene, or perhaps an enhanced malaria environment. There were also years, however, in which drought was not followed by epidemic disease, yet people (implicitly even adults, a point to which I will return below) were nevertheless reported to have died from sheer hunger (1821, 1826).

The low level of food security indicated here is all the more striking given that traditional farming systems in Gorontalo were well adapted to the unpredictable climatic situation. The practice of planting irrigated rice in stages over a period over several months, which Van Hoëvell would have liked to reform, was an example of such adaptation.[21] Gorontalese farmers no doubt realized, as did Dutch officials, that this resulted in increased losses to pests.[22] But at the same time it also reduced the more serious risk of total crop failure in the event of unfavourable weather. The staple food in nineteenth-century Gorontalo, however, was not rice but maize, and here the adaptation to climatic uncertainty was still more complete in that there was no fixed seasonal schedule at all for planting and harvesting.

> The maize of Gorontalo is planted on dry fields (*tegal*), on *sawah* fields as a second crop, and on newly cleared forest land, regardless of the time of year. If the weather is very dry or rainy, of course, the maize crop is less successful, but planting goes on nonetheless, both on the plain and on sloping or mountainous terrain.[23]

Some fields, according to an early nineteenth-century source, were planted with as many as four consecutive maize crops in the space of a single year.[24] Among the (at least) 14 maize varieties cultivated was one which took only 70 days to mature, and was therefore particularly suited to taking rapid advantage of short spells of wet weather (Riedel 1870a:80).

[20]   Res. Manado to Gov. Moluccas, 15-4-1846 (ANRI Manado 83).
[21]   CV Gorontalo 1864 (ANRI Manado 44); MV Manado 1868 and 1869 (ANRI Manado 54).
[22]   CV Gorontalo 1863 (ANRI Manado 134).
[23]   CV Gorontalo 1863 (ANRI Manado 134).
[24]   Gov. Moluccas to GG, 3-7-1824 (KITLV H142). Two or three crops per year, however, seem to have been more usual (Van Doren 1857-60, II:347; Van Hoëvell 1891:35).

Minahasa

A colonial meteorologist once remarked on 'the equanimity [*gelijkmatigheid*] of the much-praised, pleasantly cool climate of Tondano' (Smits 1909:18), and the engineer Van Marle (1922, I:43) agreed that in Minahasa, 'less than pleasant climatic situations' were 'virtually unknown'. Nineteenth-century descriptions of Minahasan agriculture, nevertheless, stress the vulnerability of the rice crop to drought and untimely wet weather, as well as pests (especially mice).[25] Selected climatic statistics from Tomohon in the short period 1895-1907 (Figure 3) confirm that even this most hospitable part of the region was not immune from dangerous climatic variations. In the Tomohon area

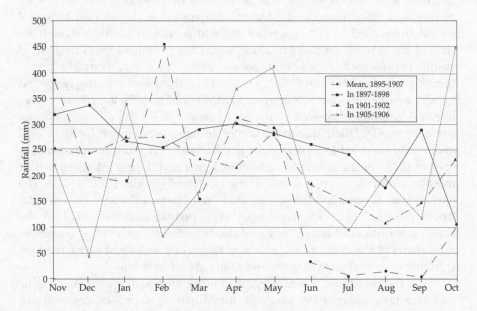

Figure 3. Monthly rainfall distribution and variability in Tomohon (Minahasa), 1895-1907 (Smits 1909:60-1)

both the northwest and southeast monsoons are rain-bearing, creating, on average, a more or less continuously (but not excessively) wet season between October and May; the months of June to September are usually relatively dry. New swiddens were cleared and burned at the beginning of this dry period and initially planted with maize, which was harvested around November; the

---

25   Francis 1860:350; Graafland 1864:18; Riedel 1872b:543.

subsequent rice crop grew during the long wet period. In 1898, however, as much rain continued to fall in June and July as in the heart of a normal wet season, and not until September did a really dry period occur. This kind of anomaly jeopardized the all-important swidden burn at the beginning of the agricultural year. In 1902, by contrast, the dry season was excessively dry, no doubt leading, as in 1853, to the failure of the maize crop. The climatic year 1905-1906 represents a third type of hazardous anomaly; here the months of December and February, in the middle of what should be the wet season, are the driest of the whole year, threatening the young rice plants.

Oral history in Minahasa, as recorded in the nineteenth century, featured stories of disastrous famines, sometimes as a consequence of drought.[26] Dramatic fluctuations in the size of the rice harvest, because these were of economic importance to the Dutch, also appear in the written historical record. In May 1669 a VOC governor of the Moluccas noted that although the state of the new *pad* crop in Minahasa seemed to promise a good harvest, 'it is still not possible to count on this, because too little rain can quickly change things' (De Jongh 1669). In 1707 'all *padi*' in Minahasa was reportedly spoiled by wet weather (Godée Molsbergen 1928:97), and in 1754 the rice crop was likewise 'completely spoiled by the heavy rain'.[27] In 1769, 'half' of all the rice sown reportedly failed 'due to the severe drought' (Seydelman 1769). In 1803 another drought led to a 'very poor rice harvest'.[28] An 'unprecedented' dry spell in 1824, during which no rain fell in Kema and Belang for almost seven months, resulted in 'great losses to the rice crop' (Riedel 1872b:463-4). The harvest was affected by drought in 1833 (Van Doren 1854-56, I:260), and by 'heavy rains' in 1843.[29] During the dry event of 1845-1846 (see Table 18), the Dutch authorities in Manado released rice from their warehouses 'to feed the inhabitants of the districts of Amurang, Rumo'ong and Tombasian, who are suffering a general state of want and afflicted by hot fevers'.[30]

From the middle of the nineteenth century, the quality of demographic and economic information available for Minahasa improves dramatically. Whereas the available population statistics for Gorontalo (Chapter IV) are not accurate or detailed enough to allow any sort of quantitative reconstruction of how variations in food production affected demographic change, for Minahasa we have an annual record of births and deaths from 1849 to 1872. From 1853 onward, moreover, there are also quantitative statistics regarding the annual rice and maize harvest. This makes it possible to gain an over-

---

26   Van Doren 1854-56, I:245; Graafland 1867-69, I:95, 107; Riedel 1872b:467.
27   NA VOC 2836:1180.
28   Res. Manado to Gov. Moluccas, 28-2-1804 (ANRI Manado 60).
29   Res. Manado to Res. Ternate, 17-7-1843 (ANRI Manado 80).
30   Res. Manado to Gov. Moluccas, 30-1-1846 (ANRI Manado 83).

view of how mortality levels related not only to climatic anomalies and epi-demics, but also to the production of the most important subsistence crops (Table 19). The accuracy of the quantitative data presented here is, as usual, questionable, but its uniqueness nevertheless makes an attempt at analysis worthwhile.

The link between climatic anomalies and poor harvests, first of all, is clear enough in Table 19. The dry events of 1850, 1853, 1855, and 1865 all corre-spond to more or less poor rice harvests, and those of 1853 and 1855 appear to have affected the maize harvest too, although the maize production figures for those years are particularly incomplete.[31] The long rains of 1861 and 1862 also had a marked effect on both rice and maize crops, although 1867 presents an unexplained exception in this respect. Regarding mortality, disease is clearly the pre-eminent killer, most obviously in the case of the great dysen-tery, malaria, measles and cholera epidemic of 1853-1854, but also during the malaria outbreaks of 1850-1852 and 1860.

In 1875, the government investigator A.C.J. Edeling argued that a relation-ship was also discernible in these data between food production and mortal-ity.[32] A delay of one year, he proposed, typically separated each poor harvest from its impact in the demographic statistics. The effect of the first drought in 1850, unfortunately, was hidden by the inaccurate mortality statistics for 1851, and that of the second in 1853 by the great number of deaths caused by the associated epidemic. The high mortality during 1856, however, did appear to reflect the impact of the 1855 crisis, since this was not accompanied by epidemic disease, and the death rate had been lower in 1855 following the relatively good year of 1854 between the droughts. In 1861-1862 the story was the same, with dramatically increased mortality in 1862 following the poor harvests of the previous year despite the absence of epidemic disease. The relatively low mortality of the late 1860s could also be interpreted as reflect-ing the good harvests of both rice and maize in that period.

In statistical terms, the specific relationship between the crude death rate for each year and the total size of the rice and maize harvest in each previous year is not in fact a strong one (Figure 4).[33] What is nevertheless clear from the harvest data is that taken as a whole, the crucial period of transition from high to lower mortality between about 1855 and 1870 (see Chapter VIII and Chapter X, Figure 8) was also one in which per capita food (especially maize) production in Minahasa, for reasons to be discussed below and in Chapter

---

[31] A qualitative source, however, confirms that the maize harvest of 1855 was affected by the drought (CV Manado 1855, in ANRI Manado 51).

[32] 'Memorie omtrent de Minahasa', 13-8-1875 (NA V 17-4-1877/20). More than 70 years later, Tammes (1940:192-3) reiterated the same argument using some of the same evidence .

[33] The regression line shown in Figure 4 carries an R^2 value of 0.046.

Table 19. Extreme weather, epidemic disease, food production and mortality in Minahasa, 1849-1872

Year	Extreme weather	Epidemic disease	Rice production per capita[2] (husked, kg)	Maize production per capita[3] (grain only, kg)	Combined rice and maize production per capita (kg)	Mortality[1] (per 1,000)
1849	–	–	n.a.	n.a.	–	30.3
1850	drought[4]	'terrible fevers'[5]	'mixed results'[6]	n.a.	–	30.4
1851	–	'terrible fevers'[7]	'generally favourable'[8]	'generally favourable'[9]	–	[25.3][10]
1852	–	'severe fevers'[11]	'favourable'[12]	'favourable'[13]	–	31.6
1853	'unusually long and intense drought' in second half of year[15]	'epidemic stomach disease' in August-December[14]	97	>35	>132	28.2
1854	–	dysentery, measles and malaria, January-November[16]	104	73	177	138.5
1855	'long and intense drought' in second half of year[17]	–	85	>21	>106	26.3
1856	unusually wet dry season[18]	–	169	80	249	33.7
1857	–	–	148	111	259	26.2
1858	–	–	193	177	370	25.8
1859	–	–	193	192	385	24.4
1860	–	malaria (January-April)[19]	200	131	331	32.7
1861	'unusually high rainfall throughout the entire year',[20] (interferes with burning of swiddens for 1862)[21]	–	132	128	260	27.5

1862	continuous rainy weather in first half of year[22]	–	123	94	217	38.1
1863	–	–	181	140	321	28.1
1864	–	–	166	144	310	23.0
1865	harsh drought, January-March[23]	–	150	166	316	23.9
1866	–	–	150	177	327	24.3
1867	'continuous rains throughout almost the whole year'[24]	–	185	254	439	23.4
1868	–	–	174	240	414	20.1
1869	–	–	151	223	374	25.8
1870	–	–	169	231	400	18.4
1871	–	–	177	240	417	21.5
1872	'protracted rainy weather'[25]	–	163	242	405	34.4

1   AV Manado 1849-72 (ANRI Manado 51, 52, 53).

2   CV Manado 1853-69 (ANRI Manado 39, 48, 51, 52, 53, 95, 198; Ambon 1543, 1563); A.C.J. Edeling, 'Memorie omtrent de Minahasa', 13-8-1875 (NA V 17-4-1877/20).

3   CV Manado 1853-69 (as above); A.C.J. Edeling, 'Memorie omtrent de Minahasa', 13-8-1875 (NA V 17-4-1877/20).

4   Inferred from poorer than average harvest in Minahasa (AV Manado 1850, in ANRI Manado 51), crop failure in Gorontalo (AV Gorontalo 1852, in ANRI Gorontalo 3), and reports of a 'long, intense drought' on Java in the same year (W. van Bemmelen 1916:163). Except for 1835, all of the other drought years listed by Van Bemmelen for Java in the period 1833-1870 also correspond to dry events in Minahasa.

5   AV Manado 1850 (ANRI Manado 51).

6   AV Manado 1850 (ANRI Manado 51).

7   AV Manado 1851 (ANRI Manado 51).

8   AV Manado 1851 (ANRI Manado 51).

9   AV Manado 1851 (ANRI Manado 51).

10   The mortality statistic for 1851 'was not submitted on schedule, and its accuracy is therefore doubtful' (AV Manado 1851, in ANRI Manado 51).

11   AV Manado 1852 (ANRI Manado 51).

12 AV Manado 1852 (ANRI Manado 51).
13 AV Manado 1852 (ANRI Manado 51).
14 MV Manado, August-December 1853 (ANRI Manado 54).
15 CV Manado 1853 (ANRI Manado 51).
16 MV Manado January-December 1854 (ANRI Manado 54).
17 CV Manado 1855 (ANRI Manado 51); MV Manado, 7-12-1855 (ANRI Manado 54).
18 CV Manado 1856 (ANRI Manado 52).
19 MV Manado January-April 1860 (ANRI Manado 54).
20 CV Manado 1861 (ANRI Manado 95).
21 CV Manado 1862 (ANRI Ambon 1563).
22 CV Manado 1862 (ANRI Manado 95).
23 CV Manado 1865 (ANRI Manado 52); MV Manado January-March 1865 (ANRI Manado 54).
24 CV Manado 1867 (ANRI Manado 53).
25 *Koloniaal verslag* 1872:16.

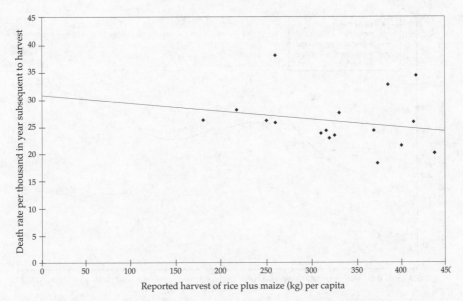

Figure 4. Food production and mortality in Minahasa, 1854-1872.
Sources: see Table 19.

XV, expanded dramatically (Figure 5).[34] Taken together with the evidence for frequent subsistence crises in Gorontalo and other parts of the region, then, the Minahasan evidence reinforces the impression there was an inverse causal relationship between food production and mortality.

That such a relationship appears to have existed even in Minahasa, the area with probably the most productive agriculture in the region, adds to its significance. Many nineteenth- and twentieth-century sources state that food is seldom or never scarce in Minahasa.[35] Alfred Russel Wallace (1987:197) described Minahasa in 1859 as a country 'with an abundance of food and necessaries', and a later visitor even called it 'the most fertile land in the world' (Bierens de Haan 1893:79). Both wet and dry rice (see Chapter II) grew well on its volcanic soils. Maize, besides complementing rice in the standard swidden cycle, was often sown as an emergency measure after the failure of an earlier rice crop, and maize cobs could be eaten in an immature

[34]   While the figures themselves are unreliable (see below), many impressionistic statements in the contemporary administrative sources confirm this trend (CV Manado 1859, in ANRI Ambon 1543; CV Manado 1864, in ANRI Manado 39; A.C.J. Edeling, 'Memorie omtrent de Minahasa', 13-8-1875, in NA V 17-4-1877/20).
[35]   AV Manado 1853 (ANRI Manado 51); A.J.F. Jansen 1861:235; Bouvy 1924:380; Hickson 1889: 208.

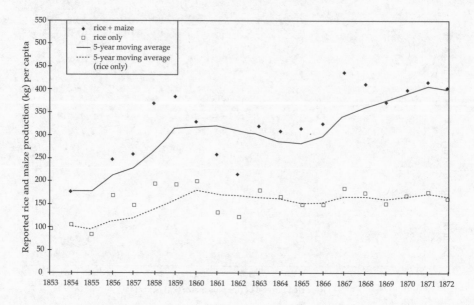

Figure 5. Staple food production in Minahasa, 1854-1872.
Sources: see Table 19.

state if there was no time to wait for them to ripen.[36] A variety of vegetables and tubers were also planted on the swiddens (Francis 1860:349; N.P.
Wilken 1870:374). Sago, finally, was available as a fallback when all else failed
(*Fragment* 1856:24; Graafland 1867-69, I:182), so that the level of food security
appeared to be very high.

Even without taking sago and other auxiliary food sources into account,
moreover, it is hard to discern any evidence for absolute scarcity in the nineteenth-century food production statistics themselves. Dietary field studies
carried out on Java around 1930 indicated that in localities where rice was
the staple food, between 250 and 300 grammes per head of the population
(including children) per day, or about 100 kg per person per year, represented
an 'adequate' level of consumption.[37] Even the worst Minahasan rice harvest

[36]   CV Manado 1862 (ANRI Ambon 1563), 1863 (ANRI Manado 52); MV Amurang October 1864
(ANRI Manado 18); 'Stukken voedingsmiddelen in de Minahassa 1877-78' (ANRI Manado 37).
[37]   *Nationaal rapport* 1937:176. In one of the two studies quoted here, about 60 g of maize and 30
g of root crops were also consumed; in the other, 50 g of root crops and no maize. Hanks (1972:
48), for Thailand, likewise gives a figure of 400 lb of *padi*, or about 200 lb (100 kg) of hulled rice,
per person per year. These are evidently nutritional minima, however, for given an 'ample' stock,
according to a study from Sarawak, adult males and females typically consume respectively 234
kg and 187 kg of hulled rice annually (Rousseau 1990:134). Ellen (1979:61) assumes a similarly
high level of consumption.

in the quantitative record, that of the drought year 1855, already produced the equivalent of 85 kg per person, yet contemporary estimates of the proportion of the Minahasan diet routinely supplied by maize rather than rice range from about one third (N.P. Wilken 1870:374) to more than half.[38] Very little food, moreover, was exported from Minahasa at this period; the compulsory rice trade initiated in VOC times was abolished in 1851 (Graafland 1898, I:89), and rice exports virtually ceased after 1855.[39]

In 1861, resident of Manado J.C. Bosch noted that the 'gigantic' proportions of the harvest statistics on paper were at odds with the 'scarcity, even want' of foodstuffs which he had personally observed in several parts of Minahasa, and concluded that at least some of the figures, presumably in order to please superior officials, must have been inflated.[40] An additional possibility, however, is that the problem lay partly in maldistribution of the available food rather than in absolute underproduction. This complex question will be considered in more detail below, but one point regarding food distribution is immediately relevant in the Minahasan context. In the historical sources for Minahasa, in sharp contrast to those for Gorontalo, I have never come across an explicit reference to famine or *hongersnood*, still less to actual deaths from starvation. The implication, already recognized by Edeling in 1875, is that by working through the medium of infant mortality, increasing the susceptibilty of the very young to disease, relative food shortages could raise mortality without becoming visible to casual observers in the form of widespread hunger among the adult population. Here and elsewhere, it was probably the very young (together, possibly, with the very old) who bore the brunt of any Malthusian 'positive checks' to population growth.

Minahasa in the mid-nineteenth century was by no means a typical part of the region, but a colonial enclave in which the economy had been transformed by state monopolies and compulsory labour services (see Chapter II).[41] In the 1850s and 1860s, moreover, its inhabitants bore an unprecedented labour burden above and beyond foodcrop farming due to an expansion in roadbuilding and coffee cultivation (see Chapter X) which some observers

---

[38] CV Manado 1856 (ANRI Manado 51).

[39] CV Manado 1855, 1856 (ANRI Manado 51). There was a brief return to rice exports, however, in the years 1872-1879 (Dirkzwager 1912:1165).

[40] CV Manado 1861 (ANRI Manado 95). This conclusion applied to the statistics for maize as well as rice. 'On the basis of personal investigations', Bosch estimated the typical consumption of maize at 4 cobs per person per day, or almost 1,500 cobs per year, at which rate the reported harvest of more than 160 million cobs should have been sufficient for all domestic needs. Yet maize, as well as rice, had been scarce in some districts during 1861. Bosch did also note, however, that much maize was used as pig fodder (see Chapter XII).

[41] Reservations also apply to the data from Gorontalo, where the early nineteenth century, as argued in Chapter II, was a time of economic decline in which trade in general, and food imports in particular, were more restricted than at either earlier or later periods.

identified as a cause of sub-optimal food production in its own right (Edeling 1919:73-4; Quarles van Ufford 1856:42-3). One reason for the comparatively poor harvests of 1861, for instance, was said to be the workload imposed on the population by intensified roadbuilding efforts in connection with an impending visit by Governor-General C.F. Pahud; this had interfered severely with agricultural activities, causing some foodcrops to be planted behind schedule.[42] It bears repeating however, that despite such competing labour demands, the general trend of per capita food production in this period was strongly upward (Figure 5). As my reconstruction of the 1853-1855 regional mortality crisis already showed, moreover, the incidence of food shortages in bad years was not limited to areas under Dutch control.

Sangir, Talaud, and Central Sulawesi

Although the historical record for areas other than Minahasa and Gorontalo is more limited, it suggests similar patterns of periodic food and disease crises induced by unfavourable weather. Food production on Sangir, as already noted with respect to the crisis of 1853-1855, was certainly vulnerable to drought, and sometimes more so than on the peninsula. During the severe dry weather of 1877-1878, there was a 'quite general lack of foodstuffs' on Sangir and Talaud following an 'almost complete' harvest failure (*Koloniaal verslag* 1878:27). In 1896, a milder dry event which was also felt in Minahasa (Van der Stok 1900:60), but which does not seem to have had much effect on the health situation there or in Gorontalo, had more serious consequences for the population of the northern islands.

> On the Sangir and Talaud Islands [...] there was a pronounced and quite general scarcity of foodstuffs in the months of September and October. The main causes here were the long drought in the first part of the year and in August, September and October, and the poor health situation of the population in some areas, which probably also resulted from the drought, and which prevented people from tending to their existing crops or planting new ones. Many root crops also failed due to the lack of rain, which, in addition, led to shortages of drinking water on some small islands.[43]

On Greater Sangir, 'hundreds' of people reportedly died in 'various epidemics' during this crisis (Coolsma 1901:645). In 1912, following another unusually severe dry season on Talaud, 'food became scarce, and drinking water

---

[42]   CV Manado 1861 (ANRI Manado 95). A rise in the birth rate during the 1850s (see Chapter X) must have placed additional pressure on the available food resources.
[43]   CV Manado 1896 (ANRI Manado 86).

unavailable or very poor'; there were many cases of 'diarrhoea, vomiting, severe constipation, headache and fever', and infant mortality rose (*Overzicht* 1914:14-5). The missionary Pennings noted that the Talaud Islands, with their thin, sandy soils, were particularly subject to food shortages despite the fact that the staple crops here were tubers rather than rice or maize.[44]

> Such a thin layer of soil, of course, dries out rapidly. If the drought is protracted, the soil cracks and when the tubers, *ubi* or *bete* [taro] (the staple food of the population of Talaud) are pulled out of the ground they are rotten, or, as local people sometimes put it, 'cooked'. In this state they are inedible, so that even the most diligent Talaud farmer is short of food. (Pennings 1908:14.)

Sources from the late nineteenth century repeatedly mention food shortages on Talaud, sometimes in connection with epidemics or wars which interfered with agricultural activities, but also as a direct result of drought.[45] 'Famine and war', lamented one missionary, 'are all that one hears of in Talaud' (Coolsma 1901:657-8).

Several accounts of famine in Sangir and Talaud are also available from earlier periods. In March 1695, a VOC sergeant stationed on Siau complained 'about the great drought which had reigned there for a very long period, so that all their *padi* and other crops had withered and died and there had been no little hunger, accompanied moreover by a great number of deaths'.[46] Another 'great drought', together with dysentery and smallpox, was involved in the severe mortality crisis of 1723-1724 (*Generale missiven* VII:694). In 1770 there was again famine and sickness on Sangir and Talaud: the coconut trees, it was said, had borne no nuts, and 'because of the famine', men could not be recruited on Talaud to help drive off a Magindanao raiding vessel.[47] In 1784 an 'unprecedented' drought hit Sangir, 'as a result of which many of the coconut trees on those islands died, and many others bore few nuts or none at all'.[48] The drought of 1824 also caused crop losses in the islands, Sangirese sailing vessels arriving in Manado 'to obtain quantities of rice and other foodstuffs'.[49]

---

[44] Also Jellesma 1911:1240. On Banggai, likewise, yams were said to be vulnerable both to drought and to excessive rain (A.C. Kruyt 1932d:483). In Minahasa, cassava also suffered during droughts ('Stukken voedingsmiddelen in de Minahassa 1877-78', in ANRI Manado 37).

[45] Coolsma 1901:655, 657, 665; CV Manado 1861 (ANRI Manado 95), 1896 (ANRI Manado 86); *Koloniaal verslag* 1861:21, 1863:18, 1888:15; Jellesma 1911:1240; MV Manado December 1863, April 1864, May 1865 (ANRI Manado 54); Tammes 1940:184-6.

[46] NA VOC 1579:132. At the same date the kings of Gorontalo and Limboto, where there had been complaints of drought and food shortages in the previous year, reported that their subjects had been afflicted by 'dysentery [*bloedgang*], of which many people have died' (NA VOC 1579: 31, 245).

[47] RPR Ternate, 27-2-1770 (ANRI Ternate 18).

[48] NA VOC 3671:99.

[49] Res. Manado to Res. Ternate, 15-11-1824 (ANRI Ternate 152).

The colonial ethnographies of Central Sulawesi all emphasize the risks to food production posed by unpredictable weather and pests.[50] In Bada, Woensdregt referred to a seasonal 'time of hunger, when people are forced to fill their stomachs with vegetables and unripe fruits', and during which stomach disease was common (A.C. Kruyt 1938, II:308). In Central Sulawesi, as in Minahasa, oral tradition included stories of disastrous droughts and famines (Adriani and Kruyt 1950-51, I:4-5; A.C. Kruyt 1938, I:116, 165, 181, 252). A few specific episodes of famine also appear in the short historical record. In 1896, when drought led to food shortages in Sangir and Talaud, 'famine reigned' in Pakambia and Onda'e too (Adriani and Kruyt 1900:136). In 1899 there was again crop failure in Pakambia, and in 1910 a group of To Napu was 'driven by hunger' to beg for food in the Poso Valley (Adriani and Kruyt 1900:208; *Brieven*, June 1910). A later source states that Napu is widely known in Central Sulawesi as a 'land of hunger'.[51] In 1911, famine threatened the coastlands around the Gulf of Tomini when the rice harvest there failed following a long drought 'during the months which are referred to as the wet season' (Boonstra van Heerdt 1914b:751).

Food storage

Despite the evidence for food shortages following poor harvests, it is clear that the most important food staple, rice, was often kept in storage from one year to the next. Threshed but unhusked, in which form it was customarily stored in the villages, Minahasan rice would keep for 'two or even three years'.[52] In Central Sulawesi, where the rice was usually stored as bound sheaves and threshed only when needed for consumption (Adriani and Kruyt 1900:208, 1912-14, II:198), it likewise remained usable, 'being now and then aired', for about two years.[53] Other foodstuffs could also be stored for shorter periods. Smoked maize cobs kept for up to six months (Tillema 1922:192; Woodard

---

[50]   Adriani and Kruyt 1912-14, II:256-63; Engelenberg 1905:139-40; Kaudern 1925:22; A.C. Kruyt 1901a, 1924:39-40, 1938, IV:52-3, 114-35; Woensdregt 1928:144, 208-19, 228, 249.
[51]   Kruyt and Kruyt 1921:407. It should be noted, however, that the imposition of corvée labour services reportedly had an adverse effect on food production in Napu after the colonial conquest (Kraan 2000:40).
[52]   Olivier 1834-37, II:30. The shorter periods mentioned in some other sources refer to husked rice as delivered to the government. In Minahasa and Gorontalo, most varieties of rice were trampled out of the plucked ears in the swiddens before being stored in the village as unhusked *padi* (Van Thije 1689; De Clercq 1873:262-3; CV Gorontalo 1854, in ANRI Gorontalo 3; CV Gorontalo 1863, in ANRI Manado 134; Graafland 1867-69, I:57, 60, 153; Pino 1920:7; N.P. Wilken 1870:385).
[53]   Woodard 1969:91. In some parts of western Central Sulawesi, such as Kulawi, there were also groups which harvested and stored only ears of rice rather than whole stems (Adriani and Kruyt 1912-14, II:289; A.C. Kruyt 1938, IV:64, 223).

1969:91), and harvested yams, laid in racks and trimmed of new shoots every two months, for up to a year (A.C. Kruyt 1932c:490-1). Dry sago powder could be kept in baskets for 'at least a month' (Tillema 1922:187), while baked sago cakes, if not used immediately, were 'laid in a brook, where the water runs over, and will there keep for six or eight months' (Woodard 1969:92). The hard sago biscuits known in the Moluccas as *sago lempeng*, which can be stored for 'many years' (Ellen 1979:53), were also manufactured in some places (*Een en ander* 1908:1046-7). Meat and fish, finally, were preserved by smoking or salting, although the supply of salt was often insufficient to permit the latter in places far from the coast (Adriani 1915:461).

One colonial source from Talaud, where taro and other tubers were important states that foodstuffs are 'hardly ever' stored: 'when the food runs out, enough for a few more days is simply fetched from the swidden' (Roep 1917: 432). Li (1991:8, 28, 41) and Barr and Barr (1993:78) describe similar situations among tuber cultivators in modern Central Sulawesi. Where grains were predominant, however, storage was essential. Minahasa was known from early times for its large reserves of harvested rice: a Spanish officer stationed in Manado in the 1640s reported that 'a ship which lies there for a month can obtain a full load, for the inhabitants always keep an abundance of rice in storage'.[54] 'For it is their custom', explained Padtbrugge in 1680, 'to keep the greater part of their *padi* in reserve for use at the funeral ceremonies of their parents, in years when the harvest is poor, as seed for sowing, for the wedding feasts of their children, for their own funerals, and so on'.[55] European visitors to Minahasa, from Padtbrugge onward, often commented on the large cylindrical vats of harvested *padi* displayed as proof of prosperity in the central galleries of the big houses.[56] Maize, preserved by smoking, was also stored in large quantities.[57] Padtbrugge (1866:324) reported that Minahasan houses were 'hung full with bundles of *padi*, maize [*Turkse tarwe*], and other grains'. In 1856, Magindanao pirates driven ashore in Minahasa reportedly burned down a single storage barn containing 18,000 maize cobs.[58]

[54]   NA VOC 1199:837v.
[55]   NA VOC 1359:153v. Another VOC source, from 1763, claims that no epidemic could lead to rice shortages in Minahasa, because 'among the Manadonese *bergboeren* there is always unstamped *padi* in reserve' (NA VOC 3119:44).
[56]   Bik 1864:168; Padtbrugge 1866:322; Reinwardt 1858:545, 565-6, 594; Van Thije 1689.
[57]   CV Manado 1857 (ANRI Manado 52); N.P. Wilken 1870:378.
[58]   MV Manado April 1856 (ANRI Manado 54).

Famine foods

Also rather difficult to square with the picture of vulnerability to crop failure emerging from the historical record is the fact that various types of emergency food were usually available to fall back on when the staple crops failed. Foremost among these was sago, obtained either from one of the three semi-domesticated palms mentioned in Chapter II (*Metroxylon sagu*, *Arenga pinnata*, and *Arenga microcarpa*), or from *Corypha utan*, the *gebang* or *silar* palm.[59] Coconuts provided another common famine food.[60] A VOC source from the mid-seventeenth century already mentions that the supply of coconut oil from Sangir is unpredictable 'because in times of infertility and crop failure, the people there must use the coconuts as food' (De Jongh 1669). Two centuries later, Steller (1866:25) claimed that the abundance of coconut and sago trees on Sangir made hunger a vitual impossibility; past stories of famine, he maintained, had been lies, 'told by the *raja* as excuses for not carrying out government orders'. In Gorontalo and Central Sulawesi, and probably elsewhere, the wild yam *Dioscorea hirsuta* was collected in the forest in times of need.[61] Other wild famine foods mentioned in the historical sources include bamboo shoots, the fleshy spadix of some palms, various types of root, wild chestnuts, and the edible leaves of a number of trees and herbaceous plants, many of which were also eaten as vegetables in normal times.[62] Tonelli (1992: 92) lists 20 wild plants still used as food today in the Tinombo area, adding that in 'times of scarcity due to crop failure or between crops, these foods become central to survival'.

Not all types of famine food were always readily accessible. Partly because of its preference for flat, wet terrain, the true sago palm (*Metroxlyon sagu*) had a restricted distribution. Rocky Siau, according to Marta in the 1580s, had 'but little sago', and what there was belonged 'exclusively to the king and some other nobles'.[63] *Metroxylon* palms were scarce until a late date in the Limboto Depression, Banggai, and many parts of upland Central Sulawesi.[64]

[59]   Hickson 1889:334; A.C. Kruyt 1895-97, V:33, 1938, I:25, IV:271.

[60]   AR Gorontalo to Res. Manado, 8-12-1826 (ANRI Manado 114); Van Dam 1931:56; Tammes 1940:188, 1949:11.

[61]   Adriani and Kruyt 1899:39, 1912-14, II:203; Li 1991:23; Stap 1919:959. The latter source (on Gorontalo) refers to *bituleh*, identified by Heyne (1950, I:458) as *Dioscorea hispida*. The same species is also mentioned by Koorders (1898:312) in his botanical work on Minahasa, although it is not clear whether it was eaten in this area.

[62]   Adriani and Kruyt 1912-14, II:199-200; A.C. Kruyt 1895-97, III:152, 1901a:1, 1938, IV:282-3, Li 1991:41.

[63]   Jacobs 1974-84, II:262. In Mori, sago stands were likewise the exclusive property of noble groups (J. Kruyt 1924:63).

[64]   Adriani and Kruyt 1900:139, 1912-14, II:204; A.C. Kruyt 1894:8, 1895-97, VI:33, 1908:1289, 1932c:257, 1938, II:110, IV:272; J. Kruyt 1933:32; Von Rosenberg 1865:28.

When foodcrop harvests failed on the neck of the northern peninsula, people came 'from far and wide' to extract sago around the swampy margins of a small lake near Baleisang on the Strait of Makasar (Boonstra van Heerdt 1914b:730). This uneven distribution, as noted in Chapter II, also made sago an important trade item. On Tagulandang, reported Kelling in 1866, 'sago, being scarce, is saved for provisioning on sea journeys, and even imported from Greater Sangir for that purpose'.[65] Siau, likewise, obtained sago from its political dependencies on Greater Sangir (Van Delden 1844:17). Gorontalo imported most of its sago from Togian and the lands around the Gulf of Tomini.[66] Balantak exported sago to the Banggai Islands (De Clercq 1890: 133). The difficulties of obtaining *Metroxylon* sago were accentuated by the fact that the coastal localities where it was concentrated, such as Paguat in Gorontalo, were often highly malarial (see Chapter VII). Workers extracting sago in coastal forests were also vulnerable to slave raiders.[67]

Other emergency food sources presented fewer problems of access. In those parts of the Poso Depression where true sago was scarce, sago from the sugar palm (*Arenga pinnata*), which grew plentifully in the wild, was used instead.[68] 'For half of the year', wrote Adriani (1901:236-7), 'the population can be said to eat rice, and for the other half maize and the sago of the *aren* [sugar] palm'. Padtbrugge noted that while there was 'not a single [*Metroxlyon*] sago tree' in the whole of the Limboto Depression, this did not apply to the sugar palm.[69] In upland Minahasa and Mongondow, *Arenga pinnata* was deliberately cultivated both for its sago and for the sugar, palm wine, and rope fibre which could be produced from it.[70] Reinwardt (1858:586) commented in 1821 on the 'great many' sugar palms in Minahasa, and De Clercq (1871b:30) wrote that whereas the sago palm 'only flourishes in swampy places', the sugar palm 'occurs everywhere'.

Outside Minahasa, the *aren* was not in fact ubiquitous.[71] Many other famine foods, it is also worth noting, were relatively indigestible, or even dangerous when consumed in large quantities or without careful preparation. Rasped

65 F. Kelling, 'Het eiland Taghoelandang en zijn bewoners' [1866] (ARZ NZG 43.2).
66 NA VOC 1366:569, 916; AR Gorontalo to Res. Manado, 17-1-1846 (ANRI Manado 119); AV Gorontalo 1824, 1829 (ANRI Gorontalo 3); 'Dagregister van den civiele gezaghebber te Gorontalo', 1845-1846 (ANRI Manado 172); Van Dam 1931:95; Van der Hart 1853:225; Res. Gorontalo to Res. Ternate, 12-3-1820 (ANRI Ternate 153); Keijzer 1856:218.
67 MV Manado April 1855 (ANRI Manado 54).
68 Adriani and Kruyt 1912-14, II:204; A.C. Kruyt 1894:8, 1895-97, VI:33.
69 NA VOC 1366:916.
70 De Clercq 1883:122; Wilken and Schwarz 1867c:363. Deliberate planting of sugar palms in the vicinity of villages was also reported by A.C. Kruyt (1938, IV:274) from western Central Sulawesi.
71 It was absent, for instance, on Talaud (Stokking 1917:346), and scarce in some parts of western Central Sulawesi (A.C. Kruyt 1938, IV:273; *Landschap Donggala* 1905:516).

coconut flesh, for instance, had to be mixed with other foods like maize or sweet potato, since otherwise it was 'difficult to digest' (Tammes 1949:11). *Corypha* sago was likewise said to cause 'all kinds of digestive disorders' (A.C. Kruyt 1938, IV:272). *Dioscorea hirsuta* is naturally poisonous, and had to be soaked, boiled, dried and stamped before it could be consumed.[72] Coconuts, as the famine record from Sangir reveals, were themselves vulnerable to dry weather (Tammes 1949:14-5), as was the wild yam.[73] The wide distribution of many potential emergency food sources, nevertheless, strengthens the impression that the episodes of hunger which occur in the historical record cannot usually be explained in terms of absolute scarcity of foodstuffs. More probable is that in some localities some people, particularly the very young, the sick, and perhaps the old, had slightly insufficient access to them in bad years. The Talaud farmer, claimed Pennings (1908:14), 'only cuts sago when he has no other food whatsoever', and among the Lauje people have died even in recent times as a result of being too slow to begin their quest for forest sago following a harvest failure (Tania Li, personal communication).

Nutrition

One of the reasons for the susceptibility of the Toraja to disease, according to Adriani and Kruyt (1950-51, I:76, II:192), was 'the poor dietary situation'.[74] Malnutrition was particularly common among men sojourning away from home to make war, collect forest products, or manufacture salt.[75] 'Toraja children', the missionaries also noted, 'do not grow quickly' (Adriani and Kruyt 1912-14, II:55). A survey of 2,517 schoolchildren between the ages of six and eighteen, carried out by the military physician De Wijn in Poso and Mori, confirmed that the development of height and weight with age was retarded even by Indonesian standards. At 15, the average Toraja male was more than ten centimetres shorter and five kilogrammes lighter than his counterpart in Jakarta. De Wijn attributed this, along with the high death and morbidity rates, to poor nutrition. The adult daily diet of two rice meals, together with 'very small quantities of fish and vegetables', was deficient in protein and

[72]   Adriani and Kruyt 1899:39, 1912-14, II:203; Li 1991:23; Whitten, Mustafa and Henderson 1987:74.
[73]   A report from Gorontalo states that it is only 'during droughts which are not too protracted and rains which are not too heavy' that wild yams can still be found 'in large quantities' in the forest (Stap 1919:959).
[74]   'Since the diet usually leaves much to be desired and the population suffers heavily from fevers', concurred Pennings (1908:15) on Talaud, 'it is not surprising that the Talaud islanders are a weak people'.
[75]   Adriani 1915:460; Adriani and Kruyt 1950-51, I:77; A.C. Kruyt 1899b:156, 1924:46, 1938, II: 124; Tillema 1926:212.

other nutrients as well as 'minimal' (at 1,850 calories) in energy terms. The real victims, however, were the children, who ate 'practically nothing but rice' (De Wijn 1952:163-4).

> In Central Celebes the people die of tuberculosis, pneumonia, influenza, following malarial fevers, chronic amoebiasis with hepatic complications, and alimentary disturbances: that is, from diseases which need not end fatally if the body is reasonably resistant to 'normal' infections. [...] I am convinced that (a.) the appallingly high death rate among the younger people and the unfavourable findings at medical examination of prospective recruits, (b.) the poor resistance to infections of the respiratory tract, and (c.) the retardation in development, especially in adolescence, are the direct results of poor nutrition in youth. (De Wijn 1952:168.)

In Sangir at the same period, Dr Blankhart saw a similarly direct relationship between poor nutrition and the slow growth of a random sample of 54 much younger children, aged between seven and twenty-one months, which he studied in Taruna on Greater Sangir (see Figure 6).

> Beyond the age of 10 months, 60 percent of the children showed a growth retardation of 5 to 8 cm compared with the Pirquet growth curve. Beyond 8 months, their weight also lagged well behind what it should have been at their age. Compared with Holt's American growth curve the discrepancy was 3 to 5 kg, while the weights mostly also fell beneath the curves from Jakarta and Jamaica, with which they shared the characteristic of levelling off between 8 and 16 months. (Blankhart 1951:99.)

The children in question were fed mainly on rice pap, fresh bananas, and sago. While breast-feeding was rarely discontinued before the age of 12 months, vegetables were seldom included in the infant diet, and fish 'almost never' (Blankhart 1951:96). Adult nutrition, too, left much to be desired.

> Sago and root crops, and to a much lesser extent rice, form the staple foods, while fish, coconut flesh, vegetables and fruits supplement the diet. The quantities consumed vary widely depending on diverse circumstances. The calorie intake (2,000 per person daily) is adequate, but the amount of protein consumed (26 grammes at most per person per day) is too low in all kinds of ways. The intake of B-group vitamins also shows significant deficiencies. (Blankhart 1951:100.)

The normal diet, in short, was 'just adequate', but the situation was 'marginal' and the population vulnerable to disease and food crises.[76] Malnutrition, particularly among infants, had been one reason for a decline in the population of

[76] This description was based partly on observations by Blankhart himself on Sangir, and partly on extrapolation from contemporary research on the dietary situation in West Seram, where the agricultural system was similar.

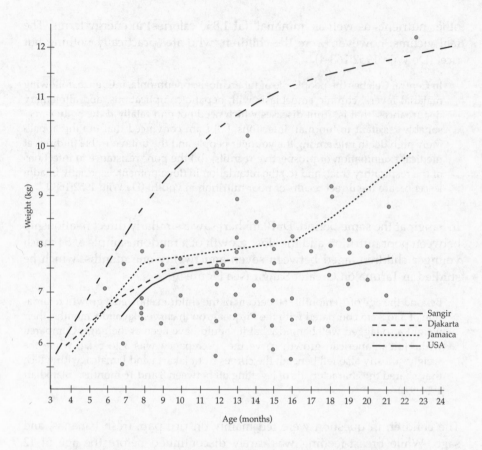

Figure 6. Growth curves for infants on Greater Sangir and elsewhere, circa 1948.
Points represent 54 randomly selected children examined at a polyclinic in Taruna.
Source: Blankhart 1951:98.

Greater Sangir during the Japanese occupation (Blankhart 1951:89-90, 99-100).

Sangir, with its heavy agricultural emphasis on root crops and sago rather than rice or maize, and its very dense population, was not typical of the region as a whole, and Blankhart's results cannot be generalized. It is worth noting, on the other hand, that the northern islands were an area where animal protein, in the form of fish, was actually available in unusually large quantities and on a more or less continuous basis (see Chapter II). In the interior of Central Sulawesi, by contrast, the principal source of protein was meat from domesticated animals, the consumption of which was almost entirely resricted to feasts and other ceremonial occasions.[77] 'Hunting also provides a meat dish now and then', commented Adriani and Kruyt (1912-14, II:200), 'but because most people do not go hunting very often, and because the prize must always be shared with the whole village, this does not happen as often as one would think'. The Toraja, consequently, lived 'most of the time as vegetarians' (A.C. Kruyt 1938, IV:282). In the mountains to the west of the Palu trench in 1910, a Dutch military officer attributed the unhealthy appearance of the local population to inadequate protein consumption.

> The main reason for this less favourable health situation must, however, be sought in the poor dietary condition of the population in general. Animal food is seldom consumed; a water buffalo or pig is only slaughtered as a sacrifice on ceremonial occasions, when it is shared among the whole community. (Boonstra van Heerdt 1914a:638.)

'Comparison of different groups in Central Celebes', found De Wijn (1952: 168-9) forty years later, 'shows that the children on the coast, who eat much fish, have a better growth curve than those of the agrarian, vegetarian groups, even though on the coast the rate of morbidity is higher'. In Minahasa, where the number of domestic animals (pigs) was probably higher than anywhere else in the region (*Fragment* 1856:19; Riedel 1872b:545-6), even 'the more well-to-do' part of the population ate meat only 'from time to time' according to an early nineteenth-century source.[78] Taken together with the evidence for poor nutrition, high infant mortality, short adult stature, and limited longevity elsewhere in the region and at earlier periods, the observations by Blankhart on Sangir and De Wijn in Poso and Mori suggest that the situation was comparable to that still found recently in remote parts of Sarawak, where, in the words of Alexander and Alexander (1993:258), 'few persons go hungry but poor nutrition reduces the strength of adults and has more serious effects on the very young and very old'.[79]

---

[77]   Adriani and Kruyt 1912-14, II:200, 1950-51, III:209; A.C. Kruyt 1895-97, IV:143; De Wijn 1952:149.
[78]   J.J. ten Siethoff, 'Topografische schetsen van een gedeelte der residentie Manado, 1845' (ANRI Manado 46). Resident Wenzel agreed that only 'well-to-do natives' ate pork other than at communal feasts (Riedel 1872b:545).
[79]   Also Baer 1999:101; Gan Chong-Yin et al. 1993:300; Kaufmann et al. 1995:547-8; Kiyu et al. 1991:211; McKay 1970:75-6. The 'potential availability of a wide range of foods', as Alexander and Alexander (1993:259) observe, 'does not mean that these are eaten regularly'.

Plate 15. Funeral feast in the Poso area with animals awaiting slaughter, circa 1918
(A.C. Kruyt 1919:55)

Moral economies?

Just as food shortages sometimes occurred in the vicinity of food sources,
the limited consumption of protein on an everyday basis did not necessarily result from any absolute scarcity of animal food. On ceremonial occasions, very large quantities of meat were often eaten in a short space of time.
Edeling (1919:7) noted in 1875 that 300 pigs and 20 cattle had recently been
slaughtered at a single feast to inaugurate the new house of a Minahasan
district chief. At funeral feasts in the Poso area (Plate 15), so much meat was
consumed by people accustomed to a largely vegetarian diet that many of
the guests typically became ill (Adriani and Kruyt 1912-14, II:200; A.C. Kruyt
1896:143) – and so much rice, according to Adriani, that 'a period of famine
[*hongersnood*] always followed'.[80] During the famine in Talaud in 1886, mem-

---

[80]   Tillema 1922:211. Aragon (1992:71), describing the festival season among the Tobaku, states
that 'people consume more meat in these few weeks than they do at any other time throughout
the remainder of the year'.

bers of the Dutch relief expedition were surprised to see 'large numbers of pigs and hens wandering through the *kampung*' on Salibabu. Asked why the livestock had not been eaten, a local man replied 'that these animals were the private property of certain persons, and were only to be slaughtered on ceremonial occasions' (Ebbinge Wübben 1889:207). De Wijn (1952:149, 164) was inclined to blame parental ignorance for the poor diet of Toraja children, and Li (personal communication) reports that there 'does not seem to be a good reason' for the barely adequate quantity, and very low protein content, of the diet on which Lauje children are still brought up today.[81] Such observations bring home the fact that patterns of food consumption reflect social and cultural circumstances as well as technological and environmental constraints.

The historical sources, unfortunately, provide little detail regarding the distribution of food within and between communities, but some speculation on this point is worthwhile. The large quantities of rice stored in Minahasan houses, first of all, served to a considerable extent for conspicuous consumption during status-boosting 'feasts of merit', and indeed also for pure display. Several observers reported that the *padi* containers, each of them individually marked for ownership (Reinwardt 1858:545), were never completely emptied.[82] Schouten (1998:26) even surmises that it was regarded as a particular honour if part of the stored grain had been kept uneaten for so long that it was in a state of decay. While this may simply indicate that there was plenty of rice to go around, it could also be interpreted in terms of unequal distribution. A VOC official in Minahasa (Van Thije 1689) described the possession of a large rice surplus as characteristic of 'anyone who is at all well-to-do' (*ijder die van enig vermogen is*), and if food stored by 'well-to-do' Minahasans also provided security for their poorer counterparts, it often did so at a daunting price: annual interest rates of 100 percent or more were charged on borrowed rice, and inability to repay such debts was reportedly a common route into slavery.[83] Descent into slavery as a result of food debts is also mentioned in sources dealing with Gorontalo and Sangir.[84] 'Sale or commendation of oneself and/or one's wife and children to a wealthier person', notes Reid (1983: 9-10) in his general discussion of Southeast Asian slavery, 'is reported in all

[81]   Also Nourse 1999:42; Tonelli 1992:57.
[82]   AV Manado 1833 (ANRI Manado 48); Pietermaat, De Vriese and Lucas 1840:119; Riedel 1872b:496-7. Guests were invited to sleep on top of the rice vats, the owners of which 'boast loudly about how many *lasten* of rice or *padi* they have provided as a bed for this or that distinguished person' (Padtbrugge 1866:322).
[83]   Dirkzwager 1912:1169-70; Graafland 1867-69, I:285, 1898, I:421-2. *Rapport* 1910:86-7; Riedel 1872b:502. Ter Laag (1920:40) specifies the same interest rate on rice and maize borrowed for seed in the Kaili area in the early twentieth century.
[84]   NA VOC 1345:350-1; AV Manado 1833 (ANRI Manado 48); Steller 1866:41; C.L. Wieling, 'Berigt omtrent het al of niet bezitten van Gorontalo', 6-2-1806 (ANRI Manado 165).

societies, especially in times of severe hardship'.

Under normal circumstances, the relatives of a needy individual would always endeavour to prevent his or her degradation to slave status (Schrauwers 2000:24). Nineteenth-century Dutch administrators noted that beggars were seldom seen because, in Riedel's words, 'custom dictates that poor and crippled people are supported as much as possible by their kin'.[85] Fishermen and hunters, certainly, were always obliged to share their prize with a wide circle of relatives.[86] 'When corn or rice is harvested', Li (1991: 16) has observed among the Lauje, 'up to one third is given away within the first few days to kin and neighbours who come to help with the work, or who are invited specifically to come and collect a share to take home'. Although Adriani and Kruyt (1950-51, I:150) reported that farming households in the Poso area were wary of unwelcome requests for charity, and always tried 'to conceal from each other how much rice they had harvested', Schrauwers, in his reconstruction of the precolonial Pamona *banua* ('longhouse'), portrays a classic 'moral economy' operating among its co-residential matrilaterally-related households (*sombori*).[87]

> Although individual *sombori* cooked their own meals, all the *sombori* within a longhouse ate together and shared their food [...]; those who had fish or other delicacies would divide these among those present. To be present while someone eats is to be obligated to join them; to leave without eating is an invitation for divine retribution (*kasalora*). Eating together is a symbol of kinship and amity. Such generalized exchange was not limited to cooked foods eaten in the presence of others. Any surplus foodstuff was distributed, with no calculation of an exact return. (Schrauwers 2000:106.)

To some extent, political leadership was also based on the provision of food security. A prospective Toraja village chief had to be 'generous enough to help a fellow villager in need' (Adriani and Kruyt 1950-51, I:114), and in times of real scarcity he would be expected to distribute rice for seed from his personal reserve (Adriani and Kruyt 1912-14, II:234, 310). In Tinombo before the Dutch conquest, comparably, one duty of the coastal *raja* (*olongiya*) was to provide seed rice 'for any highland farmers whose crops had failed'.[88]

---

[85]   AV Gorontalo 1864 (ANRI Gorontalo 3). Also AV Manado 1853, 1854 (ANRI Manado 51), 1861 (ANRI Manado 52); AV Gorontalo 1841-43 (ANRI Manado 50), 1845 (KITLV H111), 1852, 1865 (ANRI Gorontalo 3).
[86]   Adriani and Kruyt 1950-51, I:149; Van Delden 1844:22; A.C. Kruyt 1938, IV:386.
[87]   'Generalized exchange', Schrauwers (1995a:349) claims, 'marked the local economy until the 1970s' in the Poso area.
[88]   Nourse 1989:4. Also A.C. Kruyt 1938, I:324-5; Nourse 1999:64. Comparably, Heersink (1999: 42) states that a 'good regent' in South Sulawesi 'altruistically provided the population with food

The relationship between master and slave probably also involved a continuing social security function; those slaves who lived in their masters' houses, according to one description of Siau, certainly 'had the right to good food and clothing' (Van Dinter 1899:343), and it is likely that even swidden-house slaves were able to draw on their owners' food reserves in times of difficulty.[89] In the longer term, of course, the net flow of resources was nevertheless from slave to master, and the same was true in other hierarchical relationships. Van Delden (1844:16) reported in 1825 that Sangirese *raja* controlled stockpiles of food from which their subjects could borrow 'against double or triple repayment after the following harvest', and in the 1850s a Gorontalo *raja* was said to have welcomed food shortages as an opportunity 'to empty his *padi* barns at high prices'.[90]

Institutions facilitating local food redistribution in times of crisis, then, did exist in traditional society. Many of them, however, were embedded in relationships which, in the longer term, worked to concentrate food reserves (and other wealth) in the hands of relatively privileged groups. Intermittent food shortages, by forcing the poor to become indebted to the wealthy, were probably an important factor underpinning social stratification and the institution of slavery. There may also be truth in the Dutch claim that slavery, in turn, exacerbated subsistence problems by creating disincentives to surplus production.[91]

> Among the tribes which had many slaves, so that free people were [...] in the minority, much too little work was done, with the result that there was often too little to eat. The masters worked as little as possible and the slaves did likewise, because for them there was no advantage in producing more than they and their families consumed. Even if they lived in separate houses, as married slaves usually did, their masters still managed to dispossess them of any surplus. (Adriani 1921b:14.)

The conspicuous rice hoards of rich Minahasans, in this light, can be viewed as political concentrations of resources, amassed by means of bonded labour arrangements which acted to reduce the overall surplus.[92] Even in relation-

---

during famines'. Historical parallels from chiefdoms in other parts of the world are, or course, numerous (Sahlins 1963:296, 1972:255-63).

[89]   Also A.C. Kruyt 1938, I:516; Steller 1866:42. In this sense, and no doubt also in others, slavery resembled a classic 'patron-client' relationship (J.C. Scott 1972:93, 95).

[90]   CV Gorontalo 1854 (ANRI Gorontalo 3).

[91]   Adriani 1921a:22; Adriani and Kruyt 1912-14, I:164, 1950-51, I:146; A.C. Kruyt 1911:80. A report from Gorontalo in the early nineteenth century states that 'the natives plant no more than they need for daily consumption; the main reason for this is that a large part of the population consists of slaves, who work only under close supervision' (AV Gorontalo 1829, in ANRI Gorontalo 3).

[92]   In 1677 the Minahasan *walak* chiefs, interrogated by a VOC representative about the pros-

ships between equals and close kin, according to Adriani and Kruyt (1912-14, I:153-4), the pressure to share surplus food in times of difficulty, whatever its social or material compensations, also discouraged people from producing more than was sufficient for their own needs.[93]

Whether food redistribution on a non-commercial basis was effective over long distances is doubtful. Seed rice, in emergencies, could be begged from nearby villages, and sometimes even neighbouring ethnic groups, in the expectation of future reciprocity.[94] In the Poso area, moreover, travellers were traditionally fed at no (immediate) cost to themselves by the inhabitants of any (friendly) foreign settlements through which they passed.[95] This rule, however, weakened rapidly with spatial and ethnic distance. Unless they could demonstrate a kinship link with the host villagers, people from the Poso Valley travelling in Pakambia, over the watershed in the La Basin, had to make a 'gift' to the village head in order to obtain food, and were not entitled to take any with them when they left (Adriani and Kruyt 1950-51, I: 104; A.C. Kruyt 1923:152).

Commercialization and the food supply

Although it is sometimes assumed that the 'penetration' of the market tends to erode the food security of subsistence farmers, there is much evidence that in northern Sulawesi the reverse was usually true. Trading relationships, as Tania Li has shown in Tinombo, were often cultivated precisely with a view to compensating for local food shortages (see Chapter II). In Poso and Mori, Dr de Wijn was convinced that the economic isolation of the upland populations was a central reason for their poor nutritional situation:

> The sole source of food for the population was [...] the native soil. [...] So the nutritional condition was determined by what was locally grown. This meant an enforcedly vegetarian and one-sided diet. [...] Meat which could be had by hunting, and fish which abounds in the rivers and lakes, were sporadically eaten but there was no efficient distribution in the market, except perhaps on the coast. [...] As regards schoolchildren from the Central Celebes coast, who have a different mode of living and a different diet (their fathers and brothers are merchants and

---

pects for increasing the volume of rice deliveries to the Company, replied that 'this was not possible, although those people who had many slaves were also able to make many swiddens [*tuinen*], and therefore deliver more *padi*' (NA VOC 1328:163).

[93]   Compare Platteau 1991:160-2; Sahlins 1972:69-74, 114-5.

[94]   Adriani and Kruyt 1912-14, II:233-4. A source from Minahasa in 1864 notes that two needy villages in Tonsea 'will be given *padi* by the other Tonsea villages, to be paid back after the next harvest' (MV Manado June 1864, in ANRI Manado 54).

[95]   Schrauwers 1995b:21. A similar custom also existed in Minahasa until the mid-nineteenth century (Graafland 1867-69, I:72-3).

fishermen), the weight-line is much nearer the general Indonesian standard [...].
(De Wijn 1952:149-50.)

Trade, as noted in Chapter II, was always a significant element of the regional
economy, and foodstuffs were always among the goods traded. At the beginning of the nineteenth century, nevertheless, the overall volume of commerce
was still limited, markets and trading professionals few in number, and
transactions mostly non-monetized. Thereafter, a series of major new export
products – first cocoa and (in Minahasa) coffee, then *damar*, rattan, and finally
copra – combined with transport improvements, pacification, and other
changes in the political context of trade, gradually transformed most parts
of northern Sulawesi into market economies in which goods, including food,
were routinely traded for cash on a large scale.

The process of monetization can most easily be traced in the case of
Minahasa. During the British interregnum of 1810-1817, according to a
contemporary report, 'no money' circulated in the Minahasan uplands, 'the
wealth of the Alfurs' consisting exclusively of textiles, gold jewelry, brassware, iron chopping knives, and minor luxury items such as mirrors and
beads.[96] In 1824 the visiting governor-general Van der Capellen (1855:362),
although noting that 'the value of money is by no means unknown among
them', agreed that Minahasans were still 'much more interested in cloths
than in cash'. The compulsory coffee deliveries introduced in 1822 were
initially paid for 'in cash or cloth, according to the choice of the natives', but
after 1825 cash payment was the norm.[97] By 1833, the Dutch government
was also purchasing its annual contingent of Minahasan rice partly with
money instead of textiles.[98] In 1837 the *walak* chiefs requested that in future
these payments be made entirely in cash, since private traders in Manado
were now able to supply a wider assortment of textiles than the government
warehouses, 'and most natives prefer to choose their cloths for themselves'.[99]
A head tax, replacing the compulsory rice deliveries in 1852, provided an adi-
tional stimulus to monetization by forcing Minahasans to have cash on hand
when it was due to be collected. By the mid-1860s, Graafland (1867-69, II:196)
could report that 'money circulates in abundance among the population'.

[96]   P.A. van Middelkoop, 'Memorien ten vervolge van het Algemeen Verslag van de
Commissie naar de Moluksche Eilanden', 30-9-1818 (NA Schneither 128). Barter using cloths,
according to an official of the British administration in 1812, was 'the only mode of procuring
the produce of the country at Manado' (J.A. Neijs to G. Smith, 2-10-1812, in ANRI Manado 62).
[97]   A.C.J. Edeling, 'Memorie omtrent de Minahasa', 13-8-1875 (NA V 17-4-1877/20); Godée
Molsbergen 1928:185. Some coffee, however, continued to be paid for in textiles at later dates (AV
Manado 1829, in KITLV H70).
[98]   AV Manado 1833 (ANRI Manado 48).
[99]   Res. Manado to Directeur 's Lands Producten Batavia, 5-12-1837 (ANRI Manado 78).

In 1825 there were reportedly only three regular markets in Minahasa, two on the coast at Manado and Kema, where money was in use, and one in the uplands at Tondano, where barter trade was the norm (Riedel 1872b: 546). In the 1850s, attempts by the government to stimulate trade by building covered marketplaces in the interior initially failed, reportedly due to a continuing insufficiency of circulating currency.[100] In the early 1860s, however, market trade began to accelerate.[101] By the 1890s, Minahasa had five permanent and 32 periodic markets (Graafland 1898, II:242). The cash spent in these markets originated partly from compulsory coffee cultivation, which underwent a major expansion in the 1850s (see Chapter X), and from the auxiliary non-agricultural activities, particularly in the transport sector, which the coffee monopoly generated.[102] The centre of coffee production lay on the Tondano Plateau, the area praised by Hickson (1889:214) in 1886 for its 'general condition of peace and prosperity'. Beginning in about 1880 (Reyne 1948:429), a rapidly increasing volume of export income also came from the voluntary sale of copra by Minahasan smallholders. Small European coconut, coffee, and nutmeg plantations, established after 1875, also employed a growing number of Minahasans on a temporary or seasonal basis.[103]

Part of the money earned from coffee and copra was spent on imported goods, especially textiles, and the growth in the volume of imports from 1850 to 1900 (Figure 7) reflects the increasing size and market-orientation of the Minahasan economy.[104] Combined with the construction of a dense vehicular road network, the commercialization process also led to an intensification of local trade in food. In 1858, Resident Jansen argued that 'improved internal communications', in combination with a 'sufficiency of foodstuffs', were among the factors now favouring population growth.[105] Graafland (1867-69, II:195) reported a decade later that food was never scarce in Minahasa because local shortages, resulting from bad weather or pests, were always

---

[100]   AV Manado 1851-60 (ANRI Manado 51, 52); Graafland 1898, II:240-2.
[101]   AV Manado 1861 (ANRI Manado 52); MV Manado May 1862 (ANRI Manado 54).
[102]   From 1852 onward the transport of government coffee, formerly an unpaid obligation, was paid for at a standard rate according to the distance involved (Bleeker 1856:83; *Fragment* 1856:13-14). Several sources state that this was very profitable (CV Manado 1859, in ANRI Ambon 1543; Graafland 1867-69, II:114; Quarles van Ufford 1856:23). While cart owners and operators earned income by transporting the coffee, the manufacture of the oxcarts provided employment for smiths and carpenters (L. Wessels 1891:63-4).
[103]   Graafland 1898, I:165, II:174; Jellesma 1903:126; Stakman 1893:142-3.
[104]   No data are available for the years 1871-1878. The figures do not include goods imported under government auspices, but in the 1840s the value of these was only about 10% of that of private imports (Francis 1860:406). A decline in domestic textile production (see Chapter XV) was partly a cause, as well as a result, of the expansion in imports; another factor was the abolition of customs duties at Manado and Kema in 1849 (De Lange 1897:668).
[105]   AV Manado 1858 (ANRI Manado 52).

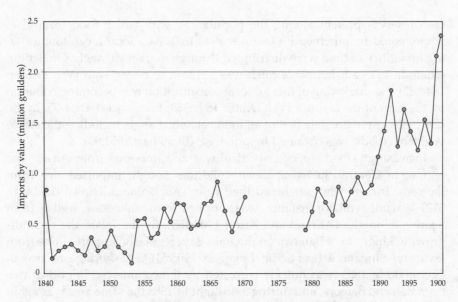

Figure 7. Minahasa: imports by value, 1840-1900.
Sources: E. Francis, 'Bijlagen behoorende bij het rapport van den kommissaris
voor Menado 1846' (ANRI Manado 50); *Overzigt handel 1846-70*;
Statistiek 1879-1900.

compensated by imports from other districts. Many other sources from the
late nineteenth century also mention trade in foodstuffs within Minahasa.[106]
In the early 1870s both rice and maize were described by Resident Van der
Crab (1875:270) as 'important articles of trade', and a *controleur* of Amurang
observed that there was 'always plenty of rice in the markets'.[107]

With the upsurge of rattan and *damar* exports around 1870, the number
of local markets in Gorontalo also began to increase.[108] Reports from the
early twentieth century describe 'lively' domestic trade and the establishment of new marketplaces everywhere in the region.[109] In Central Sulawesi,
rijksdaalder coins now tended to replace pieces of cotton cloth as standard
units of value (Adriani and Kruyt 1912-14, II:312). In 1911, trade in Bolaang
Mongondow was said to have 'profited to a great degree' from the construction of the first vehicular road into the interior (*Koloniaal verslag* 1912:34). A
shortage of food on Siau in 1912 was 'compensated to a large extent by the

[106]   CV Manado 1884, 1895 (ANRI Manado 86); De Clercq 1870c:532, 1871a:426; Gallois 1892:
43; Stakman 1893:77-8, 82; 'Stukken voedingsmiddelen in de Minahassa 1877-78' (ANRI Manado
37); N.P. Wilken 1870:374.
[107]   CV Amurang 1873 (ANRI Manado 19).
[108]   AV Gorontalo 1872 (ANRI Manado 9).
[109]   *Koloniaal verslag* 1908:66, 1911:47, 1912:34, 1914:26.

Fertility, food and fever

cash reserves present among the population, with which food from elsewhere could be purchased' (Tammes 1940:188). At a local level, too, growing quantities of food were distributed through market channels. On Sangir,
where in 1825 a fisherman's catch was 'seldom or never' sold (Van Delden
1844:22), the marketing of fish for local consumption was becoming common
by the turn of the century (Van Dinter 1899:353; Frieswijck 1902:477). In the
late 1940s approximately half of all food eaten on Sangir, including the staple
vegetable foods, was obtained by purchase (Blankhart 1951:95).

Increasingly, food (specifically, rice) was also imported from outside the
region. In Central Sulawesi, *damar* collectors bought imported rice from
the same traders who purchased their resin (Adriani and Kruyt 1912-14, II:
312). Watambayoli, for instance, was supplied from Makasar as well as from
nearby Tobungku (Adriani and Kruyt 1900:155). By the 1890s, the coconut-
growing kingdom of Banawa on the Palu Bay 'regularly' imported rice from
Java and Singapore (*Landschap Donggala* 1905:516). A shortage of rice in
Gorontalo in 1883 'was quickly corrected by the commercial import of rice
from Bali and Saigon', and during a drought in 1888 the same area was again
'spared from food shortages by substantial imports from elsewhere'.[110] In
Sangir, where 'comparatively little' rice from elsewhere was eaten in 1883,
'quite large quantities' were being imported from Makasar and Manado only
four years later.[111] During the drought of 1896, the Sangirese were able to
feed themselves partly 'by purchasing rice, which is not really a staple food
on Sangir'.[112] In 1911, similarly, rice imported by Chinese traders relieved
food shortages in the Gulf of Tomini (Boonstra van Heerdt 1914b:751).

Direct rice imports from outside the residency climbed rapidly after 1900,
a development closely associated with the simultaneous boom in the export
of copra (see Chapter II, Figure 2).[113] The imported rice was paid for largely
out of the cash earned from copra sales (Eibergen 1928:236). In 1930, 24,850
tonnes of rice were imported (W.H.M. Jansen 1990: Bijlage 2) – enough, at 100
kg per person per year, to feed almost 250,000 people, more than 20 percent
of the total population of the residency. About 60 percent of the imported rice
was apparently destined for Minahasa (Eibergen 1928:236), where by that
stage it must have amounted to almost half of all the food consumed. In the
mid-1930s, despite reduced copra prices, 'at least 30 percent' of the rice consumed in Minahasa was still said to be imported from mainland Southeast
Asia, Java, or South Sulawesi (Verkuyl 1938:106).

[110]   CV Manado 1883, 1888 (ANRI Manado 86).
[111]   CV Sangir en Talaud 1884, 1887 (ANRI Manado 146).
[112]   CV Manado 1896 (ANRI Manado 86).
[113]   The data presented for earlier years in Figure 2, it should be noted, are incomplete, since
they include only imports and exports from areas under direct Dutch control.

The existence of channels through which to buy and sell food, of course, does not automatically guarantee plentiful consumption. At the end of the eighteenth century, Woodard (1969:83-4) claimed that the people of the trading settlements on the Palu Bay 'sell their provisions indiscriminately when there is great plenty of them, and are frequently obliged to purchase from other places, and are at times reduced to great want'. Adriani and Kruyt (1912-14, II:310), at one point, even described the typical Toraja farmer in the early twentieth century as 'cash-crazy' (koopziek), 'so that shortly after the harvest, as soon as the rice may be sold (that is, after the harvest feast), a large proportion of his rice goes straight to the coast-dwellers', resulting in shortages later in the year. 'The fact that all rice must be carried down on foot from the uplands', they concluded, 'is a fortunate impediment to the sale of too much rice'. Imported rice, conversely, was not always cheap; during the drought of 1914, those who could not afford it were 'obliged to resort to sago, batata [root crops/sweet potato] and other foodstuffs' (Koloniaal verslag 1915:35).

Production for export, moreover, sometimes had a deleterious effect on subsistence production. Toward the end of the nineteenth century, Dutch officials complained that foodcrop agriculture in Gorontalo and Central Sulawesi was being neglected because of the long periods spent by the male population collecting damar and rattan in the forests.[114] During the copra boom in Minahasa, it was reported that rice imports were necessitated partly by neglect of domestic rice cultivation in favour of the new cash crop, and that coconut trees were being planted on land which would otherwise have been used for swidden farming.[115] In 1919, according to one of the few available sets of harvest statistics from Minahasa in the early twentieth century (Van Marle 1922, II:89), rice and maize production were equivalent to about 90 and 75 kg respectively per head of the population, both much lower figures than the averages of about 150 and 160 kg respectively reported between 1850 and 1870 (Table 19). As we have seen, however, the nineteenth-century statistics were probably somewhat inflated; the global influenza epidemic which reached Minahasa at the end of 1918, moreover, is known to have interfered with the following year's foodcrop harvest.[116] During the mid-1930s, according to the global figures provided by Verkuyl (1938:107), rice production within Minahasa amounted to approximately 125 kg per head, and total per capita rice availability (including imported grain) to some 180 kg.[117]

[114] Haga 1931:234-5; Van Hoëvell 1891:38, 1893b:5.
[115] Logeman 1922:66, 170; Van Marle 1922, I:66; Tideman 1926:116.
[116] Koloniaal verslag 1919:75, 1920:126. It is also possible that the decline in rice and maize cultivation was compensated by an increase in the production of other crops. The recorded cassava harvest in 1919, however, amounted to only 12 kg per head (Van Marle 1922, II:89); no other foodcrop statistics are given.
[117] These calculations are based on the population figure for 1930.

When assessing the impact of commercialization on domestic food production, it is also important to note the marked upward trend in per capita foodcrop harvests which accompanied the process of monetization and market formation in Minahasa during the 1850s and 1860s (Figure 5). Doubly striking for the fact that it occurred when compulsory coffee cultivation and roadbuilding services were making unprecedented demands on farmers' time and labour, this rise in food production was sometimes attributed by local Dutch officials to their own 'encouragement' (*aansporing*) for additional planting.[118] The economic liberal Edeling, however, was probably closer to the mark when he ascribed it to commercial incentives and to the fact that a farmer's rice and maize, unlike his coffee, was 'his own, to dispose of as he wishes'.[119] These were the same circumstances which underlay the spontaneous expansion of cash crops like cocoa and copra at different periods (see Chapter II), except that here the emerging market was domestic rather than foreign. In the final chapter of this book I will return to the question of suboptimal food production among subsistence farmers in the absence of such commercial stimuli.

Whatever the relative contributions made by greater production and better distribution, the incidence of food crises certainly appears to have declined toward the end of the colonial period. In the late nineteenth century, organized relief for the victims of local food shortages was provided on several occasions by the colonial state.[120] During the drought of 1877-1878, for instance, the residency authorities 'felt themselves obliged to offer help by setting up a brick factory in Gorontalo where everybody who so desired could work for a daily wage of *f* 0.40, to be paid either in cash or in maize imported for that purpose from Minahasa'.[121] Emergency food supplies were delivered to Talaud during the epidemic of 1886 (Ebbinge Wübben 1889:205-6, 209), and again following harvest failures in 1888 (Van Hogendorp 1890: 121) and 1896.[122] Such aid seems to have been provided for the last time during the drought of 1902, when a sum of *f* 16,300 was spent on famine relief in the residency (*Koloniaal verslag* 1903:92). The fact that it was no longer considered necessary thereafter no doubt reflects the growing effectiveness of commercial food distribution.[123] Even when rice imports briefly all but ceased in

---

[118]   CV Manado 1863, 1865 (ANRI Manado 39, 52).

[119]   'Memorie omtrent de Minahasa', 13-8-1875 (NA V 17-4-1877/20).

[120]   Such assistance seems to have been provided for the first time in 1856, when free foodstuffs were sent to Greater Sangir for refugees from an eruption of Mount Awu (MV Manado May, October and December 1856, in ANRI Manado 54).

[121]   AV Manado 1878 (ANRI Manado 53).

[122]   CV Manado 1896 (ANRI Manado 86).

[123]   The reasons were not climatic: particularly dry years after 1902 included 1911 (*Koloniaal*

1919-1920 following the imposition of export bans in Burma, Thailand and Indochina (Logeman 1922:170), no shortages were reported except as a result of insufficient harvest labour due to the concurrent influenza epidemic.[124] Minahasa, despite its own poor crop, exported 255 tonnes of locally-grown rice to other parts of the region in 1919 (Van Marle 1922, I:66).

There is also some evidence that standards of nutrition, at least in Minahasa, improved toward the end of the colonial period. Whereas at the turn of the century the diet of Minahasan peasants struck some European observers as 'inadequate' (Gallois 1892:44; Van Kol 1903:325), Tillema (1926: 202) described the Minahasans in 1924 as a 'generally well-fed' people, and Dr Kündig (1934:189), at the beginning of the 1930s, even reported having been able 'to establish personally that the population eats good solid meals, even on an everyday basis'.[125] As in the case of rice after 1870, any improvement in protein consumption probably resulted from better distribution (in space, in time, and perhaps between the individual members of communities and households) rather than from increased per capita production of meat: in 1850 there were reportedly almost 50,000 domesticated pigs in Minahasa, and in 1920, by which time the human population was more than twice as large, about 66,000.[126]

Conclusion

Scholarly opinions regarding the incidence and impact of food shortages in Indonesian history differ sharply. Metzner (1977:72, 257, 259, 1982:90) and Ormeling (1955:26, 180, 237, 240) both conclude that famine has always been a frequent event, and a significant check on population growth, in Timor and Flores.[127] The situation on these unusually dry islands, on the other hand, may not have been typical. Knapen (2001:182-3) argues that in Southeast Kalimantan the demographic significance of famine was negligi-

---

verslag 1912:31, 34), 1914 (Koloniaal verslag 1915:35, 1916:34), 1919 (Koloniaal verslag 1920:126), and probably 1925 (Quinn 1992:131).

[124]   Koloniaal verslag 1919:75; Stap 1919:810. Resident Logeman (1922:171), moreover, complained that reports of food shortages during the epidemic had been exaggerated; just 50 sacks of rice, for instance, were sufficient to relieve such a shortage on the Togian Islands in 1919.

[125]   Adam (1925b:437) makes a similar observation.

[126]   AV Manado 1850 (ANRI Manado 51); Van Marle 1922, I:92. The number of cattle in Minahasa did increase much more sharply over the same period due to rising demand for plough and draught animals (see Chapter XIV), but the meat of these animals was 'rarely eaten' (Adam 1925b:437; Van Marle 1922, I:93). One nineteenth-century source even reports a 'revulsion' for beef among Minahasans (CV Manado 1861, in ANRI Manado 95).

[127]   Also Fox 1977:18. Heersink (1999:24), in his study of Selayar, likewise reports 'periodic famines on the island in the past'.

ble, since deaths to starvation are hardly mentioned in the historical record, and emergency foods (mainly *Metroxylon* sago) were always widely available.[128] Not all of the literature on Kalimantan, however, supports this view. Freeman (1955:96-7, 104), whose anthropological fieldwork among the Iban of Sarawak in 1949-1950 happened to include an unusually bad agricultural year in which only one in three local families were able to meet their own basic rice requirements, characterizes Iban swidden cultivation as 'a highly uncertain undertaking' and concludes that 'the subsistence economy of the Iban is one of scarcity rather than plenty'. While his own account implies that most families can cope with a shortfall in rice by selling off property or supplementing their diet with sago, this author also quotes with approval a nineteenth-century colonial administrator who observed that poor harvests sometimes 'put the inhabitants to great straits to obtain means of maintaining life' (Freeman 1955:104-5, 97). Dove (1985b:149, 170, 214), during later fieldwork among the Kantu', likewise witnessed one 'disastrous' harvest after which most households were forced to beg seed rice from other longhouses up to a day's travel away, and also describes a 'hunger season' which, even in normal times, 'often precedes the rice harvest'.[129]

More importantly it would be simplistic, as Malthus long ago pointed out, to interpret even a complete absence of visible famine as an indication that food supply limitations imposed no 'positive check' upon population growth.

> This check is not so obvious to common view as the other I have mentioned, and to prove distinctly the force and extent of its operation would require, perhaps, more data than we are in possession of. But I believe it has been generally remarked by those who have attended to bills of mortality that of the number of children who die annually, much too great a proportion belongs to those who may be supposed unable to give their offspring proper food and attention, exposed as they are occasionally to severe distress and confined, perhaps, to unwholesome habitations and hard labour. (Malthus 1976:36.)

Research on the decline in European mortality which began in the eighteenth century suggests that even if actual famine accounted only for a small proportion of mortality in preindustrial Europe, much of the improvement in life expectancy after 1750 resulted from the elimination of chronic malnutrition, an achievement based on 'advances in agricultural and related technologies that permitted the per capita consumption of food to increase'.[130]

[128]   The only reported famine deaths occurred under the exceptional conditions of the Banjarmasin War (1859-1861).
[129]   Dove 1985b:219, 250-1. Also Seavoy 1986:129-32.
[130]   Fogel 1992:280. The 'nutritional' interpretation of the modern rise of population, classically formulated in the European context by McKeown (1976), has been criticized for its oversimplifi-

In an Indonesian context, medical and nutritional research on Madura has confirmed that even where 'real hunger' is never evident, infant death rates still reflect variations in the availability of food. One reason for this is that the birth weight of children born to undernourished mothers tends to be dangerously low. During an 'extremely lean season due to harvest failures' in 1981-1982, the incidence of low birth weight was 'almost twice as high' as in 'the years with regular rains'. Another is the fact that the fat and energy content of breast milk produced by undernourished women is sub-optimal. In order to 'promote infant survival and growth', conclude the authors of this policy-oriented study, 'safeguarding food security at the household level is the most appropriate intervention'.[131]

The poor quality of the earliest historical sources, unfortunately, makes it impossible to ascertain directly whether, as Reid (1990:654-6) has proposed, the mid-seventeenth century (or any other extended period) was character-ized by particulary frequent droughts or other climatic anomalies. Most of the dry years of the nineteenth century corresponded to droughts on Java (W. van Bemmelen 1916), and it is likely that the conditions which seem to have retarded the growth of teak trees in Java in the years 1645-1672 (Berlage 1931:951-2; De Boer 1951:205) were also reflected in Sulawesi. Probably more important in demographic terms than any change in the frequency of poor harvests, however, was the extent to which these were compensated by food trade and exchange. In the late nineteenth and early twentieth centu-ries, despite some local reductions in subsistence production as labour was diverted into export activities, overall food security increased considerably when food production in other areas grew in response to commercial stimuli, when large amounts of foreign rice, in a complete departure from all previ-ous conditions, were imported, and when the means of local food distribu-tion also improved thanks to rising incomes, monetization, and better trans-port facilities. In the 1920s, when almost all areas showed strong population growth, there appear to have been no significant food shortages anywhere in the region.

Many aspects of the relationship between mortality and the food sup-ply do remain problematic. The evident importance of social behaviour and

---

cation of the relationship between nutrition and mortality (Livi-Bacci 1991; Szreter 1988). Given, however, the broad correlation between economic and demographic trends which is evident at many periods in European history, most obviously the fact that the beginning of the British mor-tality decline in the eighteenth century (Wrigley et al. 1997:552-3) coincided with the onset of the industrial and agricultural revolutions but preceded major advances in scientific medicine and public health, other demographers have continued to favour an essentially Malthusian interpre-tation of secular changes in the death rate (Fogel 1997; Lee 1997).

[131]   Kusin and Sri Kardjati 1994:25-6, 34. Gopalan (1987:8-10, 66-7) makes a similar argument for Southeast Asia as a whole.

institutions in the production and distribution of food implies that cultural and political changes, such as the 'domestication' of women or the abolition of slavery, must have been central to any changes in consumption patterns. Another possible factor here is the decline of ritual feasting, and of the associated food hoarding practices, which took place in the face of missionary and government hostility (Henley 1996:50-1; Schouten 1998:108-9). In Chapter XII it will be argued that some key institutional changes of the colonial period were themselves partly the result of economic growth. No doubt this was not true in all cases: it is possible, for instance, that the political assault on slavery and the 'big house' group in early nineteenth-century Minahasa, which took place in a period of economic malaise and in a context of limited market exchange, actually contributed to that malaise by eroding traditional sources of social security. What at any rate seems clear is that the market, at least in the long term, was a more effective source of food security than were slavery, the 'moral economy', or the collection of wild famine foods, and that insofar as habits and institutions conducive to high mortality (such as poor infant feeding patterns) persisted, their effects were mitigated to a greater or lesser degree when intensive commercial exchange improved the availability of foodstuffs.

CHAPTER X
Reproductive fertility

Having investigated mortality and its determinants in Chapters VII-IX, it remains to examine patterns of fertility. This chapter summarizes what is known about fertility levels in different parts of the region at different periods, attempts to explain the observed variations, and assesses the contribution of fertility change to the patterns of population growth and decline reconstructed in Chapters IV-VI.

Fertility levels

Despite an often exaggerated concern with what they saw as the low growth rate of the indigenous population, few nineteenth-century European observers thought that low fertility was to blame for this. In 1825, Van Delden (1844:373) insisted that epidemics and other natural disasters were the only important factors limiting population growth on Sangir, 'since in normal years there are more births than deaths'.[1] 'The fertility of the women, especially those of the lower social class', reported Riedel from Gorontalo in the 1860s, 'is generally high'. 'Many', he claimed, 'have borne ten to twelve children' (Riedel 1870a:138). 'Children enough are born', echoed Graafland (1867-69, I:174) from Minahasa at the same period, 'but the great majority die in their first year of life'. The statistical data collected by Edeling in 1874 (Appendix E) showed that while this last claim was exaggerated, the reported average number of children born to date (including those who had subsequently died) per household (*gezin*), at 4.18, was indeed rather high. Completed (lifetime) fertility rates, of course, must have been higher: in 1883, an English visitor reported that Minahasan women 'often bear eight or ten' (Guillemard 1886:174).

Twentieth-century data also indicate consistently high reproductive fertility

---

[1] Steller (1866:31) also comments that the relationship between birth and death rates on Sangir is favourable, as do Von Rosenberg (1865:31) for Gorontalo and Riedel (1864b:282-3) for Bolaang Mongondow.

in Minahasa. Demographer Johanna Gooszen (1994:262), analysing the baptism and marriage registers of one Minahasan village, Woloan (near Tomohon), concludes that the average completed fertility rate among 131 women who were born between 1900 and 1915, and who ended their reproductive periods between 1945 and 1960, was 'at least 5.4'.[2] A more complex statistical reconstruction by the same researcher, using standard demographic tables, the age distribution data from the 1930 census, the mortality statistics collected by Dr Kündig in the years 1930-1932, and the recorded population growth between the censuses of 1920 and 1930, suggests an even higher average completed fertility figure of somewhere between 5.9 and 6.5 children for post-menopausal Minahasan women in the 1920s (Gooszen 1999:153). Kündig himself gives only the annual birth statistics, which for the five districts included in his study were equivalent to birth rates of 43, 44 and 42 per thousand in the years 1930, 1931, and 1932 respectively (Appendix H).[3] He describes these figures as 'very high' and comments that 'even in their periods of greatest fertility, very few European countries achieved a birth rate of 40 per thousand'.[4]

Noting that Minahasa was almost completely converted to Christianity by the end of the nineteenth century, Gooszen (1999:125) has also used the local baptism statistics published annually in the *Koloniaal verslag* as a surrogate indication of the Minahasan birth rate from 1905 onward.[5] In this way she obtains an average annual figure of 43 per thousand for the period 1925-1934, which agrees with Kündig's results. The same procedure, moreover, indicates that the annual birth rate already stood at 40 per thousand in the years 1905-1909, falling slightly to 39 in 1910-1914 and 38 in 1915-1919, then rising again to 40 in the years 1920-1924. In the single years 1900 and 1895, the equivalent figures were 38 and 40 per thousand respectively.[6] In 1890 and 1891, according to a secondary source referring to internal residency statistics, the birth rate in Minahasa apparently averaged only 34 per thousand, but the colonial doctor who quoted this figure noted that it was 'not so favourable as in earlier years' (Gallois 1892:44), and an unidentified source from the 1880s apparently mentioned a birth rate of fully 'one per 20 inhabitants', or 50 per

---

2   At the census of 1971, by comparison, the average total number of children borne by 'ever-married' Minahasan women aged 45-49 was 6.1. Equivalent figures for other areas were: Sangir-Talaud: 5.8; Bolaang Mongondow and Gorontalo: 7.0 (G.W. Jones 1977:131).

3   The number of districts included in the statistics varied from year to year.

4   Kündig 1934:175. The commentary to the 1930 census also calls these figures 'exceptionally high' (*Volkstelling* 1933-36, V:60).

5   Gooszen compares the baptism rate with the reported size of the Christian congregations in Minahasa rather than with that of the total population, so that the resulting birth rate is not greatly distorted by the fact that a small Muslim minority also existed.

6   *Koloniaal verslag* 1896, Bijlage Z:3, 1901, Bijlage Q:3. Publication of these figures in the *Kolonaal verslag* began in 1895. Almost all Minahasans had converted to Christianity by 1891 (Gunning 1924:502).

thousand (Eibergen 1928:236).

In striking contrast with these results, however, is some strong evidence for much lower fertility rates in Central Sulawesi at the beginning of the twentieth century. The 458 post-menopausal women interviewed by Albert Kruyt in the Poso area in 1902 had borne a reported total of 1,479 children, or an average of 3.23 per woman (Appendix F). The 4,349 women beyond childbearing age included in the much larger Tillema survey of 1924 (Appendix G) showed a somewhat higher average completed fertility rate of 3.90. Both figures, clearly, differ strongly from the average of five children and more indicated for post-menopausal Minahasan women at the same period. Taken as a whole, moreover, the results for all 11,969 women interviewed in Central Sulawesi in 1924, including the still-fertile majority, are in principle more or less directly comparable with those of the similar survey carried out 50 years earlier by Edeling in Minahasa, yet they show an average of only 2.80 ever-born children per married woman, against the 4.18 per household recorded by Edeling.

The question which immediately arises here is whether Minahasan women had also been less fertile in an earlier period, so that the difference between the Edeling and Tillema results can be interpreted as representative of a historical change rather than just an ethnic contrast. The annual birth statistics from Minahasa in the years 1849-1872 show that this was indeed the case (Figure 8).

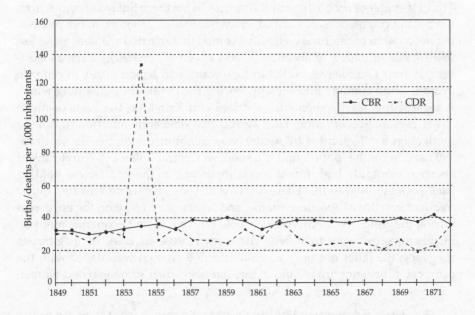

Figure 8. Recorded crude birth and death rates, Minahasa, 1849-1872.
Sources: AV Manado 1849-72 (ANRI Manado 51, 52, 53).

Compared against the reported population totals, the average annual crude birth rate was 34.9 per thousand in the period 1849-1860, but 37.2 per thousand, or 2.3 per thousand more, in the years 1861-1872. It was rising fertility almost as much as falling mortality which, by the late 1860s, had opened up a steady gap of about 15 per thousand between crude birth and death rates, producing population growth at 1.5 percent per year. The following sections aim to review, in the light of sources from this and other parts of the region, the factors which might account for such a change in fertility patterns.

Abortion, infanticide, and contraception

While children were highly valued by married couples everywhere in the region, the desire for them was not unlimited. 'Without children', wrote Graafland (1867-69, I:302), a Minahasan man 'does not consider himself fortunate', but 'too many children are not regarded as a blessing either'.[7] For women, the burden of caring for young infants was a central consideration here. 'To have many children is regarded as a blessing of the gods', noted Adriani and Kruyt (1950-51, II:335); 'nevertheless, people are not keen to have them in too rapid succession'. As in any society, there were also situations in which pregacy and childbirth were undesirable for social reasons. The best evidence for birth control practices in northern Sulawesi comes from the upland populations of Central Sulawesi. Riedel (1886:79), in his pioneering description of the Toraja, already claimed that married women 'make use of all kinds of means of abortion [*allerlei afvoerende middelen*], such as *mombayagali* (roots and leaves boiled in lime water and lemon juice), in order to avoid bearing children and thereby tearing the perineum, something which is regarded as highly shameful'. Adriani and Kruyt, on the basis of much closer personal observation, later agreed that deliberate abortion (if not the motivation for it specified by Riedel) was common among the Toraja. In his 1903 article on the 'population question' in Central Sulawesi, Kruyt ranked abortion alongside high infant mortality as one of the key factors holding back population growth. 'There are two reasons', he wrote, 'for this rather frequent practice of abortion: shame, and reluctance to take on the burden of raising the child' (A.C. Kruyt 1903b:199). Both social and economic motives, in other words, were involved. The former arose in cases of illegitimate pregacy; the latter not only when unmarried women were faced with the prospect of bringing up a child alone, but also when some married women

---

[7]   Talaud-born anthropologist Alex Ulaen remarks that even in recent times, the popular Indonesian expression *banyak anak, banyak rejeki* ('many children, many blessings') has seldom been heard on Talaud (interview, 5-9-2000).

simply felt that whether in the short or the long term, they had no need of more children.

Like at least one other colonial commentator on Indonesian abortive drugs (Persenaire 1911), Kruyt and Adriani were sceptical of the various 'medicines' reportedly used to induce abortion, many of which were applied externally rather than ingested.[8] More significant, in their opinion, were physical methods such as massage, carrying heavy burdens, or running and jumping.[9] In Bada, however, Woensdregt (1929b:353) noted the use of a crude but effective abortifacient which worked by inducing 'severe vomiting, as a result of which the foetus is expelled'. Not surprisingly, none of these methods was particularly reliable. 'I dare say', wrote Kruyt (1903b:201), 'that if nature were not so often stronger than the means of abortion, the households would be even smaller'. In demographic terms, on the other hand, the unreliability of the available techniques was counterbalanced to some extent by their dangerousness, since many attempts at abortion seem to have resulted in permanent infertility.[10] When abortion failed, infanticide was sometimes an alternative.[11] Reported methods of infanticide varied from throttling to abandonment in the forest. Adriani and Kruyt also mentioned women who, without actually abandoning their infants, nevertheless deliberately allowed them to die of hunger or exposure.[12] Woensdregt (1929b:353) confirmed that infanticide, like abortion, was practised for both social and economic reasons, adding that some women 'neglect their children because they are afraid of becoming weakened by constant suckling', and that 'even older children' were sometimes killed 'when the parents are constantly in difficulty'.[13]

Comparable reports also occur from many other parts of the region in sources from the early twentieth century. Albert Kruyt (1930a:461) noted the practice of abortion among the Loinang (Saluan) of the Luwuk Peninsula, and was told that in the Bongka River Valley, pregnant unmarried girls 'customarily hang themselves if they are not successful in procuring an abortion' (A.C. Kruyt 1903a:712). Both abortion and infanticide were reported from Balantak and Banggai, although here again only illegitimacy was explicitly

8   A.C. Kruyt 1903b:199; Adriani and Kruyt 1912-14, II:40, 1950-51, II:343.
9   Adriani 1918:390; Adriani and Kruyt 1912-14, II:40, 1950-51, II:343; A.C. Kruyt 1903b:199, 1932b:43, 1938, III:183.
10   'By applying crude and therefore often dangerous methods of abortion', stated Adriani (1915:458), 'many a slave woman has spoiled herself for later'.
11   Adriani and Kruyt 1912-14, II:55-6, 1950-51, II:344; A.C. Kruyt 1903b:201, 1911:91. One common occasion for infanticide was the birth of twins, one of which was killed to avoid both the misfortune which such an event was thought to bring with it, and 'the heavy burden which it places upon the mother' (Adriani and Kruyt 1950-51, II:369).
12   Adriani and Kruyt 1912-14, I:181, II:56; A.C. Kruyt 1903b:201, 1911:91.
13   A.C. Kruyt (1938, III:182), however, was assured 'that if a child has lived for one day, it will not subsequently be killed'.

mentioned as a motive (A.C. Kruyt 1932b:43, 1933b:65-6). Deliberate abortion (as a consequence of incest) was reported by another missionary from Sangir in 1919.[14] Tillema (1926:221), visiting Palu in 1924, was told that abortion was common there and given two reasons for this which are not mentioned in other sources. Women trapped in loveless arranged marriages, first of all, often had no desire to bear their husbands' children. By remaining childless, secondly, women, as guardians of the family inheritance (see Chapter I), could retain exclusive control of property and prestige goods to which any offspring would otherwise have a claim.

Nineteenth-century Dutch sources already mention abortion in Minahasa.[15] De Clercq (1891:225), who served as *controleur* of the Amurang division from 1866 to 1872, believed that infant mortality was no higher in Minahasa than in Java, where the population was growing more rapidly, but rather that the number of births was lower due to frequent abortion. As in Central Sulawesi, physical methods of inducing abortion often led to permanent infertility. Infanticide, according to De Clercq (1870a:133), was also 'rather common'. Whereas Albert Kruyt (1903b:201) claimed that 'ways of preventing pregnancy' were 'completely unknown among the Toraja', finally, at least one type of traditional contraception was definitely practised in nineteenth-century Minahasa. This consisted of 'certain manipulations which change the position of the uterus' (De Clercq 1870a:133) and is recognizable as deliberate retroflexion of the womb, a fairly effective contraceptive technique which was well documented on Java at the same period.[16]

Changes in the frequency of direct birth control?

Women in northern Sulawesi, then, were always capable, to a greater or lesser extent, of restricting their own fertility. But although Tammes claimed in 1940 to have found no evidence for 'extensive' birth control practices, there is in fact little direct indication that the frequency of such practices

---

[14] Kleiweg de Zwaan 1928:49. The original source reference given here is, however, incorrect. A term for deliberate abortion occurs in the dictionary of the Sangirese language compiled by Steller and Aebersold (1959:326, 532).

[15] Graafland (1867-69, I:173, 245) is the earliest.

[16] Boomgaard 1989:195. Verdoorn (1941:59) reports that among a large sample of Javanese prostitutes examined by a colonial doctor at the turn of the century, it was effective in about half of the cases in which it had been applied. Whereas Verdoorn states that the rotation was very painful and implies that it was accomplished on a single visit to the *dukun* (traditional medical specialist), in present-day Java the treatment occurs in stages, and is apparently painless (Atashendartini Habsjah, interview, 25-2-1999). Besides De Clercq, Van Kol (1903:324) also mentions the use of this technique in Minahasa.

declined under colonial conditions.[17] In Balantak, where 'much abortion' had reportedly occurred in former times as a result of permissive attitudes to premarital sex, Albert Kruyt (1933b:65-6) did think that this might have changed by the 1930s following widespread acceptance of Christianity. In nineteenth-century Minahasa, on the other hand, deliberate abortion remained so common among Christians that some observers, apparently on the basis of information from indigenous informants, blamed this precisely on 'the strict demands which Christianity makes regarding [sexual] morality' (Graafland 1867-69, I:173). Prior to conversion, it was claimed, attitudes to extramarital pregnancy had been more relaxed (De Clercq 1870a:133; Van der Hart 1853:174). In the second edition of his standard work *De Minahassa*, Graafland felt obliged to rebut this accusation by pointing out that illegitimate pregnancy had already been subject to 'heavy fines' and social penalties in pre-Christian times.[18] 'To avoid that shame', an 'old native man' reportedly recalled, 'many women resorted to means of destroying the foetus'.[19]

Abortion and contraception by traditional methods have in fact remained common in the region up to recent times.[20] Even in their responses to an official government survey carried out throughout the province of North Sulawesi in 1973 (when the use of modern contraceptives was still limited), 51 percent of married women in urban areas, and 29 percent in the countryside, admitted to knowledge of the contraceptive method involving 'deliberate inversion of the uterus'; informal interviews with midwives in the same period suggested that abortion was also 'very commonly practised'.[21] One midwife who began working in Minahasa in the 1970s has estimated that about 60 percent of 'traditional' abortions were obtained by unmarried girls for social reasons, and the remaining 40 percent by married women in the interests of family planning.[22] In the absence of direct evidence for historical changes in the frequency of deliberate fertility control, these can only be inferred on the basis of the evidence for changes in the birth rate itself, combined with speculation regarding the ways in which social and economic

[17]   Tammes 1940:184-9, 191, 195. Tammes admitted, however, that abortion was sometimes practised in Minahasa.
[18]   Meanwhile, however, De Clercq (1891:225) had already retracted his original view that extramarital pregnancy had carried no social stigma prior to conversion.
[19]   Graafland 1898, I:302. In the 1840s, extramarital pregnancy was said to be regarded as 'a very great disgrace' among the still-pagan Bantik (Van Spreeuwenberg 1845-46:33).
[20]   Schouten 1998:71; personal enquiries, Minahasa and Gorontalo, September-November 1994. Besides massage and contraceptive rotation of the uterus, contemporary informants also mention an invasive method of inducing abortion, using a sharp wooden probe, which is described in colonial sources from Java (Verdoorn 1941:61-2).
[21]   G.W. Jones 1977:147, 149. Other 'traditional' methods listed included abstinence (known to 34% of urban and 22% of rural women) and 'herbs' (55% and 28% respectively).
[22]   A.L. Kalangie-Kalalo, interview, 13-9-1994.

changes might have affected the strength of the incentives to bear more or fewer children.

Slavery

One traditional institution which tended to depress fertility, according to Adriani and Kruyt, was slavery. For several reasons, the two missionaries claimed, both the economic and the social motives for abortion were more common in slaveholding communities than elsewhere.[23] Children, first of all, were less economically important to slaveowners than to free couples without access to slave labour. 'If one has slaves', as Adriani (1915:458) put it, 'then one also has servants, so that one of the principal reasons to hope for children is eliminated'. Conversely, since slave children were 'taken away from their parents at the age of six or seven (and often even younger) and divided among their masters', many slave women had 'no desire to bear and raise children for other people' (A.C. Kruyt 1903b:201, 1911:91). These observations accord with (and partly inspire) recent interpretations of Indonesian historical demography which proceed from the assumption that slavery and childbearing can be regarded as economic alternatives (Boomgaard 1997a:8; Knapen 2001:394-5). An additional disadvantage of children for slaves was that slave mothers 'often do not have the time to look after them properly, so that in many cases they die' (Adriani 1915:458). Social factors favouring fertility control, finally, were also more significant in slave societies, since free men could easily refuse to marry slave women whom they had made pregnant, while illicit and heavily punishable liasons between free women and slave men (who in some communities outnumbered their free counterparts) provided additional demand for abortions.[24]

In 1902, Albert Kruyt presented statistical evidence for these effects in the form of a striking difference in completed fertility rates between the women of two Pamona subgroups in the Poso area: the To Lage, a large proportion of whom were hereditary slaves, and the To Pebato, among whom the number of slaves was small. In what he regarded as a representative sample of 41 To Lage women beyond childbearing age, Kruyt found that the average stated number of children ever-borne (whether or not these had survived) was 2.85. Among the To Pebato, by contrast, 155 post-menopausal women had produced a reported average of 4.03 children each (A.C. Kruyt 1903b:197).

---

[23] Adriani 1915:458, 1918:389-90, 1919:44, 1921a:22, 1921b:15; Adriani and Kruyt 1912-14, II: 40-1, 1950-51, II:338-9; A.C. Kruyt 1903b:200-1, 1911:91-2.
[24] Riedel (1886:83) also mentions abortion as a consequence of unions between free women and slave men in Central Sulawesi.

Table 20. Reported fertility and child survival rates among four Pamona subgroups in the Poso area, 1924

	Slaveholding groups		Non-slaveholding groups	
	To Lage	To Onda'e	To Pebato	To Wingke mPoso
Post-menopausal women				
Average number of births per woman	4.22	4.07	4.16	5.38
Average number of children surviving beyond infancy	3.08	3.14	3.14	3.88
All women				
Average number of births per woman	2.75	2.53	3.22	3.83
Average number of children surviving to date	1.31	1.30	1.57	2.03

Sources: Tillema 1926:46-7; Adriani and Kruyt 1950-51, II:341

Because infant mortality was also much higher among the To Lage, the discrepancy between the numbers of children surviving beyond infancy was even greater: 3.12 per woman among the To Pebato, but only 1.24 among the To Lage, who were evidently reproducing at a rate well below that necessary in order to maintain their existing population (Appendix F).

This striking result, unfortunately, was not duplicated by the much more extensive Tillema survey of 1924 (Appendix G). The 374 post-menopausal To Lage women interviewed in 1924, in fact, had borne an average of 4.22 children each, slightly more than their To Pebato counterparts either then (4.16) or in 1902 (4.03). Another slaveholding group, the To Onda'e, also showed a high average completed fertility rate of 4.07 in 1924 (Table 20). The numbers of children reported to have survived beyond infancy, moreover, were approximately equal for all three groups, although the women of a second group which had never included many slaves, the To Wingke mPoso, did report a slightly larger number of surviving children.

Kruyt himself, who republished a selection from the Tillema figures in 1951, made no comment on these discordant results, instead preferring to find support for his original view in the global statistics for all women, most of them still at fertile ages, included in the 1924 survey (Adriani and Kruyt 1950-51, II:339). These aggregate figures, mysteriously, do show a higher average number of births to date both for the To Pebato (3.22) and for another group which had never included many slaves, the To Wingke mPoso (3.83), than for the To Lage (2.75) or the To Onda'e (2.53). The numbers of children surviving to date, moreover, were also higher in both (formerly) slaveholding communities. The discrepancy between the two sets of data is very difficult to explain, the only explanation which springs to mind being that To Lage and To Onda'e women bore more of their children at a later age.[25] The post-menopausal database is smaller than that of the survey as a whole, but it remains much larger than Kruyt's 1902 samples, and while the old social relationship between master and slave often did persist after the formal abolition of slavery in the Poso area in 1907, this too seems an inadequate justification for ignoring the completed fertility figures in favour of the current statistics.[26] The former, after all, are both more directly comparable with the 1902 results (which likewise included only post-menopausal women), and refer at least partly to the same precolonial period. The global figures, by contrast, must include many mothers who were not yet born when slavery was abolished, and of course do not yet indicate completed fertility or household size.

It is conceivable that women in the slaveholding communities altered their reproductive behaviour after the abolition of slavery in anticipation of an immediate transformation in economic and social conditions, only to revert to the original patterns when this did not materialize. Short of such speculation, however, it is difficult to say that the Tillema data, in themselves, support the argument that the institution of slavery tended to lower fertility.[27] The views of Kruyt and Adriani on this subject, it should also be noted, were probably coloured to some extent by enthusiasm for population growth, and by ethical opposition to both slavery and abortion. In combination with the 1902 results, those of 1924 nevertheless remain suggestive, and although their ambiguity highlights the complexity of the problem and the number of cross-cutting factors influencing fertility behaviour, it is unlikely that the links between slavery and birth control specified in the missionary ethnographies were wholly fictitious. While comparative evidence from other parts of Southeast Asia is scarce, the proportion of children among the slave population of Dutch-controlled Ambon in the seventeenth century was certainly smaller than among non-slave groups, and a VOC governor of Ambon ascribed this explicitly to the fact that 'slave women bore few

[25]   Since only married women were interviewed, however, this cannot have been the result of later marriage. There are no arithmetical errors in the data tables.
[26]   The persistence of slavery is described by both Adriani (1915:468) and Kruyt (1911:95-6, *Brieven*, 5-3-1910).
[27]   A separate piece of quantitative evidence also contradicts the specific claim that female slaves restricted their fertility more than non-slaveowning free women. In Mori in the early 1920s, Jan Kruyt (1924:74) found that 58 of the former and 47 of the latter, in all cases women beyond childbearing age, had borne an average of 3.29 and 2.98 children respectively. The sources for these figures, however, were genealogical interviews not specifically intended to reveal fertility patterns.

children' (Knaap 1987:132). In the African literature, the association between slavery and low reproductive fertility is a commonplace; the explanations advanced here, moreover, mostly resemble those proposed by Adriani and Kruyt in emphasizing the tenuousness of economic and other ties between slaves and their children in the face of claims to those children from slave-owners.[28]

Female autonomy and the corporate kin group

Women, in general, were more strongly motivated than men to excercise family planning. One obvious reason for this was that it was women who had to provide care for infants. 'For the man', wrote Adriani and Kruyt (1912-14, II:37), 'there is no possible reason not to wish for children, since the entire burden of caring for these is borne by the mother'.[29] In most of the societies of the region, as described in Chapter I, women traditionally enjoyed a rather high degree of social and economic autonomy, and also bore a relatively heavy workload. In a study of fertility patterns on Madura in the 1970s, Niehof (1985:273, 309-12) found that contraception and abortion were more common in a fishing village where women were much involved in trading activities, and therefore had less time for motherhood and more economic automomy, than among their counterparts in an agrarian village, who enjoyed less autonomy and lower incomes. The reported prevalence of high fertility during the mid-nineteenth century in Muslim Gorontalo, where women were confined largely to domestic roles, suggests that similar factors may help explain variations in the extent of deliberate birth control in the history of northern Sulawesi.

Kruyt's 1902 fertility survey (Appendix F), because it includes women in two lowland Muslim trading communities where the pattern of gender relations was apparently similar to that found in Gorontalo (see Chapter I), once again provides some opportunity to test this proposition (Table 21). As far as the whole groups of interviewed women are concerned, the birth and infant survival rates in one of the Muslim communities, Mapane, are broadly comparable to those of the upland To Pebato, while the fertility characteristics for Tojo resemble those of the To Lage. According to Kruyt (1903b:198), on the other hand, the reason for the low birth rate in Tojo was widespread sterility due to venereal diseases introduced as a result of foreign trading contacts. Some allowance can be made for this extraneous variable by excluding

[28]   M.A. Klein 1987:56-60; Meillassoux 1986:79-85; Robertson and Klein 1983:8, 51-5, 68-76, 96, 105-9, 120-1.
[29]   See also Adriani and Kruyt 1912-14, I:86.

Table 21. Reported fertility and child survival rates among four ethnic groups in the Poso area, 1902

| | Pagan groups | | Muslim groups | |
	To Lage	To Pebato	Mapane	Tojo
All women				
Average number of births per woman	2.85	4.03	3.82	2.50
Average number of children surviving beyond infancy	1.24	3.12	3.13	1.88
Non-childless women only				
Average number of births per woman	3.25	4.19	4.16	3.16
Average number of children surviving beyond infancy	1.42	3.25	3.40	2.37

Source: A.C. Kruyt 1903b:197-8

childless (and therefore presumably sterile) women from the calculation, in which case the non-childless women of Tojo are seen to produce considerably more surviving children than those of the To Lage, and their counterparts in Mapane slightly more than those of the (by Toraja standards fertile) To Pebato. Particularly given that slavery was no doubt present in Mapane and Tojo (Adriani and Kruyt 1900:196), these results are suggestive, although once again it must be admitted that in themselves they do not justify strong conclusions.

Female autonomy in the uplands of Central Sulawesi was related to the existence of a matrifocal kinship system in which women acted as guardians of the prestige goods which the junior members of their corporate kin group needed in order to marry or stage other important ceremonies. Tillema, as we have seen, was told that reluctance to see such goods dispersed provided one direct motive for fertility control in the Palu area. This particular situation was probably never universal; in parts of Minahasa, the local equivalent of the co-residential 'big house' group which lay at the core of kinship organization in Central Sulawesi and Sangir was apparently structured along patrilineal rather than matrilineal lines (see Chapter I). There is, however, another reason to suppose that extended family structures were conducive to fertility limitation: any economic (or other) benefits of children, in the traditional situation, were typically enjoyed not only by their parents, but also by a wider circle of kin.

One straightforward economic manifestation of this 'child-sharing' tendency was the fact that within a multi-hearth, multi-generational 'big house' group, surplus food, regardless of who or whose children had produced it, was often redistributed on the basis of 'generalized exchange', with 'no calculation of an exact return' (Schrauwers 2000:106). Another was the facility and frequency of adoption. 'This custom is in fact so common', wrote Graafland (1867-69, I:323) in Minahasa, 'that one can hardly describe the life of the Alfur without having him adopted as the child of others, or adopting children himself'.[30] In Central Sulawesi, where adoption was also 'very common', the brothers and sisters of a couple with children were said to 'exercise a certain right to [adopt] their nephews and nieces, so that the father must come up with good arguments if he refuses their request'.[31] In the case of the father's siblings, this situation was related in part to bride price and debt. 'After all', noted Kruyt (1899a:86), 'they bring the bridewealth together, so they also have a right to the children'.[32]

An important insight in recent demographic anthropology is that such extra-household rights or claims to children are often major factors in the 'cost-benefit analysis' of childbearing. 'To understand fertility motivation and fertility levels', it has been observed, 'we must investigate the claims made on children, the negotiation of these competing claims, and the alternative strategies for achieving the values that are claimed from children' (Townsend 1997:110). In so far as fertility was under conscious control, both the facility of adoption as an alternative to pregnancy, and the fact that the benefits of children were shared with others or even surrendered to them, probably tended to lower the birth rate. At one level this is analogous to the (probable) effect of slavery as an economic alternative to child-rearing; at another it resembles a 'collective action dilemma' (Olson 1971; Lichbach 1996) in which the 'public good' (children), although highly valued, is under-produced because whereas its most important cost (pregnancy) is borne individually, its benefits are more or less collectivized. Both the mechanism proposed here, and the general argument that low fertility was associated with the existence of cohesive corporate kin groups, are hypothetical. But while some empirical studies have concluded that corporate kin groups are conducive to high fertility (Burch 1983:549-53; Lorimer 1954:90), others contradict this (LeVine and Scrimshaw 1983:680; Nag 1975:43), and I suspect that the former are based on situations in which the groups in question have begun to lose their original economic functions and the problem of children as public goods has become less marked. In

[30] Also Adam 1925b:467-77; Carpentier Alting 1902:106-31; *Rapport* 1910:30-42.
[31] A.C. Kruyt 1899a:81. Similar adoption customs, according to Kruyt (1899a:82, 85), existed in Talaud and Gorontalo. Reluctance to comply with adoption requests is also reported from elsewhere in Indonesia (Alexander and Alexander 1993:270) and the Pacific (Marshall 1976:34).
[32] Elsewhere Kruyt (1938, III:118) describes how one grandfather in Bada, because of the claim which he retained to the labour of his grandchildren as long as a bridewealth debt remained outstanding, tried to discourage his son-in-law from paying this off. 'What do the bride price buffalo matter to me?', the man explained; 'I would rather have my grandchildren, whom I can send here and there on errands, and use for all kinds of small jobs'.

Chapter XII I will return to the possibility that the dispersal of the traditional co-residential 'big house' groups was associated with rising fertility.

Infanticide and the sex ratio

The possibility that infanticide, as in many other societies, affected the juvenile sex ratio (Harris and Ross 1987:32; White 1976:12) provides an opportunity to search for indirect evidence of this particular type of 'fertility' control in the demographic record. The pattern of preferential female infanticide which such evidence usually reveals is not to be expected in the case of northern Sulawesi, where the central role played by women in agriculture and other spheres, together with the fact that a significant bride price was usually paid to the family of a woman when she married, meant that girl children were at least as highly valued as boys. Most sources dealing with pagan groups in Central Sulawesi, where men moved away from home upon marriage to join their wives' extended families, indicate a positive preference for female offspring.[33] A description of Minahasa in the 1840s also states that the preference (at least among grandparents) is definitely for girls, on account of the bride price which can be expected for them as adults (Van Doren 1854-56, II:142). Given this pattern, we might perhaps expect to find evidence for preferential male infanticide in the sex ratios of the populations concerned. The 1930 census shows, for eastern Central Sulawesi, a very slight surplus of girls over boys in the infant category, but boys are more numerous among older children.[34] More interesting in this respect are some early nineteenth-century population data from Minahasa and Gorontalo (Table 22).

Table 22. Reported sex ratios (males per 100 females) in the child population, Minahasa and Gorontalo, 1823-1870[35]

Minahasa		Gorontalo	
1829[36]	99	1823[37]	92
1840[38]	106	1824[39]	98
1850[40]	111	1849[41]	116
1860[42]	113	1852[43]	124
1870[44]	108	1856[45]	116

[33]   A.C. Kruyt 1903b:195; Adriani and Kruyt 1912-14, II:41, 1950-51, II:336; A.C. Kruyt 1903b: 195, 1933b:70, 1938, II:191.
[34]   *Volkstelling* 1933-36, V:63, 190. The female surplus among infants was apparently greater on Banggai, but the commentary to the census still ascribes this simply to the naturally higher mortality among male infants.
[35]   Note that the age boundary of the child category varies from estimate to estimate.

Whereas later counts show a surplus of boys, the figures from both areas in the 1820s and 1830s indicate a female majority. The reliability of the early data, of course, is low; it is not certain, moreover, that a preference for female children ever existed in Muslim Gorontalo. Muslim coast-dwellers in Central Sulawesi, in contrast to their pagan neighbours, generally preferred sons, reportedly because in Islamic areas 'the ancient *adat* [tradition] that the man goes to live with his wife has been replaced by the Mohammedan institution that the woman is the property of the husband, so that he can take her wherever he wishes' (A.C. Kruyt 1903b:196). In the case of Minahasa, however, it is interesting to note that whereas the preference in the 1840s was apparently for girls, Graafland (1867-69, I:302), writing in the 1860s, reported that the typical Minahasan husband was 'fairly indifferent as to whether he has sons or daughters: the former help him later in his work, the latter bring him money'. It remains a matter of speculation whether continuing religous conversion, a reduction in the value of bride price payments (see below), or economic and political changes affecting gender roles might account for the apparent shift in preferences and sex ratios. A decline in the rate of accidental infant mortality, allowing a greater proportion of the naturally more numerous male infants to survive, is another possible factor. If the gender imbalances shown in Table 22 do reflect the impact of infanticide, their slightness suggests either that this practice was never particularly common, or that the gender preference was never particularly strong.[46]

Age of marriage

Perhaps the most obvious indirect type of fertility control is the age at which the female members of a population tend to marry. Delayed marriage is 'the classical form of the [Malthusian] preventive check'.[47] In Central Sulawesi

36   Van Doren 1854-56, I:266.
37   AV Gorontalo 1823 (ANRI Gorontalo 3).
38   Van Doren 1854-56, I:266.
39   AV Gorontalo 1824 (ANRI Gorontalo 3).
40   AV Manado 1850 (ANRI Manado 50).
41   'Staat van de gedane zielsbeschrijving onder ultimo Augustus 1849' (ANRI Gorontalo 18).
42   AV Manado 1860 (ANRI Manado 52).
43   AV Gorontalo 1852 (ANRI Gorontalo 3).
44   AV Manado 1870 (ANRI Manado 53).
45   AV Manado 1856 (ANRI Manado 51).
46   In the United States in 1985, the equivalent ratios varied by specific age category between 105 and 106; in India in 1971, between 106 and 107 (Newell 1988:30).
47   Wrigley and Schofield 1981:459. One complication here, of course, is the fact that not all children were born to married mothers. Gooszen (1999:162) notes that more than 10% of

at the turn of the century, however, relatively early marriage was apparently the norm despite the low fertility rate. 'The average age at which the girls marry', wrote Albert Kruyt (1903b:194) in 1902, 'can be estimated at 15 years'. In 1930 this situation was said to be 'little changed' (*Volkstelling* 1933-36, V:68). A source from 1911 ascribes the high frequency of divorce on Talaud partly to 'marriage at too early an age' (*Zegeningen Gods* 1911:4); according to the missionary Stokking (1917:342), Talaud girls traditionally became 'marriageable' at 15 or 16. In mid-nineteenth century Gorontalo, according to Riedel (1870a:136), girls married 'at the age of 14 and earlier, although never before menarche'. No specific information is available regarding ages of menarche; Jan Kruyt (1937:200), however, believed that Toraja girls became sexually mature at about the same age as their Dutch counterparts.

The best evidence for delayed marriage, ironically, comes from Minahasa in the second half of the nineteenth century, when its population was growing rapidly. Among the 806 Christian couples who married in Minahasa in 1873, according to Edeling, the average age of the bride was 24, and that of the bridegroom 30 years. In one administrative division, Amurang, the female average was as high as 26, and nowhere was it lower than 22.[48] A proportion of those marrying, no doubt, were not doing so for the first time, and since Minahasa was still in the process of conversion to Christianity at this date, it is also likely that some of the recorded marriages represented only the formalization of existing unions.[49] De Clercq (1871b:33), nevertheless, noted in the same period that engagement in Minahasa 'can last several years without anything being arranged regarding the wedding' – a clear contrast with the later situation in Central Sulawesi, where marriages usually took place no more than a year after they were agreed upon by the families involved (A.C. Kruyt 1938, III:74). In 1896, moreover, the district chief of Langoan confirmed that at least in his part of Minahasa, relatively late marriage was neither a statistical illusion nor a recent consequence of conversion, but the traditional pattern. 'In the past', he wrote in his contribution to a report on Minahasan customary law, 'a young man was about 25 when he decided to get married, and a young woman had to be 20 years old or more'.[50]

Minahasan children in the period 1895-1925 were born out of wedlock, while Kruyt (1903b:194) also knew 'many women who bear child after child without marrying'. The frequency with which fear of shame apparently motivated the practice of abortion in cases of extramarital pregnancy, however, indicates that this cannot have been a normal situation.

[48]   A.C.J. Edeling, 'Memorie omtrent de Minahasa', 13-8-1875 (NA V 17-4-1877/20).

[49]   AV Manado 1860 (ANRI Manado 52); Wiersma 1872:36, 1876:92; Edeling, however, does not suggest this himself, mentioning only that 'some intercourse occurs before marriage, but marriage follows as soon as the consequences become evident'.

[50]   *Rapport* 1910:64. The main text of the report opposite this comment states that according to pagan custom, which is becoming increasingly rare as the Christianization of Minahasa

Strikingly high marital ages are also mentioned in a report from Greater Sangir at the end of the colonial period. 'The missionary of Manganitu', states the publication based on the 1930 census, 'reports: 1. that of 169 women who married in 1933, only eight were under the age of 20; 2. that it is *adat* that a girl does not marry before her twentieth year; 3. that the normal age at marriage is 24 to 25 years; reasons are not given' (*Volkstelling* 1933-36, V:67). An account of Siau at the end of the nineteenth century states that men 'usually marry between their twentieth and their thirtieth year', although 'always with women who are younger than themselves' (Van Dinter 1899:370).

It is interesting to note that both Sangir and the core area of Minahasa had long been subject to relatively high population pressure (Chapters IV and V), and that in both areas, but not usually elsewhere, bride price payments often included pieces of land.[51] The only other parts of the region for which land is mentioned as a bridewealth item in the literature are Lore (A.C. Kruyt 1938, III:110) and Banggai (A.C. Kruyt 1932d:478, 1934:125), both also areas of locally dense population. Within Minahasa, moreover, Graafland (1867-69, II:213, 1898, II:286) noted that in the northern district of Tonsea (Kema), one of the least densely populated, a custom of very early marriage ('before they have grown out of children's shoes') existed 'such as is not to be found anywhere else'. Taken together, these observations suggest a connection, perhaps mediated by a need to gain access to scarce land in order to marry, between late marriage and high population density. In Minahasa, however, this link appears to have weakened toward the end of the nineteenth century. In 1896, the chief who described late marriage as the original custom here also added that 'over the last 50 years the situation has changed' (*Rapport* 1910:64). Around 1930, according to a local church official, Minahasan women 'usually' married 'between the ages of 17 and 23' (*Volkstelling* 1933-36, V:67) – still late by Central Sulawesi or Gorontalo standards, but distinctly younger than the minimum of 20 years and the average of 22-24 suggested by the sources for Minahasa in the mid-nineteenth century. This change almost certainly helps to explain why birth rates rose in Minahasa after 1850.

As in other parts of Indonesia (Boomgaard 1996b:15), the marital age

---

approaches completion, a woman has to be 'about 15' in order to marry. Partly on this basis, Van Bemmelen (1987:183) concludes that the traditional age at marriage 'was probably quite a young one'. The chief of Langoan's statement, however, is too explicit to ignore. The apparently contradictory information in the text probably reflected a recent decline in marital ages (see below), and may also have been informed by the existing colonial legislation on Christian marriages, which specified a minimum age of 15 for women (S. van Bemmelen 1987:201).

[51]   Minahasa: Graafland 1867-69, I:318, 1898, I:467; H.E.K. 1894:359; *Rapport* 1910:67; Van Spreeuwenberg 1845-46:324; Worotikan 1910:159; Sangir (Siau): Van Dinter 1899:371; other sources for Sangir and Talaud mention coconut and sago groves, although not land as such (Brilman 1938:51; Van Delden 1844:1; Miete 1938:364; Stokking 1917:344).

was influenced by the size of the bride price. In 1847 one Dutch official complained that high bride prices in Minahasa 'make marriage difficult and so impede population growth'.[52] In 1930 the bride price was still regarded as the main reason why really young Minahasan brides were rare (*Volkstelling* 1933-36, V:67). A high bride price, it should immediately be added, is not in itself a reliable predictor of late marriage, and the link between the two can seldom be understood in purely economic terms. Bridewealth in northern Sulawesi was provided mainly by the extended kin group of the husband, who did not normally need time to save it up himself.[53] In many cases it could also be obtained on credit, often to be paid back in the form of labour services, or even circumvented altogether by means of a 'kidnap marriage' (*schaakhuwelijk*).[54] For the social elite, who often married later than their inferiors (Kaudern 1940: 47; Woensdregt 1929a:256), it was probably more a symbol of status than a real source of wealth: high-born girls in Bada, for instance, remained single 'until a candidate of equal status and wealth appears', rather than until an existing candidate had succeeded in accumulating the necessary resources.[55] The fact that the bride price was often mentioned as an advantage of having female children, nevertheless, suggests that for the bulk of the population its economic value was considerable, and a gradual decline in its reported significance (and presumably its value relative to income) in Minahasa during the late nineteenth century (S. van Bemmelen 1987:184-5, 187, 198-9) was probably among the factors which tended to facilitate younger marriages.[56]

While the erosion of bridewealth customs in Minahasa was associated partly with missionary disapproval, and possibly also with deeper changes in social organization (see Chapter XII), it seems likely that a general correlation between prosperity and nuptuality, maintained at least in part by the bride price mechanism, always existed at the whole-population level. In 1848, a Dutch official identified one of the reasons for demographic stagna-

---

[52]   J. Grudelbach, 'Gevoelen over de topographische schetsen van den Luitenant J.J. ten Siethoff', 24-12-1846 (ANRI Manado 46).
[53]   Adriani and Kruyt 1912-14, II:25; Miete 1938:365; *Rapport* 1910:67-8. Woensdregt (1929a:255), however, states that after his engagement, a Bada man usually undertook a journey of up to a year 'to earn money with which to buy all sorts of desirable things for the girl and her family'.
[54]   AV Manado 1833 (ANRI Manado 48); Adriani and Kruyt 1912-14, II:24-5; Aragon 1992:85, 87; Van Dinter 1899:375-6; Van Doren 1854-56, II:133-4; Van Hoëvell 1893b:24, 34; Kortleven 1927: 68; A.C. Kruyt 1932b:21-6, 1938, III:118; Pietermaat, De Vriese and Lucas 1840:124; Reinwardt 1858: 599; Riedel 1870a:136, 1872b:506, 1895a:93; Stokking 1917:343, 346-7; Woensdregt 1929a:262.
[55]   Woensdregt 1929a:257. Kruyt (1909:378), significantly, described the bride price in Bada as 'strikingly low'. Chabot (1950:162) denies that the bride price itself was at all significant in economic terms among elite groups in South Sulawesi, although many Bugis women remained permanently unmarried because they could not find partners of appropriate status.
[56]   At the same time, school education and the increasing importance of the marriage of love as an ideal may have had the opposite effect (S. van Bemmelen 1987:189; G.W. Jones 1977:121, 125).

tion in Minahasa as 'poverty, as a result of which marriages have become less common'.[57] Edeling later noted that in the 1850s, the number of marriages taking place in Minahasa each year seemed to have been correlated with the size of the rice and maize harvest.[58] In this light the decline in the age at marriage (and the concomitant rise in fertility) in Minahasa later in the century can probably be attributed partly to the commercialization of the domestic economy, and to the emergence of copra sales as a major new source of income after 1880. As in the context of trade (see Chapter II), it is important to note that the monetary economy was seldom clearly distinct from the sphere of traditional exchange; money is already mentioned as a component of Minahasan bridewealth payments as early as the beginning of the 1840s.[59] Meanwhile the colonization of lowland and frontier areas outside the central plateau (see Chapter V), itself partly a result of the copra boom, must also have acted to release any fertility restriction arising from the limited local availability of subsistence farmland.

Spinsterhood, divorce, and polygamy

According to the 1930 census, 21.8 percent of the adult women in the residency of Manado, compared with only 7.9 percent for Indonesia as a whole, were unmarried and had never been married before.[60] Apart from confirming that in some parts of the region the marital age was high, this also raises the possibility that many women remained permanently single. In South Sulawesi, traditionally, a significant proportion of elite Bugis and Makasarese women never married because they could not find a partner of appropriate status (H.Th. Chabot 1950:159-63; Errington 1989:261). Local people claim that a similar situation still exists in Gorontalo (interviews, October 1994) and parts of western Central Sulawesi (Aragon 1992:85). This pattern, however, does not seem to

---

[57]   J. Gansneb Tengnagel, 'Beknopte nota betrekkelijk de residentie Menado', 16-3-1848 (ANRI Manado 168).
[58]   In the poor years 1855-1857 (Chapter IX, Table 19) the recorded annual number of marriages averaged 617; in the more prosperous years 1858-1860, 1,294 (A.C.J. Edeling, 'Memorie omtrent de Minahasa', 13-8-1875, in NA V 17-4-1877/20). Tammes (1940:193) adds that the recorded birth rate was unusually low in 1856 following the drought of 1855. The official marriage statistics kept in Minahasa from 1849 onward, unfortunately, are too incomplete to be of much use for identifying longer-term trends.
[59]   Van Spreeuwenberg 1845-46:324-5. In the 1860s the value of these payments was routinely calculated in guilders (Graafland 1867-69, I:318), and by the 1920s cash had substantially replaced the old prestige goods (such as Indian textiles and brassware) as the medium of payment (Adam 1925b:445-6).
[60]   *Volkstelling* 1933-36, V:66. Gooszen (1999:145) shows that the combined average for North Sulawesi alone, 25.4%, was higher than that of any other area of comparable size in Indonesia.

have been typical. Wallace (1987:197) referred in 1859 to the 'universality of marriage' in Minahasa, and Edeling agreed that only 'a very small number' of Minahasans never married.[61] Unmarried people, moreover, were already 'relatively uncommon' in the Poso area before the Dutch conquest (Adriani and Kruyt 1912-14, II:11), and in Kulawi in 1918 there seemed to be 'no elderly bachelors or spinsters' even among the noble class (Kaudern 1940:48).

In accordance with a general Southeast Asian pattern (G.W. Jones 1994:187-8; Reid 1988-93, I:152-3), divorces were always frequent in most parts of the region.[62] Studies of Javanese women in the late twentieth century have shown that this can depress fertility by causing significant losses of 'potential reproductive time' (Hull and Hull 1977:52), and in 1902 a Bantik chief claimed that frequent divorce was among the reasons why the population of his part of Minahasa often did not increase from year to year. 'Once they are divorced', he complained (Mandagi 1914:64), 'many of them, especially men who are already over 35, remain single for a long period (in some cases for the rest of their lives)'. Other sources, however, imply, at least for men, serial marriages separated only by short intervals.[63] Frequent divorce, moreover, was not an ubiquitous pattern, and neither did the divorce rate always fall in the late colonial period of population growth.[64] Albert Kruyt (1938, III:139) noted that after the establishment of Dutch rule in western Central Sulawesi, the number of divorces rose due to the declining influence of the extended family, which had formerly helped to cement (arranged) marriages.

Royal polygamy has been suggested by Reid (1987:38-9) as another possible brake on the birth rate in precolonial Southeast Asia. In northern Sulawesi, polygamy may well have affected fertility on a small scale. 'To avoid frequent sexual intercourse', claimed Riedel (1886:79) in his description of the Toraja, 'many women encourage their husbands to take additional wives'. But while polygamous marriages were recorded in all parts of the

[61]   A.C.J. Edeling, 'Memorie omtrent de Minahasa', 13-8-1875 (NA V 17-4-1877/20).
[62]   AV Gorontalo 1841-1843 (ANRI Manado 50); NA VOC 1366:643, 650; Adriani and Kruyt 1912-14, I:344, II:34; Brilman 1938:51, 54; Cuarteron 1855:9, 23; Van Doren 1854-56, II:142; Van Eck 1882:972; F. Kelling, 'Het eiland Taghoelandang en zijn bewoners' [1866] (ARZ NZG 43.2); Graafland 1867-69, I:321, 1891:131-3; De Haan 1907:36; Hickson 1887:139, 1889:197, 281; Kortleven 1927:70; J. Kruyt 1937:197; Martens 1993:93; *Nota Toli-Toli* 1912:50; Pietermaat, De Vriese and Lucas 1840:118; L.J. van Rhijn 1851:346; Riedel 1870a:137; Robidé van der Aa 1867:242; J.J. ten Siethoff, 'Topografische schetsen van een gedeelte der residentie Menado, 1845' (ANRI Manado 46); Van Spreeuwenberg 1845-46:326; N.P. Wilken 1859:277; Wilken and Schwarz 1867c:319, 338; Woensdregt 1929a:279; *Zegeningen Gods* 1911:4-5.
[63]   Hickson (1887:139) wrote that in Sangir 'a rich man is constantly being married to different women and divorcing them again'. In 1866, Wilken and Schwarz (1867c:319, 338) met one prominent Bolaang Mongondow chief, reportedly aged 47, who had been divorced 10 times.
[64]   Van Dinter 1899:374; A.C. Kruyt 1938, II:138-9; *Nota berglandschappen* 1912:18; Riedel 1872a: 205; Stokking 1917:344; Wiersma 1876:97-8.

region, they were not particularly common, and did not usually involve large numbers of women.[65] Padtbrugge (1866:320), describing Minahasan customs in 1679, wrote that monogamy was the traditional rule, although 'various' men nevertheless had two wives. In the first part of the nineteenth century polygamy in Minahasa was restricted to a small number of high-ranking men, and no source mentions an individual with more than five wives.[66] In Banggai, traditionally, bigamy was unusual, 'a very few' men had three wives, and a single chief with twelve was remembered only in legend (A.C. Kruyt 1932b:32). On Talaud, the reported maximum was seven (Stokking 1917:347). Only nine of the 79 men included in a register of the noble families of Kulawi compiled by Kaudern (1940:45-7) were polygamous; of these the majority had two wives, and none more than four. In Bada in 1925 there were 25 polygamous men, only four of whom had more than two wives, out of a total population of about 5,000 (Woensdregt 1929a:283).

The highest rate of polygamy recorded for any part of the region at the 1930 census was found in the town of Gorontalo, where 6.7 percent of the adult male population was married to more than one woman.[67] Possibly more significant, in demographic terms, were the retinues of 'dancing girls' which traditionally attended the *raja* in some areas. On Tagulandang, for instance, a 'fairly large number' of young women were regularly selected from the *kampung* population to join this group, returning to their villages only 'when the bloom of their lives has been broken', as the missionary Kelling put it.[68] A similar custom was probably present in Gorontalo until the late nineteenth century (Tacco 1935:101; Von Rosenberg 1865, Plate 2.2), and may have survived up to the beginning of the twentieth in Tolitoli (Van Kol 1903:366).

Absence, abstinence, and amenorrhoea

Prolonged separation of married couples, according to Kruyt and Adriani, was yet another reason for the low birth rate in precolonial Central Sulawesi.[69]

---

[65]   Adriani and Kruyt 1912-14, II:31; Bosscher and Matthijssen 1854:75; Cuarteron 1855:9, 23; Van Hoëvell 1893b:26; F. Kelling, 'Het eiland Taghoelandang en zijn bewoners' [1866] (ARZ NZG 43.2); A.C. Kruyt 1930a:447-8, 1938, III:135; J. Kruyt 1924:91; De Leeuw 1937:369; Riedel 1870a:137, 1886:91; Van de Velde van Cappellen 1857:68. In many cases, moreover, the motive for taking a second wife was the infertility of the first (A.C. Kruyt 1930a:448; Woensdregt 1929a:283).
[66]   Van der Capellen 1855:362; Graafland 1867-9, I:288, 321, 1891:132; *Rapport* 1910:70; Reinwardt 1858:548; Riedel 1872b:506-7; Van Spreeuwenberg 1845-46:305.
[67]   *Volkstelling* 1933-36, V:71. For Gorontalo outside the town, the figure was 6.5%.
[68]   F. Kelling, 'Het eiland Taghoelandang en zijn bewoners' [1866] (ARZ NZG 43.2). Van Dinter (1899:349-50) and Frieswijck (1902:474) also mention this institution.

'The Toraja man', they observed, 'is naturally inclined to spend much time away from home [is van nature uithuizig]', frequently making long journeys in connection with trade and war (Adriani and Kruyt 1912-14, II:33). In Gorontalo and Bolaang Mongondow, as we have seen, similar patterns of seasonal male absence existed in connection with gold mining, and on Sangir in connection with the export of coconut oil to Manado and Ternate, which was undertaken mainly by Sangirese men themselves (Chapters I and II). Not all such absence was limited to the seasonal lull in the agricultural cycle: in 1908, Albert Kruyt (1909:378) reported that in Bada 'the number of women and girls far exceeds that of men', because 'many young men leave their land for years on end (and sometimes for good)'. Padoch (1982:93-4, 103-4) has identified the parallel custom of bejalai as a critical indirect fertility control among the Iban of Sarawak. Long-term male migration became more common on the mainland of northern Sulawesi after 1870 as a result of the growing trade in forest products (see Chapter VI); Adriani and Kruyt (1912-14, II:312) claimed that this had a 'very deleterious effect on the rate of population increase'.[70] Colonial taxation later provided an additional stimulus to seasonal migration, forcing taxpayers to earn the necessary cash by picking coconuts for coastal farmers or gathering damar and rattan.[71]

Among the Toraja there were a number of circumstances, mostly in connection with the agricultural calendar, under which sexual intercourse was prohibited for ritual reasons.[72] One reason for seasonal male emigration, in fact, was apparently that such a prohibition applied during the harvest period.[73] The periods in which intercourse was forbidden, however, seem to have been short. More importantly, there is no evidence from any part of the region for the practice of post-partum abstinence to which some authors (Alexander 1984; Santow 1987) have attributed great demographic significance in Java. This practice does exist among the Sa'dan Toraja of South Sulawesi (Hollan and Wellenkamp 1994:161, 246), and it remains possible that colonial observers in northern Sulawesi simply failed to detect or document it. The detail of

69   Adriani 1915:459-60, 465; Adriani and Kruyt 1912-14, I:88, II:312, 1950-51, I:77; A.C. Kruyt 1903b:204. It may also be worth noting in this context that in western Central Sulawesi there was some institutionalized homosexuality (Cummins 1962:109; A.C. Kruyt 1938, II:523, III:54-5).
70   A memorie van overgave from 1935 complains that the men of Kulawi are 'seldom at home, a large proportion of them wandering for years at a time in other divisions to collect rattan and damar, or to fell ebony trees' (Vorstman 1935a:14).
71   E. Gobée, 'Aanteekeningen naar aanleiding van een reis door de Possosche berglandschappen', 7-3-1926 (ARZ NZG 101A.7.2). Official policy, however, was to regulate the duration of these journeys, and ultimately to discourage them by providing alternative sources of income in the uplands (Adriani 1915:473; Adriani and Kruyt 1912-14, II:312; A.C. Kruyt 1924:46).
72   Adriani 1913b:861; Adriani and Kruyt 1950-51, II:270, 535, III:321; A.C. Kruyt 1938, IV:70, 73, 97, 107.
73   Adriani and Kruyt 1912-14, II:274, 1950-51, II:271; A.C. Kruyt 1938, IV:170.

the Central Sulawesi ethnographies, not least regarding matters of sexuality and childrearing, would nevertheless appear to make this unlikely.[74]

Many ethnographic descriptions, by contrast, mention prolonged lactation. In the seventeenth century, Padtbrugge (1866:327) already observed that Minahasan women 'breast-feed their children for long periods [*de kinderen laten zij lang zuigen*]'. Kelling noted in the 1860s that on Tagulandang a child 'usually continues to suckle until it is replaced by another', or otherwise until it was weaned at the age of three to four years.[75] Adriani and Kruyt later made similar observations in upland Central Sulawesi, and Woensdregt (1930:328) reported that in Bada a child 'usually continues to breast-feed from his mother until his fourth year, sometimes even until his sixth'.[76] A slave infant, on the other hand, was often quickly weaned by the wife of its master, who took it away from its own parents 'so that the child does not become too attached to its mother' (Adriani and Kruyt 1912-14, II:53). Particularly interesting is a statement that the influence of lactation on the likelihood of pregnancy was consciously recognized and exploited. Nursing Toraja mothers who had no desire for another baby, observed Adriani (1918: 381), 'continue to breast-feed their child for as long as possible', believing 'that they will not become pregnant again as long as they still have a child which is not yet weaned'.

The relative importance of the contraceptive effect of breast-feeding, compared with that of the sexual abstinence which accompanies it in certain traditional cultures, has sometimes been questioned (Santow 1987). The existence of a direct and strong physiological effect, caused by hormones which suppress ovulation and which are released as a response to frequent suckling, is nevertheless certain (Bongaarts and Potter 1983:24-8). Medical experts have concluded that in man as in other mammals, 'lactation serves two equally important functions: nutrition and spacing out birth intervals'.[77] Uniquely among the documented fertility-suppressing factors, moreover, it can be shown that this

---

[74] Padoch (1982:98), likewise, found no evidence for such a custom among the Iban.

[75] F. Kelling, 'Het eiland Taghoelandang en zijn bewoners' [1866] (ARZ NZG 43.2).

[76] Adriani and Kruyt 1912-14, II:53, 1950-51, II:390; A.C. Kruyt 1938, III:265-6.

[77] Delvoye et al. 1978:213. A recent study from Guatemala indicates that even if all other variables remain unchanged, the lifetime fertility of a woman who weans her children after six months will be 48 percent higher than that of one who breast-feeds for 18 months, and that of a woman who practices 'total weaning' fully 96 percent higher; the effect of variations in the frequency of lactation is also significant (Aguirre, Palloni and Jones 1998:245). Osamu Saito (1996:546), surveying the state of the art in European historical demography, concludes that 'breastfeeding, and the period of post partum infecundability that resulted from such breastfeeding practices can explain much of the observed differences in marital fertility in the European regions'. Under 'favourable conditions', according to Harris and Ross (1987:8), 'lactational practices can result in birth spacing intervals of three or more years with a degree of reliability comparable to modern mechanical and chemical contraceptives'.

one definitely became less effective in at least one part of northern Sulawesi during a period of rising birth rates and population growth.

Labour demand, breast-feeding, and fertility

Throughout much of the nineteenth century, the population of Minahasa was obliged by the colonial government to perform a fearsome array of compulsory labour services. Edeling, in his compendious *Memorie omtrent de Minahasa*, provides a description of this labour burden as it stood in 1874. Except for government officials and certain other exempted individuals, every male adult was required to perform unpaid *herendiensten* (corvée labour).[78] *Herendienst* labour was used in the first place to maintain Minahasa's extensive transport infrastructure, comprising over 1,000 kilometres of roads and more than 400 bridges. This alone took up to 60 days of work per head of the liable population each year; in 1868 a *controleur* even claimed that in the Tondano area, the repair of major roads following any particularly rainy wet season 'demands all the energy of the whole male population for months on end', so that more than once the inhabitants had been left with 'too little time to work their ricefields properly' (Edeling 1919:73-4). Another 17 days per head per year, on average, were spent on personal labour services for local officials, and an uncertain additional number on various kinds of guard and messenger duty.

Even more time-consuming for most Minahasans, however, was the burden of compulsory coffee cultivation. For Minahasa as a whole this involved an average of about 65 days' work per household per year, not including another 15 days for the shelling and preparation of the coffee beans. On the central plateau around Tomohon and Tondano, where coffee grew particularly well, the average was as high as 114 days. Because Edeling gives a breakdown of the number of days per year spent on coffee cultivation in each district, his study makes it possible to investigate the relationship between compulsory labour on the one hand, and fertility, as indicated by his parallel investigation into the numbers of children ever-born into Minahasan households (Appendix E), on the other. When the two variables are plotted against each other for all districts for which both fertility and coffee labour figures are available (Figure 9), a striking positive association is revealed.[79] Those districts subject to the greatest burden of compulsory coffee cultivation also

[78]　Corvée labourers in Minahasa, unlike some of their counterparts on Java (Boomgaard 1989a:38), received no remuneration for their work, although they were sometimes provided with food.
[79]　For many districts, unfortunately, Edeling gives no fertility data.

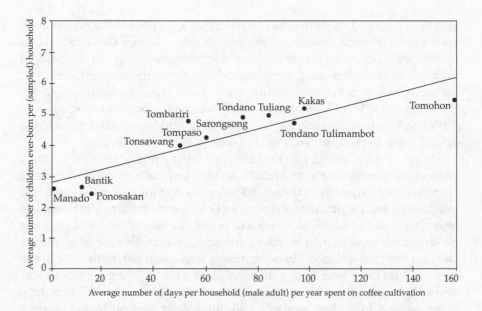

Figure 9. Female fertility and the labour burden of compulsory coffee cultivation in some Minahasan districts, 1874. Source: A.C.J. Edeling, 'Memorie omtrent de Minahassa', 13-8-1875 (NA V 17-4-1877/20).

tended to be those in which women, on average, had borne the greatest number of children. The statistical strength of this correlation means that there is virtually no chance that it is accidental.[80]

A substantial part of the compulsory labour burden was borne, directly or indirectly, by women.[81] In 1846 it was reported that because the number of men was 'insufficient for the labour which is required of them', women (and children) not only did most of the work in the swidden fields, but were

[80] The regression line shown carries an R^2 value of 0.78, and a (non-parametric) Spearman rank correlation test on the same data produces an r_s coefficient of + 0.90, which for this sample size is significant at the one percent level. A potential objection here is that the coastal districts of Manado, Ponosakan and Bantik, which grew very little coffee, were also rather different from the others in both environmental and cultural terms, so that their populations might have shown lower fertility for unconnected reasons (endemic malaria, for instance, or traditional behavioural patterns associated with paganism which were no longer present on the Christianized plateau). But even when these three districts are excluded from the analysis, the positive correlation is still strong for the upland districts alone ($R^2 = 0.61$, $r_s = + 0.81$).

[81] Bierens de Haan 1893:71-2; Edeling 1919:55; *Fragment* 1856:23; Graafland 1867-69, II:87, 1898, II:249-50; Pietermaat, De Vriese and Lucas 1840:148; Schouten 1998:68, 70; J.J. ten Siethoff, 'Topografische schetsen van een gedeelte der residentie Menado, 1845' (ANRI Manado 46); Tendeloo 1873:15; L. Wessels 1891:145.

also to be seen picking coffee and carrying rice and coffee to the government warehouses (Francis 1860:282, 349, 360). Resident Jansen (1861:230) stated in 1853 that women were themselves doing 'the greater part' of the work in the government coffee plantations, and admitted that their overall workload, including their part in foodcrop cultivation, was 'excessive'. Edeling (1919:55, 72) found in 1874 that Minahasan women 'must still work hard from dawn to dusk', and that on occasion they had probably also been forced, against the official rules, to perform *herendienst* as well as cultivation duties.[82]

Despite Paul Alexander's (1986:259) pessimistic prediction that 'archival research is most unlikely to unearth accounts of such esoteric matters as changes in the frequency of breastfeeding', a few historical sources do seem to provide just such information in the case of nineteenth-century Minahasa. The heavy workload of Minahasan women, noted Edeling in his *memorie*, 'must be one of the reasons why mothers do not have enough time to give their children their natural food'. Instead, infants were often left 'in the care of old women, who must feed them with bananas and rice'.[83] The government surveyor De Lange, after a visit to Minahasa in 1852, claimed that children there 'were weaned from their mothers' milk three days after birth, and brought up on rice, which was normally chewed for them first by old women'.[84] Early supplementary feeding with premasticated vegetable foods was also noted by several other observers.[85] Besides reflecting the fact that mothers had too little time to attend to their children, Edeling believed, this was also necessary because Minahasan women, again due to their arduous workload, produced inadequate quantities of breast milk. All of these observations are in clear contrast with Padtbrugge's statement, some two centuries earlier, that women in Minahasa breast-fed their children for 'long periods'.

There is, admittedly, some reason to be sceptical of the implication that the nineteenth-century situation reflected a radical departure from precolonial conditions. Subsistence agriculture in Minahasa, as elsewhere, had always involved much female labour (Bik 1864:169; Padtbrugge 1866: 324). Adriani and Kruyt (1912-14, II:52) heard 'very many complaints from nursing mothers about insufficient milk' in Central Sulawesi at the turn of the century, and supplementary feeding of infants with semi-solid foods also seems to have been a widespread practice.[86] There is much less cause

---

82   Also Graafland 1898, II:250; Tendeloo 1873:15.
83   A.C.J. Edeling, 'Memorie omtrent de Minahasa', 13-8-1875 (NA V 17-4-1877/20).
84   De Clercq 1891:219. A similar, but less precise, statement is found in the original report by the same official (De Lange 1897:686). Edeling, likewise, stated that feeding with chewed rice and bananas began 'within a few days of birth' ('Memorie omtrent de Minahasa', 13-8-1875, in NA V 17-4-1877/20).
85   AV Manado 1853 (ANRI Manado 51); *Fragment* 1856:23; Graafland 1867-69, I:174-5.
86   Van Dinter 1899:369; Frieswijck 1902:484; A.C. Kruyt 1932b:52; Woensdregt 1930:328.

to doubt, however, that the female labour burden in Minahasa increased greatly during the nineteenth century as a result of compulsory cultivation and other services.[87] When this observation is combined with the fragmentary direct evidence for reduced breast-feeding, and the good statistical evidence for a link between fertility and the size of the labour burden, there are clearly strong grounds for concluding that labour demand, via the medium of reduced lactational amenorrhoea and the associated shortening of the interval between successive births, was partly responsible for the population growth observed in that period. A late nineteenth-century account of the traditional customs (*alte Gebräuche*) of one Minahasan subgroup, the Tombulu, states that breast-feeding 'usually lasts one whole agricultural year [*ein ganzes Erntejahr*]', implying that this, already a short period by regional standards, is long in contemporary Minahasan terms (Riedel 1895a:99).

The interpretation of rising fertility sketched here is at odds with the common belief, inspired partly by colonial writers like Wallace (1987:70), that arduous female labour, because it tended to reduce women's reproductive fitness, was among the factors responsible for low fertility among traditional swidden cultivators in Indonesia (Alexander and Alexander 1993:264; Reid 1987:39-40). Albert Kruyt (1938, III:133) observed that Toraja women were 'quickly withered' as a result of their frequent work in the fields, and claimed, in a passage strongly reminiscent of Wallace, that birth rates were higher in coastal Mapane than in upland areas because 'women are more respected by the Muslims than by the unconverted Toraja, among whom they have to work hard' (A.C. Kruyt 1903b:198). An error in the analysis of his data, however, allowed him to exaggerate the demographic contrast; the real average completed fertility rate in Mapane (Table 21), at 3.82 children per woman, was lower than that found among the larger of the two upland groups included in his own survey, the To Pebato (4.03).[88] In so far as a systematic association did exist between 'domesticity' and fertility, moreover, it does not necessarily have to be explained in terms of infecundity, early menopause, or frequent miscarriages among swidden-farming women; a loss of female decision-making autonomy, or a reduction in deliberate birth control in response to greater freedom from agricultural tasks, could equally have been involved.

While some sources from northern Sulawesi state that pagan women had to work hard even during pregnancy (Adriani and Kruyt 1912-14, II:43; Woensdregt 1929b:356), others explicitly contradict this.[89] The evidence from

[87]   To some extent this must have been compensated by a concurrent decline in female handicraft activities (see Chapter XV); weaving and potting, however, were less arduous than agricultural work, and presumably interfered less with breast feeding.

[88]   The editors of Kruyt's demographic article pointed out this error in a footnote (A.C. Kruyt 1903b:197).

[89]   In order 'not to cause a miscarriage', pregnant women among the To Wana were reportedly for-

other regions for workloads heavy enough to have physiological consequences affecting fertility is likewise inconclusive: Padoch (1982:100), while
noting that Iban women worked hard, also observed that 'except for elderly
ones, few women appeared to be or complained of being exhausted'.[90] In
northern Sulawesi, the traditional economy probably ticked over at a relaxed
enough rate to provide even women with much free time (see Chapter XV).
There is, of course, a distinction between time-consuming and physically
demanding work: Alexander and Alexander (1993:264, 267) ascribe low birth
rates in rural Sarawak partly to 'the very hard physical labour demanded of
women in the fields', yet also report that lactation traditionally continued
for three to four years, and that 'at least in some cases, mothers of young
children did not work in the fields during breastfeeding'. The relationship
between fertility and the female labour burden was undoubtedly complex,
and conclusions drawn from one area and period cannot necessarily be
generalized. The evidence from nineteenth-century Minahasa, nevertheless,
is clear: the longer (if not necessarily the harder) women worked, the more
children they had, not the fewer.

Other interpretations of the link between labour demand and fertility

Reduced breast-feeding, as a direct consequence of heavy female workloads,
is not the only possible explanation for the observed association between
fertility and the demand for labour in Minahasa. Another is that the labour
burden affected the birth rate only indirectly, via the infant death rate. Both
because lactational amenorrhoea automatically ceases, with suckling, when
an infant dies, and because of deliberate 'child replacement' effects of various kinds, a positive correlation between the birth rate and the rate of infant
mortality is a common feature of vital rate statistics (Santow and Bracher
1984). Edeling (1919:72-3), moreover, believed that the infant death rate was
highest in those Minahasan districts where the compulsory labour burden
was heaviest, and where parents consequently had least time to care for
their children.[91] A look at his own statistics, however, shows that at least as

---

bidden to carry loads on their backs (A.C. Kruyt 1930b:573); on Talaud they were 'not permitted to
walk to far, or to perform excessively heavy work' (Stokking 1919:220); and in Minahasa, according to Riedel (1895a:96), they had traditionally been prevented from 'carrying anything heavy'.
[90]   See also Gooszen 1999:149; Knapen 2001:132.
[91]   Other sources from the same period also attribute high infant mortality in Minahasa partly
to the heavy compulsory labour burden (AV Manado 1853, in ANRI Manado 51; Bierens de
Haan 1893:72-3; *Fragment* 1856:22-3; Graafland 1867-69, I:176; A.J.F. Jansen 1861:230; Wallace
1987:197).

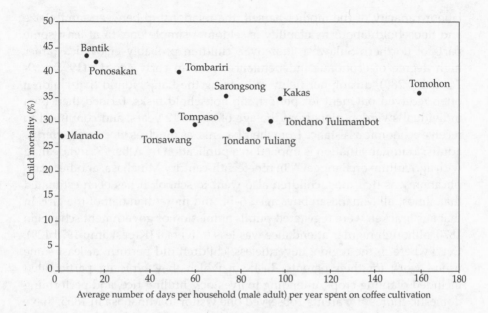

Figure 10. Child mortality and the labour burden of compulsory coffee cultivation in some Minahasan districts, 1874. Source: A.C.J. Edeling, 'Memorie omtrent de Minahassa', 13-8-1875 (NA V 17-4-1877/20).

far as coffee cultivation was concerned, this was not actually the case (Figure 10).[92]

A third possibility is that women consciously regulated their fertility according to the anticipated value of their children's labour. This kind of economic calculation forms part of the argument constructed by Kruyt and Adriani regarding the role of slavery as an indirect cause of abortion and infanticide.

> Now of course there are many To Lage women who greet the birth of a child with happiness, and Pebato women, conversely, who anticipate such an event with displeasure. But children are worth their weight in gold to the Pebato woman because later they will form her labour force, fetching water for her, cooking the rice from an early age, and, above all, quickly learning to use the rice stamper. For the To Lage woman children do not have the same great value, because after all, she already has her slaves! For this reason she is free to indulge her desire for an easy life by destroying her children, born or unborn. (A.C. Kruyt 1911:91.)

If only because frequent pregnancy and childbirth necessarily reduce the

[92] R^2 (regression line not shown) = 0.03.

labour capacity of the mother herself, the relationship between family size and household labour availability is seldom a simple one. In at least some parts of northern Sulawesi, moreover, children probably enjoyed a rather high degree of economic independence from an early age. Li (1996a:269-74, 266-7, 280), during her fieldwork among the Lauje, found that children often received payment for performing household tasks, farmed their own individual swidden plots from the age of about 12 years, and continued to receive economic assistance from their parents, as much as vice versa, even as adults; a similar situation is implied in a publication by Albert Kruyt dealing with agriculture on Banggai.[93] In nineteenth-century Minahasa, another complication was that most children also went to school; it has been estimated that almost all Minahasan boys aged 6-14, and more than half of the girls in that age bracket, were registered pupils at mission or government schools in 1870, although regular attendance was less universal (Kroeskamp 1974:129). Everywhere in the region, nevertheless, children did perform at least some useful work for their parents. Tasks in which they typically participated included planting crops, attending to livestock, hulling rice, and performing domestic chores.[94] 'Parents', observed one visitor to Minahasa in 1855, 'have much use for their children, even at quite young ages, both in the fields and for household work, and this is the primary reason why the children do not attend school as reguarly as one might desire'.[95]

Minahasan children, like their mothers, were also directly involved in compulsory coffee cultivation, and sometimes even in *herendienst* labour. Both duties, at least by the late nineteenth century, were technically incumbent upon every adult male rather than each household unit, but children and teenagers often substituted for their fathers, so that a motive for increasing the supply of labour within the household clearly existed.[96] An additional motivation was created by the tax of five guilders per household which was imposed

---

[93]   A.C. Kruyt 1932d:477. Children on Banggai likewise had their own swidden fields, distinct from those of their parents, although the age of the children concerned is not clear from this source.

[94]   NA VOC 1366:653; Adriani and Kruyt 1912-14, II:76-7, 170, 250, 253; Aragon 1992:77; Van Eck 1882:961; A.C.J. Edeling, 'Memorie omtrent de Minahasa', 13-8-1875 (NA V 17-4-1877/20); *Fragment* 1856:31; Graafland 1867-69, I:60, 161, 176, 288, II:51-2, 102; A.C. Kruyt 1911:84, 1938, I: 84, III:191, IV:72; J. Kruyt 1937:202; Padtbrugge 1866:324, 327; Riedel 1870a:130, 143, 1872:494-5; J.J. ten Siethoff, 'Topografische schetsen van een gedeelte der residentie Menado, 1845' (ANRI Manado 46); Stokking 1922:247; Tendeloo 1873:12, 14; Van Wely 1707.

[95]   Quarles van Ufford 1856:14. Graafland (1867-69, I:60) notes that schoolchildren were given several days' holiday at harvest time in order to help their parents bring in the rice.

[96]   Edeling 1919:55; Francis 1860:282, 360; Graafland 1867-69, I:81, 176; Schouten 1998:68; Wessels 1891:145. In the 1840s, according to the military officer Ten Siethoff, children began working in the coffee plantations at the age of 10 ('Topografische schetsen van een gedeelte der residentie Menado, 1845', in ANRI Manado 46).

on the Minahasan population in 1852.[97] In principle this simply replaced the compulsory rice trade through which Minahasans had already been making a less direct contribution to government coffers since VOC times, but in practice the new tax seems to have been more onerous.[98] In 1902 the visiting Dutch parliamentarian Van Kol (1903:264) estimated that for many poorer Minahasans, it represented 'ten to twenty percent of their annual income'.

Whether this undoubted increase in labour demand really led to a deliberate relaxation of fertility controls, on the other hand, cannot be ascertained directly. Edeling, in 1875, certainly claimed that the typical Minahasan woman was 'very keen on having a large family, and therefore makes no use of the means of avoiding this which are practised among other peoples'.[99] As we have seen, however, he was contradicted in the same period both by the *controleur* De Clercq, who thought that abortion and infanticide were common, and by the missionary Graafland, who wrote that Minahasan fathers (if not mothers) saw no more advantage in a very large family than in a very small one. The remarkable precision of the correlation between fertility rates and the size of the coffee labour burden also seems to tell against this version of the labour-demand theory. Even in the unlikely case that the rate of birth control was determined solely by economic considerations, it is hard to imagine that mothers could predict their future household labour needs with the kind of accuracy indicated by the Edeling data; an automatic, unconscious mechanism like reduced breast-feeding would seem better capable of accounting for such a close relationship. Given that infant mortality would presumably have been taken into account in any conscious calculation of the costs and benefits of childbearing, it is perhaps also significant that the correlation between actual household size (numbers of surviving children) and the coffee labour burden (Figure 11), while still good, is not quite as good as that obtained using the total numbers of ever-born children.[100] It remains plausible, nevertheless, that the pattern revealed by the Edeling survey reflects a combination of conscious and unconscious responses to (respectively, child and female) labour demand.

A fourth possible way of interpreting the correlation between compulsory cultivation services and fertility is to follow Boomgaard (1989a:197) in assuming that it was the income generated by these services, rather than the labour they demanded, which was the operative factor. By providing 'new economic

97   AV Manado 1852 (ANRI Manado 51). This later became a head tax paid by all male adults (Graafland 1898, I:165-6, II:248).
98   Graafland 1867-69, I:61, II:196; 1898, II:248. Edeling, however, thought that it took 'only a few days' for a taxpayer to earn the necessary sum ('Memorie omtrent de Minahasa', 13-8-1875, in NA V 17-4-1877/20).
99   A.C.J. Edeling, 'Memorie omtrent de Minahasa', 13-8-1875 (NA V 17-4-1877/20).
100    $R^2 = 0.73$.

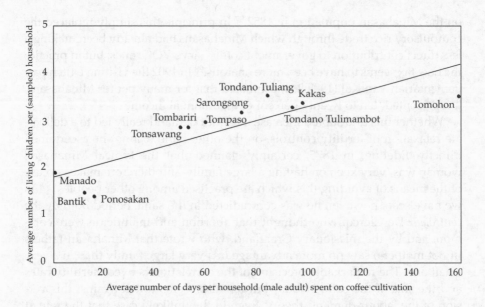

Figure 11. Household size and the labour burden of compulsory coffee cultivation in some Minahasan districts, 1874. Source: A.C.J. Edeling, 'Memorie omtrent de Minahassa', 13-8-1875 (NA V 17-4-1877/20).

opportunities', compulsory cultivation made large families either more attractive or more feasible for women who would otherwise have practised one or other form of conscious birth control; by allowing people to marry younger, the additional income also served to relax one type of unconscious fertility check. The data collected by Edeling, however, do not in themselves support this hypothesis. Compulsory coffee cultivation in Minahasa, unlike *herendienst* labour, was certainly remunerated, and as in Java it did also generate some auxiliary non-agricultural employment opportunities, particularly in the transport sector (see Chapter IX). The income earned from coffee cultivation, on the other hand, was not proportional to the time spent on it, and when average coffee earnings in the years 1873-1874 are plotted against the results of the fertility survey for all districts for which both figures are available (Figure 12), no significant correlation emerges.[101] Since coffee sales were not the only source of income in an increasingly commercialized local economy, this result does not necessarily contradict the argument that economic growth, by facilitating earlier marriage, had a broadly positive effect on the birth rate. Nevertheless, it is unlikely that a more complete income analysis

[101] R^2 (downward-sloping regression line not shown) = 0.09.

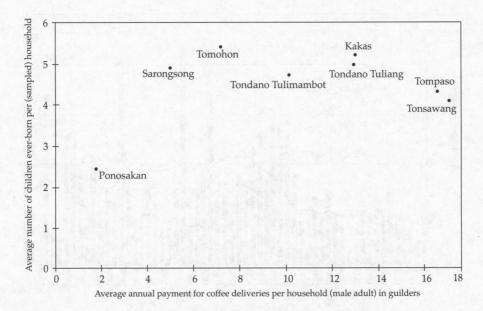

Figure 12. Female fertility and income from compulsory coffee cultivation in some Minahasan districts, 1873-1874. Source: A.C.J. Edeling, 'Memorie omtrent de Minahassa', 13-8-1875 (NA V 17-4-1877/20).

could provide a more satisfactory explanation than labour demand for the specific local variations in fertility revealed by the Edeling survey.

Labour demand and population growth in wider perspective

The chronological development of the state-imposed labour burden in Minahasa accords reasonably well with the hypothesis that fertility rates rose in the middle of the nineteenth century as a direct response to increased labour demand. Although compulsory coffee cultivation began in 1822, production rose quite dramatically after 1850 (Figure 13).[102] Roadbuilding, too, peaked in the 1850s and 1860s, which were probably the time of heaviest forced labour for the Minahasan population.[103] Graafland (1867-69, II:213)

---

[102] A 10-year moving average has been supplied in order to reveal the general trend of coffee production. Harvests of *Arabica* coffee, in Minahasa as elsewhere, fluctuated strongly according to a repetitive cycle of approximately 4 years (Paerels 1949:100).

[103] In the early nineteenth century the 'roads' of Minahasa, while exceptionally good by regional standards, still consisted almost exclusively of narrow bridle paths (AV Manado 1833,

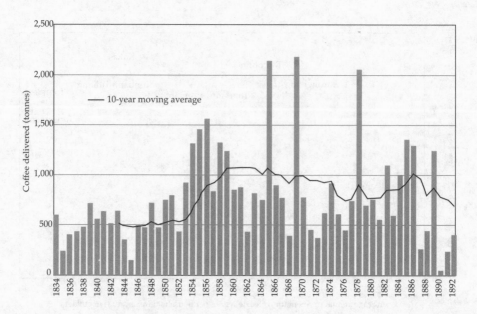

Figure 13. Compulsory coffee cultivation in Minahasa, 1834-1892 (Schouten 1995a:22)

wrote in the 1860s that in most districts 'people spend at least half of their time working on the roads or in the coffee gardens', and was later to refer to the labour burden in this period as 'extreme, degrading, and deeply unjust' (Graafland 1898, II:249). Over the next three decades, nevertheless, the pressure was only slightly relaxed.[104] In 1890 the average total compulsory labour requirement was still estimated at 155 days per liable man, including 30 days spent on main road maintenance (the *herendiensten* proper), 40 on 'village' roadworks and personal services to village headmen, and fully 85 days – no fewer than in 1874 – on coffee cultivation.[105]

---

in ANRI Manado 48). Resident Wenzel wrote in 1825 that although these were well maintained by the local population, the work involved 'cannot be regarded as heavy' (Riedel 1872b:478). The construction of wider roads suitable for carts drawn by horses or oxen began in the 1840s (AV Manado 1849, in ANRI Manado 51; Francis 1860:371-2; Schouten 1998:64; J.J. ten Siethoff, 'Topografische schetsen van een gedeelte der residentie Menado, 1845', in ANRI Manado 46).

[104]   The most important change was that after 1860, progressively fewer new roads were built (Van der Crab 1875:152; A.C.J. Edeling, 'Memorie omtrent de Minahasa,' 13-8-1875, in NA V 17-4-1877-20; Graafland 1867-69, I:75); by 1890, *herendienst* work on the transport net was mostly limited to maintenance and improvement (Stakman 1893:139-40).

[105]   Stakman 1892:728-9. Also Bierens de Haan 1893:72; Graafland 1898, II:249. In 1892, moreover, the government commissioner Gallois (1892:11) concluded that 'more or less significant deviations' from the official *herendienst* limit of 36 days per year were occurring 'almost everywhere', so that the real burden was even heavier.

At the end of the nineteenth century, however, came rapid change. After 1892, most importantly, coffee production in Minahasa all but ceased in anticipation of the formal abolition of compulsory cultivation, which eventually came in 1899 (Schouten 1995a:6, 1998:63). The *herendienst* limit was also reduced, and its enforcement improved, in 1899, while a year later new restrictions were placed upon the extent of village labour services (Van Kol 1903:254-5, 257, 259). By the beginning of the 1920s the actual corvée burden (not including village services) was thought to average around 20 days per year (Logeman 1922:128). In 1925, compulsory labour on the roads was replaced by a new transport tax of between *f* 5 and *f* 6 (Brouwer 1936:112). Meanwhile the old *f* 5 head tax, thanks to increasing prosperity among the Minahasan population, gradually became lighter in relation to the available resources.[106] In 1921, finally, a new income tax system was introduced in which all persons whose earnings were equivalent to less than *f* 120 per year – almost 20 times the amount of the former head tax – were exempt from any payment.[107] A report from 1932 describes taxation in Minahasa as 'exceptionally light' (*Verslag* 1932:2).

Whatever kept Minahasan birth rates high in the early twentieth century, then, it was not the labour burden imposed by compulsory services or taxation. The Draconian forced labour regime of late nineteenth-century Minahasa, moreover, had no parallel elsewhere in the region, yet at least one other area, Sangir, where no compulsory cultivation existed and where the government head tax did not exceed *f* 2.50 until 1905 (Encyclopaedisch Bureau 1912a:38), also saw sustained population growth during the same period. Nor can heavy female labour help to account for the high completed fertility rates reported by Riedel (1870a:136, 138) from Gorontalo, where noble women reportedly lived in 'permanent inactivity' and even the wives of 'ordinary natives' were said to perform 'no regular work' outside the home (Riedel 1870a:70, 130). The demographic significance of changes in breast-feeding practices, on this evidence, would appear to be limited to one particular geographical and historical context.

There is, however, some indication that a more widespread reduction in the duration of breast-feeding took place in the region toward the end of the colonial period. On Sangir in the late 1940s, according to Blankhart (1951:96),

---

[106] By 1912 it was thought to be equivalent to one tenth of 'the usual income of the villager' in the poorest villages of the Tondano area, itself by this stage one of the poorest parts of Minahasa (Dirkzwager 1912:1171).

[107] Logeman 1922:127. In 1930, just over 30% of the adult male population of Minahasa fell below this minimum income assessment and paid no tax (Henley 1996:104). The total tax assessment for Minahasa remained at approximately the same level as prior to the introduction of the new system, but the burden was now more fairly distributed, and incomes continued to rise. In 1913 as much as 54% of the assessed sum could not be collected, but in 1924 only 2% (Eibergen 1928:237).

'hardly a single child' was weaned before reaching the age of one year, but only 55 percent of children continued to be given breast milk thereafter. Leaving aside the improbability of the claim that so much weaning occurred precisely at the age of twelve months, this pattern clearly differs markedly from that observed 80 years earlier by Kelling, when breast-feeding, unless interrupted by the birth of another child, continued for 'three to four years'.[108]

In the 1950s, comparably, Minahasan women typically breast-fed their children for a period of two years at most, and the contraceptive effect of breastfeeding appeared largely forgotten.[109] In this case, a kind of habituation to the pattern of curtailed breast-feeding necessitated by nineteenth-century conditions may help to explain why the reversion to traditional practices was incomplete. Another possibility is that labour demand continued to affect breast-feeding practices even though this was now maintained by economic incentives rather than by political compulsion. Although the most important single commercial activity of the period 1900-1930, copra production, was not regarded as a labour-intensive activity, it still demanded (for a typical smallholder household coconut plantation of 1.4 hectare) an annual labour expenditure of 40-80 person-days per year.[110] An increase in the labour intensity of foodcrop agriculture (see Chapter XV) may also have played a role in maintaining labour demand, as may increasing participation by women in trade (Van Marle 1922, I:60). But cultural changes, such as an increased reluctance to bear the breast in public, were possibly also important here.

Conclusion

Marked differences in reproductive fertility existed between the populations of different parts of northern Sulawesi in the early twentieth century. The completed fertility rates of women in Central Sulawesi, on average, were much lower than those of their Minahasan counterparts. The birth rate in Minahasa, moreover, had risen significantly in the middle of the nineteenth

---

[108]   F. Kelling, 'Het eiland Taghoelandang en zijn bewoners' [1866] (ARZ NZG 43.2).

[109]   Dr J.J. Barten, interview, 30-10-1994. More recently, however, the Minahasan anthropologist Renwarin (2000:143) reports that Minahasan children are usually breast-fed for 'at least two years'. The contraceptive effect of breast-feeding, it must also be added, diminishes in any case after a period of one year, and only in about 20% of nursing mothers does amenorrhoea persist beyond 2 years (Delvoye et al. 1978:223).

[110]   Departement van Landbouw, Nijverheid en Handel 1925:24-5. This figure, moreover, does not include the harvesting or transport of the nuts, tasks usually carried out in Minahasa by hired immigrant workers. It is not clear how much specifically female labour was typically involved. On Sangir before the copra boom, both men and women had participated in the manufacture of coconut oil (Van Delden 1844:380; *Generale missiven* IX:530). On Selayar in South Sulawesi, women provided much of the labour involved in copra production (Heersink 1999:174).

century, contributing almost as much as falling mortality to the population growth which took place there in the period 1860-1930. Fertility rates in Central Sulawesi also seem to have risen between 1902 and 1924, although in this case the effects were initially counterbalanced by higher mortality (Chapters VI and VII). While the part played by fertility change in other episodes of demographic growth cannot be demonstrated, it was probably important. Many demographers, while continuing to debate the causal processes involved, believe that a rise in fertility is 'a common, and perhaps universal, feature of incipient modernization' (H. Jones 1990:135).

Abortion and infanticide, although missionary authors may sometimes have exaggerated their frequency, were always widespread practices in northern Sulawesi, and at least one method of contraception, retroflexion of the uterus, was also available in some areas. Deliberate sexual abstinence, at least on the part of women, is also recorded as a means of fertility control: a Toraja woman, according to Adriani and Kruyt (1912-14, II:6), sometimes had 'no objection' to her husband indulging in extramarital sex, 'for instance, if she does not wish to become pregnant again at short notice'. As far as this region is concerned, then, there is clearly every reason to follow Harris and Ross (1987: 1) in rejecting the view that demographic patterns in premodern societies reflected 'a culturally unregulated surrender to sex, hunger, and death'.

From here, however, it is still a big step to the more radical conclusion reached in colonial times by Lucieer (1924), and reiterated by some more recent authors (Boomgaard 1989a:197; White 1976:14-5, 42-3), that because fertility was always the object of active manipulation, mortality (or at least, infant and child mortality) is more or less irrelevant to the analysis of population growth in Indonesia. No improvement in health or hygiene, according to this voluntaristic argument, could in itself have caused such growth on a sustained basis, since in the absence of an increase in the parental demand for children, any reduction in mortality would simply have been cancelled out by the application of existing fertility controls 'to a correspondingly greater degree'.[111] In reality, variations in the age at marriage, the extent of male absence, and the duration and intensity of breast-feeding, none of which bore any necessary relation to conscious family planning decisions, were probably at least as important as deliberate birth control in determining fertility rates. Much abortion, moreover, was practised in order to terminate socially illegitimate pregnancies rather than to regulate marital fertility, and the means of doing either were in any case unreliable.

---

[111]   Lucieer 1924:555. 'Given the fact that Javanese women were able to manipulate their fertility', reasons Boomgaard (1989a:197) along the same lines with reference to the nineteenth-century population boom on Java, 'it must be assumed that a higher number of surviving children was accepted consciously'.

Some demographers go so far as to doubt whether 'parity-specific' fertility control (the regulation of household size as opposed to birth intervals) was ever common in 'traditional' societies, and therefore whether the (long-term) 'costs and benefits' of children were relevant to the demographic behaviour of such societies at all.[112] The most reasonable conclusion on the basis of the data from northern Sulawesi, however, is that both conscious and unconscious processes affected the birth rate, and that decisions regarding desired numbers of children were sometimes important, but not necessarily to a decisive or overriding extent. Factors limiting the demand for children, in the historically typical situation of relatively low fertility, probably included slavery, the existence of large corporate kin groups, female autonomy (which fostered both aversity to childbearing and childraising, and the power to translate this into actual birth control), and a generally low level of economic activity (which limited the need for child labour).[113] The ambiguity of the statistical evidence for the specific effects of slavery and female autonomy does not mean that these can be discounted, since many other cross-cutting influences were also at work.

Given the strong association between female labour and high fertility in nineteenth-century Minahasa, and the evidence that this was related to reductions in lactational amenhorrhoea, a certain amount of female leisure must have been conducive to the maintenance of low fertility in so far as it facilitated long and intensive breast-feeding. A central aspect of traditional female autonomy, nevertheless, was involvement in agriculture, which in itself probably tended to favour the deliberate avoidance of frequent pregnancy; the highly leisured but highly dependent women of Muslim trading and farming groups, by contrast, had less reason, and probably also less authority, to limit their fertility. Other factors favouring low fertility in the traditional situation included frequent male absence, which was related to matrilocal marriage and the existence of large matrifocal kin groups (see Chapter I). In Minahasa and Sangir there was also a pattern of delayed marriage, probably maintained by high bride prices and a relative scarcity of farmland. If only because of the bride price and the costs of marriage festivities, but possibly also in connection with conscious family planning decisions, it is likely that a more general correlation existed between levels of nuptuality and economic prosperity.

---

[112] Cleland and Wilson 1987:27; Harris and Ross 1987:13-4; Robinson 1997:70.
[113] Onerous pregnancy taboos were possibly another factor here. Throughout the region, traditionally, pregnant women (and to some extent also their husbands) were expected to observe a large number of prohibitions, often including bans on the consumption of certain animal foods (A.C. Kruyt 1933b:66; Riedel 1886:91; Stokking 1919:220-1; Woensdregt 1929b:355). It is not clear, however, whether the force of these taboos was reduced as a result of subsequent cultural change; many certainly still existed in Minahasa in the 1920s (Adam 1925b:460-1).

Reid (1988-93, I:17, 2001:56) has argued that endemic warfare provided a strong incentive for women to limit their fertility, since 'the need to be constantly ready for flight' made it useful to delay further births 'until older children were able to run by themselves'.[114] While this logic is intuitively applicable to the situation of many groups in Sulawesi, it is striking that Albert Kruyt (1903b:199-202), in his extensive discussion of birth control among the headhunting Toraja, made no mention of war or the need for mobility as a motive for birth control. Kruyt, moreover, disapproved of war at least as strongly as he disapproved of slavery, a factor which he did portray as an important indirect cause of frequent abortion. Nor did endemic warfare preclude the use of child or female labour in agriculture, as Knapen (2001:394-5) proposes. Polygamy, divorce, and the direct physiological effects of female labour likewise appear to have been relatively unimportant in terms of their effects on fertility. Some diseases, particularly malaria, probably played a role in depressing birth rates, but it should be noted that venereal disease, in stark contrast to the situation in some other parts of the world (H. Jones 1990:138), was virtually absent among the pagan, upland populations which were the least fertile (see Chapter VII). It seems unlikely, finally, that food shortages or poor nutrition had much direct effect on the birth rate. Recent comparative studies indicate that except in cases of acute starvation, female fecundity is only slightly influenced by malnutrition.[115] Subsistence crises, on the other hand, no doubt did lead to temporary reductions in the number of marriages.

[114]   Reid 1987:42. Shepherd (1995:44-7) has also suggested another link between birth control and war. For the Siraya of Taiwan in the seventeenth century, he proposes, the magical and emotional connection which existed between warriors and their wives during headhunts dictated that women were not permitted to bear children until their husbands were too old to participate in war. While such a link did also figure in Toraja beliefs and ritual practices (Adriani and Kruyt 1950-51, III:302-6; A.C. Kruyt 1938, II:123; Riedel 1886:91), there is no evidence that it was associated with fertility limitation in Sulawesi.
[115]   Aguirre, Palloni and Jones 1998:245; Bongaarts 1980:568-9; Bongaarts and Potter 1983:14-7.

CHAPTER XI

Demographic patterns

This chapter recapitulates and compares the demographic patterns reconstructed for each subregion in Chapters IV-VI, with particular reference to population density and distribution. Some recurrent distributional trends are identified, and provisionally explained in terms of geographical variations in agricultural potential, health conditions, political circumstances, and commercial opportunities. An analysis of the long-term chronological trends is attempted in the following chapter.

Crises, fluctuations, and underlying trends

In 1686 a VOC governor of Ternate, repeating (for want of more recent information) the population estimate for Minahasa made by his predecessor Padtbrugge, warned that the real figure was 'far from constant, since it is impossible to know whether there are more deaths than births, and the burning fevers, by which that nation seems to be much afflicted, carried many people to their graves last year' (Lobs 1686). Until the second half of the nineteenth century in Minahasa, and until the twentieth century in most other areas, the demographic history of northern Sulawesi was punctuated by sudden mortality crises. A few of these crises were already visible in the quantitative population record (Chapters IV-VI), and many others were described in the context of mortality and disease (Chapters VII-IX). They were caused in the first place by epidemics, in the second place by famine (itself often associated with disease outbreaks), and more rarely by war, or by natural disasters such as volcanic eruptions. Where a series of such disasters struck in rapid succession, as in Sangir between 1790 and 1825, they may sometimes have led to sustained depopulation over a considerable period.

That the population of the Sangir Islands has suffered heavy losses in the last years, and that its size has been considerably reduced as a result, is beyond doubt considering the terrible smallpox epidemic in the year 1792; the eruption of Mount Awu in 1812, so fatal for the subjects of Tabukan, Kandahar and Taruna; the unhappy year of 1817, in which hundreds of people, especially on Greater Sangir, fell victim to the cold fevers; and finally, still not so long ago, another outbreak of the deadly smallpox on these islands in 1823. (Van Delden 1844:372).

In general, however, successive mortality exacerbations were separated by more regular intervals, during which their effects were approximately cancelled out by renewed population growth. Regional smallpox epidemics, for instance, recurred at an average interval of about 25 years, killing perhaps 15-20 percent of the population each time (see Chapter VII). Significant harvest failures, with their lighter (direct and indirect) death tolls, were unpredictable in the short run, but linked in the long term with the ENSO climatic cycle (Chapter IX), the mean duration of which is between three and four years (Berlage 1931:950; Quinn 1992:121). Indigenous perceptions regarding the demographic impact of mortality crises, in the few cases where these are recorded, suggest a 'punctuated equilibrium' rather than a series of completely unpredictable changes.

> It does appear that the rate of population growth or decline is subject to strong fluctuations. When we once pointed out to a To Kadombuku chief that the statistics for that year indicated a decline in the size of his tribe, he replied: 'For years now our numbers have been growing strongly, for when I was a child the tribe was decimated by the To Napu; then the population grew, until the smallpox (in 1884) took many lives. Now we have once again recovered somewhat. So do not be concerned about this decline; we are not about to die out'. (Adriani and Kruyt 1912-14, I:88.)

At the beginning of the twentieth century, the To Tawaelia in western Central Sulawesi expressed the conviction 'that whenever their population rises above 200, a sickness comes which reduces it to 100' (A.C. Kruyt 1938, I:195). On the island of Miangas in Talaud, the botanist Lam (1932:47) was assured in 1926 that the next major epidemic, like its predecessor (that of cholera in 1885), would strike when the population of the island reached 1,000. These perceptions strengthen the hope that an attempt to screen out short-term fluctuations in order to identify the underlying demographic trends, whether flat, rising, or falling, is not futile.

The population data recapitulated

After all that has been said about the unreliability of almost every population statistic from the period before 1930, it is hardly necessary to re-emphasize how much interpretation and extrapolation must be involved in any attempt to summarize the data. Some such attempt is nevertheless unavoidable, and it is provided in Table 23. The aim of the rounded estimates given here is to

Table 23. Long-term mean population estimates (in thousands) by subregion, 1600-1930

	ca 1600	ca 1650	ca 1700	ca 1750	ca 1800	ca 1850	ca 1900	1930[1]
Talaud	–	30	35	50	45	45	25	25
Greater Sangir	25	30	30	35	25	35	60	80
Siau	5	10	10	10	10	15	25	30
Tagulandang	–	5	5	5	5	5	10	10
Sangir-Talaud	–	75	80	100	85	100	120	145
Minahasa	–	50	55	80	100	100	185	310
Bolaang Mongondow	–	–	–	–	–	55	60	70
Gorontalo	–	–	–	–	85	75	120	185
Northern peninsula	–	–	–	–	–	230	365	565
Buol and Tolitoli	–	–	–	–	–	20	25	50
Tomini	–	–	–	–	–	35	35	45
W. Central Sulawesi	–	–	–	–	–	–	120	125
Poso, Tojo and Lore	–	–	–	–	–	70	50	50
Togian Islands[2]	–	–	–	–	–	–	5	10
Mori and Tobungku	–	>50	–	–	40	–	40	40
Luwuk Peninsula	–	–	–	–	–	45	45	45
Banggai	–	–	80	–	–	–	45	50
Central Sulawesi	–	–	–	–	–	–	365	415
Northern Sulawesi	–	–	–	–	–	–	850	1140

1   Because the subregional figures are rounded to the nearest 5,000, and because those for the Sangir Islands, to preserve comparability with earlier estimates, refer to the named island only rather than to administrative divisions including smaller outliers (*Volkstelling* 1933-36, V:12, 135), this column does not add correctly.

2   Population estimates for the Togian Islands (not included as a separate unit in Chapter VI): 750 in 1854 (Bleeker 1856:135; 5,000 in 1869 (AV Gorontalo 1869, 1872, in ANRI Manado 9); 7,000 around 1920 (*Encyclopaedie* 1917-21, IV:389); 10,727 in 1930 (*Volkstelling* 1933-36, V:134).

represent the general trends behind the often dramatic short-term ups and downs. Some of the early figures for Talaud, it should be added, are particularly speculative, since speculation was particularly useful in this case in order to produce complete estimates for Sangir-Talaud as a whole.

The total population of the region, then, was a little more than 1.1 million in 1930, and probably about 850,000 in 1900. Between 1850 and 1900 the population of North Sulawesi (Sangir-Talaud and the northern peninsula) increased at an average of about 0.8 percent per year, Bolaang Mongondow and Talaud being the only areas outside Central Sulawesi which did not show strong growth in this period; Sangir, Minahasa, and Gorontalo were certainly more populous at the beginning of the twentieth century than at any time in the historical past. This was not necessarily true, however, of the region as a whole, since the population of parts of Central Sulawesi, as indicated here by the estimates for Tobungku circa 1650, Banggai circa 1700, and Poso circa 1850, had been considerably larger in earlier periods (see Chapter VI).

The data from Minahasa before 1700, while inconclusive, are not inconsistent with the 'seventeenth-century crisis' proposed by Reid (1990) for Southeast Asia as a whole. Warfare, and possibly other factors, certainly caused some depopulation in Gorontalo, for which no real quantitative record is available until the nineteenth century, between 1640 and 1680 (see Chapter V). The only series of tolerably trustworthy population figures for the seventeenth century, however, come from Siau and Greater Sangir, and here the population seems to have been larger, rather than smaller, in the middle and end of that century than at the beginning. From 1650 to 1850 the long-term mean population of the northern islands as a whole probably varied between 75,000 and 100,000, with some growth up to 1750 and a dip around 1800. After 1850 there was moderate net growth up to 1900, concealing a much faster increase (about 1.1 percent per year) in Sangir and a dramatic decline in Talaud, followed by continued overall growth at about the same rate, but with much emigration, until 1930.

The mean population of Minahasa, perhaps 50,000 in the seventeenth century, seems to have grown quite sharply in the first half of the eighteenth, and did not decline around 1800 like that of Sangir. There was little or no growth in Minahasa, however, during the first half of the nineteenth century. The colonial population boom in this area began only after 1850, with average growth rates of 1.2 percent per year in 1850-1900 (or 1.5 percent after the last mortality crisis and recovery in the 1850s), and fully 1.7 percent in 1900-1930; Kündig (1934:175), with typical colonial enthusiasm for population growth, described the ratio of births to deaths in Minahasa at the beginning of the 1930s as 'very satisfactory'. Gorontalo, where the population had been declining in the first half of the nineteenth century, also saw substantial growth (despite considerable emigration and a serious mortality

crisis between 1877 and 1885) at an average of about 0.9 percent per year in
1850-1900, then rapid growth (perhaps 1.4 percent per year) in 1900-1930.

By the late 1920s a growth trend was probably established in all parts of
the region, and at the end of the colonial period Resident Van Rhijn (1941:
134) wrote that throughout his residency there was 'practically always a surplus of births over deaths, even during the periods in which influenza and
seasonal malaria take their toll'. Except on the neck of the northern peninsula
(Buol, Tolitoli and Tomini), however, this growth began too late in Central
Sulawesi to have much impact on local population totals before 1930, especially since it was preceded in many places by a temporary decline caused
mainly by resettlement epidemics. It was the demographic inertia of this
part of the region which held the overall rate of increase down to a relatively
modest 1.0 percent per year in the period 1900-1930.

Population density and distribution

The average density of population in the region as a whole was just under 13
persons per km^2 in 1930 (*Volkstelling* 1933-36, V:7), and about 10 per km^2 in
1900. In earlier historical periods it may well have been lower, but probably
not as low as the figure of fewer than four inhabitants per km^2 implied by
Reid's estimate (1988-93, I:14), obtained by backwards projection at a hypothetical growth rate of 0.1 percent per year, that the population of Sulawesi
as a whole numbered only 1.2 million around 1600.[1] A look at the subregional
densities implied by Table 24 reveals that while the population of Central
Sulawesi was probably larger than that of the north before 1850, it can never
have been as dense, and that Sangir-Talaud, although ultimately overtaken
by other parts of North Sulawesi in terms of absolute population size, always
remained the clear leader in terms of density. In 1930 the three major Sangir
Islands were all more than twice as densely populated as Minahasa, and over
nine times more so than Gorontalo (Table 24).

The great sub-regional contrasts apparent here were also repeated on a
smaller scale. A recurrent feature of the population distribution at all levels,
especially before 1850, was its unevenness. Concealed in the colonial statistics by aggregation with sparsely populated neighbouring areas, pockets of
settlement at densities comparable to those of the Sangir Islands were also to
be found elsewhere in the region. At the beginning of the nineteenth century,
for instance, almost the whole population of Minahasa was concentrated
in the highlands around Lake Tondano, and even in 1920 this core area, at

---

[1]   This calculation assumes that the proportion of the population living in the northern half
of the island, as in 1930, was 27% (*Volkstelling* 1933-36, V:3).

Table 24. Approximate average population density, selected subregions, 1850-1930

	ca 1850	ca 1900	1930
Talaud	35	20	20
Greater Sangir	60	105	140
Siau	95	160	190
Tagulandang	80	160	160
Sangir-Talaud	50	55	70
Minahasa	20	35	60
Bolaang Mongondow	5	5	10
Gorontalo	5	10	15
Peninsular N. Sulawesi	10	15	20
W. Central Sulawesi	–	10	10
Poso, Tojo and Lore	5	5	5
Banggai	–	15	15
Central Sulawesi	–	5	5

almost 170 inhabitants per km^2, was still four times more densely populated than Minahasa as a whole (Van Marle 1922, I:48). At 100 persons per km^2, the population density on the upland plain of Mongondow was fully ten times higher than that of Bolaang Mongondow as a whole in the early twentieth century (Tammes 1940:194). The low average densities given in Table 24 for Gorontalo concealed an enclave of equally dense population in the Limboto Depression (see Chapter V). In upland Central Sulawesi vast expanses of wilderness separated tiny settled basins (A.C. Kruyt 1903b:190-1), while on the west coast the 'densely-populated Palu Valley' was an unbroken patchwork of villages and fields (Adriani and Kruyt 1898:483).

If much of the population was concentrated in enclaves of relatively dense settlement, it should be added, almost nowhere were individual settlements large enough to be described as urban.[2] The trading port of Palu, with 'perhaps five hundred houses' in 1793 (Woodard 1969:28) and an (approximately equivalent?) population of 'more than 2,000 souls' in 1850 (Van der Hart 1853:264), was the only indigenous settlement ever referred to in European sources as a 'town' (see Chapter VI). The 'big *negeri* of Tondano' in upland Minahasa, with more than 800 houses and an estimated 6-7,000 inhabitants in 1818, was actually larger, but its irrigated ricefields and largely agricultural

[2]   Historically speaking, this reflects a typical Indonesian pattern. Although Reid (1980:237-9, 1988-93, II:67-77) has argued that before the seventeenth century a relatively high proportion of Indonesia's population lived in cities, other research indicates that the great majority of the population commonly attributed to commercial towns like Makasar (Bulbeck 1992:458), Banten (Talens 1999:51) and the other major ports of Java (Christie 1991:24; Nagtegaal 1993:53) actually consisted of farmers living in politically dependent villages in the rural hinterland.

economy meant that it retained a rural appearance.[3] The prevailing land-extensive agricultural techniques tended to ensure that even in relatively populous areas, the settlement pattern at a local level remained dispersed. Where swidden farming was practised without soil preparation or other forms of intensification, a village with 300 inhabitants already required an inconveniently large circle of cultivated and fallow land around it in order to feed itself, and most had no more than 200.[4] Where more intensive farming methods were also in use, as in Minahasa, the average village population sometimes rose to 350 or more.[5] Near-urban centres like Palu or Tondano depended for a substantial part of their income on commercial activities, and Hickson (1887:140) observed that the large 'kampong' (actually a compact chiefdom) of Mengarang on Kaburuang (Talaud), with '3,500 inhabitants' in 1886, also 'carries on a considerable trade'. The generally limited extent of trade specialization (see Chapter II), then, goes a long way toward explaining why such large settlements were rare. Not until late in the nineteenth century did the population of the biggest town, Manado, exceed 10,000.[6] In 1930 Manado still had fewer than 30,000 inhabitants, and less than one percent of the total regional population lived in it and the four subordinate administrative *kota* ('towns', including Tondano) of the residency put together.[7]

Population centres: upland valleys and coastal strips

Adriani, in a lecture delivered in 1900, described the settlement pattern in Central Sulawesi as consisting of two main features: a coastal strip about 5 km wide (Adriani and Kruyt 1912-14, I:297) inhabited mainly by Muslims (often Bugis traders and their descendants), and a pagan Toraja hinterland in the mountains, separated from the shore communities by an uninhabited belt.

> Travelling southward into the uplands one reaches, at an hour or an hour and a half's journey from the coast, the end of the cultivated area and the beginning of an almost uninterrupted forest girdle [*woudgordel*] three or four hours' travel wide. On

---

[3]   P.A. van Middelkoop, 'Memorien ten vervolge van het Algemeen Verslag van de Commissie naar de Moluksche Eilanden', 30-9-1818 (NA Schneither 128).
[4]   Adriani 1916:110; Adriani and Kruyt 1912-14, II:165; Aragon 1992:42.
[5]   In 1849 the average population of the 272 administrative villages in Minahasa, according to Dutch records, was about 350 (AV Manado 1849, in ANRI Manado 51). Graafland (1867-69, I:264), writing some years later, stated that Minahasan villages ranged in size from 25 to 500 households (100-2,500 people) and that most contained between 70 and 120 households (300-600 people).
[6]   Manado had a population of fewer than 3,000 in 1850, and just over 15,000 in 1901 (AV Manado 1850, in ANRI Manado 50; Van Kol 1903:297).
[7]   *Volkstelling* 1933-36, V:123, 141-2. The five *kota* were Manado, Tondano, Gorontalo, Poso, and Donggala. The smallest of these, Poso, had a population of just 2,875.

the far side of this wooded belt begins the territory of the uplanders, where one is entirely among Toraja and can get to know their society best and in its purest form. This *woudgordel* encircles the whole of Central Sulawesi. (Adriani 1901:235.)

When the Sarasin cousins made their journeys of exploration in the years 1893-1903, they too observed that in many areas the population was divided into distinct upland (Alfur, Toraja) and lowland groups separated by a belt of uninhabited country. This applied not only to Central Sulawesi (Sarasin and Sarasin 1905, I:215), but also to Bolaang Mongondow on the northern peninsula.

> Bolaang-Mongondow owes its name to the fact that it consists of two parts, a coastal strip called Bolaang and an upland agricultural zone called Mongondow, separated from each other by a belt of virgin forest which covers the mountain slopes adjacent to the coastal plain. Such *Urwaldgürtel*, which follow the coastal mountain chains everywhere and sometimes extend far into the interior plateaux, often also form natural barriers between the culturally backward mountain people and the coast-dwellers, who are culturally more advanced thanks to their maritime commerce. (Sarasin and Sarasin 1905, I:85-6.)

Other descriptions of Bolaang Mongondow indicate the same pattern, with settled strips in the vicinity of Kotabunan on the south coast as well as Bolaang in the north, both divided from the inhabited interior by forested mountains.[8] In 1866 the missionaries Wilken and Schwarz (1867b:231, 250), setting out from Bolaang, climbed for three days through 'virgin forest' before reaching the 'fertile and relatively populous' plateau of Mongondow, then spent another two days descending to Kotabunan 'over rocks and mountains where there is no trace of any hamlet or house'. A French visitor who travelled from the town of Manado to the Minahasan uplands in 1828, comparably, described passing through a landscape of 'immense forests' and 'wild and abundant nature', with 'very little cleared and cultivated land', before finally emerging onto 'the fertile and beautiful plateau of Tondano' with its 'great expanses of ricefields' (Dumont d'Urville 1833:440, 447). Just as the upland population of Minahasa and Bolaang Mongondow was found mostly on the mountain-ringed plateaux of Tondano and Mongondow, so that of Central Sulawesi was concentrated in local depressions like those of Lindu, Kulawi, Bada, Besoa, Napu, Poso, and the upper Bongka (see Chapter VI). The altitude of the major settled basins ranged from about 500 metres (Lake Poso) to over 1,000 metres (Napu).[9]

---

[8]   De Clercq 1883:117-9, 124; Riedel 1864a:272, 275; Steup 1933:32-3, 45; Tammes 1940:194.
[9]   Kulawi lies at 570 m, the Mongondow and Tondano plateaux at about 600 and 680 m respectively, and Bada at 750 m.

The demographic sketch maps of Minahasa and Bolaang Mongondow drawn by Tammes (Chapter V, Maps 10 and 11) show that the settled coastal strip was actually less continuous than Adriani and Sarasin and Sarasin implied. Even in 1940, after several decades of migration from the mountains to the lowlands, large stretches of the south coast of the northern peninsula remained almost uninhabited, and on the north coast, where the littoral plain was wider, settlement was still localized around bays and river mouths rather than forming an unbroken strip along the shore. In precolonial times, the great bulk of the population in Bolaang Mongondow and Minahasa was probably found on their respective central plateaux, while the lowland settlements were small and widely spaced. In Central Sulawesi, by contrast, the mountain basins, while often densely settled, were mostly much less populous in absolute terms (at least by the late nineteenth century) than those of Tondano and Mongondow, while the population of some lowland areas, especially the Palu Bay and Valley, was relatively large (see Chapter VI).

Not all aspects of the population distribution fit neatly into the upland valley/coastal strip model. The populous Limboto depression, lying almost at sea level and connected with the coast by the short Gorontalo trench, is difficult to classify either as a mountain basin or as part of a coastal settlement zone, although it might perhaps be regarded as a combination of both. In Central Sulawesi, especially in the area to the west of the Palu trench, there were some groups of settlements located in rugged mountain country rather than on or around valley floors (Kaudern 1925:20, 34). In Tobungku during the late nineteenth century, most of the settlements on the coastal strip were actually located a short distance inland for protection against seaborne slave raiders and malaria (see Chapter VI). The distance between the coastal and interior population centres also varied considerably: on the Luwuk Peninsula, the *Urwaldgürtel* separating the interior populations from the 'culturally more advanced people of the coast' was only 5-10 km wide (Wanner 1914:136).

Despite these variations, however, the descriptions by Adriani and the Sarasins do capture two cardinal features of the population distribution: much of the mainland population, especially at earlier periods, was concentrated in (for outsiders) rather remote inland depressions or plateaux, while the remainder mostly lived on or near the coast. It is also noteworthy that in four cases (Tondano, Limboto, Poso, and Lindu) the settled inland basins contained major lakes. A similar pattern, as Reid (1997) has observed, was originally typical of many other parts of Indonesia, particularly Sumatra, with the demographic balance tipping rapidly in favour of the coastal lowlands in the course of the twentieth century. In precolonial New Guinea, with its higher mountains, there was likewise a 'fairly consistent correlation' between high population density and 'open valleys above 1,500 m' (Brookfield and Hart 1971:68).

Population centres: islands

Another recurrent pattern was a tendency for offshore islands, and small islands in particular, to be important in demographic terms. In North Sulawesi, as we have seen, it was the Sangir Archipelago, rather than Minahasa or Gorontalo, which stood out at all periods as the most densely populated area. In 1920 the forester Heringa (1921b:733) noted that the Sangir Islands were 'among the most densely populated parts of the East Indian Archipelago', and had been 'completely cleared for cultivation'.[10] By this date Talaud, with an overall density of just under 20 people per km^2, was less conspicuously populous but at earlier periods the contrast with Sangir had been smaller. The Banggai Archipelago, lastly, was also more densely settled in 1930 than all but one or two small areas on the mainland of Central Sulawesi, and in the eighteenth century its population had been larger still.

Among the individual Sangir Islands, little Siau (156 km^2) and Tagu-landang (62 km^2) were always more densely populated than much larger Greater Sangir (562 km^2). Within Talaud, likewise, it was not the main island of Karakelang (1,000 km^2), but its smaller neighbours Kaburuang (94 km^2) and Salibabu (156 km^2), and especially the even smaller outliers to its north, Miangas (2 km^2) and the Nanusa group (27 km^2), which stood out as densely settled. The northern islands of the Talaud Archipelago, in fact, provide (to anticipate for a moment the subject matter of Chapters XIII and XIV) some of the region's most striking examples of environmental change as a result of pure population pressure. The original flora of Miangas, noted the botanist Lam (1932:26) after visiting this tiny island in 1926, had 'completely vanished' to make way for 'coconut groves and other plantations of the natives, whose large number (nearly 700) requires an intensive cultivation of the ground available'. On Merampi in the Nanusa group, one of the wettest places in the whole region and one without grazing animals to motivate the creation of fire-climax grasslands (see Chapter XIV), the same author observed a vegetation which he characterized as 'fire savannah'.[11] A few years later a colonial administrator wrote that there was 'perhaps reason to speak of overpopulation' in Nanusa, where more than 3,500 people lived on less than 30 km^2 of rugged and largely infertile coral rock (Tamawiwy 1934). Yet in 1775, according to Forrest (1779:317), the same islands had already supported 1,300 'male inhabitants', corresponding to an even larger total of perhaps 4,500 people.[12]

---

[10]   Blankhart (1951:89), in the late 1940s, also commented on the very high population densities ('up to 105 per km^2') on Greater Sangir.

[11]   Lam 1950:583 (see also the photograph opposite p. 581).

[12]   Valentijn (Keijzer 1856:192), writing half a century before Forrest and basing himself upon less complete VOC sources, also located 510 *weerbare mannen*, or 18% of his total for the whole Talaud Archipelago, on the Nanusa Islands, which make up just 2% of the Talaud land area (Appendix D).

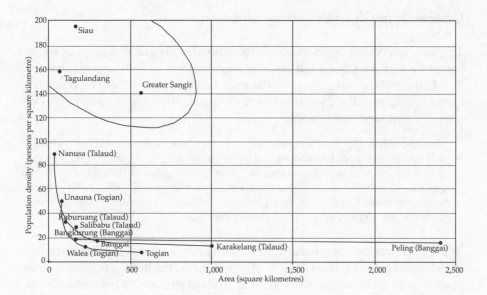

Figure 14. Population density and island size, 1930.
Sources: *Tabel* 1895:67 (for areas of Togian Islands); *Volkstelling* 1933-36, V:8, 134.

If the evidence was limited to unreliable early population counts, it would
be tempting to dismiss the concentration on small islands as an illusion
caused by less complete enumeration of the interior population on the larger
ones. The same pattern, however, is evident even in the latest and most accurate demographic sources. Figure 14 shows the relationship between area
and population density for the larger members of the four main offshore
island groups (Sangir, Talaud, Banggai, and Togian) according to the census
of 1930. Except for Sangir, where Tagulandang is out of line and only Siau
and Greater Sangir fit the general pattern, all four groups show a consistent
inverse relationship between island size and population density. A single
asymptotic curve, in fact, could have been plotted for all of the Talaud,
Togian and Banggai Islands combined, although here again Sangir, with its
generally much higher population densities, is exceptional. In the case of
Talaud the vertical asymptote would be even more pronounced if Miangas,
with an area of less than two square kilometres and a staggering population
density of 470 persons per km^2 (Tammes 1940:184), more than twice that
of Siau, had been included. A similar pattern was noted by Bayliss-Smith
(1974:288-90) in Polynesia and by Fox (1977:23) in the outer arc of the Lesser
Sundas, where the main islands of Timor and Sumba were never as densely
populated as smaller Roti or Savu, and these in turn were surpassed in population density by Ndao, a tiny island off the northwestern coast of Roti.

Localizing factors: agriculture and the natural environment

Tammes, surveying a selection of data on the historical demography of Sangir-Talaud, Minahasa and Bolaang Mongondow in 1940, argued that the distribution of the population had always reflected that of the available economic resources – the most important of which, given the agrarian focus of the economy, were fertile soils.[13]

> The first thing which strikes one here, as elsewhere, is the correlation between soil fertility and population density. The fertile Sangir Islands, the so-called *bovenlanden* [uplands] in Minahasa, and the plain of Mongondow have long been the centres of relatively dense population. Fewer people, correspondingly, live in the less fertile areas. Karakelang, and the infertile mountains of western Mongondow, are relatively thinly populated. (Tammes 1940:196.)

In the same period the soil scientist Mohr (1938b:493), noting that a similar correlation held for Indonesia as a whole, and that the best soils were almost always volcanic in origin, went so far as to conclude that 'in the Netherlands Indies the population density is a function of the nature of the soil, and this is a function of the presence of active volcanoes'.

The active volcanoes of the Sangir Islands, it has been noted, often killed large numbers of people during eruptions (see Chapter VII). In terms of soil fertility, however, they were a great blessing, and for local farmers this attraction outweighed the risks attending settlement in their vicinity. The ash ejected by Mount Awu on Greater Sangir, for instance, formed an excellent agricultural soil even in a virtually unweathered state. One year after a major eruption of this volcano in 1856, Resident Jansen already noted that 'fields which were not too deeply buried under ash and lava have yielded food crops once more, some of them in abundance'; the fact that the volcano was still smoking had not deterred the population from returning to cultivate its slopes.[14] A decade later, according to the missionary Steller, the ash from the 1856 eruption was still exceptionally fertile.

> In some places, such as Kolongan, the ash ejected from the volcano, and spread for miles around as far as the coast, raised the ground level by four to seven feet, and was so fertile in the first years after the eruption that people who have not seen such a thing before find it almost unbelievable. To this day the inhabitants of Taruna, Kolongan, Kandahar, Tariang and Sawang live mainly on the root crops which they cultivate without much effort in the layer of loose sand and ash, and which reach an exceptional size. (Steller 1866:12-3.)

[13]   G.W. Jones (1977:51-5), writing almost 40 years later, reached a similar general conclusion.
[14]   MV Manado June 1857 (ANRI Manado 54).

The island volcano of Ruang, opposite Tagulandang, held a similar attraction, although after one particularly violent eruption in 1808 it was many years before people dared to return there.[15] Not all recent volcanic material was so fertile: many sources note that the coarse, porous ejecta from Mount Soputan, which regularly blanketed a part of southwestern Minahasa in the vicinity of Amurang, were generally avoided by farmers.[16] The legendary fertility of the central plateau of Minahasa, on the other hand, was certainly due in large measure to its alkaline volcanic soils (Chapter I, Map 2).[17] 'When rice and maize are cultivated in alternation', noted the geographer Kornrumpf (1935:84-5) of this area, 'the need for land to lie fallow is eliminated in some places thanks to the fertility of the soil'.

Although volcanic soils do not occur on any scale outside Minahasa and Sangir, relatively favourable soil conditions can also help to explain the general concentration of the mainland population in upland basins. Soil quality, here as elsewhere in the tropics, tends to improve with altitude as lower temperatures slow down weathering processes (Mohr 1938a:245; Weischet and Caviedes 1993:148). This advantage can be enhanced by favourable relief; the Mongondow Plateau, as Riedel (1864b:280) observed in 1857, is a 'fine humus-rich plain' with soils enriched by alluvial deposition. In the uplands of western Central Sulawesi the situation was more complex, since the floors of the inter-montane depressions in this area were often too flat, wet, and flood-prone to be attractive for swidden farming purposes.[18] Particularly at their margins, however, they were well suited for irrigation, which was already widespread here in precolonial times.[19] The combination of wet rice cultivation on the valley floor and swiddening on the adjacent hillsides was a good one in terms of food security, and this, as Reid (1997:78) has argued, was probably an additional reason for the attractiveness of mountain valleys for agricultural settlement. In Minahasa, another area where supplementary wet fields were always common, a third farming strategy was also available in the form of swamp rice cultivation on the seasonally flooded margins of Lake Tondano (see Chapter II).[20]

[15]   Van Delden 1844:362-3; Frieswijck 1902:430; A.J.F. Jansen, 'Missive Sangir en Talaut Eilanden', 26-8-1857 (ANRI Manado 166).
[16]   AV Manado 1829 (KITLV H70); A.J.F. Jansen 1861:222; Koorders 1898:4; Van Marle 1922, I: 33-4; Pietermaat, De Vriese and Lucas 1840:113; Riedel 1872b:464. Ulfers (1868:3), however, noted that the fertility of this material increased over time as a result of weathering.
[17]   Van Doren 1854-56, I:261; Eibergen 1928:228-9; G.W. Jones 1977:3; Kemmerling 1923-24, I: 95; Mohr 1938:250; Pietermaat, De Vriese and Lucas 1840:113; RePPProT 1988, I:259; Whitten, Mustafa and Henderson 1987:15. Hardjono (1971:92-3) discusses the considerable variations in fertility which exist between different volcanic soils in Indonesia.
[18]   Grubauer 1913:496, 503; A.C. Kruyt 1908:1286, 1328, 1909:357-8.
[19]   Most of the settlements, correspondingly, tended to be located at the edges of the plain near the intersection with the mountain slopes (Grubauer 1913:406; A.C. Kruyt 1908:1286).
[20]   In Mongondow, by contrast, no irrigation seems to have been practised until the twentieth century (Van Marle 1922, II:83; Wilken and Schwarz 1867c:364).

In a few places, the association between soil quality and population density appears to break down. The best soils of the Gorontalo area, colonial writers believed, were to be found not in the populous Limboto Depression, but in the surrounding hills (Van Hoëvell 1891:32; Riedel 1870a:68, 78, 80), and particularly on the almost uninhabited Bawangio (Bone) Plateau in the east (Korn 1938:3). Because Tammes (1940:189, 196) had little historical data for the Talaud group, secondly, he was able to attribute the relatively sparse population of these islands in his time mainly to their thin, non-volcanic soils, but the more complete demographic reconstruction presented in Chapter IV reveals that while Talaud was probably never as densely populated as Sangir, it was nevertheless more so, until the middle of the nineteenth century, than Minahasa (Table 24). The island of Peling in Banggai, thirdly, was also one of the more densely settled areas, yet it consists mostly of weathered limestone, and its soils are shallow and leached (Schrader 1941:107, 109). Some climatic, political, and medical reasons for the Gorontalo 'anomaly' will be suggested below. The cases of Talaud and Banggai are more problematic, but it is striking that both of these areas also differed from almost all other parts of the region in that their foodcrop farming systems were based largely on tubers rather than rice and maize (see Chapter II). The possibility that the relatively high population densities on Banggai and Talaud were related to this eccentric agriculture will be discussed in Chapter XV.[21]

Climatic conditions in the areas of dense population range from the driest in the region (the Palu Valley) to the wettest (Sangir), and Tammes (1940:196), looking only at North Sulawesi minus Gorontalo, concluded that there was no link between climate and population density. At least outside Sangir and Talaud, however, some correlation is in fact evident (rather surprisingly, at first sight, given what has been said in Chapter IX about the demographic consequences of drought) between dense settlement and relative aridity. Because approaching monsoon winds deposit most of their moisture on the surrounding mountains before reaching the Palu and Limboto valleys, neither of these densely populated areas receives an annual average rainfall total in excess of 1,500 mm. To a lesser extent, the Mongondow Plateau, the Poso Valley, and the upper Bongka basin also stand out on the regional precipitation map as areas of local rainshadow (Chapter I, Map 3), and similar effects were probably present on a smaller scale in the mountain basins of western Central Sulawesi. The surprising dryness of the Tomini coastlands, resulting partly from obstruction of the northwest monsoon by the mountain spine of the northern peninsula, and partly from the extended rainshadow

---

[21] It is not clear, on the other hand, whether root crops are less sensitive than grains to soil quality; taro tolerates soils of low base saturation, but 'good yields require high fertility', while yams are also said to 'need fertile soils' (Flach and Rumawas 1996:70, 89).

cast by the Luwuk Peninsula during the southeast monsoon, also brings to mind the fact that Tomini seems to have an important population centre before the nineteenth century (see Chapter VI). Although the central plateau of Minahasa is not particularly dry as a whole, finally, it is nevertheless distinctly more so than the adjacent west coast, and in the vicinity of Tondano town the local yearly average falls just below the 2,000 mm mark.[22]

A positive association between aridity and population density is by no means unique to this region. Many of the major early civilizations of Southeast Asia, it has often been pointed out, were located in relatively dry areas like the middle Irrawady basin, Central and East Java, northeastern Thailand and Cambodia.[23] Perhaps less widely appreciated is the fact that dry, drought-prone Nusa Tenggara and South Sulawesi were among the most densely populated parts of the Indonesian outer islands at the time of the 1930 census (*Volkstelling* 1933-36, V:7, VIII:4). Reid (1987:78-9), finally, has linked dense settlement in the upland basins of precolonial Sumatra (especially the Toba plateau) with the rainshadow cast by the surrounding mountains, which assured their inhabitants of dry weather during at least part of each year.

A relatively dry climate, and especially a pronounced and reliable dry season, is beneficial to farmers in at least three important respects. Nutrient leaching and mechanical erosion of the soil by rain, firstly, are minimized under dry conditions (Mohr 1938a:245-6). The risk that the vegetation felled to open a new swidden field will fail to dry out properly before it is burned, secondly, is also reduced; in northern Sulawesi as elsewhere, incomplete burning was a common cause of swidden failure.[24] Farmers on the central plateau of Minahasa, thanks to the rainshadow of the mountains to their west, were able to clear and burn their swiddens earlier in the year than their counterparts on the wetter west coast (Edeling 1919:57; Graafland 1864:8, 19), and since the new fields could be planted with a preliminary crop of maize before the onset of the rainy west monsoon, this meant that agricultural productivity was greater in the uplands than in the lowlands. Sun and heat, thirdly, are also good for ripening rice (Bellwood 1997:242; Dove 1985:41), especially if it can be protected from the accompanying drought by means of irrigation (MacKinnon et al. 1996:532; Mohr 1938b:262). Extensive wet ricefields, despite the difficulties involved in lowland irrigation, were

[22]   Braak 1946:75; Van Marle 1922, II:100. Other parts of the central plateau, including Tomohon, Langoan and Kakas, receive over 2,500 mm (Van Marle 1922, II:100; Smits 1909:60). In the vicinity of Amurang on the west coast, however, annual averages exceed 4,000 mm (Van Marle 1922, II:100).
[23]   Dobby 1956:349; Missen 1972:22; Mohr 1938a:245; Pelzer 1963:5; Reid 1995:94-5; Robequain 1946:108; Stargardt 1992:60.
[24]   Adriani and Kruyt 1950-51, III:41; CV Manado 1862 (ANRI Ambon 1563); Francis 1860:350; A.C. Kruyt 1924:47; Li 1991:40.

present from the seventeenth and eighteenth centuries respectively in Palu and Gorontalo, and where dry and wet rice were grown in tandem, the latter was usually planted at a later stage in the agricultural calendar, maturing during the dry season when swidden rice cultivation was impossible (see Chapter II). In addition to their beneficial effects on foodcrop farming, dry conditions are also particularly favourable for the cultivation of at least one important non-food crop, cotton. The weaving of cotton cloth for intra-regional export was an important domestic industry in Gorontalo at the beginning of the nineteenth century, and probably also much earlier.[25] Other

Table 25. Mean annual precipitation (mm) and interannual rainfall variation at 16 locations in northern Sulawesi

	Mean	In driest year	In wettest year	Coefficient of variation[26]
Pendolo (Lake Poso)[27]	3995	2490	5216	0.129
Poso (coast)	2403	1720	3114	0.136
Mapanget (Minahasa, west coast)	3278	2009	4420	0.174
Unauna (Togian)	3237	2083	4440	0.195
Masarang (Minahasa, plateau)	2342	1337	3384	0.197
Beo (Talaud)	3118	4164	1333	0.198
Taruna (Sangir)	3897	2435	6093	0.201
Modayak (Mongondow)	2462	1327	3366	0.212
Tinombo (Tomini)	1287	844	1695	0.214
Parigi	1749	860	2823	0.225
Luwuk (Luwuk Peninsula, south coast)	1001	617	1888	0.230
Banggai	2194	1240	3328	0.261
Dampelas (northern peninsula, west coast)	2041	1149	2696	0.280
Donggala	1428	634	2229	0.283
Kuandang (Gorontalo, north coast)	2725	1260	3568	0.301
Tolitoli	2212	737	3696	0.319

Sources: ASEAN 1982: 15, 133-5, 137-9, 143, 145-9, 151-3; *Regenwaarnemingen* 1882-1933 (Masarang)

[25] Jasper and Pirngadie (1912:230), Riedel (1870a:91) and Scherius (1847:416-7) give some details on the process of cotton production and weaving in nineteenth-century Gorontalo. An administrative document from 1864 states that cotton has been cultivated in this area for 'more than 100 years' (CV Manado 1864, in ANRI Manado 39), and a VOC source from 1683 mentions that '20 pieces of Gorontalese cloth [*Gorontaalse kleden*]' had been included in the periodic tribute formerly paid by Gorontalo to the sultan of Ternate (*Generale missiven* IV:517).

[26] CV = Standard Deviation / mean for all years on record.

[27] The high annual rainfall average given here for this station is in disagreement with the precipitation map by Fontanel and Chantefort (1978: Indonésie III) reproduced in Chapter I (Map 3); possibly it results from a very local climatic effect of Lake Poso, on the shore of which Pendolo lies.

dry areas which traditionally exported at least some cotton textiles included Tomini, Mandono on the south coast of the Luwuk Peninsula, and probably the Palu Valley.[28]

Wet areas, conversely, were no doubt at an advantage if there was a long succession of particularly dry years, and this may help to explain why the population of the Sangir Islands was apparently unaffected by the climatic perturbation of the 'seventeenth-century crisis'. If a regular dry season could be beneficial to agriculture, moreover, unpredictable periods of drought and rain clearly were not. Table 25, based on twentieth-century (and in some cases late nineteenth-century) precipitation records from the 16 meteorological stations in northern Sulawesi for which more than 20 years of data are available, provides an overview of interannual rainfall variability in different parts of the region. The locations are arranged according to the predictability of their annual rainfall totals, from the least variable to the most.

Any conclusions drawn from this table can only be very tentative, since rainfall patterns within a single subregion varied widely according to altitude and other local factors, and since the figures given here say nothing about the seasonal distribution of precipitation. Some positive association between population density and climatic stability or predictability, nevertheless, does seem to be apparent. Beo (Talaud), Taruna (Sangir), Mapanget and Masarang (Minahasa), and Modayak (Mongondow), firstly, all show relatively low levels of interannual variation, as does Pendolo in upland Central Sulawesi. Tinombo on the Gulf of Tomini, interestingly, also displays quite a low coefficient of variation despite its very dry climate. The most severe variability, conversely, is found on the sparsely-populated northern and western coasts of the mainland (Kuandang, Tolitoli, Dampelas, and Donggala).

On a much smaller scale, the population distribution was also influenced by the problem of pest control. An important and time-consuming aspect of swidden farming in most areas was the construction of fencing to protect the crops from wild pigs and deer. In the Kaili area, according to one Dutch *controleur*, fencing was 'a task which actually dominates the whole business of opening a swidden' (Ter Laag 1920:41); in Mongondow, accordingly, swidden fields 'which had already become unsuitable for rice cultivation as a result of repeated use' reportedly continued to be farmed for as long as the surrounding fence remained intact (Wilken and Schwarz 1867c:365). On very small islands, however, large mammal pests were either absent, or could be hunted to extinction, so that food crops could safely remain unfenced (Broch 1998:210; A.C. Kruyt 1932d:484). Along the coasts of the northern peninsula, some farmers whose permanent homes were on the mainland chose for

---

[28]   Tomini: NA VOC 2132:230; *Generale missiven* IV:517. Mandono: Bosscher and Matthijssen 1854:105; Van der Hart 1853:113. Palu: Holmgren and Spertus 1989:68-9.

Plate 16. Men (dibbling) and women (sowing) plant rice on a newly cleared and burned swidden complex in Central Sulawesi, 1912 (ARZ photograph collection, Land- en Volkenkunde Celebes 403)

this reason to make their swiddens on nearby islets (Boonstra van Heerdt 1914b:730). Descriptions of Sangir also mention swidden gardens on small islands opposite littoral settlements, and it is likely that the same rationale was involved here.[29] The Nanusa Islands, further north, were free of wild pigs in the early twentieth century, as was Miangas.[30] The unusual pattern of dispersed, isolated swiddens reported from Sangir (Steller 1866:17) and Banggai (A.C. Kruyt 1932d:477) may also be indicative of a relatively limited pest problem (although pigs were definitely present on these larger islands, and fences were built to keep them out).[31] Swidden fields in mainland areas, by contrast, were almost always laid out in large contiguous complexes (Plate 16), partly for military security and to facilitate the labour exchange

[29] Van Delden 1844:357, 360; Van Dinter 1899:331; Encyclopaedisch Bureau 1912a:14; Stokking 1910:16-7.
[30] Lam 1932:49; A. Ulaen, interview, 5-9-2000. Rats, interestingly, were also absent from Miangas (Lam 1932:34).
[31] Another possibility is that this pattern was associated with state formation and the absence of war (see Chapter I).

involved in planting and harvesting, but mainly in order to share and lighten the work of fencing and guarding against pests.[32]

Although flat terrain was generally avoided by conventional swidden farmers, the wider pieces of level coastland did provide ideal conditions for both wild and cultivated stands of *Metroxylon* sago. One coastal plain, that of Parigi, was also brought under irrigation at an early date (see Chapter II). Another potential attraction of the sea coast was the availability of fish. Where hunted and domesticated animals were the main sources of protein, the everyday diet was often poor in nutritional terms (see Chapter IX). In coastal areas, however, and especially in the Sangir, Talaud, and Banggai Islands, where large numbers of swidden farmers lived close to the shore, sea fishing provided a more reliable supply. The inhabitants of small, mountainous islands with little or no coastal plain, such as Siau and Tagulandang, were at a particular advantage in that they could fish regularly at sea while still making their swiddens in the preferred hillside locations.

The big inland lakes, as already noted in Chapter II, were also important sources of fish and shellfish. Farmers living around the shores of Lake Poso fished extensively, sometimes selling part of their catch to travellers from elsewhere (Adriani and Kruyt 1912-14, II:200, 371). In western Central Sulawesi, likewise, smoked fish was traded from Lake Lindu to Kulawi and the Palu Valley.[33] Lake Limboto, as Padtbrugge already observed in 1677 (Robidé van der Aa 1867:167), was also intensively fished.[34] Particularly important here was the freshwater shrimp *Caridina nilotica*, a staple source of protein for the local poor (Williams 1940:62). In Lindu, freshwater mussels played a similar role (Bonne and Sandground 1939:2125). Lakes were doubly attractive in nutritional terms because in addition to fish and other marine animals, they also harboured large numbers of water birds.[35] In many cases,

[32] Adam 1925b:493; Adriani and Kruyt 1950-51, III:25-6; Atkinson 1989:261; Dutrieux 1931b:3; Graafland 1864:19; A.C. Kruyt 1930a:413, 431; 1938, III:30; Ter Laag 1920:41; Li 1991:22; Rapport adat kebiasaan 1910:85; Veenhuizen 1903:58. There were, however, some exceptions to this rule even on the mainland (Van Andel and Monsjou 1919:117; Van der Hart 1853:113), and in Balantak some swiddens were left unfenced (A.C. Kruyt 1934:131).
[33] Adriani and Kruyt 1898:510; A.C. Kruyt 1938, IV:144, 399; Logeman 1922:71; Sarasin and Sarasin 1905, II:48; Tillema 1926:221.
[34] AV Gorontalo 1823, 1864 (ANRI Gorontalo 3); Van Hoëvell 1891:36-7; Korn 1939:24; Morison 1931:56; Reinwardt 1858:517; Riedel 1870a:92; Von Rosenberg 1865:29, 68; R. Scherius 1847:415-6.
[35] Adriani and Kruyt 1950-51, I:12; Bonne 1941:1141; Buddingh 1860:367, 369; Van der Capellen 1855:361; Dumont d'Urville 1833:453; P.A. van Middelkoop, 'Memorien ten vervolge van het Algemeen Verslag van de Commissie naar de Moluksche Eilanden', 30-9-1818 (NA Schneither 128); Godée Molsbergen 1928:42; Guillemard 1886:208-9; Reinwardt 1858:517; Von Rosenberg 1865:58, 65; Van de Velde 1845:51.

the concentration of population in inland basins was probably related to the presence of such lakes and the animal food which they provided.

Localizing factors: disease

Where areas of what seemed to be reasonable agricultural potential had remained sparsely populated, Tammes was inclined to explain this in terms of malaria. It was endemic malaria, he suggested, which had discouraged settlement outside the central plateau in Minahasa and prevented population growth in the Dumoga Valley of western Bolaang Mongondow (Tammes 1940: 193, 195-6). More recently, Knaap (1987:120-1) and Metzner (1977:239-48, 1982: 106, 108-9) have used malaria to explain aspects of the population geography of other Indonesian regions. In some parts of northern Sulawesi, the densely populated areas certainly corresponded well with the malaria-free zones. Most of the Minahasan plateau lay neatly above the 600 metre altitude limit of the main local malaria vector, *Anopheles minimus* (Chapter I, Map 6), and the comparatively dense lowland population around Amurang (Chapter V, Map 10), in one of the few malaria-free coastal zones, could be interpreted in the same way.[36] Presumably thanks to its almost complete lack of level terrain with standing or gently-flowing water, Siau, the most densely populated of the Sangir Islands, harboured little or no malaria (Tammes 1940:188) and consequently was always regarded as the healthiest (Coolsma 1901:628; Van Dinter 1899:345). Miangas too, according to Dr Weck in 1926, was largely malaria-free (Lam 1932:50). In Gorontalo, endemic malaria in peripheral areas (Paguat, Kuandang, that part of the Limboto Depression to the west of the lake, and the Bone Valley in the east) may well have contributed to the pronounced concentration of the population in the immediate hinterland of Gorontalo town.

The epidemiology of malaria also seems to provide an attractive partial explanation for the *woudgordel* pattern noted by Adriani and the Sarasins, in which settled coastlands were separated from interior population centres by belts of uninhabited forest. Among populations native to endemic malaria zones most adults were immune, and only infants regularly died of the disease. To live close to the edge of such a zone and to enter it frequently, then, was far more dangerous for adults than to be settled permanently within it. Where the coast was malarial but the interior free of the disease, this must have tended over time to result in two distinct population groups, one adapt-

[36]   The malaria parasite itself is also affected by altitude, since the rate at which it develops and reproduces is sensitive to temperature (Gilles and Warrell 1993:126). But because a mean temperature of 20-30 °C is optimal, altitude only begins to provide any relief in Sulawesi above about 850 m (Whitten, Mustafa and Henderson 1987:499). Only one of the major settled basins, Napu, was higher than this, and conditions there were still strongly malarial (see Chapter VII).

ed to coastal conditions and the other, without the protection of immunity, avoiding the lowlands as much as possible. An insuperable problem with malaria as a general explanation for the *woudgordel*, however, is that only one of the major upland population centres, the Minahasan plateau, was definitely malaria-free. Many others, in fact, definitely were not: Tammes himself (1940:195) admitted that 'much malaria' occurred on the Mongondow Plateau (yet apparently 'without affecting the vitality of the population'), and because *A. maculatus*, unlike *A. minimus*, breeds easily at altitudes above 600 metres, the high mountain basins of western Central Sulawesi were extremely malarial. The fact that populous Banggai was always notorious for its endemic malaria, finally, is also difficult to square with the idea that this disease was a key factor in the population geography of the region.

That the geography of disease did have at least some effect on the population distribution, on the other hand, is clear from the fact that for fear of becoming sick, people living in upland Minahasa (Riedel 1872b:462, 465-6), and in the malaria-free interior of the Luwuk Peninsula (Kleiweg de Zwaan 1929:783), were reluctant to visit the nearby malarial coasts. It is possible that as Knapen (1998:88) has described for Kalimantan, this fear was also partly inspired by other diseases, especially contagious infections like smallpox and cholera which were brought to the region from outside by sea travellers. Remoteness from harbour settlements, and from other major population centres, certainly seems to have afforded some protection against such outbreaks. Poigar, in the far southwest of Minahasa on the border with Bolaang Mongondow, was known in the mid-nineteenth century as 'a very healthy place', since 'the epidemics which raged through Minahasa did not reach it' (De Clercq 1870c:536). In Central Sulawesi in the early twentieth century, cholera was apparently still unknown in remote Bada (A.C. Kruyt 1938, II: 308), and the Napu valley was said to have been safe in the past even from smallpox epidemics (see Chapter VII).

The fact that smallpox has an incubation period of 10 days or more (Breman 1991:167; Fenner et al. 1988:188, 202-3) makes it unlikely that geography alone was decisive here, since Napu, while isolated by Sulawesi standards, is still only about 40 km from the sea, and less than 20 km from the neighbouring settled basin of Besoa, where the disease did occur (A.C. Kruyt 1938, II:310). Without the benefit of acquired immunity, furthermore, a population which had successfully avoided infection over a number of smallpox cycles was certain to be devastated if a subsequent epidemic finally did penetrate its defences, so that in the long term net mortality was not necessarily lower among more remote groups (see Chapter VII). Relative isolation, nevertheless, did no doubt facilitate the application of deliberate measures to avoid contact with infected individuals and areas, while the sheer perception that there was safety in distance from epidemic hearths was probably another factor favouring the *woudgordel* pattern of coastal avoidance.[37]

In northern Sulawesi, as in precolonial Sumatra (Reid 1997:80), water-borne diseases like cholera and dysentery generally seem to have been more common in coastal areas than in the uplands. Pollution of drinking water during periods of drought was a frequent problem in Banggai, Donggala, Sangir and Talaud, while flooding, as in the case of the 1854 cholera outbreak (see Chapter IX), sometimes had the same effect in Gorontalo. It should also be noted, however, that all of these lowland areas were already densely populated, a circumstance which favoured disease transmission and placed pressure on limited local water supplies. Especially prior to colonial pacification, moreover, many upland settlements, being constructed in defensive hilltop locations, had severe hygiene and drinking water problems of their own. Coast-dwellers, in fact, were at a positive advantage when it came to the disposal of human waste, which was deposited in stream or river estuaries or on the beach, where it was quickly washed away by the sea. In some places pile dwellings, partly for this purpose, were built directly on the shore over land which was flooded at high tide (Sarasin and Sarasin 1897).

Localizing factors: politics and violence

Since not all potential village sites were equally defensible, the prevalence of warfare tended to favour settlement in areas of accidented terrain. Coastal villages were vulnerable to seaborne raids unless there was a nearby 'refuge hill' (*vluchtheuvel*) to which their inhabitants could flee if danger threatened.[38] Inland lakes, on the other hand, sometimes offered rather good defensive possibilities (Reid 1997:82). Tondano, until its destruction by the Dutch and reconstruction on the nearby shore under British direction in 1812 (Mangindaän 1873:370), was built partly on piles over the lake of the same name (Van Dam 1931:77; Riedel 1872c), most of its approaches on the landward side protected by swamps (Plate 17). Any aggressors were obliged to attack it by boat from the open water, where surprise was impossible.[39] The Tondanese, consequently, regarded themselves as 'untouchable [*ongenaakbaar*]',[40] and when they revolted against the colonial government in 1808-1809, it was in this stronghold that they were able to withstand a nine-month siege before their eventual defeat. On Lake Lindu the natural island of Bola

[37]   In Tawaelia (near Napu) at the beginning of the twentieth century, there were said to be few inhabitants who had ever seen the sea (A.C. Kruyt 1908:1331).

[38]   A.C. Kruyt 1895-97, IV:122; Keijzer 1856:222; Robidé van der Aa 1867:253.

[39]   Godée Molsbergen 1928:64; Supit n.d.:vii, 1986:89, 177-83, 190.

[40]   AV Ternate 1807 (ANRI Ternate 141).

Plate 17. Tondano town from the lake, 1679 (NA VEL 1305)

was used as a refuge in times of war, and this was said to be why the nearby lakeside villages, unlike others in the area, were not individually fortified (Adriani and Kruyt 1898:519).

Very small marine islands probably offered the same kind of defensive advantage. The more convex the coastline, the more difficult it was for an attacker to approach undetected, and the shorter the distance from the shore settlements to the higher ground, the less time the islanders needed to concentrate in the best defensive location. On tiny Miangas, a stone fort on the summit of a 100-metre hill commanded views over the whole island (Lam 1932, Plate 2); the remains of a larger fortification of the same kind, enclosing a freshwater spring and even agricultural land, can still be seen on Merampi in Nanusa.[41] A Spanish expedition sailing between Mindanao and Sangir in 1543 visited 'a small island', probably one of the Kawio group, where 'the natives had fortified themselves on a rock [...] in the sea, with an entrance on only one side'. When the inhabitants refused to provide food, the Spaniards 'fought with them, the combat lasting four hours', and eventually 'carried the place'. The houses within the fortification 'were raised up high on posts, and the sea quite surrounded the rock' (Blair and Robertson 1903-09, II:70).

[41] A. Ulaen, interview, 11-9-2000.

On the Togian Islands in the nineteenth century the main Bugis settlement, Balabatang, enjoyed a different kind of natural protection in the form of 'a labyrinth of coral reefs'.[42]

Reid (1997:80-1) has proposed that tribal populations deliberately isolated themselves in the interior of the larger Indonesian islands in order to preserve their independence from the centres of state power in the lowlands; Adriani (1919:5-6), writing on Central Sulawesi, agreed that the forest girdle surrounding the Toraja was left intact partly 'as a barrier between their territory and that of the coastal people'. To say that upland people avoided contact with outsiders would in fact be an oversimplification, since almost every 'Alfur' group was linked to one or other coastal 'kingdom' together with which it formed, in some respects, a single political, economic, and ritual unit (see Chapter I). The intervention of the *raja* in judicial matters, for instance, was actively sought by the uplanders on frequent occasions (Li 2001:46-52). 'People say', noted Albert Kruyt (1938, I:177), 'that the advantage of this *mepue* [formal submission to a coastal lord] lay in the fact that because the ruler now came between the opposing parties in all kinds of conflicts, the tribes were no longer free to fine and attack each other arbitrarily'. In order to play his judicial role effectively, on the other hand, the ruler had to remain an impartial outsider, and could not become an integral part of the community.[43] There were other reasons, too, for keeping the state at arm's length. If royal intervention was useful when upland conflicts threatened to get out of hand, few highlanders were keen to give up violence or the right to revenge altogether, still less to accept far-reaching trade monopolies or onerous labour services.[44] They were also aware, it seems, that their own lack of solidarity was likely to cost them their liberty if they came into close contact with groups endowed with greater economic and organizational resources. 'It was as if the Toraja instinctively knew', wrote Adriani and Kruyt (1950-51, I:106), 'that their society was based on too weak a foundation to withstand the influence of the outside world; the only way to preserve it was to isolate it'.

[42]   AV Manado 1854 (ANRI Manado 51).

[43]   In Dutch Minahasa, for instance, the leaders of rival groups were reportedly prepared to respect the judgement of the European resident 'because they know that he is impartial' (Watuseke and Henley 1994:360). At a more local level, likewise, disputes were often resolved through the arbitration of prominent individuals from uninvolved, neutral settlements (Adriani and Kruyt 1950-51, I:118; A.C. Kruyt 1938, II:64, 217; Padtbrugge 1866:315). This perceived need for impartial authority is a key reason for the prominence of foreigners, especially Bugis and Dutch, in the history of northern Sulawesi (Henley 2002, 2004).

[44]   Despite constant attempts to ban headhunting, the Dutch played the role of *raja* in Minahasa for 150 years before the Tondano War finally put an end to internal violence in 1809 (Henley 1996: 37). The principal reasons for the anticolonial revolt with which this war began were the rice tax imposed at the end of the eighteenth century (see Chapter V), and the low price now paid by the Dutch (in textiles) for Minahasan rice (Mambu 1986:37).

Whether by means of economic manipulation, or via the threat and application of violence, some of the lowland societies of the region certainly had considerable success in inducting and absorbing the population of the less well organized groups around them. A case in point is the movement of 'thousands of captured men, women, and children' (Riedel 1870b:556), as well as many refugees, from the Tomini coastlands to Gorontalo during the eighteenth century, and the concentration of the large resulting population in the immediate vicinity of the political capital.

> A glance at the map [Chapter V, Map 12], in conjunction with the figures indicating the distribution of population over the various districts, immediately shows that most of the population is concentrated on the plain of Gorontalo. This has occurred not because the most fertile land is located there (much better land, in fact, is to be found in the mountains), but because the *raja* have forced the population to settle there in order to control and exploit it better. (Van Hoëvell 1891:32.)

Until late in the nineteenth century, comparably, the political power and monopolistic trading activities of the Sangirese *raja* ensured that the population of the Sangir Islands was constantly augmented by slaves imported from Talaud. In Chapter IV it was speculated that each year about 300 Talaud slaves might have been delivered as tribute – a figure equivalent, other things being equal, to an annual population gain of about 0.5 percent for Sangir, and to a substantial drain of almost 0.7 percent per year for Talaud.

Political power, then, had both a centrifugal and a centripetal effect. In so far as they were able, the lowland and island *raja* concentrated their subjects, whose labour, conspicuous deference, and military services they valued, in the core areas of their kingdoms; to the extent that they failed, the population tended to settle at a sufficient distance from them to minimize their fiscal impositions while still taking advantage of their judicial services. This polarization no doubt contributed to the geographical separation of upland and lowland population centres. The unevenness of the population distribution was further reinforced by the fact that there was a degree of safety, and strength, in numbers, so that localities which were already densely settled tended to become more so. On the east coast of Central Sulawesi in the eighteenth and nineteenth centuries, a combination of raiding, forced relocation, and the quest for security gave rise to large harbour settlements ruled by warlords who protected their own flock while actively depopulating adjacent areas (Velthoen 1997b:371, 379, 381). The various slight advantages of small islands over other localities in environmental, military, and also commercial terms (see below) often led to their selection as political capitals, which amplified the demographic effect of those advantages by promoting both forced and voluntary immigration. In eastern Indonesia, Albert Kruyt (1931:616) once wrote, the most powerful rulers always seemed to have 'isolated themselves on small islands, from which they exercised their power over the surrounding peoples'. Kruyt cited Banggai (Gapi), Ternate, Tidore, and Bacan as examples of this 'remarkable phenomenon'; he might also have added Siau, historically the most powerful kingdom in Sangir, and also the most densely populated island.[45]

The demographic effects of slave raiding and trading were not limited to redistribution of the population within the region. Until the end of the nineteenth century, constant exports of slaves to other parts of Indonesia also took place. Many allochthonous groups, from the well-known pirates of the southern Philippines (Warren 1981) to the Tobelo of Halmahera (Riedel 1885a: 58, 65-6) and the obscure Tidong people from the east coast of Kalimantan (*Corpus diplomaticum* V:567; Warren 1981:84-6), were involved in this activity over long periods. The most active slave exporters up to about 1760 were Mandar and Bugis immigrants from South Sulawesi (see Chapter II), whose methods combined violence, purchase, and political extortion.[46] In the second half of the eighteenth century, however, a new period of intensified raiding began under the auspices of the increasingly powerful Sulu sultanate, a predatory state with its capital in the archipelago of the same name between Borneo and Mindanao (Riedel 1864a:511; Warren 1981:147). In 1777 the Magindanao, as the multi-ethnic raiding groups backed by Sulu were known, even attacked the Dutch stronghold of Manado, although they were eventually driven off by artillery fire from the fort.[47] 'There is no place along the whole length of the coast from Kotabunan to Bolaang', wrote VOC resident of Manado G.F. Dürr in 1794, 'where they have not landed and stolen a greater or lesser number of people' (Godée Molsbergen 1928:152). In the early nineteenth century, onshore colonies in Tolitoli and Tobungku enabled Magindanao pirates to maintain a permanent presence in Sulawesi waters.[48]

Until the 1850s the Dutch naval forces in Sulawesi were too weak, and their technological advantage too slight, to achieve any lasting success against the slave raiders.[49] When Governor-General A.J. Duymaer van Twist

---

[45]   At the very beginning of the European period, comparably, the kingdom of Manado, which for a time may have overshadowed even Siau in political importance, was apparently centred on the very small island of Manado Tua ('Old Manado') across the bay from the modern town of the same name (Graafland 1868; Padtbrugge 1866:306).

[46]   Van Brandwijk van Blokland 1749; Claaszoon 1710; Cloek 1726; Roselaar 1706; NA VOC 1579:29, 76, 81, 1608:617-8, 2099:995, 1081, 1084, 1093, 2649:116; *Generale missiven* IV:325, 796, V:611, VI:191-2, 349, 353, VII:489-90, 521, 612, IX:139-41, 149, 262. In 1729, for instance, 2,000 seaborne warriors under the leadership of a Mandar prince extorted a 'contribution' of 125 slaves from three coastal settlements in the Gulf of Tomini (NA VOC 2132:229-30).

[47]   Godée Molsbergen 1928:132; Riedel 1864a:520-2; Valckenaer 1778.

[48]   Velthoen 1997b:378. A Tobelo pirate colony, Velthoen notes, was also established in the Bay of Tolo around 1790.

[49]   The base in Tolitoli was destroyed by a Dutch raid in 1765, and again in 1822, but in both

visited the Moluccas and Minahasa in 1855, he was told that 'the pirates had once again committed the greatest atrocities, especially in the vicinity of Manado, carrying away hundreds of coast-dwellers to sell as slaves or to chain up as oarsmen in their boats' (Quarles van Ufford 1856:2). A year later, however, a Dutch steam gunboat succeeded for the first time in cornering a fleet of six raiding vessels, and destroying part of it, off the north coast of Minahasa.[50] In 1862, and again in 1865, similar routs took place in Talaud.[51] In 1875 it was reported that 'thanks to years of vigilance on the part of the government steamships', no Magindanao pirates had been seen off the Sangir coasts for more than a decade (Van der Crab 1875:333). After 1880 there was little raiding in the Gulf of Tomini either (Van Hoëvell 1893a:68). Not until the end of the century, however, were the more exposed eastern and western coastlines of Central Sulawesi thought to be safe (Boonstra van Heerdt 1914b:727; Goedhart 1908:486), and an isolated attack by a Sulu vessel on a fishing boat off Sangir took place as late as 1920 (Logeman 1922:160-1; *Zeeroof* 1921).

The uncoerced commercial sale of slaves by their indigenous masters, although technically forbidden by the European authorities in Indonesia after 1813 (*Encyclopaedie* 1917-21, III:804), also continued throughout the nineteenth century in areas outside direct Dutch control. Banggai, for instance, was still a significant exporter of purchased slaves (as well as enslaved captives) to Ternate and South Sulawesi around 1850.[52] In western Central Sulawesi the export of slaves by Bugis traders, mainly to East Kalimantan (*Landschap Donggala* 1905:521), continued to take place at the beginning of the twentieth century (Sarasin and Sarasin 1905, II:12), probably ending only with the official abolition of all slavery in this part of the region in 1907 (Encyclopaedisch Bureau 1912b:104).

Warren (1981:165, 180), in his classic study of the 'Sulu Zone' in the heyday of the Sulu sultanate from 1768 to 1898, estimates that a single bishopric on Luzon lost between 750 and 1,500 inhabitants each year to slave raids during the early nineteenth century, and points out that Dutch officials identified similar raids as one cause of the demographic decline in Gorontalo at the same

cases it was quickly re-established (Pietermaat, De Vriese and Lucas 1840:164; Van Schoonderwoert 1766; Velthoen 1997b:378; Vosmaer 1839:130; A.J. van Delden, 'Verslag van de Rijkjes en Negorijen ten westen van Menado gelegen, 1833', in ANRI Manado 48; Res. Manado to Gov. Moluccas, 18-8-1835, in ANRI Manado 78).
[50]   Graafland 1867-69, I:33; MV Manado April 1856 (ANRI Manado 54); PV Manado 1856 (ANRI Manado 48).
[51]   Coolsma 1901:655; Encyclopaedisch Bureau 1912a:35; MV Manado, May-June 1865 (ANRI Manado 54).
[52]   A. Revius, 'Algemeen Verslag omtrent de oostkust van Celebes', 10-2-1851 (ANRI Ternate 180).

period.[53] In 1807, likewise, 'the constant depradations of the Magindanao' were blamed, alongside epidemics and volcanic eruptions, for the 'enormous' reduction in the size of the population which was thought to have taken place in recent years on Sangir.[54] Other sources, however, cast doubt on the idea that slave raiding made a significant impression on overall population totals. In his extensive report on the Sangir Islands in 1825, Van Delden (1844:373) dismissed 'the loss of some natives from time to time' in pirate attacks as too slight to compare with disease or other natural disasters as a check on population growth.[55] Quantitative evidence confirms that the rate of demographic depletion attributable to slave raiding was much lower than in Luzon. The total number of people abducted by pirates from the coasts of Minahasa and Gorontalo in the year 1830, according to detailed contemporary reports by local officials, was 98.[56] In 1832, reported losses from Minahasa, Bolaang Mongondow and Gorontalo combined amounted to 88.[57] In the 12 months from July 1845 to June 1846, 62 people were abducted from Minahasa alone (Francis 1860:386). More fragmentary reports from other years indicate lower rather than higher figures.[58] Some undercounting no doubt occurred, and the army officer Ten Siethoff may well have been right when he estimated in 1845 that on average, Minahasa was losing about 100 people to slave raiders each year.[59] This, however, was still only about one in every thousand inhabitants; throughout the period of sustained population growth later in the nineteenth century, by comparison, colonial military recruitment alone accounted for at least as high a rate of emigration (see Chapter V).

Even allowing, then, for the fact that the proportion of the population inhabiting the vulnerable coastlands was smaller in Minahasa than in some other parts of the region, it does not seem likely that slave raiding by outsiders was ever a key reason for low population growth in North Sulawesi. Like

---

53   AV Gorontalo 1841-1843 (ANRI Manado 50).

54   AV Ternate 1807 (ANRI Ternate 141).

55   This comment refers to attacks on fishermen and traders at sea; Van Delden makes no mention of coastal raids. Half a century earlier, slave raiding was likewise thought to be of minor importance on Greater Sangir, although more significant for Siau and Tagulandang (Valckenaer 1778).

56   The raiders arrived in April, and were not seen again after June. During this period what appears to be a meticulous count, broken down by subregion, was kept (Res. Manado to Gov. Moluccas, 17-4-1830, 28-4-1830, 27-5-1830, 3-6-1830, 5-6-1830, in ANRI Manado 76).

57   Res. Manado to troop commander Manado, 9-5-1832 (ANRI Manado 77). The figure includes 10 subjects of the *raja* of Bolaang Mongondow.

58   Res. Manado to opzieners Minahasa, 28-1-1844 (ANRI Manado 81); AV Manado 1852 (ANRI Manado 51). Occasionally, however, there were bigger raids. In 1801, according to a contemporary British source, 40 raiding vessels 'reduced the principal settlement on Sangi to ashes and brought about the death of its Raja and the captivity of nearly two hundred women' (Warren 1981:164).

59   J.J. ten Siethoff, 'Topografische schetsen van een gedeelte der residentie Menado 1845' (ANRI Manado 46).

the sustained slave trade between Talaud and Sangir, the 'hundreds' of slaves (according to Revius) exported or abducted from Banggai each year in the mid-nineteenth century may well have represented a more significant drain at a local level.[60] In this context, however, it must be noted that not all of the slaves exported via Banggai actually originated there; a Dutch report from 1875 states that the 'more than one hundred women and children' seized by Tobelo pirates in the Gulf of Tomini during the previous year were 'sold in the Banggai Archipelago, and elsewhere in the territory of the sultan of Ternate on the east coast of Celebes'.[61]

Whatever its impact upon absolute population totals, slave raiding clearly provided a strong disincentive to settlement in the immediate vicinity of the sea. Until the Dutch naval success off Manado in 1856, coastal swiddens in Minahasa were 'dangerous to work in because of the Magindanao people-thieves', and as in Tobungku, what lowland villages there were mostly lay a kilometre or so inland for safety.[62] If the threat of seaborne violence grew, as on the east coast of Central Sulawesi during the early nineteenth century, existing coastal settlements were sometimes abandoned altogether in favour of new sites in the interior (see Chapter VI). Many of the people who left the Tomini coastlands for Gorontalo during the eighteenth century did so not in captivity, but in search of safety from seaborne raids (Van Mijlendonk 1756). Patterns of coastal avoidance in other parts of Indonesia have also been linked with slave raiding (Metzner 1982:106; Reid 1997:81-2). On the whole, however, the extent to which the coast was avoided during the era of seaborne violence is still less striking than the extent to which it was settled despite the attendant risks. The establishment of the Pax Neerlandica at sea, together with the extension of colonial control to the highlands (which then lost their attraction as fiscal refuges) and the simultaneous boom in lowland coconut cultivation, did result in an increase in coastal population densities in the late nineteenth and early twentieth centuries. Long before this shift, however, the exposed Sangir and Talaud Islands were already the most densely populated parts of the region, Banggai and the Palu Bay probably the two largest population centres in Central Sulawesi, and the remaining coasts of the mainland also scattered with settled strips and enclaves. The inverse correlation between population density and island size, indeed, partly reflects the prevalence of coastal settlement, since the smaller the island, the longer its coastline in relation to its surface area.

---

[60]   A. Revius, 'Algemeen Verslag omtrent de oostkust van Celebes', 10-2-1851 (ANRI Ternate 180). The total population of Banggai was probably comparable to that of Talaud. The slaves exported from Peling, Revius added, were transported under such bad conditions that more than half of them perished en route.

[61]   AR Gorontalo to Res. Manado, 10-6-1875 (ANRI Manado 13).

[62]   S. van de Velde van Cappellen to directors NZG, 13-4-1852 (ARZ NZG 19.1).

Localizing factors: trade

Access to the sea and its commerce was vital to the small professional trading communities of the region, and also to many of its indigenous political leaders, who derived income and prestige from the exchange of imported luxury goods for saleable commodities like *damar*, beeswax and rice produced in the interior. 'In Indonesia', argues Reid (1997:80), 'the state has always been essentially coastal and sustained by foreign resources'. Part of the reason for this, it was suggested in Chapter I, was simply that trade strengthened the economic incentive to eliminate violence and reduced the amount of free time available for war. Where small groups could gain relatively exclusive control of trade flows, however, commerce also created relationships of dependency and debt which contributed directly to the emergence of political hierarchy.[63] While trade wealth enabled such groups to attract followers and purchase slaves, state formation simultaneously improved their ability to threaten or force other people into joining them or resettling in their vicinity.

In northern Sulawesi, where rivers were mostly too small and fast-flowing for navigation, and where no place was more than a few days' walk from the sea, there were no compelling geographical 'choke points' of trade to compare with the big estuaries controlled by the coastal sultanates of Sumatra and Kalimantan.[64] Lowland political centres like Manado, Bolaang, or Tojo, nevertheless, were all located at or near the termini of well-worn trade routes leading to the uplands.[65] The port of Gorontalo controlled the narrow valley linking the Limboto Depression with the sea, and Parigi the strategic land route across the neck of the northern peninsula to the Palu Bay, itself a natural gateway to the uplands of western Central Sulawesi. Due to the greater area of their commercial hinterlands and the greater distances which uplanders there had to travel to the sea in order to do their trading themselves, the trade-orientated lowland population centres of Central Sulawesi were often larger than their equivalents on the northern peninsula.

---

[63]   Watuseke and Henley 1994:361. Most trade was conducted on the basis of credit (Adriani and Kruyt 1912-14, II:303; AV Manado 1829, in KITLV H70; Broersma 1931b:231; Van Dam 1931:80; Van der Hart 1853:99; NA VOC 1775:232-3; A. Revius, 'Algemeen Verslag omtrent de oostkust van Celebes', 10-2-1851, in ANRI Ternate 180; Steller 1866:37).
[64]   Far from providing means of transport, noted Van Marle (1922, I:8), the rivers of Minahasa and Bolaang Mongondow, with their steep headwater valleys and flood-prone lower reaches, were 'natural impediments to commerce'. In Central Sulawesi, however, two rivers, the Gumbasa in the Palu Valley (Hissink 1912:60), and the La in Mori (Maengkom 1907:862), were navigable for some 30 km upstream.
[65]   In Bolaang Mongondow, Dutch observers believed, the coastal *raja* deliberately discouraged improvement of the path to the uplands in order to safeguard their trading privileges (De Clercq 1884:117-8).

Some islands were naturally suitable for trading establishments due to their geographical position. Bugis traders found themselves conveniently 'in the centre of their commercial terrain' on the Togian Islands, from which they could sail in any direction to the coasts of the Gulf of Tomini.[66] The possibility of 'island hopping', as Heersink (1999:44) points out for South Sulawesi, eased the considerable dangers of navigation, and this may have been a factor encouraging settlement on Siau and Tagulandang, which formed stepping stones along the route between Greater Sangir and Manado. An additional advantage of islands and coasts for the purposes of local trade (and political centralization) was the relative ease of movement which they made possible between neighbouring villages – not so much by sea (coastal *prahu* traffic in Sangir was particularly contingent on weather conditions) as on foot along the beach, which in many areas provided the closest approximation to a road.[67] The main commercial advantage of the Sangir Islands, however, was not their geography but their coconut plantations, the luxuriance and productivity of which was ensured by the presence here of fertile, well-drained volcanic soils in the low-altitude coastal locations favoured by this crop (Tammes 1949:14).

At a local level the population distribution always reflected a combination of commercial, environmental, and political factors. That trade alone was seldom decisive is illustrated by the situation in the vicinity of the most important commercial 'choke point' in the region, the path from Tawaeli on the Palu Bay to Toboli on the Gulf of Tomini.[68] On the Tomini side, as already noted, this crossing was controlled by the kingdom of Parigi, where many traders were based. Toboli itself, however, was a minor settlement, and the capital of Parigi was located not where the path came down to the sea, but some 20 km – a four-hour row (Adriani and Kruyt 1898:440) – further south along the coast, on a 'broad, level coastal plain'.[69] Van der Hart (1853:205) described this plain as 'a very fertile and pleasant country' abounding in horses and water buffalo, and Jansen found it to be 'a very populous and

[66]   AV Manado 1854 (ANRI Manado 51). Togian exported turtleshell in the seventeenth century (Von Rosenberg 1865:145-6), and was the site of an important Bugis colony by the early nineteenth (AR Gorontalo to Res. Manado, 29-1-1825, in ANRI Manado 114).
[67]   Boonstra van Heerdt 1914b:731-2; Van Delden 1844:30, 367. Inland lakes, likewise, were also much used for transport between the settlements on their shores (Adriani and Kruyt 1950-51, III:335; Bleeker 1856:75; A.C. Kruyt 1938, I:141).
[68]   There were also three other routes across the peninsula around this point, including one from Parigi itself to Palu and Biromaru. The path from Tawaeli to Toboli, however, was the shortest and 'by far the most frequently followed' (Adriani and Kruyt 1898:440).
[69]   A.C. Kruyt 1938, I:85. Further north, comparably, the other historically important overland trade route across the northern peninsula began not at Tolitoli, but in the much smaller satellite kingdom of Dondo (Boonstra van Heerdt 1914b:763; *Generale missiven* IX:146).

apparently prosperous land'.[70] Other sources reveal that at least part of it was under irrigated rice cultivation.[71] At Toboli, by contrast, there was too little flat terrain between the mountains and the shore to favour this kind of land use (Wichmann 1890:989). While income and political power associated with the Tawaeli-Toboli trade no doubt made possible the enclave of intensive agriculture and dense population at Parigi, environmental factors dictated that it could not be located in the immediate vicinity of the trade route.

Conclusion

A very uneven population distribution was always characteristic of northern Sulawesi. This distribution featured concentrations of settlement on volcanic soils, in dry valleys and on high plateaux, around large lakes, on small islands, and in coastal trading centres. It was conditioned by a complex of environmental, political, and commercial factors which, although sometimes unclear in detail, is fairly transparent as a whole. In themselves, however, these localizing influences do not necessarily say much about fertility, mortality, or long-term demographic change. Clusters of population in defensive localities, for example, are not necessarily the result of genocide elsewhere. Nor do concentrations in areas with fertile soils necessarily demand explanation in terms of famine elsewhere; they could equally reflect the tendency of a stable population, the size of which is governed by other factors (disease, for instance, or low reproductive fertility), to gravitate toward those places where it can grow its food with minimum effort and maximum chance of success (Mohr 1945:254).

The overall dimensions of the population and the long-term trends, then, remain to be explained. The most common chronological pattern, to recapitulate, seems to have been one of crisis-ridden quasi-equilibrium, with epidemics and other disasters regularly killing substantial fractions of the population, but with little or no net growth in the long term. Sustained population growth, on the other hand, took place in Minahasa during the eighteenth century, in both Minahasa and Sangir after 1860, and in Gorontalo after 1885. The population of Tobungku and Banggai on the east coast of Central Sulawesi, conversely, declined substantially between the end of the seventeenth century and the beginning of the twentieth, while Talaud saw a very sharp decline in the last part of the nineteenth which was not compensated by subsequent growth.

[70]   AV Manado 1854 (ANRI Manado 51).
[71]   CV Gorontalo 1864 (ANRI Manado 44); Van Hoëvell 1893a:71.

CHAPTER XII

The causes of population growth

Tammes (1940:176) began his discussion of the demography of North Sulawesi with the apt observation that at a 'by our standards normal' growth rate of one percent per annum, a population originating from a single couple will contain more than a thousand million people within 2,000 years. Since the Austronesian ancestors of the present population of northern Sulawesi almost certainly arrived there well over 2,000 years ago (Bellwood 1997:118), this means that if their numbers had grown as fast before 1900 as they did between 1900 and 1930, they would have had ample time to populate not just the whole region, but the whole world.[1] Here, then, is emphatically a case of what Reid (1987) refers to as 'low population growth in precolonial Southeast Asia', and of course it also represents part of a much wider demographic puzzle. Between the beginnings of agriculture and the onset of the modern period of global population growth around 1750, the average rate of increase of the total human population appears to have been well below 0.1 percent per annum (H. Jones 1990:8). This lack of long-run growth, it has been said, constitutes the 'single most significant fact of historical demography' (Wilson 2001:24).

Explaining the exceptionality of growth

The general complex of factors restricting population growth in northern Sulawesi under most historical conditions, if not their relative importance, is reasonably clear. In the first place mortality was high, and the most important direct reason for this was disease (Chapter VII). At least one fifth of all children born, and in most places probably many more, died in infancy, and at least one third before reaching adulthood. Once in every generation a small-pox epidemic killed about one person in every six, and often more. Where malaria was fully endemic it pushed the child mortality rate up beyond 40 percent; where it occurred in the form of occasional epidemics, it weakened

---

[1]   The global population in 1900 stood at about 1,500 million (Osborn 1960:88).

the adult population and increased the frequency of stillbirths and abortions. Dysentery epidemics regularly killed adults as well as children, and the incidence of debilitating diseases other than malaria was also very high. Poor nutrition and periodic food shortages were a second factor behind the high death rates (Chapter IX). Although the proximate cause of death was almost always disease, mild malnutrition (particularly protein deficiencies) and occasional absolute shortages of food, by reducing the resistance of the population to sickness, contributed both to the high death rate among children and to the generally short stature and limited life expectancy of adults.

The significance of a third factor often regarded as a key reason for high mortality in precolonial Southeast Asia, war, is much more doubtful see (see Chapter VII). While warfare and other types of violence were endemic in most parts of the region, they did not usually take large numbers of lives. Their effects on agriculture, trade, medical hygiene, and reproductive behaviour, while perhaps more important, are difficult to isolate from other limitations in these areas, and doubts here are strengthened by a review of the long-term population trends reconstructed in Chapters IV-VI. Although the populations of the least violent areas, Sangir, Gorontalo and Banggai, were all relatively dense, that of Sangir does not seem to have grown much during almost two centuries of peace from 1680 to 1860, while that of Banggai declined over the same period. Both Gorontalo and Minahasa saw demographic stagnation during the very peaceful decades from 1820 to 1850, and the population of Bolaang Mongondow does not seem to have grown significantly in the period 1850-1900, following the establishment of internal peace as a result of indigenous state formation. In Minahasa, conversely, violence was still endemic (Godée Molsbergen 1928:98-101, 124-7, 132, 135-9, 143, 145, 153), or even escalating (Schouten 1998:49), during what appears to have been a period of sustained population growth in the eighteenth century.

These comparisons, of course, are very crude, and ignore many extraneous variables; the continual export of slaves, for instance, may well have been a factor in the long demographic stagnation on Banggai, while the arrival of Asiatic cholera, combined with economic problems, no doubt led to heightened mortality in Minahasa and Gorontalo during the first half of the nineteenth century. The conclusion that endemic low-level warfare was not a very important check on population growth in sparsely-populated, stateless areas, however, is supported by parallel evidence from Kalimantan (Knapen 1997:445-7). Historically speaking, the demographic impact of war appears to have been much greater in the populous states of Java and mainland Southeast Asia (Reid 1987:42-3, 1988-93, I:17-8).

High mortality was not usually offset by high fertility (Chapter X). In Central Sulawesi (the best documented area in this respect) on the eve of colonial rule at the beginning of the twentieth century, the reported number of children borne by the average woman during her whole reproductive life-time was between three and four, or just enough to ensure the replacement of the existing population (Appendices F and G). Even allowing for some exaggeration on the part of missionary authors regarding the frequency of deliberate abortion and infanticide, it is clear that as in many other parts of Indonesia (Kleiweg de Zwaan 1925, 1928), both were widely practised. Very long periods of breast-feeding, which depress fertility via the mechanism of lactational amenorrhoea, were probably the norm everywhere in the region until the nineteenth century (although post-partum sexual abstinence appar-ently was not). Frequent separation of married couples as a result of male absence was an important complementary factor in many areas and periods. In Minahasa and Sangir, finally, there was also a tradition of relatively late marriage, both men and women typically marrying above the age of 20 years.

Demographic equilibrium and carrying capacity

Tammes (1940:196) believed that the lack of sustained population growth in North Sulawesi (outside Minahasa) before 1850 had reflected a state of equilibrium (*evenwicht*) between population and economic resources. In the first place this meant that population densities were systematically related to the productivity of local farming systems, which was determined mostly by soil characteristics (see Chapter XI). Outside the fertile upland basins and volcanic islands, Tammes argued, concentrated settlement was possible only on the basis of commerce, the extent of which in the traditional economy had been limited.

> Only where other sources of income are available, such as trade and fishing, is the population somewhat denser. This is the case, for instance, in the larger settlements and on some of the small islands. Where no economic opportunities are present [*niets te halen valt*], the population is extremely sparse. (Tammes 1940:196).

As we have seen, Tammes, partly because his historical data were incom-plete, underestimated the magnitude of past demographic changes. Nevertheless the indigenous perception that such fluctuations concealed a long-term equilibrium, the evident sluggishness of population growth over a period of millenia, the fact that food shortages did affect the death rate, and the observed geographical correlation between population density and agricultural resources, all lend credibility to the idea of a demographic 'car-rying capacity' determined by the productivity of the local economy. Knaap (1987:99-123, 1995) has provided some statistical evidence for this kind of limit in his detailed study of late seventeenth-century Ambon, where population growth in the aftermath of war seems to have ceased once the average population density reached 25-30 persons per km^2.[2]

The maintenance of a demographic equilibrium must depend on homeostatic mechanisms which lower fertility, or raise mortality, or both, as the size of the population approaches the stable level. The existence of such mechanisms, of course, cannot simply be assumed. While some historians of other Indonesian regions have not hesitated to link deliberate abortion with limitations in the availability of farmland (Dobbin 1983:16), and patterns of delayed marriage with 'the delicate ecological balance between environment and demography' (B.W. Andaya 1993b:21), it is striking that the conscious motives for birth control specified in historical sources from northern Sulawesi (see Chapter X) do not suggest any connection with environmental conditions.[3] In so far as economic considerations were important, these related either to the short-term costs of childbearing for women, or to the projected medium-term benefits of children within the household, as determined by political factors affecting parental demand for, and access to, child labour. Nowhere does the long-term ability of the local economy to support the children themselves seem to have entered into the parental calculation.[4]

The fertility control commonly practised by individual women in Central Sulawesi, moreover, was directly at odds with the prevailing public values, which (albeit mainly for military rather than economic reasons) apparently favoured unlimited reproduction.[5] According to Adriani (1917:454), one of the 'three duties of public life' among the Toraja (the others were courage in the military or supernatural defence of the community, and generosity) was 'the production of many children, through which the tribe was strengthened'.[6] Abortion and infanticide, correspondingly, were not openly condoned, and in some areas even attracted heavy traditional penalties if their

[2]   Knaap's assumption that demographic stability continued after 1690, however, is based mainly on a few widely-spaced eighteenth- and nineteenth-century population estimates. Continuous data are available only for the first few years of the 'stable' period.
[3]   It is interesting to note that the original source cited by Dobbin on abortion among the Minangkabau attributes this form of birth control simply to the heavy female labour burden, which is difficult to combine with caring for infants (Verkerk Pistorius 1871:56-7).
[4]   According to W.H. Scott (1994:118), however, early Spanish sources from the Philippines do indicate that some women practised abortion 'because of poverty or poor prospects for their children'.
[5]   Coleman (1986:14-6, 35) notes the complexity of the relationship between the costs and benefits of children as seen from the perspective of individual women, and those accruing to the community at large.
[6]   Elsewhere, however, Adriani and Kruyt (1912-14, I:86) acknowledged that this was predominantly a male ideal. In the second edition of *De Bare'e sprekende Toradjas*, the duty to have many children is softened to an obligation to marry, the aim of marriage being 'none other than to produce children, and in this way to contribute to the continuation of the family' (Adriani and Kruyt 1950-51, I:109).

practice became public knowledge.[7] No doubt it was partly as a result of these attitudes that Toraja abortionists were not able to perfect their skills to the degree reported from some other parts of Southeast Asia (Shepherd 1995: 5-7), so that despite the demand for birth control, the means of achieving it remained unreliable and dangerous.[8]

Another immediate objection to any interpretation of the observed population distribution in terms of limits to food production is that large parts of the region were (and are) not only sparsely populated, but completely uninhabited, so that their carrying capacity, following the ecological/economic argument to its logical conclusion, would have to be interpreted as zero.

> It is striking how sparsely populated this part of Central Sulawesi is. The villages are all small and the distances between them great. Many settled areas are separated from each other by great stretches of virgin forest which cannot be crossed in less than two or three days' travel. These extensive forests are found between the valleys of all the major rivers, because like many other peoples of the archipelago the Toraja tend to cluster in the vicinity of important watercourses. It takes three days, for instance, to traverse the wild and densely-forested mountain country which divides the Poso depression, where most of the Bare'e-speaking tribes live, from the valley of the Tawaelia, home of the To Besoa, To Banahu and To Bada. From there it is once again several days' journey through the mountains to the To Lindu and To Kulawi in the Palu drainage basin, and to the tribes of the Palu Valley. (A.C. Kruyt 1903b:190-1.)

In 1903, the anthropologist and historian H.J. Nieboer used the demographic data published by Albert Kruyt (1903b) to cast doubt on the theory, already popular in his time, that birth control among '*Naturvölkern*' should be interpreted as a form of Malthusian preventive check.

> That this 'obvious' explanation is not entirely correct [...] is evident from the fact that these practices are found mainly among farming peoples in areas where there is an ample availability of land, and where the food supply is therefore capable of further expansion. Mr Kruyt has provided us with details of precisely such a situation. The country is very sparsely populated, the unused land is available to everyone, the areas depopulated by war remain empty, and yet population growth is still subject to deliberate restriction. It is clear that no Malthusian motivation can be involved here. (H.J. Nieboer 1903:715-6.)

For several reasons, however, this argument, although probably correct as far as the conscious motives for fertility control are concerned, is not conclu-

---

[7]   Adriani and Kruyt 1950-51, II:344; A.C. Kruyt 1903a:712, 1903b:200, 1930a:461, 1930b:559; 1938, III:184.

[8]   Particular women 'known for their skill at producing abortion', nevertheless, did exist 'everywhere' in Central Sulawesi (A.C. Kruyt 1938, III:183).

sive as a refutation of the broader argument that sparse population reflected limited economic opportunities. While there was much unoccupied land, it is striking that almost all of those areas with the potential, under existing farming systems, for high agricultural productivity – the upland basins, the dry valleys, the volcanic islands – were not only populated, but densely so. The evident precariousness of the subsistence food supply (see Chapter IX) even under favourable conditions makes it likely that many of the uninhabited areas could not in fact have been cultivated productively enough by existing methods (and at existing levels of labour investment, of which more below and in Chapter XV) to maintain food security in crisis years. Political and medical factors, secondly, also made large areas of land inaccessible, or at least highly unattractive, for farming purposes. Within Minahasa, for instance, the prevalence of malaria in the lowlands, and the desire to maintain a degree of autonomy from coastal power centres, probably worked alongside differences in agricultural potential to concentrate the bulk of the population on the central plateau (see Chapter XI). Preventive checks to population growth, then, may conceivably have operated not with respect to the potential carrying capacity of the total land area, but only within the boundaries of such existing centres of relatively dense population.

Tammes, who did not believe in the effectiveness of traditional fertility control, saw only two processes, both operating via mortality, which could account for his proposed equilibrium:

> 1. The direct effect of food shortages which in times of increasing population density, and mainly following particularly poor harvests, lead to reduced birth rates and increased mortality (especially child mortality as a result of reduced disease resistance); 2. Emigration of the surplus population from healthy areas to malarial locations, where it ultimately dies out. (Tammes 1940:197.)

Regarding the second of these possibilities it must be said that while very high death rates, especially among non-immune newcomers, undoubtedly prevailed in zones of endemic malaria, there is not much evidence for sustained emigration from malaria-free to malarial areas other than on a seasonal basis. In malarial Napu during the late nineteenth century, admittedly, routine mortality was said to be so high, and the birth rate so low, that a stable population was maintained only by constant imports of enslaved war captives from neighbouring parts of Central Sulawesi.[9] But if Adriani and Kruyt were right to imply a causal relationship here, then it evidently resulted from perceived 'underpopulation' in Napu rather than from population pressure elsewhere.

Also interesting from the point of view of interpreting migration as an

9   Adriani and Kruyt 1912-14, I:87; A.C. Kruyt 1903b:203, 1908:1292, 1309.

aspect of demographic homeostasis is the situation of the Talaud and Banggai Islands, both of which exported large numbers of slaves over long periods on a commercial basis (Chapters IV and VI). Both areas, strikingly, were also characterized by an unusual combination of quite dense population and relatively infertile soils, a predicament which may have combined with their lack of other commercial resources to make this last-ditch export strategy both attractive to local political leaders, and necessary if import goods, including essential iron, were to be obtained in adequate quantities.[10] During a Dutch visit to Talaud in 1854, some of the chiefs who acted as slave suppliers for their overlords in Sangir candidly explained 'that for them the slaves were a necessary medium of exchange, because they did not have much else with which to pay for the goods they needed'.[11] In the sparsely populated Poso area, by contrast, Adriani (1915:468) observed that 'to sell a slave was regarded as a disgrace, because it meant that the tribe lost another member'. But if slave exports acted to stabilize population levels on Banggai and Talaud, they cannot have contributed much to the maintainance of any broader equilibrium, since most of the exported slaves (at least in the Talaud case) remained within the region, and since neither area was malaria-free or otherwise healthier than the destinations (for Talaud, Sangir) to which the slaves were transported.

The more credible of the two feedback mechanisms proposed by Tammes is the effect of rising population densities on in situ mortality. Unless farming practices change or the food supply is augmented by trade, per capita food availability must inevitably decline if a population grows to the point where less productive land has to be brought under cultivation (Henley 1997a:105). Especially where water supply problems exist or where floods create a frequent health hazard, the incidence of infectious disease is also likely to rise as a population becomes more dense (Cohen 1989:47-51). Agricultural techniques were not in fact fixed and immutable, and there is evidence that in Minahasa, intensification of labour inputs in response to population growth already allowed some increase in the areal productivity of the existing farmland during the eighteenth century. Had the soils been less fertile or the preferred farming methods different, however, this might not have been possible, and there are indications that unsustainable farming practices, leading to land degradation and falling foodcrop yields, were directly involved in the nineteenth-century depopulation of the Poso and Mori areas. Both agricultural intensification in Minahasa, and the evidence for an ecological crisis with demographic consequences in Central Sulawesi, will be discussed in Chapter XV.

---

[10] Schoorl (1994:50), comparably, writes that on Buton in Southeast Sulawesi, the export of slaves 'was seen as a necessity to boost income for the ruling estates' even though the resulting depopulation inevitably meant a 'weakening of the sultanate'.
[11] A.J.F. Jansen, 'Missive Sangir en Talaut Eilanden', 26-8-1857 (ANRI Manado 166).

The agricultural 'carrying capacity' of a given area is not determined solely by environmental conditions, but also by the farming techniques to which a population is accustomed (Brookfield 1984), and by the amount of labour which it is prepared or able to expend in the pursuit of a plentiful harvest (Bayliss-Smith 1980). In northern Sulawesi, the general preference for labour-efficient agricultural methods and intensive, short-fallow swidden cycles (Chapters XIII-XIV) placed a particularly high premium on soil quality. Moreover food production, if only because of a rather marked 'leisure preference' in economic behaviour (see Chapter XV), was not always maximized, and given the evidence for maldistribution of food and underfeeding of infants even under favourable conditions, it would be naive to assume that this behaviour was automatically modified whenever mortality rose.

Whatever the precise combination of environmental and behavioural limitations involved, it does appear that the scope for spatial expansion of traditional agriculture was much more limited than early Western observers like Kruyt and Nieboer believed. Landuse in eastern central Sulawesi concluded a survey of Sulawesi's land resources carried out in connection with the national transmigration programme in the 1980s, is 'strongly influenced by difficult growing conditions over ultrabasic and limestone soils and the traditional agricultural lands have become confined to the larger valleys and plains where crop growth is acceptable' (RePPProT 1988:123). Even in fertile Minahasa, there were said at the beginning of the twentieth century to be localities 'the infertility of which makes them completely unsuitable for farming, and which were therefore abandoned by the first people to clear them of forest' (Jellesma 1903:83-4). The colonization of the lowlands and southern borders of Minahasa in the late nineteenth and early twentieth centuries (see Chapter V) was based not on a geographical extension of subsistence agriculture as already practised in the old settled areas, but on the exploitation of a new commercial resource, copra. It also coincided with a dramatic expansion in domestic market exchange, which both stimulated production and reduced the vulnerability of individual farming communities to local subsistence crises. The colonists were probably forced to employ longer fallow cycles than were customary on the central plateau (see Chapter XIV), and at Modoinding, a specially chosen site for organized transmigration on the border with Bolaang Mongondow, irrigation turned out to be essential 'for an adequate improvement of the soil, which quickly becomes exhausted by the current *ladang* cultivation' (Weg 1938:94).

Similar arguments, of course, can be applied to the population history of Indonesia as a whole. Despite the by now almost universal realization that the rainforests of Indonesia, like their equally sparsely-populated counterparts elsewhere in the world, mostly grew on very poor soils and in permanently humid climates hostile to most types of agriculture, the myth that precolonial

Southeast Asia offered its inhabitants 'an abundance of rich agricultural land' (Junker 1999:134) has been slow to die.[12] The historically uninhabited areas of the outer islands, as many transmigrants from Java and Bali have found to their cost, are seldom well suited for agricultural colonization. Where frontier settlement projects have been successful in colonial and post-colonial Southeast Asia, they have usually involved either the transformation of the landscape by means of labour- and capital-intensive irrigation, drainage, and terracing, or, more often, the cultivation of new cash crops for previously inaccessible or non-existent export markets (Levang 1997; Uhlig 1984). Sophistry aside, as recent authors continue to point out (Boomgaard 1997a:3-4; Rigg 1991:83), it is hardly conceivable that the persistent geographical correlation between relatively high population densities and naturally fertile soils, especially with respect to the broad contrast between Java/Bali and the outer islands, is a historical accident.[13] At this archipelagic scale, moreover, it also becomes very difficult to believe that the generally denser population of the more economically productive areas resulted from constant migration flows, rather than from in situ processes affecting birth and death rates.

Observations like these, in my opinion, cast fundamental doubt on the attempts of some demographers and anthropologists to ascribe traditional patterns of low reproductive fertility to a quasi-universal 'two-child psychology' (Carey and Sopreanto 1996:621), or to other accidents of society and culture which bear no relation to environmental conditions (Cleland and Wilson 1987; Shepherd 1995). Indirect links, in other words, must in fact have existed between the institutional and behavioural patterns leading to low fertility, and the economic factors limiting the scope for population growth. Following the recognition among ecologists that non-human populations are not 'self-regulating' as collectivities, and that '[reproductive] strategies that enhance individual success will always be favoured by natural selection, regardless of their effects on others and on the population' (Low, Clarke and

---

[12]   It is interesting to note that although Knapen (1997:449, 2001:390-1) has described population densities in precolonial Borneo as 'far below the carrying capacity of the environment', surveys of agricultural potential carried out by the Food and Agriculture Organization in the 1970s still identified huge areas of Kalimantan as unsuitable even for the cultivation of swidden rice (Löffler 1982:131). See also Hardjono 1971:102.

[13]   Even if we accept that the total population of Java (with Madura) in 1800 was only 7.5 million (Boomgaard and Gooszen 1991:82), its average population density was already over 55 persons per km^2, or at least five times that of northern Sulawesi in the same period. While a great expansion of the area under irrigation and permanent fields undoubtedly took place on Java in the course of the nineteenth century, it is worth noting that Raffles (1978, I:108), contrary to common belief, did not state in 1817 that only one eighth of the island was inhabited and cultivated. What he wrote was that over the remaining seven-eighths, 'the soil is either entirely neglected or badly cultivated, and the population scanty'; for 'bad' cultivation here, and very possibly also for 'neglect', read: swidden farming or livestock rearing.

Lockridge 1992:24), it has become more difficult to explain cultural patterns and social institutions conducive to fertility restriction in terms of analogies with what Harris and Ross (1987:14) called 'optimizing relations established through selection-by-consequences in the evolution of species, in the behaviour patterns of a single species of organism, and in the behaviour of communities of diverse species organized into ecosystems'.[14] The establishment of population equilibria, in most current thinking, must be explained not by identifying 'special adaptive mechanisms whose function is to restrain population growth', but rather in terms of 'the ultimate inability of individuals and economies to overcome the inherent finitude of resources' (Wood 1998: 120). Without wanting to give the impression that the answers are clear, certain, or complete, I would like to suggest some ways in which low fertility in northern Sulawesi did reflect this 'finitude of resources' despite the fact that its immediate causes at the level of individual women were mostly cultural and political.

The most obvious evidence for such a link, firstly, is the correlation between delayed marriage and high population densities in Minahasa and Sangir. The fact that bride price payments in both of these areas often included pieces of farmland arguably also makes visible at least part of the specific mechanism by which relative scarcity tended to depress fertility: the implied need to wait until such land became available in order to marry and raise children. It is possible that the size of other bridewealth demands was also affected by the knowledge that not all potential marriage partners enjoyed access to the means of subsistence necessary to feed a family. In Central Sulawesi, where early marriage was the norm, its effects on fertility were counteracted by frequent male absence, and here too a link with economic conditions can be discerned. Padoch (1982:115, 117), who identifies male absence as an important indirect fertility control among the Iban of Sarawak, notes that its frequency and duration are determined partly by the productivity of subsistence agriculture. Where long, continuous settlement in the same locality has led to land degradation, Iban men compensate for declining foodcrop yields by spending more time away from home earning income from commercial activities (wage labour and forest product collection) which can be exchanged for food produced elsewhere. The fact that temporary male emigration was least highly developed in the most agriculturally productive part of northern Sulawesi, Minahasa, and most common in less fertile Central Sulawesi, suggests a similar pattern. In so far as male absence underpinned matrifocal kinship organization, it also reproduced itself by creating social

---

14   Well-known (and much-criticized) attempts to interpret aspects of cultural behaviour as mechanisms for the maintenance of stable population/resource ratios include those of Vayda (1976) on the subject of war, and Rappaport (1984) on ritual feasting in New Guinea.

incentives for men to spend much time away from home (see Chapter I), and at the same time reinforced the patterns of female autonomy which favoured deliberate birth control (see Chapter X).

To the extent that slavery was conducive to fertility control, it too may have constituted a homeostatic link between subsistence production and the birth rate. Slavery, it has been noted, often had its origin in food debts, and was probably also underpinned on a long-term basis by the food security provided by masters to their slaves in times of hardship (see Chapter IX). Other things being equal, then, we might expect to find most slaves in those areas where subsistence crises were most common, and there is some evidence that this was indeed the case. The proportion of slaves in the population of drought-prone Gorontalo was large (Chapter III), and in Central Sulawesi the slaveholding To Lage, To Onda'e, and To Pada groups all inhabited areas where unusually large amounts of land were unsuitable for swidden agriculture as a result of conversion, probably at least partly in connection with declining soil fertility, to permanent grassland (see Chapters XIII-XV).[15] Albert Kruyt (1899c:608) even referred in one publication to 'overpopulation' among the To Lage, who were obliged by the spread of grasslands in their territory to 'migrate steadily further toward the north' (A.C. Kruyt 1911:80). Comparable evidence that geographical variations in the prevalence of slavery were related to differences in levels of economic security can be found in an early twentieth-century ethnography of the Ifugao of upland Luzon in the Philippines:

> Before the American occupation, except in those few parts of the habitat that were prosperous and in which the obtaining of the daily ration was not a serious problem, the selling by parents who found themselves poverty stricken of one of their children was not at all uncommon (Barton 1969:28).

Slavery, in this light, can be viewed partly as an institutional consequence of (periodic) scarcity – and so, by extension, can the strengthening of incentives to deliberate birth control which it entailed.[16] In so far as it weakened the incentives to surplus production, slavery also tended to reproduce its own economic preconditions by increasing the frequency of food crises. An almost

[15]   Kruyt (1911:75) observed that the social position of slaves among the To Pada, who inhabited the largest stretch of continuous grassland in the region (see Chapter XIII), was particularly disadvantageous. It is also interesting to note that To Lage men were more strongly involved than their non-slaveholding neighbours in seasonal *damar* collection (A.C. Kruyt 1911:83), leading to more frequent male absence.
[16]   This interpretation, it will be noted, differs radically from the traditional view, inspired by the classic work of H.J. Nieboer (1900), of Southeast Asian slavery as a mode of labour control or surplus extraction conditioned by the abundance of available land relative to the labour supply (Reid 1983:8) – a view which has long been questioned in the literature on slavery in Africa (Kopytoff and Miers 1977:68-9).

exactly parallel argument can be constructed with respect to the corporate kin group and its (possible) effects on fertility behaviour; more will be said about this below.

Long and intensive breast-feeding, finally, may likewise have been related to economic (specifically, dietary) conditions. Children born to malnourished mothers, several studies have suggested, 'tend to suckle more frequently and more intensively to obtain adequate amounts of breastmilk' (Aguirre, Palloni and Jones 1998:234), and this tendency is strengthened when the infant diet is also deficient in other sources of protein (Lesthaeghe 1986:214). There are, then, grounds for interpreting several of the cultural patterns conducive to low fertility as consequences of economic scarcity. This interpretation is reinforced by a comparative review of what the demographic evidence from different parts of the region implies regarding the root causes of population growth.

Population growth: Minahasa, 1855-1930

At the beginning of the nineteenth century, about 100,000 people probably lived in Minahasa. Smallpox killed at least 15,000 of them in 1817, cholera, dysentery and malaria perhaps another 10,000 in the early 1830s (Graafland 1867-69, II:157), and the evidence (Chapter V) suggests that the total did not reach 100,000 again until the early 1850s, when it was promptly cut back once more by about 10,000 in 1854 due to a combined epidemic of dysentery, cholera, measles and malaria. This time, however, the recovery was rapid, and the rather accurate figures which are available from 1860 onward (Figure 15) show a remarkably steady increase (the dip in 1877 is almost certainly an error) from 100,000 in 1860 to 180,000 in 1900, followed after 1905 by acceler-ated growth, the detailed course of which cannot be reconstructed for want of data, to a population of more than 300,000 in 1930. Both a fall in mortality and a rise in fertility were responsible for the pattern of sustained growth from 1855 to 1930.[17]

A striking feature of the almost continuous population record from the period 1860-1905 is the absence of the dramatic mortality crises which had periodically affected Minahasa in earlier times. The most obvious (indeed, the only immediately obvious) reason for this was vaccination against small-pox, the level of which was reportedly 'as high as could be wished for in any civilized country' by 1860.[18] Thanks to the vaccine, Minahasa was completely spared from the smallpox epidemics which raged beyond its borders in 1860-

---

[17]   The effects of considerable immigration (from Sangir, Talaud and Gorontalo) were almost exactly cancelled out by emigration of Minahasans to other parts of Indonesia (see Chapter V).
[18]   AV Manado 1860 (ANRI Manado 52).

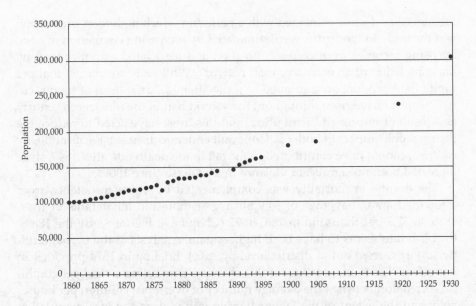

Figure 15. Population growth in Minahasa, 1860-1930.
Sources: AV Minahasa 1860-69 (ANRI Manado 52, 53); *Koloniaal verslag* 1871-97, 1902,
1907; *Uitkomsten* 1922:216-19; *Volkstellling* 1933-36, V:xi.

1861, 1883-1884 and 1908-1909. Vaccination, on the other hand, had begun
here as early as 1822, and since the regional epidemic of 1839-1841 also took
few lives in Minahasa, it could be argued that if smallpox was really a crucial
limiting factor, then the total population in 1860 would already have been
much larger than at the beginning of the century, which it was not. Also difficult to explain is the limited impact of the cholera epidemics of 1866-1867,
1874, and 1885-1886, the last of which seems to have caused a considerable
population decline in Gorontalo and Talaud, yet was 'only sporadic, and did
not last long' in Minahasa (Graafland 1898, I:96) despite the absence of an
effective medical treatment. The annual mortality statistics from the period
1849-1872, moreover, show that besides the disappearance of the sudden
crises, the routine background death rate also fell from an annual average of
28.6 per thousand in 1849-1860 (excluding the epidemic year 1854) to 25.7 per
thousand in 1861-1872 (Chapter VIII, Table 17).

Colonial quarantine measures may well have been a factor reducing the
impact of cholera and other infectious diseases in late nineteenth-century
Minahasa, as may improved hygiene and other changes in behaviour associated with European influence and conversion to Christianity. From 1855
onward, quinine was also distributed on a surprisingly large scale for the
treatment of malaria. What is probably more significant, however, is that

the mortality decline coincided with a period in which both food production and the trade in foodstuffs were stimulated by increasing circulation of cash, by rising incomes from coffee cultivation and associated activities, and by the completion of an extensive road network. While it is not certain that per capita food production continued to grow after 1872, the level of food security seems to have risen throughout the second half of the nineteenth century as a result of improved distribution, and this must have acted to reduce the demographic impact of both epidemic and endemic diseases. Pacification, by contrast, cannot have contributed to the fall in the death rate after 1849, since there had been no significant violence in Minahasa since 1809.

The decline in mortality was complemented by a rise in natality, from a reported annual average of 34.9 births per thousand inhabitants in 1849-1860, to 37.2 per thousand in 1861-1872 (Chapter X, Figure 8). By the 1880s, the birth rate seems to have been higher again. Analysis of the partial fertility survey carried out at district level by A.C.J. Edeling in 1874 provides an important clue to the reasons for this change by revealing a clear geographical correlation between the average number of ever-born children per household, and the extent of the labour burden imposed on the local population by compulsory coffee cultivation. Explaining this association, however, is no straightforward matter.

Thanks to the near-invisibility of the immediate causes of fertility change in the historical record, the relationship between labour demand and the birth rate, when recognized at all, has been subject to divergent interpretations. In Java, according to Alexander (1986:257), fertility rose under the Cultivation System because 'increased participation of women in arduous and sustained work' meant that infants had to be weaned more quickly. This led to shorter intervals between successive pregnancies, both because breastfeeding itself inhibits fertility (lactational amenorrhoea) and because of a custom, well documented in modern Java (although not in older sources), of avoiding sexual intercourse for as long as breastfeeding continues.[19] Javanese women, in other words, were forcibly worked into producing more children. Boomgaard, by contrast, attributes the correlation between fertility rates and compulsory labour services to 'the growth of the non-agricultural sectors of the Javanese economy, generated by the Cultivation System, which created new economic opportunites'. Thanks to additional income from the compulsory cultivations, and especially from transport, handicraft and other ancillary economic activities stimulated by the System, increasing numbers of people were able to support larger families, and also 'to marry earlier than they could have

---

[19]   Boomgaard (1989a:194-5), while acknowledging some of the evidence for longer periods of post-partum abstinence in modern Java, believes that in the nineteenth century such abstinence lasted 'no more than 40 days'.

done if they had had to wait for a piece of land' (Boomgaard 1989a:197). Far from forcing peasant women to have more children, in this analysis, colonialism enabled them to do so by raising their incomes.

The conclusions reached by Alexander and Boomgaard have been described by Hull (2001:159) as 'diametrically opposed'. In terms of their implications for the broad outlines of demographic history, this may be an exaggeration; in both cases, after all, a rise in fertility is elicited by an increase in economic activity. For obvious Malthusian reasons, it should also be noted, the combination of population growth and declining welfare implicit in the Alexander model could not be sustained indefinitely. Partly with this in mind, and partly because they presume that patterns of economic activity are not subject to the kind of political constraints imposed by the Cultivation System, macro-demographers tend to follow Adam Smith (1870:77) in treating labour demand and income (food) supply as more or less identical quantities (Lee 1997:1064-5; Wrigley and Schofield 1981:465). But in view of the unresolved disagreement between Boomgaard and Alexander over the specific nature of the agreed link between aggregate economic growth and fertility increase on Java, it is clearly important here not to go further down any single explanatory path than the direct historical evidence permits.

In the case of Minahasa, a reduction in the duration and intensity of breast-feeding, as a result of (direct and indirect) female involvement in compulsory labour services, is definitely attested to in contemporary sources. The precision of the statistical relationship (at least on a geographical basis) between the birth rate and the size of that burden arguably also points to an unconscious mechanism rather than to a conscious fertility adjustment, the correlation of which with the demand for labour is more likely to be clouded by other locally varying social and cultural factors. While there is no evidence for long periods of post-partum sexual abstinence in Minahasa (or anywhere else in the region), the significance of extended breast-feeding alone in depressing the birth rate is widely recognized among demographers (see Chapter X). Since child labour was undoubtedly useful in reducing or compensating for the compulsory labour burden, it is possible that a deliberate relaxation of existing fertility controls (abortion, infanticide, traditional contraception, and delayed marriage are all attested to from Minahasa) was also involved (Alexander and Alexander 1979).

There was no correlation on a district level between fertility rates and the income earned from compulsory coffee cultivation, which was not proportional to the amount of labour involved. During the late nineteenth century, however, many other sources of income also emerged or expanded in Minahasa, including carting, cattle breeding, the production of food for the domestic market, and later copra sales and wage labour in the private sector. Although it is not likely that a complete income analysis would provide a more satisfactory explanation than labour demand for the specific geographical variations in fertility revealed by the Edeling survey, the general increase in prosperity caused by the commercial expansion probably contributed to the chronological trend toward higher fertility in so far as this was linked with the slight but significant decline which took place toward the end of the nineteenth century in the age at which Minahasan women married. The increased availability of economic opportunities outside subsistence agriculture, the exploitation of new agricultural resources outside the central plateau, and rising cash incomes in general, all facilitated marriage, if only by making the associated festivities more affordable.

A link between economic activity and fertility which operates via income rather than via labour demand certainly seems called for in order to help explain why annual birth rates in Minahasa were seldom lower than 38 per thousand, and often above 40 per thousand, during the early twentieth century. Compulsory coffee cultivation was discontinued in 1899, and by the 1920s the tax burden, effectively another form of compulsory labour, was also light. It remains possible, on the other hand, that coconut cultivation and copra production, although less labour-intensive than coffee growing, combined with the general acceleration of other economic sectors, and possibly the labour-intensification of foodcrop agriculture (Chapter XV), to keep the demand for both child and adult female labour high. The duration of breast-feeding, although it probably lengthened somewhat, does not appear to have resumed its traditional proportions, and a kind of habituation to the changes of the nineteenth century may have been involved here alongside economic choices.

Food distribution, on the mortality side, continued to improve (despite a probable decline in domestic food production) after 1900, when Minahasa began to import very large quantities of foreign rice while at the same time its domestic transport and market networks were consolidated (Plate 18). Some further improvements in the medical situation were also brought about by species sanitation measures against malaria, the introduction of a cure for yaws, the gradual elimination of skin disease, and the increasing popularity of Dutch-trained midwives. These developments were no doubt mutually reinforcing; while better nutrition improved resistance to disease, better health had a positive effect on nutrition, not only because it led to increased labour productivity, but also because frequent illness is a key cause of inadequate food consumption, and hence malnutrition, among infants (Floud, Wachter and Gregory 1990:245; Kusin and Sri Kardjati 1994:32). While there is not much evidence that poor nutrition (barring actual starvation) affects fertility, medical care (malaria control and professional midwifery) probably had some positive effect upon the birth rate, as did mortality improvements themselves, which, by reducing the incidence of widowhood, tend to produce higher fertility rates among older women of reproductive age.

Plate 18. Public market in Tomohon (Minahasa), 1945, showing horse- and ox-carts (KITLV Photograph 6679)

No long series of mortality figures, unfortunately, is available for Minahasa after 1870. In the years 1931 and 1932, however, the death rates in the districts surveyed by Dr Kündig (Appendix H) were 23.2 and 23.3 per thousand respectively, figures well below the average for the 1860s. In 1930, on the other hand, an epidemic of influenza and dysentery killed many infants and raised the overall crude death rate to 29.6 per thousand, a level reminiscent of the 1850s. The mortality figures collected during Kündig's intensive survey were probably more complete (especially with respect to infant deaths) in relation to the recorded population totals than their nineteenth-century predecessors, so that the real contrast between the two periods may have been greater than his results suggest. It does seem likely, nevertheless, that the mortality reduction in the second half of the nineteenth century was at least as great as that in the early years of the twentieth, and this strengthens the impression that economic rather than medical factors were of primary importance here.[20]

[20]   Some fragmentary data from the late 1940s, on the other hand, suggest a second pronounced decline in mortality after 1930. In Mori in the years 1947-1948, the reported average crude death

Population growth: Minahasa, 1700-1800

The modern episode of sustained population growth in Minahasa, beginning in 1855, does not seem to have been the first. In the course of the eighteenth century, according to the global estimates presented in Chapter XI (Table 23), the Minahasan population had already almost doubled, from perhaps 55,000 in 1700 to approximately 100,000 in 1800, suggesting an average increase of about 0.6 percent per year. The dimensions of this growth, it must be repeated, are rather hypothetical, and there is even some residual doubt as to whether any of it was real. Having presumed to make the estimates, however, an attempt must be made to explain them. Medicine, obviously, can be ruled out here, and while the relatively long interval between successive smallpox epidemics in the eighteenth century (see Chapter VII) was no doubt conducive to population growth, it is difficult to see why this should have had more effect in Minahasa than in Sangir. Any reduction in internal warfare, despite the continuous Dutch presence, also seems to have been slight, and although it is possible that other important cultural changes took place which affected fertility and mortality, the absence of missionary activity or Western schooling makes it unlikely that these were to any degree independent of the economic environment.[21] The causes of the growth prior to 1800, in fact, can only reasonably be sought in economic changes, two of which seem dramatic enough to be regarded as candidates: an increase in agricultural productivity, and an increase in external trade.

Tammes (1940:192) proposed that the growth of the Minahasan population between the seventeenth century and the nineteenth had resulted mainly from the gradual incorporation of a productive new food plant, maize, into the swidden farming system.[22] By the nineteenth century, as we have seen, maize was certainly a very important crop in this area, perhaps equalling rice in terms of quantities produced and consumed (see Chapter IX). Much maize was also fed to pigs, the main domestic animals in Minahasa, and to horses.[23] Its resistance to drought, short maturation period and limited labour requirements (Heyne 1950:143) made it an ideal complement to swidden *padi*, raising

---

rate was 16.5 per thousand (De Wijn 1952:165). On Greater Sangir in 1949 it was just 14 per thousand, having fallen from 23 per thousand immediately after the Second World War; Blankhart (1951:89) attributed this in part to the restoration of medical services on the island.

[21]   Some conversions to Christianity did occur in Minahasa during the VOC period, but in 1821, according to the (probably rather complete) Dutch records, there were still only 4,048 Minahasan Christians (Reinwardt 1858:583).

[22]   Wigboldus (1988:54) also believes that maize became progressively more important in this period, but sees this more as a response to population growth than as one of its causes.

[23]   Edeling 1919:73; N.P. Wilken 1870:374; J.J. ten Siethoff, 'Topografische schetsen van een gedeelte der residentie Menado 1845' (ANRI Manado 46). Purseglove (1972, I:302) calls maize grain 'an outstanding feed for livestock'.

both the level of food security in times of unfavourable weather, and the total productivity of each field.[24] Maize yielded much better than rice on ground cleared of *alang-alang* grass rather than secondary forest (Appendix K), and may therefore have helped to make possible shorter fallow periods and a more intensive cultivation cycle (see Chapter XIV). In combination with rice, it probably also helped to maintain the fertility of the better soils: according to a source from the beginning of the twentieth century, it was the alternation (*wisselbouw*) of rice with maize which 'spared the ground from exhaustion' in those areas of fertile volcanic soil where unirrigated fields were in continuous cultivation without fallow (Worotikan 1910:153). While maize may to some extent have displaced existing secondary crops, it is unlikely that these had been as productive.[25]

An immediate objection to the idea that maize powered the population growth of the eighteenth century, however, is that this New World crop, introduced to nearby Sangir as early as the mid-sixteenth century (see Chapter II), was already common in Minahasa by the 1670s. Padtbrugge (1866:324) observed in 1679 that Minahasan houses were 'hung full with bundles of rice, *turkse tarwe* [maize] and other grains', and later recorded that maize was grown 'in great abundance, so that 15,000 cobs can usually be obtained in exchange for one blue *salempuris*' (Van Dam 1931:78). A different source, on the other hand, suggests that at this stage maize cultivation was not yet universal in Minahasa: in 1677, the assembled *walak* chiefs told a VOC official that 'except for *oubijs* [tubers] and *pattaten* [sweet potatoes], which they live on for the most part', their subjects grew little food other than rice.[26] While this statement should probably be interpreted in terms of the declared reluctance of the chiefs to promise higher rice deliveries in the future, it does raise the possibility that the importance of maize continued to grow after 1680. It is also tempting to link the growth trend suggested by the early seventeenth-century population figures from Sangir with a similar consolidation of New World crops, in this case sweet potato as well as maize. A second difficulty with the maize hypothesis, however, is the underlying assumption that higher productivity must have resulted in bigger harvests. Schouten (1998:47) argues that maize was exploited not primarily in order to increase the food surplus, but in order to create more free time; this possibility will be discussed in Chapter XV.

---

[24] The local varieties which emerged in Minahasa after its introduction were said to be of very high quality (Graafland 1898, I:152). In the twentieth century one of these was chosen by the colonial government for further selective breeding on Java (Van der Veer 1948:139).

[25] In Central Sulawesi maize may well have taken the place of Job's tears (*Coix lachryma-jobi*), the indigenous name of which it often inherited, in local farming systems (Adriani and Kruyt 1950-51, III:147; A.C. Kruyt 1938, IV:230).

[26] NA VOC 1328:163r. I am grateful to Jouke Wigboldus for pointing out this source to me.

A different approach to the population growth between 1700 and 1800 has been proposed by Wigboldus (1988:37), who argues that this growth must be attributed at least partly to a process of commercialization. In Minahasa, the eighteenth century was a period in which foreign trade expanded. Annual rice sales to the VOC increased from some 60 tonnes around 1690 to 170 tonnes by 1730, and averaged about 300 tonnes in the 1740s (Brandwijk van Blokland 1749; Godée Molsbergen 1928:87, 106, 113). By reducing the distances over which the rice had to be transported, the construction of additional VOC outposts at Amurang in 1719 and Kema in 1751 (Wigboldus 1988:37) no doubt encouraged farmers to sell a greater proportion of their surplus.[27] At the same time there was also an increase in the number of private vessels loading Minahasan rice, beeswax, and nautical rope manufactured from *gumutu*, a fibre product of the sugar palm.[28] By the 1750s this free trade was described as 'lively' (Godée Molsbergen 1928:122), and in subsequent years it included the export of rice to Sulu by Bugis traders (Warren 1981:12). In the 1770s a significant number of ethnic Chinese merchants decided to settle permanently in Manado (see Chapter V), causing a further shift in favour of the private sector. In 1782 the Dutch resident attributed a recent decline in official VOC trade to 'the many Chinese in Manado, each of whom has at least three wives at different places in the uplands, collecting rice to be exported privately'.[29] In 1804, another official complained that the amount of beeswax entering official Dutch trade had also declined as the number of Chinese residents had grown (Watuseke and Henley 1994:368).

In the immediately following period, by contrast, private commerce stagnated. 'The amount of shipping activity in Manado', reported Resident Wenzel in 1825, 'has remained stable, or at least has not increased, for many years' (Riedel 1872b:549). The correspondence here between commercial trends and population growth, which also stagnated in the early nineteenth century, is striking. To some extent, of course, the volume of trade must have been determined by the size of the population, rather than vice versa. It also remains to be shown how the export of a proportion of the main subsistence food, mostly in return for luxury textiles and in the context of a weakly devel-

---

[27]   By the beginning of the nineteenth century, there were also coastal outposts at Bentenan and Tanawangko (Watuseke and Henley 1994:377-9).
[28]   In 1729 (*Generale missiven* VIII:21) it was reported that many inhabitants of the Tombariri area 'have moved down to Tanawangko on the coast, and set up new villages in order to sell their rice more easily to the private traders whose vessels put in there' (also NA VOC 2132:29). Whereas the map of Minahasa drawn by Padtbrugge in 1679 shows Tombariri ('Tomriri') as an upland settlement south of Tomohon (Henley 1995:47), Tanawangko itself was the capital of the *walak* by the nineteenth century (Chapter I, Map 5).
[29]   Gov. Moluccas to GG, 28-9-1782 (ANRI Ternate 91).

oped domestic market, could have been conducive to population growth in Minahasa during the eighteenth century. One part of the answer is that commercial demand probably stimulated total rice production (see Chapter XV), so that the sale of the resulting surplus did not mean reduced domestic consumption.[30] Before returning to the question of exactly how commerce and population growth were articulated, however, it is important to establish that the population increase in eighteenth-century Minahasa is not the only case of a demographic change for which commercial developments seem to provide the most convincing explanation.

Population growth: Sangir, 1850-1900

If the population of Minahasa grew rapidly in the late nineteenth century, so did that of the Sangir Islands to its north (Greater Sangir, Siau and Tagulandang). Sangir, combining exceptionally fertile soils with the various advantages of coastal settlement and the availability of a lucrative export product in the form of coconut oil, was already very densely settled by regional standards long before 1850. In the second half of the nineteenth century, nevertheless, its population, according to my estimates (Chapter XI, Table 23), suddenly grew from perhaps 55,000 to some 95,000, a proportional increase not far short of that which took place in Minahasa over the same period. Yet in terms of its concurrent political and economic development, Sangir, a 'self-governing' area never subject to compulsory cultivation, and without any permanent Dutch administrative presence before 1882, differed radically from its neighbour.

One circumstance conducive to population growth which Sangir did share with Minahasa, admittedly, was widespread smallpox inoculation. Although Tammes (1940:197) claimed that rapid growth had begun in Sangir 'before there was any question of vaccination on a significant scale', more than 14,000 Sangirese were in fact treated by travelling government vaccinators during the smallpox epidemic of 1860 alone, and by 1864 the vaccine was said to be 'permanently established' on the islands.[31] As in the

---

[30] Schouten (1998:47) and Wigboldus (1988:55) have also suggested that an increase in the availability of iron, as a result of trade, might have led to greater agricultural productivity. It must be noted, however, that Minahasan farmers already used iron chopping knives in the seventeenth century (Padtbrugge 1866:365), and apparently preferred spades made of hard *woka* (*Livistona rotundifolia*) wood over iron hoes (P.A. van Middelkoop, 'Memorien ten vervolge van het Algemeen Verslag van de Commissie naar de Moluksche Eilanden', 30-9-1818, in NA Schneither 128). Not surprisingly given the presence of a very old ironworking centre in Central Sulawesi, there is no historical evidence from any part of the region for a 'transition from stone to steel' of the type proposed by Dove (1989) for Kalimantan.

[31] MV Manado, October 1860 and December 1864 (ANRI Manado 54).

Minahasan case, however, freedom from smallpox can hardly be a complete explanation for the substantial growth of this period. Much less quinine, moreover, was available in Sangir than in Minahasa during the nineteenth century, and apart from slave raiding, which did decline rapidly after 1860 but which probably never had a great demographic impact even before that date (see Chapter XI), Sangir had already been an unusually peaceful part of the region since the end of the seventeenth century (see Chapter I). Protestant missionaries arrived in the islands in 1858, but since by that stage a large part of the population had been nominally Christian for more than 200 years, it is unlikely that cultural change as a direct consequence of religious conversion was as pronounced as in Minahasa. Immigration from Talaud may have accelerated after 1870, but contemporary descriptions of the Sangir Islands do not mention such a movement, and neither is Sangir named as a destination in the sources describing the late nineteenth-century exodus from Talaud, which saw a demographic collapse just as the population of the neighbouring islands was soaring. The traditional import of slaves from Talaud to Sangir, moreover, came to a halt in the same period.

Given the scarcity of convincing alternative explanations, the main factor behind population growth in Sangir during the late nineteenth century, as Tammes (1940:190) surmised, must have been 'the expansion of economic opportunities [*bestaansmogelijkheden*] – specifically, the cultivation of commercial crops'. Although Sangir had exported coconut oil to Manado and Ternate since the seventeenth century, the copra boom, which began earlier here than in Minahasa, gave unprecedented commercial importance to the already extensive coconut stands on the islands, and led to the planting of many more. The export of copra from Siau dates from 1862 (Van Dinter 1899: 334), and in 1880 a German trading firm established an agency on Greater Sangir in order to buy up this product directly (Encyclopaedisch Bureau 1912a:48; Matthes 1881). By the beginning of the twentieth century Sangir as a whole was probably exporting at least 5,000 tonnes of copra, or 50 kg for every inhabitant, each year (Encyclopaedisch Bureau 1912a:49). Starting in about 1860, secondly, nutmeg trees were planted on Greater Sangir and later also Siau, where they produced 'outstanding' yields, although nutmeg always remained less important than copra as an export product.[32] The rather precise correlation here between the onset of demographic growth on the one hand, and the emergence of completely new export products on the other, means that in the case of Sangir the possibility that it was a growing population which led to more trade (rather than vice versa) can effectively be ruled out.

[32]   Van Dinter 1899:335-7; Janse 1898:19-20; Tergast 1936:132.

Demography and export production

Given the clear correspondence between commercial expansion and population growth in Sangir after 1860, it is also tempting to attribute part of the decline in the Sangirese population between 1750 and 1800, a development tentatively associated in Chapter XI with an unusually rapid succession of natural disasters, to the impact of Magindanao pirate activity on seaborne trade. A two-way link between commercial and population trends is certainly evident in the case of Gorontalo, where demographic stagnation or decline in the first half of the nineteenth century coincided with the exhaustion of many gold mines, the decline of the important local weaving industry in the face of competition from European imports, and the introduction of colonial customs duties, which caused much Bugis transit trade to shift to the Togian Islands (see Chapter II). 'The level of prosperity in this division', wrote an assistant resident of Gorontalo in 1843, 'has fallen steadily over a number of years, and continues to decline today'.[33] The conspicuous poverty of the Gorontalese (Von Rosenberg 1865:23) was further exacerbated, at least temporarily, when a monetary head tax was imposed in 1850 despite the continuing scarcity of sources of monetary income.[34]

After 1870, by contrast, the fortunes of the area were transformed by the rise of rattan (Plate 19), *damar* and copra as lucrative export products. The inclusion of Gorontalo town as a port of call for the regular steamship services of the KPM in 1873 (*Koloniaal verslag* 1874:101), and the relaxation of customs restrictions there in 1879 (Matthes 1881), allowed it once more to overtake Togian and Parigi as the main commercial centre for the whole Gulf of Tomini, from the coasts of which many forest products, and eventually much copra, also came.[35] By 1890, Gorontalo was said to be the most important trading port in eastern Indonesia after Makassar (Van Hoëvell 1891:43). It was in this period of commercial expansion that the population of its hinterland, despite a rather unfavourable disease environment and a still inadequate level of vaccination coverage (see Chapters VII and VIII), began to climb rapidly (Chapter V).[36]

More interesting still is that the clear decline in the population of Tobungku between 1700 and 1900, which cannot easily be explained simply

[33] AV Gorontalo 1841-1843 (ANRI Manado 50).
[34] AV Gorontalo 1852, 1854 (ANRI Gorontalo 3).
[35] Broersma 1931b:229-35; Van der Crab 1875:442-4; Gonggrijp 1915:1336; Van Hoëvell 1891: 38, 42-3; Hunger 1920:293; Van Kol 1903:334-5; Van Musschenbroek 1880:97.
[36] Rattan and *damar* did not occur in the densely populated and entirely deforested Limboto Depression, but the male population of this core area became involved in the seasonal collection of these forest products elsewhere (Haga 1931:234-5; Van Hoëvell 1891:38). Coconut palms, by contrast, grew in large numbers on the plain (Riedel 1870a:88).

Plate 19. Rattan being dried for export, Gorontalo, circa 1930
(KITLV Photograph 18.822)

in terms of movements to neighbouring areas (see Chapter VI), corresponds
with the long-term demise of eastern Central Sulawesi as a centre of iron
production. In the sixteenth century, Tobungku, thanks to the availability of
readily-smelted ore in the adjacent interior, was an important source of iron
implements and weapons for the whole of eastern Indonesia (see Chapter II).
Like other ironworking centres in the archipelago, however, it may already
have been in decline by the end of the seventeenth century due to competition
from metal imported from China and Europe (Reid 1988-93, I:112). Another
problem (this time specific to eastern Central Sulawesi) was that from the
seventeenth century onward, most of the metal produced in the particularly
iron-rich Matano area was no longer exported via the east coast, but via Bugis
colonies in the neighbourhood of Malili on the Gulf of Bone (Bulbeck and
Caldwell 2000:96-100). Although the course of the decline cannot be reconstructed, it is interesting to note that during the 1840s the number of large
Bugis sailing vessels (*paduakang*) visiting Tobungku and Banggai each year to
load iron and *tripang* reportedly fell from 'twenty or thirty' to 'four or five'.[37]

---

[37]   A. Revius, 'Algemeen Verslag omtrent de oostkust van Celebes', 10-2-1851 (ANRI Ternate
180).

While a series of local wars was said to be the primary reason for this, it is possible that falling overseas demand for Tobungku iron was another factor – and also, in view of the pacifying effects of trade (see Chapter II), that the political instability was itself related to a reduction in export earnings. The demise of the Central Sulawesi iron industry in the late nineteenth century was certainly rapid (A.C. Kruyt 1901b:150; Sarasin and Sarasin 1905, I:312), and by 1930 the export of this metal from the east coast seems to have ceased altogether (Broersma 1931a:1042-4).

It is also possible to construct an argument linking the depopulation of Talaud, in the period 1875-1900, with concurrent economic changes. American and British whaling ships, operating in the Pacific and eastern Indonesia, frequently visited the Talaud Islands during the mid-nineteenth century to make repairs and take on water and provisions.[38] These supplies, along with the sexual services of local women, were paid for in clothing and textiles, iron, distilled alcohol, and sometimes silver coins.[39] Sperm whale teeth, worn by the islanders as ornaments (Cuarteron 1855:101), were another item obtained from the whaling crews, and it is possible that as in some Pacific island societies at the same period (Thomas 1991:110-7), these also became important in local trade and exchange. Some Talaud men enlisted, temporarily or permanently, as sailors on the British and American vessels, and many of the chiefs, who had little or no knowledge of the Dutch claim to their islands, spoke fluent English. At its peak in the 1850s the number of whaling ships visiting Talaud each year may have been as high as 50, implying an extensive commerce with the local population.[40] Thereafter, however, these visits became less frequent, occurring only 'now and then' in the 1870s (Van der Crab 1875:359), and ceasing altogether by the 1890s (Jellesma 1911:1242). In the same period, moreover, the centuries-old trade in slaves

---

[38]   E. Francis, 'Aantekening van den kommissaris voor Menado 1846' (ANRI Manado 167); AV Manado 1854 (ANRI Manado 51); Bleeker 1856:96; Buddingh 1860:344-9; Coolsma 1901:655; Van der Crab 1875:357-9; Cuarteron 1855:102-3, 108-10; A.J.F. Jansen, 'Rapport betrekkelijk het oppergezag over en den toestand van de Talaut Eilanden', 12-8-1857 (ANRI Manado 166).

[39]   Buddingh 1860:344; A.J.F. Jansen, 'Missive Sangir en Talaut Eilanden', 26-8-1857 (ANRI Manado 166).

[40]   A.J.F Jansen, 'Missive Sangir en Talaut Eilanden', 26-8-1857 (ANRI Manado 166). Even outside Talaud, the scale of the trade engaged in by the whalers seems to have been considerable (Olivier 1834-37, II:41). One Dutch official, writing in 1846, described them as smugglers who, 'on the pretext of requiring water and provisions, visit all the harbours of the Moluccas and supply these lands with English goods without paying customs duties' (Francis 1860:413). At Kema in Minahasa, also a common port of call for British whalers until the 1850s (AV Manado 1853, 1854, in ANRI Manado 51), the value of these clandestine imports was rumoured to have reached *f* 100,000 in some years (Francis 1860:413). The total value of official annual imports to Minahasa in the 1840s, by comparison, was only about *f* 300,000 (Chapter IX, Figure 7). The rumours, on the other hand, may well be exaggerated; a later report by Jansen states that 'very few' goods are imported by the whalers (AV Manado 1853, in ANRI Manado 51).

from Talaud to Sangir (see Chapter IV) also came to an end, partly under
Dutch pressure (Encyclopaedisch Bureau 1912a:25). On the face of things it
would seem unlikely that the cessation of an annual emigration flow could
have contributed to a depopulation trend, but since slaves were an important export commodity for Talaud, in this case such an idea is clearly in line
with the general correlation between demographic and commercial trends
observed elsewhere in the region.

The whaling activity in the vicinity of Talaud became extensive only at the
beginning of the nineteenth century, and cannot explain why the population
of this island group was already dense in earlier times.[41] Whether the decline
in the Tobungku iron trade can help to account for the parallel long-term
population decline in Banggai, which was originally involved in that trade,
but already seems to have lost political control of Tobungku to Ternate by
the end of the seventeenth century (Reid 1988-93, I:110), is also unclear. The
population of many parts of Central Sulawesi, moreover, declined in the late
nineteenth century (Chapter VI) despite an increasingly intensive involvement in the production of *damar* resin for export. More will be said about
these anomalies in Chapter XV. In general, however, it appears that population totals, even in the absence of medical improvements or major changes
in subsistence agriculture, were sensitive to any growth or decline in the volume of external trade. This association is the more striking considering that
trade itself was often a significant health hazard: during the seaborne trading
expeditions beloved of Sangirese men, claimed the missionary Steller (1866:
37), 'a number of people always die, while the remainder, who in many cases
are all sick, bring infectious diseases with them when they return home'.

Commercialization and population growth

In the absence of serial data on birth and death rates other than those from
Minahasa after 1849, it is seldom possible to say for certain how commercial
and demographic processes were articulated. One factor, however, was no
doubt the generally positive effect of commerce on the size and reliability of
the food supply. Gorontalo, for instance, imported little food (see Chapter
II), and experienced frequent shortages and epidemics (Chapter IX), in the
period 1820-1870, but was reportedly saved from such shortages in the
1880s by rice from Bali and Saigon.[42] By 1920 it had become 'dependent on

---

[41]   Forrest (1779:159-62, 314-8), in his description of Talaud in 1775, makes no mention of visits
by whaling ships, and in 1821 it was reported that English whalers had been active in Moluccan
waters only for 'some years' (Van Graaf and Meijlan 1856:257).
[42]   CV Manado 1883, 1888 (ANRI Manado 86).

imports from elsewhere' for its food supply (Pino 1920:7). When incomes increased as a result of rattan collection after 1870, internal market exchange also accelerated.[43] In this particular case, there is even some evidence for a direct link between the volume of commerce and the physical stature of the population. Dutch observers of the mid-nineteenth century attributed the short stature, weak appearance, and poor health of the Gorontalese partly to undernourishment.[44] Although they remained rather small in later, apparently more prosperous times (see Chapter VII), their height may well have declined during the period of precarious self-sufficiency: Reinwardt (1858: 520), in contrast to all subsequent visitors, described them in 1821 as 'very well-built' and 'larger and more muscular than the Javanese', while his colleague Bik (1864:154) agreed.[45]

In Gorontalo, as in Minahasa and Sangir, the local economy became monetized to an unprecedented degree during the period of population growth in the late nineteenth century. The fluidity of exchange which this made possible no doubt enhanced the effects of economic growth on the availability of food. It is not likely, however, that the moderation of subsistence crises by food purchases had been impossible for structural reasons under earlier conditions. Barter trade was always a feature of the traditional economy, and the prestige goods (textiles, brassware, livestock) which formed its most important currency were exchangeable for foodstuffs (see Chapter II). Among the Iban of Sarawak, according to Freeman (1955:103), such goods were sought partly with an explicit view to exchanging them for rice in the event of a food shortage within the household. The fact that they were also used for making bride price payments, moreover, indicates a likely link between income and fertility under non-monetized conditions: if the influx of cash into Minahasa in the nineteenth century tended to facilitate earlier marriage, then the influx of Indian textiles as a result of increasing rice exports during the eighteenth century probably had the same effect.[46]

Prosperity, as the demography of post-industrial societies reminds us, need not necessarily have a positive effect on fertility, and neither was this

---

[43]   AV Gorontalo 1872 (ANRI Manado 9).
[44]   Francis 1860:289; *Landbouw in Gorontalo* 1871:367; Riedel 1870a:69.
[45]   Once again, however, it must be stressed that descriptions of this kind are always highly subjective (see Chapter VII). In the 1860s, when Riedel (1870a:68) characterized the Gorontalese as 'small and weak', the naturalist Von Rosenberg (1865:31-3) found them to be 'of medium height, well-proportioned', and 'accustomed to withstanding fatigue'.
[46]   These texiles probably formed the most important component of bridewealth payments in Minahasa (De Clercq 1871c:33; Van Doren 1854:131; Graafland 1898, I:466-7; Olivier 1834-37, II: 32; Padtbrugge 1866:320; Pietermaat, De Vriese and Lucas 1840:122; Reinwardt 1858:599; Riedel 1872b:485, 557; Van Spreeuwenberg 1845-46:324).

always the case in earlier times.[47] The (to my knowledge) oldest description of 'family planning' in Indonesia, written by VOC governor-general Laurens Reael in the Moluccas in 1618, attributes the high rate of abortion and infanticide among Moluccan women partly to increases in the cost of living caused by 'the many needs which they have learned from the European nations' (*Generale missiven* I:88). Nuptuality, nevertheless, was not the only mechanism by which increased economic activity tended to favour high birth rates. The statistical evidence from nineteenth-century Minahasa indicates that it was the increased demand for labour which, via the automatic effects of reduced breast-feeding among hard-worked women, and perhaps also via conscious changes in reproductive behaviour aimed at increasing the availability of child labour within the household, formed the most important link between economic change and rising fertility. It is possible to argue that a parallel development had already occurred during the earlier period of demographic growth in the eighteenth century. In 1689, the *walak* chiefs told the Dutch resident of Manado that Minahasans were 'completely incapable' of providing the labour needed to hull the rice which they sold to the Company, since 'their wives and children already had enough productive work to do outside farming'.[48] In the first half of the eighteenth century, nevertheless, the VOC exported progressively larger quantities of husked rice instead of *padi* (Godée Molsbergen 1928:106, 113), implying that the female and child labour burden was increasing even at this early date.[49]

The relationship between economic and fertility change was complex, and to combine labour demand and income growth under the single heading of 'commercialization' is inherently dangerous. The very heavy demand for labour in nineteenth-century Minahasa resulted as much from political compulsion as from economic choice, so that in some districts rising fertility, as Paul and Jennifer Alexander (1979, 1984, 1986) have argued for the whole of Java under the Cultivation System, may well have coincided with diminishing rather than rising incomes. The role of labour demand in boosting fertility during more typical episodes of increasing commercial activity, moreover, cannot be demonstrated conclusively, and it does not seem likely that the involvement of women and children in copra or iron production,

---

[47]   The reverse assumption, indeed, has been predominant in twentieth-century demography. For Java, however, Hull and Hull (1977) demonstrated that a positive relationship between 'economic class' and fertility existed as late as the 1970s.

[48]   Van Thije 1689. Original wording: *'hun vrouwen en kinderen buiten den landbouw echter genoeg te doen vonden om aan de kost te komen'*. A decade earlier, Padtbrugge had likewise been told that Minahasan farmers could not provide hulled rice to the Company because the work of stamping the *padi* was 'too onerous' (Godée Molsbergen 1928:54).

[49]   The fact that the proportion of the rice crop sold for export was limited (see Chapter II), on the other hand, should be borne in mind here, since all *padi* ultimately had to be stamped anyway before it was cooked and eaten.

whether direct or indirect, was ever as intensive as their exploitation for the purposes of compulsory coffee cultivation in Minahasa. There are, however, ways in which increases in the availability of economic resources might have increased the 'demand for children' without necessarily involving those children directly in production, and here the concept of commercialization, understood as a social as well as an economic process, remains useful.

Two of the most important and widespread institutions in the traditional societies of the region, slavery and the corporate kin group with its multi-household co-residential core, can be understood partly as adaptations to economic scarcity. In the case of slavery some of the reasons for this, relating to food debts and the provision of food security, have already been discussed. The parallel utility of the corporate kin group as a source of subsistence security resided in the fact that extensive sharing of food was practised among its constituent households (see Chapter IX). In another respect, too, kin solidarity was underpinned by scarcity. Schrauwers (1995b:18) characterizes the principal corporate kin group among the Pamona, the matrifocal *santina*, as a gerontocratic organization in which 'genealogical seniors control their juniors politically through their control of the elite goods required for bridewealth'. Here again there is a parallel with slavery: slaves were, as Schrauwers (1997:368) puts it, 'permanent juniors', and the (reduced) bride prices which changed hands when they married were usually provided not by the kin of the groom, but by his masters.[50] A precondition for social control via control of elite goods, however, was presumably that juniors enjoyed limited independent access to such goods: that is, that bridewealth items, most of which always originated ultimately from foreign trade, could not be obtained too easily via trade itself.

The disintegration of the corporate kin groups, at least as residential units, was a widespread phenomenon in the late nineteenth and early twentieth centuries (see Chapter I). At least one contemporary observer, the naturalist Sydney Hickson, linked this development directly with increases in trade income. Whereas Chabot (1969:98-9), writing in the mid-twentieth century, retrospectively attributed the dispersal of the 'big house' groups on Siau to the political intervention of the colonial government and the cultural influence of the Protestant mission, Hickson, who visited Sangir and Talaud while that change was still in progress in the 1880s, saw it more as a spontaneous response to an increase in wealth and commerce.

A more important point [...] is the gradual diminution, or to use a Dutch word, the 'verkleining' of houses as the civilization or wealth of the inhabitants increases. This struck me particularly in my return journey from Nanusa, as we gradually

---

50 Adriani and Kruyt 1950-51, II:314; A.C. Kruyt 1938, III:109; Schrauwers 1995b:24.

got within touch of civilization and the wealth of the inhabitants increased. The largest houses I saw were in Nanusa where foreign vessels very rarely call. In Lirung [Salibabu] the houses were somewhat smaller, none of them I should think capable of holding more than 200 persons. At Manarang [Kaburuang], also in Talauer [Talaud], a kampong which contains 3,500 inhabitants, and carries on a considerable trade, the houses were still smaller, but nevertheless some of them must have been able to accommodate 60 or 100 persons. In Taroena and Manganitu, the two most important places in Great Sengir [Greater Sangir], and the centre of the cocoa-nut trade, places where money is used and cocoa [coconut] trees cultivated, &c., &c., the houses were not large enough for more than ten or twenty persons (except the houses of the rajahs, whose numerous followers all claim shelter under their roofs). One step further in this process and we arrive at mere hovels only capable of holding a man, his wife, and two or three children, such as we find in such a place as Menado, where natives and Europeans live and freely trade and mix together. (Hickson 1887:140-1.)

The disintegration of the Sangirese *bale* into individual households did not mean the definitive end of the extended family as a basis for economic organization, and collective land ownership remained typical until the end of the colonial period. The collectivities involved, however, were now vaguely defined, overlapping, weakly corporate bilateral kin groups, and 'the lack of definite precepts as to who belongs to the group' led to increasingly frequent land ownership conflicts (H.Th. Chabot 1969:100). A similar pattern was evident in Minahasa, where the traditional big house groups likewise 'gradually fell apart into [nuclear] families [*gezinnen*]' (Holleman 1930:49).

This weakening and blurring of the corporate kin groups occurred not only because their political functions were usurped by the colonial state (which in many cases also applied direct pressure to demolish the big houses), but also because their economic functions, with respect both to the supply of prestige (exchange) goods and to the distribution of food, were replaced by the market. A similar combination of political and economic factors was very likely responsible for the disappearance of slavery. In Minahasa, admittedly, the formal abolition of slavery by the colonial government in 1819 was apparently effective despite the fact that it occurred during a period of little or no economic growth. Elsewhere, however, the surprising efficacy of this drastic intervention in indigenous society probably reflected the fact that the economic foundations of the relationship between master and slave were already being undermined by alternative, commercial sources of income and subsistence security. The relationship between trade on the one hand, and slavery and other forms of dependency on the other, was no doubt complex; in Chapter I it was argued that the use of trade goods to create debts was probably an important means of political centralization, and one nineteenth-century source, referring to resource-poor Banggai, mentions descent into slavery as a specific result of trade debts.[51] But where trade was intensive enough to create generalized prosperity, it almost certainly tended to have the opposite effect.

The demographic implications of these developments stem from the fact that although the magnitude of their influence on fertility is uncertain, both slavery and the corporate kin group created incentives to practise birth control (see Chapter X). The former, other things being equal, tended to reduce the demand for children among both slaves and slave-owners; the latter, in its typical matrifocal form, underpinned patterns of female autonomy and authority which were likewise conducive to deliberate fertility restriction. One source, recalling Mary Douglas' conclusion (1966:272) that population control in 'primitive groups' tends to be undertaken more in relation to resources conveying social advantages than to those crucial to survival, even mentions that a female custodian of family heirlooms (prestige goods) sometimes wished to remain childless simply in order to 'keep the *pusaka* [inheritance] undivided in her possession'.[52] Both slavery and the corporate kin group, moreover, may also have created significant disincentives to surplus production, thereby tending to reproduce the economic conditions for their own existence by limiting the quantity of both subsistence and prestige goods available. Matrifocal social organization, finally, reinforced patterns of male absence, and on Sangir its decay probably combined with the increasing role of professional merchants (rather than Sangirese men themselves) in transporting trade goods to raise fertility rates in the late nineteenth and early twentieth centuries.[53]

In Chapter X, I suggested that the frequency of adoption and other 'child-sharing' behaviour in traditional society was a further factor reducing the incentives to bear children. Adoption remained a characteristic custom up to the end of the colonial period, the *adat* law specialist Adam (1925b:473) noting in the 1920s that even in Minahasa there was 'no question' of it disappearing. Transfer of children (and child labour) between households, in fact, has remained common up to the present day.[54] The weakening of extended family structures, nevertheless, must have entailed some 'privatization' of the benefits of children, since it was no doubt within the old corporate kin

---

51   A. Revius, 'Algemeen Verslag omtrent de oostkust van Celebes', 10-2-1851 (ANRI Ternate 180).
52   Tillema 1926:221. Some early Spanish sources from the Philippines, according to W.H. Scott (1994:118), likewise indicate that family planning (abortion) was 'practised by ranking ladies to limit their lineage and preserve their heritage'.
53   Neither of these arguments, however, applies to Minahasa, where male absence was always limited, and traditional social organization partly patrifocal (see Chapter I).
54   Schouten 1995b:2-3; Schrauwers 1995a:342, 350. Schrauwers (1995a:351), however, notes that these transfers now tend to take the form of 'fosterage', in which the children concerned do not necessarily share in the inheritance of their foster parents, rather than the more far-reaching 'adoption' described in earlier sources.

group that the labour of juniors, if only because surplus food was redistrib-uted among the constituent households of such a group 'with no calculation of an exact return' (Schrauwers 2000:106), was most effectively shared. The dissolution of this institution made it easier for parents to monopolize the benefits of their own children, and at the same time also rendered them more exclusively dependent on those same children for security in their old age.[55] Both developments, in principle, strengthened the incentive to increase the size of the individual household by bearing and raising more children.[56]

Were the effects of commercialization on patterns of reproductive behav-iour reversible, or did they reflect, as Lesthaeghe (1980:539-42) has argued in the context of sub-Saharan Africa, the once-only destruction of traditional social systems embodying fertility control mechanisms which could not easily be reconstructed? Where such effects were supported by ideological changes like those influencing the social position of women following conversion to Islam, the latter interpretation may be the more accurate. Changes in breast-feeding practices, too, seem to have been relatively inelastic, and if slavery and the corporate kin group tended to reduce the availability of resources as well as the birth rate, then their demise must have been to some extent self-perpetuating. More than one documented episode of commercial decline, on the other hand, was clearly associated with in situ depopulation, and the historical and anthropological data examined in the previous chapters suggest that the boundary between the subsistence-focused, non-monetized traditional economy on the one hand, and the market economy on the other, was seldom sharp or absolute. In this chapter, more generally, I have tried to show that the traditional social institutions affecting fertility must be viewed partly as contingent products of their economic environment.

Conclusion

Despite dramatic short-term and local fluctuations, something approaching a long-term equilibrium probably characterized the demography of most parts of northern Sulawesi before 1850. Both high mortality and low fertility contributed to this situation. Two different kinds of low-fertility regime can arguably be discerned: one resting partly on delayed marriage (Minahasa and Sangir), and another in which women married young, but this was counter-balanced by much male absence and deliberate abortion (Central Sulawesi).

[55]　White (1976:311-31) emphasizes the importance of this second consideration as a factor affecting desired family size in modern Java.
[56]　A possible parallel is suggested by Graafland's observation (1898, II:268-9) that the rapid increase in livestock numbers in Minahasa during the late nineteenth century (see Chapter XIV) was caused partly by a strengthening of individual ownership rights to animals.

Social institutions conducive to fertility limitation reflected economic scarcity, and to some extent their occurrence in time and space was inversely correlated with economic opportunity. If there was any conscious attempt to optimize the ratio of population to resources, however, it manifestly failed to produce an equilibrium at which everyone always had enough to eat, and some of the processes restricting population growth worked via the food supply and its influence on the death rate.

However systematic or unsystematic the mechanisms maintaining the quasi-equilibrium, more importantly, they were readily overridden, or at least radically readjusted, by the exploitation of new economic opportunities, particularly with respect to lucrative export products such as iron and copra. Where trade income diminished, conversely, the demographic response was also clear. This sensitivity of population trends to the level of external trade seems to have existed even in circumstances where almost the whole population was engaged primarily in subsistence farming and concentrated in upland areas, where the internal market was weakly developed and the level of monetization low, and where endemic warfare was still present. While medical advances, improvements in hygiene, and (possibly) autonomous cultural changes accelerated the population growth trend of the late colonial era, they were not necessary preconditions for such growth. Despite his failure to recognize the importance of traditional fertility checks, it seems that Tammes (1940:197) was ultimately right to argue, with Malthus, that 'population always increases where the means of subsistence increase' – a principle which, appropriately qualified and modified, still forms the ultimate theoretical context for much modern work in macro-historical demography (Caldwell 2001:5-7; Lee 1997:1107-9). Neither in the sphere of trade nor in that of food production were all potential 'means of subsistence' exploited, and the cultural factors affecting economic behaviour, in so far as these are amenable to historical analysis, will be re-examined in the concluding chapter. First, however, I will attempt to reconstruct how the existing economic activities affected the natural environment.

CHAPTER XIII

Vegetation and deforestation

The history of man's impact on the natural environment in northern Sulawesi is in the first place the history of deforestation. This is not to deny that people at all periods also planted trees on a greater or smaller scale. The focus of their agricultural activities in our period, however, was usually on swidden foodcrops, and it will be argued that in most cases the arboreal vegetation which they created on swidden fallow land and elsewhere was radically different from the natural forest which it replaced. The human presence also had other effects on the environment: one of these, soil erosion as a result of deforestation, is touched on below, and the human impact on some animal populations will be examined in Chapter XV. Of course it cannot simply be assumed that all deforestation was a result of human activity; the contribution of natural factors is discussed in Chapter XIV. The first task, however, is to reconstruct the pattern of vegetation cover as it appears in the historical sources from different periods.

Cartographic and statistical sources

Because the quantity and quality of the relevant sources, even more than in the case of the demographic statistics, increase dramatically from the past toward the present, it is not feasible to write a history of deforestation in this region in strictly chronological sequence. To begin with the oldest scraps of landscape description would create a misleading impression of historical change as more and more geographical detail subsequently came into focus. In practice it is the relatively well-known recent past which must provide a point of reference for the more distant past, not vice versa. The best starting point for such historical extrapolation is, of course, an actual vegetation map. But while the descriptive sources on landscape and vegetation in northern Sulawesi are often quite rich, maps showing forest cover are scarce and mostly late. From the nineteenth century there are just a handful covering particular subregions, and although a forest map of the Manado residency as a whole was reported to be in preparation by the forestry service in 1922

(*Verslag Dienst Boschwezen* 1921-22:40), the oldest surviving specimen dates only from 1932, and was first published in 1935 (Van Steenis 1935).

This map, reproduced here in slightly simplified form (Map 14), is part of the well-known vegetation chart of Indonesia as a whole produced by the botanist C.G.G.J. van Steenis for inclusion in the *Atlas van Tropisch Nederland* ('Atlas of the Tropical Netherlands') of 1938.[1] Although Van Steenis (1935:26) warned that it is a first attempt and had 'no pretensions of any sort', it was compiled with the help of forestry officials with local experience and is the only map of its kind from the colonial period. This small (1:10 million) sketch provided the basis for several other contemporary and later vegetation maps of Sulawesi, including, apparently, the much larger-scale drawings produced for use by the Allied military forces during the Second World War.[2] In 1950 it underwent a major revision – on what basis is not clear – and was republished in 1958 (Van Steenis 1958b) on the larger scale of 1:5 million as part of a new vegetation map of island Southeast Asia.[3] From the descriptive evidence presented below it will be evident that this later version, included here in modified form (Map 15), is much more accurate than its predecessor for some parts of the region (notably the central and western interior of Central Sulawesi), but mysteriously less so for others, including Sangir and the Luwuk Peninsula.[4] The reason for these discrepancies is unknown, but they do not appear to result from actual land use changes between 1932 and 1950, so that the two Van Steenis maps can best be regarded as parallel, complementary views of the situation around 1930.

The possibility that the differences between Maps 14 and 15 (for instance, the apparent reforestation on the Luwuk Peninsula) reflect real changes in the vegetation cover after 1932 can be ruled out partly thanks to the independent (but unfortunately much more recent) point of comparison provided by Map 16, an extract from a 'land cover' chart compiled from completely different primary sources by the Indonesian government's Regional Physical

---

[1]   The coastal mangrove belts shown in the original, some of which are incorrectly positioned, have been omitted here.
[2]   Section of Military Geology 1944:140; Allied Geographical Section 1945: Map 4. The first of these is explicitly derived from the *Atlas van Tropisch Nederland* map, and from the *Waldkarte* in a 1935 dissertation which was in fact copied from a pre-publication version of the same Van Steenis map (Kornrumpf 1935:91, Karte VI). The stated sources for the second are enigmatic, but the near-identical vegetation boundaries, especially on the northern peninsula, cannot be coincidental.
[3]   The 1950 revision was carried out by L.W. Hannibal for the Indonesian Forest Service (FWI/ GFW 2002:8; Van Steenis 1958a:2).
[4]   Two faults in the original have not been reproduced here: the 'plantations' (presumably smallholder coconut plantations, but in that case much too localized) shown by Van Steenis on the coastlands and in the Dumoga Valley of Bolaang Mongondow, and the exaggerated areas of wet ricefields on the east coast of Bolaang Mongondow and to the east of Lake Poso.

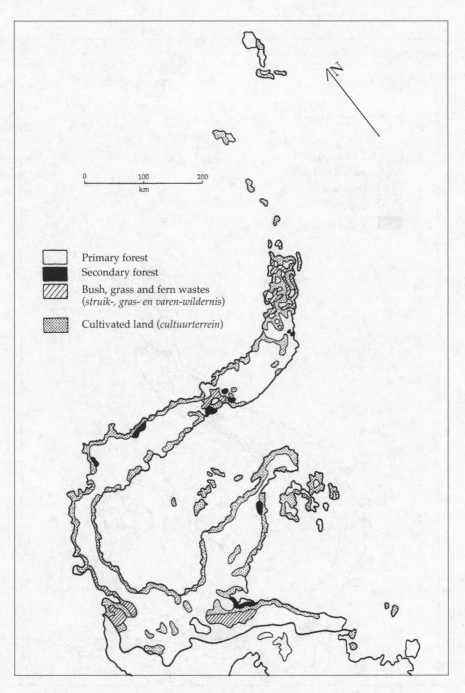

Map 14. Northern Sulawesi: vegetation cover according to G.G.G.J. van Steenis in 1932. Redrawn from Van Steenis (1935, map) and *Atlas van Tropisch Nederland* (1938: Blad 7a).

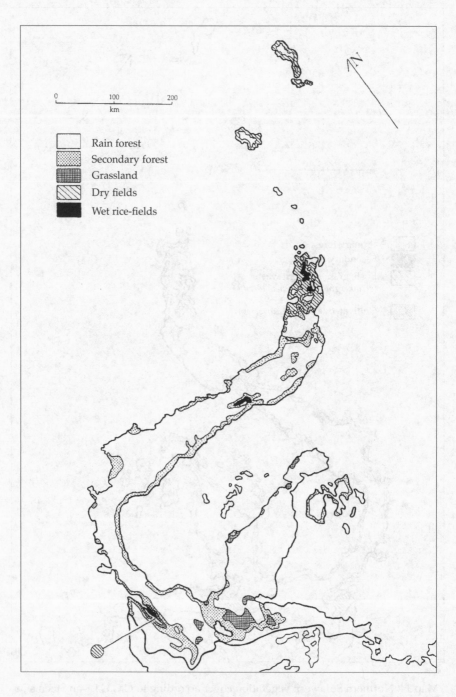

Map 15. Northern Sulawesi: vegetation cover according to G.G.G.J. van Steenis
in 1958 (redrawn from Van Steenis 1958b)

Rain forest

Secondary forest

Grassland

Dry fields

Wet rice-fields

0 100 200
km

N

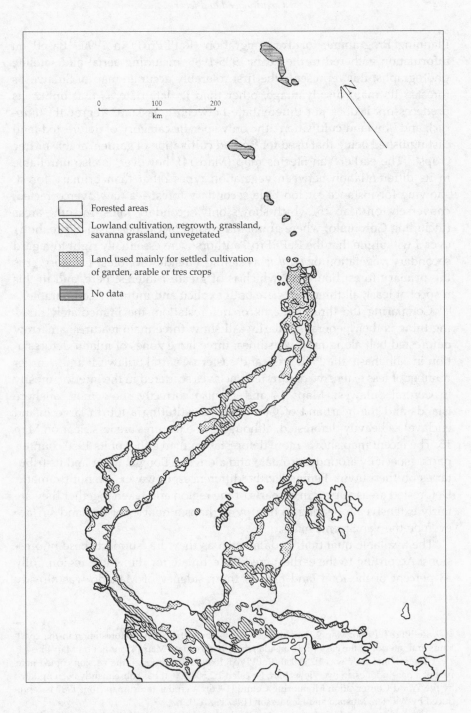

Map 16. Northern Sulawesi: vegetation cover, circa 1985 (redrawn from
RePPProT 1990b: Map 9)

Planning Programme for Transmigration (RePPProT) in 1990.[5] Based on information gathered in the years 1985-1988, including aerial and satellite photographs, this represents the first tolerably accurate map of Sulawesi's forests.[6] Its main disadvantage, other than its late date, is that unlike its predecessors it does not differentiate between grassland, 'regrowth' (*belukar*), and 'lowland cultivation', the only specific category of deforested land distinguished being that used for 'settled cultivation of garden, arable or tree crops'.[7] The earlier Van Steenis map (Map 14), however, is also unreliable in its differentiation between vegetation types other than primary forest, showing for instance far too little secondary forest – a flaw overcorrected, conversely, on Map 15, which shows only secondary forest in some areas (including Gorontalo) where grassland was in fact widespread. Since, however, I will argue that the RePPProT authors were essentially right to regard secondary vegetation or *belukar* as falling outside the forest category, it is the primary forest boundary which is of greatest interest here, and in this respect at least, all three maps are both explicit and mutually comparable.

Comparing the three patterns of deforestation, the immediately striking thing is their general similarity. All show three main features: a narrow deforested belt along most coastlines; three large zones of inland deforestation in Minahasa, the Palu area, and eastern Central Sulawesi; and a larger number of less extensive deforested enclaves scattered in the interior, mostly in Central Sulawesi. Maps 14 and 16 also correctly show most offshore islands and the heartland of Gorontalo (constituting a fourth large inland enclave) as heavily deforested, although these features are less clear on Map 15. The recent map shows more deforestation than either of its 1930 counterparts, especially around Gorontalo and along the Bongka River and its tributaries on the Luwuk Peninsula; the differences, however, are not dramatic. Deforested areas appear in all parts of the region and taken together they are fairly extensive, appearing to occupy perhaps a quarter of the land surface even on the Van Steenis maps.

The available quantitative data, such as they are, support these impressions. According to the earliest credible estimate for the whole region, fully 33 percent of the total land area of the residency of Manado was already

---

[5]   RePPProT 1990b: Map 9. This map confirms, for instance, the deforestation in the coastlands and interior of the eastern peninsula which is shown on Map 14, but not on Map 15.

[6]   The original scale was 1:250,000 (RePPProT 1990a:149), although the version copied here, part of a pan-Indonesian overview chart, is scaled 1:2,500,000. It has subsequently been updated by the World Conservation Monitoring Centre (1996). A cruder forest map from 1982 is reproduced by Whitten, Mustafa and Henderson (1987:99, 103).

[7]   The nature of the distinction between the latter category and 'lowland cultivation' is also unclear.

without forest cover in 1925.[8] In 1931, however, the initial estimate of 60,000 km^2 under forest was raised to 67,000, bringing the official deforestation figure down to 26 percent, and in 1941, the last year of the colonial statistics, it stood at 27 percent.[9] The land use survey accompanying the 1990 map, by comparison, gives a proportion of 32 percent, five percentage points higher than in 1941 (RePPProT 1990a:105).

Qualitative sources

Both maps and statistics, then, indicate that in the six decades between 1925 and 1985, the overall proportion of deforested land in northern Sulawesi increased from about a quarter to about a third. Qualitative historical sources, however, suggest that the real change was smaller, since some of the discrepancies between the colonial and recent survey result simply from inaccuracies in the older data.[10] Landscape descriptions from the early twentieth century frequently reveal areas of deforestation where none, or too little, appears on the Van Steenis maps, but the existence of which was nevertheless confirmed by the aerial and satellite surveys of the 1980s. Where usable evidence is available from earlier times, it often suggests that the same continuity can also be traced back further into the past. In the following review by subregion, the evidence from the earliest period for which a reasonably complete picture can be assembled will in each case be presented first, followed by a more tentative survey of earlier clues, and where appropriate a summary of later developments. For some parts of North Sulawesi the 'baseline' date can be pushed back to the middle of the nineteenth century; for Central Sulawesi, however, no general descriptions are available until the end of that century or later. The subregional division applied below, it should be noted, is somewhat different from that used in the preceding demographic chapters, and not all parts of the region are discussed in detail.

Although Central Sulawesi in particular is often characterized today as a region of dense tropical forest (Acciaioli 1992:155; Metzner 1981a:42), this was not how it was perceived in colonial times. In 1911, the ethnographer

---

8   *Verslag Dienst Boschwezen* 1925:49. Estimates for the two immediately preceding years are also available (*Verslag Dienst Boschwezen* 1923:19, 1924:34), but in 1923 the residency still excluded the east coast of Central Sulawesi, while the figure for 1924 (15%) is too far out of line with subsequent estimates to be taken seriously.

9   *Verslag Dienst Boschwezen* 1931:167; Boomgaard 1996a:166. It should be added, however, that the criteria used to define forest in the Forestry Service statistics are unclear.

10   For this reason the map presented by Durand (1994:128-9), in which the Van Steenis and RePPProT data are superimposed, gives an exaggerated impression of the speed of recent deforestation in Sulawesi.

Grubauer (1913:443) even called it 'a land in which merciless destruction of the forest has become the rule'. Kaudern, who travelled there in the years 1917-1920, also portrays a landscape heavily influenced by man:

> The vegetation and the animals of Central Celebes are about the same as in the rest of the island. The primeval forest however has here extensively given place to grounds cleared with fire by the natives. This is especially the case in the eastern part, where vast grounds at present are overgrown by the steppe grass called alang-alang. In all the cultivated basins the primeval forest has of course long ago yielded to the chopping knife of the native. (Kaudern 1925:24.)

The geologist Koperberg (1929, I:6), surveying the Poso area and a part of the Luwuk Peninsula at the beginning of the twentieth century, was relieved to find 'wide panoramas' and 'much more open terrain' than in the sites of his previous and more difficult explorations in the forested interior of the northern peninsula.

Poso and Mori

Such open landscapes prompted concern as well as appreciation. Not long after his arrival in Poso in 1892, Albert Kruyt (1895-97, II:117, III:131) became worried about what he saw as excessive forest clearance by swidden farmers. 'Huge quantities of valuable timber', he warned, 'are lost each year, so that whole areas are already devoid of trees and replaced by long grass (*kusu-kusu*, *alang-alang* [*Imperata cylindrica*]) or brushwood [*kreupelhout*]'.[11] In the basin of the Tomasa, the largest tributary of the Poso River, the entire landscape was already 'bare, covered with grass and low wood, wherever the eye looks' (A.C. Kruyt 1899c:604). In 1912, Kruyt wrote from Lake Poso that if deforestation continued at the same rate for another 25 years there would be 'no wood left', and that one benefit of irrigated farming, recently imposed on the population by the Dutch, would be to protect 'this already not very well-forested land' from further clearance (*Brieven*, 5-7-1912, 15-12-1912).

---

[11]   A.C. Kruyt 1895-97, III:153. Lay sources like this one, where they are specific, invariably refer to the grasses of northern Sulawesi either as *alang-alang* (*Imperata cylindrica*), known in the local (Moluccan) dialect of Malay as *kusu-kusu*, or, more rarely, as *glagah* (*Saccharum spontaneum*), *kano-kano* in Moluccan Malay. Expert sources confirm that in peninsular North Sulawesi, these were indeed the commonest species (Koorders 1898:15, 26, 273-4, 278; Von Rosenberg 1865:12, 57, 63, 90). In Central Sulawesi, however, it appears that *alang-alang* proper was relatively uncommon, and that particularly on regularly burned and grazed grasslands (in the Palu Valley, for instance) other types, including *Andropogon* and *Themada* species, were dominant (Steup 1929: 590, 1933-36 IV:31, 1938:286-8; Whitten, Mustafa and Henderson 1987:397, 494). In view of this diversity, the names *alang-alang* and *glagah* will be used here only in quotations, or where their accuracy is certain.

While these statements reflected a conventional colonial prejudice against shifting cultivation, the deforestion lamented by Kruyt is confirmed by other contemporary descriptions.[12] Walking from the Gulf of Bone to the Gulf of Tomini in 1895, Sarasin and Sarasin (1905, I:237-40, 243) found that the rain-forest gave way to scrub, grassland, and cultivated fields more than a day's march south of Lake Poso, the eastern shore of which was also 'covered with fields and grass- and woodland patches'. Immediately north of the lake, an undulating 'parkland' of grass, interspersed with small wooded hills, stretched almost a third of the way to the sea. This was followed by a more variegated landscape of bush and grassy patches, which did not yield to a final band of primary forest until the Gulf of Tomini coast was only three hours away (Sarasin and Sarasin 1905, I:255-7, 272-82). The first European to travel to the Poso interior, the *controleur* Van der Wyck, did so in 1865. He reported that there were many settlements and swiddens along the path from Poso to the lake, that the last part of the journey led 'through a *padang* [open field]', and that it would be easy to make a survey of the route, 'since the trees which grow on the mountains have all been felled, the Alfurs hav-ing their cultivations mostly on the slopes' (Adriani 1913b:851-4, 858). Such descriptions are at odds with the first Van Steenis map (Map 14), which only shows two small deforested enclaves between Lake Poso and the sea. They correspond well, however, with the revised Van Steenis map (Map 15) and the 1990 RePPProT map (Map 16), on both of which the extensive north-south corridor of deforestation, and the bare Tomasa Valley, are clearly visible.

An even more extensive zone of deforestation appears on all three vegeta-tion maps in the basin of the La River, between the Poso Valley and Mori. Although hardly mentioned in recent literature, this is well described in earlier sources, and Van Steenis may have been right to portray it as the largest single expanse of open landscape in the whole region.[13] The grassland plain at its heart, stretching almost unbroken over perhaps 350 km^2, was certainly the big-gest of its kind. Kruyt, who walked across this grassland in 1899 and estimated its length at 'two days' march' (A.C. Kruyt 1900b:439), provided a unique sketch map of its boundaries in his account of the journey for the Netherlands Missionary Society (Map 17). Apart from small copses, often of bamboo, only narrow strips of woodland or swamp along the watercourses interrupted its grassy expanses (Plate 20).[14] The local population knew this plain simply as

---

[12]   Abendanon 1915-18, II:610, 676-80, 693, 728; Adriani 1915:460; Adriani and Kruyt 1912-14, I: 33, 55; A.C. Kruyt 1894:9, 11, 1898:89-92, 1899c:594-5, 601-9; Grubauer 1913:420-2, 426, 436, 443.
[13]   Photographs of this area in 1988 (Hegener 1990:146, 235, 236) show more forest cover than is suggested by the earlier accounts, and it is probable that some reforestation had occurred in the intervening period due to reduced burning (see Chapter XIV).
[14]   Adriani and Kruyt 1900:200-9; Abendanon 1915-18, II:615-6, 621; Hegener 1990:123-4; Horsting 1924:216-7; Steup 1931:1133.

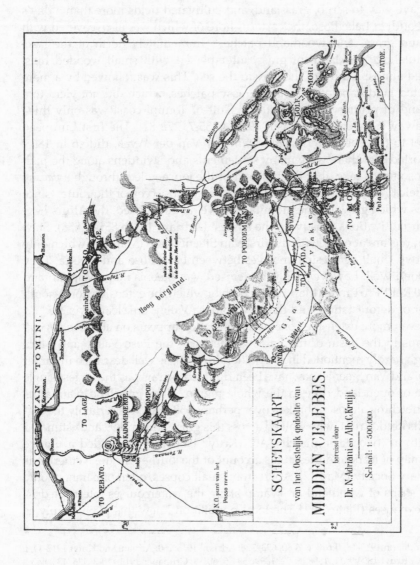

Map 17. 'Sketch map of the eastern part of Central Sulawesi travelled through by Dr N. Adriani and Albert C. Kruyt', 1899. Shows the approximate extent of the Pada grassland ('Gras vlakte', to right of title box). (Map reproduced from Adriani and Kruyt 1900.)

Plate 20. A colonial survey expedition crossing the Pada grassland, 1910 (Abendanon
1915-18, II: Plate CXVIII; original drawn from a photograph)

Pada, 'the Grassfield' (Adriani and Kruyt 1912-14, I:63). The hilly territories
of the To Onda'e and To Pakambia, immediately to the west and northwest of
the plain, were also substantially treeless.[15] Beyond the wooded hills which
formed the eastern rim of the Pada, the flanks of the La were once again covered mostly with grass as far downstream as Tompira, about 15 km from the
sea (Adriani and Kruyt 1900:170; A.C. Kruyt 1900b:445). Immediately south of
the lower La, finally, the Lembo depression was described by the Sarasins in
1896 as an 'open parkland' of alternating grass and trees.[16] This appears clearly
on the 1958 and 1990 maps as a separate deforested area.

Tobungku, Banggai, and the Luwuk Peninsula

In Tobungku, Maps 14 and 16 show only a narrow coastal strip of cleared
land, and Map 15 no deforestation at all. In the early twentieth century, the
mountains visible from the sea along the Tobungku coast were certainly

---

[15]   Adriani and Kruyt 1900:210, 1912-14 I:55, 60; A.C. Kruyt 1900b:464; Steup 1931:1132-3.
[16]   Sarasin and Sarasin 1901:211, 1905, I:326-7. Also J. Kruyt 1924:33.

heavily forested (Van Vuuren 1920, I:313-4). When Padtbrugge sailed along this coast in 1678, by contrast, he was surprised to see 'many hamlets spread along the mountains, which are mostly bare thanks to the hard work and diligent cultivation of the farmers, making them a pleasant sight in these wild and desolate parts' (Van Dam 1931:100). Sources from the intervening centuries, unfortunately, are few, and do not reveal at what period this once populous land was reclaimed by forest (see Chapter VI).

Although one early description of Peling mentions 'numerous clearings' on the hillsides (De Clercq 1890:129), other accounts (Bosscher and Matthijssen 1854:99; Goedhart 1908:484) do not seem to confirm the partial but extensive deforestation depicted on the Banggai Islands by Map 14. A geographical study from 1941, however, provides an explanation for this discrepancy. Unlike most of their counterparts on the Central Sulawesi mainland, the 'deforested' areas in Banggai represent a low woody vegetation rather than grassland, farmland, or savanna.

> On the islands, *alang-alang* is almost absent. Abandoned *ladang* quickly acquire a vegetation of ferns, which gives way after a few years to young wood, thin, hard and tenacious. Thicker forest is not common here, so that shortages of wood occur locally. (Schrader 1941:109.)

In this light, the words of a Dutch sea captain who described Peling in 1850 as 'densely vegetated with forest and brushwood [*kreupelhout*]' (Van der Hart 1853:101) take on a new significance, and at the same time it becomes easier to understand how a military source could still describe the Banggai Islands as 'mostly jungle-covered' in 1944.[17]

In the eastern part of the Luwuk Peninsula, Maps 14 and 16 indicate a simple pattern of purely coastal deforestation, while Map 15 shows almost no unforested land. Neither view, however, is correct for earlier periods. Descriptions from 1905 and 1906 show that some coastal areas were indeed deforested; the vegetation on the north side of the narrow neck of the terminal section of the peninsula near Pagimana, for instance, consisted of 'open savanna' in which 'the savanna grass which the natives call "cuscusu" [*kusu-kusu = alang-alang*] is almost the only thing which flourishes' (Wanner 1914: 81). In some places on the south coast there were also 'extensive fields of grass'.[18] The main zones of forest clearance, however, were two long cultivated strips running parallel to the coast, but 5-10 km inland, on both sides of the peninsula (see Chapter VI).

---

[17]　Section of Military Geology 1944:20. The statement in another reconnaissance study that the islands 'are rich in timber' (Allied Geographical Section 1945:21) must, however, be erroneous.
[18]　Goedhart 1908:485. Also Wanner 1914:80.

Plate 21. The Bada Valley, circa 1912 (ARZ photograph collection,
Land- en Volkenkunde Celebes 39)

Lore and upland western Central Sulawesi

When Central Sulawesi is described as a region of vast forests, it is often with reference to the mountain country which lies to the west of the Poso lake and river, and part of which now forms the Lore-Lindu National Park (Whitten, Mustafa and Henderson 1987:103). Even those colonial writers most prone to worry about deforestation admitted that this area still contained large reserves of completely virgin forest.[19] Yet here too, there were significant cleared enclaves. The roughness of the Van Steenis maps, especially the earlier version (Map 14), makes it difficult to identify these with particular topographic features or with their equivalents on Map 16, which shows many more. Once again, however, it is the recent map which better corresponds to the situation revealed in the descriptive sources from around the beginning of the twentieth century.

Many of the deforested enclaves in 1990, firstly, still coincided with the 'cultivated basins' of which Kaudern remarked 70 years earlier that their forests had 'long ago yielded to the chopping knife'. Kaudern's own map of these basins, in which most of the population of Lore and upland western

---

[19]   A.C. Kruyt 1903b:190-1; Heringa 1921a:796; Steup 1931:1127-8.

Central Sulawesi was concentrated, was reproduced in Chapter VI (Map 13). One of them, the Napu Depression, was so deforested that the few copses still standing on its grassland floor were 'carefully preserved by the inhabitants in order to have firewood and rattan to hand in this treeless land'.[20] It was perhaps to Napu that Padtbrugge was referring when he recorded in 1682 that the 'fine plains' in the mountains behind Poso were said to be 'so populous that in many places there is even a shortage of firewood around the villages, so that they have to make their fires with dried manure'.[21] The Bada Valley, too, contained extensive grasslands (Plate 21). If the forest clearances on Map 16 are rather larger than the settled areas as Kaudern sketches them, the same was probably already true in his time and before: early travellers noted that while the settlements themselves were usually concentrated on or around the cultivated, grassy, or swampy valley floors, the surrounding mountainsides were often also deforested up to high altitudes.[22]

A feature of Map 16 which neither appears on the Van Steenis maps, nor corresponds to any of Kaudern's settlement concentrations, is the long strip of unforested land running from north to south along the peaks of the Tineba (Fennema) mountains immediately to the west of the Poso Depression. This too, however, is described in some detail in early twentieth-century sources.[23] It consisted of an unusual high-altitude moorland vegetation of *Sphagnum* moss and low shrubs, interspersed with mossy woodland (Steup 1931:1129-30). Grubauer (1913:461), who crossed it at the north end in 1911, observed that at this point it merged directly into the grassy slopes of the Napu Depression, exactly as indicated on the 1990 land cover map.

The Palu Valley

One case of deforestation in Central Sulawesi which has not escaped the attention of post-colonial scholars is that of Palu Valley, the celebrated 'driest place in Indonesia' and one of the principal woodless areas on all three vegetation maps.[24] A continuous patchwork of *sawah*, pastures and villages

[20]   A.C. Kruyt 1908:1285. Also Adriani and Kruyt 1912-14, II:199.
[21]   Van Dam 1931:93. 'Tonappo' (To Napu) is one of the toponyms mentioned by Padtbrugge. Kruyt (1908:1285), however, commented that he had never seen manure being used as a fuel in the area.
[22]   Abendanon 1915-18, II:751, 757, 868; Adriani and Kruyt 1898:505; Boonstra van Heerdt 1914a: 627; Grubauer 1913:461-2, 529, 534, 548; A.C. Kruyt 1908:1283-4, 1336, 1909:357, 374, 1938, I:262, 309; Kruyt and Kruyt 1921:405; Sarasin and Sarasin 1905, II:89; Schuyt 1913:349; Steup 1931:1125.
[23]   Abendanon 1915-18, II:594, 737-8; Grubauer 1913:460-1; A.C. Kruyt 1909:354; Schuyt 1911: 4-5.
[24]   Metzner 1981a, 1981b; Whitten, Mustafa and Henderson 1987:495-6.

Plate 22. The Palu Valley with the deforested western range in the background, 1910
(Abendanon 1915-18, II: Plate CLX)

set in a spectacular mountain trench, this was the country hailed by Adriani
and Kruyt (1898:483) in 1897 as 'one of the most beautiful landscapes in
Sulawesi'. The houses in Biromaru, southeast of Palu, were made exclusively
from coconut palm trunks and bamboo 'since there is virtually no timber on
this grassy plain' (Adriani and Kruyt 1898:467). A zoological collector who
had visited Donggala a year earlier reported that the mountainsides on the
western flank of the trench (Plate 22) were also 'absolutely bare up to 5000 or
6000 feet [1,500 or 1,800 metres]'.[25]

In accordance with the dry climate, those parts of the valley floor which
were not under irrigation had a semi-arid appearance. For the Sarasins (1905,
II:14), the spectacle of herders coralling sheep at sunset on a 'dry grey steppe'
near Bora in 1902 was 'an almost African scene'.[26] *Opuntia* (prickly pear) cactus bushes in particularly dry spots strengthened the impression of desertifi-
cation, and in subsequent years this plant multiplied to become a plague in
the valley.[27] The observation that the terrain on which the cactus grew often
consisted of abandoned *sawah*, and that one reason for the abandonment of

[25]   Hartert 1897:154. Not, as Metzner (1981a:47) and Whitten, Mustafa and Henderson (1987:
495) state, the eastern side; the report quoted by the Sarasins refers to the eastern flank not of
the Palu Valley, but of the mountain chain terminating in the Donggala Peninsula. The mountains east of the valley were more heavily wooded (Abendanon 1915-18, II:845, 909; Sarasin and
Sarasin 1905, II:17).
[26]   Metzner (1981a:43) draws a similar parallel.
[27]   Sarasin and Sarasin 1905, II:12, 14; Steup 1929:583-7; Van der Goot 1940.

such fields was the deposition of eroded sediments brought down by streams from the adjacent mountainsides (Steup 1929:587, 588; Verhoef 1937:222), fed a conviction among Dutch observers that the Palu Valley was in the grip of a man-made ecological crisis (A.C. Kruyt 1938, I:24, 97; Tillema 1926:217, 222). Some colonial officials were convinced that 'reckless' deforestation by indigenous farmers (Steup 1929:588) was to blame for the dryness of the climate itself, and that this too had adversely affected wet rice agriculture in recent times.[28] 'I think there is indeed nowhere else in the archipelago', declared the government forester Bruinier in 1923, 'where deforestation has had such a fatal influence as in this land, which could otherwise have been a little Egypt, lavishly watered by rivers flowing from wooded mountains' (Steup 1929:590).

Proponents of this apocalyptic view, both then (Tideman 1926:3; Kornrumpf 1935:67) and more recently (Metzner 1981a:51; Whitten, Mustafa and Henderson 1987:495), have supported it with reference to an older description of the Palu Valley first published in François Valentijn's *Oud en Nieuw Oost-Indien* in 1724. This originates once again from Padtbrugge and is based on information provided to him by a VOC soldier, Joannes Franszoon, whom he sent to reconnoitre the nearby land route over the base of the northern peninsula in 1681.[29] It portrays 'the country around Palu, all the way to the mountains' as 'a fine land like Holland', flat and fertile, with paddies worked by buffalo and 'pleasant fields, full of all kinds of livestock' (Keijzer 1856: 214). But while this may indeed seem a far cry from what Bruinier (1924:7) called 'a telling example of how man can ruin a land through ignorance and mismanagement', the landscape of the Palu Valley has always been diverse enough to describe in apparently contradictory ways.

More than two centuries later, Adriani and Kruyt (1898:461) were also struck by its 'Dutch appearance' and even commented that in this respect things were 'just as in Valentijn's day'.[30] Some parts of the landscape, however, were more Dutch than others. 'The strip of land along the edge of the mountains', the two missionaries noted, 'is dry and stony, while that along the banks of the river is fertile and well-cultivated'.[31] In many places, streams flowing from the mountains had left flood deposits of sand in the plain or incised it with small ravines (Adriani and Kruyt 1898:469, 483). Abendanon (1915-18, II:884-7, 906, 910) also described dry, grassy, or cactus-covered allu-

---

[28]   Hissink 1912:63; A.C. Kruyt 1938, I:21; Ter Laag 1920:21; Logeman 1922:31.
[29]   Van Dam 1931:91. The original diary of this remarkable journey has been preserved (NA VOC 1366:690-718), although it contains rather less landscape information than Padtbrugge's *memorie van overgave*.
[30]   Also Kruyt and Kruyt 1920:201.
[31]   Ironically, one of the things which most reminded them of Holland ('the Dutch heaths') was 'a herd of sheep peacefully grazing on the dry fields' – perhaps the same sheep and the same fields which the Sarasins were to find so African (Adriani and Kruyt 1898:469).

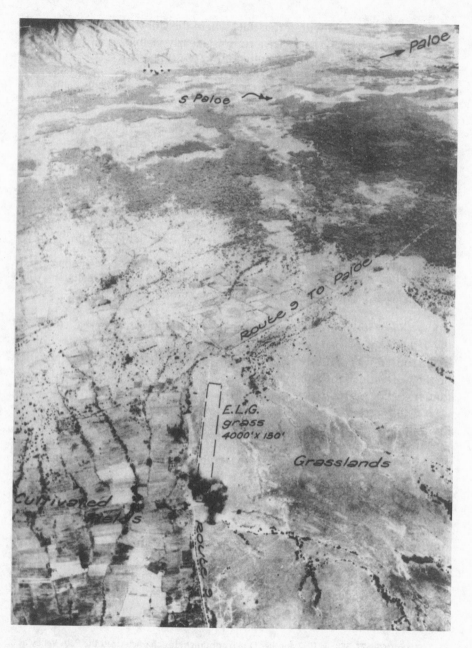

Plate 23. The Palu Valley, showing cultivated fields on the lower part of the valley floor and grasslands on the adjacent porous sediments, 1944 (Allied Geographical Section 1945: Photograph 11)

vial deltas, juxtaposed with fertile flats where the soil was less porous or the
water table closer to the surface – a contrast clearly visible on an aerial photograph of the eastern part of the valley from 1944 (Plate 23).

> The ground consists of detrital material from the adjacent mountain chains, and is
> not homogeneous in composition. Clay, sand, powder, gravel and conglomerate
> layers alternate with each other across the surface, so that in some places the soil
> is fertile and fit for cultivation, in others stony or infertile. The result is that exten-
> sive complexes of bountiful *sawah* alternate with dark coconut plantations, swamp
> forests, and areas of dry, barren terrain. (Abendanon 1915-18, II:910.)

'It is important', confirmed a Dutch administrator in 1925, 'not to form the
wrong image of the most arid area in the Netherlands Indies'.

> One would expect to be confronted here with a region of great scarcity, a more
> or less desert-like landscape. But while such areas are present here and there (the
> strikingly prominent mountains, for instance, are completely bare), nothing could
> be less true. Much of the terrain is exceptionally suitable for *sawah* cultivation, and
> much maize is planted as a secondary crop. (Voorn 1925:5.)

A few years later, a colleague of Bruinier's in the forestry service compared
the valley floor as seen from a distance not to African steppes, but to 'English
park landscapes', and estimated that the maximum altitude of deforestation
on the west side of the valley was 'about 2,000 metres', or only slightly higher
than in 1896.[32]

It is also striking that Abendanon (1915-18, II:906), who studied the geomorphology of the valley more intensively than anyone else before or since,
attributed its many abandoned *sawah* fields not to sedimentation problems or
climatic change, but to 'conflicts between the local chiefdoms [*landschappen*]'.
The first Dutch *controleur* of Palu, Hissink (1912:63), also mentions 'the great
insecurity and consequent turmoil during a period of many years before our
arrival', alongside environmental degradation, as a reason for the neglected
state of local irrigation systems. European explorers at the turn of the century, moreover, reported abandoned *sawah* from several other parts of Central
Sulawesi besides the Palu Valley, and in these other cases there was no suggestion that erosion and deforestation problems were to blame. Instead, the
explanations proposed included recent depopulation, disease among the buffalo used to work the irrigated fields, and, once again, political instability.[33]

---

[32]   Steup 1929:577, 588. In 1937 another Dutch administrator characterized the Palu Valley as 'a
very fertile area where *sawah* farming is practised on a large scale', only to add that those parts of
the plain not under cultivation 'are covered with sparse secondary forest, interspersed with extensive and rather dry grassland on which large numbers of cactuses grow' (Ansingh 1937:1, 3).
[33]   Boonstra van Heerdt 1914a:626; A.C. Kruyt 1908:1313-5, 1334, 1938, I:195, 228, IV:18; Kruyt
and Kruyt 1921:406-9; *Koloniaal verslag* 1906:59; Schuyt 1911:15, 1913:365; Engelenberg 1906:10-1.

All this is not to argue that the environmental situation in the Palu area was necessarily static at the time of the Dutch conquest, or in the first years of Dutch rule. The sudden spread in this period of the *Opuntia* cactus, a plant already present in Indonesia since the seventeenth century (Van der Goot 1940:414-5), suggests that significant changes may indeed have been underway.[34] What is certain, however, is that deforestation itself was well advanced in much earlier times. Thomas Forrest, who travelled in Indonesia in the period 1764-1784, already described treeless landscapes around Kaili, a toponym identified by Albert Kruyt (1938, I:46) with a village on the east side of the Palu Bay, but also used as a general designation for the Palu area (see Chapter VI).

> At a place called Kyly or Kyela, north of Macassar, and in the Mandar division, there is said to be a spacious harbour; there are also said to be some hills free from wood, and covered with grass, near the harbour, and many sheep are bred there: this is unusual in a Malay country, where trees in general have possession of the soil, and sheep are therefore universally scarce (Forrest 1792:81).

Unexpectedly, a Dutch report from another century earlier paints the same picture in more detail. In 1669, the steersman of a VOC ship sent to survey the west coast of Sulawesi compiled sailing instructions for the Bay of Palu in which considerable landscape information has been preserved.[35] The tip of the western peninsula, near modern Donggala, was 'a medium-high promontory without trees', whereas over the water the 'north or east shore outside the bay' consisted, as in the early twentieth century, of 'high land with trees'. Further south within the bay, however, the eastern coast too became treeless (Plate 24). 'From Kaili to Palu', states the report, 'the high land or mountains a little inland rise gradually in stages from the shore toward the mountaintops, but bare and without trees, covered only with grass, like a series of dunes'.[36] Two and a half centuries later Abendanon was to describe, in the more clinical language of geomorphology, what was clearly still the same landscape:

> Further to the north, sloping at an angle of 8° toward the west, the bare, infertile, steeply-faced terraces of loose eroded material, into which water sinks away so quickly, descended from the irregularly-peaked, wooded eastern range. From a little southeast of Palu to a point east of Mamboro, this hilly strip has a dry and desert-like character. (Abendanon 1915-17, II:891.)

---

[34] Adriani and Kruyt (1898) do not mention the cactus at all in their account from 1897, while the Sarasins, in 1902, saw cactus bushes only 'now and again' in particularly dry places (1905, II: 12). Grubauer (1913:576), by contrast, reported 'dense stands' of them covering 'whole fields' in 1911, and by 1928 they had become the characteristic vegetation over a large area to the east of the Palu River.

[35] NA VOC 1276:1022r-3v.

[36] NA VOC 1276:1023v.

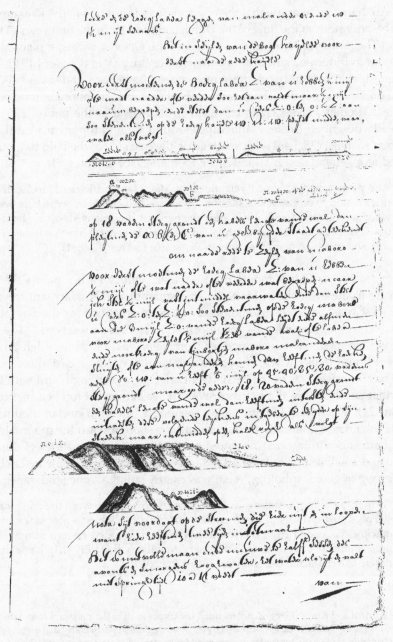

Plate 24. Deforested landscapes around the Bay of Palu (Kaili), as seen from a VOC ship in 1669. The second drawing from the bottom shows a 'bare ridge' (*kale rugh*) with isolated trees on the eastern shore of the bay near Mamboro. (NA VOC 1276:1023.)

In the seventeenth century as in Abendanon's day, then, what Valentijn (Keijzer 1856:214) called the 'blessed land' of the Palu Valley was already overlooked by bare, deforested hills.[37]

Gorontalo

Populous Gorontalo always formed a major interruption in the almost continuous forests which, apart from some small settled upland enclaves near Tinombo and Tolitoli (see Chapter VI), covered the interior of the northern peninsula from Palu all the way to the Mongondow Plateau.[38] In 1821, Reinwardt (1858:508-9) described the floor of the Limboto Depression as a level plain, eight hours' travel long and four hours' wide, on which there were 'no wild trees or forest of any significance'. The surrounding mountain sides were also partly cultivated, some of them 'to a high altitude' (Reinwardt 1858:510, 517). 'Completely devoid of forest', echoed Von Rosenberg (1865: 6) after his own visit in 1863, the part of the plain near Gorontalo town consisted of 'farmland and pasture' interrupted only by stands of deliberately planted or preserved tree crops like banana, coconut and sugar palm. At its northern rim it merged into a landscape of alternating grass- and woodland with 'the appearance of a park', while the higher land around it was a patchwork of cultivated fields, grasslands, brushwood, and coconut groves (Von Rosenberg 1865:2, 60-1, 76, 100). The vegetation of Gorontalo's 'worn-out grasslands', noted Riedel, was 'extremely thin and scanty'.[39] To the west of the Limboto Depression, the similar but smaller Paguyaman Basin also contained a grassy plain – once again, a feature which shows up better on the 1990 RePPProT forest map than on either of the earlier sketches by Van Steenis. Smaller stretches of grassland existed in Paguat and on the Bawangio (Bone) Plateau.[40]

Descriptions from before the nineteenth century are few, but documents from the 1681 VOC military expedition to Gorontalo mention a 'coes-coes

---

[37]   A marked tendency in colonial and post-colonial sources to underestimate the antiquity of deforestation, and to exaggerate its environmental consequences, has also been demonstrated by Fairhead and Leach (1996, 1998) in West Africa.

[38]   Bik 1864:153; Boonstra van Heerdt 1914b:727, 752, 756, 759; Heinrich 1932:49-83; Kortleven 1927:10; Morks 1931:1; *Nota Toli-Toli* 1912:31; Riedel 1872a:191; Sarasin and Sarasin 1905, I:79-85, 97-9, 111-15, 121-6, 149-64, 187; Schwarz and De Lange 1876:157; Reinwardt 1858:505, 523, 536; Von Rosenberg 1865:88, 90; Steup 1933; Tammes 1940:193-4; Veenhuizen 1903:37; Verhoef 1938. Along many stretches of coast even the cleared littoral strip was missing, and virgin forest reached down to the sea (Boonstra van Heerdt 1914b:729; Sarasin and Sarasin 1905, I:132).

[39]   CV Gorontalo 1864 (ANRI Manado 44); Riedel 1870a:52.

[40]   Bik 1864:153; Van Doren 1857-60, I:368; Reinwardt 1858:523; Von Rosenberg 1865:109.

veld' (*alang-alang* field) near the harbour, and state that the path to Dumoga, a now-vanished settlement on the eastern rim of the depression, led 'mostly through open fields and across a fine plain'.[41] Padtbrugge also observed that the country was 'full of wild buffalo, many of which have been domesticated', and that Limboto 'produces many sheep', strong indications that grasslands were already extensive.[42] In 1744, an irrigation canal was constructed 'over some *coes-coes* fields' between two of the rivers flowing across the eastern part of the plain.[43]

Despite the evident antiquity of deforestation in Gorontalo, it was not until the appointment of specialized forestry officials in 1919 (Tideman 1926: 128) that the issue became a matter of active concern for the Dutch administration. The forester Heringa (1921a:795) now spoke of Gorontalo's 'devastated forests', and his ever-zealous colleague Bruinier (1924:7) warned that while Palu represented the residency's most serious case of deforestation, 'Gorontalo too is already in dire danger and demands restorative measures'. These were duly taken, beginning in 1930 with attempts at artificial reforestation on some of the high land northeast of the Limboto Plain (Grondijs 1931:7-8; *Verslag Dienst Boschwezen* 1931:163). By 1939 more than 2,300 km^2 of existing forest in Gorontalo had also been placed under state protection (Korn 1939:25-7).

As in Palu (Tideman 1926:134), deforestation was often blamed for the flash floods or *banjir* which regularly destroyed crops in low-lying areas (Moolenburgh 1921:4; Morison 1931:8). Siltation in the Gorontalo estuary, and the deposition of river sediments on flooded farmlands, were related concerns (A.Ph. van Aken 1932:170; Gonggrijp 1915:1363). On this point, however, there were also dissenting voices. The '*banjir* phenomenon', one official pointed out in 1923, was 'just as strongly evident in the Boalemo area, where there is no question of any watershed deforestation, as in Gorontalo proper'; the most important causes of flooding, in his view, were simply the shortness and steepness of the rivers and the variability of the climate (Edie 1923:5). Whether or not flooding was a natural phenomenon in Gorontalo, it certainly was not a new one. In 1842, one *banjir* had swept away 56 houses along the Bone River, drowned more than 300 head of livestock, and even destroyed a small stone fort near the harbour.[44] While this particular event was excep-

---

[41]   NA VOC 1366:682, 780. This Dumoga is not to be confused with the area and river of the same name in Bolaang Mongondow (see below).
[42]   Robidé van der Aa 1867:166-7. The point at the southern gateway to the depression where Gorontalo town now lies was then called Padang (Padengo), meaning, like the Pada of the La basin, an expanse of flat, grassy terrain (Van Dam 1931:96).
[43]   NA VOC 2649:111.
[44]   AR Gorontalo to Res. Manado, 10-7-1842 (ANRI Manado 117).

tional (the biggest, it was said, since 1805 or 1806), less dramatic floods were common. Von Rosenberg (1865:5-6) noted in 1863 that the houses in Gorontalo town were all built on high stilts to avoid regular inundation, and in the 1880s a large part of the town was said to flood at least once a year (Van Hoëvell 1891:34). In 1843, moreover, the Gorontalo estuary was already reported to be 'silting up from year to year', and sand deposited by floodwater in fields and irrigation channels was a problem for farmers in the 1850s.[45]

The flood problem in Gorontalo, in fact, can also be traced back much further in the historical record. Padtbrugge wrote in 1677 that *banjir* in the Bone River were sometimes so violent 'that the narrow outlet to the sea cannot contain the torrent, and the water backs up the other stream [the Bolango River] toward Gorontalo and the lake, and even floods all the surrounding land'.[46] In 1694 a Gorontalese chief, albeit doubtless with some exaggeration, complained to another Dutch visitor that 'each year the water shoots down from the mountains with such force that all the crops in the fields are destroyed, and we can find nothing to eat'.[47] If flood intensity is indeed a good measure of watershed deforestation, then, the watersheds were probably just as deforested in the seventeenth century as in the early twentieth.

In recent reports (Abdussamad 1987; P3SU 1994, I:2.2-2.3), and implicitly in at least one colonial source (Korn 1939:3), the changing size of Lake Limboto is identified as another indirect measure of deforestation. Accelerated siltation by eroded sediments certainly seems to have been partly responsible for a quite dramatic shrinkage of this lake since the Second World War. But while some observers (Van Kol 1903:341; Sarasin and Sarasin 1905, I:141) believed that it was already shrinking in the nineteenth century, the evidence for this is not strong (Table 26). Most of the estimates in the table are obviously very impressionistic, and the considerable seasonal changes in the extent of the lake also complicate the issue.[48] Reinwardt's visit in 1821,

[45] AV Gorontalo 1841-1843 (ANRI Manado 50); AV Gorontalo 1854 (ANRI Gorontalo 3); 'Dagregister van den civiele gezaghebber te Gorontalo', 10-3-1850 (ANRI Manado 27). In 1852, the process of siltation in the estuary was described as 'very rapid' (AV Gorontalo 1852, in ANRI Gorontalo 3).

[46] Robidé van der Aa 1867:163. The capital of Gorontalo, at that time, was located inside the depression near Lake Limboto. It was moved to its present location in the 1750s following the completion of a stone VOC fort on the estuary, which made the site more secure from seaborne raids (Bastiaans 1939:25; Von Rosenberg 1865:17).

[47] NA VOC 1579:31. In 1686, Gorontalo had been temporarily relieved of its tribute obligations to the VOC partly in consideration of the 'flood damage' which it had recently suffered (NA VOC 1428:172v).

[48] Another complication is the possibility that the water level changed as a result of alterations in the channel which provided the sole outlet from the lake to the Bolango River and the sea. Riedel (1870a:55) describes this outlet, which certainly controls the level of the lake surface today (G. Rose, interview, 25-9-1994) as 'an artificial canal', and Padtbrugge, in his diary of the

Table 26. Reported dimensions of Lake Limboto, 1682-1993

Year	Time of year	Reported size	Equivalent surface area	Reported depth	Other details
ca 1682[1]	estimate based on visits in September (end of dry season) 1677 and (possibly) March 1681[2]	'at a guess, about [22 km] in circumference, not including the low, muddy, broken lands'	ca 40 km²	–	–
1821[3]	September (after unusually severe dry season)	Tondano Lake (Minahasa) 'far exceeds that of Limboto in size'[5]	< 50 km²[4]	–	–
ca 1840[6]	?	'at a guess, [22 km] long and [about 7 km] wide'	ca 100 km²	–	possibly a garbled reproduction of the 1682 estimate[7]
1854[8]	May (dry season)	'has a circumference of [22 km]'	ca 40 km²	–	–
1863[9]	August (dry season)	'the length can be estimated at [18 km], the width at [7.5 km]'	'can be estimated at [...] [80 km²]'	'varies between [4.5 m] and [about 1 m]' of rainfall in the mountains'	lake level 'subject to a periodic rise and fall according to the amount
ca 1870[10]	?	'has a length of about [15 km], a breadth of [9 km], and an almost round, or rather elliptical, shape'	ca 100 km²	–	'According to old reports, the circumference of this lake used to be greater in the past'
1883[11]	Sept. (dry season)	'about [11 km] long'	?	–	–
1895[12]	March (end of wet season)	'length about 11 km, breadth about 7 km'	ca 70 km²	'The average depth is 2 m at most'	'larger in the rainy season than in the dry monsoon'; 'a lake on the point of extinction, gradually drying up and being overgrown by a thick layer of water plants'

1922[13]	?	'Length and breadth are 11 km and 6.5 km.'	ca 70 km²	–	'gives the impression of a swamp more than that of a lake'
ca 1934[14]	?	[ca 14 km long by an average 5 km wide, tapered]	ca 70 km²	'max. depth 14 m'	source is a topographic sketch map
1939[15]	?	'9 by 15 km in size and elliptical in shape'	ca 100 km²	–	'slowly but surely silting up and being overgrown'
1993[16]	'dry season'	'about [30 km²], approximately [6 by 6 km, approximately circular]'		'max. depth 3.5 m'	'One of the most significant properties of the lake is the seasonal fluctuation of the lake perimeter [...]'
1993[17]	'wet season'	'± [45 km²]'		–	

1 Van Dam 1931:96.
2 Padtbrugge sailed across the lake in 1677, but not in 1681.
3 Reinwardt 1858:562.
4 Lake Tondano was approximately 12 km long and 4-6 km wide (Grudelbach 1849:401; Horsting 1917:227).
5 Reinwardt's statement elsewhere (1858:508) that Lake Limboto 'must occupy almost one third of the plain' (or about 150 km² according to Von Rosenberg's estimate of the area of the depression) can be discounted in view of this very specific comparison.
6 Van Doren 1857-60, II:324.
7 Padtbrugge's description was published in 1724 by Valentijn (Keijzer 1856:219), on whom Van Doren undoubtedly draws, and Padtbrugge and Valentijn both give a figure of about one geographical mile (7 km) for the distance across the lake in one direction.
8 Buddingh 1860:367.
9 Von Rosenberg 1865:62-3.
10 Riedel 1870a:55.
11 Guillemard 1886:208.
12 Sarasin and Sarasin 1905, I:141.
13 Logeman 1922:9.
14 Algemeene schetskaart van Nederlandsch-Indië 1941 (compiled 1939). Depth information from P3SU 1994, I:2.5), reproduced from a 1984 fisheries service report quoting an unknown source dated 1934.
15 Korn 1939:3.
16 P3SU 1994, I:2.3, 2.14.
17 P3SU 1994, I:2.3.

for instance, coincided with a major drought, and Padtbrugge's equally low estimate from 1682 probably also refers to the situation at the end of the dry monsoon (although unlike later writers, Padtbrugge does explicitly exclude the swampy margins of the lake). Comparability problems aside, however, it is still striking that this earliest historical description is the one which most closely resembles the state of the lake in 1993, and that whether the figures from the nineteenth and early twentieth centuries show a significant down-ward trend is an open question. To the extent that the size of Lake Limboto is determined by changes in forest cover within its catchment area, then, it can be concluded that such changes probably were not great during this period.

For one part of Gorontalo, the narrow range of barrier hills separating the Limboto Depression from the Gulf of Tomini coast, there is nevertheless direct evidence for progressive deforestation in the course of the nineteenth century. Reinwardt (1858:506) reported in 1821 that the steep slopes on either side of the Gorontalo Bay were 'partly cultivated with cotton and maize, partly covered with tall forests'; the artist Bik (1864:153) who accompanied him on his journey, also commented that from the sea, Gorontalo had a 'very fertile' appearance. In 1863, however, Von Rosenberg could already paint a distinctly different picture of the same hills. 'On both the landward and the seaward sides', he wrote, 'the slopes are covered with gardens, interrupted only here and there by wood- and grassland, the area of which shrinks from day to day' (Von Rosenberg 1865:6). By 1883, according to a British visitor, the seaward slopes near Gorontalo were almost bare, and it was 'only some distance inland, or in the deeper gullies, that any patches of woodland occur'. The coastal land-scape, he added, was 'utterly untropical in appearance'.[49] In the early years of the twentieth century this untropical scene was further enhanced, as in the Palu Valley, by the spread of the *Opuntia* cactus (Edie 1923:9).

Bolaang Mongondow

The deforested and settled enclave on the Mongondow Plateau was even more sharply delineated than that of the Limboto Depression, and made

---

1681 VOC expedition, mentions it as 'the place where they had channelled, defined and drained the lake' (NA VOC 1366:829). Several small fortifications had been built close to this point, and by analogy with a similar strategic site at Tonsea Lama in Minahasa, where a river barrage could be used to flood the shores of Lake Tondano upstream (Van Dam 1931:77), it is possible that its military importance stemmed partly from its water control function. According to Gorontalese oral tradition (Riedel 1895b:1729-30), Lake Limboto had no outlet to the sea until the canal was constructed; the Sarasins (1901:133), however, believed that this was impossible given the volume of runoff entering the lake.

49   Guillemard 1886:209. Also Sarasin and Sarasin 1905, I:136.

a dramatic impression on nineteenth-century visitors. Jansen, after a hard two-day climb over the densely forested mountains separating it from the north coast, gave a lyrical description of 'the plain of Mongondow, with its thousands of coconut trees, its many *kampung* and its fine farm- and grass-lands [*weilanden*], stretched out at our feet under a bright sun'.[50] Wilken and Schwarz 1867a:238), likewise, portrayed it as 'a pleasant patchwork of small woods and open areas, fields and gardens, ponds and streams'.[51] Strongly reminiscent of the densely-settled highland basins of western Central Sulawesi, it covered less than five percent of the area of the subregion, but contained more than half of the population (see Chapter V).

A significant difference between the Van Steenis vegetation maps (Maps 14 and 15) on the one hand, and the recent RePPProT map (Map 16) on the other, is that the latter shows a more continuous westward extension of the Mongondow clearance zone along the valley of the Dumoga River. Descriptive sources show that this time, the discrepancy is not an illusion caused by inaccuracy in the earlier maps. When the Sarasins (1905, I:111-5) walked through the Dumoga Valley in 1893 the small settlements which they passed were still separated by long stretches of forest, and as late as 1935 a visiting Dutch forestry official came to the uncharacteristic conclusion that there was 'no need to be afraid of deforestation' in this area (Verhoef 1938:16). At the 1930 census its population was only 5,000 souls, or seven percent of the Bolaang Mongondow total (*Volkstelling* 1933-36, V:122, 135). Beginning in about 1940, however, the accessibility of the Dumoga area from the Mongondow heartland and from Minahasa made it a target for migration from increasingly overpopulated areas elsewhere. Local settlers were later joined by official transmigrants from Java and Bali, and the population of the valley increased sixfold between 1961 and 1981. By the end of this period, some 45 percent of the area of the Dumoga administrative district was esti-mated to be 'in use for *ladang* farming' (Ulaen-Hoetagaol 1985:50, 73).

Minahasa

The sources for the landscape history of Minahasa are much better than those for other parts of the region. A credible and quite detailed vegetation map of this area, first of all, was drawn up by the botanist Koorders in 1895 (Map 18). Compiled from 'data provided by the district chiefs', and doubtless also

---

50   A.J.F. Jansen, 'Uittreksel uit het dagboek [...] gehouden op zijne reis naar de landen op de noord en westkust van Celebes [...] September en Oktober 1857' (ANRI Manado 167).
51   Other comparable descriptions are Riedel 1864b:275; Sarasin and Sarasin 1905, I:87, 95; Wilken and Schwarz 1867a:234.

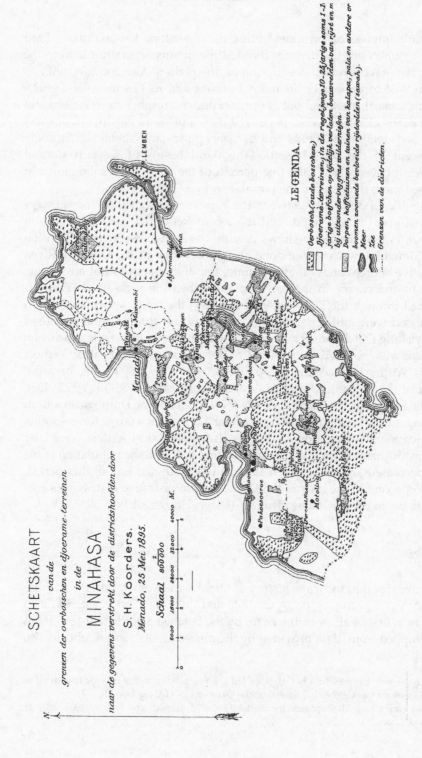

Map 18. Minahasa: vegetation cover in 1895 according to S.H. Koorders ('Sketch map by S.H. Koorders showing the distribution of primary [oerbosschen] and secondary [jurame] forest in Minahasa, according to information supplied by the district chiefs'). (Map reproduced from Koorders 1898.)

Plate 25. Part of the central plateau of Minahasa to the west of Lake Tondano, with
grassland much in evidence, 1920 (Van Marle 1922, I: Figure 9)

benefiting from Koorders' personal observations during his five-month in
situ botanical investigation, this shows virgin forests (*oerbosch*) covering
somewhere between a third and a half of the total area. Villages, tree crops
and irrigated ricefields occupy another fraction, but the dominant vegetation consists of secondary forest (known in Minahasa as *jurame*) growing
'on temporarily abandoned rice- and maizefields', together with 'occasional
grasslands' (*bij uitzondering gras wildernissen*) and (presumably) currently
cultivated fields.

Rapid population growth (see Chapter V) led to accelerating forest
destruction in Minahasa during the early twentieth century. In 1919, 28 percent of Minahasa (see Appendix J) technically consisted of *domeingronden* or
'state lands', comprising 'forest reserves' together with 'all land on which
no [cultivation] rights are exercised' (Van Marle 1922, I:67-8). Some of these
lands, however, were almost certainly under illicit swidden cultivation: in
1922, the forestry service noted that in many parts of Minahasa the *domein*
boundaries would have to be redefined because 'conversion of state land to
private land is already very far advanced' (*Verslag Dienst Boschwezen* 1921-22:
41). By 1925, according to one source, actual forest cover had already fallen to
just 12 percent (Lam 1950:575), although this may well be an underestimate.

Map 19, reproduced from a 1944 military reconnaissance study (Allied
Geographical Section 1944: Map 3), purports to show the situation at the end
of the colonial period. Its exaggerated depiction of the forest area, in which
secondary regrowth has evidently been included, is not very informative;
Van Steenis (Maps 14 and 15), more accurately, shows 'dry fields' and 'bush,
grass and fern wastes' as the dominant types of land cover. The 1944 map,
however, does highlight an important change which had taken place in the
nature of the deforested part of the Minahasan landscape since the turn of

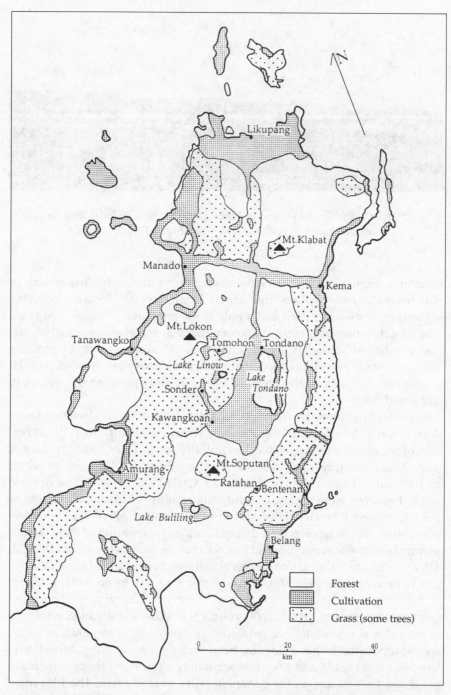

Map 19. Minahasa: vegetation cover according to a military reconnaissance study, 1944 (redrawn from Allied Geographical Section 1944: Map 3)

the century. Whereas Koorders (1898:261, 274) had judged the proportion of grassland in Minahasa to be even lower than in Java, here almost a third of the land area is labelled 'grass (some trees)', and while this is probably exaggerated, there is no doubt that the area under grass increased rapidly in the first part of the twentieth century (Plate 25).[52]

Nineteenth-century records do not include explicit estimates of forest cover in Minahasa, and the vegetation map by Koorders is the oldest reasonably reliable cartographic aid here.[53] Beginning in 1862, however, the Dutch authorities, with the help of recently trained Minahasan land surveyors, did attempt to measure the total area under rice cultivation.[54] Combined with contemporary data on tree crops and fallow periods, this makes it possible to construct a rough minimum estimate of the amount of 'waste land' under neither permanent or periodic cultivation in Minahasa in the middle of the nineteenth century (Appendix I). In 1862 some 154 km^2 were thought to be occupied by swidden ricefields, and another 22 km^2 by *sawah*. No comparable information is available for maize and other secondary crops, but most of these, as we have seen (Chapters II and IX), were planted consecutively in the same year and on the same land as the dry rice.[55] At the end of 1861 there were reportedly some 5.9 million coffee trees in Minahasa, and the Cultivation Report for that year estimates on the basis of standard planting distances that these occupied a total area of about 65 km^2. Similar, but probably less reliable, calculations indicated an additional 24 km^2 planted with cocoa trees, and 28 km^2 with coconut palms.[56]

Estimates of fallow periods in Minahasan foodcrop agriculture during the nineteenth century are bewilderingly diverse. One source from 1833 first states that swidden rice is usually grown 'on high ground, preferably in places where there are thick forests [*zware bosschen*]', only to add that 'districts which have plenty of land usually let their fields lie fallow for three or four years, while others are obliged to plant them every alternate year'.[57] There were also some places where unirrigated land was in continuous use without any fallow interval, as what are known in Java as *tegalan*, permanently cultivated dry fields (Edeling 1919:48; Tammes 1940:192). The busi-

---

[52] The same study also provides descriptions of some particular grassland areas (Allied Geographical Section 1944:34, 43-4), as does the botanist Lam (1931:210, 215).
[53] One much earlier land use map, dating from around 1830, also exists, but this is very schematic and shows little more than the location of the main coffee gardens and rice-growing areas (Henley 1995:35-6, 49).
[54] CV Manado 1862 (ANRI Ambon 1563).
[55] Some maize was also planted on separate maize swiddens (CV Manado 1857, in ANRI Manado 52; Edeling 1919:58); a cultivation report from 1861 (CV Manado 1861, in ANRI Manado 95), however, states that this was only done 'occasionally' (*bij uitzondering*).
[56] CV Manado 1861 (ANRI Manado 74, 95).
[57] AV Manado 1833 (ANRI Manado 48).

ness of reconstructing the 'typical' swidden cycle is also complicated by the fact that some true swiddens were planted with main crops (rice and maize) for two or more consecutive years before being left fallow. Since these data on swidden cycles are of central importance not only to the reconstruction of deforestation levels in nineteenth-century Minahasa, but also to the general argument developed below regarding the causes of deforestation, they are reproduced here in full (Table 27).

In the early nineteenth century (Table 27: 1825, 1833?) an ideal preference, probably connected with the establishment of permanent land ownership rights by pioneer cultivators (Riedel 1869a:6; G.A. Wilken 1870:110), apparently existed for the clearance of virgin forest. How often this happened in practice, given the concentrated, sedentary settlement pattern (see Chapter V) and the need to lay out swiddens in large contiguous complexes (Chapter XI), is unclear; by 1870 it had certainly become rare (Table 27: ca 1870c). It is possible that the increased external demands placed on the supply of male labour in the course of the nineteenth century made the clearance of primary forest less feasible. Evidence from other parts of the region, however, indicates that rotational cultivation was both the normal and the preferred precolonial pattern (see Chapter XIV); within Minahasa, moreover, the colonization of uninhabited areas was undoubtedly more common at the end of the nineteenth century than at the beginning (Chapter V).

The great majority of the data in Table 27, at any rate, indicate a main cropping period of either one or two years, followed by recultivation after a fallow period of between three and ten years. The typical ratio of cultivated to fallow land areas, on this evidence, ranged from 1:10 to 2:3, and the fallow period was usually only just long enough to allow regrowth of woody vegetation. The practice of planting fruit trees and other perennial crops on the 'abandoned' swiddens after the end of the main cropping period, moreover, meant that the secondary regrowth itself was partly man-made. A description of fallow land on the southwestern border of Minahasa in 1869, in a place where the fallow interval was a rather typical five to eight years, brings home the implications for the landscape.

> This fallow land, or *jurame* as it is known here, has a monotonous appearance. Invariably it is characterized by a great number of ferns and copses of bamboo together with papaya and *tagalolo* [*Ficus septica*] trees, and by *lingkuwas* [*Alpinia Galanga*] and *galoba* [*Costus* species] bushes, among which a coconut palm or a banana tree rises up here and there. (De Clercq 1870c:527.)

Koorders (1898:26) described a different vegetation with a more closed canopy for *jurame* on the more fertile central plateau of Minahasa. But the height of the secondary forest was still only five to six metres, and instead of the 30-50 species of large tree typical of virgin hill forest (see Chapter I), here

Table 27. Swidden cycle data, Minahasa, 1821-1901

Year	Locality	Cultivation and fallow period indications
1821[1]	not specified	'a field lies fallow for 5 or 6 years after each harvest'
1824a[2]	not specified	'land which has been planted for one year has to lie fallow for 5 years before it will yield another harvest'
1824b[3]	not specified	apart from *sawah* on the shores of Lake Tondano, ricefields are 'all high [dry] fields which are cultivated only for 1 year and then left fallow again'
1825[4]	not specified	'The native prefers to make his *padi* gardens mainly where he is obliged to fell tall, heavy timber [*groot en zwaar hout*], and ideally in places where there have never been gardens in the past [...] [he] lets the ground lie fallow for 3 years at least, but more often for 5 years and more'
1833[5]	not specified	'The rice is usually grown on high ground, and preferably in places where there are thick forests, because weeds grow less fast there. [...] The districts which have plenty of land usually let their fields lie fallow for 3 or 4 years, while others are obliged to plant them every other year'
ca 1840[6]	not specified	'if the present area under rice cultivation was more than doubled, there would quickly be a shortage of land, since the native lets his dry ricefields lie fallow for 3 to 5 years before he regards them as suitable for that grain once more'
1846a[7]	not specified	'forested land is chosen by preference' for swidden cultivation; 'most fields can only be cultivated for 1 or 2 years, and the abandoned fields must lie fallow for at least 3 years to regain their lost fertility from a new vegetation cover'
1846b[8]	environs of Lake Tondano	dry rice 'is planted with good results for 2 consecutive years, and then the fields are left fallow for 3 to 5 years, or else planted once or twice in this period with various vegetables'
1846c[9]	along path from Manado (western Minahasa)	local landscape is 'almost nine-tenths covered by a wilderness of vegetation 6 to 15 years old which to Likupang (north) was formerly cultivated'
1855[10]	Tanawangko (west coast)	'The rice land in the neighborhood of the villages lay fallow, in which state it remains for 5 years [...]'
1860[11]	vicinity of Manado	'after the forest is cleared the land is usually planted with *padi* only once, sometimes twice, and then abandoned so that young wood (*belukar*) can grow up on it once more, making it suitable for rice cultivation again after about 7 to 10 years'
1861[12]	coffee-growing districts (central uplands)	*jurame* (fallow) land 'is land which has been used for *padi* and maize cultivation and has lain fallow for 4 to 6 years'

Year	Locality	Cultivation and fallow period indications
1862[13]	'many districts' in coffee-growing area (central uplands)	shortage of forest lands for coffee planting 'in the vicinity of villages' means that 'land which has lain fallow for 3 to 6 years now has to be used for that purpose'
1863[14]	not specified	land chosen for rice swiddens is 'mostly forest land, or *jurame* of 3 to 10 years'
1864[15]	not specified	land preferred for maize swiddens is 'forest land or *jurame* of 3 to 10 years, together with land on which long grass (known as *kusut kusut* [= *kusu-kusu, alang-alang*]) grows'
ca 1864a[16]	Minahasa in general	'the laboriously-cleared fields can only be used for a single season, after which, if other land is available, they are left to fallow for from 2 or 3 to 5 years'
ca 1864b[17]	Sonder (central uplands)	'And those farmers living in areas where land is abundant are the fortunate ones. Where this is not the case – in the vicinity of the *negeri* Sonder, for instance – work in the fields yields but poor returns, since the old farmlands (*jurame*) have to be re-used year in, year out, or else with excessively short fallow intervals'
1866a[18]	not specified	'Every year [...] new forest or *jurame* land is cleared, and after the harvest this land lies fallow for 4 to 7 years before being cultivated again [...]'
1866b[19]	Tondano area only	'in some places in the Tondano division shortage of land often forces the population to grow rice on the same field 4 to 5 times in succession, which is possible here because of the greater fertility of the soil'
1869[20]	southwestern Minahasa	'New land must, however, be used each year; in the second year it serves only for planting with maize, whereafter it lies fallow for 5-8 years before it is ready for cultivation once more'
ca 1870a[21]	'in most districts'	'after use for a single year, the fields must lie fallow for 2, 3, 4, or more years'
ca 1870b[22]	Tomohon district (central uplands)	'Only in a few districts, such as Tomohon, can some land be cultivated with good results for 2 or 3 consecutive years'
ca 1870c[23]	not specified	'Where completely new lands or forests are brought into cultivation, which very rarely happens now [...]'
1872a[24]	Minahasa in general	'the prevailing custom in Minahasa [is] never to cultivate the fields for two consecutive seasons, but to let them lie fallow for 2, 3, 4 or more years'; however: 'Newly-cleared forest land can also be used with success for a second year'
1872b[25]	Pasan and Ratahan	'Where plentiful land is available, the fields are even left fallow for 9, 10 or more years [...]'

1875[26]	(southeast Minahasa) various (specified); Negeri Baru = Manado; Langoan, Remboken, Sarongsong, Tulimambot, Tuliang = vicinity of Lake Tondano; Kawangkoan, Sarongsong, Sonder, Tomohon = western part of central uplands	Among other places, this occurs in the districts of Pasan and Ratahan' 'The period for which the fields lie fallow varies between districts and is mostly determined by the amount of land available for agricultural use; if there is sufficient land, farmers usually wait until the *alang-alang* or *glagah* has been suffocated by the rising undergrowth. Usually the dry fields are abandoned after one year and then lie fallow for 2 or 3 to 10 years and more. In some districts, however, the land remains in use for longer – 2 years, for instance, at some places in Tonsea, 2, 3 or 4 years in Negeri Baru, Langoan, Kawangkoan, Remboken and Sarongsong, and in Sonder even up to 10 years, while in the districts of Tulimambot, Tuliang and Tomohon some land is in continuous use'
1879[27]	not specified	'only very few fields are planted every year, and as a rule no fields lie fallow for fewer than 3 years, and some for up to 10 years'
1881[28]	not specified	'Almost everywhere here the native has a superabundance of land which has been brought into cultivation at some point in the past, so that he can farm in different places each year and only has to re-use the same piece of land after an interval of at least 3 years, and usually much longer.'
1882[29]	not specified	'In some parts of Minahasa, where the soil is sufficiently fertile, *padi* is planted on the same land for 2 consecutive years [...]. Thereafter the land is left fallow for several years.'
1895a[30]	vicinity of Kakaskasen (central uplands)	'Local experience shows that after the ground has been covered for 3-4 years with this [already 3-4 year-old] wood, it is once again fertile enough to be cleared and cultivated, usually with rice or maize, for 2-3 consecutive years.'
1895b[31]	Minahasa in general	*jurame* (fallow) land is 'generally young forest of 10 to 25, or sometimes 1 to 10 years old on temporarily abandoned fields of rice and maize'
1896[32]	not specified	'After the *padi* is harvested the fields are usually left fallow for a time, sometimes only for a few months, in other areas for a few years.'
1901[33]	contrasts uplands / lowlands	'In the uplands, where the soil is very fertile, such gardens [swiddens] are planted every year on the same land, the rotation of rice and maize guarding against soil exhaustion. But by the sea, where the soil quality is lower, cultivation cannot be repeated since the returns already become inadequate in the second year. Here it is therefore necessary to move the gardens to new locations every year'

1   Reinwardt 1858:585.
2   Olivier 1834-37, II:35.
3   Van der Cappelen 1855:358.
4   Riedel 1872b:539, 540.
5   AV Manado 1833 (ANRI Manado 48).
6   Van Doren 1857-60, II:362.
7   Francis 1860:349, 350.
8   Grudelbach 1849:406
9   E. Francis, 'Aantekeningen van den kommissaris voor Menado 1846' (ANRI Manado 50).
10 *Fragment* 1856:150.
11 Teysman 1861:344.
12 CV Manado 1861 (ANRI Manado 95).
13 CV Manado 1862 (ANRI Ambon 1563).
14 CV Manado 1863 (ANRI Manado 52).
15 CV Manado 1864 (ANRI Manado 39).
16 Graafland 1864:8.
17 Graafland 1864:8.
18 CV Manado 1866 (ANRI Manado 52).
19 CV Menado 1866 (ANRI Manado 52).
20 De Clercq 1870c:526-7.
21 N.P. Wilken 1870:374.
22 N.P. Wilken 1870:374.
23 N.P. Wilken 1870:376.
24 G.A. Wilken 1873:134.
25 G.A. Wilken 1873:134.
26 Edeling 1919:48.
27 CV Manado 1879 (ANRI Manado 86).
28 Matthes 1881.
29 CV Manado 1882 (ANRI Manado 86).
30 Koorders 1898:26.
31 Koorders 1898: vegetation map (reproduced here as Map 19).
32 CV Manado 1896 (ANRI Manado 86).
33 Worotikan 1910:153.

there were just a handful.[58]

> This secondary forest consists almost exclusively of four or five types of tree, of which a single species usually dominates locally. These are fast-growing trees which do not reach a large size, and have poor-quality wood. [...] The principal tree species are the following: *Boehmeria moluccana* [...] *Homalanthus populifolius* [...] *Melochia indica* [...] *Ficus ribes* [...] and *Ficus minahasa* [...]. Among them grows here and there an *aren* (*Arenga saccharifera*) or an elegant *wanga* palm (*Metroxylon elatum*) [...]. The undergrowth, in so far as it has not already been killed by the shade of the closely-spaced little trees and reduced to a half-rotten state, consists of *alang-alang* (*Imperata*) [...]. (Koorders 1898:26.)

It was precisely in this fertile upland area, moreover, that such well-developed *jurame* was scarce, since *tegalan* and very intensive short-fallow swidden cycles were common (Table 27: ca 1864b, 1866b, 1875, 1901), and grasslands were sometimes brought back into cultivation before they had reverted to woody regrowth of any description.[59] Even the oldest secondary forests, notably, were still clearly distinct from the remaining natural vegetation; 'reversion of cultivated land to the wild state', observed the Dutch Resident Van der Crab in 1873, 'does not occur' (Van Kol 1903:239).

Where rotations longer than ten years are mentioned or implied in Table 27 (1846c, 1872b, 1875, 1895b), it is mostly in relation to the more sparsely populated parts of Minahasa outside the central plateau. The Dutch sources, proportionally speaking, are weighted against these peripheral areas, since colonial interest during the nineteenth century focused mainly on the central uplands where most of the exportable crops (coffee and rice) were grown. Koorders' comment (Table 27: 1895b) that the *jurame* on his vegetation map is 'generally' 10-25 years old, although somewhat at odds with his own descriptions, also suggests a need for caution here. So do the land use data from 1919 presented by Van Marle (1922:86-9), according to which currently cultivated fields occupied only nine percent of the total area of swidden land in Minahasa as a whole, and less than five percent in the Kema and Belang administrative divisions (Appendix J). On balance it seems reasonable to select a figure of eight years (more justification for this figure will be provided in Chapter XIV) as an approximation to the average length of the fallow period in the middle of the nineteenth century, and to assume an average main crop cultivation period of just one year. Given a nine-year cycle, then, the total amount of land involved in swidden cultivation according to the

---

[58]   A generic term for bush fallow in Minahasa was *sawukow* (*Rapport* 1910:49; Worotikan 1910: 152-3), which is identified in a dictionary of the Tontemboan language with a single species of *Ficus* (Schwarz 1908b:420).

[59]   N.P. Wilken 1870:376; CV Manado 1864 (ANRI Manado 39).

1862 land use figures was nine times 154 km², or roughly 1,400 km².

Besides the foodcrop swiddens, the coffee 'gardens' were also subject to a rotation of sorts. The productivity of coffee trees in Minahasa, according to an early report, began to decline once they reached an age of six or seven years, 'after which they are no longer worth maintaining, so that the native is continually obliged to lay out new gardens'.[60] Other sources, however, give production periods of 12 years and more (*Fragment* 1856:20; Francis 1860: 358). Abandoned gardens, if located on *jurame* land previously included in the swidden fallow cycle, were generally returned to their original owners (L. Wessels 1891:139). After an unknown interval they were apparently suitable once more for foodcrop cultivation, although in 1859 a regulation was issued stipulating that non-productive coffee lands were to be left fallow 'so that they can be used again for coffee cultivation at a later date'.[61] The length of the effective average fallow period in nineteenth-century Minahasa cannot be reconstructed, but it will probably not be exaggerated to put the amount of land directly or indirectly involved in coffee production in 1862 at 150 km² instead of the recorded 65 km². Adding this, the other tree plantations (28 km² of coconuts and 24 km² of cocoa) and the small area of *sawah* (22 km²) to the land involved in swidden cultivation (1,400 km²) gives a total of about 1,600 km² under either periodic or permanent cultivation, implying that by 1862 about one third of the land area of Minahasa had been cleared of natural vegetation (Appendix I).[62] By 1895, it will be remembered, that proportion had risen to about 60 percent, and in 1920 it probably stood somewhere between 75 and 85 percent.

Descriptive sources from the first half of the nineteenth century often give the impression of a much more complete forest cover than existed in 1862. 'The whole region', states one administrative report from the 1820s, 'is covered with thick woods'.[63] The government investigator Francis (1860:319) judged that 'hardly one-tenth' of Minahasa was 'occupied and cultivated' in

---

60   AV Manado 1833 (ANRI Manado 48). Dumont d'Urville (1833:458) also states that coffee plantations in Minahasa 'quickly become exhausted, and are abandoned in order to plant others'.
61   CV Manado 1858, 1859 (ANRI Ambon 1528, 1543). A description of swidden coffee cultivation in early twentieth-century Sumatra states that after 5 years the plantations are allowed to revert to secondary forest, whereupon 'the terrain lies fallow for between 7 and 15-20 years, before being cleared again as a *ladang* and planted with food crops and coffee' (Paerels 1949: 111).
62   The land area figure used in this calculation, like that employed by Van Marle, is somewhat lower than that which forms the basis for the demographic calculations elsewhere in this book (Appendices E, F, I). In this context, however, it is probably justified in so far as many swiddens were probably missed by the pioneer survey of 1862: in 1864 the recorded total area under dry rice reached 185 km², and in the years 1865-1870 it averaged 189 km² (A.C.J. Edeling, 'Memorie omtrent de Minahasa', 13-8-1875, in NA V 17-4-1877/20).
63   AV Manado 1829 (KITLV H70).

1846.[64] As late as 1853, Resident Jansen (1861:252) described Minahasa as an area 'of which as yet only a very small part is cultivated, the rest being blanketed, as it were, by thick forests containing many useful types of timber'. A closer look at the descriptions from this period, however, shows that despite the scrawny character of most of the swidden-fallow vegetation in Minahasa, such judgements reflected a failure to differentiate between secondary and primary forest. The diary of Francis' visit in 1846, for example, reveals that what he understood as 'wilderness' included forest regrowth of six to fifteen years old on former swiddens.[65] A year earlier the army officer and amateur naturalist Ten Siethoff had stated that 'the whole of Minahasa is covered, as it were, by a single forest', only to add that in places that forest 'varies in density and uniformity, and takes on the appearance of many woods which merge into the more open vegetation between them'.[66] Reinwardt (1858:543), by contrast, was well able to distinguish secondary from primary vegetation, noting that in the lowlands between Kema and Manado the vegetation was 'mostly of the kind that quickly grows up on land which is cleared of trees'.

Nineteenth-century visitors to the most densely populated parts of the central plateau, where fallow periods were shortest, were in any case unanimous in describing intensively cultivated landscapes almost devoid of forest.[67] For the area of particularly fertile volcanic soils around Tomohon, one of Padtbrugge's travel diaries even provides such a description from the seventeenth century.[68] Walking from Kakaskasen to Tomohon in January 1679, the governor and his party 'travelled mostly through fine cultivated hills [*schoone saij-heuvelen*], as only swidden rice [*berg-rijs*] is grown in these parts'. 'From there', Padtbrugge continues, 'we wandered this day through the whole country of Tomohon, Tombariri and Sarongsong, [...] passing always through fields of young and pleasant crops which promise a rich harvest'. Next day the 15-kilometre march from Tomohon to Tondano also led 'through cultivated lands as before'. While a considerable further intensification of farming practices probably took place even in this most thoroughly cultivated subregion during the intervening period (see Chapter XV), a strong echo of Padtbrugge's account can still be heard in a description of the Minahasan agricultural landscape written fully two and a half centuries later.

---

64   Also Olivier 1834-37, II:36; Riedel 1872b:539.
65   'Aantekeningen van den kommissaris voor Manado 1846' (ANRI Manado 50).
66   'Topografische schetsen van een gedeelte der residentie Menado, 1845' (ANRI Manado 46).
67   *Fragment* 1856:21, 94; Guillemard 1886:181; Hickson 1889:225; Reinwardt 1858:550, 554-5, 566; Scalliet 1995:412.
68   NA VOC 1345:546-7.

Rice has been strongly displaced by *milu* (maize) and coconuts (copra) as an agricultural product in Minahasa, but because the rice here is grown mainly in dry
ladang, it still dominates the landscape in many places. These rice *ladang* have a
very characteristic appearance; whole hills are covered with them. If it were not
for the fact that the vegetation is much lower and less dense, at first sight they
could be taken for *alang-alang* fields. (Lam 1931:211.)

Padtbrugge also provides the earliest report of real grassland in Minahasa,
on the coastal plain near Manado. Leaving the VOC fort for his trip to the
interior, he was obliged to set out at three o'clock in the morning 'across
the reed fields [*liesvelden*, probably *alang-alang*], which would have been too
exhausting to cross in the heat of the sun'. These fields were apparently not
very extensive, for by sunrise the 'reeds' were 'mostly' behind him, and the
climb to the plateau had begun.[69] Nineteenth-century sources also mention
fields of *alang-alang* and *glagah* (*Saccharum spontaneum*) grass both on the
coastal plain and in parts of the interior, but not on the same scale as the
grasslands described from Gorontalo and Central Sulawesi.[70] The only really
sizeable expanse of old permanent grassland in Minahasa was found in its
southeastern corner around Ratahan, in what became the Belang administrative division. In 1681 a VOC officer, marching inland from Bentenan to
Ratahan, passed first through a 'brush-bamboo forest' (*kreupel-bamboese-*
bosch) and a sago wood before emerging 'onto the grassy hills [*liesbergen*],
under and over which we marched for a long time before arriving in the
village'.[71] This landscape was not much changed in 1939, when an American
National Geographic correspondent 'rolled down from the buffalo-grass hills
near Ratahan to the Molucca Sea' in his hired car.[72]

Sangir

On the earliest Van Steenis map (Map 14) the Sangir Islands are shown
as almost competely deforested, whereas the revised version (Map 15)
erroneously shows considerable areas of rain forest. Even the first map,
however, is misleading in that the natural vegetation on Sangir had been

---

[69]   NA VOC 1345:539.
[70]   De Clercq 1870c:530; Edeling 1919:53, 57; *Fragment* 1856:21; Graafland 1867-69, I:299, II:164;
Hickson 1889:225; Reinwardt 1858:551, 563; L.J. van Rhijn 1851:306; Sarasin and Sarasin 1905, I:5,
8-10, 30, 37, 53, 77; Scalliet 1995:411; 'Instructie voor de koffij cultuur in de Residentie Menado',
5-11-1844 (ANRI Manado 37); J.J. ten Siethoff, 'Topografische schetsen van een gedeelte der residentie Menado, 1845' (ANRI Manado 46).
[71]   NA VOC 1366:790-1.
[72]   Williams 1940:63. Lam (1931:215) also mentions this grassy landscape, part of which is
shown from the air in Plate 33 (Chapter XIV).

replaced notaby grasslands, annual crops, or even (for the most part) second-ary regrowth, but by a new type of man-made permanent forest dominated by coconut palms, which blanketed large parts of Tagulandang and Greater Sangir 'up to the highest mountaintops'.[73] Nutmeg and *sagu baruk* (*Arenga microcarpa*) trees (Tammes 1936a:43, 48) were planted under the coconuts, forming a second canopy layer in many places, while *Metroxylon* (true) sago grew in groves on wet ground. Other important foodcrops included bananas and tubers (see Chapter II), both of which, like *sagu baruk* and nutmeg, could be grown underneath the coconut trees; open swiddens, planted in their first year with rice and maize, were found mainly on high slopes (Tergast 1936:131, 135-9, 141).

Although nutmeg was introduced to Sangir only in the middle of the nineteenth century (Janse 1898:19-20), and coconut cultivation received a crucial extra stimulus from the growing international market for copra from 1862 onward (see Chapter II), the basic combination of coconuts and food-crop agriculture was already well established prior to these developments. 'Everywhere on and along the mountains', reported Van Delden (1844:362) in 1825, 'the land appears covered with coconut trees, between which banana and rice swiddens have been laid out'.[74] In 1855 an NZG missionary compared the numerous mountaintop *ladang* huts of the Sangirese farmers to 'Swiss cot-tages', nestling picturesquely in 'fertile gardens' surrounded by 'tall coconut forests', and observed that the coconut palm was present 'in greater numbers than perhaps anywhere else in the whole of the Indies' (Van de Velde van Cappellen 1857:45). 'Sangir', agreed Hickson (1889:174) thirty years later, 'may be considered to be the home of the coconut in these parts'.

Coconuts already seem to have been present on Sangir in the mid-sixteenth century (De Sá 1955:328), but since they are not mentioned in Marta's fairly detailed description of food and agriculture on Siau in the 1580s (Jacobs 1974-84, I:262), it is possible that they did not become common until the early sev-enteenth century.[75] By the 1650s both Siau and Tagulandang certainly had an abundance of coconut palms (Colin 1900-02, I:110), and Tabukan, on Greater Sangir, was exporting coconut oil to Ternate (Hustaart 1656). In view of the demonstrable link between commercial and demographic trends in other contexts, including that of Sangir itself during the copra boom of the late nineteenth century, it is in fact tempting to link the apparent increase in the population of Siau and Greater Sangir between 1600 and 1650 (see Chapter

---

[73] Heringa 1921b:733. Tergast (1936:135), however, states that the 'coconut belt' reached no higher than 700 m above sea level, whereas Siau and Greater Sangir both have peaks of 1,000 m and more.

[74] Also Steller 1866:17; E. Francis, 'Aantekeningen van den kommissaris voor Menado 1846' (ANRI Manado 167).

[75] By 1630 there were definitely coconuts on Siau (Jacobs 1974-84, III:476).

IV) with the rise of coconut oil as an export product; local economic growth may have been an additional reason, alongside the very wet local climate, why the demography of Sangir was unaffected by the presumed 'crisis' of the mid-seventeenth century (Chapter XII).

Like nineteenth-century visitors Padtbrugge, who visited the islands in 1677 and 1680, observed that 'even the biggest and highest' mountains of Greater Sangir were planted with coconut trees (Robidé van der Aa 1867:253-4). An illustration in his diary of the 1677 expedition includes some of the coconut forests of Siau (Plate 26). More surprisingly, Padtbrugge also mentioned that there were at least 300 head of cattle on Greater Sangir and that at an earlier date there had been more than 1,000.[76] Cattle ('bullocks') were still present both here and on Tagulandang in 1775 (Forrest 1779:312, 318), but by 1825 the only livestock in the Sangir Archipelago were pigs, goats and chickens (Van Delden 1844:21), and despite a Dutch attempt to reintroduce them (Steller 1866:21), large animals remained either absent or very rare thereafter.[77] Padtbrugge wrote that the cattle on Greater Sangir 'wander in the wild and live in the woods', some of them 'grazing on the slopes of the mountains' (Robidé van der Aa 1867:254-5). In his time, then, there must have been grass for them to eat.[78] Later sources, however, rarely mention grass on Sangir.[79] Possibly the cattle grazed among the coconut palms, the canopy of which, unlike that of other trees, can be thin enough not to prevent the growth of grass on the ground below (Departement van Landbouw, Nijverheid en Handel 1925:15; Tammes 1949:29).

The population growth of the late nineteenth and early twentieth centuries all but destroyed what was left of the natural vegetation on Sangir. In the 1850s, the 'small but dense woods' of the Sangir Archipelago still provided 'a generous supply of the best and finest sorts of timber' (Van de Velde van Cappellen 1857:45). By 1884, however, there were 'very few forests, due to the dense population'.[80] In 1912 it was reported that 'the virgin forest [*oerbosch*] has as good as vanished to make way for regularly laid-out gardens' (Encyclopaedisch Bureau 1912a:22). The supply of wood was now insufficient for local construction needs, so that despite deliberate planting of fast-grow-

---

[76]   Robidé van der Aa 1867:255. These figures, moreover, refer only to the chiefdom of Taruna, whereas there were also cattle in Tabukan (Robidé van der Aa 1867:254).

[77]   Bastiaan 1930:5; Encyclopaedisch Bureau 1912a:23; Francis 1860:354; Steller 1866:21.

[78]   A local source attributed the reported decline in cattle numbers, which had occurred well within living memory, to a volcanic eruption rather than to any shortage of pasture (Padtbrugge 1867:254-5).

[79]   Van Delden (1844:17), however, did note in 1825 that swidden clearing sometimes involves the cutting of 'high grass', and Hickson (1889:176) described a field of *alang-alang* and other grasses on the west coast of Greater Sangir in 1885.

[80]   CV Sangir- en Talaudeilanden 1884 (ANRI Manado 146).

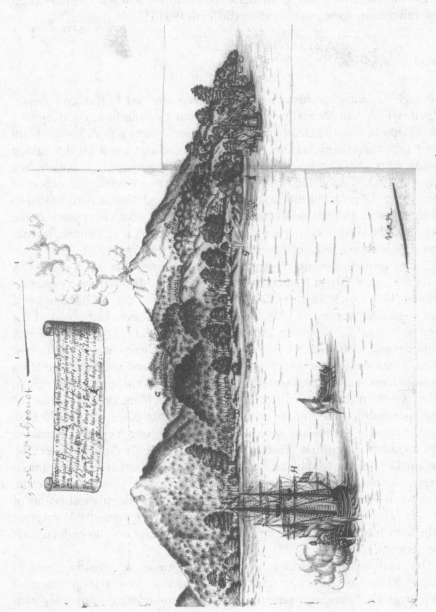

Plate 26. Siau in 1677, showing coconut stands (NA VOC 1337)

ing timber species, wood also had to be imported from elsewhere (Heringa 1921b:734, 741). By the 1930s, 'virtually all terrain' on Siau and Greater Sangir was under some form of cultivation (Brilman 1938:15).

Talaud

Although its landscape history cannot be reconstructed in the same depth, Talaud, which Van Steenis portrayed as about two-thirds forested around 1930 (Maps 14 and 15), clearly presents a different picture from Sangir. Until about 1885 there were said to be 'almost no coconut trees' on the Talaud Islands.[81] Possibly this was because the Sangirese kingdoms to which they were subject had succeeded up to that point in discouraging the export of oil or copra.[82] Thereafter the crop spread rapidly, and Talaud participated in the copra boom. In 1920, nevertheless, it was still 'only the lower parts' of the larger islands which were occupied by coconut gardens, while timber, including valuable ebony, remained plentiful elsewhere (Heringa 1921b:734).

Early twentieth-century observers, in fact, believed that much of the forest on the larger Talaud Islands consisted of undisturbed natural vegetation (Brilman 1938:13, 15; Tergast 1936:129). The botanist Lam, on the basis of a brief vegetation survey in 1926, was also of this opinion, but noted at the same time that 'the forest in Talaud is not more than moderately heavy' (Holthuis and Lam 1942:99). At one location on the east coast of the largest island, Karakelang, he was surprised to find what resembled an 'alpine' flora of grass, ferns, bushes and small trees at a low altitude, and apparently in a place where no signs of cultivation were evident (Lam 1927). A 'savanna' vegetation with partial tree cover was also present in places (Lam 1950:583). In other parts of Karakelang there were secondary forests clearly associated with swidden agriculture (Holthuis and Lam 1942:101; Tergast 1936:136). The smaller Talaud Islands of Kaburuang and Salibabu were more intensively cultivated than Karakelang, and here the forest had retreated to the point where 'there are only some small groves left on the highest points of the hills' (Holthuis and Lam 1942:101). This agrees with Forrest's description of the same islands in 1775, when Salibabu in particular was 'in high cultivation' (Forrest 1779:316).

The small northern outliers of the Talaud group, as already noted in Chapter XI, featured some spectacular examples of deforestation, albeit on a tiny scale. On Miangas, where the natural vegetation had 'completely van-

[81]   CV Manado 1895 (ANRI Manado 86).
[82]   E. Francis, 'Aantekening van den kommissaris voor Menado 1846' (ANRI Manado 167); A.J.F. Jansen, 'Missive Sangir en Talaut Eilanden', 26-8-1857 (ANRI Manado 166); Keijzer 1856:174.

ished' by 1926 (Lam 1932:26), some timber trees were intentionally planted to offset the shortage of wood (Holthuis and Lam 1942:127) and timber imports also occurred (Lam 1932:47-8). Merampi (Mengampit), in Nanusa, had an almost treeless vegetation which Lam (1950:581, 583) characterized as 'fire savannah'.[83] Most of the inhabited islands of the Nanusa and Kawio groups, in fact, were 'competely cleared and converted into coconut and banana gardens', while coconuts had been planted on some of the uninhabited islets too (Heringa 1921b:734).

Summary

If tree crops and fallow regrowth are excluded from the forest category, then about one quarter of the land area of northern Sulawesi was unforested in 1930. Most of the major foci of deforestation corresponded to areas of dense population: Sangir-Talaud, Minahasa, Mongondow, Gorontalo, the Palu Valley, the upland valleys of Lore and western Central Sulawesi, Banggai, and the settled coastal strips in all parts of the region. In Poso and Mori, however, very extensive forest loss coincided with areas of moderate to low population density. This part of interior eastern Central Sulawesi was also unusual in that much, if not most, of its deforested landscapes consisted of open grassland or savanna. Although some grasslands were also found in other parts of the mainland, particularly Gorontalo and the Palu Valley, the typical man-made landscape elsewhere was characterized by a combination of cultivated fields and bush-fallow vegetation of low stature and limited botanical diversity. No significant grasslands, at least after the end of the eighteenth century, were found in Sangir or Banggai. Foodcrop farming on Sangir was substantially integrated with coconut cultivation, giving rise to a light but permanent man-made arboreal vegetation dominated by coconut palms.

Both the Palu Valley and the Limboto Depression were already heavily deforested in the seventeenth century, and there is little evidence that the problems of flooding, soil erosion and siltation experienced here in the early twentieth century resulted from the kind of recent environmental crisis proposed by colonial sources. Some progressive deforestation, nevertheless, did occur in the hills around the Limboto Plain during the second half of the nineteenth century. In Minahasa and Sangir, sustained population growth after 1860 was certainly accompanied by rapid loss of primary forest; in the Minahasan case it also coincided with a progressive expansion of grasslands, which had previously been rare in this area, at the expense of secondary woodland.

---

[83] The flat summit of this island was already deforested in 1886, although the slopes around it were wooded (Ebbinge Wübben 1888:136-7).

CHAPTER XIV

The making of the landscape

This chapter attempts to relate the observed vegetation patterns to the specific human activities involved in landscape change: subsistence agriculture, animal husbandry and hunting, cash crop farming, and timber exploitation. In order to minimize the risk of attributing man-made landscapes to natural processes, the influence of climate, soil, geology, and natural fires is discussed at the end of the chapter rather than at the beginning.

Foodcrop agriculture

In all of its forms, including those based mainly on root crops (Plate 27), subsistence agriculture involved the clearance of the natural vegetation. Although tubers and bananas were tolerant of shade to the extent that they could be planted underneath coconut palms (Lam 1932:27, 52; Tammes 1949: 28-9), or remain productive for some years as part of a light secondary forest on old swiddens, they were never cultivated underneath a thick leaf canopy. Even the wild yam (*Dioscorea hirsuta*), a common famine food (see Chapter IX), was found among secondary vegetation rather than in natural forest (Li 1991:5, 23). It is not certain that natural forests in Southeast Asia contain sufficient wild tubers to support even the sparsest hunter-gatherer population (Bailey et al. 1989; Headland 1987). *Metroxylon* sago stands were the only mature arboreal vegetation which, in places, afforded an important food source, and these too were often deliberately planted rather than wild-growing.[1]

In the period up to 1930, permanent-field agriculture was always the exception rather than the rule in regional terms. In Minahasa some dry fields, thanks to exceptionally fertile soils and the seasonal rotation of rice and maize, were in annual use by the late nineteenth century (Chapter XIII, Table

---

[1]   Adriani and Kruyt 1912-14, II:203-4; Dormeier 1947:252; Kortleven 1927:90. Tergast (1936: 137), however, reported in 1935 that deliberate planting of *Metroxlyon* sago 'does not seem to occur' on Sangir and Talaud.

Plate 27. A taro swidden on Talaud, 1979 (YMB Talaud/Minahasa Photograph 67)

27: ca 1864b, 1875, 1901). Ploughing and manuring made possible continuous maize cultivation in the most densely settled part of Gorontalo at the same period (see Chapter II). In neither case, however, were very large areas of land involved. Wet ricefields, always planted on an annual basis, were rather more common, but even after decades of promotion by the colonial state, these still occupied less than 0.5 percent of the total land area of the region in 1926 (Table 28).

The fact that permanently cultivated fields were always less common than swiddens, on the other hand, does not mean that the impact of agriculture on the natural vegetation was slight. As the data from nineteenth-century Minahasa already suggest, swidden cycles were seldom long enough to allow the forest to regenerate in anything approaching its original form. The 'typical' Minahasan fallow interval, it was surmised in Chapter XIII, lasted about eight years, so that the largest trees to be seen were perhaps ten metres tall, less than half the height of the natural climax forest. The predominant secondary vegetation consisted of shrubs, ferns, bananas, various other deliberately planted fruit trees and palms, saplings with stem diameters of five or six centimetres (Koorders 1898:26), and often also *alang-alang* grass on the most recently abandoned swiddens. Where the fallow period was shorter

Table 28. Reported extent of irrigation (km^2) in northern Sulawesi, 1926[2]

Minahasa[3]	99
Bolaang Mongondow	1
Gorontalo	29
Donggala	64
Poso, Tojo and Lore	24
Total	217

Source: Tideman 1926:118

than eight years, or the main cropping period longer than a single year, the number of tall trees was of course smaller still. Contiguous blocks of land under various stages of more or less woody regrowth, rather than swidden clearings scattered through high forest, characterized the agrarian landscape under these conditions.

> The land in the neighbourhood of the *negeri* is usually divided into sections, the number of which depends on the number of years for which the land is left fallow, such that each farmer always returns to the same location after the cycle has elapsed. Usually there are five sections, sometimes more, sometimes fewer – three, for instance, in the capital *negeri* of the district Remboken [Tondano area]. The larger landowners have land of their own in each of these sections. (Edeling 1919:51.)

Although Minahasan foodcrop agriculture in the nineteenth century was intensive by regional standards, there is no evidence from other areas to support the suggestion by Whitten, Mustafa and Henderson (1987:575-7) that 'traditional swidden cultivation' in Sulawesi typically involved fallow periods of '15-30 years'.[4] While such long intervals may have occurred in places, they were certainly unusual (Table 29).

One source here (Table 29: upland western Central Sulawesi ca 1900) mentions the clearance of primary forest in order to establish preferential use

[2]   Including both '*sawah* irrigated by running water' and (in Minahasa) 'rain-dependent *sawah*'. The data 'must be viewed with the appropriate reserve' (Tideman 1926:118), and probably represent minima; the figure given in the same source for dry fields in 'regular' or 'irregular' cultivation, 'more than 100,000 *bau* [ca 700 km^2]' is certainly much too low.

[3]   It is not entirely clear why the figure for Minahasa is so much lower than that of 133 km^2 given by Van Marle (1922, II:89) in 1919 (Table 30 and Appendix J). Rice production, however, did decline in Minahasa during the 1920s due to increasing concentration on copra (see Chapter IX). In 1940 the reported figure was 105 km^2 (M. van Rhijn 1941:41), and in 1953, 139 km^2 (Ormeling n.d.:5).

[4]   None of the sources which these authorscite, significantly, is specifically concerned with Sulawesi. It is worth adding that even a fallow period of 30 years would still be far too short to allow regeneration of the climax forest (Cant 1973:13). Virgin forest in Borneo, for instance, consists of trees ranging from a minimum of 110 to a maximum of 720 years old (Dove 1983a:126).

Table 29. Swidden cycle data for areas outside Minahasa, 1825–1949

Area	Year	Cultivation and fallow period indications
Sangir Islands[1]	1825	'After rice has been grown on it, [a field] lies fallow for 4 to 5 years, or is planted with banana trees, *batata* [sweet potato] and *bete* [taro]'
Tagulandang[2]	1866	Land borrowed by missionaries for foodcrop cultivation is abandoned after '3–4 years', to be 'converted into a swidden again by its owner perhaps 10 years later'
Sangir and Talaud[3]	1935	'When a piece of forest land is converted into a *ladang* it is used for several years in succession, first for annual crops like rice [...], later for perennial crops including [...] bananas. After the first few years the forest is allowed to grow back until it shades out these food crops, at which point the *ladang* is abandoned. On Talaud the soil gets a long rest period, but elsewhere the interval is short in connection with the scarcity of cultivable land. [...] In practice the exploitation of such a *ladang* generally goes on for 5 or 6 years, and sometimes – depending on fertility and maintenance – even longer'
Siau[4]	1941	'In *ladang* farming the general rule is that a piece of land is cultivated for 3 to 5 years in succession, and then lies fallow for 5 to 8 years'
Greater Sangir[5]	ca 1949	'*Ladang* cultivation is usually employed, the land being used for 1 year and abandoned for 5 to 7 years'
Bolaang Mongondow (coastal slopes near Bolaang)[6]	1857	terrain 'is used by the inhabitants of the Pasisir Bolaang [Bolaang coast] for making their dry *padi* fields – to judge, at least, by the monotonous signature of the 3- to 5-year-old *jurame* vegetation'
Bolaang Mongondow (coast and uplands)[7]	1866	'after being used for one year on the coast, and 2 to 3 years in Mongondow, [swidden fields] must lie fallow for some years [*enige jaren*]'
Boalemo (Gorontalo)[8]	1912	'The swiddens are cultivated for 1 to 2 years with maize or *padi*, after which the not very intensive methods employed make it necessary to clear new pieces of land. Once land has been abandoned for 5 years or more it is considered to have reverted to government ownership. Only the coconut gardens near the coast are no longer abandoned'
Kuandang (Gorontalo)[9]	1917	'Woodland is cleared mainly for the creation of rice *ladang*, which are not normally planted with *padi* (in alternation with maize as a supplementary crop) for more than two successive years. Thereafter the land is planted once or twice more with maize alone, and then temporarily abandoned [...]. After 4 or 5 years, or sometimes only after 10 years, these lands, as so-called *jurame* which have gradually been reoccupied by bush and young trees, are worked and planted again by the original cultivator

for as long as the fertility of the soil permits [...] This is repeated until ultimately the ground becomes completely exhausted [...]'

Tolitoli[10]	1927	'A *ladang* is planted and harvested 2 or 3 times, with intervals of 2 or 3 years'
Donggala area[11]	1888	'Abandoned farmland is usually allowed to lie fallow for 2 to 3 years'
Palu Bay and west side of neck of northern peninsula[12]	1931	'A *ladang* usually lasts for a single harvest [*een planttijd*], which can be equated with ± 6 months. [...] The fallow period here usually lasts 3 to 6 years on the coastal plains, and 5 to 8 years in the mountains'
Upland western Central Sulawesi[13]	ca 1900	'[A farmer] has the choice between land which was last farmed 5 or 6 years ago, and where the trees are not yet very large, and land which is covered by virgin forest [*oerbosch*]. Families which cultivate a piece of virgin forest obtain a certain right to make their swiddens on the same land again after it has lain fallow for a few years'
vicinity of Lake Lindu, western Central Sulawesi[14]	1939	'A given piece of land is always worked as a *ladang* for just a single year, after which it is allowed to lie fallow for 6 years. Rice and maize are planted simultaneously [...]'
Poso area[15]	1895a	'A piece of good land can be cultivated again after lying fallow for 3 years, so the fact that in practice a used piece of ground is generally left fallow for 6 to 8 years indicates that there is an abundant supply of land'
Poso area[16]	1895b	'Fallow land is preferred [when selecting swidden sites], since the vegetation there is not so thick and heavy as on forest land. After 3 or 4 years of fallow a piece of ground can be recultivated with hope of a good harvest'
Banggai[17]	ca 1932	'land which has lain fallow for about 5 years, and has therefore become suitable for recultivation, is called [...]'

1   Van Delden 1844:18.
2   F. Kelling, 'Het eiland Taghoelandang en zijn bewoners' [1866] (ARZ NZG 43.2).
3   Tergast 1936:136.
4   M. van Rhijn 1941:42.
5   Blankhart 1951:86.
6   Riedel 1864b:272.
7   Wilken and Schwarz 1867c:364.
8   *Regeeringsrapport Boalemo* 1914:169.
9   Van Andel and Monsjou 1917:118-9.
10   Kortleven 1927:88.
11   *Landschap Donggala* 1905:522.
12   Dutrieux 1931b:3.
13   A.C. Kruyt 1938, IV:35.
14   Bloembergen 1940:390.
15   A.C. Kruyt 1895-97, II:117.
16   A.C. Kruyt 1895-97, III:131.
17   A.C. Kruyt 1932d:477.

rights during subsequent farming cycles. Two others, describing sparsely-populated areas late in the colonial period (Kuandang 1917, Tolitoli 1927), suggest that short-fallow swiddening was unsustainable in the long term due to declining soil fertility; more will be said about this below and in Chapter XV. The maximum fallow period specified for land already brought into cultivation, however, is ten years (Tagulandang 1866, Kuandang 1917), and the norm about six years.[5] On this evidence, then, fallow intervals everywhere in the region, and at all documented periods, were just as short as those prevailing in nineteenth-century Minahasa. In Sangir, moreover, the production period of some swiddens was also much longer than in Minahasa, so that the ratio of productive to fallow areas approached 1:1.

These short cycles are consistent with accounts of many comparable swidden cultivation systems elsewhere in Indonesia. Van Steenis (1937:638) characterized Indonesian *ladang* in general as 'semi-permanent agricultural fields', cultivated 'once every so many (usually five to ten) years'.[6] Seavoy (1973b:219) states that in West Kalimantan, 'mature trees are never allowed to grow again' after the initial clearance, since secondary forest 'is preferred for slashing because it is much easier to cut' – a consideration which was equally important, according to colonial sources, for swidden farmers in northern Sulawesi.[7] A fallow period of five to eight years was sufficient to produce secondary vegetation shady enough to kill a substantial proportion of the weed growth which had usually motivated the abandonment of the swidden (Seavoy 1973a), and to provide sufficient ash to fertilize the soil after burning, but not so long that heavy axework was required to re-open the field for the next cultivation cycle.[8] 'If the land has been out of agricultural production for eight years or less', notes Seavoy (1973b:219), 'all of the trees can be felled with a large bush knife'. In modern Tinombo, where fallow intervals in the interior average between five and ten years, farmers emphasize that besides being harder to fell, older forest is also much more difficult to burn, entailing a high risk that the cleared plot will have to be abandoned until the large trunks have rotted (Li 1991:37, 40; Tonelli 1992:73-4).

The highly agrarian landscapes produced by short-fallow swiddening

5   Another source from western Central Sulawesi states that with 'few exceptions', swiddens are opened in secondary rather than primary forest ('Commentaar op concept bepalingen AR Midden Celebes om branden van bosschen en alang-alang tegen te gaan', 27-12-1913, in ARZ NZG 101A.7).
6   Also Missen 1972:41; Palte and Tempelman 1978:97.
7   Adriani and Kruyt 1912-14, II:239; Graafland 1864:20. See also Table 29 above (Poso area, 1895b).
8   It is possible that beyond the eight-year threshold there was a decline in the rate at which the amount of labour involved in forest clearance continued to increase with the length of the fallow cycle, so that the age of the secondary forest was no longer so critical. If so, the distinction between short-fallow and long-fallow systems was probably clear-cut rather than gradual.

(Plates 28-31) are at odds with the persistent myth that under conditions of traditional 'shifting' cultivation, 'the interaction of humans with the Southeast Asian rainforest was primarily one of interdependence', and that 'population pressures were low enough for routine regeneration' (Reid 1995:93). Average population densities in most parts of precolonial northern Sulawesi were indeed low, but the result was seldom that the natural vegetation was able to re-establish itself between episodes of cultivation. Rather, the area of per-manently modified secondary vegetation (and sometimes grassland) tended in such cases to remain small, and that of largely undisturbed natural forest correspondingly large. Combined with the advantages of farming adjacent swiddens rather than isolated fields, the positive preference for short swid-den cycles was no doubt an additional reason, alongside those enumerated in Chapter XI, for the very uneven distribution of the population.

Demography and deforestation

Minahasa is almost the only part of the region for which figures are avail-able regarding the amount of land cleared and cultivated by each farming household. Dutch sources from 1872 and 1875 give the typical size of a single swidden as respectively 0.7 hectare and 1.1-1.8 hectares.[9] If the aver-age was approximately one hectare, and if the typical Minahasan household, as indicated by administrative sources from the same period (see Chapter III), counted five individuals, then the amount of land cleared and planted with main annual crops by the 100,000-strong population of Minahasa in 1862 would have been 20,000 hectares, or 200 km^2. Allowing for some under-counting, this agrees quite well with the 154 km^2 actually planted with dry rice according to the land use survey of that year. The same assumption, one hectare of secondary forest clearance per family of five individuals per year, was also arrived at by Van Beukering (1947:9) as a general rule-of-thumb on the basis of a 'ladang enquiry' into swidden farming practices in many parts of Indonesia held at the beginning of the 1930s. The only part of northern Sulawesi for which the results of this enquiry are available is Donggala, and here they support Van Beukering's rule. 'On the coastal plains', states the report in question, 'a ladang-farming household works approximately one hectare, while this is the maximum size of an upland ladang' (Dutrieux 1931b:3). An annual cultivated area of 0.2 hectare per individual implies that

---

[9]   G.A. Wilken 1873:117; Edeling 1919:52. The Cultivation Reports from the early 1860s also give some equivalent figures derived indirectly from the land use surveys and population counts. These vary by administrative division from 0.70 to 1.75 ha per farming household (CV Manado 1862-1865, in ANRI Ambon 1563, Manado 39, 52).

Plate 28. Swidden landscapes, I: Sonder (Minahasa), 1824 (RMV Collectie A. Payen, Calpin A, Sketch 36). Reproduced by permission of the Rijksmuseum voor Volkenkunde, Leiden.

Plate 29. Swidden landscapes, II: the Gorontalo trench, circa 1880. KITLV Photograph 26.755 (Woodbury and Page collection).

Plate 30. Swidden landscapes, III: northeast coast of Minahasa, 1944. The cleared patches include some grassland. Old forest is visible for comparison on the far right. (Allied Geographical Section 1944: Photograph 45.)

Plate 31. Permanent and short-fallow unirrigated fields near Tomohon (Minahasa), 1944 (Allied Geographical Section 1944: Photograph 38)

a swidden farming population like that of Minahasa in 1862, practising fallow cycles averaging nine years' duration at a density of about 20 persons per km^2, will inevitably clear 36 percent of its habitat of natural forest. At 50 persons per km^2 only 10 percent of the natural vegetation will be left, and at 55 per km^2, theoretically, none at all.

In Minahasa, had the agricultural pattern remained unchanged, complete deforestation would have occurred as a result of foodcrop farming alone by 1930, when the population density stood at 58 persons per km^2. The area devoted to food production, however, did not increase as rapidly as the population. In the previous chapter it was estimated that the deforested proportion of Minahasa grew from about one third in 1860, when the population numbered 100,000, to about four fifths in 1920, by which time the population was over 240,000. Nine percent of all land, moreover, was permanently occupied by coconut trees in 1920, against less than one percent in 1860 (Appendices I and J), so that the real growth in the food-producing area, given that subsistence crops were seldom planted under mature coconut trees in Minahasa, was about 75 percent, against a demographic increase of 140 percent.[10]

It is not possible to explain this discrepancy in terms of shortening swidden cycles. A striking feature of the nineteenth-century Minahasan swidden cycle data presented in Chapter XIII (Table 27) is that the stated fallow periods show no discernible downward trend toward the end of the century. In the Tondano administrative division, according to the land use survey of 1919, currently cultivated fields accounted for 18 percent of all non-irrigated farmland (Appendix J), and a description of agriculture in various parts of the central plateau in the 1930s mentions no fallow period longer than five years (Weg 1938:147-54); in this area, then, there may well have been some shortening of swidden cycles after 1900.[11] In the Manado division, on the other hand, the areal ratio of uncultivated *jurame* to cultivated swiddens in 1919 was 1:12, in Kema (Tonsea) only 1:20, and in Belang even lower, so that the overall proportion of non-irrigated farmland under current main-crop cultivation for Minahasa as a whole was nine percent, implying an average fallow interval of ten years, slightly *longer* than the eight-year mean proposed in Chapter XIII for the middle of the nineteenth century. Two circumstances lend credibility to this surprising result. The internal distribution of the population, firstly, had become somewhat more even in the intervening period (see

[10] In contrast to the situation in Sangir (see Chapter XIII), maize, root crops and bananas were typically intercropped among the young coconut trees only for the first 3 years after planting, disappearing as the palms approached maturity (Departement van Landbouw, Nijverheid en Handel 1925:15).

[11] Little other quantitative information on swidden cycles in Minahasa is available for the early twentieth century, although one source from 1912 states that 'dry fields, in those places where much land is still available, are cultivated only once every 3 years, and sometimes once every 7 years' (Dirkzwager 1912:1165).

Chapter V), and colonization of previously uncultivated areas, particularly in Tonsea, probably allowed – or, given the lesser fertility of the soils outside the central plateau, obliged – the settlers to employ longer fallow periods. In order to support a rapidly growing livestock population, secondly, many farmers had incorporated a new grassland phase into the swidden succession, which delayed the reversion to secondary woodland (see below).

The real reasons why the rate of deforestation as a result of foodcrop agriculture lagged behind that of population growth were threefold. After 1880, firstly, Minahasa was no longer self-sufficient in food, and after 1900 imported rice always met a substantial proportion of local food needs (see Chapter IX). Probably in connection with this reliance on imported food, secondly, the amount of land cultivated each year by the typical farming household appears to have declined. In 1875, according to Edeling (1919:52), only the smallest swiddens, belonging to 'unmarried persons', covered an area of less than 0.35 hectare. In 1896, however, a report by local chiefs implied that there were few swiddens which exceeded that size.[12] Tammes (1940:192), in the 1930s, agreed that a Minahasan family (*gezin*) 'can work about one third of a hectare of forest, or one quarter of a hectare of *alang-alang* terrain'.[13] A third factor was a substantial increase in the area under permanent-field cultivation, including irrigation (Table 30).

Table 30. Expansion of irrigation in Minahasa, 1860-1920

Year	Approximate area under irrigation (km^2)	Irrigated area as proportion of total area planted with rice (%)	Rice production from irrigated fields as proportion of total rice production (%)
ca 1860[14]	20	10	25
ca 1880[15]	60	25	40
ca 1920[16]	135	35	60

[12]   *Rapport* 1910:53. It should also be noted, however, that Graafland (1898, I:150), writing in the 1890s, still gives a range of 0.35-1.4 ha.
[13]   Given that grassland swiddens required more labour than swiddens cleared from secondary forest, it is possible that the spread of grasslands in Minahasa after 1895 automatically led to some decline in the ratio of farmland area to population.
[14]   Areas: Appendix I; production (5,100 tonnes of hulled rice from *sawah*, 14,700 tonnes from dry fields): CV Manado 1859 (ANRI Ambon 1543).
[15]   Areas (60 km^2 under irrigation, 200 km^2 planted with dry rice): CV Manado 1879 (ANRI Manado 86); production: Matthes 1881 (proportional figure only).
[16]   Areas: Appendix J; production (12,820 tonnes of hulled rice from *sawah*, 8,290 tonnes from dry fields): Van Marle 1922, II:89.

Although foodcrop yields from *sawah* fields were not always higher than those from swiddens in terms of the areas actually under cultivation (Appendix K), the fact that they did not require a fallow rotation enabled them to support a much higher density of population. The area of annually cultivated dry fields also increased in Minahasa between 1860 and 1930. Ox-drawn ploughs, almost unknown in this area before 1850 (Francis 1860: 348, 354; A.J.F. Jansen 1861:234) were in use on dry as well as irrigated fields by the 1870s.[17] In 1938 it was estimated that two thirds of the unirrigated farmland around Tomohon (Plate 31), and almost half of that in the Tondano area, consisted of *tegalan*.[18] In combination with food imports, then, it was a partial transition from shifting to permanent-field agriculture, rather than a consistent shortening of swidden cycles, which enabled the rapid population growth which took place in late colonial Minahasa to be absorbed without a fully proportional increase in the area devoted to food production. The extent to which this transition was actually a result of the concurrent population growth will be discussed in Chapter XV.

The virtual absence of quantitative land use data makes it impossible, for other parts of the region, to attempt the kind of close analysis of the relationship between demography and deforestation made here in the case of Minahasa. In broad qualitative terms, a comparison between the distribution of the population and the distribution of deforested areas at different periods should nevertheless provide a rough guide to the relationship between food-crop agriculture and vegetation change. Throughout North Sulawesi, that relationship was clearly strong. Given that all of the major Sangir Islands already had population densities in excess of 100 persons per km[2] by 1900, it is hardly surprising that they had been 'completely cleared for cultivation' by 1920 (Heringa 1921b:733). Volcanic soils, together with an intensive swidden system in which crops continued to be harvested from the same plot for five or six consecutive years, and with considerable food imports, allowed such high densities to be supported here without either irrigation or the use of the plough. On Siau, where the population density was aready close to 100 per km[2] in 1850, almost all land was probably under periodic cultivation even before the copra boom, farmers working swiddens 'on and among rocks where one would think hardly a tree or a plant could gain a hold' (Van Delden 1844:362). Yet the ability of tubers and bananas to grow underneath coconut palms meant that this ubiquitous subsistence agriculture could still be combined with a lucrative cash crop which both fuelled further population growth, and paid for imported food.

---

[17] A.C.J. Edeling, 'Memorie omtrent de Minahasa', 13-8-1875 (NA V 17-4-1877/20).
[18] Weg 1938:152. It is not clear, however, whether the *ladang* areas given in this source include fallow land.

The depopulation of Talaud in the last quarter of the nineteenth century (see Chapter IV) may help to explain why in 1926 the forest cover on Karakelang was 'in general, not higher than about 30-35 m, interspersed with occasional lofty trees', whereas the forests of nearby Morotai, in the North Moluccas, reached 'a height of 40 or 50 m, with many heavy trees' (Holthuis and Lam 1942:99). While the botanist Lam, who was not aware of the demographic background, thought that the relatively light forest cover on Talaud was probably 'a consequence partly of edaphic factors, partly of floristic differences', it is possible that what he assumed to be mature primary forest was in fact an advanced, but not yet complete, state of regrowth on land which had still been under cultivation only half a century earlier.[19] In 1848, according to Cuarteron (1855: Quadro 4), 23,450 people, or 23 per km^2, lived on Karakelang, compared to only 13 per km^2 in 1930 (*Volkstelling* 1933-36, V: 8). If swidden cycles were similar to those practised in Minahasa at the same period, then over 40 percent of the island must have been under periodic cultivation before the demographic collapse.

In Bolaang Mongondow, the 'huge, impressive garden' (Riedel 1864b:275) of the Mongondow Plateau and the separate deforested strips on the coasts corresponded exactly with the distribution of the farming population.[20] In Gorontalo, where the great bulk of the population was always concentrated in the Limboto Depression, the correspondence, at least in general terms, was equally good. The progressive deforestation of the barrier hills between Lake Limboto and the Gulf of Tomini in the second half of the nineteenth century, moreover, was caused by emigrants from the densely populated plain, many of whom settled as swidden farmers on the adjacent slopes (Van Kol 1903:337-8; Gonggrijp 1915:1363-4). This exodus, described in more detail in Chapter XV, was stimulated partly by population growth, and partly by the emancipation of the slaves in 1859, which gave them freedom of movement but left their masters in possession of the irrigated farmland on the floor of the depression.

In western Central Sulawesi the distribution of the precolonial population, in so far as it can be reconstructed, also corresponded closely with that of the deforested areas. The populous Palu Valley, as we have seen, was already heavily deforested in the seventeenth century, and except for the mountaintop marshes of the Tineba range, all of the areas shown as devoid of primary forest

[19] It is not clear whether the patches of savanna and 'alpine' vegetation also observed by Lam on Karakelang can likewise be connected with denser human settlement in the past. However, Piapi, the name of the largest treeless area, suggests a link with fire (Lam 1927:396), and since Karakelang is not volcanic and not known to contain other natural fire sources, it is tempting to interpret this as a reference to deliberate burning.
[20] The role of agricultural settlement in opening up a new deforestation zone in the Dumoga valley after 1930 was discussed in Chapter XIII.

on recent vegetation maps correspond to what Kaudern called the 'cultivated basins' of the Toraja. Napu, Besoa and Bada, for instance, were 'three inhabited and cultivated spots amid the steep mountains' (A.C. Kruyt 1909:349), while further west the Kulawi basin was also 'densely populated by the standards of Central Sulawesi' (Kruyt and Kruyt 1920:196). Other settled enclaves, all of them corresponding to zones of deforestation on Map 16 (Chapter XIII), included Pekawa in the mountains to the west of the Palu Trench, and Lindu to its east. The limited size of these upland agricultural clearances, at least in comparison with their counterparts in Minahasa and Mongondow, is explained by the fact that their populations were also smaller.

Disproportionate deforestation in Poso and Mori

The more widespread deforestation observed in the Poso Valley at the beginning of the twentieth century, by contrast, is more difficult to account for in terms of demography alone. While this area was more evenly settled before the turn of the century than the mountains to its west, its population, at about 25,000 people or nine per km^2, was not dense.[21] Yet the extent of forest loss here, especially to the north and east of Lake Poso, seems to have been comparable with that observed in very populous areas like the Palu Valley or the Limboto Depression. In marked contrast to the situation in Sangir or nineteenth-century Minahasa, moreover, grassland and savanna were common here alongside secondary woodland.

A close look at descriptions of precolonial farming and settlement in the Poso Valley reveals an unusual pattern. Foodcrop agriculture, as in many other areas, was based on rice and maize, and took place exclusively on dry swidden fields. The reported fallow period, at six to eight years (Table 29: Poso area 1895a), was also unexceptional. Here, however, this rotation was apparently unsustainable, so that whole villages, and not just their outlying swidden houses, were periodically forced to shift to new locations.[22]

> When the area of land which such a village needed to feed itself had become completely deforested and exhausted, the villagers chose a site for a new settlement

[21]   This early population estimate (Gallas 1900:813) originates from Albert Kruyt. Most later estimates for 'Poso' actually include neighbouring areas like Tojo and Napu; those which do not (Adriani and Kruyt 1912-14, I:88; *Volkstelling* 1933-36, V:134) accord well with the one cited here. Adriani and Kruyt (1912-14, I:89) put the density at almost 15 inhabitants per km^2, but their area figure is a severe underestimate. The figure used here (2,700 km^2 for 'Pamona Selatan' and 'Pamona Utara' combined) comes from a modern administrative source (*Sulawesi Tengah* 1992:7).
[22]   Adriani and Kruyt 1950-51, I:167; Gallas 1900:813; Van Hoëvell 1893b:30; A.C. Kruyt 1895-97, III:131, 1899:608-9, 1911:81; *Brieven*, 5-7-1912.

within the territory of their tribe, and founded a new village there. The old village
was abandoned to its fate; the houses quickly became derelict, the protective pal-
lisade decayed, and only the coconut palms remained to mark the hill as the site
of a former village. The traveller in this land saw at least as many such abandoned
villages as inhabited ones. (Adriani 1919:9-10.)

This particular description probably exaggerates the extent to which farming
practices were responsible for the large number of deserted settlements in the
Poso area, since warfare and epidemics could also trigger the abandonment
of existing village sites.[23] Where a shortage of usable farmland was indeed
the cause, moreover, the abandoned site was sometimes reoccupied after a
number of years, 'when the forest has grown up again and the soil is therefore
fit for cultivation once more' (Adriani and Kruyt 1950-51, I:167). At least some
cases of village movement, in other words, can be seen as the consequence
of a high-level fallow rotation (Bellwood 1997:248), above and beyond that
applied by individual households within a single village territory, rather than
as an indication that local agriculture constituted an unplanned and destructive system of *roofbouw* or 'robber farming', as Albert Kruyt (1895-97, III:153,
1924:41) often alleged. Permanent or not, however, the wholesale abandonment of nuclear settlements as a result of local deforestation is not reported
from other parts of the region in the historical sources, and suggests an unusually high rate of forest clearance per head of the population.[24]

Another reason for the disproportionate extent of deforestation in the
Poso Valley can be found in past demographic change. The population of
this part of Central Sulawesi, it was surmised in Chapter VI, declined significantly in the second half of the nineteenth century, and possibly also over a
much longer period. Some of its abandoned villages, then, reflected not just
local migration, but absolute depopulation. Talaud, on the other hand, also
saw a substantial demographic decline in the same period, and although the
relative sparseness of the forests on Karakelang in the early twentieth century arguably still bore witness to their former clearance and cultivation, such
barely noticeable traces were hardly comparable with the extensive grasslands and savannas of Central Sulawesi. Even if the extent of forest clearance
in the Poso Valley must ultimately be attributed to a denser past population,
then, the fact that it was sustained through a long period of demographic
decline, whereas on Talaud almost all of the abandoned farmland quickly
reverted to forest, still requires further explanation.

Still more problematic from a demographic point of view is the existence
of the great grassland of Pada, in the basin of the La River and its tributaries

---

[23]   Adriani and Kruyt 1950-51, I:166-7; Van Hoëvell 1893b:30; A.C. Kruyt 1894:13, 22, 1895-97,
II:117-8, 1899c:614.
[24]   One implicit parallel from Minahasa, however, will be mentioned below.

in Mori and Pakambia. Albert Kruyt (1900b:462-3), at the end of the nine-teenth century, estimated the total population of this plain at just 600 souls, or fewer than two per km^2. While some deserted villages ('mostly abandoned due to disease') were in evidence (Adriani and Kruyt 1900:204), the inhabit-ants of the Pada insisted that it had already been a grassland when their ancestors first settled there.[25] The forester Steup (1931:1133), walking across it in 1930, was baffled by the bareness of this 'seemingly endless plain':

> The grassy vegetation, dry at that time, gave the plain very much the appearance of a heath. A tree is a great rarity in this region, and the Pompangeo mountains to the north also looked badly deforested [...]. It is and remains a mystery how such a small population can devastate such an enormous area of land. (Steup 1931:1133.)

One part of the solution to Steup's 'mystery' may be that this largest grass-land in northern Sulawesi contained the region's only known natural fire sources, which will be described presently. The Pada, however, also offers the clearest example of how human activities associated with animal husbandry and hunting could contribute to deforestation.

Grassland origins

Besides planting rice and other crops on the narrow strips of less deforested land along the rivers (Adriani and Kruyt 1912-14, I:63), the inhabitants of the Pada owned large herds of water buffalo and were keen hunters of the numerous wild deer with which they also shared the plain.[26] In order to provide grazing for these animals they were in the habit of setting fire to the grasslands which blanketed most of the landscape, periodically burning off the high, coarse adult grass to make way for a regrowth of more succulent young shoots. When Adriani and Kruyt (1900:201) looked down on the Pada from its eastern rim after dark one evening during their visit in 1899, they saw 'many great fires burning at various points on this plain, where the dry grass had been set alight'. These fires were intrinsically less controllable than swidden burns: the following day the two missionaries were witness to one which had spread to the trees surrounding the village in which they were staying, and had to be fought with water to prevent it from destroying the

---

[25]   A.C. Kruyt 1900b:442. No earlier population statistics of any kind are available for this area, which remained virtually unknown to the Dutch until Adriani and Kruyt's visit.
[26]   Adriani and Kruyt 1900:203-4, 206-7, 1912-14, I:136; Goedhart 1908:539-40; Hegener 1990: 124; Horsting 1924:219; A.C. Kruyt 1900b:465. One indication of the special significance of the buffalo in Pada is that here, but apparently not elsewhere, these animals were kept overnight in stalls underneath the stilt houses (Adriani and Kruyt 1912-14, II:170).

houses.[27] Such blazes must have spread over very large areas of the plain, and besides rejuvenating the grass itself, they also had the effect of preventing its eventual replacement by trees.

Some historical sources on northern Sulawesi suggest that under certain conditions, abandoned swiddens could become permanent grasslands by a process of purely natural succession. In 1845 Ten Siethoff wrote that in Minahasa, *alang-alang* and *glagah* 'sometimes spread and grow with such speed that they destroy most of the woody plants before these have had a chance to come up, and so become the masters of extensive fields'.[28] 'Poor soils', agreed Graafland (1898, II:265) later in the century, 'quickly become overgrown with coarse grasses', whereas abandoned swiddens on more fertile land 'are occupied in the space of a single year by shrubs, which soon become young trees, and in three to five years a low woodland vegetation has developed'. The forester Bruinier (1924:12) believed that in Minahasa it was above all steep slopes prone to soil erosion which tended to become 'hot *alang-alang* fields' once their forest cover was felled by farmers. Colonial complaints about the effects of shifting cultivation in Bolaang Mongondow, Gorontalo and Central Sulawesi often assumed a still more direct and inevitable relationship between *roofbouw* and the spread of *alang-alang*.[29]

More detailed descriptions, however, tend to support the conclusion of most of the secondary literature on the subject that grassland in Indonesia is a 'fire-climax' vegetation, and that repeated burning is necessary in order to prevent its reversion to forest.[30] Koorders (1898:26, 261) noted at the end of the nineteenth century that although fallow land in Minahasa was often colonized in the first instance by *alang-alang*, the resulting grasslands were seldom permanent. Under natural conditions, woody vegetation was gradually able to establish itself despite the competition, and ultimately shaded the grass to death in the shadow of its thickening canopy. 'In most parts of Minahasa', he concluded, 'these grasslands are transformed into forest within the space of a few years' (Koorders 1898:274). Two decades earlier, Edeling had also acknowledged this process of natural succession from grassland fallow to secondary forest when he mentioned that Minahasan farmers only needed to dig grass root mats out of their intented swiddens 'when the *jurame* is being re-used after a short interval, so that the *alang-alang* (*kusu*) and *glagah* (*kano-*

[27]   Adriani and Kruyt 1900:206-7. Also Horsting 1924:217.
[28]   J.J. ten Siethoff, 'Topografische schetsen van een gedeelte der residentie Menado, 1845' (ANRI Manado 46).
[29]   Van Andel and Monsjou 1919:119; Dutrieux 1930:17; A.C. Kruyt 1895-97, III:153, 1924:41; Morison 1931:24; Weg 1938:160.
[30]   Brookfield, Potter and Byron 1995:181; Brosius 1990:109-10; Dove 1986:165; Masipiqueña, Persoon and Snelder 2000:184-7; Pelzer 1945:19-20; Seavoy 1975:49; Terra 1958:170.

kano) have not yet been entirely suffocated [*verstikt*]'.[31]

In Central Sulawesi it was a similar story. 'The abandoned swiddens', observed a Dutch *controleur* in Donggala, 'become overgrown with *alang-alang*, and spontaneous reforestation follows – at least, that is, when the bushy regrowth [...] is not repeatedly set on fire' (Ter Laag 1920:43). Jan Kruyt, travelling near the headwaters of the Bongka River in 1932, also concluded that the 'extensive *alang-alang* fields' which he saw there could not be explained purely in terms of swidden agriculture.

> When trees are felled to clear a swidden and the land is left to its fate once more after the harvest, young forest grows up again spontaneously, and there is no question of *alang-alang* fields being formed. This species of tough grass, which has a subterranean rhizome, does come up, but is subsequently overwhelmed by shrubs and trees. If people burn off the *alang-alang*, however, they destroy the young trees while actually promoting the growth of the grass, which burns only to ground level and then immediately puts up young shoots from its rhizomes, while the bushes and trees need a much longer recovery period. (J. Kruyt 1933:38.)

Brown patches in the grassy expanse indicated that such deliberate grassland fires had indeed been lit. As on the Pada, this was done partly 'to attract deer, which come to feed on the young shoots' (J. Kruyt 1933:38). In an earlier source, the Bongka Valley is also identified as a habitat of feral (*verwilderde*) water buffalo, which were regarded as the property of the *raja* of Tojo and could be hunted only with his permission (Adriani and Kruyt 1912-14, II:170). This suggests parallels with grasslands in South Sulawesi (Heersink 1995:49-50), Sumba (Dove 1984:115), and South Kalimantan (Brookfield, Potter and Byron 1995:190) which originated as royal hunting grounds.

The upper Bongka was partially depopulated as a result of Dutch military actions at the beginning of the twentieth century (A.C. Kruyt 1930b:404), and the early reference to feral buffalo perhaps suggests that as in neighbouring parts of Central Sulawesi, its population had already been declining before the colonial conquest. Jan Kruyt, then, was probably right to assume that most of the cleared land had in fact been cultivated in the past. The fact that the Bongka grasslands have been preserved up to the present day despite very low population densities, however, must be attributed in large measure to the sustained impact of hunting and fire.[32]

---

[31]   'Memorie omtrent de Minahasa', 13-8-1875 (NA V 17-4-1877/20). Van Kol (1903:316-7) records a similar statement from the turn of the century, and the modern Lauje distinguish between permanent *alang-alang* grasslands (*gio*) and 'grassy sucession during the first year after fallow' (*abo*) (Tonelli 1992:71).

[32]   This interpretation differs from that of Whitten, Mustafa and Henderson (1987:578), who attribute them simply to 'shifting cultivation on poor soils' (also Alvard 2000:430). In 1975, a total of approximately 5,000 To Wana people lived in the upper Bongka Valley (Atkinson 1989:5).

Hunting and the introduction of the deer

Deer, together with wild pigs, were the focus of most hunting activity in
northern Sulawesi during the colonial period. In the Palu Valley, as in South
Sulawesi (Heersink 1995:49-51) and perhaps as a result of cultural influence
from Bugis immigrants, massive deer drives were held in which the animals
were flushed out of cover by beaters and pursued across the grass- and farmland on horseback (Voorn 1925:10-1; Woodard 1969:123). Elsewhere the hunt
took place on foot with the help of dogs and its social significance was not as
great, but large drives, on fields specially burned off for the occasion, were
nevertheless reported.[33] The abundance of deer observed in the deforested
areas of Central Sulawesi at the beginning of the twentieth century certainly
hints at deliberate landscape management. The Bada Depression was 'very
rich in deer' (A.C. Kruyt 1909:358), and the less densely populated Gimpu
Valley, south of Kulawi, 'a paradise for whole herds' (Boonstra van Heerdt
1914a:644). In 1895 the Sarasins (1905, I:255, 273) saw many deer in the grassy
'parkland' north of Lake Poso, where they also observed 'thick, black columns
of smoke in several places, revealing where stretches of grassland had been
set on fire'.[34] Deer were numerous in similar terrain along the Gulf of Tomini
coast (Boonstra van Heerdt 1914b:756), and deer hunting (with firearms) in
Gorontalo is already mentioned in sources from the first half of the nineteenth
century (De Boudyck-Bastiaanse 1845:152; Van der Hart 1853:226).

Surprisingly the deer, which may not be native to Sulawesi at all (Van
Bemmel 1949:254), seems to have become widespread in the region only
during the course of the nineteenth century. Deer were present in Palu in the
1790s (Woodard 1969:94) and in the Poso Valley by 1865 (Adriani 1913b:861).
But in Bada the appearance of the first one was still remembered by middle-
aged people in 1908 (A.C. Kruyt 1909:358), and in Napu, Besoa, and Bongka
it was an even later event (Adriani and Kruyt 1912-14, II:355; A.C. Kruyt
1930b:502). In Balantak, on the tip of the Luwuk Peninsula, no deer were
seen until 1914 (A.C. Kruyt 1932a:363). In 1920 there were still some mountain areas over the 'border' in South Sulawesi where none were yet present

[33]   Adriani and Kruyt 1950-51, III:368. Descriptions of more conventional hunting methods in
Central Sulawesi are provided by Adriani and Kruyt (1950-51, III:352-66; A.C. Kruyt 1938, IV:
320-91); Riedel (1872b:503) reproduces a shorter account for Minahasa. The use of fire as an actual
hunting tool, to flush out and drive the animals (Conklin 1957:60; Seavoy 1975:49), is not specifically reported from northern Sulawesi, although it probably occurred. Schwarz (1908b:455), in
his dictionary of the Tontemboan language, gives a term meaning 'to set fire to wood or reeds in
order to drive out the animals which are found there', although the single illustration which he
provides involves flushing rats out of *alang-alang*. Dutrieux (1931b:5) mentions the use of fire 'for
hunting purposes' around the Palu Bay.
[34]   Sarasin and Sarasin 1905, I:257. The Sarasins do not specify the purpose of this burning,
however, and it is possible that buffalo rather than deer were the intended beneficiaries.

(Kruyt and Kruyt 1920:98, 106). Oral history suggested that Palu and Tojo, both foci of Bugis settlement, had been important centres of deer dispersal in Central Sulawesi.[35] While the deer was already common in Gorontalo in 1821 (Reinwardt 1858:513), it was definitely absent at that date in Minahasa, where its introduction (this time by the Dutch) took place somewhere between the years 1831 and 1842 – probably closer to 1831, since by 1855 it was already said to be present 'in large numbers' and providing 'much venison' for local hunters.[36] Around 1870 a visiting artist chose a group of deer in a grassy clearing as the centrepiece for his portrayal of the landscape around Lake Tondano (Plate 32). In 1944, the Allied reconnaissance study of Minahasa attributed the by now extensive grasslands of this area partly to burning of the vegetation for hunting as well as farming purposes (Allied Geographical Section 1944:34).

The spread of the deer in the nineteenth century, then, probably led to an increase in the extent of man-made grasslands. Two caveats, however, must be added here. To some extent, firstly, the deer may simply have displaced another grazing animal, the indigenous *anoa* or dwarf buffalo (*Bubalus depressicornis*), to attract which hunters almost certainly also used fire to create meadows (Whitten, Mustafa and Henderson 1987:504, 542). The grassy patches reported by the Sarasins (1905, I:24) on the higher slopes of the (extinct) Klabat volcano in Minahasa were probably linked with the hunting of *anoa*, trails of which were numerous in the vicinity.[37] Hunting, secondly, was seldom the sole reason to create grasslands. A stronger motive in most areas was provided by domesticated or semi-domesticated grazing animals, of which the most important, at least until the twentieth century, was the water buffalo.[38]

---

[35] The first deer on the upper Bongka, however, were thought to have arrived through the forest from the Sumara Valley in Mori (A.C. Kruyt 1930b:502).

[36] Quarles van Ufford 1856:40. Accounts from 1821 (Reinwardt 1858:591) and 1825 (Riedel 1872b:503) state with a clarity rare in such sources that there are no deer in Minahasa. Although I have not found references to the introduction in contemporary documents, Graafland (1898, I:43) and the Sarasins (1905, I:67) later stated that the first deer were imported by Resident Cambier (in office 1831-1842).

[37] See also Chapter XIII, Map 19. *Anoa* are also capable of living in undisturbed montane forest, and at present this is their main habitat (Whitten, Mustafa and Henderson 1987:412, 540). They may, however, have been more widespread in the past; the Kruyts (1920:98) certainly implied that there was a competitive relationship between *anoa* and deer.

[38] On the Pada (Adriani and Kruyt 1900:203-4) and on some islands off the coast of Tolitoli (Kortleven 1927:97) there were also deer which were partly tame, although these were not rounded up at intervals as described below for the buffalo.

Plate 32. Artist's view of Lake Tondano with deer and meadow in the foreground,
circa 1870 (KITLV Print 20.639)

Swidden/grazing combinations: Poso and Minahasa compared

In the Poso Valley the water buffalo was a creature of great cultural importance, used for sacrifice and feasting, as a measure of wealth, and as a currency for the payment of bridewealth and traditional fines. Since there were
no wet ricefields to be ploughed or trampled, however, it played no role in
foodcrop agriculture. The buffalo spent most of each year wandering freely,
but were caught and kept in captivity for one or two months to prevent them
from becoming fully wild (Adriani and Kruyt 1912-14, II:170-3). The obvious
way for swidden farmers to create grazing for large numbers of livestock is to
convert their abandoned swiddens, where the forest has already been felled
for agricultural purposes, into fire-climax grasslands. If this conversion is
sustained, whether deliberately or by the accidental spread of grassland fires
to secondary woodland, the farmers will ultimately be obliged to move on in
search of new forest land, leaving behind them a trail of deforestation which
may be perpetuated by further fires lit to maintain the existing pasture for
grazing or hunting purposes.[39] The unusual pattern of frequent settlement

---

[39]   Seavoy (1975), although he emphasizes hunting rather than livestock grazing, has proposed
that a similar combination of swidden farming and grassland conversion is typically responsible
for cases of progressive forest destruction by indigenous peoples in West Kalimantan.

movement noted above is clearly consistent with such a pattern of progressive grassland formation, and grasslands in the Poso area, as Adriani and Kruyt made clear in an emphatic if logically somewhat inconsistent passage, were seldom brought back into cultivation once they had been created.

> The Toraja [Pamona] farmer leaves grasslands unused, because he has no tools which would allow him to cultivate such fields, and also because they provide regular grazing places for the buffalo, which will keep trying to return to them by breaking through the surrounding fences. Only in cases of extreme necessity will he resort to working them. (Adriani and Kruyt 1912-14, II:239.)

Although an explicit statement regarding the conversion of abandoned swiddens into grazing land is not available, deliberate burning of existing grasslands, as already noted, certainly occurred (Sarasin and Sarasin 1905, I:257). Such burning, of course, could also have maintained a grassy vegetation on farmland abandoned as a result of depopulation rather than migration, and this would explain why the pattern of forest clearance created by a denser population in the past was preserved in the Poso Valley rather than being erased by natural reforestation as it was on Talaud.

Whether or not it was the combination of livestock grazing with swidden cultivation which led to progressive deforestation in the Poso area, the counter-example of Minahasa, where more than 40,000 grazing animals were integrated into swidden farming systems during a period of rapid population growth, shows that this was not an inevitable process. At the beginning of the nineteenth century there were very few large livestock in Minahasa; here it was almost exclusively the pig, kept within the village and fed partly with maize and other swidden products, which was slaughtered or exchanged on ceremonial occasions.[40] Goats and horses were also present, but only in small numbers, and water buffalo were restricted to the southeastern corner of Minahasa near Belang and Ratahan (Graafland 1898, II:V) – the same area, significantly, where grasslands were already uncharacteristically extensive in the seventeenth century (see Chapter XIII) and where a report from 1871, in the only clear parallel with the unstable settlement pattern of the Poso Valley which I have come across from another part of northern Sulawesi, mentions a 'continual abandonment and relocation of *negeri*'.[41] The reported areal ratio

---

[40]   Reinwardt (1858:589) stated in 1821 that no Minahasan family was without a pig, and according to Dutch figures there were a total of almost 50,000 of them in 1850, or approximately one for every two members of the human population (AV Manado 1850, in ANRI Manado 51). Common pig foods, other than maize (Edeling 1919:73; N.P. Wilken 1870:374), included papaya (De Clercq 1873:267; Quarles van Ufford 1856:40), taro, and sweet potato (Schwarz 1907, III:42, 58, 106).

[41]   'Stukken omtrent aanleggen van sawa's velden door Tonsawang in het district Ponosakan', 24-8-1871 (ANRI Manado 101).

of cultivated swidden fields to *jurame* (fallow) land in the Belang administrative division in 1919 was an uniquely low 1:40 (Appendix J), and it can safely be assumed that most of the *jurame* here actually consisted not of fallowed swiddens, but of grasslands which had been permanently removed from the swidden cycle.

In the course of the nineteenth century, nevertheless, increasing numbers of grazing livestock also appeared in other parts of Minahasa. As horse transport replaced human porters during the early years of compulsory coffee cultivation, firstly, the number of these animals rose from a few hundred in 1820 (Reinwardt 1858:588) to more than 8,000 in 1845 (Francis 1860:372), although it was cut back severely by livestock disease in the decade 1845-1855.[42] After the introduction of ox-carts in 1852, secondly, the place of horses as beasts of burden was increasingly taken by cattle, the number of which tripled in the following five years and continued to soar thereafter as the road network was completed, local trade accelerated, and the use of the plough became more common (Chapter XV, Plate 36).[43] Meanwhile the number of horses – which unusually in Indonesia were also used for ploughing (Van Leeuwen 1951) – increased too. Between 1850 and 1920 the total number of grazing livestock in Minahasa grew from perhaps 10,000 to more than 50,000 – a proportional increase far greater than that of the human population over the same period (from 100,000 to 240,000).[44]

Table 31. Reported livestock numbers, Minahasa, 1850-1920

Year	Horses	Water buffalo	Cattle	All large livestock
1850[45]	6,649	n.a.[46]	1,648	(>) 8,297
1900[47]	13,836	0	28,430	42,266
1920[48]	14,591	1	38,681	53,273

[42] *Fragment* 1856:4; De Lange 1897:689; Quarles van Ufford 1856:16.
[43] AV Manado 1852 (ANRI Manado 51); Wessels 1891:63. Initial stocks of cattle were apparently obtained by import from the Philippines (Riedel 1870a:60).
[44] It should of course be added that the livestock statistics, especially for the nineteenth century, are not reliable.
[45] AV Manado 1850 (ANRI Manado 51).
[46] The water buffalo in Belang, which like those of the Poso Valley lived in a semi-wild state, seem to have been exterminated by hunting on Dutch orders in the second half of the nineteenth century (Graafland 1898, II:V). In 1920 the district of Ratahan, like the rest of Minahasa, contained many cattle (Van Marle 1922, I:91).
[47] *Koloniaal verslag* 1902, Bijlage A:7.
[48] Van Marle 1922, I:91.

The expansion of grasslands outside Belang after 1850 was due mainly, if not entirely, to this explosion in the numbers of grazing livestock. In the first half of the nineteenth century, *belukar* dominated the landscape in the settled areas; almost the only grasslands were recently abandoned swiddens temporarily overgrown with *alang-alang*, together with some *sawah* land on which grass was allowed to grow in the off-season. 'After the harvest', noted Resident Jansen in 1853, the *sawah* fields 'are used as pasture, for which there is great demand, and of which a shortage sometimes exists due to the increasing numbers of cattle'.[49] As the livestock continued to multiply, however, more and more swidden fallow land was also brought into use as temporary pasture.[50] Graafland (1898, II:265, 402) observed at the beginning of the 1890s that the *jurame* were 'much used for horse and cattle grazing', since 'fallowed maize and *padi* swiddens offer an excellent opportunity to maintain whole herds at no expense'.

Fire was often employed to prolong the grassland phase of the swidden cycle. By 1924 the deliberate burning of *alang-alang* fields had become a source of official concern (Bruinier 1924:9, 15), and the Allied reconnaissance study from 1944, which identifies the vegetation of almost one third of Minahasa as 'Grass (some trees)' (Chapter XIII, Map 19), explains that a 'considerable area' has been 'converted into grass, thicket, and bracken wastes by repeated burning of the vegetation for agriculture, cattle-breeding and hunting'.[51] In the Tonsea division, where only five percent of the swidden land was reportedly under foodcrop cultivation in 1919 (Appendix J), it is likely that some *jurame* had by this stage become permanent grasslands like those of Belang (Bruinier 1924:9). In many places, however, it appears that the swidden cycle was simply lengthened somewhat to accommodate the new or extended grassland phase, and that natural regrowth of woody vegetation continued to occur. In 1920, Van Marle (1922, I:68) still referred to the whole of the area not currently planted with food or cash crops as 'woodlands [*bosterreinen*], in which cultivation rights are recognized and the positions of the *ladang* change from year to year'. The fact that this was not the case in the Poso area, then, must be attributed at least partly to differences in the intentions and priorities of the farmers concerned.

---

49   A.J.F. Jansen 1861:235. In Gorontalo too, horses grazed the grass which grew on off-season *sawah* fields after the rice harvest (Van Hoëvell 1905:178).
50   Dirkzwager 1912:1168; Edeling 1919:12; Eibergen 1928:233.
51   Allied Geographical Section 1944:34. Also Van Marle 1922, I:80. Off-season *sawah*, meanwhile, continued to be used for grazing purposes, while some cattle also grazed in coconut plantations (Departement van Landbouw, Nijverheid en Handel 1925:15; Tammes 1949:29).

Livestock and the landscape in other areas

In Minahasa the use of animals to work irrigated fields was an innovation
of the colonial period, but there were other areas where it had long been
traditional (see Chapter II). The water buffalo of Lore and western Central
Sulawesi, unlike those of the Poso Valley or the Pada, were driven in herds
through wet ricefields in order to turn the soil by trampling in preparation
for planting (A.C. Kruyt 1938, IV:93-7) – a procedure which required a greater
number of animals than did the use of the plough (Ansingh 1937:9; Lanting
1939:70). The amount of livestock in the areas where irrigated fields existed
was therefore considerable, and a piece of local oral tradition recorded by
Albert Kruyt (1908:1328-9), according to which the grassy highland basins of
Napu, Besoa and Bada had been cleared of forest in legendary times by the
rolling of a giant buffalo, perhaps hints allegorically at the real role played by
this animal in shaping the landscape.

Not all of the buffalo in the uplands of western Central Sulawesi were
used in rice agriculture (*Nota berglandschappen* 1912:23), and even those
which were typically wandered freely, like their counterparts in Poso, for
most of the year (A.C. Kruyt 1938, IV:298). The immobility of the *sawah* fields,
however, precluded the pattern of shifting settlement and very extensive
grazing found further east, so that local livestock densities were greater. A
description of pasture land in the Bada Valley in 1910 suggests that in some
places there were so many water buffalo that grazing alone, without the help
of man-made fires, was sufficient to prevent reversion of the grassland to
forest.

> Here the footpath led through beautiful fields of fresh green grass, constantly
> kept short by large herds of *kerbau* which graze here every day; sometimes it was
> as if we were walking through Dutch pastures. In some places these fields even
> reminded us of a Dutch park, especially where small groups of trees and multi-
> tudes of chrysanthemums made a pretty effect. (Schuyt 1911:21.)

In Gorontalo, by contrast, the animals used to plough the *sawah* and permanent maize fields originally seem to have grazed mainly on fire-climax grassland. If the Limboto Depression as a whole was already populous, the bulk of
its population was concentrated to the east of the lake in the immediate hinterland of Gorontalo town. Whereas this core area was 'covered with villages
and fields of rice and maize' (Riedel 1870a:78), further west the landscape
was more varied, and included much grass (see Chapter XIII). Von Rosenberg
(1865:76) noted in 1863 that the *woka* (*Livistona rotundifolia*) palms scattered
over the savanna near Limboto 'lose their leaves almost every year when
the grass is burned off', and two twentieth-century administrative reports
identify '*alang-alang* burning', without specifying its cause, as an obstacle to

reforestation (Morison 1931:25; Korn 1939:27). Van Rhijn, the penultimate prewar Dutch resident of Manado, eventually confirmed that the numerous livestock in Gorontalo were 'the indirect cause of the fires, since their owners burn off the old grass to provide them with fresh pasturage'.[52]

At the same time, however, Van Rhijn (1941:480) also claimed that the cattle themselves 'systematically destroy [...] the young trees which grow up naturally'. Grazing densities certainly must have increased in the late nineteenth and early twentieth centuries, since the growth in the number of large livestock in Gorontalo after 1860 was almost as dramatic as in Minahasa.[53]

Table 32. Reported livestock numbers, Gorontalo, 1860-1930

Year	Horses	Water buffalo	Cattle	All large livestock
1860[54]	4,929	5,282	113	10,324
1900[55]	7,929	6,273	8,148	22,350
1930[56]	4,474	1,518	34,594	40,586

As in Minahasa, the main cause of this growth was an increase in the use of draught animals for transport. After 1920 there was also an extension of the area under irrigation (Chapter XV), leading to more ploughing (Grondijs 1931:13). Again as in Minahasa, neither the increase in livestock nor the simultaneous growth of the human population (from perhaps 70,000 in 1860 to 185,000 in 1930) seems to have led to a fully proportional extension of the deforested area.[57] The area under grass, in fact, actually shrunk as old grasslands were encroached upon by foodcrop cultivation (Morison 1931:54); by 1939, pasture had reportedly become so scarce that except in the off-season, when they could graze on the dry *sawah*, plough animals were forced to find a 'lean meal' on dykes and roadsides (Korn 1939:22).

Another interesting feature of the livestock figures from Gorontalo is the almost complete replacement of water buffalo by cattle between 1860 and 1930, a development also parallelled elsewhere in Indonesia (Merkens 1927:

---

[52] M. van Rhijn 1941:480. In the early twentieth century, some grassland was apparently also burned specifically in order to kill ticks which carried livestock disease (Logeman 1922:60).
[53] Here again, it should be added that the livestock statistics are probably not reliable.
[54] CV Gorontalo 1860 (ANRI Manado 95).
[55] *Koloniaal verslag* 1902, Bijlage A:7.
[56] Grondijs 1931:12.
[57] As already noted, however, emigration did lead to additional deforestation on the hills between the Depression and the Gulf of Tomini. After the completion of a road across the peninsula from Gorontalo to Kuandang in 1925, new settlements were also established in the interior to the north of Lake Limboto (Morison 1931:11-2).

118-25). The reasons for this change included road improvements, which meant that the superior ability of the buffalo to cross difficult terrain was less of an advantage than in the past. The most important factor, however, was livestock disease. The water buffalo in Gorontalo were repeatedly hit by disease outbreaks during the second half of the nineteenth century, and in the years 1914-1916 a disastrous epidemic of pyroplasmosis killed fully 80 percent of the stock, forcing the population to turn to cattle, which were much less affected.[58] This experience also made farmers receptive to the improved cattle (but not buffalo) breeds introduced by the Dutch authorities in 1922 (Edie 1923:22; Grondijs 1931:13). The decreasing availability of pasture, finally, may itself have favoured cattle over buffalo (Merkens 1927:122-3), although stall-feeding of cattle, often resorted to in Java where grazing land was scarce, was not found in Gorontalo even at the end of the colonial period (Korn 1939:23).

The heavily deforested Palu Valley always supported a large population of grazing animals. Padtbrugge, in the late seventeenth century, described it as 'crawling with all kinds of livestock: cattle [*runderen*], buffalo, horses, sheep, goats, and much wild game' (Van Dam 1931:91). Woodard (1969: 94), having spent two years there as a captive a century later, agreed that Sulawesi was 'well stocked with horses, buffaloes, cattle, deer, sheep'.[59] Both buffalo and sheep, unusually in the region, were corralled every night rather than being allowed to roam freely for much of the year, and it is likely that as in Bada, some of the Palu grasslands were maintained solely by intensive grazing.[60] Seavoy (1975:50) notes that in Kalimantan, such high-density grazing is rare because it requires 'constant supervision'; in the Palu Valley, this supervision was provided as a labour service by dependants and slaves of the noble livestock owners (Hissink 1912:109; A.C. Kruyt 1938, I:508). Like their counterparts elsewhere, however, Kaili farmers also routinely used fire to create fresh pasture.[61]

Also rich in livestock was the west coast of the Gulf of Tomini (from Parigi in the south to Moutong in the north), an area estimated in 1865 to contain more water buffalo than the Limboto Depression.[62] Parigi, in addition, was well known throughout the region for its horses, which in the early nine-

---

[58]   AV Gorontalo 1872 (ANRI Manado 9); CV Gorontalo 1860, 1863 (ANRI Manado 95, 134); Edie 1923:18-9; *Landbouw in Gorontalo* 1871:363; Van Hoëvell 1891:39-40; *Koloniaal verslag* 1863:11, 1915:35, 1916:34, 1917:35; Moolenburgh 1921:19-20; MV Manado February 1861 (ANRI Manado 54); Von Rosenberg 1865:6; Riedel 1870a:60; Tillema 1926:221.

[59]   Also Forrest 1792:81. The numbers of livestock given in the earliest sources after the Dutch conquest (Hissink 1912:123; Tideman 1926:197-8) are almost certainly too low. In 1935 there were (at least) 5,784 buffalo, 3,763 cattle, and 1,877 horses in the valley (Vorstman 1935:25).

[60]   A.C. Kruyt 1938, IV:298; Sarasin and Sarasin 1905, II:13-5; Woodard 1969:94.

[61]   Dutrieux 1931b:5-6; Steup 1929:588; Vorstman 1935:15.

[62]   AV Gorontalo 1865 (ANRI Gorontalo 3). Also Van der Hart 1853:205; Van Hoëvell 1892:353, 357.

teenth century were regularly exported to Gorontalo.[63] Before the coconut
boom, correspondingly, the Tomini coastal strip contained much grassland.
'All of these low plains', wrote a Dutch military officer after exploring the area
in 1912, 'are covered with high *alang-alang*, interspersed here and there with
small patches of woodland' harbouring 'many deer and wild pigs' (Boonstra
van Heerdt 1914b:755-6). At this date the population of the Tomini coast was
small, but before the migrations to Gorontalo in the eighteenth century it had
probably been much larger (see Chapter VI). As in the case of the Poso Valley,
then, it is possible that deforestation originally caused by swidden cultivation had been preserved through a long period of demographic decline by
continued burning for hunting and grazing purposes. Where depopulation
was more complete and burning ceased altogether, conversely, the forest did
regenerate. While Padtbrugge attributed the extensive deforestation which
he saw in Tobungku in 1678 to the 'hard work and diligent cultivation of the
farmers' (Van Dam 1931:100), he also noted that the area was also 'full of buffalo'.[64] In this light it is likely that the 'bare hills' of Tobungku were kept that
way largely by fire, so that less work was involved than he assumed. By the
twentieth century, nevertheless, the sparsely populated Tobungku coastline
was heavily forested (see Chapter XIII).

No grazing, no grass?

On the offshore islands of Sangir, Talaud and Banggai, for most of the period
covered by this study, large grazing animals were scarce or absent. Some
cattle, as already noted, were present on Sangir in the seventeenth and eighteenth centuries, but by 1825 they had disappeared, and water buffalo are
not reported from Sangir or Talaud at any period. Neither the *anoa* nor the
deer, moreover, reached these islands either; in the early twentieth century,
the only large mammals here were pigs (Bastiaan 1930:5; Brilman 1938:17-8)
and goats (Logeman 1922:62). Banggai, despite its proximity to the mainland of Central Sulawesi, never obtained the water buffalo, and while cattle
were introduced from Gorontalo at the end of the nineteenth century, their
numbers remained small.[65] Both the deer and the *anoa* were also absent in
Banggai until shortly before the Japanese invasion, when some deer appar-

[63]   AV Gorontalo 1845 (KITLV H111); AV Ternate 1807 (ANRI Ternate 141); Bleeker 1856:138;
Van der Hart 1853:205; Van Hoëvell 1905:177; Von Rosenberg 1865:41. In Moutong, too, horses
'wandered wild' on the slopes (Buddingh 1860:377).
[64]   NA VOC 1345:286.
[65]   Bosscher and Matthijssen 1854:100; Goedhart 1908:485; Schrader 1941:127. In 1906 there
were about 200 cattle in the archipelago, all on Banggai proper; by 1938 the number had risen to
almost 800. Goats, however, were present in larger numbers.

ently swam over to Peling from the mainland (Schrader 1941:127).

The fact that all three of these populous island groups were almost com-pletely devoid of grassland, then, confirms the close link between grass and livestock. In the absence of an incentive to create pastures for grazing, foodcrop swiddens were always allowed to revert quickly to woody veg-etation after cultivation, and the use of fire was limited to the re-opening of secondary forest swiddens. In Banggai the result was 'jungle' (Section of Military Geology 1944:20) in the true sense of what the geographer Schrader (1941:109) called 'young wood, thin, hard and tenacious'. Had the coconut palm not been so ubiquitous on Sangir, its landscapes would no doubt have been similar.[66] On the mainland, too, it is striking that grasslands were rare before 1850 to the north and east of the 'buffalo line' reconstructed in Chapter II (Map 8), and that where they did occur it was almost always in places where some buffalo were in fact present: Belang in Minahasa, the plateau of Mongondow, and Mandono on the south coast of the Luwuk Peninsula. One exception, the coastal savanna near Pagimana, probably represents another old piece of agricultural deforestation preserved by subsequent hunting activity (A.C. Kruyt 1930a:339-48; Schrader 1941:127).

The correlation between the occurrence of grassland and the use of fire in hunting and animal husbandry was not perfect. In Minahasa in 1824, before the introduction of either deer or cattle, one part of the country between Sonder and Tomohon on the densely-populated central plateau was already 'covered with the grass called kouskous [kusu-kusu = alang-alang]' (Scalliet 1995: 411). Lam (1950:581, 583), moreover, found 'fire savanna' on one of the popu-lous Nanusa Islands, where grazing livestock were likewise absent, in 1926. In these exceptional cases very short swidden rotations, combined perhaps with inadvertent burning as a result of insufficiently controlled swidden fires, were apparently enough to maintain a grassy landscape despite the absence of a reason for doing so deliberately. It should also be noted that large grasslands, especially of alang-alang (Conklin 1959:61-2), were naturally more persistent than small ones, since any fires spread easily across them, and since relatively few seeds of woody vegetation reached their centres (Van Steenis 1937:638). This may explain why the mountainsides to the east of the Napu Valley were covered with grass 'up to a very high altitude' in 1930 despite the fact that 'nowhere on the slopes was any ladang farming or livestock grazing to be seen' (Steup 1931:1125), and why many colonial officials failed to appreciate the link between livestock and grassland formation at all. It is clear, neverthe-less, that the great majority of large grasslands ultimately owed their existence

---

[66]   'Large areas', states Hardjono (1971:77), describing the effects of shifting cultivation in Indonesia as a whole, 'became converted into jungles as distinct from forests, as abandoned clearings were left to a secondary growth of low bushes and trees'.

to the deliberate creation of pasture for grazing.

Less clear are the reasons why the type and number of grazing livestock varied so much from area to area. Except in the case of the deer, species introductions are unlikely to have played an important role here, since all of the other major grazing livestock types were definitely present in the Palu Valley in the seventeenth century.[67] Nor do variations in the density of the human population seem to have been a very significant factor. While the inhabitants of the Poso Valley or the Pada were no doubt in a better position to reserve land for grazing than those of a very densely populated area like Sangir, it is striking that the disappearance of cattle on Sangir between 1775 and 1825 coincided with a period of demographic decline rather than growth. The population boom in late colonial Minahasa and Gorontalo, conversely, was combined with an even greater proportional increase in the number of grazing livestock.

Animal skins and horns were exported from Central Sulawesi on a small scale at the beginning of the twentieth century (Adriani and Kruyt 1912-14, II:309; Logeman 1922:93). The abundance of large livestock on the Pada may have resulted to some degree from commercial specialization, since the To Pada paid a tribute of buffalo to Mori (A.C. Kruyt 1900b:464-5; Maengkom 1907:868), and by analogy with other cases of tributary trade (see Chapter II), this was probably only part of a larger flow.[68] Commercial factors, however, can hardly explain the complete absence of the buffalo from large parts of the region. Nor did the position of the buffalo line bear much relation to the distribution of wet rice farming, which was absent in Mori, Poso east of Lore, and the Tomini lands north of Parigi, but present on the Minahasan plateau from an early date despite the absence of the buffalo. Gorontalo, moreover, already had many buffalo before the spread of irrigation there in the eighteenth century; Padtbrugge reported in 1682 that these were used 'only as beasts of burden and for riding on'.[69] On the whole it is difficult to avoid the impression that the distribution of grazing livestock, at least before the transport improvements which made cattle popular in Minahasa and Gorontalo, was determined largely by cultural preferences and historical accident. The natural environment, however, affected the facility with which grasslands could be created, and this factor is considered separately below. In the case

[67]   In Minahasa, where water buffalo never spread outside the Belang area, they were nevertheless already present in the mid-seventeenth century (Colin 1900-02, I:111).
[68]   Elsewhere, too, buffalo were sometimes traded over long distances overland (Adriani and Kruyt 1950-51, III:367; Sarasin and Sarasin 1905, II:12). Donggala, at least in late colonial times, also exported live sheep and goats to Kalimantan (Logeman 1922:62; M. van Rhijn 1941:79).
[69]   Van Dam 1931:97. Transport, alongside ploughing, remained an important function of the water buffalo in Gorontalo in the early nineteenth century (AV Gorontalo 1845, in KITLV H111; Van der Hart 1853:226).

of the Poso Valley it is also possible that the importance of grazing reflected
the unsuitability of local soils for sustained short-fallow swidden cultivation,
and that periodic village relocation was necessary not in the first place due to
grassland expansion itself, but simply in order to maintain the level of food
production. This important point will be discussed in Chapter XV.

Cash crops

A systematic assessment of the amount of land involved in commercial
agriculture is possible only in the case of colonial Minahasa, where by 1862,
according to the earliest Dutch survey, coffee, coconut, and cocoa trees occupied a total of 65, 28, and 24 km^2 respectively (Appendix I).[70] Even when
allowance is made for fallowed coffee gardens (see Chapter XIII), it does not
seem likely that much more than five percent of the total land area, or 15
percent of the area under (periodic or permanent) cultivation, was devoted to
cash crops at this date.[71] In 1919, by which time coffee and cocoa were insignificant but coconut cultivation had expanded greatly as a result of the copra
boom, the equivalent figures were 11 and 15 percent respectively (Appendix
J). Unless these figures are radically inaccurate, then, cash crops in Minahasa,
despite their great economic (and demographic) importance, were always a
rather minor factor in terms of land use.

While coffee and cocoa (as well as cotton and tobacco for local trade) were
also grown in other parts of the region at various periods, it is not likely that
their relative significance with respect to foodcrop agriculture was anywhere
greater than in nineteenth-century Minahasa. The case of the coconut palm,
on the other hand, is different. On Sangir, as we have seen, coconuts already
seem to have formed the dominant vegetation in Padtbrugge's time, and in
1922 a Dutch official complained that because of intensive coconut planting
by Sangirese farmers during the copra boom, 'not half a *bau* [0.35 hectare] of
land is left for rice or maize cultivation' (Logeman 1922:66).

Forest land was seldom cleared solely for the purpose of coconut planting. The vast majority of coconut trees were planted on foodcrop swiddens,
either simultaneously with the main annual subsistence crops, or immedi-

---

[70]   In 1890, by comparison, the area planted with coffee in Minahasa was about 50 km^2 (*Gouvernements-koffiecultuur* 1894:462). Coconuts, it should be added, did not actually become an
export crop in Minahasa until the 1880s, but have been included here for the sake of comparison
with the situation in later periods.
[71]   Cocoa trees only come into full production at the age of about 10 years (Van Hall 1949:
287-8), and in northern Sulawesi their lifespan was 20-30 years (A.J.F. Jansen, 'Aantekeningen
betreffende de kakao-cultuur in de residentie Menado', 23-4-1859, in ANRI Manado 167); it is
unlikely that cocoa plantations were often left fallow in the manner of coffee gardens.

ately after the last harvest.[72] In this way, as Resident Van Rhijn (1941:42) succinctly put it at the end of the colonial period, 'the coconut plantations come into being via foodcrop agriculture'. Unlike the secondary vegetation which they replaced, however, they could not be felled after eight years or so to allow a new cycle of foodcrop production, since at that age they were only just beginning to produce nuts (Tammes 1949:39). Farmers therefore had the choice between replanting tubers and bananas in the shadow of the trees, as in densely-populated Sangir, or seeking new sites for more productive food-crop swiddens elsewhere, in which case coconut planting, like livestock graz-ing in the Poso Valley, blocked the fallow rotation and led to a progressive expansion of the cultivated area. Some such expansion occurred everywhere in late colonial Indonesia where swidden foodcrop cultivation was combined with the planting of perennial cash crops:

> The coconuts are planted in the *ladang*, mixed with annual crops. The normal procedure is that the germinated coconuts or other perennial crops are planted out among foodcrops such as rice and maize. After a certain length of time the garden is abandoned; at most, the planter returns now and again to clear away weed growth. Once the coconut trees begin to bear nuts the garden is usually a lit-tle better maintained, but in all cases the crop is ultimately obtained at a very low cost. Whole regions have been planted and transformed in this way, the original *ladang* cultivation being replaced upon its reversion to forest with coconut, rubber or coffee plantations. (Tammes 1949:7.)

Rubber, important in Sumatra and Kalimantan, was never significant in northern Sulawesi, while coffee gardens, with their short productive lifespan, seldom made a very permanent impression on the landscape. Coconuts, by contrast, could preserve patterns of past forest clearance almost indefinitely. The production period of this crop is extremely long: coconut palms reach full productivity only after 10 or 20 years, sometimes continue to yield good harvests of nuts after 75 years, and can live for up to 160 years (Tammes 1949:17, 39). Under favourable conditions, moreover, the lifespan of a coco-nut plantation, even without deliberate replanting, is not limited to a single generation of trees. Padtbrugge already observed that in at least one place on Greater Sangir the coconuts were reproducing themselves naturally without human intervention (Van Dam 1931:67), and later writers confirm that this was common in the nineteenth and early twentieth centuries (Steller 1866:19; Heringa 1921b:733). The coconut forests of Sangir, in other words, were hold-

---

[72] Departement van Landbouw, Nijverheid en Handel 1925:13; Dutrieux 1930:17, 1931a:11; Ter Laag 1920:42; *Militaire memoire Parigi* 1929:5; Schrader 1941:126. One late source (Lanting 1939:65) does state that part of the population 'devoted itself exclusively to coconut cultivation, and only made *ladang* in order to plant coconuts on them later'; but even here it is clear that foodcrops were grown on the newly-cleared swiddens first.

ing their own against rainforest regeneration, and had effectively become part of the natural vegetation.

During the copra boom millions of new coconut trees were planted outside the old oil-exporting centres of Sangir and Kaili, especially in Tomini and Minahasa where many coastal districts were transformed into continuous carpets of smallholder coconut plantations (Plate 33). Copra export statistics, nevertheless, suggest that in regional terms the amount of land devoted to coconut cultivation remained quite small. A recorded average of 103,000 tonnes of copra was exported from northern Sulawesi in the years 1928-1931 (A.Ph. van Aken 1932:158), and in 1939, by which time the residency of Manado was producing about one third of all Indonesian copra (Tammes 1949:8), approximately 214,000 tonnes, less than a quarter of which now came from Sangir and Donggala/Palu.

Table 33. Approximate copra exports (tonnes) by subregion, 1939

Sangir and Talaud	35,000
Minahasa and Bolaang Mongondow	63,000
Gorontalo (Limboto Depression and south coast only)	12,000
Togian and the Gulf of Tomini coasts	60,000
Luwuk and Banggai	12,000
Donggala (and Palu)	16,000
Tolitoli, Buol and Kuandang	16,000
Total	214,000

Source: M. van Rhijn 1941:32

According to Tammes (1936b:146, 1949:39), 10 kg per tree was a normal annual copra yield in eastern Indonesia. In 1930, then, there were probably about 10 million productive trees in northern Sulawesi, and in 1939, 21 million. Many of the additional 11 million trees which came into production by 1939 must already have been planted nine years earlier, and local consumption of oil and other coconut products, on the basis of a conventional Indonesian ratio of one tree for every human inhabitant (Tammes 1949:11), probably accounted for a further million or so.[73] Allowing for some undercounting, then, it seems reasonable to suppose that the real total in 1930, including young trees, was about 20 million.[74] Typical coconut planting intervals in northern Sulawesi varied from six metres on parts of the Gulf of

[73]   In Sangir, as in other parts of Indonesia (Tammes 1949:11), it was customary to plant one coconut tree for domestic use on the birth of each child (Van Dinter 1899:368; Frieswijck 1902:484).
[74]   According to Kemmerling (1923-24, I:6) there were some 8 million coconut trees on Greater Sangir alone around 1920, but Blankhart (1951:83) gives a figure of only 3.5 million for the same

Plate 33. Part of southeastern Minahasa between Belang and Ratahan, showing continuous coconut plantations near the coast and grassy hills inland, 1944 (Allied Geographical Section 1944: Photograph 8)

Tomini coast, to nine metres in parts of Minahasa (Tammes 1936b:149-50). If the average was eight metres, each hectare of coconut forest in the region contained approximately 160 trees (Reyne 1948:470). At 20 million trees, then, the total area under coconuts in 1930 was roughly 1,250 km^2.

This figure, equivalent to less than 1.5 percent of the land area of the residency and perhaps six percent of the deforested area, may well be an underestimate, since the Sangir Islands alone have a combined area of more than 800 km^2 (Appendix D) but produced less than 15 percent of the region's copra in 1939 (Table 33). Even at the end of our period, nevertheless, it is clear that this most important of commercial crops was still much less significant than foodcrop and livestock farming as an agent of landscape change.[75] In 1953, by which time Minahasa alone produced one quarter of all Indonesian copra exports, coconut trees were estimated to occupy 16 percent of its land area.[76] Before the rise of the copra trade the area occupied by coconut palms, however significant locally, must have been negligible in regional terms.[77] The key role in natural forest clearance which Reid (1995:98-103) attributes to the cultivation of pepper and other cash crops in precolonial Sumatra, then, had no parallel in northern Sulawesi before the end of the nineteenth century.[78]

Timber production for export

As far as international trade was concerned, the forests of northern Sulawesi became commercially significant only toward the end of the nineteenth century, and then mainly for their rattan (*Calamus* species) and *damar* (the resin of conifers of the genus *Agathis*) rather than for their timber. While cases of unsustainable rattan exploitation are on record from the late colonial period (Tideman 1926:129-30; Dutrieux 1930:10), the nature of this plant, a small

---

island in the late 1940s. In Minahasa there were said to be about 6 million productive trees in 1938 (Weg 1938:144), which, at 10 kg of copra per tree, corresponds well with the 1939 export figure (Table 33).

[75]   A limitation of the coconut palm as a cash crop was that it did not produce an economic yield of copra above an altitude of somewhere between 300 (Ormeling n.d.:2) and 500 metres (Tammes 1949:14). In Minahasa, this meant that it could not be grown commercially on the central plateau.

[76]   Ormeling n.d.:2-3. This estimate (750 km^2) is based on a reported total of 7.5 million trees, and assumes an average planting interval of 10 metres.

[77]   It should perhaps be added that especially before the 1860s, coconuts were only partly a cash crop; in Sangir, for instance, they were also an important emergency food source when subsistence crops failed (see Chapter IX). In Minahasa, conversely, rice was partly an export crop until the 1850s (Chapter II).

[78]   Even in Sumatra, it is worth adding, less than 2% of the total land area was apparently cleared for pepper cultivation over the three centuries from 1600 to 1900 (Reid 1995:102).

climbing palm which could be harvested without felling its host trees (Heyne 1950, I:342), meant that such episodes did not lead to destruction of the forest as a whole even on a local scale. *Agathis*, by contrast, was often a major component of the forests in which it occurred, and *damar* tapping did sometimes (though not always) lead to the death of the tree (Van der Vlies 1940:624, 637). The distribution of the species involved, however, was restricted, and despite earlier warnings that 'slaughter tapping' (*rooftap*) was causing 'terrific destruction' in Central Sulawesi, there were still 'several million' *damar* trees in Central Sulawesi in 1940.[79]

The only timber valuable enough to be exported in significant quantities from northern Sulawesi, a mountainous region remote from major commercial, industrial and population centres, was ebony (*Diospyros* species), of which the residency of Manado had become Indonesia's most important producer by the 1930s (Steup 1935:45). The depletion of this very slow-growing wood was rapid and in many places almost complete, at least as far as adult trees were concerned.[80] In Minahasa, where ebony had still been 'rather widespread' in the middle of the nineteenth century (Graafland 1898, I:31), it was 'already scarce' by 1895 (Koorders 1898:522) and present only in 'insignificant' quantities 25 years later.[81] On Sangir and Talaud, reported a forestry official in 1920, 'felling has been so heavy that within one or two years all further ebony exploitation there will probably have to be halted, since except in a few parts of Talaud no trees of more than 50 centimetres in diameter are left' (Heringa 1921a:798). By 1934, felling had been forbidden in the Palu area too. Only the eastern part of Central Sulawesi was now producing ebony for export, and even here exhaustion was imminent at some of the more accessible sites (Steup 1935:53, 62). *Diospyros*, like *Agathis*, was often found in relatively homogenous stands, so that the effect of such exhaustion on the local landscape was quite dramatic.[82] On the one island of the Sangir group which still had some natural forest, Biaro, 'some hills' were 'completely bare'

---

[79]   Van der Vlies 1940:617, 619. At the turn of the century, according to Van Kol (1903:335), tappers were already having to travel 'deeper and deeper into the interior' to find 'the good sorts of *damar*'; this, however, probably had to do more with the customary system of exclusive rights to each tree (Nieboer 1929:83; Steup 1931:1131) than with the exhaustion of the supply.

[80]   The forestry department ultimately prohibited the cutting of trees with a diameter of less than 60 cm (Steup 1935:53). Ebony trees must grow for 80 years before they are mature enough for felling (Heringa 1921b:743).

[81]   Heringa 1921a:798. Two centuries earlier, Padtbrugge had claimed that in some parts of Minahasa the wood was 'so plentiful that there is almost no household equipment which is not made of ebony' (Van Dam 1931:78). In 1873, the Minahasan districts of Tonsea and Belang were still able to provide quite large quantities for a government export order (Res. Manado to chief telegraphic engineer Batavia, 13-12-1873, in ANRI Manado 101).

[82]   In the purest stands of Central Sulawesi, ebony trees locally made up as much as 90% of the forest (Steup 1935:51, 63). Elsewhere, however, the proportion was much lower (Heringa 1921a:800).

by the beginning of the twentieth century as a result of ebony felling and the additional damage caused in the process of transporting the logs.[83] The distribution of this tree, on the other hand, was even more restricted than that of *Agathis* (hence, in part, its high commercial value), so that the areas involved were very small.[84] Steup (1935:51) calculated that the total amount of ebony wood exported in 1932 corresponded to just 30 hectares of the purest ebony forest (although the area actually felled was no doubt greater).

Another case of selective overexploitation is possibly that of the sandalwood tree (*Santalum album*), which seems to have formed part of the natural climax vegetation of the arid zone around Palu (Whitten, Mustafa and Henderson 1987:486-7). The valuable wood of this species was exported as early as the first half of the sixteenth century from 'the archipelago of the Celebes', where at that time it was said to be abundant.[85] In the early twentieth century, by contrast, Dutch botanists had some difficulty finding any specimens at all in the Palu area (Bloembergen 1940:380; Heyne 1950, I:590). If this was a case of unsustainable human exploitation, however, then the depletion of the sandalwood reserve, as on Java (Boomgaard 1996b:9), must have taken place at a very early date. In 1708, a VOC mission to Kaili was already disappointed to find that 'single sandalwood trees were growing here and there, but they were of small girth', and that 'everybody whom we questioned on the subject agreed that they are so thinly distributed as to be hardly worth mentioning'.[86] The Palu Valley, it should also be added, was an area of dense population and much animal husbandry, so that commercial exploitation was probably not the only reason for the depletion of its sandalwood reserves.

Timber consumption for domestic and construction purposes

While there were no large towns in the region to provide commercial demand for building timber, the rural mass of the population used much wood for housebuilding, fencing, and cooking. Light timber and firewood

---

[83]   Frieswijck 1902:431. By 1920, 'only a few adult trees' were left on Biaro following intensive felling by Dutch companies (Heringa 1921a:798, 1921b:735, 738).
[84]   Ebony stands were limited mainly to dry ravines at low altitudes and other steep lowland terrain with thin, well-drained soils (Heringa 1921a:800, 1921b:735; Steup 1930:862, 866-9, 1935: 48-50).
[85]   De Urdaneta 1837:429. In some early European sources, Timorese sandalwood is mistakenly identified as originating from Makassar in South Sulawesi. This particular report, however, comes from the Moluccas and almost certainly refers to the indigenous sandalwood of Central Sulawesi as also described by Rumphius (1750, II:44, 46-7).
[86]   NA VOC 1775:109-10, 234. It is, however, likely that local informants were keen to play down the importance of this product for political reasons (Noorduyn 1983:117; Rumphius 1750, II:46-7).

came mostly from the vegetation cut in the process of swidden clearance, and the need to wait until regrowth had progressed sufficiently to provide fencing material was sometimes one factor determining the minimum length of the fallow period.[87] Thicker forest, however, also provided wood, particularly the heavier pieces used for housebuilding. Where the population was relatively dense, as in Minahasa, those parts of the uncultivated forest closest to the farmed and fallow land sometimes became visibly depleted by timber extraction.

> Before the *domeinverklaring* [the formal designation of all 'waste' lands as colonial state domain in 1877], almost every family or *negeri* claimed a particular section of the forests located in its vicinity (this right was called *palow* or *apar*) in which it could collect forest products such as timber, rattan, *nibung* [*Oncosperma filamentosum*, a palm supplying auxiliary housebuilding materials] and the like. Sometimes such sections of forest were rather intensively exploited, so that the tree cover gradually became very thin and the forest was no longer intact; land in such a condition was called *rokrok* or *rombe*. (Worotikan 1910:153.)

Selective felling for indigenous domestic and construction purposes probably explains the impoverished forest landscapes which Reinwardt described in some parts of Minahasa in 1821. Climbing the Lokon volcano on the western rim of the central plateau, Reinwardt found that although the mountainsides were 'thickly forested', the trees were 'not of any great height or girth'. The heavier timber, he surmised, 'has mostly been cut out' (Reinwardt 1858:551). On a trip over the lower watershed on the eastern rim of the plateau, he was once again surprised how little intact primary forest was to be seen.

> Since the mountains behind Papakelang appeared from a distance to be very thickly wooded, I had expected to find an old, extensive forest here. But although I walked on for quite a long way up the path to the village of Rerer, I still found that most of the heavy timber had everywhere been felled. The only tall trees were a few fine, lofty *wanga* [*Metroxylon elatum*] palms; the rest of the vegetation consisted mostly of younger, or naturally smaller, bushes and trees. (Reinwardt 1858:563-4.)

Later in the nineteenth century, indigenous timber consumption was both boosted by population growth, and supplemented by Dutch construction activity as large numbers of wooden bridges and coffee warehouses were built in rural areas. In the 1890s Koorders (1898:328, 386-7, 415, 522-3) identified several timber tree species which had become scarce due to 'constant felling', and (Graafland 1898, I:31) attributed the disappearance of the 'best sorts of wood' from accessible parts of Minahasa to the fact that these 'were

---

[87]   Adriani and Kruyt 1912-14, II:251. In more densely populated areas, some firewood was also deliberately planted (Holthuis and Lam 1942:127; N.P. Wilken 1870:374).

used in the past as building timber for houses and bridges'.[88] The fact that Reinwardt unhesitatingly described the *rok-rok* or selectively felled woods as forests, on the other hand, suggests that these were clearly distinct from the fallow or *jurame* lands, and that little of the deforestation described in later accounts, or shown on the Koorders map of 1895 (Chapter XIII, Map 18), resulted from timber exploitation alone. Rather, the use of wood for construction purposes should be regarded as a supplementary activity leading to selective forest depletion beyond the limits of the swidden-fallow area.

Timber consumption for industrial purposes

Iron manufacture, the region's earliest and historically most important export industry (see Chapter II), involved melting down iron ore on woodpile fires before smelting and working it in charcoal-burning forges.[89] Large quantities of wood were required for both processes, and given that the iron industry has been held responsible for early episodes of deforestation both in Europe (Pounds 1990:282) and in other parts of Indonesia (Colombijn 1997c:432), it is worth investigating whether such a link can be also established in the case of Central Sulawesi.

Some of the areas identified in historical sources as ironworking centres were indeed foci of early deforestation. The richest source of iron ore in northern Sulawesi, for instance, was apparently the territory of the To Pakambia (Chapter I, Map 5; Chapter XIII, Map 17) in the valley of the Yaentu, a tributary of the La (Adriani and Kruyt 1950-51, III:326). At the end of the nineteenth century the floor of this valley formed an extension of the Pada grassland, while the surrounding mountains were also covered largely by grass (Adriani and Kruyt 1900:210; A.C. Kruyt 1900b:464). Another ore-producing area, Onda'e (A.C. Kruyt 1901b:149), located between Pakambia and Lake Poso, was likewise a land of 'bare mountains' and 'total deforestation' (Adriani and Kruyt 1912-14, I:55). The most historically important ironworking region on the whole island, not far over the 'border' with South Sulawesi near the modern nickel mine of Soroako on the shore of Lake Matano, was also quite extensively deforested (Abendanon 1915-18, I:467; Grubauer 1913:39, 58).

---

[88] The Manado Cultivation Report for 1862 already mentions 'large areas of forest' in the less densely populated parts of Minahasa 'from which the best and most useful sorts of timber have disappeared as a result of long and continuous felling' (CV Manado 1862, in ANRI Ambon 1563).
[89] A.C. Kruyt 1901b:151-3. Usually, although not always (Sarasin and Sarasin 1905, I:312), the manufacturing process was completed in the immediate vicinity of the ore sources, and only finished products were exported to other regions.

The correspondence between deforestation and ironworking activity was not, however, clear-cut. On the headwaters of the Kaya, a river feeding into the western side of Lake Poso, another ore source mentioned by A.C. Kruyt (1901b:149) lay in an area described in 1910 as 'thickly forested'.[90] The Poso area as a whole, moreover, had supported a denser population in the more or less distant past (see Chapter VI), so that the possible effect of woodcutting for smelting purposes is impossible to isolate from that of agricultural deforestation.[91] Extensive cattle grazing on deliberately fired grasslands had preserved, if not extended, the scope of earlier forest clearance, and the name Pakambia apparently meant 'place of pasture' (Adriani and Kruyt 1912-14, I: 60). No important ironworking sites, conversely, were present on the largest grassland, the Pada of Mori, at the end of the nineteenth century. By that date, admittedly, the iron industry in Central Sulawesi was in deep decline as a result of competition from foreign imports (Chapter XII); at earlier periods it had been much more significant, and perhaps also more geographically widespread. While many European sources comment on the extent of deforestation in the areas in question, however, none link this with the iron industry or mention any indigenous tradition which did so. The fact that only certain selected types of timber seem to have been used for charcoal manufacture (A.C. Kruyt 1901b:152-3, 1938, IV:410) also suggests that wholesale deforestation is unlikely to have resulted from felling for this purpose alone.

The only other local industries which stand out as potential causes of deforestation in the period before 1930 are gold mining and boatbuilding. Wooden pit props were used in some of the deep gold mines on the north coast of the northern peninsula from an early date (Duhr 1781:111), but there is no evidence that this led to any significant forest clearance, as Colombijn (1997c:432) has suggested for parts of Sumatra.[92] More destructive locally were the open-cast hydraulic mining methods (Henley 1997:426-7, 429)

---

[90]   Abendanon 1915-18, II:733. The fact that the water of the lower Kaya was clear and without suspended sediment (Abendanon 1915-18, II:728) confirms that its headwaters must have been forested.

[91]   The dangers of confusing these two factors are illustrated by a potentially misleading piece of indirect evidence for iron-related deforestation from the mid-nineteenth century. When Van der Wyck passed the confluence of the Tomasa River with the Poso on his pioneering journey to Lake Poso in 1865, he was told that it was 'on that branch that a mass of villages is located, and that the best iron is found; there are also a multitude of forges there, something which I could not find at the lake' (Adriani 1913b:859). It was the Tomasa Valley which was memorably described by Albert Kruyt (1899c:604) as treeless 'wherever the eye looks' in 1899. Kruyt also noted, however, that the swords traded through this valley to the lowlands were not in fact manufactured in Tomasa itself (which he did not include in his list of ore sources), but imported from other areas further south and east (A.C. Kruyt 1899c:602, 1901b:149).

[92]   Most of the gold mines were found along the northern peninsula between Tomini and Gorontalo and between Tolitoli and Bolaang (Henley 1997b:429), in areas which were heavily forested.

used by the European mining companies which worked some sites in North Sulawesi, without much success, between 1896 and 1931 (Van Bemmelen 1949, II:131). Here again, however, only a few small areas were affected.

Boats were built for local use in coastal settlements throughout the region, but only a few places, notably the Nanusa Archipelago in Talaud and the island of Manui off the southernmost part of the Tobungku coast, ever seem to have specialized in this industry to the extent that vessels built there were regularly exported over long distances (see Chapter II). Manui, in the middle of the nineteenth century, was said to be heavily forested – although the presence of buffalo (Bosscher and Matthijssen 1854:79) suggests that it was not entirely so – and sent rafts of unworked timber, as well as finished craft, to the Tobungku mainland.[93] Later sources, unfortunately, give no indication as to whether progressive deforestation of this island resulted. Most of the Nanusa Islands were heavily deforested in the early twentieth century, but how closely this was related to the boatbuilding industry is uncertain, since they were also densely settled and intensively cultivated. Considering the 'overpopulation' (Tamawiwy 1934) of these islands as a group, in fact, it is perhaps more surprising that one of them, Garete, was described in 1926 as 'an uninhabited flat coral island' which served as 'the forest reserve of the Nanusa Islands' (Holthuis and Lam 1942:101, 127).

Natural factors: earth movements, geology, and hydrology

A few localities in northern Sulawesi were naturally without tree cover. In places, for instance, geological features and recent tectonic movements produced slopes too steep and unstable for forest growth (Abendanon 1915-18, II:594, 737, 742; Schrader 1941:109), and where earthquakes were frequent, landslides and subsidences resulted in large treeless patches.[94] The name of the Bada Valley, meaning 'yellow', may have referred to the colour of the landslide scars on its slopes (A.C. Kruyt 1938, I:279). Abendanon (1915-18, II: 844-5, 849-50, 882-3, 885) noted that the whole Palu area was being uplifted at a (geologically speaking) very rapid rate, and that at the same time the valley floor was subsiding relative to the mountains around it.[95] This led to accelerated stream erosion both on the steep trench sides, which were dis-

---

[93]   Bosscher and Matthijssen 1854:78-9. Although there are also extensive forests on the mainland, this source notes, timber is scarce in the immediate vicinity of the coastal settlements, and more easily transported there by sea from Manui than carried overland from the interior.

[94]   Abendanon 1915-18, II:879; A.C. Kruyt 1909:356-7, 1938, I:208, 279.

[95]   The terraces on the east side of Palu Bay, which a VOC steersman compared to a series of sand dunes (see Chapter XIII) represented successive phases of past uplift and compensatory erosion (Abendanon 1915-18, II:885).

sected by dramatic ravines (Plate 34), and on the higher ground behind them, which became 'badlands' (Surastopo Hadisumarno 1977:50) of short, incised stream valleys separated by narrow ridges. While the unstable, landslide-prone slopes made it difficult for trees to become established on the mountains, the heavy load of eroded material carried by the streams was deposited as coarse, porous sediments around the edges of the trench floor, helping to create the 'steppe' conditions described by the Sarasins (Abendanon 1915-18, II:847-8, 884-5, 888). A similar process of tectonic uplift and stream incision has been identified as one factor contributing to deforestation in Timor (Brookfield 1997:36). As in Timor, however, it cannot provide a complete explanation here, since some steep parts of the Palu Valley had retained their forest cover, and since the deforested area clearly coincided with a zone of intensive human interference. When measures to control this interference were taken by the colonial government in the 1920s, moreover, the erosion gullies were among the first parts of the landscape to be recolonized by forest (Steup 1929:594).

Bedrock geology, by influencing the composition and thickness of the soil mantle, affects both the type and luxuriance of the forest growing above it (Whitten, Mustafa and Henderson 1987:463-71, 473-84), and the attractiveness of an area for agricultural clearance (see Chapter II). Only twice in the literature on northern Sulawesi, however, is the claim made that bedrock characteristics can in themselves preclude forest growth, and in both cases it is dubious. In Talaud, firstly, Lam (1927:388) attributed the low 'alpine' vegetation of Gunung Piapi, on the east coast of Karakelang, to the fact that this mountain consisted of serpentine, a hard ultrabasic rock which weathered so slowly that only a very thin soil could develop.[96] Large expanses of similar rocks and soils, on the other hand, also occur in eastern Central Sulawesi (Van Bemmelen 1949, I:403; Whitten, Mustafa and Henderson 1987:463-71), and here they were almost entirely forested. The geographer Schrader (1941: 109), secondly, argued that on Peling in Banggai it was the rugged limestone landscape, with infertile soils and underground drainage, which, in combination with a relatively dry climate, prevented the development of dense forest cover. Part of the Pada grassland, interestingly, is also a karst area with underground drainage (Kaudern 1938:124-5). No general correlation between limestone geology and deforestation can however be deduced, since Abendanon (1915-18, I:468) noted that in other parts of Central Sulawesi it was 'almost always the limestone rocks which carry the thickest forest'.

---

[96]   The name of this mountain suggests a volcano, and in 1910 a Dutch missionary described it as such and implied that this accounted for its thin vegetation cover (Zwaan 1910:6). The geologist Kemmerling (1923-24, I:94), however, denied that there was any trace of recent vulcanism on Talaud.

Plate 34. Unforested, steeply-incised stream valley on the western flank of the Palu Trench, circa 1913 (Abendanon 1915-18, II: Plate CLXII)

Grasses and reeds probably form the natural vegetation on some types of terrain which are subject to frequent flooding (Whitten, Mustafa and Henderson 1987:454). Sources from the colonial period describe periodically inundated grasslands on the banks of Lake Limboto (Riedel 1870a:55; Frohwein 1933:29) and around the smaller Tonsawang (Buliling) lakes in the south of Minahasa.[97] In what Abendanon dubbed the grassy 'Sahara' of the Sumara Valley in Mori, local people reported that 'at times of very high water, the whole plain is flooded'.[98] The same factor may also have contributed to the maintenance of grasslands around the Tondano, Lindu and Poso lakes, in the Palu Valley, and in some deforested localities on the coast. In most of these places, on the other hand, both human settlement and grazing animals were also present. Other flood-prone areas, moreover, were occupied by swamp forest rather than grassland (Steup 1933:35; Whitten, Mustafa and Henderson 1987:454).

A somewhat less disputable case of naturally sparse tree cover is that of the long, flat plateau stretching along the 2,000-metre summit of the Tineba (Fennema) range, where early twentieth-century explorers were surprised to find a vegetation which reminded them of European moorlands.[99] As with similar flora in parts of upland Sumatra (De Wilde and Duyfjes 2001:377), a combination of topographic and geological factors which impede drainage, together with a very wet mountain climate, must provide at least part of the explanation for these high-altitude marshes.[100] Since, however, the moors were 'extremely rich in game', and (although themselves uninhabited) bordered in at least one place on grasslands surrounding a settled highland basin (Grubauer 1913:396, 461), the influence of man-made fires cannot be ruled out even here.[101] In Sumatra and Kalimantan, even swamp forests have been known to burn 'in especially dry years' (Van Steenis 1937:637).

[97]   *Fragment* 1856:81; J.J. ten Siethoff, 'Topografische schetsen van een gedeelte der residentie Menado 1845' (ANRI Manado 46).
[98]   Abendanon 1915-18, II:648. The same was said of another low-lying grassland adjacent to Lake Matano, further south in what is now South Sulawesi (Abendanon 1915-18, I:475).
[99]   Grubauer 1913:460-1; Steup 1931:1129. A smaller mountaintop marsh was reported on the watershed above the Sumara Valley in eastern Central Sulawesi (Abendanon 1915-18, II: 654-5) and another on the summit of Mount Nokilalaki (Ngilalaki) in the western highlands (Bloembergen 1940:401), although in the latter case there was low but apparently continous tree cover.
[100]   The annual rainfall on these mountaintops exceeds 2,500 mm, there is no dry season, and the mean temperature of the coldest month is under $20°C$ (Fontanel and Chantefort 1978: Indonésie III). The surface rock on the plateau is a 'quartzite schist' (Abendanon 1915-18, II:593, 737).
[101]   There were 'countless paths made by deer and pigs' on the plateau (Grubauer 1913:396). It is also interesting to note that signal fires were regularly lit by travellers on its rim above the Napu Depression (Hofman 1909:33-4).

Climate

Nowhere in the region was the climate so dry that in the absence of regular burning, it would not support forest cover (Lam 1950:572-3; Whitten, Mustafa and Henderson 1987:486). Palu, with an average annual rainfall of just 547 mm over the period 1908-1941, appears to be the driest place in the whole of Indonesia (Metzner 1981a:45-6), yet *johar* (*Cassia siamea*) and mahogany trees planted in the town during the 1920s grew well when protected from fire and grazing animals (Verhoef 1937:221). Reforestation experiments on the slopes of the Palu Valley, initiated by the colonial forestry department in 1923 (Steup 1929:591), also gave rapid results (*Verslag Dienst Boschwezen* 1929:298). The most effective method of reforestation, in fact, proved to be the simple exclusion of farmers from designated protected zones.

> The results yielded by this method are truly dazzling. It turns out that even in dry areas like these, the natural vegetation is still forest. Everyone who has known the region for any length of time is amazed at the speed with which the forest spreads to reclaim the lands which are naturally its own. (Steup 1929:593-4.)

'Natural reforestation', confirmed a *controleur* of Palu with rather more caution in 1935, 'is proceeding slowly but surely in the reserved areas'. Where setbacks occurred, these usually resulted from man-made fires:

> The guilty parties are usually livestock holders, who set fire to the grasslands in order to stimulate the growth of young grass. If the wind is strong and the farmer careless, the fire spreads to the forests. Heavy penalties are called for here. (Vorstman 1935:15.)

The natural climax vegetation of the Palu Valley, then, was not grassland, but a 'monsoon forest' of drought-tolerant trees like sandalwood (Whitten, Mustafa and Henderson 1987:486-7). In dry Gorontalo, likewise, Riedel observed in the 1860s that what was left of the natural forest 'does not generally have that majestic, imposing appearance characteristic of a tropical vegetation'.[102]

Climatic conditions, of course, did affect the ease with which fires could be lit and the amount of damage which they did if they spread. In dry areas, the frequency with which swidden and grassland fires got out of control may well have promoted the extension of grass at the expense of secondary forest.[103] This, moreover, might also have been a factor favouring animal husbandry and hunting, leading in turn to further deliberate grassland burning. Examples of relatively dry areas where grazing livestock were numerous, and grasslands extensive, include not only the Palu Valley and the Limboto

[102] Riedel 1870a:52. Also Von Rosenberg 1865:6-7.
[103] Dutrieux 1931b:5; Ter Laag 1920:40; Vorstman 1935:15.

Depression, but also the Tomini coastlands, and to a lesser extent the area around Mandono on the south coast of the Luwuk Peninsula. A glance at the precipitation map (Chapter I, Map 3), on the other hand, shows that eastern Central Sulawesi, where the extent of deforestation was greatest in relation to the population density and grassland and savanna most widespread, is among the wettest parts of the region, with average annual rainfall totals in excess of 2,500 mm. Much of this area, moreover, experiences no clearly distinct dry season (Kornrumpf 1935:76; Oldeman and Darmiyati Sjarifuddin 1977: map). Given that grass is often easier to burn than felled secondary forest, it is in fact tempting to speculate that grassland management and livestock farming on the Pada were precisely adaptations to the very wet climate of this area, which made swidden cultivation a more precarious undertaking than elsewhere.[104]

Natural fires

Not quite all vegetation fires were man-made. Periodic eruptions maintained girdles of grass- and brushland around the higher slopes of Minahasa's active volcanoes.[105] Although forest fires ignited by lightning strikes appear to be rare in wet tropical climates, they do occur (Burger 1936:882; Lam 1950: 575). On the Pada, more permanent natural fire sources also existed. In the prehistoric past this plain had been a swamp, with the result that there was a layer of lignite (*bruinkool*) not far beneath its surface. Adriani and Kruyt (1912-14, I:63) reported in 1912 that at two locations this lignite layer was on fire. In one place an exposed section had been ignited by a swidden fire in 1904, 'with the result that the ground continued to burn'; the second fire had been burning 'for as long as anyone can remember'. Abendanon (1915-18, II:618-9) provides a more detailed description of one of these fires, together with a photograph (Plate 35). The side of a low hill appeared to have been torn off by an explosion, revealing a thick seam of lignite about eight metres below the crest. Jets of steam, hot enough to bake the surrounding clay, emerged at several points from the face of the scar, and rose to form a plume visible from a great distance. Abendanon believed that having been exposed to the air by erosion, the lignite 'must have ignited spontaneously', perhaps due to marsh gas.

Even if all lignite fires were in fact started by human activity, they clearly

---

[104]   Pelzer (1945:19) notes that *alang-alang* and other tropical grasses 'burn very rapidly and with a hot flame, even when still green'.
[105]   Bik 1864:169; Dumont d'Urville 1833:429; Graafland 1867-69, I:143; Kemmerling 1923-24, I: 127; Koorders 1898:14-5; Van Marle 1922, I:13; Reinwardt 1858:555-6.

represented a more permanent hazard than other fires of man-made origin. And if, by analogy with similar fires in exposed coal seams in Kalimantan (Goldammer and Seibert 1989:518), the burning edge of the seam tended to retreat as the exposed lignite was consumed, then there must have been occasions on which the fire spread. The Pada, it will be recalled, was the largest stretch of unbroken grassland in the region; lignite deposits, moreover, also occurred in the deforested basins of Napu and Besoa (Abendanon 1915-18, II:750). Neither Abendanon nor Adriani and Kruyt, on the other hand, actually mention the ignition of vegetation by the lignite fires on the Pada, and Abendanon's photograph shows trees growing in the immediate vicinity of the fire source.

Conclusion

There is no doubt that subsistence agriculture, and more specifically swidden farming, was the most important agent of landscape change in North and Central Sulawesi before 1930. Although there was much local variation, swidden farmers in northern Sulawesi typically planted about 0.2 hectare of land per head of the population with primary foodcrops (usually rice and maize) each year, and required about nine times that area, or just under two hectares, per individual in order to maintain the preferred swidden rotation. Where almost all land was suitable for cultivation and the settlement pattern concentrated, this resulted in a local population density of about 50 persons per km^2. The higher densities already found in the mid-nineteenth century in places like Sangir, Mongondow, the Palu Valley, and some parts of Minahasa and Gorontalo were made possible by various combinations of more intensive swidden cycles, supplementary irrigated farming, and food imports. Even the normal pattern of swidden farming, with its fallow interval of eight years or less, produced a highly agrarian landscape dominated by brushwood and low secondary forest, and cannot usefully be regarded as having a limited or temporary impact on the natural vegetation.[106] Longer fallow intervals, or itinerant settlement patterns, were associated with the cultivation of poor soils, often in conjunction with extensive animal husbandry, by sparse populations outside the major centres of settlement.

The occurrence of grassland was very strongly correlated with that of large grazing animals, and most grasslands were former swiddens deliber-

---

[106] Even the term 'degradation', sometimes favoured in the literature to describe the impact of traditional swidden cultivation on natural forest (L. Chabot 1996:91; Potter 1993:108), would be misleading here and is better reserved for the effects of selective felling of useful timber species outside the swidden-fallow areas.

ately fired to provide pasture for buffalo, cattle, or deer.[107] In some places this
was an integral part of the swidden cycle, elsewhere a permanent or semi-
permanent conversion. During episodes of demographic decline, repeated
grassland burning for the purposes of animal husbandry and hunting sometimes preserved patterns of deforestation originally created by the foodcrop
farming activities of larger populations. In the Poso Valley, unusually, the
systematic permanent conversion of abandoned swiddens into grazing land
in the late nineteenth century probably led to a progressive expansion of
the deforested area despite a declining population. More intensively grazed
permanent pastures, on some of which the livestock density may have been
high enough to prevent reforestation even without the use of fire, were found
in areas where large numbers of water buffalo were used to work irrigated
ricefields. The possibility of intensification, and the fact that grazing could be
integrated into a stable swidden cycle, meant that although grasslands were
almost always associated with animal husbandry or hunting, there was no
direct or inevitable relationship between the total extent of deforestation and
the number of livestock present.

Compared to that of foodcrop production, the impact of cash crops on
the landscape was slight. Coconut plantations were very extensive in some
localities by 1930, but as a whole they probably did not account for more than
10 percent of the area transformed by human activity. The consumption of
timber for domestic and construction purposes affected the density and composition of the uncultivated forest in the vicinity of populous areas, and two
commercially important types of tree, sandalwood and ebony, were almost
completely felled out by the end of the colonial period. Timber exploitation,
however, never caused forest destruction or depletion on anything approaching a modern scale. The use of wood in ironworking may have contributed
to the deforestation of parts of Central Sulawesi in the more distant past, but
was not the only factor here.

On occasion forest fires, whether ignited by natural causes or spreading
from deliberately fired swiddens and grazing lands, affected primary as well
as secondary vegetation:

> During the unprecedentedly long drought in 1902, a great area of *damar* forest on
> the eastern peninsula (in the hinterland of Tojo) was destroyed by fire. The for-
> est burned for months on end, and the fire extended to the Gulf of Tomini. The
> air was filled with smoke and ash particles, so that visibility at sea was severely
> reduced. (Adriani and Kruyt 1912-1914, II:306-7.)

[107] Bracken and ferns, reported alongside grasses and fire-resistant trees on open landscapes in
Minahasa and Central Sulawesi, also reflected intermittent burning (Steup 1938:288-9; Whitten,
Mustafa and Henderson 1987:397, 401, 542).

Plate 35. Burning lignite outcrop near Tomata on the Pada grassland, 1910
(Abendanon 1915-18, II: Plate CXVIII)

In the case of the Pada grassland, where fires lit by pastoralists and hunters spread uncontrolled across the plain every year, and especially where permanent fire sources in the form of burning lignite outcrops were also present, it is possible that the surrounding forest was pushed back over a long period without ever being felled for farming purposes.[108] Elsewhere, however, the relatively good correspondence between the extent of deforestation and the (contemporary or former) distribution of the human population supports the conclusion reached by Brosius (1990:119) in upland Luzon that because fire damage to primary forest was seldom lasting, 'it cannot be said that grassland burning has actually been a cause of deforestation'; rather, fire 'served as an instrument of maintenance, preventing the return [...] to later stages of succession'.[109]

Climatic factors affected the composition of the natural vegetation, and perhaps also the likelihood that swiddens or secondary forest would be

[108]   Regular burning at favoured hunting sites is apparently sufficient to carve grasslands, albeit very slowly, out of uncultivated tropical forest (Pelzer 1945:19; Van Steenis 1937:636; Whitten, Mustafa and Henderson 1987:504, 542).
[109]   Occasional fires, on the other hand, may well have had an important influence on the composition and ecology of the natural forests (Goldammer and Seibert 1989; Goldammer, Seibert and Schindele 1996).

converted to grazing land, although it seems that both very wet and very dry conditions were favourable to animal husbandry. On the Tineba Plateau, high rainfall, heavy cloud cover, and relatively low temperatures probably combined with poor drainage to create conditions conducive to marsh formation rather than forest growth. Volcanic summits, earthquake scars, cliffs, and possibly some areas of seasonal flooding were also naturally unforested, while tectonic movements may have contributed, alongside human activity, to the deforestation of the Palu Valley. Steup (1936:42), nevertheless, was no doubt right to conclude that 'almost the whole surface area of Sulawesi' would have been occupied by some form of forest in the absence of human interference.

CHAPTER XV

Population and environment

This final chapter addresses some systematic topics in the study of environmental history, including the sustainability of farming systems and the question of agricultural intensification in relation to demographic change. The available evidence regarding the human impact on wild animal populations, and on climatic conditions, is also summarized. A possible case of environmental degradation with demographic consequences is described, and the social and environmental preconditions for sustainable resource use are discussed in so far as the historical sources allow. The last part of the chapter returns to the central issue of demography, describing some aspects of economic behaviour which complicate the broadly positive relationship between resource availability and population growth described in Chapter XII and identifying 'positive feedback' mechanisms by which an imbalance between population and agricultural resources, once established, may sometimes have led to further demographic growth. A concluding section recapitulates the main findings of the whole study both with respect to the factors controlling demographic change, and regarding the human impact on the natural environment.

Agricultural sustainability

The typical swidden fallow period of about eight years was short – shorter, in fact, than that of twelve years identified by Van Beukering (1947:9) as the minimum necessary for 'proper forest recovery' and the 'undisturbed practice of *ladang* cultivation'. Yet traditional farming practices in northern Sulawesi did not usually lead to serious soil erosion, falling foodcrop yields, or other signs of unsustainable land use. In Minahasa, even Dutch administrators were forced to admit this despite their instinctive antipathy to swidden farming. Resident Jansen, having alleged that besides entailing a 'loss of valuable timber resources', swiddening inevitably caused 'land degradation [*het bederven van den grond*] as a result of erosion [*wegvloeiing*] of the topsoil layer on mountains and slopes', nevertheless went on to concede that 'the fertile soil and extensive forests of Minahasa indisputably lend themselves very well to such use, and the Alfur possesses a certain degree of skill in this type of agriculture, which can be practised in a sustainable [*duurzaam*] way, and with good results, thanks to the abundant supply of land'.[1] 'The cultivation of rice and maize on dry fields', confirmed another resident 25 years later (by which time the Minahasan population was already some 40 percent larger), 'has not yet led to the slightest exhaustion of the soil' (Matthes 1881).

Since the locations of both swidden complexes and nuclear settlements were chosen with considerable care, farmers were concerned, under most circumstances, to ensure that it would not be necessary to abandon them in the foreseeable future. One manifestation of this concern was the care taken to prevent swidden fires from getting out of control and rendering adjacent land 'unfit for cultivation' (Tillema 1922:205) by destroying the fallow vegetation.[2] Perimeter firebreaks, consisting of cleared strips around the slashed swiddens, served to contain the annual burn.[3] This precaution was supported by supernatural sanctions. Farmers in Bada, according to Woensdregt (1928:165), believed 'that the spirits will punish humans if the trees around the swidden complex, in which they have taken refuge, are also burned'.[4] Dutch sources mentioning careless or recreational burning almost always refer to grassland areas which had already been permanently deforested for grazing or hunting purposes.[5]

Tonelli (1992:3-4, 38, 69, 74, 111) and Li (1991:26, 30) describe how under increasing population pressure, shortening fallow periods have led to soil erosion and declining crop yields in the modern Tinombo highlands.[6] Similar accounts from earlier times, however, are not easy to find. At the very end of the colonial period, Resident Van Rhijn (1941:42) did report that fallow periods on Sangir were shortening as a result of overpopulation, warning that such a trend 'leads in the long term to reduced production per unit area'. The cycle of 3-5 years under cultivation and 5-8 years of fallow which he describes for Siau, however, is not particularly short in Sangirese terms even by nineteenth-century standards (Chapter XIV, Table 29: Sangir 1825, Tagulandang 1866). On Sangir, moreover, the practice of cultivating food

---

[1]   CV Manado 1856 (ANRI Manado 51).
[2]   Such accidental fires, however, did occur on occasion (Adriani and Kruyt 1912-14, I:190; MV Manado, August 1864, in ANRI Manado 54; Steup 1931:1132-3).
[3]   Adriani and Kruyt 1950-51, III:43; A.C. Kruyt 1938, IV:54; Woensdregt 1928:164-5.
[4]   A similar belief demanded that farmers left at least one tall tree standing on each swidden as a spirit refuge, 'in order to ensure themselves of good weather' (Woensdregt 1928:165).
[5]   Ter Laag 1920:43; Steup 1931:1121, 1125; Van Steenis 1935:48; J. Kruyt 1933:38.
[6]   Also Nourse 1989:59, 61, 1999:66. The unusual preference for flat rather than sloping land, inspired by a fear of landslides, which Li (1991:41) reports from Tinombo may also be related to this degradation.

Plate 36. Sustainable land use, 1945: wet ricefields (with ox-drawn plough) and coconut groves in Minahasa (KITLV Photograph 6676)

crops underneath coconut and nutmeg trees, reminiscent of modern 'agro-forestry' systems (Huxley 1998), afforded considerable protection against soil erosion and flooding. In 1920 the forester Heringa observed that for this reason the hydrological situation on the islands, despite their dense population and mountainous relief, gave 'no cause for alarm'.

> The original forest has almost entirely made way for a vegetation of perennial tree crops – coconuts, nutmeg and sago – which, because they are mostly planted (or have grown) in an irregular and rather dense pattern, have taken over the [water-retaining] function of the original forest quite effectively (Heringa 1921b:741).

In Minahasa, as we have seen, average fallow periods appear to have lengthened slightly, rather than shortened, between 1850 and 1920 (although an increasing proportion of the fallow land came under grass in order to provide grazing for livestock). Irrigation, food imports, and an expansion of the total area under cultivation enabled the rapidly-growing Minahasan population to feed itself without affecting the fertility of its rich agricultural soils.[7] The

---

[7]   The areal rice yields specified by Tammes (1940:192) as typical for Minahasan swidden

combination of *sawah* – an ecologically very stable farming system (Geertz 1963:29; Greenland 1998:188) – and coconut cultivation which character-ized much of Minahasa in the early twentieth century (Plate 36) approached the ideal of intensive, sustainable smallholder agriculture celebrated by Robert Netting in *Smallholders, householders* (1993). The positive relationships which can emerge under favourable natural conditions between population growth, per capita income, and sustainable use of the environment have been well described in an African context by Tiffen, Mortimore and Gichuki in their book *More people, less erosion* (1994).[8] Further Indonesian parallels are suggested by the work of Nibbering (1991, 1997) in upland Java and Metzner (1982) in Flores.

There were some exceptions, however, to the rule of sustainable land use. The dry limestone hills to the south of the Limboto Depression, for instance, appear badly eroded in an aerial photograph from 1945 (Plate 37). Still partly forested in 1820, they were almost bare by 1880 following large-scale agricultural settlement, and infested with cactus by 1920 (see Chapter XIII). Although deforestation had a very long history in the Palu Valley, secondly, there is some indication that the problem of soil erosion was becoming par-ticularly serious there by the beginning of the twentieth century, at least for farmers on the valley floor where the eroded material was deposited during flash floods. The swidden cycle data from areas outside Minahasa (Chapter XIV, Table 29), thirdly, also include two twentieth-century reports which suggest unsustainable farming practices. In Tolitoli, a *ladang* was said to be planted and harvested only two or three times, at intervals of two or three years, before its (implicit) abandonment (Kortleven 1927:88); in Kuandang on the sparsely-populated north coast of Gorontalo, fallow lands were reported-ly cultivated in a four to ten-year cycle 'until ultimately the ground becomes completely exhausted, and only *alang-alang* will still grow there' (Van Andel and Monsjou 1917:119).

While the direct causal association proposed here between soil exhaus-tion and grassland formation is almost certainly inaccurate (see Chapter XIV), limited soil fertility certainly made short swidden cycles more difficult to maintain outside the traditional centres of dense agricultural settlement, most of which were located on particularly good land (Chapter XI). A report from the 1930s, for example, states that at the new local resettlement site

---

farming in the 1930s are higher, rather than lower, than those obtained on test plots during a supervised investigation by local Dutch officials in 1861 (Appendix G).

[8]   The mechanisms involved here include increased availability of labour and capital for investment in land improvements such as irrigation or terracing, and the consolidation of per-manent individual land ownership rights which often takes place under conditions of commer-cialization and population pressure (also Platteau 2000:75-92).

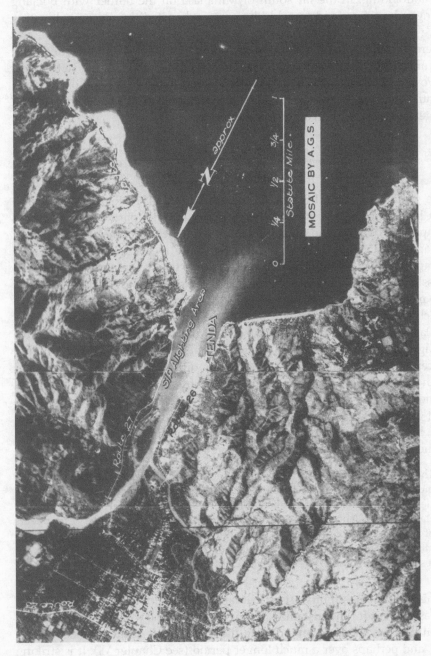

Plate 37. Unsustainable land use, 1945: deforested, eroded limestone hills between Gorontalo town (top left) and the Gulf of Tomini coast (Allied Geographical Section 1945: Photograph 19)

of Modoinding, in the far south of Minahasa on the border with Bolaang
Mongondow, farmland 'quickly becomes exhausted' by *ladang* cultivation
(Weg 1938:94). Situations like this were unusual in northern Sulawesi, and
where they did occur as a result of migration to previously uninhabited frontier areas, mostly late and localized. The grasslands and shifting settlements
of Poso and Mori as described by Adriani and Kruyt at the end of the nineteenth century, however, may reflect a comparable process operating over a
longer timespan and on a much larger scale.

Poso and Mori: unsustainable land use with demographic consequences?

'The ground in Central Sulawesi', noted Adriani (1915:460), 'is for a large
part limestone [*kalkbodem*], and therefore dry and not particularly fertile'. A
comparison between the vegetation maps from the end of the colonial period
(Chapter XIII, Maps 14 and 15) and the more recent RePPProT soil map
(Chapter I, Map 2) confirms that the area of extensive secondary forest and
grassland in Poso and Mori corresponded quite closely to the distribution of
two particular soil types: acid soils developed on ultrabasic parent materials,
which are notoriously difficult to cultivate wherever they occur (RePPProT
1990a:148), and shallow calcareous soils, which, although often favourable
for agriculture in terms of their chemical properties, are porous and highly
susceptible to erosion under Indonesian conditions.[9]

In Chapter XIV, the unusual pattern of frequent settlement movement
found in the Poso Valley was linked with the deliberate creation of permanent grasslands on which to graze water buffalo. One contemporary description, however, implies that soil exhaustion, rather than grassland conversion
as such, was often the stimulus for village relocation.

> The farmland available to a *kampung* which has remained in the same place for
> more than 20 years consists entirely of fallow land, or *yopongura*; forest lands to be
> cleared for the first time are called *pangalo*. Fallow land is preferred, since the veg-
> etation there is not so thick and heavy as on forest land. After three or four years
> of fallow a piece of ground can be recultivated with hope of a good harvest. If a
> *kampung* is located in a place where the soil is generally infertile, then this always
> results in a migration [*verhuizing*]. (A.C. Kruyt 1895-97, III:131.)

In this light the possibility arises that land degradation was also responsible,
at least in part, for the sustained demographic decline which appears to have
taken place in the Poso area during the second half of the nineteenth century, and perhaps over a much longer period (see Chapter VI). It is striking

---

[9]   T.W.G. Dames 1955:95; Hardjono 1971:94; Uhlig 1980.

that Albert C. Kruyt (1899c:608), despite his insistence that the area as a whole was sparsely populated, mentions 'overpopulation and the resulting lack of arable land' as one reason for the recent emigration of many To Lage from the grassy Tomasa Valley.[10] One piece of indigenous oral tradition, from Onda'e, also seems to point in the direction of depopulation as a consequence of permanent land degradation. This relates to Wawo nTolo, one of several abandoned village sites on the deforested slopes overlooking the Walati Valley to the east of Lake Poso.[11]

> According to the present generation, a curse rests upon the land of Wawo nTolo. This curse manifests itself in the fact that no maize will grow there. In former times things were different, and the inhabitants had an abundance of maize. This made them so arrogantly carefree that they no longer used only the discarded core of a maize cob to clean themselves after defaecating, but the whole cob instead. Then the gods became enraged, and since that time the land will no longer yield any maize. Wawo nTolo has not been inhabited within living memory. (Adriani and Kruyt 1912-14, I:54.)

It is not certain, of course, that there is any kernel of truth in this myth. But an ecological explanation for the depopulation trend in terms of falling food production as a result of soil exhaustion is especially attractive here given that the last part of the demographic decline occurred at a time of increasing involvement in the lucrative *damar* export trade, whereas elsewhere, increasing commerce was rather consistently associated with population growth. Declining foodcrop harvests, moreover, might also help to explain the enthusiasm with which Toraja men participated in *damar* collection (see Chapter XII). In the same context, finally, it is also interesting to recall that at the beginning of the twentieth century the inhabitants of the Poso Valley were described as small in stature compared to their western neighbours (Chapter VII).

If the broad dynamics of precolonial demography were Malthusian (Chapter XII), and if soil quality was typically an important determinant of population density (Chapter XI), then the relatively unfavourable pedology of Poso and Mori immediately raises the question of how and why a larger population had ever become established there in earlier times. One possible answer is that land degradation was a very long, progressive process which did not immediately affect either the initial settlers' perception of the area's agricultural potential, or the demography of their communities. Another

---

[10] Also Adriani and Kruyt 1912-14, I:38; A.C. Kruyt 1911:81.
[11] It may also be significant here that Onda'e, together with nearby (and equally deforested) Pakambia, was affected by famine in 1896, and Pakambia to harvest failure in 1899, although neither year was disastrous in most other parts of the region (Adriani and Kruyt 1900:136, 208).

possiblility, however, is that at the period of denser population the local economy had been more commercialized, permitting both imports of agricultural produce from elsewhere, and a more efficient distribution of locally-grown food (see Chapter IX). Several parts of the Poso and Mori area, notably Onda'e (see Chapter XIV), were once important sources of valuable iron ore, and although this was not true of the Tomasa and Poso river valleys, some iron was certainly exported via these valleys to the Gulf of Tomini coast.[12] As the iron industry declined from the seventeenth century onward, conceivably, the population was increasingly thrown back on inadequate local agricultural resources, leading both to the spread of unsustainable farming practices, and to a secular decline in population as nutrition deteriorated, debt-slavery spread (depressing reproductive fertility), and emigration increased.

While this neat ecological model is attractively simple and comprehensive, other interpretations of the best-documented part of the demographic decline in Central Sulawesi, that of the Poso area during the late nineteenth century, are also possible. The *damar* export boom of this period, although it probably led to an increase in prosperity, also involved a great deal of male absence, which must have had a negative effect on fertility rates. Many upland men, in fact, migrated for years on end to the coastal entrepôts and to the *Agathis* forests, a movement which was of some demographic significance in its own right (see Chapter V). Another possibility is that the prevalence of malaria increased in this period, raising the death rate. As in Gorontalo (see Chapter XIV), the water buffalo population of Central Sulawesi was strongly reduced by disease in the late nineteenth and early twentieth centuries.[13] Boomgaard (1987:57), quoting Bruce-Chwatt (1980:163) to the effect that *Anopheles maculatus* is more attracted to cattle than to man, has suggested major outbreaks of livestock disease on Java were associated with malaria epidemics: when the numbers of cattle fell, the mosquitos fed more often on human blood. *A. maculatus*, strikingly, also seems to have been the main vector in upland Central Sulawesi (see Chapter VII).[14] Land degradation, finally, is not a necessary component of any articulation between commercial and demographic decline (see Chapter XII), and neither is there any evidence that it was involved in the rather clear association between long-term depopulation and the decline of the iron trade on the east coast of Central Sulawesi in Tobungku and Mori.

Even if soil exhaustion was not an important factor behind demographic change, however, it certainly helps to explain the unusual willingness of farm-

[12]   AV Manado 1852 (ANRI Manado 51); Van Hoëvell 1893b:27; Riedel 1886:80.
[13]   A.C. Kruyt 1908:1293-4, 1938, IV:18; Schuyt 1911:15; Tillema 1926:221.
[14]   Other sources, however, suggest that *A. maculatus*, at least in Indonesia, is not zoophilic (Bonne-Wepster and Swellengrebel 1953:457).

ers in precolonial Poso and Mori to convert abandoned swiddens into pasture land, and move their settlements (temporarily or permanently) to new locations near old forest, rather than attempting to maintain a short-fallow cultivation cycle in situ. This, in turn, may shed light on the surprising importance of the water buffalo in Poso and Mori, where there were no wet ricefields, and where these animals therefore played no role in foodcrop agriculture. Despite their apparent lack of integration, swidden and livestock farming did not necessarily 'coexist without fusion', as Ormeling (1955:189) said of Timor. The soils of this part of Central Sulawesi, it can be surmised, were often simply unsuitable for long-term cultivation by the customary short-fallow methods, and if whole swidden complexes had to be abandoned anyway after a period of years or decades, then conversion to grassland for grazing may simply have represented a rational use for the already degraded land.

Access and ownership

The social and political factors which mediate between agricultural technology and the sustainability of farming systems, unfortunately, are barely amenable to investigation on the basis of historical sources from northern Sulawesi. Some comments on the ownership and distribution of land, nevertheless, are in order. Land rights in swidden farming, firstly, varied considerably from area to area. In the Poso Valley, fallow land was reallocated each year by a process of consultation and consensus within the village (Schrauwers 1998:116). Conflicts arising between households were referred to the arbitration of the village elders, and since any decision applied only to 'a single planting season', a disadvantaged party could be 'contented with the hope that next year, more allowance will be made for his preference for a particular piece of land' (Adriani and Kruyt 1950-51, III:27). In nineteenth-century Minahasa, by contrast, the right to re-cultivate a given piece of swidden land tended to remain in the hands of a single household from year to year.

> The swiddens [...] are not scattered and isolated on mountaintops and valleys, or hidden away in the forest, but adjoin each other on a single chosen terrain, where there is space for all inhabitants of the *negeri*. This land is regarded as communal, but some people have recognized personal rights there, obtained by original clearance of the forest or by inheritance. They mark these rights by planting *tawa'an* (*Dracaena terminalis*), which does not die off, at the corners of their piece of land, and prefer to occupy that plot themselves. (Graafland 1898, I:149.)

Another source from the same period goes so far as to claim that in Minahasa, land once cleared of forest remains in possession of its first cultivator and his descendants 'even in the event that he leaves the ground uncultivated for so long that it reverts to wilderness'.[15]

In view of this contrast, it is tempting to link the evidence for profligate land use and environmental degradation in the Poso Valley with the absence of permanently recognized land rights like those which were apparently traditional in Minahasa. Uncertainty of future access to any given swidden plot, might have made farmers less careful in their use of fire, and more indifferent to the spread of uncultivable grasslands. In Poso, on the other hand, the agricultural process was clearly still under effective community control; the land within each village territory was a 'governed commons' (Ostrom 1990). A more likely example of a 'tragedy of the commons' (Hardin 1968) is perhaps the rapid degradation of the barrier hills of Gorontalo, where pioneer swidden-farming settlement, by freed slaves formerly engaged in permanent-field agriculture in the Limboto Depression (see below), probably took place in the absence of any relevant cooperative rules or conventions. The abovementioned report of declining crop yields at the local transmigration site of Modoinding in Minahasa also suggests a link between pioneer settlement and unsustainable land use. In both cases, however, it must be repeated that the (previously uninhabited) sites involved were naturally less fertile than those from which their settlers came.

Whatever the role of community sanctions against unsustainable practices, it is clear that the scarcer a resource and the more continuous its exploitation, the more likely it was to be under relatively private and exclusive control. As in many other parts of the world (Boserup 1965:78-87; Pingali 1990:249-50), in the case of farmland there was a clear correlation between the exclusivity of use or ownership rights and the density of the population.[16] Minahasa, for example, was more thickly populated than the Poso Valley, and Banggai, where pieces of privately-owned swidden farmland were often bought and sold, more so than neighbouring Balantak, where such transactions were unknown.[17] The most exclusive land ownership rights of all were found in the very densely settled and largely irrigated eastern section of the Limboto Depression, where there were 'thousands of people whose very homes are built on land belonging to the nobles, and who have no land of their own

[15]   G.A. Wilken 1873:110. Also Francis 1860:345; Holleman 1930:1-2; A.J.F. Jansen 1861:238; *Rapport* 1910:9, Stakman 1893:153; Worotikan 1910:162.
[16]   'Population pressure', agrees Metzner (1982:225) in his study of another Indonesian region, 'can be assumed to have accelerated the process of individualization of land tenure'.
[17]   A.C. Kruyt 1932d:478, 1934:125. In Poso, too, the selling of land was regarded as 'an absurdity' before the Dutch conquest (Adriani and Kruyt 1912-14, II:232), whereas in Minahasa it already occurred in the early nineteenth century (see Chapter II). Li (1991:56) reports that in modern Tinombo, where the population density is high, 'the individual who first cleares land and his descendents have perpetual use rights'.

whatsoever'.[18] Elsewhere, too, irrigated land in particular tended to be the property of narrowly defined kin groups (A.C. Kruyt 1938, III:154). Because wet ricefields were 'used every year', according to Albert C. Kruyt (1924:49), farmers in the Poso Valley 'automatically began to feel that they had personal rights to these' when they were forced to create them by the Dutch after 1905. Besides their permanence and scarcity, another factor here was no doubt the considerable labour investment involved in laying them out: the automatic lapse of personal rights to swidden land in Balantak, by contrast, was said to occur when the cultivator had 'eaten his sweat from it' (A.C. Kruyt 1934:125) – that is, when a field had repaid the labour invested to clear it.[19]

Exclusive rights to *Agathis* (*damar*) trees and stands, turning to commercial resources, were traditionally claimed by particular individuals and kin groups respectively. Recognition of these claims, despite the high degree of political decentralization, initially seems to have been strong and broad enough to prevent competitive (and therefore unsustainable) tapping.[20] In the course of the *damar* export boom, however, serious conflicts arose over some *Agathis* forests in Central Sulawesi, and these were further exacerbated in the 1920s by counterproductive Dutch intervention in the allocation of the exploitation rights (Steup 1931:1131; Van der Vlies 1940:622-4). The most localized and exhaustible resources of all tended to be under direct monopoly control by political leaders. In Sangir swift nesting sites supplying edible birds' nests, a lucrative export product, were each regarded as the property of a particular *raja* (Van Delden 1844:20-1, 360; Steller 1866:12). When the *walak* chief of Kema (Tonsea) in Minahasa requested VOC support for his claim to a similar site on the offshore island of Lembeh in 1770, the Company authorities in Ternate agreed on the grounds that 'if everybody is able to collect the nests at will, then nobody has any significant benefit from them, since the birds are continually disturbed' (Edeling 1919:33). Control of the Lembeh birds' nests remained in the hands of the same family throughout the nineteenth century (Lengkong 1981), and Graafland (1867-69, I:3, 1898, I:22) observed that the site was kept under constant guard. In Gorontalo and Bolaang Mongondow nesting areas of the maleo (*Macrocephalon maleo*), a bird which incubates its large, edible eggs by burying them in beach sand, were controlled by local *raja*, whose representatives guarded the eggs against poachers.[21] The lake of Moat, not far from the populous Mongondow plain, was likewise a private domain of the Bolaang *raja*, guarded by his slaves for

---

[18]   CV Gorontalo 1864 (ANRI Manado 44).

[19]   Li (1996b:511) refers to this principle as 'an indigenous labour theory of value'.

[20]   F.J. Nieboer 1929:83; Steup 1931:1131, 1933:36; Van der Vlies 1940:621-2. In the case of rattan, by contrast, open access seems to have been the norm (Riedel 1870a:79; Siebert 1995:214-5).

[21]   *Corpus diplomaticum* VI:671; Von Rosenberg 1865:114-5. A comparable arrangement may have existed in parts of Banggai (Argeloo and Dekker 1996:60; Goedhart 1908:462).

the sake of its eels, from the flesh of which oil was manufactured (Riedel 1901:226; Schwarz and De Lange 1876:155).

In Bolaang Mongondow, Buol, and Banggai, similar arrangements also applied to *Metroxylon* sago stands.[22] In this case there was an explicit obligation on the part of the *raja* to guarantee the availability of sago to his subjects in times of famine when other crops failed.

> That the sago stands [*sagobossen*] were shown to the young ruler [on the occasion of his inauguration] is explicitly mentioned in the myth [of Buol kingship]. Here the myth is referring to the communal [*gemeenschappelijke*] sago stands, which are the property of the whole community and which may only be exploited in times of need. The ruler is the nominal owner of these stands. Their management is an integral aspect of the institution of kingship, and can in fact be regarded as one of the most important symbols of royal power. (Van Wouden 1941:378.)

Although this mythical formulation is no doubt idealized, it does show that the royal sago monopoly was perceived not (only) as one of the spoils of power, but (also) as a collective solution to the problem of managing a vital common property resource. No doubt the same was often true to a greater or lesser degree even in those cases where less essential resources were under elite control. Sustainable management of maleo nesting sites under a royal monopoly, for instance, may at least have helped ensure that maleo eggs remained on sale year after year at the public markets in Gorontalo (Von Rosenberg 1965:114).

Forest conservation

Besides protecting secondary vegetation from accidental fire, indigenous groups sometimes also conserved permanent forest stands in a deliberate way. Here again, the clearest examples come from localities where the scarcity and high value of timber made such conservation most necessary. In the 'treeless land' of the Napu Valley, the few surviving copses were 'carefully preserved by the inhabitants in order to have firewood and rattan to hand' (A.C. Kruyt 1908:1285). The 'forest reserve of the Nanusa Islands' (Holthuis and Lam 1942:127), Garete, may well have been excluded from agricultural use in order to meet the demand for boat- and housebuilding timber which existed on its densely populated neighbours. Cuarteron (1855:22) identified

---

[22] *Corpus diplomaticum* VI:671; Dormeier 1947:252-3; A.J.F. Jansen, 'Uittreksel uit het dagboek [...] gehouden op zijne dagboek reis naar de landen op de noord en westkust van Celebes [...] September en Oktober 1857' (ANRI Manado 167); Schrader 1941:125; Wilken and Schwarz 1867a:40; Van Wouden 1941:378.

Garete as the source of the wood used by Nanusa boatbuilders in the 1840s, and in the early twentieth century wood from Garete was also exported to Miangas.[23] Further south in Sangir, it appeared to the forester Heringa (1921b:733) in 1920 that while the original vegetation on Tagulandang and Greater Sangir had completely made way for coconut groves, Siau, the most densely populated member of the group, still had a few natural forest remnants, 'albeit in a substantially depleted state'. Here again, it was probably the very high local demand itself which ensured that no complete timber exhaustion was allowed to occur.

Not all instances of indigenous forest protection, on the other hand, were motivated by such directly economic considerations. 'Everywhere in the homeland of the West Toraja', wrote Albert C. Kruyt (1938, II:467), 'there are small woods [*bosjes*] where no timber may be cut, and spots which are avoided, because they are thought to be the dwelling-places of *to i kau* [tree spirits]'. Such 'ritually reserved' forest zones, unfortunately, are rarely mentioned elsewhere in the regional literature, although one source (Holthuis and Lam 1942:101) does state that on otherwise deforested Miangas there was 'a very small grove' on the refuge hill in the centre of the island which was 'preserved as a sort of sanctuary'. By analogy with traditional swidden farming systems elsewhere in Southeast Asia, it is likely that such sanctuaries were in fact widespread.[24] A fearful respect for individual trees was certainly common. 'Some tall trees', noted Woensdregt (1928:162) in Bada, 'may not be felled under any circumstances, since they are regarded as the particular dwelling-places of spirits'.[25]

Dutch forest protection measures in northern Sulawesi began at a rather early date, but were characterized by false starts, a false perception that swidden farming led automatically to progressive destruction of old forest, and limited effectiveness. In 1858, local chiefs in Minahasa were already

[23] Lam 1932:47-8. A report from 1906 notes that one type of boat customarily built in Nanusa is 'mainly used for the transport of planks and suchlike' (AV Manado 1906, in ANRI Manado 30).
[24] Conklin (1957:34) estimated that as much as one third of the primary forest within the territory of the Hanunoo community which he studied in Mindoro was protected by 'religious taboos'.
[25] Other sources, however, suggest that as in Java (Boomgaard 1992:48), such supernatural protection was seldom very absolute (Adriani and Kruyt 1950-51, II:55; A.C. Kruyt 1932d:480). A small offering (betel, a chicken) and an appropriately phrased invitation were usually enough to persuade the guardian spirit to move elsewhere, whereupon the tree in question was promptly 'cut down all the same' (A.C. Kruyt 1934:129). It can never be assumed that religious taboos protecting plants or animals were effective. While Kruyt (1935:7) reported that crocodiles in Lake Poso, being regarded as blood relatives of man, were never hunted, a nineteenth-century report from Gorontalo states that although local people 'worship' the crocodiles of Lake Limboto, they are also 'very skilled in the capture of these voracious animals, and even torture them once they are caught' (AV Gorontalo 1841-43, in ANRI Manado 50).

instructed 'to discourage the burning of forest for opening new agricultural fields, and to make this practice conditional upon the acquisition of a special licence'.[26] Experiments with active reforestation began at the same period, and by 1862 more than 50,000 ironwood, teak, and other saplings had been planted 'in order to meet the increasing demand for good timber'.[27] This very labour-intensive activity, however, was quickly abandoned, and despite some renewed interest in the twentieth century, deliberate planting of timber trees never again occurred on a large scale in colonial Minahasa (Steup 1932:146; Weg 1938:172-3). State control of swidden clearance and burning, meanwhile, also proved impossible for the time being, and by 1891 a complementary restriction on timber extraction for domestic purposes had likewise fallen into disuse (*Uittreksel* 1914:3). Not until the turn of the century (Van Kol 1903:248) did state forest protection in Minahasa begin to take effect, and not until the years 1923-1929 were definitive boundaries established beyond which, in order to safeguard the remaining watershed forests, no further farming or felling was permitted.[28] In 1919, meanwhile, two small dedicated nature reserves (*natuurmonumenten*) were also established in sparsely populated Tonsea (*Verslag Dienst Boschwezen* 1921-22:30). Eleven percent of the land area of Minahasa, or virtually all of the remaining primary forest, had protected status in the 1930s (Stuurman 1936:88).

Attempts at forest protection outside Minahasa did not begin until the 1920s, when reservation and reforestation projects were undertaken in Palu and Gorontalo. Farmers on the hillsides around the Limboto Depression were obliged, for a time, to plant their swiddens after a single year of food-crop production with teak, *johar* and other saplings (Frohwein 1933:18). Protecting the young trees from drought, fire, grazing animals, and the apparent indifference of the farmers, however, proved difficult, and like the earlier attempts at active reforestation in Minahasa, this scheme was not a success.[29] In Palu, as we have seen, the natural reforestation of zones from which farmers were completely excluded gave more promising results. In this area there were very significant consequences for local communities, some of which were permanently relocated to non-protected areas (Vorstman 1935b:21). Overall, however, state forest protection had little influence on the extent of cultivation and deforestation during the colonial period. In 1941 only 4.2 percent of the area of the residency, or 5.7 percent of the estimated forest area, had reserved status (Boomgaard 1996a:166), and only a part of

---

26   CV Manado 1858 (ANRI Manado 48).
27   CV Manado 1862 (ANRI Ambon 1563).
28   Holleman 1930:6; *Verslag Dienst Boschwezen* 1921-22:41, 1923:34.
29   A recurrent problem with active replanting schemes was that the saplings required much care and were very sensitive to drought (*Verslag Dienst Boschwezen* 1923:34; Grondijs 1931:7-12).

the reserve forest would have been much affected by human activity had it been unprotected.

Climate change as a result of deforestation?

As in the Palu Valley in the twentieth century (see Chapter XIII), the reasons for early forest protection attempts in Minahasa included the conviction that the clearance of forest was harmful to the local climate. According to its designer, Resident Jansen, the swidden licence system abortively introduced in 1858 was intended 'to prevent further destruction of timber and excessive deforestation of the uplands, which has such a deleterious effect upon the climate, and hence upon agriculture'.[30] Despite its disconcerting resonances with the modern environmental awareness, this was not in fact an unusual view in colonial circles at that date; 'ideas about deforestation, desiccation and climatic change', Grove (1997:5) has shown, had already been popular in Europe since the middle of the eighteenth century, 'often as a basis for proposing large scale forest conservation'.

The strength of the relationship between forest cover and climate is still a matter of considerable debate, but it appears that deforestation must occur over very large areas before its effect on precipitation patterns becomes significant.[31] Rainfall statistics recorded between 1882 and 1933 at Masarang, in the centre of the Minahasan plateau, certainly do not indicate that annual precipitation averages declined during this period of considerable deforestation; if anything, the trend is slightly upward (Figure 16).[32] Nor does there seem to have been any downward trend in annual precipitation in dry Palu between 1909, when records began there, and 1941 (Metzner 1981a:47). Since a relatively dry climate, in Sulawesi, offers a number of distinct advantages for agricultural purposes (Chapter XI), it is perhaps worth adding that any such decline which did take place in earlier periods would not necessarily have been problematic for the human population.

---

[30]   CV Manado 1858 (ANRI Manado 48). Reinwardt (1858:582), writing in 1821, also believed that the 'densely forested mountains' of Minahasa ensured reliable rainfall.
[31]   Ward and Robinson 1990:47. Knapen (2001:35) shows that deforestation has apparently led to declining average annual rainfall in Southeast Borneo during the twentieth century.
[32]   The regression line shown carries an R^2 value of 0.01. Masarang, at about 900 m altitude, is the weather station in the Minahasan uplands where measurements began at the earliest date.

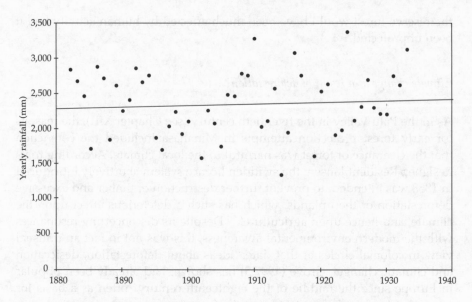

Figure 16. Annual rainfall at Masarang (Minahasa), 1882-1933.
Source: *Regenwaarnemingen* 1882-1933; some missing months filled
in with monthly averages given by Boerema (1931:204).

Human activity and wild animal populations

Destruction of natural forest habitats, although still limited in regional
terms prior to 1930, was no doubt already disastrous for wild animal species
restricted to particular localities. Given that the Cerulean paradise-flycatcher
(Eutrichomyias rowleyi), for example, lived only in natural forest on populous
Sangir, it is surprising that small numbers of these birds have managed to
survive up to the present (Whitten, Mustafa and Henderson 2002:xvi). The
construction of coastal roads and the agricultural settlement which this
encouraged, together with incipient overexploitation of the eggs in response
to growing demand in local markets, led to a serious reduction in the maleo
population of the Gorontalo area in the 1920s.[33] The conversion of forest to
secondary woodland and grassland, conversely, was favourable, and often
intentionally so, for other animals, particularly deer and wild pigs.[34] Possibly
the indigenous babirusa or 'pig-deer' (Babyrousa babirussa) also benefited
here. In the 1930s, the size of the game stock (wildstand) in heavily deforested

[33]   Uno 1949:151. In 1938, consequently, a reserve was established in Gorontalo to protect the
bird (Uno 1949:153).
[34]   Boomgaard (1997b) and Kathirithamby-Wells (1997) note that throughout colonial
Indonesia and Malaya, large herbivores were most numerous in areas of swidden cultivation
and forest disturbance.

Minahasa was said to be 'not unfavourable; wild pigs, deer, and babirusa even cause much damage [to crops] here and there' (Stuurman 1936:92).

If hunting made little impact on the growing pig and deer population, it had serious consequences for some other species. The crocodiles of Lake Limboto, for instance, seem to have been exterminated within a decade after the colonial government began to pay a bounty for every animal killed there, or crocodile egg dug up, in 1858.[35] Overhunting of birds, using firearms, was reported in Minahasa from the middle of the nineteenth century onward.[36] Sea turtles, in the same period, reportedly became scarcer in Sangir (Steller 1866:21) and Togian (Van Musschenbroek 1880:98) as a result of hunting for their shells.[37] Fishing practices, by contrast, mostly seem to have been sustainable. 'Since time immemorial', wrote Riedel (1895b:1730) regarding the important shrimp fishery in Lake Limboto, 'more than 6,000 kg have been hauled out every day for food, without causing any perceptible reduction of the stock'. Overfishing using traditional fish poison may nevertheless have been a problem in places (Van Doren 1854-56, I:256; Van Spreeuwenberg 1845-46:195), and in the early twentieth century there was also some dynamite fishing at sea (Ter Laag 1920:55). Little information, unfortunately, exists regarding traditional fishery management practices. Privately-owned fish pens were found along the margins of Lake Limboto and Lake Tondano, where exclusive fishing rights to some stretches of unenclosed water perhaps also existed.[38] No such rights, however, applied on Lake Poso (Adriani and Kruyt 1950-51, III:381), and open access was probably also the norm at sea, although particular communities did make exclusive claims to some fishing grounds in Sangir and Banggai.[39]

Several non-native species of fish were introduced into the lakes and rivers of northern Sulawesi in late colonial times (Schuster 1950:72-5), in some cases with disastrous consequences for the populations of indigenous fresh-

---

[35]   A total of 71 crocodiles and 250 eggs were destroyed in the first six months (AV Manado 1858, in ANRI Manado 52), 470 animals were killed in a single month in December 1864, and after 1865 there were no more reports of bounty payments (MV Manado, December 1864 and February-April 1865, in ANRI Manado 54). No crocodiles are mentioned in a description of the lake from 1883 (Guillemard 1886:208-9).

[36]   *Fragment* 1856:33; Graafland 1898, I:44; Grudelbach 1849:403.

[37]   At the end of the eighteenth century, by contrast, Woodard (1969:96) claimed that turtle-shell was obtained without killing the turtles: 'There are plenty of turtle: though the natives do not eat them, they catch them for the sake of their tortoiseshell, which they can scale off without injury to the animal, and let it escape again.'

[38]   Tondano: Adam 1925b:489; J. Grudelbach, 'Gevoelen over de topografische schetsen van den Luitenant J.J. ten Siethoff', 24-12-1846 (ANRI Manado 46). Limboto: S.R. Nur, interview, 4-5-1995. The *raja* of Limboto and Gorontalo levied a tax on fishing in Lake Limboto; it is not clear whether any further intervention was also involved here (Riedel 1870a:92; R. Scherius 1847:416).

[39]   Adhuri 1993:146-8; Thufail 1994:5-6; A.C. Kruyt 1932c:271.

water fish and molluscs (Whitten, Mustafa and Henderson 1987:50-2, 293-4). One such introduction, that of the *mujair* (*Tilapia mossambica*) to Lake Lindu, brought an unexpected benefit for the local human population. Apparently because the new fish either preyed on the molluscan intermediate hosts of the responsible parasite, or competed with it for phytoplankton food, the debilitating disease echinostomiasis disappeared entirely from the Lindu valley between 1956 and 1971 (Carney, Sudomo and Purnomo 1980).

Agricultural intensification and disintensification

The relationship between demography and deforestation, it was noted in Chapter XIV, was critically mediated by the extent to which increases in population were accompanied by shifts from swidden to permanent-field farming systems, particularly wet rice cultivation. At least in its simpler forms, without the use of the plough or the construction of large water control works, wet rice farming was indigenous to northern Sulawesi (see Chapter II). In the twentieth century a certain amount of technical irrigation, using large engineered dams, was provided under Dutch direction in Gorontalo (Korn 1939:14; Morison 1931:49-50) and in the Palu Valley (Dutrieux 1931a:11; Vorstman 1935:21-2). Some authors (Acciaioli 1989:66; Metzner 1981a:47) have suggested that the original introduction of wet rice cultivation to Palu between 1660 and 1680 was also associated with foreign influence, this time in the form of Bugis immigration; the great exodus from South Sulawesi, which led to the establishment of Bugis colonies in many parts of Indonesia, was initiated by the Dutch conquest of Makasar in 1669 (L.Y. Andaya 1995; Reid 1992:501-2). With these exceptions, however, there is little reason to think of the distribution of irrigated farming in terms of technological diffusion or culture contact.

While colonial observers, who invariably regarded irrigation as a superior system, tended to attribute it to past contacts with 'higher' cultures, indigenous informants disagreed. In Tondano farmers claimed that the usefulness of irrigation had been discovered accidentally in situ – an interpretation which derives credibility from the fact that some of the local rice varieties could be grown on both dry and flooded fields (De Clercq 1871d:4).

> *Sawah* cultivation, according to local stories, originated when a certain Tondanese laid out a dry ricefield next to a patch of muddy ground. Desiring to keep his field as square as possible, he sowed *padi* on part of the wet area, and to his surprise it grew better there than on the dry ground. After that people began to make *sawah* fields systematically, and became progressively more proficient at doing so. Although there is nothing imposssible about this story, it is surely more probable that the Tondanese learned this technique from foreigners. (N.P. Wilken 1870:373.)

In Napu, likewise, one farmer told Albert C. Kruyt (1938, IV:18) that irrigation there had developed by trial and error following the observation that rice planted on swampy ground produced better yields than swidden rice during a drought; another man stated that *sawah* farming had in fact been the original system, and swiddening a later development.[40] Knowledge of irrigation techniques, significantly, was a good deal more widespread than their actual practice. Adriani (1915:470) noted that although farmers in the Poso Valley had never made irrigated fields themselves, they nevertheless 'knew perfectly well what was involved in wet rice cultivation' as a result of long contact with their *sawah*-farming neighbours in Lore.[41]

One common way of thinking about the relationship between these two farming systems is based on the assumption that swidden cultivation, although profligate in its use of land, is more efficient in terms of returns to labour. Swiddening, in this analysis, always represents the most rational choice of farming technique unless land becomes scarce, in which case farmers have little choice but to adopt the more labour-intensive irrigated system. Scarcity of land might arise either because of in situ population growth, as classically proposed by Ester Boserup in *The conditions of agricultural growth* (1965:59-61), or alternatively due to centripetal migration, resulting in a local concentration of the existing population. In the Indonesian historical context, according to an influential argument by Michael Dove (1985a:12-35), one common reason for such demographic concentration has been political pressure from state elites seeking more effective control over subject populations and their agricultural surplus.

The empirical basis for the orthodox assumption that the transition from swidden to *sawah* must inevitably involve a decline in labour productivity is surprisingly fragile. In an early comparison of field studies from several parts of Southeast Asia, Hanks (1972:64) already showed that although swidden farmers did tend to work fewer hours in the fields than their *sawah*-farming counterparts, their labour, at least when the initial investment needed to create irrigation infrastructure was left out of consideration, was often less productive. Wet-rice farmers who sowed their seed by direct broadcasting, in fact, produced up to twice as much rice as swidden cultivators for each day of work performed.[42] Padoch (1985:282, 286) later found that under the favourable topographic and soil conditions provided by some upland val-

---

[40]   These origin stories, unusually, feature no mythological elements; farmers clearly regarded the possibility of irrigation as a matter of common sense.

[41]   In the past, indeed, immigrants from elsewhere had repeatedly practised wet rice farming on a small scale in the Poso area itself (Adriani and Kruyt 1950-51, III:7).

[42]   A limitation here is that Hanks considers only the production of rice, whereas in fact almost all swiddens (and some irrigated fields) also produce many secondary crops. The same applies to the comparable recent survey by Knapen (2001:200) using data from Kalimantan.

leys in Kalimantan, irrigation was more labour-efficient than swiddening even when *sawah* farmers used the more laborious technique of transplanting seedlings from nursery beds. Recently, Robert Hunt (2000) has re-assessed the existing Southeast Asian evidence for the orthodox view and concluded that according to all of the field studies which permit rigorous comparison in this respect, *sawah* farming actually has a much higher labour productivity than swiddening in terms of rice yield per person-day of routine cultivation work invested.[43] As other writers have pointed out, moreover, rice grown in wet fields often has the additional advantage of being less vulnerable to adverse weather, so that its yields are more stable and reliable from year to year.[44]

These observations support the suggestion by Reid (1988-93, I:20) that until quite recent times, the distribution of wet rice farming in Southeast Asia was 'determined primarily by the physical conditions of each area and only secondarily by population pressure'.[45] In northern Sulawesi, certainly, early wet fields were mostly found in those places where they could be construct-ed without much elaborate terracing, fed by small streams which were easily diverted and controlled without the aid of major earthworks, and practised in tandem with swiddening as a way of diversifying the farming system (see Chapters II and XI). The restricted distribution of such ideal natural sites for wet fields, on the other hand, seems to have set tight limits to the amount of land which farmers were prepared to bring under irrigation in the absence of political or demographic pressure. During the mid-nineteenth century, repeated Dutch orders to expand the area under irrigation in Minahasa were certainly unpopular.[46] A report from 1862 states that except in a few places around the Tondano and Tonsawang (Buliling) lakes where marshy ground 'automatically forces the population to grow its *padi* on wet fields', irrigation is practised only 'in proportion to the fear which exists for the unpleasant consequences of disobedience'.[47]

Most often this resistance was ascribed to conservatism or, strangely in view of the antiquity of wet rice farming in Minahasa, to ignorance. Some

[43]   Again, however, it should be noted that the production data used by Hunt do not include non-rice crops, and that his labour data do not include initial infrastructural investments.
[44]   Conelly 1992:213; Hanks 1972:56; Terra 1952:17, 19, 1958:160, 162, 169, 175. One reason for this is of course a more constant supply of water (even on the simplest rain-fed diked fields) to the growing plants (Christiansen 1986:17). Another is that wet rice farming involves no burning of slashed fallow vegetation, a stage in the swidden cycle which is vulnerable to disruption by wet weather (Padoch 1985:284).
[45]   Leach (1999:318-21) has provided a detailed critique of demographic explanations for the spread of irrigation in the Pacific area.
[46]   AV Manado 1833 (ANRI Manado 48); CV Manado 1856, 1861, 1862, 1864, 1866 (ANRI Manado 39, 51, 52, 95; Ambon 1563); Francis 1860:355; Graafland 1898, I:148; A.J.F. Jansen 1861: 232; MV Manado, September 1853 (ANRI Manado 54); N.P. Wilken 1870:374.
[47]   CV Manado 1862 (ANRI Ambon 1563).

European observers, however, recognized that one practical concern here was the maintenance of cropping diversity: unlike *sawah*, 'the dry fields, besides *padi*, also yield many other products including firewood, vegetables, pumpkins, *patatas* [sweet potato], and above all maize'.[48] Resident Jansen (1861:232), moreover, concluded that 'wet fields, where these are not formed by nature, demand a quantity of labour, both in order to create them and in order to maintain the water channels and suchlike, which in many places exceeds the capacity of the local population'.[49] On this point he was at odds with many other Dutch officials, who believed that swiddening, because it involved the constant clearance of forest, was more laborious (at least in the long run) than irrigated farming.[50] What does seem clear is that the initial labour investment required to construct bunded or terraced fields and water channels in less than optimal locations, as Conelly (1992:218, 220) has confirmed in a field study from the Philippines, formed a major disincentive to this form of intensification.[51]

The area under irrigation in Minahasa, nevertheless, increased rapidly during the late nineteenth and early twentieth centuries, from about 20 km^2 in 1860 to over 130 km^2 by 1920 (Chapter XIV, Table 30). To what extent this was a strictly 'Boserupian' response to population growth and the resulting scarcity of land is difficult to say, since Dutch officials, convinced that wet rice farming was superior to swiddening in terms of productivity, reliability, and timber conservation, and also concerned for political reasons to prevent Minahasans from living for long periods in scattered swidden huts (Schouten 1998:59), continued to apply direct pressure on the population to lay out *sawah* complexes regardless of whether or not swidden land was in short supply.[52] At least at the aggregate level, as already noted, there does not seem to have been a decline in swidden yields or a shortening of fallow periods significant enough to make a transition to permanent-field farming necessary for reasons of sustainability alone. Another complication here is that part of the *sawah* expansion took place not on former dry fields, but on new land reclaimed

[48]   N.P. Wilken 1870:374. Also A.J.F. Jansen 1861:232; Wilken and Schwarz 1867c:364.
[49]   Also CV Belang 1873 (ANRI Manado 19).
[50]   CV Manado 1856 (ANRI Manado 51), 1859 (ANRI Ambon 1543); Edeling 1919:46, 58; N.P. Wilken 1870:374; Wilken and Schwarz 1867c:364.
[51]   The additional pressures of compulsory coffee cultivation and roadbuilding (see Chapter X) must have made this especially so in nineteenth-century Minahasa.
[52]   In 1871, for instance, such pressure was exercised in the still sparsely-populated southeastern district of Ponosakan on two grounds: that 'the chances of a successful harvest are much better on wet than on dry fields', and that a village built in the vicinity of *sawah* is 'permanently inhabited', whereas for a population which 'lives for the greater part of the year in swidden huts', the construction and maintenance of the large nuclear villages favoured by the government is 'a heavy burden' ('Stukken omtrent aanleggen van sawa's velden door Tonsawang in het District Ponosakan', 24-8-1871, in ANRI Manado 101).

specifically for that purpose from Lake Tondano: at least four times during the colonial period (in 1862, 1875, 1895, and 1913) the water level in the lake was artificially lowered, by state public works projects involving the deepening of the outlet channel, in order to create additional lakeside *sawah*.[53]

Yet a more or less direct causal link between population pressure and the adoption of wet rice farming does seem to have existed in some places and periods. Certainly political compulsion was not the only factor: a cultivation report from 1864 notes the beginnings of a 'gratifying' trend toward 'more passive and obedient' attitudes to state-sponsored agricultural innovation among the Minahasan population, and in general Dutch sources from after 1870 no longer portray the degree of local resentment toward irrigation initiatives which is evident from earlier documents.[54] The missionary Wilken (1870:374) observed in the 1860s that if all the inhabitants of Tondano were to cultivate swiddens (like most other Minahasans) instead of *sawah*, they 'would quickly run short of ricefields, or at least be compelled to make these at a great distance from the *negeri*'. A report from the same area in 1873 is explicit that one (though not the only) reason for the popularity of wet rice cultivation was the growing scarcity of land for swidden farming:

> Ignorance of the advantages of the wet over the dry cultivation method, together with a very understandable attachment to practices followed since olden times, still form obstacles here and there to the spread of wet *padi* cultivation. Progress, however, is definitely evident in this respect: witness the construction of substantial waterworks in the district of Langoan, where in the past there was a marked aversion to creating *sawah* fields but where in the last year the population, acting entirely of its own accord, has made some 300 *bau* [200 ha] of additional land fit for *sawah* cultivation. This is an increasingly desirable and necessary course of action in the [Tondano] division both because of the [economic] advantages which it offers, and because woodland in which to open new dry fields is becoming more and more scarce.[55]

If the factor of increasing land scarcity is consistent with Boserup's demographic interpretation of agricultural intensification, the second consideration cited here in relation to the desirability of irrigation, economic advantage, recalls the alternative view of Netting (1993:288-94) and others that a more common reason for farmers to raise per hectare labour and capital inputs is 'market pull' in the form of increased commercial demand for agricul-

---

[53]   *Adatvonissen* 1914:84; CV Manado 1862 (ANRI Ambon 1563); Dirkzwager 1912:1164; Graafland 1898, II:188-9; Horsting 1917:229; Logeman 1922:63; MV Manado, 4-1862 (ANRI Manado 54); Schouten 1998:58.
[54]   CV Manado 1864 (ANRI Manado 39); CV Manado 1879 (ANRI Manado 86); Van Geuns 1906:81; Graafland 1898, I:148; Wattendorf 1883.
[55]   CV Tondano 1873 (ANRI Manado 19).

tural products.[56] The second half of the nineteenth century, it was argued in Chapter IX, saw a dramatic improvement of the domestic market system in Minahasa, including the market for foodstuffs, as a result of social changes, road improvements, and an influx of cash income from compulsory coffee cultivation and (in lowland areas) free smallholder copra production. Whether or not it was routinely more labour-efficient to grow rice on wet than on dry fields, *sawah* certainly permitted a greater total production per unit area given a willingness to maximize labour investments. In this light, the expansion of irrigation in densely populated parts of Minahasa after 1860 might be interpreted partly as an attempt by farmers to take advantage of the growing commercial demand for rice by increasing their total production of this crop under conditions of local land scarcity (which precluded areal expansion).

A look at the recorded harvest statistics, on the other hand, shows that most of the production increase was accounted for my maize, at that period still almosts exclusivel a swidden crop, rather than rice (Chapter IX, Fig. 5). Per capita rice production, in fact, remained approximately stable after 1860, suggesting either that for technical reasons rice cultivation was less able to keep pace with the growing commercial demand for food than was maize production, or that the expansion of irrigatin, in accordance with the Boserup model, was dictated less by price incentives to surplus production than by an endeavour to maintain rice harvests at existing levels under conditions of growing land scarcity. The transition from dry to wet rice farming, nevertheless, was no doubt facilitated by the simultaneous expansion of trade i non-rice foodstuffs (especially maise), which reduced the advantages associateed with the greater variety of crops which could be grown on swiddenfields.

Whatever the relative contributions of demographic pressure and commercial demand to the intensification process in Minahasa, irrigated farming itself certainly took increasingly labour-intensive forms as the population continued to grow. Noting that Tondanese farmers still sow their rice seed directly onto their *sawah* rather than in separate nursery beds as was customary on Java, a cultivation report from 1879 predicts that they will neverthe-

---

[56]   Examples of this alternative interpretation can be found in the Indonesian literature. In this detailed study of agriculture and population pressure on Flores in the 1970s, Metzner (1982: 205) concluded that although labour-intensive intercropping techniques had allowed unirrigated farmland to support a rapidly growing population at surprisingly high densities, quantitative variations in the labour-intensity of agriculture from place to place were correlated less with population density itself than with the degree to which the local economy was 'commercialized' (his own term). Scholz (1988:215), in his comprehensive agrarian geography of Sumatra in the 1980s, agreed that recent trends toward irrigated rice forming and 'intensive planting of perennial crops' had been 'the result of the invading money economy rather than of population pressure'.

Plate 38. Women transplanting rice seedlings on an irrigated field, Minahasa, 1945 (KITLV Photograph 6660)

less adopt the more laborious technique as soon as 'the limited availability
of land forces them to cultivate in a more intensive way'.[57] By 1906 the use
of seedbeds and transplanting had indeed begun to replace broadcast sowing (Van Geuns 1906:80), and by the 1940s it was standard practice (Plate
38). In addition, *sawah* which had formerly lain fallow in the dry season (see
Chapter II) were now planted after the rice harvest with maize and other
secondary crops, and by 1920 there were also some wet fields which produced two rice harvests every year (Van Marle 1922, I:73, 75). At the end of
the colonial period, by which stage the population density on one part of the
Tondano plateau had risen to 400 persons per km^2 (see Chapter V), the level
of interest in wet rice cultivation among Minahasans was at last described by
a Dutch Resident as 'adequate' (M. van Rhijn 1941:42).

When Dutch efforts to promote irrigation were extended to Sangir,
Talaud, and Central Sulawesi after the beginning of the twentieth century,
they encountered the same initial resistance as in Minahasa.[58] On Sangir,
where suitable terrain was said to be scarce and most of it 'already occupied
by sago palms' (Tergast 1936:139), these efforts remained completely unsuc-

---

[57]   CV Manado 1879 (ANRI Manado 86).
[58]   Adriani 1915:470; Adriani and Kruyt 1912-14, I:150, 1950-51, III:8; *Brieven* 5-7-1912; Dutrieux

cessful despite the very high local population densities, which in principle should have made the areal productivity of *sawah* attractive. In sparsely-populated Central Sulawesi, by contrast, a considerable expansion of irrigation did occur under Dutch pressure. Both the motivation and the method here, to an even greater extent than in Minahasa, was to resettle the population in large new villages where it could more easily be supervised and controlled:

> In the old days, people only lived permanently in the village if their farmland happened to be very nearby. For most of the year they lived in their houses on the swiddens, visiting the village only for festivities and meetings, or when there were rumours of war. Now, however, this freedom was gone, since in the new villages everybody was under regular supervision. If the old type of agriculture had been continued, the now much larger villages would obviously have required a very great area of farmland around them. Naturally there could be no more question of moving constantly to and fro; the houses were now more solidly built, the plots of land around them well planted, most villages had a school and a teacher's residence, and it was desirable to concentrate the farmland in their immediate vicinity. It is, therefore, very fortunate that the Government has forced the Toraja to lay out irrigated ricefields. (Adriani 1915:470.)

This, then, was a classic example of the kind of intensification process described by Dove (1985a) in which the state, partly by direct means and partly by concentrating the population in settlements so large that swidden farming is no longer practical, brings about a shift to permanent-field cultivation which facilitates taxation and political control.

A more complex illustration of the links between political factors, population density, and intensive agriculture is provided by Gorontalo. In the seventeenth and eighteenth centuries power-holders in this area consistently endeavoured to concentrate the population, 'in order to control and exploit it better' (Van Hoëvell 1891:32), on the eastern part of the Limboto Depression in the immediate hinterland of the capital.[59] By the early nineteenth century, no doubt at least partly as a consequence of this concentration, Gorontalo was one of the main centres of wet rice agriculture in the region and also the only area where ploughing and manuring were applied to continuously cultivated dry fields (see Chapter II). After 1860, however, much of the farmland on the floor of the Depression was suddenly abandoned and its irrigation systems fell into disuse. From about 25 km^2 in 1854, the area under *sawah* declined to only 7 km^2 in 1916.[60]

1931a:11; De Haze Winkelman 1935:4; A.C. Kruyt 1924:41-7, 1932d:474; *Militaire memorie Parigi* 1929:6; Roep 1917:432; Schrader 1941:125; Tergast 1936:138.

[59]   After 1729, the resident Dutch officials seem to have been involved in this endeavour (Riedel 1870a:68) as well as the indigenous *raja*.

[60]   The estimate for 1854 is based on a reported total of 10,179 irrigated fields or *panimbang*,

Several changes were responsible for this remarkable disintensification process, the opposite of what was happening in Minahasa at the same period. Repeated outbreaks of lethal disease, firstly, affected the water buffalo used for ploughing throughout the second half of the nineteenth century (see Chapter XIV). Increased temporary emigration, in connection with forest product collection, may also have played a role after 1870 (Haga 1931:234). The main factor, however, was the emancipation of the Gorontalese slaves in 1859. 'The sole owners of land', states a Dutch report from that year, 'are the nobles, who force their slaves, or the commoners, to work it in return for an insignificant wage'.[61] Once freed from bondage to their masters and land-lords, large numbers of slaves abandoned the *sawah* for the hills surrounding the depression, where unclaimed land was apparently available for swidden farming (Gonggrijp 1915:1363-5; Van Kol 1903:337-8). Others left the Gorontalo area entirely (Monoarga 1937:367), many migrating to Minahasa. The labour supply on the plain was now insufficient to sustain the existing agricultural activities and in fact much of the land here, which remained in the possession of its original owners, fell into complete disuse (Van Geuns 1906:26).

After 1915 the disintensification trend was reversed and the abandoned *sawah* brought back into cultivation, mostly under a system of sharecropping (Peddemors 1935:29-30). Under Dutch supervision an area of 29 km^2 was supplied with technical irrigation between 1920 and 1931; at the end of that period, the total irrigated area in Gorontalo stood at almost 40 km^2 (Morison 1931:50, 53). A recovery of livestock numbers following the replacement of water buffalo by cattle (see Chapter XIV) probably played a role here, but another factor was no doubt accelerated population growth, which, despite continuing centrifugal migration, tipped the political balance in favour of the landowners once more.

The extent of irrigation, then, was determined by a combination of environmental, demographic, economic and political factors. Topography, hydrology and soil characteristics made wet fields attractive propositions in some localities even at low population densities, and effectively ruled them out in others regardless of demography: in the 1930s the agricultural extension officer Tergast (1936:138) advised against any attempt to promote *sawah* farming on Talaud partly on the grounds that 'since the soil is not very fertile, good harvests, which are surely desirable when making propaganda

---

of which about 7,000 had an area of about 112, and the rest about 312, square Rhineland roods each (CV Gorontalo 1854, in ANRI Gorontalo 3). Other sources from the same period suggest a similar total area (Res. Manado to GG, 30-9-1849, in ANRI Gorontalo 18; CV Gorontalo 1860, in ANRI Manado 95). The stated figure for 1916 was 1,000 *bau* (Moolenberg 1921:18). Other sources (Van Geuns 1906:26; Gonggrijp 1915:1363-5; Haga 1931:234; Van Kol 1903:337-8) describe the abandonment of *sawah* and other farmland without giving quantitative details.
[61]   CV Manado 1859 (ANRI Ambon 1543).

for something new, cannot be guaranteed'. Rising population densities, nevertheless, sometimes resulted in the extension of irrigation to less naturally
favourable areas as a response to increasing scarcity of land. Demographic
dispersals, conversely, could have the opposite effect, as in Gorontalo after
1859. The decline in *sawah* cultivation in Napu in the second half of the nineteenth century (see Chapter II), comparably, seems to have been caused partly by male emigration in connection with warfare and *damar* collection (A.C.
Kruyt 1908:1313-4; Kruyt and Kruyt 1921:409). Enhanced economic incentives to maximize rice production may have worked in tandem with population pressure to stimulate the spread of irrigation in colonial Minahasa; on
Sangir, conversely, the profitability of the (already established) smallholder
coconut and nutmeg plantations combined with topographic factors to prevent a similar development from occurring in the early twentieth century.
Political centralization favoured intensification both indirectly, by giving rise
to dense concentrations of population, and directly, since some power-holders, whether simply in order to make these demographic concentrations possible, or in order to facilitate the control and transport of the food surplus by
keeping the ricefields tightly grouped, organized the provision of irrigation
infrastructure themselves.[62] Such direct intervention was not unique to the
colonial government. A Gorontalo *raja* apparently ordered the construction
of a major irrigation canal in 1744, and in the Palu Valley around 1900 the
raja of Sigi was himself the owner of extensive irrigated fields, worked by his
subjects as a form of taxation.[63]

In the complex web of historical interactions between irrigation, demography, economics and politics, directions of causality are often ambiguous.
It is possible that in some places the existence of wet rice farming, because it
encouraged concentrated settlement and facilitated surplus extraction, was a
cause, rather than a consequence, of social stratification and political centralization.[64] On the whole, however, the evidence suggests that state formation
in northern Sulawesi was associated in the first place with maritime trade
rather than foodcrop agriculture (see Chapter I). The upland valleys which
offered the best natural opportunities for irrigation did not give rise to large
centralized polities, while the expanses of laboriously constructed lowland

[62]   Albert C. Kruyt (1938, I:501) attributed the formation of large nuclear settlements in the
Palu Valley to 'the guiding power of members of the aristocracy' and also noted a 'close association' in local oral tradition between social stratification, which was more pronounced here than
further east, and *sawah* cultivation.
[63]   NA VOC 2649:111; A.C. Kruyt 1938, I:508.
[64]   Other mechanisms are also conceivable here. In upland western Central Sulawesi, according to Albert C. Kruyt (1938, I:502, 508), members of the social elite were able 'to make the common people dependent upon them' thanks to their monopoly control of the water buffalo used
to till the wet fields.

sawah in Parigi, the Palu Valley, and the Limboto Depression were there primarily due to the activities of local kingdoms which derived their wealth and
power largely from trade in gold, slaves, coconut oil, and forest products.[65]

A final case of intensification which deserves discussion here concerns not
a shift to irrigated or permanent-field cultivation, but a change in the technology of swidden farming. As Wigboldus (1988:54-7) has pointed out, a significant increase in both labour inputs and areal yields appears to have taken
place in Minahasan agriculture between the seventeenth century and the
beginning of the nineteenth. Padtbrugge (1866:324-5), describing Minahasan
farming practices in 1679, paints a picture familiar from many other parts of
the region two centuries later: the soil 'is neither turned nor ploughed', and
the rice seed is planted in individual holes made using dibbling sticks. By
the 1820s, however, an unusual system of broadcast sowing was also in use
on some swiddens.[66] This involved the preparation of the whole field, to a
depth of about 10 cm, with a hard, narrow wooden spade called (in Tombulu)
a *wahi*.[67] Dibbling, according to a later description by Graafland (1864:8-9),
demanded 'less work' than the combination of shallow tillage and broadcast
sowing, but also gave 'a less abundant harvest'.[68]

Edeling observed in 1875 that the two methods were typically applied in
different locations: sowing 'in the mountains', dibbling 'near the coast, and
also on sloping ground'.[69] It is possible, then, that Padtbrugge's description applies only to coastal areas, and that sowing was already practised
elsewhere in Minahasa in his time. Padtbrugge, however, had visited the
central plateau himself, and the remainder of his account appears to relate

[65]   It is worth noting, nevertheless, that Palu also exported rice (to nearby Donggala) in the
nineteenth century (Hissink 1912:121; *Landschap Donggala* 1905:516) and that Gorontalo, according to Rumphius (1750, V:198), exported some specifically *sawah*-grown rice in the seventeenth
century.
[66]   The use of tools to till the soil on swidden fields is also mentioned, or implied, in sources
dealing with several other areas (Adriani 1901:236; Boonstra van Heerdt 1914a:638; Van Hoëvell
1893b:41; A.C. Kruyt 1938, I:183; Woensdregt 1928:188-90; Woodard 1969:91). Except on *sawah*,
however, broadcast sowing is not. Outside Minahasa dibbling was apparently employed even
on prepared soil (Van Delden 1844:17-8; Tergast 1936:136; Woensdregt 1928:195, 200), which suggests that tillage was less thorough.
[67]   AV Manado 1833 (ANRI Manado 48); Riedel 1872b:540. A fuller description of this technique is given by Wilken (1870:376), who adds that tillage was often repeated after planting
in order to eliminate weeds. As on broadcast-sown wet fields (see Chapter II), some plants
were shifted and replanted as they grew in order to even out the distribution of the crop in
the field. The earliest available description of the *wahi* appears in a source from 1818 (P.A. van
Middelkoop, 'Memorien ten vervolge van het Algemeen Verslag van de Commissie Moluksche
Eilanden', 30-9-1818, in NA Schneither 128).
[68]   By the 1860s, it should be added, the metal *pacol* had largely replaced the wooden *wahi*
(Graafland 1864:21).
[69]   A.C.J. Edeling, 'Memorie omtrent de Minahasa', 13-8-1875, in NA V 17-4-1877/20.

mostly to the upland population. The idea that Minahasan farming became more labour-intensive in the course of the eighteenth century, moreover, is in neat accordance, following the Boserup model of demographically-driven agricultural intensification, with the population growth of the same period (see Chapter V). An argument can also be made that a complementary factor here was 'market pull' in the form of enhanced commercial demand for rice. Although domestic market exchange was still weakly developed at this period (see Chapter IX), rice production does seem to have been somewhat responsive to changes in export demand. An increase in the price paid by the VOC for Minahasan rice at the beginning of the 1670s reportedly had the effect that 'everyone went most industriously to work making ricefields', and an attempt to ban private (non-VOC) exports from Minahasa in 1753 led to a reduction in the amount of rice planted as well as sold, for which reason it was discontinued three years later (Godée Molsbergen 1928:30, 122). In assessing the proposition that a combination of demographic and export growth already led to an increase in the areal and labour-intensity of Minahasan agriculture during the eighteenth century, on the other hand, it is also necessary to consider another feature of Minahasan agriculture at that time which, while even more unusual than the system of swidden farming with soil tillage and broadcast sowing, suggests anything but high labour inputs: the unique practice of planting the principal crop, rice, only once every other year.

Biennial farming in Minahasa

In his *memorie van overgave* of 1803, Resident of Manado G.F. Duhr noted that the *walak* or district of Langoan (on the southern part of the Minahasan plateau), delivered rice to the government only at two-year intervals. The reason for this, in Duhr's amazed words, was that 'since olden times, the people of this district have had the custom of making swiddens and planting *padi* only once every other year!'. The same was also true of 'most' districts in the southwestern quarter near Amurang (the Tontemboan language area); the remainder of Minahasa, by contrast, produced a rice harvest every year (Godée Molsbergen 1928:159-60). Not much later the biennial system seems to have disappeared entirely, for it is not described at first hand in any subsequent source.[70] Graafland (1864:6-7), writing at the beginning of the 1860s,

---

[70] This applies not only to the compendious report written by Resident Wenzel in 1825, which contains a detailed account of Minahasan agriculture (Riedel 1872b:539-43), but also to the earlier *memories* of 1804 (Watuseke and Henley 1994) and 1809 ('Memorie door den afgaande Manados onderprefect Carl Christoph Prediger', 15-9-1809, in ANRI Manado 61).

stated that Minahasans in general ('the people of this country') had 'in former times' been accustomed to planting rice only once every two years, but that at a certain point 'the government informed them that they could in fact do this every year, and so [from then on] they did'. Enough local knowledge of the old system was still present among the Tontemboan in the late nineteenth century to make possible a retrospective account of how it had worked by missionary-ethnographer J.A.T. Schwarz.[71]

> *Lumoang* refers here to the real agricultural year, *ta'um bangko'*, the 'big year', or *ta'un ailoang*, 'the year for which the *lumoang* or [swidden] consecration ceremony is held'. After the harvest for this year is complete, there follows the 'little' or false year, *ta'un toya'ang*. In this little year, at least officially, no farming is done and no swidden sacrifices are made; the men construct fishponds, manufacture salt, collect forest products, build houses and suchlike, while the women weave cloth and make baskets, or perform other work. (Schwarz 1907, III:266.)

Another term for the 'little year' was *wawalen*, literally 'the time of staying at home'.[72] How the Minahasans arrived at this 'rather irrational arrangement', Schwarz declared, 'is impossible to say with certainty'. According to his account the biennial cycle had been discontinued not by government fiat but because of conversion to Christianity, as a result of which people 'lost their fear' of farming in the previously forbidden 'small year' (Schwarz 1907, III:266-7).

The origin and history of the biennial system are indeed obscure. Edeling (1919:45-6), writing in 1875, and recently Wigboldus (1978:23-4, 1988:15), have both assumed that it dated from before the period of European contact. Schouten, however, argues that the luxury of a biennial rice harvest was probably made possible only by the introduction of a very productive secondary crop in the form of maize.[73] The consecutive planting of separate maize and rice crops on the same swiddens apparently meant that the agricultural cycle, from the initial clearance of fallow vegetation to the completion of the rice harvest, often lasted a full twelve months or more, leaving no time within the same calendar year for the post-harvest festivities. This was probably the origin of the 'big' and 'small' years: together, noted Schwarz

---

[71]   J.A.T. Schwarz, an NZG missionary, arrived in Sonder in 1861 (Graafland 1898, II:LXXXI).
[72]   'Sometimes a swidden is opened surreptitiously', Schwarz added, 'but in that case they say it is worked by hired labourers from another tribe, such as the Tombulu'.
[73]   Schouten 1998:47. 'Was there', Schouten asks, 'such fertile land available [before the advent of maize] that each harvest of rice and (probably) of root crops was abundant enough for two years' consumption?'. As additional support for her hypothesis she cites the fact that later in the nineteenth century the southern part of Minahasa, where the biennial system had formerly been practised, was described as an area where 'maize was better accepted than elsewhere as a substitute for rice as a staple food'.

(1907, III:266), 'the *ta'un ailoang* and the *wawalen* add up to two years, but they are not of equal length'.

According to Schouten (1998:46) the lengthening of the big year occurred because it included two maize harvests, 'one before and one after the rice harvest'. At least in the nineteenth century, however, the second maize crop was in fact planted simultaneously with the rice, to be picked before the latter had reached maturity (see Chapter II). Schwarz (1907, III:255), moreover, describes only a single preliminary maize planting. Edeling (1919:59), on the other hand, does mention that 'sometimes, as in Kawangkoan [a Tontemboan district]', Minahasans planted maize 'twice in succession, and then rice'. More importantly, it is probably not necessary to invoke a series of three consecutive crops in order to explain the 'big year'. Minahasan maize took up to four months to ripen (Graafland 1864:7, 22) and dry rice up to seven months (De Clercq 1871d), while the preliminary clearing, drying, and firing of the swiddens, by analogy with comparable systems elsewhere (Conklin 1957:63; Kunstadter 1978:83), must also have taken some weeks. A description of farming practices in Bolaang Mongondow at the same period suggests a similar, but incomplete, development in the direction of a biennial cycle based on dry-season maize cultivation.

> As in many places in Minahasa, the swidden year is distinguished into a big and a small year (or alternatively, two small years). In a big year new fields which have been lying fallow are opened up, while in a small year the same field is planted with maize immediately after the harvest, and later sown with *padi*. (Wilken and Schwarz 1867c:364.)

Here rice is planted every year, and there is no suggestion that the big and small years are of unequal length. The labour-intensive opening of new swiddens, however, takes place only every other year, while maize is planted both before the first rice crop (Wilken and Schwarz 1866c:365), and as a catch crop between the big and small years.

One possible interpretation of the biennial cycle is that it served to maintain a relatively long fallow interval, and therefore preserve soil fertility, in areas of concentrated settlement and local population pressure. After the disappearance of the old system Graafland (1864:8) reported that the Tontemboan district on which Schwarz based his description, Sonder, was short of farmland, so that 'work in the fields yields but poor returns, since the old farmlands (*jurame*) have to be reused year in, year out, or else with excessively short fallow intervals'. If such frequent recultivation was necessary in the 1860s due to population pressure, on the other hand, it is difficult to see why similar pressure should have had precisely the opposite effect at an earlier period. It could be argued that areal crop yields had fallen as a result of the abandonment of the biennial system, or because of frequent compulsory labour duties which reduced the time available for intensive preparation and maintenance of the swiddens. Equally likely, however, is that the 'little year' had been valued for reasons unconnected with food production.

The only reference to biennial agriculture which I know of in a contemporary source from before 1803 appears in the *memorie van overgave* of a seventeenth-century VOC Resident of Manado, Isaac van Thije.[74] This, surprisingly, refers exclusively to wet rice farmers on the shores of Lake Tondano, who are said to 'plant only once every two years, always letting their land lie fallow for a year even though they can cultivate it better than any other *negeri* by draining or flooding it at will'; 'all other' Minahasans, by contrast, 'plant every year' (Van Thije 1689). Here, then, there is no doubt that the biennial farmers in question could potentially have produced an annual rice crop on a sustainable basis. If the two-year cycle was indeed restricted to Tondano in 1689, then it must have become widespread only in the course of the eighteenth century – a conclusion which is arguably in accordance with Schouten's 'maize hypothesis' as outlined above, and with her view that Minahasan farmers took advantage of this new crop more in order to provide themselves with 'more leisure time' than in order to maximize their food supply.[75]

To some extent, no doubt, the adoption of maize and the biennial cycle simply involved the redistribution of already available 'leisure time' in a new and less even way: during their 'big year' Tontemboan farmers probably worked more continuously in agriculture, and perhaps also made larger swidden fields, than their counterparts elsewhere. Yet the very existence of such a time surplus, however distributed, seems to confirm that the traditional economy operated well below its potential food-producing capacity. Another pointer in the same direction is the remarkable fact that in the nineteenth century the colonial government was able to extract upwards of 100 person-days per year of labour on roads and coffee plantations from the average Minahasan household (see Chapter X) without importing any food to compensate for lost subsistence production. Domestic foodcrop harvests, in fact, increased considerably during the period of heaviest compulsory labour (Chapter IX).

[74]   I am grateful to Jouke Wigboldus for first drawing my attention to this source.
[75]   Schouten 1998:47. For Wigboldus (1988:129), Van Thije's statement simply indicates that in 1689 'the Tontemboan were not yet noticeable rice deliverers to the Dutch East Indies Company'. 'Lower Tongkimbut [Tontemboan]', however, certainly sold rice to the VOC in 1680 (NA VOC 1366:224), and several Tontemboan groups were 'accustomed' to doing so by 1695 (NA VOC 1579:150-1).

Economic behaviour revisited

Not all of the time traditionally spent on non-agricultural activities in Minahasa, it must be stressed, was unproductive in economic terms. During the Tontemboan 'little year', as Schwarz noted, housebuilding, salt manufacture and hunting were common male activities, while women produced textiles and other handicraft manufactures. The huge colonial redeployment of labour into coffee production and roadbuilding, accordingly, was made possible partly by the 'de-industrialization' of the Minahasan economy. In the early part of the nineteenth century Minahasan women were still heavily involved in manufacturing textiles for domestic use from a variety of materials including tree bark, cotton, and bamboo fibres.[76] Bamboo fabric, used as sailcloth and sacking material as well as for clothing, was also exported on a small scale.[77] In the 1860s, however, Graafland (1867-69, I:224) noted the 'gradual disappearance' of this product 'as a result of the greater use of [imported] cotton clothing'.[78] By 1874 'only a few women' were still said to be weaving any kind of cloth,[79] and by the turn of the century virtually all domestic textile production had ceased.[80] The manufacture of clay pots, also a significant female handicraft until the mid-nineteenth century, had likewise disappeared by the beginning of the twentieth.[81] It would be too simplistic, then, to conclude that the precolonial economy was characterized in all respects by 'underproduction' and that subsequent economic growth was achieved solely by taking up the existing labour slack.

Other evidence nevertheless confirms that both here and elsewhere in the region, time not spent producing either food or other material goods was highly valued. The agricultural calendar in Minahasa was punctuated by numerous time-consuming ritual activities (Schwarz 1907, III:246-67). During some of these ceremonies, known generically as *foso*, 'all work in the *negeri* ceases; it is forbidden to go to the swiddens or even to leave the village, and no sounds of woodcutting or rice pounding may be heard' (Graafland 1867-

---

[76]   AV Manado 1833 (ANRI Manado 48); Francis 1860:318; Graafland 1867-69, I:195, 224-5, 1898, I:319, 351-2; Meyer and Richter 1903:2-5; Palm 1958:10-2, 1961:62-5; Pietermaat, De Vriese and Lucas 1840:144; Reinwardt 1858:602; Riedel 1872b:549-50; J.J. ten Siethoff, 'Topografische schetsen van een gedeelte der residentie Menado 1845' (ANRI Manado 46); Van Spreeuwenberg 1845-46:315.

[77]   AV Manado 1833 (ANRI Manado 48); Riedel 1872b:549-50; Schwarz 1908a:57.

[78]   Meyer and Richter (1903:5-6) stress the influence of missionary attitudes here, alongside the 'enormous quantity' (Graafland 1898, I:116) of imported textiles.

[79]   AV Manado 1874 (ANRI Manado 53).

[80]   Dirkzwager 1912:1163; Jasper and Pirngadie 1912:3-4; Kluiver 1894:167; Palm 1958:11, 1961: 64; Schwarz 1908a:57.

[81]   Francis 1860:318; Graafland 1867-69, I:226; Kluiver 1894:167; Padtbrugge 1866:323; Riedel 1872b:551.

69, I:112). An elaborate system of personal 'feasts of merit', moreover, existed alongside the communal *foso* (Schouten 1998:22-4; Tauchmann 1968:215-26). During the early nineteenth century, Dutch officials in Minahasa regularly complained about the amount of time spent on ceremonial feasting rather than on agriculture and other (in their eyes) more productive activities.[82] In 1856 Resident Jansen, discovering that the ritual experts in Tonsea had prescribed a nine-day ceremony during which all labour in the fields or for the government was to cease, summarily banned all *foso* lasting more than three days, thereby triggering a mass conversion to Christianity in that part of Minahasa (Graafland 1898, II:279). On Sangir, the missionary Steller (1866:35) alleged that farmers were forced by their chiefs 'to abandon all of their activities for days and weeks on end in order to prepare and participate in bacchanalia'. In the Poso area, where ceremonial feasting was largely restricted to weddings and funerals, agricultural activities were nevertheless ritually prohibited on as many as eight or nine days each month.[83] Even local people, apparently, sometimes found the ritual labour proscriptions excessive. 'If we really kept strictly to all of the forbidden days connected with our feasts', one Bada farmer told Woensdregt (1928:248), 'there would be no time left over for agricultural work'.[84]

The existence of the non-agricultural 'little year' in precolonial Minahasa, and the more widespread importance of time-consuming ceremonial activities and agricultural taboos (not to mention wars) suggest that the restriction of labour inputs was typically a more important consideration in economic behaviour than the rigorous maximization of food production. Dove (1985b:379) describes the maximization of returns to labour as 'a basic and pervasive aspect' of the traditional agricultural economy which he studied among the Kantu' of West Kalimantan, and Knaap (1987:127), on the basis of historical sources, concludes that farmers in seventeenth-century Ambon displayed a 'leisure preference' (Wilkinson 1973:84) which meant that they were only prepared to invest additional labour in agriculture if the 'marginal returns' to such investment were high.[85] Whether it is interpreted as resulting from a simple preference for leisure on the part of food producers, from cultural and religious prescriptions against full deployment of the available labour resources,

---

[82]   AV Manado 1833 (ANRI Manado 48); Res. Manado to Res. Ternate, 20-6-1807 (ANRI Manado 60); Watuseke and Henley 1994:358, 373.
[83]   Adriani and Kruyt 1912-14, II:265; A.C. Kruyt 1895-97, III:141. Other types of work, however, were permitted on these days.
[84]   Also Aragon 1992:71; Kraan 2000:40; Nourse 1999:169-70.
[85]   The fact that it was the relatively undemanding cultivation of coconuts, denigrated by European planters as a 'lazy man's crop' (Heersink 1999:173), which came to provide the bulk of northern Sulawesi's export income in the late colonial period (see Chapter II) could also be seen in this light.

or (as suggested in Chapter IX) from the disincentives to surplus production experienced by all but the most socially ambitious members of a community in which any such surplus must be shared, the paradox of sub-optimal food production and consumption in subsistence-oriented farming communities has been a topic of frequent comment in Indonesia (Seavoy 1977, 1986:9-27) as in many other parts of the world (Sahlins 1972:51-74).

That traditional constraints on labour investment in food production could nevertheless be overcome either by opportunity (commercialization) or by necessity (population pressure) is sufficiently clear from the economic history of Minahasa in the late nineteenth century. To the extent that the 'failure' of Minahasans to deploy more of their labour in rice and maize production during the VOC period can be interpreted as a rational economic choice, then, it can only be concluded that despite the incipient demographic and economic growth, neither land scarcity nor commercial incentives were yet sufficiently pronounced to make such deployment attractive or necessary.

Not all of the economic choices which people made, on the other hand, can easily be explained in terms of rational calculations regarding the returns to labour. The sheer fact that most subsistence farmers ate more rice and maize than sago, for instance, already suggests that they were not exclusively concerned to minimize the amount of time which they spent producing food, since field studies in Borneo and New Guinea have shown that sago 'can be around two to four times as productive as hill [swidden] rice when translated into energy (calorific) terms'.[86] In 1845 a Dutch observer in Minahasa noted that for this reason the population of Tonsawang, where more sago was eaten than in other districts, was at an advantage in terms of food security.

I have also heard tell that the sago palms which are numerous in Tonsawang insure its inhabitants against scarcity, not because of the food (sago) which they supply, but because of the time which the native saves by making use of them, since these trees grow without requiring any human attention, and the sago can be obtained more quickly and easily than rice.[87]

Although the distribution of true sago (*Metroxlyon sagu*) was restricted by its preference for flat, wet terrain (see Chapter IX), at least some additional scope for planting this tree seems to have existed almost everywhere.[88] Two other

[86]   Strickland 1986:131. Also A. Brouwer 1998:350-1; Ellen 1979:49; Persoon 1988:43; Whitten and Whitten 1985:33.
[87]   J.J. ten Siethoff, 'Topografische schetsen van een gedeelte der residentie Menado 1845' (ANRI Manado 46).
[88]   In 1844, for instance, the resident of Manado instructed every Minahasan household to plant 6 sago trees 'in muddy places' (Res. Manado to opzieners, 20-1-1844, in ANRI Manado 81), and beginning in 1857 (CV Manado 1857, in ANRI Manado 52) thousands of additional *Metroxylon sagu* trees were planted in all parts of Minahasa on government orders. In the 1860s

sago-yielding trees, moreover, could be grown on dry and sloping ground: the *aren* or sugar palm (*Arenga pinnata*) and the *sago baruk* (*A. microcarpa*) of Sangir. Both were somewhat more arduous to process than true sago, but probably still more labour-efficient as a food source than any field crop.[89] Wilken and Schwarz (1867c:363) estimated that in Bolaang Mongondow two people working for 'four or five days' could extract enough sago from a single sugar palm to feed a household of six for a month.[90]

Besides demanding little labour, sago also had another characteristic which, judging by other aspects of farming behaviour (Chapter II), should in principle have been highly valued: year-round availability and an almost complete invulnerability to pests or climatic irregularities.[91] To a lesser extent, some other subsidiary food plants were also superior to rice and maize in terms of reliability of yields. Bananas were said to 'hold out longer than other crops during protracted droughts' (Jellesma 1911:1240-1), while taro, in a suitably moist environment, could be planted and harvested throughout the year regardless of the season, and was also relatively little affected by mammal pests like wild pigs.[92] In this light it is interesting to recall that the three parts of the region where tubers did play a central role in foodcrop agriculture, Sangir, Talaud, and Banggai, were all densely populated, and that Talaud and Banggai both produced an annual population surplus which they exported in the form of slaves. As in the case of the maize/rice combination in Minahasa (see Chapter XII), the productivity and reliability of tuber-based farming systems may have been a factor favouring high population densities in these areas. As usual, however, the direction of causality is unclear. Given that taro, yams and sweet potato apparently tend to produce higher carbohydrate yields per unit area than swidden rice, and that at least one of these tubers, the yam, is generally very labour-intensive to grow (Purseglove 1972, I:98), it is also possible that the heavy emphasis on root crop cultivation was a form of intensification necessitated precisely by existing population pressure.[93] In Banggai, the initial intensification process might conceivably have

the same policy was followed, apparently with success, in the heartland of Gorontalo, where previously there had been no *Metroxylon* sago at all (CV Gorontalo 1864, 1867, in ANRI Manado 44, 53; Riedel 1870a:89).

[89]   Adriani and Kruyt 1912-14, II:204; Aragon 1992:76; *Een en ander* 1908:1045-6; Tammes 1936b: 47.

[90]   Adriani (1901:242) made a similar estimate for sago production from unspecified trees in the Luwu area of South Sulawesi.

[91]   A. Brouwer 1998:350; Ellen 1979:50; Persoon 1988:44.

[92]   A.C. Kruyt 1924:38; Li 1991:8, 28, 41; Purseglove 1972, I:64; Roep 1917:432; Tammes 1940: 192. Pigs, states Li (1991:41), do root up taro, but apparently 'never manage to finish it'. Wild pigs, on the other hand, were certainly a threat to root crops on Banggai (A.C. Kruyt 1932d:483), and drought did sometimes kill tubers on Talaud (see Chapter IX).

[93]   Tuber yields mentioned by Purseglove (1968, I:86, 1972, I:64, 114) for other parts of the

occurred during the political and commercial heyday of the Banggai sultanate before the seventeenth century. On the Sangir Islands, another important factor favouring root crops was undoubtedly their ability to grow underneath a canopy of coconut palms (see Chapter XIII).

Sago, compared to rice and maize, is a poor source of protein, vitamins and minerals (Anderson 1977:71), and its bland taste means that a sago meal, as Persoon (1988:45) observes, 'begs more than does rice for fish, vegetables or meat'. Sago-eaters, then, are at both a nutritional and a gastronomic disadvantage in areas where animal food is scarce. This may help to explain why sago tended to be most important in coastal areas where fish was readily available (Seavoy 1986:149) – and, conversely, where the desire to spend much time fishing made the labour-efficiency of sago production doubly attractive. On the whole, however, it seems prudent to accept that cultural preference and historical accident were sometimes as important as either environmental adaptations or rational economic choices in determining the distribution of farming systems. Just as the distribution of the water buffalo reflected a broad geographical divide between southwestern and northwestern sections of the region (Chapter II, Map 8) as well as an affinity with wet rice cultivation and (in Poso and Mori) itinerant swidden farming on poor soils, it is striking that the tuber-growing islands of Banggai, Sangir and Talaud are also those parts of northern Sulawesi which lie closest to the Moluccas and New Guinea, where rice has always been less important than in central and western Indonesia (Spencer 1966:110-9).

Population density and population growth: positive feedback?

It is possible that in some circumstances a high population density was itself conducive to population growth, so that a growth trend, once initiated, was self-reinforcing. One potential 'positive feedback' mechanism of this type has to do with the fact that although it was not unusual for farmers to respond quickly to off-farm commercial opportunities, they tended to do so most wholeheartedly when a scarcity of land on which to grow their own food left them with less choice in the matter.[94] This was the case, for instance,

---

world (no statistics are available from Sulawesi) range from 7 tonnes per hectare upwards, whereas rice swiddens in nineteenth-century Minahasa produced less than one tonne of hulled rice per hectare (Appendix K). All three tubers consist for about 70% of water, whereas the water content of husked rice is about 10% (Purseglove 1968, I:85, 1972, I:63, 111, 178).

[94]   This argument has some parallels with that of Heersink (1998), who proposes that in 'marginal' areas of South Sulawesi, such as the island of Selayar, low agricultural productivity inspired compensatory strategies of commercial specialization (weaving, shipbuilding, trading,

during the nineteenth century in the densely-populated vicinity of Tondano, an area well known throughout Minahasa for its fish market, its carpenters, and its female handicraft products, particularly bamboo-fibre cloth and basketwork.[95] In the 1850s, with the completion of the vehicular road network, Tondano also became the main centre of the profitable new carting and cart manufacturing industries.[96] This continuing economic diversification was directly stimulated by local population pressure.

> Not everybody is in possession of *sawah*, and many must seek their fortune from the dry fields on the slopes of the mountains to the east and west of Tondano. [...] But these lands too are insufficient to provide farming opportunities for everyone; some people must therefore hire out their labour to owners of *sawah* fields who do not cultivate these themselves, or on the private coffee plantation at Masarang. Some go fishing on a regular basis, which provides them with a good living. Others hunt ducks, cut and transport grass [as fodder for horses], and so on. Still others go elsewhere to work in nutmeg gardens, drive their carts to and from Manado as freight carriers, hire out their services in other districts as carpenters, and even undertake the construction of whole houses. Tondano town, meanwhile, provides abundant work for carpenters, smiths, and cobblers. In short, this is a community in which many other sources of income besides agriculture provide in a satisfactory way for the needs of all. (Graafland 1898, II:174.)

In the seventeenth century, when biennial farming was practised in Tondano, it was only during the alternate non-agricultural years that the Tondanese were said to 'support themselves by making pots and selling fish' (Van Thije 1689). At this stage, then, there cannot yet have been any question of enforced diversification. By the beginning of the nineteenth century, however, seasonal labour migration had become a necessity 'because the people of Tondano possess more water than land, so that foodstuffs are relatively scarcer there than elsewhere'.[97] Many later sources also associate other forms of economic diversification in Tondano with the limited availability of land for farming.[98] As recently as the 1980s, research by economic

---

and coconut cultivation) which were so successful that they ultimately gave rise to concentrations of dense population. I suspect, however, that the dry climate of Selayar was less of a disadvantage for foodcrop farmers (see Chapter XI) than Heersink supposes.

[95] Buddingh 1860:44; Graafland 1867-69, I:217, 221, 224, 1898, I:348-9; Kluiver 1894:167; Riedel 1872b:550-1; Van Spreeuwenberg 1845-46:166, 169. In 1821, '20 or 30' Tondano men were even employed by the *raja* of Gorontalo as 'craftsmen, particularly carpenters' (Reinwardt 1858:511).

[96] Graafland 1867-69, II:114; Quarles van Ufford 1856:23; L. Wessels 1891:64.

[97] P.A. van Middelkoop, 'Memorien ten vervolge van het Algemeen Verslag van de Commissie naar de Moluksche eilanden', 30-9-1818 (NA Schneither 128).

[98] Van Kol 1903:316; Kündig 1934:188; Van Marle 1922, I:58-9; N.P. Wilken 1870:374. It is possible that lower transport and transaction costs in local trade, one of the 'virtuous interactions' between population density and economic growth identified in contemporary Kenya by Tiffen, Mortimore and Gichuki (1994:261-73) and in a broader context by Platteau (2000:34-51), were also involved here.

anthropologists in the vicinity of Kakas (to the south of Lake Tondano) found that the extent to which individual households were involved in trading was 'very much dependent on land ownership', indicating that off-farm activities had retained their original 'supplementary character' with respect to agriculture: 'the less land that is available to a household, the more important it is to trade'. 'Trading', the authors of this study (Mai and Buchholt 1987) went so far as to conclude, 'is an extension of agriculture, that is, it has to compensate for the inadequacy of agriculture to provide for household reproduction'.[99]

Tondano's experience of accelerated commercialization as a result of population pressure was not unique. The inhabitants of a second Minahasan district identified in the mid-nineteenth century as short of farmland, Sonder, later 'became heavily engaged in small-scale trading', and were 'omnipresent in Minahasan marketplaces' by 1900 (Schouten 1998:175). In 1920 there were also unusually large numbers of part-time carpenters, cartwrights, and blacksmiths in Sonder (Van Marle 1922, I:60). A possible parallel from an earlier period is provided by Nanusa in Talaud, the population of which specialized for centuries in the manufacture of sailing vessels for export (see Chapter II) and supplied dried fish to the larger Talaud Islands in exchange for vegetable food.[100] In the 1850s, warriors elsewhere in Talaud were also reported to be using swords 'forged by the diligent inhabitants of Nanusa'.[101] While the small Nanusa Islands offered some natural advantages for boatbuilding and fishing purposes, this is less conceivable in the case of ironworking. Possibly it was the persistently high density of population on these islands (see Chapter XI), itself partly a result of the existing commercial specialization, which encouraged their inhabitants to seek additional sources of trade income. A similar development is evident in the history of Ndao, a tiny and very densely populated island off the coast of Roti in the Lesser Sundas. 'All of the men of Ndao', reported Fox (1977:29), 'are goldsmiths and silversmiths, and they leave their island at the beginning of each dry season to fashion jewelry for the people of the Timor area'.

In nineteenth-century Tondano, off-farm activities generated more than sufficient income to compensate for the scarcity of farmland which made them necessary. One Dutch visitor stated in the 1840s that because 'the best carpenters' came from Tondano, 'a greater prosperity is visible among the population here than elsewhere' (Van Spreeuwenberg 1845-46:166). In 1855

---

[99]   Mai and Buchholt 1987:108, 113. In the title of their monograph, Mai and Buchholt refer to this supplementary commercial activity as 'subsistence trade'.
[100]   A. Ulaen, interview, 5-9-2000.
[101]   A.J.F. Jansen, 'Rapport betrekkelijk het oppergezag over en de toestand van de Talaut Eilanden', 12-8-1857 (ANRI Manado 166).

another wrotethat a 'haze of prosperity' hung over Tondano town.[102] In later periods this no longer seems to have been the case: by the 1930s the area around Lake Tondano, partly due to 'overpopulation', was said to be among the poorest parts of Minahasa.[103] In so far as the link between commercial activity and population growth appears to be very general, and to involve some mechanisms (household labour demand and efficient food distribution, for example) which are only indirectly related to levels of income, we can nevertheless surmise that where population pressure promoted market involvement, it was also conducive to further population growth.

To the extent that the expansion of irrigation in Minahasa was necessitated by rising population densities, it too may have set up positive feedback mechanisms leading to further population growth. Whether the shift from swidden to wet rice farming as such had a positive effect on levels of reproductive fertility, as proposed by Reid (1987:39-41), is unclear.[104] But if Hunt (2000) is right to conclude that *sawah* cultivation was more productive than swiddening in terms of labour efficiency (after the initial infrastructural investments had been amortized) as well as areal yields, then the creation of 'landesque capital' (Blaikie and Brookfield 1987:9) in the form of level fields, dikes, terraces, dams and irrigation channels automatically tended to boost per capita food production in the long term. And even if the Hunt thesis is wrong, colonial officials in Sulawesi were undoubtedly correct to point out that the yields from irrigated ricefields varied less from year to year than those from swiddens.[105] If only by boosting the reliability of the food supply, then, the transition to wet rice probably still depressed mortality to some degree.

Conclusions

The principal way in which the human population of northern Sulawesi affected its environment in the period prior to 1930 was by removing the natural vegetation. Settlement was concentrated in areas which, for reasons of climate, soil, and topography, were suitable for intensive short-fallow swidden cultivation and/or the construction of wet ricefields. Here the origi-

---

[102]   Bleeker 1856:78. Also Graafland 1867-69, I:181, II:114, 195, 1898, II:174-5; Hickson 1889:208.
[103]   Brouwer 1936:60; Kündig 1934:188. Another factor here was the absence from the plateau of the coconut palms which brought much export income to other districts.
[104]   Certainly this shift was not automatically associated with a drastic reduction in the female agricultural workload, as Reid suggests. In early twentieth-century Minahasa women were much involved in irrigated farming (Beck 1922:65), not least in the laborious task of transplanting rice seedlings from nursery beds (Plate 38). In many parts of Java in the 1970s, at least half of all labour inputs in *sawah* farming were provided by women and girls (White 1976:158). The nineteenth-century Minahasan fertility data, in any case, show that the harder women worked, the more children they had, not the fewer (see Chapter X).
[105]   Several Dutch sources confirm that although farmers objected to the work involved in creating irrigated fields, they did appreciate the reliability of the yields which these produced even in dry years (Adriani and Kruyt 1950-51, III:8; *Brieven* 5-7-1912 and 15-12-1912; CV Manado 1866, in ANRI Manado 52; A.C. Kruyt 1924:43).

nal forest was almost entirely replaced by agrarian landscapes dominated by cultivated fields, bush and young woodland consisting of a few pioneer tree species, and sometimes also coconut palms and livestock pastures. The farming systems found in these areas of dense settlement, nevertheless, were usually sustainable, producing more or less stable yields and not requiring periodic population movements or the progressive destruction of additional virgin forest. During periods of population growth, moreover, they often proved amenable to further intensification, whether via the application of tillage and broadcast sowing techniques on swidden fields, or via the extension of irrigated and permanent dry-field farming. There are indications that the well-defined land rights associated with dense, sedentary populations were conducive to the prevention of land degradation.

Soil exhaustion, expansionary shifting cultivation, and the creation of large semi-permanent grasslands, in so far as they occurred, were associated not with dense settlement or demographic growth, but with the exploitation of poor soils by sparse (and even declining) populations practising swidden farming in combination with extensive livestock grazing. Land degradation may well have been a particular risk in periods of disengagement from commerce, when groups which had depended partly on imported food were thrown back on purely local agricultural resources. In some areas, the rapid expansion of coconut cultivation on swidden land toward the end of the colonial period also promoted progressive destruction of the natural forest. Around 1930, however, the effects of this land-hungry commercial activity were balanced out by the extent of area-efficient permanent-field systems in the main centres of settlement, and by a partial replacement of locally-produced food by imported rice. At this date the total extent of deforestation, at one quarter of the land area of the region, was almost exactly that which would have been needed to support the population of just over 1.1 million souls on the basis of a typical subsistence swidden-farming land requirement of about two hectares (including bush-fallow land) per individual.

The distribution of the population was in the first place a function of economic geography. In so far as it did not reflect variations (determined mostly by natural conditions, partly by cultural preferences for particular food crops) in the productivity of subsistence agriculture, it reflected the distribution of commercial resources (iron, gold, coconuts) and the lowland political systems based on the control of those resources. More importantly for the interpretation of demographic processes, long-term population change also seems to have been determined mainly by economic factors. Episodes of economic expansion, stimulated by demand for export products like rice, coffee, and copra, were usually accompanied by population growth, and there are indications that the incorporation of maize and other New World crops into subsistence farming systems may have had the same effect. Economic dislocation, conversely, was associated with low or negative population growth (Gorontalo and Minahasa in the first half of the nineteenth century), and at least one case of long-term demographic decline (that of eastern Central Sulawesi between the seventeenth century and the beginning of the twentieth) coincided with the protracted collapse of an important export industry (iron). Although migration from poorer to richer areas was sometimes an important factor here, it cannot fully account for the observed association between economic and demographic change, which usually also involved in situ processes affecting fertility and mortality. These processes operated despite very low levels of occupational specialization and despite the persistence of a subsistence-focused economic system. They also predated colonial intervention: medical and hygiene improvements under colonial rule, although sometimes effective, and in one case (vaccination against smallpox) extremely so, were not necessary preconditions for demographic growth.

The historically typical demographic situation of crisis-ridden quasi-equilibrium was maintained by a combination of both high mortality and low fertility, and episodes of population growth appear to have been accompanied both by reductions in the death rate and by increases in the birth rate. The traditionally low levels of reproductive fertility, however, were maintained by a complex of behavioural patterns which at first sight appear to bear little relation to economic conditions: prolonged breast-feeding, frequent male absence, bridewealth customs leading to delayed marriage, and various forms of deliberate birth control practised in connection with female autonomy, slavery, and probably also the existence of large, organized extended kin groups. High death rates, maintained by disease, periodic food shortages, and to a much lesser extent by war and other forms of human violence, were also conditioned partly by practices which do not appear to have stemmed from economic necessity: deficient infant diets, poor hygiene, hoarding of food for bursts of conspicuous consumption, a 'leisure preference' in economic behaviour, a widespread cultural aversion to some of the most reliable crops (sago and tubers), and probably also some systematic underproduction and maldistribution of food in connection with ritual, slavery, and political decentralization.

Some of the ways in which economic and demographic processes were articulated are nevertheless clear and others can be inferred with greater or lesser degrees of confidence. Although the immediate cause of most mortality was disease, firstly, death rates were sensitive to the level of food availability, and the incidence of food shortages was reduced, even without increases in local production, when levels of prosperity (in terms of exchange goods like textiles, brassware, and cash) rose, when local trade intensified, and when foodstuffs were imported. This effect was most pronounced in the late colonial period (though not only in the areas actually under colonial control) when income from coffee and copra cultivation promoted extensive monetization, led to the appearance of regular and permanent markets where few had previously existed, and financed the import of large quantities of rice from outside the region. The extent of commercial exchange under non-monetized conditions, however, should not be underestimated either, and it is likely that demographic significance had already attached to the trade in foodstuffs in earlier times. Trade, once initiated, tended to erode one of the obstacles to further commercial development by promoting pacification and political integration.

The age at which people married, turning to the factors affecting fertility, was determined to some extent by the relationship between population and resources. Traditional patterns of delayed marriage were found only in Minahasa and Sangir, where population densities were always high and where the supply of accessible, high-quality farmland was restricted. A decline in the average marital age which took place in Minahasa toward the end of the nineteenth century was probably associated partly with rising income from cash crops and non-agricultural activities, and partly with the colonization, in connection with coconut cultivation, of formerly marginal areas where climate and soil conditions were unfavourable for foodcrop agriculture. Where economic change involved increased demands for adult female labour, as in Minahasa during the period of compulsory coffee cultivation, it also led directly to reduced birth intervals by interfering with the traditional practise of prolonged and intensive breast feeding. In so far as it entailed increasing demands for child labour, it weakened the incentives to practise deliberate fertility control by means of abstinence, abortion, or infanticide.

There are reasons to think, finally, that two traditional institutions which affected fertility behaviour, slavery and the corporate kin group, were also eroded by commercialization in so far as both were partly adaptations to economic scarcity, and therefore became redundant when levels of prosperity rose and their 'social security' functions were taken over by the market. By providing an economic alternative to children for slave-owners and by weakening the ties between slaves and their own offspring, slavery, which was often underpinned by food debts, encouraged women in both groups to limit their fertility. By 'collectivizing' the benefits of children (including the provision of old-age security), the corporate kin group, which derived its cohesion partly from the security provided by the sharing of food and partly from the control of scarce prestige goods by its leaders, probably had a similar effect. Because it was usually structured along matrilineal lines, the politically autonomous extended family was also a bastion of female autonomy, another feature of traditional society which favoured effective fertility control. By promoting the disintegration of these units, then, commercialization itself, as well as the outside cultural influences which often accompanied it, may have favoured increasing realization of the (predominantly male) desire for a large number of children. It must be stressed, however, that these processes are inferred rather than proven on the basis of historical sources.

Many other uncertainties also surround the details of the relationship between demography and economic conditions. It is, for instance, difficult to say exactly to what extent the 'punctuated equilibrium' which characterized the demographic situation at times of limited or stable commercial involvement reflected a systematic balance between population and agricultural resources, or the behavioural patterns which restricted population growth under these conditions resulted from a process of environmental adaptation. The existence of large areas of uninhabited land would at first sight seem to tell against any explanation in terms of environmental 'carrying capacity'. The fact that most of these uninhabited areas were poorly suited for traditional subsistence farming without supplementary cash crops, however, raises important doubts here, as does the evidence that settlement outside the most fertile valleys, plateaux and islands was associated with land degradation, a process which in one case (that of Poso and Mori) seems to have contributed to a progressive decline in population.

Not all economic resources were utilized, and of those which were, not all necessarily served to raise production. In Minahasa, for instance, the productivity of maize may well have been exploited partly in order to increase the availability of free time. There are indications, conversely, that population pressure, once established, set up processes of economic change which tended to generate further population growth. On the whole, however, the historical evidence from North and Central Sulawesi does not support the Boserupian view of demographic change as an independent variable. In the long run it was what Malthus called the 'means of subsistence' which, as mediated by cultural and political preferences among the range of such means potentially available, determined the broad outlines of demographic history.

Appendices

APPENDIX A

Abbreviations

ANRI	Arsip Nasional Republik Indonesia (National Archive of the Republic of Indonesia, Jakarta)
App.	Appendix
AR	Assistant Resident
ARZ	Archief van de Raad voor de Zending der Nederlandse Hervormde Kerk (Archive of the Council for Missions of the Dutch Reformed Church, Het Utrechts Archief, Utrecht)
AV	Algemeen/Administratief Verslag (General/Administrative Report)
CBR	Crude Birth Rate (annual births per 1,000 inhabitants)
CDR	Crude Death Rate (annual deaths per 1,000 inhabitants)
COIHB	Comité Oost-Indische Handel en Bezittingen (Comittee for East Indies Trade and Possessions, collection in NA)
CV	Cultuur Verslag (Cultivation Report)
GG	Governor-General
Gov.	Governor
H	Handschrift (Western manuscripts collection, KITLV)
KIT	Koninklijk Instituut voor de Tropen (Royal Tropical Institute, Amsterdam); see also MvO
KITLV	Koninklijk Instituut voor Taal-, Land- en Volkenkunde (Royal Dutch Institute of Southeast Asian and Caribbean Studies, Leiden)
KPM	Koninklijke Paketvaart Maatschappij (Royal Dutch Packet Boat Company)
MMK	see MvO
MR	Mailrapport (Mail report, in NA)
MV	Maand Verslag (Monthly Report)
MvO	Memorie van Overgave ('Memoirs of transfer'; NA collection, divided into two series: KIT and MMK)
NA	Nationaal Archief (National Archive, The Hague)
n.a.	not available
PV	Politiek Verslag (Political Report)
R^2	In regression analysis, a measure of the tightness of the association between two variables (range: 0-1)
Res.	Resident
r_s	Spearman's Rank Correlation Coefficient (range: -1 to +1)
RMV	Rijksmuseum voor Volkenkunde (National Ethnological Museum, Leiden)
RPR	Resoluties Politieke Raad (Resolutions of the Political Council)
VKI	Verhandelingen van het Koninklijk Instituut voor Taal-, Land- en Volkenkunde (KITLV monograph series)
V	Verbaal (class of document in NA)
VOC	Verenigde Oostindische Compagnie (Dutch East Indies Company)
YMB	Yayasan Mitra Budaya (Mitra Budaya Foundation, Jakarta)
NZG	Nederlandsch Zendeling Genootschap (Netherlands Missionary Society)
VEL	NA map collection (inventory 1867)

Glossary

adat	custom, tradition
alang-alang	coarse grass species (*Imperata cylindrica*)
Alfur	uplander (see Chapter I)
anoa	dwarf buffalo (*Bubalus depressicornis*)
aren	sugar palm (*Arenga pinnata*)
bangsa	nobility
belukar	secondary forest vegetation
beras	husked rice
burger	'citizen' or 'townsman' subject directly to Dutch authority (see Chapter II)
damar	resin from certain trees, used for manufacturing varnishes (see Chapter II)
dapur	household or nuclear family; literally, 'hearth'
dorp	village
controleur	'controller' (Dutch colonial administrative official)
glagah	species of grass (*Saccharum spontaneum*)
hombres de armas	'fighting men'; see *weerbare man*
huisgezin	'household' (usually: nuclear family)
jurame	see *belukar*
kabupaten	modern administrative division below the province (residency) level
kampung	village
kerbau	water buffalo
kora-kora	type of (usually military) sailing vessel
kota	town
kusu-kusu	see *alang-alang*
ladang	dry swidden field
landschap	area, chiefdom
memorie van overgave	'memoir of transfer', report compiled by departing colonial official for use by his successor
negeri	village
padi	unhusked rice
raja	king, chief
resident	colonial administrative official in charge of a residency
rijksgroten	chiefs of state
sawah	wet ricefield
tegalan	dry fields under permanent cultivation
volkstelling	census
walak	village confederacy (in Minahasa)
weerbare man	'fighting man'; in practice, often a unit of fiscal or demographic measurement (see Chapter III)

APPENDIX C

Weights and measures[1]

Amsterdam pound	0.5	kg
bau (*bouw*)	0.7	ha
English mile	1.6	km
vadem (fathom)	1.8	m
gantang	20	kg
Duitse ('geographical') mile	7.4	km
korgi = *kadi* = *kodi* (cloth)	20	pieces
kati	0.6	kg
koyang	1.5	tonne[2]
kula (coconut oil, Sangir)	5	litres[3]
last	1.5	tonne[4]
paal	1.5	km
pikul	60	kg
Rhineland foot	0.314	m
Rhineland rood	3.8	m
real (gold)	0.027	kg
tektek (farmland, Minahasa)	0.35	ha[5]
tuman (sago)	12.5	kg[6]
weight ratio of hulled rice to unhusked *padi* (Minahasa)	0.5[7]	

[1] Most units, in view of the limited accuracy of almost all sources, have been considerably rounded. Bulbeck, Reid, Lay and Yiqi (1998:182-3) employ a similar level of rounding, equating for instance 1 *pikul* with 60 kg in place of the more conventional 62.5 kg.

[2] Technically 80 *gantang* or 26.5 *pikul*, about 1.6 tonne. In the early ninteenth century, however, the *koyang* was regarded as interchangeable with the *last* of 1.5 tonnes (P.A. van Middelkoop to A.A. Buijskens, 4-10-1817, in NA Schneither 128).

[3] Van Dinter 1899:334.

[4] Some writers state that the *last* used to measure Minahasan rice in the seventeenth century contained 4,000 (Van Doren 1854-56, I:260) or even 4,400 (Wigboldus 1988:15) Amsterdam pounds of 0.5 kg. By 1728, however, one last definitely weighed 3,000 pounds, or 1.5 tonne, as far as the VOC authorities in Ternate were concerned (NA VOC 2099:242), and this is consistent with later sources on Minahasa (Godée Molsbergen 1928:141, 147). Knaap (1996:192) notes that while the *last* used to measure the cargo capacity of sailing vessels in Java during the eighteenth century contained 4,000 Amsterdam pounds, a *last* of rice weighed only 24.5 *pikul*, again about 1.5 tonne.

[5] Standardized at 0.5 *bau* in 1861, before which its size was apparently variable (Riedel 1872b: 567).

[6] Reinwardt 1858:513.

[7] NA VOC 1345:651; Van Dam 1931:79; Francis 1860:350; Godée Molsbergen 1928:17, 30, 54, 67; A.J.F. Jansen 1861:237; Lobs 1686; J.J. ten Siethoff, 'Topographische schetsen van een gedeelte der residentie Menado 1845' (ANRI Manado 46); Van Marle 1922, I:67.

weight ratio of stripped maize grain to maize on the cob 0.4^{8}
average weight of maize cob (Minahasa) 0.2 kg^{9}

Sources (unless otherwise indicated): *Encyclopaedie* 1917-21, II:686-8; 'Stukken maten en gewichten 1884' (ANRI Manado 14).

---

[8] Van Marle 1922, I:67.
[9] Van Marle 1922, I:67.

Areas of major islands and 1930 administrative divisions (km²)

Miangas			2
Nanusa group			27
Karakelang			1,000
Salibabu			156
Kaburuang			94
	Talaud		1,281
Greater Sangir			562
Siau			156
Tagulandang			62
	Sangir		813
		Sangir and Talaud	2,093
Minahasa			5,274
Bolaang Mongondow			8,172
Gorontalo			12,227
		Peninsular N. Sulawesi	25,673
Buol and Tolitoli			7,429
W. Central Sulawesi[1]			10,336
Tomini area (Parigi)			6,359
		North Sulawesi	27,766
Una-una[2]			71
Togian[3]			563

Walea[4]		211
Togian group		845
	Poso area[5]	11,859
	Mori and Tobungku[6]	12,805
	Luwuk Peninsula	8,859
Peling		2,406
Banggai (Gapi)		289
Bangkurung		156
	Banggai Islands	3,164
	Central Sulawesi	60,813
	Northern Sulawesi	88,579

Sources: Lam 1932:15 (Miangas); *Tabel* 1895:66-7 (Nanusa, Togian); *Volkstelling* 1933-36, V:8, 156 (other).

Note: Because many very small islands have not been included individually, the areas of the various island groups do not add correctly.

1   Palu and Donggala.
2   Binang Unang.
3   Batu Daka, Togian, Malenge, and Talata Koh.
4   Walea Kodi, Walea Bahi, Puah, and Buka.
5   Poso, Lore and Tojo (including Togian).
6   Kolonodale.

APPENDIX E

The Edeling fertility survey, Minahasa, 1874[1]

District	Number of house-holds included in survey[4]	Number of ever-born children per household[5]	Number of living children per household[6]	Child mortality[2] (%)	Childless marriages[3] (%)
[Satellite] subdistricts beyond Ranoiapo River	484	4.23	3.30	21.81	6.2
Likupang	–	–	–	23.45[7]	–
Manado	50	2.60	1.90	27.10	33.8
Tonsea	–	–	–	27.28[8]	–
Tonsawang	220	3.99	2.87	27.94	9.09
Tondano Tuliang	674	4.97	3.57	28.08	5.04
Tompaso	714	4.25	3.00	29.23	25.21
Tondano Tulimambot	1,402	4.72	3.31	29.65	5.21
Kakas	1,223	5.20	3.40	34.43	5.81
Sarongsong	148	4.90	3.20	35.00	16.20
Tomohon	1,287	5.40	3.51	35.13	7.85
Tombariri	1,012	4.78	2.88	39.72	4.35
Ponosakan	153	2.44	1.42	41.98	20.30
Bantik	1,152	2.64	1.50	43.20	29.86
All districts	[> 8,519[9]]	4.18	2.82	31.72	14.08
Chinese [in Minahasa]	306	4.40	3.30	24.50	?[10]

Source: A.C.J. Edeling, 'Memorie omtrent de Minahasa', 13-8-1875, in NA V 17-4-1877/20

1   All figures are reproduced exactly as in the original table, and to the same number of decimal places. There are some minor inconsistencies, but since the reasons for these cannot be reconstructed, no attempt has been made at correction.
2   *Pct. overleden kinderen*
3   *Huwelijken zonder kinderen, pct.*
4   *Aantal gezinnen*
5   *Geheel aantal kinderen per gezin*
6   *Aantal levende kinderen per gezin*
7   It is not clear why this proportional figure is given here, but not the data from which it is derived.
8   See previous footnote.
9   This is the total for all districts for which a figure is given (excluding, therefore, Likupang and Tonsea). No combined figure is included in the original source.
10 Question mark in original text.

APPENDIX F

The Kruyt fertility survey, Poso area, 1902

Group Characteristics	To Lage Pagan, slaveholding	To Pebato Pagan, non-slaveholding	Mapane Muslim, coastal	Tojo Muslim, coastal, much venereal disease	All groups
Number of post-menopausal women interviewed	41	155	62	200	458
Total number of children ever-born	117	625	237	500[1]	1479
Average number of children ever-born per woman	2.85	4.03	3.82	2.50	3.23
Number of women who had remained childless	5	6	5	42	58
Rate of childlessness[2] (%)	12.2	3.9	8.1	21.0	12.7
Average number of children ever-born per non-childless woman	3.25	4.19	4.16	3.16	3.70
Total number of offspring who had died 'as small children'	66	141	43	125[3]	375
Infant mortality (%)	56.4	22.6	18.1	25.0	25.4
Average number of children surviving beyond infancy per woman	1.24	3.12	3.13	1.88	2.41
Average number of children surviving beyond infancy per non-childless woman	1.42	3.25	3.40	2.37	2.76

Source: A.C. Kruyt 1903b:197-8

1 Implied from the statement that for 'each woman' the average number of children was 2.5 (A.C. Kruyt 1903b:198), on the assumption that this refers to the total number of women rather than the number of non-sterile women.

2 It is possible that some of the childless women had never married, although Kruyt's account does not suggest this.

3 Implied from the stated mortality rate of 25% (A.C. Kruyt 1903b:198).

The Tillema fertility survey, Central Sulawesi, 1924 (extract and summary)

	Number of women interviewed	Average number of children ever-born per woman	Infant mortality[1] (%)	Average number of children surviving beyond infancy per woman	Total mortality among offspring to date (%)	Average number of surviving children per woman
Post-menopausal women						
Selected groups:						
To Lage	374	4.22	26.9	3.08	57.6	1.79
To Ondae	185	4.07	22.8	3.14	47.2	2.15
To Pebato	415	4.16	24.4	3.14	53.8	1.92
To Wingke-mposo	321	5.38	27.9	3.88	52.4	2.56
All groups	4,349	3.90	19.6	3.14	43.3	2.22
All women						
Selected groups:						
To Lage	1,107	2.75	–	–	52.4	1.31
To Ondae	530	2.53	–	–	48.6	1.30
To Pebato	869	3.22	–	–	51.2	1.57
To Wingke-mposo	868	3.83	–	–	47.0	2.03
All groups	11,969	2.80	–	–	40.6	1.14

Source: Tillema 1926:46-7

1 At ages '0-2' according to one column in the original table; described in another column as *zuigelingensterfte*.

The Kündig fertility and mortality survey, Minahasa, 1930-1932

	Airmadidi	Tondano	Kawangkoan	Kakas	Langoan	All districts	Birth and death rates per thousand (all districts)
1930							
Population	10,326	19,102	26,371	–	–	55,799	
Births	442	841	1,114	–	–	2,397	43.0
Deaths	291	650	712	–	–	1,653	29.6
Deaths at ages 0-1	84	243	173	–	–	500	
1931							
Population	10,782	19,722	27,101	18,742	17,278	93,625	
Births	454	907	1,192	755	792	4,100	43.8
Deaths	291	467	597	438	382	2,,175	23.2
Deaths at ages 0-1	100	146	156	136	106	644	
1932							
Population	11,263	20,535	–	19,116	17,937	68,851	
Births	397	877	–	787	808	2,869	41.7
Deaths	252	465	–	490	398	1,605	23.3
Deaths at ages 0-1	102	182	–	133	120	537	

	Airmadidi	Tondano	Kawangkoan	Kakas	Langoan	All districts	Birth and death rates per thousand (all districts)
All years							
Births	1,293	2,625	2,306	1,542	1,600	9,366	
Deaths at ages 0-1	286	571	329	269	226	1,681[1]	
Infant mortality (%)	22.1	21.8	14.3	17.4	14.1	17.9[2]	

Source: Kündig 1934:175

[1] The figure of 1837 given in the original table is erroneous.
[2] The figure of 19.6% given in the original table is erroneous.

APPENDIX I

Land use (km²) in Minahasa, 1862[1]

	Dry rice	Swidden fallow (estimate)	Wet rice	Coffee gardens	Coffee fallow (estimate)	Cocoa plantations	Coconut plantations	Total area under perman-ent or periodic cultivation
Administrative divisions:								
Manado	29	–	0.2	–	–	–	–	–
Kema	31	–	0.2	–	–	–	–	–
Tondano	44	–	16.9	–	–	–	–	–
Amurang	43	–	0.8	–	–	–	–	–
Belang	7	–	3.4	–	–	–	–	–
Minahasa	154	1,230	22	65	85	28	24	ca 1600
Minahasa totals as % of total land area[2]	3	26	0.5	1	2	0.5	0.5	33

Sources: AV Manado 1862 (ANRI Ambon 1563); AV Manado 1863 (ANRI Manado 52)

1 The figures given here for Kema, which were missing in the 1862 report, and those from Tondano, which were incomplete in 1862, are from 1863.
2 In order to maintain comparability with Appendix F, the area figure used to calculate these proportions was 4,787 km² rather than the 5,274 km² given for Minahasa in the 1930 census (Appendix I) and used as a basis for demographic calculations elsewhere in this book.

APPENDIX J

Land use in Minahasa, 1919

Administrative divisions (1862)[4]	Land area[1] (km²)	Cultivated swiddens[2] (km²)	Swidden fallow (juramei) (km²)	Cultivated swiddens as proportion of all swidden land (%)	Wet ricefields (km²)	Coconut plantations (km²)	Other cultivated land[3] (km²)	State ('waste') land and nature reserves (km²)
Manado	568	28	329	7.8	4	106	20	67
Kema	1,190	29	599	4.6	21	146	5	390
Tondano	804	104	476	17.9	81	22	18	103
Amurang	1,403	83	603	12.1	10	106	20	580
Belang	850	12	514	2.3	18	52	21	233
Minahasa	47,87[5]	253	2,484	9.2	133	428	96	1,354
Minahasa totals as % of total land area	100	5.3	51.9	-	2.8	8.9	2.0	28.3

Source: Van Marle 1922, II:86-9

1 Due to rounding errors and an error in the original table, the component areas do not add up exactly to the totals given here.
2 Implicitly: swiddens planted with main food crops (rice and maize).
3 Coffee, nutmeg, sago, tobacco, cloves, cocoa, cassia.
4 The 1862 administrative divisions have been reconstructed in order to facilitate comparison with Appendix I.
5 This figure differs considerably from that of 5,274 km² given in the 1930 census (Appendix I), but has been retained here in order not to affect Van Marle's proportional results. It refers only to the mainland of Minahasa; if offshore islands were included, according to Van Marle (1922, II:5), the total area would be 4956 km². It is not clear whether the remaining discrepancy with respect to the later figure reflects a boundary change, or an improvement in measurement. The use of the lower figure here and in Appendix E is probably justified in so far as the land use statistics are more likely to be understated than exaggerated.

APPENDIX K

Areal foodcrop yields in Minahasa

	Dry rice: average (hulled, tonnes/ha)	Dry rice: most productive variety (hulled, tonnes/ha)	Wet rice: average (hulled, tonnes/ha)	Wet rice: most productive variety (hulled, tonnes/ha)	maize (grain only, tonnes/ha)
1861 (on test plots of ca 0.3 ha)[1]					
Administrative division:					
Manado	0.90	1.37	–	–	–
Tondano	0.90	1.29	0.86	1.29	–
Amurang	0.45	0.69	0.34	0.43	–
Belang	0.28	0.34	0.41	0.64	–
ca 1940 (global estimates for single farming household)					
on primary forest (*oerbosch*) swidden (0.33 ha)	1.50	–	–	–	2.10
On 'young forest' (*jongbosch-gronden*) swidden (0.33 ha)	1.20	–	–	–	1.50
On grassland (*alang-alang*) swidden (0.25 ha)	0.48	–	–	–	1.20

Sources: CV Manado 1862 (ANRI Ambon 1563); Tammes 1940:192

1 These tests were supervised by the *controleurs* of each administrative division (CV Manado 1861, in ANRI Manado 95); where exactly they were carried out, and according to what procedure, is unclear. In each test, 2 or 3 different rice varieties were planted; it is not clear whether indigenous farmers would have planted the same combination.

Bibliography

Abdussamad, K.
1987   'Kompleksitas permasalahan Danau Limboto serta beberapa alternatif
            acuan keseimbangan ekosistem Alo-Molowahu-Biyonga Kabupaten
            Dati II Gorontalo'. Paper, Seminar regional kecenderungan kerawa-
            nan ekosistem Sulawesi Utara dan alternatif penanggulangannya
            pada Pelita V, Manado, 12-13 November.
Abendanon, E.C.
1915-18   *Geologische en geographische doorkruisingen van Midden-Celebes (1909-
            1910)*. Leiden: Brill. Four vols.
Acciaioli, Greg
1989   *Searching for good fortune; The making of a Bugis shore community at Lake
            Lindu, Central Sulawesi*. [PhD thesis, Australian National University.]
1992   'Introducing Central Sulawesi', in: Toby Alice Volkman and Ian Cald-
            well (eds), *Sulawesi; The Celebes*, p. 155. Hong Kong: Periplus. [Periplus
            Travel Guides.]
Adam, L.
1925a   'Uit en over de Minahasa V. Bestuur', *Bijdragen tot de Taal-, Land- en
            Volkenkunde* 81:390-423.
1925b   'Uit en over de Minahasa VI. Zeden en gewoonten en het daarmede
            samenhangend adatrecht van het Minahassische volk', *Bijdragen tot de
            Taal-, Land- en Volkenkunde* 81:424-99.
Adas, Michael
1981   'From avoidance to confrontation; Peasant protest in precolonial and
            colonial Southeast Asia', *Comparative Studies in Society and History*
            23:217-47.
Adatvonissen
1914   'Adatvonnissen (1898-1910)', *Adatrechtbundels* 9:84-96.
Adhuri, Dedi Supriadi
1993   'Hak ulayat laut dan dinamika masyarakat nelayan di Indonesia
            bagian Timur; Studi kasus P. Bebalang, Desa Sathean dan Demta',
            Masyarakat Indonesia 20:143-63.
Adriani, N.
1901   'Mededeelingen omtrent de Toradjas van Midden-Celebes', *Tijdschrift
            voor Indische Taal-, Land- en Volkenkunde (TBG)* 44:215-54.
1913a   'De reis van den heer W.J.M. Michielsen naar het Posso-Meer, 12-17
            Juli 1869', *De Indische Gids* 35-2:1612-8.

1913b 'Verhaal der ontdekkingsreis van Jhr. J.C.W.D.A. van der Wyck naar het Posso-Meer, 16-22 October, 1865', *De Indische Gids* 35-2:843-62.
1915 'Maatschappelijke, speciaal economische verandering der bevolking van Midden-Celebes, sedert de invoering van het Nederlandsch gezag aldaar', *Tijdschrift van het Koninklijk Nederlandsch Aardrijkskundig Genootschap* 32(Second Series):457-75.
1916 'De Hoofden der Toradja's in Midden-Celebes', *Verslagen der Algemeene Vergaderingen Indisch Genootschap* 1915-16:107-26.
1917 'De Toradja'sche vrouw als priesteres', *Verslagen en Mededeelingen der Koninklijke Akademie van Wetenschappen, Afdeeling Letterkunde* 5-2:453-78.
1918 'Zwangerschap en geboorte bij de Toradja's van Midden-Celebes'. *Nederlandsch Maandschrift voor Verloskunde en Vrouwenziekten en voor Kindergeneeskunde* 7:380-90.
[1919] *Posso (Midden-Celebes)*. Den Haag: Zendingsstudie-Raad. [Onze Zendingsvelden 2.]
1921a 'De bewoners van Midden-Celebes', in: J.C. van Eerde (ed.), *De volken van Nederlandsch Indië in monographieën*, vol. 2, pp. 1-32. Amsterdam: Elsevier.
1921b *Korte schets van het Toradja-volk in Midden-Celebes*. Oegstgeest: Zendingsbureau.

Adriani, N. and A.C. Kruyt
1898 'Van Posso naar Parigi, Sigi en Lindoe', *Mededeelingen van wege het Nederlandsch Zendelinggenootschap* 42:369-535.
1899 'Van Posso naar Todjo', *Mededeelingen van wege het Nederlandsch Zendelinggenootschap* 43:1-46.
1900 'Van Posso naar Mori', *Mededeelingen van wege het Nederlandsch Zendelinggenootschap* 44:135-214.
1901 'Geklopte boomschors als kleedingstof op Midden-Celebes en hare geographische verspreiding in Indonesië', *Internationales Archiv für Ethnographie* 14:139-91.
1912-14 *De Bare'e-sprekende Toradja's van Midden-Celebes*. Batavia: Landsdrukkerij. Four vols.
1950-51 *De Bare'e sprekende Toradjas van Midden-Celebes (de Oost-Toradjas)*. Amsterdam: Noord-Hollandsche Uitgevers Maatschappij. Four vols. [Verhandelingen der Koninklijke Nederlandse Akademie van Wetenschappen, Afdeeling Letterkunde, Nieuwe Reeks 54, 55, 56.]

Aernsbergen, A.J. van
1925 'Uit en over de Minahasa III. De katholieke kerk en hare missie in de Minahasa', *Bijdragen tot de Taal-, Land- en Volkenkunde* 81:8-60.

Aguirre, Guido Pinto, Albert Palloni, and Robert Jones
1998 'Effects of lactation on post-partum amenorrhoea; Re-estimation using data from a longitudinal study in Guatemala', *Population Studies* 52:231-48.

Aken, A.Ph. van
1932 'Memorie van overgave van de residentie Manado.' [NA MvO MMK 306.]

Aken, Gerrit van
1694   'Bericht aangaande de staat der kerken en scholen op Manado,
            Bolaang, Kaidipan etc. alsmede in de Sangihe-Talaud archipel, 18-
            8-1694', in: H.E. Niemeijer (ed.), forthcoming, *Bronnen betreffende de
            Protestantsche kerk in de Molukken, 1605-1795*. [Original source: NA
            VOC 1556.]

Alexander, Jennifer and Paul Alexander
1979   'Labour demands and the "involution" of Javanese agriculture',
            Social Analysis 3:22-44.
1993   'Economic change and public health in a remote Sarawak commu-
            nity', *Sojourn* 8:250-74.

Alexander, Paul
1984   'Women, labour and fertility; Population growth in nineteenth-cen-
            tury Java', *Mankind* 14:361-71.
1986   'Labour expropriation and fertility; Population growth in nineteenth
            century Java', in: W. Penn Handwerker (ed.), *Culture and reproduction;
            An anthropological critique of demographic transition theory*, pp. 249-62.
            Boulder, Colorado: Westview.

Algemeene memorie Poso
[1925]   'Algemeene memorie inzake de onderafdeeling Poso.' [NA MvO KIT
            1208.]

Algemeene schetskaart van Nederlandsch-Indië
1941   *Algemeene schetskaart van Nederlandsch-Indië*. Blad 84-85/XVI-XVII.
            Topografischen Dienst. [Scale: 1: 200,000.]

Allen, Bryant, Harold Brookfield and Yvonne Byron
1989   'Frost and drought through time and space. Part II: The written, oral
            and proxy records and their meaning', *Mountain Research and Devel-
            opment* 9:297-305.

Allied Geographical Section, Southwest Pacific Area
1944   *Menado (Celebes)*. N.p.: Allied Geograpical Section. [Terrain Study
            83.]
1945   *Central Celebes*. N.p.: Allied Geograpical Section. [Special Report 82.]

Alvard, Michael S.
2000   'The potential for sustainable harvests by traditional Wana hunters
            in Morowali Nature Reserve, Central Sulawesi, Indonesia', *Human
            Organization* 59:428-40.

Andaya, Barbara Watson
1993a   'Cash cropping and upstream-downstream tensions; The case of
            Jambi in the seventeenth and eighteenth centuries', in: Anthony Reid
            (ed.), *Southeast Asia in the early modern era; Trade, power, and belief*, pp.
            91-122. Ithaca, New York: Cornell University Press. [Asia, East by
            South.]
1993b   *To live as brothers; Southeast Sumatra in the seventeenth and eighteenth
            centuries*. Honolulu: University of Hawaii Press.

Andaya, Leonard Y.
1981   *The heritage of Arung Palakka; A history of South Sulawesi (Celebes) in the*

seventeenth century. The Hague: Nijhoff. [KITLV, Verhandelingen 91.]

1993   *The world of Maluku; Eastern Indonesia in the early modern period*, Honolulu: University of Hawaii Press.

1995   'The Bugis-Makassar diasporas', *Journal of the Malaysian Branch of the Royal Asiatic Society* 68:119-38.

Andel, W.J.D. van

1921   'Memorie van overgave van de onderafdeling Bwool.' [NA MvO KIT 1186.]

Andel, W.J.D. van and M.A. Monsjou

1919   'Bestuursinrichting en grondenrecht in de afdeeling Gorontalo (1917)', *Adatrechtbundels* 17:114-22.

Anderson, A.J.U.

1977   'Sago and nutrition in Sarawak', *The Sarawak Museum Journal* 25:71-80.

Ansingh, W.

1937   'Nota inzake het landschap Sigi-Dolo.' [NA MvO KIT 1206.]

Aragon, Lorraine V.

1990   'Barkcloth production in Central Sulawesi; A vanishing textile technology in outer island Indonesia', *Expedition; The University Museum magazine of archaeology and anthropology, University of Pennsylvania* 32-1:33-48.

1992   *Divine justice; Cosmology, ritual, and protestant missionization in Central Sulawesi, Indonesia*. [PhD thesis, University of Illinois.]

1996   'Twisting the gift; Translating precolonial into colonial exchanges in Central Sulawesi, Indonesia', *American Ethnologist* 23:43-60.

2000   *Fields of the lord; Animism, Christian minorities, and state development in Indonesia*. Honolulu: University of Hawaii Press.

Argeloo, Marc and René R.J. Dekker

1996   'Exploitation of megapode eggs in Indonesia; The role of traditional methods in the conservation of megapodes', *Oryx* 30:59-64.

Argensola, Bartolomé Leonardo de

1992   *Conquista de las Islas Malucas*. Madrid: Miraguano/Polifemo. [Originally published 1609; Biblioteca de Viajeros Hispánicos 7.]

Arts, Job and Nol van Beurden

1982   Goud en geloof; De invloed van de goudmijnbouw en de zending op het moderne imperialisme in Celebes 1880-1915. [MA thesis, Rijksuniversiteit Utrecht.]

ASEAN [Association of South-East Asian Nations]

1982   *The ASEAN compendium of climatic statistics*. Jakarta: ASEAN Sub-committee on Climatology, ASEAN Committee on Science and Technology, ASEAN Secretariat.

Atkinson, Jane Monnig

1989   *The art and politics of Wana shamanship*. Berkeley: University of California Press.

Atlas van tropisch Nederland

1938   *Atlas van tropisch Nederland*. Batavia: Koninklijk Nederlandsch Aardrijkskundig Genootschap/Topografischen Dienst in Nederlandsch-Indië.

Avink, K.F.
1935   'Aanvullende bestuursmemorie onderafdeling Kolondale'. [NA MvK
            KIT 1214.]

Baak, B. van
1919   'Bestuur van het rijk Gorontalo (1867)', *Adatrechtbundels* 17:112.

Babcock, Tim G.
1989   *Kampung Jawa Tondano; Religion and cultural identity.* Yogyakarta:
            Gadjah Mada University Press.

Baer, A.
1999   *Health, disease, and survival; A biomedical and genetic analysis of the Orang
            Asli of Malaysia.* Subang Jaya: Center for Orang Asli Concerns.

Bailey, Robert C., Genevieve Head, Mark Jenike, Bruce Owen, Robert Rechtman and
Elzbieta Zechenter
1989   'Hunting and gathering in tropical rain forest; Is it possible?', *Ameri-
            can Anthropologist* 91:59-82.

Barr, Donald F. and Sharon G. Barr
1993   'Ritual and belief in Da'a', in: Marilyn Gregerson (ed.) *Ritual, belief,
            and kinship in Sulawesi*, pp. 25-90. Dallas, Texas: International Museum
            of Cultures.

Barton, R.F.
1969   *Ifugao law.* Berkeley: University of California Press.

Bastiaan, A.A.
1930   'Nota behoorende bij de acte van verband dd. 13 September 1930 van
            het landschap Kendahe-Tahoena,' [NA MvO KIT 1180.]

Bastiaans, J.
1938   'Het verbond tusschen Limbotto en Gorontalo', *Tijdschrift voor Indische
            Taal-, Land- en Volkenkunde (TBG)* 78:215-47.
1939   'Batato's in het oude Gorontalo, in verband met den Gorontaleeschen
            staatsbouw', *Tijdschrift voor Indische Taal-, Land- en Volkenkunde (TBG)*
            79:23-72.

Bayliss-Smith, T.P.
1974   'Constraints on population growth; The case of the Polynesian outlier
            atolls in the precontact period', *Human Ecology* 2:259-95.
1980   'Population pressure, resources and welfare; Towards a more realistic
            measure of carrying capacity', in: H.C. Brookfield (ed.), *Population-
            environment relations in tropical islands; The case of eastern Fiji.* Paris:
            UNESCO.

Beck, W.J.
1922   'Mapaloes', *Koloniale Studiën* 6:64-8.

Belcher, Edward
1848   *Narrative of the voyage of H.M.S. Semarang, during the years 1843-46;
            Employed surveying the islands of the eastern archipelago; Accompanied by
            a brief vocabulary of the principal languages.* London: Reeve, Benham,
            and Reeve. Two vols.

Bellwood, Peter
1976   'Archaeological research in Minahasa and the Talaud islands, north-
            eastern Indonesia', *Asian Perspectives* 19:240-88.
1997   *Prehistory of the Indo-Malaysian archipelago*. Second edition. Honolulu:
            University of Hawaii Press. [First edition 1985.]
Bemmel, A.C.V. van
1949   'Revision of the rusine deer in the Indo-Australian archipelago', *Treu-
            bia* 20:191-262.
Bemmelen, R.W. van
1949   *The geology of Indonesia*. The Hague: Government Printing Office. Three
            vols.
Bemmelen, Sita van
1987   'The marriage of Minahasa women in the period 1861-1933; Views and
            changes', in: Elsbeth Locher-Scholten and Anke Niehof (eds), *Indone-
            sian women in focus; Past and present notions*, pp. 181-204. Dordrecht:
            Foris. [KITLV, Verhandelingen 127.]
Bemmelen, W. van
1916   'Droogte-jaren op Java', *Natuurkundig Tijdschrift voor Nederlandsch-
            Indië* 75:157-79.
Benda-Beckmann, F. von, K. von Benda-Beckmann and A. Brouwer
1995   'Changing "indigenous environmental law"' in the Central Moluccas;
            Communal regulation and privatization of sasi', *Ekonesia* 2:1-38.
Berg, B.J. van den,
1935   'Nota inzake het landschap Tawaeli.' [NA MvO KIT 1204.]
Berlage, H.P.
1931   'Over het verband tusschen de dikte der jaarringen van djatiboomen
            (*Tectona grandis Lf.*) en den regenval op Java', *Tectona* 24:939-53.
Besten, Gerhardi â,
[1757]   'Rapport van een visitatie van kerken en scholen in Noord-Sulawesi, de
            Sangir-Talaud eilanden, en Makian, 1-9-1757', in: H.E. Niemeijer (ed.),
            forthcoming, *Bronnen betreffende de Protestantsche kerk in de Molukken,
            1605-1795*. [Original source: ANRI Ternate 429.]
Beukering, J.A. van
[1947]   *Het ladangvraagstuk; Een bedrijfs- en sociaal economisch probleem*. [Bata-
            via]: Departement van Economische Zaken. [Mededeelingen van het
            Departement van Economische Zaken in Nederlandsch-Indië 9.]
Bickmore, Albert S.
1868   *Travels in the East Indian Archipelago*. London: Murray.
Bierens de Haan, A.
1893   'De Minahasa', *Nederlandsch Zendingstijdschrift* 5:65-97.
Bik, J.Th.
1845   'Aanteekeningen over de goudmijnen van Gorontalo op Celebes',
            Tijdschrift voor Nederlandsch Indië (TNI) 7-2:90-104.
1864   'Aanteekeningen nopens eene reis naar Bima, Timor, de Moluksche
            eilanden, Menado en Oost-Java, gedaan in 1821 en 1822 met den
            hoogleeraar C.G.C. Reinwardt', *Tijdschrift voor Indische Taal-, Land- en
            Volkenkunde (TBG)* 14:125-83.

Blaikie, Piers and Harold Brookfield (eds)
1987   *Land degradation and society*. London: Methuen.

Blair, Emma H. and J.A. Robertson (eds)
1903-09   *The Philippine Islands, 1493-1898*. Cleveland: Clark. 55 vols.

Blankhart, David Meskes
1951   *Voeding en leverziekten op het eiland Sangir in Indonesië*. [PhD thesis, Rijksuniversiteit te Utrecht.]

Bleeker, P.
1856   *Reis door de Minahassa en den Molukschen archipel, gedaan in de maanden September en October 1855 in het gevolg van den gouverneur-generaal Mr. A.J. Duymaer van Twist*. Batavia: Lange. Two vols.

Bloembergen, S.
1940   'Verslag van een exploratie-tocht naar Midden-Celebes (Lindoe-meer en Goenoeng Ngilalaki ten zuiden van Paloe) in Juli 1939', *Tectona* 33:377-418.

Blok, Roelof
1848   'Beknopte geschiedenis van het Makassarsche Celebes en onderhoorigheden', *Tijdschrift voor Nederlandsch Indië (TNI)* 10-1:3-77.

Boer, H.J. de
1951   'Treering measurements and weather fluctuations in Java from AD 1514', *Koninklijke Nederlandse Akademie van Wetenschappen, Proceedings of the Section of Sciences, Series B, Physical Sciences* 54:194-209.

Boerema, J.
1931   *Regenval in Nederlandsch-Indië. Deel I: Gemiddelden van den regenval voor 3293 waarnemingsplaatsen [...]*. Batavia: Landsdrukkerij. [Verhandelingen Koninklijk Magnetisch en Meteorologisch Observatorium 24-1.]
1933   *Regenval in Nederlandsch-Indië. Deel IV: Kaarten van den gemiddelden jaarlijkschen en maandelijkschen regenval op Celebes*. Batavia: Koninklijk Magnetisch en Meteorologisch Observatorium. [Verhandelingen Koninklijk Magnetisch en Meteorologisch Observatorium 24-4.]

Bohigian, Gary William
1994   *Life on the rim of Spain's Pacific-American empire; Presidio society in the Molucca Islands, 1606-1663*. [PhD thesis, University of California, Los Angeles.]

Bongaarts, John
1980   'Does malnutrition affect fecundity? A summary of evidence', *Science* 208:564-9.

Bongaarts, John and Robert G. Potter
1983   *Fertility, biology, and behaviour; An analysis of the proximate determinants*. San Diego: Academic.

Bonne, C.
1941   'Echinostomiasis aan het Lindoemeer in Centraal-Celebes', *Geneeskundig Tijdschrift voor Nederlandsch-Indië* 81:1139-67.

Bonne, C. and J.H. Sandground
1939   'Echinostomiasis in Celebes veroorzaakt door het eten van zoetwatermosselen', *Geneeskundig Tijdschrift voor Nederlandsch-Indië* 79:2116-34.

Bonne, C., A.J.P. Borstlap, Lie Kian Joe, W.J. Molenkamp and W. Nanning
1942a   'Voortgezet bilharzia onderzoek in Celebes', *Geneeskundig Tijdschrift voor Nederlandsch-Indië* 82:21-36.

Bonne, C., A.J.P. Borstlap, Lie Kian Joe, W.J. Molenkamp, C.E. de Moor and W. Nanning
1942b   'Voortgezet onderzoek over echinostomiasis in Celebes', *Geneeskundig Tijdschrift voor Nederlandsch-Indië* 82:3-20.

Bonne-Wepster, J. and N.H. Swellengrebel
1953   *The anopheline mosquitoes of the Indo-Australian region.* Amsterdam: De Bussy.

Boomgaard, Peter
1981   'Female labour and population growth on nineteenth-century Java', *Review of Indonesian and Malaysian Affairs* 15-2:1-31.
1987   'Morbidity and mortality in Java, 1820-1880; Changing patterns of death and disease', in: Norman G. Owen (ed.), *Death and disease in Southeast Asia; Explorations in social, medical and demographic history*, pp. 48-69. Singapore: Oxford University Press. [Asian Studies Association of Australia Southeast Asia Publications Series 14.]
1988   'Forests and forestry in colonial Java: 1677-1942', in: John Dargavel, Kay Dixon and Noel Semple (eds), *Changing tropical forests; Historical perspectives on today's challenges in Asia, Australasia and Oceania*, pp. 59-87. Canberra: Centre for Resource and Environmental Studies, Australian National University.
1989a   *Children of the colonial state; Population growth and economic development in Java, 1795-1880.* Amsterdam: Free University Press. [CASA Monographs 1.]
1989b   'Pokken en vaccinatie op Java, 1780-1860; Medische gegevens als bron voor de demografische geschiedenis', in: G.M. van Heteren, A. de Knecht-van Ekelen and M.J.D. Poulissen (eds), *Nederlandse geneeskunde in de Indische Archipel 1816-1942*, pp. 115-27. Amsterdam: Rodopi.
1992   'Sacred trees and haunted forests – Indonesia, particularly Java, 19th and 20th centuries', in: Ole Bruun and Arne Kalland (eds), *Asian perceptions of nature; Papers presented at a workshop, NIAS, Copenhagen, Denmark, October 1991*, pp. 39-53. Copenhagen: Nordic Institute of Asian Studies. [Nordic Proceedings in Asian Studies 3.]
1996a   *Forests and forestry 1823-1941.* Amsterdam: Royal Tropical Institute. [Changing Economy in Indonesia 16.]
1996b   *Historicus in een papieren landschap.* Leiden: KITLV Uitgeverij. [Inaugurele rede, Universiteit van Amsterdam.]
1997a   'Introducing environmental histories of Indonesia', in: Peter Boomgaard, Freek Colombijn and David Henley (eds), *Paper landscapes; Explorations in the environmental history of Indonesia*, pp. 1-26. Leiden: KITLV Press. [Verhandelingen 178.]
1997b   'Hunting and trapping in the Indonesian archipelago, 1500-1950', in: Peter Boomgaard, Freek Colombijn and David Henley (eds), *Paper landscapes; Explorations in the environmental history of Indonesia*, pp. 185-213. Leiden: KITLV Press. [Verhandelingen 178.]

1998a   'Environmental impact of the European presence in Southeast Asia, 17th-19th centuries', *Illes i Imperis* 1:21-35.

1998b   'The VOC trade in forest products in the seventeenth century', in: Richard H. Grove, Vinita Damodaran and Satpal Sangwan (eds), *Nature and the Orient; The environmental history of South and Southeast Asia*, pp. 375-95. Delhi: Oxford University Press.

1999   'Shame or savings? Patterns of migration and family formation in colonial Sumatra and Java (Indonesia), 1800-1950'. Paper, ESF workshop on leavers and stayers in Eurasian societies, The Hague, 18-20 June.

2001   'Crisis mortality in seventeenth-century Indonesia', in: Ts'ui-jung Liu, James Lee, David Sven Reher, Osamu Saito and Wang Feng (eds), *Asian population history*, pp. 191-220. Oxford: Oxford University Press.

2003   'Smallpox, vaccination, and the Pax Neerlandica; Indonesia, 1550-1930', *Bijdragen tot de Taal-, Land- en Volkenkunde* 159:590-617.

Boomgaard, Peter, Freek Colombijn and David Henley (eds)
1997   *Paper landscapes; Explorations in the environmental history of Indonesia*. Leiden: KITLV Press. [Verhandelingen 178.]

Boomgaard, P. and A.J. Gooszen
1991   *Population trends 1795-1942*. Amsterdam: Royal Tropical Institute. [Changing Economy in Indonesia 11.]

Boonstra van Heerdt, R.
1914a   'De berglandschappen behoorende tot de onderafdeeling Paloe van Midden-Celebes', *Tijdschrift van het Koninklijk Nederlandsch Aardrijkskundig Genootschap* 31(Second Series):618-44.

1914b   'De noorderarm van het eiland Celebes, van Paloe tot Bwool', *Tijdschrift van het Koninklijk Nederlandsch Aardrijkskundig Genootschap* 31(Second Series):725-65.

Booth, Anne
1988   *Agricultural development in Indonesia*. Sydney: Allen and Unwin. [Asian Studies Association of Australia Southeast Asia Publications Series 16.]

Boserup, Ester
1965   *The conditions of agricultural growth; The economics of agrarian change under population pressure*. London: Allen and Unwin.

Bosscher, C. and P.A. Matthijssen
1854   'Schetsen van de rijken van Tomboekoe en Banggai, op den oostkust van Celebes', *Tijdschrift voor Indische Taal-, Land- en Volkenkunde (TBG)* 2:63-107.

Boudyck-Bastiaanse, J.H. de
1845   *Voyages faits dans les Moluques a la Nouvelle-Guinée et a Célèbes, avec le comte Charles de Vidua de Conzano, a bord de la goëlette royale Viris*. Paris: Bertrand.

Bouvy, A.C.N.
1924   'Uit en over de Minahasa I. De Minahassa en de geneeskunst', *Bijdragen tot de Taal-, Land- en Volkenkunde* 80:365-96.

Braak, C.
1946   'Klimaat', in: C.J.J. van Hall and C. van Koppel (eds), *De landbouw in den Indischen Archipel*, vol. I, pp. 63-82. 's-Gravenhage: Van Hoeve.

Bracher, M.D. and Gigi Santow
1982   'Breast-feeding in Central Java', *Population Studies* 36:413-29.

Brandes, J.L.A.
[1894]   'Taalkaart van de Minahasa; Schaal 1:375000.' [KIT map collection.]

Brandwijk van Blokland, Gerard
[1749]   'Memorie weegens den teegenwoordigen toestand van saaken in de Moluccos, 20-8-1749', in: H.E. Niemeijer (ed.), forthcoming, *Memories van overgave van gouverneurs van de Molukken (Ternate) in de zeventiende en achttiende eeuw*. [Original source: NA VOC 2740.]

Breman, Joel G.
1991   'Viral infections with cutaneous lesions', in: G. Thomas Strickland (ed.), *Hunter's tropical medicine*, pp. 162-71. Seventh edition. Philadelphia: Saunders. [First edition 1945.]

Breton, Hendrik
[1767]   'Memorie wegens den presenten staat der Moluccos, 3-8-1767', in: H.E. Niemeijer (ed.), forthcoming, *Memories van overgave van gouverneurs van de Molukken (Ternate) in de zeventiende en achttiende eeuw*. [Original source: ANRI Ternate 78.]

Brieven
1908-31   *Brieven van den zendeling Alb. C. Kruyt en zijne vrouw aan hunne vrienden.* Leeuwarden: Onderafdeeling "Leeuwarden" van het Nederlandsch Zendeling Genootschap. Three vols.

Brilman, D.
1938   *De zending op de Sangi- en Talaud-eilanden.* N.p.: Zendingsstudie-Raad.

Broch, Harald Beyer
1998   'Local resource dependency and utilization on Timpaus', in: Arne Kalland and Gerard Persoon (eds), *Environmental movements in Asia*, pp. 205-26. Richmond, Surrey: Curzon. [Nordic Institute of Asian Studies Man and Nature Series 4.]

Broersma, R.
1931a   'De beteekenis van Selebes' oostkust voor den handel', *Tijdschrift van het Koninklijk Nederlandsch Aardrijkskundig Genootschap* 48(Second Series):1039-49.
1931b   'Gorontalo, een handelscentrum van Noord Selebes', *Tijdschrift van het Koninklijk Nederlandsch Aardrijkskundig Genootschap* 48(Second Series):221-38.

Brookfield, Harold C.
1972   'Intensification and disintensification in Pacific agriculture; A theoretical approach', *Pacific Viewpoint* 13-1:30-48.
1984   'Intensification revisited', *Pacific Viewpoint* 25-1:15-44.
1997   'Landscape history; Land degradation in the Indonesian region', in: Peter Boomgaard, Freek Colombijn and David Henley (eds), *Paper landscapes; Explorations in the environmental history of Indonesia*, pp. 27-59. Leiden: KITLV Press. [Verhandelingen 178.]

Brookfield, Harold C. and Doreen Hart
1971   *Melanesia; A geographical interpretation of an island world*. London: Methuen.

Brookfield, Harold C., Lesley Potter and Yvonne Byron
1995   *In place of the forest; Environmental and socio-economic transformation in Borneo and the eastern Malay Peninsula*. Tokyo: United Nations University Press.

Brosius, J. Peter
1990   *After Duwagan; Deforestation, succession, and adaptation in upland Luzon, Philippines*. Michigan: Centre for South and Southeast Asian Studies, University of Michigan. [Michigan Studies of South and Southeast Asia 2.]

Brouwer, Arie
1998   'From abundance to scarcity; Sago, crippled modernization and curtailed coping in an Ambonese village', in: Sandra Pannell and Franz von Benda-Beckmann (eds), *Old World places, New World problems; Exploring issues of resource management in eastern Indonesia*, pp. 336-87. Canberra: Centre for Resource and Environmental Studies, Australian National University.

Brouwer, Marten
1936   *Bestuursvormen en bestuursstelsels in de Minahassa*. Wageningen: Veenman.

Brown, Colin
1987   'The influenza pandemic of 1918 in Indonesia', in: Norman G. Owen (ed.), *Death and disease in Southeast Asia; Explorations in social, medical and demographic history*, pp. 235-56. Singapore: Oxford University Press. [Asian Studies Association of Australia Southeast Asia Publication Series 14.]

Bruce-Chwatt, Leonard Jan
1980   *Essential malariology*. London: Heinemann.

Brug, Peter Harmen van der
1995   *Malaria en malaise; De VOC in Batavia in de achttiende eeuw*. Amsterdam: De Bataafsche Leeuw.

Brug, S.L.
1926   'De geographische verspreiding van muskieten in den Oost Indischen archipel', *Mededeelingen van den Dienst der Volksgezondheid in Nederlandsch-Indië* 15:525-36.

Brug, S.L. and J.W. Tesch
1937   'Parasitaire wormen aan het Lindoe Meer (oa. Paloe, Celebes)', *Geneeskundig Tijdschrift voor Nederlandsch-Indië* 77:2151-8.

Bruinier, J.B.H.
1924   *De bosschen van de Minahasa en boschreserveering*. Manado: Liem Oei Tiong. [Noord-Selebes-Instituut Publicatie 1.]

Buddingh, S.A.
1860   *Neêrlands-Oost-Indie; Reizen over Java, Madura, Makasser, Saleijer, Bima, Menado, Sangier-eilanden, Talau-eilanden, Ternate gedaan gedurende het tijdvak van 1852-1857*, vol. 2. Rotterdam: Wijt.

Bulbeck, Francis David
1992   *A tale of two kingdoms; The historical archaeology of Gowa and Tallok, South Sulawesi, Indonesia*. [PhD thesis, Australian National University.]

Bulbeck, David, Anthony Reid, Lay Cheng Tan and Yiqi Wu
1998   *Southeast Asian exports since the fourteenth century; Cloves, pepper, coffee and sugar*. Singapore: ISEAS. [Sources for the Economic History of Southeast Asia 4.]

Bulbeck, David, and Ian Caldwell
2000   *Land of iron; The historical archaeology of Luwu and the Cenrana valley; Results of the Origin of Complex Society in South Sulawesi Project (OXIS)*. Hull: Centre for South-East Asian Studies, University of Hull.

Burch, Thomas K.
1983   'The impact of forms of families and sexual unions and dissolution of unions on fertility', in: Rodolfo A. Bulatao and Ronald D. Lee (eds), *Determinants of fertility in developing countries. Vol. 2: Fertility regulation and institutional influences*, pp. 532-61. New York: Academic.

Burger, D.
1936   'Bliksem als oorzaak van boschbrand', *Tectona* 29:881-93.

Burkill, I.H.
1935   *A dictionary of the economic products of the Malay Peninsula*. London: Crown. Two vols.

Bushnell, Andrew F.
1993   '"The horror" reconsidered; An evaluation of the historical evidence for population decline in Hawai'i, 1778-1803', *Pacific Studies* 16:115-61.

Caldwell, John C.
2001   'What do we know about Asian population history? Comparisons of Asian and European research', in: Ts'ui-jung Liu, James Lee, David Sven Reher, Osamu Saito and Wang Feng (eds), *Asian population history*, pp. 3-23. Oxford: Oxford University Press.

Calkins, Richard
1994   *Indonesia; Environment and development*. Washington, DC: World Bank. [A World Bank Country Study.]

Campo, J.N.F.M. à
1992   *Koninklijke Paketvaart Maatschappij; Stoomvaart en staatsvorming in de Indonesische archipel 1888-1914*. Hilversum: Verloren. [Publikaties van de Faculteit der Historische en Kunstwetenschappen 3.]

Cant, R.G.
1973   *A historical geography of Pahang*. Singapore: Malaysian Branch of the Royal Asiatic Society. [MBRAS Monograph 4.]

Capellen, [G.A.G.P.] van der
1855   'Het journaal van den Baron van der Capellen op zijne reis door de Molukko's', *Tijdschrift voor Nederlandsch Indië (TNI)* 17-2:281-313, 357-96.

Carey, Arlen D. and Joseph Sopreanto
1996   'The evolutionary demography of the fertility-mortality equilibrium', *Population and Development Review* 21:613-30.

Carney, W. Patrick, Sjahrul Masri, Salludin and J. Putrali
1974   'The Napu Valley, a new schistosomiasis area in Sulawesi, Indonesia',
            Southeast Asian Journal of Tropical Medicine and Public Health 5:246-51.

Carney, W. Patrick, J. Putrali and J.M. Caleb
1974   'Intestinal parasites and malaria in the Poso Valley, Central Sulawesi,
            Indonesia', *Southeast Asian Journal of Tropical Medicine and Public Health*
            5:368-73.

Carney, W.P., Sjahrul Masri, M. Sudomo, J. Putrali and George M. Davis
1975   'Distribution of *Oncomelania hupensis* in the Napu Valley of Central
            Sulawesi, Indonesia', *Southeast Asian Journal of Tropical Medicine and
            Public Health* 6:211-8.

Carney, W.P., M. Sudomo and Purnomo
1980   'Echinostomiasis; A disease that disappeared', *Tropical and Geograph-
            ical Medicine* 32:101-5.

Carpentier Alting, J.H.
1902   *Regeling van het privaatrecht voor de inlandsche bevolking in de Minahassa-
            districten der residentie Menado. Vol. 1: Burgelijke stand, huwelijk afstam-
            ming, adoptie.* Batavia: Landsdrukkerij.

Chabot, H.Th.
1950   *Verwantschap, stand en sexe in Zuid-Celebes.* Groningen: Wolters.
1969   'Processes of change in Siau 1890-1950', *Bijdragen tot de Taal-, Land- en
            Volkenkunde* 125:94-102.

Chabot, Lyne
1996   Le défi forestier en Indonésie; Entre l'expansion agricole et l'exploi-
            tation forestière; Le cas de Jambi, Sumatra. [MA thesis, Université
            Laval.]

Christiansen, Sofus
1986   'Wet rice cultivation; Some reasons why', in: Irene Norlund, Sven
            Cederroth and Ingela Gerdin (eds), *Rice societies; Asian problems and
            prospects*, pp. 15-27. London: Curzon. [Studies on Asian Topics 10.]

Christie, Jan Wisseman
1991   'States without cities; Demographic trends in early Java', *Indonesia*
            52:23-40.

Claaszoon, Jacob
1710   'Memorie over den tegenwoordigen staat en stand der zaken in de
            provincie Molocco, 14-7-1710', in: H.E. Niemeijer (ed.), forthcoming,
            *Memories van overgave van gouverneurs van de Molukken (Ternate) in de
            zeventiende en achttiende eeuw.* [Original source: ANRI Ternate 80.]

Clarence-Smith, William Gervase
1993   'From Maluku to Manila; Cocoa production and trade in maritime
            South East Asia, from the 1820s to the 1880s'. Paper, Conference on
            cocoa production and economic development in the nineteenth and
            twentieth centuries, London, 15-17 September.
1994   'The impact of forced coffee cultivation on Java, 1805-1917', *Indonesia
            Circle* 64:241-64.
1998a   'The economic role of the Arab community in Maluku, 1816 to 1940',
            Indonesia and the Malay World 26:32-49.

1998b   'The rise and fall of Maluku cocoa production in the nineteenth century; Lessons for the present', in: S. Pannell and F. von Benda-Beckmann (eds), *Old World places, New World problems; Exploring resource management issues in eastern Indonesia*, pp. 94-112. Canberra: Centre for Resource and Environmental Studies, Australian National University.

Clark, Colin, and Margaret Haswell
1967   *The economics of subsistence agriculture*. Second edition. London: Macmillan. [First edition 1964.]

Cleland, John, and Christopher Wilson
1987   'Demand theories of the fertility transition; An iconoclastic view', *Population Studies* 41:5-30.

Clercq, F.S.A. de
1870a   'Boekaankondiging', *Tijdschrift voor Nederlandsch Indië (TNI)* 4-1:124-37.
1870b   'Iets over het bijgeloof in de Minahasa', *Tijdschrift voor Nederlandsch Indië (TNI)* 4-2:1-11.
1870c   'De overzijde der Ranojapo', *Tijdschrift voor Indische Taal-, Land- en Volkenkunde (TBG)* 19:521-39.
1871a   'De afdeeling Amoerang in de jaren 1861-1868', *Tijdschrift voor Nederlandsch Indië (TNI)* 5:422-7.
1871b   'Allerlei over de residentie Manado; Opmerkingen naar aanleiding van verschillende beschrijvingen', *Tijdschrift voor Nederlandsch Indië (TNI)* 5-2:23-34.
1871c   'Over eenige maatschappelijke instellingen bij de inlandsche Christenen in de Minahasa', *Tijdschrift voor Nederlandsch Indië (TNI)* 5-1:211-6.
1871d   'De voornaamste padisoorten geteeld op de droge velden in de Minahasa', *Tijdschrift voor Nederlandsch Indië (TNI)* 5-1:1-7.
1872   'De huizen in Bolaang Mongondow', *Tijdschrift voor Indische Taal-, Land- en Volkenkunde (TBG)* 18:282-3.
1873   'Het strand der Minahasa', *Tijdschrift voor Nederlandsch Indië (TNI)* 1873-1:249-72.
1883   'Schets van het landschap Bolaäng-Mongondow', *Tijdschrift van het Koninklijk Nederlandsch Aardrijkskundig Genootschap* 7:116-25. [Second Series.]
1890   *Bijdragen tot de kennis der residentie Ternate*. Leiden: Brill.
1891   'De hervorming van het Minahasa-stelsel', *Verslagen der Algemeene Vergaderingen Indisch Genootschap* 1891:203-31.
1898   'De nieuwe bewerking van het boek van den heer Graafland over de Minahasa', *De Indische Gids* 20-2:843-51.
1909   *Nieuw plantkundig woordenboek voor Nederlandsch Indië*. Amsterdam: De Bussy.

Cloek, Jacob
1726   'Berigt in 't kort van de jegenwoordigen staat en stand der Moluccos met het geene daer verder onder gehoort, 15-6-1726', in: H.E. Niemeijer (ed.), forthcoming, *Memories van overgave van gouverneurs van de Molukken (Ternate) in de zeventiende en achttiende eeuw*. [Original source: NA VOC 2050.]

Cluijsenaer, Joachim Petrus
1720   'Rapport van een visitatie van kerken en scholen in Noord-Sulawesi, 1-9-1720', in: H.E. Niemeijer (ed.), forthcoming, *Bronnen betreffende de Protestantsche kerk in de Molukken, 1605-1795*. [Original source: NA VOC 1979.]

Cohen, Mark Nathan
1989   *Health and the rise of civilization*. New Haven: Yale University Press.

Coleman, David
1986   'Population regulation; A long-range view', in: David Coleman and Roger Schofield (eds), *The state of population theory; Forward from Malthus*, pp. 14-41. Oxford: Blackwell.

Colenbrander, H.T.
1898   'Officieele berichten omtrent het opheffen van den Compagnie's post te Parigi', *Mededeelingen van wege het Nederlandsch Zendelinggenootschap* 42:587-95.

Colin, Francisco
1900-02   *Labor evangelica; Ministerios apostolicos de los obreros de la Compañia de Iesus, fundacion, y progressos de su provincia en las Islas Filipinas*. Second edition. Barcelona: Henrich. Three vols. [First published 1663.]

Colombijn, Freek
1997a   'The ecological sustainability of frontier societies in eastern Sumatra', in: Peter Boomgaard, Freek Colombijn and David Henley (eds), *Paper landscapes; Explorations in the environmental history of Indonesia*, pp. 27-59. Leiden: KITLV Press. [Verhandelingen 178.]
1997b   'Een milieu-effect rapportage van de gambircultuur in de Riau-archipel in de negentiende eeuw', *Tijdschrift voor Geschiedenis* 110:290-312.
1997c   'Van dik hout en magere verdiensten; Houtkap op Sumatra (1600-1942)', *Spiegel Historiael* 32:431-7.

Conelly, W. Thomas
1992   'Agricultural intensification in a Philippine frontier community; Impact on labor efficiency and farm diversity', *Human Ecology* 20:203-23.

Conklin, Harold C.
1957   *Hanunóo agriculture; A report on an integral system of shifting cultivation in the Philippines*. Rome: Food and Agriculture Organization of the United Nations. [FAO Forestry Development Paper 12.]
1959   'Shifting cultivation and succession to grassland climax', in: *Proceedings of the Ninth Pacific Science Congress of the Pacific Science Association*, vol. 8, pp. 60-2. Bangkok: Chulalongkorn University, Department of Science. [Pacific Science Congress 9.]

Coolsma, S.
1893   'De zending op de Sangir- en Talaut-eilanden', *Nederlandsch Zendingstijdschrift* 5:193-298.
1901   *De zendingseeuw voor Nederlandsch Oost-Indië*. Utrecht: Breijer.

Corpus diplomaticum
1907-55   *Corpus diplomaticum Nederlando-Indicum*. Uitgegeven door J.E. Heeres en F.W. Stapel. 's-Gravenhage: Nijhoff. Six vols.

Cortesão, Armando (ed.)
1944		*The Suma Oriental of Tomé Pires; An account of the East, from the Red Sea to Japan, written in Malacca and India in 1512-1515 [...], vol. 1*. London: The Hakluyt Society. [Works issued by the Hakluyt Society, Second Series 89.]

Coté, Joost
1996		'Colonising Central Sulawesi; The 'Ethical Policy' and imperialist expansion 1890-1910', *Itinerario* 20-3:87-107.

Crab, P. van der
1862		*De Moluksche eilanden; Reis van Z.E. de Gouverneur-Generaal Charles Ferdinand Pahud, door den Molukschen archipel*. Batavia: Lange.
1875		'Memorie van overgave van de residentie Menado.' [NA MvO MMK 229.]

Crawfurd, John
1856		*A descriptive dictionary of the Indian islands and adjacent countries*. London: Bradbury and Evans.

Cribb, Robert
2000		*Historical atlas of Indonesia*. Richmond, Surrey: Curzon.

Cross, John H., Michael D. Clarke, W. Patrick Carney, J. Putrali, Arbain Joesoef, H. Sadjiman, Felix Partono, Hudojo, and Sri Oemijati
1975		'Parasitology survey in the Palu Valley, Central Sulawesi (Celebes), Indonesia', *Southeast Asian Journal of Tropical Medicine and Public Health* 6:366-75.

Cuarteron, D. Carlo
1855		*Spiegazione e traduzione dei XIV quadri relativi alle isole di Salibaboo, Talaor, Sanguey, Nanuse, Mindanao, Celebes, Bornèo, Bahalatolis, Tambisan, Sulu, Toolyan, e Labuan presentati alla Sacra congregazione de propaganda fide nel mese Settembre 1852*. Roma: Tipografia della S.C. di Propaganda Fide.

Cuff, Timothy
1995		'Introduction; Historical anthropometrics – theory, method, and the state of the field', in: John Komlos (ed.), *The biological standard of living on three continents; Further explorations in anthropometric history*, pp. 1-15. Boulder, Colorado: Westview.

Cullinane, Michael, and Peter Xenos
1998		'The growth of population in Cebu during the Spanish era; Constructing a regional demography from local sources', in: Daniel F. Doeppers and Peter Xenos (eds), *Population and history; The demographic origin of the modern Philippines*, pp. 71-138. Madison: Center for Southeast Asian Studies, University of Wisconsin. [CSAS Monograph 16.]

Cummins, J.S.
1962		*The travels and controversies of Friar Domingo Navarrete, 1618-1686*. Cambridge: Cambridge University Press. Two vols. [Works issued by the Hakluyt Society, Second Series 118, 119.]

Daghregister
1896-1931	*Daghregister gehouden in 't Casteel Batavia* [1642-1682]. 's-Gravenhage: Nijhoff, Batavia: Landsdrukkerij, Kolff.

Dam, Pieter van
1931   *Beschrijving van de Oostindische Compagnie*, vol. 2-1. 's-Gravenhage: Nijhoff. [Rijks Geschiedkundige Publicatiën 74.]

Dames, Mansel Longworth (ed.)
1921   *The book of Duarte Barbosa; An account of the countries bordering on the Indian Ocean and their inhabitants [...]*, vol. 2. London: The Hakluyt Society. [Works issued by the Hakluyt Society, Second Series 49.]

Dames, T.W.G.
1955   *The soils of East Central Java*. Bogor: General Agricultural Research Station. [Pemberitaan Balai Besar Penelitian Pertanian 141.]

De Bevoise, Ken
1995   *Agents of apocalypse; Epidemic disease in the colonial Philippines*. Princeton, New Jersey: Princeton University Press.

[Delden, A.J. van]
1844   'De Sangir-eilanden in 1825', *Indisch Magazijn* 1(4-6):356-83, 1(7-9):1-32.

Delvoye, Pierre, Mohamed Badawi, Marc Demaegd and Claude Robyn
1978   'Long lasting lactation is associated with hyperprolactinemia and amenorrhoea', in: C. Robyn and M. Harter (eds), *Progress in prolactin physiology and pathology; Proceedings of the International Symposium on Prolactin held in Nice, France, 20-23 October, 1977*, pp. 213-32. Amsterdam: Elsevier, North-Holland Biomedical Press. [Developments in Endocrinology 2.]

Departemen Pendidikan dan Kebudayaan
1983   *Adat istiadat daerah Sulawesi Utara*. Jakarta: Proyek Inventarisasi dan Dokumentasi Kebudayaan Daerah, Departemen Pendidikan dan Kebudayaan.

Departement van Landbouw, Nijverheid en Handel
1925   *Een en ander over de volksklappercultuur in* de Minahassa. Weltevreden: Landsdrukkerij.

Dinter, B.C.A.J. van
1899   'Eenige geographische en ethnographische aanteekeningen betreffende het eiland Siaoe', *Tijdschrift voor Indische Taal-, Land- en Volkenkunde (TBG)* 41:324-89.

Dirkzwager, N.
1912   'Het Nederlandsch-Indisch gouvernement en zijne tekortkomingen tegenover de Minahassa', *De Indische Gids* 34-2:1160-73.

Dobbin, Christine
1983   *Islamic revivalism in a changing peasant economy; Central Sumatra, 1784-1847*. London: Curzon. [Scandinavian Institute of Asian Studies Monograph Series 47.]

Dobby, E.H.G.
1956   *Southeast Asia*. Third edition. London: University of London Press. [First edition 1950.]

Doeppers, D.F.
1999   'Feeding Manila in the 19th century; The changing rice trade'. Paper, Centre for Asian Studies Amsterdam, 26 April.

Domsdorff, A.M.
1937   'De Minahassische dorpsgemeenschap in haar genetisch verband (1928)', *Adatrechtbundels* 39:344-59.

Donner, Wolf
1987   *Land use and environment in Indonesia*. Honolulu: University of Hawaii Press.

Doren, J.B.J. van
1854-56   *Fragmenten uit de reizen in den Indischen Archipel*. Amsterdam: Sybrandi. Two vols.
1857-60   *Herinneringen en schetsen van Nederlands Oost-Indië*. Amsterdam: Sybrandi. Two vols.

Dormeier, J.J.
1947   *Banggaisch adatrecht*. 's-Gravenhage: Nijhoff. [KITLV, Verhandelingen 6.]

Douglas, Mary
1966   'Population control in primitive groups', *The British Journal of Sociology* 17:263-73.

Dove, Michael R.
1983a   'Forest preference in swidden agriculture', *Tropical Ecology* 24:122-42.
1983b   'Theories of swidden agriculture, and the political economy of ignorance', *Agroforestry Systems* 1:85-99.
1984   'Man, land and game in Sumbawa; Some observations on agrarian ecology and development policy in eastern Indonesia', *Singapore Journal of Tropical Geography* 5:112-24.
1985a   'The agroecological mythology of the Javanese and the political economy of Indonesia', *Indonesia* 39:1-36.
1985b   *Swidden agriculture in Indonesia; The subsistence strategies of the Kalimantan Kantu'*. Berlin: Mouton.
1986   'The practical reason of weeds in Indonesia; Peasant vs state views of *Imperata* and *Chromolaena*', *Human Ecology* 14:163-90.
1989   'The transition from stone to steel in the prehistoric swidden agricultural technology of the Kantu' of Kalimantan, Indonesia', in: David R. Harris and Gordon C. Hillman (eds), *Foraging and farming; The evolution of plant exploitation*, pp. 667-77. London: Unwin Hyman. [One World Archaeology 13.]

Downs, Richard Erskine
1955   'Head-hunting in Indonesia', *Bijdragen tot de Taal-, Land- en Volkenkunde* 111:40-70.
1956   *The religion of the Bare'e-speaking Toradja of Central Celebes*. 's-Gravenhage: Excelsior.

Dozier, Edward P.
1966   *Mountain arbiters; The changing life of a Philippine hill people*. Tucson: The University of Arizona Press.

Driessen, P.M., P. Buurman and Permadhy
1976   'The influence of shifting cultivation on a "podzolic" soil from Central Kalimantan', in: Soil Research Institute, *Peat and podzolic soils and their potential for agriculture in Indonesia; Proceedings ATA 106 Midterm*

Seminar, Tugu, October 13-14, 1976, pp. 95-115. Bogor: Soil Research Institute. [Soil Research Institute Bulletin 3.]

Duhr, George Fredrik
1781   'Berigt aangaande de goudmynen op de kust van Celebes', *Verhandelingen van het Bataviaasch Genootschap van Kunsten en Wetenschappen* 3:105-16.

Dumont d'Urville, M.J.
1833   *Voyage de la corvette l'Astrolabe exécuté par ordre du Roi, pendant les années 1826-1827-1828-1829 [...]*, vol. 5. Paris: Tastu.

Dunnebier, W.
1907a   'De zending in Bolaäng-Mongondow', *Mededeelingen van wege het Nederlandsch Zendelinggenootschap* 51:1-21.
1907b   'Zielental van Bolaäng Mongondow, medio 1906', *Mededeelingen van wege het Nederlandsch Zendelinggenootschap* 51:24-5.
1919   'Laatste berichten uit Bolaäng-Mongondow', *Maandblad der Samenwerkende Zendings-Corporaties* 2:119.
1949   'Over de vorsten van Bolaang Mongondow', *Bijdragen tot de Taal-, Land- en Volkenkunde* 105:219-74.

Durand, Frédéric
1994   *Les forêts en Asie du sud-est; Recul et exploitation; Le cas de l'Indonésie*, Paris: L'Harmattan.

Dutrieux, F.B.
1930   'Aanvullende memorie van overgave van de onderafdeling Boalemo.' [NA MvO KIT 1189.]
1931a   'Gewijzigde en aanvullende memorie van overgave van de onderafdeling Donggala.' [NA MvO KIT 1197.]
1931b   'Toelichtingen op het ladangvraagstuk betreffende de onderafdeeling Donggala.' [NA MvO KIT 1197, Bijlage B.]

Dijk, L.C.D. van
1862   *Neêrland's vroegste betrekkingen met Borneo, den Solo-archipel, Cambodja, Siam en Cochin-China*. Amsterdam: Scheltema.

Ebbinge Wübben, F.A.
1888   'Die Nanusa-Inseln', *Dr. A. Petermanns Mitteilungen aus Justus Perthes' Geographischer Anstalt* 34:136-8.
1889   'Naar de Talaut-eilanden', *Tijdschrift van het Koninklijk Nederlandsch Aardrijkskundig Genootschap* 6(Second Series):201-12.

Echols, John M. and Hassan Shadily
1992   *Kamus Indonesia-Inggris*. Third edition. Jakarta: Gramedia. [First edition 1976.]

Eck, R. van
1882   'Schetsen uit het volksleven in Nederl. Oost-Indië', *De Indische Gids* 4-2:105-30, 566-78, 956-83.

Eckenhausen, H.
1930   'Memorie van overgave van de onderafdeling Parigi.' [NA MvO KIT 1201.]

Edeling, A.C.J.
1919   'Memorie omtrent de Minahasa', *Adatrechtbundels* 16:5-95.

Edie, J.E.
1923   'Memorie van overgave van de afdeling Gorontalo.' [NA MvO KIT
                1188.]
Een en ander
1908   'Het een en ander over de sagoe-bereiding op Noord-Celebes', *Week-
                blad voor Indië* 4-52:1045-7.
Eeuwijk, Peter van and Brigit Obrist van Eeuwijk
1993-94   'Professionalisierte und volkstümliche Basisgesundheitsversorgung
                bei den Minahasa (Nord-Sulawesi, Indonesien); Konkurrenz oder
                Ergänzung', in: Marc-Olivier Gonseth (ed.), *Les frontières du mal;
                Approches anthropologiques de la santé et de la maladie,* pp. 435-57. Berne:
                Société Suisse d'Ethnologie. [Ethnologica Helvetica 17-18.]
Eibergen, P.
1928   'De Minahassa', *Tijdschrift voor Economische Geographie* 19:228-38.
Ellen, Roy F.
1978   *Nuaulu settlement and ecology; An approach to the environmental relations
                of an eastern Indonesian community.* The Hague: Nijhoff. [KITLV, Ver-
                handelingen 83.]
1979   'Sago subsistence and the trade in spices; A provisional model of eco-
                logical succession and imbalance in Moluccan history', in: Philip C.
                Burnham and Roy F. Ellen (eds), *Social and ecological systems,* pp. 43-74.
                London: Academic. [Association of Social Anthropology Monograph
                18.]
Elson, R.E.
1994   *Village Java under the Cultivation System 1830-1870.* Sydney: Allen and
                Unwin. [Asian Studies Association of Australia Southeast Asia Publi-
                cation Series 25.]
1997   *The end of the peasantry in Southeast Asia; A social and economic history of
                peasant livelihood, 1800-1990s.* Basingstoke, Hampshire: Macmillan.
Encyclopaedie
1917-21   *Encyclopaedie van Nederlandsch-Indië.* Leiden: Brill, 's-Gravenhage:
                Nijhoff. Eight vols.
Encyclopaedisch Bureau
1912a   'De zelfbesturende landschappen Tahoelandang, Siaoe, Taboekan,
                Kandhar-Taroena en Manganitoe op de Sangi- en Talaud-eilanden',
                Mededeelingen van het Bureau voor de Bestuurszaken der Buitenbezittingen
                2:5-82.
1912b   'De zelfbesturende landschappen van de residentie Menado, gelegen
                op den vasten wal van Celebes', *Mededeelingen van het Bureau voor de
                Bestuurszaken der Buitenbezittingen* 2:85-205.
Engelenberg, A.J.N.
1905   'Bespreking van het bestuursbeleid in Nederlandsch Oost-Indie,
                toegelicht in verband met beschouwingen over de behoeften van de
                verschillende deelen van Indie en meer speciaal van Midden-Celebes',
                *Indisch Genootschap; Verslagen der Algemeene Vergaderingen van 8 Januari
                1901 - 29 Mei 1905*:121-56.

1906   'Bijdrage voor de memorie van overgave van den resident S.J.M. van Geuns, voorzover betreft de afdeeling Midden-Celebes, bevattende een overzicht van de gebeurtenissen van 13 Mei 1903 - 1 Juni 1906.' [NA MvO MMK 302 (Appendix).]

Errington, Shelly
1989   *Meaning and power in a Southeast Asian realm*. Princeton, New Jersey: Princeton University Press.

Esser, S.J.
1934   *Handleiding voor de beoefening der Ledo-taal; Inleiding, teksten met vertaling en aanteekeningen en woordenlijst*. Bandoeng: Nix. [Verhandelingen van het Bataviaasch Genootschap van Kunsten en Wetenschappen 72-1.]

Fairhead, James and Melissa Leach
1996   *Misreading the African landscape; Society and ecology in a forest-savanna mosaic*. Cambridge: Cambridge University Press. [African Studies Series 90.]
1998   *Reframing deforestation; Global analysis and local realities; Studies in West Africa*. London: Routledge.

Falkus, Malcolm
1990   'Economic history and environment in Southeast Asia', *Asian Studies Review* 14-1:65-79.

Feachem, Richard G.A.
1977   'Environmental health engineering as human ecology; An example from New Guinea', in: Timothy P. Bayliss-Smith and Richard G. Feachem (eds), *Subsistence and survival; Rural ecology in the Pacific*, pp. 129-82. London: Academic.

Fenner, F., D.A. Henderson, I. Arita, Z. Jezek and I.D. Ladnyi
1988   *Smallpox and its eradication*. Geneva: World Health Organization. [History of International Public Health 6.]

Ferguson, C.
1912   'Uit een brief van Br. C. Ferguson te Kaloewatoe, eiland Groot-Sangir', *Mededeelingen vanwege het Comité tot Voorziening in de Godsdienstige Behoeften van de Gevestigde Inlandsche Protestantsche Christengemeenten op de Sangi- en Talauer Eilanden* 13:5-8.

Fisher, Charles A.
1966   *South-East Asia; A social, economic and political geography*. Second edition. London: Methuen. [First edition 1964.]

Flach, M. and F. Rumawas (eds)
1996   *Plant resources of Southeast Asia. Vol. 9: Plants yielding non-seed carbohydrates*. Bogor: PROSEA.

Floud, Roderick, Kenneth Wachter and Annabel Gregory
1990   *Height, health and history; Nutritional status in the United Kingdom, 1750-1980*. Cambridge: Cambridge University Press.

Fogel, Robert William
1992   'Second thoughts on the European escape from hunger; Famines, chronic malnutrition, and mortality rates', in: S.R. Osmani (ed.),

            Nutrition and poverty, pp. 243-86. Oxford: Clarendon.

1997   'New findings on secular trends in nutrition and mortality; Some
            implications for population theory', in: Mark R. Rosenweig and Oded
            Stark (eds), *Handbook of population and family economics*, vol. 1A, pp.
            433-81. Amsterdam: Elsevier.

Fontanel, J. and A. Chantefort

1978   *Bioclimats du monde Indonésien*. Pondichéry: Institut Français de Pon-
            dichéry. Two vols. [Travaux de la Section Scientifique et Technique 16.]

Forrest, Thomas

1779   *A voyage to New Guinea and the Moluccas [...]*. London: Scott.

1792   *A voyage from Calcutta to the Mergui Archipelago [...]*. London: Robson.

Fox, James J.

1977   *Harvest of the palm; Ecological change in eastern Indonesia*. Cambridge,
            Massachusetts: Harvard University Press.

Fragment

1856   'Fragment uit een reisverhaal', *Tijdschrift voor Nederlandsch Indië (TNI)*
            18-1:391-432, 18-2:1-38, 69-100, 141-60.

Francis, E.

1860   *Herinneringen uit den levensloop van een' Indisch' ambtenaar van 1815 tot
            1851*. Vol. 3. Batavia: Van Dorp.

Freeman, J.D.

1955   *Iban agriculture; A report on the shifting cultivation of hill rice by the Iban
            of Sarawak*. London: HMSO. [Colonial Research Studies 18.]

Frieswijck, E.

1902   'Aanteekeningen betreffende den geografischen en ethnografischen
            toestand van het eiland Tagoelandang (afdeeling Sangi- en Talaut
            Eilanden)', *Tijdschrift van het Binnenlandsch Bestuur* 22:426-38, 469-89.

Frohwein, A.O.

1933   'Memorie van overgave van de onderafdeling Gorontalo.' [NA MvO
            KIT 1194.]

Furukawa, Hisao

1994   *Coastal wetlands of Indonesia; Environment, subsistence and exploitation*.
            Kyoto: Kyoto University Press.

FWI/GFW

2002   *The state of the forest: Indonesia*. Bogor: Forest Watch Indonesia, Wash-
            ington DC: Global Forest Watch.

Gallas, P.A.

1900   'Bijdrage tot de kennis van het landschap Poso', *Tijdschrift van het Konink-
            lijk Nederlandsch Aardrijkskundig Genootschap* 17(Second Series):801-14.

Gallois, W.O.

1892   *Rapport nopens den staat van zaken in de Minahassa*. Batavia: Lands-
            drukkerij.

Gan Chong-ying, Chin Bin, Teoh Soon-teong and Michiel K.C. Chan

1993   'Nutritional status of Kadazan children in a rural district in Sabah,
            Malaysia', *Southeast Asian Journal of Tropical Medicine and Public Health*
            24:293-301.

Gardiner, Peter and Mayling Oey
1987   'Morbidity and mortality in Java 1880-1940; The evidence of the colonial reports', in: Norman G. Owen (ed.), *Death and disease in Southeast Asia; Explorations in social, medical and demographic history*, pp. 70-90. Singapore: Oxford University Press. [Asian Studies Association of Australia, Southeast Asian Publications Series 14.]

Geertz, Clifford
1963   *Agricultural involution; The process of ecological change in Indonesia.* Berkeley: University of California Press. [Association of Asian Studies Monographs and Papers 11.]

Geestelijke en stoffelijke dingen
1911   'Van geestelijke en stoffelijke dingen', *Mededeelingen vanwege het Comité tot Voorziening in de Godsdienstige Behoeften van de Gevestigde Inlandsche Protestantsche Christengemeenten op de Sangi- en Talauer Eilanden* 12:1-4.

Generale missiven
1960-97   *Generale missiven van gouverneurs-generaal en raden aan Heren XVII der Verenigde Oostindische Compagnie.* 's-Gravenhage: Nijhoff. Eleven vols.

Geuns, S.J.M. van
1906   'Memorie van overgave van de residentie Menado.' [NA MvO MMK 302.]

Gilles, Herbert M. and David Warrell
1993   *Bruce-Chwatt's essential malariology.* Third edition. London: Arnold. [First edition 1980.]

Glamann, Kristof
1981   *Dutch-Asiatic trade, 1620-1740.* Second edition. 's-Gravenhage: Nijhoff. [First edition 1958.]

Godée Molsbergen, E.C.
1928   *Geschiedenis van de Minahassa tot 1829.* Weltevreden: Landsdrukkerij.

Goedhart, O.H.
1908   'Drie landschappen in Celebes', *Tijdschrift voor Indische Taal-, Land- en Volkenkunde (TBG)* 50:442-548.

Goldammer, J.G. and B. Seibert
1989   'Natural rain forest fires in eastern Borneo during the Pleistocene and Holocene', *Naturwissenschaften* 76:518-20.

Goldammer, Johann G., Berthold Seibert and Werner Schindele
1996   'Fire in dipterocarp forests', in: Andreas Schulte and Peter Schöne (eds), *Dipterocarp forest ecosystems; Towards sustainable management*, pp. 155-85. Singapore: World Scientific.

Gonggrijp, G.F.E.
1915   'Gorontalo', *Koloniaal Tijdschrift* 4:1361-72.

Gooszen, A.J.
1994   *Een demografisch mozaïek, Indonesië 1880-1942.* [PhD thesis, Landbouwuniversiteit Wageningen.]
1999   *A demographic history of the Indonesian archipelago 1880-1942.* Leiden: KITLV Press. [Verhandelingen 183.]

Goot, P. van der
1940   'De biologische bestrijding van de cactus-plaag in het Paloe-dal
             (Noord-Celebes)', Landbouw 16:413-29.
Gopalan, C.
1987   Nutrition problems and programmes in South-East Asia. New Delhi: World
             Health Organization Regional Office for South-East Asia. [SEARO
             Regional Health Papers 15.]
Gouvernements-koffiecultuur
1894   'Gouvernements-koffiecultuur in de residentie Menado', Tijdschrift
             voor Nederlandsch Indië (TNI) 23-1:434-66, 23-2:161-218.
[Graaf, H.J. van and G.J. Meijlan]
1856   'De Moluksche eilanden', Tijdschrift voor Nederlandsch Indië (TNI) 18-
             1:73-137, 167-96, 231-65, 315-59.
Graafland, N.
1864   'Fragment eener onuitgegevene beschrijving van de Minahassa', Mede-
             deelingen van wege het Nederlandsch Zendelinggenootschap 8:1-23.
1868   'De Manadorezen', Bijdragen tot de Taal-, Land- en Volkenkunde 15:382-
             93.
1867-69   De Minahassa; Haar verleden en haar tegenwoordige toestand (eene bijdrage
             tot de taal- en volkenkunde). Rotterdam: Wijt. Two vols.
1891   'De huwelijksvoltrekking van inlandsche Christenen in de Molukken
             en de Minahassa', Nederlandsch Zendingstijdschrift 3:129-49.
1898   De Minahassa; Haar verleden en haar tegenwoordige toestand. Batavia:
             Kolff. Second edition. Two vols. [First edition 1867-1869.]
Greenland, D.J.
1998   'Rice and rice-based farming systems', in: C.C. Webster and P.N. Wil-
             son (eds), Agriculture in the tropics, pp. 178-99. Third edition. Oxford:
             Blackwell Science. [First edition 1966.]
Grist, D.H.
1955   Rice. Second edition. London: Longmans and Green.
Grondijs, Th.W.
1931   'Vervolg-memorie van overgave van de afdeling Gorontalo.' [NA
             MvO KIT 1190.]
Grove, Richard H.
1997   Ecology, climate and empire; Colonialism and global environmental history,
             1400-1940. Cambridge: White Horse.
Grove, Richard H., Vinita Damodaran and Satpal Sangwan (eds)
1998   Nature and the Orient; The environmental history of South and Southeast
             Asia. Delhi: Oxford University Press.
Grubauer, Albert
1913   Unter Kopfjägern in Central-Celebes; Ethnologische Streifzüge in Südost-
             und Central-Celebes. Leipzig: Voigtländer.
Grudelbach, J.
1849   'Het meer van Tondano en omstreken', Indisch Archief 1-1:399-407.

Guillemard, F.H.H.
1886   *The cruise of the Marchesa to Kamschatka and New Guinea; With notices
            of Formosa, Liu-Kiu, and various islands of the Malay Archipelago*, vol. 2.
            London: Murray.

Gullick, J.M.
1958   *Indigenous political systems of western Malaya*. London: Athlone. [Lon-
            don School of Economics Monographs on Social Anthropology 17.]

Gunning, J.W.
1924   'Uit en over de Minahasa II. De Protestantsche zending in de Mina-
            hassa', *Bijdragen tot de Taal-, Land- en Volkenkunde* 80:451-520.

Haan, J.G. de
1907   'Een en ander over Bantik', *Mededeelingen van wege het Nederlandsch
            Zendelinggenootschap* 51:34-44.

Haga, B.J.
1931   'De Lima-pahalaä (Gorontalo); Volksordening, adatrecht en bestuurs-
            politiek', *Tijdschrift voor Indische Taal-, Land- en Volkenkunde (TBG)*
            71:186-314.

Hall, C.J.J. van
1949   'Cacao', in: C.J.J. van Hall and C. van de Koppel (eds), *De landbouw in
            de Indische Archipel*, vol. IIB, pp. 272-346. 's-Gravenhage: Van Hoeve.

Hanks, Lucien M.
1972   *Rice and man; Agricultural ecology in Southeast Asia*. Chicago: Aldine
            Atherton.

Hardin, Garrett
1968   'The tragedy of the commons', *Science* 162:1243-8.

Hardjono, J.
1971   *Indonesia, land and people*. Jakarta: Gunung Agung.

Harris, Marvin and Eric B. Ross
1987   *Death, sex, and fertility; Population regulation in preindustrial and develop-
            ing societies*. New York: Columbia University Press.

Hart, C. van der
1853   *Reize rondom het eiland Celebes en naar eenige der Moluksche eilanden*.
            's-Gravenhage: Fuhri.

Hartert, Ernst
1897   'Mr William Doherty's bird-collections from Celebes', *Novitates Zoolo-
            gicae; A journal of zoology in connection with the Tring Museum* 4:153-66.

Haze Winkelman, A.W. de
1935   'Algemene gegevens Afdeling Poso.' [NA MvO KIT 1213.]

Headland, Thomas N.
1987   'The wild yam question; How well could independent hunter gather-
            ers live in a tropical rain forest ecosystem?', *Human Ecology* 15:463-91.

Heersink, Christiaan G.
1995   'Interactie tussen mens en landschap in Zuid-Sulawesi tijdens de
            vroeg-moderne periode'. [Paper, KITLV Eden Project.]
1998   'Environmental adaptations in southern Sulawesi', in: Victor T. King
            (ed.), *Environmental challenges in South-East Asia*, pp. 95-120. Rich-

mond, Surrey: Curzon. [Nordic Institute of Asian Studies Man and Nature in Asia Series 2.]

1999   *Dependence on green gold; A socio-economic history of the Indonesian coconut island Selayar*. Leiden: KITLV Press. [Verhandelingen 184.]

Hegener, Michiel

1990   *Guerilla in Mori; Het verzet tegen de Japanners op Midden-Celebes in de tweede wereldoorlog*. Amsterdam: Contact.

Heinrich, Gerd

1932   *Der Vogel Schnarch; Zwei Jahre Rallenfang und Urwaldforschung in Celebes*. Berlin: Reimer/Vohsen.

H.E.K.

1894   'Het huwelijk in de Minahassa', *Tijdschrift voor Nederlandsch Indië (TNI)* 23-1:357-65.

Hekker, H.W.M.

1988   'Vooroudercultus en sjamanisme in de Minahasa; Syncretisme van de Minahassische religie', *Bijdragen tot de Taal-, Land- en Volkenkunde* 144:64-83.

1991   'Vooroudercultus en sjamanisme in Bolaang Mongondow', *Bijdragen tot de Taal-, Land- en Volkenkunde* 147:445-53.

1993   *Minahassers in Indonesië en Nederland; Migratie en cultuurverandering*. [PhD thesis, Universiteit van Amsterdam.]

Hengel, J. van

1910   'Memorie van overgave van de residentie Menado.' [NA MMK 303.]

Henley, David

1989   *The idea of Celebes in history*. Clayton, Victoria: Monash University Centre of Southeast Asian Studies. [CSEAS Working Paper 59.]

1993   'A superabundance of centers; Ternate and the contest for North Sulawesi', *Cakalele* 4:39-60.

1994   'Population and environment in precolonial northern Sulawesi'. Paper, 13th biennial conference of the Asian Studies Association of Australia, Perth, 13-16 July.

1995   'Minahasa mapped; Illustrated notes on cartography and history in Minahasa, 1512-1942', in: Reimar Schefold (ed.), *Minahasa past and present; Tradition and transition in an outer island region of Indonesia*, pp. 32-57. Leiden: Research School CNWS. [CNWS Publications 28.]

1996   *Nationalism and regionalism in a colonial context; Minahasa in the Dutch East Indies*. Leiden: KITLV Press. [Verhandelingen 168.]

1997a   'Carrying capacity, climatic variation, and the problem of low population growth among Indonesian swidden farmers; Evidence from North Sulawesi', in: Peter Boomgaard, Freek Colombijn and David Henley (eds), *Paper landscapes; Explorations in the environmental history of Indonesia*, pp. 92-120. Leiden: KITLV Press. [Verhandelingen 178.]

1997b   'Goudkoorts; Mijnbouw, gezondheid en milieu op Sulawesi (1670-1995)', *Spiegel Historiael* 32:424-30.

2002   *Jealousy and justice; The indigenous roots of colonial rule in northern Sulawesi*. Amsterdam: VU University Press. [Comparative Asian Studies 22.]

2004   'Conflict, justice, and the stranger-king; Indigenous roots of colonial rule in Indonesia and elsewhere', *Modern Asian Studies* 38:85-144.

Heringa, P.K.

1921a   'Rapport over de begroeiing van de onderafdeelingen Posso en Parigi van de Afdeeling Midden-Celebes, speciaal met het oog op de bosschen en houtstand', *Tectona* 14:795-810.

1921b   'Rapport over de begroeiing van de Sangi- en Talaud-eilanden', *Tectona* 14:733-46.

Heyne, K.

1950   *De nuttige planten van Indonesië.* 's-Gravenhage: Van Hoeve. Two vols.

Hickson, Sydney J.

1887   'Notes on the Sengirese', *The Journal of the Anthropological Institute of Great Britain and Ireland* 16:136-43.

1889   *A naturalist in North Celebes; A narrative of travels in Minahassa, the Sangir and Talaut islands, with notices of the fauna, flora and ethnology of the districts visited.* London: Murray.

Hirschmann, F.Ch.H.

1934   'Vervolg-memorie inzake de afdeling Donggala.' [NA MvO KIT 1202.]

Hissink, [C.]

1912   'Nota van toelichting, betreffende de zelfbesturende landschappen Paloe, Dolo, Sigi en Beromaroe', *Tijdschrift voor Indische Taal-, Land- en Volkenkunde (TBG)* 54:58-128.

Historische verhael

1646   'Historische verhael vande treffelijcke reyse, gedaen naer de Oost-Indien ende China, met elf schepen, door den Manhaften Admirael Cornelis Matelief de Ionge, in den jaren 1605, 1606, 1607, ende 1608', in: Isaac Commelin, *Begin ende voortgangh der Vereenighde Nederlandsche geoctroyeerde Oost-Indische compagnie* [...], vol. 2. Amsterdam: Jansz.

Hoëvell, G.W.W.C. Baron van

1891   'De assistent-residentie Gorontalo, voor zoover die onder rechtstreeksch bestuur is gebracht', *Tijdschrift van het Koninklijk Nederlandsch Aardrijkskundig Genootschap* 8(Second Series):26-43.

1892   'Korte beschrijving van het rijkje Mooeton (Bocht van Tomini)', *Tijdschrift van het Koninklijk Nederlandsch Aardrijkskundig Genootschap* 9(Second Series):349-60.

1893a   'Bijschrift bij de kaart der Tomini-bocht', *Tijdschrift van het Koninklijk Nederlandsch Aardrijkskundig Genootschap* 10(Second Series):64-72.

1893b   'Todjo, Posso en Saoesoe', *Tijdschrift voor Indische Taal-, Land- en Volkenkunde (TBG)* 35:1-47.

1905   'Het paard in de Gorontalosche landschappen', *Internationales Archiv für Ethnographie* 17:177-82.

Hoff, A.

1938   'Vervolg-memorie van overgave van de onderafdeling Bolaäng-Mongondo.' [NA MvO KIT 1179.]

Hofman, Ph.H.C.

1906   'De zending in Posso, gedurende 1906', *Mededeelingen van wege het Nederlandsch Zendelinggenootschap* 51:336-52.

1909   'Napoe en Besoa', *Mededeelingen van wege het Nederlandsch Zendeling-genootschap* 53:30-47.

Hogendorp, W. van
1890   'De Sangir- en Talauteilanden', *Nederlandsch Zendingstijdschrift* 2:113-22.

Hollan, Douglas W. and Jane C. Wellenkamp
1994   *Contentment and suffering; Culture and experience in Toraja.* New York: Columbia University Press.

Holleman, F.D.
1930   *Verslag van een onderzoek inzake adatgrondenrecht in de Minahasa.* Weltevreden: Landsdrukkerij. [Mededeelingen van de Afdeeling Bestuurszaken der Buitengewesten van het Departement van Binnenlandsch Bestuur, Serie A, 11.]

Holmgren, Robert J. and Anita E. Spertus
1989   *Early Indonesian textiles from three island cultures; Sumba, Toraja, Lampung.* New York: The Metropolitan Museum of Art.

Holthuis, L.B. and H.J. Lam
1942   'A first contribution to our knowledge of the flora of the Talaud islands and Morotai', *Blumea* 5:93-145.

Hopkins, Donald R.
1983   *Princes and peasants; Smallpox in history.* Chicago: The University of Chicago Press.

Horridge, G. Adrian
1978   *The design of planked boats in the Moluccas.* Greenwich: National Maritime Museum. [Maritime Monographs and Reports 38.]

Horsting, L.H.G.
1917   'Het meer van Tondano en zijne omgeving', *Jaarverslag van den Topographischen Dienst in Nederlandsch-Indië* 12:224-34.
[1924]   *Pawiro; Zwerftochten door Indië.* [Batavia]: Kolff.

Hull, Terence H.
1987   'Plague in Java', in: Norman G. Owen (ed.), *Death and disease in Southeast Asia; Explorations in social, medical and demographic history*, pp. 210-34. Singapore: Oxford University Press. [Asian Studies Association of Australia Southeast Asia Publications Series 14.]
2001   'Indonesian fertility behaviour before the transition; Searching for hints in the historical record', in: Ts'ui-jung Liu, James Lee, David Sven Reher, Osamu Saito and Wang Feng (eds), *Asian population history*, pp. 152-75. Oxford: Oxford University Press. [International Studies in Demography.]

Hull, Terence H. and Valerie J. Hull
1977   'The relation of economic class and fertility; An analysis of some Indonesian data', *Population Studies* 31:43-57.

Hunt, J.
1837   'Some particulars relating to Sulo, in the Archipelago of Felicia', in: J.H. Moor (ed.), *Notices of the Indian Archipelago, and adjacent countries; Being a collection of papers relating to Borneo, Celebes, Bali, Java, Sumatra,*

Nias, the Philippine Islands, Sulus, Siam, Cochin China, Malay Peninsula,
appendix, pp. 31-60. Singapore: n.n.

Hunger, F.W.T.
1920   *Cocos nucifera; Handboek voor de kennis van den cocos-palm in Neder-
            landsch-Indië, zijne geschiedenis, beschrijving, cultuur en producten.* Sec-
            ond edition. Amsterdam: Scheltema and Holkema. [First edition
            1916.]

Hunt, Robert C.
2000   'Labor productivity and agricultural development; Boserup revisited',
            Human Ecology 28:251-77.

Hustaart, Jacob
1656   'Schriftelijk vertoog van den tegenwoordigen staat der Vereenigde
            Nederlandsche Oostindische Comp:e in 't gouvernement der Moluxe
            eijlanden', in: H.E. Niemeijer (ed.), forthcoming, *Memories van overgave
            van gouverneurs van de Molukken (Ternate) in de zeventiende en achttiende
            eeuw.* [Original source: KITLV H454e.]

Huther, Georg Jacob
[1781]   'Rapport van een visitatie van kerken en scholen in Noord-Sulawesi
            en op de Sangir-Talaud eilanden, 27-4-1781', in: H.E. Niemeijer (ed.),
            forthcoming, *Bronnen betreffende de Protestantsche kerk in de Molukken,
            1605-1795.* [Original source: NA VOC 3597.]

Hutterer, Karl L.
1984   'Ecology and evolution of agriculture in Southeast Asia', in: A. Terry
            Rambo and Percy E. Sajise (eds), *An introduction to human ecology
            research on agricultural systems in Southeast Asia,* pp. 75-97. Honolulu:
            East-West Center.

Huxley, P.A.
1998   'Agroforestry', in: C.C. Webster and P.N. Wilson (eds), *Agriculture in
            the tropics,* pp. 222-56. Third edition. Oxford: Blackwell Science. [First
            edition 1966.]

Inventaris Arsip Gorontalo
1976   *Inventaris Arsip Gorontalo 1810-1865.* Jakarta: Arsip Nasional.

Jacobs, H.
1974-84   (ed.) *Documenta Malucensia.* Roma: Institutum Historicum Societatis
            Iesu. Three vols.
1992   'The insular kingdom of Siau under Portuguese and Spanish impact,
            16th and 17th centuries', in: Bernhard Dahm (ed.), *Regions and regional
            developments in the Malay-Indonesian world,* pp. 33-43. Wiesbaden: Har-
            rassowitz.

Janse, J.M.
1898   *De nootmuskaat-cultuur in de Minahassa en op de Banda-eilanden.* Batavia:
            Kolff. [Mededeelingen uit 's Lands Plantentuin 28.]

Jansen, A.J.F.
1856   'Uitbarsting van den Awoe op Groot-Sangir', *Natuurkundig Tijdschrift
            voor Nederlandsch Indië* 10:3-77.
1861   'De landbouw in de Minahasa van Menado, in 1853', *Tijdschrift voor
            Taal-, Land- en Volkenkunde van Nederlandsch-Indië (TBG)* 10:221-58.

Jansen, W.H.M.
1989   'De economische ontwikkeling van Celebes 1900-1938', *Jambatan* 7-
            2:65-79.
1990   De economische ontwikkeling van de residentie Menado, 1900-1940;
            Een onderzoek naar de economische structuur, de handel en de con-
            junctuur, en het inheemse ondernemersgedrag. [MA thesis, Rijksuni-
            versiteit Leiden.]

Jasper, J.E. and Mas Pirngadie
1912   *De inlandsche kunstnijverheid in Nederlandsch Indië. Deel II: De weefkunst.*
            's-Gravenhage: Mouton.

Jellesma, E.J.
1903   *De Minahassa en eenige andere streken der residentie Menado* […]. Amster-
            dam: De Bussy.
1911   'De Talauer-eilanden (Residentie Menado)', *De Indische Gids* 33-2:1236-
            43.

Jones, Gavin W.
1977   *The population of North Sulawesi.* Yogyakarta: Gadjah Mada University
            Press. [Department of Demography, Australian National University,
            Indonesian Population Monograph Series 1.]
1994   *Marriage and divorce in Islamic South-East Asia.* Kuala Lumpur: Oxford
            University Press.

Jones, Huw
1990   *Population geography.* Second edition. London: Chapman. [First edition
            1981.]

Jongh, Maximiliaen de
1669   'Rapport wegens den toestand in de provintie Molucco, 14-5-1669',
            in: H.E. Niemeijer (ed.), forthcoming, *Memories van overgave van gou-*
            verneurs van de Molukken (Ternate) in de zeventiende en achttiende eeuw.
            [Original source: NA VOC 1271.]

Junker, Laura Lee
1999   *Raiding, trading, and feasting; The political economy of Philippine chief-*
            doms. Honolulu: University of Hawaii Press.

Kam, Joseph
1821   'Account of a visit to Celebes and Sangir islands & c. in the Malayan
            Archipelago, by the Rev. Joseph Kam, missionary at Amboyna, in the
            Autumn of 1817', *Quarterly Chronicle of Transactions of the London Mis-*
            sionary Society 1:280-5, 298-300.

Kamus besar
1988   *Kamus besar bahasa Indonesia.* Jakarta: Balai Pustaka.

Kartodirdjo, A. Sartono
1971   (ed.) *Laporan politik tahun 1837.* Djakarta: ANRI. [Penerbitan Sumber-
            Sumber Sedjarah 4.]
1973   *Ikhtisar keadaan politik Hindia-Belanda tahun 1839-1848.* Jakarta: ANRI.
            [Penerbitan Sumber-Sumber Sejarah 5.]

Kathirithamby-Wells, Jeya
1997   'Human impact on large mammal populations in peninsular Malaysia
            from the nineteenth to the mid-twentieth century', in: Peter Boom-

gaard, Freek Colombijn and David Henley (eds), *Paper landscapes; Explorations in the environmental history of Indonesia*, pp. 217-41. Leiden: KITLV Press. [Verhandelingen 178.]

Kaudern, Walter

1925   *Structures and settlements in Central Celebes*. Göteborg: Elanders Bok-
            tryckeri Aktiebolag. [Ethnographical studies in Celebes; Results of the
            author's expedition to Celebes 1917-1920; 1.]

1938   *Megalithic finds in Central Celebes*. Göteborg: Elanders Boktryckeri
            Aktiebolag. [Ethnographical studies in Celebes; Results of the author's
            expedition to Celebes 1917-1920; 5.]

Kaufmann, Silvia, Rainer Gross, Werner Schultink, Soemilah Sastroamidjojo, and
Klaus Leitzmann

1995   'Nutritional situation and food consumption pattern among selected
            areas of West-Kalimantan, Indonesia', *Southeast Asian Journal of Trop-
            ical Medicine and Public Health* 26:541-9.

Kelling, P.

1906   'Uit eene brief van Br. P. Kelling', *Mededeelingen vanwege het Comité tot
            Voorziening in de Godsdienstige Behoeften van de Gevestigde Inlandsche
            Protestantsche Christengemeenten op de Sangi- en Talauer Eilanden* 1:12-
            6.

1907   'Enkele bijzonderheden omtrent de Christengemeenten op het eiland
            Siauw', *Mededeelingen vanwege het Comité tot Voorziening in de Gods-
            dienstige Behoeften van de Gevestigde Inlandsche Protestantsche Chris-
            tengemeenten op de Sangi- en Talauer Eilanden* 3:6-11.

Kemmerling, G.L.L.

1923-24   *De vulkanen van den Sangi-archipel en van de Minahassa*. Weltevre-
            den: Landsdrukkerij. Two vols. [Dienst van den Mijnbouw in Neder-
            landsch-Oost-Indië, Vulkanologische Mededeelingen 5.]

Keijzer, S. (ed.)

1856   *François Valentijn's Oud en nieuw Oost-Indien*, vol. 1. 's-Gravenhage:
            Susan. [First edition 1724.]

Kielstra, J.C.

1921   'De bewoners van Noord-Celebes', in: J.C. van Eerde (ed.), *De volken
            van Nederlandsch Indië in monographieën*, vol. 2, pp. 35-56. Amsterdam:
            Elsevier.

Kiliaan, J.Th.E.

1908   'Oudheden aangetroffen in het landschap Besoa (Midden-Celebes)',
            Tijdschrift voor Indische Taal-, Land- en Volkenkunde (TBG) 50:407-51.

King, Victor T. (ed.)

1998   *Environmental challenges in South-East Asia*. Richmond, Surrey: Curzon.
            [Nordic Institute of Asian Studies Man and Nature in Asia Series 2.]

Kisman, M.

1941   'Over nier- en uretersteenen en het voorkomen daarvan in de Mina-
            hassa', *Geneeskundig Tijdschrift voor Nederlandsch-Indië* 81:2682-93.

Kiyu, Andrew, Bibiana Teo, Stalin Hardin and Flora Ong

1991   'Nutritional status of children in rural Sarawak, Malaysia', *Southeast
            Asian Journal of Tropical Medicine and Public Health* 22:211-5.

Klein, Martin A.
1987   'The demography of slavery in western Soudan', in: Dennis D. Cordell
            and Joel W. Gregory (eds), *African population and capitalism; Historical
            perspectives*, pp. 50-61. Boulder: Westview.
Klein, W.C.
1932   'Bestuursmemorie van de onderafdeling Bwool.' [NA MvO KIT 1193.]
Kleiweg de Zwaan, J.P.
1925   'Kindermoord in den Indischen archipel', *Mensch en Maatschappij* 1:22-
            39.
1928   'Abortus provocatus in den Indischen archipel', *Mensch en Maatschap-
            pij* 4:33-50.
1929   'Bijdrage tot de anthropologie van Celebes', *Tijdschrift van het Koninklijk
            Nederlandsch Aardrijkskundig Genootschap* 46(Second Series):782-91.
Kluiver, J.
1894   'De inlandsche kunstnijverheid in de Minahasa', *Tijdschrift voor Nijver-
            heid en Landbouw in Nederlandsch-Indië* 48:166-9.
Knaap, Gerrit J.
1987   *Kruidnagelen en christenen; De Verenigde Oost-Indische Compagnie en de
            bevolking van Ambon, 1656-1696*. Dordrecht: Foris. [KITLV, Verhande-
            lingen 125.]
1995   'The demography of Ambon in the seventeenth century; Evidence
            from colonial proto-censuses', *Journal of Southeast Asian Studies* 26:227-
            41.
1996   *Shallow waters, rising tide; Shipping and trade in Java around 1775*. Leiden:
            KITLV Press. [Verhandelingen 172.]
Knapen, Han
1997   'Koortsachtig koppen tellen in de binnenlanden van Zuidoost-Borneo
            (1700-1900)', *Spiegel Historiael* 32:444-9.
1998   'Lethal diseases in the history of Borneo; Mortality and the interplay
            between disease environment and human geography', in: Victor T.
            King (ed.), *Environmental challenges in South-East Asia*, pp. 69-94. Rich-
            mond, Surrey: Curzon. [Nordic Institute of Asian Studies Man and
            Nature in Asia Series 2.]
2001   *Forests of fortune? The environmental history of Southeast Borneo, 1600-
            1880*. Leiden: KITLV Press. [Verhandelingen 189.]
Kol, H. van
1903   *Uit onze koloniën; Uitvoerig reisverhaal*. Leiden: Sijthoff.
Koloniaal verslag
1848-1941   *Koloniaal verslag*. 's-Gravenhage.
Kopstein, F.
1926   'Hygiënische studieën uit de Molukken', *Mededeelingen van den Dienst
            der Volksgezondheid in Nederlandsch-Indië* 15:1-88.
Koorders, S.H.
1898   *Verslag eener botanische dienstreis door de Minahasa; Tevens eerste overzicht
            der flora van N.O. Celebes uit een wetenschappelijk en praktisch oogpunt*.
            Batavia: Kolff. [Mededeelingen uit 's Lands Plantentuin 19.]

Koperberg, M.
1929   *Bouwstoffen voor de geologie van de residentie Manado.* Weltevreden:
            Landsdrukkerij. Two vols.

Kopytoff, Igor and Suzanne Miers
1977   'African "slavery" as an institution of marginality', in: Suzanne Miers
            and Igor Kopytoff (eds), *Slavery in Africa; Historical and anthropological
            perspectives*, pp. 3-81. Madison: The University of Wisconsin Press.

Korn, B.
1939   'Nota van de onderafdelingen Gorontalo en Boalemo.' [NA MvO KIT
            1195.]

Kornrumpf, Martin
1935   *Mensch und Landschaft auf Celebes.* Breslau: Hirt.

Kortleven, K.S.
1927   'Nota van toelichting betreffende het zelfbesturend landschap Toli-
            Toli.' [NA MvO KIT 1199.]

Kotilainen, Eija-Maija
1992   *'When the bones are left'; A study of the material culture of Central Sulawesi.*
            Helsinki: Suomen Antropologinen Seura. [Transactions of the Finnish
            Anthropological Society 31.]

Kraan, Nol
2000   *Twee blijde boodschappers; Brieven uit Bada van Jacob en Elisabeth
            Woensdregt 1916-1928.* Zoetermeer: Boekencentrum.

Kroeskamp, H.
1974   *Early schoolmasters in a developing country; A history of experiments in
            school education in 19th century Indonesia.* Assen: Van Gorcum.

Kruyt, A.C.
1892   'Mijne reis van Gorontalo naar Poso (Posso), met den Gouverne-
            mentsstoomer "Zeeduif", 4-16 Februari 1892', *Mededeelingen van wege
            het Nederlandsch Zendelinggenootschap* 36:225-56.
1893   'Mijn tweede reis van Gorontalo naar Poso', *Mededeelingen van wege
            het Nederlandsch Zendelinggenootschap* 37:101-14.
1894   'Naar het meer van Poso', *Mededeelingen van wege het Nederlandsch
            Zendelinggenootschap* 38:1-23.
1895-97   'Een en ander aangaande het geestelijk en maatschappelijk leven van
            den Poso-Alfoer', *Mededeelingen van wege het Nederlandsch Zendeling-
            genootschap* 39:1-36 (I), 106-128 (II), 129-53 (III), 40:121-60 (IV), 41:1-22
            (V), 23-42 (VI), 42-52 (VII).
1898   'Van Paloppo naar Posso', *Mededeelingen van wege het Nederlandsch
            Zendelinggenootschap* 42:1-106.
1899a   'De adoptie in verband met het matriarchaat bij de Toradja's van Mid-
            den-Celebes', *Tijdschrift voor Indische Taal-, Land- en Volkenkunde (TBG)*
            41:80-92.
1899b   'Het koppensnellen der Toradja's van Midden-Celebes, en zijne
            beteekenis', *Verslagen en Mededeelingen der Koninklijke Akademie van
            Wetenschappen, Afdeeling Letterkunde* 4-3:147-229.
1899c   'Het stroomgebied van de Tomasa-rivier', *Tijdschrift van het Koninklijk
            Nederlandsch Aardrijkskundig Genootschap* 16(Second Series):593-618.

1899d   'De weerwolf bij de Toradja's van Midden-Celebes', *Tijdschrift voor Indische Taal-, Land- en Volkenkunde (TBG)* 41:548-67.

1900a   'Eenige ethnografische aanteekeningen omtrent de Toboengkoe en de Tomori', *Mededeelingen van wege het Nederlandsch Zendelinggenootschap* 44:215-48.

1900b   'Het rijk Mori', *Tijdschrift van het Koninklijk Nederlandsch Aardrijkskundig Genootschap* 17(Second Series):436-66.

1901a   'Regen lokken en regen verdrijven bij de Toradja's van Midden Celebes', *Tijdschrift voor Indische Taal-, Land- en Volkenkunde (TBG)* 44:1-11.

1901b   'Het ijzer in Midden-Celebes', *Bijdragen tot de Taal-, Land- en Volkenkunde* 53:148-60.

1903a   'Beobachtungen an Leben und Tod, Ehe und Familie in Zentral-Celebes', *Zeitschrift für Socialwissenschaft* 6:707-14.

1903b   'Gegevens voor het bevolkingsvraagstuk van een gedeelte van Midden-Celebes', *Tijdschrift van het Koninklijk Nederlandsch Aardrijkskundig Genootschap* 20(Second Series):190-205.

1908   'De berglandschappen Napoe en Besoa in Midden-Celebes', *Tijdschrift van het Koninklijk Nederlandsch Aardrijkskundig Genootschap* 25(Second Series):1271-344.

1909   'Het landschap Bada in Midden-Celebes', *Tijdschrift van het Koninklijk Nederlandsch Aardrijkskundig Genootschap* 26(Second Series):349-80.

1911   'De slavernij in Posso (Midden-Celebes)', *Onze Eeuw; Maandschrift voor Staatkunde, Letteren, Wetenschap en Kunst* 11-1:61-97.

1919   'Het gedenken der dooden op de tweede Paaschdag', *Maandblad der Samenwerkende Zendingscorporaties* 2-4:55.

1923   'Koopen in Midden Celebes', *Mededeelingen der Koninklijke Akademie van Wetenschappen, Afdeeling Letterkunde* 26-B:149-78.

1924   'De beteekenis van den natten rijstbouw voor de Possoërs', *Koloniale Studiën* 8-2:33-53.

1926   'Pakawa, een landstreek in de onderafdeeling Paloe (Midden Celebes)', *Tijdschrift van het Koninklijk Nederlandsch Aardrijkskundig Genootschap* 43(Second Series):526-44.

1930a   'De To Loinang van den oostarm van Celebes', *Bijdragen tot de Taal-, Land- en Volkenkunde* 86:327-536.

1930b   'De To Wana op Oost-Celebes', *Tijdschrift voor Indische Taal-, Land- en Volkenkunde (TBG)* 70:397-627.

1931   'De vorsten van Banggai', *Koloniaal Tijdschrift* 20:505-28, 605-23.

1932a   'Balantaksche studiën', *Tijdschrift voor Indische Taal-, Land- en Volkenkunde (TBG)* 72:328-90.

1932b   'Banggaische studiën', *Tijdschrift voor Indische Taal-, Land- en Volkenkunde (TBG)* 72:13-102.

1932c   'De bewoners van den Banggai-archipel', *Tijdschrift van het Koninklijk Nederlandsch Aardrijkskundig Genootschap* 49(Second Series):66-88, 249-71.

1932d   'De landbouw in den Banggai-archipel', *Koloniaal Tijdschrift* 21:473-92.

1932e   'Ziekte en dood bij de Banggaiers', *Bijdragen tot de Taal-, Land- en Volkenkunde* 89:141-71.

1932f   'De zwarte kunst in den Banggai-archipel en in Balantak', *Tijdschrift voor Indische Taal-, Land- en Volkenkunde (TBG)* 72:727-41.

1933a   'Lapjesgeld op Celebes', *Tijdschrift voor Indische Taal-, Land- en Volkenkunde (TBG)* 73:172-83.

1933b   'Van leven en sterven in Balantak (oostarm van Celebes)', *Tijdschrift voor Indische Taal-, Land- en Volkenkunde (TBG)* 73:57-95.

1934   'De rijstbouw in Balantak (oostarm van Celebes)', *Tijdschrift voor Indische Taal-, Land- en Volkenkunde (TBG)* 74:123-39.

[1935]   *De krokodil in het leven van de Posoërs.* Oegstgeest: Zendingsbureau.

[1937]   *Het leven van de vrouw in Midden-Celebes.* Oegstgeest: Zendingsbureau.

1938   *De West-Toradjas op Midden-Celebes.* Amsterdam: Noord-Hollandsche Uitgeversmaatschappij. Four vols. [Verhandelingen der Koninklijke Nederlandse Academie van Wetenschappen, Afd. Letterkunde 40.]

Kruyt, A.C. and J. Kruyt

1920   'Een reis door het westelijk deel van Midden-Celebes', *Mededeelingen; Tijdschrift voor Zendingswetenschap* 64:3-16, 97-112, 193-216.

1921   'Verslag van een reis naar het landschap Napoe in de onderafdeling Posso (Celebes)', *Tijdschrift van het Koninklijk Nederlandsch Aardrijkskundig Genootschap* 38(Second Series):400-14.

Kruyt, J.

1924   'De Moriërs van Tinompo (oostelijk Midden-Celebes)', *Bijdragen tot de Taal-, Land- en Volkenkunde* 80:33-217.

1933   'Een reis door To Wana', *Mededeelingen; Tijdschrift voor Zendingswetenschap* 77:19-48.

1937   'Iets over de geestesstructuur der inheemschen van Midden-Celebes', *Nederlandsch Tijdschrift voor Psychologie* 5:194-214.

1970   *Het zendingsveld Poso; Geschiedenis van een konfrontatie.* Kampen: Kok.

Kükenthal, Willy

1896   *Forschungsreise in den Molukken und in Borneo, im Auftrage der Senckenbergischen naturforschenden Gesellschaft.* Frankfurt a. M.: Diesterweg.

Kündig, A.

1934   'Eenige statistische gegevens uit de Minahasa', *Mededeelingen van den Dienst der Volksgezondheid in Nederlandsch-Indië* 23:167-94.

Kunstadter, Peter

1978   'Subsistence agricultural economies of Lua' and Karen hill farmers, Mae Sariang district, northwestern Thailand', in: Peter Kunstadter, E.C. Chapman and Sanga Sabhasri (eds), *Farmers in the forest; Economic development and marginal agriculture in northern Thailand*, pp. 74-133. Honolulu: University Press of Hawaii.

Kusin, J.A. and Sri Kardjati

1994   'Summary and overview of main findings', in: J.A. Kusin and Sri Kardjati (eds), *Maternal health and nutrition in Madura, Indonesia*, pp. 23-36. Amsterdam: Royal Tropical Institute.

Laag, C.M. ter

1920   'Nota van overgave van de onderafdeling Donggala.' [NA MvO KIT 1196.]

Laarhoven, Ruurdje
1989   *Triumph of Moro diplomacy; The Maguindanao sultanate in the 17th century.*
            Quezon City: New Day.

Lakehinila, Domingo
[1782]   'Rapport van een visitatie van kerken en scholen op de Sangir-Talaud
            eilanden, 30-5-1782', in: H.E. Niemeijer (ed.), forthcoming, *Bronnen
            betreffende de Protestantsche kerk in de Molukken, 1605-1795.* [Original
            source: ANRI Ternate 23.]

Lam, H.J.
[1927]   'Een plantengeografisch Dorado', in: *Verhandelingen van het Vierde Neder-
            landsch-Indisch Natuurwetenschappelijk Congres, gehouden te Weltevreden
            op 22-26 September 1926,* pp. 386-97. Weltevreden: Kolff.
1931   'Botanische aanteekeningen over de Minahasa', *De Tropische Natuur*
            20:209-19.
1932   *Miangas (Palmas).* Batavia: Kolff.
1950   'Proeve ener plantengeografie van Celebes', *Tijdschrift van het Koninklijk
            Nederlandsch Aardrijkskundig Genootschap* 67(Second Series):566-604.

Landbouw in Gorontalo
1871   'De landbouw in Gorontalo', *Tijdschrift voor Nederlandsch Indië (TNI)*
            5-2:361-8.

Landschap Donggala
1905   'Het landschap Donggala of Banawa', *Bijdragen tot de Taal-, Land- en
            Volkenkunde* 58:514-31.

Lange, S.H. de
1853   'Berigten betreffende de wetenschappelijke reis in de residentie Mana-
            do van den geographischen ingenieur S.H. de Lange', *Natuurkundig
            Tijdschrift voor Nederlandsch-Indië* 4:165-78.
1897   'Menado en Kema als vrijhaven', *Tijdschrift voor Nederlandsch Indië
            (TNI)* 1897:667-707.

Lanting, H.T.
1939   'Vervolg memorie van overgave van de afdeling Donggala.' [NA MvO
            KIT 1207.]

Lapian, A.B.
1980   (ed.) *Ternate; Memorie van overgave J.H. Tobias (1857); Memorie van over-
            gave C. Bosscher (1859).* Jakarta: ANRI.
1987   *Orang laut, bajak laut, raja laut; Sejarah kawasan laut Sulawesi abad XIX.*
            [PhD thesis, Universitas Gadjah Mada.]

Leach, Helen M.
1999   'Intensification in the Pacific; A critique of the archaeological criteria
            and their application', *Current Anthropology* 40:311-39.

Lee, Ronald D.
1997   'Population dynamics; Equilibrium, disequilibrium, and consequences
            of fluctuations', in: Mark R. Rosenzweig and Oded Stark (eds), *Hand-
            book of population and family economics,* vol. IB, pp. 1063-115. Amster-
            dam: Elsevier. [Handsbooks in Economics 14.]

Leeuw, P. de
1937   'Huwelijksrecht in Bolaang-Mongondow (1933)', *Adatrechtbundels* 39:368-76.
Leeuwen, A. van
1951   'Sawahbewerking met behulp van paarden in de Minahassa', *Hemera Zoa* 58:567.
Lengkong, B.
1981   *Sejarah ke pemilikan Pulau Lembeh.* Manado: Jajasan PAKXDO.
Lesthaeghe, R.
1980   'On the social control of human reproduction', *Population and Development Review* 6:527-48.
1986   'On the adaptation of sub-Saharan systems of reproduction', in: David Coleman and Roger Schofield (eds), *The state of population theory; Forward from Malthus*, pp. 212-38. Oxford: Blackwell.
Leupe, P.A.
1865   'De verdediging van Ternate, onder den Gouverneur Johan Godfried Budach 1796-1799; Eene bijdrage tot de geschiedenis onzer Oost-Indische bezittingen', *Bijdragen tot de Taal-, Land- en Volkenkunde* 12:262-374.
Leur, J.C. van
1960   *Indonesian trade and society; Essays in Asian social and economic history.* Second edition. Bandung: Sumur Bandung. [First edition 1955.]
Levang, Patrice
1997   *La terre d'en face; La transmigration en Indonésie.* Paris: Orstrom.
LeVine, Robert A. and Susan C.M. Scrimshaw
1983   'Effects of culture on fertility; Anthropological contributions', in: Rodolfo A. Bulatao and Ronald D. Lee (eds), *Determinants of fertility in developing countries. Vol. 2: Fertility regulation and institutional influences*, pp. 666-95. New York: Academic.
Li, Tania Murray
1991   *Culture, ecology and livelihood in the Tinombo region of Central Sulawesi.* Jakarta: Environmental Management Development in Indonesia Project. [EMDI Environmental Report 6.]
1996a   'Household formation, private property, and the state', *Sojourn* 11:259-87.
1996b   'Images of community; Discourse and strategy in property relations', *Development and Change* 27:501-27.
2001   'State, space, and difference; Relational histories on Sulawesi's upland frontier', *The Journal of Asian Studies* 60:41-66.
Lichbach, Mark Irving
1996   *The cooperator's dilemma.* Ann Arbor: University of Michigan Press.
Livi-Bacci, Massimo
1991   *Population and nutrition; An essay on European demographic history.* Cambridge: Cambridge University Press. [Cambridge Studies in Population, Economy and Society in Past Time 14.]

Lobs, Jacob
[1686]   'Berigt van den jegenwoordigen staat, en stant der Molluccos, 5-10-
            1686', in: H.E. Niemeijer (ed.), forthcoming, *Memories van overgave van
            gouverneurs van de Molukken (Ternate) in de zeventiende en achttiende eeuw.*
            [Original source: NA VOC 1428.]

Löffler, Ernst
1982   'Übersichtsuntersuchungen zur Erfassung von Landresourcen in
            West-Kalimantan, Indonesien', in: E. Meynen and E. Plewe (eds), *For-
            schungsbeiträge zur Landeskunde Süd- und Südostasiens; Festschrift für
            Harald Uhlig zu seinem 60. Geburtstag*, pp. 122-31. Wiesbaden: Steiner.

Logeman, F.H.W.J.R.
1922   'Memorie van overgave van de residentie Menado.' [NA MvO MMK
            304.]

Lorimer, Frank
1954   *Culture and human fertility; A study of the relation of cultural conditions
            to fertility in non-industrial and transitional societies.* Paris: UNESCO.
            [Population and Culture 1.]

Low, Bobbi S., Alice L. Clarke and Kenneth A. Lockridge
1992   'Toward an ecological demography', *Population and Development Review*
            18:1-31.

Lubbers, A.E.H.
1893   'Eene bijdrage tot de anthropologie der bevolking in de assistent-resi-
            dentie Gorontalo (Residentie Menado)', *Geneeskundig Tijdschrift voor
            Nederlandsch-Indië* 32:775-806.

Lucieer, A.I.
1924   'Het kindertal bij de volkeren van Ned.-Indië (buiten Java)', *Tijdschrift
            van het Koninklijk Nederlandsch Aardrijkskundig Genootschap* 41(Second
            Series):540-63.

MacKinnon, Kathy, Gusti Hatta, Hakimah Halim, and Arthur Mangalik
1996   *The ecology of Kalimantan.* Hong Kong: Periplus. [The Ecology of Indo-
            nesia Series 3.]

MacKnight, C.C.
1983   'The rise of agriculture in South Sulawesi before 1600', *Review of Indo-
            nesian and Malaysian Affairs* 17:92-116.

Maengkom, F.R.
1907   'Dagboek van een tocht uit Todjo naar Mori (Midden-Celebes), en terug
            naar het Poso-Meer (11-27 April 1906)', *Tijdschrift van het Koninklijk
            Nederlandsch Aardrijkskundig Genootschap* 24(Second Series):855-71.

Mai, Ulrich, and Helmut Buchholt
1987   *Peasant pedlars and professional traders; Subsistence trade and rural markets
            of Minahasa, Indonesia.* Singapore: Oxford University Press.

Malthus, Thomas Robert
1976   *An essay on the principle of population; Text, sources and background criti-
            cism.* New York: Norton.

Mambu, Eddy
1986   'Jalannya Perang Tondano'. Paper, Seminar Perang Tondano, Jakarta,
            17 November.

Mandagi, P.A.
1914   'Over het huwelijk, de verwantschap en het erfrecht bij de Bantiks
              (1902)', *Adatrechtbundels* 9:53-83.
Mangindaän, L.
1873   'Oud Tondano', *Tijdschrift voor Indische Taal-, Land- en Volkenkunde
              (TBG)* 20:364-77.
Marle, V.J. van
1922   *Verslag eener spoorwegverkenning in de afdeeling Menado*. Weltevreden:
              Landsdrukkerij. Two vols. [Dienst der Staatsspoor- en Tramwegen,
              Mededeelingen, Opname 18.]
Marshall, Mac
1976   'Solidarity or sterility? Adoption and fosterage on Namoluk Atoll',
              in: Ivan Brady (ed.), *Transactions in kinship; Adoptation and fosterage in
              Oceania*, pp. 28-50. Honolulu: The University Press of Hawaii.
Marten, Gerald G. and Daniel M. Saltman
1986   'The human ecology perspective', in: Gerald G. Marten (ed.), *Tradi-
              tional agriculture in Southeast Asia; A human ecology perspective*, pp. 20-
              53. Boulder, Colorado: Westview.
Martens, Martha Anne
1993   'Uncovering the widow among the Uma', in: Marilyn Gregerson (ed.),
              Ritual, belief, and kinship in Sulawesi, pp. 91-7. Dallas, Texas: Interna-
              tional Museum of Cultures.
Martin, Petra
1993   'Zur Faserweberei auf Sangihe und Talaud', in: Marie-Louise Nab-
              holz-Kartaschoff, Ruth Barnes and David J. Stuart-Fox (eds), *Weaving
              patterns of life; Indonesian textile symposium 1991*, pp. 377-91. Basel:
              Museum of Ethnography.
Masipiqueña, Andres B., Gerard A. Persoon and Denyse J. Snelder
2000   'The use of fire in northeastern Luzon (Philippines); Conflicting views
              of local people, scientists, and government officials', in: Roy F. Ellen,
              Peter Parkes, and Alan Bicker (eds), *Indigenous environmental know-
              ledge and its transformations; Critical anthropological perspectives*, pp.
              177-211. Amsterdam: Harwood Academic. [Studies in Environmental
              Anthropology 5.]
Matthes, P.A.
1881   'Memorie van overgave van de residentie Menado.' [NA MvO MMK
              300.]
McKay, David A.
1970   'Nutrition, environment and health in the Iban longhouse', *Southeast
              Asian Journal of Tropical Medicine and Public Health* 1:68-77.
McKeown, Thomas
1976   *The modern rise of population*. London: Arnold.
McLaren, Angus
1990   *A history of contraception; From antiquity to the present day*. Oxford:
              Blackwell. [Family, Sexuality and Social Relations in Past Times.]

Meade, Melinda
1976   'Land development and human health in West Malaysia', *Annals of the*
            Association of American Geographers 66:428-39.
Meillassoux, Claude
1981   *Maidens, meal and money; Capitalism and the domestic community.* Cam-
            bridge: Cambridge University Press. [Themes in the Social Sciences.]
Menopo, Johannis Manuel
1893   'Menambahi deri kaoel dan perdjandjian diboeat pengakoewan dan di
            bertegoehken segala hal-hal diantara oleh akoe Padoeka Radja Johan-
            nis Manuel Menopo serta mantri[2] koe jang bergoena sekarang soedah
            mengakoe dan mengarti hadat[2] di tanah Karadjaan Bolaang Mon-
            gondo [...]', *Tijdschrift voor Indische Taal-, Land- en Volkenkunde (TBG)*
            35:481-97.
Merkens, Jan
1927   *Bijdrage tot de kennis van den karbouw en de karbouwenteelt in Nederlandsch*
            Oost-Indië. Utrecht: Schotanus en Jens.
Metzner, Joachim K.
1977   *Man and environment in eastern Timor; A geoecological analysis of the Bau-*
            cau-Viqueque area as a possible basis for regional planning. Canberra: Aus-
            tralian National University. [Development Studies Centre Monograph
            8.]
1981a   'Palu (Sulawesi); Problematik der Landnutzung in einem klimatischen
            Trockental am Äquator', *Erdkunde* 35:42-54.
1981b   'Palu (Sulawesi); Problems of land utilization in a climatic dry valley
            on the equator', *Applied Geography and Development* 18:45-62.
1982   *Agriculture and population pressure in Sikka, isle of Flores; A contribution to*
            the study of agricultural systems in the wet and dry tropics. Canberra: Aus-
            tralian National University. [Development Studies Centre Monograph
            28.]
Meyer, A.B. and O. Richter
1903   *Celebes I: Sammlung der Herren Dr Paul und Dr Fritz Sarasin aus den*
            Jahren 1893-1896. Dresden: Stengel. [Publikationen aus dem König-
            lichen Ethnographischen Museum zu Dresden 14.]
Meyer, A.B. and L.W. Wiglesworth
1898   *The birds of Celebes and the neighbouring islands.* Berlin: Friedländer.
Miete, A.
1938   'Het adatrecht der Sangihe- en Talaudeilanden', *Koloniaal Tijdschrift*
            27:356-71.
Militaire memorie Parigi
[1929]   'Militaire memorie inzake de onderafdeling Parigi.' [NA MvO KIT
            1200.]
Missen, G.J.
1972   *Viewpoint on Indonesia; A geographical study.* Melbourne: Nelson.
Mohr, E.C.J.
1938a   'Climate and soil in the Netherlands Indies', *Bulletin of the Colonial*
            Institute of Amsterdam 1:241-51.

1938b   'The relationship between soil and population density in the Nether-
             lands East Indies', in: *Comptes rendus du Congrès International de Géo-
             graphie Amsterdam 1938. Vol. 2: Géographie Coloniale*, pp. 478-93. Leiden:
             Brill.

Molt, Jan Hendrik
[1726]   'Rapport van een visitatie van kerken en scholen in Noord-Sulawe-
             si en op de Sangihe- en Talaud-eilanden, 11-12-1726', in: H.E. Nie-
             meijer (ed.), forthcoming, *Bronnen betreffende de Protestantsche kerk in
             de Molukken, 1605-1795*. [Original source: NA VOC 2072.]

Monoarga, R.
1937   'Zoogenaamde verjaring van grondbezitsrechten gebaseerd op de
             Gorontalosche adat (1932)', *Adatrechtbundels* 34:365-7.

Moolenburgh, P.E.
1921   'Memorie van overgave van de afdeling Gorontalo.' [NA MvO KIT
             1187.]

Morison, H.H.
1931   'Memorie van overgave van de onderafdeling Gorontalo.' [NA MvO
             KIT 1191.]

Morks, C.J.
1931   'Aanvullende memorie van overgave van de onderafdeling Boalemo.'
             [NA MvO KIT 1192.]

Moulin, D. de
1989   'Teaching of medicine in the Dutch East Indies', in: G.M. van Heteren,
             A. de Knecht-van Eekelen and M.J.D. Poulissen (eds), *Nederlandse
             geneeskunde in de Indische Archipel 1816-1942*, pp. 23-31. Amsterdam:
             Rodopi.

Müller, H. and J.W. Tesch
1937   'Autochtone infectie met Schistosoma japonicum op Celebes', *Genees-
             kundig Tijdschrift voor Nederlandsch-Indië* 77:2143-50.

Musschenbroek, S.C.J.W. van
1878   *Kaart van de Minahassa*. 's-Gravenhage: Topographische Inrichting.
1880   'Toelichtingen behoorende bij de kaart van de bocht van Tomini of
             Gorontalo en aangrenzende landen', *Tijdschrift van het Koninklijk Neder-
             landsch Aardrijkskundig Genootschap* 4(Second Series):93-110.

Mijlendonk, Jan Elias van
[1756]   'Memorie wegens den presenten staat van saken in de Moluccos, 20-
             7-1756', in: H.E. Niemeijer (ed.), forthcoming, *Memories van overgave
             van gouverneurs van de Molukken (Ternate) in de zeventiende en achttiende
             eeuw*. [Original source: NA VOC 2882.]

Nag, Moni
1975   'Marriage and kinship in relation to human fertility', in: Moni Nag
             (ed.), *Population and social organization*, pp. 11-54. The Hague: Mou-
             ton.

Nagtegaal, Luc
1993   'The pre-modern city in Indonesia and its fall from grace with the
             gods', *Economic and Social History in the Netherlands* 5:39-59.

1995   'Urban pollution in Java, 1600-1850', in: Peter J.M. Nas (ed.), *Issues in urban development; Case studies from Indonesia*, pp. 9-30. Leiden: Research School CNWS. [CNWS Publications 33.]

Nalin, David R. and J. Glenn Morris, Jr.
1991   'Cholera and other vibrioses', in: G. Thomas Strickland (ed.), *Hunter's tropical medicine*, pp. 305-13. Seventh edition. Philadelphia: Saunders. [First edition 1945.]

Nanoesa-eilanden
1905   'De Nanoesa-eilanden', *De Indische Gids* 27-1:314-6.

Nationaal rapport
1937   'Nationaal rapport van Nederlandsch-Indië voor de Intergouverne-menteele Conferentie van Landen in het Verre Oosten voor Landelijke Hygiëne, 3-13 Augustus 1937', *Mededeelingen van den Dienst der Volksgezondheid in Nederlandsch-Indië* 26:100-216.

Netherlands Indies Medical and Sanitary Service
1929   *Control of endemic diseases in the Netherlands Indies*. Weltevreden: Landsdrukkerij.

Netting, Robert McC.
1993   *Smallholders, householders; Farm families and the ecology of intensive, sustainable agriculture*. Stanford, California: Stanford University Press.

Newell, Colin
1988   *Methods and models in demography*. London: Belhaven.

Newson, Linda A.
1998   'Old World diseases in the early colonial Philippines and Spanish America', in: Daniel F. Doeppers and Peter Xenos (eds), *Population and history; The demographic origins of the modern Philippines*, pp. 17-36. Madison, Wisconsin: Center for Southeast Asian Studies, University of Wisconsin-Madison. [CSEAS Monograph 16.]

Nibbering, Jan Willem
1991   'Crisis and resilience in upland land use in Java', in: Joan Hardjono (ed.), *Indonesia; Resources, ecology, and environment*, pp. 104-31. Singapore: Oxford University Press.
1997   'Upland cultivation and soil conservation in limestone regions on Java's south coast; Three historical case studies', in: Peter Boomgaard, Freek Colombijn and David Henley (eds), *Paper landscapes; Explorations in the environmental history of Indonesia*, pp. 153-83. Leiden: KITLV Press. [Verhandelingen 178.]

Nieboer, F.J.
1929   'Gegevens over Parigi (1926)', *Adatrechtbundels* 31:80-4.

Nieboer, H.J.
1900   *Slavery as an industrial system; Ethnological researches*. 's-Gravenhage: Nijhoff.
1903   'Der "Malthusianismus" der Naturvölker', *Zeitschrift für Socialwissenschaft* 6:715-8.

Niehof, Anke
1985   *Women and fertility in Madura (Indonesia)*. [PhD thesis, Rijksuniversiteit Leiden.]

Noorduyn, J.
1983   'De handelsrelaties van het Makassaarse rijk volgens de notitie van Cornelis Speelman uit 1670', in: *Nederlandse historische bronnen*, vol. 3, pp. 97-123. Amsterdam: Verloren.
1991   *A critical survey of studies on the languages of Sulawesi*. Leiden: KITLV Press. [Bibliographical Series 18.]

Noot, Petrus
1703   'Rapport van een visitatie van kerken en scholen in Noord-Sulawesi en op de Sangir-Talaud eilanden, 3-1-1703', in: H.E. Niemeijer (ed.), forthcoming, *Bronnen betreffende de Protestantsche kerk in de Molukken, 1605-1795*. [Original source: NA VOC 1675.]

Nota Toli-Toli
1912   'Nota betreffende het landschap Toli-Toli', *Tijdschrift voor Indische Taal-, Land- en Volkenkunde (TBG)* 54:27-57.

Nota berglandschappen
1912   'Nota van toelichting over de berglandschappen boven het Paloedal', *Tijdschrift voor Indische Taal-, Land- en Volkenkunde (TBG)* 54:1-26.

Nourse, Jennifer Williams
1989   *We are the womb of the world; Birth spirits and the Lauje of Central Sulawesi*. [PhD thesis, University of Virginia.]
1999   *Conceiving spirits; Birth rituals and contested identities among Laujé of Indonesia*. Washington: Smithsonian Institution Press. [Smithsonian Series in Ethnographic Inquiry.]

Nouwens, A.L.
1932   'Nota inzake landschap Boengkoe.' [NA MvO KIT 1210.]

Nur, Samin Rajik
1979   *Beberapa aspek hukum adat tatanegara kerajaan Gorontalo pada masa pemerintahan Eato (1673-1679)*. [PhD thesis, Universitas Hasanuddin.]

Oldeman, L.R. and Darmiyati Sjarifuddin
1977   *An agroclimatic map of Sulawesi*. Bogor: Central Research Institute for Agriculture. [Contributions CRIA 33.]

Olivier, J.
1834-37   *Reizen in den Molukschen archipel naar Makassar, enz. in het gevolg van den gouverneur-generaal van Nederland's Indië, in 1824 gedaan*. Amsterdam: Beijerinck. Two vols.

Olson, Mancur
1971   *The logic of collective action; Public goods and the theory of groups*. Cambridge, Mass.: Harvard University Press. [Harvard Economic Studies 124.]

Ormeling, F.J.
1955   *The Timor problem; A geographical interpretation of an underdeveloped island*. Djakarta: Wolters.
n.d.   'Minahasa; Producent van kopra en kruidnagel.' [Unpublished article, KITLV library.]

Osamu Saito
1996   'Historical demography; Achievements and prospects', *Population Studies* 50:537-53.

Osborn, Frederick
1960   'Population; An international dilemma', in: *On population; Three essays*.
            pp. 85-138. New York: The New American Library.

Ostrom, Elinor
1990   *Governing the commons; The evolution of institutions for collective action*.
            Cambridge: Cambridge University Press. [The Political Economy of
            Institutions and Decisions.]

Overname van Ternate
1879   'Overname van Ternate van de Engelschen in 1803', *Bijdragen tot de
            Taal-, Land- en Volkenkunde* 27:202-23.

Overzicht
1914   'Een overzicht van den arbeid op de Sangi- en Talauer-eilanden', *Mede-
            deelingen vanwege het Comité tot Voorziening in de Godsdienstige Behoeften
            van de Gevestigde Inlandsche Protestantsche Christengemeenten op de Sangi-
            en Talauer Eilanden* 16:1-17.

Overzigt handel [1846-70]
1850-71   *Overzigt van den handel en de scheepvaart in de Nederlandsche bezittingen
            in Oost-Indië buiten Java en Madura*. 22 vols. Batavia: Landsdrukkerij.

P3SU [Proyek Pembinaan Pengairan Sulawesi Utara]
1994   *Integrated watershed management and development plan for the Limboto-
            Bolango-Bone basins*. N.p.: n.n. Two vols. [Technical Report 15.]

Pabbruwe, H.J.
[1994]   *Dr Robertus Padtbrugge (Parijs 1637-Amersfoort 1703), dienaar van de
            Verenigde Oost-Indische Compagnie, en zijn familie*. Kloosterzande: Due-
            rinck.

Padoch, Christine
1982   *Migration and its alternatives among the Iban of Sarawak*. The Hague:
            Nijhoff. [KITLV, Verhandelingen 98.]
1985   'Labour efficiency and intensity of land use in rice production; An
            example from Kalimantan', *Human Ecology* 13:271-89.

Padtbrugge, Robert
1866   'Beschrijving der zeden en gewoonten van de bewoners der Mina-
            hassa', *Bijdragen tot de Taal-, Land- en Volkenkunde van Nederlandsch-Indië*
            13:304-31.

Paerels, B.H.
1949   'Bevolkingskoffiecultuur', in: C.J.J. van Hall and C. van de Koppel
            (eds), *De landbouw in de Indische Archipel*, vol. IIB, pp. 89-119. 's-Graven-
            hage: Van Hoeve.

Palm, C.H.M.
1958   'Ancient art of the Minahasa', *Madjalah untuk Ilmu Bahasa, Ilmu Bumi
            dan Kebudajaan Indonesia* 86:1-59.
1961   'Oude Minahasische kunst', *Kultuurpatronen* 3/4:55-101.

Palte, J.G.L. and G.J. Tempelman
1978   *Indonesië; Een sociaal-geografisch overzicht*. Second edition. Bussum:
            Romen. [First edition 1975.]

Pastells, P. Pablo
1936   'Historia general de Filipinas (1644-1662)', in: Pedro Torres y Lanzas
            and Francisco Navas del Valle (eds), *Catálogo de los documentos relativos
            a las Islas Filipinas existentes en el Archivo de Indias de Sevilla*, vol. 9. Bar-
            celona: Tasso.

Pearson, Richard D. and Richard L. Guerrant
1991   'Hookworm infections', in: G. Thomas Strickland (ed.), *Hunter's tropi-
            cal medicine*, pp. 700-11. Seventh edition. Philadelphia: Saunders. [First
            edition 1945.]

Peddemors, M.
1935   'Iets over landbouw, leven en gewoonten in Gorontalo', *Mededeelingen
            Vereeniging van Gezaghebbers BB* 29:25-33.

Pelras, Christiaan
1972   'Notes sur quelques populations aquatiques de l'archipel Nusan-
            tarien', *Archipel* 3:133-68.
1981   'Célèbes-sud avant l'Islam selon les premiers témoingnages étrangers',
            Archipel 21:153-84.
1996   *The Bugis*. Oxford: Blackwell. [The Peoples of South-East Asia and the
            Pacific.]

Pelzer, Karl J.
1945   *Pioneer settlement in the Asiatic tropics; Studies in land utilization and
            agricultural colonization in Southeastern Asia*. New York: American Geo-
            graphical Society. [Special Publications of the American Geographical
            Society 29.]
1963   'Physical and human resource patterns', in: Ruth T. McVey (ed.), *Indo-
            nesia*, pp. 1-23. New Haven: Human Relations Area Files. [Survey of
            World Cultures 12.]

Pennings, A.
1908   'Mededeelingen van de Talauer-eilanden', *Mededeelingen vanwege het
            Comité tot Voorziening in de Godsdienstige Behoeften van de Gevestigde
            Inlandsche Protestantsche Christengemeenten op de Sangi- en Talauer Eilan-
            den* 4:13-20.

Pérez, P. Lorenzo O.F.M.
1913-14   'Historia de las misiones de los Franciscanos en las islas Malucas y
            Célebes', *Archivum Franciscanum Historicum* 6:45-60 (I), 681-701 (II),
            7:198-226 (III), 424-46 (IV), 621-53 (V).

Perine, Peter L.
1991   'Syphilis and the endemic treponematoses', in: G. Thomas Strickland
            (ed.), *Hunter's tropical medicine*, pp. 301-10. Seventh edition. Philadel-
            phia: Saunders. [First edition 1945.]

Persenaire, J.B.C.
1911   'Over Indische abortiva', *Geneeskundig Tijdschrift voor Nederlandsch-
            Indië* 51:230-6.

Persoon, Gerard A.
1988   'Sago en rijst op Siberut (Indonesie); Een vergelijking', *Antropologische
            Verkenningen* 7-4:36-49.

Peta rupabumi Indonesia
1992   *Peta rupabumi Indonesia 1:50.000; Lembar 2114-64; Podi*. Cibinong: Bako-
           surtanal.

Pielat, Jacob Christiaen
1731   'Memorie ofte berigt soo van den jegenwoordigen staat en stand der
           Moluccos als andere zaken meer, 9-6-1731', in: H.E. Niemeijer (ed.),
           forthcoming, *Memories van overgave van gouverneurs van de Molukken
           (Ternate) in de zeventiende en achttiende eeuw*. [Original source: ANRI
           Ternate 74.]

[Pietermaat, D.F.W., De Vriese and E. Lucas]
1840   'Statistieke aanteekeningen over de residentie Menado', *Tijdschrift voor
           Nederlandsch Indië (TNI)* 3:109-67.

Pingali, Prabhu L.
1990   'Institutional and environmental constraints to agricultural intensifi-
           cation', in: Geoffrey McNicoll and Mead Cain (eds), *Rural development
           and population; Institutions and policy*, pp. 243-60. New York: Oxford
           University Press. [Population and Development Review 15.]

Pino, J.J.F.
1920   'Vervolg memorie van overgave van de afdeling Gorontalo.' [NA MvO
           KIT 1185.]

Pirie, Peter
1984   'Human populations and agroecosystems', in: A. Terry Rambo and
           Percy E. Sajise (eds), *An introduction to human ecology research on
           agricultural systems in Southeast Asia*, pp. 111-40. Honolulu: East-West
           Center.

Platt, A.L.
1933   'Algemene gegevens inzake de afdeling Poso.' NA MvO KIT 1211.

Platteau, Jean-Philippe
1991   'Traditional systems of social security and hunger insurance; Past
           achievements and modern challenges', in: Ehtisham Ahmad, Jean
           Drèze, John Hills and Amartya Sen (eds), *Social security in developing
           countries*, pp. 112-70. Oxford: Clarendon.
2000   *Institutions, social norms, and economic development*. Amsterdam: Har-
           wood.

Pleyte, C.M.
1891   'Sumpitan and bow in Indonesia', *Internationales Archiv für Ethno-
           graphie* 7:265-81.

Potter, Lesley
1987   'Degradation, innovation and social welfare in the Riam Kiwa Valley,
           Kalimantan, Indonesia', in: Piers Blaikie and Harold Brookfield (eds),
           Land degradation and society, pp. 165-76. London: Methuen.
1993   'The onslaught on the forests in South-East Asia', in: Harold Brook-
           field and Yvonne Byron (eds), *South-East Asia's environmental future;
           The search for sustainability*, pp. 103-23. Kuala Lumpur: United Nations
           University Press/Oxford University Press.

Pounds, N.J.G.
1990   *An historical geography of Europe.* Cambridge: Cambridge University Press.

Ptak, Roderich
1992   'The northern trade route to the spice islands; South China Sea-Sulu Zone-North Moluccas (14th to early 16th century)', *Archipel* 43:27-55.

Purseglove, J.W.
1968   *Tropical crops; Dicotyledons.* London: Longman. Two vols.
1972   *Tropical crops; Monocotyledons.* London: Longman. Two vols.

Putrali, J., W. Patrick Carney, E.E. Stafford, and Saluddin Tubo
1977   'Intestinal and blood parasites in the Banggai kabupaten, Central Sulawesi, Indonesia', *Southeast Asian Journal of Tropical Medicine and Public Health* 8:375-9.

[Quarles van Ufford, H.]
1856   *Aanteekeningen betreffende eene reis door de Molukken van zijne excellentie den Gouverneur-Generaal Mr A.J. Duymaer van Twist, in de maanden September en October 1855.* 's-Gravenhage: Nijhoff.

Quinn, William H.
1992   'A study of Southern Oscillation-related climatic activity for AD 622-1900 incorporating Nile river flood data', in: Henry F. Diaz and Vera Markgaf (eds), *El Niño; Historical and paleoclimatic aspects of the Southern Oscillation,* pp. 119-49. Cambridge: Cambridge University Press.

Raffles, Thomas Stamford
1978   *The history of Java.* Kuala Lumpur: Oxford University Press. Two vols. [First published 1817.]

Rappaport, Roy A.
1984   *Pigs for the ancestors; Ritual in the ecology of a New Guinea people.* Second edition. New Haven: Yale University Press. [First edition 1968.]

Rapport adat kebiasaan
1910   'Rapport over de 'adat kebiasaan, uitgebracht door een inlandsche commissie', *Adatrechtbundels* 3:1-113.

Regeeringsrapport Boalemo
1914   'Regeeringsrapport nopens de toestanden in de onderafdeeling Boalemo der afdeeling Gorontalo (1912)', *Adatrechtbundels* 9:169.

Regenwaarnemingen
1880-1934   *Regenwaarnemingen in Nederlandsch-Indië [1879-1933].* 55 vols. Batavia: Landsdrukkerij.

Regerings-almanak
1817-1942   *Regerings-almanak voor Nederlandsch-Indië.* Batavia: Landsdrukkerij.

Reid, Anthony
1980   'The structure of cities in Southeast Asia; Fifteenth to seventeenth centuries', *Journal of Southeast Asian Studies* 11:235-50.
1983   'Introduction; Slavery and bondage in Southeast Asian history', in: Anthony Reid (ed.), *Slavery, bondage and dependency in Southeast Asia,* pp. 1-43. St. Lucia: University of Queensland Press.
1984   'The pre-colonial economy of Indonesia', *Bulletin of Indonesian Economic Studies* 20:151-67.

1987	'Low population growth and its causes in pre-colonial Southeast Asia', in: Norman G. Owen (ed.), *Death and disease in Southeast Asia; Explorations in social, medical and demographic history*, pp. 33-47. Singapore: Oxford University Press. [Asian Studies Association of Australia, Southeast Asia Publications Series 14.]
1988-93	*Southeast Asia in the age of commerce, 1450-1680.* New Haven: Yale University Press. Two vols.
1990	'The seventeenth-century crisis in Southeast Asia', *Modern Asian Studies* 24:639-59.
1992	'Economic and social change, c. 1400-1800', in: Nicholas Tarling (ed.), *The Cambridge history of Southeast Asia. Volume 1: From early times to c. 1800*, pp. 460-507. Cambridge: Cambridge University Press.
1995	'Humans and forests in pre-colonial Southeast Asia', *Environment and History* 1:93-110.
1997	'Inside out; The colonial displacement of Sumatra's population', in: Peter Boomgaard, Freek Colombijn and David Henley (eds), *Paper landscapes; Explorations in the environmental history of Indonesia*, pp. 61-89. Leiden: KITLV Press. [Verhandelingen 178.]
2001	'South-East Asian population history and the colonial impact', in: Ts'ui-jung Liu, James Lee, David Sven Reher, Osamu Saito and Wang Feng (eds), *Asian population history*, pp. 45-62. Oxford: Oxford University Press.

Reinwardt, C.J.C.

1858	*Reis naar het oostelijk gedeelte van den Indischen Archipel, in het jaar 1821.* Amsterdam: Muller.

Renwarin, P.R.

2000	*Matuari wo tonaas Minaesa; Dinamika budaya Tombulu di Minahasa.* [Draft PhD thesis, Leiden University.]

RePPProT [Regional Physical Planning Programme for Transmigration]

1988	*Review of Phase I results; Sulawesi.* Jakarta: Government of the Republic of Indonesia/Overseas Development Administration, Foreign and Commonwealth Office, UK. Two vols.
1990a	*The land resources of Indonesia; A national overview* [text]. Jakarta: Government of the Republic of Indonesia/Overseas Development Administration, Foreign and Commonwealth Office, U.K.
1990b	*The land resources of Indonesia; A national overview* [atlas]. Jakarta: Government of the Republic of Indonesia/Overseas Development Administration, Foreign and Commonwealth Office, U.K.

Reyne, A.

1948	'De cocospalm', in: C.J.J. van Hall and C. van Koppel (eds), *De landbouw in de Indische Archipel*, vol. IIA, pp. 426-525. 's-Gravenhage: Van Hoeve.

Rhijn, L.J. van

1851	*Reis door den Indischen Archipel, in het belang der evangelische zending.* Rotterdam: Wijt.

Rhijn, M. van

1941	'Memorie van overgave van de residentie Menado.' [KITLV H1179.]

Ricklefs, Merle C.
1986   'Some statistical evidence on Javanese social, economic and demo-
            graphic history in the later seventeenth and eighteenth centuries',
            Modern Asian Studies 20:1-32.
2001   *A history of modern Indonesia since c. 1200*. Third edition. Basingstoke,
            Hampshire: Palgrave. [First edition 1981.]

Riedel, J.G.F.
1862   *Pada menjatakan babarapa perkara deri pada hhikajatnja tuwah tanah Mina-
            hasa sampej pada kadatangan orang kulit putih Nederlanda itu*. Batavia:
            Landsdrukkerij. [Inilah Pintu Gerbang Pengatahuwan Itu Apatah
            Dibukakan Guna Orang-Orang Padudokh Tanah Minahasa Ini 5.]
1864a   'Bijdrage tot de geschiedenis der zeerooverijen op de kusten der
            Minahasa. [1776 en 1777]', *Tijdschrift voor Indische Taal-, Land- en
            Volkenkunde (TBG)* 14:511-23.
1864b   'Het landschap Bolaäng-Mongondouw', *Tijdschrift voor Indische Taal-,
            Land- en Volkenkunde (TBG)* 13:266-84.
1869a   'Iets over het landbezit in de Minahasa, (Residentie Menado)', *Tijd-
            schrift voor Nijverheid en Landbouw in Nederlandsch-Indië* 14:1-9.
1869b   'Het oppergezag der vorsten van Bolaang over de Minahasa (bijdrage
            tot de kennis der oude geschiedenis van Noord-Selebes)', *Tijdschrift
            voor Taal-, Land- en Volkenkunde van Nederlandsch-Indië (TBG)* 17:505-
            24.
1870a   'De landschappen Holontalo, Limoeto, Bone, Boalemo en Katting-
            gola, of Andagile, geographische, statistische, historische en ethno-
            graphische aanteekeningen', *Tijdschrift voor Indische Taal-, Land- en
            Volkenkunde (TBG)* 19:46-153.
1870b   'De vestiging der Mandaren in de Tomini-landen', *Tijdschrift voor
            Indische Taal-, Land- en Volkenkunde (TBG)* 19:555-64.
1871   'De volksoverleveringen betreffende de voormalige gedaante van
            Noord-Selebes en den oorsprong zijner bewoners', *Tijdschrift voor
            Nederlandsch Indië (TNI)* 1871-1:288-303.
1872a   'Het landschap Boeool; Korte aanteekeningen', *Tijdschrift voor Indische
            Taal-, Land- en Volkenkunde (TBG)* 18:189-208.
1872b   'De Minahasa in 1825; Bijdrage tot de kennis van Noord-Selebes',
            Tijdschrift voor Indische Taal-, Land- en Volkenkunde (TBG) 18:458-568.
1872c   'Nord-Selebesche Pfahlbauten', *Zeitschrift für Ethnologie* 4:192-7.
1872d   'De vroegere regten en verpligtingen der vrije Alifoeroes van Noord-
            Selebes', *Tijdschrift voor Indische Taal-, Land- en Volkenkunde (TBG)*
            18:157-63.
1885a   'Galela und Tobeloresen; Ethnographische Notizien', *Zeitschrift für
            Ethnologie* 17:58-89.
1885b   'De oorsprong en de vestiging der Boalemoërs op Noord-Selebes',
            Bijdragen tot de Taal-, Land- en Volkenkunde 34:495-521.
1886   'De Topantunuasu of oorspronkelijke volksstammen van Centraal
            Selebes', *Bijdragen tot de Taal-, Land- en Volkenkunde* 35:77-95.
1895a   'Alte Gebräuche bei Heirathen, Geburt und Sterbefällen bei dem Tom-
            buluh-Stamm in der Minahasa (Nord Selebes)', *Internationales Archiv
            für Ethnographie* 7:89-109.

1895b   'Het Meer van Poso en de "Binnenseen" van Noord- en Centraal-
             Selebes', *De Indische Gids* 17-2:1724-34.
1901   'De Poïgar-rivier in het landschap Bolaäng Mongondou, Noord-
             Selebes', *Tijdschrift van het Koninklijk Nederlandsch Aardrijkskundig
             Genootschap* 18(Second Series):225-8.

Rigg, Jonathan
1991   *Southeast Asia; A region in transition; A thematic human geography of the
             ASEAN region.* London: Unwin Hyman.

Robequain, Charles
1946   *Le monde malais; Péninsule malaise, Sumatra, Java, Bornéo, Célèbes, Bali et
             les petites îles de la Sonde, Moluques, Philippines.* Paris: Payot.

Robertson, Claire C. and Martin A. Klein (eds)
1983   *Women and slavery in Africa.* Madison: The University of Wisconsin
             Press.

Robidé van der Aa, [P.J.C.B.] (ed.)
1867   'Het journaal van Padtbrugge's reis naar Noord-Celebes en de Noor-
             dereilanden (16 Aug.-23 Dec. 1677)', *Bijdragen tot de Taal-, Land- en
             Volkenkunde* 14:105-340, 558-65.

Robinson, Warren C.
1997   'The economic theory of fertility over three decades', *Population Studies*
             51:63-74.

Robson, Stuart (ed.)
1995   *Deśawarṇana (Nāgarakṛtāgama) by Mpu Prapanca.* Leiden: KITLV Press.
             [Verhandelingen 169.]

Rodenwaldt, Ernst
1926   'Entomologische notities III', *Mededeelingen van den Dienst der Volks-
             gezondheid in Nederlandsch-Indië* 15:89-108.

Roep, B.
1917   'Hygiëne op de Talaudeilanden', *Tijdschrift voor het Binnenlandsch
             Bestuur* 53:414-33.

Roorda van Eysinga, S.
[1831]   *Verschillende reizen en lotgevallen van S. Roorda van Eysinga [...].* Kam-
             pen: Roorda van Eysinga.

Rootselaar, F.J. van
1957   'Pinta in Indonesia', *Documenta de Medicina Geographica et Tropica* 9:33-44.

Roselaar, Pieter
1706   'Korte beschrijving van soodanige landen, eijlanden en plaatsen als
             onder de Moluccos gelegen sijn, 11-6-1706', in: H.E. Niemeijer (ed.),
             forthcoming, *Memories van overgave van gouverneurs van de Molukken
             (Ternate) in de zeventiende en achttiende eeuw.* [Original source: NA VOC
             1727.]

Rosenberg, C.B.H. von
1865   *Reistogten in de afdeeling Gorontalo, gedaan op last der Nederlandsch
             Indische regering.* Amsterdam: Muller.

Rousseau, Jérôme
1990   *Central Borneo; Ethnic identity and social life in a stratified society.* Oxford:
             Clarendon.

Ruibing, Aaldrik Hendrik
1937   *Ethnologische studie betreffende de Indonesische slavernij als maatschap-*
            pelijk verschijnsel. [PhD thesis, Rijksuniversiteit Utrecht.]
Rumphius, Georgius Everhardus
1705   *D'Amboinsche rariteitkamer* [...]. Amsterdam: Halma.
1750   *Het Amboinsch kruid-boek* [...]. Six vols. Amsterdam: Uytwerf.
Sá, Artur Basílio de (ed.)
1955   *Documentação para a história das missões do padroado Português do Ori-*
            ente. Vol. 3: Insulíndia, 1563-67. Lisboa: Agência Geral do Ultramar,
            Divisao de Publicaçoes e Biblioteca.
Sahlins, Marshall
1963   'Poor man, rich man, big man, chief; Political types in Melanesia and
            Polynesia', *Comparative Studies in Society and History* 5:285-303.
1972   *Stone age economics.* Chicago: Aldine Atherton.
Santow, Gigi
1987   'Reassessing the contraceptive effect of breastfeeding', *Population*
            Studies 41:147-60.
Santow, Gigi and M.D. Bracher
1984   'Child death and time to the next birth in Central Java', *Population*
            Studies 38:241-53.
Sarasin, Fritz
1906   *Versuch einer Anthropologie der Insel Celebes. Vol. 2: Die Varietäten des*
            Menschen auf Celebes. Wiesbaden: Kreidel. [Materialen zur Naturge-
            schichte der Insel Celebes 5-2.]
Sarasin, Paul and Fritz Sarasin
1897   'Über den Zweck der Pfahlbauten', *Globus; Illustrierte Zeitschrift für*
            Länder- und Völkerkunde 72:277-8.
1901   *Entwurf einer geographisch-geologischen Beschreibung der Insel Celebes.* Wies-
            baden: Kreidel. [Materialen zur Naturgeschichte der Insel Celebes 4.]
1905   *Reisen in Celebes ausgeführt in den Jahren 1893-1896 und 1902-1903.*
            Wiesbaden: Kreidel. Two vols.
Scalliet, Marie-Odette
1995   *Antoine Payen; Peintre des Indes orientales; Vie et écrits d'un artiste du xixe*
            siècle. Leiden: Research School CNWS. [CNWS Publications 34.]
Schefold, Reimar
1988   *Lia; Das große Ritual auf den Mentawai-Inseln (Indonesien).* Berlin: Reimar.
1995   'The heroic theft; Myth and achievement in Minahasan society', in:
            Reimar Schefold (ed.), *Minahasa past and present; Tradition and transi-*
            tion in an outer island region of Indonesia, pp. 22-31. Leiden: Research
            School CNWS. [CNWS Publications 28.]
Schelle, C.J. van
1890   'Opmerkingen over de geologie van een gedeelte der afdeeling
            Gorontalo (residentie Menado)', *Jaarboek van het Mijnwezen in Neder-*
            landsch Oost-Indië 18-2:115-58.
Scherius, Johannes
[1735]   'Rapport van een visitatie van kerken en scholen in Noord-Sulawesi
            en op de Sangir-Talaud eilanden, 30-7-1735', in: H.E. Niemeijer (ed.),

forthcoming, *Bronnen betreffende de Protestantsche kerk in de Molukken, 1605-1795.* [Original source: NA VOC 2344.]

[Scherius, R.]
1847   'Eenige bijdragen tot de kennis en den toestand der afdeeling Gorong-
                talo (eiland Celebes)', *Verhandelingen en Berigten betrekkelijk het Zeewezen
                en de Zeevaartkunde* 7(Second Series):399-421.

Schippers, M.H.
1886   'Iets over den stam der Bantiks', *Mededeelingen van wege het Neder-
                landsch Zendelinggenootschap* 30:94-105.

Schnitger, F.M.
1989   *Forgotten kingdoms in Sumatra.* Singapore: Oxford University Press.
                [First published 1939.]

Scholz, F.M.
1988   *Agrargeographie von Sumatra.* Giessen: Selbstverlag des Geographischen
                Instituts der Justus Liebig, Universität Giessen. [Giessener Geogra-
                phische Schriften 63.]

Schoonderwoerdt, Jacob van
1766   'Memorie wegens den presenten staat der Molukkos, 24-7-1766', in:
                H.E. Niemeijer (ed.), forthcoming, *Memories van overgave van gou-
                verneurs van de Molukken (Ternate) in de zeventiende en achttiende eeuw.*
                [Original source: ANRI Ternate 79.]

Schoorl, J.W.
1994   'Power, ideology and change in the early state of Buton', in: G.J.
                Schutte (ed.), *State and trade in the Indonesian Archipelago*, pp. 17-59.
                Leiden: KITLV Press. [Working Paper 13.]

Schouten, Mieke J.C.
1978   De veranderende positie van het walakhoofd in de Minahasa gedurende
                de 19e eeuw; Ukung, volkshoofd, ambtenaar. [MA thesis, Vrije Univer-
                siteit Amsterdam.]
1988   'The Minahasans; Eternal rivalry', in: N. de Jonge, V. Dekker and R.
                Schefold (eds), *Indonesia in focus; Ancient traditions, modern times*, pp.
                116-21. Meppel: Edu'Actief.
1992   'Heads for force; On the headhunting complex in Southeast Asia and
                Melanesia', *Anais Universitários, Universitade da Beira Interior, Série Ciên-
                cias Socias e Humanas* 3:113-28.
1995a   'Exports and areas; Export crops and subsistence in Minahasa, 1817-
                1985'. Paper, First conference of the European Association for South-
                East Asian Studies, Leiden, 29 June-1 July.
1995b   'From *anak piara* to PKK: ideologies and history of Minahasan women's
                household duties'. Paper, Third international workshop of the Interdis-
                ciplinary Study Group on Indonesian Women (WIVS), Leiden, 25-29
                September.
1998   *Leadership and social mobility in a Southeast Asian society; Minahasa, 1677-
                1983.* Leiden: KITLV Press. [Verhandelingen 179.]
1999   'Quelques communautés intermédiaires et Insulinde Orientale', in:
                R.M. Loureiro and S. Gruzinski (eds), *Passar as frontieras; II Colóquio*

internacional sobre mediadores culturais - seculos XV a XVIII, pp. 245-64. Lagos: Centro de Estudos Gil Eanes.

Schrader, R.

1941 'Het landschap Banggai', *Nederlandsch-Indische Geografische Mededeelingen* 1:103-9, 125-32.

Schrauwers, Albert

1995a 'The household and shared poverty in the highlands of Central Sulawesi', *The Journal of the Royal Anthropological Institute, incorporating Man* 1:337-57.

1995b *In whose image? Religious rationalization and the ethnic identity of the To Pamona of Central Sulawesi*. [PhD thesis, University of Toronto.]

1997 'Houses, hierarchy, headhunting and exchange; Rethinking political relations in the Southeast Asian realm of Luwu', *Bijdragen tot de Taal-, Land- en Volkenkunde* 153:356-80.

1998 "Let's party'; State intervention, discursive traditionalism and the labour process of highland rice cultivators in Central Sulawesi, Indonesia', *The Journal of Peasant Studies* 25:112-30.

2000 *Colonial 'reformation' in the highlands of Central Sulawesi, Indonesia, 1892-1995*. Toronto: University of Toronto Press. [Anthropological Horizons 14.]

Schuster, W.H.

1950 *Mas'alah tentang pemasukan dan pemindahan ikan di Indonesia*. Bandung: Vorkink. [Pengumuman dari Urusan Perikanan Darat 3.]

Schuyt, P.

1911 'Van dag tot dag op reis naar de landschappen Napoe, Besoa en Bada', *Mededeelingen van wege het Nederlandsch Zendelinggenootschap* 55:1-26.

1913 'Langs oude en nieuwe wegen', *Mededeelingen van wege het Nederlandsch Zendelinggenootschap* 57:341-70.

Schwarz, J.A.T.

1903 'Manêwas', *Mededeelingen van wege het Nederlandsch Zendelinggenootschap* 47:101-23.

1907 *Tontemboansche teksten*. Leiden: Brill. Three vols.

1908a 'Ethnographica uit de Minahassa', *Internationales Archiv für Ethnographie* 18:44-61.

1908b *Tontemboansch-Nederlandsch woordenboek met Nederlandsch-Tontemboansch register*. Leiden: Brill.

Schwarz, J.A.T. and A. de Lange

1876 'De landweg uit de Minahassa naar Bolaäng-Mongondou', *Mededeelingen van wege het Nederlandsch Zendelinggenootschap* 20:145-79.

Scott, James C.

1972 'Patron-client politics and political change in Southeast Asia', *The American Political Science Review* 66:91-113.

Scott, William Henry

1985 *Cracks in the parchment curtain, and other essays in Philippine history*. Second edition. Quezon City: New Day. [First edition 1982.]

1992 *Looking for the prehispanic Filipino, and other essays in Philippine history*. Quezon City: New Day.

1994   *Barangay; Sixteenth-century Philippine culture and society.* Quezon City: Ateneo de Manila University Press.

Seavoy, Ronald E.

1973a   'The shading cycle in shifting cultivation', *Annals of the Association of American Geographers* 63:522-8.

1973b   'The transition to continuous rice cultivation in Kalimantan', *Annals of the Association of American Geographers* 63:218-25.

1975   'The origin of tropical grasslands in Kalimantan, Indonesia', *Journal of Tropical Geography* 40:48-52.

1977   'Social restraints on food production in Indonesian subsistence culture', *Journal of Southeast Asian Studies* 8:15-30.

1986   *Famine in peasant societies.* New York: Greenwood. [Contributions in Economics and Economic History 66.]

Section of Military Geology, Geological Survey, U.S. Department of the Interior

1944   *Celebes; Terrain intelligence.* [Strategic Engineering Study 97.]

Sell, Dominicus

[1724]   'Rapport van de kerk- en schoolvisite op de noorder eijlanden en Celebes, 1-11-1724', in: H.E. Niemeijer (ed.), forthcoming, *Bronnen betreffende de Protestantsche kerk in de Molukken, 1605-1795.* [Original source: NA VOC 2029.]

Semmelink, J.

1885   *Geschiedenis der cholera in Oost-Indië vóór 1817.* Utrecht: Breijer.

Seydelman, Bernard Sebastian

1769   'Memorie van den tegenwoordigen staat van Manado en aangrenzende rijken, 20-10-1769', in: H.E. Niemeijer (ed.), forthcoming, *Memories van overgave van gouverneurs van de Molukken (Ternate) in de zeventiende en achttiende eeuw.* [Original source: NA VOC 3301.]

Shepherd, John Robert

1995   *Marriage and mandatory abortion among the 17th-century Siraya.* Arlington, Virginia: American Anthropological Association. [American Ethnological Society Monograph Series 6.]

Sherman, George

1980   'What "green desert"? The ecology of Batak grassland farming', *Indonesia* 29:113-48.

Siebert, Stephen F.

1995   'Prospects for sustained-yield harvesting of rattan (*Calamus spp.*) in two Indonesian national parks', *Society and Natural Resources* 8:209-18.

Siemonsma, J.S. and Kasem Piluek (eds)

1994   *Plant resources of Southeast Asia. Vol. 8: Vegetables.* Bogor: PROSEA.

Sinderen, U. van

1901   'Rapport van de kerk- en schoolvisite [...] begonnen in den Jaare 1761, op de eylanden van Batchian, de Noordcust van Celebes, en het Noordereyland van Tagulanda [...]', *Mededeelingen van wege het Nederlandsch Zendelinggenootschap* 45:349-402.

Slamet-Velsink, Ina E.
1995   *Emerging hierarchies; Processes of stratification and early state formation in the Indonesian Archipelago; Prehistory and the ethnographic present.* Leiden: KITLV Press. [Verhandelingen 166.]

Smiet, A.C.
1990   'Forest ecology on Java; Conversion and usage in a historical perspective', *Journal of Tropical Forest Science* 2:286-302.

Smith, Adam
1870   *An inquiry into the nature and causes of the wealth of nations.* London: Murray. [First published 1776.]

Smith, R.M.
1986   'Transfer incomes, risks and security; The roles of the family and the collectivity in recent theories of fertility change', in: David Coleman and Roger Schofield (eds), *The state of population theory; Forward from Malthus*, pp. 188-211. Oxford: Blackwell.

Smits, P.J.
1909   'Het klimaat der hoogvlakte van Tondano', *Natuurkundig Tijdschrift voor Nederlandsch-Indië* 68:18-109.

Sneddon, J.N.
1978   *Proto-Minahasan; Phonology, morphology and wordlist.* Canberra: Department of Linguistics, Research School of Pacific Studies, Australian National University. [Pacific Linguistics Series B-54.]
1981   'Northern part of Celebes (Sulawesi)', in: Stephen A. Wurm and Shirô Hattori (eds), *Language atlas of the Pacific area*, Map 43. Canberra: Australian Academy of the Humanities / Japan Academy. [Pacific Linguistics Series C-66.]

Snellen, W.B.
1990   'Success and failure of malaria control through species sanitation; Some practical examples', in: W. Takken, W.B. Snellen, J.P. Verhave, B.G.J. Knols and S. Atmosoedjono, *Environmental measures for malaria control in Indonesia; An historical review on species sanitation*, pp. 81-127. Wageningen: Wageningen Agricultural University. [Wageningen Agricultural University Papers 90-7.]

Son, E.L. van
1935   'Aanvullende memorie inzake de onderafdeling Poso.' [NA MvO KIT 1212.]

Sopher, David E.
1965   *The sea nomads; A study based on the literature of the maritime boat people of Southeast Asia.* Singapore: National Museum. [Memoirs of the National Museum 5.]

Spencer, J.E.
1963   'The migration of rice from mainland Southeast Asia into Indonesia', in: Jacques Barrau (ed.) *Plants and the migrations of Pacific peoples; A symposium*, pp. 83-9. Honolulu: Bishop Museum Press.
1966   *Shifting cultivation in Southeastern Asia.* Berkeley: University of California Press. [University of California Publications in Geography 19.]

1975   'The rise of maize as a major crop plant in the Philippines', *Journal of*
                Historical Geography 1:1-16.

Spreeuwenberg, A.F. van
1845-46   'Een blik op de Minahassa', *Tijdschrift voor Nederlandsch Indië (TNI)* 7-
                4:161-214, 301-33, 8-1:23-49.

Stafford, E.E., D.T. Dennis, S. Masri and M. Sudomo
1980   'Intestinal and blood parasites in the Torro Valley, Central Sulawesi,
                Indonesia', *Southeast Asian Journal of Tropical Medicine and Public Health*
                11:468-72.

Stakman, M.C.E.
1892   'Het rapport van den resident van Menado over het verslag der koffie-
                commissie; Met eenige kantteekeningen', *De Indische Gids* 14-1:720-44.
1893   *De Minahassa; Bezwaarschrift opgemaakt naar aanleiding van het rapport*
                nopens den staat van zaken in de Minahassa uitgebracht door W.O. Gallois.
                Amsterdam: Van Holkema en Warendorf.

Stampioen, Joannes
[1696]   'Rapport van een visitatie van kerken en scholen op de Noorderei-
                landen en in Noord-Celebes, 18-9-1696', in: H.E. Niemeijer (ed.),
                forthcoming, *Bronnen betreffende de Protestantsche kerk in de Molukken,*
                1605-1795. [Original source: NA VOC 1579.]

Stap, [H.W.]
1919   'Eene regeling betreffende het uitleenen van gelden voor landbouw-
                en andere doeleinden aan de inlandsche bevolking door een plaatse-
                lijk fonds (districtskas) en het Gouvernement', *Koloniaal Tijdschrift*
                8:797-813, 957-71.

Stargardt, Janice
1992   'Water for courts or countryside; Archaeological evidence from Burma
                and Thailand reviewed', in: Jonathan Rigg (ed.), *The gift of water; Water*
                management, cosmology and the state in South East Asia, pp. 59-70. Lon-
                don: School of Oriental and African Studies.

Statistiek
1877-1909   *Statistiek van den handel, de scheepvaart en de in- en uitvoerrechten in Neder-*
                landsch-Indië. Batavia: Landsdrukkerij. 35 vols.

Stavorinus, John Splinter
1798   *Voyages to the East-Indies. Vol. 2: Voyage to the Cape of Good Hope, Batavia,*
                Samarang, Macasser, Amboyna, Surat, &c. in the years 1774-1778. London:
                Robinson.

Steenis, C.G.G.J. van
1935   'Maleische vegetatieschetsen I; Toelichting bij de plantengeografische
                kaart van Nederlandsch Oost Indië', *Tijdschrift van het Koninklijk Neder-*
                landsch Aardrijkskundig Genootschap 52(Second Series):25-67.
1937   'De invloed van den mensch op het bosch', *Tectona* 30:634-53.
1958a   *Commentary on the vegetation map of Malaysia.* Groningen: Noordhoff/
                UNESCO Humid Tropics Research Project.
1958b   *Vegetation map of Malaysia.* N.p.: UNESCO. [Flora Malesiana Series I,
                Vol. 2.]

Steller, E.

1866   *De Sangi-archipel*. Amsterdam: De Hoogh.

Steller, K.G.F. and W.E. Aebersold

1959   *Sangirees-Nederlands woordenboek met Nederlands-Sangirees register*. 's-Gravenhage: Nijhoff.

Sterren, Anke van der, Alison Murray and Terry Hull

1997   'A history of sexually transmitted diseases in the Indonesian archipelago since 1811', in: Milton Lewis, Scott Bamber and Michael Waugh (eds), *Sex, disease, and society; A comparative history of sexually transmitted diseases and HIV/AIDS in Asia and the Pacific*, pp. 203-30. Westport, Connecticut: Greenwood. [Contributions in Medical Studies 43.]

Steup, F.K.M.

1929   'Plantengeografische schets van het Paloedal', *Tectona* 22:576-96.

1930   'Bijdragen tot de kennis der bosschen van Noord- en Midden Celebes I. Het ebbenhout in de onderafdeeling Poso', *Tectona* 23:857-73.

1931   'Bijdragen tot de kennis der bosschen van Noord- en Midden Celebes II. Een verkenningstocht door Midden-Celebes', *Tectona* 24:1121-35.

1932   'Bijdragen tot de kennis der bosschen van Noord- en Midden-Celebes III. Het zoogenaamde tjempaka-hoetan complex in de Minahasa', *Tectona* 25:119-47.

1933   'Bijdragen tot de kennis der bosschen van Noord- en Midden-Celebes IV. Over de boschgesteldheid in de onderafdeeling Bolaang Mongondow', *Tectona* 26:26-49.

1933-36   'Botanische aanteekeningen over Noord Celebes', *De Tropische Natuur* 22:109-11, 23:61-3, 24:186-9, 25:29-31.

1935   'Het ebbenhout in de dienstkring Manado', *Tectona* 28:45-65.

1936   'Vegetatieschetsen uit Celebes', *De Tropische Natuur* 25:41-5.

1938   'Over vegetatietypen op Celebes', *Natuurkundig Tijdschrift voor Nederlandsch-Indië* 98:283-93.

Stok, J.P. van der

1900   'Het klimaat der Minahassa', *Natuurkundig Tijdschrift voor Nederlandsch-Indië* 59:44-71.

Stokking, H.G.

1910   'Naar Miangas en Nanoesa', *Mededeelingen vanwege het Comité tot Voorziening in de Godsdienstige Behoeften van de Gevestigde Inlandsche Protestantsche Christengemeenten op de Sangi- en Talauer-eilanden* 7:12-20.

1917   'Over het oud-Talaoetsche huwelijk', *Mededeelingen van wege het Nederlandsch Zendelinggenootschap* 61:342-8.

1919   'Gebruiken bij zwangerschap en geboorte op Talaoet', *Mededeelingen van wege het Nederlandsch Zendelinggenootschap* 63:219-29.

1922a   'Gebruiken bij den rijstbouw op Talaoet', *Mededeelingen; Tijdschrift voor Zendingswetenschap* 66:242-54.

1922b   'Gebruiken der Talaoereezen bij de zeevaart', *Mededeelingen; Tijdschrift voor Zendingswetenschap* 66:149-60.

Strickland, G. Thomas
1991   'Malaria', in: G. Thomas Strickland (ed.), *Hunter's tropical medicine*, pp. 586-617. Seventh edition. Philadelphia: Saunders. [First edition 1945.]

Strickland, G. Thomas and M. Farid Abdel-Wahab
1991   Schistosomiasis', in: G. Thomas Strickland (ed.), *Hunter's tropical medicine*, pp. 781-809. Seventh edition. Philadelphia: Saunders. [First edition 1945.]

Strickland, S.S.
1986   'Long term development of Kejaman subsistence; An ecological study', *Sarawak Museum Journal* 36:117-71.

Stuurman, A.
1936   'Memorie van overgave van de afdeling Menado.' [NA MvO KIT 1177.]

Sudomo, Mohammad and W. Patrick Carney
1974   'Precontrol investigation of schistosomiasis in Central Sulawesi', *Bulletin Penelitian Kesehatan* 2-2:51-60.

Sulawesi Tengah
[1992]   *Sulawesi Tengah dalam angka 1991*. N.p.: Biro Pusat Statistik/Badan Perencanaan Pembangunan Daerah, Propinsi Sulawesi Tengah.

Supit, Bert
n.d.   *Sejarah Perang Tondano (Perang Minahasa di Tondano)*. Jakarta: Yayasan Lembaga Penelitian Sejarah dan Masyarakat.
1986   *Minahasa dari amanat Watu Pinawetengan sampai gelora Minawanua*. Jakarta: Sinar Harapan.

Surastopo Hadisumarno
1977   'The geomorphology of the Palu area; Sulawesi from Landsat-1', *The Indonesian Journal of Geography* 7-34:45-59.

Swellengrebel, N.H.
1937   'Malaria in the Netherlands Indies', *Bulletin of the Colonial Institute of Amsterdam* 1:37-45.

Szreter, Simon
1988   'The importance of social intervention in Britain's mortality decline c. 1850-1914; A re-interpretation of the role of public health', *Social History of Medicine* 1:1-37.

Tabel
1895   *Tabel van de resultaten eener, met behulp van den planimeter, verrichte meting van den vlakken inhoud der Nederlandsche bezittingen in Oost-Indië*. Batavia: Landsdrukkerij.

Tacco, Richard
1935   *Het volk van Gorontalo (Historisch, traditioneel, maatschappelijk, cultureel, sociaal, karakteristiek en economisch)*. Gorontalo: Yo Un Ann.

Takken, W. and B.G.J. Knols
1990   'A taxonomic and bionomic review of the malaria vectors of Indonesia', in: W. Takken et al. (eds), *Environmental measures for malaria control in Indonesia; An historical review on species sanitation*, pp. 9-62. Wageningen: Wageningen Agricultural University. [Wageningen Agricultural University Papers 90-7.]

Talens, S.H.
1999   *Een feodale samenleving in koloniaal vaarwater; Staatsvorming, koloniale expansie en economische onderontwikkeling in Banten, West-Java (1600-1750)*. Hilversum: Verloren.

Tamawiwy, M.S.
1934   'Nota behoorende bij de acte van verband van het landschap Talaud-eilanden.' [NA MvO KIT 1183.]

Tammes, P.M.L.
1936a   'De cultuur van een weinig bekende palm voor sago-winning op Sangihe', *Landbouw* 12:43-9.
1936b   'Productiecijfers van klappers', *Landbouw* 12:147-50.
1940   'De biologische achtergrond van het bevolkingsvraagstuk op Noord-Celebes en de Sangihe- en Talaud-archipel', *Tijdschrift voor Economische Geographie* 31:177-98.
[1949]   *De bevolkingscultuur van klapper in het bijzonder in Oost Indonesië*. [Mededelingen van het Departement van Economische Zaken in Nederlandsch-Indië 11.]

Tauchmann, Kurt
1968   *Die Religion der Minahasa-Stämme (Nordost-Celebes/Sulawesi)*. [PhD thesis, Universität zu Köln.]

Tenckink, Wouter Hendrik
[1784]   'Rapport van een visitatie van kerken en scholen van het gouvernement Ternate en onderhorige eilanden, 23-9-1774', in: H.E. Niemeijer (ed.), forthcoming, *Bronnen betreffende de Protestantsche kerk in de Molukken, 1605-1795*. [Original source: NA VOC 3440.]

Tendeloo, H.J.
1873   'De toestand der vrouw in de Minahasa', *Mededeelingen van wege het Nederlandsch Zendelinggenootschap* 17:10-31.

Terburgh, J.T.
1919   'Malaria-bestrijding bij de inlandsche bevolking door middel van chininisatie', *Mededeelingen van den Burgerlijken Geneeskundigen Dienst in Nederlandsch-Indië* 9:72-139.

Tergast, G.C.W.C.
1936   'Schets van den landbouw op de Sangihe- en Talaud-eilanden', *Landbouw* 11:125-45.

Terra, G.J.A.
1952   *Cultuurtype, landbouw en welvaart in Indonesië*. Djakarta: Wolters. [Inaugural lecture, University of Indonesia.]
1958   'Farm systems in South-East Asia', *Netherlands Journal of Agricultural Science* 6:157-82.

Tesch, J.W.
1936   'Iets over lepra in Midden-Celebes en de leprozenkampong bij Paloe', *Geneeskundig Tijdschrift voor Nederlandsch-Indië* 76:2829-40.
1939   'Voorloopige aanteekeningen over anthropologisch onderzoek bij de bewoners van Midden-Celebes', *Geneeskundig Tijdschrift voor Nederlandsch-Indië* 79:2374-83.

Teysmann, J.E.

1861   'Verslag van den honorair-inspecteur van kultures J.E. Teysmann, over
            de door Z.Ed. in 1860 gedane reizen in de Molukken', *Natuurkundig
            Tijdschrift voor Nederlandsch-Indië* 23:290-369.

Thije, Isaac van

1689   'Instructie voor Harman Jansz. Steenkuijler, boekhouder en subaltern
            hooft tot Manado, waar na zig voor eerst en tot nader order sal regu-
            leren, 18-7-1689', in: H.E. Niemeijer (ed.), forthcoming, *Memories van
            overgave van gouverneurs van de Molukken (Ternate) in de zeventiende en
            achttiende eeuw.* [Original source: NA VOC 1461.]

Thomas, Nicholas

1991   *Entangled objects; Exchange, material culture, and colonialism in the Pacific.*
            Cambridge, Mass.: Harvard University Press.

Thufail, Fadjar Ibnu

1994   'The evolution of marine tenure systems in Para and Kei island; Social
            and ecological perspectives'. Paper, International seminar on indig-
            enous knowledge, Padjadjaran University, Bandung, 11-15 July.

Tideman, J.

1926   'Memorie van overgave van de residentie Menado.' [NA MvO MMK
            305.]

Tiele, P.A.

1877-86   'De Europeërs in den Maleischen Archipel', *Bijdragen tot de Taal-, Land-
            en Volkenkunde* 25:321-420 (I), 27:1-69 (II), 28:261-340 (III), 395-482 (IV),
            29:153-214 (V), 30:141-242 (VI), 32:49-118 (VII), 35:257-355 (VIII).

Tiele, P.A. and J.E. Heeres (eds)

1886-95   *Bouwstoffen voor de geschiedenis der Nederlanders in den Maleischen Archi-
            pel.* 's-Gravenhage: Nijhoff. Three vols.

Tiffen, Mary, Michael Mortimore, and Francis Gichuki

1994   *More people, less erosion; Environmental recovery in Kenya.* Chichester:
            Wiley.

Tillema, H.F.

1922   *'Kromoblanda'; Over 't vraagstuk van 'het wonen' in Kromo's groote land.*
            Vol. 5-1. 's-Gravenhage: Masman.

1926   *Zonder tropen geen Europa!* Bloemendaal: Tillema.

Tonelli, Lise

1992   Case study of changing land use in the middle hills of Lombok, Cen-
            tral Sulawesi. [MA thesis, Dalhousie University, Halifax.]

Touwen, Jeroen

2001   *Extremes in the archipelago; Trade and economic development in the Outer
            Islands of Indonesia, 1900-1942.* Leiden: KITLV Press. [Verhandelingen
            190.]

Townsend, Nicholas

1997   'Reproduction in anthropology and demography', in: David I. Kertzer
            and Tom Fricke (eds), *Anthropological demography; Toward a new syn-
            thesis*, pp. 96-114. Chicago: The University of Chicago Press.

Uhlenbeck, O.A.
1861   'De Tomori-expeditie in 1856', *Mededeelingen betreffende het Zeewezen* 1:1-61.

Uhlig, Harald
1980   'Man and tropical karst in Southeast Asia; Geo-ecological differentiation, land use and rural development potentials in Indonesia and other regions', *GeoJournal* 4:31-44.
1984   (ed.) *Spontaneous and planned settlement in Southeast Asia; Forest clearing and recent pioneer colonization in the ASEAN countries and two case-studies on Thailand.* Hamburg: Institute of Asian Affairs. [Giessener Geographische Schriften 58.]
1990   'Der Trockenlandreisbau – ein wenig bekanntes Potential der tropischen Entwicklungsländer', in: M. Domrös, E. Gormsen en J. Stadelbauer (eds), *Festschrift für Wendelin Klaer zum 65. Geburtstag,* pp. 375-98. Mainz: Geographisches Institut der Johannes Gutenberg-Universität. [Mainzer Geographische Studien 34.]

Uitkomsten
1922   *Uitkomsten der in de maand november 1920 gehouden volkstelling. Vol. 2: Tabellen.* Batavia: Ruygrok.

Uittreksel
1914   'Uittreksel uit het Rapport-Gallois (Javaasche Courant 29 juli 1892)', *Adatrechtbundels* 9:3-4.

Ulaen-Hoetagaol, Sophia
1985   Manalun dan mamarut jurame; Kajian tentang aktivitas perladangan di sekitar kawasan taman nasional Dumoga Bone, Bolaang-Mongondow, Sulawesi Utara. [MA thesis, Universitas Indonesia.]

Ulfers, S.
1868   'Het Rano-i-Apo gebied en de bevolking van Bolaäng Mogondou', *Mededeelingen van wege het Nederlandsch Zendelinggenootschap* 12:1-26.

Uno, A.
1949   'Het natuurmonument Panoea (N. Celebes) en het maleohoen (*Macrocephalon maleo* SAL. MÜLLER) in het bijzonder', *Tectona* 39:151-65.

Urdaneta, Andres de
1837   'Relacion escrita y presentada al Emperador por Andres de Urdaneta de los sucesos de la armada del Comendador Loaisa, desde 24 de Julio de 1525 hasta el año 1535', in: Martin Fernandez de Navarrete (ed.), *Coleccion de los viages y descubrimientos, que hicieron por mar los Españoles desde fines del siglo XV, Vol. V,* pp. 401-39. Madrid: Imprenta Nacional.

Valckenaer, Paulus Jacob
[1778]   'Memorie overgegeven door den heer Paulus Jacob Valckenaer afgaande gouverneur aan zijn Eds successeur den heer Mr Jacob Roeland Thomaszen, aankomend gouverneur van Ternaten, 20-8-1778', in: H.E. Niemeijer (ed.), forthcoming, *Memories van overgave van gouverneurs van de Molukken (Ternate) in de zeventiende en achttiende eeuw.* [Original source: ANRI Ternate 78.]

Vandermeer, Canute
1967   'Population patterns on the island of Cebu, The Philippines, 1500 to
               1900', Annals of the Association of American Geographers 57:315-37.
Vayda, Andrew P.
1976   War in ecological perspective; Persistence, change, and adaptive processes in
               three Oceanic societies. New York: Plenum.
Veenhuizen, A.C.
1903   'Aanteekeningen omtrent Bolaäng-Mongondo', Tijdschrift van het Konin-
               klijk Nederlandsch Aardrijkskundig Genootschap 20(Second Series):35-74.
Veer, K. van der
1948   'Mais', in: C.J.J. van Hall and C. van de Koppel (eds), De landbouw in
               de Indische archipel, vol. IIA, pp. 111-56. 's-Gravenhage: Van Hoeve.
Velde, C.W.M. van de
1845   Gezigten uit Neêrlands Indië, naar de natuur geteekend en beschreven.
               Amsterdam: Buffa.
Velde van Cappellen, D. van de
1857   'Verslag eener bezoekreis naar de Sangi-eilanden', Mededeelingen van
               wege het Nederlandsch Zendelinggenootschap 1:27-83.
1858-59   'Uittreksels uit eenen brief van S. van de Velde van Cappellen, in
               leven zendelingleeraar te Amoerang', Mededeelingen van wege het Neder-
               landsch Zendelinggenootschap 2:309-68, 3:215-50.
Velthoen, Esther J.
1997a   'A historical perspective on Bajo in eastern Sulawesi'. Paper, Interna-
               tional seminar on maritime communities in a changing world, Univer-
               sitas Sam Ratulangi, Manado, 23-27 September.
1997b   '"Wanderers, robbers and bad folk"; The politics of violence, protec-
               tion and trade in eastern Sulawesi, 1750-1850', in: Anthony Reid (ed.),
               The last stand of Asian autonomies; Responses to modernity in the diverse
               states of Southeast Asia and Korea, 1750-1900, pp. 367-88. Basingstoke:
               Macmillan.
Verdoorn, Johannes Adrianus
1941   Verloskundige hulp voor de inheemsche bevolking van Nederlandsch-Indië.
               's-Gravenhage: Boekencentrum.
Verhoef, L.
1937   'Typen van stervend land in den Nederlandsch Indischen archipel; het
               Paloedal (Midden Celebes)', Tectona 30:220-2.
1938   'Bijdragen tot de kennis der bosschen van Noord- en Midden-Celebes
               V. Het boschgebied Ongkak Doemoga (Bolaang Mongondow)', Tec-
               tona 31:7-29.
Verkerk Pistorius, A.W.P.
1871   Studien over de inlandsche huishouding in de Padangsche bovenlanden.
               Zalt-Bommel: Noman.
Verkuyl, A.H.
1938   'De Minahasa. IV (Slot)', Tropisch Nederland 11:105-9.

Verschuer, F.H. van
1883   'De Badjo's', *Tijdschrift van het Koninklijk Nederlandsch Aardrijkskundig Genootschap* 7(First Series):1-7.

Verslag
1932   'Verslag resultaat van plaatselijke onderzoekingen op Menado ingevolge gouvernementsbesluit van 5 januari 1932, No. 3.' [MvO KIT 1173.]

Verslag Dienst Boschwezen
1901-48   *Verslag van den Dienst van het Boschwezen in Nederlandsch-Indië over het jaar* [1900-1948]. Batavia: n.n.

Vink, G.J.
1941   *De grondslagen van het Indonesische landbouwbedrijf.* Wageningen: Veenman.

Visser, Leontine
1989   *My rice field is my child; Social and territorial aspects of swidden cultivation in Sahu, eastern Indonesia.* Dordrecht: Foris. [KITLV, Verhandelingen 136.]

Vlies, A.P. van der
1940   'De agathisbosschen in de afdeeling Poso', *Tectona* 33:616-40.

Volkstelling
1933-36   *Volkstelling 1930.* Batavia: Departement van Economische Zaken. Eight vols.

Voorn, M.C.
1925   'Aanvullende memorie van overgave inzake de onderafdeling Paloe.' [NA MvO KIT 1198.]

Vorderman, A.G.
1899   'Aanteekeningen bij het opstel van den aspirant controleur B.C.A.J. van Dinter over het eiland Siaoe sub aardvruchten', *Tijdschrift voor Indische Taal-, Land- en Volkenkunde (TBG)* 41:390.

Vorstman, J.A.
1935a   'Aanvullende memorie van overgave inzake de onderafdeling Paloe.' [NA MvO KIT 1203.]
1935b   'Zout en water in de Paloe-vlakte', *Mededeelingen van de Vereeniging van Gezaghebbers B.B.* 31:19-23.
1936   'Belastingbetaling in arbeid', *Mededeelingen van de Vereeniging van Gezaghebbers B.B.* 34:40-5.

Vosmaer, J.N.
1839   'Korte beschrijving van het zuid-oostelijk schiereiland van Celebes, in het bijzonder van de Vosmaers-baai of van Kendari; Verrijkt met eenige berigten omtrent den stam der Orang Badjos, en meer andere aanteekeningen', *Verhandelingen van het Bataviaasch Genootschap van Kunsten en Wetenschappen* 17:63-184.

Vreede, E.A.A. de
[1950]   *Luwuk-Banggai en Drenthe.* N.p.: Provinciaal Zendingscomité der Nederlands Hervormde Kerk in Drenthe.

Vries, Ruard Wallis de
1996   *D.H. de Vries; Een Amsterdamse koopman in de Molukken, 1883-1901.*
              Baarn: Ambo.

Vuuren, L. van
1920   *Het gouvernement Celebes; Proeve eener monographie.* [Weltevreden]:
              Encyclopaedisch Bureau. Two vols.

Wallace, Alfred Russel
1986   *The Malay archipelago; The land of the orang-utan and the bird of paradise;
              A narrative of travel with studies of man and nature.* Singapore: Oxford
              University Press. [First edition 1869.]

Wanner, Johannes
1914   'Eine Reise durch Ostcelebes', *Dr. A. Petermann's Mitteilungen aus Jus-
              tus Perthe's Geogr. Anstalt* 60-1:78-81, 133-6.

Ward, R.C. and M. Robinson
1990   *Principles of hydrology.* London: McGraw-Hill.

Warren, James Francis
1981   *The Sulu Zone, 1768-1898; The dynamics of external trade slavery, and eth-
              nicity in the transformation of a Southeast Asian Maritime state.* Singapore:
              Singapore University Press.
1998   *The Sulu Zone; The world capitalist economy and the historical imagination.*
              Amsterdam: VU University Press. [Comparative Asian Studies 20.]

Watson, C.W.
1992   *Kinship, property and inheritance in Kerinci, Central Sumatra.* Canterbury:
              Centre for Social Anthropology and Computing and Centre of South-
              East Asian Studies, University of Kent. [CSAC Monographs 4.]

Wattendorf, F.L.
1883   'Memorie van overgave van de residentie Menado.' [NA MMK 301.]

Watuseke, F.S. and D.E.F. Henley
1994   'C.C. Predigers verhandeling over het plaatselijk bestuur en de
              huishouding van de Minahasa in 1804', *Bijdragen tot de Taal-, Land- en
              Volkenkunde* 150:357-85.

Waworoentoe, A.L.
1894   'De oude geschiedenis der Minahasa volgens de legenden en sagen
              van het volk', *Verhandelingen van het Bataviaasch Genootschap van Kun-
              sten en Wetenschappen* 47:85-99.

Weber-Van Bosse, A.
1904   *Een jaar aan boord H.M. Siboga.* Leiden: Brill.

Weg, U.J.
1938   'Memorie van overgave van de afdeling Menado.' [NA MvO KIT
              1178.]

Weischet, Wolfgang, and Cesar N. Caviedes
1993   *The persisting ecological constraints of tropical agriculture.* Harlow, Essex:
              Longman.

Weitzel, A.W.P.
1883   'Geschiedkundig overzicht van de expeditie naar Tomorie op Celebes
              in het jaar 1856', *Bijdragen tot de Taal-, Land-, en Volkenkunde van
              Nederlandsch-Indië; Uitgegeven vanwege het Koninklijk Instituut voor de*

Taal- Land- en Volkenkunde van Nederlandsch-Indië ter gelegenheid van het Zesde Internationale Congres der Oriëntalisten te Leiden. Vol. 2: Land- en Volkenkunde, pp. 35-56. 's-Gravenhage: Nijhoff.

Wely, Wilhelmus van
[1707] 'Rapport van een visitatie van kerken en scholen in Noord-Sulawesi en op de Sangir-Talaud eilanden, 2-11-1707', in: H.E. Niemeijer (ed.), forthcoming, *Bronnen betreffende de Protestantsche kerk in de Molukken, 1605-1795*. [Original source: NA VOC 1758.]

Werndly, Jan Thomas
[1729] 'Rapport van een visitatie van kerken en scholen op Makian, Bacan, in Noord-Sulawesi en op de Sangir- en Talaud-eilanden, 6-4-1729', in: H.E. Niemeijer (ed.), forthcoming, *Bronnen betreffende de Protestantsche kerk in de Molukken, 1605-1795*. [Original source: NA VOC 2132.]

Wessels, C.
1933 'De katholieke missie in Noord-Celebes en op de Sangi-eilanden, 1563-1605', *Studiën; Tijdschrift voor Godsdienst, Wetenschap en Letteren* 65:365-96.
1935 *De katholieke missie in de Molukken, Noord-Celebes en de Sangihe-eilanden gedurende de Spaansche bestuursperiode 1606-1677*. Tilburg: Bergmans. [Historisch Tijdschrift Serie Studies 3.]

Wessels, L.
1891 'De gouvernments-koffiecultuur in de Minahassa, residentie Menado', *Tijdschrift voor Nederlandsch Indië (TNI)* 20-1:50-71, 123-46.

White, Benjamin
1973 'Demand for labour and population growth in colonial Java', *Human Ecology* 1:217-36.
1976 *Production and reproduction in a Javanese village*. [PhD thesis, Columbia University.]

Whitten, Anthony J., Muslimin Mustafa and Gregory S. Henderson
1987 *The ecology of Sulawesi*. Yogyakarta: Gadjah Mada University Press.
2002 *The ecology of Sulawesi*. Hongkong: Periplus. [The Ecology of Indonesia Series 4.]

Whitten, Anthony J. and Jane J. Whitten
1985 'Tanaman sagu dan pengolahannya di pulau Siberut', in: Gerard Persoon and Reimar Schefold (eds), *Pulau Siberut; Pembangunan sosio-ekonomi, kebudayaan tradisional dan lingkungan hidup*, pp. 30-6. Jakarta: Bhratara Karya Aksara.

Wichmann, Arthur
1890 'Bericht über eine im Jahre 1888-89 im Auftrage der Nederländischen Geographischen Gesellschaft ausgeführte Reise nach dem Indischen Archipel', *Tijdschrift van het Koninklijk Nederlandsch Aardrijkskundig Genootschap* 7(Second Series):907-94.

Wiersma, J.N.
1871 'Geschiedenissen van Ratahan en Passan van de vroegste tijden tot op den tegenwoordigen tijd, volgens de geheime overleveringen der ouden van dagen', *Bijdragen tot de Taal-, Land- en Volkenkunde* 18:204-27.

1872   'Het huwelijk in de Minahassa', *Tijdschrift voor Nederlandsch Indië (TNI)*
                1872-2:4-40.
1876   *Ervaringen gedurende mijn twaalfjarig zendingsleven.* Rotterdam: Storm
                Lotz.

Wigboldus, Jouke S.
1979   'De oudste Indonesische maiscultuur', in: Francien van Anrooij, Dirk
                H.A. Kolff, Jan T.M. van Laanen and Gerard J. Telkamp (eds), *Between
                people and statistics; Essays on modern Indonesian history presented to P.
                Creutzberg*, pp. 19-31. The Hague: Nijhoff.
1987   'A history of the Minahasa c. 1615-1680', *Archipel* 34:63-101.
1988   A history of the Minahasa (northeasternmost Sulawesi, Indonesia) c.
                1680-1825. [Manuscript.]
1996a   Demografie en economie van noordelijke gebieden in continentaal en
                insulair Celebes (excl. Minahasa) vóór 1850. [Manuscript.]
1996b   Demografie van Minahasa 1563-1695; Gegevens en analyses voor
                onderzoek. [Manuscript.]

Wilde, W.J.J.O. de and B.E.E. Duyfjes
2001   'On the special botanical character of the Leuser Park and vicinity,
                with emphasis on the high mountain blang vegetation of northern
                Sumatra', *Flora Malesiana Bulletin* 12:377-91.

Wilken, G.A.
1873   'Het landbezit in de Minahasa', *Mededeelingen van wege het Neder-
                landsch Zendelinggenootschap* 17:107-37.
1883   'Over de verwantschap en het huwelijks- en erfrecht bij de volken van
                het Maleische ras', *De Indische Gids* 5-1:656-764.

Wilken, N.P.
1849   'De godsdienst en godsdienstplegtigheden der Alfoeren in de Mena-
                hassa op het eiland Celebes', *Tijdschrift voor Nederlandsch Indië (TNI)*
                11-2:387-402.
1859   'Brief van den zendeling N.P. Wilken, te Tomohon, Menahasse van
                Menado', *Mededeelingen van wege het Nederlandsch Zendelinggenootschap*
                3:262-80.
1870   'Iets over den landbouw in de Minahassa en de daarbij gebruikelijke
                benamingen', *Tijdschrift voor Nederlandsch Indië (TNI)* 4-2:373-85.

Wilken, N.P. and J.A. Schwarz
1867a   'Verhaal eener reis naar Bolaäng Mongondou', *Mededeelingen van wege
                het Nederlandsch Zendelinggenootschap* 11:1-41, 225-54.
1867b   'Het heidendom en de Islam in Bolaang Mongondow', *Mededeelingen
                van wege het Nederlandsch Zendelinggenootschap* 11:255-83.
1867c   'Allerlei over het land en volk van Bolaäng Mongondou', *Mededeelin-
                gen van wege het Nederlandsch Zendelinggenootschap* 11:284-398.

Wilkinson, Richard G.
1973   *Poverty and progress; An ecological model of economic development.* Lon-
                don: Methuen.

Willer, T.J.
1861   *Volkstelling in Nederlandsch Indie.* 's-Gravenhage: Nijhoff.

Williams, Maynard Owen
1940   'The Celebes; New man's land of the Indies', *The National Geographic Magazine* 78-1:51-82.

Wilson, Chris
2001   'Understanding the nature and importance of low-growth demographic regimes', in: Ts'ui-jung Liu, James Lee, David Sven Reher, Osamu Saito and Wang Feng (eds), *Asian population history*, pp. 24-44. Oxford: Oxford University Press.

Wiltenaar, Ericus Johannes
[1769]   'Rapport van een visitatie van kerken en scholen in Noord-Sulawesi en op de Sangir-Talaud eilanden, 25-1-1769', in: H.E. Niemeijer (ed.), forthcoming, *Bronnen betreffende de Protestantsche kerk in de Molukken, 1605-1795*. [Original source: ANRI Ternate 19.]

Woensdregt, Jac.
1928   'De landbouw bij de To Bada' in Midden-Celebes', *Tijdschrift voor Indische Taal-, Land- en Volkenkunde (TBG)* 68:125-255.
1929a   'Verloving en huwelijk bij de To Bada' in Midden Celebes', *Bijdragen tot de Taal-, Land en Volkenkunde* 85:245-90.
1929b   'Zwangerschap en geboorte bij de To Bada' in Midden-Celebes', *Koloniaal Tijdschrift* 18:352-66.
1930   'Het kind bij de To Bada in Midden Selebes', *Koloniaal Tijdschrift* 19:321-35.

Wood, James W.
1998   'A theory of preindustrial population dynamics; Demography, economy, and well-being in Malthusian systems', *Current Anthropology* 39:99-121.

Woodard, David
1969   *The narrative of Captain David Woodard and four seamen who lost their ship while in a boat at sea, and surrendered themselves up to the Malays in the island of Celebes; Containing an interesting account of their sufferings […], and their escape from the Malays, […] also an account of the manners and customs of the country*. London: Dawsons of Pall Mall. [First published 1805.]

World Conservation Monitoring Centre
1996   *Tropical forests of Sulawesi and the Moluccas*. Cambridge: World Conservation Monitoring Centre. [Map, 1:2,000,000.]

Worotikan, J.A.
1910   'Landbezit in de Minahasa', *Adatrechtbundels* 3:152-63.

Wouden, F.A.E. van
1941   'Mythen en maatschappij in Boeol', *Tijdschrift voor Indische Taal-, Land- en Volkenkunde (TBG)* 81:333-410.

Wrigley, E.A. and R.S. Schofield
1981   *The population history of England 1541-1871; A reconstruction*. London: Arnold. [Studies in Social and Demographic History 2.]

Wrigley, E.A., R.S. Davies, J.E. Oeppen and R.S. Schofield
1997   *English population history from family reconstitution 1580-1837*. Cambridge: Cambridge University Press. [Cambridge Studies in Population, Economy, and Society in Past Time 32.]

Wylick, Carla van
1941   *Bestattungsbrauch und Jenseitsglaube auf Celebes.* [PhD thesis, Universität Basel.]

Wijn, J.F. de
1952   'A nutritional survey of the Toradja population (Central Celebes) compared with other agrarian populations in Asia', *Documenta de Medicina Geographica et Tropica* 4:149-70.

Zacot, François
1978   'To be or not to be Badjo – this is our question', *Prisma; Indonesian Journal of Social and Economic Affairs* 10:17-29.

Zakelijk verslag
1860   'Zakelijk verslag van de verrigtingen der Nederlandsche Marine in Oost-Indië, gedurende het jaar 1857', *Verhandelingen en Berigten betrekkelijk het Zeewezen, de Zeevaartkunde, de Hydrographie, de Koloniën en de daarmede in verband staande Wetenschappen* 1860-62:96-130.

Zeeroof van Groot Sangi
1921   'De zeeroof van Groot Sangi', *Koninklijke Nederlandsche Vereeniging Onze Vloot* 13:23-6, 54-9.

Zeerooverijen
1850   'De zeerooverijen der Soeloerezen', *Tijdschrift voor Nederlandsch Indië (TNI)* 1850-2:99-105.

Zegeningen Gods
1911   'Zegeningen Gods. (Uit het Jaarverslag over het ressort Salibaboe)', *Mededeelingen vanwege het Comité tot Voorziening in de Godsdienstige Behoeften van de Gevestigde Inlandsche Protestantsche Christengemeenten op de Sangi- en Talaud Eilanden* 12:4-7.

Zending
1895   'De zending van twee Minahassasche hoofden naar Java', *Tijdschrift van het Binnenlandsch Bestuur* 11:349-83.

Zwaan, [W.J.A.]
1910   'Talaud. (Uit een brief van Br. Zwaan)', *Mededeelingen vanwege het Comité tot Voorziening in de Godsdienstige Behoeften van de Gevestigde Inlandsche Protestantsche Christengemeenten op de Sangi- en Talauer Eilanden* 6:6-7.

General index

Abendanon, E.C. 484, 486-7, 556-7, 559, 561-2
Acciaioli, Greg 30, 48
Adam, L. 465
Adriani, N. 28, 64, 70, 114, 222, 225, 227-8, 232-3, 247, 252-3, 255, 261, 263, 281-2, 290-1, 307, 343, 347-8, 350, 356, 366-7, 370, 372-3, 383-5, 388, 411, 426, 438, 440-1, 483-4, 487, 531, 534, 537, 561-2, 572, 585, 602
Aken, A.Ph. van 46, 272, 304
Alexander, Jennifer 462
Alexander, Paul 388, 448-9, 462
Allen, Bryant 320
Alsteijn, P. 168
Andaya, Leonard Y. 235
Andel, W.J.D. van 266
ANRI see Arsip Nasional Republik Indonesia
Aragon, Lorraine V. 48, 77, 256, 348
Archief van de Raad voor de Zending (ARZ) 44
Argensola, Bartolomé Leonardo de 106, 114, 213, 216, 232, 243
Arsip Nasional Republik Indonesia (ANRI) 44
Avink, K.F. 266

Baak, B. van 201
Banjarmasin War 360
Bayliss-Smith, T.P. 413
Bemmelen, R.W. van 379
Berwouts, Rogier 45
Beukering, J.A. van 521, 567
Bik, J.Th. 461, 494
Blankhart, David Meskes 48, 274, 280, 345-7, 397, 412, 452, 548

Bleeker, P. 187, 204
Blok, Roelof 233
Boerema, J. 582
Boomgaard, Peter 7-8, 116, 297, 393, 399, 448-9, 574, 582
Boonstra van Heerdt, R. 218
Bosch, J.C. 337
Boserup, Ester 585, 588-9, 595
Bosscher, C. 46, 243-4, 246, 259, 300
Bouvy, A.C.N. 274, 280-1, 283, 290-1, 299, 301, 304, 308, 312
Brilman, D. 262, 306
Brookfield, Harold C. 320
Brosius, J. Peter 564
Bruce-Chwatt, Leonard Jan 270, 574
Brug, Peter Harmen van der 273
Bruinier, J.B.H. 484, 486, 490
Buchholt, Helmut 605
Byron, Yvonne 320

Cambier, J.P.C. 535
Capellen, G.A.G.P. van der 169, 353
Catholic 41, 45, 118, 133-4, 144, 165
Chabot, Hendrik Th. 48, 105, 106-7, 114, 380, 463
Christian, Christianity 23, 28, 31, 37, 39, 42, 45, 47, 94, 110, 128-9, 133-7, 144-5, 147, 150, 152, 169, 184, 216, 275, 302, 307, 364, 369, 378-9, 387, 447, 452, 596, 600
Clercq, F.S.A. de 46, 178, 188, 193, 235-6, 240, 243, 246, 254, 290, 307, 343, 368-9, 378, 393
Coleman, David 438
Colin, Francisco 179

Conelly, W. Thomas 587
Conklin, Harold C. 579
Coté, Joost 257
Crab, P. van der 355-500, 505
Cuarteron, D. Carlo 129, 137, 148, 152, 155, 157, 160, 162, 528, 578
Cultivation System 5-6, 94, 448-9, 462, 499

Dam, Pieter van 45
Delden, A.J. van 46, 106, 112-3, 116, 120, 129, 132, 137, 145, 148, 152-3, 186, 213, 259, 263, 283, 290, 351, 363, 430, 509-10
Dobbin, Christine 35, 438
Doren, J.B.J. van 493
Douglas, Mary 465
Dove, Michael R. 80, 360, 585, 591, 600
Dozier, Edward P. 287
Dürr, G.F. 428
Duhr, George Fredrik 168, 176, 309, 595
Dumont d'Urville, M.J. 506
Dutch Reformed Church 127
Dutrieux, F.B. 534
Duynmaer van Twist, A.J. 428

Edeling, A.C.J. 46, 249-50, 262, 273-4, 331, 337, 348, 358, 363, 365, 378, 381-2, 386, 388, 390, 393-5, 448, 450, 526, 594, 596
El Niño/Southern Oscillation (ENSO) 320
Elson, R.E. 297
ENSO *see* El Niño/Southern Oscillation

Fairhead, James 489
Falkus, Malcolm 8
Faria, M. de 135
Food and Agriculture Organization 443
Forrest, Thomas 148, 156, 159-60, 162, 412, 460, 487
Fox, James J. 605
Francis, E. 129, 132, 137, 145, 148, 151, 153, 156, 186, 200, 204, 213, 265, 270, 506-7
Franszoon, Joannes 484
Freeman, J.D. 360, 461

Gallois, W.O. 396
Gardiner, Peter 297

Goedhart, O.H. 243, 247
Goens, Rycklof van 111
Gichuki, Francis 570, 604
Gooszen, A. Johanna 111, 115, 364, 378, 381
Graafland, Nicolaas 46-7, 264, 272, 274-5, 279, 285, 293, 306-8, 312, 353, 363, 366, 369, 375, 377, 379, 392-3, 395, 409, 466, 535, 539, 594-5, 597, 599
Grove, Richard H. 581
Grubauer, Albert 292, 476, 482, 487
Grudelbach, J. 269

Hanks, Lucien M. 585
Hannibal, L.W. 470
Hardjono, J. 415, 544
Harris, Marvin 385, 399, 444
Hart, C. van der 86, 232, 240, 246, 272, 433
Heersink, Christiaan G. 350, 359, 433, 603-4
Henderson, Gregory S. 483, 517, 533
Hendrik Kraemer Instituut 44
Heringa, P.K. 47, 412, 490, 569, 579
Heyne, K. 290
Hickson, Sydney J. 47, 160, 263, 290, 308-9, 311, 315, 354, 382, 409, 463, 509-10
Hissink, C. 290, 486
Hoëvell, G.W.W.C. van 101, 111, 219, 225, 320, 328
Hoff, A. 281
Horst, W.A. van der 206-8
Hull, Terence H. 449, 462
Hunt, Robert C. 586, 606

Indische Kerk 43
Iranzo, Juan 167, 178-9
Islam, Islamic 23, 27-8, 31, 36-7, 184, 377

Jacobs, H. 135, 139
Jansen, A.J.F. 46, 76, 81, 91, 94, 107, 111, 134, 142, 151-4, 157, 159-60, 187, 191, 206, 293, 307, 311, 354, 388, 414, 433, 495, 507, 539, 567, 581, 587, 600
Jasper, J.E. 418
Jellesma, E.J. 159
Jones, Gavin W. 414
Jongh, Maximiliaen de 146

Kam, Joseph 134
Kathirithamby-Wells, Jeya 582
Kaudern, Walter 234, 260, 383, 476, 481-2, 529
Kelling, P. 79, 133, 142, 343, 383, 385, 398
Kemmerling, G.L.L. 548, 557
Knaap, Gerrit J. 106, 119, 422, 437-8, 600
Knapen, Han 125, 258, 287, 312, 359, 401, 423, 443, 585
Kol, H. van 368, 393, 533, 551
Koninklijk Instituut voor de Tropen (KIT) 44
Koorders, S.H. 289, 342, 495, 497, 499-500, 505, 553-4
Koperberg, M. 90, 476
Kornrumpf, Martin 415
KPM 457, *see also* Royal Dutch Packet-Boat Company
Kruyt, Albert C. 27, 30, 47, 64, 70, 73, 78, 106, 114, 118, 222, 225, 227-8, 232-3, 247, 250, 252-3, 256, 261-3, 267, 281-2, 284, 290-1, 297, 307, 312, 347, 350, 356, 365-73, 375, 378, 380, 382-5, 388-9, 392, 401, 426-8, 438-40, 442, 445, 476, 482-4, 487, 529-31, 534-5, 537, 540, 555, 561-2, 572-3, 577, 579, 585, 593
Kruyt, Jan 47, 378, 533, 535
Kündig, A. 48, 249-50, 262, 266, 268-9, 273-4, 280, 306, 359, 364, 406, 451

Laag, C.M. ter 349
Lam, H.J. 404, 412, 499, 508, 513, 528, 544, 557
Lange, S.H. de 187, 388
Leach, Helen M. 489, 586
Lesthaeghe, R. 466
Leur, J.C. van 91
Li, Tania Murray 48, 350, 392, 568, 576-7, 602
Lima lo Pohala'a 31, 196
Logeman, F.H.W.J.R. 359
Lopes, A. 135
Lucieer, A.I. 399

Magalhães, D. de 135, 139
Mai, Ulrich 605
Malthus, Thomas Robert 360, 610
Malthusian 377, 439, 449, 573

Marle, V.J. van 48, 329-500, 505-6, 517, 539
Marta, Antonio 45, 256, 509
Matthijssen, P.A. 46, 243-4, 246, 259
McKeown, Thomas 360
Merkus, P. 199
Metzner, Joachim K. 359, 422, 483, 570, 576, 589
Meyer, A.B. 599
Michielsen, W.J.M. 224, 233-4
Mohammedans 169, 377
Mohr, E.C.J. 414
Mortimore, Michael 570, 604
Muslim 27, 36-7, 85, 127, 137, 144, 148, 151-2, 235, 364, 373-4, 377, 389, 400, 409
Mustafa, Muslimin 483, 517, 533

NA *see* Nationaal Archief
Nationaal Archief (NA) 44-5
Navarette, Domingo 63, 77, 84
Nederlandsch Bijbelgenootschap 47
Nederlandsch Zendelinggenootschap (NZG) 42-3, 46-7, 60, 250, 509, 596
Netherlands Missionary Society 477
Netting, Robert McC. 570, 588
New World 65, 99, 453
Newson, Linda A. 115
Neijs, J.A. 92
Nibbering, Jan Willem 570
Nieboer, H.J. 439, 442, 445
Niehof, Anke 373
Nourse, Jennifer Williams 48
NZG *see* Nederlandsch Zendelinggenootschap

Oey, Mayling 297
Ormeling, F.J. 287, 359, 575

Padoch, Christine 384, 390, 444, 585
Padtbrugge, Robert 45, 51, 58, 60, 63, 67, 69, 72, 82, 90, 105-6, 112-3, 116, 128, 136, 142, 146, 165, 168, 175, 178, 181, 185, 192, 195, 197-8, 205, 213, 215-7, 228, 232, 236, 238, 243-4, 253, 258, 266, 279, 341, 343, 383, 385, 388, 403, 421, 453-4, 462, 480, 482, 484, 490-1, 493-4, 507-8, 510, 542-3, 545-7, 551, 594
Pahud, C.F. 338

Pax Neerlandica 431
Pelzer, Karl J. 561
Pennings, A. 339, 344
Persoon, Gerard A. 603
Pietermaat, D.F.W. 46, 66, 262, 289
Pirngadie 418
Platteau, Jean-Philippe 604
Protestant, Protestantism 42-4, 47, 127,
  129, 133, 138-40, 144-5, 148, 151, 155,
  184, 188, 296, 463
Purseglove, J.W. 602

Raffles, Thomas Stamford 443
Rappaport, Roy A. 444
Reael, Laurens 462
Regional Physical Planning Programme
  for Transmigration (RePPProT) 470,
  474-5, 477, 489, 495, 572
Reid, Anthony 8, 33, 107, 175, 180, 205,
  254, 258, 278, 285, 307, 349, 361, 382,
  401, 406, 408, 411, 415, 426, 432, 435, 550,
  586, 606
Reinwardt, C.J.C. 47, 198, 258, 275, 343,
  461, 489, 491, 494, 507, 537, 553-4
RePPProT see Regional Physical
  Planning Programme for
  Transmigration
Revius, A.F.J.J.G. 46, 74, 77, 88, 243, 246,
  272, 431
Rhijn, M. van 46, 304, 407, 541, 547, 568
Richter, O. 599
Ricklefs, Merle C. 112
Riedel, J.G.F. 46, 91, 187-8, 197, 215, 260,
  262, 350, 363, 366, 370, 378, 397, 415,
  418, 461, 489, 491, 534, 583
Roep, B. 312
Roselaar, Pieter 128, 136, 147, 156, 168,
  236, 238, 244
Rosenberg, C.B.H. von 47, 59, 363, 461,
  489, 491, 494, 540
Ross, Ronald 294, 385, 399, 444
Royal Dutch Packet-Boat Company 92,
  see also KPM
Rumphius, Georgius Everhardus 82, 594

Saito, Osamu 385
Salvation Army 43
Sarasin, Fritz 47, 222, 232, 256, 258, 260,
309, 410-1, 422, 479, 483-4, 487, 494-5,
  534-5, 557
Sarasin, Paul 47, 222, 232, 256, 258, 260,
  309, 410-1, 422, 479, 483-4, 487, 494-5,
  534-5, 557
Scalamonti, Joannes 179-80
Schefold, Reimar 287
Schelle, C.J. van 270
Scherius, Johannes 176, 418
Schofield, Roger 449
Scholz, F.M. 589
Schoorl, J.W. 441
Schouten, Mieke J.C. 48, 349, 453, 455,
  596-8
Schrader, R. 544, 557
Schrauwers, Albert 48, 463, 465
Schwarz, J.A. 77, 184, 190, 193, 382, 410,
  495, 534 596-7, 599, 602
Scott, William Henry 438, 465
Seavoy, Ronald E. 520, 536, 542
Second World War 265, 270, 452, 470,
  491
Sell, Dominicus 152
Seydelman, Bernard Sebastian 128, 137,
  147, 156, 160, 168, 175, 177-8, 185
Shepherd, John Robert 401
Siethoff, J.J. ten 392, 430, 507
Smith, Adam 449
Speelman, Cornelis 77
Spreeuwenberg, A.F. van 605
Steenis, C.G.G.J. van 470, 474-5, 477, 481-
  2, 489, 495, 497, 508, 512, 520
Steller, E. 81, 110, 133, 142, 307-8, 342,
  363, 414, 460, 600
Steup, F.K.M. 47, 531, 552, 565
Stokking, H.G. 378

Tammes, P.M.L. 6-7, 48, 115, 139, 163, 193,
  368-9, 381, 411, 414, 416, 422-3, 435, 437,
  441, 452, 455-6, 467, 526, 548, 569
Tergast, G.C.W.C. 509, 515, 592
Thije, Isaac van 56, 598
Tiffen, Mary 570, 604
Tillema, H.F. 47, 230, 250, 261, 272, 274,
  282, 308-9, 311-3, 359, 365, 368, 371-2,
  374
Tondano War 256
Tonelli, Lise 342, 568

Ulaen, Alex 366

Valckenaer, Paulus Jacob 198
Valentijn, François 45, 112, 118, 136, 147, 150, 158-9, 163, 189, 412, 484, 489, 493
Velde van Cappellen, D. van de 88, 153-4
Velthoen, Esther J. 428
Verdoorn, Johannes Adrianus 368
Vereenigde Oost-Indische Compagnie (VOC) 31, 39, 41-2, 45-6, 56, 67, 72, 86, 92, 98, 105, 116, 119-20, 127-8, 132-4, 136-7, 142, 144, 146-7, 156, 160, 162, 165-8, 172, 175, 183-5, 195-6, 198, 205, 210, 213, 216-8, 221-2, 232-3, 235, 238, 240, 244, 250-1, 257, 265-6, 268, 273, 275, 305, 452, 454, 462, 488-9, 491, 494, 508, 577, 595, 601
VOC *see* Vereenigde Oost-Indische Compagnie

Wallace, Alfred Russel 47, 258, 335, 382, 389

Warren, James Francis 429
Weck 266, 269, 422
Weddik, A.L. 189, 200, 215
Wenzel, J. 46, 176, 185, 262, 269, 275, 289-90, 300, 347, 396, 454, 595
Wessels, C. 158, 172, 189
Whitten, Anthony J. 483, 517, 533
Wieling, C.L. 169
Wiersma, J.N. 268
Wigboldus, Jouke S. 48, 59, 172, 177, 275, 452, 454-5, 594, 596
Wilken, G.A. 180-1
Wilken, N.P. 77, 184, 190, 193, 382, 410, 495, 588, 594, 602
Willer, T.J. 110, 112
Woensdregt, Jac. 262, 308, 340, 367, 380, 385, 568, 579, 600
Woodard, David 45, 232, 256, 260, 307, 356, 542, 583
Wrigley, E.A. 449
Wijck, J.C.W.D.A. van der 210, 222, 224, 477, 555
Wijn, J.F. de 48, 261, 263, 344, 347, 349, 352

Index of geographical names

Africa, African 9, 371, 445, 570
Africa, West 489
Airmadidi 272-4
Alfur, Alfurs 19, 31, 33, 76, 101, 115, 179,
    198, 218, 221, 225, 235-6, 239, 259, 308,
    353, 410, 426, 477, 568
Ambon, Ambonese 3, 7, 60, 90, 106, 119,
    127, 144, 205, 210, 250, 372, 437, 600
America, American 45, 345-6, 459, 508,
    see also USA
America, North 84
America, South 297
Ampana 224
Ampibabo 218-9, 221
Amsterdam 44
Amurang 165, 172, 267, 294, 299, 330,
    355, 368, 378, 415, 417, 454, 595
Arab, Arabs 37, 86, 99, 166, 215
Arabs, Hadhrami 86
Asia, Asian 86, 95, 98
Asia, Southeast 1-2, 4, 6-8, 19-20, 23, 26,
    33, 89, 101, 107, 176, 254, 258, 285-7,
    307, 349, 356, 361, 372, 382, 406, 417,
    435-6, 439, 443, 445, 470, 515, 521, 579,
    585-6
Atinggola 195, 199, 202
Austronesian 19, 37, 60, 68, 435
Awu, Mount 250, 358, 403, 414

Bacan 161, 428
Bada 69, 83, 104, 222, 224-7, 229, 231,
    233, 261-62, 271, 308, 310, 340, 367,
    380, 383-4, 410, 423, 529, 534, 540, 542,
    568, 579, 600
Bada Depression 534
Bada Valley 47, 481-2, 540, 556

Bajau, see Bajo
Bajo 39, 86-8, 236, 244
Balabatang 426
Balantak 60, 75, 239-40, 242, 246, 343,
    367, 369, 421, 534, 576-7
Baleisang 343
Banawa 216, 231-3, 356
Banda 60, 144
Bandung 295
Banggai 2, 15-6, 33-4, 41, 51, 62, 67, 69,
    71, 74, 77, 99, 104, 114, 210, 235-43,
    245-6, 248, 252, 255-46, 265, 271, 281-3,
    290, 294-5, 301, 303, 309-10, 342, 367,
    376, 383, 392, 405-6, 413, 416, 418, 420,
    423-4, 428-9, 431, 436, 441, 458, 460,
    464, 479-80, 513, 519, 542, 544, 548,
    557, 576, 578, 583, 602-3, see also Gapi
Banggai Archipelago 13, 235, 238, 412
Banggai Islands 62, 68, 259, 265, 343,
    413, 421, 441, 480
Banggai Peninsula 237
Bangkurung 236
Bantik 18, 26, 273, 286, 369, 382, 387
Bare'e 37, 225, 439
Batavia 71, 92-3, 273, 291, 297, 305
Batui 240
Bawangio Plateau 267, 416, 489
Belang 181, 266, 270, 298-9, 315, 330, 505,
    508, 525, 537-9, 544-5, 549, 551
Bengal 74, 278
Bentenan 454, 508
Beo 162, 271, 418-9
Besoa 119, 121, 222, 224-9, 277, 280, 410,
    423, 529, 534, 540, 562
Biaro 133, 551-2
Bintauna 183-5, 190

Biromaru 229, 431, 483

Boalemo 196, 200, 202, 208, 242, 490, 518

Bola 422

Bolaang 104, 183-5, 187-90, 192, 293, 410, 428, 432, 518, 555, 577

Bolaang Itang 110

Bolaang Mongondow 31, 33-4, 37, 46-8, 53, 62, 72, 77, 80, 82-3, 99, 104, 119-20, 143, 165, 181, 183-96, 208, 210, 216, 257, 267, 271, 279, 281, 283, 285, 290, 293, 297, 302, 305, 319, 355, 363-4, 382, 384, 405-6, 410, 414, 422-3, 430, 432, 436, 442, 470, 490, 494-508, 517-8, 528, 532, 548, 572, 577-8, 597, 602

Bolang Bangka 189

Bolang Itang 183

Bolang Uki 183, 188, 190, 196

Bolango 183, 186, 189, 196

Bolango River 491

Bolukan 235

Bone 195-6, 202, 208, 239, 416, 489

Bone, Gulf of 232, 458, 477

Bone River 490-1

Bone Valley 267, 422

Bongka 224, 410, 534

Bongka River 13, 222, 227, 231, 239, 303, 367, 416, 474, 533, 535

Bongka Valley 13, 69, 102, 367, 533

Bora 231, 483

Borneo 26, 68, 276, 287, 311, 428, 443, 517, 581, 601

Britain, British 42, 47, 130, 148, 156, 176, 195, 217, 260, 267, 300, 302, 312, 353, 361, 363, 424, 459, 494

Bugis 27, 31, 37, 39, 41, 80, 86-7, 98-9, 101, 169, 196, 199-200, 202, 213, 215-6, 232-3, 238, 244, 247, 304, 380-1, 408, 426, 428-9, 433, 454, 457-8, 534-5, 584

Bulan [Bolaang] River 172

Buliling 559, 586

Bungku 245

Bunta 266

Buol 21, 33, 37, 62, 186-7, 195, 197, 204, 208, 213-7, 242, 258, 265, 278-80, 306, 405, 548, 578

Burma 30, 359

Buton 60, 74, 441

Buyu mBajau 102

Caile 232, *see also* Kaili

Cambodia 417

Celebes 60-1, 169, 186, 243, 258, 260, 431, 476, *see also* Sulawesi

Celebes Sea 16

Celebes, Central 263, 345, 347, 352, 552, *see also* Sulawesi

China, Chinese 67, 71, 84-7, 95, 98, 156, 158-9, 162, 166, 169-71, 201-2, 204-5, 230, 266, 279, 294, 304, 356, 454, 458

Dago 134

Dampelas 418-9

Dayak 216

Dolangon 80

Dolo 231

Dondo 214, 216, 433

Donggala 60, 83, 216, 231, 233, 249, 260, 280, 306, 310, 409, 418-9, 424, 483, 487, 517, 519, 521, 533, 548, 594

Donggala Peninsula 483

Dua Saudara, Mount 250

Dumoga 490, 495

Dumoga River 495

Dumoga Valley 193, 267, 424, 470

Dutch 3-5, 17, 20, 25, 27, 30, 33-4, 36-7, 41-2, 44-7, 56, 61, 63, 66-8, 70, 73-4, 77, 82-6, 88, 92-4, 96-9, 104-6, 108-16, 118-21, 123, 127, 129-30, 132-3, 137-9, 143-5, 148-9, 152, 154-8, 160-1, 166, 169-72, 176-9, 181-4, 186-8, 190-1, 193, 195-203, 205-6, 208, 210, 213-4, 217-8, 221-2, 227-8, 230, 232, 234-6, 243-4, 246, 249, 256-7, 269-71, 284, 291, 293, 296, 299-300, 302-3, 305, 311, 320, 328, 330, 337-8, 349-51, 353, 356, 358, 372, 382, 424, 426, 428-9, 431, 441, 452, 454-5, 459-61, 476, 480, 484, 487, 495, 499, 505, 509, 531, 533, 535, 537-8, 540, 542-3, 546, 552-3, 567, 576-7, 579, 584, 586-8, 591-2, 600-1, 605

Dutch East Indies Company 3, 23, *see also* Verenigde Oost-Indische Compagnie

English, *see* British

Ensa ndau 257

Eurasian 95, 166

Europe, European 7-8, 19-20, 31, 36, 42-
    3, 47, 61, 66, 75, 83-4, 91-5, 98, 100-1,
    105, 107, 111, 113-6, 123, 127, 133, 139,
    144, 149, 153, 155, 158, 161, 166, 169-
    72, 179, 183, 189, 195-204, 206, 210,
    213, 215, 220, 222, 224, 226, 228-9, 232,
    234, 237, 240, 246-7, 254-5, 257-8, 260,
    262, 264, 285-7, 291, 293, 296, 301, 305,
    308, 341, 354, 359-60, 363-4, 385, 426,
    428-9, 447, 457-8, 462, 464, 477, 486,
    552, 554-6, 559, 581, 587, 596, 600

Flores 4, 359, 570, 589

Gapi 235, 238, *see also* Banggai
Garete 556, 578-9
German 456
Gimpu 232
Gimpu Valley 229, 534
Gorontalo, Gorontalese 2, 13, 20, 27,
    30-1, 33-5, 39, 41-4, 46, 53, 59-60, 63-
    4, 67-74, 81-3, 86-7, 89-90, 93, 95-100,
    105, 107-9, 111, 119, 121, 165, 167, 172,
    177, 181, 183, 193, 195, 198-200, 209,
    211, 214-6, 218-9, 221, 242, 248-9, 252,
    257, 259-62, 265, 267, 269-70, 272-3,
    275, 277-81, 284, 290, 296, 299, 302,
    310-1, 314, 317-28, 330, 333, 335, 338,
    340, 342-4, 349, 351, 355, 357-8, 363-4,
    369, 373, 375-9, 381, 383-4, 397, 405-
    9, 411-2, 416, 418, 422, 424, 427, 429,
    430, 432, 436, 445-7, 457-8, 460-1, 474,
    489-95, 508, 513, 516-8, 522, 528, 532,
    534-5, 539-43, 545, 548, 555, 560, 562,
    570-1, 576-80, 582-4, 591-2, 593-4, 602,
    604, 608
Gorontalo Bay 494
Guatemala 385
Gumbasa 432
Gunung Piapi 557

Hague, The 44
Halmahera 31, 428
Hambu 228
Hanunoo 579
Hispanic, *see* Spain
Holland, *see* Dutch, Netherlands

India, Indian 73-4, 98, 294, 377
Indochina 359
Irrawady basin 417

Jakarta (Djakarta) 44, 344-6
Jamaica 345-6
Japan 41, 44
Java, Javanese 3, 5-9, 16, 30, 71-2, 94, 98,
    112, 116, 130, 181, 254, 270, 276, 278-
    80, 297, 300, 313, 333, 336, 356, 361,
    368-9, 382, 386, 394, 399, 408, 417, 436,
    443, 448, 453, 461-2, 466, 495, 499, 542,
    552, 570, 574, 579
Java, Central 13
Java, East 13

Kaburuang 155, 159, 409, 412, 464
Kaidipang 110, 183-5, 189, 195
Kaili 39, 63, 71, 84, 215-6, 232-3, 256, 286,
    349, 419, 487-8, 542, 548, 552
Kakas 181, 273, 417, 605
Kakaskasen 503, 507
Kalimantan 3, 9, 31, 41, 52, 112, 258, 291,
    360, 423, 428-9, 432, 436, 455, 520, 533,
    536, 542, 547, 559, 562, 585-6, 600
Kalimantan, Southeast 3, 6, 125, 276, 359
Kalinga 287
Kalongan 150
Kalongan-Taruna 146
Kandahar 113, 121, 144-9, 153, 403, 414
Kantewu 15, 65
Kantu 360
Karakelang 155, 160, 256, 263, 265, 412,
    414, 528, 530, 557
Karaton 308
Kawangkoan 172, 179, 273, 503, 597
Kawio 425, 513
Kaya, River 555
Kema 90, 181, 266, 270, 279, 293-4, 298-9,
    330, 354, 379, 454, 459, 505, 507, 525,
    577
Kendari 243, 246, 278, 293
Kenya 604
Kerinci 115
Klabat 37, 535
Kolongan *see* Taruna
Kolonodale 13, 242, 267, 310
Koro-Lariang 13, 234

Kotabangon 193
Kotabunan 80, 187, 193, 428
Kuandang 195, 197, 208, 217, 320, 418-9,
     422, 518, 520, 541, 548, 570
Kulawi 39, 56, 114, 224, 229, 232-5, 268,
     280, 340, 382-4, 410, 420, 529, 534
Kyela 487
Kyly, *see* Kyela

La 432, 479, 481, 554
La Basin 352, 490
La River 13, 247, 267, 477, 530
Langoan 180, 273, 379, 417, 503, 595
Lauje 48, 75, 349-50, 392, 535
Ledo 39
Lembo Depression 247, 479
Lembunu 218, 268
Leron *see* Lirung
Lesser Sundas 3, 7-9, 413, 605
Likupang 179-80, 266, 273
Lima lo Pohala'a 33, 35, 39
Limboto 30-1, 33, 63, 97, 108-9, 195-200,
     202-3, 206, 219, 242, 269, 339, 411, 416,
     490, 492
Limboto Depression 13, 43, 59, 63-4, 97,
     99, 194-5, 206-8, 212-3, 249, 265, 340-1,
     406, 409, 414, 420, 430, 457, 489, 494,
     513, 528-9, 540-2, 548, 560-1, 570, 576,
     580, 591, 594
Limboto, Lake 31, 69-70, 251, 421, 491-2,
     494, 528, 541, 559, 579, 583
Limboto Plain 490, 513
Lindu 224, 232-3, 268, 284, 410-1, 529,
     559
Lindu, Lake 261, 283, 296, 421, 424, 519,
     584
Lindu Valley 234, 584
Lirung 161, 163, 464
Loinang 261, 367
Lokon, Mount 180, 553
Lolayan 193
Lore 58, 69, 121, 222-31, 234, 252, 261,
     379, 405, 408, 481-2, 517, 540, 545, 585
Luwu 104, 232, 241, 243, 418, 602
Luwuk Peninsula 13, 41, 60, 68-9, 74,
     106, 235-6, 239-42, 261, 265-6, 367, 405,
     411, 417-9, 423, 470, 474, 476, 479-80,
     534, 544, 548, 561

Luzon 3, 429-30, 445, 564

Madura 361, 373
Magindanao 152, 156, 159, 217, 246, 339,
     341, 428-31, 457
Makasar, Makasarese 3, 27, 41, 71-2, 77,
     86, 92, 167, 195, 213, 216, 233, 238,
     243-4, 278, 356, 381, 408, 457, 487, 552,
     584
Makasar Strait 228, 343
Malabar 135
Malaka Straits 72
Malay 20, 31, 39, 73, 109, 259, 476, 487
Malaya 582
Malili 458
Maluku Sea 13, 16
Mamboro 487-8
Mamuju 228
Manado 2, 34, 41-6, 48, 66-7, 74-5, 81,
     84, 90, 92, 95, 98, 106, 119, 127-9, 134-
     5, 137-9, 143, 147-9, 151, 156-9, 161,
     165-6, 168-9, 172, 178-9, 185, 205,
     213-4, 233, 244-5, 254, 264, 266, 269,
     275, 278-9, 286, 290, 294-6, 298-9, 302,
     305-6, 311, 315, 317, 319, 321, 330, 339,
     341, 353-4, 356, 381, 384, 409-10, 428-9,
     431-3, 454, 456, 469, 474, 501, 503, 507-
     8, 525, 541, 548, 551, 595, 604
Manado River 294
Manados 29, 167
Manarang 464
Mandar 39, 86-7, 98, 196-7, 213, 215-6,
     218, 239, 428, 487
Mandono 85, 216, 237, 239-40, 387, 419,
     544, 561
Manganitu 62, 121, 145-9, 151-3, 275, 379
Magindanao 213
Mangondo 172, *see also* Monondo
Manila 90, 143, 167, 178
Manui, island 81, 243, 556
Mapane 373-4, 389
Mapanget 15, 418-9
Marundu 247
Masarang 418-9, 581-2, 604
Mata ndau 119, 121, 267
Matano 82, 458
Matano, Lake 269, 291, 554, 559
Mataram 113

Mengampit 513
Mengarang 409
Mentawai 287
Merampi 412, 425, 513
Miangas 80, 155-6, 161, 251, 413, 420,
    422, 425, 579, 404
Minahasa 13, 15-6, 18-20, 24, 26-31, 33,
    37-8, 40-8, 51, 53, 55-60, 62, 64-71, 73,
    75, 80, 82-4, 86-7, 91-6, 98, 100, 104-6,
    109, 111-2, 115-8, 120, 123, 143, 154,
    161, 165-84, 191-3, 195, 205-7, 210-1,
    234, 247, 249-60, 262-9, 271-6, 278-81,
    283-6, 289, 292-302, 305-15, 317-9,
    329-43, 347, 349, 351-59, 362-6, 368-9,
    374-83, 386-95, 397-8, 400, 403, 405-12,
    414-5, 417-9, 422-3, 426, 429-32, 436-7,
    440-2, 444, 446-52, 456, 459-66, 474,
    492, 495-508, 513, 515-8, 520-30, 532,
    534-40, 544-6, 548-51, 553, 561-3, 567-
    70, 572, 575-7, 580-3, 586-606, 608-10
Minangkabau 37, 438
Mindanano 157, 217
Mindanao 61, 77, 425, 428
Mindoro 579
Mintu 80
Moat, Lake 577
Modayak 418-9
Modoinding 442, 572, 576
Molibagu 183, 186, 190
Moluccas, Moluccan 3-4, 19, 31, 39, 41,
    60, 63, 66-8, 71, 93, 101, 119, 128, 146,
    239, 255, 275, 295, 330, 341, 429, 459-
    60, 462, 476, 552, 603
Moluccas, North 30, 41, 59, 163, 528
Moluccas, South 115-6, 144
Moluccas Sea 508
Mongondow 13, 16, 34, 36, 46, 69-70, 80,
    83, 91, 94, 104, 172, 177, 183, 185-8,
    192-3, 210, 234, 258-9, 343, 410-1, 414,
    418-9, 495, 513, 518, 529, 544, 562, 577
Mongondow Plateau 267, 415-6, 423,
    489, 494, 528
Monondo 172, *see also* Mangondo
Mori 2, 34-6, 39, 51, 63, 74, 76, 79, 88,
    111, 121, 225, 227, 229, 242-8, 253, 257,
    261, 267, 284-5, 344, 347, 352, 372, 405,
    432, 441, 476-9, 513, 529-31, 535, 545,
    555, 559, 572-5, 610

Mori Atas 247
Mori Bay 228
Mori, Gulf of 83
Morotai 528
Moutong 86, 195, 208, 218-20, 278, 318,
    542-3

Nanusa 155, 157, 159, 161, 251, 308, 412,
    425, 513, 579, 605
Nanusa Archipelago 556
Nanusa Islands 81, 412, 420, 544, 556,
    578
Napu 64, 69, 118-9, 121, 222, 224-5, 228-
    30, 233, 253-4, 268, 271, 277, 283, 340,
    410, 422, 424, 440, 482, 529, 534, 540,
    562, 585, 593
Napu Depression 482, 559
Napu Valley 64, 106, 423, 544, 578
Ndao 413, 605
Negeri Baru 119, 503
Netherlands, the 44, 262-3
Netherlands Indies 130, 139, 486
New Guinea 60, 81, 311, 411, 444, 601,
    603
Ngilalaki 559
Nokilalaki, Mount 559
Nusa Tenggara 417

Oegstgeest 44
Onda'e 253-4, 340, 573

Pacific 90, 115, 375, 459
Pada 290, 479, 530-1, 533, 535, 540, 545,
    554-5, 557, 562, 564
Pagimana 480, 544
Paguat 67, 96-8, 195, 199, 204, 208, 242,
    265, 268-70, 343, 422, 489
Paguyaman 199, 208
Paguyaman Basin 267, 489
Paibatu 224
Pakambia 340, 352, 531, 554, 573
Paleleh 195
Palu 13, 16, 36, 39, 45, 59, 63, 73-4, 85,
    100, 104, 229, 231-5, 258, 260, 265, 271,
    278, 286, 347, 368, 374, 408-9, 416, 418,
    433, 439, 474, 489-90, 534-5, 542, 548,
    551-2, 556, 560, 580-1, 584, 594
Palu Bay 36, 86, 91-6, 231-3, 280, 356-7,

411, 431-3, 488, 519, 534, 556
Palu River 487
Palu Trench 62, 231-2, 411, 529, 558
Palu Valley 20, 30, 39, 58, 63-4, 69-72, 76-7, 110, 227-8, 232-4, 248, 254-5, 257, 281, 286, 304, 307, 309, 409, 411, 416, 419, 421, 432, 439, 476, 482-9, 494, 513, 528-9, 534, 542, 545, 552, 557, 559-60, 562, 565, 570, 581, 584, 593-4
Pamona 22, 36-7, 39, 48, 107, 225, 350, 370-1, 463, 537
Papakelang 553
Papuan 166
Parigi 34, 41, 64, 72, 78, 92, 94, 218-20, 222, 227, 233, 278-9, 418, 421, 432-3, 457, 542, 545, 594
Parigi, North 220
Parigi, South 220
Pasan 166, 502-3
Pasi 193
Pasisir Bolaang 518
Pebato 391
Pekawa 62, 234, 261, 286, 529
Peling 104, 235-9, 259, 309, 416, 431, 480, 544, 557
Pendolo 418-9
Petasia 247
Philippines 3, 13, 19, 34, 68, 77, 82, 115, 166, 217, 271, 276, 287, 428, 438, 445, 465, 538, 587
Piapi 528
Poigar 423
Pokobondolong 242
Polynesia 413
Pompangeo 531
Ponosakan 166, 268, 273, 387, 587
Portuguese 25, 41, 61, 65, 83, 86, 213
Poso 20, 25, 29, 36-7, 47-8, 74-8, 105, 210, 219, 222-32, 234, 250, 256-7, 261, 263, 267, 272, 274, 276, 281, 285, 292, 303, 343-4, 347-8, 350, 352, 365, 371-2, 382, 405-6, 408-11, 418, 441, 476-9, 482, 513, 517, 519-20, 529-31, 536-40, 545, 555, 559, 572-6, 600, 610
Poso Depression 39, 228, 439, 482
Poso, Lake 13, 16, 115, 210, 222, 224, 229, 231, 233, 251-2, 263, 291, 410, 418, 421, 470, 476-7, 481, 529, 534, 554-5, 573,

579, 583
Poso River 107, 229, 231, 476, 574
Poso Toraja 263
Poso Valley 21, 39, 246-8, 252, 284, 340, 416, 477, 529-30, 536-8, 540, 543, 545-7, 563, 572-3, 575-7, 585
Pulo 232
Punan 68

Ranoiapo River 179-81
Raranggonao 234
Ratahan 166, 502-3, 508, 537-8, 549
Remboken 503, 517
Rerer 553
Romo'ong 172
Roti 7, 9, 412, 605
Ruang 131, 415
Ruang, volcano 251
Rumo'ong 37, 119, 330

Sa'dan Toraja *see* Toraja
Sa'dang 31
Sahendaruman, volcano 251
Saigon 356, 460
Sakkudei 287
Salibabu 157, 163, 277, 349, 412, 464
Saluan 242, 261, 286, 367
Sangi 430
Sangir, Sangirese 13, 16, 20-1, 23-9, 34-7, 39, 41-2, 45, 47-8, 53, 60, 62, 65, 68-9, 71-2, 76-7, 79-81, 84, 88-90, 93-4, 99, 104-5, 107, 109-13, 116, 127-65, 175, 177, 179, 181, 183, 191-2, 205, 248, 250-2, 258-9, 262-3, 270-5, 277, 279-80, 292, 294, 297, 299-300, 302-4, 306-10, 319, 338-9, 342, 344-7, 349, 356, 363-4, 368, 374, 379, 382, 384, 397-8, 400, 403, 405-8, 413-6, 418-21, 424-5, 428-31, 433, 436-7, 441, 444, 446, 452-3, 455-7, 460-1, 463-6, 470, 513, 515, 518, 520, 525, 529, 543-8, 550-1, 562, 568, 577, 579, 582-3, 590, 600, 602-3, 609
Sangir, Greater 62, 68, 110, 119-20, 127, 130, 133-4, 140, 144-55, 165, 179, 249-51, 265-6, 277, 280, 283, 297-8, 301-3, 338, 343, 345-6, 358, 379, 403, 405-6, 408, 412-3, 430, 433, 452, 455, 508-12, 509-10, 518, 547-8, 579

Sangir Archipelago 33, 61, 152, 319, 412, 509

Sangir Islands 16, 46, 49, 76, 82, 106, 129, 143, 152, 181, 265, 283, 290, 303, 403, 407, 412, 414, 422, 427, 430, 433, 455-6, 518, 527, 550, 603

Sangkup 183

Sarawak 336, 347, 360, 384, 390, 444, 461

Sarongsong 273, 503, 507

Sausu 196, 218-9

Savu 413

Sawang 145-6, 414

Sawu 7, 9

Sea-Sea 309

Selayar 77, 360, 398, 603-4

Semarang 278

Seram 115

Seram, West 345

Siau 24, 41, 45, 48, 59, 65, 68, 73, 76, 84, 105-7, 114, 119-20, 127, 132-45, 152-4, 156, 165, 216, 256, 265, 277, 302, 339, 342-3, 351, 355, 379, 405-6, 408, 412-3, 421-2, 428, 430, 433, 455-6, 463, 509-11, 518, 527, 568, 579

Siau Island 135-9

Sidoan 197, 218, 221

Singapore 93

Sigenti 221

Sigi 77, 104, 231, 233, 593

Simpang 261, 266, 269

Siraya 401

Sonder 172, 179-80, 273, 504-5, 522, 544, 596-7, 605

Soputan, Mount 415

Soroako 554

Spain, Spaniard, Spanish, Hispanic 36, 41, 66, 69, 77, 105-6, 115, 127, 129, 133-4, 137, 143-4, 148, 157, 165, 167, 175, 178, 255, 425

Sulawesi 13, 41, 47, 60, 65, 68, 71, 74, 85-6, 90, 97, 101, 106, 112, 161, 187, 195, 210, 213, 232, 237, 251, 254-5, 260, 271, 2786, 280, 297, 307-9, 361, 368, 384, 389, 401, 407, 417, 422-3, 428, 442, 470, 474-5, 483, 517, 520, 537, 542, 548, 565, 581, 603, 606

Sulawesi, Central 2, 13, 17, 20, 23-8, 31, 34-5, 37, 39, 41-3, 46-9, 53, 55, 57-61, 64-5, 68-9, 71-4, 76-9, 83, 85-92, 95, 100, 104, 106, 111, 114, 118-9, 121, 181, 213-48, 223, 231-5, 250-3, 255-63, 267-9, 271-2, 274, 277, 279-86, 290-2, 294-6, 299, 303-7, 309, 312-3, 320, 338-43, 346, 355, 357, 365-6, 370, 374-9, 381-5, 388, 398-9, 404-12, 415-6, 419-21, 423, 426-7, 429, 431-2, 436, 438-40, 442, 444-5, 453, 455, 458-60, 466, 470, 474-6, 478, 480-2, 486, 495, 508, 513, 517, 519-20, 528-30, 532-5, 540, 543, 545-6, 551-2, 554-5, 557, 559, 561-3, 572, 574-5, 577, 590-1, 593, 608, 610

Sulawesi, North 2, 6, 23, 39, 41, 45, 47-9, 61, 67, 69, 81, 83, 86, 90, 109, 115, 154, 160, 165-211, 248, 294, 320, 369, 381, 406-8, 416, 430, 435, 437, 475-6, 527, 556, 562, 610

Sulawesi, northern 1-2, 11-48, 51, 54, 59, 61, 68, 71-3, 83, 85, 93, 99, 101, 107, 111, 119, 123-4, 125, 127, 175, 233, 252, 256, 258, 262, 264, 273, 275-6, 281, 285, 289, 293, 295, 313, 352-3, 366, 373, 376, 380, 382, 384, 386, 390, 392, 398-400, 403, 405, 412, 418-9, 422, 424, 426, 432, 435, 438, 442-4, 466, 469, 471-3, 475-6, 513, 517, 521, 531-2, 534, 547-8, 550-1, 554, 556-7, 562, 567, 572, 575, 579, 583-4, 586, 593, 600, 603, 606

Sulawesi, South 7, 9, 27, 30-1, 41, 48-9, 61, 72, 77, 82, 86-7, 90, 107, 225, 239, 243, 270, 350, 356, 380-1, 384, 398, 417, 428-9, 433, 533-4, 552, 554, 559, 584, 602

Sulawesi, Southeast 49, 293, 441

Sulu 35, 89, 217, 428-9, 454

Sumalata 202, 208

Sumara 228

Sumara River 227

Sumara Valley 35, 83, 535, 559

Sumatra 3, 8, 27, 31, 58, 115, 181, 230, 270, 276, 411, 417, 424, 432, 506, 547, 550, 555, 559

Sumatra, North 9

Sumatra, West 35

Sumba 413, 533

Suwawa 196

Sweden, Swedish 260

Swiss 47

Tabukan 113, 121, 145-52, 266, 275, 301, 403, 509-10
Tagalog Philippines 110
Tagulandang 68, 79, 119-20, 127-34, 142, 145, 152-4, 159, 251, 285, 310, 343, 383, 385, 405, 408, 412, 415, 421, 430, 433, 455, 509-10, 518, 520, 579
Taiwan 401
Talaud 13, 21, 25, 36, 46, 52-3, 55, 57, 61-2, 65, 72, 76-7, 80-1, 89, 92, 99, 111, 127-65, 181, 183, 191-2, 207, 238-9, 248, 252, 256, 262-3, 265, 271, 277, 279, 283, 292, 294, 296, 303, 308-10, 312-4, 338, 341, 343-4, 348, 358, 363, 375, 378-9, 383, 390, 404-6, 408-9, 412-4, 416, 418-9, 421, 424, 427, 429, 431, 441, 446-7, 456, 459-60, 463-4, 512-3, 515-6, 518, 528, 530, 537, 543, 548, 551, 556-7, 590, 592, 602-3, 605
Talaud Archipelago 412
Talaud Islands 49, 104, 160, 179, 191, 265, 431
Talauer 464
Tamaduë 228
Tamako 134, 137-8, 142, 145-9, 151, 153, 275
Tanawangko 179, 454, 501
Tariang 414
Taruna 249, 266, 275, 277, 302, 345-6, 403, 414, 418-9, 510
Taruna (Kolongan-) 145, 153-5
Tawaelia 13, 58, 222, 228, 231-3, 263, 267-8, 283, 297, 424, 433, 439
Ternate, Ternatan 35, 41, 45-6, 66-7, 81, 92, 106, 114, 127, 133, 135, 145-6, 156, 158, 160-2, 166, 168-9, 176-8, 184-6, 195, 198, 205, 210, 213-4, 216, 219, 221, 236-40, 242-4, 246, 257, 269, 276, 278, 302, 384, 428-9, 431, 456, 460, 509, 577
Tewulu 234
Thailand 336, 359, 417
Tidong 428
Tidore 177, 428
Tilamuta 242
Timor 8, 287, 359, 413, 557, 575, 605
Tineba mountains 484, 528, 559

Tineba Plateau 565
Tinombo 48, 62, 77, 82, 197, 217-8, 220-1, 274, 342, 350, 352, 418-9, 489, 520, 568, 576
To Bada 439
To Banahu 439
To Bau 119, 121
To Besoa 439
To Kadombuku 404
To Kulawi 439
To Lage 107, 224, 370-4, 391, 445, 573
To Lindu 439
To Loinang 269
To Napu 107, 252, 404
To Onda'e 252, 371-2, 445, 479
To Pada 445, 545
To Pakambia 479, 554
To Pebato 102, 107, 370-1, 373-4, 389
To Rau 224
To Tawaelia 268, 404
To Wana 103, 227, 303, 389
To Wingke mPoso 371
Toba 417
Tobaku 256, 348
Tobelo 246, 428, 431
Toboli 433
Tobungku 2, 34, 41, 60, 62, 65, 71-2, 74, 77, 82, 85, 116, 239, 242-8, 253, 265, 269, 272, 278, 290, 356, 405-6, 411, 428, 431, 457-60, 479-80, 543, 556, 574
Togian 303, 310, 343, 413, 418, 433, 457, 548, 583
Togian Archipelago 16
Togian Islands 13, 62, 84, 96, 98, 125, 204, 225-7, 277, 280, 301, 318, 358, 405, 426, 433, 457
Tojo 13, 76, 83, 85-6, 101-3, 110, 114, 155, 217, 220-9, 248, 371-2, 403, 406, 430, 517, 529, 535, 563
Tolitoli 27, 33, 62, 186, 189-90, 197, 213-7, 232-3, 265, 270, 292, 294, 303, 383, 405, 407, 418-9, 428, 433, 489, 519-20, 535, 548, 555, 570
Tolo, Bay of 430
Tomaiki 242
Tomasa 555, 574
Tomasa Valley 477, 555, 573
Tomasa River 476, 555

Tomata 564
Tombariri 180, 273, 454, 507
Tombasian 37, 172, 330
Tombuku 242
Tombulu 389, 594, 596
Tomini 62, 85, 197, 205, 208, 210, 218-21,
    248, 278, 318, 405, 407, 416-9, 427, 431,
    433, 457, 543, 545, 548, 550, 555, 561
Tomini, Gulf of 13, 33-4, 41, 68-9, 72-4,
    81, 83-4, 91-2, 96, 98-9, 101-2, 195-8,
    204, 210, 219, 221-3, 233, 242, 268, 318,
    320, 340, 343, 356, 419, 428-9, 431-3,
    477, 494, 528, 534, 541-2, 548, 563, 571,
    574
Tomohon 67, 180-91, 273, 298, 318, 329,
    363, 386, 417, 454, 502-3, 507, 524, 527,
    544
Tomori Bay 16-7, 72, 243, 246, 267
Tompaso 172
Tompira 479
Tondano, Tondanese 16, 26, 37, 43, 56-7,
    75, 80, 92, 180-91, 257, 269, 273, 276,
    283, 298-9, 311, 315, 329, 354, 386, 397,
    408-11, 417, 424-5, 502, 507, 517, 525,
    527, 559, 584, 586, 588-8, 590, 598,
    604-6
Tondano Plateau 354
Tondano, Lake 56, 180-91, 271, 315, 407,
    415, 492-4, 497, 501, 503, 535-6, 583,
    588, 598, 605-6
Tongkimbut 598
Tongko River 256

Tonsawang 58, 62, 66, 166, 559, 586, 601
Tonsea 29, 95, 119, 180-91, 266, 273, 352,
    379, 525-6, 539, 551, 577, 580, 600
Tonsea Lama 494
Tontemboan 505, 534, 595, 597-9
Toraja 22-3, 26-7, 31, 35, 42, 75, 78-9, 85,
    88, 102, 114, 225, 227, 250, 253, 256,
    258, 260-1, 263, 285, 290-1, 296, 304,
    344, 347, 349, 357, 366, 368, 374, 378,
    382, 384-5, 389, 399, 401, 409-10, 426,
    438-9, 529, 537, 573, 579, 591
Torau 224
Tua 428
Tuliang 503
Tulimambot 503

Unauna 16, 418
USA, *see* America
Utrecht 44

Verenigde Oost-Indische Compagnie
    (VOC), *see* Dutch East Indies
    Company

Walati Valley 573
Wana 533
Watambayoli 83, 227, 356
Woloan 364
Wawo nTolo 573

Yacua 232
Yaentu Valley 229, 554